MW01348281

By the People

A History of the United States

SECOND EDITION

AP® Edition

James W. Fraser
New York University

 **Pearson** 330 Hudson Street, NY 10013

Portfolio Manager: Ed Parsons
Managing Editor: Debbie Coniglio
Development Editor: Mary Gawlik
Director, Product Management and Marketing: Elaine Shema
Marketing Manager: Michele Gillis
Content Specialist: Jean Woy
Program Manager: Joanne Dauksewicz
Project Manager: Jennifer Thomas, Lumina Datamatics
Project Coordination, Text Design, and Electronic Page Makeup: Lumina Datamatics
Cover Designer: Jennifer Hart Design
Cover Illustration/Photo: Main photo: American flag popularly attributed to Betsy Ross (David Smart/Shutterstock); **Insert photos, left column (top to bottom):** Alison Turnbull Hopkins with banner (American Photo Archive/Alamy Stock Photo); Mechanic during maintenance, 1873 (ZU_09/DigitalVision Vectors/Getty Images); American Civil War Generals and their officers (National Archives/Stocktrek Images/Getty Images); Voters voting (Blend Images, Hill Street Studios/Brand X Pictures/Getty Images) Gold washing in California (duncan1890/E+/Getty Images); **Insert photos, right column (top to bottom):** Battle of Bunker's Hill 1775- Colonel Prescott (SOTK2011/Alamy Stock Photo); Picket, oil workers' union, Seminole, Oklahoma (Prints and Photographs Division, Library of Congress. Russell Lee, [LC-USF34- 034063-D]); Engraving, 1870, Group of Native Americans (Grafissimo/E+/ Getty Images); Stamp printed in USA showing Rosa Parks, circa 2013 (neftali/Shutterstock); Students picketing in front of White House, April 17, 1965 (Everett Collection Historical / Alamy Stock Photo)
Manufacturing Buyer: Mary Ann Gloriande
Printer/Binder: LSC Communications
Cover Printer: LSC Communications

Acknowledgments of third-party content appear on pages S1–S9, which constitute an extension of this copyright page.

2   18

Cataloging-in-Publication data is on file with the Library of Congress.

Student Edition ISBN-13: 978-0-134-67210-6 (High School Binding)
Student Edition ISBN-10: 0-134-67210-0 (High School Binding)

Dedication

To my children and grandchildren and all the students of their generations.
May they find the American story in all its complexity as fascinating as I do.

Brief Contents

Contents

PART 4 Crafting A Nation, People, Land, And A National Identity, 1800–1848

8 Creating a New People, Expanding The Country, 1801–1823 220

9 New Industries, New Politics, 1815–1828 249

10 Democracy in the Age of Andrew Jackson, 1828–1844 280

11 Manifest Destiny: Expanding the Nation, 1830–1853 307

Maps

List of Tables and Figures

Special Features

American Voices

Thinking Historically

When Historians Disagree

To the Teacher

I hope you and your students enjoy reading *By the People* and that your students learn history and learn to value the study of American history and historical thinking skills as well as preparing well for the AP® exam, as a result of reading it.

In writing *By the People* I have had several key goals in mind:

- **To create a book that is interesting.** I have used stories to try to give students a flavor of the developments that have created the United States as it is. Too many students say "history is my most boring subject." All of us involved with the teaching of high school and college history courses need do to all we can to help our students emerge liking what they have learned and with a thirst for more historical knowledge. I hope *By the People* is a contribution to that goal.

- **To focus on all of the lands that eventually became the United States and the people who eventually became part of this country and culture.** Thus the fact that different and competing Europeans established Santa Fe, New Mexico (by the Spanish), Quebec, Canada (by the French), and Jamestown, Virginia (by the English), in the same three-year time span, 1607–1610, says a lot about what was happening in Europe and in different parts of North America that one would miss by focusing only on English settlements. The fact that the rapid expansion of cotton production after the War of 1812 shaped the face of southern slavery, northern industrialism, and new developments in transportation and communications worldwide would be missed if one studies different regions in isolation. The United States was a much smaller country when it declared independence in 1776 than it is today, but developments in areas such as California and Texas are as important as developments in original colonial areas of Virginia and Massachusetts in shaping the modern nation.

- **To provide a history of the many different peoples who have shaped the United States as it is today, as reflected in the title of this book—*By the People*.** Whenever possible, I have focused on the stories of average everyday women and men who have created this country. In a survey of U.S. History, it is essential to tell the stories of the leaders—the people from George Washington to Donald Trump and from Benjamin Franklin to Andrew Carnegie to Jane Addams—who have been the best-known leaders of their generations. At the same time, I believe it is equally important to tell the story of some of those whose names have been forgotten—women and men who fought in the Revolutionary army, enslaved people who ran away or found other ways to resist and ultimately gain freedom, women who worked for decades to win the right to vote, immigrants who came to the United States in the hope of building a better life, American Indians of many different tribes who found ways to maintain their cultures in spite of formidable obstacles. These and many other people are essential to the story that is told in this book.

- **To foster a sense of agency—as well as historical knowledge—in our students by focusing on the stories of the active roles in history played by diverse peoples of this country.** When history becomes one thing after another, it gets just plain boring. When history becomes only a celebration of the good and greats among us, it is unbelievable. And when history is only a story of the bad things that some Americans have done to others, it is just plain depressing. On the other hand, if American history can be the story of those who fought back against injustice, who organized to win new rights, who found ways to build a better society, then our students can ask, "why not me?" And, I believe that such a history of people who made a difference can lead our students in their time to join the list of those who have helped build a better and more hopeful country.

- **Finally, and very important to all of us, in every step in the development of *By the People*, to be mindful of the changing standards that the College Board established for AP® U.S. History, starting with the revisions for the May 2015 exams and further changes that impacted exams for 2017 and 2018.** My editors and I have worked hard to ensure that this second edition is fully up to date with the latest changes in these standards, including those finalized in the summer of 2017. These newest standards focus on analyzing historical evidence and on argument development. Every chapter is organized around these skills with questions and suggestions that help a student think about the information that is presented in the same way historians think about evidence. My goal is to prepare students so that, well before the exam, the kinds of questions that are asked and the responses to information that are required will be second nature to them based on their work with this book.

No book alone can do the job of teaching students what they need to know, fostering a lifelong love of history, or creating a can-do spirit that American students need so badly. Nevertheless I hope that *By the People* can be a useful resource that, in the hands of an expert teacher, can help create a learning experience that develops the knowledge and skill we want our students to have.

Please let me know what your experience—and that of your students—is like. E-mail me at jim.fraser@nyu.edu. I am anxious to hear, to learn, and to be a partner with you in creating the education that our students deserve.

Jim Fraser
New York City

To the Student

I hope you enjoy reading *By the People* and that you learn the value of the study of American history and historical thinking skills as a result of reading it.

The title of this book—*By the People*—describes one of my key goals. This text is a history of the many different peoples who have shaped the United States as it is today. Whenever possible, I have focused on the stories of average everyday women and men who have created this country. In a survey of U.S. History, it is essential to tell the stories of the leaders—the people from George Washington to Donald Trump and also from Benjamin Franklin to Andrew Carnegie to Jane Addams—who have been the best-known leaders of their generations. At the same time, I believe it is equally important to tell the story of some of those whose names have been forgotten—women and men who fought in the Revolutionary army, enslaved people who ran away or found other ways to resist and ultimately gain freedom, women who worked for decades to win the right to vote, immigrants who came to the United States in the hope of building a better life, American Indians of many different tribes who found ways to maintain their cultures in spite of formidable obstacles. These and many other people are essential to the story that is told in this book.

In focusing on the stories of the diverse peoples of this country, I have also sought to foster a sense of agency—as well as historical knowledge. When history becomes a listing of one thing after another, it gets boring. When history becomes only a celebration of the good and greats among us, it is unbelievable. And when history is only a story of the bad things that some Americans have done to others, it is just plain depressing. On the other hand, if American history can be the story of those who fought back against injustice, who organized to win new rights, who found ways to build a better society, then our students can ask, "why not me?" And, I believe that such a history of people who made a difference in the past can lead today's students in your time to join the list of those who have helped build a better and more hopeful country.

Please let me know what your experience is like. E-mail me at jim.fraser@nyu.edu. I am anxious to hear and to learn.

Jim Fraser
New York City

Highlights and Features of *By the People*, Second Edition

Written with a single author voice, *By the People* seeks to spark students' interest in historical inquiry through an integrated social and political history narrative.

New to This Edition

Extensive updating and revising have been completed for this edition, with attention throughout the book to the latest AP® History Disciplinary Practices and Reasoning Skills. Specifically, this edition includes new and more in-depth coverage on:

- New research on earliest migration patterns of the first peoples of the Americas
- The place of women in early American Indian societies
- Changes in sailing and navigation
- New information on the Columbian exchange in a global context
- Early development of slavery up to the 1808 ban on international slave trade
- Differences in state constitutions and forms of government
- Technological innovations in textile machinery, steam engines, interchangeable parts, the telegraph, agricultural inventions, and transportation networks
- Liberal social ideas from abroad and Romantic beliefs in human perfectibility and its influence on literature, art, philosophy, and architecture
- Changes in political parties over time
- Lincoln and Reconstruction, especially on the debate about Lincoln's vision for the United States and commitment to emancipation
- Internal immigration, child labor, and women creating the middle class as producers and consumers
- LGBTQ contributions to history

In addition, this edition offers insightful information about the influence of technological innovation on economic development and society:

- Employment trends increasing in the services and decreasing in manufacturing
- Divided government and hostility
- Increasing environmental concerns
- Fear of terrorism and ISIS
- Continuing wars in Iraq and Afghanistan
- Black Lives Matter
- Influence of greater technological connectivity
- The long presidential election of 2016

Program Highlights

By the People enriches the AP program mission in these specific ways:

- Gives attention to continuity and change over time, organizing the past to foster historical understanding of how history actually unfolds and the ways in which people living through an era experience it. The text is organized into nine parts that reflect the basic periods of U.S. history: Contact and Exploration, 1491–1607; Settlements Old and New, 1607–1754; A New Birth of Freedom—Creating the United States of America, 1754–1800; Crafting a Nation, People, Land, and a National Identity, 1800–1848; Expansion, Separation, and a New Union, 1844–1877; Becoming an Industrial World Power—Costs, Benefits, and Responses, 1865–1914; War, Prosperity, and Depression, 1890–1945; Fears, Joys, and Limits, 1945–1980; and Certainty, Uncertainty, and New Beginnings, 1980 to the Present.
- Uses a narrative approach that covers the essential core content of U.S. history, integrating stories that allow students to learn some aspects more deeply and ponder material more critically.
- Tells the story of U.S. history by examining the relationship of the United States to the rest of the world, noting not only the impact of the American experience on other nations and cultures but also the impact of those cultures on the United States, whether that impact be through immigration, the worldwide exchange of ideas through media and commerce, or official foreign policy.
- Highlights the diversity of the American people as an essential element in the nation's history.
- Incorporates extensive AP content and pedagogy:
  - A correlation of chapters to the AP U.S. History Course Framework Key Concepts opens each part of the text.
  - AP Practice Tests at the end of each part include multiple-choice questions, short-answer questions, a long essay question, and a document-based question that can be completed on MyHistoryLab.
  - A chapter-based pedagogical structure is designed to improve historical thinking skills and foster student engagement and success on the AP exam.

Features

The pedagogical approach of *By the People* is designed to provide numerous opportunities for students to engage in historical inquiry and to focus on analyzing historical evidence and argument development. Each feature connects to the historical thinking skills that are an essential part of the study of history and essential to success on the AP exam. They are intended to serve as points of discovery through which students learn and understand the past and its significance. Three features appear throughout the text: American Voices, Thinking Historically, and When Historians Disagree.

The American Voice features share viewpoints from many different types of people, all of whom were participants in this country's history. From Native Americans, slaves, and immigrants to farmers, laborers, and soldiers to mothers, activist women, and service providers to politicians, social leaders, and presidents, these accounts bring to life vital pieces of our history in contexts that bring new perspectives. For example, one account by Mary Rowlandson describes an attack on her colonial village and her abduction by Indians. Another account by Charles Ball relates his days as a slave. Later, letters by Paul Coe provide an intimate view of life as a solider in Vietnam, and a memoir by Artie Van Why relates not only the horror of 9/11 but also the profound humanity he experienced that day.

The Thinking Historically features present ways in which historians try to interpret and analyze events and developments in U.S. history. Students can begin to get a sense of how important this interpretation and analysis is to represent history in ways that reflect the actual contexts of the events. Questions after these features challenge students to practice thinking historically for themselves. "How the Other Half Lives" relates the difficulties Jacob Riis encountered as he tried to publicize his writings about the population in New York City living in abject poverty. "Limiting Free Speech" discusses the tensions throughout society as people differed strongly on the issue of participating in World War I. Other features share analysis of issues such as the civil rights movement, same-sex marriage, and more.

Finally, the When Historians Disagree features juxtapose two different takes on history by historians with varying perceptions of the same issues or events. These features introduce students to the lively and dynamic nature of history, and the questions for students at the end allow them to practice the critical thinking and analysis that is necessary to engage in the study of history. Some of the questions explored in these features include How should Columbus be remembered? What was the impact of the New Deal? Could, or should, have the United States won in Vietnam?

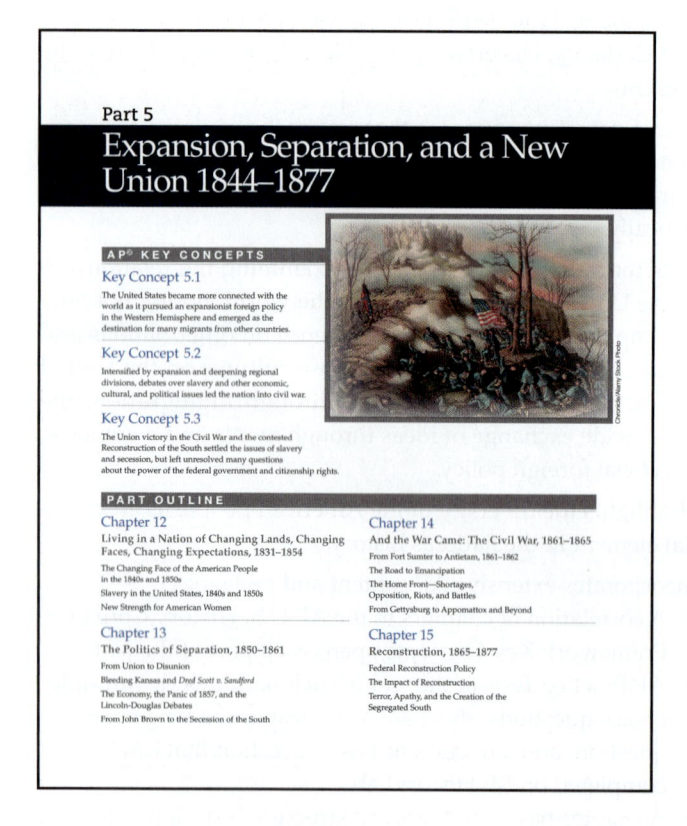

Part Opening Outlines

Each of the nine parts opens with an outline of the text chapters and the AP U.S. History Course Framework Key Concepts covered in the part.

Chapter Learning Objectives

Objectives for each main section of the chapter correlate to the Key Concepts of the AP U.S. History Course Framework. These objectives serve as a guide for the student learner to the chapter's main topics and themes.

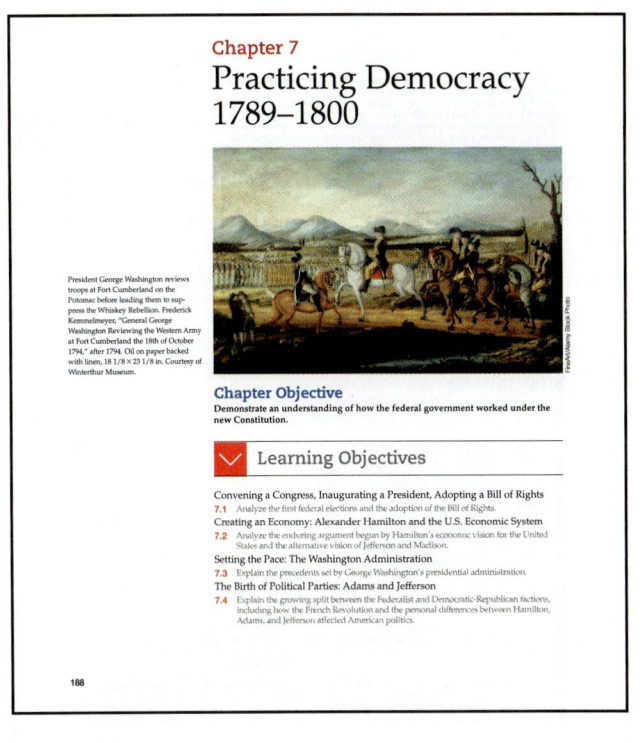

Quick Review Questions

Questions that ask students to use historical thinking skills necessary for the practice and study of history conclude each main section of the chapter. These questions ask students to construct arguments, consider cause-and-effect, evaluate patterns of change, and evaluate comparisons and contrasts. Students are asked to use these skills as they relate to both the content of the section and the overall themes in the AP U.S. History Course Framework.

When Historians Disagree

This new feature—one for each of the nine parts of the book—focuses on Analyzing Secondary Sources. In each of these, short segments give the description of the same event from the pens of two different historians. Students are then asked to describe the claim that each historian has made, the evidence that they used, and the differences between them. Finally the student is asked to provide his or her own explanation of the topic.

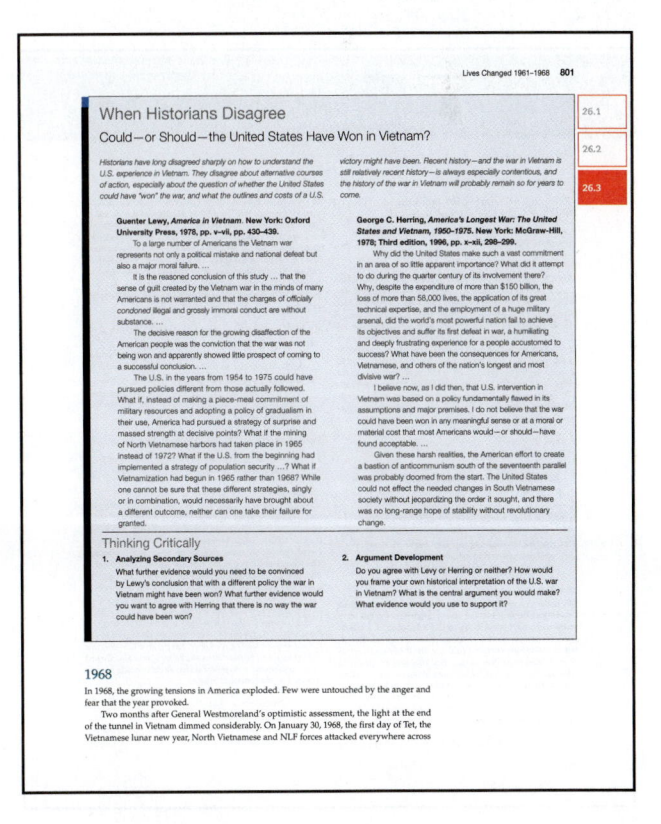

American Voices

Primary source document excerpts bring history alive by introducing students to the words, thoughts, and ideas of people who lived and experienced the events of the time. Each document includes a brief head note and critical analysis questions to help students put the sources in their historical context.

Thinking Historically

This feature continues the emphasis of providing ample opportunity for the practice of historical thinking skills. These brief document excerpts relate the themes of the new AP U.S. History Course Framework to content within the chapter. The feature includes questions that connect to the skills.

Chapter Summary and Review

An extensive set of review questions based on the chapter learning objectives, key concepts and themes from the AP U.S. History Course Framework, and writing about history continue the focus of the pedagogical program in the text on critical thinking and writing skills.

AP Practice Tests

Each of the nine parts of the text conclude with a full AP Practice Test. Using primary source documents, images, and cartoons, the tests include multiple-choice questions, short essays, and long essays to mirror the AP exam. The content of each Practice Test focuses on the content within the part, giving students a broad introduction to the test and the chance to review the content in the context of an AP exam. A full Document-Based Question is available on the Pearson MyHistoryLab website to complete the Practice Test for each part.

Exceptional Art and Illustration Program

A full complement of maps, photographs, and illustrations support the discussions within the text and provide geographic context as well as many iconic images of the past.

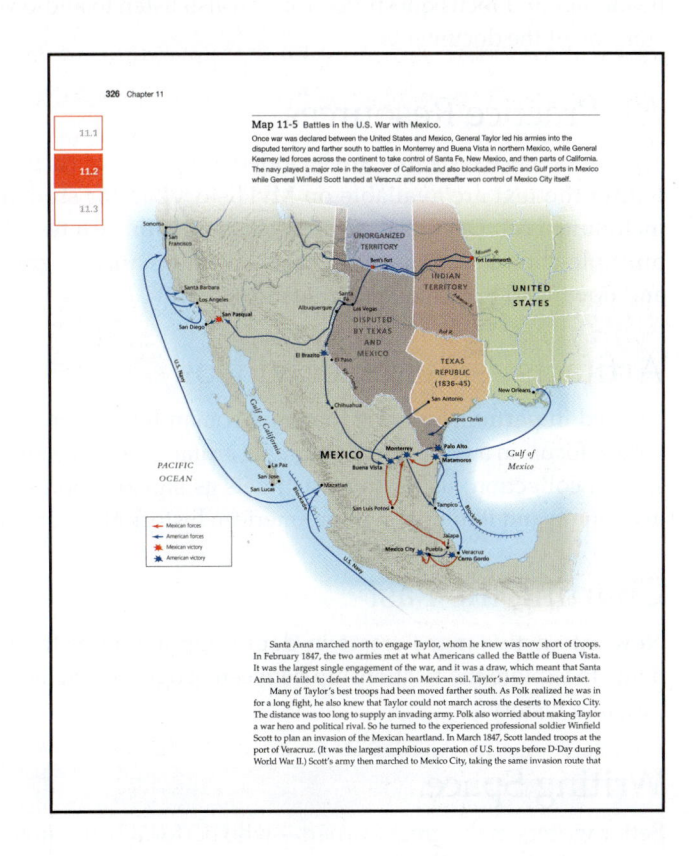

Teaching and Learning Materials

MyHistoryLab™

A fully integrated learning program, MyHistoryLab for *By the People* helps students better prepare for class, quizzes, and exams—resulting in more dynamic experiences in the classroom and improved performance in the course. The immersive Pearson eText—with videos and interactive activities just a click away—engages students in their study of history, and fosters learning within and beyond the classroom.

Pearson eText with Audio

Contained within MyHistoryLab, the Pearson eText enables students to access their textbook online—through laptops, iPads, and tablets. Download the free Pearson eText app to use on tablets. Students may also listen to their text with the Audio eText.

MyHistoryLibrary

The new MyHistoryLibrary contains more than 700 of the most commonly assigned *primary source documents*, complete with headnotes and focus questions. You can also listen to audio versions of all the documents.

AP Practice Resources

The AP practice tests that are included at the end of each part within the text are available on MyHistoryLab for students, including a full Document-Based Question with each test. The multiple-choice sections of the tests are automatically graded and download to the student gradebook.

Artifacts as Evidence Videos

Created in partnership with the Smithsonian Institution, these videos focus on a wide range of unique artifacts from the Smithsonian collection, using these artifacts as starting points for explaining and illuminating the American historical experience.

Charting the Past

New interactive maps create in-depth opportunities for students to explore the relationship between geography, demography, and history.

Writing Space

Better writers make great learners—who perform better in their courses. To help students develop and assess concept mastery and critical thinking through writing, we created the Writing Space in MyHistoryLab. It's a single place to create, track, and grade writing assignments, provide writing resources, and exchange meaningful, personalized feedback with students quickly and easily. Plus, Writing Space includes integrated access to Turnitin, the global leader in plagiarism prevention.

Preview and Adoption Access

Upon textbook purchase, students and teachers are granted access to MyHistoryLab with Pearson eText. High school teachers can obtain preview or adoption access for MyHistoryLab in one of the following ways:

Preview Access

- Teachers can request preview access online by visiting www.PearsonSchool.com/Access_Request. Select Social Studies, choose Initial Access, and complete the form under Option 2. Preview Access information will be sent to the teacher via e-mail.

Adoption Access

- With the purchase of this program, a Pearson Adoption Access Card with Instructor Manual will be delivered with your textbook purchase. (ISBN: 978-0-13-354087-1)
- Ask your sales representative for a Pearson Adoption Access Card with Instructor Manual. (ISBN: 978-0-13-354087-1)

OR

- Visit PearsonSchool.com/Access_Request, select Social Studies, choose Initial Access, and complete the form under Option 3—MyLab/Mastering Class Adoption Access. Teacher and Student access information will be sent to the teacher via e-mail.

Students, ask your teacher for access.

Pearson reserves the right to change and/or update technology platforms, including possible edition updates to customers during the term of access. This will allow Pearson to continue to deliver the most up-to-date content and technology to customers. Customer will be notified of any change prior to the beginning of the new school year.

For Teachers

New! Annotated Teacher's Edition

A new comprehensive Teacher's Edition with detailed annotations authored by Stacie Brensilver. Annotations appear in the text next to the topic under discussion. There are three forms of annotations for the teacher: teaching the History Disciplinary Practices (three types) and History Reasoning Skills (four types); Classroom Activities (usually three per chapter); and A Deeper Look (websites and questions for more detailed study). In addition, Key Concepts and Subtopics, along with the associated Thematic Learning Objectives, appear in each chapter at the appropriate point.

Instructor's Resource Manual

The Instructor's Resource Manual for *By the People*, contains key concepts, learning objectives from the text, chapter outlines and summaries that cover each section in the text, additional discussion questions, suggested activities, videos for flipped classes, suggested readings, and a quick review and chapter review answer key. This resource is a downloadable for teachers within MyLab History.

AP® Exam Style Test Bank

A new AP Exam Style Test Bank is a downloadable resource for teachers within MyLab History. Questions in this Test Bank are formatted to mirror the AP Exam, containing an abundance of document- and image-based multiple-choice questions correlated to each chapter and part in the textbook, Short- and long-answer questions are also included at the end of each part. Answers are tagged according to topic, AP concept, and Learning Objective, with page numbers provided for easy reference.

PowerPoint™ Presentations

Strong PowerPoint presentations make lectures more engaging for students. Correlated to the chapters of your Pearson textbook, each presentation includes a lecture outline and images and maps from the textbook. This resource is a downloadable for teachers within MyLab History.

Test Generator

This easy-to-use test generation software program provides the multiple-choice and essay questions from the printed test item file and allows users to add, delete, and print tests.

For Students

The following supplements are available for purchase.

Pearson Test Prep Series: AP® U.S. History

Completely revised and updated by Stacie Brensilver of New York Univeristy, this Test Prep Workbook for AP® United States History, includes a review of the content of the course, along with Multiple Choice, Short Answer, and Long Essay Questions (with answers and explanations) for all 30 chapters of By the People, updated with the June 2017 changes to the AP® U.S. Course. Also included are 12 Document Based Questions, with suggested answers. In this second edition there two complete practice tests with answers and explanations and a new introduction to strategies for taking the exam.

Reading and Note Taking Study Guide

This supplement by John Reisbord provides a chapter-by-chapter guide to help students read their textbook effectively, using various critical reading skills and strategies for an organized approach to reading and studying.

DBQ Workbook

For additional practice, this workbook by Ted Dickson and Michael Linquist of Providence Day School provides document-based and free-response questions for students to use to strengthen critical-thinking and essay-writing skills.

New! Historical Practices, Skills, and Course Themes Workbook for AP® United States History

This new workbook by Ted Dickson of Providence Day School, Charlotte, NC introduces students to the practices, skills, and course themes that they will need for the course and the exam. Organized according to the 9 periods of the course, each chapter has an introduction to the period, 6-8 individual activities, and a set of practice questions in AP® format. This is the practical, affordable, focused help students need to learn historical thinking and writing and to prepare for the exam.

Acknowledgments

It is with a great deal of gratitude that I thank the many reviewers whose insightful comments and suggestions have helped shape this text during its development:

Lee Annis, Montgomery College; Joyce Baird, Dripping Springs High School; Stacie Brensilver, New York University; Gwendolyn Cash, Clear Creek High School; Peggy Cashion, The Woodlands High School; Catherine Cluck, Westlake High School; Matt Cone, Plano Senior High School; Kevin Conforti, Lexington Christian Academy; Thomas Conway, Westlake High School; Lorraine Dumerer, R.L. Turner High School; Zach Dziedzic, Loyola Blakefield; John Eckerson, Milton High School; Susan Elliot, Viewpoint School; Greg Feldmeth, Polytechnic School; Rebeca Kelley, Washington High School; Kurt Knierim, Rocky Mountain High School; Sue Ikenberry, Georgetown Day School; Christopher Lee, Zephyrhills High School; Stephen Ludlam, John A. Rowlands High School; Pamela Marquez; Sue Masty, North Penn High School; Dr. Louisa Bond Moffitt, Marist School; Sara Romeyn, Bullis High School; Penny Rosas, Mayde Creek High School; Rick Rosenberg, Main South High School; Margaret Sargent, Great Valley School District; James L. Smith, Arrowhead Park Early College High School; Jennifer Snoddy, George Walton Comprehensive High School; Matt Tassinari, Palmdale High School; Kevin Varano, Sci Tech High School; Dan Wagenberg, Brien McMahon High School; Cherry Whipple, S.F. Austin High School; Samuel Wilson, Southwest High School.

I also wish to thank the following people for their invaluable assistance with the AP practice tests and chapter review material: Zach Dziedzic (Practice Tests 2, 3, 4, and 5), Laura Gordon (Practice Test 7), Sue Ikenberry (Practice Test 9), Karen Johnson (Practice Test 8), Cherry Whipple (Practice Tests 1 and 6), Stacie Brensilver Berman (Quick Reviews), and John Reisbord (Chapter summaries and reviews) and especially Rod Franchi for an extraordinary effort to review, revise, and update all the Practice Tests to fit with the latest College Board standards.

By the People has been a long time in the making. It began when Lesley Henderson of Lawrence King Publishers showed up in my office at Northeastern University and asked me to think about writing such a book. Since that time, many people have contributed to the making of this book. My NYU colleagues Diana Turk and Stacie Brensilver Berman have been a never-ending source of ideas, critique, and encouragement; Alexandra Wood then a doctoral candidate and now a member of the faculty offered research help, and my former colleague William Fowler offered advice at crucial moments as has Amy Karwoski, a more recent NYU graduate student. My NYU graduate students in Social Studies Curriculum: U.S. History read and critiqued the manuscript and have contributed more than they will ever know. The staff of the College Board have been generous with their time in explaining the many changes in the AP standards over recent years. I also want to thank the many AP teachers and the staff of the College Board who have attended my annual sessions at the summer AP teacher conferences or other AP workshops have shared critical ideas all along the way. Warren Goldstein of the University of Hartford and Ted Dickson of Providence Day School have shared many ideas along the way. My superb editor for the first edition, Charlyce Jones-Owen has supported—and challenged—me every step of the way. Other editors and marketers including especially Caroline Grauman-Boss, the late Gerald Lombardi, Ed Parsons, Joanne Dauksewicz, Jean Woy, Stacie Brensilver Berman, and Rod Franchi have been a terrific team for the second edition. It has been my good fortune to work with the extraordinary Mary Gawlik who reviewed and edited every word of both editions. Elaine Shema, Michele Gillis, and Cheryl Keenan at Pearson have shaped this manuscript in essential ways and made it much better for their efforts. And my wonderful family—my wife Katherine Hanson and our children and grandchildren—have been a never-ending source of support whether it is Katherine's reminder that "writing this book is what you have always wanted to do" or another generation wondering if Grandpa ever got up from his desk.

James W. Fraser
New York University

About the Author

James W. Fraser is Professor of History and Education and Chair of the Department of Applied Statistics, Social Science, and Humanities at the Steinhardt School of Culture, Education, and Human Development at New York University. His teaching includes a survey course in U.S. History for future Social Studies teachers and courses in the History of American Education, Religion & Public Education, and Global Culture Wars. He holds a PhD from Columbia University. Dr. Fraser was the 2013–2014 President of the History of Education Society and is a former member of the Editorial Board of the *History of Education Quarterly*. He served as Senior Vice President for Programs at the Woodrow Wilson National Fellowship Foundation in Princeton, New Jersey from 2008 to 2012. He has also served as NYU liaison to the New Design High School, a public high school in New York's Lower East Side, and to Facing History and Ourselves.

Before coming to New York University Dr. Fraser taught in the Department of History and the School of Education at Northeastern University in Boston where he was the founding dean of Northeastern's School of Education. He was also a member and chair of the Commonwealth of Massachusetts Education Deans Council, the Boston School Committee Nominating Committee, and other boards. He was a lecturer in the Program in Religion and Secondary Education at the Harvard University Divinity School from 1997 to 2004. He has taught at Lesley University; University of Massachusetts, Boston; Boston University; and Public School 76 Manhattan. He is an ordained minister in the United Church of Christ and was pastor of Grace Church in East Boston, Massachusetts, from 1986 to 2006.

In addition to *By the People*, Dr. Fraser is the author or editor of twelve books including *Between Church and State: Religion and Public Education in a Multicultural America* (second edition, 2016); *The School in the United States: A Documentary History* (third edition, 2014), *Preparing America's Teachers: A History* (2007), and *A History of Hope: When Americans Have Dared to Dream of a Better Future* (2002). He lives in New York City with his wife Katherine Hanson and their dog, Pebble.

Correlation of By *the People* to the AP U.S. History Course and Exam Description

Upon publication, this text was correlated to the most current College Board's U.S. History Course Framework. We continually monitor the College Board's AP Course and Exam Descriptions for updates. For the most current correlation for this textbook, visit PearsonSchool.com/AdvancedCorrelations.

AP U.S. HISTORY CURRICULUM		Chapter and Page References
Period 1 **1491–1607**	**On a North American continent controlled by American Indians, contact among the peoples of Europe, the Americas, and West Africa created a new world.**	**Chapters 1, 2, 3, 4**
Key Concept 1.1	As native populations migrated and settled across the vast expanse of North America over time, they developed distinct and increasingly complex societies by adapting to and transforming their diverse environments.	Chapter 1
	I. Different native societies adapted to and transformed their environments through innovations in agriculture, resource use, and social structure.	pp. 3–17
Key Concept 1.2	Contact among Europeans, Native Americans, and Africans resulted in the Columbian Exchange and significant social, cultural, and political changes on both sides of the Atlantic Ocean.	Chapters 1, 2
	I. European expansion into the Western Hemisphere generated intense social, religious, political, and economic competition and changes within European societies.	pp. 17 21, 31 34, 41–43
	II. The Columbian Exchange and development of the Spanish Empire in the Western Hemisphere resulted in extensive demographic, economic, and social changes.	pp. 31–41, 43–51
	III. In their interactions, Europeans and Native Americans asserted divergent worldviews regarding issues such as religion, gender roles, family, land use, and power.	pp. 34–41, 43–54
Period 2 **1607–1754**	**Europeans and American Indians maneuvered and fought for dominance, control, and security in North America, and distinctive colonial and native societies emerged.**	**Chapters 2, 3, 4**
Key Concept 2.1	Europeans developed a variety of colonization and migration patterns, influenced by different imperial goals, cultures, and the varied North American environments where they settled, and they competed with each other and American Indians for resources.	Chapters 2, 3, 4
	I. Spanish, French, Dutch, and British colonizers had different economic and imperial goals involving land and labor that shaped the social and political development of their colonies as well as their relationships with native populations.	pp. 31–41, 43–54, 82–89
	II. In the 17th century, early British colonies developed along the Atlantic coast, with regional differences that reflected various environmental, economic, cultural, and demographic factors.	pp. 63–82, 94, 96–120
	III. Competition over resources between European rivals and American Indians encouraged industry and trade and led to conflict in the Americas.	pp. 78–88
Key Concept 2.2	The British colonies participated in political, social, cultural, and economic exchanges with Great Britain that encouraged both stronger bonds with Britain and resistance to Britain's control.	pp. 94–120
	I. Transatlantic commercial, religious, philosophical, and political exchanges led residents of the British colonies to evolve in their political and cultural attitudes as they became increasingly tied to Britain and one another.	pp. 94–120
	II. Like other European empires in the Americas that participated in the Atlantic slave trade, the English colonies developed a system of slavery that reflected the specific economic, demographic, and geographic characteristics of those colonies.	pp. 97–104
Period 3 **1754–1800**	**British imperial attempts to reassert control over its colonies and the colonial reaction to these attempts produced a new American republic, along with struggles over the new nation's social, political, and economic identity.**	**Chapters 4, 5, 6, 7**
Key Concept 3.1	British attempts to assert tighter control over its North American colonies and the colonial resolve to pursue self-government led to a colonial independence movement and the Revolutionary War.	Chapters 4, 5
	I. The competition among the British, French, and American Indians for economic and political advantage in North America culminated in the Seven Years' War (the French and Indian War), in which Britain defeated France and allied American Indians.	pp. 129–135
	II. The desire of many colonists to assert ideals of self-government in the face of renewed British imperial efforts led to a colonial independence movement and war with Britain.	pp. 135–156

Key Concept 3.2	The American Revolution's democratic and republican ideals inspired new experiments with different forms of government.	Chapters 4, 5
	I. The ideals that inspired the revolutionary cause reflected new beliefs about politics, religion, and society that had been developing over the course of the 18th century.	pp. 95–96, 135–145, 161–175
	II. After declaring independence, American political leaders created new constitutions and declarations of rights that articulated the role of the state and federal governments while protecting individual liberties and limiting both centralized power and excessive popular influence.	pp. 161–162
	III. New forms of national culture and political institutions developed in the United States alongside continued regional variations and differences over economic, political, social, and foreign policy issues.	pp. 165–167, 176–185, 189–112
Key Concept 3.3	Migration within North America and competition over resources, boundaries, and trade intensified conflicts among peoples and nations.	Chapters 6, 7
	I. In the decades after American independence, interactions among different groups resulted in competition for resources, shifting alliances, and cultural blending.	pp. 165–167, 198–200
	II. The continued presence of European powers in North America challenged the United States to find ways to safeguard its borders, maintain neutral trading rights, and promote its economic interests.	pp. 202–209
Period 4 **1800–1848**	**The new republic struggled to define and extend democratic ideals in the face of rapid economic, territorial, and demographic changes.**	**Chapters 8, 9, 10, 11, 12**
Key Concept 4.1	The United States began to develop a modern democracy and celebrated a new national culture, while Americans sought to define the nation's democratic ideals and change their society and institutions to match them.	Chapters 8, 10, 11
	I. The nation's transition to a more participatory democracy was achieved by expanding suffrage from a system based on property ownership to one based on voting by all adult white men, and it was accompanied by the growth of political parties.	pp. 221–225, 268–277, 281–294
	II. While Americans embraced a new national culture, various groups developed distinctive cultures of their own.	pp. 226–230, 295–297
	III. Increasing numbers of Americans, many inspired by new religious and intellectual movements, worked primarily outside of government institutions to advance their ideals.	pp. 226–230, 297–304
Key Concept 4.2	Innovations in technology, agriculture, and commerce powerfully accelerated the American economy, precipitating profound changes to U.S. society and to national and regional identities.	Chapters 9, 12
	I. New transportation systems and technologies dramatically expanded manufacturing and agricultural production.	pp. 250–254, 258–268
	II. The changes caused by the market revolution had significant effects on U.S. society, workers' lives, and gender and family relations.	pp. 254–258, 300–304
	III. Economic development shaped settlement and trade patterns, helping to unify the nation while also encouraging the growth of different regions.	pp. 343–344, 346–349, 258–261, 266–268, 275–277
Key Concept 4.3	The U.S. interest in increasing foreign trade and expanding its national borders shaped the nation's foreign policy and spurred government and private initiatives	Chapters 8, 9, 11, 12
	I. Struggling to create an independent global presence, the United States sought to claim territory throughout the North American continent and promote foreign trade.	pp. 231–246, 283–288
	II. The United States' acquisition of lands in the West gave rise to contests over the extension of slavery into new territories.	pp. 351–362, 269–272
Period 5 **1844–1877**	**As the nation expanded and its population grew, regional tensions, especially over slavery, led to a civil war—the course and aftermath of which transformed American society.**	**Chapters 11, 12, 13, 14, 15, 16**
Key Concept 5.1	The United States became more connected with the world, pursued an expansionist foreign policy in the Western Hemisphere, and emerged as the destination for many migrants from other countries.	Chapters 9, 10, 11, 12, 16
	I. Popular enthusiasm for U.S. expansion, bolstered by economic and security interests, resulted in the acquisition of new territories, substantial migration westward, and new overseas initiatives.	pp. 299–300, 308–335, 468–483
	II. In the 1840s and 1850s, Americans continued to debate questions about rights and citizenship for various groups of U.S. inhabitants.	pp. 343–350
Key Concept 5.2	Intensified by expansion and deepening regional divisions, debates over slavery and other economic, cultural, and political issues led the nation into civil war.	Chapters 9, 11, 12, 13
	I. Ideological and economic differences over slavery produced an array of diverging responses from Americans in the North and the South.	pp. 254–258, 330, 351–362
	II. Debates over slavery came to dominate political discussion in the 1850s, culminating in the bitter election of 1860 and the secession of Southern states.	pp. 370–394
Key Concept 5.3	The Union victory in the Civil War and the contested reconstruction of the South settled the issues of slavery and secession, but left unresolved many questions about the power of the federal government and citizenship rights	Chapters 14, 15
	I. The North's greater manpower and industrial resources, the leadership of Abraham Lincoln and others, and the decision to emancipate slaves eventually led to the Union military victory over the Confederacy in the devastating Civil War.	pp. 399–426
	II. Reconstruction and the Civil War ended slavery, altered relationships between the states and the federal government, and led to debates over new definitions of citizenship, particularly regarding the rights of African Americans, women, and other minorities.	pp. 431–453

Period 6 **1865–1898**	**The transformation of the United States from an agricultural to an increasingly industrialized and urbanized society brought about significant economic, political, diplomatic, social, environmental, and cultural changes.**	**Chapters 16, 17, 18, 19**
Key Concept 6.1	**Technological advances, large-scale production methods, and the opening of new markets encouraged the rise of industrial capitalism in the United States.**	**Chapters 17, 18**
	I. Large-scale industrial production — accompanied by massive technological change, expanding international communication networks, and pro- growth government policies — generated rapid economic development and business consolidation.	pp. 490–504, 507–508
	II. A variety of perspectives on the economy and labor developed during a time of financial panics and downturns.	pp. 513–516, 521–522, 535–545
	III. New systems of production and transportation enabled consolidation within agriculture, which, along with periods of instability, spurred a variety of responses from farmers.	pp. 529–535
Key Concept 6.2	**The migrations that accompanied industrialization transformed both urban and rural areas of the United States and caused dramatic social and cultural change.**	**Chapters 16, 17, 19**
	I. International and internal migration increased urban populations and fostered the growth of a new urban culture.	pp. 501–504, 509–516, 553–561
	II. Larger numbers of migrants moved to the West in search of land and economic opportunity, frequently provoking competition and violent conflict.	pp. 461–486
Key Concept 6.3	**The Gilded Age produced new cultural and intellectual movements, public reform efforts, and political debates over economic and social policies.**	**Chapters 16, 17**
	I. New cultural and intellectual movements both buttressed and challenged the social order of the Gilded Age.	pp. 499–501, 504–505, 521, 550–552, 559, 563–564
	II. Dramatic social changes in the period inspired political debates over citizenship, corruption, and the proper relationship between business and government.	pp. 505–507, 524–528, 559–565
Period 7 **1890–1945**	**An increasingly pluralistic United States faced profound domestic and global challenges, debated the proper degree of government activism, and sought to define its international role.**	**Chapters 19, 20, 21, 22, 23, 24**
Key Concept 7.1	**Growth expanded opportunity, while economic instability led to new efforts to reform U.S. society and its economic system.**	**Chapters 19, 21, 22**
	I. The United States continued its transition from a rural, agricultural economy to an urban, industrial economy led by large companies.	pp. 625–631, 626–627
	II. In the Progressive Era of the early 20th century, Progressives responded to political corruption, economic instability, and social concerns by calling for greater government action and other political and social measures.	pp. 552–553, 565–576, 620–624, 647–649
	III. During the 1930s, policymakers responded to the mass unemployment and social upheavals of the Great Depression by transforming the U.S. into a limited welfare state, redefining the goals and ideas of modern American liberalism.	pp. 650–666
Key Concept 7.2	**Innovations in communications and technology contributed to the growth of mass culture, while significant changes occurred in internal and international**	**Chapters 20, 21, 24**
	I. Popular culture grew in influence in U.S. society, even as debates increased over the effects of culture on public values, morals, and American national identity.	pp. 603–604, 606, 617–620, 625–636, 638–639, 722
	II. Economic pressures, global events, and political developments caused sharp variations in the numbers, sources, and experiences of both international and internal migrants.	pp. 628–631, 634–636, 719–722
Key Concept 7.3	**Participation in a series of global conflicts propelled the United States into a position of international power while renewing domestic debates over the nation's proper role in the world.**	**Chapters 20, 21, 22, 23**
	I. In the late 19th century and early 20th century, new U.S. territorial ambitions and acquisitions in the Western Hemisphere and the Pacific accompanied heightened public debates over America's role in the world.	pp. 585–597
	II. World War I and its aftermath intensified ongoing debates about the nation's role in the world and how best to achieve national security and pursue American interests.	pp. 598–612, 640–642, 666–671, 676–680
	III. U.S. participation in World War II transformed American society, while the victory of the United States and its allies over the Axis powers vaulted the U.S. into a position of global, political, and military leadership.	pp. 678–703
Period 8 **1945–1980**	**After World War II, the United States grappled with prosperity and unfamiliar international responsibilities, while struggling to live up to its ideals.**	**Chapters 24, 25, 26, 27**
Key Concept 8.1	**The United States responded to an uncertain and unstable postwar world by asserting and working to maintain a position of global leadership, with far-reaching domestic and international consequences.**	**Chapters 24, 25, 26, 27**
	I. United States policymakers engaged in a Cold War with the authoritarian Soviet Union, seeking to limit the growth of Communist military power and ideological influence, create a free-market global economy, and build an international security system.	pp. 722–730, 734–737, 745–752, 795–802, 811—815, 828–830
	II. Cold War policies led to public debates over the power of the federal government and acceptable means for pursuing international and domestic goals while protecting civil liberties.	pp. 731–734, 745–750, 798–800, 812–813, 830–834
Key Concept 8.2	**New movements for civil rights and liberal efforts to expand the role of government generated a range of political and cultural responses.**	**Chapters 24, 25, 26, 27**
	I. Seeking to fulfill Reconstruction-era promises, civil rights activists and political leaders achieved some legal and political successes in ending segregation, although progress toward racial equality was slow.	pp. 762–773, 792–794, 802–803

	II. Responding to social conditions and the African American civil rights movement, a variety of movements emerged that focused on issues of identity, social justice, and the environment.	pp. 778–780, 815–820, 830–31
	III. Liberalism influenced postwar politics and court decisions, but it came under increasing attack from the left as well as from a resurgent conservative movement.	pp. 737–739, 752–753, 778–795, 803–805, 809–811, 823–834
Key Concept 8.3	**Postwar economic and demographic changes had far-reaching consequences for American society, politics, and culture.**	**Chapters 24, 25, 27**
	I. Rapid economic and social changes in American society fostered a sense of optimism in the postwar years.	pp. 713–719, 793, 824–826
	II. New demographic and social developments, along with anxieties over the Cold War, changed U.S. culture and led to significant political and moral debates that sharply divided the nation.	pp. 753–762, 822–823
Period 9 1980-Present	**As the United States transitioned to a new century filled with challenges and possibilities, it experienced renewed ideological and cultural debates, sought to redefine its foreign policy, and adapted to economic globalization and revolutionary changes in science and technology.**	**Chapters 28, 29, 30**
Key Concept 9.1	**A newly ascendant conservative movement achieved several political and policy goals during the 1980s and continued to strongly influence public discourse in the following decades**	**Chapters 28, 29, 30**
	I. Conservative beliefs regarding the need for traditional social values and a reduced role for government advanced in U.S. politics after 1980.	pp. 843–848, 858–861, 879–883, 898–899, 914–932
Key Concept 9.2:	**Moving into the 21st century, the nation experienced significant technological, economic, and demographic changes.**	**Chapters 28, 29, 30**
	I. New developments in science and technology enhanced the economy and transformed society, while manufacturing decreased.	pp. 861–863, 877 , 889–896, 924–926
	II. The U.S. population continued to undergo demographic shifts that had significant cultural and political consequences.	pp. 863–869, 878, 883—884, 921, 923–932
Key Concept 9.3	**The end of the Cold War and new challenges to U.S. leadership forced the nation to redefine its foreign policy and role in the world.**	**Chapters 28, 29, 30**
	I. The Reagan administration promoted an interventionist foreign policy that continued in later administrations, even after the end of the Cold War.	pp. 848–857, 873–877, 884–887
	II. Following the attacks of September 11, 2001, U.S. foreign policy efforts focused on fighting terrorism around the world.	pp. 904–924

Part 1

Contact and Exploration 1491–1607

AP® KEY CONCEPTS

Key Concept 1.1

As native populations migrated and settled across the vast expanses of North America over time, they developed distinct and increasingly complex societies by adapting to and transforming their diverse environments.

Key Concept 1.2

Contact among Europeans, Native Americans, and Africans resulted in the Columbian Exchange and significant social, cultural, and political changes on both sides of the Atlantic Ocean.

PART OUTLINE

Chapter 1
The World before 1492

Jacques Le Moyne, an early French explorer, recorded Native American women cultivating crops. Within the cultures of most North American tribes, women were the prime cultivators of crops, while men were hunters.

Snark/Art Resource, NY

Chapter Objective

Demonstrate an understanding of the migrations, daily life, and changing cultures among the diverse groups of the first North Americans and explain the independent developments of cultures among Native Americans, Europeans, and Africans before the encounters of 1492.

Learning Objectives

The Peopling of North America

1.1 Describe what the archaeological record tells about the arrival, development, and cultures of the first peoples of North America.

The Diverse Communities of the Americas in the 1400s

1.2 Describe the diversity of American Indian cultures in the United States on the eve of their encounter with Europeans.

A Changing Europe in the 1400s

1.3 Describe the changes in Europe that led to Columbus's voyages and that shaped European attitudes when encountering the peoples of the Americas.

Africa in the 1400s

1.4 Describe the political, cultural, and religious developments in Africa that would shape contact between Europeans and Africans in the Americas.

Asia in the 1400s

1.5 Contrast developments in Asia with those in Europe at the time when Europeans first reached the Americas.

The Navajo people, or Dine as they prefer to be called, tell a story of their coming into this world. The story begins in a world of darkness (Nihodilhil):

> Because of the strife in the First World, First Man (Atse Hastin), First Woman (Atse Estsan), and the Coyote called First Angry, followed by all the others, climbed up from the World of Darkness and Dampness to the Second or Blue World.

From this dark or black world, the people emerged through the blue and yellow worlds before finally making their way to the bright white world where they live today:

> Soon, First Man and First Woman began to make things the way they were supposed to be. The Holy People helped them. Their first job was to rebuild the mountains. … Then, the people made a fire. To start it, they used flint. … First Man and First Woman wanted a hogan. … Talking God helped to build the first hogan. … This was the place where the people lived and worked.
>
> By now First Man and First Woman had become human. They were like us.
>
> After this, there were four seasons. In the spring, the plants came up from the ground. In the winter, the plants died and were hidden under the snow. Then in the spring, they came up again. The plants grew into crops such as corn, beans, and squash.

> Source: There are many versions of the Navajo creation story. This account was provided by Harry Benally, a Navajo carver and silversmith from Sheep Springs, New Mexico, and Harold Carey, a Navajo historian from Malad City, Idaho. http://navajopeople.org/blog/navajo-creation-story-nihalgai-the-glittering-or-white-world/ downloaded February 14, 2013.

Other North American tribes had their own stories of how their people emerged onto the earth from a region below, or arrived through the water, or came down from the clouds. All believed that some ancient pilgrimage had brought them to the place where their tribe resided and would, with divine favor, reside forever.

In many cases, creation stories help people understand the meaning and purpose of their lives and the ordering of their world. Thus, in a version of the Cherokee creation story, among the first inhabitants of the world were a man, Kana'ti, who provided meat, and his wife, Selu, who ensured the family had corn and beans. Not surprisingly, later Cherokee society reflected a similar division of labor, and social life, based on gender in which men

North Wind Picture Archives / Alamy Stock Photo

Navajo art regularly portrayed the many different gods that in Navajo tradition accompanied human beings in their emergence into the world. The Navajo believed that these gods could help, hinder, or occasionally play tricks on people in their daily lives.

Significant Dates

Approx. 30,000 years ago	Earliest signs of settlement in western Alaska and California; Stone Age carvings dating to this era have been found in France and North Africa
711–732	North African Muslims conquer most of Spain; though slowly pushed back by Christian kingdoms, they maintain control of parts of southern Spain until 1492
c. 750	Mound-building cultures expand in the Mississippi River Valley
c. 800	Beginning of caravan trade across the Sahara between sub-Saharan Africa and Mediterranean world that would continue well past 1900
800	Charlemagne is crowned emperor in Europe; beginning of generally unsuccessful efforts to unite Christian Europe's many independent units
850–1100s	Rise and decline of the Anasazi in Chaco Canyon; founding of Acoma Pueblo
950–1400	Rise and decline of Cahokia
1101	Norse colony of Vineland is established in North America
1142	Possible date for the founding of the Iroquois Confederacy
1324	Pilgrimage of Mansa Musa, emperor of Mali, to Mecca
1325	Rise of Aztec Empire Founding of Tenochtitlán (Mexico City)
1348–1350s	Bubonic plague begins in Europe
1415	Portuguese begin exploration of the Atlantic coast of Africa
1421–1423	Chinese explore the Indian Ocean and East Africa
1453	Ottoman Turks capture Constantinople End of the Hundred Years' War between France and England
1458	Songhay Empire captures Timbuktu
1469	Marriage of Isabella of Castile and Ferdinand of Aragon

(continued)

were often away hunting, while women managed the farming of corn, beans, squash, pumpkins, sunflowers, watermelons, potatoes, and peas without consulting with men, who knew little of their business.

Modern anthropologists tend to trace the path of early human immigration from Asia either on foot across what was sometimes dry land between what is now Russian Siberia and Alaska or by small boats that hugged the coast of the two continents beginning some 25,000 or even 35,000 years ago. Hunters from Siberia may have followed their animal prey across solid land and then fanned out across the Americas. Seafaring travelers might have followed the fish from Alaska down the coast of North and South America. Perhaps both forms of migration took place. From the early migrations, human communities spread across much of North and South America. Recent discoveries point to successful human hunts for mastodons in Florida some 14,500 years ago.

While the ancestors of modern American Indians were building their communities, establishing their culture, and engaging in extended trade with other Native Americans, other humans in other parts of the world were developing their own often quite different cultures. Carvings found in southern France and North Africa date from the same period as the earliest settlements of the Americas. Although contact between the rest of the world and the Americas was at best minimal, the people who lived in Africa, Asia, and Europe maintained trade and contact with one another over thousands of years, even as they developed their own languages as well as agricultural and social systems. The arrival of Europeans in the Americas after 1492 led to dramatic transformations of the cultures of all of these places. Peoples who had developed very different cultural norms as well as different ways of viewing the world suddenly came into contact with one another. Understanding the independent development of people and cultures on both sides of the Atlantic is essential to understanding how contact between them would significantly change them all.

The Peopling of North America

1.1   **Describe what the archaeological record tells about the arrival, development, and cultures of the first peoples of North America.**

While the Navajo told the stories of First Man and First Woman journeying up through various worlds to finally emerge in the place where they now lived and the Cherokee told of the division of labor between Kana'ti and Selu, other Native Americans had their own creation stories. To the residents of the Jemez Pueblo in northern New Mexico, Fotease (chief of the war society) planned a journey to come to this world to test the people's power, and when they arrived at the site of their pueblo, they knew they had found the right place, saying, "This will be the place for us forever; from here we are not going to move the pueblo to any other place." For the Shasta of what is now the Northwest United States, their world began when Old Man Above bored a hole through the sky and came down to Earth to plant the first trees and to create birds and fish and all the animals, including the grizzly bear, and then continued to live in his tepee, Mount Shasta. In the Zuni story, the sun was lonely, so he sent for the people who lived below the ground and invited them to come out and live in the sunlight and gave them corn. Indeed, the gift of corn—a staple food for many native peoples throughout the Americas—is one of the consistent themes in many diverse creation stories.

While storytellers in every tribe keep these creation stories alive, modern anthropologists have their own differing explanations of the way the various tribes arrived in the places where they lived. Anthropologists continue to debate among themselves and with some American Indians about their conclusions. During an ice age, more of the world's water is stored in glaciers. As a result, the oceans are lower; sometimes much lower. Geological evidence indicates that between thirty-six thousand and thirty-two thousand years ago and again between twenty-five thousand and fourteen thousand years ago, substantial dry land existed between the northern tip of Asia in Siberia and North America (see Map 1-1). This land was wide enough for animals, including mammoths and the human hunters who followed them, to

Map 1-1 The Earliest Americans.

There is ongoing debate about just when and how the first Americans migrated from Asia. Some evidence shows that cold periods during which glaciers stored water, thus lowering sea levels, made migration possible over land. Migrants may have walked from Siberia across what is now the Bering Sea into North America and then down through passageways in the glaciers. Perhaps many more migrants may have traveled by small boats down the Pacific coasts of North and South America.

Polar view shows that glaciers blocked movement from Beringia (B) into North America (A) 20,000 years ago. By 14,000 years ago (large map) melting had created an access corridor.

cross. But when the glaciers melted, oceans rose, and what anthropologists now refer to as the **Bering Land Bridge** disappeared under what is now the Bering Sea. Any further human migration had to be by boat, which would explain the rapid expansion of human communities from Alaska to the southern tip of South America. Indeed some scientists now posit that most if not all migration from Asia to the Americas was by boat, with the Bering Land Bridge accounting for only a minority of the migrants, if any. Whether by land through what is now Alaska or by boat down the Pacific coast, peoples from Asia arrived and populated many parts of the Americas some fourteen thousand to fifteen thousand years ago.

Bering Land Bridge

The name given to the land that connected Alaska and Siberia thousands of years ago, which is now under the current Bering Sea.

1.1

1.2

1.3

1.4

1.5

Clovis people

The name of early residents of North America whose spear points were found near what is now Clovis, New Mexico, in 1929.

The Land Bridge, Clovis Culture, and Recent Discoveries

Most anthropologists used to believe that the first immigrants to the Americas were the **Clovis people** who might have come to North America around thirteen thousand years ago. The Clovis people took their name from a site near what is now Clovis, New Mexico, where a trove of thirteen-thousand-year-old arrow and spear points was found in 1929. The points, which were fluted so they could be attached to spears, were obvious signs of human activity and were the oldest human artifacts found in the Americas up to that time.

Recent excavations in central Texas, however, found primitive spear tips that are at least 15,500 years old, much older and less sophisticated than those found at Clovis. The mammoth hunters of Florida also predated the Clovis people by a thousand years. Archaeologists have discovered similar evidence at many sites elsewhere in the Americas. Because no Clovis-like spear tips have ever been found in Siberia, most anthropologists now believe that the Clovis spear point was an invention that early Americans developed long after they had lost contact with Asia.

Newer anthropological evidence also suggests that not all of the first peoples of the Americas walked to get there. Other peoples may have crossed the oceans thousands of years before the first Europeans ever set foot in the Western Hemisphere. Whenever and however the first inhabitants of the Americas came, their descendants adapted to their new lands, spread out across the Americas, and created a wide range of languages and civilizations. By fourteen thousand years ago, various peoples were living in every part of North and South America.

Changing Climate and Cultures—Anasazi and Cahokia

Before the arrival of Columbus, the largest and most sophisticated civilizations in the Americas were found in Mexico and South America. Nevertheless, hundreds of years before Columbus crossed the ocean, complex communities could be found in the present-day United States—among the ancient residents of Chaco Canyon in New Mexico, known as the Anasazi, and among the Cahokia people of the Mississippi River Valley.

W.Scott McGill/Fotolia

Spear points found near Clovis, New Mexico. The human workmanship on these points is obvious, and though earlier spear points have now been found, these examples show the development of Native American hunting skill at an early time.

American Voices

The Natchez Tradition, c. 800

Many American Indian tribes moved often to seek better hunting or farming or to escape more belligerent neighbors. The Natchez of Louisiana are related linguistically and culturally to the pyramid builders of Mexico and Guatemala. They tell a story of their movement north to Louisiana that fits with the archaeological evidence of such a movement around the year 800 CE. A Keeper, or priest, of the Natchez told the following story to a Frenchman in Louisiana in the 1700s of the CE.

Before we came to this land we lived yonder under the sun [pointing with his finger nearly southwest, by which I understood that he meant Mexico]; we lived in a fine country where the earth is always pleasant; there our Suns [chiefs] had their abode, and our nation maintained itself for a long time against the ancients of the country, who conquered some of our villages in the plains but never could force us from the mountains. Our nation extended itself along the great water [the Gulf of Mexico] where this large river [the Mississippi] loses itself; but as our enemies were become very numerous, and very wicked, our Suns sent some of their subjects who lived near this river, to examine whether we could retire into the

country through which it flowed. The country on the east side of the river being found extremely pleasant, the Great Sun, upon the return of those who had examined it, ordered all his subjects who lived in the plains, and who still defended themselves against the ancients of the country, to remove into this land, here to build a temple, and to preserve the eternal fire.

Source: From Judith Niles, *Native American History* (New York: Ballantine Books, 1996), p. 43.

Thinking Critically

1. **Causation**

   How does the storyteller explain the migration patterns of his people some nine hundred years earlier? Given what we know of the historical record, how accurate might this explanation be?

2. **Contextualization**

   What light does the story shed on relations between different American Indian peoples before the arrival of Columbus in the Americas?

THE ANASAZI OF THE SOUTHWEST   The **Anasazi**, or "ancient ones," began building communities in New Mexico and Arizona perhaps seven hundred years before the arrival of Columbus. They cultivated crops such as corn (or maize), beans, squash, and chilies that were cultivated for centuries farther south in modern-day Mexico. Long before Columbus, these crops had been brought to the Anasazi and other tribes of what is now the American Southwest either through a slow exchange of information from one small band to another or through a larger migration of Central American farmers into the regions farther north such as in the story of the Natchez people's migration to the Mississippi River Valley (see American Voices, The Natchez Tradition, above). These crops were needed to feed a settled, urbanized community, and the Anasazi and other early peoples used them all. In time, the Anasazi began developing Chaco Canyon in northwest New Mexico as the hub of a widespread trade and ceremonial-religious network. Chaco Canyon was a large city built of logs and adobe (mud bricks) with buildings as high as five stories. It included more than a dozen pueblos (large buildings) in an area measuring eight miles by two miles. Facing the main plaza, with its underground kivas where religious rites were conducted, Pueblo Bonito contained eight

Anasazi

Anasazi, meaning "ancient ones," lived in modern-day New Mexico, Arizona, and Colorado some seven hundred years before Columbus.

Natalia Bratslavsky/Fotolia

hundred rooms and may have housed two thousand people. It was the largest "apartment" building in North America until the construction of new high-rises in New York in the 1880s. Roads from Chaco Canyon allowed trade to develop in many directions. Turquoise and other valuable goods were traded, perhaps as far south as central Mexico.

The Anasazi built housing or palaces into the cliffs to provide protection from the weather and from other tribes who might try to attack.

After a prolonged drought in the early 1100s, the Anasazi abandoned Chaco Canyon. Their descendants created small farming communities across the Southwest. Some built the cliff dwellings that can still be seen at Mesa Verde in southwestern Colorado. While smaller than Chaco Canyon, Mesa Verde includes some two hundred rooms. Built into the side of the canyon wall, the rooms offered protection from enemies, since they could be reached only by ladders. By 1300, the Anasazi, faced with another great drought, abandoned Mesa Verde also and seem to have disappeared from history, though the founders of Acoma Pueblo may have been Anasazi. Acoma, not far from Albuquerque, New Mexico, was established sometime in the 1100s. Still functioning today, it may be the oldest continuously inhabited city in the current United States.

Other peoples, known as the Hohokam, settled on lands farther west near present-day Phoenix, Arizona. While the Hohokam communities existed for hundreds of years, the high point of their civilization is estimated to have been between 1150 and 1450. They developed an extensive agricultural system using canals to irrigate crops that included cotton, tobacco, corn, beans, and squash. But like the Anasazi, they slowly declined. Ruins of Hohokam communities may be seen in Casa Grande, Arizona. Slowly, Hopi, Zuni, Pueblo, and Navajo peoples moved into the older Anasazi and Hohokam territories of New Mexico, Arizona, Utah, and Colorado and built the pueblos and villages that the first Spanish explorers encountered in the 1500s.

CAHOKIA AND THE MISSISSIPPI RIVER VALLEY The Cahokia people of the Mississippi Valley, also known as the **Mound Builders**, created a flourishing culture between 900 and 1350. If one could go back one thousand years and visit Cahokia, the center of this culture, one would find a city surrounded by strong wooden walls with thatch-covered houses that were home to twenty thousand to forty thousand people, near what is now East St. Louis, Illinois. Cahokia was probably the largest settlement in what is now the United States, and one thousand years ago its "Mississippian culture" flourished throughout the Mississippi Valley and beyond. Archaeologists have found similar mound-building communities at Coosa and Etowah, Georgia; Moundville, Alabama; and Natchez, Mississippi.

At the center of Cahokia, a series of wide earth mounds up to one hundred feet high led to the people being called the Mound Builders. These mounds were used to bury the most prominent leaders. Atop the central mound was a temple and a wide plaza used for ceremonies centered on the seasons and the sun. The plaza was located on a perfect north–south axis, and a massive circle of wooden posts functioned as a kind of observatory to trace the sun's path.

Mound Builders

A name given to Native American tribes that built large burial and ceremonial mounds on which religious and sports activities took place.

Cahokia Mounds State Historic Site, painting by William R. Iseminger

This artist's rendition of ancient Cahokia shows the large city on the banks of the Mississippi River.

Priests and chiefs at Cahokia tracked the sun, conducted rituals, and dispensed gifts that displayed their power, while nearby hamlets grew the food that fed the city's inhabitants. Such large, settled communities with differentiated roles and a social hierarchy were possible because complex agricultural practices had replaced the earlier hunting and gathering economy. By about 900, a warming trend in the earth's climate made new forms of agriculture possible. Instead of being limited to what foods they could find or hunt, residents of Cahokia were now able to begin farming. They developed flint hoes which, unlike the digging sticks that had been used in the past, allowed them to not only plant corn but also keep a field free of weeds year after year, expanding yield. Fields filled with rows of corn or beans allowed a larger population to be fed than ever before. Like the Hohokam of the Southwest, they cultivated squash, corn, and beans, which they could grow on a seasonal basis, store as a surplus through the winter, and thereby support an urbanized culture. When eaten together, maize and beans form a complete protein diet, and as a result, the population could be well nourished.

In Cahokia, and in most settled Native American cultures, farming was women's work. Men hunted to add animal protein and flavor to the diet. Together, they produced a rich supply of food, enough to sustain not only themselves but also a much larger community that included many—priests, chiefs, and the workers who built the mounds—who neither farmed nor hunted.

Aztec cultivation of corn before the arrival of the first Europeans.
Ms Palat. 218-220 Book IX An Aztec man planting maize, from the 'Florentine Codex' by Bernardino de Sahagun, c.1540-85, Spanish School, (16th century) / Biblioteca Medicea-Laurenziana, Florence, Italy / Bridgeman Images

1.1   Quick Review

Describe in what ways the Anasazi and Cahokia cultures changed over time and adapted to their environments through innovations in agriculture, resource use, and social structures. What unique features did each culture develop? What did they have in common?

The Diverse Communities of the Americas in the 1400s

1.2   **Describe the diversity of American Indian cultures in the United States on the eve of their encounter with Europeans.**

The native peoples of North America were a remarkably diverse group.* They spoke many different languages, some more different from each other than English is from Chinese. These languages were spread among five hundred to six hundred independent societies with different approaches to hunting and farming, different social structures and gender relationships, varying creation stories, and diverse understandings of the spiritual (see Map 1-2, p. 10). While often seen as a unified ethnic and cultural group by Europeans, native peoples did not see themselves that way. For example, one Ojibwe wrote that his people did not see themselves having anything in common with the Dakotas since they are so different in language and religious beliefs and are mortal enemies.

Nevertheless, Native American tribes also tended to share some things in common. Though their lives have sometimes been romanticized beyond anything they would recognize, it was true that they tended to live comfortably with nature and in harmony with the sacred, which they found in every aspect of life. Most saw time as circular—not a steady line from creation to the present and future, but a reoccurring series of events to be celebrated in rituals that involved the retelling of ancient stories linked to the annual growth of the crops and to animal life. They honored shamans and priests who were considered visionaries and who were expected to have contact with the supernatural and keep the stories alive. These shamans and priests had the special responsibility of helping restore harmony when it was disrupted by disease, war, or climactic changes that brought famine. Most native North Americans saw the community and not the individual as the focus of life and labor. Community members won fame and respect by what they gave away more than by what they kept for themselves. The accumulative spirit of autonomous Europeans, gaining ever more possessions—especially land and the status in European society that came from land ownership—made no sense to most American Indians.

---

*There is considerable debate today about the terms *American Indian* and *Native American*. In fact, most of the descendants of the first peoples of North America prefer to be identified by their specific tribe—Navajo or Mohawk or Cherokee or whatever specific group—when possible. When speaking of larger groups of native peoples, some think that *Native American* is a more respectful term, while many others prefer to be called *American Indian* or *Indian*. In Mexico, most prefer *indigenous*, while many Canadian tribes prefer *first nations*. In keeping with that diversity of preferences, this book uses tribal names when relevant and otherwise uses the terms *American Indian* or *Indian* and *Native American* interchangeably.

Map 1-2 North American Culture Areas, c. 1500.

The lands that would become the United States include significantly different climate zones, and in the 1500s, when many Native American tribes had their first contact with Europeans, these different climates produced significantly different tribal cultures depending on where the people lived.

Although precise measurement is impossible, scholars estimate that approximately 7 million Indians lived in what is now the United States and Canada, although some argue that the number was much higher. In any case, larger numbers of native peoples lived in Mexico and Central and South America. The total native population for all of the Americas was probably 50 to 70 million, perhaps as high as 100 million, when the first Europeans arrived. Europe's population at the time was approximately 70 to 90 million, and Africa's population was 50 to 70 million. If these numbers are correct, then although North America was relatively sparsely populated, the Americas as a whole had as many or more people than either Europe or Africa in 1492. Asia, it is worth noting, had a far larger population, perhaps in the range of 200 to 300 million people (Figure 1-1).

North American Indians also lived in a land of extraordinary physical diversity, from the tundra of Alaska to the forests of New England, from the prairies and grasslands of the Midwest to the lush Pacific Coast and the dry Southwest. In these diverse environments, climatic changes led to seasons of plenty and seasons of famine. Different environments also led to radically different ways of life. While the settled farmers of Cahokia and their descendants in the Southeast and the pueblo peoples of the Southwest left the clearest records, many nomadic tribes roamed the heart of the continent and the Pacific coast, depending much more on their skills as hunters and their ability to gather abundant plant foods than on settled agriculture. Success and failure in war or the spread of disease caused American Indian populations to ebb and flow long before the first European encounters.

The Pueblo People of the Southwest

Some of the largest American Indian settlements in what is now the United States were in the Southwest. In place of the abandoned Anasazi centers, Pueblo and Hopi people created thriving settlements in New Mexico and Arizona, some of which exist to this day.

In the Pueblo and Hopi Southwest, an intricate maze of canals, dams, and terracing allowed agriculture to flourish in a dry climate. Like the Anasazi, the Pueblo and Hopi relied on corn, brown beans, and various forms of squash. They had domesticated turkeys and used dogs to hunt, so wild game, in addition to turkey, added animal protein to their diet.

In both Hopi and Pueblo communities, members of special societies wore ritual masks called kachinas and danced in ceremonies designed to connect the community with its ancestors while seeking their presence and blessing on the crops. The Pueblo people eventually spread out over Arizona and New Mexico, speaking different languages yet connected to each other by trade and common religious practices.

The Tribes of the Mississippi Valley

In the mid-1300s, Cahokia and the mound-building culture began to disappear. No one knows all of the reasons for this decline, but climate almost certainly had a role in it. Around 1350, a relatively rapid colder climate shift known as the "Little Ice Age" began and lasted until 1800. As the climate got colder, agriculture suffered. Europeans abandoned their settlements in places like Greenland. If the power of the priests and kings in Cahokia depended on their seeming control of the sun and the seasons, the Little Ice Age likely sapped that power. The change in weather drastically reduced the supply of food from outlying hamlets on which their large cities depended. Whatever the reasons, by 1400, Cahokia was abandoned.

With the decline of Cahokia and the mound-building culture, the population of the Mississippi Valley shrank. The most direct descendants of Cahokia, the people later known as the Creeks, Choctaws, and Chickasaws, settled on the eastern side of the Mississippi River and the southern Appalachian Mountains.

Other tribes dominated other parts of Cahokia's former territory. The Cherokees and Tuscaroras settled in parts of Georgia, Tennessee, and North Carolina. They are connected linguistically with the Iroquois of the Great Lakes and New York more than with the Creeks and Choctaws. Yet other tribes dominated the Piedmont area of what would be the Carolinas. Whatever their language or background, most of these tribes lived in small communities of five hundred to two thousand people. None lived in cities that were anything like

Figure 1-1 Population of the Americas, Europe, Africa, and Asia.
Any report on the population of different parts of the world in the 1400s is only an educated guess since there was nothing like a modern census to depend on. Nevertheless, anthropological and historical records allow somewhat accurate estimates. Certainly Asia had the most people in the time of Columbus, while the Americas, Europe, and Africa were fairly well matched in terms of population.

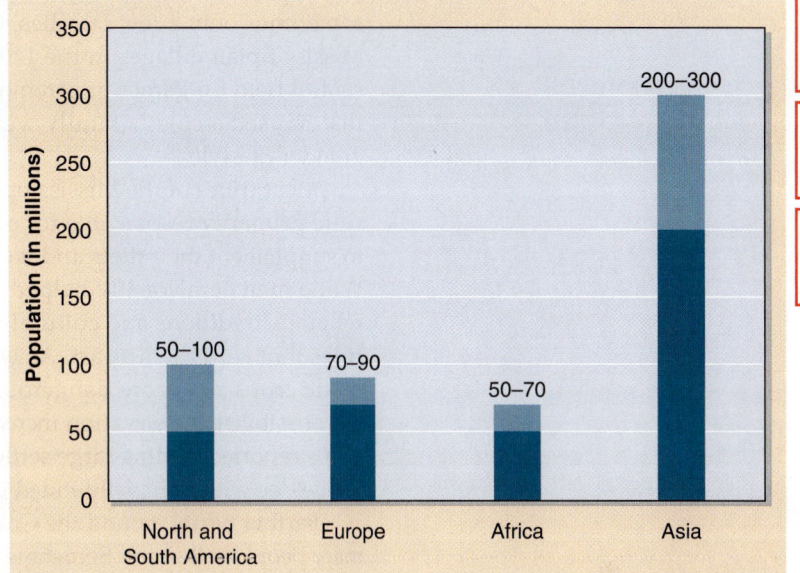

1.1
1.2
1.3
1.4
1.5

Cahokia. Neighboring villages might exchange corn or meat. Longer-distance exchange—and there was considerable long-distance exchange—was generally limited to things that were rare and easy to carry: copper implements, beads and shells from the Atlantic Coast, or quartz from the Rocky Mountains. Artifacts uncovered in almost any native settlement in North America attest to the lively long-distance trade among all of the continent's tribes.

Archaeological evidence also suggests that as Cahokia declined, smaller chiefdoms developed and often fought with each other and with other tribes. These communities, sometimes only a few families, built places of refuge throughout the Mississippi Valley. Mississippian villages in the 1400s included a half dozen to several dozen houses with a central field for games or ceremonies, all surrounded by a sturdy wooden wall. Structures that housed a chief's family were somewhat larger but do not seem to have reflected a grander lifestyle.

Most tribes of the Mississippi Valley followed the Cherokee tradition in which women were primarily responsible for planting and harvesting crops, while men hunted for meat to supplement their diets and were responsible for warfare whether defensive or offensive. While men occasionally helped in the fields and women, less often, joined in the hunts, religious traditions and cultural norms meant that men's and women's lives had different rules that kept them apart. As weather and war made food scarcer (it was harder to cultivate crops and more dangerous to hunt game if human enemies were lurking nearby), the possibility of starvation increased. Still, the first European explorers who arrived in the 1540s reported finding large settlements in modern South Carolina, Georgia, Alabama, and Tennessee with rich well-tended fields and well-designed houses and villages.

Farther north, around the Great Lakes, the Dakota Sioux and the Fox tribes were the primary people in the area. Sometime in the 1600s, after the arrival of the first Europeans but before the tribe had any contact with them, the Ojibwe (also known as Chippewa) immigrated from the Atlantic coast to the Great Lakes, making their tribal center on an island—now known as Madeline Island—about two miles off the southern coast of Lake Superior. According to one tribal tradition recorded in the 1880s, "Our forefathers, many strings of lives ago, lived on the shores of the Great Water in the east. Here it was, that while congregated in a great town, and while they were suffering the ravages of sickness and death, the Great Spirit … [led them] from the shores of the great water and [they] proceeded westward." The sickness was possibly from European disease, which often traveled far faster than any European explorers, but certainly a primary cause of death was Ojibwe battles with the powerful Iroquois from whom they were happy to escape, though in the new country they found themselves at war with the Dakota and Fox tribes.

In their new homes, the Ojibwe created a new culture, fishing Lake Superior's rich resources; hunting moose, bear, elk, and deer; and cultivating corn and pumpkins. They dressed in shirts and leggings of deer and elk skins, lived in birch-bark houses, and fished in birch-bark canoes. Around a sacred fire, they gathered and maintained traditions in which governance, healing, and religious rites were closely mixed. By the end of the 1600s, they had experienced their first contact with Europeans—the "black gowned priests," as they called the Jesuit missionaries, and occasional trappers who came west from French Canada.

The Pacific Coast—From the Shasta to the California Indians

In the Pacific Northwest, the Shasta and other tribes lived in towns of several hundred people, constructing houses as long as sixty feet built of cedar and richly decorated with painting and sculpture. These Pacific Coast Indians lived primarily on the abundant salmon in their rivers, which could be smoked or dried for year-round consumption. As a result of plentiful food and good housing, these tribes developed a settled community life with their own art and culture.

Farther down the Pacific Coast in California, the Yokut, Miwok, Maidu, and Pomo represented one of the largest concentrations of American Indians north of Mexico, perhaps 700,000 or 10 percent of the Indians north of the Rio Grande. These Native Americans lived in clans of extended families rather than larger tribal units. Their economy was based on gathering wild plants and on fishing and hunting. They did not engage in settled agriculture, probably because the wild foods in California were so abundant and settled agriculture offered little improvement in their diet or way of life.

Onondaga village attacked in 1615 by Samuel de Champlain (1567–1635), French explorer and founder of Canada. Onondaga: Iroquoian-speaking people inhabiting villages of bark and wood longhouses occupied by related families, situated in what is now New York. / Universal History Archive/UIG/The Bridgeman Art Library

This drawing shows an Iroquois Onondaga village under an attack led by the French explorer Samuel de Champlain. It also shows the longhouses that provided homes to several families, all surrounded by a stockade fence.

The Iroquois Confederacy and the Tribes of the Atlantic Coast

In the Northeast, the original five nations of the Iroquois (or the Haudenosaunee as they call themselves)—the Mohawks, Oneidas, Onondagas, Cayugas, and Senecas—developed an alliance and a united front against other tribes, an approach that would also serve them well in their encounters with Europeans. The Iroquois Confederacy's central meeting place and council fire was near present-day Syracuse, New York. In Iroquois communities, several families would live in a single sturdy longhouse made of posts and poles covered with bark, but the house itself and the land around it belonged to the community. As many as one thousand people lived in some Iroquois towns made up of many longhouses. Iroquois legends tell of a great peacemaker, Dekanawidah, who convinced the warring tribes to live together under the Great Law of Peace. An eclipse of the sun around the year 1142 supposedly strengthened his plea for unity. Clans led by women governed the five nations. The women leaders chose the sachems, male leaders who attended the council meetings and led in war but who were also accountable to the clans.

On the Atlantic Coast and the eastern slopes of the Appalachians were Algonquian-speaking tribes, the largest of which, the Powhatans, may have included sixty thousand or more people. For these tribes—some of the first to encounter Europeans and to be decimated by European disease and warfare—hunting and fishing as well as farming corn, beans, and squash provided the major food sources. They lived in permanent towns and villages. Like other tribes, the Atlantic Coast Indians did not keep written records, but even as late as the 1670s, an English trader described a Cherokee town of many houses along crisscrossing streets, surrounded by a stockade two feet thick and twelve feet high. Creek homes sometimes included separate kitchens, storerooms, and summer and winter dwellings. Social life centered on the ceremonies of the seasons that gave thanks for the harvest and to celebrate the start of a new year, especially the green corn dance held in late summer, which might attract several hundred Indians from surrounding villages.

1.1

1.2

1.3

1.4

1.5

Res fuerat quondam prestans, & Gloria summa
Orbis subiectus Cesaris Imperio,
Hic longe prestat, cuius nunc Orbis Eous,
Et Nouus, atq, alter panditur Auspitijs.

Quilibet punctus magnus continet leucas duode
cim cū dimidia, ita q̃ duo magni puncti continent
viginti quinq; leucas, Cōtinet autē leuca quatuor
Italica miliaria, ita q̃ omnes puncti qui hic cōſpi
ciuntur continent centum leucas.

A map of the Aztec capital of Tenochtitlán on site of what is now Mexico City. The Aztec built Tenochtitlán on an island with only a few easy-to-defend causeways linking it to the mainland and built beautiful floating gardens along the waterways.

The Aztec, Mayan, and Inca Empires

If one were to travel south in the mid-1400s from what is now the United States, one would come to the great Aztec city of Tenochtitlán. With a population of 200,000, it was as large as or larger than any contemporary city in Africa or Europe. The Aztecs founded Tenochtitlán on an island in the middle of Lake Texcoco in 1325, connected it to the mainland by three broad causeways, and supplied the city with fresh drinking water through a carefully designed aqueduct. When the Aztecs first arrived in central Mexico, the people who then ruled the region, known as the Toltecs, looked down on them as barbarians. That soon changed. The Aztecs conquered the Toltecs and destroyed their capital. The Aztec's Tenochtitlán used Toltec designs, but was a new and grander capital. Led by their emperor, Aztec society was highly stratified; the emperor and priests at the top ruled a powerful empire with a population of ten to twenty million that dominated subjugated tribes in surrounding areas.

The huge markets of Tenochtitlán in which forty thousand or fifty thousand traders met to exchange gold and jewelry, pottery and baskets, meat, fish, fruits, and vegetables amazed the first Spaniards who described it as "thrice as large as the celebrated square in Salamanca [in Spain]." Aztec art included the creation of plates of gold and jewelry encrusted with pearls and precious stones along with mosaics of feathers and small stones—art that would be greatly admired by the Spanish when they first saw it. Aztec agriculture, largely based on the practices of groups who had come before them, produced maize as the staple crop (made into tortillas that fed everyone), cacao or chocolate, fruit, beans, and cactus (from which they produced an alcoholic drink). The Aztecs maintained an extensive trade network with other peoples but also made war on them to expand their empire and ensure a steady stream of prisoners for the human sacrifices they believed their gods demanded. While the Aztecs built their empire by making strategic alliances with other tribes, by the mid-1400s, they relied on their own large army and attacked former allies, creating enemies who would help the Spanish conquer the Aztecs in the early 1500s.

American Voices

Richard Hakluyt, The True Pictures and Fashions of the People in That Part of America Now Called Virginia, 1585

When Sir Walter Raleigh founded the short-lived colony of Roanoke, Richard Hakluyt—who never left England—used Raleigh's reports to create a "true picture" of the American Indians. Since the Indians themselves did not keep such records, Hakluyt's accounts provide some of the best examples available of what Native American life was like at the time of their first contacts with Europeans even if it is certainly distorted by Hakluyt's perspective.
Note: The Elizabethan English of the original is hard to follow. The text below has been rendered in contemporary English.

The Princes of Virginia … wear the hair of their heads long. … They wear a chain about their necks of pearls or beads of copper, which they much esteem, and they wear bracelets of the same material on their arms. … They carry a quiver made of small rushes holding their bow ready bent in one hand, and an arrow in the other, ready to defend themselves. In this manner they go to war, or to their solemn feasts and banquets. They take much pleasure in hunting deer whereof there is great store in the country. … The women … are of reasonably good proportion. In their going they carry their hands dangling down and wear a deer skin excellently well dressed, hanging down from their navel unto the middle of their thighs, which also cover their hinder parts. The rest of their bodies are all bare. …

At a certain time of the year they make a great, and solemn feast whereunto their neighbors of the towns adjoining repair from all parts. … [T]hey dance, sing, and use the strangest gestures. … All this is done after the sun is set for avoiding of the heat. …

The towns of this country … are compassed about with poles stuck fast in the ground, but they are not very strong. The entrance is very narrow. There are but few houses therein, save those which belong to the king and his nobles.

This people therefore void of all covetousness live cheerfully and at their hearts ease. But they solemnize their feasts in the night, and therefore they keep very great fires to avoid darkness and to testify their joy.

Source: Richard Hakluyt, The True Pictures and Fashions of the People in That Part of America Now Called Virginia, 1585.

Thinking Critically

1. **Analyzing Primary Sources**

   Based on this document, what picture might an Elizabethan reader have formed about conditions in Virginia?

2. **Argument Development**

   In your opinion, how useful is this document as evidence of the true nature of American Indian societies in Virginia? What argument can you make to support your opinion?

To the east and southeast of the Aztec Empire was the once great empire of the Maya. The Mayan Empire had been at its height long before the Aztecs emerged on the scene. Indeed, the Mayan culture had been developing for thousands of years when Mayans first came into contact with Europeans.

The Mayans dominated what is now the Yucatan Peninsula of Mexico and much of modern Honduras, Belize, and Guatemala. The Mayans were the only American culture to develop a fully functional written language. They also developed sophisticated systems of mathematics and a calendar that projected time far into the future. Like the Aztecs, they practiced human sacrifice and subjugated other nearby tribes in pursuit of people and goods. They had an extensive agricultural system, producing not only food but also cotton, which was a source of trade and wealth.

While in decline from their peak or "classical period," by the time of their encounter with Europeans, the Mayans, some 800,000 people divided into sixteen to eighteen independent kingdoms, were still a strong presence in western Mexico and Central America in the 1400s. The remains of their greatest architecture could be seen all around them. They still produced and traded cotton, and their trade routes connected them with the other empires of the Americas.

Farther south, the Inca Empire was even larger than that of the Aztecs. It extended along the Pacific coast of South America from southern Colombia to northern Chile, and included almost all of what is today Peru, Ecuador, and Bolivia (see Map 1-3, p. 16). The Incas ruled some 32 million people from their capital of Cuzco, another city of 200,000, in what is now Peru, and from the mountain fortress and religious center of Machu Picchu. The empire had a vast bureaucracy and army as well as twenty-five thousand miles of roads and bridges, rivaling those of ancient Rome, all supported by heavy taxes. Inca religion was centered on the sun and its seasons; human and animal sacrifice was common. The Inca emperor and his

Map 1-3 Inca Empire in 1500.

The Inca Empire was perhaps the largest empire in the world, stretching down nearly all of the Pacific coast of South America, connected by roads and reporting to a single centralized government based in modern-day Peru.

family were considered divine. Like the Aztecs, the Inca Empire was relatively new when Europeans encountered it in the early 1500s. The main Inca conquests had occurred only in the 1400s.

American Indian Cultures, Trade, and Initial Encounters with Europeans

While the peoples living in North and South America before 1492 were divided by significant language differences and great distances, they still knew quite a bit about each other and traded regularly with far distant communities. Trade networks stretched from the Aztec Empire across all parts of North America. Long before the rise of the Aztecs, corn production had spread from Central America to many parts of North America. The presence of sea shells in Native American communities a thousand miles from the ocean and copper implements hundreds of miles from the nearest copper mine attests to the trade in goods that was rich and varied by the 1400s (see Map1-4).

Not all exchanges between tribes were friendly. There was certainly warfare also, sometimes to settle matters of honor and sometimes in the search for valuables. Hunting peoples seem to have raided farming communities, and farming communities fought with each other over land. Bows and arrows were deadly weapons, and scalping an enemy to gain a trophy, and perhaps a part of the enemy's spirit, was well known before 1492.

Even though the native peoples of North and South America maintained their trade networks and fought with other tribes, each tribe saw itself as the center of its own world. Their different stories, cultures, and spiritual traditions reflected that. Although trade might be of value, trading partners were not seen as part of a tribe's community. To understand Indian responses to the arrival of the Europeans, it is essential first to understand that no Indians thought of themselves as being American Indians or Native Americans as opposed to white Europeans. Instead, they thought of themselves as Senecas or Creeks or Hopi or some other discrete population. They did not see much in common with other distinct native peoples. This mind-set prevented any unified resistance to the first European aggressions in the 1400s and, later, in the 1500s and even 1600s. If a particular tribe thought it made sense to ally with the Europeans against another tribe or trade with the Europeans for new goods that would give them an advantage over another tribe, they saw no reason not to do so. If the Europeans could become part of well-established trade networks or allies in attacking long-standing enemies, so much the better. It took several hundred years before most American Indians realized that the Europeans did not look on them as they looked on themselves and that any equality in trade or warfare was to be short-lived.

While different tribes were happy to make alliances with different groups of Europeans, Native American culture tended to understand warfare in ways radically different from most Europeans. War among tribes was usually a way to settle specific issues or achieve honor and, most of all, to restore the balance that was essential to Indian life. The European model of total conquest was a concept that would have been foreign to most American Indian cultures. In this way as in so many other ways, the Europeans who began arriving in the 1490s could not have been more different.

At the same time, and unknown to the people of the Americas, other peoples, living in Europe, Africa, and Asia, were developing their own societies, creation stories, and worldviews. The world was never the same once representatives from these diverse peoples—Spanish explorers, slaves and free servants from West Africa, and those who followed them across the Atlantic—met and mingled with the native peoples of the Americas. But to understand the mingling, one must understand the development of separate cultures in other parts of the world.

Map 1-4 Native North American Cultural Areas and Trade Networks, c. 1400 CE.
While the peoples of North America were divided by climate, customs, and languages, they established complex trade networks in which goods produced in one region were traded over significant distances and found in regions far from their origin.

1.1

1.2

1.3

1.4

1.5

1.2   Quick Review

What are some unique cultural developments among specific American Indian tribes that were influenced by the geography or climate in which those tribes lived? What other factors impacted the development of different Native American communities?

A Changing Europe in the 1400s

1.3   Describe the changes in Europe that led to Columbus's voyages and that shaped European attitudes when encountering the peoples of the Americas.

Europeans had been sailing on the Atlantic long before Columbus was born. Well before the 1400s, most educated Europeans believed that the earth was round, though they debated its size. Norse sailors, commonly known as Vikings, came from modern-day Norway and Denmark and settled in Iceland in the late 800s. In 980, they expanded their territory to

Greenland where they interacted—not always peacefully—with the local Inuit people and exported lumber to Scandinavia while maintaining themselves with successful farms. In 1001, a Norse party led by Leif Erickson established a colony farther west that it named Vineland. No one is sure where Vineland was, though tradition places it in North America. Modern excavations show the remains of a Norse colony in the modern Canadian province of Newfoundland. Some claim Norse settlements as far south as the modern state of Maine. But while Iceland maintained contact with Europe and the Greenland colony survived until the early 1400s, when the same colder weather that undermined Cahokia also brought the Greenland colony to an end, Vineland was never permanent, and by the time Columbus was born, all earlier European contact with North America was long forgotten.

In the two hundred years before Columbus sailed across the Atlantic, Europe went through a series of extraordinary changes. Some of the most important changes had to do with seafaring—changes in shipbuilding, navigation, and the spread of information. By the 1200s, trade was growing all along the coasts of Europe from the Mediterranean to the Atlantic coasts of France and England and the Baltic coasts of northern Europe. A new kind of ship, known as a "cog," which carried a single sail and was steered with a centerline rudder, was developed in Europe around 1200 and dominated the coastal trade for the next century. By the late 1200s, a larger ship known as a "carrack" or sometimes simply "ship" was developed first in the Mediterranean. Unlike cogs, carracks had two or three masts and up to five sails, enabling them to carry more and travel farther faster, even in the face of less friendly winds. The *Santa Maria* that carried Columbus in 1492 was a carrack. Navigational instruments also became much more sophisticated between the 1200s and the 1400s. Early compasses, developed around 1250, showed sailors the direction in which they were sailing, even when out of sight of land. And by 1481, the Portuguese had developed a mariner's astrolabe, which helped determine latitude—distance north or south of the equator. (Longitude—east–west position—could not be measured until the 1700s.) Finally, the invention of the printing press by Johannes Gutenberg in the 1440s led to the production of not only Bibles but also detailed navigational information that was shared across Europe. As a result, by the 1490s, if not before, goods and ideas—even diseases—were being transmitted all across Europe from German and Russian ports on the Baltic to Italian and North African ports on the Mediterranean. Those changes not only set Columbus on his travels but also shaped the beliefs and expectations with which the first Europeans arrived in the Americas.

If a time-traveler were to go back to the Europe of the 1400s—to London, England, or Seville, Spain, or Paris, France, or the rural countryside where most people lived—they would find a world that would seem strange and primitive. There were not a lot of people around. Europe was still recovering from the devastating **Black Death**, the bubonic plague that arrived in 1348 on rats carried by ships trading in the Black Sea. In a few years after it first arrived, at a time when much of Europe was already facing unusually cold weather and famine, the plague wiped out at least one-third, perhaps even one-half, of Europe's population. About seventy million people lived in Europe in 1300. By the late 1350s, the plague had reduced the population to perhaps forty-five million. Whole families and villages disappeared. Through the late 1300s, there were empty fields or forests where people had once lived or farmed. The loss of so many people traumatized the survivors who looked for someone to blame for the disaster. Jews, religious nonconformists, and foreigners made good scapegoats, and there were massive persecutions across Europe.

A unified Roman Catholic Christian Church dominated the religious life of Europe in the 1400s. The Protestant Reformation was still a century in the future. Distance between cities, the difficulty of travel, and political divisions resulted in a Catholic Church that was far less centralized than it later became. Nevertheless, the church with its liturgy, creeds, and clergy—the pope, bishops, priests, monks, and nuns—was the strongest institution in Europe, unifying people who had different languages and leaders. Literacy, learning, and the preservation of culture rested mostly with the church. The church also provided what social services there were for the aged, sick, and poor. Jews lived in most parts of Europe, sometimes tolerated, sometimes savagely repressed, and occasionally honored for their contributions to medicine, commerce, and scholarship, but they were a small minority. There were also Muslim strongholds across southern Europe from Spain to the Balkans. Nevertheless, in most cities, a great Christian cathedral was the largest building, and everywhere church spires marked the center of both secular and religious life.

Black Death

The bubonic plague that devastated Europe in the 1300s, reducing the population by as much as half.

Life in this period would seem primitive to modern eyes. Most people were dirty, poorly clothed, and illiterate. Life expectancy was in the thirties, especially because infant mortality and deaths from childbirth were high. Trade was limited because transporting most things was difficult and expensive. The church taught that seeking wealth, especially charging interest for loans, was sinful. People were encouraged to stay where they were—in the community and in social class where they were born, whether they were peasants or nobles.

The Ottoman Empire Changes Eastern Europe

In 1453, when Christopher Columbus was two years old, Muslim Ottoman Turks conquered the city of Constantinople, the most important city in Eastern Europe. From their new capital, renamed Istanbul, the Ottomans ruled an empire that stretched from Hungary to include the Balkans and most of the Middle East and North Africa. The Ottoman Empire controlled the eastern Mediterranean for the next four centuries.

The fall of Constantinople shocked Europe. Constantinople had been at the crossroads of the trade routes between Europe and Asia and was considered the equivalent of Rome as a religious and political center. The Ottomans encouraged trade within their empire, but restricted others from using the land and sea routes across the eastern Mediterranean. Suddenly Christian Europe was cut off from the lucrative land-based trade in spices and luxury goods with Asia that had existed since Italy's Marco Polo had traveled to China in the late 1200s. The Mediterranean, which had been the great unifying conduit of the Roman Empire, was now as divided as the lands surrounding it. The city-states of Italy—Venice, Genoa, and Florence especially—which had dominated the Mediterranean and trade with Asia and grown wealthy from it, began a slow decline. Other Europeans on the Atlantic Coast, especially those in Portugal and Spain, began to seek new ways to reach Asia—without the need to deal with the Ottomans.

The Rise of Portuguese Exploration

The first and in many ways the most adventurous European to seek a new way of connecting with Asia was Prince Henry of Portugal (1394–1460). Even before the Ottoman conquest of Constantinople, Henry, a younger son of the king of Portugal, decided that Portugal, with its strategic location on Europe's southern Atlantic Coast, should try to establish a new trade route to Asia by sailing around Africa.

Although he is known to history as "the Navigator," Henry's personal seagoing was modest. In 1415, he commanded a Portuguese fleet, but for the rest of his life, he stayed at his castle at Sagres on the Portuguese coast and commissioned others to make voyages and report back to him. These voyages not only generated geographical information about the African coast but also led to better navigational instruments and charts as well as better-designed ships that could travel greater distances in bad weather and good.

In 1424, Prince Henry organized a long series of expeditions—in which others did the actual travel—that sailed farther and farther south along the coast of Africa. Once they learned how to navigate the currents off the African coast, a skill greatly helped by the new designs in shipbuilding and navigational instruments, Portuguese explorers moved quickly. In 1444, Portuguese ships reached Senegal, long fabled as a source of gold, and established a slave-trading company in Lagos. They reached Sierra Leone around 1460 as well as claimed and settled the previously uninhabited Cape Verde Islands. Finally, in 1488, Bartolomeu Dias rounded the Cape of Good Hope on the southern tip of Africa. A decade later, in 1498, Vasco da Gama followed Dias's route and reached India. These successful expeditions led to flourishing trade with Asia and Africa by the early 1500s. The Portuguese not only established a string of trading colonies in India, Indonesia, and China but also developed a massive new African trade. Portuguese merchants virtually reinvented slavery in Western Europe, and Portugal became the first and most significant player in the African slave trade as well as in the spice trade with Asia. By 1504, at least one ship a month sailed from Lisbon to Asia, and the wealth from Asian spices and other luxury goods and from African gold and slaves was making Portugal the richest nation in Europe.

Historians have argued about Henry's, and by extension Portugal's, motives. Henry certainly wanted to find a route that would put Portugal at the center of the trade with Asia. Asian goods—porcelain, silk, spices—had long been popular and profitable luxury goods in Europe.

RMN-Grand Palais/Art Resource, NY

In the 1400s, the vast majority of the people of Europe were poor peasants who worked long days in the fields with little economic gain to show for their work. At the top of society were nobles, who lived in grand castles like the one pictured, and the clergy, who reminded nobles and peasants of their responsibility to stay in the class to which they were born and not seek economic or social advancement.

1.1

1.2

1.3

1.4

1.5

1.1

1.2

1.3

1.4

1.5

Technological advances in the development of new navigational instruments and in sailing ship construction, like the building of the three-masted carrack shown here, allowed sailors to travel much farther and more safely across the Atlantic.

North Wind Picture Archives / Alamy Stock Photo

The nation that could secure access to these goods after the Ottomans restricted the eastern Mediterranean routes would become rich. Old animosity between Christian Europe and the Muslim world fueled the quest to defy Ottoman trade obstacles. Legends of a Christian presence in the heart of Africa also motivated expanded contact with that continent. If the Christians of Europe could ally with Christians who might be in Africa, their armies would surround the Muslim world and weaken its power. Perhaps most important to Henry, however, was the wealth to be made in Africa itself. Portugal could obtain African gold and slaves from every voyage whether or not it made discoveries or alliances with far-off Christians.

Slavery was an ancient institution. It was sanctioned in the Bible and other ancient texts thousands of years before the days of Prince Henry. The Roman Empire had slaves, including some from Africa. But while slavery had died out in most of Europe during the Middle Ages—although serfs in Russia were only semi-free—it persisted in the Middle East and Africa. Arab traders brought African slaves across the Sahara to sell in markets in the Middle East. In fact, various African peoples routinely captured and enslaved their rivals. And Muslim conquerors and pirates enslaved captured European Christians. Europeans developed new forms of slavery along with the exploration of Africa. As early as 1336, King Alfonso IV of Portugal reported, and probably sponsored, slave raiding in the Canary Islands off the coast of West Africa. Indeed, the Canary Islands would be an important base for further exploration of Africa, one often contested between Portugal and Spain. After 1500, slavery would transform European commerce, most of all in the trade with European colonies in the Americas, while also transforming and weakening the economies of Africa and—in particular—utterly changing the lives of millions of Africans.

England and France

While Portugal was establishing its ocean routes to Asia and growing fabulously wealthy in the process, most of the rest of Europe remained poor and distracted with more immediate worries. France and England fought the Hundred Years' War (1337–1453) with each other, depleting both nations' resources. When the war ended, France was divided by a bitter civil war until 1477 as the royal government sought to assert its control of the kingdom. England was also torn by a civil war, the War of the Roses, as the Lancaster and York branches of the royal family fought until Henry VII defeated Richard III of York in 1485. The destruction wrought by war and plague left little time, money, or energy for either France or England to engage in exploration.

Despite all their troubles, England and France were relatively unified kingdoms. In contrast, other areas of Europe were not united at all during this period and, in fact, would not be until the mid-1800s. For centuries before its unification, most of what is now Germany was considered part of the Holy Roman Empire, but the empire was actually a very loose confederation divided into a number of much smaller entities. No Italian state existed. Until the 1800s, what is now modern Italy was divided into many competing, independent free cities, principalities, and small kingdoms that spoke different and often mutually incomprehensible versions of Italian. These groups were also often at war with each other. As a result, these areas did not initiate much organized external exploration. Even though many sailors from what is now Italy were among the most important European explorers of the era, they worked for other governments.

The Unification and Rise of Spain

Unlike some other parts of Europe, Spain, however, achieved a dramatic new unity in the late 1400s, and this unified Spain would be a powerful force in the Americas. The political, cultural, and religious unification of Spain—known as the *Reconquista*, or "reconquest"—was an extraordinary development given the seven centuries during which unity of any sort had seemed impossible. In 711, Muslim invaders from North Africa conquered most of the Iberian Peninsula (modern Spain and Portugal) and remained in control of parts of it for almost eight hundred years. While the rest of Europe remained Christian, much of Medieval Spain was in African Muslim (Moorish) hands.

Reconquista
The long struggle (ending in 1492) during which Spanish Christians reconquered the Iberian Peninsula from Muslim occupiers, who first invaded in the 700s.

Christian monarchs gradually reconquered Portugal and most of Spain from the Muslims, but the struggle took centuries. While some areas were ruled by Christians, many others remained Muslim. Yet the very divisions of Spain resulted in some of the richest cultural developments in Europe. While armies fought, people mingled, producing new ideas and some of the scientific developments that would later enrich all of Europe. It was through Spain that the culture of Islam came into Europe, including Arabic numerals, algebra, paper, cotton, rice, and sugar. It was in Muslim Córdoba that Greek philosophy, Roman law, and eastern art and architecture mixed. It was also in Spain, far more than elsewhere in Europe, that Jews were treated with respect, even honor, as "peoples of the book" who shared sacred scriptures with Christians and Muslims. It was also on the border lands between Christianity and Islam that some of the great medieval cities of Spain—León, Zamora, Burgos, and Ávila—emerged, creating an independent class of citizens who were neither nobles nor serfs but free women and men. As the medieval saying went, "the air of the city makes you free."

Spain's long-standing divisions ended in the late 1400s. By 1400, the Iberian Peninsula was divided into four Christian kingdoms—Castile, Aragon, Portugal, and Navarre—and one Muslim kingdom in the south—Granada. In 1469, Isabella of Castile married Ferdinand of Aragon. This marriage united the two most powerful Spanish thrones. The joint monarchs then began a long campaign to finish the reconquest of Spain. In January 1492, their armies defeated Muslim Granada, adding its territory to their kingdom. When Granada surrendered, it ended eight hundred years of Islamic power in Spain. That same year, in the name of religious uniformity, Ferdinand and Isabella expelled all Jews from Spain, a move that cost them some of their most innovative citizens. But Isabella and Ferdinand wanted their nation to be unified, and like most Europeans at the time, they saw religious uniformity as key to that goal. And in that same eventful year, after a long hesitation, Isabella commissioned an Italian sailor named Christopher Columbus to try to find a route to Asia that would be different from the African one Portugal was exploring.

1.1
1.2
1.3
1.4
1.5

1.3 Quick Review

How did changes in Europe in the 1400s determine European states' ability to launch expeditions of discovery in the Atlantic? How did changes in seafaring, the unification of Spain, and the fall of Constantinople to the Ottomans affect this process?

1.1

1.2

1.3

1.4

1.5

Map 1-5 African Trade Networks.

Like American Indians, Africans traded over great distances. The major trade routes made trade centers such as Timbuktu and Gao rich and powerful as goods—and often people being sold as slaves—were transported through these cities from one region to another.

▲	Salt
▇	Gold
—	Major trade routes
●	Major cites
—	Present-day boundaries

0   800 MILES

0   800 KILOMETERS

Africa in the 1400s

1.4 **Describe the political, cultural, and religious developments in Africa that would shape contact between Europeans and Africans in the Americas.**

In the late 1400s, parts of Africa were also undergoing changes that would influence the cultural interactions that would take place in the "New World" in the 1500s. Just as in Europe and the Americas, none of the people in Africa knew that they were living on the edge of events that would turn their world upside down. Yet events were under way that would change the lives, economies, cultures, and worldviews of almost everyone.

Ancient Ties between Africa and Europe

Contact between Africa and Europe did not begin with Prince Henry's voyages. North Africa had been part of Mediterranean civilization for at least three thousand years. What are today the nations of Egypt, Libya, Algeria, Morocco, and Tunisia were some of the richest provinces of the Roman Empire. As Christianity spread throughout the Roman Empire, some of the strongest Christian centers were in North Africa. One of the most influential of all early Christian thinkers was St. Augustine (354–430), born in what is now Algeria, who served as bishop of the Algerian city of Hippo. Farther south, Christianity took root quickly in Ethiopia, and that part of east Africa has remained predominantly Christian for two thousand years. In addition, southern Europe and parts of Africa south of the Sahara shared a long history of trade (see Map 1-5). This trade was never entirely interrupted, even when Arab armies conquered North Africa in the 600s and Islam replaced Christianity as the dominant religion across North Africa and from there into Spain. Between about the year 800 and the establishment of railroads in the mid-1900s, camel caravans crossed the Sahara on a regular basis, bringing gold, slaves, and information about sub-Saharan Africa to North Africa, Europe, and the Middle East, while bringing European cloth, glassware, armaments, housewares, and other trade goods along with European and Middle Eastern ideas to central Africa.

The Empires of Ghana, Mali, and Songhay

sub-Saharan Africa

All parts of the African continent south of the Sahara—about two-thirds of the landmass of Africa.

South of the Sahara (known as **sub-Saharan Africa**), the Africans differed in customs, ethnicity, and economic life from Muslim North Africa. On the coast of sub-Saharan Africa, Africans met Portuguese traders and quickly took an interest in particular European goods, including iron and cloth, acquiring them through exchanges of hides, copper, ivory, and slaves in easier ways than the long Saharan caravans had allowed. The European voyages of the mid-1400s provided an alternative international trade route that increased trade, producing a greater variety of goods on both continents and, for the African elite, added the prestige of owning goods from far away. The Africa that first began major economic and cultural contact with Europe in those years was a continent that met its northern neighbor on terms of equality in military, cultural, and technological terms, its population not yet decimated by the massive trade in slaves that was to come or by attacks by industrialized European colonial forces.

Just south of the Sahara, the kingdom of Ghana governed much of West Africa for hundreds of years. Ghana's power was based on trade and its mastery of metalworking to make weapons and tools. Ghana was at the northern end of African trade routes that brought gold, ivory, and slaves out of the African interior and at the southern end of the desert routes by which Muslim traders brought the slaves, gold, and ivory from south of the Sahara to North Africa, the Middle East, and Europe in exchange for salt, silk, and other goods. Control of that trade made Ghana rich. Royal and religious officials, soldiers, merchants, and iron workers dominated Ghana.

As early as 1050, King Barmandana of Mali began to extend his kingdom, and the empire of Mali slowly dominated and replaced Ghana as the leading power in the region. The inner delta of the Niger River where it splits into multiple branches made Mali a rich agricultural district as well as a center of trade. Barmandana converted to Islam and made a pilgrimage to Mecca, the Muslim holy city in Arabia. Some two hundred years later, another Malian king, Sundiata, made Mali the master of West Africa. When one of Sundiata's successors, Mansa Musa, made his pilgrimage to Mecca in 1324, his lavish caravan and generous gifts spread gold so freely that "the value of Cairo's currency was depressed for many years." Until much larger sources of gold were found in the Americas in the 1500s, African gold was highly prized in Europe for a thousand years. Mansa Musa built new mosques and schools and established an Islamic university at Timbuktu that was respected throughout the Muslim world for its scholarship.

To the east of Mali, another empire, Songhay, grew stronger, capturing Timbuktu in 1458 just as the Portuguese were exploring the African coast. In the late 1400s, under two of its greatest kings, Sunni Ali (r. 1464–1492)—who died in the year of Columbus's first voyage—and Askia Muhammad (r. 1493–1528), Songhay became the strongest military and economic power in West Africa. When Sunni Ali became king of Songhay in 1464, he quickly established himself as an effective military leader. Sunni Ali also understood the religious divisions of his lands. The urban inhabitants, who controlled trade, were mostly Muslim. But in the countryside, most people held to traditional beliefs, and they were the source of the agricultural wealth of the kingdom. Though himself a Muslim, Sunni Ali treated both groups with respect and brought stability and prosperity to his kingdom. When Sunni Ali died in 1492, his son and heir, Sunni Baru, rejected Islam but was overthrown, and a new leader, Askia Muhammad (r. 1493–1528), came to power. Askia Muhammad was a devout Muslim, but like Sunni Ali, he respected traditional customs.

This mosque in Djenne, Mali, was originally built in the 1300s of mud hardened by the sun and was restored in the early 1900s to look much as it did at the height of the Mali Empire.

As with Mali and Ghana, Songhay's power was based on trade. Gold, ivory, and slaves could be collected from the south and east. In exchange, silks and other fine goods were brought in caravans across the Sahara from Egypt, the Middle East, and Europe. Trade created wealth, which allowed both lavish lifestyles and military power that extended the empires. And trade also facilitated the exchange of ideas and scientific information. Askia Muhammad's control was such that he was able to make his own pilgrimage to Mecca in 1494–1497, trusting subordinates to maintain his rule in his absence.

Kongo, Benin, and Central Africa

South of Songhay, in the kingdoms of Kongo, Benin, and surrounding areas, government was less far reaching than in the empires of Mali and Songhay. In the 1490s, Portuguese missionaries converted the king of Kongo to Catholicism. Close ties developed between Kongo and the papacy in Rome despite the enormous distances between them. More than a century later, slaves from Kongo would confuse English and Spanish authorities who could not comprehend the origin of their Christian beliefs and knowledge of the Catholic Mass.

While Kongo kings were Catholic, most other Central Africans practiced traditional religions that included belief in a world after death, ancestor worship, and a central role for priests and other intermediaries between divine and human affairs. The Africans who were taken across the Atlantic to the Americas as slaves brought these religious and cultural traditions with them.

Kongo kings generally inherited the throne from their father or brother, but a group of nobles or electors could choose a different ruler. A similar system was found in much of Central Africa. In Ndongo, election ratified succession within a reigning family. In Biguba,

1.1

1.2

1.3

1.4

1.5

in what is now Guinea-Bissau, the king was elected from among a group of elite families. In Sierra Leone, the ruler was elected, but once in office could dismiss the electors, and a similar system was followed in Benin. Europeans reported that, to maintain their own power, nobles sometimes deliberately selected weak monarchs. In 1601, one European wrote, "a village mayor in our country has more authority than such a king." In these West African kingdoms, a person or family could cultivate land, secure in the knowledge that they would truly "own" the crops or goods produced on the land and could sell or trade them, but they could never sell the land itself. Indeed, if the family stopped working the land, any claim they might have to it disappeared.

Centralized government and the wealth generated by trade also led to military power that allowed West Africans to resist not only the first Portuguese attempts at conquest but also many subsequent ones. In 1446, when Portuguese explorers, seeking slaves and gold, reached the Senegal River (which is now the northern border of Senegal), African canoes attacked their ship, and nearly all of the European raiders were killed. A year later, the same thing happened to another crew near the island of Goree. Similar types of resistance would continue for the next two centuries.

African boats were small compared with European ships. They tended to be canoes dug out of a single log, but their small size gave them power. They could navigate shallow areas where the Europeans could not go and could move quickly between rivers, estuaries, and the ocean. These canoes carried as many as fifty to one hundred fighters each. Facing such effective resistance at sea, before they ever landed on unknown shores or attempted to travel up uncharted and hostile rivers, the earliest Portuguese travelers quickly decided that it was better to seek peaceful trade agreements with African kings than to do battle. The result was that as early as 1456, Diogo Gomes represented the Portuguese crown in negotiating treaties of peace and commerce with African rulers of several states.

Slavery in Africa

Slavery was a significant part of the African economy in the 1400s. It was important in the empires of Mali and Songhay and in Kongo long before the Portuguese arrived. In an economic system where the community, not an individual, owned land in common, as it did in West Africa, owning people who could work the land was a way to accumulate wealth.

When the Portuguese began their African trade in the 1400s, African slaves had been brought across the Sahara to Europe and the Middle East for over one thousand years. Most female slaves became domestic workers and concubines in urban households in North Africa, the Middle East, and Europe, while many male slaves served in the armed forces, and some—women and men—were later freed. Benin City had seen slaves parade through for centuries. The Portuguese simply shifted part of this trade to Europeans on the coast and away from the Arab-dominated overland routes across the Sahara. Although the voracious demand for enslaved Africans in the Americas would disrupt the African economy in the 1600s and 1700s, that was a later story. As many slaves were transported across the Atlantic in the two hundred years between 1650 and 1850 as were transported across the Sahara in a thousand years. When the Portuguese first became involved in the slave trade, they merely built on existing trade and cultural traditions. Far fewer people were involved than would be the case in the future, but for those who were enslaved, the new patterns created huge dislocations.

An African could be enslaved for many reasons—as punishment for crime or as payment for debt—but most slaves were captured in war from other communities. Those who sold them considered the slaves aliens, not people like themselves. Like the American Indians, Africans did not think of themselves as Africans but as members of a specific tribe—Ashanti, Yoruba, Kru—and enslaving members of another tribe did not distress them. The economic advantages of capturing slaves in war and then selling them also made war itself a profitable commercial venture and exacerbated other tensions.

Nevertheless, just because slavery and the slave trade were already part of the economic systems of West Africa when the Portuguese arrived in the mid-1400s does not change the horror of the institution. Being captured in war, losing one's freedom, and then being sent away from home must always have been terrifying. It was even worse if one was forced to march across the terrible Sahara or loaded onto a ship controlled by strange-looking people who spoke a totally different language and who considered slaves not merely aliens but subhuman. Although the earliest African and European slave traders did not recognize it— or probably care about it—a more terrible form of slavery was being born in the 1400s. For the first time, not only the slaves' freedom but also their language, culture, and identity were being destroyed. The Africans unlucky enough to become American slaves already knew about slavery as an institution, but they had never encountered conditions in which they were stripped of everything familiar to them.

Africans, as slaves or as free people hired for the work, would accompany some of the earliest Portuguese, Spanish, and English explorers of North and South America in the 1500s, helping explore Florida, Virginia, Texas, and New Mexico. Descendants of Europeans and Africans have lived together with American Indians for five hundred years in the land that would eventually be the United States. But after the first generation, very few African slaves gained their freedom in the Americas as opposed to the many from the Saharan slave trade who were able to eventually blend into the various societies where they ended up.

1.4 Quick Review

How were African political units similar to or different from European ones in the 1400s? How did the earliest European contact with Africa change, or not change, the nature of African slavery?

Asia in the 1400s

1.5 **Contrast developments in Asia with those in Europe at the time when Europeans first reached the Americas.**

While the Americas, Africa, and Europe were all divided into many small tribes, cities, and nation-states in the 1400s, China was united in a single empire and had been for more than two thousand years. When Columbus sailed from Spain to the Americas in 1492, Europe had some five hundred independent states. A single emperor governed perhaps 150 to 200 million people in China. Of course, China is not all of Asia. The Indian subcontinent included 75 to 150 million people living in many independent principalities. The Philippine Islands were a quilt of small kingdoms, some Hindu, some Buddhist, and (after 1380) some Muslim. Korea and Japan were independent kingdoms, while Tibet and Vietnam struggled to maintain their independence from China. But most of the peoples of Asia were in contact with one another and enriched one another's cultures.

In 1421, the Chinese emperor Zhu Di celebrated the completion of the Forbidden City, his new palace and temple complex in Beijing. Envoys from as far away as East Africa and Arabia were present. Twenty-six thousand guests feasted at a ten-course banquet. In the same month, England's King Henry V celebrated his wedding to a French princess with six hundred guests. Zhu Di's army included one million soldiers armed with gunpowder, while Henry had five thousand soldiers armed with bows and arrows. But then, Zhu Di's new capital of Beijing had a population that was fifty times larger than Henry's London.

Zhu Di (r. 1402–1424) also commissioned Chinese fleets that sailed to South Asia, India, and East Africa and well into the Pacific Ocean. These treasure fleets mapped the Indian Ocean and brought back exotic animals, trade goods, and knowledge that made China a center of geographic studies in the early 1400s.

But Chinese oceanic exploration came at high cost. Huge forests in China and Vietnam were cleared to provide the teak to build the fleets' ships. Thousands of artisans labored to build the ships, and many more left as sailors, most of whom never returned. The expensive ocean voyages also distracted China's attention from its vulnerable land frontiers in the northwest. And the mandarins, China's professional, highly educated bureaucrats, despised and resented the naval officers who were in charge of the fleets.

In 1424, a new emperor, Zhu Gaozhi, issued an edict:

> All voyages of the treasure ships are to be stopped. ... Those officials who are currently abroad on business are ordered back to the capital immediately. ... The building and repair of all treasure ships is to be stopped immediately.

For the next two hundred years, China became increasingly isolated from the rest of the non-Asian world. As a result, China played no role in the initial creation of the new world that came into being as people of the Americas, Europe, and Africa interacted.

By the 1490s, China was prospering but quite inward looking. South Asia, especially India, was just beginning to be engaged in what would be a growing trade with Europe through the new trade routes that Portuguese explorers were establishing. Sub-Saharan Africa, dominated by the Songhay Empire and the kingdom of Kongo, was also trading with Europeans via a newly established Atlantic trade route dominated by the Portuguese, as well as their long-established trade routes across the Sahara that connected them with the Muslim world, increasingly dominated by the Ottoman Empire. American Indians had their own long-distance trade relationships that spanned thousands of miles, even though they never contemplated trade that might cross the oceans that bounded them. As all of this interaction was taking place, the newly united kingdom of Spain took the lead in seeking yet another way to expand trade in the world that they knew. At the beginning of the year 1492, no one living anywhere on the planet knew how eventful that effort to seek new pathways for trade would be.

1.5 Quick Review

Why did European sailors reach the Americas when Asian sailors did not?

Conclusion

The world that existed before the Columbian encounter of 1492 was rich and dynamic in cultures, civilizations, and diversity. The first peoples of North America had settled the continent long before Columbus set sail in 1492. Perhaps as early as thirty thousand years ago, the ancestors of today's American Indians began to people North and South America. Whether they came by land or water, these original groups of people established agrarian and hunter–gatherer cultures over the centuries. North American Indians established diverse forms of agriculture, depending on their environments and different social and political systems, some of which involved sophisticated trading empires and cities that rivaled those of medieval Europe. Their cultural heritage would be changed forever by the impact of European arrival and colonization.

While the first peoples of North America had been establishing their communities, Europeans in the 1400s were on the move, recovering from the wars and the bubonic plague that had decimated the continent in the late 1300s. European contact with North America was motivated in part by the 1452 Muslim conquest of Constantinople, which placed the Eastern Mediterranean under the control of the Ottoman Empire and closed off traditional land and sea routes to India and other centers of trade in Asia. The kingdom of Portugal led the way in exploring sailing routes around Africa. Eventually, new trade relationships gradually developed between Europeans and the many African empires and kingdoms. The Portuguese adopted and exploited the institution of slavery and the slave trade, which had generally disappeared in Europe, and brought African slaves back to Europe even before the first slaves were transported to the Americas.

Even before Portugal's Prince Henry the Navigator dispatched his sailors to explore the African coast, the Chinese emperor Zhu Di ordered the construction of the "treasure fleets," which explored and established trade routes in the Indian and Pacific oceans. His ships and sailors at least matched those of Europe; however, Zhu Di's successor ordered the end of the treasure fleets, which were seen as a drain on China's wealth. For this reason, Europeans had no serious rivals when they first encountered the Americas.

While Portuguese sailors sailed around Africa to reach Asia, an Italian sailor, Christopher Columbus, was commissioned by the king and queen of a newly unified Spain to try a different route, sailing west across the Atlantic rather than south and east around Africa. The result was an encounter between civilizations in Europe, Africa, and the Americas that knew nothing of each other—a world-changing event for everyone involved.

Chapter Review

What was life and culture like for Native Americans, Europeans, and Africans before the encounters of 1492?

Chapter 1 Summary and Review

The Peopling of North America

1.1 **Describe what the archaeological record tells about the arrival, development, and cultures of the first peoples of North America.**

Summary

Most anthropologists believe the native inhabitants of the Americas walked on dry land between Siberia and Alaska during ice ages that created a land bridge between the continents or came by water in small canoes that stayed close to the coasts of both continents. Until recently, scholars believed that the first immigrants to the Americas were the so-called Clovis people who might have come to North America approximately thirteen thousand years ago. New evidence, however, suggests that humans arrived much earlier. Whenever and however the first Americans came, their descendants adapted to their new lands, spread out across the Americas, and created a wide range of languages and civilizations. The largest and most sophisticated pre-Columbian civilizations emerged in Mexico and South America. Nonetheless, complex societies also developed in North America, perhaps most notably the Anasazi of the Southwest and the Cahokia of the Mississippi River Valley.

Review Question

1. Argument Development
   How did the adoption of settled agriculture help shape the development of Cahokia society?

The Diverse Communities of the Americas in the 1400s

1.2 **Describe the diversity of American Indian cultures in the United States on the eve of their encounter with Europeans.**

Summary

The early native peoples of North America were a diverse group of peoples who spoke many languages and formed five hundred to six hundred independent societies. The diversity of the Native American population reflected the physical diversity of the Americas; the wide range of geographical conditions influenced the various cultures of these groups. The Aztecs and the Incas created the largest pre-Columbian empires. After conquering the Toltecs, the Aztecs built an increasingly aggressive empire in central Mexico. The Incas built an even larger empire along the Pacific coast of South America. A vast bureaucracy and army, along with a well-developed infrastructure, helped the Incas maintain control of their territory. In what is now the U.S. Southwest, the Pueblo and Hopi peoples used sophisticated agricultural techniques to farm in a dry climate. A slightly smaller yet sophisticated culture of Mound Builders established Cahokia. Cahokia flourished for centuries, but after its demise, the population of the Mississippi Valley shrank. The inhabitants of the Pacific Northwest, including the Shasta, took advantage of an abundant food supply to develop a settled community life with well-developed art and culture. In the Northeast, the five nations of the Iroquois—the Mohawks, Oneidas, Onondagas, Cayugas, and Senecas—formed a powerful confederacy. On the Atlantic Coast and the eastern slopes of the Appalachians, many tribes lived in permanent towns and villages. Hunting, fishing, and farming provided the major food sources for these peoples. For all of the differences among American Indian communities, the extensive trade networks between them encouraged common ways of looking at the world.

Review Questions

2. Argument Development
   How would you explain the fact that after the demise of Cahokia, no urban center of similar size and sophistication emerged to take its place?

3. Comparison
   What common features characterized the worldview of most American Indian peoples?

A Changing Europe in the 1400s

1.3 **Describe the changes in Europe that led to Columbus's voyages and that shaped European attitudes when encountering the peoples of the Americas.**

Summary

In the century before Columbus sailed across the Atlantic, Europe went through extraordinary changes. Those changes not only set Columbus on his travels but also shaped the beliefs and expectations with which the first Europeans arrived in the Americas. In 1400, Europe was still recovering from the devastation of the Black Death, while the Catholic Church was the most unifying force in Europe. From a modern point of view, life in this period would seem primitive. Most people were dirty, poorly clothed, and illiterate. Europe's limited trade was further disrupted by the fall of Constantinople, a key trading hub, to the Ottomans in 1453. This event prompted Europeans to seek new ways to reach Asia for more direct trading opportunities. At the same time, advances in seafaring made it possible for Europeans to explore beyond the Mediterranean.

Prince Henry the Navigator spearheaded Portugal's efforts in this regard, and during the 1400s, Portuguese explorers sailed around Africa and into the Indian Ocean. Internal divisions and conflicts left England, France, Germany, and Italy ill-equipped to follow Portugal's lead. The completion of the *Reconquista* and the unification of Spain under Isabella and Ferdinand, however, enabled Spain to emulate—and eventually surpass—Portugal's accomplishments.

Review Questions

4. Causation
What short-term and long-term consequences did the fall of Constantinople have for Europe?

5. Comparison
Compare and contrast Spain, England, and France on the eve of the Age of Exploration. Why did Spain take the lead in westward expansion?

Africa in the 1400s

1.4 **Describe the political, cultural, and religious developments in Africa that would shape contact between Europeans and Africans in the Americas.**

Summary

By the 1400s, North Africa had been part of Mediterranean civilization for at least three thousand years. In addition, parts of Africa south of the Sahara had a long history of trade with southern Europe. In West Africa, Ghana's power, which enabled it to gain control of much of West Africa, was based on trade and its mastery of metalworking to make iron weapons and tools. Ghana's successors, Mali and Songhay, built similar regional empires. Like Ghana, each drew its power from trade and technological advantages. In all three kingdoms, Islam was the religion of the cities and the ruling class. South of Songhay, in the kingdom of Kongo and surrounding areas, government was powerful but far less structured. Centralized government and the wealth generated by trade also led to military power that allowed West Africans to resist not only the first Portuguese attempts at conquest but also many subsequent ones. Slavery was a significant part of the African economy long before the Portuguese arrived. But during the 1400s, a more terrible form of slavery was born through which not only a slave's freedom but also his or her language, culture, and identity were destroyed.

Review Question

6. Causation
How did the Portuguese impact the practice of African slavery when they arrived in the 1400s?

Asia in the 1400s

1.5 **Contrast developments in Asia with those in Europe at the time when Europeans first reached the Americas.**

Summary

While the Americas, Africa, and Europe were all divided into many small tribes, cities, and nation-states in the 1400s, much of the heart of Asia was united under Chinese imperial control. In the 1400s, Chinese wealth, cities, technological sophistication, military power, and population dwarfed those of Europe. While the Chinese launched significant exploration initiatives, such voyages were quickly halted, and China turned inward. For the next two hundred years, China became increasingly isolated from the rest of the non-Asian world.

Review Question

7. Comparison
Compare and contrast Europe and Asia on the eve of European exploration. What is the significant difference that helps determine the course of history?

1. Preparing to Write: Plan Your Argument

Long Essay Question—Evaluate the extent in which the environment shaped the development of pre-Columbian civilizations north of Mexico.

To help you master the details before you begin to write, create a five-column table, with one column for each of the major regions discussed in this section. Use the table to identify specific ways each adapted to their respective environments. What is bubbling up from your table? Write a "first draft" thesis that answers the long essay question above. When writing an AP U.S. History essay, the most common mistake students make is addressing the right topic but failing to answer the question asked, so be sure you understand your "mission" based on the question assigned to you.

2. Preparing to Write: Establish Context in Your Introduction

Long Essay Question—Evaluate the primary factors that contributed to European exploration and settlement of the New World in the 1400s and 1500s.

Before making an effective argument about specific historical developments, students need to establish the context in which the Age of Exploration began. Start by listing the major developments in Europe during this time period. Then write a four- to seven-sentence introduction that uses these major developments to establish context for the argument you will make in your thesis.

Chapter 2
First Encounters, First Conquests 1492–1607

Many of the islands on which Columbus landed, including the Bahamas, Hispaniola, and Cuba, were inhabited by Taino Indians, the first people in the Americas to interact with Columbus. Shown here is a re-creation of a Taino village in modern-day Cuba.

Ian Nellist/Alamy

Chapter Objective

Demonstrate an understanding of the initial encounters of Europeans, Africans, and American Indians in the Americas and how this "Columbian Exchange" led to social, cultural, and political changes for all involved.

 ## Learning Objectives

Columbus, the Columbian Exchange, and Early Conquests

2.1 Explain the reasons behind the voyages of Columbus and describe early Spanish encounters with the peoples of the Caribbean, Mexico, and South America.

A Divided Europe: The Impact of the Protestant Reformation

2.2 Explain how the Protestant Reformation and the development of the nation-state changed Europe and European ideas about how best to settle and govern America.

Exploration and Encounter in North America: The Spanish

2.3 Analyze early Spanish exploration of America north of Mexico.

Exploration and Encounter in North America: The French

2.4 Analyze early French exploration and claims in North America.

Exploration and Encounter in North America: The English

2.5 Explain motivations of English explorers, privateers, and reasons for settlement.

After sixty-six days of sailing, the last half on uncharted open seas, an Italian sailor commissioned by Queen Isabella and King Ferdinand of Spain, Christopher Columbus, and his crew landed on a small Caribbean island on October 12, 1492. Columbus named the island San Salvador. No one is sure on which island in the Bahamas Columbus first landed. But there was a Taino village on the shore, and human contact came quickly. Columbus and his crew received a friendly greeting from the Tainos of whom Columbus said,

> I recognized that they were people who would be better freed [from error] and converted to our Holy Faith by love than by force—to some of them I gave red caps, and glass beads … and many other things of small value, in which they took so much pleasure and became so much our friends that it was a marvel. Later they came swimming to the ships' launches where we were and brought us parrots and cotton thread in balls and javelins. … In sum, they took everything and gave of what they had very willingly. … All of them go around as naked as their mothers bore them. …

The world was never the same again.

Although Columbus did not know it, that encounter represented the beginning of an extraordinary change in worldwide human contact. Columbus claimed that he had achieved his mission to reach Asia. The Europeans who came after him quickly realized that they had encountered not Asia but an unknown continent filled with unfamiliar peoples. The Columbian encounter led to unimagined power and wealth for many Europeans. It also led to the creation of new ethnic groups as offspring of American Indian–European couples came to be known as Latinos or Hispanics. And it shifted the balance of trade and commerce around the world from land to the world's oceans.

For the American Indians, the encounter that began with Columbus was even more of a surprise, and much more devastating. Suddenly, from across the ocean, unimagined people arrived, with a strange way of talking and dressing, a strange religion, and a different way of looking at the world. In part because of differences in technology, in part because of differences between European and indigenous people's understandings of war and conquest, and, most of all, because of differences in the two groups' ability to withstand European diseases, the encounter led to conquest, disease, and death for many Indians.

Everett Historical/Shutterstock

This image shows Columbus taking his leave from the king and queen of Spain to journey across the Atlantic.

Significant Dates

1492	Columbus lands on an island in the Bahamas
1497	John Cabot explores the coast of North America for England
1507	A German mapmaker names the new continent "America" in honor of Amerigo Vespucci
1509	Juan Ponce de León founds San Juan, Puerto Rico
1513	Juan Ponce de León leads an expedition that includes Europeans and Africans to explore Florida—first encounter of Europeans, Africans, and Native Americans in the future United States
1514–1566	Bartolomé de Las Casas's fifty-two-year campaign for the rights of the Indians
1517	Martin Luther begins Protestant Reformation
1519–1521	Hernán Cortés conquers the Aztec Empire in Mexico
1524	Giovanni da Verrazano explores the Atlantic coast of North America for France
1528–1536	Cabeza de Vaca travels from Florida to Texas to Mexico
1532	Francisco Pizarro conquers the Inca Empire
1534–1536	Jacques Cartier explores the St. Lawrence River
1534	Parliament names Henry VIII head of the Church of England
1540–1542	Coronado expedition to the Southwest
1539–1542	Hernando de Soto explores the Mississippi River Valley
1542–1543	Juan Rodriguez Cabrillo explores the coast of California
1565	St. Augustine, Florida, is founded, oldest European city in what is now the United States
1579	Francis Drake sails along California coast

(continued)

| 1587 | Roanoke, Virginia, first English settlement in North America; Filipino sailors from a Spanish ship land in Morro Bay California—first Asians known to arrive in the future United States |
| 1598 | First Spanish settlement in New Mexico |

Understanding what happened in future United States over the next five hundred years depends on understanding the differences between those who arrived from Europe—especially from Spain, France, and England—as well as from Africa—and the diverse peoples who lived in the Americas when they arrived. With the arrival of Columbus and the many Europeans who later followed him, something new in human history took place: a massive transit and mixing of peoples in North and South America.

Columbus, the Columbian Exchange, and Early Conquests

2.1 **Explain the reasons behind the voyages of Columbus and describe early Spanish encounters with the peoples of the Caribbean, Mexico, and South America.**

As delighted as Columbus was by the Tainos' generous welcome and what seemed to him the easy opportunity to convert them to Christianity, Columbus also noted other things that would be more ominous for their future:

> They do not carry arms nor are they acquainted with them, because I showed them swords and they took them by the edge and through ignorance cut themselves. They have no iron. Their javelins are shafts without iron and some of them have at the end a fish tooth.

Conquest, Columbus came to believe, would be easy.

Columbus described what would be the terms of much of the European contact with American Indians: "They should be good and intelligent servants." Columbus also looked closely at the gold ornaments and jewelry that some of the Indians were wearing. The effort to subjugate the Indians and the search for gold had begun.

Christopher Columbus's Exploration through Four Voyages

In spite of the friendly welcome he received, Columbus took some Tainos as captives. He wanted to teach them Spanish and show them to his sponsors in Spain. Columbus also wanted guides to the gold he was sure could be found since he had seen gold ornaments.

American Voices

The Dedication of Columbus's Log to the King and Queen of Spain, 1493

Returning from his first voyage in early 1493, Columbus spelled out the links between his voyage and Ferdinand and Isabella's efforts to unify Spain in his report to the rulers.

This present year of 1492, after your Highnesses had brought to an end the war with the Moors who ruled in Europe and had concluded the war in the very great city of Granada, where this present year on the second day of the month of January I saw the Royal Standards of Your Highnesses placed by force of arms on the towers of the Alhambra …and Your Highnesses, as Catholic Christians and Princes, lovers and promoters of the Holy Christian Faith, and enemies of the false doctrine of Mahomet and of all idolatries and heresies, you thought of sending me, Christóbal Colón, to the said regions of India to see the said princes and the peoples and the lands, and the characteristics of the lands and of everything, and to see how their conversion to our Holy Faith might be undertaken. … So, after having expelled all the Jews from all of your Kingdoms and Dominions,

in the same month of January Your Highnesses commanded me to go, with a suitable fleet, to the said regions of India.

Source: Oliver Dunn and James E. Kelley, Jr., translators, *The Diario of Christopher Columbus's First Voyage to America, 1492–1493*, abstracted by Fray Bärtolomé de Las Casas (Norman: University of Oklahoma Press, 1988), pp. 17–19.

Thinking Critically

1. **Causation**

   Columbus made a strong link between Spain's defeat of Muslim Granada, the expulsion of Jews from Spain, and his own voyage across the Atlantic. To what degree do you think the first two events led to the third?

2. **Analyzing Primary Sources**

   What does the document suggest about the role of religion in motivating Spain's efforts at overseas exploration and expansion? Do you find the argument compelling? Why or why not?

2.1

2.2

2.3

2.4

2.5

Led by native guides, he sailed on to Cuba and sent a party inland to find the local chief (or *cacique* as the Tainos called their leaders) who his guides said had access to gold. When Columbus did not find the leader or the gold, he sailed to another island he named Hispaniola (modern Haiti and the Dominican Republic). He built a fort and left part of his crew there with instructions to search for gold. In January 1493, Columbus, with six Taino prisoners, turned back to Spain.

Columbus never fully understood the importance of his voyage. He set out to discover a route across the Atlantic directly to Asia, and he thought he had indeed reached an unknown part of Asia, perhaps Japan or Korea. Thinking the people he met looked like those who came from the part of south Asia Europeans called "the Indies," he called them *Indians*. Of course, he did not really discover them because the Indians were already there. Columbus certainly discovered a new route across the Atlantic, but it led to a continent filled with people unknown to Europeans and to whom Europeans were equally as unfamiliar.

The rest of Columbus's life was a tragedy, for himself and much more so for the peoples he had encountered. To impress the Spanish court, Columbus exaggerated what he had found, especially the gold. Isabella and Ferdinand gave him seventeen ships and 1,200 men for a second voyage to seek slaves and gold in this supposed part of Asia, just as the Portuguese were finding both in Africa and India.

When he returned to Hispaniola in 1494, Columbus found that the native residents had killed the sailors he had left behind in 1492. A local chief initially offered protection to the Europeans, but when the sailors sought to make the Tainos slaves, they rebelled. Columbus ordered retribution, and many Tainos were killed. As word spread of the harsh ways of the Europeans, the Indians became less friendly, and Columbus found himself "discovering" deserted villages. The Caribbean had little gold despite Columbus's desperate efforts to force the natives to find it, and many Tainos died from Spanish swords or from forced labor that the Spanish instituted.

Columbus himself was a better explorer than administrator and less vicious than many of his successors (see Map 2-1). During his third voyage to the Caribbean in 1498, he tried to set up a government on Hispaniola. But many Spaniards complained about hard lives there with little reward. A new governor sent Columbus back to Spain in chains. Although the Spanish monarchs forgave him and allowed him a fourth voyage in 1502, he never governed again.

Exploration and Naming of a Continent

Columbus was not the first European to reach the Americas. Archaeologists have discovered evidence of a short-lived Norse settlement called L'Anse aux Meadows on Newfoundland somewhere between 900 and 1000, but the settlement was quickly forgotten on both sides of the Atlantic. If others crossed the Atlantic, or the Pacific, their voyages were also soon forgotten. What was different about the voyage of Columbus was that so much of Europe took interest and so many Europeans followed in his wake.

In the earliest exploration and conquest of the Americas, Spain was the unquestioned leader. Portugal's king, Joao II, whom Columbus had approached before Ferdinand and Isabella, was deeply disappointed when Columbus, forced by a storm to stop in Portugal on his return voyage in 1493, told the king of his successful travels. While Portugal was just beginning to reap the economic rewards of its new contact with India and was focused primarily on its rich trade routes around Africa and into the Indian Ocean, the Portuguese king did not want to lose out on any claims to the lands across the Atlantic. Portuguese explorers quickly set out across the Atlantic, exploring and claiming much of South America. In 1494, Spain and Portugal agreed to the **Treaty of Tordesillas** in which a line drawn by the pope separated Spanish and Portuguese claims in South America. To this day, Brazil, east of the line, is a Portuguese-speaking country, while the rest of South America is Spanish-speaking.

In April 1495, Isabella and Ferdinand authorized a young Italian merchant, Amerigo Vespucci, to make three or four trips—the historical record is not clear—between 1497 and 1504. Sailing along the coast of Brazil, much farther south than Columbus ever ventured, Vespucci concluded that the land mass on the other side of the Atlantic was much larger

Treaty of Tordesillas

Treaty confirmed by the pope in 1494 to resolve the claims of Spain and Portugal in the Americas.

Map 2-1 Columbus's Voyages.

Columbus made a total of four voyages starting and ending in Spain and enabling him to see and describe the islands of the Bahamas where he first landed, Hispaniola (modern-day Dominican Republic and Haiti), Cuba, Jamaica, and the lower coast of Central America.

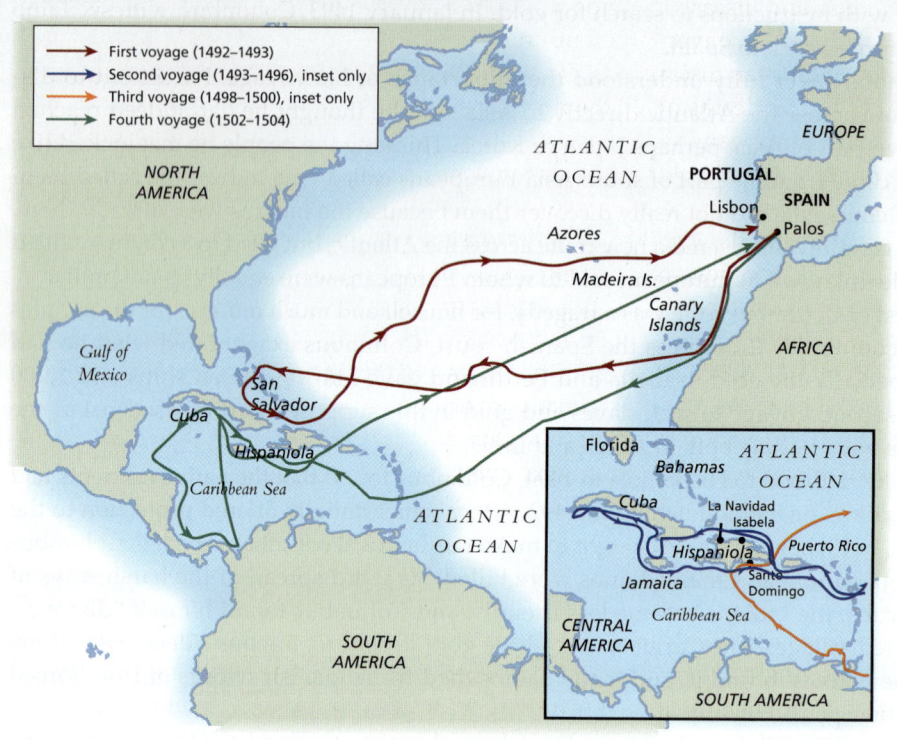

than the first reports indicated. Unlike Columbus, Vespucci was convinced that Europeans had reached a new continent, rather than Asia. As a result, a German publisher, Martin Waldseemüller, produced a new map of the world in 1507. He called the new continent that Vespucci described **America** in his honor.

The Impact of European Arms and Disease

America

The name given to the lands Europeans encountered across the Atlantic after 1492, in honor of the explorer Amerigo Vespucci.

The Spanish governors who came after Columbus were more efficient and more cruel. Ferdinand and Isabella not only ordered that the Indians be treated well and not be enslaved but also pressed hard for gold. Spanish governors, however, focused on the gold and ignored the command to show kindness. Nicolás de Ovando, who was appointed governor on Hispaniola in 1502, set a pattern. He brought 2,500 Spanish settlers—families, not just male explorers—to build a permanent settlement. In the future, many Spanish explorers also married native women, creating new families of mixed ethnic heritage. Ovando attacked the Tainos ruthlessly. In 1502, he responded to a rebellion in Higüey by capturing six hundred to seven hundred Indians and then ordering them all to be knifed to death and their bodies displayed. Later, in 1503, he convened an ostensibly friendly meeting of the caciques, the district chiefs, and when some eighty of them had assembled in one building, he ordered the doors locked and the building burned with them in it. With that act, the last independent chiefdoms of Hispaniola were ended.

However, the most devastating thing that Columbus and his successors did was unintentional. They brought European diseases. The Tainos, like all natives of the Americas, had no immunity to smallpox, measles, or other diseases they had never known. In Europe where these diseases were common and had been for hundreds of years, many people had developed immunity to them or at least to their worst effects. American Indians had no such immunity. As a result, while Indians died by the hundreds from Spanish swords, they died by the thousands from disease. There were probably one million people on Hispaniola when Columbus landed in 1492. By the early 1500s, only one thousand Tainos were left. Within a century, all were gone. The European destruction of the first people of the Americas had begun.

From a total population of perhaps 70–100 million (no one really knows) when Columbus arrived, the population of native peoples in all of the Americas dropped to 4.5 million as a result of war and disease in the decades after the first encounter. However unintentional the introduction of European disease was, the staggering number of Indian deaths made their conquest easy, and many Europeans were happy to take advantage of their already cleared land. For the Indians, tragedy followed tragedy.

Soon, on the islands where Columbus first landed, the only Indian descendants were people of mixed races. A Spanish census of 1514 indicated that 40 percent of the Spanish men had native wives. The arrival of African slaves in the 1500s added African blood to the mix. Today, many of the peoples of the Americas are descendants of all three of the groups that met in the Columbian encounter.

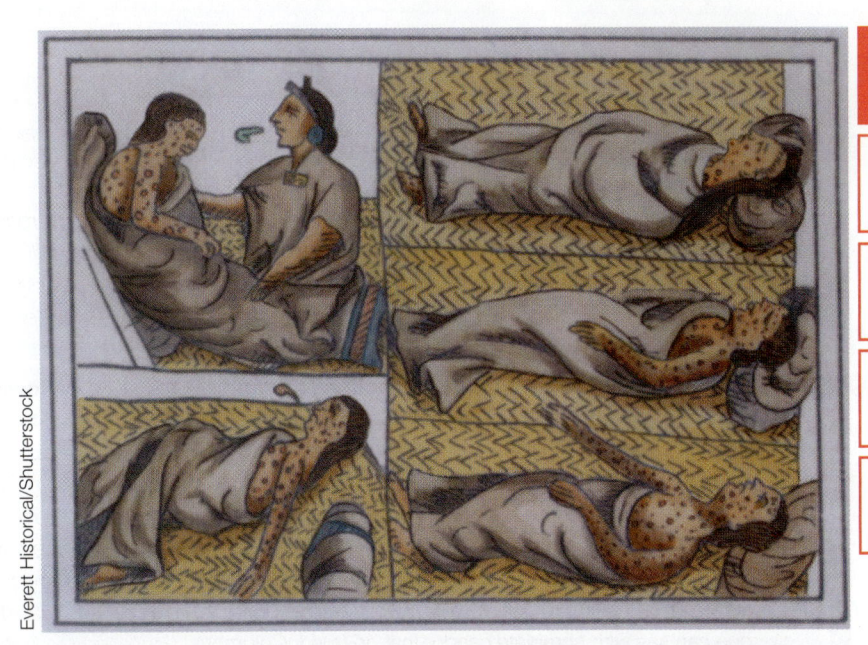

Everett Historical/Shutterstock

European diseases, especially smallpox, killed more of the original inhabitants of the Americas than any other cause. This illustration, originally done by Aztec scribes before their conquest, described "a great sickness" that came with sores "so terrible that the victims could not lie face down, nor on their backs, nor move from one side to the other."

The Making of an Ocean World—The Atlantic and the Columbian Exchange

News of the new contact with the Americas changed the way many people looked at the world. Most educated Europeans already believed that the world was round and not flat. But until 1492, they were concerned primarily with the land. Traders had long gone over land on the **Silk Road** between Venice and China. A series of peace agreements made such trade relatively safe, if still arduous, in the 1200s and 1300s. The well-publicized travels by Marco Polo—over fifteen thousand miles between 1271 and 1295—brought luxury goods to Europe from Asia while his account *The Travels of Marco Polo* built even greater interest and demand for Asian goods. From ancient times, sailors traded across the Mediterranean, and by the 1300s, there was trading all along the coast of Europe. Portuguese sailors stayed close to the coast of Africa as they sailed around that continent to Asia. Norse sailors had explored the far North Atlantic—hopping from Iceland to Greenland, and on to the nearest parts of North America—seeking new fishing opportunities. But Columbus and his crew did something different; they sailed directly across the ocean, with no landmarks to guide their journey. Soon, the oceans—the Atlantic, the Indian, and the Pacific—became the primary trade routes for Europeans, Americans, and increasing numbers of unwilling Africans. Nations that had ports on the Atlantic, especially Spain, Portugal, France, Holland, and England, moved from the margins of a land-focused Europe to become the key points of contact with an ocean-focused world. The shift from primarily land-based, or near-shore, sea trade to trade spanning the world's oceans was a revolution in the way people thought, and it had winners and losers.

The trade and cultural exchanges across the interconnected continents of Europe, Asia, and Africa did not end after 1492, but the relationships were different. Portugal and Spain replaced Genoa and Venice as the primary European links to Asia. Portuguese ships dominated the Indian Ocean. Many others followed Columbus in very short order. In addition to those who explored the Atlantic coast, Vasco Nunez de Balboa reached the Isthmus of Panama in 1513 and became the first European to view the Pacific. In 1519, five ships and their crews commanded by Ferdinand Magellan began a journey around the tip of South America in 1520 and across the Pacific to the Philippines, where Magellan himself was killed. Three years after they had departed, a handful of Magellan's original crew became the first people to circumnavigate the globe, arriving back in Spain in 1522.

More important for Spain's imperial ambitions, a Spanish priest and navigator, Andres de Urdaneta, established the trade route from Manila in the Philippines across the Pacific to Acapulco on Mexico's Pacific coast beginning in 1565. Between 1565 and 1815, Spanish ships known as Manila galleons brought silver mined in the Americas across to Manila.

Silk Road

The overland trading route first established by the Venetian trader Marco Polo in the late 1200s.

2.1

2.2

2.3

2.4

2.5

When Historians Disagree

How Should Columbus Be Remembered?

For most of American history, Christopher Columbus was a hero— the man who "discovered America." No one challenges that his voyages established new contact between the peoples of Europe and the Americas. But many recent historians are challenging other claims regarding Columbus. Columbus's voyage took courage and skill and it changed the world forever, but Columbus and his successors were also devastating to the people of the Americas. Consider the two points of view below.

Lincoln Paine, *The Sea and Civilization: A Maritime History of the World*. New York: Vintage Books, 2013, p. 390.

Christopher Columbus, conceived a bold plan "that he would sail south and west … and that, sailing in this direction he would eventually come to the land of India, with the noble island of Cipangu [Japan] and the realms of the Grand Khan." He was not the first to believe such a voyage was possible, and one can say with complete candor that he failed: Columbus underestimated the size of the earth; he did not reach Asia; and he did not tap into the great spices of the orient. None of this diminishes his epochal accomplishment in establishing an unbroken link between Eurasia and Africa in the east and the Americas in the west. If he excelled his contemporaries, it was not necessarily in navigational ability or intuition, but in his persistent vision and relentless pursuit of the financial and political support without which the honor of bridging the Atlantic would have fallen to another.

Howard Zinn, *A People's History of the United States, 1492–Present*, New York: HarperCollins, 1980, 1999, pp. 9–10.

To emphasize the heroism of Columbus and his successors as navigators and discoverers, and to deemphasize their genocide, is not a technical necessity but an ideological choice. It serves—unwittingly—to justify what was done.

My point is not that we must, in telling history, accuse, judge, condemn Columbus *in absentia*. It is too late for that; it would be a useless scholarly exercise in morality. But the easy acceptance of atrocities as a deplorable but necessary price to pay for progress … that is still with us. One reason these atrocities are still with us is that we have learned to bury them in a mass of other facts. … This learned sense of moral proportion, coming from the apparent objectivity of the scholar, is accepted more easily than when it comes from politicians at press conferences. It is therefore more deadly.

Thinking Critically

1. **Argument Development**

   Paine and Zinn look at different evidence as primary. How would you argue that one is right and one is wrong?

2. **Analyzing Secondary Sources**

   How important is it that Paine's analysis is part of a maritime history of the world, while Zinn's is part of a political history of the United States?

New Spain

The name of Spain's first empire in the Americas.

Manila galleons also brought porcelain, spices, furniture, silk, and other fabrics from all of Asia to **New Spain**, as the Spanish called their empire in Mexico and Central America. Many of these goods were then shipped across the Atlantic to Spain itself and traded to the rest of Europe. Silver from Spain's American empire became a worldwide currency, and the trade across the Atlantic and Pacific oceans created a new worldwide commerce. The Manila galleons also brought people across the Atlantic; in 1587, some of the Filipinos on the crew of the galleon *Nuestra Senora Esperanza* anchored in what was later known as Morro Bay, California, and established a community there—the first Asians known to settle in what would, centuries later, be the United States.

The world of the 1500s was becoming an oceanic world. The Atlantic Ocean that had been the great barrier on the western edge of Europe suddenly became the great highway connecting known and previously unknown continents, facilitating trade and the movement of people on a scale never before imagined. Portugal and Spain were the first European states to establish trading routes across the oceans, but during the 1500s, England, France, and Holland also assumed major roles in the new trade. Looking at this world in 1615, the English explorer and adventurer Sir Walter Raleigh wrote "whosoever commands the sea commands the trade; whosoever commands the trade of the world commands the riches of the world, and consequently the world itself." No one would have said such a thing before 1492, but by little more than a century later, Raleigh was describing a commercial revolution and a quest for power and profit that would intensify the tensions between European nation-states in the decades to come.

The interactions between Europeans and the native people of the Americas transformed the lives of both populations. What became known as the **Columbian Exchange**—the interchange of diseases, plants, animals, and human cultures between New and Old Worlds after 1492—reflected some of these changes. The most tragic loss occurred with the transmission of disease-bearing microbes that devastated populations in the Americas. New populations began to emerge after 1492, when the peoples who met in the Americas produced offspring that carried the biological traits and the cultures of their ancestors from vastly different parts of the world. **Mestizo** people—or people of mixed Indian, European, African, and occasionally Asian bloodlines—increased all across the Americas.

The exchange also changed the eating habits of almost every person on the planet. In Europe, Asia, and Africa, corn, beans, peanuts, potatoes, cassava, sweet potatoes, avocados, pineapples, tomatoes, chilies, vanilla, and cocoa from the Americas enriched people's diets. Sweet potatoes alone became a major food source for generations in Africa. Rice, wheat, barley, oats, and many new fruits and vegetables from Europe, Africa, and Asia fed the American Indians, as did chickens, cattle, sheep, and pigs (see Table 2-1). Horses changed the way many American Indians lived. Because of the introduction of new crops from across the ocean into the Americas and into Europe, Asia, and Africa, people were healthier and lived longer, and the world's population increased. A world without this variety is unimaginable today.

Columbian Exchange

The transatlantic exchange of plants, animals, and diseases that occurred after the first European contact with the Americas.

mestizo

People of mixed Indian, European, African, and occasionally Asian bloodlines.

2.1

2.2

2.3

2.4

2.5

The Conquest of the Aztec and Inca Empires

Besides European diseases, the peoples of the Americas faced another threat: armed conquest. Hernán Cortés sailed from Cuba to Mexico with six hundred soldiers in 1519. Within two years, he conquered Tenochtitlán, the Aztec capital, and renamed it Mexico City. When he first arrived, some of the Aztecs thought Cortés might be their lost god Quetzalcoatl. In their initial encounter, the Aztec emperor Motecuhzoma (often written as Montezuma) welcomed Cortés. They exchanged gifts, which Cortés saw as a sign of submission to Spain. The relationship soured quickly. Cortés took the emperor prisoner but allowed him to maintain a façade of rule.

In July 1520, the Aztecs turned on Cortés, and he and his soldiers fled the capital. But they did not go far. With support from non-Aztec peoples who hated Aztec dominance and especially hated being used for the human sacrifices that Aztec religion demanded, the Spanish army regrouped and began a bloody siege of Tenochtitlán. Motecuhzoma himself was killed, probably by his own people, and Cortés completed his conquest of the city in August 1521.

With Tenochtitlán destroyed, Cortés set about building a new and grander city on the same spot. On the site of the main Aztec temple, he ordered the building of a massive new Catholic

Table 2-1 The Columbian Exchange

From the Americas to Europe, Africa, and Asia	From Europe, Africa, and Asia to the Americas
Plants	
Corn (maize), Potatoes, Sweet potatoes, Peanuts, Pumpkins, Pineapples, Guava, Squash, Tomatoes, Peppers, Papayas, Avocados, Beans, Cassava, Blueberries, Tobacco, Cocoa, Vanilla, Cranberries	Wheat, Barley, Rye, Oats, Apples, Peaches, Pears, Plums, Apricots, Cherries, Bananas, Coffee, Tea, Sugar cane, Melons, Lemons, Oranges, Cabbage, Carrots, Grapes, Lettuce, Onions, Garlic, Eggplant, Spices, Coconuts, Almonds, Walnuts, Cucumbers, Lentils
Animals	
Turkeys, Llamas	Chickens, Donkeys, Cattle, Goats, Horses, Pigs, Sheep, Cats, Rats
Disease	
Tuberculosis, Syphilis (Syphilis was also known in the ancient Eurasian world and has been found in Egyptian mummies, but a new and virulent form of the disease was brought to Europe from the Americas.)	Smallpox (the single most deadly disease among American Indians), Measles, Influenza, Yellow fever, Typhus, Scarlet fever, Diphtheria, Chickenpox, Mumps, Whooping cough, Plague (Sometimes multiple diseases from this list affected an American Indian community at the same time.)

De Agostini Picture Library/The Bridgeman Art Library

One of the earliest images of Hernán Cortés, on horseback, fighting with Aztec warriors.

Viceroyalty of Peru

After the conquest of the Inca Empire, the Spanish crown created a second administrative unit based in the Inca city of Lima and separate from Mexico-based New Spain to govern most of what is today South America and called it the Viceroyalty of Peru.

repartimiento

A Spanish policy that required the conquered people of the Americas to work in the service of someone of Spanish descent who in return would teach them the core of Christianity.

encomienda

In the Spanish colonies, the grant to a Spanish settler of a certain number of American Indian subjects, who would pay him tribute in goods and labor.

cathedral modeled on the one at Granada, which had recently been built in the former Muslim stronghold in southern Spain. In both cases, the religious architecture symbolized the defeat of the "infidels" and the victory of European Catholic Christianity. Within a generation, a thriving new Mexico City, filled with great churches and government palaces, had become the home of the Spanish viceroy—the king's representative—and the capital of New Spain.

In 1532, in Peru, Francisco Pizarro and his army of 168 Spanish soldiers defeated the Inca emperor Atahuallpa and his army of eighty thousand soldiers. Within a few years, the Inca Empire of thirty-two million people, much larger than the Aztec Empire, had become the **Viceroyalty of Peru**, a second major outpost of distant Spain. In the eyes of the Spanish, Peru's primary purpose was to supply gold and silver to finance Spain's European ambitions. At Potosí in Bolivia, forty-five thousand slaves—at first Indians and then also Africans—worked the mines that created the wealth that made King Charles V and his son Philip II the richest and most powerful rulers in Europe.

The swiftness of the Spanish conquest of the Aztec and Inca Empires was possible for many reasons. Aztec resistance was undermined by a sense of fatalism fueled by early visions of their own defeat. Many non-Aztecs joined with Cortés, more than happy to be rid of the Aztecs. The Incas could not imagine, and therefore did not fear, Pizarro's attack since he claimed to come in the name of friendship. Pizarro's surprise attack was simply inconceivable to people reared in Inca ways. And both empires found Spanish horses, swords, and armor terrifying. The ruthless military skill of Cortés and Pizarro and the Spanish mastery of guns, steel swords, and horses created an enemy who was simply unimaginable to Aztec and Inca armies and therefore very difficult to resist. The Aztecs and the Incas could not match the Spanish strategies and tools of war.

Perhaps the most significant Spanish advantage was smallpox. The Aztecs may have lost half of their population to smallpox during the two years of attack by Cortés on their capital, and the Incas faced the same terrifying losses. An Inca emperor had died from smallpox shortly before Pizarro arrived. Disease traveled far faster along the continent's vast trading routes than even Spanish armies could march. For people used to living in harmony with nature, the terrible ravishing of the disease that occurred along with the arrival of these frightening white-skinned, bearded, and horse-mounted soldiers tore apart their world—militarily, culturally, and spiritually—all in a very short time.

Borrowing from what he saw as successful Spanish efforts to subdue the people of Hispaniola, Cortés set out to create a permanent Spanish empire in the lands he conquered. Like Spain itself after 1492, Cortés believed that New Spain should be united by a single Catholic Christian faith. He also wanted to be sure that the victories he had won were permanent. He was critical of other Spanish conquistadors, especially in Panama, where the Spaniards simply devastated the country while searching for wealth. Cortés wrote, "Without settlement there is no good conquest, and if the land is not conquered, the people will not be converted." From his victory in 1521 on, Cortés built his empire on the ideas of *repartimiento* and *encomienda*. Repartimiento was a Spanish policy that required the conquered people of the Americas to work in the service of someone of Spanish descent who in return would teach them the core of Christianity. And the encomienda system was essentially a grant of native peoples to a Spaniard to help him settle the land. Encomienda was a grant of people, not specifically of land, but the people who were forced to work the land created the basis of a new stable economy for the empire that was arising. For those who lost their freedom, the system forced them to labor to make others rich and learn a faith that was not their own. But

Snark/Art Resource, NY

Although he never left Europe, Theodore de Bry (1528–1598) spent many years drawing illustrations of European–Indian encounters based on firsthand reports, including this one showing the attack by Spanish soldiers on an Indian village.

for the masters of the Spanish empire, the encomienda system meant that the fruits of a stable society were greater than those to be gained simply by stealing everything of value and departing. Within another century, the same economic system had spread throughout the Spanish-controlled Americas—from New Mexico and California to the tip of South America.

While the vast new Spanish empires produced immense wealth that transformed Spain from a relatively weak feudal economy to a prosperous one moving quickly toward modern capitalism, they also transformed life for everyone—Spanish and Indian—living in them. Spanish authorities quickly created a rigid caste system in which Spaniards of pure Spanish descent ruled over both a large population of mestizo peoples and, at the bottom, the virtually enslaved native peoples and African slaves.

Bartolomé de Las Casas and the Voices of Protest

Spain's treatment of the American Indians did not occur without protest. In 1511, on a Sunday before Christmas, Antonio de Montesinos, a Dominican priest on Hispaniola, asked his Spanish congregation, "Tell me, by what right do you keep these Indians in cruel servitude? … You are in mortal sin for the cruelty and tyranny you deal out to these innocent people."

Bartolomé de Las Casas (1484–1566) may have heard Montesinos's sermon, or heard of it. Las Casas edited the log of Columbus's journey and moved to Hispaniola to make his own fortune in 1502. Although he became a priest in 1510, he participated in the conquest of Cuba in 1512 and was rewarded with a large ranch worked by Indian slaves or encomienda. But his conscience bothered him. In 1514, he gave up the land and the slaves and began preaching and writing against the oppression of the Indians, which he continued to do for the next fifty years. Las Casas documented the cruelty of the Spanish conquerors, begging the Spanish crown to stop the **conquistadores**, the soldiers who were establishing the Spanish Empire in the Americas.

conquistadores

The name given to the early Spanish conquerors of Mexico and Peru.

New Spain quickly developed a rigid caste system based primarily on family lines tracing back to Spain. At the top was a small elite of Spanish immigrant families who ruled in state and church. Lower were those of mixed Spanish and Indian families and, at the bottom, were the remaining native peoples.

Museo Nacional del Virreinato Tepotzotlán

John Mitchell / Alamy Stock Photo

This statue of Bartolomé de Las Casas stands in a prominent place in modern Mexico City as recognition of the respect in which he is held by many of the indigenous people of Mexico and the Americas.

Las Casas also left an important record of the life and customs of the first peoples of the Americas. He wrote that among them, "marriage laws are nonexistent: men and women alike choose their mates and leave them as they please, without offense, jealousy, or anger." They live, he wrote, in

> large communal bell-shaped buildings, housing up to 600 people at one time … made of very strong wood and roofed with palm leaves. … They prize bird feathers of various colors, beads made of fish bones, and green and white stones with which they adorn their ears and lips, but they put no value on gold and other precious things. … They are extremely generous with their possessions and by the same token covet the possessions of their friends and expect the same degree of liberality.

The purpose of all of Las Casas's writings was to ask the Spanish authorities to protect the Indians. He described seeing native people worked to death in the mines when "'moderate labor' turned into labor fit only for iron men: mountains are stripped from top to bottom and bottom to top a thousand times; they dig, split rocks, move stones and carry dirt on their backs to wash it in rivers, while those who wash gold stay in the water all the time with their backs bent so constantly it breaks them."

Las Casas always hoped that if the Spanish monarchs only knew the truth, they would intercede. At times, the distant monarchs seemed to heed him. Shortly before her death, Isabella had ordered that the Indians must be treated "as freemen and not as slaves, they must be given wages, they must be treated well." Las Casas was determined to show how far reality departed from these orders. In 1550 at the call of King Charles V (Ferdinand and Isabella's grandson and heir), de Las Casas engaged in a debate at the Spanish court with another priest, Juan Gines de Sepulveda, in which Sepulveda defended Spain's right of conquest and argued that the peoples of the Americas were "a children … whose condition is such that their function is the use of their bodies and nothing better can be expected of them," while Las Casas insisted that the Indians were fully human and should be treated with all the dignity any human deserved. King Charles did not officially adopt either view.

2.1 Quick Review

Which factor do you believe was most responsible for the destruction of native populations? Justify your answer with evidence from the chapter.

American Voices

Bartolomé de Las Casas, *The History of the Indies*, 1550

In The History of the Indies, *Las Casas documented just how cruel the first Europeans could be in their treatment of the indigenous people of the Americas.*

The men were sent out to the mines as far as eighty leagues away while their wives remained to work the soil, not with hoes or plowshares drawn by oxen, but with their own sweat and sharpened poles that were far from equaling the equipment used for similar work in Castile. Thus husbands and wives were together only once every eight or ten months, and when they met they were so exhausted and depressed on both sides that they had no mind for marital communication and in this way they ceased to procreate. As for the newly born, they died early because their mothers, overworked and famished, had no milk to nurse them, and for this reason, while I was in Cuba, 7,000 children died in three months. Some mothers even drowned their babies from sheer desperation, while others caused themselves to abort with certain herbs that

produced stillborn children. In this way husbands died in the mines, wives died at work, and children died from lack of milk, while others had not time or energy for procreation, and in a short time this land, which was so great, so powerful and fertile, though so unfortunate, was depopulated. If this concatenation of events had occurred all over the world, the human race would have been wiped out in no time.

Source: Bartolomé de Las Casas, *The History of the Indies*, 1550.

Thinking Critically

1. **Analyzing Primary Sources**
   What kinds of abuses did Las Casas identify?

2. **Contextualization**
   Who might Las Casas have been hoping to influence by publicizing Spanish abuses in the New World?

A Divided Europe: The Impact of the Protestant Reformation

2.2 Explain how the Protestant Reformation and the development of the nation-state changed Europe and European ideas about how best to settle and govern America.

When Columbus sailed in 1492, he did so with a commission from the rulers of a newly unified, Catholic Spain. Spanish explorers and conquerors brought the same quest for unity to the Americas. In 1492, nearly all Western Europeans shared that sense of religious unity. Soon, however, Europe's religious unity would disappear.

Less than thirty years after Columbus made his voyage across the Atlantic, the Protestant Reformation changed the way Europeans thought about the world. The initial European encounter with the Americas was led by representatives of a religiously united Europe. But nearly all of the subsequent exploration and settlement of North America was conducted by Europeans from a continent deeply divided by religious hostility. That divide shaped attitudes toward the Americas on both sides of the Atlantic.

The Birth of Protestantism

In 1517, before Hernán Cortés began his conquest of Mexico, a young German monk, Martin Luther (1483–1546), asked for a debate about religious doctrine by posting his

Ninety-Five Theses

A document with ninety-five debating points that a young monk, Martin Luther, hoped would lead to a series of reforms within the Catholic Church.

Protestant Reformation

The process that began with Martin Luther's efforts to reform the Catholic Church's practices in the early 1500s and that eventually led followers of Luther, Calvin, and others to completely break from the Catholic Church.

North Wind Picture Archives / Alamy Stock Photo

Martin Luther's challenge to Catholic teachings and practices in his day led to a decisive split in the unity among Christians that had been known in Western Europe for centuries. Soon thereafter, John Calvin also challenged some of Luther's teachings, leading to a three-way split between Catholics, Lutherans, and Calvinists—followed by further splits among Protestants.

nation-state

A relatively new development in Europe during the 1300s and 1400s in which nations became the major political organizations, replacing both the smaller kingdoms and city-states.

Peace of Augsburg in 1555

An agreement among different smaller kingdoms in Germany that no ruler would attack the kingdom of another on religious grounds.

Treaty of Westphalia of 1648

A 1648 peace treaty between a number of European powers that significantly extended the ideas of the Peace of Augsburg.

Ninety-Five Theses on the door of a church in Wittenberg in the small independent German-speaking state of Saxony. At this time, others within the Roman Catholic Church began to challenge some of the church's practices and questioned the Catholic Church's insistence that bishops and not everyday Christians should interpret the Bible and the idea that one could reach salvation through "good works." Luther's challenges quickly led to a religious split, first in Germany, and then across Europe. That split, known as the **Protestant Reformation**, would shape the cultural and political development of the future United States.

As word of Luther's protests spread, many Germans, including significant members of the nobility who controlled many of the small independent states of Germany, were drawn to the Lutheran cause. In the century that followed, new splits developed among Protestants as they cultivated their own religious ideas. Followers of the French-Swiss reformer, John Calvin (1509–1564), were known as Calvinists, while other Protestants went in other directions.

At its core, Protestantism was a rejection of the authority of the pope and bishops in matters of religious faith and morals in favor of the judgments of individuals and small communities of Christians. Most Protestants turned to the individual's reading of the Bible, especially the writings of St. Paul that stressed faith ahead of efforts to earn salvation. Calvinists also rejected Lutheran maintenance of the Catholic creeds and the Catholic-like Mass, preferring a form of worship centered on a Bible-focused sermon.

One of the things that fueled the extraordinary response to Luther's challenge was the technology of printing that had developed during the previous sixty-two years. Johannes Gutenberg's creation of a printing press that used moveable type in 1455 and the subsequent rapid spread of printing hugely expanded literacy beyond a small educated elite, mostly clergy, who had monopolized literacy in the medieval world. By 1500, at least ten million books had been printed, and many people learned to read; thus, new ideas could spread with a swiftness not known before. Modern translations of the Bible and sermons and pamphlets by Catholics, Lutherans, and Calvinists circulated quickly—a free flow of ideas that most people in Europe had not experienced before.

Religion and the Nation-State

The idea of the **nation-state** developed more or less at the same time as the Protestant–Catholic split and the two developments reinforced each other. The idea that the world should be governed by independent nations, or nation-states, was new in the Europe of the 1500s. Indeed, a world divided into separate independent nations clashed with a long-standing ideal, held by many, of a Europe unified in religion and government. In reality, the Europe of the 1400s was not united in any political way. Real power rested in local territories. Frederick, Elector (or Duke) of Saxony, had enough power to ensure Luther's safety in spite of hostility from the Holy Roman emperor, the pope, and the kings of nearby France. Most of Europe's modern nations did not exist. Even within the church, distance and the difficulty of travel gave local Catholic bishops great independence from papal authorities in Rome.

By the late 1400s, however, something new was emerging in European views of the best forms of government. Ferdinand and Isabella united Spain by 1492. Kings in France, Sweden, Scotland, and England had done the same earlier in the 1400s. The idea of being part of a nation was taking on new importance (see Map 2-2).

Virtually no one argued in favor of religious freedom for the citizens of these nations. Instead, different religious parties, Catholics and assorted Protestant groups, sought to impose their religious beliefs on others. Each party argued that it was defending truth and saw no reason to tolerate those they believed were defending error. This belief in the absolute rightness of one's cause led to more than a century of bloody persecution and religious wars from Ireland and Scotland to France, Germany, and Hungary. The **Peace of Augsburg in 1555** and the **Treaty of Westphalia of 1648** finally ended the long warfare between Catholics and Protestants in Europe. The treaties provided that, in each nation covered by the treaty, the ruler would decide the faith of the people and that foreign armies would no longer intervene in the religious affairs

Map 2-2 Europe on the Eve of the Columbian Encounter.

In the years before Columbus made his 1492 voyage across the Atlantic, Western Europe was being divided into nation-states, including England, France, and Spain. Central Europe remained a series of separate states loosely united in the Holy Roman Empire.

of another state. It was a long way from religious freedom, but it brought an end to the worst religious bloodshed while linking national unity and religious uniformity more tightly than ever.

Religious divisions had a huge impact on European settlement in the Americas. Protestant nations did not want Catholic ones to dominate the colonies, while Catholic nations did not want Protestant colonies. Different nations from a divided Europe battled with each other for control of those new lands. In addition, the wars and divisions in Europe that were fueled by the Reformation led many to seek asylum in a new place, preferably as far away from the old as possible.

2.2 Quick Review

How might religious changes and new ideas about national unity have inspired people in Europe to look at the world differently than they had before 1517?

Exploration and Encounter in North America: The Spanish

2.3 **Analyze early Spanish exploration of America north of Mexico.**

Columbus claimed the lands he found for Spain, and for a long time, only Spain among the European powers showed much interest in the lands of Central or North America, although sailors and adventurers working for both France and England explored the North

American coast and made their own counterclaims to the lands and rivers they saw. In addition, Portuguese adventurers quickly settled the east coast of South America and called it Brazil. Conquests of the Aztec and Inca Empires produced extraordinary wealth for Spain. Exploration farther north in the Americas—in the future United States—was secondary. Most Europeans showed more interest in getting through or around North America and on to Asia than in exploring the lands north of New Spain. Nevertheless, the unknown lands north of Mexico beckoned to some Spaniards in the 1500s, even if they were often considered a consolation prize for those who were not chosen for activities farther south (see Map 2-3).

Ponce de León in Florida, 1513–1521

Juan Ponce de León, who had been part of the Spanish army that conquered Muslim Granada in 1492, led the first known European expeditions to Puerto Rico and Florida. In 1508–1509, he founded the first Spanish community near what would become San Juan and was named Governor of Puerto Rico. In 1513, he led an expedition from Puerto Rico that arrived in what he thought was another island, which he named La Florida. Legend says he was seeking a "Fountain of Youth" that would keep him forever young. Certainly he was seeking an expansion of Spain's empire in the Americas and greater wealth for himself. Ponce de León was accompanied by free Africans whose families were slaves in Spain. Europeans, Africans, and the native peoples of the Americas first met on the soil of the future United States when Ponce de León landed.

In 1521, Ponce de León returned to Florida with some two hundred followers from Puerto Rico. The Native Americans in Florida did not welcome them. Ponce de León was wounded by a poisoned arrow and died soon thereafter. But the first of many contacts between native peoples and travelers from Europe and Africa in what are now the fifty United States had been made in Florida.

Map 2-3 North American Exploration.

In the first one hundred years after Columbus, European explorers traveled along both the Atlantic and Pacific coasts and through much of the interior of what almost two hundred years later would become the United States. By 1592, however, most Europeans had concluded that there was no easy route through North America to Asia and little gold to be found so they lost interest in the regions north of Mexico.

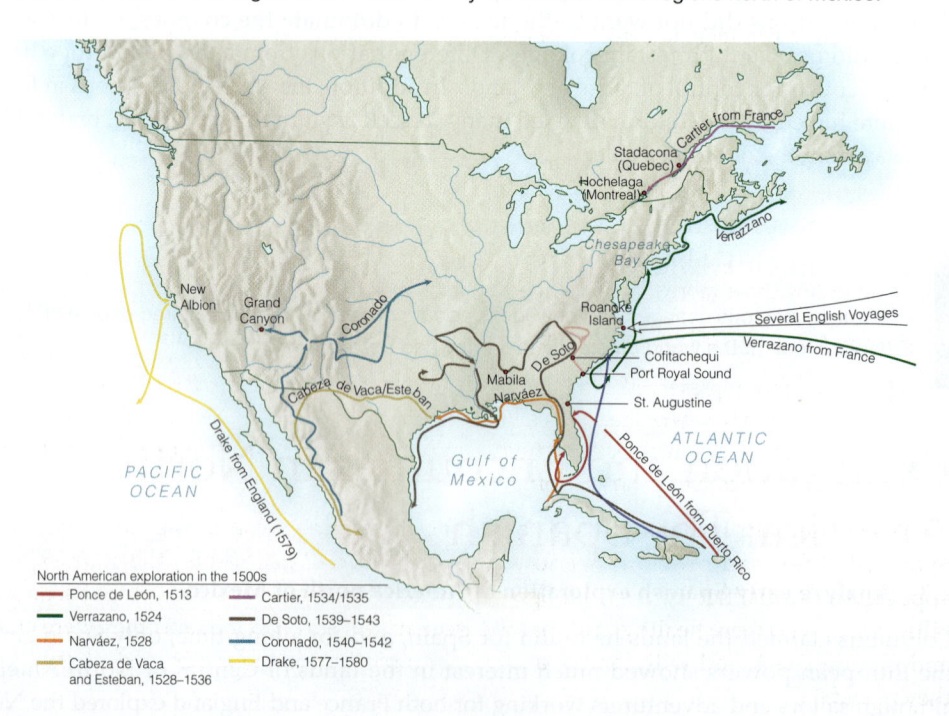

Exploring Texas by Accident: Cabeza de Vaca, 1528–1536

In 1528, there was another ill-fated effort to colonize Florida. Pánfilo de Narváez sailed to Tampa Bay with about four hundred men—Europeans and a few Africans. The Narváez expedition was a disaster. Leaving the ships in Tampa Bay, they spent months tramping through swamps, wearing fifty to sixty pounds of heavy armor, seeking gold. Soon, they sought merely food and water. Along the way, American Indians attacked them, shooting arrows that penetrated their armor, and then vanished into the forests and swamps.

Finally, ill, under attack, and starving, the survivors decided to build new boats and leave. Years later, one of the few survivors remembered:

> This seemed impossible to all, because we did not know how to build them, nor were there … one of all the things that are necessary, nor anyone who would know any way to apply ingenuity. And above all there was nothing to eat.

Nevertheless, they built five barges, and 250 men set out for what they hoped would be a rescue in New Spain (Mexico). Instead, the currents, winds, and a hurricane took them west. Many drowned in storms, but two or three of the five barges survived the storm and came ashore near what is now Galveston, Texas.

American Indians gave the survivors food, water, and shelter. Of the eighty explorers who survived the journey across the Gulf of Mexico, only fifteen lived through the first winter on the Texas coast (see Map 2-3). The others died of cold and disease. Many of the American Indian hosts also died of European diseases that the Spanish brought with them, and the surviving Indians grew hostile to these intruders.

While others from the Narváez expedition may have lived out their lives among the American Indians of the Texas coast, four of them, three Spaniards—Alvar Nunez Cabeza de Vaca, Andres Dorantes, Alonso del Castillo Maldonado—and an enslaved African Muslim from North Africa, named Esteban, decided to literally walk to Spanish territory in Mexico. Thus, like Florida, Texas was explored by Europeans and Africans together, providing the Indians there with their first exposure to both. The foursome's eight-year adventure took them through southern Texas, the northern states of Mexico, and eventually to the Pacific coast and on to Mexico City.

The four travelers developed a reputation as healers and traders as they collected a trove of information about American Indians who lived in permanent houses and had a good supply of corn and beans. Later, Cabeza de Vaca described the ways of the people he met:

> When Indian men get into an argument in their villages, they fist-fight until exhausted, then separate. Sometimes the women will go between and part them, but men never interfere. No matter what the disaffection, they do not resort to bows and arrows. …
>
> All these [plains] tribes are warlike, and have as much strategy for protection against enemies as if they had been reared in Italy in continual feuds. … Whoever fights them must show no fear and no desire for anything that is theirs. …
>
> I believe these people see and hear better and have keener sense in general than any in the world. They know great hunger, thirst, and cold, as if they were made for enduring these more than other men, by habit and nature.

De Vaca also described "a big copper rattle" that was given to them:

> It had a face represented on it, and the natives prized it highly. … It had been brought from the north, where there was a lot of it, replied the natives, who considered copper very valuable. Wherever it came from, we concluded the place must have a foundry to have cast the copper in hollow form.

The American Indians refused to believe these men were of the same race as the Spaniards they had previously known. As Cabeza de Vaca wrote, the four explorers appeared to be distinct from earlier Spanish invaders because, "we cured the sick and they killed those who were healthy, and that we came naked and barefoot and they were clothed and on horseback and with lances, and … had no other purpose but to steal everything they found."

2.1

2.2

2.3

2.4

2.5

When the four explorers finally reached Mexico City in 1536, their story inspired further exploration. The expeditions that followed, however, did not heed the four explorers' peaceful approach to interactions but were, instead, motivated by suggestions of astounding riches.

Exploring the Southwest: Esteban, de Niza, and Coronado, 1539–1542

When the four Texas explorers told their story in Mexico City, they were met with great interest. In their years living with American Indians, they heard stories of seven wealthy and powerful cities on the Rio Grande with buildings of four or five stories and copper, silver, and gold everywhere. For the Spaniards, stories of fabulous wealth were alluring.

An old Spanish legend was about seven Christian bishops who had fled from the Muslim invasion of Spain in the 700s and established seven wealthy cities far to the west. As the Spanish community in Mexico City heard the stories from Texas, many of them remembered this legend and the wealth that Cortés had found. The Texas survivors showed the copper rattle they had been given, which added to the allure. Many in Mexico City now wanted to explore the territory to their north.

In 1539, a Franciscan brother, Marcos de Niza, led an expedition to find the fabled cities. De Niza asked Esteban, the African who had walked across Texas, to scout for him. Thus an African was the first non-Indian that many of the Pueblo peoples met. Drawing from his experiences, he decided to dress with feathers, bells, and turquoise to seem godlike. His messages back to de Niza indicated that he had come to wealthy towns. When he came to the Zuni Pueblo of Hawikuh, they told Esteban to leave. When he threatened them, they killed him. De Niza came far enough north to see Hawikuh from a distance, but he did not want to risk Esteban's fate. He returned to Mexico City and reported to the viceroy that the city "is better seated than any I have seen in these parts," and he said, "I was told that there is much gold there." De Niza's report was carefully worded to avoid exaggerating. Nevertheless, such a report was enough to launch further expeditions. De Niza had also heard a name for the region—Cibola. From then on, the search for the **Seven Cities of Cibola** became the stuff of legend.

Seven Cities of Cibola

The name given by early Spanish explorers to a number of Native American pueblos.

In 1540, Francisco Vázquez de Coronado led a large expedition into what is now modern Arizona. At the Zuni pueblo of Hawikuh, Zunis resisted the demand that they submit to previously unheard of Spanish authority. Coronado's men attacked the village, primarily to gain access to food, and then turned east to central New Mexico. Residents of other villages along the Rio Grande were no more enthusiastic about submitting to Spanish power or supplying food and provisions than the Zuni had been. The Pueblos quickly found that, rather than fight, the best solution was to keep the Spanish moving by assuring them that the real wealth was just over the horizon.

In 1541, the expedition set off into what are now northern Texas, Oklahoma, and Kansas. The Spaniards met Teya Indians but did not find gold or European-style cities. Finally, discouraged and with their supplies gone, they returned to Mexico City in 1542 with little to show for their efforts. It was decades before Spanish authorities would try again to settle in Arizona or New Mexico.

Exploring the Mississippi River Valley: The de Soto Expedition, 1539–1542

While Coronado was roaming the Southwest, another Spanish adventurer, Hernando de Soto, was exploring even more of the future United States. De Soto had won fame and gold through military exploits in Panama in the 1520s and had been a part of Pizarro's conquest of the Inca Empire in the 1530s. He was then given a royal charter to settle La Florida and the lands beyond. He would try again where Ponce de León and de Narváez had failed. In 1539, he sailed to Florida with some five hundred to six hundred Spaniards and about one hundred captive American Indians and Africans.

In 1540, the expedition moved from northern Florida into what would be Georgia and the Carolinas. In a place they called Cofit-achiqui, probably a Creek Indian village, the ruler, a young woman, greeted de Soto and "presented unto him great store of clothes of the country … and took from her own neck a great cordon of pearls, and cast it about the neck of the Governor, entertaining him with very gracious speeches of love and courtesy." De Soto responded by taking the princess prisoner and demanding that she guide his expedition over the Appalachian Mountains to the gold he sought. She did lead them over the mountains, but then escaped, taking home with her the pearls that she had given de Soto. Other Indians who happened to be in de Soto's path would not be so fortunate.

As the expedition crossed the Appalachian Mountains into what would become Tennessee, Alabama, and Mississippi, they were met by Native Americans bringing gifts; the Spaniards quickly tried to make the natives into guides and slaves. But as word of the Spaniards spread, they found fewer gifts and more hostility. De Soto reported well-populated lands throughout the expedition. Later European explorers, however, found far fewer Indians. Indeed, the single most significant impact of the de Soto expedition may have been a massive depopulation of the American Southeast resulting from European diseases that spread far beyond any of the peoples the expedition met directly.

In 1541, de Soto crossed the Mississippi River, exploring what is now Arkansas and, probably, modern-day Texas. When they turned back to the Mississippi River, de Soto demanded that a nearby Native American town provide supplies and porters to help with the river crossing. The village chief refused, so de Soto ordered his soldiers to destroy the town; his journal reports that "the cries of the women and children were such as to deafen those who pursued them."

De Soto himself died of fever on June 20, 1542. His fellow explorers sank his body in the Mississippi River so the now-hostile Indians would not know their leader was gone. Then they built rafts and drifted down the river. After considerable hardship, 311 survivors—about half the original group—reached Mexico. They had not found much in North America that interested them.

Library of Congress, Prints & Photographs Division [LC-USZ62-79801]

Jacques Le Moyne, an early French colonist in Florida, drew this picture of an Indian queen being carried by high-ranking men. While the picture is from the later 1500s in Florida, the princess that the de Soto expedition met a few years earlier may well have been treated with similar respect.

Exploring California: The Cabrillo Voyage, 1542–1543

While Coronado and de Soto explored on land, the Spanish authorities commissioned Juan Rodriguez Cabrillo to investigate the Pacific Coast. In 1542, Cabrillo sailed north from Mexico along the Pacific Coast with three ships "to discover the coast of New Spain" and continue until he reached China, which was assumed to be not far distant. Cabrillo's ships left Navidad, Mexico, in June 1542, and by September had reached San Diego Bay in California. They exchanged gifts with friendly American Indians and reported seeing a beautiful land of valleys, savannas, high mountains, and smoke that indicated a large native population. Cabrillo called California a "good country where you can make a settlement."

He continued north along the Pacific Coast as far as the Russian River in northern California. Like many after him, Cabrillo overlooked the entrance to what is now San Francisco Bay because of the heavy fog. He did, however, realize that in Monterey Bay—the future capital of Spanish and Mexican California—there was a fine harbor. After Cabrillo died of an injury, the expedition returned to Mexico. They had found neither China nor the gold they sought.

2.1

2.2

2.3

2.4

2.5

Early Settlements in Florida: Fort Caroline and St. Augustine, 1562–1565

After all these failed efforts, Spanish interest in the lands north of Mexico waned. The first actual European settlements in North America reflected the growing divisions in Europe itself. Catholic Spain now had to compete with France—a nation divided between Catholicism and Protestantism—and with Protestant England and Holland. Only when these other European powers showed an interest in North America did Spain set up permanent settlements there.

No nation was more deeply split by the Protestant–Catholic divide than France, which had a large Protestant minority and a strong Catholic majority. In 1562, Gaspard de Coligny, a French Protestant nobleman and admiral, commissioned expeditions to Florida. Although there was no European settlement in Florida, it seemed to be a strategic location on the sea lanes between Spain's empire in Mexico and South America and Spain itself. As a loyal subject of the French king, Coligny wanted to secure lands for France. He also wanted to create a safe haven for his fellow Protestants. In 1562, Coligny commissioned Jean Ribault to make an initial trip to Florida, followed by a larger French expedition, including many families with their livestock in 1564. The settlers moved to the mouth of the St. Johns River where Jacksonville, Florida, is today and built a town they named Fort Caroline after King Charles IX of France. It would be a useful outpost for France, yet far enough away to avoid the political and religious turmoil of their homeland.

The Spanish, however, considered this colony a major religious, political, and commercial threat to Spain's control of the Americas. Pedro Menéndez de Avilés was given jurisdiction of a new Spanish colony to reach from Florida to Newfoundland and was told to establish cities in Florida and oust the French Protestants. He did both.

In 1565, Menéndez de Avilés founded St. Augustine, Florida, today the oldest city of European origin still inhabited in the United States. All the lands north and west of it, he declared, now belonged to the king of Spain. He began a friendly trade with the Timuca Indians who lived in northern Florida and sought to convert them to Catholicism. The Timucas valued Spanish goods and provided the colony with food, root vegetables, wild

This illustration by Jacques Le Moyne shows the French, led by Jean Ribault, landing at the St. Johns River in Florida in May 1562 and being greeted by friendly Timuca Indians.

fruit, fish, oysters, game, and corn but resisted religious conversion. Having established St. Augustine, de Avilés attacked Fort Caroline, killing all its inhabitants. When the French fleet coming to aid Fort Caroline was shipwrecked along the coast by a hurricane, de Avilés killed the survivors, too. Florida would remain in Spanish hands for centuries, and its bloody European beginnings mirrored Europe's divisions.

The founders of Spain's first colonies in North America, like those who settled in Latin America, reflected the spirit of the *Reconquista*, or "reconquest," of Spain itself when Muslims and Jews were driven out of the country and religious and national unity were seen as one and the same. For hundreds of years, soldiers of Christian Spain fought against Muslims, whom they considered infidels, seeking to win military glory, wealth, and spiritual honor on the battlefield. It was a world-view in which religious fervor and military bravery were united in the service of the nation. After the victory over the last Muslim stronghold in Spain in 1492, the next generation of Spanish men could not hope for the success of their fathers, grandfathers, and great-grand-fathers in Spain itself, but they brought the same mixture of military heroics and religious fervor to the Americas. In the 1500s, a way of looking at the world and especially at conquest that had been reshaping Spain itself for hundreds of years became the key to creating an ever-expanding empire in the Americas.

Sean Pavone/Shutterstock

St. Augustine, Florida, was settled as a Spanish outpost in 1565 to ensure control of North America. While Acoma and other Pueblos in the Southwest are older, St. Augustine is the oldest continuously inhabited community established by Europeans in North America.

Cultural practices in Spain and other parts of Europe at the time may have also played a role in how ruthless the early Europeans were. Under a system of primogeniture, land was typically passed on to the oldest son. Younger sons would not have the same opportunities to acquire land and the wealth that went with it. Some would opt to spend their lives in the church, but many would opt to spend their lives as soldiers where, through conquest of new lands, they might be rewarded.

Unlike the empires in Mexico and Peru, the Spanish colonies in Florida were settled by people who did not want to create a vast empire but valued the independence that distance gave. As citizens on the border between European settlement and American Indian territory, these settlers wanted to avoid the tightly ordered hierarchical society that was evolving in Mexico. The cities and the farms in Florida prospered. One settler recorded, "I have planted with my own hands grapevines, pomegranates, orange trees and figs, wheat, barley, onions, garlic and many vegetables that grow in Spain." The colonists quickly took to the corn that was the staple of the Indian diet.

There were also slaves in St. Augustine from the beginning. Although his royal commission had authorized him to bring up to five hundred African slaves to St. Augustine, De Avilés actually brought only about fifty. In time, Spanish Florida had a black militia and included both African slaves and free Africans.

There was also intermarriage and more casual sexual encounters among Europeans, Native Americans, and Africans in Spanish Florida. In this outpost, the races blended, creating a new culture and new bloodlines. St. Augustine became a place where Europeans from other nations settled. Some settled of necessity after their ships were wrecked on the Florida coast. Others came to escape legal problems, military commitments, or families. Despite strict rules issued in Madrid, isolated places like St. Augustine reflected considerable diversity, including Jews escaping an increasingly intolerant Europe as well as French, Flemish, and German immigrants escaping religious persecution or simply wanting a new start in life.

The Spanish also sent Franciscan missionaries into the surrounding Native American territories. The Franciscans who traveled into the interior of Florida and Georgia to make converts also sought alliances with the Indians. Indian leaders came to St. Augustine to

2.1
2.2
2.3
2.4
2.5

2.1

2.2

2.3

2.4

2.5

trade and negotiate, and they accepted, however casually, Spanish rule. Eventually, about eighty mission centers were established from the Savannah River in Georgia to as far south as modern Daytona Beach. The Franciscans also brought European diseases along with their preaching, and the American Indian population fell drastically. Nevertheless, for a century, Native Americans, missionaries, and soldiers traded religious and cultural ideas as well as the tools of commerce and war.

Despite occasional battles with the American Indians, raids by European navies, and hurricanes, life in Spanish Florida continued more or less uninterrupted from the 1500s well into the 1700s. Except for a brief period of British rule between 1763 and 1784, Florida remained a Spanish colony until it was ceded to the United States in 1821, 256 years after the founding of St. Augustine.

Settling New Mexico: 1598

After Coronado's expedition returned to Mexico City in 1542, there was little further exploration of New Mexico for over half a century. Then in 1598, the Spanish viceroy in Mexico City decided it was time for another look at the lands of the north and appointed a new governor for what was called "New Mexico." The rumors that great wealth existed there had never died. More pragmatically, the Spanish were worried about the Protestant English. In 1579, Francis Drake, an English privateer (a pirate working for the government), sailed up the coast of California, duplicating Cabrillo's route (and his failure to find San Francisco). Drake then turned west and duplicated the route of an earlier Spanish explorer, Ferdinand Magellan, sailing across the Pacific and on around the world before returning to London in 1580. To the authorities in Spain, this achievement was a real threat. They considered the Pacific to be their ocean and they certainly considered all of North America to be their land. Settling the interior of North America before someone followed Drake back to the Pacific coast suddenly seemed imperative.

Don Juan de Oñate was appointed governor of New Mexico with instructions to "endeavor to attract the natives with peace, friendship, and good treatment … and to induce them to hear and accept the holy gospel." Oñate's expedition included families, a few Spanish soldiers, Franciscan friars, and Indians, along with supply wagons, cattle, sheep, and mules. Oñate's wife, Isabel Tolosa Cortés Montezuma, was herself a granddaughter of Cortés and a great-granddaughter of the Aztec emperor Montezuma. On April 30, 1598, the expedition stopped on the banks of the Rio Grande and claimed all of the lands and peoples to the north for Spain. Oñate named the place where he crossed the river El Paso del Norte the "pass to the north." With the Oñate expedition, unlike earlier ventures, Spanish occupation of New Mexico would come closer to being permanent.

Oñate asked Pueblo chiefs to swear allegiance to Spain and convert to Christianity. Oñate chose to interpret their lack of hostility as agreement. He also built a capital, which he named San Gabriel. Something resembling a permanent settlement of four hundred Europeans in the middle of thousands of Pueblo Indians began to take shape.

At first, all was peaceful. Oñate divided New Mexico into administrative districts, each with a priest to try to convert the American Indians to Christianity. He allowed self-government to continue in each pueblo—he had little choice—but insisted that each one must have a political governor. He was more interested in exploring for the gold, silver, or pearls, which he was sure were just over the horizon, and did not try to force the Native Americans to labor for the Spanish.

The peace did not last, however. Zutucapan, the leader of the Acoma Pueblo, had avoided meeting Oñate because he did not want to cede any authority to the Spaniards. Late in 1598, he attacked a Spanish scouting party, and in 1599, Oñate struck back. After a fierce battle, the Spaniards, whose guns, swords, and horses gave them a huge advantage, burned Acoma to the ground. One thousand of its residents were killed, and the remaining five hundred were taken as slaves. When the Jumano Indians also resisted Oñate, he hanged their chiefs and burned their village.

Oñate's cruelty and his failure to find riches led to his recall in 1609. The new royal governor Don Pedro de Peralta moved the capital farther north to a new town that he created and named Santa Fe, in 1610. There, Peralta built the oldest public building still standing in the United States—the governor's mansion. The colony's attention turned from gold to farming. Churches were built at the center of each pueblo. The Spanish hoped these churches would become new centers of Indian life and faith, though tensions also continued.

2.1

2.2

2.3

2.4

2.5

> ### 2.3 Quick Review
>
> Why did Spanish authorities have so little interest in North America for so long? What eventually increased their interest?

Exploration and Encounter in North America: The French

2.4 **Analyze early French exploration and claims in North America.**

King Francis I of France (r. 1515–1547) did not want to leave the Americas to Spain or Portugal. He certainly did not want England to get a foothold in the Americas. In 1524, some thirty years after Columbus, the French king commissioned an Italian sailor, Giovanni da Verrazano, to explore the Atlantic coast and find a sea route to Asia for France. Verrazano concluded that an entire continent divided the Atlantic from the Pacific. After Verrazano, French interest in North America focused farther north, on the St. Lawrence River Valley and what became Canada, especially after Jacques Cartier's visit of 1534 to that region. After the destruction of Fort Caroline in 1565, there were no French settlements along the Atlantic coast of what is now the United States, though the French did establish colonies on islands in the Caribbean. Eventually however, the French explored the Mississippi River from north to south and created their own inland empire from what is now Chicago and Detroit to St. Louis and New Orleans—today's U.S. Midwest. For most of the 1600s and 1700s, France claimed much more of the land of the future United States than either Spain or England.

First French Visit to the Atlantic Coast of the United States—Verrazano, 1524

Verrazano's ship *La Dauphine* left France in January 1524 and landed on what is now Cape Fear, North Carolina, two months later. He described the people he met there as, "of color russet, and not much unlike the Saracens; their hair black, thick, and not very long." He wondered if they might be Chinese.

On April 17, 1524, Verrazano became the first European to sail into New York Harbor, describing how the inhabitants of Manhattan "came towards us very cheerfully, making shouts of admiration, showing us where we might come to land most safely with our boat." He continued north, visiting Rhode Island's Narragansett Bay, Maine, and Newfoundland, and he mapped much of the Atlantic coast of the future United States and Canada before returning to France.

Jacques Cartier Seeks a Sea Route to Asia, 1534

Ten years later, in 1534, France authorized Jacques Cartier to seek a northern sea route to Asia. Cartier did not find the route—which did not exist except through then-frozen Arctic ice—but he explored Newfoundland and the gulf of the St. Lawrence River, laying the basis for future French claims to these lands. He also began a trade in furs that would have great significance for French and English relations with American Indians.

On a second voyage in 1535–1536, Cartier explored the St. Lawrence River far upstream (see Map 2-3, p. 44), coming to the sites of present-day Quebec and Montreal. More than a thousand friendly Indians came to the river to greet him. He traded European goods, including knives, for food, beginning a trading relationship that would transform the lives of native tribes and Europeans. But Cartier stayed too long, and when winter closed in, he could not return to France because the river froze over. Cartier spent a terrible winter on the St. Lawrence, buried in deep snow and losing a quarter of his crew to disease and cold. Although Cartier's travels would be the basis for future French land claims, it would be another half century before the French developed a serious interest in North America, after they discovered that there was no quick way around it to the Asian lands they really wanted to find.

> ### 2.4 Quick Review
>
> How did early French exploration differ from the Spanish? How was it similar?

Exploration and Encounter in North America: The English

2.5 **Explain motivations of English explorers, privateers, and reasons for settlement.**

Although Spanish explorers reached the Americas first, an English expedition was quick to follow. King Henry VII of England commissioned another Italian, Giovanni Caboto, or John Cabot, to sail across the Atlantic in 1497. Cabot made landfall in North America, most likely in Newfoundland, and may have traveled as far south as Maine. He did not meet any people, but erected a cross and banner to claim the lands for England. When he returned to London, he was given a rich reward.

In 1498, Cabot set out on a second voyage, but he and his companions disappeared—most likely their ships were sunk in a storm—and there is no clear evidence of further English discoveries or claims in the Americas until more than fifty years later when a very different England found new reasons to look more carefully across the Atlantic.

England's Reformation Shapes the Country

In the early years of the Protestant Reformation, few would have predicted that England would break with the Roman Catholic Church. When he became king in 1509, Henry VIII was a good Catholic. He even wrote a defense of traditional Catholic doctrine that led the pope to give him the title "Defender of the Faith." He had married Catherine of Aragon, daughter of the devoutly Catholic Ferdinand and Isabella of Spain. But Henry's marriage problems would eventually reshape the country and the Atlantic World.

By the late 1520s, Henry wanted to end his marriage with Catherine. Five of their six children had died. Only a daughter named Mary survived, and Henry wanted a male heir. He had also fallen in love with the young Anne Boleyn. Under pressure from the king, the English clergy agreed to dissolve the marriage. But Pope Clement VII needed political support from Catherine's nephew, Charles V, king of Spain and Holy Roman emperor, who opposed the divorce. The pope stalled and refused to approve the divorce.

A century, even a decade, earlier Henry would have had little room to maneuver. Now the Protestant Reformation gave him an opening. In 1534, Parliament passed legislation ending papal authority in England and declared Henry and his successors to be "the only Supreme Head in earth of the Church of England." Henry annulled his marriage to Catherine, married Anne, and celebrated the birth of a new daughter, Elizabeth, though he still longed for a son. He closed monasteries and sold off church land or used it to reward loyal followers. Henry did not embrace many Protestant teachings. Other than substituting his own authority for that of the pope, official Christianity in England remained closer to Catholicism than to the Protestantism of Luther or Calvin, a fact that would become especially significant in the next century.

When Henry died in 1547, England had three major religious groups. Some, known as **Anglicans**, were perhaps a majority and supported Henry's arrangement, including independence from the pope and preserving traditional Catholic religious forms. However, a growing minority of Protestants, known as Puritans, wanted more radical religious change to "purify" the Church of England of Catholic practices, especially the leadership of bishops. In addition, many Roman Catholics could not agree to the break with Rome and remained loyal to the Catholic Church.

Henry's successor was his nine-year-old son Edward VI (r. 1547–1553) from the king's marriage to his third wife, Jane Seymour, after he got tired of Anne and had her executed. In the end, Henry had six wives but only three children. The boy-king's regents sought to make the English church more Protestant in its doctrines and rituals. But when Edward died at age fifteen, his half-sister Mary became queen and returned England—briefly—to Catholicism. However, Mary also died after a reign of only five years. In 1558, Elizabeth I (r. 1558–1603), daughter of Henry VIII and Anne Boleyn, succeeded her.

Elizabeth's reasons for embracing Protestantism were strong. If England were Catholic, then Henry's marriage to her mother would be illegal, and Elizabeth would be an illegitimate child and unable to assume the throne. If England were Protestant, she had every right to be queen of England. And Elizabeth meant to be queen. She did not want her subjects fighting with each other, however. In the Act of Uniformity of 1559, Parliament declared that she was "Supreme Governor" of the Church of England. Worship should follow the *Book of Common Prayer*, which preserved many Catholic rituals within a Protestant theology, and bishops continued to lead the church. Every person in England was required to attend church once a week or face a fine. Catholics who refused to break with Rome were persecuted. But as long as Protestants agreed to the Act of Uniformity and to attend church services that followed the *Book of Common Prayer*, Elizabeth's government left them free to disagree about their beliefs to their heart's content.

During Elizabeth's long reign, England became a major power in Europe and the world. Spain, under King Philip II, great-grandson of Ferdinand and Isabella, was at the center of a Catholic revival, and Philip's Spain and Elizabeth's England became bitter rivals. Queen Elizabeth subsidized Protestant rebels against Spain's rule of the Netherlands and even engaged in a correspondence with Ottoman Sultan Murad III about a possible joint Protestant–Muslim attack on Catholic Spain. King Philip, in return, plotted Elizabeth's overthrow and made plans to invade England to secure Spain's power and protect Catholic unity.

When Spain attacked England in July 1588, Spain's navy—the Spanish Armada—was defeated by the English navy and destroyed by storms. After 1588, England's navy dominated the Atlantic and eventually all of the world's oceans. English sailors grew more skilled, the country's shipbuilders became more sophisticated in their designs, and its navigators gained new understanding of winds and currents as well as their charts and instruments. For Elizabeth and many of her subjects, the defeat of the threatened Spanish Catholic invasion linked the Protestant religion and English patriotism indissolubly in their minds. A small nation, on the margins of Europe, was suddenly a major player in an emerging Atlantic World.

Elizabethan Explorers and Pirates

While Elizabeth I ruled England, English adventurers, with her support, set out to make a place for themselves and their country in the new oceanic world. English and other European fishermen had fished off the North Atlantic coast of North America since the early 1500s. By the 1580s, however, warfare and piracy became the dominant role of the English who visited the Americas. Building settlements at that time was not a priority. If powerful Catholic Spain was exploiting the continents for gold and silver, England saw no reason not to relieve the Spanish ships of some of their treasure without going to the trouble of mining it themselves.

Anglicans

Within the Church of England, one group of Protestants who wanted to establish a church that was led by the English monarchy.

2.1
2.2
2.3
2.4
2.5

Private Collection/The Bridgeman Art Library

Queen Elizabeth ruled England from 1558 to 1603 during which time the country prospered internally and emerged as a major sea power in the world.

Francis Drake was perhaps the most famous pirate—or *privateer* as they were known when their exploits were commissioned by the government. Drake was licensed for piracy by Queen Elizabeth. Licensing individual captains to harass the Spanish treasure fleets was far cheaper than supporting a large navy, and the English government, at minimal risk, kept a fifth of whatever the pirates brought to England. Indeed, pirates may have supplied 10 percent of English imports in the 1590s. The decades of legalized piracy also helped expand the technical knowledge of English mariners as they used some of their ill-gotten gains to build stronger and better ships. The role of this piracy was instrumental in laying a foundation for England's sea power.

Francis Drake was an explorer as well as a privateer. During his voyage around the globe from 1577 to 1580—the first commander of such an expedition to survive—he confirmed the contours of the Americas for the English. He then continued across the Pacific and around Africa before returning to London. In 1585, he attacked and burned St. Augustine, Florida. In 1588, he helped defeat the Spanish Armada. His exploits brought considerable wealth to Queen Elizabeth's England while weakening Spanish control of the seas. By the time Drake died in 1596, while again harassing the Spanish in Central America, English sailors were confident that they could travel anywhere without trouble, even if Spain still controlled the most valuable land in the Americas.

Walter Raleigh and the "Lost Colony" of Roanoke

In 1584, Queen Elizabeth authorized Walter Raleigh to use his own funds to settle a permanent English colony in North America. At the time, England and Raleigh himself were most interested in establishing a base from which privateers like Drake could easily operate and profit financially. Raleigh organized a reconnaissance trip to identify potential sites in 1584. The small group discovered Roanoke Island and was received warmly by the Algonquian people, two of whom (Manteo and Wanchese) returned to England with the crew. In 1585, Raleigh sent one hundred young men back to Roanoke on the Outer Banks of North Carolina along with the two Algonquian emissaries. It was the first English colony in what is now the United States. It was also short lived. When the men landed, one of their ships ran aground, and most of the food they had brought was ruined. The Roanoke Indians were not happy to feed the colonists, whom they began to suspect of trying to dominate them, and a battle broke out in 1586 in which the Roanoke chief, Wingina, was killed. When Francis Drake arrived later that spring to rest his crews and refit his ships, he found the survivors in disarray. Instead of refitting, he agreed to take the survivors back to England when they decided to abandon the colony.

Raleigh was not discouraged, however. If a colony of men could not succeed, then perhaps one composed of families could. In 1587, he convinced English investors to create a new colony in a location on the Chesapeake Bay, which would have more navigable waters than the shallows around Roanoke. Colonists were promised five hundred acres per family, a huge estate for the times, though one might question England's authority to give away land claimed by the Algonquians. Some one hundred people left England to create this new colony, but events along the way landed them instead back at Roanoke, amid the Algonquians who had fought their predecessors. Nevertheless, the colony was established, houses built, and the settlers began their new lives in this isolated place. Virginia Dare was born and baptized in this colony—the first English child known to be born in what is now the United States.

But Roanoke came to be known as the "Lost Colony." The settlers had been left in what seemed like reasonably good shape with a promise that resupply ships would arrive the following spring. However, no ships were allowed to leave England in 1588 because of the threatened Spanish attack. The government commandeered every ship to oppose the mighty Spanish Armada. Nor did weather help the colony. Between 1587 and 1589, the worst drought in eight hundred years struck. If the experience of later colonies is any guide, drought increased tensions with nearby American Indians who became much more reluctant to provide food when they faced their own shortages. When John White finally returned to Roanoke with the promised supplies in 1590, he found the colony abandoned. Whether the colonists were massacred or simply had melted into the surrounding Indian tribes is unknown.

John White, himself an early English settler, drew this picture of a "woman and child of Pomeiooc" in an effort to describe the Algonquians with whom the first English explorers came into contact.

2.5 Quick Review

How did Francis Drake contribute to English wealth and power? How were English activities in the Americas different from and similar to that of the Spanish or the French?

Conclusion

Through most of the 1500s, Cabrillo's, de Soto's, and Coronado's expeditions for Spain; Verrazano's and Cartier's voyages for France; and Raleigh's colonizing efforts for England were considered failures, though Drake's exploration and piracy were much admired. Fortunes had been spent, but few permanent settlements had been made. The explorers of North America found no gold and failed to find a quick route to China. Nevertheless, by the end of the 1500s, Spain, France, and England had a much clearer picture of the geography of North America than earlier. Many of the native peoples of North America also had at least a vague knowledge of the militaristic Europeans whose presence would change everything for future generations. Half a century after Columbus first landed, the Atlantic and Pacific coasts and most of the southern half of the United States had been the scene of many interactions between American Indians, Europeans, often Africans, and occasionally Asians. Yet even one hundred years after Columbus, settlement was limited to a few Spanish posts in Florida and New Mexico. For the American Indians, Europeans were people who came quickly and left almost as quickly. While disease decimated some tribes, most of the surviving native peoples of North America continued daily life in the early 1550s, even through 1600, with few differences from life centuries before. They might have a few new trade goods or an occasional skirmish with Europeans, but that was about it. That situation would change quickly after 1600 as three great European powers, Spain, France, and England—and smaller ones including the Netherlands and Sweden—established permanent settlements and vied for control of North America.

Chapter Review

How did European politics, economics, and religious issues lead to exploration and settlement in America? Of these three, which would you argue was the single most important category? Why? What evidence would you use for your argument?

Chapter 2 Summary and Review

Columbus, the Columbian Exchange, and Early Conquests

2.1 **Explain the reasons behind the voyages of Columbus, and describe early Spanish encounters with the peoples of the Caribbean, Mexico, and South America.**

Summary

Columbus's voyages to the Americas represented the beginning of an extraordinary change in worldwide human contact. Building on Columbus's exploits, Spain was the unquestioned leader in the early exploration and conquest of the Americas. Because of disease and warfare, Spanish exploration and conquest of the Americas decimated the native peoples with whom they came in contact. The Columbian encounter also led to an ocean-focused world trade system and the exchange of disease, plants, animals, and human culture between the New and Old Worlds. Within decades of Columbus's arrival in the New World, the two most important American Indian empires, the Aztecs and the Incas, had succumbed to disease and Spanish aggression, and eventually all other American tribes suffered the same fate, if not from the Spanish then from another European power. For the first one hundred years after Columbus, little permanent European settlement took place north of Mexico, but Spanish, French, and English explorers mapped the coastlands and much of the interior of the future United States and Canada while they mostly sought a sea route around it. By 1600, however, future settlement of North America came quickly.

Review Questions

1. Contextualization
   What do Columbus's words and actions on arriving in the New World tell us about his motives for making his voyages?

2. Argument Development
   In what ways did the global economy shift toward an ocean-based trade system that created winners and losers?

A Divided Europe: The Impact of the Protestant Reformation

2.2 **Explain how the Protestant Reformation and the development of the nation-state changed Europe and European ideas about how best to settle and govern America.**

Summary

The Protestant Reformation changed the way Europeans thought about the world, whether they were Protestant or Catholic. The religious divide produced by the Reformation would have a profound impact on the European expansion and settlement in the Americas. Martin Luther's protests sparked the Reformation. Luther and John Calvin developed the most important religious ideas of Protestantism. The idea of the nation-state developed at the same time as the Protestant–Catholic split, and a new sense of the relationship between national and religious identity emerged. In a divided Europe, nation-states competed to control both new lands in the Americas and battled in old lands in Europe. The disruption that wars and divisions brought to Europe led many to seek asylum in the New World of the Americas, as far away from the old one as possible.

Review Question

3. Causation
   How did political and religious developments in Europe of the 1500s shape the course of European settlement in the Americas?

Exploration and Encounter in North America: The Spanish

2.3 **Analyze early Spanish exploration of America north of Mexico.**

Summary

Although less appealing to Spanish adventurers than Mexico and South America because it was colder and because there was virtually no gold or silver there, North America attracted its share of would-be conquerors and colonists. Juan Ponce de León led the first official European expeditions to Puerto Rico and Florida. In 1528, Pánfilo de Narváez led another ill-fated effort to colonize Florida. The tales brought back by survivors of that expedition inspired Spanish exploration of the Southwest in search of fabled cities of enormous wealth, including an expedition led by Francisco Vazquez de Coronado. While Coronado was roaming the Southwest, Hernando de Soto was exploring the Mississippi River Valley. A third expedition led by Juan Rodriguez Cabrillo investigated the Pacific Coast of California. After all these seemingly fruitless efforts, Spanish interest in the lands north of Mexico waned. Only when other European powers showed an interest in North America did Spain set up permanent settlements. When French Protestants attempted to settle in Florida, the Spanish countered by killing them and creating the city of St. Augustine. Later, Spanish efforts to establish New Mexico were fueled by fears of English exploration along the Pacific coast.

Review Questions

4. Argument Development

How do you account for the failure of the Spanish government to follow up the expeditions of de Soto, Coronado, and Cabrillo with more exploration? Why did Spanish authorities remain uninterested in the region north of Mexico?

5. Contextualization

How did the Pueblos respond to early Spanish efforts to find gold in their territory? What does their response tell us about their strategies for dealing with these newcomers?

Exploration and Encounter in North America: The French

2.4 **Analyze early French exploration and claims in North America.**

Summary

French interest in North America focused on the St. Lawrence River Valley and what became Canada as well as on islands in the Caribbean. In 1524, King Francis I of France commissioned Giovanni da Verrazano to explore the Atlantic coast and find a sea route to Asia for France. Verrazano was the first European to sail into New York Harbor, and he mapped much of the Atlantic coast of the future United States, but he found no route to Asia. In 1534, France tried again to find a sea route to Asia, this time launching another unsuccessful expedition led by Jacques Cartier. On a second voyage in 1535–1536, Cartier explored the St. Lawrence River. Although Cartier's travels would be the basis for future French land claims, it would be another half century before the French developed a serious interest in North America.

Review Question

6. Causation

How do you account for France's lack of success in the New World during the 1500s?

Exploration and Encounter in North America: The English

2.5 **Explain motivations of English explorers, privateers, and reasons for settlement.**

Summary

English exploration and settlement in North America during the 1500s was shaped by England's break with the Catholic Church. King Henry VIII's desire to secure the annulment of his marriage to Catherine of Aragon led him to renounce papal authority. Under Henry's successor, Edward VI, the English church became more Protestant in its beliefs and rituals. When Catherine's daughter Mary I came to the English throne, she returned the country to Catholicism. Her successor Elizabeth I reestablished Protestantism and sought religious consensus. During Elizabeth's long reign, England became a major Protestant power in Europe and the world. Conflict between England and Spain brought English adventurers and privateers to the Americas, the most famous of whom was Francis Drake. Walter Raleigh sponsored two failed attempts to establish English settlements in North America.

Review Questions

7. Causation

How did events in the decades before Elizabeth I's reign help shape her religious policies?

8. Contextualization

Why did contemporaries see most of the European expeditions in North America during the 1500s as failures?

1. Preparing to Write: Support Your Assertion

Short-Answer Question—Use "When Historians Disagree" from Section 2.1 to answer (a).

a. Briefly explain ONE major difference between Paine's and Zinn's historical interpretations of Columbus.

Short-Answer Questions come in three parts, but for now you are asked to take on only one. Short-Answer Questions demand direct assertions and then specific evidence to support them. Respond to the question above in three sentences. The first sentence should identify a major difference, and the next two should explain that difference.

2. Preparing to Write: Establish Context in the Introduction

Long Essay Question—Evaluate the extent of change in England's New World goals during the 1500s.

Before making an effective argument about specific historical developments, students need to establish the context in which England's colonization efforts shifted to a family-based model. With this need to establish context, write an introduction of four to seven sentences—including a rough thesis—that briefly discusses England's rise to power during this time period. Your rough thesis should address what is staying constant in England's New World aspirations as well as why it shifted to a colonization model based on family settlement.

Section I: Multiple-Choice Questions

Questions 1.1–1.2 refer to the excerpt below.

"The men were sent out to the mines as far as eighty leagues away while their wives remained to work the soil. … Thus husbands and wives were together only once every eight or ten months and when they met they were so exhausted and depressed on both sides that they had no mind for marital communication and in this way they ceased to procreate. As for the newly born, they died early because their mothers, overworked and famished, had no milk to nurse them, and for this reason, while I was in Cuba, 7,000 children died in three months. Some mothers even drowned their babies from sheer desperation, while others caused themselves to abort with certain herbs. … In this way husbands died in the mines, wives died at work, and children died from lack of milk, while others had not time or energy for procreation, and in a short time this land which was so great, so powerful and fertile, though so unfortunate, was depopulated."

—Bartolomé de Las Casas, *The History of the Indies*, 1550

1.1   The Spanish treatment of Native Americans as described in the excerpt led most directly to

    a. a debate about the proper treatment of Native Americans

    b. widespread praise of Spain's American policies

    c. a more humane treatment of indigenous peoples by other European nations

    d. repudiation by Spain of its vast American empire

1.2   Before becoming a priest, Las Casas helped in the conquest of Cuba and was rewarded with an encomienda. The encomienda system implemented by the Spanish in the New World was designed to

    a. assist in the discovery of gold that could be shipped back to Spain

    b. establish a social system with Spanish citizens at the top

    c. provide housing for Spanish colonists

    d. provide labor for the Spanish colony

Questions 1.3–1.4 refer to the excerpt below.

The Dedication of Columbus's Log to the King and Queen of Spain

"This present year of 1492, after your Highnesses had brought to an end the war with the Moors who ruled in Europe and had concluded the war in the very great city of Granada, where this present year on the second day of the month of January I saw the Royal Standards of Your Highnesses placed by force of arms on the towers of the Alhambra … and Your Highnesses, as Catholic Christians and

Princes, lovers and promoters of the Holy Christian Faith, and enemies of the false doctrine of Mahomet and of all idolatries and heresies, you thought of sending me, Christóbal Colón, to the said regions of India to see the said princes and the peoples and the lands, and the characteristics of the lands and of everything, and to see how their conversion to our Holy Faith might be undertaken. … So, after having expelled all the Jews from all of your Kingdoms and Dominions, in the same month of January Your Highnesses commanded me to go, with a suitable fleet, to the said regions of India."

—The *Diario* of Christopher Columbus's First Voyage to America, 1492–1493

1.3   Beyond his stated goal of converting the residents to Christianity, why did Columbus specifically want to reach the regions of India?

    a. Columbus was seeking new technology to replace the loss of innovation that resulted from the ouster of the Jews.

    b. King Ferdinand and Queen Isabella hoped to form a political alliance with the Muslims.

    c. The fall of Constantinople had closed land routes to the lucrative trade with the East.

    d. Spain desired to conquer kingdoms in Asia and take over their trade routes to Europe.

1.4   Columbus's colonization of Hispaniola set a precedent for the Spanish

    a. adopting Indian customs

    b. abandoning Indian lands quickly

    c. establishing mutually beneficial trade networks

    d. converting the Indians to Christianity

Questions 1.5–1.6 refer to the excerpt below.

The Princes of Virginia … wear the hair of their heads long.

"… They wear a chain about their necks of pearls or beads of copper, which they much esteem. … They carry a quiver made of small rushes holding their bow ready bent in one hand, and an arrow in the other, ready to defend themselves. In this manner they go to war, or to their solemn feasts and banquets. They take much pleasure in hunting deer whereof there is great store in the country, for it is fruitful, pleasant, and full of good woods.…

At a certain time of the year they make a great, and solemn feast whereunto their neighbors of the towns adjoining repair from all parts, every man attired in the most strange fashion. … Then being set in order they dance, sing, and use the strangest gestures."

—Richard Hakluyt, *The True Pictures and Fashions of the People in That Part of America Now Called Virginia*, 1585

1.5 Hakluyt, the author of the excerpt above, used stories of North America to create a "true picture" of the Indians. What was a direct result of Hakluyt's description of the New World?

   a. England decided to put off establishing settlements in the New World for several decades.

   b. English colonization efforts that attracted a large number of males and females.

   c. The promotion of English colonies that, through trade alliances with American Indians, exported fur.

   d. Calls for war with Spain, which eventually led to the English destruction of the Spanish Armada.

1.6 Which of the following was true of Native Americans before the arrival of Europeans in the Americas?

   a. They had developed a large variety of cultures and languages.

   b. They were mostly members of small, hunter-gatherer groups.

   c. They lived in agricultural communities with a strong central government.

   d. They built elaborate networks connected to their religious practices.

Questions 1.7–1.9 refer to the excerpt below.

What Exactly Is the Spanish Legacy? What Is the Spanish Imprint on the United States?

"The period from Columbus's first landfall in 1492 to 1607, when the English made their settlement at Jamestown, has traditionally been a blank spot in American history books. The historian Howard Mumford Jones also compared Spain's sixteenth-century achievements to those of antiquity:

> The Spaniards invented a system of colonial administration unparalleled since the days of ancient Rome; in religion they launched the most sweeping missionary movement since the Germanic tribes accepted Christianity. … As for culture, the Spaniards transplanted dynamic forms of Renaissance art, thought, and institutions to the Americas with amazing quickness.

> The Spanish established a college for the sons of Indian chiefs, in Mexico in 1536. … and, as Jones observed, 'When in 1585 a forlorn little band of Englishmen were trying to stick it out on Roanoke Island, three hundred poets were competing for a prize in Mexico City.'"

— From Henry Wiencek, historian, "The Spain among Us," 1993

1.7 Besides the items in the excerpt, such as the establishment of new colleges, which of the following statements is true regarding Spain's colonial empire in the sixteenth century?

   a. Local governments were given autonomous control over their regions.

   b. Many young families migrated to New Spain.

   c. A caste system was established that incorporated the diverse populations.

   d. Most of the wealth extracted from the colony was used to build up the colony's emerging economy.

1.8 Which region of the future United States was most influenced by the Spanish in the sixteenth century?

   a. New England   **c.** Southwest

   b. Great Plains   **d.** Northwest

Questions 1.9–1.10 refer to the image below by Theodore de Bry from the 1500s.

1.9 Which of the following was a significant factor spurring European exploration in the fifteenth and sixteenth centuries?

   a. A competition for trade following the closing of overland trade routes

   b. The fragmentation of nation-states

   c. The desire to assist new peoples in building modern, autonomous communities

   d. A population seeking refuge because of the Black Plague

1.10 The scene shown in the image reflects the

   a. beginning of a mutually beneficial trade network between the American Indians and the Spanish

   b. lack of resources the Spanish encountered in the New World

   c. American Indian domination of the Spanish in the early years of colonization

   d. desire of the Spanish to spread Christianity

Section II: Short-Answer Questions

1.11 Answer (a), (b), and (c).

  a. Briefly explain why ONE of the following represents the most significant factor that led to European involvement in the New World.
   • a search for new sources of wealth
   • economic and military competition
   • desire to spread Christianity
  b. Provide AT LEAST one piece of evidence from the period to support your explanation.
  c. Briefly explain why ONE of the other options you considered for answer (b) is not as persuasive as the one you chose.

Question 1.12 refers to the chart below showing the Columbian Exchange.

1.12 Using the chart below, answer (a), (b), and (c).

  a. Briefly explain ONE historical event or development that accounts for the new Atlantic exchanges in the sixteenth and seventeenth centuries.
  b. Briefly explain ONE specific historical effect of the new Atlantic exchanges in the sixteenth and seventeenth centuries.
  c. Briefly explain a SECOND specific historical effect of the new Atlantic exchanges in the sixteenth and seventeenth centuries.

Section III: Long Essay Questions

Directions: Answer Question 1.13 **or** 1.14. (Suggested writing time: 40 minutes) In your response you should do the following.

• Respond to the prompt with a historically defensible thesis or claim that establishes a line of reasoning.
• Describe a broader historical context relevant to the prompt.
• Support an argument in response to the prompt using specific and relevant examples of evidence.
• Use historical reasoning (e.g., comparison, causation, continuity or change over time) to frame or structure an argument that addresses the prompt.

• Use evidence to corroborate, qualify, or modify an argument that addresses the prompt.

1.13 Evaluate the extent to which there were similarities in how native peoples of the Northeast and Southwest adapted to their respective environments.

1.14 Evaluate the extent to which there were differences in how the Columbian Exchange impacted the Americas and Europe.

Section IV: MyHistoryLab

Document-Based Question: Native American Peoples

Part 2

Settlements Old and New 1607–1754

AP® KEY CONCEPTS

Key Concept 2.1

Europeans developed a variety of colonization and migration patterns, influenced by different imperial goals, cultures, and the varied North American environments where they settled, and they competed with each other and American Indians for resources.

Key Concept 2.2

The British colonies participated in political, social, cultural, and economic exchanges with Great Britain that encouraged both stronger bonds with Britain and resistance to Britain's control.

PART OUTLINE

Chapter 3

Settlements, Alliances, and Resistance 1607–1718

Trade in goods for furs from Native Americans and in colonial products, especially barrels of tobacco to Europe, was key to the success of European colonies in the 1600s, as illustrated by this encounter between an American Indian trapper and a French trader.

Timewatch Images / Alamy Stock Photo

Chapter Objective

Demonstrate an understanding of the motivations for and results of the European settlements in North America.

 ## Learning Objectives

The English Settle in North America

3.1 Explain why the English began to settle in North America; what regional differences reflected various environmental, economic, cultural, and demographic factors; and how slavery was introduced in the English colonies.

England's Wars, England's Colonies

3.2 Analyze the relationships between competition among European rivals and American Indians over resources, politics in England, internal colonial tensions, and life in the English colonies in North America during the 1600s.

France Takes Control of the Heart of a Continent

3.3 Explain how French, Spanish, Dutch, and British colonizers had different economic and imperial goals and, in particular, how France's growing role and power in North America affected English and Spanish colonies.

Developments in Spanish Colonies North of Mexico

3.4 Analyze the impact of the expansion of other European colonies on Spain's colonies in New Mexico, Texas, and California.

For over one hundred years after Columbus, Europeans spent more time trying to get around or through North America to reach Asia than they spent paying attention to the lands that would become the United States or Canada. Spain's vast American empire was based in Mexico and Peru. The Spanish found Mexico, Central and South America, and the Caribbean more rewarding than they did North America, which lacked gold or silver and which they considered barren and icy.

For decades, most European contact with North America was focused on the demand for codfish. Fishermen from France, England, and the Basque regions of Spain spent summers off the coast of Canada and Maine. They set up temporary stations in Newfoundland, repaired their boats, and dried their fish. Few stayed the winter, and no permanent colonies were founded. The Native Americans found the fishermen intrusive. The fishermen resented the Indians who plundered stores left behind over the winter. But most of the time, both sides simply avoided each other. Nevertheless, occasional contact was all it took to begin the spread of European diseases among the tribes of North America, well in advance of more sustained settlement.

By the late 1500s, however, some in England and France as well as Spain were developing new interests in North America. In 1585, Richard Hakluyt the elder wrote *Pamphlet for the Virginia Enterprise* in an effort to convince his English countrymen that a settlement, or planting as he called it, was in their interests. He recognized that the native peoples might not welcome them, but he said:

> We may, if we will proceed with extremity, conquer, fortify, and plant in soils most sweet, most pleasant, most strong, and most fertile, and in the end bring them all in subjection and to civility.

For Hakluyt, subjection and conversion of the Native Americans to Protestant Christianity meant a rich profit and a military base for England against Catholic Spain. Others agreed, including King James I, who succeeded Elizabeth I in 1603. With the settlement of Jamestown, Virginia, in 1607, the English came to America to stay. Only one year later, France established a permanent settlement at Quebec on the Saint Lawrence River. In 1610, Spanish authorities also moved to a new permanent capital for their vast New Mexico territory that they named Santa Fe. In a three-year span between 1607 and 1610, Europe's three largest powers had all established permanent North American colonies.

From the settlements of Jamestown and Quebec, England and France claimed huge tracts of lands that they would eventually come to dominate. The English expanded from tiny Jamestown to control most of the Atlantic coast north of Florida and west toward the Allegheny Mountains. From Quebec, the French built trade and military centers all along the Saint Lawrence River and down the Mississippi to New Orleans on the Gulf of Mexico, a vast region they called New France. After 1610, the Spanish expanded their settlements from New Mexico west to California while maintaining those in Florida.

In the 1500s, explorers had come and quickly departed from North America. In the 1600s, some Europeans began to stay. Initially some Indian tribes saw Europeans as welcome trading partners or military allies against other tribes. Especially in the later 1600s when settlements grew too quickly, disease spread too rapidly, or the Europeans became too demanding, Indian resistance stiffened. The story of the growth of European communities in North America and the responses by American Indian tribes—sometimes through friendly trade and sometimes in open warfare—is the heart of this chapter.

The English Settle in North America

3.1 **Explain why the English began to settle in North America and how slavery was introduced in the English colonies.**

When James I became king of England in 1603, he was anxious to make peace with Spain. He quickly ended the royal support for legalized piracy that Queen Elizabeth I had provided—though piracy itself flourished throughout the 1600s. But many in England wanted a larger

Significant Dates   3.1

1607	Jamestown, Virginia, founded by English as a joint stock company
1608	Quebec founded by French
1610	Santa Fe founded as Spanish capital of New Mexico
1618	Headright system established in Virginia, expanded in Maryland, giving each settler one hundred acres and more for a family
1619	African slaves sold in Jamestown
1620	Plymouth, Massachusetts, is founded by English Pilgrims
1624	Fort Orange (later Albany), New York, is founded by the Dutch
1626	New Amsterdam (later New York City) is founded by Dutch
1630	Massachusetts Bay Colony is founded by English Puritans
1634	Maryland is founded by Lord Baltimore as a haven for English Catholics
1636	Rhode Island is founded
1637	Pequot War in New England
1638	First African slaves are brought to Boston, Massachusetts
1639	Fundamental Orders of Connecticut confirm government for Hartford-based colony (founded in 1637)
1642–1649	English Civil War
1649–1658	England is governed as a Puritan Commonwealth
1660	Charles II begins to rule in England
1661	Maryland law defines slavery as lifelong and inheritable
1663	Carolina colony is founded by England
1664	English capture New Netherlands colony, rename it New York
1675	King Philip's War in Massachusetts
1676	Bacon's Rebellion in Virginia
1680	Pueblo Indian Revolt in New Mexico

(continued)

3.2

3.3

3.4

joint stock company
A new kind of financial institution that emerged in Europe in the 1500s. The design allowed many different investors to buy and sell shares of an enterprise. It allowed the accumulation of more resources than any one person might have, yet reduced risk for each individual involved. The joint stock company is the forerunner of the modern corporation with stock traded on Wall Street.

role in the Americas. If they were not going to steal America's wealth from the Spanish on the seas, then they would need to find other ways to gain from contact with America. Investors created the Virginia Company. They told those they sent to America "to try if they can find any mineral" and to seek "passage to the Other Sea," the longed-for shortcut to China. The investors also advised them to build settlements at some distance from the coast to avoid a Spanish attack and to gain as much knowledge and food from the Indians as possible "before that they perceive you mean to plant among them." Within about thirty years, England had settled or claimed large territories, and their claims continued to expand into the 1700s (see Map 3-1).

Colonizing Virginia: Jamestown

Although most Spanish colonizing efforts were sponsored by rich individuals, a larger number of English investors came together to begin the settlement of North America. In April 1606, King James I gave a formal charter to the Virginia Company, a London-based **joint stock company** that had many investors who pooled their resources, shared the risks, and, they hoped, reaped the financial rewards of the venture. A joint stock company resembled a modern corporation with many investors, limited risk, and potentially huge resources. It became the model for subsequent English colonizing efforts for the next quarter century. In 1607, 105 men from the Virginia Company, under the command of Christopher Newport who had served and fought with Drake, arrived in North America. They named their new community Jamestown in honor of King James. The company appointed a council of six to govern the colony and left it to the council to elect its own president. They called themselves planters, not conquerors, because they meant to plant—or establish—a permanent colony, though the distinction was limited. But things in Jamestown did not go well.

The unhealthy conditions at the site the colonists selected along the James River probably killed more of them than any other cause. Although they thought they had selected "a very fit place," they had in fact chosen land with a terrible water supply. The water from the James River was tidal. At high tide, it was salt water. At low tide, it was "full of slime and filth." The years 1607 and 1608 were drought years leading to a severe shortage of food. The winter of 1607–1608 was extremely cold. The Indians were suffering from the same drought and cold and were reluctant to trade food with the colonists. Waterborne disease and starvation weakened bodies, and few of the English escaped terrible bouts of sickness.

The members of the council constantly disagreed— they ended up executing one of the councilors as a Spanish spy—and the rest of the colonists fought each other bitterly. Although the colony's purpose was to enrich investors in London, those who were actually in Virginia found little reason to care whether the investors were enriched or not. England seemed far away. John Smith, the only member of the council not from the British nobility, complained, "Much they blamed us for not converting the Savages, when those [colonists] they sent us were little better if not worse." By 1608, only 38 of the 105 colonists were still alive.

The founders of Jamestown faced a different situation from what Columbus had encountered in 1492 when the Indians of Hispaniola gasped in awe at the ships, swords, and men with beards. By 1607, generations of Atlantic coast Indians

Map 3-1 Spread of Settlement: Atlantic Coast European Colonies, 1607–1639.

The earliest European colonies on the Atlantic coast north of Florida began as very small settlements close to the coast and then spread into the interior. New Sweden became the core of Delaware, while New Netherland, stretching along the Hudson River, later became the core of both New York and New Jersey. Massachusetts Bay and Plymouth were separate colonies until merged with Massachusetts in 1686.

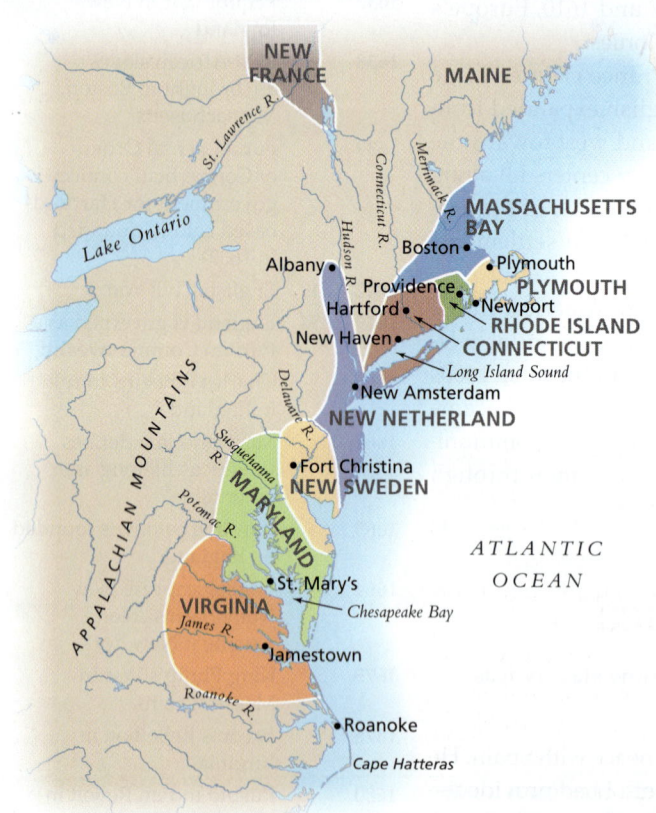

had substantial experience with Europeans. They had seen their ships, traded with them, and fought them. Some had even traveled to Europe and brought back reports of how these white adventurers lived. Europeans who were shipwrecked or from failed colonies—perhaps even from Roanoke—had melded into the Indian tribes and shared their knowledge with them. The Spanish at St. Augustine had tried to establish a northern outpost in the region. The Indians' opinion of Europeans was not favorable. For the Paspahegh tribe, on whose land Jamestown was built, the English were trespassing. And relationships between Jamestown and all of the local Indians, a confederation of Algonquian-speaking tribes of thirteen thousand to fifteen thousand people, were tense.

During its first weeks, the colony was attacked, and only after that did the settlers build a stockade. The English came to understand that the Paspahegh and some thirty other nearby tribes were under the rule of an overlord they called Powhatan whom the English described as functioning something like an emperor over the tribal chiefs. If the colonists wanted to make a lasting accommodation, it needed to be with him.

By his own account—in his autobiography, *The True Travels, Adventures, and Observations of Captain John Smith*, published in 1630—John Smith saved the colony. Smith was an experienced soldier who had fought in Austria against the Muslim Turks, had been captured and sold into slavery in Istanbul, had escaped, and had made his way through Russia, Germany, and North Africa before coming home to England. He brought all of this experience to Virginia.

Early in his Virginia career, Smith had one of the most famous Indian encounters in American history. During the early months of the settlement, while Powhatan was trying to understand what these Englishmen wanted, Smith was exploring the countryside. He was taken prisoner by the Algonquians and brought before Powhatan. In Smith's telling, he was about to be executed—he was laid on the ground with his head on a rock, and men with clubs stood around him. Then Powhatan's daughter, Pocahontas, already known to Smith for her work as a negotiator with Jamestown, suddenly "got his head in her arms, and laid her own upon his to save him from death." Powhatan granted Smith a reprieve. Most historians now believe that Powhatan scripted the whole event. After his rescue, Powhatan told Smith that "now they were friends" and gave him an Algonquian name. Far from being executed, Smith had been adopted. Perhaps Powhatan aimed to make Smith one of the many chiefs who reported to him.

Smith did not accept Powhatan's offer of a place within the Algonquian confederation though he did not formally reject it either. The English offered Powhatan an English crown that would symbolize his place in a world ruled by King James. Each side was jockeying for signs of submission from the other. In the early years, Powhatan could easily have destroyed Jamestown either by a direct attack or simply by withholding food. Instead, the Powhatan confederation fed the English and saw benefit in trading with them. The English brought valuable new goods. Powhatan meant to use the English to strengthen his position against other tribes. The English avoided war and starvation and survived only by making an alliance with Powhatan.

Smith's success in dealing with Powhatan was only part of his contribution to the colony. After he became governor in 1608, he instituted a policy that "he who does not work, does not eat." In a tiny colony, far from home, there could be no leisure class and no slackers. To survive, the colony needed the back-breaking labor of farming and stockade building. Smith set everyone to it. Jamestown would have gone the way of Roanoke or other failed ventures without his leadership.

But Smith returned to England in 1609. As a result, he was not in Jamestown for the "starving time" of the winter of 1609–1610 when the colony was almost wiped out by star-

Library of Congress Prints and Photographs Division [LC-USZ62-8104]

Pocahontas gained fame first as the young woman who rescued Virginia's leader, John Smith, and later as the wife of tobacco planter, John Rolfe. She is shown here as she was seen in London, as Rebecca Rolfe, the first Native American to be seen by many in England.

3.1

3.2

3.3

3.4

vation and disease. Realizing that the peaceful trade he hoped for was not materializing, Powhatan withdrew from contact with the Europeans. Consequently, the English could not rely on the Indians for food. The English attacked the Indians, burned their houses, plundered their sacred sites, and stole their valuables. But the English could not eat the valuables, and another party seeking food was found dead with their mouths stuffed with bread by the Indians.

In the spring of 1610, the surviving colonists decided to abandon Jamestown. They burned the town and sailed down the James River. However, before they reached the sea, they were met by an English fleet with four hundred men led by the newly appointed governor, Lord de la Warr, and enough supplies to last a year. The colony was rebuilt where it had been.

While the colonists in Virginia had been starving, the Virginia Company in London had reorganized itself and sold significantly more stock to raise funds. It also enlisted clergy across England to preach on the importance of colonizing Virginia. The venture was no longer described as a way to acquire quick riches but as a kind of national mission. It was England's duty, the ministers said, to send missionaries and build a permanent Protestant base in the Americas that would convert Indians and serve England in future confrontations with Spain.

Jamestown survived. But for another decade, life remained precarious. Thousands of colonists arrived in Virginia, having fled England after being thrown off their land, but disease and limited food decimated their numbers. A new economic foundation for the colony's survival had to be found.

Jamestown was saved by a product that Columbus had discovered—tobacco. Before 1492, no Europeans knew anything about tobacco, though the peoples of North and South America had used it for medicinal and religious purposes for hundreds of years. But Columbus took some tobacco leaves with him on his first return voyage. Within a few decades, smoking tobacco became popular in Europe. Spaniards smoked tobacco from Cuba. King James, who found smoking tobacco "loathsome to the eye, hateful to the nose, harmful to the brain, dangerous to the lungs," also saw in it a way to make significant profits and created a royal

This illustration was published in 1624 as part of John Smith's book about his time in Virginia showing, among other things, his battles with the American Indians, his rescue by Pocahontas, and his map of the colony.

MPI/Getty Images

3.1

3.2

3.3

3.4

monopoly. And Virginia, its settlers discovered, had the ideal climate and conditions for producing tobacco. The settlers might have preferred to find silver or gold, but tobacco quickly became valuable.

Meanwhile, the Indians had lost patience with the continual encroachment of the English. In 1622, led by Opechancanough, Powhatan's brother and the tribe's new leader, the Algonquians attacked and killed some 300 of the 1,200 English settlers. Attacks continued for more than a decade. The conflict eventually bankrupted the Virginia Company, and in 1624, in the last year of his reign, King James converted Virginia into a royal colony controlled directly by himself. With Virginia as a royal colony, efforts to settle the area continued.

The shift from trade with Indians to tobacco-based agriculture in the 1620s sealed the fate of the Indians who had been essential to the colony's early survival. Indian land became more valuable to the English than the Indians themselves, while disease decimated Indian populations. The new emphasis on agriculture also meant that many from England would settle and farm the land. The shift from trade to tobacco production also changed the lives of thousands of Africans who were brought to the Americas as slaves to produce the new crop. Tobacco was a key factor in reshaping who would be a part of this new English-speaking nation and the role they would play in the society that emerged.

Smoking tobacco quickly became a popular symbol of sophistication in Europe, making the production of tobacco in Virginia very profitable.

INTERFOTO/Alamy Stock Photo

3.1

3.2

3.3

3.4

The Massachusetts Colonies: Plymouth, Boston, and Beyond

The settlement of New England was a different story from that of Virginia. By the first two decades of the 1600s, many in England thought their country was overpopulated. Changes in agriculture were forcing people out of subsistence farming and into cities. England's economy was stagnating. What better outlet for excess population, some said, than the new colonies across the ocean? It was a great service, some argued, to ship the poor to do the agricultural work that was so badly needed across the sea. Early on, there was interest in establishing other colonies beyond Jamestown.

King James especially wanted to see one group on its way across the ocean—the Protestant extremists—known as Puritans or in some cases Separatists—who were forever agitating for more change, a more thorough reformation, they said, within the Church of England (which was also known as the Anglican or Episcopal Church).

Queen Elizabeth I sought religious peace by tolerating differences in viewpoints as long as people accepted her religious authority and that of the bishops she appointed as well as agreed to use the form of worship prescribed in the *Book of Common Prayer*, which outlined a form of worship very similar to the Catholic mass. But the Puritans wanted change—much more change. They believed that the office of bishop had no base in the Bible and that each individual congregation should be self-governing. They believed each individual was responsible for reading and understanding the Bible. They did not want to follow a prayer book, Catholic or Anglican.

Those who opposed demands for religious uniformity also had major differences among themselves. Some believed it was their duty to stay within the Anglican Church and work for change. Others thought that change could come only from leaving the established church. The former tried to "purify" the Church of England and were known as Puritans. The latter group, called Separatists, thought that the church was hopelessly corrupt and that they needed to form their own separate religious communities. The Separatists were constantly in trouble with the authorities since everyone in England was expected to belong to the Anglican Church and attend its worship every Sunday. To separate oneself from the church, to worship in a place or form not authorized by the church, was treason. No wonder King James wanted to "harry them out of the land," and that so many of the Separatists wanted to leave.

3.1

3.2

3.3

3.4

This modern re-creation of the Pilgrim Village at Plimoth Plantation (note old-style spelling) has been built using extensive original records from 1627—seven years after the colony's founding when life had reached a bit of stability—on the site of the first Pilgrim colony in Plymouth, Massachusetts.

Version One/Alamy Stock Photo

Pilgrims

A name given to the Separatists within the Church of England who settled Plymouth, Massachusetts.

Mayflower Compact

The 1620 agreement made among the Pilgrims and others (whom the Pilgrims called "Strangers") on board the ship that brought them to Plymouth.

Separatists, also known as **Pilgrims**, founded the second permanent English colony in North America at Plymouth, Massachusetts, in 1620. The origins of Plymouth colony lay in a small community of Separatists who left England for Holland in 1607 where they were safe.

But the Separatists worried that their children raised in Holland would become more Dutch than English. Eventually, they decided that English North America would be a happier place for them. In 1619, these Separatist Pilgrims secured a grant of land from the Virginia Company, got financial backing from their own investors in a separate joint stock company, and hired a ship. After many delays, the *Mayflower* sailed from Plymouth, England, on September 6, 1620, with 102 passengers. Half the passengers were members of the congregation. The others were "strangers" along for adventure or profit. As William Bradford, who became Plymouth's historian, wrote of this congregation, "they knew they were pilgrims" as they set out for a long and dangerous journey.

After a stormy two-month voyage, they reached land far north of where they meant to go. Realizing that they were outside of the Virginia territory and that their new community was split between its religious members and others, they agreed to "combine ourselves together into a civil body politic, for our better ordering and preservation." Future generations would see the **Mayflower Compact** as the beginning of government by the consent of the people. But historians have seen it as something more modest: an agreement among a diverse group of people to try to get along with each other through what they knew would be a hard winter in a strange land.

The Pilgrims' first landing in November 1620 was at what is now Provincetown, Massachusetts. By December, however, they had moved across Cape Cod Bay to a place they named Plymouth where a high hill offered protection, and a large level area leading down to the harbor seemed a good place to build a town. Plymouth was empty when the Pilgrims landed. As recently as 1616, one thousand or more Indians had lived around Plymouth, but an epidemic had wiped them out. Elsewhere in the Americas, disease traveled faster than people. Enough European fishermen and traders had been traveling along the coast to ensure a plentiful supply of microbes. The new community quickly built on the now empty land protected by European immunity to diseases but vulnerable to much else.

The Pilgrims had arrived too late to build the kind of shelter they needed for a New England winter. During the winter of 1620–1621, about half the community died from disease, cold, and malnutrition. Some families were wiped out altogether. They had no contact with Native Americans, but they knew they were being watched constantly.

Then, in spring 1621, an Indian walked "very boldly" into the heart of the small Plymouth community. And when he arrived, to their utter amazement, he said, "Welcome, Englishmen!" The visitor was Samoset, a native of what is now Maine, where English fishermen had been landing for a century, hence his knowledge of the language. More important, he had been sent to visit them by Massasoit, the ruler of the Wampanoag Indians of the area. Massasoit was also familiar with English ships that had sailed along the coast and had sent exploring parties ashore. He was now ready to make contact.

Soon after Samoset's visit, Massasoit himself arrived with many warriors and a translator named Squanto who had been captured by previous English explorers and who had lived in London. He became a go-between for Massasoit with the Pilgrim community, even though neither side ever fully trusted him.

Squanto surprised the Pilgrims when he described parts of London and, more important, when he taught them how to find hibernating eels in nearby creeks. They had their best meal in months that evening. He also taught them to catch herring in the town brook and use them as fertilizer for planting corn. It proved to be the salvation of the colony. The Pilgrims concluded an agreement with Massasoit that led to fifty-four years of peace, an amazing development in the Americas.

In the fall of 1621, with peace concluded and the first successful harvest accomplished, Governor Bradford announced that it was time to "rejoice together" with the people who had helped, indeed allowed, them to survive. The first Thanksgiving (the Pilgrims never actually used that word) was a weeklong time of feasting on the fruits of the harvest and on turkeys, ducks, geese, deer, and stews. The Pilgrims were re-creating something they knew well, a traditional English harvest festival. Most of those present at "the first Thanksgiving," however, were Wampanoags, including Massasoit himself who brought gifts of freshly killed deer to the festivities.

Another group of religious dissidents from England were not far behind Plymouth's Pilgrims. **Puritans** who wanted to stay within the Church of England and change it were also having a hard time in the 1620s. James's son and successor, King Charles I (r. 1625–1649), was extremely hostile to the Puritans. Advocating reform within the established church became more difficult and dangerous. However, a group of Puritans controlled the Massachusetts Bay Company, a joint stock company that was organized to explore and settle North America. It was similar to the Virginia Company except that Puritans led it. They planted their first colony in Salem in 1629, just north of present-day Boston, and wanted to expand. In late 1629, someone realized that they could move the whole company—its charter and

Puritans

A name given to those Protestants within the Church of England who wanted to stay in the church but "purify" it of what they saw as Roman Catholic ways.

American Voices

Of Plymouth Plantation, by William Bradford, 1630–1651

William Bradford wrote his classic book over a period of many years to inform an English audience—and English investors—of the state of the new colony or plantation.

Being thus arrived in a good harbor and brought safe to land, they fell upon their knees and blessed the God of heaven, who had brought them over the vast and furious ocean, and delivered them from all the perils and miseries thereof again to set their feet on the firm and stable earth. …

Being thus passed the vast ocean and a sea of troubles before in their preparation … they had now no friends to welcome them, nor inns to entertain or refresh their weather-beaten bodies, nor houses or much less towns to repair to, to seek for succor. …

And for the season it was winter, and they that know the winters of that country know them to be sharp and violent and subject to cruel and fierce storms. … Besides, what could they see but a hideous and desolate wilderness, full of wild beasts and wild men, and what multitudes there might be of them they knew not. …

But that which was most sad and lamentable was that in two or three months' time half of their company died … being infected with the scurvy and other diseases, which this long voyage … had brought upon them; so there died sometimes two or three of a day in the aforesaid time, that of 100 and odd persons scarce fifty remained. …

The spring now approaching, it pleased God the mortality began to cease amongst them, and the sick and lame recovered. … Afterwards they … began to plan their corn, in which service Squanto stood them in great stead, showing them both … how to set it, and after how to dress and tend it … and where to get other provisions necessary for them, all which they found true by trial and experience. …

They began now to gather in the small harvest they had, and to fit up their houses and dwellings against winter, being well recovered in health and strength, and had all things good plenty.

Source: William Bradford, *A History of Plymouth Plantation* (Boston: Massachusetts Historical Society, 1856)

Thinking Critically

1. **Analyzing Primary Sources**

   According to Bradford, what challenges did the first Plymouth settlers face? What helped them?

2. **Contextualization**

   What does Bradford's account tell us about the importance of Native American peoples to the initial survival of the settlement?

3.1

3.2

3.3

3.4

the control that went with it—out of England and into their new colony. With such a move, the Massachusetts Bay Company could shift from being a corporation to a form of colonial government and chart a course for itself very different from Virginia. If successful, this move would create a self-governing Puritan company thousands of miles from the king and his bishops who were making things so difficult for Puritans in England.

John Winthrop, an ardent Puritan, was invited to be the governor of the new colony. In spring 1630, fourteen ships left England for Massachusetts Bay with their charter on board. By the end of the summer, more than one thousand people and two hundred cattle had landed in Massachusetts. In the next decade, known as the Great Migration, some twenty thousand people followed. Puritan Massachusetts soon had more people than Plymouth and Jamestown combined.

The Massachusetts Puritans also had a clear sense of purpose. As Winthrop said: "Our immediate object is to seek out a new home under a due form of Government both civil and ecclesiastical. … we shall be as a City upon a hill. The eyes of all people are upon Us." The Puritan's hoped that their new Commonwealth in New England could be a model of how society should operate for old England.

The Pilgrims had written their Mayflower Compact as a simple basis for the colony's government. The Puritan migrants of 1630 meant to use the more detailed **Charter of the Massachusetts Bay Company** to organize a permanent self-governing colony in Massachusetts.

The first meeting on New England soil of the Great and General Court—the colony's governing body (as the state legislature in Massachusetts is still called)—took place in August 1630. What had started as a business venture in England was transformed into a government in Massachusetts. Annual elections chose the governor, deputy governor, and members of the legislature. When King Charles I realized what the Puritans had done, he sent a ship to recover the charter. Winthrop called out the militia and mounted cannons at the entrance to Boston harbor. Those under royal command who had come for the charter decided that it would be wiser to sail back to England without it. A full 140 years before the American Revolution, British citizens in North America were engaged in armed resistance of British authorities based in London.

The Puritans valued literacy. If salvation depended on a personal encounter with the Christian faith, then Puritans needed to be able to read the Bible. In 1636, only six years after Boston was founded, the colony's legislature ordered the creation of a college that would soon be named Harvard after an early benefactor. They created Boston Latin School to prepare young men for college, and in 1647, the legislature required every township in the colony to provide for a school.

The Puritans of Massachusetts Bay, however, had their differences with one another. In 1637, Puritans on the Connecticut River found the government in Boston too restrictive and created their own independent colony of Connecticut based at Hartford. Two years later, the Hartford colonists established a formal government for their colony, crafting the **Fundamental Orders of Connecticut**. The document offered more men the right to vote than did Massachusetts Bay. Some have considered it as the first written constitution in the Americas, though others, looking at the Massachusetts charter and other such documents, dispute that claim. Other Puritans found the Boston government not strict enough and created a more theocratic colony at New Haven the following year.

More troublesome to the Puritans was Roger Williams, whose advocacy of freedom of conscience for every individual was almost unique in the 1600s. Williams was a Puritan. He arrived in Boston in 1631 only a year after the town's founding. But he quickly got into trouble because he asserted that civil authority could not enforce religious laws, including a law against blasphemy. In 1635, he was convicted of "erroneous" opinions. In the winter of 1636, to avoid arrest, he walked from his old home in Salem, Massachusetts, through snow-covered forest to Narragansett Bay (more than sixty-five miles) and soon established a new colony called Providence where he invited all those "distressed of conscience" to the first colony that would separate church and state and grant full liberty to people of any religious opinion, a direct slap at Puritan efforts at religious uniformity. Williams established

The Charter of the Massachusetts Bay Company

The legal charter given to the London-based corporation that launched Massachusetts Bay Colony.

Fundamental Orders of Connecticut

The 1639 charter that Massachusetts authorities allowed a new separate colony based in Hartford to adopt, which confirmed its independence from Massachusetts.

close working relationships with both the Wampanoag and Narragansett tribes—and insisted on paying them for the land on which he established his colony, unlike the settlers of Boston or Plymouth. Under Williams' leadership Rhode Island became a haven for religious dissenters.

In addition, Anne Hutchinson caused a stir with her charismatic preaching and her belief that God's inspiration could be more immediate than most Puritans believed. While Puritans insisted that every man and woman should read and interpret the Bible, they expected the interpretation to follow certain paths. In addition, only men were supposed to preach. When Hutchinson said that she herself received direct revelations from God, she had moved beyond what the Puritans would tolerate and was banished from the colony. She and her followers made their way, first to Roger Williams's colony in Rhode Island, and then to Dutch New Amsterdam where she was killed in an Indian attack in 1643.

While the first generation of New England's founders argued about whose version of Protestant theology was correct, their American-born children and grandchildren sometimes wandered quite far from the theological interests of the founders. The first Massachusetts Puritans saw themselves as being on an "errand into the wilderness," as a 1670 sermon put it. Religious fervor and conversions were less common in the next generations as the tight-knit colony expanded its commerce and prosperity.

In Massachusetts in the 1600s, only those who could convincingly demonstrate that they had a true religious conversion could be church members, and only church members could vote. Since one had to convince a congregation that he or she had truly been converted to become a church member, many, including the children of devout church members, could not qualify for either church membership or the right to vote. People who were excluded from these privileges did not make for happy colonial residents.

In 1662, Massachusetts clergy adopted the **Halfway Covenant**, which allowed adults who had been baptized as children, because their parents were church members, to have their own children baptized, even if they were not among the members of a congregation. The compromise was a significant one for a community in which church membership was central to all else. In time, that compromise also led to many Massachusetts churches allowing any who could demonstrate familiarity with Christian doctrine and led a good life to be church members—and therefore also voters. The Halfway Covenant and other such moves represented an important compromise with reality and created a more diverse and inclusive society even as they diluted the religious focus on which Massachusetts had been founded.

Kevin Fleming/Corbis/VCG/Getty Images

This 1922 statue of Anne Hutchinson at the Massachusetts State House commemorates a woman who caused considerable difficulties for the authorities who ruled in Boston during her own time.

Halfway Covenant

Plan adopted in 1662 by New England clergy that allowed adults who had been baptized because their parents were church members, but who had not yet experienced conversion, to have their own children baptized.

Maryland

After Virginia and the New England colonies, the next English colony to be established on the mainland of North America was Maryland. Earlier English colonies had been founded by corporations or were royal colonies ruled by governors appointed by the king. Maryland represented something new, a proprietary colony. A **proprietary colony**—of which Maryland was the model—was essentially owned by one person and heirs who were, as the Maryland charter said, "true and absolute lords and proprietaries." The proprietor might allow others to own land and might take advice from local officials, but the whole colony was private property and, as such, could be passed from generation to generation within the proprietor's family. King Charles I established this model when he offered to give Maryland to George Calvert, the first Lord Baltimore.

Maryland was also different in another way. Lord Baltimore was a devout Catholic, and Catholics were persecuted in England. But King Charles was sympathetic despite popular opposition. Lord Baltimore, with the king's support, was determined to establish Maryland as a haven for English Catholics. After George Calvert died, his son, Cecil Calvert, the second Lord Baltimore, developed the colony. He realized that he had to recruit more people than a Catholic-only colony would attract. So, in 1649, Maryland granted freedom of worship to all Christians, including Protestants of any persuasion.

proprietary colony

A colony created when the English monarch granted a huge tract of land to an individual as his private property.

headright system
A system of land distribution during the early colonial era that granted settlers a set amount of land for each "head" (or person) who settled in the colony.

While the proprietors retained final authority in Maryland, Lord Baltimore's charter required the calling of a representative assembly, which he agreed to do in 1635. Thus by 1640, eight colonies—Virginia, Massachusetts Bay, Maryland, Connecticut, Plymouth, New Haven, and the island colonies of Bermuda and Barbados—had some form of representative assembly at a time when King Charles I was attempting to rule England without calling Parliament into session.

After initially establishing a colony of large estates, Maryland's proprietors felt they needed many more settlers to make the colony a success, so they decided to follow Virginia's lead and give every European settler one hundred acres, another one hundred for each additional adult member of the family, and fifty acres for each child as a means of attracting many more immigrants. This **headright system**—as it came to be called because it gave land to each "head," or person, who settled in the colony—made moving to Maryland very popular. From the beginning, Marylanders also knew that, as in Virginia, tobacco would be the key to their economic success. With tobacco came the need for more workers than even the headright system could attract. Thus, African slavery came early to Maryland. In 1661, Maryland was the first colony to formalize laws governing slavery. The laws included the stipulations that slaves inherit their status from their mother and that slavery for those born into it was for life.

Additional Colonies: Continued Settlement and Development

Later English colonies borrowed ideas from earlier ones. Plymouth and Boston learned from mistakes made at Jamestown. Those who established later English colonies studied Jamestown, Plymouth, and Boston, borrowing what they liked and ignoring the rest. In addition, those colonies also studied the prosperous English colonies that were developing on the island of Bermuda and in the Caribbean. Those island colonies attracted their own settlers from England and brought far more slaves from Africa than did the mainland colonies. On the islands, slaves worked on the expanding sugar plantations. Table 3-1 shows all of the English colonies that were eventually established in North America and in the islands.

CONNECTICUT AND NEW HAMPSHIRE   After the creation of the colonies at Plymouth, Massachusetts Bay, Connecticut, and New Haven, the New England colonies continued to be reshaped. Connecticut was united with New Haven in 1662. Massachusetts Bay Colony merged with Plymouth in 1685. New Hampshire became a separate colony under a royal governor in 1691. (Vermont did not separate from New York until after the American Revolution, and Maine was part of Massachusetts until 1820.)

NEW YORK   New York was settled before Maryland, but not by the English. What is now New York and New Jersey was settled by the Netherlands, or Holland, a new Protestant country carved out of what had been Spanish possessions in the late 1500s. Sailing for the Dutch, Henry Hudson had explored much of the Atlantic coast in 1609. His voyage gave the Netherlands the basis for its claim to land in North America. The Dutch West India Company was set up in 1621, and it built a Dutch trading post at Fort Orange (now Albany, New York) in 1624. The economic base of the Dutch colony was the fur trade. The Iroquois were happy to trade with the Dutch. They benefited from fostering competition between Dutch and French traders to see who would offer the best price for furs and be the best military allies.

In 1626, the Dutch built a settlement and commercial center called New Amsterdam on Manhattan Island, which, according to legend, was purchased from local Indians for sixty Dutch guilders (calculated at approximately $24 by an historian in the 1840s, over $1,000 today but still exceedingly cheap). There is some debate about which tribe actually received any payment. The payment, however, reflected a European understanding of landownership. Most Native American tribes did not think in terms of someone actually owning land; to them, the land, air, and water were open to all.

Despite efforts by its longtime governor Peter Stuyvesant to enforce religious uniformity and ban Jews, New Amsterdam soon became a haven for religious dissenters including Jews, Catholics, Quakers, and Muslims. It was also home to Dutch, German, French, Swedish, Portuguese, and English settlers. The Dutch were active in the slave trade. New Amsterdam

Table 3-1 England's American and Island Colonies

Colony	Founded	Official Religion	Government
Virginia	1607	Anglican	Corporation; Royal after 1625
Bermuda (island colony)	1612	Anglican	Corporation
Plymouth	1620 Merged with Massachusetts, 1685	Puritan	Corporation
St. Christopher (island colony)	1624	Anglican	Royal
Barbados (island colony)	1627	Anglican	Royal
Nevis (island colony)	1628	Anglican	Royal
Massachusetts (included Maine)	1630	Puritan	Corporation (based in Boston)
New Hampshire	1630	Puritan	Corporation; Royal after 1679
Antigua (island colony)	1632	Anglican	Royal
Montserrat (island colony)	1632	Anglican	Royal
Maryland	1634	Haven for Roman Catholics with no established church; Anglican after 1692	Proprietary 1634–1690; Royal 1691–1715; Proprietary again after 1715
Rhode Island	1636	Haven for dissenters, especially Baptists	Corporation
Connecticut (Hartford)	1636	Puritan	Charter
New Haven	1638; became part of Connecticut in 1665	Puritan	Charter
Jamaica (island colony)	1655 (captured from Spanish)	Anglican	Royal
Carolina	1663; split into North and South Carolina, 1729	Anglican	Proprietary
New York	Settled by Dutch 1624–1626; became English, 1664	None	Proprietary, 1684; Royal after 1685
New Jersey	1664 (split from New York)	None	Proprietary
Pennsylvania	1681	None, established as a haven for Quakers	Proprietary
Delaware	1701 (split from Pennsylvania)	None	Proprietary
Georgia	1732	None	Proprietary; Royal after 1751

Based on from David Goldfield, et al., *The American Journey: A History of the United States*, 6th ed. (New York, NY: Pearson Prentice Hall, 2011), p. 56.

had the largest number of African slaves in North America in the 1600s. As a trading center, New Amsterdam also saw many Native Americans who came to the city to sell furs and buy European goods. Successive Dutch governors banned sexual contact between the Dutch residents and Indians, but the ban was not always honored.

While the heart of the Dutch colony remained on Manhattan Island, the Dutch authorities offered large tracts of land to wealthy Dutch citizens, known as **patroons**, to develop the lands along the Hudson River between New Amsterdam and Albany. Dutch investors who promised to settle at least fifty people on their land were given huge tracts of land, which they controlled as private fiefdoms. Nevertheless, New Netherlands never had more than ten thousand European and African residents. In the Americas, Dutch colonial efforts did not so much focus on building a large colony as on building a small nucleus of Europeans, mostly men, who could develop trade partnerships and alliances with American Indians and often intermarry with them.

In 1664, King Charles II gave New Amsterdam to his younger brother, the duke of York (who later became King James II). That the Dutch already had a settlement on the land did not bother either brother. Having been "given" the colony, the duke sent a fleet to New Amsterdam to take it. There was little resistance to the English takeover; Governor Peter Stuyvesant was unpopular, and the English promised to respect Dutch property. The Dutch briefly recaptured the colony in 1673, but it returned to English rule permanently the following year. The heart of the Dutch oceanic empire was in Asia. They were not going to fight the English over this remote outpost.

The duke of York divided the colony, keeping New York for himself and giving New Jersey to two political allies. For the rest of the 1600s, New Jersey remained a colony of small farms of limited profit to its proprietors, although it attracted a diverse group of European

patroons

Dutch settlers who were given vast tracts of land along the Hudson River between New Amsterdam and Albany in return for bringing at least fifty immigrants to work the land.

This map of New Amsterdam just at the time the English first took control (note the English flag flying on the fort) shows the site of the fort at the tip of Manhattan and the British ships off shore.

Private Collection/Ken Welsh/The Bridgeman Art Library

settlers because its proprietors offered land at low prices and gave settlers significant religious and political freedom. But New York, with its great harbor and access to the interior via the Hudson River, grew quickly in population and wealth to become one of the most valuable English colonies.

PENNSYLVANIA AND DELAWARE The next English colony to be created was Pennsylvania. Like Maryland, Pennsylvania was established as a proprietary colony and a haven for a persecuted religious group while being open to all. Pennsylvania's proprietor was William Penn, the son of Sir William Penn, an admiral in the Royal Navy with close connections to King Charles II. The younger William Penn inherited the right to collect a substantial debt that the king owed to the Penn family. King Charles II repaid the debt in the form of land in North America. But while William Penn inherited both fortune and royal connections, he was a member of a dissident religious community known as Quakers because they supposedly trembled—quaked—at the name of God. Quakers broke with much of the religious practice of the day. When they gathered for worship, Quakers sat in silence until someone was moved by the Spirit to speak. They did not have formal clergy and gave women equal standing with men in their community, known as the Society of Friends. In addition, they were absolute pacifists who would not serve in the military. Because of their refusal to serve in the military and attend the services of the Church of England, they were constantly in legal trouble. Penn himself was briefly jailed for following Quaker practices.

Penn received his land grant from King Charles II in 1681, and the next year he sailed to Pennsylvania and founded Philadelphia (the City of Brotherly Love). Penn recruited settlers widely, in Britain and on the European continent, especially in Germany. By 1700, eighteen thousand Europeans had arrived. In keeping with his Quaker beliefs, Penn insisted on peaceful trade with the Indians. Although he had been granted land from the king, Penn also paid the Indians for their land. During his lifetime, Pennsylvania was generally a peaceful place.

All did not remain peaceful on the Pennsylvania frontier, however. As the colony grew, frontier tribes felt threatened by the rapid expansion, and the English colonists felt threatened by the Indians. Despite the increasing levels of threat, the colonists' Quaker beliefs kept them from forming a militia. In 1720, James Logan, William Penn's primary representative in the colony, had an idea. The Scots Irish of northern Ireland were Protestant and were fighters, having fought both the English and the Irish Catholics for land and religious freedom for themselves. Logan offered large tracts of land in central Pennsylvania, near today's Lancaster, to Scots Irish who would settle between the pacifist Quakers of Philadelphia and the frontier Native Americans.

Gift of Edgar William and Bernice Chrysler Garbisch/National Gallery of Art, Washington, DC

Although this painting was done long after the 1682 treaty shown here was concluded, it portrays Penn's commitment to negotiate with the tribes in Pennsylvania, including these negotiations to purchase the land on which Philadelphia was built.

Logan wrote that, as he became "apprehensive from the Northern Indians," he "therefore thought it might be prudent to plan a settlement of such men as those who had so bravely defended Londonderry [northern Ireland] … as a frontier in case of any disturbance." It was the beginning of a major Scots Irish migration to the mountains of Pennsylvania and later Virginia and the Carolinas that would bring some 250,000 from northern Ireland to the backcountry of the colonies and shape the ethnic and cultural roots of the Appalachian mountains for generations, even as it represented an odd ethical compromise that kept the Quakers protected in their pacifist ways.

While maintaining peace with, or at least distance from, the Indians, Penn allowed slavery in his colony. As early as 1684, two years after its founding, 150 African slaves arrived in Philadelphia. Slaves quickly came to have a key role as household servants, and by the early 1700s, slaves made up one-sixth of the city's population. In rural communities, slaves worked not only on farms but also in iron furnaces, mines, tanneries, and salt works.

Penn tried to create a prosperous colony based on high ideals. But he was also an aristocrat who held absolute power. By the 1690s, many in the colony, Quakers and non-Quakers, demanded more political freedom. In 1701, Penn reluctantly agreed to a Charter of Liberties that established an elected legislature, though the legislature and the Penn family would continue to argue until the beginnings of the American Revolution.

The 1701 charter also allowed the three most southern counties of Pennsylvania to create their own assembly, which became the core of the separate colony of Delaware. The first Europeans to settle in Delaware were from Sweden and Finland, creating the small and short-lived New Sweden colony at Fort Christina—today's Wilmington, Delaware—in 1638. The Dutch of New Amsterdam conquered the Fort Christina colony in 1655 before themselves being defeated by the English in 1664. The area was included in the land grant given to William Penn, but its separate history and geographical distance limited its relationship to the rest of Pennsylvania.

CAROLINA   South of Virginia, the land was contested between England and Spain, to say nothing of the Indian tribes who lived there. But England meant to win control of the area. Soon after coming to the throne, Charles II rewarded eight of his supporters, and sought to secure England's land claims by creating a colony named Carolina (based on the Latin for *Charles*). The proprietors developed an elaborate system of government that prescribed a hierarchical society with themselves at the top followed by the local gentry, and then poor white servants, with African slaves at the bottom. The city of Charles Town, later Charleston, became the colony's capital.

Carolina was a divided colony. In the north, most of the settlers were relatively poor white farmers from Virginia. Farther south, large-scale rice growing created a rich colony. Much of the colony's commercial success focused on the city—and harbor—at Charleston and on trade with the British Caribbean colonies, especially Barbados where large slave populations were fed Carolina rice. Many of the early immigrants to Charleston were from Barbados, both wealthy Europeans who became the elite of the mainland colony and African slaves who did the actual work of the rice farming. Following the model of Barbados, the southern part of Carolina became one of the earliest plantation economies on the mainland of North America. The split between the north and south was formalized when King George II officially divided the colony into North and South Carolina in 1729.

GEORGIA   The last English colony that would later be part of the United States was Georgia, founded in 1733 for idealistic reasons. James Oglethorpe, a war hero in England, wanted to create a place where the poorest of England's poor, those in debtor's prisons because they could not repay what they owed, could find new lives. Oglethorpe also believed that England needed a strong frontier colony on the border with Spanish Florida. These settlers, people whose alternative might well be prison, would be inspired to be not only farmers but also soldiers within this frontier border. Given this focus, Oglethorpe excluded Catholics—who might be secretly loyal to Catholic Spain—and Africans, free or slave—since they might be tempted to run away. With Georgia, the thirteen colonies that went on to unite in 1776 were in place.

African Slaves and Indentured Servants in England's Colonies

In 1619, a Dutch ship arrived at Jamestown. John Rolfe, anxious to expand the workforce for his tobacco farm, traded food supplies to the Dutch in return for twenty African slaves. Rolfe's 1619 purchase of other humans is usually given as the date for the beginning of slavery in what is now the United States. In fact, the Spanish had African slaves in Florida during the 1500s (see Chapter 2). A census of Virginia in 1620 that did not count Indians listed

This early picture of a Virginia tobacco plantation shows the role of African slave labor in doing the work of the plantation and the role of the English elite in managing the work.

indentured servants

An individual who contracted to serve for a period of four to seven years in return for payment of passage to America.

32 Africans—17 women and 15 men—out of a total population of 982. Nevertheless, the exchange of American-grown foodstuffs for African people that took place in 1619 was significant. Although it would have been impossible to predict it then, slave labor would become the economic foundation of the colonies and of the new nation that emerged from them.

The slavery that existed in British North America in the early 1600s was profoundly different from what slavery had been in the early 1500s or from what it became in the colonies in the early 1700s. Many think of slavery as a static institution, but the nature of slavery changed often. For many Americans, the image of slavery is that of the large plantations that existed in the South between 1800 and the 1860s. But understanding the development of slavery in the United States requires more careful observation. Slavery, though always terrible, meant different things at different times.

In the earliest years, slavery, though very difficult, was less harsh and hopeless than it became after about 1680. When John Rolfe purchased those twenty African slaves in 1619, it was not clear what their status would be. Slavery had not been codified either as a permanent lifelong status or as something associated always with race.

The first generation of African slaves in Virginia often worked side by side not only with English and Irish servants—many of whom also had little choice about coming to America—but also with captured Indians. Race was always a factor, but racial lines were blurred. Servants and slaves lived together, created new families together, and resisted together when they felt ill-treated.

In the small farms of the Chesapeake, in the Middle Colonies, and in New England, slaves also worked side by side with those who owned the land and with **indentured servants** who were working for a specified number of years to pay off the cost of their travel from Europe to America. Some of these indentured servants came seeking a better life; others came as an alternative to prison in England. During a term of indenture, a servant was treated much like a slave. Indentured servants could be bought and sold and were often whipped. The difference between indentured servanthood and slavery, and it was significant, was that at the end of their term, ranging from four to seven years, indentured servants were set free. Until the late 1640s, the majority died before completing their term, and even after earning their freedom, most of the newly freed were not able to earn much, although a few prospered and joined the elite. Since an English indentured servant costs about half as much as an African slave, and since neither tended to live long, many Virginians initially preferred indentured servants. Servants and slaves often intermarried and saw themselves as a united group.

The Africans, like the European servants, dreamed of a day when they might be free to own their own land. That dream was not an impossible one in the early 1600s. For example, Anthony Johnson was sold as a slave in Jamestown in 1621. He worked on the farm of the Bennett family and became known for his "hard labor and … service." After more than a decade of labor on the Bennett property, he was allowed to farm independently, while still a slave. He married a woman named Mary. Their children were baptized with the blessings of the authorities. Eventually, he gained his freedom and changed his name. When the Bennetts moved to eastern Virginia, the Johnsons moved with them. By 1651, Anthony Johnson owned a 250-acre farm with his own servants and at least one slave. His son John owned 550 acres, and another son owned 100 acres. The Johnson family, if not viewed as the equals of their white neighbors, were in many ways part of Virginia's landed gentry. During the 1600s, the Johnsons were not the only former slaves to achieve this status.

However, slaves in Virginia, Maryland, or the Carolinas could not repeat this success in the 1700s or 1800s.

There was more to the experience of the Johnsons than the freedom they gained to own and work their own land. They were free to travel. They were members of Christian churches and participated in the financial and religious activities of the colony. The total number of Africans, slave and free, remained relatively small in Virginia before 1680. On the eastern shore where the Johnsons lived, there were some forty free blacks out of a total black population of three hundred. While most Africans remained in slavery, 30 percent of the people of African descent in parts of Virginia were free in 1668. Race was not insignificant, but neither race as a marker of slavery nor slavery as an institution was as static as they would later become.

Slavery also developed in the northern colonies, coming to Massachusetts soon after it came to Virginia. By the 1660s, Boston's elite lived in a slave-owning world. One-third of the slaves in Massachusetts lived in Boston. In the North, slavery was more urban than rural. In the cities, slaves worked as household servants, cooking, cleaning, sewing, tending gardens and stables, and running errands. They also worked on wagons and wharves. Northern slaves, like many southern slaves of the 1600s, were much more fully integrated into European-American society, had less contact with fellow Africans and African traditions, and had much more freedom than later generations of slaves.

> **3.1 Quick Review**
>
> Compare the reasons for founding the different English colonies in North America during the 1600s. How might these different reasons lead to different developments in the colonies?

England's Wars, England's Colonies

3.2 Analyze the relationship between competition among European rivals and American Indians over resources, politics in England, internal colonial tensions, and life in the English colonies in North America during the 1600s.

The tensions that led Pilgrims and Puritans to flee England erupted into a full-scale civil war in England in the 1640s. The Puritans won and a Puritan Commonwealth ruled the country for eleven years (1649–1660) before Parliament restored the monarchy. The religious and political battles in England fueled settlement in North America. Puritans sought refuge in Massachusetts when they were feeling oppressed in England, supporters of the royal cause sought refuge in Virginia when the Puritans dominated at home, while Catholics moved to Maryland, and other dissidents found tolerant places such as Rhode Island or Pennsylvania. England's American colonies were often violent places. In the 1670s, internal tensions burst into violence in the colonies. King Philip's War in Massachusetts was one of the most vicious wars ever fought in North America. In Virginia, backcountry farmers took up arms against the royal governor in 1679. The growth, the tensions, and the violence all helped create the political and cultural structures of the colonies of British North America in the 1700s.

Civil War and Revolution in England

When King James died in 1625, his son became King Charles I (r. 1625–1649). King Charles was known for his religious sincerity and lack of political skill. The king and his advisors pursued religious Anglican uniformity far more strictly than his predecessors. The Puritan movement, however, grew despite royal opposition. By 1640, Parliament was overwhelmingly Puritan and passed laws that favored the Puritans and limited royal authority.

By 1642, England was in a civil war between king and Parliament. Parliament's army defeated the king, who was executed in 1649. Oliver Cromwell ruled England as a Puritan Commonwealth from 1649 to 1658. By the time Cromwell died in 1658, many in England were tired of Puritan rule. In 1660, Parliament invited the son of Charles I to reign as King Charles II (r. 1660–1685). The Anglican Church again became the official state church, but

3.1

3.2

3.3

3.4

the new king, determined to avoid another civil war, was more tolerant of religious differences than his father had been. Charles II also took an interest in expanding his North American colonies. Almost half of the colonies of the future United States—New York, New Jersey, Pennsylvania, North and South Carolina—date to his reign.

Wars in New England—Pequot War, 1637, and Metacom's War (King Philip's War), 1675–1676

The half century of peace that the Pilgrims of Plymouth and the Wampanoag Indians experienced was unusual in North America. It seemed that the two cultures could live side by side in relative harmony. But while there was harmony in Plymouth between 1620 and 1675, there were also tensions, sometimes sharp ones.

Early in Plymouth's history, one incident showed just how violent the Pilgrims could be. Massasoit let Governor Bradford know that another tribe, the Massachusetts Indians, who lived north of Plymouth, was preparing to attack Plymouth. Whether the wily Massasoit was reporting the truth or using the Pilgrims to settle an old score is unclear, but Bradford took him seriously. Under the command of Miles Standish, Pilgrim soldiers killed two of the tribe's leaders. The Massachusetts Indians decided not to antagonize these violent Europeans and moved farther north. Other tribes saw that, for good or ill, the alliance between Massasoit and the Pilgrims ran deep. But from Holland, the Pilgrim's spiritual guide Pastor John Robinson condemned "the killing of those poor Indians," warning, "where blood is once begun to be shed, it is seldom staunched of a long time after."

The Massachusetts Bay Puritans did not maintain peace for as long as the Plymouth settlers. Massachusetts Bay was larger, stronger, and less tolerant of outsiders than Plymouth. The Massachusetts Bay Puritans often traded with Indian tribes, especially the Pequots of the Connecticut River Valley. But when the captain of a trading vessel was killed in 1637, the Puritans responded harshly. Building an alliance with the Mohegans and Narragansetts, they attacked a Pequot fortress on the Mystic River, set the houses on fire, and attacked anyone who fled. In the short **Pequot War**, four hundred Pequots were killed and their village annihilated. Surviving Pequots were sold into slavery. From the Mohegans' perspective, this conflict was an opportunity to expand their influence. From the perspective of the Narragansetts, it was horrifying. They were accustomed to Indian warfare that focused on the skill and bravery of a few, not the annihilation of the many. Europeans, they discovered, fought differently.

Other tensions between the English settlers and Indian tribes were also evident. The English did not tend to intermarry or engage in sexual liaisons with Indians as frequently as the Spanish, French, and Dutch. Many parts of New Spain and New France were conquered by unmarried men who quickly developed intimate relationships with native women and created a mestizo (mixed European and Indian blood) community. These relationships often helped strengthen ties between cultures and reduce tensions. But New England was settled by English families, and their descendants tended to produce children within the community. Mixed-race people were rarer in English colonies.

Especially in New England, the English wanted to convert the Indians to their religion. But most Indians resented and resisted missionaries, whether English, Spanish, or French. For all of his friendship with the Pilgrims, Massasoit distrusted Christianity. He saw the conversion of Indians on Cape Cod as a rejection of his role as their supreme chief.

What fostered the most tension, however, was the constant growth of the European community. The forty miles between Plymouth and the heart of Massasoit's world provided a sufficient barrier for people who generally walked everywhere, but the European population was expanding. By the 1660s, English settlements were springing up in every direction and were beginning to dominate much more land. European livestock ate Wampanoag corn. Land sales that had once seemed wise now seemed to confine a new generation of Wampanoags.

A new generation of Pilgrims and Wampanoags were coming to power, people who did not remember their early friendship. In 1657, Governor Bradford, who had led Plymouth for thirty-seven years, died. At about the same time, Massasoit was succeeded, first by his son Wamsutta, known as Alexander, and shortly after by his other son Metacom (who was known to the Pilgrims as King Philip).

Pequot War

Conflict between English settlers and Pequot Indians over control of land and trade in eastern Connecticut.

Throughout the 1670s, rumors circulated that Metacom was preparing for war. He denied that he had anything but peaceful intentions, but he was also buying arms and ammunition. In January 1675, a Christian Indian, John Sassamon, told Josiah Winslow, Bradford's successor as governor, that Metacom was indeed preparing for war. Winslow refused to believe Sassamon and sent him on his way. Soon thereafter, Sassamon's body was discovered. Metacom denied any role in his death and asked the authorities to allow the Wampanoags to settle what he saw as an internal matter. But instead, the Plymouth authorities hanged three of Metacom's associates.

The first skirmishes of what was known as **Metacom's War (King Philip's War)**—using Metacom's English name—took place within two weeks of the executions, in June 1675. People in outlying towns took refuge in fortresses. Abandoned homes were burned. When a father and son left the Swansea garrison and found Indians vandalizing their home, they fired on them. The Wampanoags did not want to draw the first blood, but once shots had been fired, they fought furiously. Within days, at least ten of the English were killed. When the Plymouth militia gave chase, the Indians simply melted into the woods and lived to fight another day—and fight they did. Early encounters between Europeans and natives of the Americas had pitted matchlocks (difficult-to-fire guns that were unusable in the rain) against Indian bows and arrows. However, in this war, both sides were armed with more modern flintlocks that each side could use with deadly aim against the other.

As the war escalated, Europeans throughout New England lived in terror and died in isolated settlements or larger towns. Colonial troops who did not understand Indian wars marched into ambushes and died by the scores. Indians died in even larger numbers, and the Wampanoag community was destroyed. Other tribes, even those that sought to remain

Metacom's War (King Philip's War)

Conflict in New England (1675–1676) between Wampanoags, Narragansetts, and other Indian peoples against English settlers.

3.1

3.2

3.3

3.4

American Voices

Mary Rowlandson, The Sovereignty and Goodness of God, 1682

The journal of Mary Rowlandson describes an Indian attack on Lancaster, Massachusetts, in 1676, the death of her daughter and many friends, and her subsequent experience as an Indian captive. Despite the terror and loss, Rowlandson provided one of the first accounts of an American Indian war dance—just before her captors' successful attack on the town of Sudbury, Massachusetts. It also relates her relatively friendly conversations with Metacom (Philip) himself.

On the tenth of February, 1676, came the Indians with great numbers upon Lancaster. ... Hearing the noise of some guns, we looked out; several Houses were burning. ... There were five persons taken in one house. The Father and the Mother and a sucking Child they knocked on the head; the other two they took and carried away alive. ... Some in our house were fighting for their lives, others wallowing in their blood, the House on fire over our heads ... yet the Lord by his Almighty power preserved a number of us from death, for there were twenty-four of us taken alive and carried Captive. ...

But now, the next morning, I must turn my back upon the Town, and travel with them into a vast and desolate Wilderness, I knew not whither. It is not my tongue or pen can express the sorrows of my heart and bitterness of my spirit that I had at this departure, but God was with me in a wonderful manner, carrying me along, and bearing up my spirit that it did not quite fail. One of the Indians carried my poor wounded Babe upon a horse; it went moaning all along, "I shall die, I shall die." I went on foot after it with

sorrow that cannot be expressed. ... This day in the afternoon, about an hour by Sun, we came to ... An Indian Town called Wenimessett [today New Braintree, MA] ... About two hours in the night, my sweet Babe like a lamb departed this life. ...

During my abode in this place [after several moves], Philip spoke to me to make a shirt for his boy, which I did, for which he gave me a shilling ... and with it I bought a piece of Horse flesh. Afterwards he asked me to make a Cap for his boy, for which he invited me to Dinner. I went, and he gave me a Pancake about as big as two fingers; it was made of parched wheat, beaten, and fried in Bear's grease, but I never tasted pleasanter meat in my life.

[Rowlandson was released by her captors in April as part of an unsuccessful peace initiative.]

Source: Mary Rowlandson, "The Sovereignty and Goodness of God, 1682," in Nathaniel Philbrick and Thomas Philbrick, editors, *The Mayflower Papers: Selected Writings of Colonial New England* (New York; Penguin Books, 2007), pp. 166–211.

Thinking Critically

1. **Analyzing Primary Sources**
   While Rowlandson describes her own experience, how accurate or inaccurate do you think her report might be?

2. **Argument Development**
   How would you use evidence from the documents to explain the Indians' decision to take captives rather than simply killing all of the town's inhabitants? Might there be another explanation?

neutral, were decimated. In western Massachusetts, after Indians burned the town of Springfield, colonists turned on friendly or neutral tribes. Despite pleas from the missionary John Eliot to protect the "Praying Indians"—converts to Christianity who were loyal to the Massachusetts authorities—the converts were taken to relocation centers in Boston Harbor where many died of exposure and malnutrition.

In one of the bloodiest battles of the war, known as the Great Swamp Fight of December 1675, a Plymouth force attacked the Narragansetts after tracking through swamps. Even though the Narragansetts had remained neutral throughout the warfare, the English force destroyed their fort, killing perhaps three hundred Narragansett warriors and burning alive another three hundred women, children, and old people. Humanity seemed to have vanished from these descendants of those who sought to build a new Christian community.

Throughout the winter of 1675–1676, the outcome of the war was unclear. The European communities in New England risked being wiped out that winter. But in the summer of 1676, the Indians were running out of food. Some of the tribes that had been allied with Metacom drifted away or shifted their allegiance. The end came in August when Metacom and a few dedicated supporters were cornered in a swamp and killed.

In a grisly end to the war, King Philip's head was displayed on a pole in Plymouth for the next twenty years. Authorities in Plymouth and Boston expelled many of the Indians from New England. Over one thousand Wampanoags and their allies, including Philip's wife and son, were sold into slavery in the Caribbean. John Eliot, the longtime pastor to Christian Indians wrote, "To sell souls for money seems a dangerous merchandise." But in the hatreds created by the war, these voices were not heard.

Of the seventy thousand people of all races living in New England at the beginning of the war, some five thousand were killed—one thousand of the English and at least four thousand Native Americans. King Philip's War was one of annihilation; each side sought to destroy the other. In fact, the percentage of people killed in King Philip's War was larger than corresponding percentages for the American Revolution, the Civil War, or World War II. For the Wampanoags, the war ended the independent nation that Metacom and his father Massasoit had led (see Map 3-2).

Bacon's Rebellion in Virginia, 1676

As King Philip's War was being fought in New England, Virginia was also engulfed in violence. Like the war in Massachusetts, **Bacon's Rebellion** illustrated the instability of early colonial life and alliances that were constantly shifting. King Philip's War was a battle between Europeans and Indians. In Virginia, the conflict was more complex.

By 1660, Virginia had forty thousand colonists, including a small elite and many poor workers—Africans and Indians, some slave, some free, and European indentured servants or others who had finished their time of indenture. At this time, there were at least as many Indian as African slaves in Virginia. However, most of the Virginia tribes kept their distance from the white settlements, except for occasional trade.

Sir William Berkeley was the royal governor of Virginia for most of the time from 1642 to 1677. He brought order to the colony, but it was an aristocratic order. He and an inner circle ran the government and retained most of the profits from the tobacco trade no matter who actually grew the crop. The wide disparity of wealth and power generated increasing tension between rich whites and poor whites, between established landowners and newly arrived colonists (who could acquire land only along the western frontiers of the territory—closer to hostile tribes), and among Europeans, Africans, and Indians. Even if slaves and indentured servants did earn their freedom, land was increasingly difficult to acquire, and many were limited to becoming tenant farmers for wealthier landowners.

In 1675, resentment came to a head. The economy was in the doldrums. Neither the corn crop, which was essential for food, nor the tobacco crop, which was essential for money, was doing well. When Indians from the Doig tribe raided Thomas Mathew's plantation, because Mathew supposedly had not paid for items obtained from the tribe, area colonists retaliated with an attack of their own. However, the colonists mistakenly attacked the Susquehanaug tribe instead of the Doigs. Violence was flaring.

Bacon's Rebellion

A 1676 rebellion in Virginia, led by a recent immigrant from England, Nathaniel Bacon, in which a militia attacked not only Indian villages but also the royal governor before being defeated.

Map 3-2 King Philip's War in New England in 1675–1676.

As the map shows, King Philip's—or Metacom's—War involved all of New England in brutal conflict, not only in Plymouth where it began but throughout Rhode Island, Massachusetts, and the Connecticut River towns.

At that point, Nathaniel Bacon, recently arrived in Virginia from a prosperous English family and already one of the largest landowners in the western part of the colony, organized a militia to attack the Indians. Bacon and his followers had heard news of King Philip's War where many tribes had united. They feared unity among Virginia's tribes and had no intention of discriminating between friendly and unfriendly Indians. Bacon's militia began attacking Indians indiscriminately, seeing every Indian as an enemy. Governor Berkeley, however, believed that Virginia needed friendly tribes on its frontier to protect it from hostile tribes who lived farther west. He refused to support Bacon's militia, and Bacon refused to disband his militia. Berkeley had Bacon arrested and then released him. Bacon marched his ragtag army of free Africans, slaves, and poor whites into Jamestown and set the town on fire. In the face of the militia, Governor Berkeley fled, calling for help from England. The crown sent one thousand English troops; it had no patience with rebels. Most rebels surrendered and were pardoned. In 1676, Bacon died at age twenty-nine from dysentery. Twenty-three leaders of the short-lived rebellion were hanged. Virginia's poor had been crushed.

Bacon's Rebellion illustrates the complexity of American history. Berkeley was an overbearing aristocrat. During his more than thirty years as governor, he made evident his dis-

Thinking Historically

The Declaration of the People by Nathaniel Bacon, General, 1676

While Virginia Governor Berkeley complained about trying to govern people who were poor, discontented, and armed, Bacon had the support of most of the people, white and black, who were poor, indebted, unhappy, and well armed. Bacon issued a Declaration of the People, stating the many reasons—from high taxes to elite control of the fur trade to lack of support in his Indian wars—for the rebellion.

For having upon specious pretences of public works, raised unjust taxes upon the commonality for the advancement of private favourites and other sinister ends, but no visible effects in any measure adequate. …

For having wronged his Majesty's prerogative and interest by assuming the monopoly of the beaver trade. …

For having protected, favoured and emboldened the Indians against his Majesty's most loyal subjects, never contriving, requiring, or appointing any due or proper means of satisfaction for their many invasions, murders, and robberies committed upon us.

For having the second time attempted the same thereby calling down our forces from the defence of the frontiers, and most weak exposed places, for the prevention of civil mischief and ruin amongst ourselves, whilst the barbarous enemy in all places did invade, murder, and spoil us, his Majesty's most faithful subjects.

Of these … we accuse Sir William Berkeley, as guilty.

Source: Selections from Louis B. Wright and Elaine W. Fowler, *Documents of Modern History: English Colonization of North America* (New York: St. Martin's Press), pp. 163–165.

Thinking Critically

1. **Analyzing Primary Sources**
   What does the excerpt from Bacon's declaration tell us about the underlying causes of social tensions during the mid-1600s in Virginia? How do you think Berkeley would have answered the charges?

2. **Contextualization**
   What role did Bacon and his followers believe the colonial government should play in Virginia? How might their views have differed from those of Berkeley and his supporters? (Note how both sides called on the king to side with them.)

respect for the majority of people in his colony. Bacon's militia represented a racially diverse army of the dispossessed. But even as the rebels were demanding more equal treatment for themselves, they were also demanding the right to kill Indians indiscriminately and steal their land. In the end, poor whites, enslaved Africans, and Native Americans all lost. While Bacon and his followers were defeated, the arrival of so many well-trained British troops reduced the power of the tribes to bargain.

3.2　Quick Review

Identify similarities and differences between the conflicts in New England and Virginia. How did the population and past events of each colony lead to the violence that occurred?

France Takes Control of the Heart of a Continent

3.3 Explain how French, Spanish, Dutch, and British colonizers had different economic and imperial goals and, in particular, how France's growing role and power in North America affected English and Spanish colonies.

French explorers had been among the earliest Europeans to see much of the northern Atlantic coast of North America in the early 1500s. Little came of their discoveries, however, until the European demand for beaver fur led French traders to set up trading outposts that became the towns of Quebec and Montreal. During the long reign of King Louis XIV (r. 1643–1715), New France expanded from a tiny isolated community around Quebec to dominate the St. Lawrence River Valley. French communities were founded throughout the heartland of North America from Detroit and Chicago to New Orleans. By 1715, New France claimed far more of North America than either the English or the Spanish (see Map 3-3).

Map 3-3 France in the American Interior, 1670–1720.

As this map shows, French exploration and claims to Montreal, the St. Lawrence River Valley, the Great Lakes, and the Mississippi River all the way to the Gulf of Mexico gave it claim to the heart of North America and also completely encircled the English colonies on the Atlantic coast and challenged the Spanish for control of Texas.

Early French Settlement—Quebec, Montreal, and the Fur Trade

With the news that there seemed to be no way around North America, France, like England, lost interest in the land that Verrazano and Cartier had explored in the 1520s and 1530s. Later in the 1500s, however, trade between Europeans and Native Americans grew in importance. Beaver pelts were becoming popular for fur hats in Europe. Trade in beaver fur transformed the economies of Europe and the tribes of North America as surely as the greed for gold and silver transformed South America. As Montagnais and Hurons developed trading partnerships with the French, and the Iroquois with the English, trade and warfare became more intense. Ancient rivalries among the Indians escalated as each tribe fought to control the supply of beaver furs that seemed in insatiable demand in Europe. While these tribes had long fought each other for honor, living space, and captives, they now had

European weapons, acquired through trade, that further fueled the warfare. Tribes seemed bent on annihilating their opponents, a goal that had not been part of Indian warfare in the past. Even though the French and British fur traders preferred to make alliances with the Indians rather than enslave them, the results for many tribes were nevertheless disastrous.

The trade in beaver pelts also encouraged Europeans to make permanent settlements. Samuel de Champlain began exploring the St. Lawrence River in 1603 and founded the city of Quebec in 1608 as a representative of a private fur company—just one year after the English founded Jamestown. With only twenty-eight men in his colony, Champlain knew that he needed alliances if Quebec was to succeed. So he joined the Montagnais and Hurons in a war against the Iroquois and solidified an alliance that would be the foundation of Quebec's trade. The Huron alliance also allowed Champlain to travel farther west. He spent 1615–1616 exploring the Great Lakes.

After 1612, Champlain was appointed as the king's Viceroy for New France, uniting commercial and governmental positions. As late as 1635, when Champlain died, Quebec had a population of only three hundred, but it was there to stay. Montreal was settled in 1642 to expand trade farther west along the St. Lawrence River. Jesuit missionaries arrived and lived among the Hurons, learning their ways and seeking to convert them to Catholic Christianity. New France, and the missions it sponsored, were as deeply Catholic as most of the English settlements were Protestant, adding to tensions between the French and English colonies over Indian alliances and the quest for larger territory that would last throughout their histories.

During the early 1600s, Quebec and Montreal were small French towns, thousands of miles from any other such town, but with their own European families, parishes, and culture. New France came close to being wiped out in the late 1640s when the Iroquois Confederation overran Huron villages, torturing, killing, or taking prisoner everyone in sight. Jesuit missionaries died along with their Huron hosts. Once a nation of over 10,000 people, the Hurons disappeared as a recognizable group after 1648. The defeat of the Hurons was a huge blow to French missionaries and to the fur trade that was the economic anchor of New France.

The Iroquois attacked French villages, and besieged Montreal itself. Two hundred French settlers were killed and more left for France as quickly as they could. The future of New France was far from clear in 1650. Montreal and Quebec, however, remained militarily secure, and the Algonquians replaced the Hurons as the major French allies and the source of access to the fur trade.

Exploring and Claiming the Mississippi River Valley

In 1663, Louis XIV made New France into a royal province and sent one thousand French soldiers to protect Quebec from Iroquois attack and establish it once and for all as the seat of what he expected to be a vast French empire. Plans were laid to make this expansion happen.

In 1672, Governor Louis de Frontenac sent Louis Joliet, who spoke a number of Indian languages, and Father Jacques Marquette, a Jesuit missionary, to find and explore a great waterway spoken of in Indian stories—the Mississippi (or *Mitchisipi*, "great water"), which he hoped might be the route to China. In June 1673, Marquette and Joliet paddled into the Mississippi, the first Europeans known to do so. Early in their trip, they were welcomed by the Illinois tribe and given a great feast. The encounter was the beginning of a long-term French-Indian alliance in the region.

Joliet and Marquette determined that the Mississippi flowed south into the Gulf of Mexico, not west to the Pacific and China as had been hoped. But they understood that they were in the midst of a land of great potential. They could develop a French colony that would allow a rich trade with the Indians and block the expansion of the English.

Fear of hostile tribes and of being captured by the Spanish led Joliet and Marquette to turn back before reaching the mouth of the Mississippi. On the return trip, they visited other Indian villages, including a Miami Indian village of *Checagou* or Chicago. Joliet returned to Quebec to report and draw maps of their travels. Marquette continued his missionary work until he died in 1675. What would, some two centuries later, become the Midwest of the United States was first described for Europeans and mapped by these two explorers. While the authorities in France wanted to strengthen the settlements in the St. Lawrence River Valley, Governor Frontenac had no patience with such caution. In young Robert de La Salle, he found a per-

American Voices

Journal of the Voyage of Father Jacques Gravier, of the Society of Jesus [Jesuits], in 1700, from the Country of the Illinois to the Mouth of the Mississippi River

The Jesuit Relations was a publication of reports on Jesuit missionary work that provided an extraordinary glimpse of the countryside and of the people who lived along the Mississippi from modern-day Wisconsin to the Gulf of Mexico between the 1690s and the mid-1700s. One Jesuit priest, Father Jacques Gravier, described his journey down the Mississippi to the fort that would become New Orleans.

I started in 1700, on the 8th of September, to come here. … I was accompanied by 5 Canoes manned by Frenchmen. … We made only 4 leagues the 1st day, because one of our canoes was split by a snag hidden in the water, and we had to halt in order to repair it. … I embarked in my Canoe to visit Monsieur Davion, a missionary priest, who was sick. … In his mission, 3 different languages are spoken: the Iakou, with thirty Cabins; the Ounspik, with ten or twelve Cabins, and the Toumika, who are in seven hamlets, consisting in all of fifty or sixty small Cabins. …

[Another] village is on the crest of a steep mountain, precipitous on all sides. There are eighty Cabins in it, and in the middle of the Village is a fine and very level open space, where from morning to night, young men exercise themselves.

Since we have left the Natches, we have lived only on Indian corn with a few Squashes—For it is a long time since either wild oxen, Deer, or bears have been seen in this quarter; and if we have found a few bustards or wild geese, they have been so lean that they were as tasteless as wood. … The navigation of the Mississippi is very slow and tedious, and very difficult—especially in ascending it. It is also very troublesome on account of the gnats and other insects called Mosquitoes, midges, And black flies. … At last, on the 17th of December, I reached fort Mississippi, after 68 Days of navigation in descending the river. … The Commandant, Monsieur de Bienville, has there a small and very neat house.

Source: Reuben Gold Thwaites, editor, *Travels and Explorations of the Jesuit Missionaries in New France, 1610–1791,* Vol. LXV, *Lower Canada, Mississippi Valley, 1696–1702* (Cleveland: The Burrows Brothers, 1900), pp. 101–105, 127–129, 145–147, 159–161.

Thinking Critically

1. **Causation**
   What does Father Gravier's 1700 report relate about French exploration along the Mississippi in the 1600s?
2. **Analyzing Primary Sources**
   What does Father Gravier's account suggest about the nature of French settlement along the Mississippi River in 1700?

fect ally for exploring the Mississippi Valley.

La Salle led a much larger expedition than that of Joliet and Marquette down the Illinois and Mississippi Rivers in 1679. La Salle's goals were to build an alliance with the Illinois and other tribes against the Iroquois and to establish a permanent French presence throughout the Mississippi Valley that would ensure limits on English and Spanish expansion. In 1681–1682, he and his men traveled down the Mississippi to the Gulf of Mexico. In the name of King Louis XIV, he claimed "possession of this country of Louisiana" and of "the seas, harbors, ports, bays, adjacent straits, and all the nations, peoples, provinces, cities,

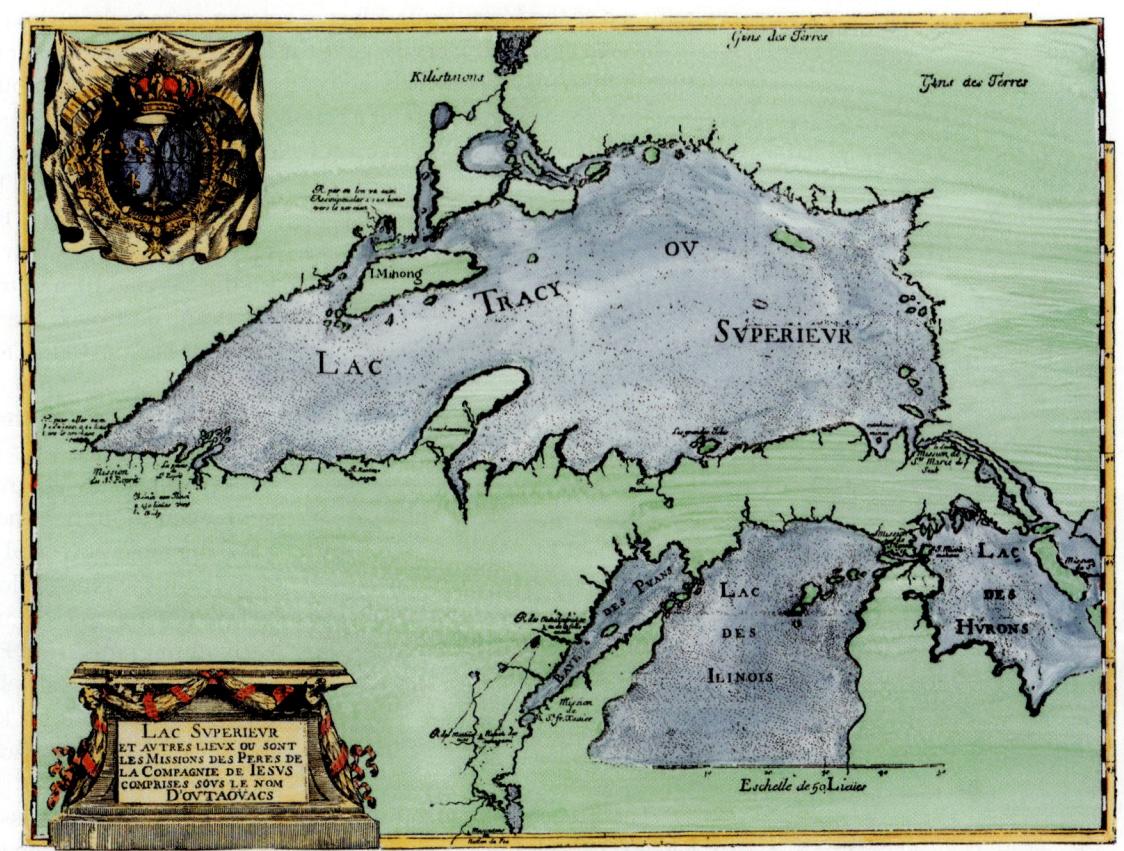

French Jesuit missionaries explored west as well as south of the French capital of Quebec. By the late 1600s, the Jesuits were mapping Lake Superior and the other Great Lakes with surprising accuracy.

North Wind Picture Archives/Alamy Stock Photo

towns, villages, mines, minerals, fisheries, streams, and rivers within it." It was a claim to more than one-third of North America.

Not content with reaching the mouth of the Mississippi, La Salle then continued as far west on the Gulf of Mexico as Texas. Eventually, he pushed his followers too hard, and some of them murdered him in 1687.

Other French explorers and settlers followed in La Salle's wake. French trappers and traders (known as *coureurs de bois* or "runners of the woods") established relationships with various Native American tribes as well as personal relationships with native women and brought wealth back to New France. Some of them established a base called Fort Arkansas at the confluence of the Arkansas and Mississippi Rivers. French Jesuits built a mission at Chicago. In 1698, the Bishop of Quebec appointed missionary priests to a new mission at the Natchez Post on the Arkansas River. The French communities that dotted the Mississippi in the late 1600s and early 1700s were small. They included American Indians and French trappers, families, and missionaries. They never matched the English settlements in size or in isolation from the American Indian tribes that surrounded them. But they were there to stay.

Creating the French Gulf Coast—Biloxi, Mobile, and New Orleans

As a result of the reports from explorers and missionaries, Louis XIV decided to secure the French claim to the mouth of the Mississippi. Pierre d'Ibreville was commissioned in 1698 to scout the area.

D'Iberville landed on the east bank of the Mississippi River and built a fort near a Bilochi Indian settlement, which came to be called Biloxi. D'Iberville and his crew moved up the Mississippi River until they found a trail connecting the Mississippi to Lake Ponchartrain and promised to return. To his surprise, d'Iberville also found a group of free blacks who were living with Indians and who did not take kindly to the arrival of Europeans.

Queen Anne's War of 1702–1713 (see Chapter 4) made travel difficult and dangerous. With the coming of peace in 1713, d'Iberville's younger brother Jean-Baptiste de Bienville returned to the Mississippi. When a veteran of La Salle's trip down the Mississippi arrived in the area in 1713, d'Iberville gave the intrepid French explorer command of another French city on the Gulf coast, which they named La Mobile (now Mobile, Alabama).

In 1718, de Bienville built a colony that he called New Orleans on the land between the Mississippi and Lake Pontchartrain. New Orleans appeared on French maps, and stock was sold to develop it, well before any town existed. In March and April 1718, Bienville led some fifty men in tearing out cypress swamps and laying out a town on the crescent turn in the Mississippi River. After a hurricane destroyed the village in 1722, a new street grid was laid out—the French Quarter for which New Orleans is famous today.

The only contact the residents of New Orleans had with France was the occasional arrival of supply ships. Few volunteers moved to this isolated spot, even though French speculators, led by John Law, the most powerful banker in France, invested heavily in the New Orleans venture and were desperate for the new colony to succeed. Most of the early immigrants from France were prostitutes and criminals who literally left France in chains. Many died in transit, but by 1721, New Orleans had 178 European residents who enjoyed the freedom their isolation gave them.

A French visitor to New Orleans painted this view of Illinois Indians engaged in trade with the Europeans in 1735. Note that one of the tribe is most likely an escaped African slave.

The French also introduced African slavery into the Mississippi Valley. While there had been slaves in Quebec, none of the early explorers coming south from Canada brought African slaves with them. But after 1700, slavery grew in French Louisiana. The first slave ships arrived in New Orleans in 1719. In 1721, ships brought 925 slaves from Haiti (then called Saint-Dominque). A census in 1732 indicated that, of the 471 people living in the French towns in the Illinois River country, 168 were Africans.

Most slaves brought to New Orleans were from Senegal in West Africa. These Africans, if not Muslim themselves, were familiar with Islam and Muslim music that used chanting accompanied by stringed instruments. This music became part of the culture of New Orleans. The Senegalese also knew how to cultivate indigo, which thrived in Louisiana, and how to process it into dye. In addition, early slave ships brought sugar and rice, which the slaves also knew how to grow. Europe and Africa had been shaping each other's cultures for generations by the time New Orleans was founded, but the mix was especially deep in that city. With the French securely in control of both the headwaters and the mouth of the Mississippi River, France was in a strong position to be the dominant European power in North America, just as Spain was dominant farther south.

3.3 Quick Review

How did France's role in North America evolve from small settlements in Canada to become the "dominant European power"? Justify your answer.

Developments in Spanish Colonies North of Mexico

3.4 **Analyze the impact of the expansion of other European colonies on Spain's colonies in New Mexico, Texas, and California.**

Spain had established the first permanent settlements in the future United States—Florida in 1565 and New Mexico in 1598. Both remained isolated, but while St. Augustine, Florida, remained small, Spain claimed vast lands in New Mexico surrounding the new capital they built at Santa Fe in 1610. From Santa Fe, the Spanish ruled Indian pueblos with an iron hand, demanding more and more work and trying to stamp out traditional Indian religious practices. The Spanish also brought the *encomienda* system (see Chapter 2) north from Mexico, assigning large numbers of Indians to work the land of Spanish estate or *hacienda* owners in return for the owners' obligation to instruct the Indians in the Christian faith. The Indians resented the forced labor and did not want to be instructed in the Christian faith. In 1680, seventy years after the establishment of Santa Fe, to the surprise of the Spanish, a large-scale rebellion erupted in New Mexico. Although the Spanish authorities eventually reasserted their presence in New Mexico, they governed with a lighter hand the second time around. Spanish authorities also worried about the territorial claims that England and France were making to other parts of North America. To counter those claims, the government of New Spain established small but permanent colonies beyond New Mexico across the Southwest from Texas to California (see Map 3-4).

hacienda

A large tract of land or ranch given to an individual by the Spanish crown. Where the earlier encomienda system was a grant of *individuals*—nearly always Indians—the hacienda system that replaced it was a grant of *land*, which the owner was then expected to staff with laborers, sometimes through an encomienda and sometimes by hiring people for wages.

The Pueblo Revolt—New Mexico, 1680

In August 1680, an uprising of the normally peaceful Pueblo Indians of northern New Mexico led by a charismatic leader, Popé, resulted in the greatest defeat of a European colony in the history of the Americas. In the **Pueblo Revolt**, nearly all of the Spanish who lived on isolated ranches and farms were killed. Survivors from the outlying communities poured into Santa Fe, which was then besieged. The Indians cut the city's water supply and burned outlying buildings. On August 21, Governor Antonio de Otermin decided to retreat to Mexico with the survivors.

During the retreat, one Indian told Otermin that the revolt happened because his people were "tired of the work they had to do for the Spaniards and the clergy [who] did not allow them to plant, to do other things for their own needs." Another old man told the governor that it was because the Spaniards had tried to take away "the ways of their ancestors, the faith by which they have lived and thrived." Both of these grievances—the harsh workloads and religious repression demanded in the encomienda system—were crucial in fueling the revolt, as was hope that life might return to a happier day before the Spanish arrived.

Pueblo Revolt

Rebellion in 1680 of Pueblo Indians in New Mexico against their Spanish overlords, sparked by Spanish suppression of native religious activity and excessive Spanish demands for Indian labor.

Map 3-4 Changes in the Southwest.

The heart of Spain's empire in the Americas always remained south of the future United States in Mexico and Peru. However, by the 1600s, authorities based in Mexico had authorized the development of an important Spanish colony in territory they called New Mexico, among the Pueblo Indians in the area around Santa Fe and Taos. Spanish settlers also established a mission near the future Tucson, Arizona, though it would be after 1700 before there was Spanish settlement in Texas or California.

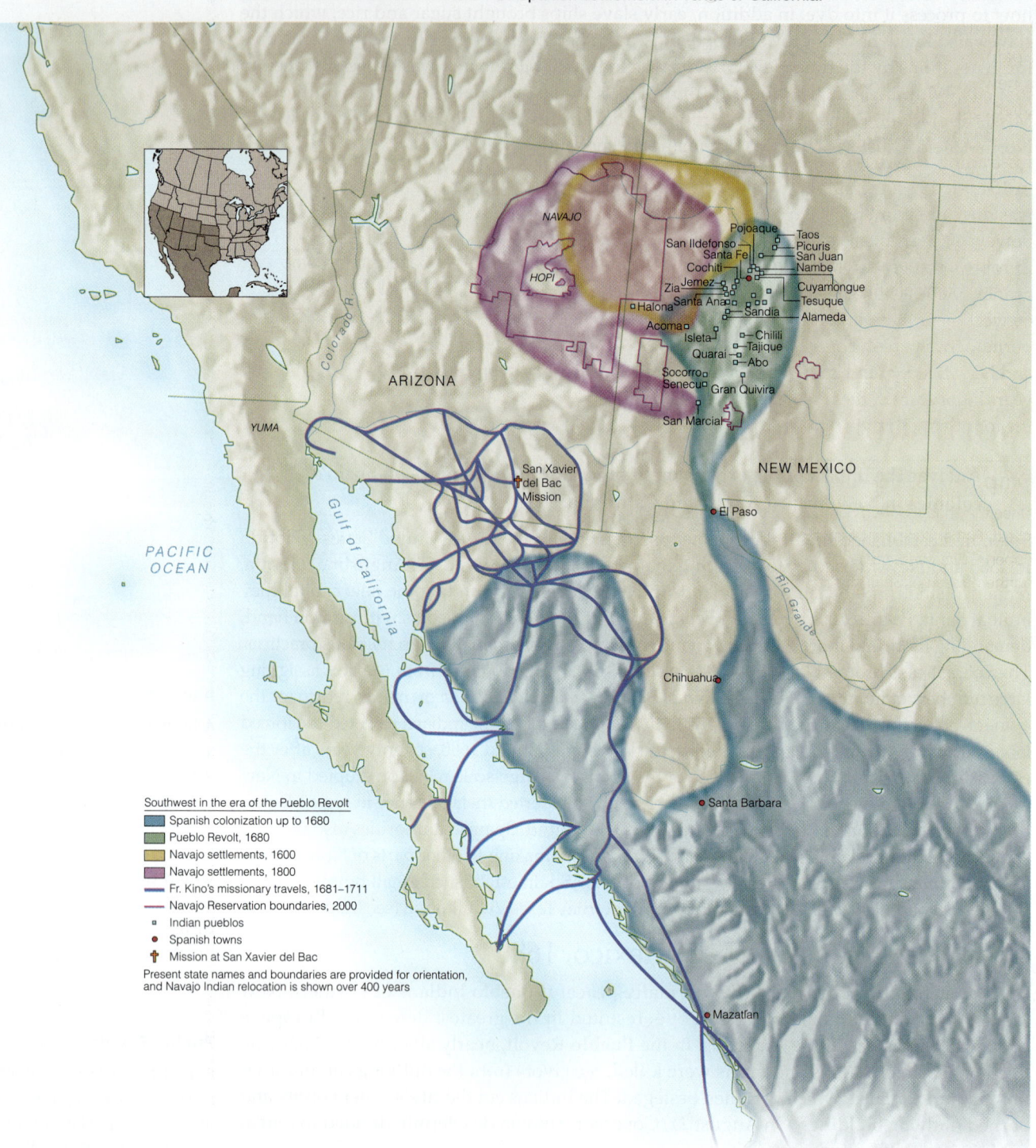

After the success of the revolt, Indian leaders lived in the governor's mansion in Santa Fe. Churches were leveled, statues destroyed. Pueblo life returned more or less to what it had been before 1598. The distant and defeated Spanish were mocked.

The Spanish eventually regained control of New Mexico, but it took twelve years. Nowhere else in the Americas, not even among the powerful Aztecs and Incas, was a revolt so successful or long lasting. In 1690, the Spanish viceroy in Mexico City appointed a new governor for New Mexico, Don Diego de Vargas, who had an ability to compromise that many of his predecessors had lacked. Vargas left El Paso with his army in 1692. He offered each pueblo a full pardon in exchange for their reconversion to Christianity, but he did not try to stamp out tribal religion. The Indians could retain both faiths and agreed to his terms.

Spain's Response to France and England—San Antonio, Texas, and the Missions of California

Word that La Salle had claimed the coast of Texas for France frightened authorities in New Spain. When the French founded New Orleans in 1718, the Spanish decided to act. They built a new city of their own, San Antonio, to assert their claims to Texas. Although small and isolated, San Antonio was the first permanent European settlement in present-day Texas.

By the mid-1700s, the Spanish were also worried about English explorations and Russian fur-trading activities on the Pacific coast. While Cabrillo had explored the coast of California in 1542–1543 and small temporary Spanish settlements had followed, nothing permanent was developed in the 1500s or 1600s. In response to their worries about England and Russia, however, the Spanish established a fort and then a mission in San Diego, the first permanent European settlement in what is now the U.S. state of California in 1769. From there, Spanish Franciscan missionaries created a string of missions from San Diego to San Francisco to convert the Indians and develop the economy of California. Before the American Revolution, permanent Spanish communities could be found on the Atlantic coast in Florida, in Texas and New Mexico, and on the Pacific Coast in California (see Map 3-5). It would be many more years before any of these were much more than small dusty outposts. Nevertheless, they were the foundation for the much more extensive settlement that would follow.

Map 3-5 California Missions.

Once they had founded San Diego in 1769, the Spanish authorities in Mexico commissioned a Franciscan priest, Father Junipero Serra, to create a string of missions along the Pacific Coast of what they called Alta (or upper) California. Serra and his successors created these missions as far north as San Francisco, the farthest northern reach of Spanish settlement into the Americas. Present state boundaries are provided for orientation.

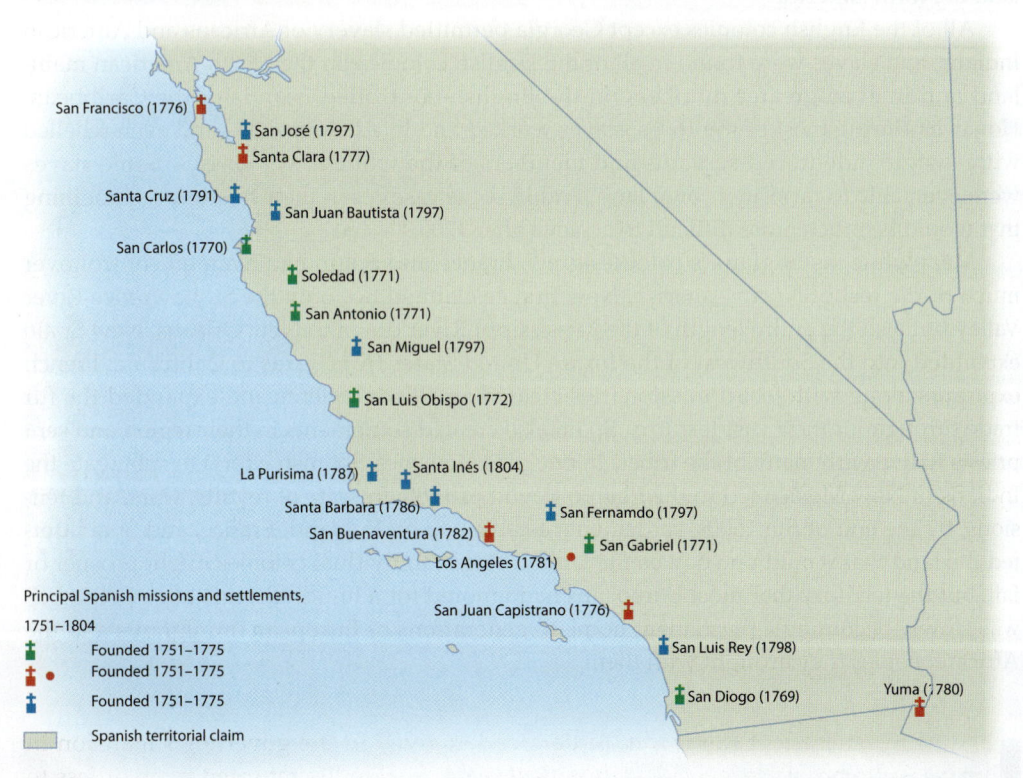

Why was Spain so concerned about English and French colonization?

Conclusion

The nations of Europe showed little interest in establishing settlements north of Mexico until the early 1600s. After 1600, some English investors sensed the merit of establishing colonies in North America, not only to trade with the Indians but also to Christianize them and enlist them as an ally against England's rival Spain. The first successful English colony was established at Jamestown, Virginia, in 1607. The colony would not have been lasted without the leadership of the English adventurer John Smith or the assistance of Powhatan, an Algonquian leader, who saw an advantage in establishing trade with the English and using them as allies against other Indian tribes.

While Jamestown was established as a commercial enterprise, the New England colonies were established as refuges for England's diverse and restive religious nonconformists, including the Puritans and Pilgrims.

The New England colonies coexisted for some time with nearby Indian groups. However, as the New England colonies grew in size and encroached on Indian lands, growing hostility ultimately led to the vicious Metacom's War, or King Philip's War, in the 1670s. A different kind of violence engulfed Virginia. White immigrants, mostly poor people, living at a distance from the coast, made alliances with Africans, slave and free, in attacks on the nearby Native American tribes. These allied groups also attacked the royal government based on the Atlantic coast. The revolt was soon defeated, but it resulted in the expulsion of most tribes from Virginia and a decision by the authorities to limit the immigration of poor whites and rely more on African slave labor in the colony.

After the establishment of Virginia and the New England colonies, other English colonies developed in quick succession. Maryland became a haven for Catholics, who were also being persecuted in England. Carolina began to expand production of rice and tobacco. New York was acquired from the Dutch, and New Jersey split off of New York. Pennsylvania was established initially for the Quakers, and Delaware eventually split from that colony. Finally, Georgia was founded, thus establishing England's thirteen colonies on the mainland of North America.

All of the English colonies except Georgia permitted slavery of Africans and American Indians, and slaves were found in all of the English colonies on the North American mainland and in even greater numbers on the English-controlled islands of the Caribbean. However, during most of the 1600s, slaves worked and lived alongside—and even rebelled with—white indentured servants and members of the white lower classes. Some slaves were even able to farm their own land, and in some cases earn their freedom—something that would be much more difficult to achieve after 1700.

Meanwhile, as England's colonies grew, France and Spain had claimed control over much of the rest of North America. New France claimed not only the St. Lawrence River Valley but also the entire length of the Mississippi River down to New Orleans. New Spain expanded into the Southwest of the future United States from Texas to California. French explorers along with Jesuit missionaries created small settlements and expanded the fur trade throughout their vast territory. Spain also created settlements in their region and sent priests to live with many of the tribes. In one case, however, Spanish efforts to subjugate the Indians of New Mexico led to the Pueblo Revolt of 1680. In spite of revolts, wars, and tensions, by the end of the 1600s, settlements established by England, France, and Spain dotted the land that would one day be the United States. Individual colonies might prosper or fail, but the territory that most Europeans had ignored for a hundred years after Columbus was slowly becoming a permanent home to generations of European immigrants and the African peoples they brought with them.

Chapter Review

How did the English, French, and Spanish interaction with American Indians and Africans differ?

Chapter 3 Summary and Review

The English Settle in North America

3.1 **Explain why the English began to settle in North America and how slavery was introduced in the English colonies.**

Summary

In 1607, Jamestown, the first permanent British settlement in North America, was established in what would become the colony of Virginia. The settlement's early years were marked by poor planning, disease, and tense relations with local Indians. The shift from trade with Indians to tobacco-based agriculture in the 1620s ensured the colony's survival and also meant increased conflict between colonists and Indians. Many in England came to see settlement of North America as a solution to England's overpopulation and religious conflicts. Puritans established settlements in Massachusetts in the 1620s and 1630s. The government and society they created reflected their religious beliefs. The first slaves arrived in Virginia in 1619. Slavery in British North America before the 1680s, although still difficult, was neither as harsh nor as absolute as later forms of American slavery.

Review Questions

1. Continuity and Change over Time
   How did Jamestown's economic focus change over its first two decades?

2. Contextualization
   What kind of society did the Puritans of Massachusetts hope to establish? In this context, why did North America seem like a good place to settle?

England's Wars, England's Colonies

3.2 **Analyze the relationship between politics in England, internal colonial tensions, and life in the English colonies in North America during the 1600s.**

Summary

The tensions that led Pilgrims and Puritans to flee England erupted into a full-scale civil war in the 1640s in which King Charles I lost his head and a Puritan Commonwealth ruled the country for eleven years. The religious and political battles in England fueled settlement in North America. Puritans sought refuge in Massachusetts, supporters of the royal cause fled to Virginia, Catholics moved to Maryland, and other dissidents found such tolerant places as Rhode Island. When King Charles II was put on the throne in 1660, he also rewarded supporters with grants of new colonial charters, including New York and Pennsylvania. In the 1670s, long-simmering tensions burst into violence in the colonies. Metacom's (King Philip's) War in Massachusetts was one of the most vicious wars ever fought in North America. In Virginia, poor farmers, as well as slaves and indentured servants, took up arms against the royal governor in Bacon's Rebellion. The uprising was a major turning point in the history of slavery in Virginia.

Review Questions

3. Causation
   How did civil war in England shape the development of British North America?

4. Comparison
   Compare and contrast the economies of New York and Carolina in the 1600s. Predict how this difference would shape these respective colonies.

France Takes Control of the Heart of a Continent

3.3 **Explain France's growing role and power in North America and its impact on English and Spanish colonies.**

Summary

The fur trade transformed New France, attracting French settlers and leading to conflict among Indian peoples. During the long reign of King Louis XIV (r. 1643–1715), New France expanded from a tiny isolated community around Quebec to dominate the St. Lawrence River Valley. As the result of French expeditions into the interior of North America, French communities were founded around the Great Lakes and down the Mississippi River to New Orleans. With the French in control of both the headwaters and the mouth of the Mississippi River, France was in a strong position to be the dominant European power in North America, just as Spain was dominant in Mexico and South America.

Review Question

5. Causation
   How did the fur trade reshape the way American Indians lived?

Developments in Spanish Colonies North of Mexico

3.4 Analyze the impact of Indian uprisings and the expansion of other European powers on Spain's colonies in New Mexico, Texas, and California.

Summary

Spanish efforts to impose a harsh colonial regime on the Pueblos of New Mexico led to a large rebellion. While the Spanish were eventually able to reassert their presence in New Mexico, they also worried about the claims that England and France were making to other parts of North America. To counter those claims, the government of New Spain established small but permanent colonies across the Southwest from Texas to California.

Review Question

6. Comparison
   What did the Pueblo Revolt and King Philip's War have in common in terms of causes? And how were they different in terms of effects?

1. Preparing to Write: Plan Your Argument

Long Essay Question—Evaluate the extent of change in relations between New England Puritans and American Indians during the period 1620 to 1700.

Draw a timeline from 1620 to 1700. Was there less Puritan reliance on American Indians over time? More conflict? After reviewing important events related to this question, take notes above the timeline on what is changing. Below the timeline, take notes on what is remaining constant. Was there an English need for land? After you take notes, write a first-draft thesis and then proceed with an outline of your argument.

2. Preparing to Write: Develop Your Thesis

Long Essay Question—Evaluate the extent of change in the role of labor for the Southern plantation economies from 1607 to 1754.

When you write a thesis as an apprentice-historian, you are offering your unique interpretation after studying the topic. For every question you encounter, think about why the historical development at its core is significant. This question is a great example. Think about why the shift from indentured servitude to enslaved Africans is significant. What impact did this shift have on the social hierarchies of Southern communities? Once you unlock this answer, you will have rich material to discuss, which will make your writing more analytical.

Chapter 4
Creating the Culture of British North America 1689–1754

Raw materials, most of which were produced with slave labor from Britain's colonies in North America and the Caribbean, were bringing great wealth to the nation as illustrated in this picture of sailing ships from North America unloading at London's Old Custom House dock.

Chapter Objective

Demonstrate an understanding of how local and global developments shaped the lives and thoughts of those residing in British North America from the Glorious Revolution to the beginnings of the American Revolution.

 ## Learning Objectives

England's Glorious Revolution and "the Rights of Englishmen," 1689

4.1 Analyze the impact of England's Glorious Revolution on the thinking and political organization of British colonists in North America.

The Plantation World: From a Society with Slaves to a Slave Society

4.2 As the English colonies, like other European empires, participated in the Atlantic slave trade and developed a system of slavery that reflected the specific economic, demographic, and geographic characteristics of the colonies, explain why and how slavery developed as it did in North America in the late 1600s and early 1700s.

Stability and Instability in the American and British Worlds

4.3 Analyze the changes in the ideas and daily lives of the people in British North America in the 1700s as colonial residents also participated in political, social, cultural, and economic exchanges with Great Britain that encouraged both stronger bonds with Britain and resistance to Britain's control.

4.1

4.2

4.3

ClassicStock/Alamy Stock Photo

The *New England Courant*, one of the early colonial newspapers, was published from 1722 to 1726, but both its publisher James Franklin and his younger brother Benjamin continued to publish newspapers in the 1720s and 1730s.

In 1733, a young apprentice, John Peter Zenger, was hired to start a new newspaper in New York, the *New York Weekly Journal*. Newspapers, though long popular in England, were still fairly new in British North America. The first regularly published colonial newspaper, *The Boston News-Letter*, began publication in 1704, but it was subsidized by the British government. Later newspapers, including James Franklin's *New England Courant* that began publication in 1722, were more independent. The *Journal*'s New York backers were part of a political faction in the colony that opposed Royal Governor William Cosby. Zenger quickly began printing stories about official corruption and government actions he considered to be dictatorial. Within a year, he was indicted for printing seditious libel. British law at the time made it a crime to print attacks on public officials that challenged their authority—whether the articles were false or true—and Zenger had clearly printed attacks on Governor Cosby. But Zenger and his backers fought back, defending themselves in court.

In a well-publicized trial that lasted into 1735, Zenger's attorney argued for rights of speech and the press that far exceeded what then existed in Britain. He asked the jury, "Shall the press be silenced that evil governors may have their way?" The trial, the attorney said, was not about Zenger but "every free man that lives under a British government on the main of America." The jury acquitted Zenger in spite of the law.

Zenger's acquittal has been celebrated ever since as a key victory for freedom of speech and freedom of the press. In part it *was* a victory. Zenger was free to keep up his critique, and other publishers were emboldened by the result. On the other hand, the laws against seditious libel were not repealed, and every editor of Zenger's day knew that there was a danger of arrest and trial before a jury that might not be as sympathetic as the one Zenger faced. Nevertheless, by the 1730s, there were more than twenty newspapers in the North American colonies. They offered critiques of royal governors and republished articles from the English press demanding freedom and calling attention to what they called "the rights of Englishmen." These newspapers also published news from other colonies and began to create a stronger sense of unity among Americans—a name that residents of the British colonies were starting to call themselves.

Zenger's defense reflected the views of a growing number of English inhabitants of North America at the time. The great divisions over religious and political authority, which had created turmoil and uprisings in England and in the colonies, were receding into the dim past. In spite of numerous new tensions, many who lived in America between 1690 and 1760 were feeling a strong sense of pride in being British—enjoying the prosperity that the British Empire was creating and appreciating an elected Parliament that was playing a dominant role in asserting individual liberties. However, that pride in British institutions and British rights slowly changed as some colonists began to shift their loyalties. Over time, many came to distrust the British government and began to talk of a way to protect their own rights as colonists. Understanding that shift is key to understanding the decades before the American Revolution.

Significant Dates

1662	Halfway Covenant in Massachusetts
1689	The Glorious Revolution, James II is replaced by William and Mary
1692	Salem witch trials
1701–1713	Queen Anne's War
1704	Mohawk Indians destroy Deerfield, Massachusetts
	Esther Williams is taken hostage
	First regular colonial newspaper begins publication in Boston
1707	Act of Union between England and Scotland
1715–1716	Yamasee War in South Carolina
1721	First smallpox inoculations advocated by Cotton Mather and administered in Boston
1730s	Jonathan Edwards leads religious revivals
1732	Georgia is established
	Benjamin Franklin begins publication of *Poor Richard's Almanack*
1734	Beginning of First Great Awakening
1735	John Peter Zenger is acquitted in trial for libel
1739	Stono slave rebellion in South Carolina
1739	War of Jenkins' Ear between England and Spain in the Caribbean
1741	Slave conspiracy in New York City
1744–1748	King George's War between Britain and France
1754	Albany Plan of Union advocates unifying the colonies for war with France

England's Glorious Revolution and "the Rights of Englishmen," 1689

4.1 **Analyze the impact of England's Glorious Revolution on the thinking and political organization of British colonists in North America.**

The twenty-five years between 1675 and 1700 were times of turmoil in England and its North American colonies. A little more than a decade after King Philip's War and Bacon's Rebellion convulsed the colonies, and a half century after their own Civil War, the English

Parliament came to distrust King James II who they believed was centralizing too much authority and who they suspected of privately supporting Catholicism in spite of a law that required the monarch to defend the Protestant faith. They ousted him in 1689 in what was known as the **Glorious Revolution**. For many in England and its colonies, it was an exciting time, an assertion of "the rights of Englishmen" and the authority of elected assemblies to control their destiny. Initially, news of the overthrow of James II brought rebellions in many of the colonies. Royal governors were arrested, and popular assemblies demanded new authority, just as Parliament had done in London. Soon enough, a new English government asserted its authority in colonial matters. Nevertheless, the Glorious Revolution created a new sense of rights on both sides of the Atlantic Ocean.

4.1
4.2
4.3

Glorious Revolution

Bloodless revolt that occurred in England in 1688 when parliamentary leaders invited William of Orange, a Protestant, and his wife, Mary, the daughter of King James II, to assume the English throne in place of James II.

Parliament's Decision to "Elect" a New King and Queen

King James II (r. 1685–1688), who came to the English throne at the death of his brother Charles II, expanded religious freedoms for Catholics and appointed some to high office. His actions led many to suspect he was a Catholic and aroused serious opposition in Britain's Protestant majority, many of whom associated Protestantism with British independence and Catholicism with Spanish and French foreign domination.

James also wanted to assert royal authority, especially in England's increasingly independent colonies. He appointed a single royal governor, Sir Edmund Andros, over a newly designated Dominion of New England, which comprised Plymouth, Massachusetts, New Hampshire, Connecticut, Rhode Island, as well as New York and New Jersey. He also abolished most of the local autonomy that the colonies had enjoyed.

The colonists resented the unwanted merger of their colonies as well as the new king and governor who were enforcing it, but they could do little about it. However, in England, Parliament turned against James II. Rather than risk losing his head like his father, James fled the country. Parliament invited James's Protestant daughter, Mary, and her husband, Prince William of Orange, rulers in the Netherlands, to come to England as joint sovereigns. This move by Parliament was a dramatic change that would have far-reaching effects. The concept of the **divine right of kings**, by which the sovereign—good or bad—inherited the throne from the previous sovereign and ruled with unquestioned authority, was already in decline. But now, Parliament, had decided not only to limit royal authority but also to take some control over the choice of a king or queen themselves.

To justify the ouster of one king and the virtual election of new monarchs, English people had to rethink how they understood themselves and their system of government. Kings and queens retained power after 1689, but their supremacy was now bound by law. After 1689, it was clear that Parliament, as representative of the people, was a deciding force in England.

divine right of kings

A belief that the king—or queen—was selected by God through birth in the royal family and that it was irreligious to question either a monarch's fitness to serve or a monarch's decisions. During the 1600s, England overthrew two monarchs, and afterward, few still held such a belief.

John Locke—Defending the Right to Revolution

The most famous English philosopher at the time of the Glorious Revolution, John Locke, justified the revolution by insisting that all government rested on the **natural rights** of the governed. This concept was a novel idea in 1689, but Locke, who was living in exile in Holland because of his opposition to James's rule, wrote that humans were born free in a state of nature and agreed to a social compact only when it suited their purposes. If the people no longer agreed, then monarchs had no right to continue to rule. The basic "rights of all Englishmen" to accept or reject their government came to be the dominant political ideology of the English nation—as it then existed on both sides of the Atlantic. Locke was one of a number of the early thinkers of the **European Enlightenment**, including René Descartes in France and Baruch Spinoza in Holland, who were coming to believe that reason was superior to either faith or deference to authority as a way to organize society and advance ideas of human liberty and happiness—ideas that in the 1700s would explode into revolutions in ideas and government across the world.

In his *Second Treatise on Government*, Locke described civil society as a social contract made by free people to live together, but one in which everyone retained "his natural freedom, without being subjected to the will or authority of any other man." Neither kings

natural rights

Political philosophy that maintains that individuals have an inherent right, found in nature and preceding any government or written law, to life and liberty.

European Enlightenment

A continent-wide intellectual movement that began with a rejection of the unquestioned authority of religious institutions and faith and substituted a belief in human reason, rational self-interest, and the discoveries of science.

nor Parliament was supreme. The people were. Locke insisted, "There remains still in the people a supreme power to remove or alter the legislative [power] when they find the legislative act contrary to the trust reposed in them." Locke's revolutionary ideas helped justify the Glorious Revolution of 1689. A hundred years later, his ideas would be cited often in North America.

North American Responses

In England's American colonies, news of the Glorious Revolution brought rejoicing. In New England, the colonists arrested Governor Andros and sent him back to England, though he later returned as Governor of Virginia. The new monarchs, William and Mary, allowed the New England colonies to return to their former separate existences. However, when the king and queen reestablished the governments of Massachusetts and Connecticut, they included a clause in the royal charters granting "liberty of Conscience" to all Protestants—but not Catholics. Baptists, Anglicans, and others were now free to build their own churches and worship as they wished. Some Puritans protested against this "tolerance for error," as they called allowing other churches to conduct their own services, but the rules stuck in spite of their protests and Baptist and Episcopal churches began to spring up where they had previously been prohibited. All Protestants were free to build churches—at their own expense—and worship freely, but everyone paid taxes to support the Congregationalists, and Catholic worship was not allowed in New England.

After the Glorious Revolution, England insisted on "liberty of conscience" for all Protestants, forcing the Puritan authorities in Massachusetts to allow new churches, including St. Michael's Episcopal Church, shown here, founded in Marblehead in 1714.

In New York, news of the change in England brought a general uprising. Those on the bottom of the social order—merchants, dockworkers, and traders—seized power under the leadership of a German immigrant, Jacob Leisler. Leisler held power for two years, but when he was slow in ceding power to the new royal governor appointed by William and Mary, he was arrested and executed for treason. However, those loyal to Leisler remained a faction in New York politics for a generation to come.

In Maryland, there was also an uprising. The Catholic proprietor was driven from office and lost ownership of the colony. Maryland became a royal colony with a governor appointed by the king and queen, and the Anglican Church of England became the colony's official church. After the Glorious Revolution, Maryland, a colony that had been chartered in 1632 to protect Catholics, excluded Catholics from public office.

In the Americas, the Glorious Revolution produced winners and losers. After 1689, independent corporations like the Virginia Company and the Massachusetts Company as well as colonial proprietors like Lord Baltimore or William Penn faced a decline in power. Catholics in England and Maryland lost hard-won political rights as the new monarchs asserted England's status as a Protestant nation. But Protestants who were not part of the established church gained rights, and Protestant men who had been excluded from the voting lists because they belonged to a dissenting religious group could now vote. Elected legislatures (elected by landowning white males) competed with royal governors to make the laws for each colony. In spite of moves that made colonial society somewhat more democratic, changing one's social and economic status was becoming more difficult in all of the colonies. An English colonial elite, many in the third and fourth generation of Americans, supported by English military authority, now dominated colonial life. The British communities became larger, more secure, and wealthier.

4.1   Quick Review

How do the colonists' reactions to the Glorious Revolution reflect their sense of connection to ideas and events in England and to ideas circulating in the early years of the European Enlightenment?

   2. Based on what you read, for whom in the British colonies did the Glorious Revolution have a positive effect? A negative effect?

The Plantation World: From a Society with Slaves to a Slave Society

4.2   As the English colonies, like other European empires, participated in the Atlantic slave trade and developed a system of slavery that reflected the specific economic, demographic, and geographic characteristics of the colonies, explain why and how slavery developed as it did in North America in the late 1600s and early 1700s.

Amid all the talk of "the rights of Englishmen," one group of North American residents lost rights after the 1680s—African slaves. All of the British colonies had slaves in the late 1600s, but the institution of slavery changed most dramatically in the southern colonies—Maryland, Virginia, and, soon, also the Carolinas. Bacon's Rebellion brought great changes to Virginia and its neighbor Maryland after 1676. Once the planter elite had defeated Bacon's ragtag militia, they quickly consolidated their power. They did not want another rebellion like the one they had just lived through in which poor whites allied with Africans, slave and free. Having decided that African slaves would make better and more dependable workers than either Indian slaves or white indentured servants, this planter elite wrote new slave codes that clearly made slavery an inherited and permanent status. They also imported many more African slaves and reduced the numbers of English indentured servants allowed into these colonies. Historian Ira Berlin described this shift: "A society with slaves gave way to a slave society." It was a significant change—from a society in which slavery existed to a society in which the institution of slavery dominated all aspects of society—particularly for those who were enslaved. Although this shift began in Virginia and Maryland, its effects would eventually extend to other southern colonies.

Seeking Stability by Creating a Slave Society

As the institution of slavery came to be more rigidly defined, it also came to be linked more closely to race. Africans were seen as slaves. Europeans—even the poorest Europeans—were free. More and more Indians were simply excluded from the colonies. Those Africans who had already achieved their freedom, and those few who did so during the 1700s, lived in a dangerous world. While Anthony Johnson had moved from slavery to freedom and prosperity in the Virginia of the mid-1600s (see Chapter 3), his children and grandchildren fled from Virginia in the late 1600s to avoid the risks of slavery, some of them living with the Nanticoke Indians in a small community of African, European, and American Indian origin.

   Children of mixed race were marginalized or simply declared to be African slaves. Any child born to a black woman was automatically considered to be African even if, as was often the case, the father was a European slave-owner. But mixed-race children born to white mothers were more problematic, so stringent efforts were made to prohibit sexual liaisons between white women and males of other races.

   While there were slaves in all of England's North American colonies, as slavery became institutionalized, the numbers of African slaves in the southern colonies rose dramatically. In the 1680s, approximately two thousand Africans were shipped to Virginia. Between 1700 and 1710, approximately eight thousand arrived. In 1668, white indentured servants

Map 4-1 Enslaved People in British North America in 1750.

Between 1700 and 1750, there were growing numbers of slaves in all thirteen of the mainland British colonies in North America, but hardly in equal numbers. By 1750, the percentage of slaves in most of New England was 2–3 percent of the population, while in Rhode Island and New York—the northern colonies with the most slaves—they represented 10–14 percent. But there was a much higher proportion of slaves in the southern colonies, ranging from 27 percent of the population of North Carolina to 61 percent of the population of South Carolina.

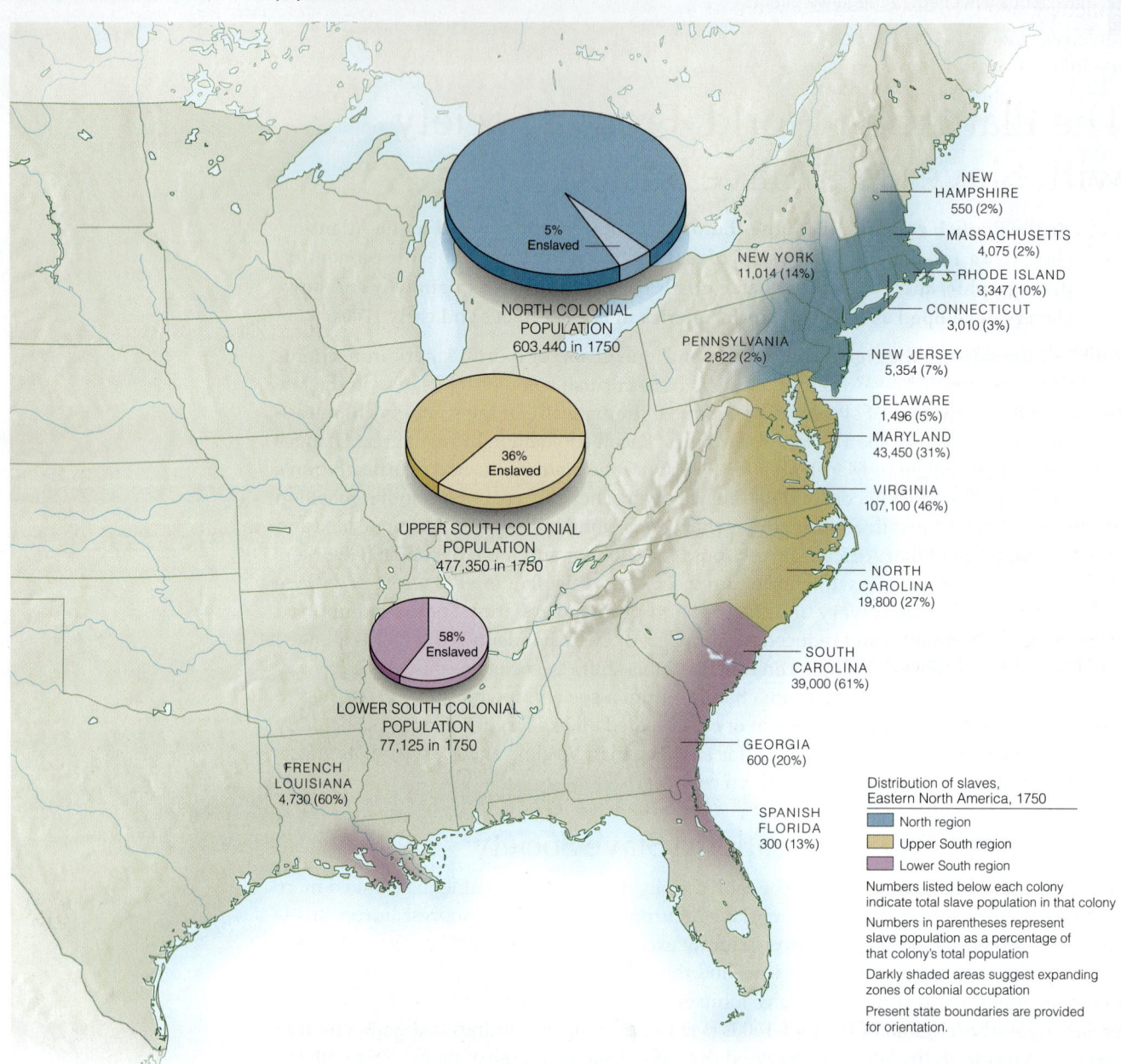

5%
Enslaved

NORTH COLONIAL
POPULATION
603,440 in 1750

36%
Enslaved

UPPER SOUTH COLONIAL
POPULATION
477,350 in 1750

58%
Enslaved

LOWER SOUTH COLONIAL
POPULATION
77,125 in 1750

FRENCH
LOUISIANA
4,730 (60%)

NEW
HAMPSHIRE
550 (2%)

MASSACHUSETTS
4,075 (2%)

RHODE ISLAND
3,347 (10%)

CONNECTICUT
3,010 (3%)

NEW YORK
11,014 (14%)

PENNSYLVANIA
2,822 (2%)

NEW JERSEY
5,354 (7%)

DELAWARE
1,496 (5%)

MARYLAND
43,450 (31%)

VIRGINIA
107,100 (46%)

NORTH
CAROLINA
19,800 (27%)

SOUTH
CAROLINA
39,000 (61%)

GEORGIA
600 (20%)

SPANISH
FLORIDA
300 (13%)

Distribution of slaves,
Eastern North America, 1750

North region

Upper South region

Lower South region

Numbers listed below each colony
indicate total slave population in that colony

Numbers in parentheses represent
slave population as a percentage of
that colony's total population

Darkly shaded areas suggest expanding
zones of colonial occupation

Present state boundaries are provided
for orientation.

outnumbered African slaves by five to one, and there were about equal numbers of Indian and African slaves. By 1700, nearly all tobacco and rice workers in Virginia and the Carolinas were African slaves (see Map 4-1).

The Atlantic Slave Trade, the Middle Passage, and the Nature of Colonial Slavery

North American slavery was always a relatively small part of the Atlantic slave trade. The sugar plantations of the Caribbean, Brazil, and New Spain needed many more slaves—and slaves there died much more quickly—so there was a constant flow of slaves to islands con-

Middle Passage

The horrendous voyage in which slaves were taken from West Africa to slave colonies in the Americas during which as many as a quarter died.

trolled by the English, French, Dutch, Danish, and Spanish and to the South American mainland. Some ten to fifteen million Africans were forced across the Atlantic between 1500 and 1900, but only a fraction came to the mainland British colonies (see Map 4-2).

New states in West Africa—Asante, Dahomey, and Oyo—emerged along the African coast, fueled by the transfer of slaves from the interior of Africa to the coast for sale and shipment to the Americas. Some African states such as Benin refused to engage in the slave trade. But those that did grew rich. What had been a limited, if brutal, business now seemed to have no limit. For most West Africans, the huge growth of the African slave trade was a disaster. In addition to the internal warfare and fear among Africans that the slave trade inspired, the continent lost millions of people, which sapped its strength.

Once slaves arrived on the African coast, they were kept naked in cramped quarters in what were called slave factories. They were fed only bread and water. Those found to be fit were "marked on the breast, with a red-hot iron, imprinting the mark of the French, English, or Dutch companies, that so each nation may distinguish their own." Sorted and branded, the slaves were held for sale to ship captains who would take them across the Atlantic.

The **Middle Passage**—the transit of slaves from Africa to the Americas—was a horrifying experience. One slave ship captain said that slaves were packed "like books upon a shelf … so close that the shelf would not easily contain one more," up to four hundred on a ship. Men were chained shoulder to shoulder. Women were generally not chained but packed just as tightly for a voyage that took seven weeks in a filthy ship's hold that stank of human waste. The rate of disease was high: 25 percent of slaves died on the voyage. Slaves were force fed to reduce the loss of valuable cargo to starvation. One slave trader noted the tendency of slaves "to revolt aboard ships." Slaves would, he said, "watch all opportunities to deliver themselves, by assaulting a ship's crew, and murdering them all." Slaving was a dangerous and dirty but profitable business.

The first generation of slaves in North America, those arriving in the early 1600s, came from the coast of West Africa. They were familiar, at least in a general way, with each other and with European culture and languages since Europeans had been trading along the coast for more than one hundred years. Those who

North Wind Picture Archives/Alamy Stock Photo

As economic developments in all of North and South America came to depend more and more on slavery, the hunt for slaves went deeper and deeper into the African continent, leading to slave coffles—as they were known—in which newly captured people were marched hundreds of miles to the coast for transport across the Atlantic in numbers never before seen.

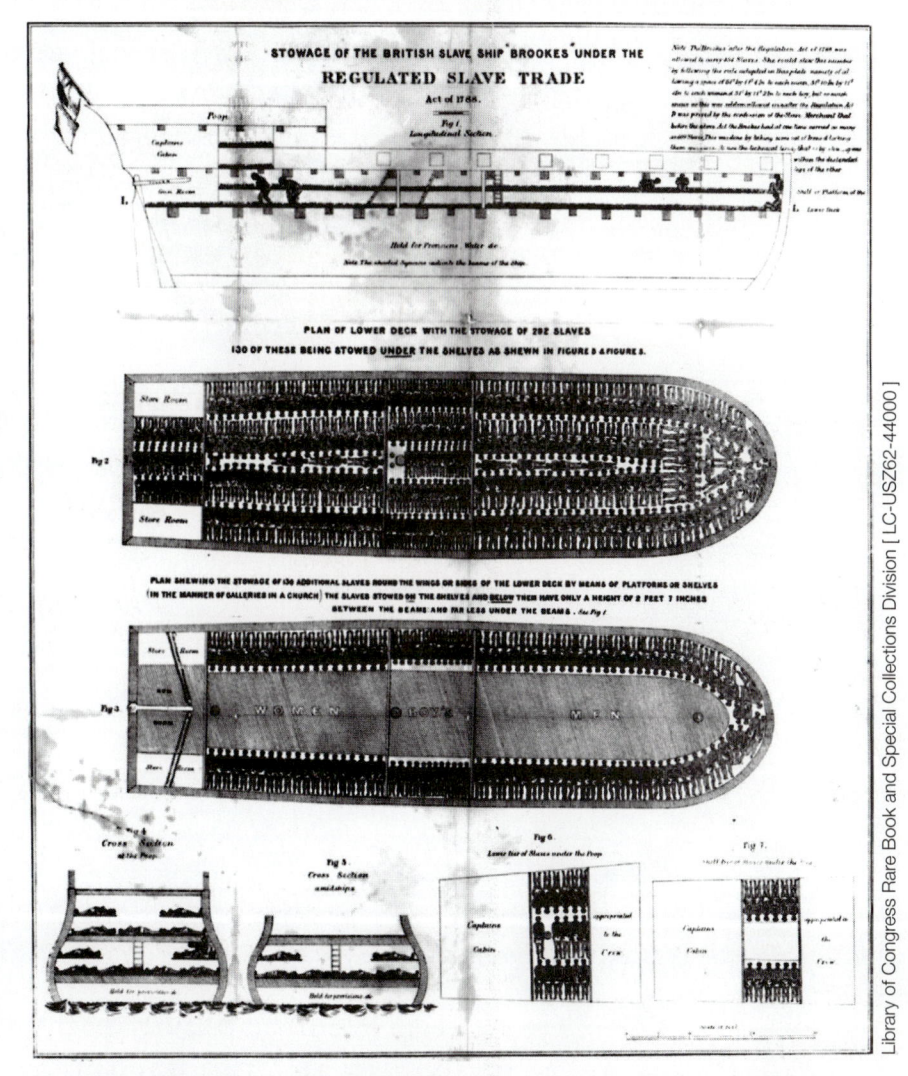

Library of Congress Rare Book and Special Collections Division [LC-USZ62-44000]

This sketch of the inside of a slave ship and the chart showing British rules for the slave trade shows how tightly slaves were packed for the horrendous Middle Passage from Africa to the Americas. Not surprisingly, a quarter of the slaves often died on the voyage, and survivors never forgot the trauma.

4.1

4.2

4.3

Map 4-2 Origin and Destinations of Enslaved Africans, 1700–1800.

This map shows not only the places of origin in Africa for most of the slaves transported across the Atlantic between 1700 and 1800 but also their destinations in the Americas. While perhaps half a million humans were sold into slavery in British North America, almost three times as many people were sold into the British Caribbean colonies and an equal number to Portuguese Brazil.

Chesapeake

4% 15% 11% 16% 16% 38%

Origin of Africans, 1700–1800
- Senegambia
- Windward Coast
- Gold Coast
- Bight of Benin
- Bight of Biafra
- West Central Africa
- Mozambique

Carolinas

23% 18% 9% 3% 7% 40%

The Atlantic Slave Trade during the 18th Century

Over 5,800,000 Africans arrived in the Americas (1700–1800)

9% 25% 25% 1% 3% 18% 19%

Africans reaching the New World, 1700–1800
- British North America (522,400)
- British Caribbean (1,439,500)
- Spanish Americas (1,114,460)
- French Americas (1,044,800)
- Dutch Americas (208,960)
- Danish Americas (46,450)
- Portuguese Brazil (1,427,900)

NORTH AMERICA

SOUTH AMERICA

ATLANTIC OCEAN

PACIFIC OCEAN

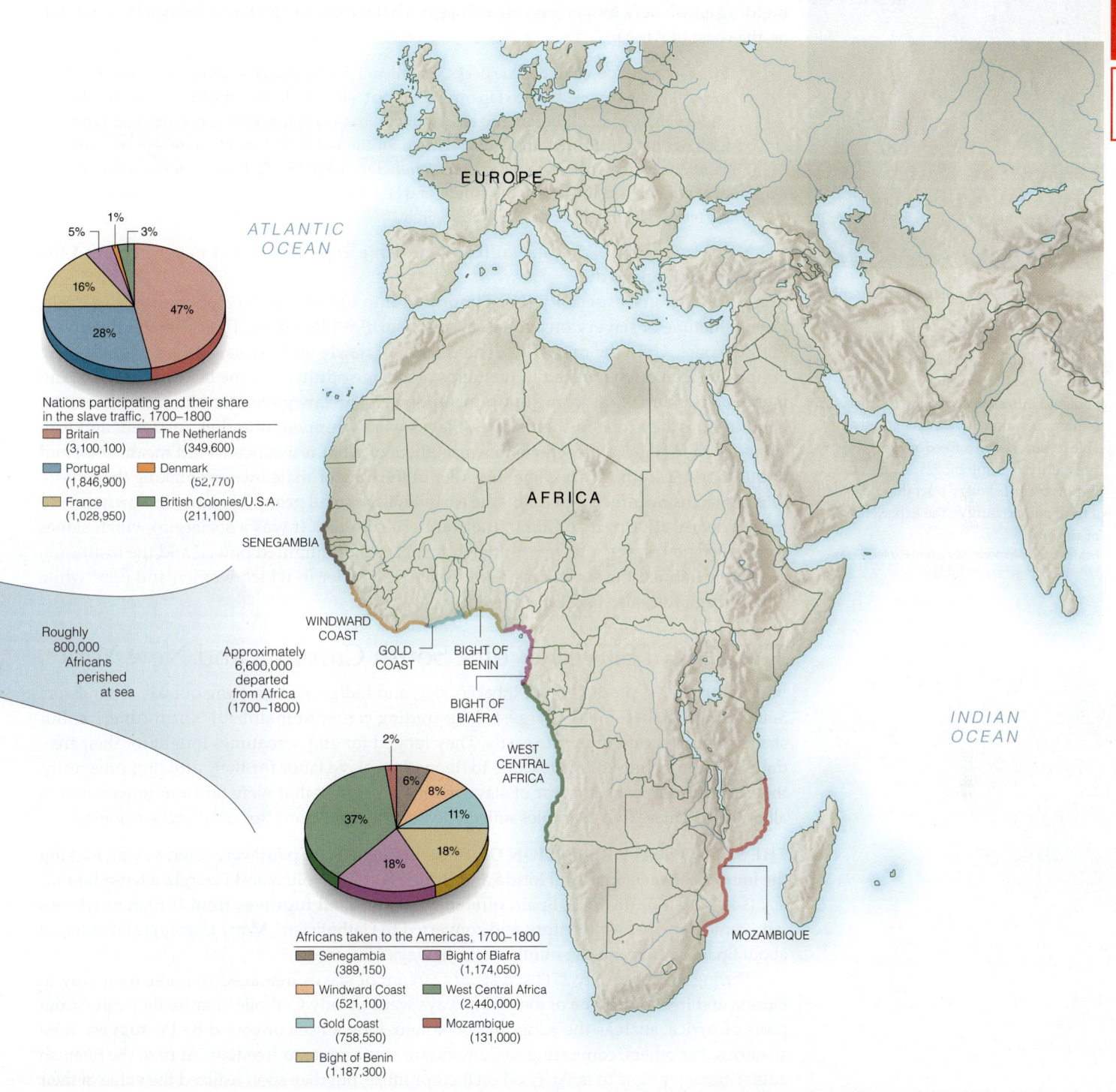

Nations participating and their share in the slave traffic, 1700–1800

- Britain (3,100,100)
- The Netherlands (349,600)
- Portugal (1,846,900)
- Denmark (52,770)
- France (1,028,950)
- British Colonies/U.S.A. (211,100)

Roughly 800,000 Africans perished at sea

Approximately 6,600,000 departed from Africa (1700–1800)

SENEGAMBIA
WINDWARD COAST
GOLD COAST
BIGHT OF BENIN
BIGHT OF BIAFRA
WEST CENTRAL AFRICA
MOZAMBIQUE

Africans taken to the Americas, 1700–1800

- Senegambia (389,150)
- Bight of Biafra (1,174,050)
- Windward Coast (521,100)
- West Central Africa (2,440,000)
- Gold Coast (758,550)
- Mozambique (131,000)
- Bight of Benin (1,187,300)

arrived later often had been captured much farther inland. They knew little about European ways or about each other.

The first generation of slaves were allowed some dignity, but by the late 1600s, every effort was made to rob slaves of their self-respect. Slaves were inspected like animals by those who bought and sold them. Masters used names as part of an effort to break the slaves' spirits. New slaves were named Sukey or Jumper or Hercules. Slave marriages were not recognized by law, and a master could sell husband away from wife or children from parents.

4.1

4.2

4.3

According to his popular autobiography, *The Interesting Narrative of the Life of Olaudah Equiano*, published in 1789, Olaudah Equiano was captured in Nigeria in 1756 when he was eleven years old and sold into slavery. Unlike most slaves of his generation, he was eventually able to purchase his freedom and rise to prosperity. His autobiography became an important antislavery tract that provided a firsthand account of the experience of slavery.

Royal Albert Memorial Museum, Exeter, Devon, UK/The Bridgeman Art Library

Olaudah Equiano was born around 1745. According to his autobiography, he was captured when he was eleven years old, shipped to America, and put to work first as a domestic servant in Virginia. He had much better luck than most slaves, eventually purchasing his freedom and writing a description of his experiences that became an early tract for the budding antislavery movement. He reported what it meant to be taken onboard a slave ship on the coast of Africa:

> I was soon put down under the decks, and there I received such a salutation in my nostrils as I had never experienced in my life: so that, with the loathsomeness of the stench, and crying together, I became so sick and low that I was not able to eat, nor had I the least desire to taste anything. I now wished for the last friend, death, to relieve me; but soon, to my grief, two of the white men offered me eatables; and, on my refusing to eat, one of them held me fast by the hands, and laid me across I think the windlass, and tied my feet, while the other flogged me severely.

Millions of other Africans suffered the same experiences but never achieved the freedom that Equiano did.

Most Africans, especially those imported into the southern colonies after the 1680s, faced a lifetime of slavery on a tobacco, cotton, or rice plantation. Their difficult lives were not long ones. Until the mid-1700s, one-quarter of newly arrived slaves died within a year. Young children often worked in the fields alongside adults, and the labor for women and men was backbreaking from sunup to sundown. The law gave plantation owners a free hand in how they treated their slaves. Slaves were whipped, branded, tortured, and executed for the smallest infractions to warn others of what resistance would mean. Total and unquestionable authority became the order of the day for male owners, making them absolute monarchs over their slaves. By the early 1700s, a small group of plantation owners controlled nearly all aspects of life in the southern colonies. It was a society in which slaves were given no respect, a few wealthy white males had unlimited power, and the institution of slavery defined the social order—a hierarchical order in which women and poor white men, though free, also had little power.

The Fear of Slave Revolts: South Carolina and New York

In the early 1700s, production of tobacco, rice, and indigo was growing quickly. Charleston, South Carolina, became the largest slave-trading center in mainland North America. But slaves did not accept their fate easily. They longed for and sometimes fought for their freedom. As more white colonists came to depend on slave labor for their growing prosperity, they also lived in constant fear of slave revolts, uprisings that were far from uncommon in all of the colonies. Two examples reflect the volatile conditions throughout the colonies.

THE STONO SLAVE REBELLION OF 1739   England and Spain were often at war, making the border between Spanish Florida and British South Carolina and Georgia a tense boundary (see Map 4-3). In 1693, Spain offered freedom to all fugitives from British territories who came into Spanish territory and converted to Catholicism. Many Carolina slaves heard about Spain's offer, and the number of runaways increased.

Throughout the early 1700s, a steady stream of slaves managed to make their way to Florida and freedom. Some of these runaways were already Catholic because they came from parts of Africa, such as the Kingdom of Kongo, long since converted by Portuguese missionaries. For others, converting to Catholicism was a route to freedom. At first, the Spanish authorities were slow to make good on their promise, but they soon realized the value of their policy. The runaway slaves were a drain on the Carolina economy and an embarrassment to the British. In addition, the newly freed slaves were a strong first line of defense on the Spanish side of the border. After all, as newly free people in Spanish Florida, they had special reason to defend the territory from the British, who wanted to perpetuate their slavery.

One of these former Carolina slaves, Francisco Menendez, won a special commendation from the Spanish in 1728 for his heroism in defending St. Augustine from English attack. When the Spanish authorities decided to create a separate settlement they called Mose—to the north of St. Augustine—as a buffer against further attacks, the Spanish governor placed

Map 4-3 British-Spanish Competition and the Expansion of Slavery into Georgia.

While the border between Georgia and Florida was considered an international boundary between the British and Spanish colonies, the reality was that most of the unguarded territory was filled with forest and swamp, and for slaves the path from South Carolina to Spanish Florida was a path from slavery to freedom.

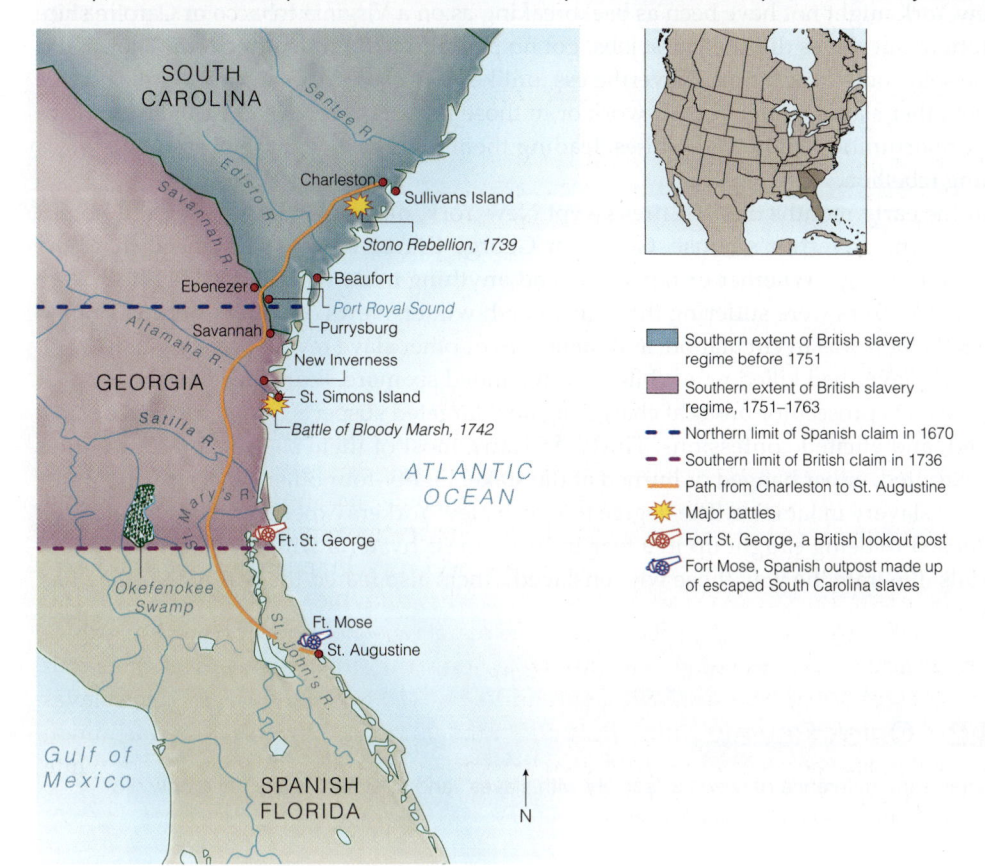

Menendez in charge. Mose was more a fort than a town, but it was home to approximately one hundred Africans who defended Florida and organized attacks on the British in South Carolina.

A large effort by Carolina slaves to gain freedom in Spanish Florida in 1739 came to be called the **Stono Rebellion**, the largest slave uprising in the colonies before the American Revolution. It terrified slave masters throughout the British colonies. The rebellion began when some sixty slaves from the South Carolina rice plantations, led by a slave named Cato, armed themselves, burned buildings of the slave owners, and killed whites who got in their way as they sought freedom in Spanish Florida. Fearful slave owners sent the South Carolina militia to stop them. In a battle at Stono, South Carolina, fifty miles from what was then the Florida border, many of the rebels and their white pursuers were killed. Other slaves were captured and returned to slavery. But some made it to freedom in Florida. In response, the white planter government of South Carolina temporarily restricted the importation of more African slaves and permanently curtailed the rights of slaves to assemble with one another.

After the Stono Rebellion was crushed, individual slaves continued to escape south across the border. Menendez, the former slave, had further adventures. Traveling to Spain, he was captured by the British and threatened with execution, but he eventually escaped and, by 1752, was again back leading the militia in Florida. By 1763, Mose had a population of three thousand, mostly escaped slaves. When Spain ceded Florida to Britain in that year, the Spanish did not abandon the community but moved the Mose Africans to Cuba, where they were given land, tools, a subsidy, and ironically, a slave for each leader in the community.

Stono Rebellion

Uprising in 1739 of South Carolina slaves against whites; inspired in part by Spanish officials' promise of freedom for American slaves who escaped to Florida.

TENSIONS IN NEW YORK CITY, 1741   In the 1700s, slavery was not limited to the southern colonies. New York City and Providence, Rhode Island, had some of the largest concentrations of slaves in North America at that time. New York's African American community included approximately two thousand out of the city's ten thousand residents. Slave labor in New York might not have been as backbreaking as on a Virginia tobacco or Carolina rice plantation, but slaves did the worst jobs, got no pay, and had limited freedom. They could also be sold south at any time. Nevertheless, unlike rural slaves, urban slaves had a chance to meet other slaves, either at their work or in those taverns that welcomed them. Some of these opportunities frightened whites, leading them to react to what they assumed was a pending rebellion.

In the early months of 1741, fires swept New York, destroying businesses and homes including the governor's house. Governor George Clarke became convinced that "the Negros are rising." Whether or not slaves had anything to do with it, the 1741 fires were real. New Yorkers were suffering through a harsh winter. News of South Carolina's Stono Slave Rebellion was in circulation, and memories of other slave revolts were fresh. In 1712, New York slaves had killed nine whites and wounded six more. Fear spread easily.

A zealous prosecutor brought charges against targeted suspects, pitted accused against accused, and elicited confessions. Thirty Africans, most of them slaves, and four whites were executed, either hanged or burned at the stake. Eighty-four other suspects were transported to slavery in Jamaica. The degree to which New Yorkers experienced an actual revolt as opposed to being caught up in a fear-induced mass hysteria will never be known, but the trials illustrate the way those who enslaved others also feared the reality that they had created.

4.2 Quick Review

What is the difference between a "society with slaves" and a "slave society," and how did part of North America become the latter?

Stability and Instability in the American and British Worlds

4.3   **Analyze the changes in the ideas and daily lives of the people in British North America in the 1700s as colonial residents also participated in political, social, cultural, and economic exchanges with Great Britain that encouraged both stronger bonds with Britain and resistance to Britain's control.**

Act of Union

The 1707 vote by the Scottish and English Parliaments to become one nation of Great Britain.

In 1706–1707, the English and Scottish Parliaments passed the **Act of Union**, formally uniting England and Scotland to create Great Britain. Although the two countries had been ruled by a single monarch since 1603, they were separate nations with separate Parliaments, and the American colonies were English colonies. After 1707, England and Scotland were one country, and the English colonies became British North America. The act extended the political stability of the Glorious Revolution. By 1707, third and fourth generations of people living in the American colonies had never seen Britain, even though they were of English and occasionally Scottish descent. They were being joined by other Europeans, especially immigrants from Germany and Ireland—mostly Scots-Irish Protestants from the north of Ireland—along with increasing numbers of unwilling and unfree Africans.

The British economy on both sides of the Atlantic was changing, and people were prospering. Although many people were still poor, the desperate starving time in Virginia and similar early struggles elsewhere were far behind. In British cities on both sides of the Atlantic and on the great plantations developing in the southern colonies, a growing social and economic elite lived comfortable lives, largely made possible by the slave trade and the backbreaking work of African slaves. The wealthiest colonial residents were those who lived on the tobacco, rice, and indigo plantations of Virginia and the Carolinas, including people like Charles and Anne Byrd Carter, whose families owned thousands of acres as well as many slaves and produced some of the goods most in demand in Great Britain and Britain's other colonies around the world.

Recent arrivals from Europe went to work in the cities or moved deeper and deeper into the interior. After 1730 when Queen Anne's government passed the Test Act that stripped non-Anglican Protestant clergy in Britain and Ireland of their status and forbade their followers from any government position, thousands of Scots-Irish Presbyterians, who were heavily impacted by the act and by the poverty of their homes, left northern Ireland for eventual settlement far in the back woods of Pennsylvania, Virginia, and the Carolinas.

As their dress and the picture's background illustrate, Charles and Anne Byrd Carter of Virginia were among the colonial elite when these pictures were painted in the 1730s.

Colonial life was still full of uncertainty. The hysteria that led to the Salem witch trials in the 1690s reflected these deep-seated fears that were just under the surface of much of colonial society. Rural women were often isolated, and even urban women were confined to domestic worlds, which could be lonely. The ever-present danger of Indian raids continued to threaten British colonies, just as raids by settlers were a constant danger for tribes living near the colonies. The wealthy elite, whose wealth depended on slaves, feared slave revolts. In addition, wars in Europe often led to battles in North America.

By the early 1700s, England was the world's dominant sea power, bringing great financial benefits to those who controlled the trade in goods and people across the Atlantic and bringing prosperity to those who lived in port cities on both sides of the ocean. As trade and prosperity grew, the quest for commercial success began to replace religious devotion as the prime focus of many people's lives.

The Salem Witch Trials of 1692

Underlying tensions in colonial life surfaced in Massachusetts during the harsh, unrelenting winter of 1691–1692. The residents of Salem and the surrounding Massachusetts communities also lived in fear because New England was under siege from Indians allied with French Canada. In midwinter, Indians killed fifty residents of York, Maine, and took more hostage. Residents of other Maine communities fled in terror and were living in or near Salem. Exiles from Maine may have been especially traumatized, but all of the residents heard their stories and feared further attacks. Moreover, other tensions were brewing in the port city of Salem. Many poorer residents resented their neighbors who formed a more prosperous commercial elite. In addition, women in Salem, like in all English colonies, lived within strict submissive gender roles. Women who were unusually assertive, especially women who lived alone or were of non-English backgrounds, were not trusted.

As these tensions simmered, Salem fell into a kind of mass hysteria late that winter. Two young girls in the home of the Reverend Samuel Parris of Salem Village—his daughter, Betty, and her cousin Abigail—began to suffer fits. They seemed to be "bitten and pinched by invisible agents." The town doctor wondered if their disease might be a result of witchcraft. In March, the girls accused Tituba, the family's Indian slave, of bewitching them. Thus began the **Salem witch trials**, one of the best-known episodes of mass hysteria in the English colonies.

Soon other young women came forward with tales similar to those of Betty and Abigail. As a result, formal charges were brought, and court proceedings began. In time, some of

Salem witch trials

The 1692–1693 hysteria in Salem, Massachusetts, during which women and men were accused of being witches who had made a pact with the devil, some of whom were executed for the crime.

those accused, including Tituba, "confessed" to being witches. Witnesses turned against one another, and convictions for witchcraft became common.

Between February 1692 and May 1693, legal action was taken against 144 people—106 women and 38 men. Six men and fourteen women, including Tituba, were executed. That so many people in Salem believed their illnesses and troubles were the work of witches was not strange in the 1600s. Most people in Europe believed that there were witches—people who had made a compact with the devil and could appear as ghosts and make other people and animals sick. Hundreds of supposed witches were executed in England in that century, and many other accusations of witchcraft had surfaced in New England, although never on the scale of what happened in Salem. In Salem, the whole community became involved as the accusations spread quickly from one household to another. Virtually all of the accusers were young women under age twenty-five, and most of the victims were also women—though often older and sometimes, like Tituba, not white.

The hysteria ended almost as quickly as it had begun. By the fall of 1692, Massachusetts authorities—clergy and political leaders—were starting to have doubts about the trials and executions. Most people in the colony probably still believed in witchcraft, but they were increasingly uneasy about what was happening in Salem. By spring 1693, it was all over. One of the judges, Samuel Sewall, publicly apologized for his role and asked God's pardon. Reverend Parris was forced to leave Salem, and the Massachusetts authorities voted compensation for families of victims. The Salem witch trials were one of the last times that people were executed for explicitly religious reasons in North America.

Women's Lives

By the middle of the 1700s, the white culture of British North America was generally divided between the public and private realms. Because women were generally relegated to the private realm, many of them lived cut off from society.

Urban women had much more opportunity for social contact than those living in more isolated regions. In Williamsburg, Virginia, two women—Anne Shields and Jane Vobe—ran their own taverns. Mary Channing ran a large store in Boston, and Lydia Hyde had her own shop in Philadelphia. While these women may have been the exception, city women did have more opportunities to interact than rural women.

However, more than 90 percent of the British residents of North America lived on farms, sometimes very isolated farms, and the lives of rural women could be frighteningly lonely. In settled farm communities, especially in southern New England, women could often find limited contact with other women in ways that allowed them to build friendships, such as gathering to trade soap, candles, cheese, and butter, or attending church. Growing commercial prosperity also meant that some women were able to purchase imported goods including tea, china, and—for a few—even silk.

Mehetabel Chandler Coit, who lived in New England from 1673 to 1758, left one of the oldest diaries of a colonial woman to be found. Coit was more fortunate than many, living most of her adult life with her shipbuilder husband in the bustling town of New London, Connecticut. Her diary reflected family life; reporting births and deaths and the comings and goings of children or her worries about a daughter whose "foot burnt with a warming-pan," or a son on whom a "plank fell … but got no grate mater of hurt." Reflecting more travel than was possible for many, she reported that in September 1707, "My Husband and I went to Middletown," and later "we come Home and mother Coit came with us," apparently to live with her son and daughter-in-law. However, there were occasional musings, including one undated entry that said, "for the few Hours of Life Alotted to me, Grant me great God but bread and liberty, I'll ask no more."

As the American population expanded, finding land often required moving to more isolated rural areas, which could make contact and community life more difficult, especially for women. While male farmers also lived very isolated lives, they traveled to town to sell goods and buy necessities more often

Everett Historical/Shutterstock

WITCHCRAFT AT SALEM VILLAGE.

In the witch trials in Salem, Massachusetts, in 1692 and 1693, the full extent of the hysteria was on display in the courtrooms of the state where even the most respected judges were caught up in it.

When Historians Disagree

What Caused the Hysteria in Salem?

Historians have offered many different reasons for the prosecutions for witchcraft that took place in and around Salem, Massachusetts, in 1692. Looking at some of the same events, Jane Kamensky and Mary Beth

Norton came to very different conclusions. There are no right or wrong answers here. There are, however, fascinating and important differences, as the material from these two distinguished historians illustrates.

Jane Kamensky, "The Colonial Mosaic, 1600–1660," in Nancy F. Cott, editor, *No Small Courage: A History of Women in the United States* (New York: Oxford University Press, 2000), pp. 95–98.

In Salem, Massachusetts, women confronted a range of perils and possibilities during the social upheaval of the late-seventeenth century. … The crisis at Salem belonged, in part, to a very old Puritan pattern in which the Devil almost always seemed to appear in the shape of a woman.

But there were different things about Salem. For one thing, there appeared in Salem new sorts of "devils" to fight against: the rapid growth of the population, the spread of commerce, the feuding of neighbor against neighbor. … Perhaps [most of the accusers], like Mary Rowlandson, … were eager to claim a larger space for women's voices in a changing world. Perhaps they truly were suffering—not from what we today would understand as witchcraft, but from some other mental or physical illness. To their audiences, however, the explanation was readily at hand in the shape of three local women whom the girls accused of tormenting them.

Mary Beth Norton, *In the Devil's Snare: The Salem Witchcraft Crisis of 1692* (New York: Random House, 2002), pp. 3–5.

Salem. The word alone evokes persistent images in the minds of twenty-first-century Americans…

What I found has led me to develop a new interpretation of the witchcraft crisis, one that places it firmly in the context of its very specific time and place: Essex County, Massachusetts, in the early 1690s. The county's residents were then near the front lines of an armed conflict that today is little known but which at the time commanded their lives and thoughts, as was demonstrated by the ubiquity of the subject in the letters and diaries I was reading. They called it the Second Indian War [or] King William's War. *In the Devil's Snare*, though, contends that the dramatic events of 1692 can be fully understood only by viewing them as intricately related to concurrent political and military affairs in northern New England. … When I started my research … I had no idea that this book would become what it has: an exploration of the history of frontier warfare and its impact on the collective mentality of an entire region.

Thinking Critically

1. **Contextualization**

   Norton makes the case that the specific context of events around Salem, Massachusetts, in 1692 is crucial to understanding the witchcraft hysteria. How convincing do you find that argument in comparison with others she rejects or those that Kamensky makes?

2. **Causation**

   Two modern distinguished historians provide very different answers to the question of what caused the hysteria in Salem. Which do you find more convincing? Using evidence to support your answer, why do you make that argument?

than women. These trips provided men far more opportunity to meet neighbors and participate in the social and political discussions. In contrast, women were limited not only by assumptions that they should stick to household matters and leave political discussion and trade to their husbands but also by the physical demands of pregnancy, birth, nursing, and child rearing as well as by the daily chores of a farm—taking care of the animals, raising the vegetables, preserving food, preparing meals, spinning wool, weaving cloth, and making clothes.

Women's work also included playing the role of physician or pharmacist because most farm families did not have access to more formal medical care. Women had to be familiar with medical information and herbal medicines. Manuals such as *Aristotle's Complete Masterpiece: Displaying the Secrets of Nature in the Generation of Man* provided many women with detailed information on sexual matters, childbirth, and child rearing. In addition, the opportunities women had to share medical and child-rearing information, provide medical care, and support each other through medical emergencies and childbirth were extremely important to women's community life. Midwives and healers had special status, but any nearby farm wife might be summoned to attend a birth, and a woman in labor might well have six to ten female attendants. The times surrounding a birth were an important social occasion as women had time to sew, tell stories, and catch up with each other.

At the bottom of the social hierarchy were enslaved women. For women living in slavery, the usual gender distinctions of white society had less meaning. On farms and plantations, male and female slaves all worked long hours in the fields. In urban areas, where there might be greater gender distinctions in specific forms of work, enslaved women were still afforded few of the protections that were expected—if not always enforced—for white women.

There were, of course, exceptions to the general isolation that women living outside of cities experienced. Eliza Lucas (1722–1793) was born to a wealthy English sugar-growing family on the island of Antigua in 1722. She was educated in London and then joined her family in South Carolina in 1738. She quickly became a popular member of Charleston's elite. However, in 1739, war between England and Spain required her father to return to Antigua. She was left in charge of three Carolina plantations at the age of sixteen. In 1744, Eliza married Charles Pinckney. He also traveled a great deal and left her in charge of the plantations. Like male plantation owners, Eliza Pinckney supervised a large labor force of slaves whose labor was the basis of her wealth and leisure. Her position gave her time and opportunity to develop her agricultural ideas and cultivate her intellect, which she did throughout her life. She experimented with new crops and crop rotations. She also helped develop cultivation of the indigo plant, which was used to create a blue dye that was popular in England and which soon rivaled rice as a source of wealth in South Carolina.

The Growth of Cities: Philadelphia, New York, Boston, Charleston

In 1700, British North America had a population of approximately 250,000, including both Europeans and Africans, but not Indians. Boston was the largest city in the colonies with 8,000 inhabitants, followed by New York City with 6,000. Philadelphia and Charleston were both under 3,000, but Philadelphia was growing fast. By contrast, the capital of New Spain, Mexico City, had 100,000 residents, and London had over 500,000 in 1700. With growing trade and prosperity, the British North American population would dramatically increase (see Table 4-1). By the 1770s, on the eve of the American Revolution, Philadelphia would have about 30,000 residents, followed by New York with almost 25,000, Boston with a little more than 16,000, and Charleston with almost 12,000. The total colonial population would be 2.5 million, including 500,000 slaves of African origin.

Many colonists responded to the growing trade and prosperity with pride in being part of the British Empire. In the 1690s, Virginia moved its capital from Jamestown to Williamsburg, complete with a new capitol building that reflected this pride. The structure had two wings—one for the elected legislature, the House of Burgesses, and one for the royally appointed council—just as the Parliament that sat in London had places for the elected House of Commons and the hereditary House of Lords. The governor's elegant Williamsburg residence reflected the status of the crown's representative in the colony.

Although most people still lived on farms or in small towns, the port cities were becoming significant centers of trade and culture for the whole British Empire. Between 1701 and 1754, the cities of British North America moved from being rude outposts to cities that looked and felt very much like similar cities in Britain. In the early 1700s, New York City, Philadelphia, Boston, and Charleston all emerged as significant trading centers for

Table 4-1 Estimated Populations of the Four Largest Cities in British North America between 1700 and 1775

City	1700	1720	1750	1775
Boston	8,000	12,000	16,000	17,500
Philadelphia	2,000	10,000	15,000	31,000
New York	6,000	7,000	14,000	21,500
Charleston	2,000	3,500	6,500	11,000

4.1

4.2

4.3

American Voices

Benjamin Franklin, The Way to Wealth, 1757

Benjamin Franklin (1706–1790) was born in modest circumstances in Boston, Massachusetts, in 1706. At age twelve, after two years of schooling, Franklin became an apprentice—an indentured servant—to his older brother, James, a printer in Boston. In 1723, at the age of seventeen—and four years before his indenture expired—Benjamin took advantage of a loophole in the contract and left Boston for Philadelphia. By 1729, at the age of twenty-three, he was sole owner of a printing business. While he made money printing government documents and publications for private businesses, Franklin also produced Poor Richard's Almanack, *which predicted the weather for the coming year and shared friendly advice. By 1748, when he was forty-two years old, Franklin was one of the richest people in the northern colonies and decided that it was time to retire from work, live the life of a gentleman, and devote himself to public service. Public service had always been important to Franklin, and it was a measure of the status he sought. He had already helped launch the Library Company of Philadelphia. Soon after he retired, Franklin engaged in his famous experiment with a kite to prove that lightning was, indeed, electricity. In 1755, he helped found the College of Philadelphia that would become the University of Pennsylvania. In 1757, Franklin published* The Way to Wealth, *one of Franklin's most enduring works, which reflected a changing colonial culture, one in which religious orthodoxy and national loyalties mattered less and individual commercial success mattered much more.*

I stopped my horse lately where a great number of people were collected at a vendue [sale] of merchant goods. The hour of sale not being come, they were conversing on the badness of the times, and one of the company called to a plain, clean old man with white locks: "Pray, Father Abraham, what think you of the times? Won't these heavy taxes quite ruin the country? How shall we be ever able to pay them? What would you advise us to? …"

"Friends," says he, "and neighbors, the taxes are indeed very heavy, and if those laid on by the government were the only

ones we had to pay, we might more easily discharge them; but we have many others, and much more grievous to some of us. We are taxed twice as much by our idleness, three times as much by our pride, and four times as much by our folly; and from these taxes the commissioners cannot ease or deliver us by allowing an abatement. However, let us hearken to good advice, and something may be done for us; 'God helps them that help themselves,' as Poor Richard says in his almanac of 1733. …

"'If time be of all things the most precious, wasting time must be,' as Poor Richard says, 'the greatest prodigality'; since as he elsewhere tells us, 'Lost time is never found again'; … and 'Early to bed and early to rise, makes a man healthy, wealthy, and wise.' … 'Diligence is the mother of good luck,' as Poor Richard says … and 'Little strokes fell great oaks,' as Poor Richard says in his almanac—the year I cannot just now remember.' …

"And now to conclude, 'Experience keeps a dear school, but fools will learn in no other, and scarce in that'; for it is true, 'We may give advice, but we cannot give conduct,' as Poor Richard says. …"

Thus the old gentleman ended his harangue. The people heard it and approved the doctrine, and immediately practiced the contrary, just as if it had been a common sermon.

Source: Benjamin Franklin, *The Works of Benjamin Franklin, with Notes and a Life of the Author by Jared Sparks* (London: Benjamin Franklin Stevens, 1882).

Thinking Critically

1. **Contextualization**
   How did Poor Richard's values reflect the mid-1700s? How might people in the mid-1600s or mid-1800s have responded?

2. **Comparison**
   What groups in colonial society would have been most likely to see Franklin's values as their own? What groups would not? Why the differences?

the British world. Their good harbors supported ocean-based commerce, based on Britain's growing dominance of the world's oceans, and industries that included Britain's naval building, the tea trade, and the slave trade. Ships based in North America carried food—cornmeal, pork, and beef—and naval stores—tar, pitch turpentine, lumber—to the great sugar plantations of the British West Indies. These prosperous plantations on Barbados, Jamaica, and other British-controlled islands were far richer than anything on the mainland of North America. They also had many more slaves than any plantation on the mainland. But they depended on North America to supply their food and building supplies. The ships returned to North American ports with slaves, sugar, rum, molasses, cotton, and fruit from the Caribbean; manufactured goods from Great Britain; and letters of credit that expanded the cash in circulation in the colonies and in London.

Cities also became safer places to live after Boston clergyman Cotton Mather championed the first vaccinations against smallpox in 1721. While smallpox had been a major cause of death among Indians who had never developed immunity to the disease, many Europeans also died of it. Mather, a Puritan theologian and pastor, was also an acute scientific observer. He had read about a Turkish doctor who had produced light cases of smallpox by deliberately infecting healthy people with the disease, which produced immunity in them against more lethal strains.

When the smallpox epidemic of 1721 hit Boston, Mather advocated using that doctor's inoculation approach, and a physician, Zabdiel Boylston, tried it. Mather collected the statistics. Of some three hundred people inoculated, only five or six died compared with nine hundred deaths among the five thousand who were not inoculated. The statistics were compelling. Smallpox inoculations spread throughout the colonial world, though it was another thirty years before smallpox inoculations were common in England.

Commercial Attitudes, Commercial Success— Mercantilism and the New Trading Economy

Since at least the time of Queen Elizabeth I, the Western world's economy, and certainly the economy of Britain and Britain's possessions, had been organized around an economic system known as **mercantilism**. But as trade developed in the colonies, the seeds of what would later be described as **capitalism** were already taking hold. Advocates of mercantilism believed that economic transactions should be directed to increase the nation's wealth, that the world's wealth was finite, and that for any nation to grow in wealth some other nation needed to be the loser. Using this mercantile approach, the British Empire closely guarded the colonies so that their wealth went exclusively to Britain and not to other European countries. Economists of the time believed that it was critical that the colonies be used only to produce raw materials that would enrich the European nation that claimed them and that colonies also consume manufactured products from their mother country. Any trade outside of this closed loop, they feared, ran the risk of diluting the nation's wealth. Advocates for capitalism saw the economic world very differently. Economists who favored capitalism believed there was no limit to the world's wealth because it was trade, not the goods that were being traded, that was the ultimate key to wealth. Thus, trade between individuals and between nations allowed continuing growth for all parties.

mercantilism

Economic system whereby the government intervenes in the economy for the purpose of increasing national wealth.

capitalism

Economic system best described by Adam Smith in 1776 in which trade is seen as the source of wealth rather than as exchange of goods themselves; as a result, wealth can continually expand as trade expands.

The prime example of mercantilism in the Americas was the British Navigation Acts of 1650 and 1660. The 1660 Navigation Act proclaimed that "from thenceforward, no goods or commodities whatsoever shall be imported into or exported out of any lands, islands, plantations, or territories to his Majesty belonging or in his possession ... but in such ships or vessels as do truly and without fraud belong only to the people of England or Ireland, dominion of Wales or town of Berwick upon Tweed." In other words, anything shipped *to* North America or to other British colonies had to be transported in English ships, and everything shipped *from* the colonies had to be transported in English ships bound for England. The goal was clear: the colonies would produce raw goods—as the act stipulated, "sugars, tobacco, cotton-wool, indigoes, ginger, fustic, or other dyeing wool"—and ship them only to England. England would produce manufactured goods, and the colonies would be limited to buying goods only from England. The arrangement was a closed economic system, and it was designed to ensure that

WASHINGTON AS A SURVEYOR.

As colonial life became more settled in British North America between the 1680s and the 1750s, economic patterns became more established. In the early 1700s, a British study reported the kinds of trades practiced in the colonies, including this illustration of a male master and apprentice surveyors.

North Wind Picture Archives/Alamy Stock Photo

wealth from the colonies flowed only to London, not back to the colonies and certainly not to any other country. Britain had little interest in cultivating wealth within the colonies themselves.

The problem with mercantilism was that it focused too much on ownership of *things* and too little on the *trade* of things. The efforts on the part of Spain to maintain its wealth by controlling the world's supply of silver and gold are illustrative of that problem as was the effort of British pirates to steal the same gold. Many European wars of the era were fought over issues related to mercantilism as each European power sought to control the greatest amount of what they saw as the world's limited wealth. As the Navigation Acts made clear, for much of the 1600s and 1700s, even as Britain itself was beginning to focus on developing an economy based on trade, its government attempted to use mercantile principles to control that trade with the American colonies.

The **Triangle Trade** that developed in response to British mercantile policies involved the shipment of slaves from Africa to the West Indies and North America in exchange for rum (see Map 4-4). Sugar and rum (made from sugar) were also shipped to Britain, and goods manufactured in Britain were shipped to Africa, the West Indies, and the mainland of North America. But there was also significant trade directly between North America and Britain.

Triangle Trade

A pattern of trade that developed in the 1700s in which slaves from Africa were sent to the West Indies and mainland North America while goods and other resources were shipped between the West Indies and North America and Britain.

Map 4-4 The Triangle Trade.

As this map shows, the so-called triangular trade was not a perfect triangle. But for the British colonies, the most significant trade focused on England from which manufactured products were shipped to the Americas and to Africa. In return, African slaves were shipped to the Caribbean and to North America, Caribbean rum was shipped to Africa and to England, and raw materials—including fish, fur, grain, rice, indigo, and tobacco—were shipped directly from North America to England which, according to mercantile laws, was the only place where raw materials could be turned into finished manufactured goods.

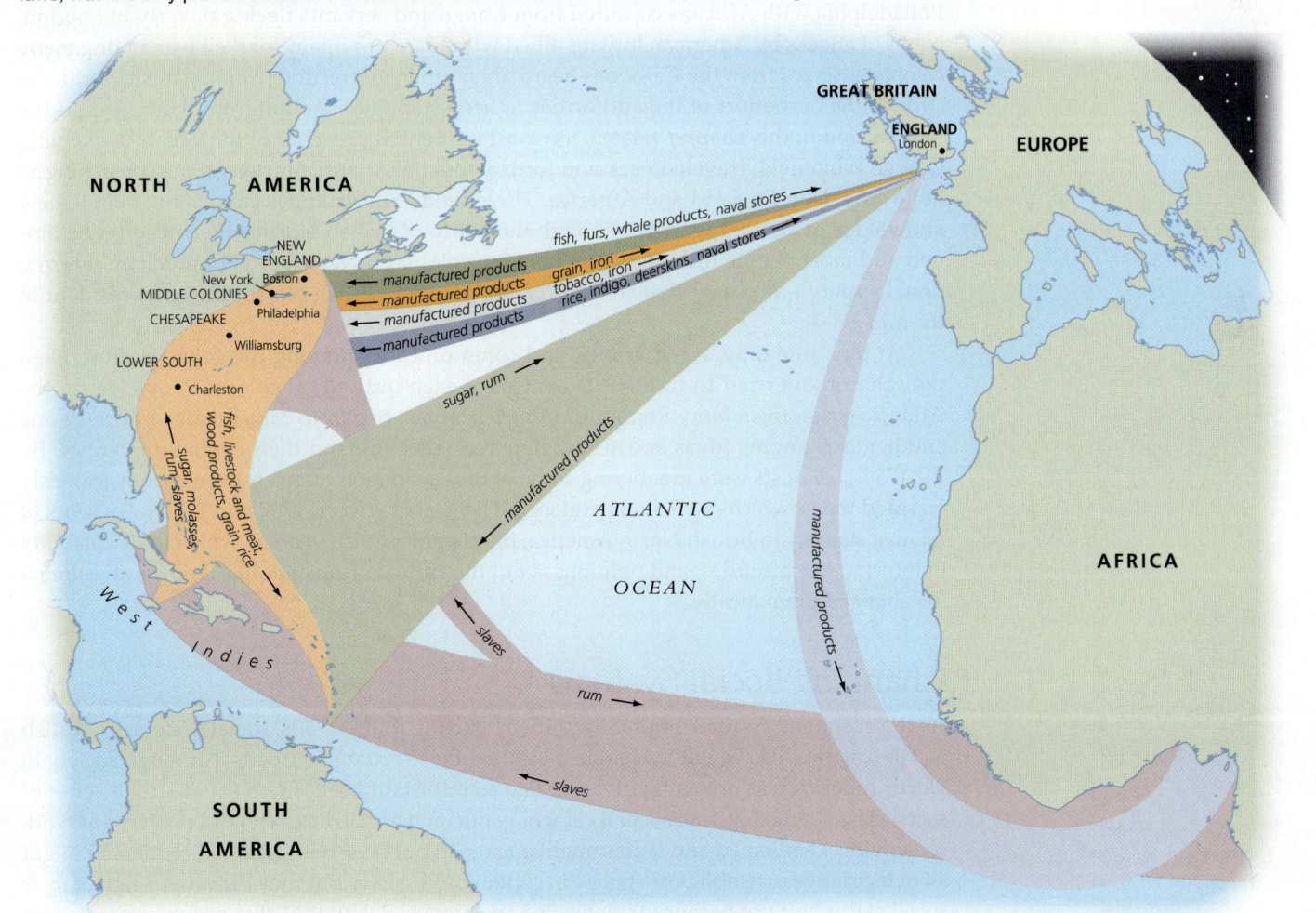

Raw materials, including fur, grain, tobacco, rice, and indigo—the last three all produced by slave labor—were shipped directly to Britain in return for manufactured products that by law—though not always in reality—could be produced only in Great Britain.

For British colonists living in North America, the trade problems were more real than theoretical. They hated mercantilism and the Navigation Acts, not because they opposed slavery or the introduction of slave labor into the colonies or because they thought capitalism was a better economic theory but because the British policies were keeping them from getting rich. Molasses could be bought more cheaply from French colonies than from British. Slaves could sometimes be bought more cheaply from Dutch traders than from English. Similarly, goods produced in the colonies—tobacco, rice, food stuffs, and ship stores—could often fetch higher prices elsewhere in the world than in Britain. Trading with a wider world, especially the rich colonies of the Caribbean, made more sense and produced greater profit than limiting trade to England alone.

Circumventing the Navigation Acts, through either finding legal loopholes or simply sailing off in a different direction from what British laws allowed, became a major enterprise and source of wealth throughout all of the British colonies. Many of the richest merchants in North America were adept at evading British trade laws and customs duties. The involvement of the colonies in worldwide trade—even when that trade was illegal—foreshadowed not only American independence but also a shift in economic systems from the closed world of mercantilism to a more open and elastic world in which trade and commerce, rather than simply ownership of things, was the key to wealth.

Trade was also increasing the exchange of information. Cotton Mather learned about smallpox inoculations from Turkish physicians through contacts in London. New York's traders interacted with merchants in Jamaica and Barbados as well as Africa and England. Jews whose forbearers had been exiled from Spain mingled on the streets of New York and Philadelphia with Africans captured from Kongo and servants fleeing poverty in London. News of attacks by American Indians allied with France or Spain sparked fear among many colonists. Slaves from the Carolinas heard about offers of freedom from Spanish Florida, in spite of the best effort of the authorities to keep such information from them. And as the next section in this chapter relates, the most influential preacher of the Great Awakening, George Whitefield, traveled back and forth across the Atlantic thirteen times, preaching to huge crowds in England and America. These kinds of exchanges gave many people new knowledge of a wider world. Although the world of British North America could be limited and most people did not travel very far, colonial society was very much an international society—a context that shaped the life of every British North American resident in the mid-1700s.

At the same time, trade, travel, and communication among the colonies grew, even though London tried to tighten its control of each individual colony. People along the Atlantic coast, from New England to the Carolinas, began to take greater notice of one another, exchanging ideas and seeing new reasons to defend their common interests. By the 1750s, colonists were identifying some of those common interests even as they jealously guarded their own colony's independence. The years between 1707 and 1754 were years of relative stability in British North America, but they were also years in which the availability of information, attitudes, and opinions about the value of British political power in colonial life changed dramatically.

Changing Social Systems

As the economic systems gradually shifted, starting in the 1730s, social systems in British North America also began to change, reflecting those economic trends. Although society in North America was not as highly stratified as in Britain itself, there was a strong sense of social class. At the top was a small class of gentlemen and ladies, who did not have to work for a living. Gentlemen and ladies might engage in public service, and the gentlemen might sit in legislative assemblies or engage in certain professions, but they did so as a sign of their social status and not because they needed the money. Below that elite group, separated by

4.1

4.2

4.3

a great gulf, were those who had to work for a living—farmers and tradespeople known as "mechanics" and, below them, the servants and slaves. However prosperous the mechanics and farmers might become, they were still stigmatized. They were expected to know their place and maintain proper deference to society's elite. At the very bottom were those in varying degrees of unfreedom—slaves, indentured servants, or simply desperately poor people. Members of this group were disregarded in terms of having any say or influence. People in these classes typically acknowledged duty to those above them and expected deference from those below.

By the 1720s, however, some of the mechanics and farmers were becoming a new social class: the "middling sorts." These prosperous working people earned their success through hard work and frugality, both of which the elite scorned. Over generations, this group would evolve into what we now call the middle class. The middling social class, including printers, most physicians, small farmers, and those who sailed on ships, differentiated themselves from working people in the less prosperous trades and the servants and slaves. A new perspective was taking shape. People began to question the notion of a society that expected deference to those of higher status. The assumption that one stayed in the class to which one was born was quickly disappearing. Benjamin Franklin, though much more successful than most, was far from the only resident of colonial America to move from one class to another. Of course, social movement was not only in an upward direction.

As class roles weakened, some also moved downward or moved outside of the class system altogether, such as the most famous outlaw of the mid-1700s, Thomas Bell. If one depended on colonial newspapers, then the best-known American of the first half of the 1700s was not Benjamin Franklin or Jonathan Edwards (see next section on religion) but Thomas Bell. This "famous American traveler" was the subject of much fascination. He was known for his thefts, swindles, and escapes in Massachusetts, New York, New Jersey, Virginia, Maryland, the Carolinas, and island colonies including Barbados and Jamaica, and his exploits were followed with great interest.

A Changing Religious Landscape—From the Halfway Covenant to the First Great Awakening

From the time of the first settlement in British North America, there was a sense that this new land was a divinely planned opportunity to begin the world again and make it right. In 1702, Cotton Mather, perhaps the best-known minister in Boston at the time, published a book that claimed that New England had a special divine mission. Mather praised God that Europe had made contact with the Americas after the Protestant Reformation so British North America was being built by Protestants and not by Roman Catholics. At the same time, some Catholics saw their mission from the opposite side of the Reformation divide. Giovanni Botero wrote in 1595 that it was only divine providence that led the kings of France and England to reject overtures from Columbus so that his initial "discovery" could be made while sailing for Catholic Spain.

Not all Europeans accepted their mission as a special part of divine providence, however. Roger Williams, who founded Rhode Island as a haven for religious tolerance, insisted that God did not choose special elect nations—not England and not New England. A group of settlers in northern New England reminded one missionary who spoke of their divine mission, "Sir, … our main end is to catch fish." Nevertheless, the notion that America was part of a divine drama of salvation was widespread.

By the early 1700s, however, the sense of being on a divine mission declined. The grandchildren and great-grandchildren of the original Puritan settlers were living increasingly comfortable lives in the commercially prosperous British Empire. Religious fervor and religious conversions were less and less common, and many were much more tolerant of the growing religious diversity in all of the colonies. This growth of religious toleration in the 1700s—something not imagined in the 1600s—prompted more Europeans to come to the British colonies in search of religious freedom that they could not find in their homelands, including German-speaking immigrants who found themselves on the wrong side of the Protestant–Catholic divide in their homeland or Scots-Irish Presbyterians whose clergy and values were not recognized by the British government after 1703.

Increasingly, more of those who already lived in the colonies began to consider alternatives to the religious dogmas of their parents and communities. The growth of new philosophical ideas in Europe led many to look more to science and human reason than to faith in trying to understand their world. They called the time in which they were living the Age of Enlightenment or the European Enlightenment. Ideas that thinkers such as Locke and Descartes had tested in the 1600s blossomed into a full-fledged intellectual and political movement in the 1700s. Some in this period rejected all religious teachings, while others simply placed less emphasis on matters of faith and more on reason. In the colonies as in Europe, some people began to take religion with a large grain of salt, being convinced that most religious matters were mere superstitions that were, at best, unprovable by the scientific tools of the new age. Some simply turned their attentions to other matters, especially their short-term prosperity and comfort.

Describing his travels in Pennsylvania between 1750 and 1754, the German Protestant minister Gottlieb Mittelberger described a scene not at all to his liking. After describing the wide range of religious beliefs, he continued, "Many pray neither in the morning or in the evening, neither before nor after meals. No devotional book, not to speak of a Bible, will be found with such people."

Mittelberger may have been happy to leave Pennsylvania and return to his ministry in Germany. However, while many ministers expressed similar worries about a religious decline in the colonies in the early 1700s, especially New England, other preachers sought ways to foster religious energy. By the 1720s, Solomon Stoddard, who served as the minister of the Congregational church in Northampton, Massachusetts, and who had been one of the authors of the Halfway Covenant, was leading a resurgence of religion in much of western Massachusetts and Connecticut.

Stoddard's grandson and successor, Jonathan Edwards (1703–1758), led even larger religious revivals. Edward's sermons in western Massachusetts, like those of John Wesley in England, led many to report that their "hearts were strangely warmed" and that they were experiencing a new sense of divine presence. In the **First Great Awakening**, religious revivals swept all of the North American colonies in the late 1730s.

First Great Awakening

A significant religious revival in colonial America begun by the preaching of Solomon Stoddard and Jonathan Edwards in the 1720s and 1730s and expanded by the many tours of the English evangelical minister George Whitefield that began in the 1730s.

The religious fervor of the First Great Awakening swept all the American colonies. George Whitefield, an English preacher shown here, was its most prominent leader. Whitefield crossed the Atlantic thirteen times beginning in 1739 and was probably heard by more Americans than any other individual before the Revolution.

SOTK2011/Alamy Stock Photo

Edwards prided himself on preaching in a low voice and seeking to convert people solely by the logic of his words. He rejected anti-intellectual religion as "heat without light." But by the 1730s, these logical sermons were creating their own dramatic results. Many in Edwards's congregation were undergoing deeply emotional conversion experiences and taking religion seriously in a way that they never had before. In a short period of time, three hundred conversions were reported, increasing church membership considerably.

In perhaps his best-known sermon, Edwards said, "The God that holds you over the pit of hell, much as one holds a spider, or some loathsome insect, over the fire, abhors you, and is dreadfully provoked; his wrath towards you burns like fire … yet it is nothing but his hand that holds you from falling into the fire every moment." Edwards was urgently pleading with his hearers to rethink the direction of their lives.

Later in the 1730s, George Whitefield (1714–1770) became the most powerful preacher of the Great Awakening. Whitefield lived in Britain but preached to huge audiences in both Britain and North America. His first trip to North America began in Georgia in 1738. In 1739 and 1740, he crossed the Atlantic again, making a preaching tour that started in Georgia, moved through the middle colonies (including Philadelphia, where his preaching impressed Benjamin Franklin who became a lifelong friend if not a convert), and progressed to Boston where huge audiences attended a series of sermons, including one on Boston Common that drew a crowd of thirty thousand listeners. Whitefield also visited Northampton and preached at Edwards's church to great acclaim.

Whitefield had high regard for Edwards and Presbyterian ministers like Gilbert Tennent. He had a much lower opinion of some other preachers and said that "the reason why congregations have been so dead, is because dead men preach to them." Timothy Cutler, an Episcopal priest in Boston, responded by describing Whitefield's sermons as "his beastly brayings."

Cutler was not the only minister to resist the emotionalism of Whitefield and Edwards. The leaders at Harvard and Yale did not like the revivalists whom they saw as emotional and divisive. Churches were split. The Presbyterian Church was split into New Light (pro-Awakening) and Old Light (anti-Awakening) bodies. Many Congregational churches were split, and towns that had supported one church for much of the past century now supported two, or three, or even four. In contrast, the Baptists, who generally sided with the Awakening, grew dramatically.

The Great Awakening changed American society. Many who had previously shown little interest in religion became converted. The revivals of the Great Awakening cut across many of the traditional divides of class and race, even gender. While more women than men responded to the religious energy, some of the rules segregating classes and races seem to have been suspended for these revivals. Africans—slave and free—and American Indians were also converted and became enthusiastic members of religious bodies. Samson Occom, a Mohegan Indian from Connecticut, was a convert in the Awakening who went on to be a revival leader, preaching to white and Native American audiences.

The Awakening transformed American higher education, which at that time was closely connected to the churches. Harvard resisted the movement while Yale, first split by it, eventually moved into the Awakening camp. Prorevival ministers founded Dartmouth—initially meant to serve American Indians—and Princeton to support the revival cause and help prepare a new generation of revival-oriented ministers.

Ongoing Wars in Europe and British North America

Between 1689 and 1815, England and France were engaged in more or less continual war with each other for control of global empires. Spain was often allied with France in these wars. For those living in North America, each war involved not only international struggles but also local battles, especially with Indian tribes that were in their own shifting alliances with European powers. From Europe's perspective, the American Revolution itself could be seen as just one battle in that long ongoing war. But long before the Revolution, colonial life in Britain's colonies, as well as in colonies claimed by France and Spain, was shaped by these wars.

4.1

4.2

4.3

American Voices

Jonathan Edwards, *A Treatise Concerning Religious Affections*

In his book, A Treatise Concerning Religious Affections, *published in 1746 after the Great Awakening had run its course, Edwards asked a fundamental question about any religious experience: "How does one judge if it is real or not?" He answered that the key was found in the way a person lived.*

What is the nature of true religion? ... Gracious and holy affections have their exercise and fruit in Christian practice. ... Slothfulness in the service of God, in his professed servants, is as damning, as open rebellion. ... Christ nowhere says, ye shall know the tree by its leaves or flowers, or ye shall know men by their talk, or ye shall know them by the good story they tell of their experiences, or ye shall know them by the manner and air of their speaking, and emphasis and pathos of expression, or by their speaking feelingly, or by making a very great show by abundance of talk, or by many tear and affectionate expressions, or by the affections ye feel in your heart towards them: but by their fruits you shall know them. ... "Let your light so shine before men, that others

seeing your good works, may glorify your Father which is in heaven" (Matt. 5:16). ... Hypocrites may much more easily be brought to talk like saints, than to act like saints. ... [W]e should get into the way of appearing lively in religion, more by being lively in the service of God and our generation, than by the liveliness and forwardness of our tongues.

Source: Jonathan Edwards, *A Treatise Concerning Religious Affections* (Boston: S. Kneeland and T. Green, 1746, reprinted and edited by John E. Smith, New Haven: Yale University Press, 1959).

Thinking Critically

1. **Contextualization**
   How does this passage reflect the ideas of the Great Awakening? What might he have said differently if he had been opposed to the Awakening?

2. **Analyzing Primary Sources**
   Referring to this passage, who is Edwards arguing with? Why do you say so?

For most of the 1700s, France claimed the St. Lawrence River Valley and the Mississippi Valley from what is now Minnesota to New Orleans—an area spanning more of North America than England's colonies. In 1724, Cadwallader Colden, an English surveyor, reminded the governor of New York that "the French plainly shew their intention of enclosing the British Settlements and cutting us off from all Commerce with the numerous Nations of Indians." Despite the larger population of the British colonies, many colonists shared his fear that Britain's colonies were encircled by French ones. They also worried because Spain controlled Florida, many Caribbean islands, and the rich lands of Central and South America, giving Spain great power and wealth in its confrontations with Britain on both sides of the Atlantic. In addition, Indian tribes, many allied with the French, were often the dominant power in territory from western New York through Pennsylvania and into the western portions of the Carolinas and Georgia (see Map 4-5).

It was not always clear who was winning and who was losing in the ongoing struggles, but war was a fact of daily life for much of the colonial era, sometimes devastatingly close to home. When William and Mary came to the throne in England in 1689, King Louis XIV of France objected to their elevation and he fought what colonists called King William's War from 1689 to 1697. The war's outcome was inconclusive, but the battles had devastating consequences for northern New England as Indian tribes allied with France attacked English settlements including York, Maine, perhaps helping provoke the Salem witch hysteria. European settlement of Maine was delayed for a generation.

Soon after that war ended, the War of the Spanish Succession began over rival claimants to the Spanish throne, one backed by France and one supported by Britain. The war lasted from 1701 to 1713. The British colonists in North America called this war Queen Anne's War for the British monarch who ruled during this time. During this conflict, major battles took place between Spanish and British forces in Florida and the Carolinas. In the same period, battles continued to erupt between French and British forces in Canada and New England, with various Indian tribes allied on all sides.

Throughout the 1600s, the five nations of the Iroquois were firmly allied with the English against the French and France's Indian allies. In 1689, a leader of the Mohawks—one of the five Iroquois nations—said of his people that, "as they are one hand and soul

Map 4-5 French, English, and Spanish Claims, 1608.

Although it did not have the European population of the British colonies, New France, which was settled along the St. Lawrence River to the north and the Mississippi River to the west, was much larger than the British colonies. The large areas of land claimed by France along with the area of Florida claimed by Spain prevented British colonies from growing further and created hostile tensions.

with the English, they will take up the ax with pleasure against the French." By the beginning of Queen Anne's War, however, some Iroquois were beginning to believe that their alliance with the English meant that the Iroquois did all the fighting but received little in return. In 1701, Iroquois leaders signed a separate treaty of peace with the French that gave them new trading rights, especially at French-owned Detroit.

For the next several decades, most of the Iroquois tried to keep clear of the continuing British–French tensions. Some Mohawks had different ideas, however. Despite their long alliance with the English, a group of Mohawks settled near Montreal in French Canada and converted to Catholicism. Among these settlements were also settlements of refugees from non-Iroquois tribes who had been defeated in King Philip's War (1675–1676). These refugees harbored an intense dislike of the English, especially the English in Massachusetts. They and their Canadian-based Iroquois allies nurtured a desire to show their support for France and seek revenge on Massachusetts for the loss of Indian lives in King Philip's War.

In February 1704, Canadian-based Mohawks destroyed the town of Deerfield, Massachusetts. Fifty colonists were killed, and perhaps seventy more were taken captive. By the end of the day, the town was a burning ruin. Deerfield's Congregational minister, Reverend John Williams, as well as his wife and remaining children, were taken hostage after one of the children was killed in the attack. His wife died on the forced march to Canada where the captives were taken. Eventually, Massachusetts officials ransomed Williams and most of the captives. The minister wrote an account of the attack and his captivity that became a best seller at the time.

To the utter surprise of Rev. Williams and the Massachusetts officials, however, some of the Deerfield captives preferred to stay in Canada with the Mohawks. Among them was Eunice Williams, the minister's daughter. She married a Mohawk, changed her name to A'ongote Gannenstenhawi, converted to Catholicism, and was the mother of three children raised in the Mohawk community. She lived a long life among her adopted community and died there in 1785 at the age of ninety-five.

Even when there were periods of relative peace among the European powers, Indian tribes fought their own battles with the colonists. As white settlement expanded in the Carolinas, the Tuscarora tribe began to resist. In 1711, the Tuscaroras captured a leader of Swiss and German immigrants, Christoph von Graffenried, and the Carolina surveyor-general, John Lawson. Graffenried was freed, but the Tuscarora executed Lawson. In response, the South Carolina authorities declared war on the Tuscarora and enlisted another tribe, the Yamasee, as their allies. Within two years, most Tuscarora villages were burned, and a thousand of its tribe were killed. The remaining Tuscaroras moved west to avoid white settlement and, seeking further protection, affiliated with the Iroquois in 1722, enlarging the Iroquois League to six nations rather than five.

After the war, the Yamasees expected to be rewarded by the Carolina authorities for supporting their efforts. When no rewards were forthcoming, and when whites continued taking Yamasees as slaves, the Yamasees, in alliance with the Creeks, attacked Carolina plantations, killing settlers and traders in one of the bloodiest wars in colonial history. For a time, it was unclear whether the Carolina colony would survive, but officials sought an alliance with the powerful Cherokees, who had become dependent on trade with the British for the clothes and rifles. The Cherokees quickly defeated the Yamasees. Those Creeks and Yamasees who survived fled to Spanish Florida, leaving virtually no Yamasees or Creeks in the Carolinas. The British community also suffered significant loss of life in the **Yamasee Wars**, but it was clear they were the victors.

In 1739, after twenty-five years of peace between the major European powers that held claims in North America, Britain and Spain again went to war—the so-called War of Jenkins' Ear—when Spain claimed a right to search British ships in the Caribbean for contraband goods and Britain objected. (The odd nickname for the war referred to a British ship's captain, Robert Jenkins, whose ear was cut off by a Spanish boarding party.) The British defeated Spain in this war, which confirmed the dominance of British sea power in the Atlantic and Caribbean and made colonial trade with Britain and Britain's Caribbean colonies much easier for American colonists.

Before the war of 1739 with Spain had ended, Britain and France were fighting again in the War of the Austrian Succession (referred to as King George's War in North America). Much of New York and New England was engulfed in that war. The result, again, was modest victories and land transfers, but with considerable loss of life to British and French colonists and to their Indian allies.

By 1754, another war erupted, known in Europe as the Seven Years' War and in British North America as the French and Indian War. Unlike the previous wars, the British would be decisively victorious at the end of the French and Indian War in 1763 (see Chapter 5). However, as you will see, the consequences of expanding the British Empire in North America would be significant.

The many wars between 1689 and 1763 (see Table 4-2) disrupted life in North America. Colonial militias were called up. Colonial shipping was attacked. Settlements of colonists and Indians were damaged or ruined. Indian alliances shifted. Various tribes were either

Yamasee Wars

Yamasee Wars (1715–1717) involved a federation of several tribes, many of whom had previously been allied with the British, in an effort to drive all whites out of South Carolina. After huge losses on both sides, some of the Yamasee allies sought peace while most others fled much farther south and west.

Table 4-2　Wars in British North America between 1689 and 1763

Dates	Who Fought	Name of War in North America	Name of War in Britain	Impact/Outcome
1689–1697	English and British colonies allied with Iroquois against France, New France, and Indian allies	King William's War	War of the League of Augsburg or War of the Grand Alliance	Considerable devastation, especially in Maine; no border changes as a result
1702–1713	Same as King William's War, with Spain joining as an ally of France	Queen Anne's War	War of Spanish Succession	Primarily fought in Europe, also in New England (against French Canada) and the Carolinas (against Spanish Florida); France and Spain determine to create Gulf colonies—New Orleans and San Antonio
1739–1742	Britain against Spain; France remained neutral	War of Jenkins' Ear		Fought mostly in the Caribbean, though Georgia-based forces attacked Saint Augustine in Spanish Florida
1744–1748	Britain against France	King George's War	War of Austrian Succession	French forces attacked and destroyed communities in New York; significant loss of life in New York and New England
1754–1763	Britain against France and Spain with important Indian allies	French and Indian War	Seven Years' War	Largest war; Britain wins control of all of French Canada

4.1

4.2

4.3

decimated or fled their homelands. Many colonists and Indians died, and for many of those who survived, life was far from secure.

The Unifying Effects of the Wars on British Colonies

During the wars of the 1700s, many English colonists developed a deep sense of patriotism to the British cause, often linked to an equally strong dislike of all things French and of the Indian nations allied with France. At the same time, they came to realize that the British army was sometimes far away when it was most needed and that they needed to develop their own militias to protect themselves. The British monarchs were distracted by these wars and were inclined to neglect the colonies in the intervening years. As a result, colonial governments grew stronger and more independent.

For most of his life, Benjamin Franklin was a loyal subject of the British Empire. In 1754, Franklin wrote that his greatest desire was for the people of Great Britain and the people of Britain's American colonies to "learn to consider themselves, not as belonging to different

Even as late as 1774, Benjamin Franklin, shown here with members of Parliament, considered himself a loyal British subject, trying his best to reduce tensions between the colonies and the authorities in London.

Huntington Library/SuperStock

Communities with different Interests, but to one Community with one Interest." In 1754, many colonists agreed with Franklin.

By the early 1750s, it was also clear to many in British North America that the tension between England and France, which was playing out on both sides of the Atlantic, would soon lead to another war. In the early summer of 1754, several of the North American colonial governments appointed commissioners to meet in Albany, New York, to negotiate stronger mutual defense treaties with the Six Nations of the Iroquois and to discuss the common defense of the British colonies. Benjamin Franklin, one of Pennsylvania's four commissioners, wanted far more. He arrived in Albany with a plan for "one general government [that] may be formed in America, including all the said colonies." The particulars of the **Albany Plan of Union**, as it came to be known, included a provision that each colony would retain its own government, but that the new united colonies would be led by a council of representatives from the thirteen colonies and a single "president general" appointed by the crown. The unified government would have authority to raise soldiers, build forts, and regulate trade with the Indians. It would help the thirteen colonies realize Franklin's dream of being "one community with one interest." Franklin said, if the Iroquois "should be capable of forming a Scheme for such an Union," he could not understand why "a like Union should be impracticable for ten or a Dozen English Colonies."

In fact, Franklin's proposed plan, though supported by the commissioners who met in June and July 1754, was defeated resoundingly by the colonies. Every colonial legislature rejected the plan, fearing it meant giving up too much control to other colonies and especially to the crown, who would appoint the leader. At the same time, officials in London rejected the plan because they saw it giving too much power to the colonies. They preferred to have each colony accountable separately to London. Nevertheless, quite a few colonial leaders met each other for the first time at the Albany gathering, and the possibility of union had been mentioned and considered.

Tensions continued to grow between Britain and France and between Britain's Iroquois allies and the tribes allied with the French forces. As the British colonies saw the world moving toward a war between Great Britain and France—a war they knew would be fought in large part on the border between British North America and New France—colonial legislatures sought to raise taxes to provide for their defense. This need was especially urgent in Pennsylvania where Indians, allied with France, had defeated several western settlements and were within a day's distance of Philadelphia itself.

Even in this desperate situation, however, the Penn family, which still controlled the colony, refused to allow their own lands to be taxed. Although William Penn had founded the colony as a refuge for persecuted Quakers, his son Thomas saw it mostly as a source of income. By 1757, the Pennsylvania legislature decided to send a delegation to England to negotiate directly with Thomas Penn to get him to pay his fair share of the funds to protect his colony or, if that failed, to request the English government to give them a royal governor rather than one appointed by the Penn family. The obvious representative for Pennsylvania to send was Benjamin Franklin. The fifty-one-year-old Franklin sailed for England that summer and, except for brief trips home, lived there until 1775. He did not get the funds from Penn but enjoyed London and, for many years, remained a very loyal British subject, even attending the coronation of King George III in 1760. However, beginning in the early 1760s, the pressure of war as well as issues of politics, trade, and taxes began to drive Britain and the colonists apart.

Albany Plan of Union

Plan put forward in 1754 by Massachusetts governor William Shirley, Benjamin Franklin, and other colonial leaders, calling for an intercolonial union to manage defense and Indian affairs.

4.3 Quick Review

How did multiple wars between Great Britain, France, and Spain affect life in British North America? To what degree did they draw colonists closer to Britain? How did they make colonists more independent and distrusting of Britain?

Conclusion

The Glorious Revolution of 1689 changed the balance of power in England's government. Although kings and queens continued to be much more than figureheads, Parliament assumed much greater control. In 1707, England united with Scotland to become Great Britain, and over the course of the 1700s, the wars Britain conducted around the world with its old enemies France and Spain would, in North America, involve Native Americans allied with each one of them. Great Britain enforced mercantilism, a closed economic system that allowed for trade only between the colonies and the mother country. This system was designed to ensure the colonies supplied Great Britain with raw materials; in return, the colonies did not manufacture their own goods or buy them on a world market but, rather, purchased manufactured goods only from Great Britain. Nevertheless, Britain's American colonies grew and prospered with thriving port cities and an emerging colonial elite who sometimes became quite good at evading the British government's regulations.

After the 1680s, the wealthy elite of Virginia and Maryland began to use more slaves and fewer indentured servants. The southern colonies, where the greatest growth of the slave population was taking place, enacted laws that created a slave society in which African slaves could expect a lifetime of servitude while the slave-plantation economy created a rigid social hierarchy with a few white men at the top and almost everyone else living in various degrees of dependence on them.

At the same time, diverse underlying tensions in New England led to the Salem witch trials that involved an entire community in hysterical accusations, legal actions, and twenty executions.

Women's roles were largely relegated to the private realm—raising children and working in the home. Rural women often led lonely lives with few opportunities to connect with other women. Urban women had more options to socialize, particularly in the trade of household necessities such as preserved foods, soap, and candles. Some women joined their husbands as part of the privileged social and economic elite of the colonies.

From the first settlement in British North America onward, many colonists maintained a sense that somehow their new land was a divinely planned opportunity to begin the world again and make it right. By the early 1700s, however, the sense of being on a divine mission had declined, and tolerance for religious diversity was growing. With the coming of the European Enlightenment, people in Europe and in the colonies began to look more to science and human reason than to faith in trying to understand their world. Many ministers worried about a religious decline in the colonies, and some sought ways to release religious energy, spawning the First Great Awakening. Yet other colonists came to a growing regard for other forms of self-improvement and interest such as those championed by Benjamin Franklin in his *Poor Richard's Almanack*. Increasingly, in spite of philosophical differences, colonists came to regard themselves as Americans and less as British subjects living on a different side of the Atlantic Ocean.

Chapter Review

How did events throughout the 1700s transition the North American colonies from separate entities into colonies with more common pursuits and new and conflicted ideas about their relationship with Great Britain itself?

Chapter 4 Summary and Review

England's Glorious Revolution and "the Rights of Englishmen," 1689

4.1 **Analyze the impact of England's Glorious Revolution on the thinking and political organization of British colonists in North America.**

Summary

The twenty-five years between 1675 and 1700 were times of turmoil in England and its North American colonies. King James II expanded religious freedom for Catholics and moved to assert royal authority in the colonies. In 1689, Parliament forced James II from the throne and invited his daughter, Mary, and her husband, the Dutch prince William of Orange, to take his place, an event known as the Glorious Revolution. One effect was that Parliament emerged as the supreme political force in England after 1689. The philosopher John Locke justified the revolution by insisting that all government rested on the rights of the governed. In England's American colonies, news of the Glorious Revolution brought general rejoicing. Nonetheless, the Glorious Revolution produced winners and losers in the colonies. Independent corporations and colonial proprietors faced a decline in power. Catholics lost political rights, and all Protestants gained rights. In all colonies, social and economic mobility declined, and an English colonial elite came to dominate colonial life.

Review Question

1. Causation
   What impact did the Glorious Revolution have on the political landscape of British North America?

The Plantation World: From a Society with Slaves to a Slave Society

4.2 **As the English colonies, like other European empires, participated in the Atlantic slave trade and developed a system of slavery that reflected the specific economic, demographic, and geographic characteristics of the colonies, explain why and how slavery developed as it did in North America in the late 1600s and early 1700s.**

Summary

An important effect of Bacon's Rebellion was that the planter elite began to replace indentured servants with slaves. At the same time, they wrote new slave codes that more clearly made slavery an inherited and permanent status. As the institution of slavery came to be more rigidly defined over time, it also came to be linked more closely to race. In addition, the numbers of African slaves rose dramatically as slavery became institutionalized. All in all, some ten to fifteen million Africans were forced across the Atlantic between 1500 and 1900; most were sent to island plantations and only a fraction came to the mainland British colonies. The Middle Passage—the transit of slaves from Africa to the Americas—was a horrifying experience. Slaves were treated as property, not as people. By the early 1700s, a small group of plantation owners controlled nearly all aspects of life in the southern colonies. It was a society in which slaves were given no respect, a few wealthy whites had unlimited power, and the institution of slavery defined the social order. As more white colonists came to depend on slave labor for their growing prosperity, they also lived in constant fear of slave revolts, revolts that were far from uncommon in all of the colonies.

Review Questions

2. Continuity and Change over Time
   How and why did the relationship between slavery and race in British North America change between 1650 and 1750?

3. Contextualization
   Describe the sequence of events that took the typical African slave from his or her homeland to the Americas. What physical and psychological hardships did slaves experience during this journey?

Stability and Instability in the American and British Worlds

4.3 **Analyze the changes in the ideas and daily lives of the people in British North America in the 1700s as colonial residents also participated in political, social, cultural, and economic exchanges with Great Britain that encouraged both stronger bonds with Britain and resistance to Britain's control.**

Summary

Colonial life, though far more settled in the 1700s than it had been in the 1600s, was still full of uncertainty and change. The hysteria that led to the Salem witch trials in the 1690s reflected deep-seated fears that were just under the surface of much of colonial society. By the middle of the 1700s, the white culture of British North America was generally divided between the public and private realms. Many white women, generally relegated to the private realm, lived particularly isolated lives, especially in rural areas. Although most Americans lived on farms, colonial America's cities were quickly growing. What had largely been a mercantilist economy began to shift over time toward a capitalist economy during the first half of the 1700s. In contrast, the British economy remained firmly rooted in mercantilist principles, which created tensions between colonists and British officials. The changing colonial economy led to the emergence of a middle class. During this period, religious enthusiasm declined as the colonies became more religiously diverse. The Great Awakening, a series of religious revivals that swept all of the North American colonies in the late 1730s, reflected the desire of many for a more direct and emotional Christian experience. Adding to the uncertainty of the period was the fact that, between 1689 and 1815, England and France were engaged in more or less a continual series of wars with each other for control of global empires. For those living in North America, each war involved not only international struggles but also local battles with Indian tribes that were in their own shifting alliances with European powers. During the 1700s, these wars deepened the patriotic commitment of many English colonists to Britain. At the same time, those wars led to a growing sense of independence in colonial governments.

Review Questions

4. Contextualization

How would you characterize the lives of women in British North America—both free and enslaved—in the first half of the 1700s? What are the limits of those generalizations?

5. Causation

How do you explain why the Great Awakening emerged as a religious movement in the 1730s? And what effects does it have on American colonists?

1. Preparing to Write: Support Your Assertion

Short-Answer Question—Use Map 4-2 to answer (a) and (b).

a. Briefly explain ONE major economic cause that contributed to the emergence of the patterns depicted in the map.

b. Briefly explain ONE major social effect that resulted from the patterns depicted in the map.

Short-Answer Questions come in three parts, but for now you are asked to take on only two. You can write all parts in one paragraph if you think that would be a stronger response, but most students separate their response to answer each question individually. Short-Answer Questions demand direct assertions and then specific evidence to support them. For each question above, start by responding to the question with specific evidence in one sentence. Then add about two more sentences to explain your assertion.

2. Preparing to Write: Develop Your Thesis

Long Essay Question—Evaluate the extent of differences in British and American colonial views of mercantilism from 1689 to 1754.

When a prompt asks you to evaluate the extent of anything, imagine a continuum running from "Not at all" to "Totally." Then you are to pick a point along the continuum that reflects the historical reality. For this prompt, what seems to be driving such a difference in perspective? This answer might be the basis of your argument.

Section I: Multiple-Choice Questions

Questions 2.1–2.2 refer to the following excerpt.

"[I]t is a great result that the French have won the confidence and friendliness of the Savages, through the great familiarity and frequent intercourse which they have had with them. … At first they fled from us, and feared us; now they wish us with them … [T]hese Savages, having (as they supposed,) some advantage over the English, threw themselves upon them with fury, thinking, I believe, to get revenge for the injury that had been done us. … Likewise, towards the end of the year 1611, the Hollanders merely wishing to land at Cap de la Heve to take in some fresh water, our Savages assailed them fiercely, and made away with six of them, among whom was the Captain of the ship. It seems to me that we will be unworthy of this friendliness, if we do not so act that it may avail them in learning to love him, from whom we receive all our blessings. … Thank God this much has already been accomplished, that they do not wish to die without baptism …"

— *The Jesuit Relations of New France,* 1616

2.1 The excerpt best reflects which of the following developments from this time period?

 a. The goals and interests of European leaders and colonists diverged at that time.

 b. Conflicts over land and resources led to King Philip's War.

 c. Interactions between Europeans and American Indians often led to alliances.

 d. The resistance of American Indians to Dutch colonizing efforts led to major Dutch concessions.

2.2 In highlighting that "they do not wish to die without baptism," the text was referring most directly to

 a. successful French efforts to convert American Indians to Christianity

 b. hopes of including American Indians in the Great Awakening

 c. American Indian insistence on maintaining their traditional religion

 d. an American Indian custom when it comes to military conflicts

Questions 2.3–2.4 refer to the following excerpt.

"The first object which saluted my eyes when I arrived on the coast, was the sea, and a slave ship. … These filled me with astonishment, which was soon converted into terror, when I was carried on board. … I have seen coals of fire, glowing hot, put on a shovel and placed so near lips [of Negroes] as to scorch and burn them. And this has been accompanied with threats of forcing them to swallow the coals if they any longer persisted in refusing to eat. … As very few of the Negroes can so far [tolerate] the loss of their liberty and the hardships they endure, they are ever on the watch to take advantage of the least negligence in their oppressors. Insurrections are frequently the consequence. … They are likewise always ready to seize every opportunity for committing some acts of desperation to free themselves from their miserable state and notwithstanding the restraints which are laid, they often succeed."

— Olaudah Equiano, "The Interesting Narrative of the Life of Olaudah Equiano," or "Gustavus Vassa, The African," 1789

2.3 In the excerpt, Equiano was directly referring to a trend from the period in which

 a. the Columbian Exchange passed along disease in great numbers

 b. Africans developed overt and covert means to resist

 c. the Atlantic economy resulted in African traders receiving raw goods in exchange for enslaved Africans

 d. Europeans debated how people from other continents should be treated

2.4 What was the most common initial destination of Africans in the 1700s?

 a. New England

 b. New York

 c. West Indies

 d. South America

Questions 2.5–2.6 refer to the following excerpt.

"For the increase of the shipping and the encouragement of the navigation of this nation, which under the good providence and protection of God is so great a means of the welfare and safety of this Commonwealth: be it enacted by this present Parliament, and the authority thereof, that from and after the first day of December, one thousand six hundred fifty and one, and from thence forwards, no goods or commodities whatsoever of the growth, production or manufacture of Asia, Africa or America, or of any part thereof; or of any islands belonging to them … as well of the English plantations as others, shall be imported or brought into this Commonwealth of England, or into Ireland, or any other lands, islands, plantations, or territories to this Commonwealth belonging, or in their possession, in any other ship or ships, vessel or vessels whatsoever, but only in such as do truly and without fraud belong only to the people of this Commonwealth, or the plantations thereof, as the proprietors or right owners thereof. …"

— Scobell's Acts of Parliament, *Goods from Foreign Parts by Whom to Be Imported,* 1651

2.5 This document is most likely excerpted from which of the following documents?

   a. Mayflower Compact

   b. Fundamental Orders of Connecticut

   c. Molasses Act

   d. Navigation Act

2.6 This document is most closely associated with

   a. the Glorious Revolution

   b. mercantilism

   c. Bacon's Rebellion

   d. salutary neglect

Questions 2.7–2.8 refer to the following excerpt.

"Then one morning all on a Sudden, about 8 or 9 o'clock there came a messenger and said Mr. Whitefield preached at Hartford and Weathersfield yesterday and is to preach at Middletown this morning [October 23, 1740] at ten of the Clock. … When I saw Mr. White-field come upon the Scaffold he looked almost angelical, a young, slim slender youth before some thousands of people with a bold undaunted countenance, and my hearing how God was with him everywhere as he came along it solemnized my mind, and put me into a trembling fear before he began to preach; for he looked as if he was Cloathed with authority from the Great God, and a sweet solemn solemnity sat upon his brow. And my hearing him preach gave me a heart wound; by Gods blessing my old foundation was broken up, and I saw that my righteousness would not save me; then I was convinced of the doctrine of Election and went right to quarrelling with God about it, because all that I could do would not save me; and he had decreed from Eternity who should be saved and who not."

— **"The Spiritual Travels of Nathan Cole," 1741**

2.7 The quoted passage is associated with which colonial movement?

   a. Glorious Revolution

   b. Enlightenment

   c. Great Awakening

   d. Great Migration

2.8 Which of the following factors contributed most directly to the movement described in the excerpt?

   a. Increased American Indian attacks

   b. Decline in faith brought on by the Enlightenment

   c. Salutary neglect

   d. Glorious Revolution

Questions 2.9–2.10 refer to the following excerpt.

"Demographic conditions also shaped Chesapeake society during the seventeenth century. For one thing, life was short. A substantial number of immigrants died soon after they arrived, victims of a now vague complex of diseases that contemporaries called 'seasoning.' How many failed to live through the first year is unknown, but the figure was high enough to provoke frequent comment. And, although the chances of survival increased as the seventeenth century progressed, the Chesapeake colonies were considered dangerous to new arrivals as late as 1700, particularly during late summer. Many … who survived seasoning, furthermore, did not live to complete their terms."

— **Louis Green Carr and Russell R. Menard, historians, "Immigration and Opportunity," 1979**

2.9 Which group of immigrants is referred to in the excerpt?

   a. Puritans

   b. Indentured servants

   c. Africans

   d. Jesuit priests

2.10 Which crop was especially relevant to these immigrants?

   a. Sugar

   b. Rice

   c. Wheat

   d. Tobacco

Section II: Short-Answer Questions

Question 2.11 is based on the following two excerpts.

"If other colonies sought to escape from English vices, Virginians wished to fulfill English virtues. Let other colonies dazzle the world with a City upon a hill, inspire by a commonwealth of brotherly love, or encourage with a vast humanitarian experiment. The model in Virginians' heads was compounded of the actual features of a going community; the England, especially the rural England, of the 17th and 18th century. If Virginia was to be in any way better than England, it was not because Virginians pursued ideals which Englishmen did not have; rather that here were novel opportunities to realize the English Ideals."

— **Daniel J. Boorstin, historian, *The Colonial Experience*, 1958**

"The Plantation revolution came to the Chesapeake with the thunder of cannons and the rattle of sabers. Victory over the small holders, servants and slaves who composed Nathaniel Bacon's motley army in 1676 enabled planters to consolidate their control over Chesapeake society. In quick order, they elaborated a slave code that singled out people of African descent as slaves and made their status hereditary. In the years that followed, as the number of European servants declined and white farmers migrated west, the great planters turned to Africa for their work-force. During the last decades of the seventeenth century, the new order began to take shape. The Chesapeake's economy stumbled into the eighteenth century, but the grandees prospered, and the profits of slave labor filled their pockets. A society with slaves gave way to a slave society around the great estuary."

— **Ira Berlin, historian, *Many Thousands Gone: The First Two Centuries of Slavery in North America*, 1998**

2.11 Using the Boorstin and Berlin excerpts, answer (a), (b), and (c).

   a. Briefly explain ONE major difference between Boorstin's and Berlin's historical interpretations of colonial America.

   b. Briefly explain how ONE specific historical event or development during the 1600s and 1700s that is not mentioned directly in the excerpts could be used to support Boorstin's interpretation.

   c. Briefly explain how ONE specific historical event or development during the 1600s and 1700s that is not mentioned directly in the excerpts could be used to support Berlin's interpretation.

Question 2.12 refers to the image to the right.

2.12 Using the image above, answer (a), (b), and (c).

   a. Briefly explain the point of view expressed through the image about ONE of the following.
- Work, Exchange, and Technology
- Migration and Settlement
- Geography and the Environment

b. Explain how ONE element of the image expresses the historical theme you identified in part a.

c. Explain how the historical theme you identified in part (a) shaped patterns of colonial settlement from 1607 to 1754.

Library of Congress Prints & Photographs Division [LC-US262-45595]

Cartouche from map showing the inhabited part of Canada, 1777

Section III: Long Essay Question

Directions: Answer Question 2.13 **or** 2.14. (Suggested writing time: 40 minutes) In your response you should do the following.

- Respond to the prompt with a historically defensible thesis or claim that establishes a line of reasoning.
- Describe a broader historical context relevant to the prompt.
- Support an argument in response to the prompt using specific and relevant examples of evidence.
- Use historical reasoning (e.g., comparison, causation, continuity or change over time) to frame or structure an argument that addresses the prompt.

- Use evidence to corroborate, qualify, or modify an argument that addresses the prompt.

2.13 Evaluate the extent that lax British attention to the colonies contributed to traditions of self-government that developed in American colonies in the period 1607–1754.

2.14 Evaluate the extent that British conflicts with American Indians over land, resources, and political boundaries led to military confrontations in the period 1607–1754.

Section IV: Read on MyHistoryLab

Document-Based Question: Colonial Slavery in the South

Part 3

A New Birth of Freedom—Creating the United States of America 1754–1800

Design Pics/Newscom

Chapter 5
The Making of a Revolution 1754–1783

Private Collection/The Bridgeman Art Library

The opening shots of the American Revolution were fired at the Battles of Lexington and Concord on April 19, 1775. British troops, marching from Boston, fired on members of the Massachusetts militia attempting to block their way. In the first skirmish, shown here, more militia members were killed, but by the end of the day, far more British troops had lost their lives to militia soldiers who continued to harass and shoot at them from well-guarded positions.

Chapter Objective

Demonstrate an understanding of how Britain's victory over France in the war of 1754–1763 exacerbated the grievances of many colonists and led to renewed conflict culminating in the American Revolution.

 ## Learning Objectives

Preludes to Revolution

5.1 Explain Britain's victory over France in the French and Indian War (Seven Years' War) and what conflicts followed this victory.

"The Revolution was in the Minds of the People"

5.2 Explain why, in the fifteen years before the Revolutionary War began, support for the patriot cause spread so quickly among many different groups of North Americans who by 1775 opposed Britain for different reasons.

The War for Independence

5.3 Explain how political and military strategy, ideological support for the patriot cause, and American alliances with France and Spain led to an American victory in the war for independence in spite of the presence of a large bloc of Loyalist Americans and the overwhelming military might of Britain.

On May 28, 1754, George Washington, then a twenty-two-year-old gentleman farmer recently promoted to lieutenant colonel in the Virginia militia, and Tanaghrisson, an Iroquois chief, led a force of Virginia militia and Iroquois to attack French soldiers in what is now western Pennsylvania. The French troops had been sent from Fort Duquesne—modern Pittsburgh—to look for Washington's force. Fort Duquesne was part of a string of French forts built along the Ohio and Mississippi Rivers to maintain New France's claims in the region. From the French perspective, the English were trespassing. Washington, however, was asserting the British claim to the Ohio River Valley.

The English-Iroquois force surprised the French with a dawn attack. It had been raining and the French had failed to post sentries. Ten of the French were killed and twenty-two taken prisoner. The shots fired that May morning in what came to be called Jumonville Glen, after the French commander who was killed there, were among the first in a war that would have effects worldwide.

Washington knew that the French would look for him. He built a small armed camp that he named Fort Necessity. In July, fifty French soldiers and three hundred of their Indian allies forced Washington to surrender. The French allowed the English to return to Virginia but only after Washington signed a document admitting that he had attacked and killed—or assassinated, depending on how one translated the French—French troops in the May skirmish. That skirmish in western Pennsylvania helped provoke a world war in the 1750s, and that war had a profound and long-lasting impact in British North America.

Preludes to Revolution

5.1 **Explain Britain's victory over France in the French and Indian War (Seven Years' War) and what conflicts followed this victory.**

In North America, the war that started near Pittsburgh was known as the **French and Indian War**. In most of Europe, it was called the Seven Years' War. Because of its outcome, French Canadians came to call it the War of Conquest. Whatever the war was called, it was

During the war of 1754–1763, known as the French and Indian War in British North America, British troops—some under the command of Virginia militia colonel George Washington—fighting alongside their Iroquois allies, battled French troops and their Ottawa, Delaware, and Shawnee allies. In this illustration from the late 1800s, Native Americans allied with the French, fire on British troops in one of the many battle of the war. The ultimate British victory in the war changed the face, and the politics, of North America.

Glasshouse Images / Alamy Stock Photo

Significant Dates

1754–1763	French and Indian War
1763–1766	Pontiac's Rebellion
	Paxton Boys attack Pennsylvania Indians
1765	Stamp Act crisis
Mid-1760s	Regulator movement in North and South Carolina
1770	Boston Massacre
1772	Slavery is declared illegal in England
1773	Boston Tea Party
1774	Closing of the Port of Boston, Quebec Act and other Intolerable Acts
	First Continental Congress meets in Philadelphia
1775	First battles of the Revolution at Lexington and Concord
	Second Continental Congress convenes at Philadelphia
	Battle of Bunker Hill
	British governor of Virginia, Lord Dunmore, declares freedom for slaves that join the British cause
1776	Thomas Paine's *Common Sense*
	British evacuate Boston but take New York City
	Congress adopts the Declaration of Independence
	Washington's troops capture Trenton, New Jersey

(continued)

French and Indian War

Known in Europe as the Seven Years' War and in French Canada as the War of Conquest, this war was fought in North America between 1754 and 1763 and ended with the defeat of the French.

5.1

5.2

5.3

truly a world war, fought over more of the planet than any previous war. The voyages of Columbus and subsequent maritime trade and migrations had created a vast interactive world, and in 1756, that world exploded.

The French and Indian War, 1754–1763

In North America, the formal declaration of war in 1756—two years after Washington's skirmish with the French—surprised no one. After Jumonville Glen, the English and their Iroquois allies were in constant tension with the French and their Ottawa, Delaware, and Shawnee allies. Both sides hated each other and were ready for war.

Britain and France were also sliding toward war in Europe, Asia, Africa, and the Caribbean. In January 1756, England and the German kingdom of Prussia agreed to defend each other's territory. In response, Austria signed a treaty with France. War among these countries was declared in May 1756, and the French navy defeated a British fleet in the Mediterranean the next month. Counting on his English allies to provide support, King Frederick the Great of Prussia then attacked Austria and Russia. Sweden and Saxony joined the French alliance against Prussia.

The war quickly spread to Asia. The British East India Company and the French Compagnie des Indes each controlled parts of the Indian subcontinent, either directly or through alliances with local rulers. Suraj ud Dowlah, the ruler of Bengal, who was allied with France, used the situation to attack and capture British Calcutta. A British force under Robert Clive retook the city and the French post at Chandernagor. British control of Bengal, won in that war, laid the foundation for Britain's 200-year rule in India.

The British also attacked the main African slave-trading island of Goree off the coast of Senegal and took control of it from the French, though the slave trade on the island continued as before. Goree had been the port for transshipment of slaves since the Portuguese founded it in the 1500s, and no matter which government controlled the island, merchants from many nations purchased slaves there.

Much of the war was fought in the Caribbean. British warships based in Jamaica captured the French islands of Grenada, the Grenadines, St. Vincent, Dominica, and Tobago as well as Martinique and Guadeloupe with their rich sugar plantations. At the war's end in 1763, Martinique and Guadeloupe were returned to France in exchange for concessions in North America, but the British kept the remaining islands. After Spain entered the war on the side of France in 1761, the British captured Havana, Cuba, and Manila in the Philippines, all of which were returned to Spain in 1763 in exchange for Spanish Florida.

The war changed the landscape of North America (see Maps 5-1 and 5-2). In 1758, after a French force defeated the English at Fort Ticonderoga in New York, a British force—with George Washington as one of its officers—took Fort Duquesne, renaming it Fort Pitt (today's Pittsburgh) in honor of William Pitt, who led Britain as prime minister during the war. That same year, Teedyuscung, leader of the Delaware tribe, decided that his French allies could not be trusted and sought an alliance with the English and the Iroquois. Although Teedyuscung and the Delaware did not get the Pennsylvania lands they sought, they and the Iroquois received a British promise that after the war there would be no white settlement west of the Alleghenies—a promise the British attempted to keep until the American Revolution.

In the most significant North American battle, a British army under General James Wolfe defeated a French army led by the Marquis de Montcalm and captured Quebec, the capital of French Canada, in September 1759. The British victory ended French control of all of Canada.

By the early 1760s, both Britain and France were exhausted from the fighting. Although Britain had won major victories, its new king, George III (r. 1760–1820) wanted peace, and in 1763, the two countries signed the Treaty of Paris to end the war. (Both this treaty and the later treaty ending the American Revolution in 1783 were known as the Treaty of Paris.)

The world war had many outcomes. All of the governments that fought the war emerged deeply in debt. In Europe, little land changed hands, but in other parts of the world, the changes were dramatic. Britain made concessions to bring hostilities to an end but was still the biggest winner. Its dominance of India was secure, and the British presence on the coast of Africa and in the Caribbean was enhanced. In addition, Spain ceded Florida to England. Most significantly, the war eliminated France as a North American power. Although France did regain its control of the rich sugar-producing islands of Guadeloupe and Martinique in the Caribbean, France ceded Canada and the land east of the Mississippi River to the British. To compensate its Spanish allies for their support, France also ceded its claim to the lands west of the Mississippi River, along with New Orleans, to Spain. The French threat to New England and New York ended. At the war's end, Britain controlled most of North America east of the Mississippi River.

Pontiac and Indian Responses

For American Indians living between the Mississippi River and the Atlantic, the French and Indian War was an unmitigated disaster. As a British official had said, "To preserve the balance between us and the French is the great ruling principle of the modern Indian politics." For the tribes farther south—including the Cherokee and Creeks—the Spanish presence in Florida had allowed them to play a three-way balancing act between Britain, France, and Spain. But with the French and Spanish out of eastern North America for the time being, the potential for bargaining virtually disappeared.

Although the Iroquois were allied with the British, the cost to them was high. Iroquois power had come from Britain's need for them as allies in its competition with the French. After 1763, the French were gone. At the war's beginning, the Iroquois Chief Hendrick, or Theyanoguin, had told the representatives of the British colonies who met at Albany, New York:

> Brethren—The Governor of Virginia and the Governor of Canada, are both quarrelling. … The Governor of Virginia and Pennsylvania have made paths thro' our Country … they should have first asked our consent.

Without the presence of the French in Canada, the British governors of Virginia and Pennsylvania had little reason to ask the Iroquois for consent to anything. The British general Lord Jeffrey Amherst, seeking to save money for his government, refused to provide the gifts of ammunition and gunpowder that various tribes had come to see as a kind of rent for the use of their lands. The Indians considered this refusal an insult and a fundamental threat since the tribes' survival depended on the gunpowder to hunt deer.

For the Indians who had sided with the French, the outlook was even worse. Neolin, a Delaware, living on the Ohio River, preached resistance to the "dogs clothed in red" as he called the British. His visionary message, calling on the Indians to return to the "original state that they were in before the white people found out their country," sparked a wide-ranging Indian movement to return to former Indian ways.

Pontiac, an Ottawa chief, heeded Neolin's call, sparking what came to be known as **Pontiac's Rebellion**. In the spring of 1763, only months after the Treaty of Paris was signed, Pontiac convened a meeting of Ottawa, Chippewa, Pottawatomi, and Wyandot people near Detroit. Pontiac told his listeners that, if they would cleanse themselves of the ways of the whites, they would see their lands and old powers restored. He insisted, "It is important for us, my brothers, that we exterminate from our lands this nation which seeks only to destroy us."

When Pontiac and his followers attacked, the British were able to hold Detroit and Fort Pitt, but Fort Miamis, near Fort Wayne, Indiana; Fort Ouiatenon, near Lafayette, Indiana; Fort Michilimackinac on the Great Lakes; and most of the old French posts in Indiana and

SOI-EN-GA-RAH-TA, OR KING HENDRICK.

On stone by A. Newsam.   P. S. Duval & Son's Lith. Phil.

Hendrick, a chief of the Mohawk tribe—one of the nations of the Iroquois—was a close ally of the British until killed in battle in 1755.

Pontiac's Rebellion

Indian uprising (1763–1766) led by Pontiac of the Ottawas and Neolin of the Delawares.

Map 5-1 North America before and during the French and Indian War, 1754–1763.

Maps 5-1 and 5-2 show the extraordinary changes brought about by the French and Indian War of 1754–1763. Map 5-1 shows the relatively limited range of control exercised by both the British and the French colonies in North America when the war began, as well as significant battles between the powers.

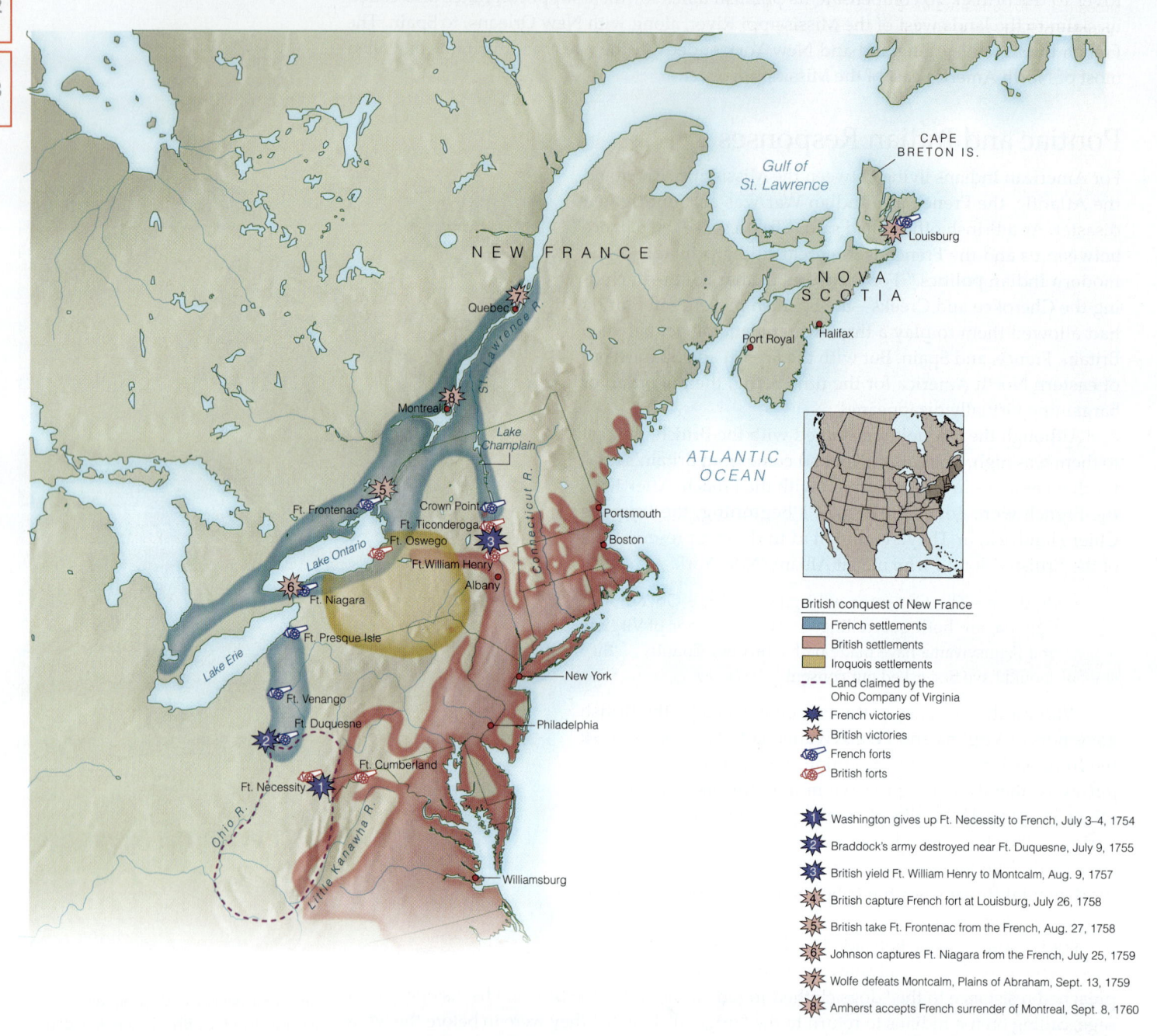

British conquest of New France

▮ French settlements
▮ British settlements
▮ Iroquois settlements
- - - Land claimed by the Ohio Company of Virginia
✴ French victories
✴ British victories
French forts
British forts

1 Washington gives up Ft. Necessity to French, July 3–4, 1754

2 Braddock's army destroyed near Ft. Duquesne, July 9, 1755

3 British yield Ft. William Henry to Montcalm, Aug. 9, 1757

4 British capture French fort at Louisburg, July 26, 1758

5 British take Ft. Frontenac from the French, Aug. 27, 1758

6 Johnson captures Ft. Niagara from the French, July 25, 1759

7 Wolfe defeats Montcalm, Plains of Abraham, Sept. 13, 1759

8 Amherst accepts French surrender of Montreal, Sept. 8, 1760

Ohio surrendered to the Indians. Most of the Ohio country was again in Indian hands. The English commander, Jeffrey Amherst, ordered his troops to put "every Indian in your Power to Death." Amherst also encouraged the distribution of smallpox-infected blankets to Indians, a move that rapidly spread the disease. In October, Pontiac received a letter from the French telling him that the French were not going to come to his aid. On receiving this news, Pontiac initiated a peace process. He met with the British authorities in Oswego, New York, in July 1766 and signed a treaty of peace. Three years later, he was murdered, probably by other Indians who resented both the deaths his rebellion had caused and his relatively quick surrender that meant the deaths were in vain.

Map 5-2 North America after the French and Indian War, 1763.

Maps 5-1 and 5-2 show the extraordinary changes brought about by the French and Indian War of 1754–1763. Map 5-2 shows the huge expanse of territory claimed by the British at the war's end in 1763, including the thirteen colonies along the Atlantic coast, the large Indian reserve of land promised to the tribes that had supported the British, the former French colonies in Canada, and the former Spanish colonies of East and West Florida that were also in British hands.

Thinking Historically

Pontiac's Vision

Seeking support for an uprising, Pontiac described a vision in which the Master of Life or the Great Spirit told him to cleanse his people and their land of the ways of the whites:

This land where ye dwell I have made for you and not for others. Whence comes it that ye permit the Whites upon your lands? Can ye not live without them? I know that those whom ye call the children of your Great Father supply your needs, but if ye were not evil, as ye are, ye could surely do without them. Ye could live as ye did live before knowing them—before those whom ye call your brothers had come upon your lands.

Thinking Critically

1. **Causation**
   How did the British victory in the war of 1756–1763 led Pontiac to fight the British?

2. **Argument Development**
   What issues and evidence would you want to include in your causation argument?

The Proclamation Line of 1763

After the long French and Indian War, the new British monarch King George III and his first minister George Grenville tried to ensure peace in North America. They meant to honor the commitments they had made in 1758 to the Delaware and Iroquois tribes and protect them from white settlement. Already embroiled in Pontiac's conflict, which largely involved formerly French allies, they did not want other rebellions, and they were wary that land-hungry settlers would quickly begin to expand into Indian-dominated areas. It was not a foolish worry. Newer European immigrants to North America, especially the Scots-Irish and Germans pushed farther into the frontier in search of new lands beyond the more settled and crowded coastal communities. They saw no reason to stop pushing and many moved well beyond the official limits of white territory in the 1760s. In October 1763, the king issued a proclamation that there should be no British settlement west of the crest of the Appalachian Mountains and that Indian rights to western lands would be protected forever. The proclamation also directed any colonists who had already settled in these lands "forthwith to remove themselves from such Settlements." For many of the tribes who lived on the western slopes of the mountains and beyond, the **Proclamation Line** fulfilled what they believed they had been promised. For white settlers on the frontier, it was a betrayal of their rights. As one said, "It was against the laws of God and nature that so much land should be idle, while so many Christians wanted to labor on it, and to raise their bread."

The Grenville administration took other steps to keep peace with the Indians. They replaced Amherst with the more conciliatory General Thomas Gage, who immediately resumed negotiations and gift giving with the tribes. The Grenville administration also strengthened the authority of the superintendents of Indian affairs, who had sought accommodations with the tribes since the 1750s.

The Proclamation Line slowed white settlement into western Pennsylvania, Ohio, and what would become Kentucky. But it also infuriated the British colonists—both land-hungry farmers and rich speculators—and did far too little to protect the Indians. Grenville and Parliament were too far away, and despite the British military outposts, their efforts to enforce the line were ineffectual, which had fateful consequences in the next decade.

Proclamation Line

Royal proclamation of 1763 designed to protect Indian tribes by setting a boundary at the peaks of the Appalachian Mountains beyond which no western white settlement was to take place.

The Paxton Boys and Rural White Responses

In the town of Paxton in Pennsylvania's Lancaster County, a group of farmers decided that the way to end warfare between whites and Indians on the frontier was to get rid of all Indians, whether they had been allied with the British or the French. Calling themselves the Paxton Boys or the Hickory Boys, these frontier vigilantes said:

We have long been convinced from sufficient evidence that the Indians that lived as independent commonwealths among us or near our borders were our most dangerous enemies.

In December 1763, the Paxton Boys attacked a Delaware village, killed six people, and burned the town. Then they killed fourteen Indian survivors who were in protective custody in the town of Lancaster. They began a march to Philadelphia to find other Indians, especially Delawares, who had taken refuge there. Before the mob got to Philadelphia, Benjamin Franklin led a delegation of the colony's leading citizens that negotiated an end to the rebellion, but the hatred of Indians would haunt the inhabitants of North America for a long time to come.

After 1763, many white residents of British North America began to lump all American Indians together as an enemy race, even though their parents and grandparents had viewed different tribes quite separately, viewing some as foes and some as friends depending on a tribe's relationship to the British cause. Even in the French and Indian War, the fighting was between the British with their Iroquois allies on one side and the French with the Ojibwa, Ottawa, Shawnee, and Wyandot as their allies. Soon after the war, the lines came to be seen quite differently and much more in racial terms, as many white residents of the British colonies came to see themselves as being united against virtually all Indians.

Threats of New Taxes

Relations between the British colonists and the American Indians were not the only concern of British authorities after 1763. Victory in the war had virtually drained the kingdom's treasury. Britain's national debt was double what it had been when the war began. In 1764, George Grenville and the majority in Parliament asked Britain's North American colonists to pay what the authorities in London thought was a fair share of the war's cost. Their argument was that the war had protected colonists far more than it had anyone living in Britain. What seemed just and equitable in London, however, was seen quite differently in the colonies. These differences on who should bear the cost of the war would soon have significant consequences.

> **5.1** Quick Review
>
> How did the war of 1756–1763 change the status and concerns of both European and Native Americans in North America?

"The Revolution Was in the Minds of the People"

5.2 Explain why, in the fifteen years before the Revolutionary War began, support for the patriot cause spread so quickly among many different groups of North Americans who by 1775 opposed Britain for different reasons.

Long after the Revolution was over, former president John Adams wrote to another former president, Thomas Jefferson, that "[t]he Revolution was in the minds of the people, and this was effected from 1760 to 1775, in the course of fifteen years before a drop of blood was shed at Lexington." He was right. For many British North Americans, a revolutionary change took place in their minds between 1760 and 1775. This change happened for many different reasons and in many different contexts.

While people like Adams and Jefferson and many of their peers moved from being loyal British subjects to revolutionary advocates of independence in those years, other colonial leaders did not. People such as Thomas Hutchinson of Massachusetts, William Franklin (Benjamin's son), and perhaps a fifth of the white colonists remained **Loyalists**— Americans who remained loyal to Great Britain and who opposed the American Revolution. For reasons of their own, a majority of African slaves were probably also Loyalists. The Loyalists lived through the same momentous changes as those who embraced the revolutionary cause, but they came to different conclusions. Still other colonists remained neutral throughout the struggle, focusing on personal matters or simply not caring who ultimately governed them.

Loyalists

The name given to those in the colonies—perhaps one-fifth to one-third of the total population—who supported the British and opposed American independence.

In addition, people in the colonies came to their own differing conclusions at varying times. Sailors and shop owners in Boston, New York, and Philadelphia as well as backwoods farmers in western Pennsylvania, Virginia, and the Carolinas were sometimes much more ready for revolution, much sooner, for their own differing reasons, than their better-known leaders.

For Africans, enslaved and free, the growing spirit of revolution held both potential and danger. Some saw in the revolutionary rhetoric the possibility of freedom and equality. In contrast, other African Americans saw the British government as a potential protector against slave owners who embraced the patriot cause, and even a liberator, although freedom was not guaranteed in any scenario.

The Iroquois, Cherokee, and other Indian tribes knew that frontier whites had little use for the king's ban on white settlement and, if freed from British authority, would stream west. As revolutionary fervor grew among frontier whites, it also fed fears among Indians, most of whom sided with the British after 1776.

In effect, during the fifteen fateful years (1760–1775) that John Adams described, many different people with wide-ranging hopes and fears considered the possibility of an American Revolution and arrived at their own conclusions. Those who embraced independence fought their own revolutions, sometimes in alliance with one another, sometimes acting at cross-purposes. Far from being clear, the goals and tactics of the revolutionaries were an ever-changing patchwork as different groups united in some ways and not in others.

Transition from the "Rights of Man" to Revolt

Many residents of the British colonies had grown up reading John Locke's defense of Britain's Glorious Revolution of 1689. Long before tensions between the colonies and the government in London reached a crisis, some colonists believed, as Locke said, that the people always retained "a supreme power to remove or alter the legislative" authority when they wanted to. Throughout the 1770s, Locke's ideas guided some of the Revolution's most articulate advocates such as Thomas Jefferson, John Adams, and Benjamin Franklin as well as backwoods rebels like Ethan Allen, a man of modest education who was the leader of Vermont's Green Mountain Boys. Using Locke's arguments in their speeches and lawsuits, they taunted royal governors, and ultimately justified armed resistance.

Revolutionary leaders also read and cited French philosophers—Voltaire, Rousseau, and Montesquieu—and authors from ancient Greece and Rome, all of whom advocated individual liberty and the need to overthrow unjust authorities. Leaders of the patriot cause became convinced that England represented the evils of empire while the colonists represented the virtues of **republicanism**, which gave much more emphasis to individual rights over hereditary privileges and supported a broad distribution of power to people, enabling them to determine how and by whom they would be governed.

Leaders on both sides of the Atlantic, those who argued for independence and those who argued to maintain the ties between Britain and the American colonies, all read the same literature. Nearly all of them believed that George III ruled only by the consent of Parliament, not from any sort of divine right. For a hundred years before the American Revolution, British subjects in the old and new worlds constituted a community of people who valued "the rights of Englishmen" and distrusted efforts to undermine those rights. When in 1776 Thomas Jefferson wrote that the colonies had a right to independence because it was a self-evident truth that "all men are created equal; that they are endowed by their creator with certain unalienable rights," he was reflecting a way of thinking that was familiar in America and Britain.

Those who shared common ideas about rights, liberty, and freedom extended beyond just residents of Britain and North America. The world that was at war in the 1750s and 1760s became a world involved in revolution in the 1770s and 1780s and beyond. Although the government of the King Louis XVI of France would play an essential role in the American victory, Louis XVI himself would lose his throne and his head to a French revolution

Republicanism

A complex, changing body of ideas, values, and assumptions that held that self-government by the citizens of a country, or their representatives, provided a more reliable foundation for the good society and individual freedom than rule by kings or any other distant elite.

within the next decade. The French and American Revolutions led to further revolutionary efforts across much of Europe as people in Germany, Poland, Scandinavia, and Italy attempted their own revolutions. Future president James Madison wrote in 1792 that "America has set the example and France has followed it, of charters of power granted by liberty."

Madison did not, however, mention another revolution that was much closer to the United States than those in Europe. In 1791, slaves in the French colony of Saint Domingue (modern Haiti) rebelled. Saint Domingue was one of the richest and most oppressive slave systems in the world, where some 500,000 African slaves grew sugar and coffee that made the 40,000 French owners very rich. A free black, Toussaint L'Ouverture—who quoted the same philosophers as North American revolutionaries—led the rebels in Haiti to win a series of victories. L'Ouverture himself was captured and died in France, but a new free Republic of Haiti was proclaimed in 1804. The rebellion was the most successful slave revolt in history and another in a long line of revolutions against distant authorities.

In addition, not long after the American Revolution, between 1810 and 1826, most of Latin America expelled its Spanish and Portuguese colonial masters. Simón Bolívar led revolutionary movements in his native Venezuela and helped establish the Republics of Colombia, Ecuador, Peru, and Bolivia. His 1812 *Manifesto of Cartagena* expressed the same philosophical ideas as those of his counterparts in North America and Europe. The American Revolution, then, was part of a worldwide revolution against distant authorities and old ideas, and it was based on a new philosophical understanding of "the rights of man" and the way the world should be organized.

The Accompanying Revolution in Religion and the Arts

In 1740, a Presbyterian minister, Gilbert Tennent, one of the leaders of the Great Awakening (see Chapter 4), preached a sermon on "The Danger of an Unconverted Ministry" in churches throughout New Jersey and Pennsylvania. Tennent's sermon, with its plea to test the personal faith of ministers, was a direct challenge to the leaders of the major Protestant denominations—Presbyterian, Congregational, and Episcopal. As a result of the Great Awakening, church members claimed permission—indeed, the responsibility—to judge their ministers as to the depth of their personal piety, not their external qualifications for office. It was not a great leap for citizens to claim the same permission, and responsibility, for judging those in civil authority.

One visiting revivalist asserted that Patrick Henry, rector of the Episcopal church in Hanover, Virginia (and uncle to the patriot leader Patrick Henry), was a "stranger to true religion." Reverend Henry, in return, demanded that Virginia's governor stop these "strolling preachers" who were, in his view, "a set of incendiaries, enemies not only to the Established Church, but also common disturbers of the peace." In a way, Henry was right. The Great Awakening disturbed the peace, split churches, and undermined all authorities, religious and secular.

In the 1740s and 1750s, artists in British North America were also asserting their independence from the Mother Country. One of the most famous colonial artists, John Singleton Copley (1738–1815), began his career in New England and New York where he quickly gained fame for English-style portraits of the commercial elite. Nevertheless, by 1768, his painting of Paul Revere carried rich symbolism of independence, showing Revere focused on his work—as a silversmith—wearing colonial-made homespun clothing, rather than a style worn in England. Although Copley himself would become a Loyalist and leave for England in 1774, his work in the 1760s reflected the quest for independence in his patrons.

Charles Willson Peale (1741–1827) briefly studied with Copley before going his own way. Unlike his teacher, however, Peale supported the revolutionary cause. From his home in Annapolis, Maryland, Peale produced heroic portraits of revolutionary heroes, including Benjamin Franklin, Thomas Jefferson, Alexander Hamilton, and probably the best known

Niday Picture Library / Alamy Stock Photo

In the 1760s and 1770s, leading artists in British North America happily mixed art and politics. John Singleton Copley was already famous for his portraits of individuals who could afford his work when in 1768 he painted this one of Paul Revere. Unlike Copley's earlier work, the Revere painting was overtly political, showing Revere as someone who worked with his hands—as a silversmith—and who wore clothing made in the colonies, not in England.

portrait of George Washington. Peale also raised troops for and fought in the revolutionary army, but his major contribution to the cause of independence was his effort to portray the best known leaders of the Revolution as larger-than-life figures.

The most famous literature of the mid-1770s included the sermons of the Great Awakening, which themselves urged individual freedom of judgment. But by the 1770s, the speeches of leaders such as Sam Adams, James Otis, Patrick Henry, and others, along with the pamphlets of Thomas Paine, were making the case for revolution quite directly.

Impressment and Taxes—Seaport Riots, the Stamp Act, the Boston Massacre, and the Boston Tea Party

The Boston Tea Party of 1773 was probably the most famous act of resistance in America before the Revolution, but it was far from the first. Between 1747 and 1774, dockworkers, sailors, and townspeople drove the leading British officials—customs officials, navy officers, and even governors—away from the docks and out of Boston five times. Similar acts of rebellion took place from New York to the Carolinas.

Impressment had been British navy policy for centuries and, since the 1690s, had been a source of riots in colonial ports. When a British warship was short of sailors, which happened often due to high rates of death and desertion, the captain had the authority to impress (or kidnap) likely sailors from merchant ships or ports and sign them up for naval service. Commercial sailors were paid higher wages than those in the navy and often had better working conditions, so impressments were, as one senior British naval officer noted, a source of "Hatred for the King's Service ... [and] a Spirit of Rebellion," for many who lived along the waterfront.

In November 1747, British Commodore Charles Knowles sent sailors in search of new recruits while his ship was in Boston Harbor. They impressed forty-six men into service. A rebellious crowd responded, taking some of Knowles's officers hostage and chasing the royal governor out of town. A successful brewer, Samuel Adams, defended the rioters as an "Assembly of People drawn together upon no other Design than to defend themselves and repel the Assaults of a Press-Gang." He insisted that they "had a natural right" to do so. Perhaps his cousin, John Adams, should have considered an earlier date than 1760 for the start of revolutionary thinking in the colonies.

British actions in the 1760s and 1770s escalated tensions in North American cities. As the British government tried to pay off the debt from the French and Indian War by imposing new taxes, colonial resistance grew. Each attempt—the Sugar and Currency Acts of 1764, the Stamp Act of 1765, the Townshend duties of 1767, and the Tea Act of 1773—led to a spiraling series of encounters. Parliament sought to raise funds, backed off in the face of colonial resistance, and then enacted new "get tough" policies that also backfired (see Table 5-1). The impact of the persistent but failed efforts to raise taxes fueled colonial resistance and the sense that resistance was effective.

The Sugar and Currency Acts of 1764 provoked limited but spirited resistance. The tax on sugar included rum and molasses, both made from sugar. The Currency Act prohibited colonies from issuing their own paper money as legal tender for either public debts, including paying taxes, or private debts, including paying merchants for goods made in Britain. In response, merchants and artisans in New York and Boston joined in a nonimportation movement in 1764 that was the beginning of a growing refusal to buy or use anything manufactured in Britain.

A year later, resistance to the Stamp Act of 1765 was stronger, and it united colonists of many social classes. The act required legal and commercial documents, including magazines, newspapers, and playing cards, to be printed on special paper showing an official stamp. Payment for the stamped paper had to be in British currency. In the spring of 1765, Patrick Henry asked Virginia's legislature, the House of Burgesses, to pass resolutions that came to be known as the Virginia Resolves opposing the tax. Middling and upper-class New Yorkers—including lawyers and merchants who would have had to pay the highest taxes if the law was enforced—began writing articles against the tax in the city's many newspapers,

Impressment

The British policy of forcibly enlisting sailors into the British navy against their will. It had long been a source of resentment toward the British government in port towns.

Table 5-1　Parliamentary Acts That Fueled Colonial Resistance

Name of Act	Description
The Sugar Act of 1764	Increased duties and strengthened collection of customs on rum and molasses, which particularly affected merchants and importers
The Currency Act of 1764	Prohibited the colonies from issuing their own paper money as legal tender for public or private debts to Britain
The Stamp Act of 1765	Taxed all legal and commercial documents, creating an immediate hardship for business leaders and building resentment in many ports where people depended on those businesses for jobs
The Declaratory Act of 1766	Repealed the Stamp Act but said Parliament could legislate for the colonies in "all cases Whatsoever"
The Revenue Act of 1766	Restricted trade in sugar, which helped British and Caribbean merchants at the expense of North American merchants
The second Revenue Act of 1767 (also known as the Townshend duties after Charles Townshend, chancellor of the Exchequer)	Placed new duties on paper, lead, paint, glass, and tea. All but the tax on tea were repealed in 1770—the same day as the Boston Massacre
The Tea Act of 1773	Allowed the British East India Company to ship tea to the colonies without having to pay normally required duties, making it cheaper than most smuggled tea. The Townshend tea tax would still apply once it reached the colonies
The "Intolerable Acts" of 1774	In response to the tea riots, Parliament closed the port of Boston, expanded the royal governor's authority, shifted control of the Ohio River country to the British governor in Quebec (the Quebec Act), and allowed British troops to use any uninhabited building as a barracks, without the owner's authorization (the Quartering Act)

which circulated widely. Some also formed a new secret organization, the **Sons of Liberty**, which sent delegates to all the colonies to build resistance to the tax. As the taxes mounted, and as colonists chafed at the insistence by Parliament that it could impose any tax it wished, the demand **"no taxation without representation"** united many across different classes. Nine colonies sent delegates to a gathering known as the Stamp Act Congress in New York City in October 1765. There they issued a Declaration of Rights and Grievances, which said that Parliament had no right to tax the colonies, and they petitioned for a repeal of the Stamp and Sugar Acts.

More important than the petition was the fact that leaders from different colonies met together and began to sense their unity. As one of the organizers of the congress said, "There ought to be no New England men, no New Yorker, etc. known on the Continent, but all of us Americans." Prior to this point, each colony had jealously guarded its independence, but Britain's parliamentary action provoked increasing unity.

While colonial leaders met and wrote petitions, some of the strongest resistance to the stamp tax developed in the working-class taverns where laborers and sailors gathered. Poor people had little reason to actually pay the tax because they did not use many legal documents or paper products that would require the stamped paper, but the tax was a symbol of British arrogance and threatened to slow the colonial economy, which could put sailors and laboring people out of work. To the poor, the haughty British authorities were becoming intolerable.

When Lieutenant Governor Cadwallader Colden placed the embossing stamps in Fort George—at the tip of Manhattan—until the new tax went into effect on November 1, 1765, public protests mounted into what came to be known as the New York Stamp Act Riot. New York merchants and groups like the Sons of Liberty agreed not to import any British goods while the Stamp Act was in force. In taverns across the city, angry citizens shared their discontent with the British. On the evening of November 1, a crowd paraded around the city with torches as well as effigies of the lieutenant governor and the devil. They dared the British troops to fire on them and burned Colden's coach. Next the crowd broke into the home of Major James of the Royal Artillery, drank his considerable supply

Sons of Liberty

Secret organizations in the colonies formed to oppose the Stamp Act. From 1765 until independence, members spoke, wrote, and took direct action against British measures, especially the Stamp Tax and the tax on tea.

"no taxation without representation"

The phrase that became a rallying cry among many colonists who protested new British taxes that were imposed by Parliament in the 1760s and 1770s, even though British North America's colonies had no representation in the Parliament that imposed them.

The Bostonian's Paying the Excise-Man, or Tarring & Feathering. Plate I.

This picture, titled "The Bostonians Paying the Excise-Man," shows many forms of resistance to British taxes that developed, including mobs that sometimes coated an offending tax collector with tar and feathers or forced him to drink boiling tea. In the background, a Liberty Tree—symbol of freedom—sports a hangman's noose, and colonists dump tea off a ship.

Boston Massacre

After months of increasing friction between townspeople and the British troops stationed in the city, on March 5, 1770, British troops fired on American civilians in Boston who were throwing projectiles at them, killing five and stirring even greater hatred toward the British army.

of liquor, and burned the house. Calling themselves the Sons of Neptune to distinguish themselves from the more middle-class Sons of Liberty, the working-class crowd resisted efforts to end the violence. Months later, when news reached New York in May 1766 that the Stamp Act had been repealed, celebrating crowds fired guns, broke windows, and erected a "liberty pole" to taunt British authorities.

Similar riots by the "lower sorts" took place in other colonial cities. In Boston, a mob ransacked the governor's home, and in Annapolis, Maryland, a crowd burned the stamp distributor's warehouse and forced him to flee the colony. In Wilmington, North Carolina, a mocking, angry crowd paraded the stamp collector through the streets. And in Charleston, South Carolina, a crowd of workers and seamen burned effigies of the stamp distributor.

In response to the unrest, British authorities under the new prime minister the Marquess of Rockingham decided not only to repeal the stamp and sugar taxes but also to show force. In 1766, while repealing the taxes, Parliament also voted the Declaratory Act, which claimed its right to tax and regulate the colonies "in all cases Whatsoever." In addition, Parliament passed the Revenue Act of 1766, restricting trade in sugar, which helped British and Caribbean merchants at the expense of colonial merchants.

A year later, Charles Townshend, chancellor of the Exchequer (treasurer) in a new British government, imposed new taxes on lead, paint, paper, and tea, known as the second Revenue Act of 1767 (also known as the Townshend duties of 1767). The new British government was desperate to find a way to pay off the war debt, and it also wanted to assert Parliament's authority over the colonies. In particular, Parliament wanted to curtail smuggling by some of the most prosperous colonial merchants and to control the mobs that kept rioting in Boston and New York. In September 1768, the warships of the Royal Navy arrived in Boston, and British troops marched through town in a show of the government's authority. According to Paul Revere, the troops "Formed and Marched with insolent Parade, Drums beating, Fifes playing, and Colours flying, up King Street." The presence of so many troops created a sense of siege in Boston.

A year and a half later, British soldiers were still stationed in Boston, creating constant tensions with residents who resented their presence. One source of the tension was the fact that off-duty soldiers were allowed to work on their own part-time, increasing competition with colonists for jobs by accepting lower wages. On the evening of March 5, 1770, an angry crowd began to throw snowballs at British soldiers. They taunted the lone British sentry at the State House, Private Hugh White. As the crowd around White grew, more people joined in the taunting or watched from the sidelines. John Adams called the crowd "a motley rabble," but they had strong support in a city tired of the presence of so many soldiers.

British Captain Thomas Preston sent more soldiers to support White while the crowd grew to three hundred or four hundred. Preston asked the crowd to disperse, assuring them that the soldiers would not fire since he himself was standing directly in front of them. However, someone threw something that knocked one of the soldiers down, and some of the soldiers started firing, even though no one heard Preston give any orders. Three men were killed—including a seaman, Crispus Attucks, a former slave who was part African and part American Indian and who would be celebrated as the first person and first among blacks to die in the Revolution. Two more later died of their wounds. The **Boston Massacre**, as colonists called it, fueled anger at the British authorities. To avoid further confrontation, the Royal Governor pulled the troops out of Boston. His action also left most of the town in the hands of an increasingly anti-British population.

In this print, designed to fuel hostility toward the British more than provide an accurate record, Paul Revere showed the British soldiers—more organized than they actually were—firing on a helpless crowd.

Some of the British troops involved were accused of murder. John Adams defended them in a subsequent trial (in which they were found not guilty). Later, Adams said that his defense of the soldiers, though highly unpopular, was "one of the most gallant, generous, manly and disinterested Actions of my whole Life." Nevertheless, Adams also said that there was "no Reason why the Town should not call the Action of that Night a Massacre." Paul Revere described the event as a deliberate military attack on a peaceful crowd. Sam Adams created a "committee of correspondence" to encourage resistance in other colonies. With such rhetoric, many Bostonians would likely never again be loyal British subjects.

In 1773, Britain decided to maintain the tax on tea, but repeal the other Townshend duties. The Tea Act of 1773 not only asserted Parliament's authority to levy whatever taxes it wished but also attempted to protect the almost-bankrupt British East India Company, which was struggling because customers were purchasing cheaper, smuggled tea elsewhere.

Under the act, the East India Company could ship large quantities of tea to the colonies without paying required duties, making the tea cheaper for the colonists, even with the Townshend tea tax. The plan was to encourage colonists to buy the taxed British East India Company tea instead of smuggled teas.

Given the tension and anger in Boston, the city's response could easily have been predicted. City residents had no intention of paying that tax, even on discounted tea. In New York, Philadelphia, and Charleston, patriotic groups, often led by the Sons of Liberty, convinced merchants not to allow the tea to land from the British ships.

In November 1773, a shipment of British tea arrived in Boston on the ship *Dartmouth*. Even before it arrived, crowds had forced the tea merchants to barricade themselves in their warehouse. Once the *Dartmouth* appeared, a crowd forced the ship to move to Griffin's Wharf where dockworkers, sailors, and merchants, not the British authorities, controlled the dock. The customs commissioners fled rather than risk getting tarred and feathered, an increasingly popular punishment by patriotic crowds for those who supported royal authority. Governor Thomas Hutchinson would not let the *Dartmouth* sail back to England, and the crowd would not let the tea be unloaded. The stand-off lasted into December.

On December 16, angry citizens met at the Old South Meeting House. When the governor would not back down, Samuel Adams said, "This meeting can do nothing more to save the country." The crowd's response—probably well rehearsed—was a series of faked Indian war whoops, a shout of "Boston harbor a tea-pot tonight," and a call to gather at Griffin's Wharf. As thousands watched from the shore, men, slightly disguised as Mohawks, boarded the *Dartmouth* and dumped the tea into Boston Harbor.

The Boston Tea Party galvanized anti-British sentiment in other colonies, and the city was seen as the incubator of revolutionary activity long before the next shots were fired. In response to the incident, the British closed the port of Boston to all shipping, creating a financial crisis that led to further anger and unrest among not only dockworkers but also the merchant elites who depended on the port for their wealth.

Robert Sayer/John Bennett/Library of Congress Prints and Photographs Division [LC-DIG-ppmsca-19468]

A British publication ridiculed American women's efforts to boycott tea, but the hostility shown in the cartoon reflects the degree to which women's protests were effective.

Daughters of Liberty

Organized as a women's response to the Sons of Liberty, the Daughters opposed British measures, avoided British taxed tea, spun their own yarn, and wove their own cloth to avoid purchasing British goods.

Women, too, became increasingly involved in leading their own protests. In response to the Stamp Act crisis of 1765, women who were determined to boycott British goods in protest began calling themselves the **Daughters of Liberty**. New England women organized spinning bees to make their own cloth so they could avoid buying English textiles. Among the elite and working people, wearing homespun clothing became a symbol of loyalty to the patriot cause. Their efforts continued to strengthen and spread, especially with the strong support they got from newspapers. In 1774, fifty-one women in Edenton, North Carolina, promised not to consume English goods, including tea, and other women organized similar boycotts elsewhere. When war broke out after 1775 and many goods became scarce, women protested when colonial merchants hoarded goods or demanded higher prices. In 1777, women in Poughkeepsie, New York, broke into the house of a merchant they thought was hoarding goods. As the war continued, women led food riots throughout the colonies.

Revolts in the Backcountry

Rural people on the frontier from New York to the Carolinas were far less concerned with impressment and taxes than those who lived in the port cities, but they were also taking matters into their own hands for different reasons. Backcountry Virginians had rebelled against royal authority since Bacon's Rebellion in 1676, and in all of the colonies, tensions mounted between coastal areas that had more access to, and more representation in, colonial governments and isolated rural inland settlements.

Farmers in the western regions of North and South Carolina felt ignored by the colonial governments and created what they called the Regulator movement in the 1760s. In South Carolina, Regulators attacked outlaws who stole from isolated farms. The governor eventually agreed to create circuit courts in the backcountry, which diminished the violence. In North Carolina, the movement protested corrupt practices of sheriffs and court officials who forced settlers to pay illegally high taxes and legal fees. Regulators rallied settlers, who refused to pay the taxes, closed the courts, and attacked officials. The governor sent in state militia, and in their largest encounter with the Regulators, 29 people were killed and 150 wounded.

Throughout the colonies, however, the most contentious issue for inland communities was relationships with Native Americans. Inland people complained that those on the coast used inland settlers as a buffer from the Indians. This strategy is exactly what the authorities had planned since the 1720s (see Chapter 3). There were also ethnic splits between the regions. Most of the inhabitants of the coastal cities were either of English backgrounds or African slaves. But between them and the Indians was a zone inhabited by Scots-Irish and Germans, many of whom had arrived a generation or two later than the Atlantic coast inhabitants and who found themselves in far greater tension with the Native Americans.

The rapid growth of the white population led to ever-increasing pressure for more land, a lot more land, that could be satisfied only by white movement into areas that belonged to Indian tribes. As whites encroached, attacks by Indians increased. Settlers wanted, and expected, the British to protect them. But after 1763, King George's Proclamation Line meant to halt further movement west and British authorities were quite unwilling to protect illegal white settlements. The British-imposed barrier caused intense anger on the frontier.

British agents sought to relieve the pressure among land-hungry white settlers and honor the king's commitment to the Indians. A 1768 treaty allowed white settlement in present-day West Virginia and Kentucky. A similar treaty opened parts of western Pennsylvania and New York to white settlement. But colonists wanted much more land than these treaties gave them and were prepared to fight to get it—whether with Indian tribes or with the king's representatives.

Violence extended all along the lines of settlement. A German immigrant, Frederick Stump, was arrested for murdering ten Indians in western Pennsylvania in 1768 and then freed from jail by a white mob. In Virginia, vigilantes who called themselves the Augusta Boys killed Cherokees.

General Thomas Gage, the senior British commander in North America, found the situation intolerable. He complained to London that "all the people of the frontiers from Pennsylvania to Virginia inclusive, openly avow, that they never find a man guilty of murder, for killing an Indian." In response to the frontier resistance, Parliament passed the Quebec Act of 1774, assigning all lands north and west of the Ohio River to the British-controlled Province of Quebec. That action effectively took Indian policy out of the hands of frontier agitators or royal governors along the coast. The Quebec Act also recognized the legal rights of the Catholic Church, which deeply offended the overwhelmingly Protestant Americans. Colonists saw the Quebec Act as one of what they called the Intolerable Acts, a series of laws that included the act that closed the port of Boston until the cost of the lost tea and the tax on it was paid, a revision of the colonial charter of Massachusetts, and a Quartering Act that allowed governors to place troops in any uninhabited building. Patriots insisted that because Parliament was enacting these laws with no representation from colonists, Britain was violating the rights of English subjects in North America. Parliament's actions were unintentionally provoking a common sense of grievance among people who had previously been quite separate in their complaints.

Growing Unity in the Colonies—The First Continental Congress

Leaders of the rebellion in Massachusetts asked those in the other colonies, from isolated inland counties to seaport towns, to join it in united action. All of them except Georgia—which was fighting Creek Indians and wanted Britain's support—sent delegates to Philadelphia in September 1774 to what became known as the **First Continental Congress**.

Most of the delegates who came to Philadelphia agreed that Parliament had no right to tax the colonies without their consent. The delegates also sought unified opposition to the British treatment of Boston. However, few were ready for a break with Britain. The Virginians wanted to continue to export tobacco, and South Carolina depended on the export of rice and indigo. Finding common ground was not easy. But the delegates did gain experience working together, even when they argued—which they did a lot.

There was little talk of war or independence at the 1774 gathering. But before they adjourned on October 26, the delegates declared that their rights were based on the laws of nature, the British constitution, and the colonial charters, and were not to be trifled with. They also agreed to a ban on British imports to take effect in December 1774, a ban on exports that would take effect in September 1775 (after the tobacco and rice crops were safely on their way to Britain), and—for symbolic reasons—an immediate ban on the consumption of tea from the East India Company. They agreed to meet again in May 1775 if relations with Britain did not improve.

First Continental Congress

Meeting of delegates from most of the colonies held in Philadelphia in 1774 in response to the British efforts to tax the colonies.

Phillis Wheatley lived an unusual life for an African slave. Before she was given her freedom, she was given considerable opportunity to learn and to write by the Wheatley family that claimed her. Her poems reflected the yearning for freedom that all colonists felt, but specifically the hopes of enslaved Africans among them.

Talk of Freedom for Slaves

For African slaves in British North America, the most revolutionary moment of the 1700s took place in London in July 1772. An American slave named James Somerset had been taken from Virginia to England as a personal servant by his master, Charles Stewart. In London, Somerset became friends with free blacks and white abolitionists. In October 1771, he ran away. He was caught and put on a ship bound for Jamaica. But Somerset's white friends petitioned for a writ of habeas corpus, requiring that Somerset be brought before a judge to determine whether he was imprisoned lawfully. They insisted that he was held against his will—which, like all slaves, he certainly was. Eventually, the Lord Chief Justice ruled that since Parliament had never legalized slavery in England itself, as opposed to the English colonies, Somerset had to be freed because "the state of slavery is of such a nature, that it is incapable of being introduced on any reason, moral or political; but only by positive law." This decision basically ended slavery in England itself, though not in England's colonies.

The **Somerset decision** caused a considerable stir in the colonies. In September 1773, the *Virginia Gazette* noted that, as news of the decision spread, running away to England was "a notion now too prevalent among the Negroes, greatly to the vexation and prejudice of their masters." Benjamin Franklin, who was living in London, had once owned slaves, but now, like many others, he was turning against the institution, calling it "this pestilential detestable traffic in the bodies and souls of men." In Massachusetts, after successfully defending a slave in a trial to obtain his freedom in the Nantucket Court of Common Pleas, John Adams said, "I never knew a jury by a verdict to determine a negro to be a slave. They always found him free."

Legal challenges were not the main ways in which slaves sought freedom before and during the American Revolution, however. Slaves heard about the protests of the Stamp Act and saw how effective mob action was. Some 107 slaves ran away from a plantation near Charleston to join other runaways in hard-to-penetrate swamps.

Whites on both sides of the Atlantic noted the absurdity of colonists protesting their own perceived enslavement by Parliament while, as one wrote, those same colonists enslaved "thousands of tens of thousands of their fellow creatures!" The most consistent voice for abolition in the 1760s and 1770s came from the Quakers, who made it mandatory for members to free their slaves or allow them to purchase their freedom. Others such as Virginia's Arthur Lee—from a powerful slaveholding family in the colony—wrote that

Somerset decision

A 1772 ruling by Britain's Lord Chief Justice in the case of James Somerset that set him free and essentially declared slavery illegal in England, though not in British colonies.

American Voices

Phillis Wheatley, Poem to the Earl of Dartmouth, 1773

Phillis Wheatley was born in West Africa in 1753. She was captured at age seven or eight and brought to Boston as a slave where she was purchased by John and Susanna Wheatley, who provided her with a good education. The young Phillis was moved by English poets, Christianity, and the talk of democracy that she heard in the 1760s and 1770s. In response, she wrote poems about religion, slavery, and freedom.

No more, America, in mournful strain
Of wrongs, and grievance unredress'd complain,
No longer shalt thou dread the iron chain,
Which wanton Tyranny with lawless hand
Had made, and with it meant t' enslave the land.
Should you, my lord, while you peruse my song,
Wonder from whence my love of Freedom sprung,
Whence flow these wishes for the common good,
By feeling hearts alone best understood,
I, young in life, by seeming cruel fate
Was snatch'd from Afric's fancy'd happy seat:
What pangs excruciating must molest,

What sorrows labour in my parent's breast?
Steel'd was that soul and by no misery mov'd
That from a father seiz'd his babe belov'd;
Such, such my case. And can I then but pray
Others may never feel tyrannic sway?

Source: Phillis Wheatley, "To the Right Honorable William, Earl of Dartmouth, His Majesty's Principal Secretary of State for North America, &c," in Herb Boyd, editor, *Autobiography of a People* (New York: Anchor Books, 2001, pp. 29–30).

Thinking Critically

1. **Analyzing Primary Sources**
   How did Wheatley's poem reflect her African roots? Her Boston experiences?

2. **Comparison**
   What light does this poem shed on Wheatley's hopes for the coming revolution? How might her vision of revolution have differed from that of her white Bostonian neighbors? From fellow enslaved Africans?

"freedom is unquestionably the birth-right of all mankind, of Africans as well as Europeans." In the 1700s, the slave trade was still a profitable institution. While some whites wrote antislavery letters and pamphlets, seven thousand slaves were imported into Charleston in 1765. The debate around slavery was as heated as the debate around British rule, and no one living through these years could fail to notice the contradiction of fighting for liberty and enforcing slavery.

5.2 Quick Review

Did Americans' revolutionary ideas contradict their attitudes toward Indians and slaves? How might colonists have answered the contradiction?

The War for Independence

5.3 **Explain how political and military strategy, ideological support for the patriot cause, and American alliances with France and Spain led to an American victory in the war for independence in spite of the presence of a large bloc of Loyalist Americans and the overwhelming military might of Britain.**

As talk of rebellion spread in 1774, not long after the Boston Tea Party, John Adams overheard rural farmers discussing the events in Boston. One insisted, "If parliament can take away Mr. Hancock's wharf and Mr. Rowe's wharf, they can take away your barn and my house." Adams realized that if isolated farmers were agreeing with a mob in Boston, revolution was possible. Beginning in 1775, what had been occasional mob actions turned into outright warfare as increasingly well-disciplined colonial militia fought against the British army. While some colonial leaders met in Congress and declared independence in 1776, other colonists, later aided by French forces, fought long and bitter battles that won the actual independence.

5.1

5.2

5.3

When Historians Disagree

Was the American Revolution Radical or Conservative? For Whom?

Respected historians Gordon S. Wood and Gary B. Nash offer quite different interpretations of the American Revolution. Neither *is necessarily completely right or wrong, and such debates remain a part of history.*

Gordon S. Wood, *The Radicalism of the American Revolution.* New York: Vintage, 1991, pp. 3–8.

The American revolutionary leaders do not fit our conventional image of revolutionaries—angry, passionate, reckless, maybe even bloodthirsty for the sake of a cause. We can think of Robespierre, Lenin, and Mao Zedong as revolutionaries, but not George Washington, Thomas Jefferson, and John Adams. They seem too stuffy, too solemn, too cautions, too much the gentlemen. We cannot quite conceive of revolutionaries in powdered hair and knee breeches. …

But if we measure the radicalism by the amount of social change that actually took place—by transformations in the relationships that bound people to each other—then the American Revolution was not conservative at all; on the contrary: it was as radical and as revolutionary as any in history. …

By the time the Revolution had run its course in the early nineteenth century, American society had been radically and thoroughly transformed. One class did not overthrow another; the poor did not supplant the rich. But social relationships—the way people were connected one to another—were changed, and decisively so. By the early years of the nineteenth century the Revolution had created a society fundamentally different from the colonial society of the eighteenth century. It was in fact a new society unlike any that had ever existed anywhere in the world.

Gary B. Nash, *The Unknown American Revolution: The Unruly Birth of Democracy and the Struggle to Create America.* New York: Viking, 2005, pp. xv–xxiv.

For more than two centuries … the great men—the founding fathers—of the revolutionary era dominate the reigning master narrative. … [W]e have not appreciated the lives and labors, the sacrifices and struggles, the glorious messiness, the hopes and fears of diverse groups that fought in the longest and most disruptive war in our history with visions of launching a new age filling their heads. Little is known, for example of Thomas Peters, an African-born slave who made his personal declaration of independence in early 1776, fought for the freedom of African Americans, led former slaves to Nova Scotia after the war, and completed a pilgrimage for unalienable rights by shepherding them back to Africa to participate in the founding of Sierra Leone. Why are the history books virtually silent on Dragging Canoe, the Cherokee warrior who made the American Revolution into a two-decade life-sapping fight for his people's life, liberty, and pursuit of happiness? We cannot capture the "life and soul" of the Revolution without paying close attention to the wartime experiences and agendas for change that engrossed backcountry farmers, urban craftsmen, deep-blue mariners, female camp followers and food rioters—those ordinary people who did most of the protesting, most of the fighting, most of the dying, and most of the dreaming about how a victorious America might satisfy the yearnings of all its peoples.

Thinking Critically

1. **Contextualization**

   Wood and Nash are both writing about the American Revolution but they focus on different evidence, different events, and most of all different people. How might the different focus change one's conclusions about the Revolution itself?

2. **Comparison**

   Which author do you find more convincing? Why?

From Lexington and Concord to Bunker Hill— Revolt Becomes War

General Thomas Gage understood the growing rebellion. After Parliament passed the Intolerable Acts, Gage recommended conciliation. But the leaders in Parliament were in no mood for conciliation, and Gage received orders to restore order at all costs. Gage kept a close eye on the Massachusetts rebels who kept an equally close eye on him. Paul Revere, who had helped lead the Boston Tea Party, now led an informal group of unemployed artisans who noted every troop movement in Boston.

THE BATTLES OF LEXINGTON AND CONCORD, APRIL 1775 The colonial militias were collecting arms in the towns of Concord and Worcester, and Gage knew it. Hoping for secrecy, he ordered troops to prepare to march to Concord to seize the arms. The colonists had been expecting such a move. Paul Revere was to report any troop movements by hanging lanterns in the steeple of Boston's North Church—one lantern if the troops moved inland and "two if by sea," meaning by boats across Back Bay. When the British troops started to move across the bay, Revere hung two lanterns in the steeple. Then he and William Dawes began their famous rides through the night to alert the colonial militia. Revere himself was arrested by British troops, but Dawes woke Sam Adams and John Hancock, who made it to Concord to organize the militia.

When the British reached Lexington Town Green at a little after 4:30 a.m. on April 19, 1775, they were met by colonial militia. Shots were fired, killing eight militiamen and wounding ten others. Only one British soldier was wounded in this first battle of the Revolution.

There was no further gunfire until the British entered the town of Concord where they found few arms. As they left to march the sixteen miles back to Boston, militiamen hidden behind trees, buildings, rocks, and fences attacked their easy targets. At the end of the day, the British had 273 casualties, the militia 95. What had been unrest was now a war.

Word of the battles of Lexington and Concord spread quickly. Many shared Thomas Jefferson's belief that "the last hopes of reconciliation" had now ended. People who were not sure about independence felt they had to make decisions. Those who remained loyal to the crown mostly did so quietly, especially in New England. But many began to commit to what they saw as a patriotic cause, some even taking matters into their own hands. Ethan Allen, who since 1770 had led his Green Mountain Boys in challenging royal authority in Vermont, and Benedict Arnold of Connecticut, then on the rebels' side, organized their own militia and captured Fort Ticonderoga on Lake Champlain on May 10, 1775. The cannons from the fort would play a large role in the coming struggle.

FROM THE BATTLE OF BUNKER HILL TO THE FORMATION OF THE COLONIAL ARMY   In the weeks after the battles at Lexington and Concord, the Massachusetts militia, fortified with recruits from Connecticut, began to dig in on the hills surrounding British-occupied Boston—Dorchester Heights to the south and Bunker Hill and Breed's Hill to the north. Colonel William Prescott of the Massachusetts militia was put in charge of fortifying the northern hills.

General Gage again felt that he had to act. On June 17, Gage ordered an attack on Breed's Hill. It was a British victory, but at a high cost—226 British dead and 828 wounded compared with 140 militia killed and 271 wounded. As one Englishman remarked, "If we have eight more such victories, there will be nobody left to bring the news."

The battle, which later became known as the Battle of Bunker Hill, even though it had taken place on Breed's Hill, was between ill-organized militia and regular units of the British army. After that battle, however, the American forces became better organized and gained support from all thirteen colonies.

African Americans in the Armies of Both Sides

The outbreak of war opened a new avenue to freedom for American slaves. While some, like Wheatley, embraced a revolution for liberty and freedom, others heeded different words. Jeremiah, a free black in Charleston, heard the rumor that the British intended to "come to help the poor negroes." He did not wait for that help but began to organize one of several slave uprisings in the Carolinas in 1775 and 1776. Jeremiah's plans for an insurrection were discovered, and he was hanged and burned at the stake in August 1775 by prorevolutionary authorities in South Carolina.

There was a good reason for the rumors among the slaves. In 1775, Lord Dunmore, the royal governor of Virginia, under attack from the rebels, fled Williamsburg. In November of that year, from his refuge on a British warship, he announced:

> I do hereby further declare all indented Servants, Negroes, or others … free, that are able and willing to bear arms, they joining His MAJESTY'S Troops as soon as may be.

The proclamation terrified whites. If Lord Dunmore promised freedom to slaves who fought for the British, then for a slave, the revolutionary struggle was very different from what it was for whites. And in South Carolina where there were eighty thousand slaves—60 percent of the population—it would be a radical revolution indeed.

5.1

5.2

5.3

Many slaves responded to the invitation. Between eight hundred and one thousand slaves joined the British army. Dunmore organized them into what he called the Ethiopian Regiment, whose members wore a sash reading "Liberty to Slaves." In one engagement, an American colonel, Joseph Hutchings, was captured by two of his own former slaves. When the British landed on Staten Island in 1776, New York and New Jersey slaves joined them. When the Royal Navy sailed up rivers in Pennsylvania and Maryland, more slaves joined them, and when the British attacked Charleston, still more joined.

Runaway slaves built forts, tended the wounded, carried supplies, and fought alongside white soldiers. British generals understood that in recruiting slaves they were also disrupting the economies of the rebellious colonies. Although disease took a terrible toll among black soldiers and their families, and though many were captured and reenslaved, the loyalty of slaves to the British cause eventually brought freedom to some of them. Approximately three hundred former slaves sailed with Dunmore when he left Virginia in 1776, and by the end of the war, British forces had relocated some three thousand more in Canada or in colonies in West Africa.

The American army was much slower to enlist free blacks or slaves than the British. African Americans, however, did serve among the colonial troops at Lexington and Concord in 1775, including Lemuel Haynes, who became one of the leading ministers in Massachusetts after the war.

Washington was reluctant to arm black soldiers, fearing not only the reaction of white troops but also the possibility that arms given to black soldiers might eventually support a slave revolt. Nevertheless, by the winter of 1777–1778, when things looked grim for the Revolution, Washington finally embraced black volunteers. Shortly after, in February 1778, Rhode Island offered freedom to "every able bodied Negro, Mulatto, or Indian Man slave in this state … to serve during the continuance of the present war with Great Britain." Perhaps one in four male slaves in the state eventually enlisted in what was known as Rhode Island's Black Regiment. Those who survived the war were given their freedom in 1783.

Moving toward Independence

Second Continental Congress

An assemblage of delegates from all the colonies that convened in May 1775 that eventually declared independence, adopted the Articles of Confederation, and conducted the Revolutionary War.

When the delegates to the **Second Continental Congress** gathered as promised in Philadelphia on May 10, 1775, the Battles of Lexington and Concord had changed everything. They knew that they had to manage a war and attempted to create the Continental Army. The obvious choice to command it was George Washington, a respected member of Congress and veteran of the French and Indian War.

Washington took command of the colonial militia, such as it was, in Cambridge, Massachusetts, on July 2, 1775, shortly after the Battle of Bunker Hill. American resistance would be more coordinated than it had been during the early skirmishes. Washington commanded between nine thousand and fourteen thousand troops—he was never sure—while Gage led about five thousand in Boston. Despite the difference in numbers, the Royal Navy controlled the water, and Gage's troops were highly disciplined soldiers. Washington's troops were a ragtag army, capable of effective guerrilla fighting and great courage, but hard to discipline, easily bored, and ready to return to their homes if fighting dragged on.

After selecting Washington and beginning to find the money—mostly in foreign loans—to support an army, the Second Continental Congress turned to another pressing question: What did they want from the war? John Dickinson of Pennsylvania wanted reconciliation with Britain if Parliament would respect the rights of the colonists. John Adams and most of the Virginia delegates wanted independence. Others were not sure. It took a year for the debate to be resolved, and before then, other matters intervened.

THOMAS PAINE'S *COMMON SENSE*   While the Congress debated independence, a new arrival from England, Thomas Paine, published a pamphlet, *Common Sense*, in January 1776. Soon, over 100,000 copies were in circulation. Paine asked, "Why is it that we hesitate? … For God's sake, let us come to a final separation. … The birthday of a new world is at hand." Paine made two basic points: that monarchy was always a bad way for people to be governed and that the time was right to declare independence. With his passionate words and exquisite timing, Paine shaped public opinion. *Common Sense* appeared on the same day

George III declared the North American colonies to be in a state of rebellion. The two events could not have contrasted more clearly. John Adams was no admirer of Paine or his pamphlet, which he saw as simple-minded and needlessly antagonistic, but Adams said that he expected *Common Sense* to become the "common faith" of the new nation.

Declaring Independence, 1776

On June 7, 1776, after months of debate in the Congress, Richard Henry Lee, a delegate from Virginia, offered a motion:

> Resolved … that these United Colonies are, and of a right ought to be, free and independent states, that they are absolved from all allegiance to the British Crown, and that all political connection between them and the state of Great Britain is, and ought to be, totally dissolved.

John Adams immediately seconded the motion.

In the debate that followed, delegates led by John Dickinson opposed the resolution. Most of the delegates had likely come to this Congress with the hope of reconciliation, not with any plan for permanent separation. But the fighting with British troops and the influence of publications like *Common Sense* had changed many minds. Congress eventually agreed to delay a vote on independence until July 1 and to appoint what became known as the Committee of Five—Thomas Jefferson, Benjamin Franklin, John Adams, Roger Sherman, and Robert Livingston—to draft a declaration in case Congress did vote for independence.

Jefferson, known for his skill with words, was chosen to write the first draft. Adams and Franklin, and ultimately the full Congress, made adjustments, which frustrated and hurt the sensitive Jefferson. The most important changes included removing Jefferson's passionate attack on the slave trade, which was hypocritical in light of the fact that Jefferson owned many slaves and made no move to free them. In addition, far too many of the others in the Congress had investments in the trade to accept Jefferson's language anywhere in the document. However, no one suggested removing Jefferson's assertion that the king "has endeavored to bring on the inhabitants of our frontiers, the merciless Indian savages," even when they all knew that it was whites on the frontiers who were invading Indian territory, and the king's government was trying to keep the two apart. Those in Congress saw the frontier whites as essential supporters of the patriot cause and were in no mood to antagonize them.

The delay until July 1 paid off. By then, no one was willing to go on record as being opposed to independence. On July 2, 1776, a unanimous Congress voted for independence, and on July 4, they adopted a declaration that began:

> When, in the course of human events, it becomes necessary for one people to dissolve the political bands which have connected them with another, and to assume among the powers of the earth, the separate and equal station to which the laws of nature and of nature's God entitle them, a decent respect to the opinions of mankind requires that they should declare the causes which impel them to the separation.
>
> We hold these truths to be self-evident, that all men are created equal; that they are endowed by their Creator with certain unalienable rights; that among these are life, liberty, and the pursuit of happiness.

The philosophical ideas that John Locke had used to defend England's change in monarchs were now, a hundred years later, used to announce to the world that monarchy itself was being abolished in England's former colonies. In Philadelphia, people celebrated with "bonfires and ringing bells, with other great demonstrations of joy." A crowd in New York tore down the statue of George III, Washington built up morale in the army by reading the Declaration to his troops, and the celebrations continued up and down the coast.

THE ARTICLES OF CONFEDERATION A year later, the Congress adopted a governing document for the new and fragile country they had created. In 1777, the **Articles of Confederation** created a national, though weak, government for what was now called the United States of America. Although eleven of the colonies ratified the Articles within a year, the last, Maryland, did not do so until 1781. Nevertheless, with the Articles of Confederation, states banded together in a formal—and ultimately successful—alliance to

Recently arrived from England, Thomas Paine took up the patriot cause with a fervor that many more established colonists lacked. In his easy-to-read pamphlet, *Common Sense*, he attacked not only the British treatment of the colonies but also the very idea of monarchy. His words were significant in fanning the flames of the independence movement.

Library of Congress Prints and Photographs Division [LC-USZ62-49366]

Articles of Confederation

Written document setting up the loose confederation of states that made up the first national government of the United States from 1781 to 1788.

When word of the Declaration of Independence reached New York City, soldiers and residents—including many African Americans in the city, slave and free—celebrated by pulling down the statue of King George III that stood on lower Broadway. The metal was eventually melted down to make bullets for the revolutionary cause.

Library of Congress Prints and Photographs Division [LC-DIG-pga-02158]

prosecute the war and govern the nation in the peace they hoped would follow. With the Articles of Confederation, the thirteen separate colonies agreed to work together for certain limited common purposes, including fighting for independence, though they remained distrustful of centralized government. Under the Articles of Confederation, there would be no national executive or court system. Congress could raise money through taxes only if every state agreed. The members of Congress squabbled as often as they agreed, and when Charles Thomson, who served as secretary to Congress from 1774 to 1789, set out to write a history of their work, he titled it "Notes of the Intrigues and Severe Altercations or Quarrels in the Congress." It was never published. Nevertheless, this government—really, an alliance of independent states more than anything that looked like a modern nation—was able to coordinate its fight and win the Revolution. Whether such a government could build a nation, however, remained to be seen.

George Washington and His Victorious Patchwork Army

The American Revolution was a long and bloody war between two strikingly different armies. On one side were Washington's patchwork Continental Army and various rebel militias—later supported by troops from France and Spain. In the course of the long war, some 200,000 of the 350,000 men who could have served participated in some military activity, but the turnover was such that no more than 25,000 served at any one time. Fighting against them was a corps of extremely well-trained British troops, supported by organized units of Loyalist colonists (as many as 8,000 Loyalists at the start of the war and increasing as the war continued) and hired soldiers from Germany. Ultimately, many factors led to the success of the rebels and their allies in their battles with the British troops (see Map 5-3), most of all, their ability to survive in spite of the British effort to eliminate them as a fighting force.

Most of the revolutionary Minute Men who fought at Lexington and Concord (called Minute Men because they had pledged to be ready to fight on a minute's notice) were farmers who owned their own weapons and knew how to shoot. In some of the early battles, the popular image of the "citizen soldier" was true as farmers and townspeople took up arms to defend their communities. But as the war continued, and as Washington and his officers created the kind of discipline necessary for an effective army, more and more of the early volunteers faded away, replaced by recently indentured servants, impoverished transients, or those who traded a jail cell for a uniform. A colonial officer called the troops "a wretched motley Crew," but Washington was an effective leader who never seemed to lose control when others started to panic, and he was deeply committed to the cause.

Despite being ill-trained, ill-fed, ill-clothed, and restless, these troops continued to fight, even after seeing the "horrors of battle … in all their hideousness," as one soldier remembered. Surprisingly, these often forgotten men are who won the independence that others celebrated.

Map 5-3 Major Battles of the American Revolution.

The Revolutionary War was fought all across British North America, not only in almost all of the thirteen colonies along the Atlantic coast but also well into British Canada and in the Mississippi River Valley.

Quebec, 1775

Montreal, 1775

Ft. Ticonderoga, 1775

Saratoga, 1777   Bennington, 1777

Ft. Stanwix, 1777   Boston, 1776

Newtown, 1777

Princeton, 1777   New York, 1776

Monmouth, 1777

Trenton, 1777

Brandywine, 1777   Germantown, 1777

Vincennes, 1779

Charlottesville, 1781   Naval Battle, 1781

Yorktown, 1781

St. Louis, 1780

Kaskaskia, 1778

Guilford Courthouse, 1781

Moore's Creek Bridge, 1776

King's Mountain, 1780

Fishing Creek, 1780

Cowpens, 1781   Camden, 1780

Charleston, 1780

Savannah, 1779

Natchez, 1778   Mobile, 1780

Pensacola, 1781

ATLANTIC OCEAN

Mississippi R.

Overview of the Revolutionary War

⚹ British victories

⚹ Patriot victories

A few women also took a direct role in the war. Armies in the 1700s usually included women known as camp followers. Some were the wives of soldiers, who could not or would not leave their husbands. Others were single women seeking adventure or simply survival in army life and army rations. Camp followers carried water to the battlefield, fed and supported the troops, nursed the wounded, and occasionally fought in battles.

American Voices

Joseph Plumb Martin, Narrative of a Revolutionary Soldier, 1775–1783

Joseph Plumb Martin was a private in the American army through eight years of war. His journal, written when he was seventy years old, makes clear that his greatest enemies were neglect and hunger.

1777—Next morning, we joined the grand army near Philadelphia, and the heavy baggage being sent back to the rear of the army, we were obliged to put us up huts by laying up poles and covering them with leaves; a capital shelter from winter storms. … About this time the whole British army left the city, came out and encamped, or rather lay, on Chestnut-hill in our immediate neighborhood; we hourly expected an attack from them; we had a commanding position and were very sensible of it. We were kept constantly on the alert, and wished nothing more than to have them engage us, for we were sure of giving them a drubbing, being in excellent fighting trim, as we were starved and as cross and ill-natured as curs. The British, however, thought better of the matter, and after several days maneuvering on the hill, very civilly walked off into Philadelphia again. Starvation seemed to be entailed upon the army and every animal connected with it. …

1780—Here was the army starved and naked, and there their country sitting still and expecting the army to do notable things while fainting from sheer starvation.

Source: Joseph Plumb Martin, A Narrative of the Adventures, Dangers, and Sufferings of a Revolutionary Soldier (originally published 1830, republished New York: Signet Classics, 2010).

Thinking Critically

1. **Contextualization**
How does Martin's description of the army as "starved and naked … fainting from sheer starvation" compare with the way you may have previously thought about the story of the Revolution?

2. **Comparison**
What does this passage suggest about the differences between the American and British armies?

A sixteen-year-old girl, Sybil Ludington, is credited with riding twice as far as Paul Revere in 1777 to warn militia troops commanded by her father that the British were on their way to attack Danbury, Connecticut. Mary Ludwig Hays, known as Molly Pitcher (for the water she carried), also supposedly loaded her husband's cannon after he was wounded at the Battle of Monmouth in 1778. Deborah Sampson disguised herself as a man, joined the army, and fought for years until a doctor discovered her identity after she was wounded.

Washington understood that though his army could fight, they could not withstand a direct battle with British regulars. He told Congress that he needed to fight a defensive war. For much of the war, his goal was not a decisive victory, but avoiding a decisive loss. The longer Washington was able to keep his army together, the better the chance that the British would tire of the war. He knew how well trained the British army was—having served in it—but he also expected that training and discipline had narrowed their conception of war and would give him the edge as long as his troops could use nontraditional tactics and avoid capture or defeat.

THE BRITISH EVACUATE BOSTON After the Battle of Bunker Hill, the British controlled Boston but were hemmed in there. Through the winter of 1775–1776, Washington commissioned Henry Knox, a young Boston bookseller, as a colonel in the Continental Army and sent him and his men to take the guns captured at Fort Ticonderoga and move them on sleds over snow-covered mountains to Boston. On the night of March 1, 1776, to the utter surprise of the British, Washington's troops assembled the guns on Dorchester Heights and then bombarded the city until March 17 when the British finally evacuated Boston.

THE WAR IN THE NORTH—MANHATTAN, TRENTON, AND VALLEY FORGE The victory in Boston was one of the few outright victories Washington would achieve. Washington's goal, however, was to wear down the British while preserving his own limited troops.

Just as the American Congress was declaring independence in Philadelphia in 1776, Sir William Howe, who had replaced Gage as the British commander, landed his army on Staten Island, across New York harbor from Manhattan. Howe had some 32,000 troops, including 8,000 German mercenaries—essentially soldiers for hire—known as Hessians (since

5.1

5.2

5.3

many were from the German province of Hesse). During the war, some 30,000 Hessians fought for the British, approximately a quarter of all of their soldiers. Hessian troops were recruited, often by force, from among the poorest Germans, and German princes would rent them out as units, especially to the British. Many Hessian soldiers had little interest in the British cause, but little choice except to fight for it. As the two sides watched each other, Washington's troops dug fortifications to defend Brooklyn and Manhattan. In late August, Howe's larger and better-trained force attacked Brooklyn. Rather than risk battle and capture, Washington abandoned Brooklyn and brought all 9,500 of his troops across the East River to Manhattan on the night of August 30. When Howe attacked Manhattan in September, Washington again retreated. Throughout the early fall, Washington continued a retreat, and the British advanced through New Jersey. As they settled down for the winter, the British held most of New Jersey, while Washington's army was across the Delaware River in Pennsylvania.

Then, on Christmas night of 1776, Washington and 2,400 troops made a daring raid across the Delaware River and captured Trenton, New Jersey. They also captured many Hessian soldiers, some of whom quickly joined the rebel side. In January, they would go on to successfully attack a British force in Princeton. By the winter of 1776–1777, Washington controlled southern New Jersey while the British held northern New Jersey and New York City, which they would control throughout the war.

In May 1777, British General John Burgoyne assembled a large army in Canada. His plan was to proceed down the Hudson River and smash the "unnatural Rebellion" by isolating New England from the other colonies. Initially, the plan went well. Burgoyne had some 8,300 men, including 3,000 German troops. He led his army across Lake Champlain, overran the Americans at Fort Ticonderoga, and continued south into New York's Hudson River Valley, an exhausting effort that involved moving a large army with heavy supplies through dense forests. As he moved through the area, Burgoyne's sometime pompous pronouncements to colonists and the German troops' inability to communicate with them bred resentment and motivated fresh volunteers for the American cause.

In September 1777, near Saratoga, New York, Burgoyne's army encountered American troops under the command of an experienced general, Horatio Gates, and Benedict Arnold (still on the American side, but soon to be caught negotiating a plan with the British to defect). The British were surprised that their bayonet charge could not break the American lines. Both armies suffered heavy losses, but neither won a decisive victory. Burgoyne's army was now cut off from its winter quarters and, shortly after, was forced to negotiate. Some 5,800 British troops were captured and held as prisoners until the end of the war. The Battle of Saratoga was a turning point for the colonial cause. It eliminated a significant British force, and it proved to the world—especially those in France and Spain who were watching the war closely—that the Americans could stand up to Britain's toughest troops.

The British wanted to split all of the northern colonies from the southern ones and to capture Washington and his army, plus the members of the Continental Congress, by overtaking Philadelphia where the Congress met. In September 1777, British troops captured Philadelphia, but the members of Congress escaped before the British arrived. Washington was able to elude them and then block supplies from getting into the city. Unable to get supplies, the British abandoned Philadelphia the following spring, and the city remained in colonial hands for the rest of the war, though there were continued riots between patriots and Loyalists in the city.

Before the British left Philadelphia, however, the American forces had to survive perhaps their most difficult winter. Washington selected Valley Forge, Pennsylvania, eighteen miles northwest from Philadelphia, as a place to make a winter camp and to keep an eye on the British in the city. His army was exhausted, cold, and hungry, and they got colder and hungrier as the winter continued. In time, however, Washington was able to appoint commissary officers who found food and clothing for the soldiers. A Prussian officer volunteering in the American cause, Baron von Steuben, began training the troops in close-order drills. Von Steuben possessed expertise in military training and hoped to make a name, and a home, for himself in a free America. In addition, a French officer, the Marquis de Lafayette, was recruited to lead forces that harassed the British. By the time the British sailed out of

Philadelphia, the American troops were better fed and clothed, better trained, and ready for new battles—preparation they would need in the next years.

In 1778, General Sir Henry Clinton replaced Howe, and a new British strategy took shape. Clinton ordered the Royal Navy to harass the colonists up and down the Atlantic coast and encouraged Britain's Indian allies to attack frontier settlements. In addition, he sent the main British land force south to overrun the Carolinas and Georgia. If he could detach those three colonies, Clinton thought, the Revolution might crumble. After 1778, the major battles of the war would be in the colonies' western and southern regions.

THE IMPORTANCE OF FRANCE AND SPAIN   The Revolution was won by the rebels for many reasons, including the key fact that France and Spain were willing to help. The two countries had their own reasons for wanting to embarrass the British and reduce Britain's power on the world stage. In particular, both France and Spain wanted greater access to trade with North America, which was highly restricted as long as the British controlled the colonies. By the 1770s, the French still resented the British victory in the Seven Years' War and wanted to ensure that France, not Britain, was the dominant power in Europe. As early as 1775, France sent agents to America to see what might be gained from assisting in the rebellion. Similarly, Spain started to supply the colonists with food and gunpowder from Spanish-held New Orleans and Cuba.

While they were willing to support the rebellion, neither France nor Spain wanted to engage in war with Britain unless the colonists were serious. In arguing for a declaration of independence in 1776, Adams told the Congress: "Foreign powers cannot be expected to acknowledge us, till we have acknowledged ourselves." He had two specific foreign powers in mind.

In 1776, Benjamin Franklin led an American delegation in Paris to seek further help. Franklin, with his simple fur cap and plain spectacles, yet sophisticated manner, charmed the French. However, Franklin needed more than charm to win real help. After the Americans not only declared independence but also defeated crack British troops at Saratoga, French leaders started to take him more seriously. His diplomatic efforts secured important supplies and, in February 1778, a full French alliance with the United States of America, the first diplomatic recognition of the new nation. A few months later, France formally declared war on Great Britain. For the rest of the war, Washington could count on the French army and navy to fight the British along with his own troops.

In 1779, Spain also declared war on Britain. Spanish forces in the South took the British forts at Baton Rouge, Natchez, Mobile, and Pensacola. Spanish attacks in the Mississippi River Valley diverted British troops from the Atlantic coast, helping the American effort.

Once France and Spain went to war with Britain, the American Revolution became a world war. The French and British navies fought in the English Channel, Spain attacked British-held Gibraltar in the Mediterranean, and all of them fought battles in the Caribbean. Most important for the American cause, the French fleet supported Washington's troops while Spanish funds and smuggling efforts provided badly needed supplies.

THE IROQUOIS AND THE BRITISH   The Iroquois were divided about how to respond to the rebellion, and at the beginning of the war most sought to remain neutral. However, many Iroquois saw Britain as the key to their own independence, especially since they knew that an independent America would never protect their territory west of the Allegheny Mountains the way George III had tried to do. As the war continued, neutrality faded. Beginning in the summer of 1777, Mohawks under the leadership of Thayendanegea, also known as Joseph Brant, attacked colonists across New York and Pennsylvania. The attacks on farms threatened not only farm families but also a crucial colonial food supply. In response, in the summer of 1779 Washington sent perhaps a third of his army to attack the Iroquois and "lay waste all the settlements around … that the country may not be merely overrun but destroyed." From Washington's perspective, the Iroquois had to be stopped. For the Iroquois, Washington's fierce response was proof that the American leadership would always be an implacable enemy. Both sides adopted brutal scorched-earth tactics that left long-lasting hatreds.

BRITISH LOYALISTS Colonists who remained loyal to Britain formed their own militia, and in the Carolinas, an army of over a thousand Loyalists challenged rebel forces. Other Loyalists joined British regiments. American rebels had nothing but contempt for them. In the New York-New Jersey area, Catherine and Phillip Van Cortland, one of the area's leading families, remained loyal to Britain. When Washington gained control of their part of New Jersey, he ordered that the Van Cortland house be used as an army hospital. With her husband away, Catherine and her children were told to leave. She described their February 1777 departure:

> Our youngest children could not pass a far yard where they were milking cows without wishing for some. My little Willing was almost in agonies, springing in my Arms and calling for milk. I therefore rode up and requested the good man to let me have some from one of his pails … the man stopped, asked who we were, and … swore bitterly he would not give a drop to any Tory Bitch. I offered him money, my children screamed; and, as I could not prevail, I drove on.

In some cities including Newark, New Jersey, in 1777 and Philadelphia in 1780, the wives of missing Loyalists were exiled by the American forces. Some Loyalist families were able to blend back into their old homes after the war, but many left for Canada or England and never returned.

WOMEN'S SUPPORT FOR WASHINGTON'S ARMY In 1780, at a particularly bad time for the Continental troops, Esther De Berdt Reed (wife of the governor of Pennsylvania) and Sarah Franklin Bache (Benjamin Franklin's daughter) asked patriot women to give up all luxuries and contribute to a fund for the Continental Army. Eventually, the women raised $300,000, a huge sum at the time.

The women's goal was to give $2 in hard currency to every soldier. Washington refused the offer and asked the women instead to buy cloth and sew shirts for the soldiers. The women agreed and produced thousands of shirts for the ill-clad troops. The experience also led to the creation of the Ladies Association, the first intercolonial organization of women in America and a model for future national organizations of women.

Stories of similar efforts abounded. For example, in Fishing Creek, South Carolina, teenage girls went from farm to farm, asking, "Is the owner out with the fighting men?" If the answer was yes, then they harvested the crops. In five or six weeks, they had completed the harvest for the whole county, saving patriot farmers from economic ruin and providing food stores for the revolutionary cause.

THE WAR IN THE SOUTH—FROM CHARLESTON TO YORKTOWN After capturing Savannah, Georgia, in December 1778, the British attacked Charleston, South Carolina, in 1780, and on May 12, that city surrendered. The loss was significant. If the British took control of Georgia and the Carolinas, it would be hard to continue the resistance in the name of the united colonies.

As the battle for control of the South continued, Washington named one of his generals, Nathaniel Greene, to lead a southern campaign. Greene divided the American forces, taking command of half and assigning others—a contingent of Maryland and Virginia militias—to Daniel Morgan, an experienced officer from Virginia. The British commander, Lord Cornwallis, also divided his army between himself and Lieutenant Colonel Banastre Tarleton, who had a reputation for exceptional cruelty, especially after one battle in which he ordered the killing of patriot troops who had already surrendered.

While the two armies maneuvered, smaller independent units fought their own battles. Loyalists fought against colonial units. Throughout 1780 and 1781, the South Carolina backcountry was filled with ugly and often personal conflicts. The civilian death toll was high.

Morgan made a stand against the British forces in a South Carolina pasture known as Cowpens in January 1781. In one of the last full-scale battles of the war, the American troops defeated Tarleton's army and captured some eight hundred British soldiers—a crucial American victory. Although the British still held Charleston and units loyal to the British harassed the revolutionaries, after Cowpens, the Americans were in control of the South Carolina countryside.

Sarah Franklin Bache, unlike her half-brother William, was a staunch defender of the patriot cause. She led an effort to raise funds for the troops in the Continental Army and later led an effort in which Philadelphia women made 2,200 shirts for the soldiers.

5.1

5.2

5.3

Library of Congress Prints and Photographs Division [LC-D415-50235]

Pleading illness, Cornwallis actually failed to show up for the surrender ceremony, which was handled by junior British officers. But everyone knew how significant the event was. Without the army that Cornwallis led, British efforts to defeat the Continental Army were at a standstill.

Cornwallis saw little chance of further success in the Carolinas and marched into Virginia in May 1781. He decided to fortify Yorktown on the York River where he thought he could count on being resupplied by water. As Cornwallis's troops dug in at Yorktown, Washington was in the North planning another attack on New York City. Greene's army was far to the south. At the prodding of the French, Washington moved quickly to take advantage of the situation. In September, the French navy blockaded the York River and cut Cornwallis off from resupply. Then, supported by French troops under the Count de Rochambeau, Washington marched his own army from New York 450 miles south at surprising speed. On September 28, Washington's sixteen thousand troops attacked Yorktown. The siege continued for the next two weeks, but after failing at an attempted escape, Cornwallis surrendered on October 17, 1781.

THE TREATY OF PARIS   The surrender of Cornwallis at Yorktown did not end the war, but it virtually guaranteed that it would eventually end favorably for the Americans. British troops still controlled New York City, Charleston, Savannah, and parts of the countryside, but the public in Britain and many in Parliament were tired of the war. In June 1780, Congress sent John Jay to join Benjamin Franklin and John Adams in Paris to negotiate peace. After news of the Yorktown surrender arrived, the British delegates agreed to a draft treaty that began, "His Britannic Majesty acknowledges the said United States … to be free Sovereign and independent States." The two sides continued to negotiate boundaries, fishing rights, and legal claims, and Britain concluded separate treaties with France and Spain. The final treaty was signed in Paris on September 3, 1783. The Revolutionary War was over, and a new nation had been born.

5.3 Quick Review

Did the French and Indian War lead directly to the American Revolution? What other factors caused the outbreak of war in 1775? Why did different groups of Americans want independence? Or want to remain connected to Britain?

Conclusion

While ideas, especially those about "the rights of man," from John Locke, fueled the conflicts, the aftermath of the French and Indian War led to some of the most decisive events of the colonies' break with Britain. While the colonists benefited from the British takeover of New France, many rebelled against Parliament's efforts to get colonists to help pay the cost of this war. Working-class residents of port cities feared impressment into the British navy and worried that new taxes would cost them jobs. Frontier colonists wanted Indian land. Slaves in the American colonies welcomed news that courts in England were moving toward outlawing slavery there; however, plantation owners, who depended on slavery and the slave trade, now had another reason for supporting an open break with the mother country. As resistances to British policies and taxes grew, Parliament responded with new taxes and sent more troops, which only inflamed colonists' passions and further united them against British rule.

In 1775, violence escalated. By mid-1775, Americans had formed their own army under George Washington. The protracted war that followed engulfed the colonies, involving not only white men but also white women, slaves, and the Indians, along with armies and aid from France and Spain. Finally, after years of avoiding capture by the British army and some successful victories by the patriot forces, new alliances with France and Spain helped the colonists win the surrender of the largest British army in North America. With the surrender of the British forces at Yorktown in 1781, and the Treaty of Paris in 1783, the independence of the United States became a reality.

Chapter Review

Which factors do you think were most important in leading to the colonists' victory against the British Empire?

Chapter 5 Summary and Review

Preludes to Revolution

5.1 **Explain Britain's victory over France in the French and Indian War (Seven Years' War) and what conflicts followed this victory.**

Summary

The Seven Years' War, known in the colonies as the French and Indian War, was fought in North America, Europe, Asia, Africa, and the Caribbean. The effects of this world war from 1754 to 1763 were far-reaching. Britain victory secured its dominance of India and enhanced the British presence on the coast of Africa and in the Caribbean. Most significantly, the 1763 Treaty of Paris that officially ended the hostilities eliminated France as a North American power. For American Indians living between the Mississippi River and the Atlantic coast, the end of the war was an unmitigated disaster, particularly because they could no longer play one country against the other to gain bargaining power. And finally, Britain's victory came at a high financial cost—soaring debt from the war itself as well as new and expensive military obligations in North America. The British government was determined that colonists should shoulder some of the burden of these costs.

Review Questions

1. Continuity and Change over Time
   How was the Seven Years' War (French and Indian War) a turning point for the European powers in North America? What changed for them and what stayed the same after the war?

2. Causation
   How did British victory in the Seven Years' War impact the relationship between American Indians and British colonists? Think about what changed when the French withdrew.

"The Revolution Was in the Minds of the People"

5.2 **Explain why, in the fifteen years before the Revolutionary War began, support for the patriot cause spread so quickly among many different groups of North Americans who by 1775 opposed Britain for different reasons.**

Summary

For a significant number of British colonists, a revolutionary change in mind-set occurred between 1760 and 1775, and it took place for many different reasons. Some were inspired by the ideas of the Enlightenment while others were moved by religion to take a more skeptical view of authority. Sailors and shop owners in Boston, New York, and Philadelphia as well as backwoods farmers in western Pennsylvania, Virginia, and the Carolinas were often much more ready for revolution, much sooner, than their better-known leaders because British actions were seriously affecting their lives. American Indians felt the pressure of an expanding white population, resulting in regular conflict and intervention by the British to stabilize the frontier. Some slaves were inspired by colonial resistance and revolted. With the growing spirit of revolution, the contradiction of slavery was not lost on slaves nor on the British on both sides of the Atlantic.

Review Questions

3. Contextualization
   Explain what John Adams meant when he said that the Revolution "was in the minds of the people, and this was effected from 1760 to 1775, in the course of fifteen years before a drop of blood was shed at Lexington."

4. Argument Development
   Do you think the revolution in religion was more a cause of patriotic fervor, or was it more of an effect?

The War for Independence

5.3 **Explain how political and military strategy, ideological support for the patriot cause, and American alliances with France and Spain led to an American victory in the war for independence in spite of the presence of a large bloc of Loyalist Americans and the overwhelming military might of Britain.**

Summary

British efforts to ensure the enforcement of the Intolerable Acts led to the first battles of the Revolutionary War at Lexington and Concord in April 1775. After these battles, the Continental Congress began to prepare for war, and by the summer of 1776, Congress was ready to declare independence. The Articles of Confederation that Congress adopted created a national government, albeit a weak one. George Washington transformed his forces into a real army and was able to survive the British leviathan. The American victory at Saratoga in 1777 was the war's turning point, leading to critical French and Spanish support. The decisive battle of the war was fought at Yorktown, Virginia, in the fall of 1781. With the Treaty of Paris in 1783, the war was over and independence was finally secured.

Review Questions

5. Continuity and Change over Time
   How and why did colonial resentment of British policies move from protest and demonstration to war and the Declaration of Independence between 1774 and 1776?

6. Causation

What factors do you think are most important in explaining the American victory in the Revolutionary War?

1. Preparing to Write: Establish Context in Your Introduction

Long Essay Question—Evaluate the extent the change in colonial relations with Great Britain from 1763 to 1775.

The AP U.S. History Exam requires students to show they can provide historical context somewhere in the essay, and an introduction is an excellent place to do this. Review the time line at the beginning of the chapter and think about the events that provide the historical backdrop during this period. Take into consideration that in the mid-1700s, most American colonists were proud to call themselves British. Then note that events like the Stamp Act, the Boston Massacre, and the Tea Party show that this sentiment changed drastically for a significant number of colonists. From that, write a four- to seven-sentence introduction, including a thesis.

2. Preparing to Write: Plan Your Argument

Long Essay Question—Evaluate the primary factors that led to American victory in the Revolutionary War in 1783.

As you consider how American forces beat the odds and won the Revolutionary War, organize a list of the leading factors that made this victory a reality. One example might be Washington's military strategy to outlast the stronger British Army. Narrow down your list to the best three factors, and for each, write a topic sentence that explains why that factor is important. Once you have written your topic sentences, develop a thesis that answers the long essay question.

Chapter 6
Creating a Nation
1783–1789

THE FOUNDATION OF AMERICAN GOVERNMENT

Library of Congress Prints and Photographs Division[LC-USZCN4-220]

After winning independence, the new United States faced many crises. In an effort to resolve some of the tensions, some of the nation's leaders proposed a new form of government and met in Philadelphia over the long hot summer of 1787 to produce a new Constitution.

Chapter Objective

Demonstrate an understanding of how the Revolution affected diverse groups of people and how independence ultimately led to the adoption of a new form of government.

 ## Learning Objectives

The State of the Nation at War's End

6.1 Explain how the outcome of the American Revolution affected different groups in the new United States.

Creating a Government: Writing the U.S. Constitution

6.2 Explain the needs, pressures, and compromises that led to writing and adopting the Constitution.

In 1787, a Philadelphia physician, Benjamin Rush, wrote, "The American war is over, but this is far from the case with the American Revolution. On the contrary, nothing but the first act of the great drama is closed." For the generation that had lived through the 1760s and 1770s, opportunities abounded to help shape the new nation they had created. When Congress adopted the official seal of the new nation (found today on the back of every dollar bill), they included the Latin phrase *Novus Ordo Seclorum*, "a new order of the ages." Thomas Paine wrote, "We have it in our power to begin the world over again." Many in the new United States of America thought they could do just that.

The revolutionary leaders—Washington, Adams, Jefferson—have become cardboard characters. Their words have been invoked too often, their deeds too sanitized. But if today's citizens are to make sense of the Revolution and the creation of a new nation, they need to see those leaders as real. In addition, people today need to realize that many other actors were also asserting their place in—or, in the case of enslaved Africans, American Indians, and Loyalists, on the margins of—the new nation. Those known as the "founding fathers" were far from the only actors. Women who had lived through the Revolution were far less willing to leave political or domestic decisions to men than their mothers and grandmothers had been. Poor farmers often felt that their grievances had not been addressed by independence, and they continued to complain. Even among those who led the Revolution itself, there were great differences of opinion, especially regarding the best ways to govern the new nation and to maintain the liberty for which they had fought. What that new order would look like depended on not only where one stood in 1783 but also where one had stood before and during the Revolution. Exploring the efforts that helped create a stable and strong nation out of thirteen very independent British colonies requires, first, understanding what the end of the Revolution meant for different groups of people who found themselves in different circumstances and, then, how they put the new nation together.

Significant Dates

1783	The Newburgh Conspiracy among Revolutionary War officers
	Treaty of Paris recognizes U.S. independence
1784	Treaty of Fort Stanwix between Iroquois and the United States
	Post–Revolutionary War economic downturn
1786	Annapolis Convention
1786–1787	Shays's Rebellion in Massachusetts
1787	Constitutional Convention in Philadelphia
	Northwest Ordinance
1787–1788	*The Federalist Papers* are published
	State conventions adopt the Constitution

The State of the Nation at War's End

6.1 Explain how the outcome of the American Revolution affected different groups in the new United States.

For people of all classes, races, and political persuasions in British North America, the Revolution brought extensive change. Great inequality remained, but few people were willing to defend inequality as they had in the colonial era. Traditional rights based on family position or inheritance, wealth, race, or gender certainly did not disappear, but rights based on heredity became much harder to defend, particularly in opposition to the rights of any individual based on talent and energy. Despite Abigail Adams's plea to her husband, John, that the Continental Congress should "remember the ladies" or Jefferson's assertions about the evils of slavery in his original drafts of the Declaration of Independence, sexism, slavery, and many forms of inequality survived the Revolution intact. Nevertheless, something had changed. Forces had been unleashed, intended or not, that would undermine oppression. Thomas Paine, ever the optimistic recorder of events, wrote, "We see with other eyes; we hear with other ears, and think with other thoughts, than those we formerly used." And he explained that freedom, to him, meant "perfect equality. … The floor of Freedom is as level as water." Not all of his contemporaries wanted "perfect equality," but widespread acceptance of inequality or hierarchy was much less common after the Revolution.

From Colonies to States

The thirteen British colonies on the mainland of North America that had banded together to fight the Revolution were nevertheless very different places from one another, with different populations, cultures, and laws. As early as 1775, as the colonists began to consider the idea of independence as a serious option, John Adams had asked the Second Continental Congress "to resolve on a general recommendation to all the states to call conventions to institute regular governments." Adams also published a pamphlet, "Thoughts on Government," outlining what he thought the new state constitutions should say. In a very short time, four states—New Hampshire, South Carolina, New Jersey, and Virginia—adopted new constitutions, even before the United States declared independence in July 1776, and before the Revolution was won, all thirteen states created their own constitutions, though in most cases they did not follow the outline that Adams recommended. Two states, Connecticut and Rhode Island, took the easy route and merely revised their colonial charter to eliminate all references to the Crown and British government.

Many people found the opportunity to write a new form of government for themselves to be exhilarating, and many wanted to include their revolutionary goals. New York, New Jersey, Maryland, and Georgia lowered the property qualifications for voting while Pennsylvania, North Carolina, South Carolina, and New Hampshire allowed all taxpayers to vote. Vermont allowed all adult males to vote whether or not they had any property or paid any tax. New Jersey alone also expanded voting rights to include women as well as men, a provision that would last until 1807.

While the Continental Congress was meeting on one side of the Pennsylvania Statehouse, the elected delegates chosen to write a new state constitution met on the other. Adams, who worried that a "spirit of leveling, as well as that of innovation," was abroad in the land, had his fears confirmed when he saw the state's constitution makers were mostly farmers, a few merchants, lawyers, artisans, shopkeepers, and schoolteachers. As historian Gary B. Nash described the group, "It was not unusual for an ironmonger born in Upper Silesia to be flanked by an Ulster-born farmer and an Alsatian-born shopkeeper as the deliberations went forward." And the deliberations produced a legislature with a single house—since the delegates were convinced that an "upper house" could certainly represent aristocratic interests they did not want a weak executive, and a broad right to vote. They also provided for annual elections so that the electorate could review the decisions of the legislature.

New York and Maryland both adopted relatively traditional constitutions that protected the power of the old elite, minus Loyalists. After a failed effort to write a state constitution and after his own return from serving the Continental Congress in Paris, John Adams himself took charge of writing a new constitution for his home state of Massachusetts in 1779. He retained the privileged role of the Congregational churches, but built in support for schools and for Harvard College. He created a two-house legislature, high property qualifications for voting for the upper house so that it would represent the elite, and perhaps the most powerful elected governor in the new nation.

The battles in the 1770s over how individual states wanted to govern themselves reflected not only very real regional differences and ideological differences about the meaning of the revolution but also significant differences in the power of local elites. They also reflected differences in ideas about how best to govern that would play out again on the national stage in future decades.

For the Revolutionary Army Officers: The Newburgh Conspiracy

democracy

A form of government in which power is vested in the people and exercised by them directly or indirectly through a system of representation.

The American experiment in creating an independent nation that would be a **democracy**, governed by the will of the majority—or at least the white male majority—almost died before it was born. During the long months between the victory at Yorktown in late 1781 and the treaty that ended the war in March 1783, the army that had won the war came close to a military takeover of the government—a *coup d'état*. Once the army had won its final battle, the Continental Congress asked the soldiers to stay on duty. And the army did not wait patiently in the year and a half that followed.

By the spring of 1783, the soldiers and officers had many reasons for complaint. The northern army was in barracks in Newburgh, New York. They were bored. By December 1782, they had not been paid for months. Pensions that the Congress had promised looked like they might never arrive. General Alexander McDougall and Colonels John Brooks and Matthias Ogden took a petition from Newburgh to the Congress in Philadelphia that said, "We have borne all that men can bear—our property is expended—our private resources are at an end, and our friends are wearied out and disgusted with our incessant applications." Borrowing money from friends to survive did not sit well with these officers. They warned that "any further experiments on their [the army's] patience may have fatal effects."

The petition arrived in Philadelphia at a crucial moment. The new nation was governed by the Articles of Confederation that had been adopted during the Revolution. Under the Articles, Congress could not levy taxes or raise funds without the unanimous approval of all the states. In late 1782, some of the states had rejected a proposal to tax imports. Alexander Hamilton wrote, "Without certain revenues, a government can have no power." The government that received the petition from the officers was in just that situation.

Those in the Congress who supported the idea of a more powerful central government used the army's petition to demand that the Congress be given the power to tax so it could raise its own funds and not have to depend on the generosity of state legislatures. These Federalists, who in the next decade formed the nucleus of the Federalist Party, led by Alexander Hamilton, made it clear to the army's representatives that they needed to support the move to give the Congress the power to tax if they were ever going to get paid. The other main faction in Congress, however—leaders who later became the Republican-Democrat Party that emerged in the 1790s—feared maintaining a standing army and opposed a larger government fueled by national taxes. They wanted to maintain the national government just as it was—as a weak alliance of individually strong states.

Deadlock followed. It was a dangerous moment. The threat by the army's officers to use force was real. They had been promised payment. Congress had now linked the payments to other agendas and postponed action. While most of those in the army were angry, there were also significant differences among them. A group of young officers were ready for action. They thought that George Washington was far too moderate. Their hero was Horatio Gates, who had led the victory at Saratoga and who disliked Washington. Some around Gates, perhaps in consultation with some Federalists in Congress, began planning for military action. In March 1783, Major John Armstrong, Jr., published the first of what were called the "Newburgh Addresses," anonymously belittling the "milk and water style" and "meek language" of the previous petitions to Congress and calling for a meeting of the officers to discuss the situation.

General Washington was horrified. Military action would undermine everything for which he and the officers had fought. But Washington was a crafty politician. He simply asked the officers to postpone their meeting by a few days, invited Gates to preside, and requested a full report, implying that he would not be there. The officers who wanted action thought they could now meet with Washington's blessing and do what they wanted.

But when Gates called the meeting to order, Washington entered the room and requested permission to speak. Though he was furious, Gates knew he could not refuse Washington in front of the other officers. Washington then attacked the anonymous "Newburgh Addresses" as "unmilitary" and "subversive of all order and discipline." He reminded the officers, "I have been … the constant companion and witness of your distresses." Would the army, he asked, contemplate attacking the Congress? "My God!" he said. "What can this writer have in view," by recommending such measures?

The speech worked. The officers cheered Washington. All threat of military action against the weak civil government was over. Congress voted to give a lump sum payment to all the officers who had been promised a pension and passed a tax on imports to pay off the national debt, including the debt to the army.

The so-called Newburgh Conspiracy was defeated. In November, the last British troops left New York City, and the American officers and their troops marched into the city and began its transition to civilian leadership. Instead of seizing power, the Continental Army began to disband, with payment as promised. Washington made a triumphal entry into the city and, on December 4, 1783, gave an emotional farewell to his officers. He then returned to civilian life at his home in Mount Vernon, Virginia. By January 1784, the army had shrunk to some six hundred soldiers.

North Wind Picture Archives / Alamy Stock Photo

Having led the American army through the hard years of the Revolutionary War and ensured a transition to civilian government, George Washington said farewell to many of the officers who had served with him. He retired from military service to Mount Vernon in December 1783.

For Poor White Farmers: Shays's Rebellion

Like the officers of the Continental Army, the poor of colonial society—now the poor of the new nation—were also unhappy, in some cases violently unhappy. Some had served as enlisted soldiers in the revolutionary army and had their own complaints about salaries. Beginning in 1784, the influx of imported goods that came with the war's end created an economic depression that hit the poor hardest. One response to this unhappiness in the first years of the new Republic took place in Massachusetts and came to be known as **Shays's Rebellion**, named for one of its leaders, Daniel Shays. Those who participated in the rebellion called themselves Regulators—not to be confused with those in the Carolinas who had taken the law into their own hands before the Revolution—but simply people who wanted to regulate the power of the new state governments.

In 1786, farmers in western Massachusetts began petitioning the state legislature for relief from economic hardships brought on by a significant increase in their taxes as the legislature tried to pay off Revolutionary War debts and by the postwar economic depression that reduced the value of farm products. For farmers who were used to being self-sufficient, the reduction in their income and demands for taxes to be paid in cash were too much to accept. In the 1780s, many rural people in Massachusetts and throughout the nation lived in what was essentially a barter economy. People traded with each other or with the occasional merchant. There was very little cash or the need for cash, which was seen as something that only more urban and wealthy people worried about. But the state's demand that taxes be paid in cash, which they did not have, threatened them with foreclosure and in the longer run challenged their whole way of life, which they saw as being destroyed because they could not raise the money demanded of them. They had to do something.

When faced with the petitions of the farmers, the Massachusetts legislature, dominated by commercial leaders from the eastern part of the state, blamed the farmers for their own plight. In response, the farmers decided on direct action. They simply stopped the courts from issuing foreclosure rulings. On August 29, 1786, 1,500 farmers armed with clubs and muskets shut down the court in Northampton as it attempted to hear cases. They also stopped courts in four other towns.

The governor and legislature reacted by passing a Riot Act that prohibited twelve or more armed persons from gathering and authorized county sheriffs to kill those who disobeyed the law. They also suspended the writ of habeas corpus and authorized the governor to arrest and hold without bail "any person or persons whatsoever."

But the farmers, many of whom had fought as soldiers in the Revolution, were prepared to fight a second time. From their perspective, the Massachusetts legislature was acting like the former royal governor. Shays and several thousand of his fellow citizens now took up arms, fearing for "our lives and families which will be taken from us if we don't defend them."

By January 1787, the Regulators had decided to overthrow the government of Massachusetts. Shays himself planned to attack the federal arsenal in Springfield and then march to Boston to "destroy the nest of devils, who by their influence, make the Court enact what they please, burn it and lay the town of Boston in ashes." He came close to succeeding.

By late January, thousands of well-armed farmers surrounded the federal arsenal in Springfield, which was defended by one thousand state militia under the command of Major General William Shepard. Unfortunately for the rebellion, different groups thought the assault was set for different days, and so on January 25, as a smaller group than expected marched on the arsenal, Shepard's troops fired over their heads but then directly into their ranks. Four or five were killed, and the rest retreated. They did not immediately give up their idea of overthrowing the state government, but no other attack came as close to doing so.

Shays's Rebellion

An armed movement of debt-ridden farmers in western Massachusetts in the winter of 1786–1787 who objected to the state's effort to tax them to pay off the Revolutionary War debt.

The Art Gallery Collection / Alamy Stock Photo

Shays's Rebellion, an uprising of poor farmers who were in danger of losing their land because of increased taxes, symbolized the discontent that many Americans felt during the economic downturn after the Revolution, but it also struck fear into many other Americans who believed the nation was on the edge of anarchy and needed a much stronger central government to deal with matters.

6.1

6.2

As 1787 wore on, the rebellion slowly ended. The Regulators were not able to establish a political base. In 1788, the economy began to recover, which made life more tolerable for farmers. Some of the rebels left Massachusetts for more remote places. Shays himself settled in Vermont. But the rebels had terrified the nation's elite and hastened the movement toward a stronger national government that could control any such uprisings in the future.

Fears of the rebellion in Massachusetts inspired other revolutionary leaders to act. When he first heard news of Shays's Rebellion, Washington told Henry Lee of Virginia that the rebellion was "proof of what our trans-Atlantic foe has predicted … that mankind when left to themselves are unfit for their own Government." But, despite their worries, men like Washington and Lee were determined not to let such a proof stand. The convention that met in Philadelphia in the summer of 1787 was a direct result, an outcome that could only deeply disappoint Shays and his followers.

For White Settlers Moving West

The new nation was huge compared with the territorial size of the European powers. The Treaty of Paris recognized the eastern border of the United States as running along the Atlantic coast from Maine to Georgia. Britain had returned Florida to Spain at the end of the Revolutionary War, so the new nation was cut off from the Gulf of Mexico by Spanish Florida, and Spain, though an ally in fighting Britain during the Revolution, was not always a friendly southern neighbor. The Treaty of Paris also made the Mississippi River the nation's western boundary. Britain essentially abandoned its Indian allies, and left them to their fate with the United States. Control of the Mississippi River itself—the right to travel on it—would remain contested, especially since the river ended at the city of New Orleans, which Spain zealously guarded (see Map 6-1).

Within this vast territory, the thirteen states hugged the Atlantic coast. Though abandoned by their British allies, American Indians still dominated the interior. More whites were crossing the mountains and claiming western lands despite the lack of government approval and the dangers of Indian attack. Some of the original royal charters gave many of the states claims to lands far into the interior. But soon after the Revolution ended, the Continental Congress began resolving conflicting land claims and creating new states and territories west of the original thirteen states, even though white settlement in some of these territories was dangerous if not impossible.

One of the first issues to be resolved was over the conflicting claims of New York and New Hampshire to the land on the eastern side of Lake Champlain. Many of the whites who had settled the region wanted independence from both. Local heroes, such as Ethan Allen and his Green Mountain Boys, had fought for the American cause in the region and wanted to control their home. As a result, Vermont became the first new state in 1791 (see Map 6-2, p. 166).

One of the most significant accomplishments of the Congress that operated under the Articles of Confederation was the creation of the Northwest Territory out of lands claimed by Pennsylvania, New York, Connecticut, and Massachusetts. Between 1784 and 1787, Congress set up territorial governments for what would become Ohio, Indiana, Illinois, Michigan, and Wisconsin.

It took years of difficult negotiations before the original states gave up their conflicting claims to the interior lands, but ordinances passed between 1784 and 1787 created a new structure for the future Midwest. In 1785, Congress ordered that the lands be surveyed, set off into a grid pattern with most sections to be sold, while some were reserved for future government needs and specifically for

Map 6-1 The American-Spanish Border, 1783–1795.

In the Treaty of Paris, Great Britain not only recognized American independence but also returned control of Florida to Spain, creating the southern border for the United States; though, as the map shows, the border was far from clear. West of the United States was the vast Louisiana Territory, for the time being also under Spanish control.

Map 6-2 State Claims to Western Lands.

The huge tract of land that the King's Proclamation Line had reserved for Indian tribes before the Revolution became part of the United States in 1783. Different original states claimed this land and one of the first duties of Congress was to sort out those conflicting claims. After 1783, no one in government spoke for the rights of the Native Americans whose land much of the territory had been.

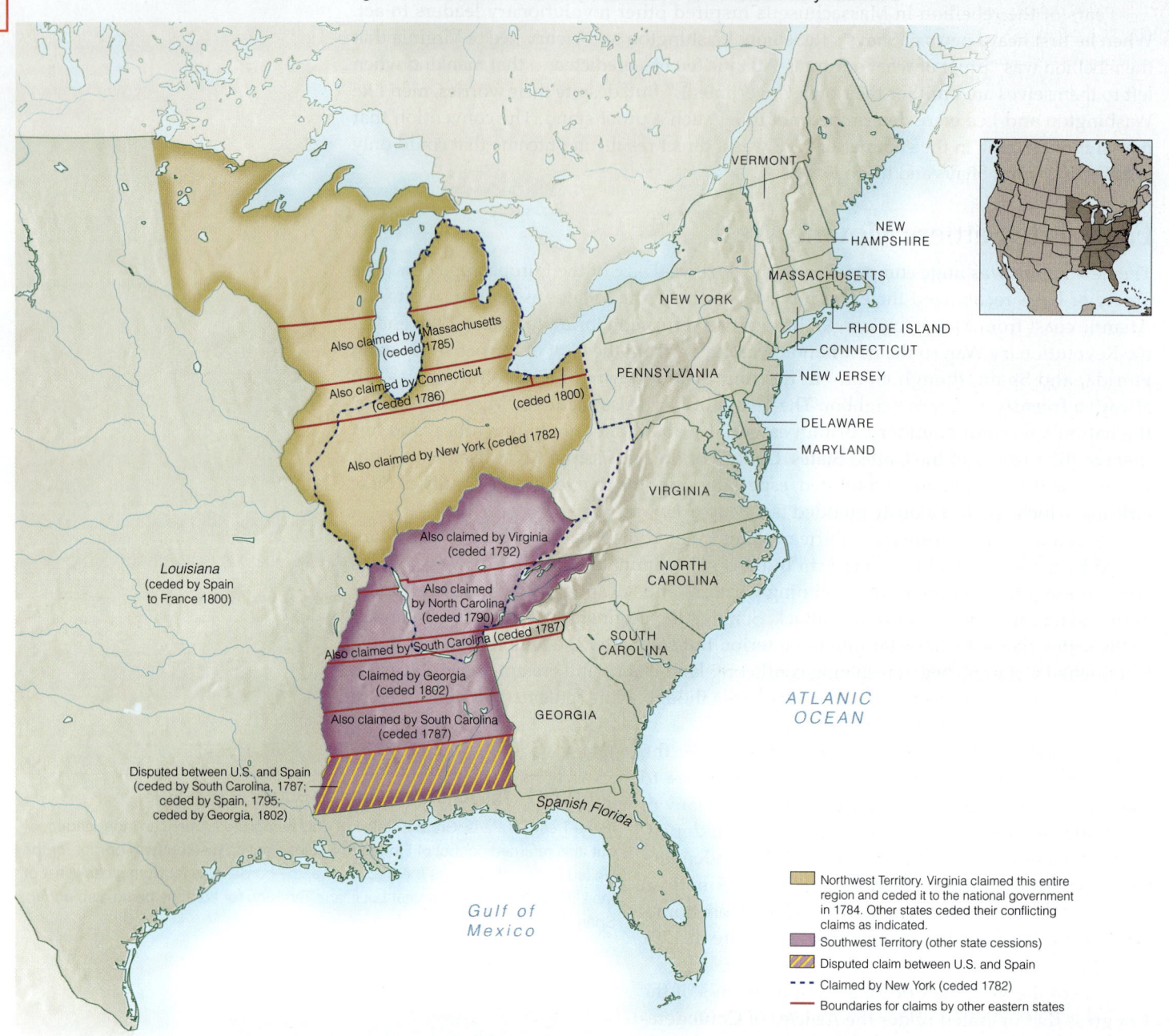

The Northwest Ordinance of 1787

Legislation passed by Congress under the Articles of Confederation that provided for public schools, authorized the sale of government land, and prohibited slavery in the Northwest Territories.

the support of schools. Earlier colonies had used rivers, mountains, and natural barriers to set off boundary lines. The grid system had the disadvantage of crossing many of these features, but had the great virtues of simplicity and clarity, which made it very popular. The grid system established in 1785 was used in future territories, creating clear and well-organized boundaries for farms and towns, but encouraging widely dispersed settlements rather than compact communities (see Map 6-3). **The Northwest Ordinance of 1787** banned slavery in these territories as well as mandated religious freedom and the development of public schools. The act also declared that "the utmost good faith shall always be observed towards the Indians; their lands and property shall never be taken from them without their consent," though little was done to enforce this provision.

Map 6-3   The Northwest Territory Grid System.

The Northwest Ordinance divided the territory into what would become five states. It also created a survey system in which the land would be divided into townships made up of thirty-six "sections," thirty-five of which would be available to settlers and one of which would be reserved to support schools.

Farther south, white settlement was, if anything, proceeding faster. An accomplished soldier, hunter, and trapper, Daniel Boone first explored the trans-Appalachian territory that would be known as Kentucky in 1767 when it was still off-limits to whites. As the Revolution was starting in 1775 and the British ability to stop settlement was ebbing, Boone blazed the "Wilderness Trail" through the Cumberland Gap in the Appalachians and established a settlement he called Boonesborough. During and after the war, many more settlers followed the Wilderness Trail. Virginia gave up its long-standing claims to the region, and the federal government, recognizing that there were already slaves in the territory, admitted Kentucky to the union as a slave state in 1792 and Tennessee in 1796.

Even farther south, the land west of Georgia that would eventually become the northern two-thirds of Alabama and Mississippi was organized as the Mississippi Territory in 1798, but the territorial government there was ineffective, and Georgia did not give up its own claims until 1802. (The southern third of Alabama and Mississippi was known as West Florida, part of the Spanish-controlled territory on the country's southern border.) While the Congress tried to settle conflicting claims to the western lands, the Indians, who had the oldest claim to the land, had no inclination to give it up.

For American Indians

For the federal Congress, the greatest threat to the new United States came from American Indians, just as the Indians' greatest threat came from the United States. For most of the tribes who lived between the Atlantic coast and the Mississippi River, the end of the American Revolution was one more in a long line of disasters. Despite the loyalty of the Iroquois to the British during the Revolution, the king's government agreed to the Treaty of Paris in 1783, which ceded all the lands between the Atlantic coast and the Mississippi and south of the Great Lakes and Canada to the new United States, without consulting with their old allies or including any provisions to protect their interests. The Proclamation Line limiting white settlement was gone. Among the many Indian tribes, even among the Iroquois, there were differing responses to the British failure to honor their loyalty. Many Indian leaders saw no reason to honor a treaty in which they had played no part and continued to act as if much of New York and Pennsylvania and all lands west of the Ohio River belonged to them.

Under the leadership of Joseph Brant, the Mohawks, who had fought so hard for the British between 1776 and 1781, petitioned the British authorities in Quebec for land on the British side of the new border and were granted a large tract in Canada. But they, like other tribes, did not let an international boundary limit their range of hunting or living. New York and Pennsylvania petitioned the Congress for help with the Indian tribes on their western frontiers, and the New York legislature considered expelling all the tribes of the Six Nations because of their alliance with the British during the war (see Map 6-4).

Through the Treaty of Paris, the British promised to withdraw from all forts south of the Great Lakes, but in fact, they were slow to honor their commitment to leave. Rather than depend on state militia, Congress in 1783 began to create the U.S. Army to occupy Fort Niagara near today's Buffalo, New York, and Fort Pitt, today's Pittsburgh. Although Congress could create an army, its difficulty in raising funds meant that the secretary of war, former general Henry Knox, had to beg for money to keep the army paid, fed, and supplied, which strengthened the hand of Indian leaders committed to resisting white expansion. And many meant to resist.

Map 6-4 Ohio in the 1780s.

The land that would later become the state of Ohio was a battlefield in the 1780s. While Great Britain included the land as part of the newly independent United States in 1783, in reality Native American tribes were the dominant force in the region and they often received aid from their Canadian-based British allies.

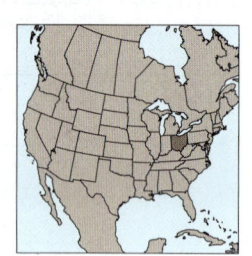

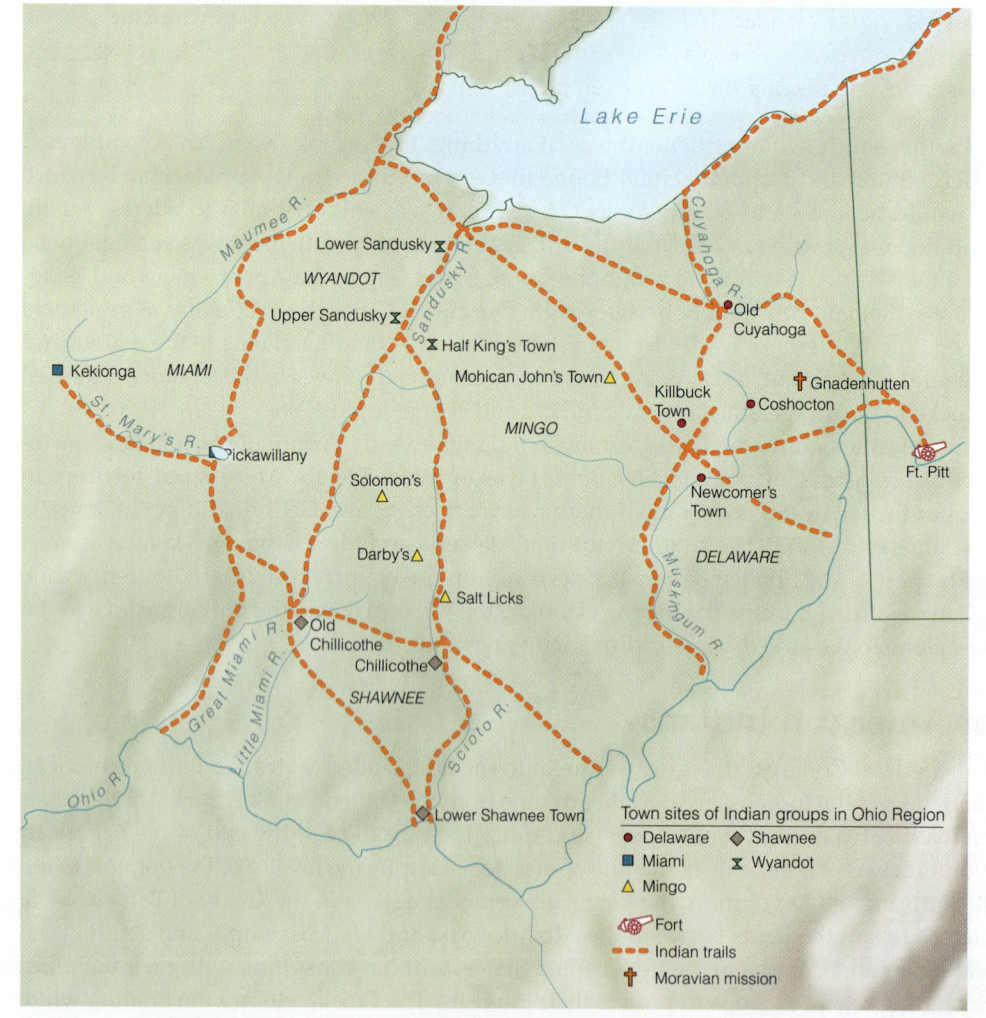

The Iroquois were far from the only Indians resisting American expansion. Many tribes had never formally agreed to peace with the new nation, and they attacked both the army and settlers. The small battles—individual attacks, kidnappings, and destruction of property—continued as they had during the Revolution. The U.S. Army was far too small, ill-trained, and ill-supplied to be much of a deterrent or to protect white settlers. Given how weak the army was, the Indians held the upper hand in the Northwest Territory and Kentucky.

A temporary peace along the New York border was secured in October 1784 by the **Treaty of Fort Stanwix** between some of the Iroquois and the U.S. government. But many, including Sagoyewatha (Red Jacket) of the Seneca and Joseph Brant of the Mohawks, opposed the treaty, and it did not hold. In fact, the Indians of the Northwest Territory would remain virtually at war with the United States from 1785 until 1795.

After the Treaty of Fort Stanwix was signed, Brant sailed for London where he met with many high-ranking British officials and had an audience with King George III. He sought financial support for his people as compensation for their role on the British side in the Revolution, and he—and his British hosts—also seem to have developed a plan for Indian resistance to the new American nation.

In 1785 and 1786, Brant began to create an Indian confederation to resist the United States. The confederation included the Iroquois, many other Indian nations who had been traditional enemies of the Iroquois, as well as Cherokees from much farther south and smaller groups who resided in the Ohio River Valley. It would be one of the most unified and effective adversaries that the United States would face. The Indians demanded that the Congress ensure that white settlement ended at the Ohio River.

While the Indians and Congress negotiated fitfully, the frontier remained a violent place. In the late 1780s, 1,500 white settlers and at least as many Indians in Ohio and Kentucky were killed (see Map 6-5, p. 170). The United States had no intention of ceding as much land to the Indians as they demanded, but under the Articles of Confederation, it was difficult to organize an army to enforce the government's claims. The perceived need to create a government strong enough to counter the Indians led many to support the Constitution in 1787.

For Slaves, Former Slaves, and Those Who Claimed Ownership of Them

In 1791, Benjamin Banneker, a free African American, wrote to Thomas Jefferson, then Washington's secretary of state, reminding him that in 1776 Jefferson had written "that all men are created equal, and that they are endowed by their creator with certain inalienable rights." Banneker continued:

> [B]ut sir, how pitiable is it to reflect that although you were so fully convinced of the benevolence of the Father of mankind ... you should ... counteract his mercies, in detaining by fraud and violence so numerous a part of my brethren, under groaning captivity and cruel oppression, that you should ... be found guilty of that most criminal act, which you professedly detested in others, with respect to yourselves.

Banneker would not let Jefferson forget the contradiction at the heart of the new American enterprise and Jefferson's own life.

As Banneker's letter indicates, many slaves and former slaves understood that the words *freedom* and *liberty* also ought to count for them. By the end of the Revolution, many whites agreed. Back in 1775, Thomas Paine asked how Americans could complain about British tyranny "while they hold so many hundreds of thousands in slavery."

The issue of freedom and liberty seemed to be gaining ground for some slaves after 1776. News traveled slowly, but word spread that in 1794, in the midst of the French Revolution, the French National Convention had abolished slavery, and then that slaves in France's most lucrative Caribbean colony had won independence for what became the black-led Republic of Haiti.

When Cornwallis surrendered at Yorktown in 1781, he had between four thousand and five thousand former slaves with his army. Many more were in other British-held areas,

Treaty of Fort Stanwix
A 1784 treaty between one faction of the Iroquois and the U.S. government that sought to end the violent battles over land in New York, Pennsylvania, and the Ohio River Valley to the west.

Joseph Brant, or Thayendanegea, was a leader among the Mohawks who convinced many in the Iroquois federation to support the British cause during the Revolution and oppose American expansion after the war as he negotiated for Native American rights. He was one of the very few people of any race to meet with both George Washington and King George III.

Map 6-5 Tribal Land Claims, 1783–1788.

Especially in the Southwest of the new United States, strong Native American tribes clamed large areas and did not much care whether the United States or Spain claimed the territory since they did not want settlers from either country.

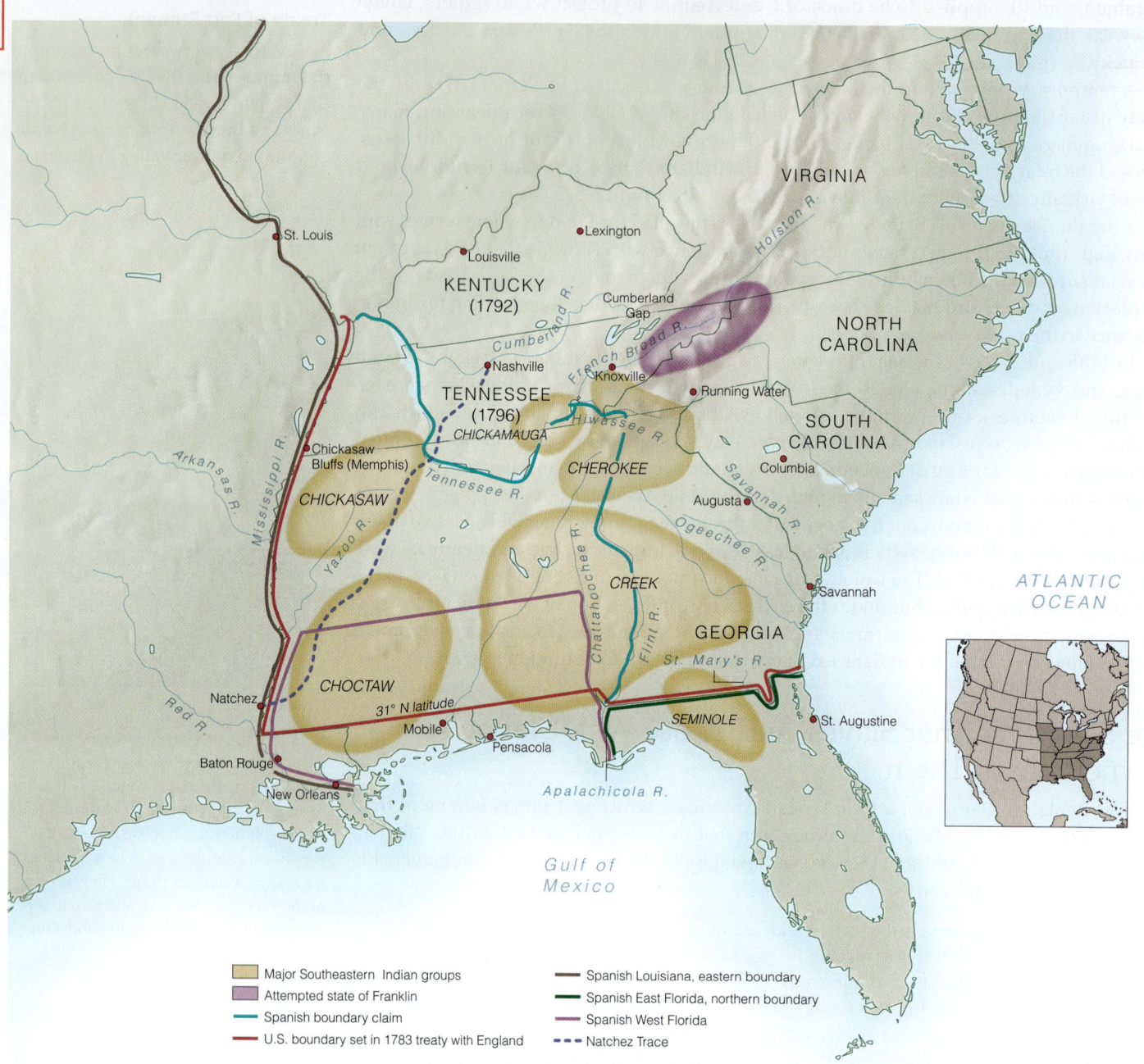

Major Southeastern Indian groups
Attempted state of Franklin
Spanish boundary claim
U.S. boundary set in 1783 treaty with England
Spanish Louisiana, eastern boundary
Spanish East Florida, northern boundary
Spanish West Florida
Natchez Trace

especially New York City. As the war ended, the British returned some slaves to old masters, gave others to new masters in the Caribbean, or simply abandoned them. But many former slaves also sailed with the British when they left the colonies, some settling as free people in Canada, England, or West Africa. A former slave named Boston King wrote that "[t]he English had compassion upon us in the day of distress. Soon after, ships were fitted out, and furnished with every necessary for conveying us to Nova Scotia." Life was not easy for African Americans in Nova Scotia, but they were free.

By the time George Washington was inaugurated president in 1789, slavery had been abolished in Massachusetts, New Hampshire, and Vermont and was dying—though slowly—throughout the north. Northern slaves worked as household help and labored in factories and farms. New York had the most slaves in the North, concentrated in

Manhattan and working on the great estates of the Hudson Valley. New Jersey and Rhode Island were next in number. In the North, however, more money was made on the slave trade than on slave labor. The Northwest Ordinance prohibited slavery in the Ohio region. Many thought slavery would also die out in Delaware, Maryland, and Virginia. Only in the Carolinas, Georgia, and the new western areas of Kentucky and Tennessee was slavery still strong.

Despite the regional differences, by 1789, one in ten African Americans was a free person. Some had won their freedom through the army. Some had won through state action. Some had been set free by individual slave owners. But in 1789, one could not assume that to be black was to be a slave. That truth was a significant change from 1776 when free blacks were a definite exception in every one of the thirteen colonies.

After Massachusetts, New Hampshire, and Vermont abolished slavery, other northern states with more slaves moved exceedingly slowly toward gradual emancipation (Table 6-1). The Pennsylvania law of 1780 declared slavery "disgraceful to any people," but then set up a system in which the first slaves would not be freed until 1808 and the last would not be emancipated until 1847. New York's abolition law of 1799 and New Jersey's of 1804, as well as similar laws in Connecticut and Rhode Island, were equally slow in their operations. Although every northern state had started the process of ending slavery before 1800, it was almost 1850 before slavery disappeared in the North.

Free blacks sometimes found work in the same households where they had been slaves. Black men worked on merchant ships, whaling vessels, or even in the navy. (The racially diverse crew of the whaling ship *Pequod* in Herman Melville's 1851 novel *Moby Dick* was not unusual.) In Philadelphia, New York, Providence, and Boston, many blacks worked on the docks. Throughout the northern states more and more free blacks referred to themselves as Africans or, as the Free African Society of Philadelphia said, "free Africans and their descendants."

In Delaware, Maryland, Virginia, and North Carolina, slavery did not die out, but slave life changed after the Revolution. Some masters heeded the revolutionary language of freedom. James Madison freed one slave named Billy because he came to fear that Billy's love

Table 6-1 The Free Black Population in the Early United States

State	Free black population in 1790	Total black population in 1790	Percentage of free blacks in total black population	Free black population in 1810	Total black population in 1810	Percentage of free blacks in total black population
New Hampshire	630	788	80%	970	970	100%
Vermont	255	271	94%	750	750	100%
Massachusetts	6,001	6,001	100%	7,706	7,706	100%
Connecticut	2,808	5,572	50%	6,453	6,763	95%
Rhode Island	3,407	4,355	78%	3,609	3,717	97%
New York	4,654	25,978	18%	25,333	40,350	63%
New Jersey	2,762	14,185	19%	7,843	18,694	42%
Pennsylvania	6,537	10,324	63%	22,492	23,287	97%
Delaware	3,899	12,786	30%	13,136	17,313	76%
Maryland	8,043	111,079	7%	33,927	145,429	23%
Virginia	12,866	305,493	4%	30,570	423,088	7%
North Carolina	4,975	105,547	5%	10,266	179,090	6%
Kentucky	114	12,544	1%	1,713	82,274	2%
Tennessee	361	3,778	10%	1,317	45,845	3%
District of Columbia	District not yet established	District not yet established	District not yet established	2,549	7,944	32%
South Carolina	1,801	108,895	2%	4,544	200,919	2%
Georgia	398	29,662	1%	1,801	107,019	2%

6.1

6.2

American Voices

Prince Hall, "From Slavery to Equality," 1797

Born a slave, Prince Hall was freed before the Revolution, and after the war he played a leading role in abolishing slavery in Massachusetts. Hall helped create the African Lodge of the Masons in Boston and delivered the following speech to that group in 1797.

Now, my brethren, nothing is stable; all things are changeable. Let us seek those things which are sure and steadfast, and let us pray God that, while we remain here, he would give us the grace of patience and strength to bear up under all our troubles, which, at this day, God knows, we have our share of. Patience, I say; for were we not possessed of a great measure of it, we could not bear up under the daily insults we meet with in the streets of Boston, much more on public days of recreation. … Helpless women have their clothes torn from their backs. … I was told by a gentleman who saw this filthy behavior in the Common that, in all places he had been in, he never saw so cruel behavior in all his life; and that a slave in the West Indies on Sundays or holidays enjoys himself and friends without molestation. …

My brethren, let us not be cast down under these and many other abuses we at present are laboring under, for the darkest hour is just before the break of day. My brethren, let us remember what a dark day it was with our African brethren, six years ago, in the French West Indies. Nothing but the snap of the whip was heard, from morning to evening. Hanging, breaking on the wheel, burning and all manner of tortures were inflicted upon those unhappy people. But, blessed be God, the scene is changed. They now confess that God hath no respect of person and, therefore, receive them as their friends and treat them as brothers. Thus doth Ethiopia stretch forth her hand from slavery, to freedom and equality.

Source: Prince Hall, "Thus Doth Ethiopia Stretch Forth Her Hand from Slavery, to Freedom and Equality" (1797), in Manning Marable and Leith Mullings, editors, *Let Nobody Turn Us Around: Voices of Resistance, Reform, and Renewal* (Lanham, MD: Rowman & Littlefield, 2000), pp. 16–18.

Thinking Critically

1. **Analyzing Primary Sources**
   What light does Hall's speech shed on race relations in Boston in the decades after the Revolution?

2. **Contextualization**
   How did the American Revolution and the revolts in Haiti shape Hall's thinking?

---

of freedom meant he was no longer "a fit companion for fellow slaves." George Washington wrote often of his wish that slavery could be gradually abolished and left instructions in his will that all his slaves should be free after he and Martha died. Other planters in the region also freed slaves. Slaves who had run away during the war managed to establish new identities and maintain their freedom, especially in cities like Baltimore, Richmond, and the new District of Columbia. By 1810, almost a quarter of the African Americans in Maryland, a third in the District of Columbia, and 6 or 7 percent in Virginia and North Carolina were free. In 1792, Thomas Brown, a black Revolutionary War veteran in Baltimore, ran, although unsuccessfully, for the Maryland legislature, promising to "represent so many hundreds of poor Blacks."

In the Virginia-Maryland region, slaves and free blacks worked in an economy that was more diverse than before the war. By 1790, slaves were growing wheat, a crop that required plows, fertilizer, and horses that needed tending. They also worked in flour mills and the ironworks, blacksmith shops, and other enterprises that were springing up in the region. Some slaves were "rented out" and moved from job to job, giving them a chance to learn more skills, travel short distances, make a little money, and gain a taste of freedom.

Other slaves were far less fortunate. In the years after the Revolution, with the plantations of Virginia and Maryland stabilized in size, slave owners needed fewer slaves. So they increased their wealth by developing a new internal market in humans. They encouraged slaves to have more children and then, as those children reached adolescence, sold them, as they sold other agricultural products, for transport to places that needed more and more slave labor. Slaves were taken to Kentucky and Tennessee. Other slaves were transported to South Carolina and Georgia. (Georgia had banned slavery at its founding in 1735, but settlers there demanded the same rights as other whites in the British colonies, and in 1751 slavery was legalized in Georgia.)

In South Carolina and Georgia, life for slaves was very different. Some of the fiercest fighting of the Revolution had disrupted almost every aspect of life there, and slaves had more opportunities to run away. With the coming of peace, however, the planter elite in these states was determined to reestablish a way of life that depended on slavery.

Slaves represented between 40 and 60 percent of the population in South Carolina and Georgia. Slave labor had produced great fortunes for the plantation owners before the war, and it would produce new fortunes for them after the war ended.

Whereas many planters in Delaware, Maryland, Virginia, and North Carolina may have felt the need to modify the tyranny of slavery, planters in South Carolina and Georgia made it clear that they had no such intentions. The few free blacks in the southernmost states, often people who had black, white, and Indian heritage, were kept as far away from the slave community as possible so the slaves would not hear the contagious language of freedom.

In the twenty years after 1790, the number of slaves doubled in South Carolina from 100,000 to 200,000, and in Georgia it more than tripled from 30,000 to over 100,000. The rapid growth of the slave population in South Carolina and Georgia at the end of the 1700s also led to a new kind of community life in the slave quarters of these large plantations. Unlike those who owned a lone slave or a single slave family, which could be closely supervised, the largest plantations in South Carolina and Georgia had hundreds of slaves in the 1790s. Slave labor created great wealth, and the owners of these plantations were the economic elite of their states, but they were often away, preferring the social life of Charleston or Savannah. Slaves, though driven by overseers, were able to develop their own community lives and norms within the slave quarters, which had not been possible on the smaller farms and plantations of an earlier era. Having their own vegetable gardens sometimes gave slaves limited economic freedom. Religious gatherings, sometimes sanctioned and sometimes secret, provided communal support.

One of the key compromises (discussed later in this chapter) among those writing the U.S. Constitution in 1787 was a clause that Congress could not ban the international slave trade until 1808. When 1808 arrived, Congress did ban the importation of any additional slaves from Africa or anywhere outside the United States. Starting with Virginia in 1778, some states banned the importation of slaves even earlier. And Great Britain banned the slave trade in 1807, one year before the United States did. The size and power of Britain's Royal Navy meant that Britain's ban, which the government was determined to enforce, was especially effective. While some traders managed the illegal smuggling of slaves into the nation until the very end of the Civil War, the 1808 action drastically curtailed U.S. participation in the international slave trade. After 1808, the major growth in the population of enslaved Africans in the United States came from births to slave mothers in the states that still allowed slavery.

For Women: The Rise of Republican Motherhood

In April 1776, Abigail Adams wrote to her husband, John, while the future president was attending the Congress that would issue the Declaration of Independence in Philadelphia and she was managing the family and farm in Quincy, Massachusetts, from which he was so often absent. She told him to "remember the ladies." And she warned, "Do not put such unlimited power into the hands of husbands. … If particular care and attention is not paid to the ladies we are determined to foment a rebellion, and will not hold ourselves bound by any laws in which we have no voice or representation." Her husband treated his wife's plea as a kind of joke, saying, "Our struggle has loosened the bonds of government everywhere; that children and apprentices were disobedient," but, he said, Abigail's letter "was the first intimation that another tribe, more numerous and powerful than all the rest, were grown discontented." We do not know how she responded to having her husband lump her plea for a voice in government with the discontent of children and apprentices. Abigail and John had a close marriage, but while she was serious about wanting the American Revolution to recognize more rights for women, he was equally determined to ignore her plea.

Women, of course, fell into all of the different groups that men did. American Indian women, most of whom like the men had supported the British, often paid a high price for their loyalty to Britain. Mary (Molly) Brant, the sister of Joseph Brant, convinced many Iroquois to support an Iroquois-British alliance during the war. When the war ended, she found a new home in Canada, reminding the British authorities that they were not providing the support they had promised her people.

Slave women also sided with the British more often than with the American Revolutionaries. With British armies operating in the southern colonies, and the British welcoming slaves to their side, women as well as men fled to freedom with the British. Of the twenty-three slaves who ran away from Thomas Jefferson's plantations during the Revolution, thirteen were female. More than 40 percent of all of the former slaves who left with the British at the end of the war were women.

Some white women—rich and poor—also supported the British cause and paid dearly for it. With the coming of the war, many Loyalist wives stayed behind to mind their homes when their husbands joined the British army or fled to Canada. These women faced hostile neighbors, and many lost their homes.

Having lived through the Revolution in Massachusetts and become a leader in the Universalist churches, Judith Sargent Murray also came to be one of the strongest voices demanding absolute equality for women in the new nation.

For white women who supported the Revolution, life was also hard, but the outcome was usually better. The Revolutionary War shaped the lives of most women who had supported it. For some, it changed virtually every aspect of life. After the war, Deborah Sampson, who had pretended to be a man and fought in the war, married and lived in Sharon, Massachusetts, but she was also entertained by President Washington, was granted a revolutionary soldier's pension by Congress, and became something of a national hero. Other women did not easily return to their old ways, limited to the private sphere of their families. With many men away for months or years, women took on household duties that were, by long tradition, men's exclusive sphere. Mary Bartlett, whose husband represented New Hampshire in Congress, reflected a changed attitude experienced by many. In her first letters in 1776, she wrote about "Your farming business," but by 1778, it had become "our farming business." The difference of one word made it clear she now included herself in the ownership of their farm—an important change.

Many women who had coped with years of isolation during the war found that the political independence of the United States brought personal independence, too. More women postponed marriage, demanded divorces from unhappy marriages, and sought higher education as well as new—if limited—political involvement in the new republic.

For many Americans, women and men, the book *A Vindication of the Rights of Woman*, written in 1792 by British writer Mary Wollstonecraft, gave words to ideas that had been taking shape since the Revolution. In her appeal for equality, Wollstonecraft called for equal education, and coeducation, for girls and boys. In America, Judith Sargent Murray expanded Wollstonecraft's arguments and insisted that women are indeed "in every respect equal to men."

Important as they were, the ideas about total equality developed by Wollstonecraft and Murray did not become the dominant ideology of the new nation. Instead, something much more moderate, **Republican Motherhood**, came to dominate public discussion. As the ideology of Republican Motherhood was developed—usually by men—in pulpits and magazines after the Revolution, women would have an important role, but a limited one—not full citizenship but also no return to a merely passive role in the domestic sphere that had been prescribed before 1776. Republican Motherhood was a kind of middle position. Its advocates suggested that women would advise their husbands and raise their sons to be active citizens and their daughters to be part of another generation of republican mothers who shaped the nation from home. But to play this role, its advocates insisted, women also needed an education, perhaps a different education from men, but a better one than that given to their mothers and grandmothers.

In 1778, Abigail Adams wrote, "I regret … how fashionable it has been to ridicule Female learning." After the war, she and many others planned to do something about it. Private academies, which had educated white male leaders for a century, began to open their doors to women, or more often, separate private academies for women were founded like the Young Ladies' Academy of Philadelphia that Benjamin Rush opened in 1787. Rush, whose views reflected the ideology of Republican Motherhood, insisted that the "attention of our young ladies should be directed as soon as they are prepared for it to the reading of history, travels, poetry, and moral essays … to the present state of society

Republican Motherhood

The belief that women should have more rights and a better education so that they might support husbands and raise sons who would actively participate in the political affairs of society.

Terra Foundation for American Art, Chicago/Art Resource, NY

American Voices

Judith Sargent Murray, "On the Equality of the Sexes," 1792

Judith Sargent Murray was born into a merchant family in Massachusetts in 1751. She was a leader of the Universalist movement in religion, which believed that all people were saved, a belief that led them to emphasize equality, including equality of the sexes. She wanted an education that would make women the equals of their brothers, husbands, and sons. Her most famous book, On the Equality of the Sexes, *was published in 1792.*

Is it upon mature consideration we adopt the idea, that nature is thus partial in her distributions? Is it indeed a fact, that she hath yielded to one half of the human species so unquestionable a mental superiority? ... May we not trace its source in the difference of education ... the one is taught to aspire, and the other is early confined and limited. As their years increase, the sister must be wholly domesticated, while the brother is led by the hand through all the flowery paths of science. Grant that their minds are by nature equal, yet who shall wonder at the *apparent* superiority, if indeed custom becomes *second nature*. ... At length arrived at womanhood, the uncultivated fair one feels a void, which the employments allotted her are by no means capable of filling. ... She experiences a mortifying consciousness of inferiority, which embitters every enjoyment. ... Now, was she permitted the same instructors as her brother, (with an eye however to their particular departments) for the employment of a rational mind an ample field would be opened. ... A mind, thus filled, would have little room for the trifles with which our sex are, with too much justice, accused of amusing themselves, and they would thus be rendered fit companions for those, who should one day wear them as their crown. ...

Should it still be vociferated, "Your domestic employments are sufficient"—I would calmly ask, is it reasonable, that a candidate for immortality, for the joys of heaven, an intelligent being, who is to spend an eternity in contemplating the works of Deity, should at present be so degraded, as to be allowed no other ideas, than those which are suggested by the mechanism of a pudding, or the sewing the seams of a garment? Pity that all such censurers of female improvement do not go one step further, and deny their future existence; to be consistent they surely ought.

Yes, ye lordly, ye haughty sex, our souls are by nature *equal* to yours; the same breath of God animates, enlivens, and invigorates us; and that we are not fallen lower than yourselves.

Source: Judith Sargent Murray, "On the Equality of the Sexes," first published in the *Massachusetts Magazine*, April 1790, reprinted in Eve Kornfeld, *Creating an American Culture, 1775–1800: A Brief History with Documents* (Boston: Bedford St. Martin's, 2001), pp. 127–132.

Thinking Critically

1. **Argument Development**
   How did Murray reflect or challenge Republican Motherhood?

2. **Contextualization**
   How did Murray's views reflect her religious faith? The fact that she lived through the Revolution? Her views of the proper education for women?

---

in America." When Priscilla Mason graduated from Rush's Young Ladies' Academy in 1794, however, she condemned the arbitrary limitations that "have denied us the means of knowledge, and then reproached us for the want of it." She continued, "The Church, the Bar, and the Senate are shut against us. Who shut them? Man, despotic man." An education that produced such a speaker may have been more than what Rush envisioned when he proposed the school.

Women also took a more direct role in politics when they could. New Jersey's 1776 Constitution gave women the right to vote, but the provision was repealed in 1807. The Bill of Rights that was added to the federal Constitution in 1791 gave all citizens—it did not exclude women—the right to "petition the government for a redress of grievances," and women regularly petitioned Congress and state legislatures. After the Revolution, women also gained significant new rights to control their own property, which they had not had before the war. It would be a long time before law and culture would support the equality that Abigail Adams or Judith Sargent Murray advocated. But attitudes had begun to change.

Within the ideology of Republican Motherhood, however, two double standards emerged. First, middle- and upper-class white women were expected to be the guardians of sexual morality. Men might stray, but, as a Philadelphia newspaper editorialized, "Ladies, much depends on you, towards a reformation in the morals of our sex." And if men did stray, it was expected they would do so only with lower-class or poor white women or with blacks, slave or free. Second, servants and working women were not included in either the rules or the opportunities for education and influence that the ideal of Republican Motherhood gave to supposedly all women, but in reality to only the increasingly well-educated and active women of higher social and economic status.

Although it is often forgotten, New Jersey's 1776 state constitution gave that state's women the right to vote, a right they exercised enthusiastically until the provision was repealed in 1807.

6.1 Quick Review

Did the Revolutionary War have a truly revolutionary effect on Britain's former colonies? How, specifically, did it impact differing groups of Americans?

Creating a Government: Writing the U.S. Constitution

6.2 **Explain the needs, pressures, and compromises that led to writing and adopting the Constitution.**

The years immediately after the Revolution were not easy ones in the new United States of America. Many Americans were unhappy. Farmers were angry about taxes. Frontier whites and Indians fought for control of the land. Many women were agitating for their own rights. Some of the most famous revolutionary leaders, including Washington, Franklin, and Hamilton, were determined to end the growing chaos and reshape the new nation they had helped to create.

The Crisis of the 1780s: The Failure of the Articles of Confederation

The problems that the nation faced in the 1780s had many sources. The Articles of Confederation were essentially a treaty among thirteen independent nations. All thirteen states needed to agree to levy any taxes, and nine states had to agree to pass a law. Real sovereignty rested with the state governments. Many Americans were happy with that arrangement. Some were not.

For present-day citizens, who live in a world in which a national government rules almost every spot on the planet, such a loose federation may seem surprising. But for the revolutionary generation, the arrangement was not strange at all. The separate colonies had experienced over a century of independent relationships with London. Until the 1760s, the links between each colony and Britain were much stronger than the ties between the various colonies. When Americans looked to Europe, they saw that small independent states and cities were the rule in what is now Germany and Italy. In that context, viewing Massachusetts, New York, and Virginia as independent states that were linked only in a loose confederation did not seem odd.

Nevertheless, leading citizens were concluding that the American confederation was not working. They believed that it was too weak, the state legislatures too strong, and that this imbalance was causing serious problems. Unlike their European models, the American confederation had acted as a united front to achieve independence, and that effort had a ripple effect on subsequent actions. Under the treaty that ended the Revolution, the United States—all of the states together—had promised to pay debts that it had incurred during the war—pensions for soldiers as well as the repayment of loans to U.S. citizens and foreign creditors. But Congress had no money and could not seem to raise any, given the requirement that all thirteen states agree to any tax. The credit rating of the new nation was dropping quickly, and the lack of faith in the government's ability to pay its debts was strangling the national economy. If the government could not pay off the loans negotiated during the Revolution, many European creditors thought, why loan any more money to either the American government or the American commercial enterprises?

The financial crisis had additional impacts. Indian tribes along the frontier were growing stronger, and the new nation risked losing control of its western lands because it could not afford a strong army to protect them. In 1785, a Shawnee leader, Piteasewa, told commissioners sent by the Congress, "We are aware of your design to divide our Councils, but we are unanimous." Although the Indians were never actually unanimous, in the 1780s they were still more than a match for the U.S. Army or the various state militias.

Moreover, many state legislatures not only failed to raise taxes or pay their state debts but often simply gave in when mobs of farmers like those in Massachusetts took control of the courthouses and stopped trials of those who had failed to pay debts or taxes. Charles Lee, one of Virginia's leading citizens, complained to George Washington in 1788 of the legislature's willingness to grant too much tax relief: "[T]he public debts and even private debts will in my opinion be extinguished by acts of the several Legislatures."

In September 1786, five states sent delegates to a convention in Maryland—known as the **Annapolis Convention**—to try to deal with yet another weakness of the Articles of Confederation—economic rivalry between the states that had led to a battle over navigation rights on the Potomac River between Maryland and Virginia and to a violent boundary dispute between New York and what would become Vermont. The convention never had a quorum and did no business, but it did give some leaders a chance to talk about the nation's problems. As a result, Alexander Hamilton wrote to the Congress asking that the states appoint delegates to meet in Philadelphia in May 1787 "to devise such further provisions as should appear to them necessary to render the constitution of the federal government adequate to the exigencies of the union."

In February 1787, five months after receiving Hamilton's letter, the Congress agreed to call a convention, but with limitations. They voted to ask the states to send delegates to Philadelphia "for the sole and express purpose of revising the Articles of Confederation, and reporting to Congress and the several legislatures such alterations and provisions therein as shall when agreed to in Congress and confirmed by the States, render the federal Constitution adequate to the exigencies of Government and the preservation of the Union." On the surface, this call was hardly a mandate for wholesale change. But it launched the Constitutional Convention of 1787, and the Convention would far exceed its authority. Some, including Madison and Hamilton, planned it that way from the beginning. The result would be a radically different form of government than the one under which the United States had won its freedom.

The Constitutional Convention of 1787

The fifty-five white men who gathered in what later came to be known as Independence Hall in Philadelphia in spring of 1787 for the **Constitutional Convention** represented the

Annapolis Convention

Conference of state delegates that issued a call in September 1786 for a convention to consider changes to the Articles of Confederation.

Constitutional Convention

Convention that met in Philadelphia in 1787 and drafted the Constitution of the United States.

In the spring of 1787, delegates from twelve of the thirteen states gathered in Independence Hall—now a national historic site—to write a new plan of government. After a summer of hard negotiations, they proposed what became the Constitution of the United States.

elite of the new nation. They had been appointed by twelve states; Rhode Island's legislature distrusted any effort to strengthen the central government and refused to send anyone. Most were fairly young. Twenty-nine had college degrees at a time when that achievement was rare. Only eight had signed the Declaration of Independence in 1776. Except for George Washington and Benjamin Franklin, some of the most prominent leaders of the Revolution were absent. Virginia's Patrick Henry and Massachusetts's John Hancock and Sam Adams refused to attend because they, too, worried that the convention would undermine the rights of individual states. Jefferson was away as U.S. ambassador to France. John Adams was ambassador to Britain. Women and the rebels of western Massachusetts who had marched with Daniel Shays, slaves and free blacks, and American Indians were not represented. But in that summer gathering in 1787, the delegates produced a frame of government that has served the United States well for more than two hundred years.

DECISIONS ON THE STRUCTURE OF A UNIFIED GOVERNMENT Coming to agreement at the Constitutional Convention involved long arguments and difficult compromises. The final result that the convention produced in September 1787 disappointed many. Surprisingly, all the delegates, even those who left in anger, kept to a pledge to keep their deliberations secret. All of the delegates wanted to be sure they had the time and freedom to talk through the difficult issues of the day without undue pressure from outside groups. No one outside the convention, including members of Congress who were still meeting in New York, had a clue what the distinguished group in Philadelphia would recommend.

A relatively young delegate from Virginia, James Madison (1751–1836), who had served in the Virginia legislature during the Revolution and had authored the Virginia Statute of Religious Freedom, was the key architect of the Constitution that emerged, although he never held a special office at the convention. In preparation for the convention, Madison privately arranged for the Virginia and Pennsylvania delegates to arrive in Philadelphia a week before the convention opened. He used that week to craft a plan that could be presented as soon as the convention got underway.

On May 29, the first day of business at the convention, Virginia's Governor Edmund Randolph, following Madison's plan, presented what came to be known as the **Virginia Plan**—the first outline of a new constitution. In Randolph's plan, a new Congress with two houses, whose members would be elected based on proportional representation reflecting the population of the various states, would replace the current Congress. The new government would represent the people, not necessarily thirteen equal states. If more people lived in certain states, especially Virginia and Massachusetts, then those states would have more votes in the Congress. The Congress would have the power to levy taxes, regulate interstate commerce, and veto state laws. Randolph also proposed creating a "national executive" and judiciary, or a set of federal courts.

The next day, May 30, the delegates endorsed a resolution from Pennsylvania's Gouverneur Morris that "a national government ought to be established consisting of a supreme legislative, executive, and judiciary." The basic outline of a strong new national government—one that included the **separation of powers** between the Congress, the executive branch, and the courts—had emerged quickly. The new system that Madison, Randolph, and Morris were proposing was also known as **federalism**, a system of government in which both the central national government and the individual state governments had real power, but in separate spheres of influence. But there would be many

Virginia Plan

The first proposal put forward at the Constitutional Convention, which included two houses of Congress, both elected by proportional representation, and a national executive and judiciary.

separation of powers

A core aspect of the Constitution by which different parts of the new national government would have their authority always limited by other parts.

federalism

A system of government in which power is clearly divided between state governments and the national—or federal—government.

days of meetings in a hot and stuffy Independence Hall before the details would be resolved and the Constitution itself would be completed.

From the opening day, there was a battle between those, generally from larger states, who wanted the new Congress to have **proportional representation**—that is, representatives elected directly by the voters of districts based on the size of a state's population—and those, generally from smaller states, who wanted Congress to be made up of representatives of the states themselves, so that each state would have an equal number of votes. The Virginia Plan called for proportional representation in both houses of the new Congress, but a subsequent plan put forward by New Jersey's William Paterson—not surprisingly known as the **New Jersey Plan**—called for a Congress in which both houses would be made up of delegates elected by state legislatures with an equal number from each state. While the delegates from the largest states, especially James Madison and Edmund Randolph, insisted that proportional representation was essential to a strong and democratic national government, Paterson, along with delegates from Delaware and surprisingly some from New York and Massachusetts, insisted that members of Congress should represent only state governments and that each state should be treated equally.

A compromise, first proposed by Connecticut's Roger Sherman—and sometimes called the **Connecticut Plan (or the Great Compromise)**—was to split the difference and create a House of Representatives, with the number of members from each state based on that state's population and elected by districts within the state, and a Senate made up of two senators from each state no matter what its population, elected by the state legislature. Adopting this Great Compromise, which was the key to the future Constitution, did not come easily.

Other issues were even more difficult to resolve. The convention came to a standstill over the office of president. Everyone assumed that the convention's presiding officer, George Washington, would be the first president in the new government, but few could agree on the details of the office or on how to select his successors. Some wanted an executive of several individuals in a cabinet of equals, while others insisted on a single leader. Most wanted to ensure that only the "wisest and best" citizens voted for the president, and almost none trusted the people to elect the president by a direct popular vote. But how to select the president—by the Congress, by state legislatures, or by some other formula—seemed impossible to resolve until Madison proposed the **Electoral College**. He suggested that each state select presidential electors according to the number of its senators and representatives in Congress by whatever method it preferred, and that these electors would then select the president. If a majority of the electors did not agree on any one candidate, the choice would fall to the House of Representatives—but with each state delegation in Congress having only one vote. This proposal seemed like a compromise that could work. The convention also decided on a four-year term for the president, with no limit on the number of terms that could be served.

There were many arguments about how much power to give the president. Delegates remembered that they had just fought a war against the tyranny of George III's government. On the other hand, after a decade of chaos, they wanted a strong executive who could make tough decisions and have the authority to make them stick. The delegates compromised and agreed that the president could veto legislation, but that a two-thirds vote of each chamber of the Congress could override a veto. Those wanting a strong executive won, though it would fall to Washington and subsequent presidents to flesh out the job.

The delegates spent almost no time on the judiciary. They created a Supreme Court and lower courts but left the details to subsequent generations. While they considered an arrangement whereby the judges of the Supreme Court and the president together might declare both federal and state laws unconstitutional, they dropped the idea. Only later, after John Marshall became chief justice in 1800, did the Supreme Court take on its role as arbiter of the constitutionality of laws.

The Effects of Slavery on a Unified Government

While the convention spent much of its time debating issues that divided large states from small ones, Madison understood that the real divide was between northern and southern

Although he held no special office at the Constitutional Convention—serving simply as one of several delegates from Virginia—James Madison planned carefully and did his best to guide the convention's deliberations. His notes on the meeting provide the best record of what happened that summer.

proportional representation

A way of selecting representatives in Congress based on the total population of a state, as opposed to having each state receive equal votes in Congress.

New Jersey Plan

A proposal of the New Jersey delegation to the Constitutional Convention by which both houses of Congress would be elected by states, with equal-size delegations for every state.

Connecticut Plan (or the Great Compromise)

Plan proposed for creating a national bicameral legislature in which all states would be equally represented in the Senate and proportionally represented in the House.

Electoral College

A system in which each state selects presidential electors according to the number of its senators and representatives in Congress by whatever method it prefers, and these electors then select the president.

states, or more specifically, between states where slavery was growing rapidly and those where it was dying out. Later, he remembered that "the institution of slavery and its implications formed the line of discrimination" on many issues. The existence of slavery in the United States embarrassed most of the framers of the Constitution. They were careful not to use the words *slave* or *slavery* even once in the final document. But they were equally careful to protect the institution and appease slaveholders.

Madison, like his fellow Virginians, Jefferson and Washington, embodied all the contradictions of slavery. Madison owned slaves, yet despised slavery. He told the convention that the "distinction of color" represented the basis for "the most oppressive domination ever exercised by man over man." Nevertheless, he later assured the Virginia convention that ratified the Constitution that the Constitution offered slavery "better security than any that now exists." He was right in his assurance.

Although many of the delegates, including some who were slaveholders, understood that slavery was incompatible with "life, liberty, and the pursuit of happiness," they were willing to live with the contradiction. The framers of the Constitution were also willing to live with slavery because of their belief that a key to securing life, liberty, and the pursuit of happiness was ensuring the inviolable right of private property. Slaves were seen, first and foremost, as the private property of their owners and only second as human beings, if as humans at all. For many at the convention, all private property, including property consisting of other humans, was sacrosanct. Without the security of property, they did not think any of their other rights were secure. They were willing to sacrifice their moral qualms about slavery to protect their rights to their own property.

The first time slavery intruded into the convention was when the delegates argued about representation in Congress. If representation was to be by population, then who would be counted as *people*? Defenders of slavery wanted slaves to be counted in equal numbers with free citizens in assigning seats to states in the House of Representatives so that slave states would have more votes in Congress. Delegates from states where slavery was shrinking or gone wanted to count only free citizens. Pennsylvania's James Wilson offered a compromise resolution, quickly seconded by South Carolina's Charles Pinckney (who owned more slaves than almost any other delegate), which said that representation in Congress would be apportioned

> [i]n proportion to the whole number of white and other free Citizens and inhabitants of every age sex and condition including those bound to servitude for a term of years, and three-fifths of all other persons not comprehended in the foregoing description, except Indians not paying taxes, in each state.

Everyone knew that "all other persons" meant slaves. After further debates, the final document kept the **three-fifths clause**.

three-fifths clause

Another compromise from the Constitutional Convention by which slaves—though the term was never used—would be counted as three-fifths of a person for purposes of establishing a state's representation under the proportional representation plan.

Pennsylvania's Gouverneur Morris condemned the three-fifths clause as creating a situation in which

> the inhabitant of Georgia and South Carolina who goes to the Coast of Africa, and in defiance of the most sacred laws of humanity tears away his fellow creatures from their dearest connection and damns them to the most cruel bondages, shall have more votes in a government instituted for the protection of the rights of mankind, than the citizen of Pennsylvania or New Jersey who views with laudable horror so nefarious a practice.

But in the end, the "nefarious practice" won.

The three-fifths clause was far from the only concession to slaveholders. When a committee was appointed to start drafting a document, Charles Cotesworth Pinckney warned them, "If the Committee should fail to insert some security to the Southern states against an emancipation of slaves, and taxes on exports, I will be bound by duty to my state to vote against the report." He need not have worried. The first draft of the Constitution included a clause that said Congress could neither tax nor prohibit "the migration or importation of such persons as the several States shall think proper to admit." "Such persons" referred to slaves, and the insistence that Congress could not tax or prohibit their "migration or importation" meant that the new government would not use its power in interstate commerce to limit the slave trade. However, the wording of the final draft did allow Congress to institute a tax and to change the policy after 1808. When 1808 arrived, the Congress did not hesitate to end the international slave trade and the importation of slaves from Africa on January 1, 1808. Nevertheless, between 1787 and 1807, over 200,000 Africans were forcibly taken from Africa and sold into slavery in the United States. In that one short 21-year period, half as many slaves were brought to the United States as the 400,000 Africans who had been brought to America over the previous 177 years between 1610 and 1787.

The final compromise about slavery came quickly. The draft of the Constitution prepared by the Committee of Detail had said that each state had an obligation to "deliver up" any person charged with a serious crime in another state. Delegates from South Carolina and Georgia asked the convention to add a clause that required "fugitive slaves and servants to be delivered up like criminals." Delegates from Pennsylvania and Connecticut objected. However, when it came time to vote, the convention embraced the request without a single dissent. It was the end of August. The delegates were tired and anxious to end their work. And the issue of slavery was just not as important to northerners as it was to southerners. As a result, the final version of the Constitution contained a clause that required states to extradite criminals from one state to another and a separate clause that stated:

> No Person held to Service or Labour in one State, under the Laws thereof, escaping into another, shall, in Consequence of any Law or Regulation therein, be discharged from such Service or Labour, but shall be delivered up on Claim of the Party to whom such Service or Labour may be due.

Once again, the word *slavery* did not appear, but everyone knew that "Person held to Service or Labour" meant slaves.

The fugitive slave clause gave slaveholders a new and powerful tool. As the 1800s wore on, it led to increasing strife because many northerners resented it, and southerners became angry at northern slowness in complying with one of the planks of the Constitution that united them.

The delegates who met in Philadelphia in 1787 compromised on many issues—slavery most of all—but one area where they did not compromise, despite the pleas of several delegates, would bedevil them for some time. On September 10, only a week before their final vote, George Mason of Virginia said he wished "the plan had been prefaced with a Bill of Rights," a guarantee of freedom of speech, press, religion, trial by jury, and so on, that would "give great quiet to the people." Mason was the author of the Virginia Declaration of Rights, and he anticipated that the lack of a guarantee of rights in the final document would create strong opposition to the Constitution. But not a single state delegation approved Mason's proposal for a constitutional Bill of Rights, though several states now had their own versions. Some delegates argued that such guarantees were unnecessary, but more of them were hot, tired, and ready to be done with their work. It was too late to add something new, but the failure to include a Bill of Rights in the original document almost derailed the whole plan.

Forty-one of the original fifty-five delegates gathered for the final vote. Edmund Randolph, who had introduced the Virginia Plan to the convention, would not sign the final document. The Constitution gave far more power to the federal government than he ever imagined it would. George Mason worried about the lack of a Bill of Rights. Elbridge Gerry of Massachusetts objected to the Constitution because he saw the three-fifths clause as giving too much power to slaveholding states and the power to raise armies as a dangerous step toward a military establishment. The remaining thirty-eight were ready to sign the document that began with these words:

> We the people of the United States, in order to form a more perfect union, establish justice, insure domestic tranquility, provide for the common defense, promote the general welfare, and secure the blessings of liberty to ourselves and our posterity, do ordain and establish this Constitution for the United States of America.

Many perhaps agreed with Benjamin Franklin, who said that there were "several parts of this Constitution which I do not at present approve," but "the older I grow the more apt

I am to doubt my own judgment and pay more respect to the judgment of others." And, he added a realistic note, "I doubt too whether any other Convention we can obtain may be able to make a better Constitution."

Debating and Adopting the Constitution

As mandated by the call to the Constitutional Convention, once the thirty-eight delegates had signed the draft Constitution, it was sent to the Congress that was meeting in New York. Ten of the delegates from the Philadelphia convention were also members of that Congress, and they transported the document. The delegates meeting in Philadelphia had far exceeded their instructions to propose amendments to the Articles of Confederation, but those members of the Congress who had not participated in drafting the new document were in no mood for a fight. They simply sent the proposed Constitution to the states for their consideration, even though they understood that it replaced rather than amended the Articles of Confederation and that it required ratification by only nine of the thirteen states. However, the members of Congress did insist that the battles about whether to adopt this radical new experiment in government would be fought on a state-by-state basis in conventions of specially elected delegates who would choose to ratify, or not ratify, the Constitution. This approach would increase the power of the voters in each state to decide instead of allowing current members of the state legislatures to do so. In the fall of 1787, the outcome was by no means clear.

Some delegates from the Constitutional Convention quickly went to work. In the fall of 1787, James Madison, along with Alexander Hamilton and John Jay—three leaders who did not normally get along with one another—wrote eighty-five newspaper articles to support the Constitution, later published as *The Federalist Papers*. In these articles, the three argued passionately that the new nation needed a strong national government and described the problems that they believed the Constitution addressed.

Federalists

Supporters of the Constitution; those who favored its ratification.

The Constitution's advocates, who called themselves **Federalists**, entered the state conventions with important advantages. They had a specific document and specific arguments on how theirs was a clear plan for improving the government. The new Constitution addressed the fears of many who would vote for delegates to the conventions and sit in them. For those afraid of another Shays's Rebellion, for those wanting a strong U.S. Army to protect them from Indians along the Allegheny frontier, and for those worried about the nation's credit rating, the Constitution provided reassurances not found in the Articles of Confederation.

Antifederalists

Opponents of the Constitution; those who argued against its ratification.

In contrast, for those known as **Antifederalists**, people who worried that a strong national government would trample on the rights of sovereign states and the liberties of individual (white, male) citizens, the Constitution offered little to calm their fears. The Constitution, which lacked a Bill of Rights and shifted significant powers from the states to the federal government, provoked attacks by many who had fought hardest against British authority in the Revolution. Many Antifederalists agreed with Virginia's Richard Henry Lee that a new "consolidated government" would be dominated by a "coalition of monarchy men, military men, aristocrats, and drones." Ratification would not be easy.

The Pennsylvania legislature, which met upstairs in the same building as the one the Constitutional Convention had met in, ordered the election of delegates even before Congress officially sent the Constitution to the states. Although backcountry farmers in Pennsylvania resisted strong government in any form, the majority of delegates to the Pennsylvania convention wanted to ratify the document and be the first state to do so, possibly securing the seat of the national government in Pennsylvania. But while Pennsylvanians debated, a convention in Delaware unanimously adopted the Constitution after only five days of discussion, beating Pennsylvania as the first state to ratify. Delegates to New Jersey's convention who liked the idea that taxes on imports arriving through New York Harbor would now be paid to the federal government instead of to the state of New York also ratified quickly. They were joined by Georgia, which wanted immediate protection from Indian raids, and by Connecticut, which had a strong Federalist party. Decisions among other states got more difficult.

American Voices

James Madison, *The Federalist Papers*, 1787, and Patrick Henry's response, 1788

James Madison, Alexander Hamilton, and John Jay published The Federalist Papers *in support of adopting the Constitution as individual pieces in newspapers in the fall and winter of 1787–1788. Hamilton wrote fifty-one of them; Madison, twenty-nine; Jay only five. In the* Federalist No. 10, *Madison insisted that a national government would reduce the danger of a political faction trampling on the liberties of others. The* Federalist Papers *remain one of the most often cited descriptions of the meaning of the new Constitution. But not everyone was convinced by them. There was opposition to adopting the Constitution in almost every state. In Virginia, Patrick Henry, one of the Constitution's staunchest opponents, gave a stirring speech against the proposed new form of government. Where Madison placed his faith in a strong federal government, Henry, a firebrand during the Revolution, trusted state governments as more accountable to the people and therefore more likely to protect their liberty.*

James Madison, *Federalist No. 10*, November 22, 1787

Among the numerous advantages promised by a well constructed Union, none deserves to be more accurately developed than its tendency to break and control the violence of faction. …

A zeal for different opinions concerning religion, concerning government, and many other points … an attachment to different leaders ambitiously contending for pre-eminence and power … have, in turn, divided mankind into parties, inflamed them with mutual animosity, and rendered them much more disposed to vex and oppress each other than to co-operate for their common good. So strong is this propensity of mankind to fall into mutual animosities, that where no substantial occasion presents itself, the most frivolous and fanciful distinctions have been sufficient to kindle their unfriendly passions. … But the most common and durable source of factions has been the various and unequal distribution of property. Those who hold and those who are without property have ever formed distinct interests in society. Those who are creditors, and those who are debtors, fall under a like discrimination. A landed interest, a manufacturing interest, a mercantile interest, a moneyed interest, with many lesser interests, grow up of necessity in civilized nations, and divide them into different classes. …

A rage for paper money, for an abolition of debts, for an equal division of property, or for any other improper or wicked project, will be less apt to pervade the whole body of the Union than a particular member of it; in the same proportion as such a malady is more likely to taint a particular county or district, than an entire State.

In the extent and proper structure of the Union, therefore, we behold a republican remedy for the diseases most incident to republican government. And according to the degree of pleasure and pride we feel in being republicans, ought to be our zeal in cherishing the spirit and supporting the character of Federalists.

Patrick Henry, "Speech against the Federal Constitution," June 5, 1788

Here is a resolution as radical as that which separated us from Great Britain. … The rights of conscience, trial by jury, liberty of the press, all your immunities and franchises, all pretensions to human rights and privileges are rendered insecure, if not lost, by this change, so loudly talked of by some, and inconsiderately by others. Is this tame relinquishment of rights worthy of freemen? Is it worthy of that manly fortitude that ought to characterize republicans? …

Guard with jealous attention the public liberty. Suspect everyone who approaches that jewel. …

The Confederation, this same despised government, merits, in my opinion, the highest encomium: it carried us through a long and dangerous war; it rendered us victorious in that conflict with a powerful nation; it has secured us a territory greater than any European monarch possesses; and shall a government which has been thus strong and vigorous, be accused of imbecility, and abandoned for want of energy? …

I am not well versed in history, but I will submit to your recollection, whether liberty has been destroyed most often by the licentiousness of the people, or by the tyranny of rulers. I imagine, sir, you will find the balance on the side of tyranny.

Thinking Critically

1. **Comparison**
   Madison and Henry represented radically differing views of the best form of government for people. Which view is more persuasive to you? Why do you think Madison's views convinced more convention delegates than Henry's views?

2. **Contextualization**
   Consider the extent to which Madison's and Henry's views on the new Constitution differed. What do their views tell you about how each man saw the challenges and dangers facing the new nation?

In Massachusetts, the outcome was far from certain. Although reaction to the rebellion of western Massachusetts farmers had helped launch the Constitution, these farmers themselves sent delegates to Boston who did not trust "these lawyers, and men of learning, and moneyed men, that talk so finely, and gloss over matters so smoothly, to make us poor little people swallow down the pill," as an Antifederalist delegate said. Two of the state's most respected revolutionaries—Governor John Hancock, whose name was at the top of the Declaration of Independence, and Sam Adams of Boston Tea Party fame—believed that the Constitution sought to solve problems that were not serious and that the states, not the national government, were best situated to protect individual liberty. In the end, the Massachusetts convention adopted the Constitution by a close vote of 187 to 168 but only on the condition, as Sam Adams insisted, that it be immediately amended to further protect the people's liberties and the rights of state governments. The Constitutional Convention's failure to add a Bill of Rights to the Constitution was already creating problems.

The next states to consider the document faced even more difficulties. The ratifying convention in New Hampshire adjourned without taking action. In addition, just as they had refused to attend the Constitutional Convention, the Rhode Island legislature refused even to call a convention. (They did, however, submit the question to town meetings in the state, and the voters rejected it, 2,708 to 237.) Maryland's convention approved the document, but also called for twenty-eight amendments to limit the power of the federal government. South Carolina approved the Constitution despite delegates' fears about "the interests of the Northern states" and the federal government's potential to limit that state's "peculiar species of property" (slaves). Because of these fears, South Carolina's convention voted for an amendment that would guarantee that states "retain every power not expressly relinquished by them."

Virginia, the largest state in the Union, was divided. Madison and Washington were strong advocates for the Constitution. But others were not enthusiastic, especially about the lack of a clear statement of state and individual rights. Patrick Henry adamantly opposed the Constitution. His loyalty was to the sovereign state of Virginia. In the end, Virginia ratified the Constitution in June 1788, partly because its opponents were split among themselves. Virginia's convention also demanded a Bill of Rights as soon as possible. With the vote in Virginia and a positive vote in a reconvened convention in New Hampshire earlier that same month, the Constitution reached its quota of nine states to support it.

Although enough states had supported ratification to launch the Constitution, no national government could thrive without New York. New York City was already emerging as the financial center of the new nation, and the state sat in a strategic location between New England and the rest of the country. The New York convention debate was long and bitter. Alexander Hamilton led the charge for the Constitution, but Antifederalists were strong. Given what was happening in other states, it would have been hard for New York

" *When opposite Bowling Green, the president and members of Congress were discovered standing upon the fort, and the Ship instantly brought to and fired a salute of thirteen guns, followed by three cheers, which were returned by the Congressional dignitaries.*" *Page 325*

As it became clear that the Constitution would be ratified and that the country would have a new and stronger government, crowds celebrated. In spite of the strong opposition to the Constitution, once it became law, most Americans supported it, though many also insisted that a Bill of Rights be added as quickly as possible.

to reject the Constitution, especially when many New Yorkers still hoped that the federal capital would remain in New York City. In the summer of 1788, the New York convention considered fifty-five possible amendments, a call for a second convention to revise the Constitution after its adoption, and a conditional vote that would ratify the document only if it were amended. In the end, however, by a slim margin (30–27), New York ratified the Constitution in July 1788, the eleventh state to do so.

The last states to ratify the Constitution, North Carolina and Rhode Island, made their choice only after the new government was already functioning. By the time they acted, there was no practical way for any state to remain outside of the new government. Refusing to ratify would have made a state a foreign government amid the United States. It remained for Americans to translate the document into an actual government and work out their complex relationships across divisions of class, race, gender, and degrees of freedom and unfreedom as well as the extraordinary distances in geography and belief that separated them.

6.2 Quick Review

What failures of the Articles of Confederation did the Constitution seek to address? What were the failures inherent in the new document? Which arguments for and against adopting the new Constitution were strongest?

Conclusion

With the end of the Revolution and the recognition of American independence, the new United States now faced the same problems that had faced the British government in the past: how to pay for a war and how to govern a restive populace. Officers in the Continental Army threatened to rebel when payment for their services was not forthcoming. Poor farmers took up arms against state taxes they could not afford. Native American tribes challenged the new United States as white settlers streamed over the Allegheny Mountains into territory that the British government had kept off-limits. At the same time, Congress began to resolve states' claims to lands far into the interior, creating new states and territories for white settlers but not the kind of army that could control the territory.

The issues of freedom and liberty led slaves and some white allies to call for an end to slavery. Northern states, where slavery was less essential to the economy, slowly began to phase out slavery, but southern states, whose economic base depended on slave labor, were adamantly against emancipation and imported record numbers of new slaves until 1808. Women in all levels of society began to expect more equal treatment and broader opportunities. Women's expectations were translated in the male-dominated society to an ideology of Republican Motherhood in which women were expected to be better educated than their mothers and grandmothers so they could support the political development of their husbands and sons.

Many believed that at the core of many of the new nation's problems was the fact that the Articles of Confederation were too weak a foundation on which to base a central government. The Constitutional Convention that met over the summer of 1787 debated and designed a completely new Constitution, laying out a new form of government with three branches of government: an executive branch, including the president and cabinet; a legislative branch, consisting of two houses of Congress; and a judicial branch, including a Supreme Court. A key purpose of this design was to balance power, preventing one person or group from dominating the government while at the same time giving the national government the authority to raise funds and to act. Although the Constitution never used the terms *slave* or *slavery*, it upheld the institution in significant ways.

When the Constitution was presented to Congress for approval, Congress mandated that each state should call a special convention to ratify, or not ratify, the document. Debate was heated. Federalists and Antifederalists (supporters and opponents of the Constitution) took strong and contentious stands. Eventually, all states ratified the document, some by

6.1

6.2

very narrow margins. No state wanted to be left behind on its own. However, demands were strong to amend it immediately, particularly by adding a Bill of Rights. Nevertheless, by 1788, even before those changes were enacted and even before the last two states had ratified the Constitution, a new form of government for the United States was ready to be launched.

Chapter Review

Does the Constitution created in Philadelphia in 1787 embody or contradict the goals of the Revolution? Why?

Chapter 6 Summary and Review

The State of the Nation at War's End

6.1 **Explain how the outcome of the American Revolution affected different groups in the new United States.**

Summary

Even before independence was won, Americans began the task to determine what concepts like freedom, equality, and democracy would look like in the new nation. In this period, colonies were becoming states; consequently, the goals for state constitutions varied. The Revolution brought extensive, though not total, change for people of all classes, races, and political persuasions. Great inequality remained, but few people were as willing to defend it as they had in the colonial era. Congress's delay in providing pay and pensions for veterans came close to sparking a military coup. Farmers in western Massachusetts were driven to rebellion by high taxes and hard economic times. The new states moved quickly to settle lands to the west of their established boundaries, sparking new conflicts and tensions with Indian peoples. Free blacks sought to create strong communities as slavery greatly declined in the northern states, but slavery became even more entrenched in the southern states. Women throughout the states began to question their roles in this newly independent nation, and many supported the idea that education for women would strengthen their contributions. Others were wary of elevating women's status and limited those trends through the ideology of Republican Motherhood, which shaped the lives of women in complex ways.

Review Questions

1. Contextualization
   What light do the Newburgh Conspiracy and Shays's Rebellion shed on the economic challenges facing the new nation at the conclusion of the Revolutionary War?

2. Comparison
   Compare and contrast the condition of African Americans, both enslaved and free, in the decades following the American Revolution. What might explain the differences you note?

Creating a Government: Writing the U.S. Constitution

6.2 **Explain the needs, pressures, and compromises that led to writing and adopting the Constitution.**

Summary

In the years after the Revolution, many came to believe that the Articles of Confederation were insufficient to meet the economic and political challenges facing the new nation. Representing the white male elite, delegates at the Constitutional Convention grappled with key issues like the structure of the national legislature, slavery, and the powers of the executive branch. After considerable debate, the delegates arrived at a new framework for the national government, which went far beyond their charged task—to revise the Articles of Confederation. Each state convened a special convention of specially elected delegates to decide whether or not to ratify the Constitution. The battle over ratification pitted Federalists against Antifederalists. The Federalist promise to move quickly to create a Bill of Rights for the Constitution helped secure ratification.

Review Questions

3. Argument Development
   Is it fair to describe the Constitution as a proslavery document? Why or why not?

4. Contextualization
   Why did Antifederalists view the Constitution as a threat to liberty? How did the experience of British colonial rule shape their views?

1. Preparing to Write: Develop Your Thesis
Long Essay Question—Evaluate the extent of change in the lives of American women during the period from 1754 to 1789.

Start by studying how the Revolution affected the mind-sets of women and how their roles changed. At the same time, in what way did their roles remain unchanged during this period? Think of a "change continuum" on which the far left represents not much change and the far right represents great change. Where on the continuum is the reality? From there you can develop a thesis.

2. Preparing to Write: Organize Your Evidence
Long Essay Question—Explain how the context of the period from 1763 to 1787 influenced the political principles included in the Constitution.

This question is concerned with the political arguments of the Revolution period and how they became codified in the Constitution. Start by identifying principles in the Constitution like popular sovereignty and separation of powers, and then tie them to the circumstances surrounding colonial resistance and the rhetoric that accompanied it. How would you organize this evidence into a two- or three-part body? After you decide your organization, develop topic sentences for each part and list the evidence you will use under each topic sentence.

Chapter 7
Practicing Democracy 1789–1800

FineArt/Alamy Stock Photo

President George Washington reviews troops at Fort Cumberland on the Potomac before leading them to suppress the Whiskey Rebellion. Frederick Kemmelmeyer, "General George Washington Reviewing the Western Army at Fort Cumberland the 18th of October 1794," after 1794. Oil on paper backed with linen, 18 1/8 × 23 1/8 in. Courtesy of Winterthur Museum.

Chapter Objective

Demonstrate an understanding of how the federal government worked under the new Constitution.

Learning Objectives

Convening a Congress, Inaugurating a President, Adopting a Bill of Rights

7.1 Analyze the first federal elections and the adoption of the Bill of Rights.

Creating an Economy: Alexander Hamilton and the U.S. Economic System

7.2 Analyze the enduring argument begun by Hamilton's economic vision for the United States and the alternative vision of Jefferson and Madison.

Setting the Pace: The Washington Administration

7.3 Explain the precedents set by George Washington's presidential administration.

The Birth of Political Parties: Adams and Jefferson

7.4 Explain the growing split between the Federalist and Democratic-Republican factions, including how the French Revolution and the personal differences between Hamilton, Adams, and Jefferson affected American politics.

When New Hampshire and Virginia voted to ratify the Constitution in June 1788, it became the law of the land. But putting that new law into effect was not easy. The old Congress as well as local and state officials in the thirteen states needed to conduct elections. Those elected to the new positions would breathe life into the words of the Constitution and set precedents based on their interpretation of its meaning—or their preferences—that would last for generations. As different Americans discovered that they interpreted the Constitution differently, and that they wanted the country to develop in diverse ways, they began long-term arguments with one another about the future.

Soon after the new Congress was elected, it created and enacted the Bill of Rights, ten amendments that many thought should have been part of the original document. With this addition, more Americans felt comfortable that they had created a government that would protect their rights and maintain their freedom. Once elected as president, George Washington quickly set out to define his role. He appointed the first members of the Supreme Court and other judges and created a presidential cabinet to carry out the work of his administration. One cabinet member, Secretary of the Treasury Alexander Hamilton, laid the foundation for the nation's economic system. Washington's secretary of state, Thomas Jefferson, disliked the emerging Hamiltonian system, and Jefferson and Hamilton would become not only bitter rivals but also symbols of two very different directions for the country. Washington himself asserted federal authority and expanded the U.S. Army to win Indian wars on the nation's frontier. The policies that were set and institutions that were created during the first years of the new government lasted for decades, but the philosophical differences about the role of government in the nation's life that emerged have persisted to the present.

Convening a Congress, Inaugurating a President, Adopting a Bill of Rights

7.1   Analyze the first federal elections and the adoption of the Bill of Rights.

In one of its last acts under the Articles of Confederation, the outgoing Congress set the dates for elections for the new House of Representatives. Elections for members of the House were held in January and February 1789. As permitted in the Constitution, different states had different rules for who could vote. Some House races were hotly contested, including the one in Virginia's fifth district that pitted two future U.S. presidents, James Madison and James Monroe, against each other. Madison won and played a crucial role in the first Congress. State legislatures elected the members of the U.S. Senate, as they would do until 1913. Presidential electors were chosen by different methods depending on the state, and they cast their ballots for the first president.

Congress and President Washington: Setting to Work

By early spring, the new Congress began to assemble in the nation's temporary capital, New York City (the location that many of its residents hoped would become permanent). Congress was supposed to convene on March 4, but it was not until April that either house of Congress could muster a quorum—a majority of the total members—which was required to do business. Much business awaited. The Constitution required each house to set up its own rules of operation. The Senate had to confirm the election of the president. The Constitution also gave the new government the power to set and collect taxes. The need for a tax law was urgent: each day that Congress delayed, thousands of dollars went uncollected.

On April 14, Charles Thomson, the secretary of Congress, arrived at Mount Vernon to officially inform George Washington of what he already knew: he had been unanimously elected president of the United States by the sixty-nine presidential electors who also elected John Adams as vice president, though by a smaller vote. Washington quickly traveled to New York where he and Adams were formally inaugurated on April 30, 1789. He then set to work creating the executive branch of the federal government.

Significant Dates

1789	New House and Senate are elected
	George Washington is elected and inaugurated as first U.S. president
	French Revolution begins
1790	Federal government assumes state Revolutionary War debts
	Washington, D.C., is selected as permanent U.S. capital (the government actually moved there in 1800)
	Judith Sargent Murray's "On the Equality of the Sexes" is published
1791	Bill of Rights is ratified
	First Bank of the United States chartered
	Ohio Indian tribes defeat U.S. Army in Northwest Territory
	Hamilton's *Report on Manufactures*
1793	Washington is reelected president
	Citizen Genêt arrives as ambassador to the United States
1793–1794	Whiskey Rebellion
1794	Western Indian Confederacy is defeated at Battle of Fallen Timbers
	Jay's Treaty is negotiated between the United States and Britain (ratified by the Senate in 1795 and effective in 1796)
1795	Treaty of Greenville ends Indian Wars on Ohio frontier
	Pinckney's Treaty with Spain
1796	John Adams is elected president
1797	Beginning of the Quasi-War with France
1798	XYZ Affair
	Congress passes Alien and Sedition Acts
	Kentucky and Virginia Resolutions declare Alien and Sedition Acts unconstitutional

(continued)

7.1

7.2

7.3

7.4

The fifty-eight-year-old George Washington had no precedents to guide him. An independent republic with an elected citizen at its head was an unprecedented development for the world of 1789. Some, led by Alexander Hamilton, who loved British models, recommended that Washington establish a court similar to that of King George III. Others, including Vice President John Adams, recommended a more egalitarian approach. Washington steered a middle course, insisting on formal state dinners and fairly formal relationships with those who came to call on him, but avoiding a throne or robes of office. He was called simply "Mr. President" instead of "your Highness." Although he was the only president never to live in the White House, he did help to design it, and African slaves did most of the work building it. While in office, he maintained a formal presidential residence in New York City and in Philadelphia when the capital moved there in 1790.

The Bill of Rights

On May 4, 1789, only a month after the House of Representatives began its work, James Madison told the House that he was planning to propose amendments to the Constitution. On June 8, he offered amendments that included line-by-line changes in the Constitution. Proposing amendments was easy. Getting them passed was not. Some of Madison's strongest partners in getting the Constitution adopted were neutral or hostile to amending it. President Washington, at Madison's request, made a brief reference to amendments in his inaugural address. Later, Washington said of the proposed amendments, "Some of them, in my opinion, are importantly necessary; others, though of themselves (in my conception) not very essential, are necessary to quiet the fears of some respectable characters and well-meaning men." It was hardly a ringing endorsement. On the other hand, some Federalists in Congress thought it was far too early to amend the Constitution, especially when other issues, like balancing the budget, were pressing.

Bill of Rights

The first ten amendments to the Constitution passed by Congress in 1789 and ratified by the states in 1791.

During the ratification process, however, Madison had promised to add a **Bill of Rights** to the Constitution. Without a promise for those added rights, key states would not have ratified the Constitution. While he was determined to fulfill his promise, Madison also knew that Antifederalists sought more far-reaching changes, and he wanted to act faster than those opponents. Representative Theodorick Bland, a close ally of Patrick Henry, proposed a second convention to consider "the defects of this Constitution." If Congress did not act to quiet this movement, Madison feared, the whole constitutional structure could unravel.

Madison quickly abandoned his original proposal for new clauses to be included throughout the body of the Constitution and decided instead to propose amendments to be added at the end of the document. The House initially passed seventeen amendments, but the Senate changed them, and on September 25, Congress sent twelve amendments to the states for ratification. It was fast work for a body that had not existed six months earlier. An amendment setting the size of the House was not ratified; neither was an amendment limiting congressional pay (it was ratified finally in 1992). The other ten amendments became the Bill of Rights, added to the Constitution in 1791 after three-fourths of the state legislatures approved them. The first of these amendments said:

> Congress shall make no law respecting an establishment of religion, or prohibiting the free exercise thereof; or abridging the freedom of speech, or the press, or the right of the people peaceably to assemble, and to petition the Government for a redress of grievances.

The Methodist church on John Street in New York City is the oldest Methodist church in the United States. Since Methodist and Baptist churches never received public support in any of the former colonies, they were among the strongest supporters of the prohibition on any congressional action to create a state church for the United States that was included in the Bill of Rights.

Other of the amendments included "the right of the people to keep and bear Arms," freedom from being required to house soldiers in private homes (a major grievance against the British before the Revolution), the right to be "secure in their persons, houses, papers, and effects, against unreasonable searches and seizures," the right to trial by jury, the right to a speedy trial, and limits on excessive bail.

Finally, the Tenth Amendment—perhaps most important to many Antifederalists, especially those who worried about federal intervention in the institution of slavery—limited the powers of the national government:

> The powers not delegated to the United States by the Constitution, nor prohibited by it to the States, are reserved to the States respectively, or to the people.

The Constitution had replaced a weak national government with a strong one, but the amendments meant that the new government would operate within clear limits. As an immediate practical matter, the Bill of Rights addressed much of the opposition to the Constitution, and the new government could proceed with less fear that its core structure would be overturned. More than 225 years later, that core structure is still intact.

7.1 Quick Review

Why was the Bill of Rights added to the Constitution? What specific rights did it protect—for states and for individuals?

Creating an Economy: Alexander Hamilton and the U.S. Economic System

7.2 Analyze the enduring argument begun by Hamilton's economic vision for the United States and the alternative vision of Jefferson and Madison.

President Washington faced difficult problems, many of them economic. The inability of the federal government under the Articles of Confederation to collect taxes meant that federal debts were not being paid and that the financial status of the United States was in serious trouble. The government could not afford an army sufficient to protect the frontier. Tensions with Britain were made worse because Britain had not withdrawn its troops from western forts as promised in the Treaty of Paris and because London merchants who were owed large sums from Americans were angry and in no mood to extend any further credit to American businesses or the government. Although the Continental Congress had adopted the dollar as the national currency in 1785, Congress, state governments, and private banks had printed a variety of paper notes, all of which could be easily counterfeited, and the ease with which they were put into circulation led to inflation. In the new United States, as during much of the colonial era, people bought and sold with an amazing variety of paper notes and coins from around the world, especially Spanish gold and silver. Solving the financial crisis and regulating the currency was essential for national prosperity. In the summer of 1789, Congress adopted a 5 percent customs tax on all imports into the United States, creating a solid financial footing for the new government. It also set up a system of federal courts and approved the establishment of four senior positions within the executive branch: secretaries of state, war, and the treasury, and an attorney general. These four officials became the first presidential cabinet.

Washington quickly appointed Thomas Jefferson, then U.S. ambassador to Paris, as his secretary of state; General Henry Knox, his deputy in command throughout the Revolution, as secretary of war; and his friend, the former governor of Virginia, Edmund Randolph, as attorney general. But given the nation's financial problems, the most important and powerful position would be secretary of the treasury, and to that office, Washington appointed New Yorker Alexander Hamilton. A brilliant and ruthless political infighter, Hamilton could handle the economic crisis better than anyone else, even if Washington also knew from bitter experience that he could never completely trust Hamilton, who had served as Washington's chief aide during the Revolution and had sometimes gone behind his commander's back or quarreled directly with him.

The Secretary of the Treasury's Key Role

On his first full day on the job, Secretary Hamilton negotiated a $50,000 loan from the Bank of New York to keep the new government solvent. He also set about creating a Customs Service to collect the 5 percent import tax that Congress had already passed, and he organized what would become the U.S. Coast Guard to be sure that imports were not smuggled into the country without being taxed. Hamilton had once said, "I hate procrastination in business," and he was not about to make a slow start on the new job. Ten days after his appointment, the House of Representatives asked him for a report on the public credit of the United States—the most pressing national issue in virtually everyone's view—and gave him until January to prepare it.

Debt and Taxes

Hamilton's *Report Relative to a Provision for the Support of Public Credit* was the foundation of the economic development of the new nation. Hamilton had read widely in philosophy and economics, as if preparing for the moment when he would be asked to design a new economic system. As he looked at the crushing debt that the nation faced from the Revolution—$54 million in federal debt and $25 million more in state debts—he knew that radical action was required (see Figure 7-1). Few people, including foreign and domestic investors and foreign governments, trusted the new country's ability to pay its bills. As a result, neither the state and federal governments nor private businesses could borrow money. The government could not finance desperately needed activities, including the creation of an army. Private businesses could not restart commerce, which had been mostly frozen since the Revolution. Revolutionary War veterans who had been paid in government promissory notes had sold them for as little as 15 cents on the dollar rather than trust a government that seemed untrustworthy to pay what it had promised. In this crisis, Hamilton saw only one solution. The federal government, he believed, needed to assume all of the Revolutionary War debt and promise to pay it all off, dollar for dollar, while establishing a tax policy that would show wary observers that the government would meet its obligations. "Credit is the entire thing," Hamilton argued.

Not everyone in Congress agreed. To Hamilton's surprise, his close ally in the fight over adopting the Constitution, James Madison, led the opposition to debt assumption in the House, and more quietly, Secretary of State Jefferson led similar opposition within the administration. States like Virginia and North Carolina that had paid off most of their own war debts were unhappy with the idea that they would now pay federal taxes to cover the debts of what they considered less responsible states like Massachusetts and South Carolina. Veterans who had sold their government promissory notes at highly depreciated rates during the 1780s to eat and live were appalled that the civilian speculators to whom they had sold them would get rich on the 100 percent payment of the debt. And for those who shared Jefferson's view of a democratic nation of small farmers, Hamilton's plan created a national government that was too big, would raise too much in taxes, would sustain a standing army, and would shift power from farmers to urban and commercial interests. They would have none of it.

Figure 7-1 Debt from the Revolutionary War, by State.

When Alexander Hamilton became secretary of the treasury, he wanted the federal government to pay off the Revolutionary War debt of each state. But states with less debt, or those that had paid their own debts (see the differences in the figure), thought the proposal was very unfair. Hamilton, however, insisted that only by guaranteeing payment for all debt could the new government establish itself as worthy of future loans that both government and business badly needed. He won.

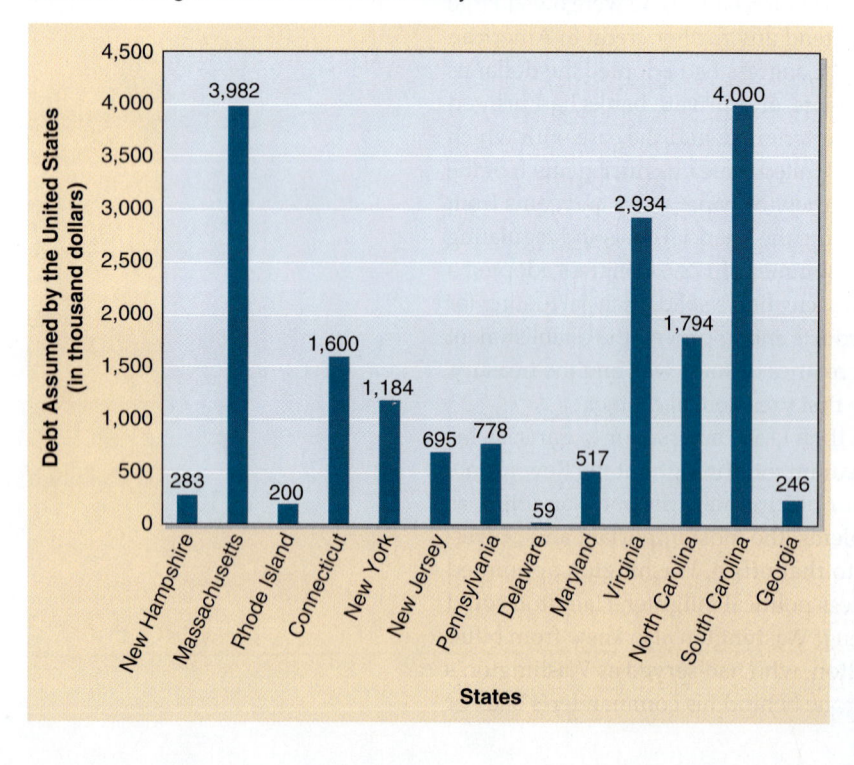

In the spring of 1790, the House, led by Madison, rejected Hamilton's proposal each of the four times he submitted it. Ever the wily politician, Hamilton sought a compromise and Secretary of State Jefferson made it happen. Many years later, Jefferson told the story of how he hosted a dinner at his home in New York at which he, Madison, and Hamilton struck a deal by which each one got something that he considered important. Hamilton wanted New York City, his home and the nation's commercial center, to be the permanent U.S. capital. But others—especially Jefferson and Madison—wanted to locate the capital farther south. They disliked the difficult travel to New York, and they also disliked urban life. They feared that a northern capital would fuel northern antislavery tendencies in Congress. Not incidentally, Madison, like George Washington, owned land on the Potomac River that would become more valuable if the capital were nearby. If Hamilton would agree to support Jefferson and Madison on the location of the capital, then the two Virginians would support Hamilton's economic plan.

In July, Congress made the compromise official. Philadelphia, not New York, was designated as the new temporary capital and the law also stipulated that a ten-square-mile site on the Potomac River between Maryland and Virginia should become the nation's permanent capital. They gave President Washington a free hand to select the specific site and plan the new center of government. The English-born architect Benjamin Henry Latrobe designed a capitol building and a presidential residence (later called the White House) in neoclassical style to assert the new nation's status. It took time to clear the land and build the first buildings. President John Adams led the move to Washington, D.C., during his last months in office, though he personally would have preferred to see the capital remain in Philadelphia or New York. Jefferson and Madison kept their part of the bargain and Congress also passed Hamilton's financial plan, including the assumption of state debts by the federal government. Henceforth, the new nation would have a government on a solid financial footing with a guaranteed credit rating, just as Hamilton wanted, and a permanent capital closer to the South, as Jefferson and Madison wanted.

The compromise solved the immediate issues, but the split on economic policy would lead to the creation of two hostile political parties—which came to be known as the Federalists and the Democratic-Republicans (known at first as Antifederalists)—that would dominate the nation's politics for the next decade. In the first years of the new government, those who supported the Constitution called themselves Federalists (wanting a strong federal government), and those opposed to the adoption of the Constitution and then Hamilton's interpretation of it were happy to be known simply as Antifederalists. But as the battle over Hamilton's plans intensified, those in the government and the newspapers who supported Madison's and Jefferson's opposition began to call themselves Democratic-Republicans, claiming that they, not those following Hamilton, were the true defenders of the republic. Almost everyone, including Hamilton, Jefferson, Madison, and especially Washington, abhorred the idea of opposing political parties, but such parties were beginning to form before Washington finished his first term in office, though at first they were merely shifting factions within the government and no one yet called them parties.

To a degree, the political divisions reflected a sectional split. Supporting Hamilton were bankers in New York and Philadelphia as well as merchants, especially those engaged in seagoing trade based in Boston or other ports. Those tending to support the Democratic-Republican cause included southern plantation owners, who always worried that the new government would move against slavery and who saw little value in banks and commercial development; farmers, ranging from supporters of Daniel Shays in Massachusetts to farmers in the backwoods of Kentucky; and small-town merchants who were less dependent on international credit. Supporters of each side also had their own newspaper. John Fenno had launched the *Gazette of the United States* in 1789 to support the Federalist cause. Two years later, Madison and Jefferson convinced Philip Freneau to launch the staunchly Antifederalist *National Gazette*. To support that paper, Jefferson, to

Library of Congress [LC-DIG-det-4a26168], Detroit Publishing Company Photograph Collection, Prints and Photographs Division

Hamilton's fiscal program was controversial from the beginning, but it launched the nation's economy in a commercial direction and created political division that continued for decades in the United States.

7.1

7.2

7.3

7.4

Bank of the United States

The first federal bank, chartered in 1781, issued currency for the country and stabilized the economy.

his later embarrassment, also put Freneau on the federal payroll as an official of the State Department. The lines between the two groups were growing stronger.

The First Bank of the United States

Once he had resolved the debt issue, Hamilton's next move widened the divide between those who, like him, wanted an activist government and a robust commercial economy and those who preferred Jefferson's vision of an agrarian nation made up of small independent farmers with a very modest national government. In December 1790, Hamilton submitted another report to Congress that called for creating a **Bank of the United States**, modeled on the Bank of England. Hamilton's fondness for British models was one reason many Americans never trusted him. But Hamilton did not want to be part of Britain. He wanted to use Britain's economic model to build a nation that would become as powerful as Britain. Achieving that vision meant creating a federal bank that would manage the economy and fund a strong government, as Britain's bank did for that country. As with the debt, not everyone agreed.

The Bank of England was a joint public–private venture. Most of its shareholders were private investors, but it played a key role in guaranteeing and repaying Britain's public debt, and its paper bank notes were accepted as official currency in Britain. Hamilton did not trust Congress or the states to issue paper currency. He feared—all too realistically, given what had happened during the Revolution—that Congress and the states would solve financial problems by printing more currency and, thus, quickly debase its value and re-create the inflation that the nation faced in the 1790s. But Hamilton was confident that no investors would risk their funds by allowing more currency to circulate than they could afford to redeem. He was anxious to have those Americans who had funds to invest become strongly attached to the new government. Currency from a semiprivate bank could be trusted because the bank would have to redeem its paper currency in gold or silver. Hamilton believed the United States could have a stable currency that everyone trusted if the Bank of the United States were chartered.

A central bank could also make loans, thus expanding the amount of credit available. With resources backed by both private investors and government guarantees, the bank could ease the credit squeeze and stimulate commerce and trade. Businesses could get loans. Investment in new enterprises could begin. Much of the bank's financing would also be promissory notes from the government itself—notes that Hamilton had just guaranteed would maintain their full value.

For southern plantation owners like Jefferson and Madison, the bank plan was much worse than the plan to assume all debt for the Revolutionary War. It would centralize power in the big northern cities—Philadelphia, New York, and Boston—where the nation's largest banks were. Jefferson did not like cities. He preferred small rural communities, which he believed were far more democratic places. He said, "I think our governments will remain virtuous for many centuries as long as they are chiefly agricultural." And, he continued, when people "get piled upon one another in large cities, as in Europe, they will become corrupt as in Europe." In addition, Jefferson, like most Democratic-Republicans of his day, did not like banks. The battle over the Bank of the United States was between those who wanted an urban commercial nation and those who wanted a nation based on independent farmers. It would not be the last such battle.

The 1799 building that was designed for the First Bank of the United States in Philadelphia reflected the solid structure and grand hopes that Hamilton had for a federal bank.

Library of Congress Prints and Photographs Division[LC-USZC4-556]

Jefferson feared that banks would keep the poor in poverty and enrich those who were already wealthy through ill-gotten gains based on speculation rather than hard work. For most farmers, who were always in debt given their need to buy seed and fertilizer before they could plant and harvest a crop, banks were the distant institutions that hounded them to repay loans. For Jefferson and Madison, and even for John Adams, the thought that the government they had worked so hard to create was now about to create a bank was galling. Hamilton and Madison now parted company forever over their interpretation of the Constitution.

Despite the opposition of some of the nation's most eloquent leaders, the bank bill sailed through Congress. Almost all northern representatives voted for it, and almost all southern ones against it. The sectional lines and the lines between the Federalist and Democratic-Republican factions (they were not yet political parties) were clearly emerging.

Once the bill passed both houses of Congress, Washington had to decide whether to sign it. Madison, who had been operating as Washington's key spokesperson in Congress, argued that the bank was an unconstitutional extension of federal power and that Washington should veto the bill. Washington then turned to his cabinet for advice. Attorney General Randolph and Secretary of State Jefferson both urged a veto. The Tenth Amendment was clear, they said, that anything not mentioned in the Constitution was left to the states, and the Constitution certainly did not authorize a federal bank. For Secretary of the Treasury Hamilton, however, the bank was essential, and the Constitution, he said, gave Congress the authority to do everything "necessary and proper" for the smooth functioning of the nation. He warned Washington that if the national government did not invoke the "necessary and proper clause," then Americans would become "a people *governed* without *government*." Washington signed the bill in February 1791, and the United States now had a bank and deeper political divisions than previously imagined.

After the bank bill, Hamilton proposed a federal mint to create uniform coins for use throughout the country. For almost twenty years after the Revolution, people had used foreign coins. Hamilton wanted U.S. coins based on the U.S. dollar, not the British pound. It was not a controversial proposal, and the federal mint was soon established.

A Blueprint for the Future of the Nation

Hamilton's last major report to Congress was his *Report on Manufactures*. Unlike the earlier reports, this one was not a plea for immediate legislation but, rather, a blueprint for the future of the nation as Hamilton saw it. Like Jefferson, Hamilton saw farming as the backbone of the economy, but he also wanted factories that would create finished goods from the products of the fields, forests, and mines for both domestic consumption and export. In addition, he wanted the nation to make everything its military might need, from uniforms to gunpowder and warships.

Hamilton regularly looked to Europe, especially Britain, for ideas, and there were many economic ideas ready for export. Hamilton greatly admired the British industrialists who were creating mechanized production on a scale never seen before. He was also influenced by the Scottish philosopher Adam Smith whose book *The Wealth of Nations* was published in 1776.

In the economic world that Smith described, wealth was generated, not by the simple ownership of things—land or gold or products—but, rather, by the free trade of goods and services and by competition to expand trade. As people competed to make a profit on their transactions, they increased the circulation of money, lowered the cost of goods, and created general prosperity—the wealth of nations and of individuals. Competition, Smith said, was the key to wealth. Thus he wrote, "It is not from the benevolence of the butcher, the brewer, or the baker that we expect our dinner, but from their regard to their self-interest." As that self-interest is satisfied through competition, there is more meat, beer, and bread at lower cost available for everyone while the butcher, brewer, and baker live well. For Smith, who called Britain "a nation of shopkeepers," it was the shopkeepers and manufacturers and traders, not the hoarders of gold and silver, who made wealth.

Smith's book was a direct attack on the earlier ideas of mercantilism that saw wealth as a matter of getting and hoarding wealth. In the new world of a capitalist system or a market economy where commerce and trade were most significant, Great Britain, with its growing factories and its Royal Navy controlling the oceans, was destined to great wealth. As Smith

7.1

7.2

7.3

7.4

7.1

7.2

7.3

7.4

was trying to describe the economic system in Great Britain, Hamilton was trying to duplicate the system in the United States.

With the bank in place and the *Report on Manufactures* completed, Hamilton resigned as secretary of the treasury in 1795, and Washington appointed Oliver Wolcott in his place. Although he remained a close presidential advisor until the end of Washington's term, Hamilton preferred to make money as a private citizen.

Thinking Historically

Hamilton's Commercial Nation versus Jefferson's Agrarian Vision

In his 1791 Report on Manufactures, *Alexander Hamilton defended "the expediency of encouraging manufacturers in the United States." Contrasting farming with manufacturing, he noted:*

> [L]abour employed in Agriculture is in a great measure periodical and occasional, depending on seasons, liable to various and long intermissions; while that occupied in many manufactures is constant and regular, extending through the year, embracing in some instances night as well as day.

Hamilton was also a harsh critic of slavery. He promoted open immigration. Immigrants from Europe would work in the emerging factories, Hamilton said, and a plentiful supply of new workers would keep wages low and factories profitable for their owners. He had no fear of child labor either, noting, "in general, women and children are rendered more useful, and the latter more early useful, by manufacturing establishments than they would otherwise be."

Hamilton wanted a federal government that would shape the nation's economy rather than leave economic development to individuals. He believed that higher tariffs should protect new industries and that government incentives should help launch those ventures when private investment was not sufficient. He saw strong patent protection as essential to invention. Moreover, he wanted to build a network of roads and canals to help commerce flow.

Hamilton knew that not everyone agreed with him. He noted that some believed that it was wrong to use the government "to accelerate the growth of manufactures." Critics, he knew, liked a

world in which "the less independent condition of an artisan can be exchanged for the more independent condition of a farmer."

Jefferson feared an activist government and thought Hamilton's plans were an antidemocratic effort to strengthen the power of the financial elite. Where Hamilton wanted the federal government to foster commerce, Jefferson and his supporters wanted a passive federal government that stayed out of people's way. While still secretary of state, Jefferson wrote, "Hamilton's financial system … had two objects; 1st, as a puzzle to exclude popular understanding and inquiry, 2nd, as a machine for the corruption of the legislature." Jefferson believed that independent farmers were far more likely to maintain a strong democratic government than paid employees, who, in giving up their economic freedom, would soon also give up their political freedom. He saw Hamilton's plan as a way to confuse the true agents of democracy. The debate from the 1790s about the proper size and role of the federal government is still alive today.

Thinking Critically

1. **Contextualization**
   What regions of the country in the 1790s best reflected Jefferson's view of America? What regions reflected Hamilton's view?

2. **Comparison**
   What groups in American society stood to gain the most if Hamilton's vision was enacted? Which groups would gain from Jefferson's vision?

7.2 Quick Review

What were the basic differences between Hamilton's ideas for the young United States and those of Jefferson?

Setting the Pace: The Washington Administration

7.3 **Explain the precedents set by George Washington's presidential administration.**

Although economic issues were the top priority, Washington also faced many others. Washington knew how fragile the new republic was. The votes to adopt the new Constitution had been close in several states, and powerful leaders, including Patrick Henry in Virginia and John Hancock in Massachusetts, would have been happy to return to a system in which the states were supreme and the national government only a weak federation. Many rural Americans, including the poor white farmers who made up most of the citizens, distrusted all governments and felt they got little benefit from them, while the tax on imports raised the cost of necessities. An obscure Massachusetts farmer, William Manning, who had fought at the battle of Concord, now wrote a pamphlet, *The Key of Liberty*, in which he argued that "friends to liberty and free government" needed to be watchful of the "few" who were dominating the new administration and needed to be prevented from destroying "free government" and "tyrannizing over" the people. While farmers like Manning complained, Britain was alert, maneuvering in military and diplomatic actions along the borders of the fledgling republic, prepared to reopen hostilities and, indeed, retake the newly independent nation if the right opportunity presented itself.

Washington was especially worried that the new nation would lose the land west of the thirteen original states. Although Britain had ceded all its claims to land east of the Mississippi River to the United States, Indians who lived in that huge territory had not agreed, and when Washington took office, the indigenous peoples were considerably stronger than the U.S. Army. In addition, the British had not removed their forces from forts in that area, even though they had agreed to in the Treaty of Paris. The British saw the Indians as a useful instrument to help them reignite a war that would end American independence and return the country to the empire.

Many western whites were so fed up with the lack of protection by the federal government that there was talk of forming a separate western nation. Between 1785 and 1788, John Sevier led settlers in the western counties of North Carolina—now the state of Tennessee—to form a state they called Franklin, or sometimes, the Republic of Franklin. They were desperate for support in their battles with local Cherokee and Chickasaw. When their petition to become a state failed, they virtually governed themselves as an independent nation. Sensing an opportunity, Spanish authorities offered financial support to the settlers if they would affiliate with Spain rather than the United States, but North Carolina authorities successfully reasserted authority in the region. When he became president in 1789, Washington wanted to be sure there were no similar interests in independence or foreign alliances in the western lands claimed by the United States.

As one of his first moves after taking office, Washington set out on a series of grand tours of the United States. People loved seeing in person this war hero, now president, and the tours were an important effort to solidify the country behind the president and the Constitution. Washington also played a major role in the wars between the U.S. government and the Native American tribes that dominated the Ohio region when he came to office. He kept pressing his case and eventually defeated the tribes that had long inhabited the Ohio River Valley. When Hamilton's efforts to raise taxes created an armed uprising of farmers along the Pennsylvania frontier—the so-called Whiskey Rebellion—Washington, showing a balanced response, took charge of the army that put down the rebellion and also treated the rebels far more leniently than some wanted. Finally, in his second term in office, Washington turned most of his attention to foreign policy, specifically the growing tension between revolutionary France and the United States, which continued even after he left office.

The President Tours the Nation

To use his personal prestige to consolidate public support for the new government, Washington went on tours of the nation, not an easy task at a time when roads were poor and horses and carriages were the only means of transport once one left the waterways. Nevertheless, between 1789 and 1791, he rode by carriage and horseback from New York through much of New England and across the South. The trips allowed him to address important issues, hear from citizens, and personalize a distant national government. Welcoming the nation's greatest hero and leader was the social event of the season for many small-town residents, and for many it consolidated the sense of belonging to one nation. Privately, Washington sometimes complained about the accommodations, but he was convinced that his speeches and meetings had done much to build goodwill and support for the nation and his administration.

7.1

7.2

7.3

7.4

American Voices

Moses Seixas and George Washington, 1790 Letters

In 1790, as part of one of his national tours, Washington visited Newport, Rhode Island, and its Touro Synagogue, the oldest synagogue in the United States. Moses Seixas, speaking for the congregation, wrote to Washington, thanking him for the visit. Washington responded with a statement of his commitment to religious freedom. In a nation that was still sorting out the meaning of democracy, and before the First Amendment was added to the Constitution, Washington's letter was an important statement of American freedom.

Letter from Moses Seixas

Permit the children of the stock of Abraham to approach you with the most cordial affection and esteem for your person and merits. … Deprived as we heretofore have been of the invaluable rights of free Citizens, we now with a deep sense of gratitude to the Almighty disposer of all events behold a Government, erected by the Majesty of the People—a Government, which to bigotry gives no sanction, to persecution no assistance—but generously affording to all Liberty of conscience, and immunities of Citizenship.

Letter from G. Washington to the Hebrew Congregation in Newport Rhode Island

While I receive, with much satisfaction, your Address replete with expressions of affection and esteem; I rejoice in the opportunity of assuring you, that I shall always retain a grateful remembrance of the cordial welcome I experienced in my visit to Newport. … The

Citizens of the United States of America have a right to applaud themselves for having given to mankind examples of an enlarged and liberal policy: a policy worthy of imitation. All possess alike liberty of conscience and immunities of citizenship. It is now no more that toleration is spoken of, as if it was by the indulgence of one class of people, that another enjoyed the exercise of their inherent natural rights. For happily the Government of the United States, which gives to bigotry no sanction, to persecution no assistance, requires only that they who live under its protection should demean themselves as good citizens, in giving it on all occasions their effectual support.

Source: George Washington Papers, 1741–1799, Library of Congress, Letterbook 39.

Thinking Critically

1. **Continuity and Change over Time**
   How does Washington's letter reflect changes in people's thinking since the 1600s or the early 1700s? How does it reflect continuity with earlier or later ideas about religious liberty?

2. **Analyzing Primary Sources**
   Washington wrote his letter before the First Amendment was added to the Constitution. What does he mean by "more than toleration" and "natural rights" to "free religious expression"?

Indian Wars: Building the U.S. Army

Washington was deeply concerned about how to handle the frontier Indians. He blamed much of the problem on the "turbulence and disorderly conduct" of settlers who would not wait for permission or protection to enter the new territories but who then complained bitterly when Indians attacked them. Still, he needed to act with caution because he wanted these new settlers to be loyal citizens despite his frustration with them. On a personal level, he himself, like many members of Congress, had speculated in western lands and stood to make money if the land could actually be opened to white settlement. But given the poverty of the federal government—including only six hundred soldiers in the army when Washington became president—the president hardly commanded a force that could make much of a difference in the vast western territory.

The chief representative of the U.S. government on the western frontier, Arthur St. Clair, was both the appointed governor of what were then the Northwest Territories of the United States—lands Indians claimed—and a major general in the army. Congress had ordered him to end all Indian titles to the lands between the Ohio and Mississippi Rivers. But St. Clair lacked the resources to do his job. His strategy, as he wrote to Washington, was to divide and conquer—to seek many treaties with individual tribes rather than one overall treaty with all the tribes. But this strategy did not go well. In 1789, just before Washington's inauguration, St. Clair negotiated several treaties with one group of Indian leaders at Fort Harmar, but most other leaders and most tribes rejected these treaties, making them virtually useless.

In 1790, Washington asked Congress to expand the army so it could force the tribes of the Ohio region to "sue for peace before a blow is struck at them." Congress agreed to expand the army to 1,000 men and added 1,500 state militia from Kentucky, Virginia, and

Pennsylvania. This increased force, however, was still not strong enough to win the victories the president thought essential.

In September 1790, 1,450 troops under General Josiah Harmar marched into the territory of the Miami and Shawnee to destroy villages and crops as a show of force that might stop the attacks on frontier settlements. In October, Harmar's army was attacked by Shawnees, Miamis, and Pottawattomies, and 500 of the Americans were killed before the rest retreated. After this defeat, attacks on white settlements continued, and attempts at negotiating peace failed. Although some Indians, led by a Seneca named Cornplanter, sought to make a separate peace for their tribes, most others rejected the proposed treaties.

In 1791, President Washington ordered a new attack. General St. Clair himself led 2,000 troops in a direct assault on the Miamis on the Wabash River in what is now Indiana. On November 4, 1791, 1,500 Indians from several tribes led by Michikinikwa—or Little Turtle—of the Miami and Blue Jacket of the Shawnee killed over 500 troops and most of the expedition's female camp followers. Washington was shocked that St. Clair had allowed his army "to be cut to pieces, hacked, butchered, tomahawked," and relieved St. Clair of his command. As 1792 began, most of the area the United States called its Northwest Territory was in Indian hands.

Throughout 1792, the Washington administration and many of the Indians tried to negotiate. In June 1792, Joseph Brant, the Mohawk leader who had earlier traveled to London to meet with King George III, went to Philadelphia and met with President Washington, becoming one of the few people to meet with both national leaders. The meeting with Washington was cordial but did not lead to any final agreements, and Brant continued to strengthen his ties with Britain. Brant and most of the Iroquois, Shawnee, and Miami leaders were determined to allow no white settlement west of the Ohio River and demanded that the United States abandon its forts in that territory. But white settlers continued to move across the Ohio River into what is today the state of Ohio. They and their government wanted more land. Some of the negotiations were good-faith efforts. Some were a sham. All failed.

While some in Congress and the press argued for peace and an end to the waste of money and lives in western military campaigns, Washington called for a full-scale war on the Indians. Secretary of War Knox began to create a more professional army of five thousand men. In late 1793, he launched a third military campaign in the Northwest Territory.

In place of the disgraced St. Clair, Washington appointed Anthony Wayne (known as "Mad" Anthony Wayne) as major general of the U.S. Army. Wayne trained his army, and during the winter of 1793–1794, they built a new base, Fort Recovery, on the site of St. Clair's defeat. In August 1794, Wayne's army defeated a large Indian force led by the Shawnee Blue Jacket at the Battle of Fallen Timbers, near present-day Toledo, Ohio. After fierce fighting among twisted tree limbs and trunks, the Indians broke ranks and retreated. British forces at the nearby Fort Miami did not support their Indian allies, and Wayne decided not to attack the British fort (see Map 7-1, p. 200).

A year later, the **Treaty of Greenville** ended major hostilities between Indians and whites in the future states of Ohio and Indiana. The treaty established Indian reserves while the Indians ceded most of the remaining lands to the government. For the tribes of the Northwest, the Battle of Fallen Timbers and the Treaty of Greenville were the end of their control of the territory. The defeated Indian leader Little Turtle was blunt, telling General Wayne, "You have pointed out to us the boundary line between the Indians and the United States, but I now take the liberty to inform you, that the line cuts off from the Indians a large portion of the country, which has been enjoyed by my forefathers from time immemorial, without molestation or dispute." But after Fallen Timbers there was little that the tribal leaders could do. Many Indians moved to British Canada or farther west into the Louisiana Territory, still formally controlled by Spain. Although groups of Indians and settlers continued minor skirmishes for another twenty years, 1795 was the end of the Indian Wars in the Ohio region. Efforts to survey settlements and create local governments came quickly.

Washington's goals for the Northwest Territory and for dealing with the Indians were mostly accomplished. White settlers got the lands they wanted, the British lost their most powerful ally in the region, and the power and prestige of the U.S. Army were enhanced. Settlement continued long after Washington left office, and tribes that were more distant from the areas of settlement were able to maintain their old ways for another generation. Ohio

7.1
7.2
7.3
7.4

Little Turtle (colour litho), American School, (19th century)/© Chicago History Museum, USA/ The Bridgeman Art Library

The battles between the U.S. military and a confederation of tribes that were fought between 1785 and 1795 were sometimes referred to as the Northwest Indian War, or Little Turtle's War, in recognition of the central role of the Miami leader, Little Turtle, in the early defeats of the U.S. forces.

Treaty of Greenville

A treaty agreed to in 1795 in which Native Americans in the Northwest Territory were forced to cede most of the present states of Ohio, Indiana, Illinois, Michigan, and Wisconsin to the United States.

Map 7-1 Indian Removals and Resistance, 1790–1814.

Between the end of the Revolution in 1783 and the Treaty of Greenville in 1795, there was almost constant warfare between Native American tribes and the U.S. Army in the Northwest Territory and further battles well into the 1800s elsewhere in what was then the West of the country.

Ceded to U.S. control before 1784 ☆ Battle
Ceded to U.S. control 1784–1809 ■ British fort
Unceded Indian lands, 1809 ■ American fort

The Treaty of Greenville on August 3, 1795 (oil on canvas), 1805, American School, (19th century)/© Chicago History Museum, USA/ The Bridgeman Art Library

was admitted as a state in 1803. Indiana followed in 1816, Illinois in 1818, but Michigan and Wisconsin much later in 1837 and 1848, respectively. In the northern portions, treaties came later, including some seventy treaties negotiated with tribes living in Wisconsin, one of which, signed in 1854 with the Ojibwe, allowed white development of northern Wisconsin and the islands in Lake Superior. But after Fallen Timbers and the Treaty of Greenville, the pattern was set and there was no large-scale resistance in the following decades.

After a series of Native American victories, the U.S. Army's victory at the Battle of Fallen Timbers in 1794 brought organized resistance to an end. A year later, in 1795, defeated tribal leaders agreed to the Treaty of Greenville, ceding most of the land of the Northwest to white settlement. This picture shows Little Turtle talking with General Anthony Wayne.

Whiskey Tax, Whiskey Rebellion

When a compromise by Hamilton, Jefferson, and Madison led Congress to pass Hamilton's economic plan in 1782, it solved one set of problems but created new ones. Paying off the debt required more income for the federal government than the customs tax alone could raise. After considering several options, Hamilton hit on the idea of taxing whiskey. If there were to be new taxes, a tax on whiskey seemed less undesirable than most options. Even Hamilton's long time opponent James Madison supported it as a way to increase "sobriety and thereby prevent disease and untimely deaths." Like the "sin taxes" of later generations, the tax on whiskey seemed an easy call. However, what seemed easy in New York and Philadelphia was seen by farmers in western Pennsylvania as a direct attack on their livelihood.

Western Pennsylvania and neighboring parts of Appalachia had been settled long before the Revolution, primarily by Scots-Irish Presbyterians who were willing to fight Indians for land and who wanted to maintain their culture, including their love for whiskey. Turning corn, their staple crop, into whiskey was also the best way to get the crop to market. A farmer could distill corn into whiskey at home and then transport a keg, or several kegs, on a horse or mule over the mountains and sell the liquid corn at $16 a keg in East Coast markets, making a considerable profit. It was much easier and more profitable than trying to transport raw corn over the mountains, and between 1783 and 1795 when Spain closed the port of New Orleans to American goods, transporting any products down the Ohio and Mississippi Rivers was not an option.

Hamilton's tax, however, ate up the profit. Moreover, the tax singled out these whiskey-making farmers and not others such as land speculators (of which Washington was one). Western farmers complained that the tax discriminated against them, and it did. They were already angry. Most frontier farmers had opposed adopting the Constitution when it was being debated in 1787 and 1788. Now only a few years later, the first administration elected under the Constitution seemed bent on destroying these farmers' best hope of economic prosperity. They rebelled.

The **Whiskey Rebellion** began with modest protests. The Pennsylvania, North Carolina, Maryland, Virginia, and Georgia legislatures passed resolutions opposing the tax. When these actions were not heeded by the administration, protests escalated. Tax collectors were shot at, tarred and feathered, or beaten and threatened with scalping. In a mass meeting in Pittsburgh, rebels agreed to fight for the repeal of the tax and to treat tax collectors with the "contempt they deserve." In 1793 and 1794, no federal taxes were collected in Kentucky or Pennsylvania's western counties. A convention of more than two hundred farmers at Parkinson's Ferry debated armed resistance to the national government. In 1794, a federal marshal, David Lennox, and John Neville, a friend of Washington's from the Revolution, were attacked by armed men when they tried to collect the tax. Neville's house was burned, and he and his family barely escaped. On August 1, six thousand rebels met outside of Pittsburgh and, modeling their behavior on revolutionaries in France, created a Committee of Public Safety, erected a guillotine, and made plans to attack the government garrison at Pittsburgh to gain weapons.

Hamilton advised Washington to "exert the full force of the Law against Offenders." But Washington worried about losing the westerners' allegiance to the United States. Throughout 1792 and 1793, he sought to negotiate with the whiskey makers. Washington's overtures were seen as weakness by some of the Whiskey Rebels. Farmers who paid the tax were attacked and their stills destroyed.

By the summer of 1794, as the riots spread and after the attack on Neville, Washington had had enough. He saw the attacks and the refusal to pay taxes as part of a plot to overthrow the Constitution. He decided to act.

7.1

7.2

7.3

7.4

Whiskey Rebellion

Armed uprising in 1794 by farmers in western Pennsylvania who attempted to prevent the collection of the excise tax on whiskey.

Whiskey rebels escorting a tarred and feathered tax collector from his burning homestead (colour litho), American School, (18th century) (after)/Private Collection/Peter Newark American Pictures/The Bridgeman Art Library

Western farmers who opposed the Whiskey Tax turned to increasingly violent means of resistance, including tarring and feathering U.S. tax agents as others had done to British tax agents before the Revolution.

7.1

7.2

7.3

7.4

Given the size of the insurgency, Washington called for twelve thousand troops to be drawn from the militias of New Jersey, Maryland, and Virginia. The president himself took command of the force and, with Hamilton at his side, marched across Pennsylvania. While Hamilton promised that every rebel they caught would be "skewered, shot, or hanged on the first tree," Washington remained "grave, distant, and austere."

In the end, the sheer size of Washington's army frightened the rebels and ended the rebellion. Most of the rebel farmers either accepted Washington's offer of amnesty if they would swear loyalty to the United States or melted away into the woods and hollows. The army arrested 150 rebel leaders, but only two were convicted of treason, and Washington pardoned both of them. But the back of the rebellion had been broken. Federal authority— loved by some, hated by others—was supreme.

The French Revolution Comes to America

News and ideas moved slowly in the 1700s. People had to wait weeks to hear about developments in another state and months to hear about foreign events. Yet to a surprising degree, Americans in the 1790s were well informed about and influenced by developments in Europe, most of all by the French Revolution about which most Americans had strong opinions.

If much of Washington's first term was taken up with economic matters and Indian wars, his second term (1793–1797) was dominated by the French Revolution (Table 7-1). Indeed, if revolution had not erupted in France, Washington might have served only one term and retired as he wanted to do.

Table 7-1 Interplay of the French Revolution and the United States, 1789–1801

Developments in the United States	Developments in France
April 1789—George Washington is inaugurated as the first U.S. president; Washington appoints Alexander Hamilton (generally pro-British) secretary of the treasury and Thomas Jefferson (generally pro-French) secretary of state.	July 1789—A Paris mob storms the Bastille Prison and sets prisoners free
September 1789—Congress approves the Bill of Rights, including freedom of religion and the press and guaranteed due process (Ratified December 1791)	August 1789—The French National Assembly issues the Declaration of the Rights of Man and Citizen—"Men are born and remain free and equal"—and affirms freedom of thought, religion, petition, and due process.
	September 1791—A new French Constitution creates a constitutional monarchy
November 1792—George Washington is elected to a second term as president after agreeing to be a candidate primarily because of concerns with the French Revolution	April 1792—The National Assembly declares war on Austria, beginning twenty-three years of war in Europe; French monarchy is overthrown
April 1793—Citizen Genêt arrives as French ambassador	January 1793—Louis XVI is executed in Paris
1793–1794—Democratic-Republican Societies spring up around United States in support of French Revolution and Jefferson-Madison policies at home; during the Whiskey Rebellion, farmers create a "Committee of Public Safety," modeled on France, and set up a guillotine	June 1793–June 1794—Reign of Terror, under a "Committee of Public Safety" in which over forty thousand people are executed; the terror ends with the execution of Maximilian Robespierre
1797—John Quincy Adams reports a French plot to create a breakaway republic in southwestern United States; President Adams fears a French-Jeffersonian plot to create a Directory in the United States	1795–1799—France is governed by a five-member Directory
1798–1800—XYZ Affair; United States fights undeclared naval war with France. In his last months in office, John Adams negotiates peace	1799—Napoleon Bonaparte stages a coup d'état and rules France until 1814
1801—Thomas Jefferson is elected president, reducing tensions with France	
1803—Jefferson purchases Louisiana Territory from France	

By 1792, Washington believed that he had stabilized the country and would have been happy to retire. However, both Hamilton and Jefferson, by then bitter enemies, told Washington that the country still needed him, in part because each saw Washington as a buffer against the other's policies. Most of their followers agreed. The most powerful argument for a second term, however, was Washington's realization that revolutionary France would soon be at war with Austria and Britain, and that war would make American diplomacy much more difficult. He could not walk away from what he saw as a coming foreign policy crisis even as he insisted "at my age, the love of retirement grows every day more & more powerful." His personal popularity exceeded any disagreement with his policies, and he was reelected unanimously.

When word of the European war reached Philadelphia in the spring of 1792, the Washington administration issued a formal Proclamation of Neutrality. Where Washington had seemed to favor Hamilton in economic matters, he favored Jefferson—and Jefferson's successor Edmund Randolph—on foreign policy. When France's revolutionary government asked America to pay off debt from the Revolutionary War earlier than negotiated, Washington agreed. When the French announced plans to send a new ambassador, just after the execution of King Louis XVI in January 1793, Washington agreed to receive him. Washington was determined to maintain neutrality. He would not let Hamilton's pro-British views draw him into a war, much as he disliked some of the news from France.

However, the new French ambassador, Edmond-Charles Genêt—Citizen Genêt as he was called, using the title that every person in France adopted if they wanted to keep their head— was as undiplomatic as a diplomat could be. He landed in Charleston, South Carolina, and immediately began commissioning American vessels to attack British shipping in direct violation of Washington's neutrality policies. He also purchased munitions for France and enlisted volunteers to attack Spanish Florida. Then he went to Philadelphia to meet the president.

Washington had long mastered the art of showing icy displeasure. Having heard about Genêt's actions in Charleston, he met Genêt with great formality, standing under a picture of Louis XVI, America's ally during its Revolution, whom Genêt's government had just executed. In the nation's capital of Philadelphia, Genêt continued to raise arms for privateers to attack the British and recruit soldiers from Kentucky to attack Florida. Washington then demanded that the French government recall Genêt, which it did early in 1794. (Fearing execution if he returned to France, Genêt then asked for asylum and settled in New York as a private citizen.) But in Genêt's brief tenure as ambassador, the **Citizen Genêt Affair**, as it came to be called, did lasting harm, inspiring hostility toward France among President Washington, Vice President John Adams, and other officials, while arousing more enthusiasm for the French Revolution among some Americans.

While Washington found it easy to dismiss Citizen Genêt, he could not as easily dismiss the fact that many Americans supported the French Revolution. In the first years of the revolution in France, most Americans strongly supported developments in the country's oldest ally. When French citizens stormed the Bastille prison in July 1789, Lafayette, who had fought beside Washington during the Revolution, sent the keys to the former prison to the president. Conservative Federalists joined with staunch Antifederalists in celebrating the emergence of a new constitutional state in Europe.

Some Federalists soon began to have doubts about the French Revolution, however. For them, news of riots and killings in France were terrifying. For the emerging republican movement, however, the news from France was more encouraging. Thomas Jefferson never stopped believing that the revolution was a grand moment in history, even if he was uncomfortable with what he viewed as its excesses. Once Britain joined the war against revolutionary France, many Americans sided with France despite official neutrality.

Democratic-Republican Societies supporting the French Revolution sprang up across the United States. The first society was established in Philadelphia, but before long there were dozens, from Maine to South Carolina and from coastal cities to backcountry hamlets. These grassroots societies were more radical than anything even Jefferson was comfortable with. Some of those who joined the Democratic-Republican Societies were farmers who were angry with the federal government and ready for some revolutionary activity of their own. But the largest societies were in East Coast cities, where anti-British sentiment still ran deep. There, small-time merchants and manufacturers, mechanics, and other citizens were

Citizen Genêt Affair

The efforts of Edmond-Charles Genêt, French ambassador to the United States (1793–1794), to stir up military support for France and the French Revolution among Americans, leading to long-term anti-French sentiment.

7.1

7.2

7.3

7.4

angry at the arrogance of an older, Federalist aristocracy and anxious to make their own place in the new nation. Members of these societies had great hopes for the ideals—if not all the tactics and the bloodshed—of the French Revolution and wanted to defend it. Not accidentally, most of the members of these societies also disliked Hamilton's economic policies as well as the expanding power of the federal government and supported the Jeffersonian opposition in elections, even if the Democratic-Republican leaders in Congress kept their distance from them.

Regardless of differences, the president was generally considered above politics, so dissenters usually avoided direct criticisms of Washington himself. Even so, the Democratic-Republican Societies became bastions of hostility to many of his policies. If the birth of the two-party system can be traced to the split between Hamilton and Jefferson over economic issues, then the deep divides over the revolution in France solidified the organization of the Federalists and the Democratic-Republicans (see Table 7-2). Ironically, given all the republican talk of liberty and equality, the groups associated with Jefferson were also much more sympathetic to slavery. Many among the Democratic-Republicans saw states' rights as a vehicle for protecting slavery. By contrast, the Federalists tended to see slavery as morally wrong and harmful to the nation's commercial development.

Washington tried hard to stay "above the fray" and unite the factions. For a time he succeeded, which explains part of the reason he was unanimously reelected in 1792, but by the end of his second term in office in 1797, more people were coming to see him as another Federalist leader. If he had run for a third term—something he had no intention of doing—the election would certainly not have been unanimous, though it is difficult to imagine a person of his enormous popularity being defeated.

U.S. anger at Britain was not fueled only by memories of 1776. In the 1790s, British soldiers still held Fort Detroit and Fort Niagara (near present-day Buffalo) in violation of the Treaty of Paris. In the summer of 1793, fearing that American neutrality was a cover for selling American grain to all sides in the European war, the British government issued Orders in Council (orders from the king through his Privy Council—the equivalent of Executive Orders in the United States) that banned all American commercial links with France or the French Caribbean islands. By 1794, the Royal Navy had taken four hundred American merchant sailors prisoner. Farmers could not sell their wheat, and dockworkers had no jobs. There were growing calls for war with Britain, which might help France, rid the frontier of the British, and end the restrictions on shipping. Washington, however, was determined to avoid war. He sent Chief Justice John Jay, who had been foreign secretary under the Articles of Confederation, to London to resolve the problems. For a short moment, Jay's appointment as U.S. representative to London quieted the calls for war.

Table 7-2 Characteristics of the Emerging Political Parties or Factions

Topic	Federalists	Antifederalists or Democratic-Republicans
Leaders	Alexander Hamilton and John Adams (personal enemies)	Thomas Jefferson and James Madison (personal friends)
Foreign policy	Generally pro-British; want to model United States on British institutions	Strongly pro-French; generally supportive of the French Revolution
Influence of federal government	Strong federal government with strong army	Weak federal government; strong states' rights
Economic policy	Commercial nation; favor building roads and canals and support the Bank of the United States	Agrarian nation; oppose federal spending for roads and canals and oppose Bank of the United States
Regional base	Strongest in New England	Strongest in the southern states
On slavery	Mildly against slavery	Favor protecting states' rights as a vehicle to protect slavery
Alien and Sedition Acts (see "The Birth of Political Parties" later in this chapter)	Sponsor and enforce Alien and Sedition Acts	Sponsor Kentucky and Virginia Resolutions declaring Alien and Sedition Acts "nullified"

But the treaty Jay negotiated with Britain late in 1794 accomplished little of what Washington wanted. Britain did agree to pay compensation for its attacks on shipping since 1793, but not to end the ban on neutral shipping to France or to pay compensation for earlier American losses. While Britain also promised again to remove its troops from the Mississippi Valley, it had been ignoring its own promises to do so for a decade, and there was little reason to assume that it would now change policy. The most Jay could say of the treaty he had negotiated was "It breaks the ice." Washington was bitterly disappointed that Jay had not accomplished more but sent **Jay's Treaty** to the Senate for ratification anyway. The Senate vote in 1795 showed the growing divisions in the country. All twenty senators identified with the Federalists in the Senate voted for the treaty, and all ten associated with the Democratic-Republicans voted against it. The public attacks against Washington, which had been muted up to this point, now became much louder.

In the final year of the Washington administration, one significant diplomatic victory helped to balance out the previous controversies. While Jay had been in London, Washington had sent Thomas Pinckney to Madrid. Where Jay had failed, **Pinckney's Treaty** succeeded beyond expectations. Worrying that Britain and the United States might settle their differences at Spain's expense, the Spanish agreed to a treaty that pushed the northern border of Florida farther south and westward to the Mississippi and, far more important, opened the Mississippi River and the port of New Orleans to U.S. commerce. Access to New Orleans was very important. During the colonial era Spain had allowed travel on the Mississippi River but, fearing the rising power of the new United States, had closed the port to all American citizens after the Revolution. With Pinckney's Treaty, western farmers could again ship goods down the Mississippi through New Orleans to world markets instead of having to struggle across the Appalachians. In addition, for all the uproar over Jay's Treaty, the British actually honored it, removing their soldiers from Niagara and Detroit. Washington believed he could now retire in confidence that the nation was secure.

Jay's Treaty

A treaty with Britain, negotiated in 1794, in which the United States made major concessions to avert a war over the British seizure of American ships.

Pinckney's Treaty

A treaty with Spain that set the border between the United States and Spanish Florida.

7.3 Quick Review

How did the Washington administration try to strengthen the nation's security between 1789 and 1796?

The Birth of Political Parties: Adams and Jefferson

7.4 Explain the growing split between the Federalist and Democratic-Republican factions, including how the French Revolution and the personal differences between Hamilton, Adams, and Jefferson affected American politics.

The framers of the Constitution feared the idea of people voting for specific candidates or a popularity contest for president and they also feared the possibility that political factions or parties with specific leaders might emerge. The Electoral College in which each state would have the number of presidential electors equal to its representation in Congress was a solution. It was designed to ensure that there was no direct election of the president but rather that wise electors would select the best person in the country. State legislatures could pick these electors any way they wished. Each elector would get two votes as long as his two candidates were from different states. Whoever got the most votes from all the electors would be president. The runner-up would be vice president. If no one got a majority of the electoral votes, then the election would be resolved in the House of Representatives. Since there had been a national consensus that George Washington should be the first president and since he was elected and reelected unanimously, only the election after Washington's retirement tested the system. The first two tests, in 1796 and 1800, did not go well.

John Adams's Difficult Presidency

The election in 1796 that made John Adams president was an odd one. By 1796, Adams, though never a close friend or political ally of Hamilton, had come to represent the Federalists, those who supported the Washington administration's foreign policy and most of Hamilton's economic policies. Most Federalists also supported Thomas Pinckney of South Carolina for vice president and a few, including Hamilton, tried to maneuver Pinckney into the presidency.

Thomas Jefferson was the logical candidate of the Democratic-Republicans, a large group—though not yet an organized political party—that sympathized with the French Revolution and thought Hamilton had shifted too much power to the federal government and to the urban economic elites of New York and Philadelphia. Although Aaron Burr of New York was not an official running mate, many Democratic-Republicans supported him as their vice presidential candidate. Advocates of these views had formed Democratic-Republican Societies in all parts of the country, organized their own newspapers, sympathized with the Whiskey Rebels, and adopted the French tricolor of red, white, and blue as their political colors. They were ready to become a political force in presidential politics.

Adams and Jefferson did not campaign in 1796—actually *wanting* to be president was considered unseemly—but many others campaigned for them. A Democratic-Republican paper in Philadelphia called Adams "His Rotundity" (he was heavy) and said that he was the "champion of kings, ranks, and titles." Federalist papers said that Jefferson was an atheist, a friend of the radical French Revolutionaries, and a danger to democracy. There were also battles within the factions. After Adams learned of Hamilton's efforts to make Pinckney president instead of him, he called Hamilton "as great a hypocrite as any in the U.S."

George Washington also entered the campaign, though without formally endorsing a candidate. In September 1796, Washington gave what he called his farewell address six months before he left office. Later generations saw the speech as the grand nonpartisan benediction of the nation's founder. Contemporaries understood it differently. In the address, Washington said he wanted to warn his country "against the baneful effects of the spirit of party generally." A political party would "distract the public councils and enfeeble the public administration. It agitates the community with ill-founded jealousies and false alarms." He also warned "that foreign influence is one of the most baneful foes of republican government."

In Washington's mind, the Democratic-Republican Societies generally embodied "the spirit of party," and he had seen how they could foment "riot and insurrection" when he had led the army against the Whiskey Rebels. He also feared that Jefferson's pro-French views represented the "insidious wiles of foreign influence." In 1796, most people took Washington's speech to mean "vote for Adams, not Jefferson." Although he would never say so directly, Washington wanted his vice president to be his successor. He got his wish.

Of the 139 electoral votes cast in the 1796 election, Adams received 71, all from New England, New York, and New Jersey, while Jefferson received 68, from Pennsylvania and the southern states. Pinckney and Burr both got fewer votes. So because of the way the Electoral College was set up, Adams and Jefferson, these two political rivals, became president and vice president, respectively.

The anger of the 1796 campaign cooled quickly. The pro-Jefferson newspaper, the *Aurora*, declared that Adams was a man "possessing great integrity." One of Jefferson's strongest supporters in Congress, William Branch Giles of Virginia, said, "The old man will make a good President, too." Jefferson and Adams exchanged cordial letters, and Adams invited the vice president to sit in the Cabinet—which Washington had never done for him—but Jefferson declined. The two dined with Washington just after Adams's inauguration, and in his inaugural address, Adams insisted that it was his "inflexible determination" to maintain peace with all nations, including France, words that surely reassured Jefferson and his followers.

But the split between the Federalists and the Democratic-Republicans went too deep for soothing words to heal. Differences came to a head in Congress in January 1798 when Matthew Lyon, a Democratic-Republican from Vermont, ridiculed the ceremonial greeting for President

Adams and insulted Federalist Roger Griswold of Connecticut. Griswold then insulted Lyon who spat in Griswold's face. Griswold attacked Lyon with his cane, and Lyon grabbed a pair of fireplace tongs to fight back on the floor of the House of Representatives. The two were pulled apart, but the incident symbolized the hatred between the two parties and the depths to which public discourse had sunk.

Nothing, however, represented the split between the two factions as much as their attitudes toward the French Revolution. Barely a week after his inauguration, Adams received troubling news that the French Directory, the five-member council then ruling revolutionary France, had refused to receive Adams's choice as U.S. ambassador to France. Adams had chosen Charles Cotesworth Pinckney (brother of the Federalist candidate for vice president) to improve the U.S.–French relationship, but the French did not see it that way. The Directory also launched an undeclared war on U.S. shipping. In the following months, the French captured three hundred American merchant ships. From his son, John Quincy Adams, who was serving as U.S. ambassador to Prussia, Adams also heard of a French plan to stir up revolt and secession in the western U.S. territories. The Federalist press called for war against France while the Democratic-Republicans claimed it was a false crisis made up by the pro-British Federalists.

Adams sought a middle ground. He sent Elbridge Gerry of Massachusetts and John Marshall of Virginia to join Pinckney in Paris and try to reopen negotiations. But he also asked Congress to establish a navy and provide funds to prepare for war if it came. The response to the new president's actions broke along partisan lines, with Federalists supporting Adams and Democratic-Republicans opposing him. But Adams won authorization for a new Department of the Navy and funds to build and support three medium-sized warships called frigates (one of which, the *U.S.S. Constitution*, is still officially on active duty).

However, Adams's peace overtures to the French did not go well. When his new delegation arrived in Paris, the French foreign minister Charles Maurice de Talleyrand arranged for agents, whom Adams identified only as "X, Y, and Z," to inform the Americans that negotiations could proceed only if Talleyrand was paid a bribe of $250,000 and the French government received a loan of $10 to $12 million as well as an apology for what the French considered Adams's belligerent tone. Pinckney's famous response was "No, no, not a sixpence." In fact, the commissioners were prepared to pay a bribe, not an unusual part of diplomacy at the time, but the amount demanded was far too high.

When word of the so-called **XYZ Affair** reached Congress and the American public in March 1798, Adams's popularity soared, and many called for a war against France to avenge U.S. honor. Federalists in Congress voted to increase the size of the U.S. Army and shift its focus from the western frontier to a presumed threat of French invasion on the Atlantic coast. Given British naval supremacy, a French invasion was improbable. Even if the British did not like the United States, they certainly did not want their archenemy France to control any territory in North America. Adams, unlike most Federalists, feared a large standing U.S. Army, especially after Hamilton won appointment as a major general within it. Adams preferred to strengthen the Navy to protect U.S. interests.

In this popular drawing that was widely circulated, Roger Griswold, a Connecticut Federalist, attacked Matthew Lyon, a Vermont Republican, who fought back with fire tongs. Few images so starkly described the state of partisan politics in the new nation.

XYZ Affair

Diplomatic incident in 1798 in which Americans were outraged by the demand of the French for a bribe as a condition for negotiating with American diplomats.

This cartoon reflects the anti-French sentiment of many Americans, showing France as having five heads (for the five-member Directory that ruled at one point), the bloody guillotine in the background, and the demand for a bribe from the upright American delegates. Note also the Africans, representative of French-owned Haiti.

Quasi-War

An undeclared war—1797 to 1800—between the United States and France.

Alien and Sedition Acts

A series of three acts passed by Congress in 1798 that made it harder for new immigrants to vote and made it a crime to criticize the president or Congress.

Kentucky and Virginia Resolutions

Resolutions written by Thomas Jefferson and James Madison that criticized the Alien and Sedition Acts and asserted the rights of states to declare federal law null and void within a state.

In 1798 and 1799, though there was no formal declaration of war, the United States engaged in what became known as the **Quasi-War** with France or, as Adams preferred to call it, the "Half-War." Treaties with France dating back to the American Revolution were repealed, and the United States began a trade embargo against France. The United States also supported the independence of Haiti, something it had not done during the Washington administration. Congress created the Marine Corps along with the Navy and armed merchant ships so they could attack French ships near the U.S. coast or in the Caribbean. Even if France had the most powerful army in Europe, Talleyrand did not really want war with the United States, and he began to make peace overtures. U.S. neutrality, if not friendship, would be important, Talleyrand thought, if France were to launch a planned invasion of England.

The war hysteria also led Congress to pass the **Alien and Sedition Acts**, actually three separate acts that irreparably hurt Adams's reputation even though he did not directly request any of them. Federalists had become increasingly fearful of pro-French agitation. Massachusetts Congressman Harrison Gray Otis asked, "Do we not know that the French nation have organized bands of aliens as well as their own citizens, in other countries?" Many Federalists wondered, could the kind of revolutionary violence seen in France happen here?

To make sure that French efforts, aided by Jeffersonian Democratic-Republicans, could not undermine the government and its Federalist leaders, Congress passed the Naturalization Act and the Alien Friends Act in June 1798, which were referred to as the Alien Acts. These laws lengthened the time to qualify for citizenship from five to fourteen years—to ensure that recent pro-French immigrants could not vote—and allowed the government to deport anyone deemed dangerous to the United States. While no one was actually deported under the acts, many French citizens left the United States on their own rather than wait and see what might happen.

A month later, on July 14, 1798, Congress passed the Sedition Act by a slim majority, and Adams signed the law. The Sedition Act targeted primarily newspaper editors like Benjamin Franklin Bache, editor of the Democratic-Republican *Aurora*, making any "false, scandalous, and malicious" speech against the government, particularly Congress or the president, a crime. Unlike the Alien Acts, the Sedition Act was vigorously enforced. Democratic-Republican Congressman Matthew Lyon—who earlier had the wrestling match with Griswold—was convicted under the law for continuing to criticize the Adams administration and spent four months in a Vermont jail. (His constituents made it clear what they thought of the act when they overwhelmingly reelected Lyon to Congress once he was released from jail.) All told, seventeen people were tried under the act, including a drunk in New Jersey who had "cast aspersions on the President's posterior" and was fined the then enormous sum of $150. But newspapers were not silenced, and the attack on free speech undermined support for the Federalists.

The Democratic-Republicans attacked the Alien and Sedition Acts. Vice President Jefferson initially counseled patience with what he saw as "the reign of the witches" in the Adams administration, but soon came to view the Alien and Sedition laws as a fundamental threat to democracy. In the fall of 1798, he drafted resolutions, and his friends and supporters in the Kentucky legislature adopted his words, that asserted a state's right to declare federal law "void and of no force" within the state's jurisdiction. Virginia's legislature adopted similar resolutions drafted by James Madison. Both legislatures invited other states to join them, but none did. Nevertheless, the **Kentucky and Virginia Resolutions** drew a sharp line between the two political factions. On the Democratic-Republican side, Madison, like Jefferson, saw the resolutions as an appropriate protest within the framework of the Constitution he had helped write, and both men saw them as the basic right of state legislatures to nullify federal law. But the Federalists saw the Kentucky and Virginia resolutions as a fundamental attack on the basic authority of the federal government and, indeed, on the Constitution itself.

While Adams never repudiated the Alien and Sedition Acts, he did end the war fever. Through emissaries, Adams received a signal that France did not want war, and after British Admiral Horatio Nelson destroyed the French fleet in the Battle of the Nile in October 1798, any remote possibility of a French invasion of the United States disappeared. Adams had become convinced that Hamilton was trying to stir up a war for his own political ambitions. The president called him "a man devoid of every moral principle." In February 1799, Adams told the Senate that he himself was committed "to embrace every plausible appearance of probability of preserving or restoring tranquility," and he also asked them to approve a new ambassador to France to replace Pinckney. Many Federalists were enraged that Adams would try yet again for peace, and he had to endure a shouting match with Hamilton— now a private citizen but an influential one. He also had to fire his own secretary of state, Timothy Pickering, who was ready for war, and replace him with a close political ally, John Marshall (who would later become chief justice of the Supreme Court). But the Senate approved William Vans Murray as the new ambassador, and the new mission worked. It took all of 1799 and 1800 to negotiate, during which time the government of France changed from the Directory to the dictatorship of Napoleon Bonaparte, but peace came. The Treaty of Mortefontaine ended the Quasi-War and protected U.S. shipping. Adams disbanded part of the army in May 1800 over the opposition of his own party. He also pardoned John Fries who had led a nonviolent rebellion against federal war taxes in Pennsylvania in 1799 and had been sentenced to death for treason. These actions cost Adams dearly, particularly among his own Federalists. But he considered the choice for peace against war his crowning achievement and ordered that his gravestone read "Here lies John Adams, who took upon himself the responsibility for peace with France in the year 1800."

American Voices

The Kentucky Resolutions of 1798

When Congress passed the Alien and Sedition Acts in 1798, a firestorm of protest broke out. Leaders of the Democratic-Republican Party saw the laws as a direct attack on freedom of speech. They also opposed the legislation because they feared it would foster war with France and expand the army, navy, and federal power in general. In response, Vice President Jefferson secretly drafted resolutions that were adopted by the Kentucky legislature in November 1798, while Madison drafted similar resolutions for Virginia. These Kentucky and Virginia Resolutions not only attacked the Alien and Sedition Acts but also declared that, since the federal government was a compact of the states, any state could declare any federal law unconstitutional within the bounds of that state. This claim would have far-reaching implications in the decades leading up to the Civil War. Although most historians see the Alien and Sedition Acts as a dangerous attack on free speech, they also see the resolutions as an equally dangerous effort to undermine national unity.

1. *Resolved,* That the several states composing the United States of America are not united on the principle of unlimited submission to their general government; but that, by compact, under the style and title of a Constitution for the United States, and of amendments thereto, they constituted a general government for special purposes, delegated to that government certain definite powers, reserving, each state to itself, the residuary mass of right to their own self-government; and that whensoever the general government assumes undelegated powers, its acts are unauthoritative, void, and of no force; that to this compact each state acceded as a state, and is an integral party; that this government, created by this compact,

was not made the exclusive or final judge of the extent of the powers delegated to itself, since that would have made its discretion, and not the Constitution, the measure of its powers; but that, as in all other cases of compact among powers having no common judge, each party has an equal right to judge for itself, as well of infractions as of the mode and measure of redress.

2. *Resolved ...* therefore, also, the same act of Congress, passed on the 14th day of July, 1798, and entitled "An Act in Addition to the Act entitled 'An Act for the Punishment of certain Crimes against the United States;'" [the Sedition Act] ... (and all other their acts which assume to create, define, or punish crimes other than those so enumerated in the Constitution,) are altogether void, and of no force; and that the power to create, define, and punish, such other crimes is reserved, and of right appertains, solely and exclusively, to the respective states, each within its own territory.

Source: Library of Congress http://lccn.loc.gov/09021366

Thinking Critically

1. **Analyzing Primary Sources**
   How did the Kentucky Resolution reflect the core beliefs of the Democratic-Republicans?

2. **Contextualization**
   Did the position that Jefferson argued in the document constitute a threat to national unity? Did the fact that he was vice president at the time make a difference one way or another in his responsibilities?

The Election of 1800

The political differences between the two leading candidates for president in 1800, President John Adams and Vice President Thomas Jefferson, could not have been clearer. But the methods for actually selecting the next president and vice president in 1800 could not have been more convoluted. None of the problems with the Electoral College that were seen in 1796 had been resolved. At that time, political parties had been informal alliances of like-minded individuals. By 1800, however, the Federalists and Democratic-Republicans were much better organized. They had come to represent two distinct philosophies and sets of personal allegiances. In December 1799, just as the maneuvering for the 1800 election was starting, news came that George Washington had died at his home in Mount Vernon, Virginia. People of all political factions mourned the loss of a unifying leader, and they knew that the next election would be more divisive than ever.

Despite the fact that most of the Constitution's authors did not want nominations of presidential candidates to occur before the selection of presidential electors, in 1800, each party's congressional delegations nominated the candidates in semisecret caucuses. When the Democratic-Republican caucus met on May 11, 1800, it was clear that Jefferson would be their nominee for president. Several candidates were considered for vice president, but the Democratic-Republicans wanted someone who would help them win New York, which they saw as the key to the White House. The man to deliver New York's votes was Aaron Burr. Few politicians, including Jefferson, trusted or respected Burr, but Jefferson did not intend to lose the presidency twice. In an ill-fated decision, the caucus and party leaders pledged that every elector would vote for both Jefferson and Burr. Everyone simply assumed that somehow Jefferson would receive the most votes and become president with Burr, the runner-up, becoming vice president, but that assumption proved to be a serious mistake.

Federalist maneuvering was equally complicated. There was general agreement that failure to support Adams would fatally split the party. But the caucus also chose Charles Cotesworth Pinckney of South Carolina, the brother of their 1796 vice presidential nominee, to be vice president, in part because he was known to be loyal to Hamilton and in part because his refusal to give a bribe to France in the XYZ Affair had made him a hero. Behind the scenes, Hamilton hoped, as he had in 1796, that he could somehow engineer Pinckney's election as president. Once again, Adams found out about Hamilton's plans and was furious.

Because the Constitution gave each state the right to choose its presidential electors any way it wished, the actual voting for those electors was spread out over most of the year. In an early but crucial test, Burr was able to ensure New York's electoral votes for the Jefferson-Burr ticket. Pennsylvania's Democratic-Republican governor also promised to deliver its electoral votes for the Jefferson-Burr ticket or, if that failed, to simply prevent a vote to choose electors from taking place in that state so Adams could not receive any votes there.

A campaign poster from the 1800 election comparing the nation's hero, outgoing President George Washington, with Thomas Jefferson who, the poster suggested, had done very little for the nation. It was designed to lead to a vote for John Adams, though he was not mentioned.

As other states continued to select their presidential electors in the summer and fall of 1800, the contest remained fierce. A Federalist newspaper said a vote for the Democratic-Republicans was a vote "for the tempestuous sea of anarchy and misrule; for arming the poor against the rich; for fraternizing with the foes of God and man" while a Democratic-Republican paper asked people to choose between, "Peace or war, happiness or misery, opulence or ruin!" The Sedition Act made direct attacks on President Adams dangerous, but the press was far from neutral, and anger at that act added fuel to the Democratic-Republican fire.

Slaves could not vote, and slavery had not been a major issue in the previous presidential campaigns, but it was in 1800. Gabriel Prosser and Jack Bowler were slaves on a Virginia plantation not far from the state capital in Richmond. Throughout the summer, they were planning a slave uprising. Prosser promised death to all whites except "Quakers,

7.1

7.2

7.3

7.4

Methodists, and French people," that is, whites known to support abolition. Over one thousand slaves were involved, forging swords from sickles, making their own bullets, and designing a flag that read "Death or Liberty." The uprising was set for Saturday, August 30, when they planned to meet at the Prosser plantation, kill the white owners, and march on Richmond. However, a terrible storm on August 30 scattered the slave army, and Governor James Monroe discovered the plan and called out the state militia. The leaders of the uprising were quickly tried and executed, but the prospect of a slave uprising terrified the southern states.

The issue of slavery complicated the presidential campaign. Both political parties were divided internally over it. Adams hated slavery, but Pinckney, his running mate, was one of the largest slave owners in South Carolina. Both Jefferson and Burr owned slaves, Jefferson many of them. But Jefferson had also written in opposition to slavery. He needed northern Democratic-Republican votes in Pennsylvania and New York where abolitionism was gaining ground. Governor Monroe and Jefferson feared that too many slave executions would spark an abolitionist upheaval and cost them votes. On the other hand, leniency could cost them votes in the fearful southern states where Adams and Pinckney suddenly looked like the forces of stability.

Some slaves saw the ironies of the situation. Most of those arrested, including Prosser, simply remained silent, knowing that nothing they said would save them. One, however, calmly told the judges:

> I have nothing more to offer than what General Washington would have had to offer, had he been taken by the British officers and put to trial by them. I have ventured my life in endeavouring to obtain the liberty of my countrymen, and am a willing sacrifice to their cause; and I beg, as a favour, that I may be immediately led to execution. I know that you have predetermined to shed my blood, why then all this mockery of a trial?

The tension between American freedom and American slavery, which was at the heart of the republic, surfaced in the 1800 contest.

Jefferson's religious beliefs also became a major election topic. Yale's president, Timothy Dwight, gave a speech asking whether the country was going to elect "men who set truth at nought … who doubt the being and providence of God." Everyone knew who Dwight was talking about, given Jefferson's liberal religious views. Many clergy and laypeople claimed that Jefferson had renounced the basic beliefs of Christianity. In fact, Jefferson was a deist who believed that God tended to leave the universe on its own. Adams himself, who tended to agree with Jefferson in religious matters, though he was more discreet and more often seen in established churches, privately expressed "indignation at the charge of irreligion," but did not say anything publically during the heat of the campaign.

The Hamilton-Adams feud could not be kept so quiet. In the summer of 1800, Hamilton wrote "A Letter from Alexander Hamilton, Concerning the Public Conduct and Character of John Adams, Esq., President of the United States." Hamilton seems to have meant the fifty-four-page document for the private use of a few electors, whom he was attempting to switch from Adams to Pinckney, but the Democratic-Republican press found the document, and it became public. In words that could, ironically, have been prosecuted under the Sedition Act, Hamilton attacked Adams for his "great intrinsic defects of character," including "his disgusting egotism," "eccentric tendencies," "bitter animosity," and "ungovernable temper." The split among the Federalists was complete. Noah Webster, a tough Federalist from Connecticut and author of the first American dictionary, wrote to Hamilton that, if Jefferson was elected as a result of this Federalist split, "the fault will lie at your door and … your conduct on this occasion will be discerned little short of insanity."

In 1800, the candidates campaigned openly, unlike 1796. The ever-diffident Adams, surprisingly, seemed to enjoy campaigning, giving speeches in key states. Jefferson considered similar campaign stops but was dissuaded by Virginia's Governor Monroe. Instead, he engaged in a nonstop correspondence with supporters and in less public forms of campaigning, offering financial and editorial advice to friendly newspaper editors.

Given the advantages that the Democratic-Republicans held, ranging from the unpopularity of the Alien and Sedition Acts to the split among the Federalists, the election

Map 7-2 The 1800 Presidential Election.

The 1800 electoral contest between incumbent John Adams and Thomas Jefferson reflected regional differences: Adams carried all of New England and Jefferson most of the South, but middle states, especially New York, decided the outcome.

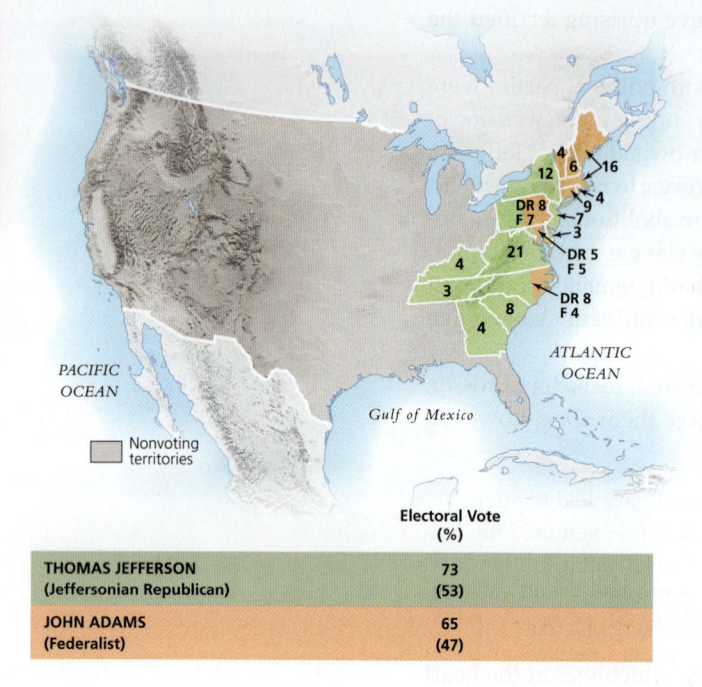

PACIFIC OCEAN

ATLANTIC OCEAN

Gulf of Mexico

Nonvoting territories

	Electoral Vote (%)
THOMAS JEFFERSON (Jeffersonian Republican)	73 (53)
JOHN ADAMS (Federalist)	65 (47)

was surprisingly close. Adams swept New England and most of the northern states while Jefferson held strong in New York and Pennsylvania and most of the southern states. The three-fifths clause, which counted slaves in the population though they were not allowed to vote, gave the southern states an advantage in the Electoral College that ultimately tipped the election for Jefferson. The last state to vote was South Carolina, and when the Jefferson–Burr ticket carried every electoral vote in that state, the new Washington, D.C., Democratic-Republican paper *The National Intelligencer* ran a headline on December 12, "Splendid Intelligence … Mr. Jefferson may … be considered as our future President." But it was not to be so simple (see Map 7-2).

Because the Democratic-Republicans had been so well organized, Jefferson and Burr each received seventy-three electoral votes, putting them well ahead of Adams and Pinckney. But because Jefferson and Burr had *each* received seventy-three votes, the two candidates had officially tied for election and the House of Representatives would now have to decide between them. Although the Democratic-Republicans had also won a majority in the new Congress, the old Congress, with a Federalist majority, would decide the election. Many Democratic-Republicans, including Jefferson, thought that Burr had engineered this outcome to make himself president. Many Federalists suddenly gave Burr a second look. As far as anyone knows, Burr did not negotiate with the Federalists. But he also did not give way to Jefferson. The country was stuck.

When Congress heard the tally of electoral votes, the outcome was seventy-three for Jefferson, seventy-three for Burr, sixty-five for Adams, sixty-four for Pinckney, and one for John Jay. The House then began to vote between the top two. But it remained deadlocked. Finally, Hamilton, who had fought for so long with Thomas Jefferson on almost every major government policy, convinced his fellow Federalists that Burr, whom he knew all too well from New York politics, was a dangerous man of too much ambition and too little morality. On February 17, Thomas Jefferson was elected president by a vote of ten state delegations to four, with two not voting. Burr became vice president. It had been a long year and a long election cycle, and it would never be repeated in quite the same form.

7.4 Quick Review

Why did factions and political parties arise in the 1790s?

Conclusion

George Washington was elected unanimously as the first president of the United States in 1789. Washington had led the army through the Revolution and presided over the convention that wrote the Constitution. His election was a forgone conclusion. However, this unity did not last.

Alexander Hamilton, Washington's secretary of the treasury, was an especially forceful advocate of a strong and activist central government. Those who agreed with this position came to be known as the Federalists. Hamilton had been charged with making the government financially solvent. He quickly convinced Congress to pass import taxes to pay off the Revolutionary War debts, to build up the national government, and especially to fund the U.S. Army. In addition, Hamilton persuaded Congress to launch the Bank of the United

States. He believed that making possible financial credit for both government and business would ensure the strength of the new republic. In time, the Federalists also became opponents of the French Revolution.

In opposition to Hamilton, Thomas Jefferson, Washington's first secretary of state, envisioned an idealized agrarian republic with a weak central government. He and the Democratic-Republicans who organized around him believed that the strongest powers should remain with the states and in the hands of the people. Jefferson distrusted banks, a standing army, and centralized authority. Led by Jefferson, the Democratic-Republicans also supported the French Revolution.

To fulfill a promise to many who ratified the Constitution, James Madison authored amendments to the Constitution that became the Bill of Rights. These amendments spelled out limits on the federal government. They guaranteed that the federal government could not establish a state religion; neither could it limit free speech or a free press. The amendments also protected the right to firearms and the right to protection from illegal search and seizure. Perhaps most important to those who initially opposed the Constitution, the Bill of Rights limited the power of the federal government to only those things that were specifically mentioned in the Constitution.

Washington's tenure as president during two terms in office was filled with conflict. He took the role of mediator and negotiator as often as possible, including efforts to balance Hamilton and Jefferson. In the Northwest Territory, he tried to control disorderly settlers whose support he also needed. At the same time, he sought a more powerful army to defeat the Native American tribes that actually controlled the territory; by the end of his first term, the tribes had been defeated and millions of acres opened for white settlements. In response to a new federal tax on whiskey, a rebellion—the Whiskey Rebellion—broke out among settlers in western Pennsylvania who had no intention of paying the tax. With a massive show of force, the Washington administration brought the rebellion to an end. The French Revolution began just as Washington was taking office, but it was during his second term (1793–1797) that it dominated the administration's interest. Washington was determined to maintain neutrality as revolutionary France went to war with Great Britain and as large numbers of Americans came to support each side in the war.

After serving as president for two terms, Washington retired. In a close race, his vice president, John Adams, defeated former secretary of state Thomas Jefferson, and under the rules then in force, Adams became president and Jefferson vice president. Four years later, the two again ran against each other, but this time, after a hard fought and exceedingly complicated election process, Thomas Jefferson became the third president of the United States.

By the time Jefferson was inaugurated, the factions that Washington abhorred had begun to harden into two political parties. The Federalists who supported a strong central government, a national bank, and the development of commercial enterprise were represented in the presidential contests by John Adams, but Alexander Hamilton, who privately feuded constantly with Adams, drove the party's ideas. On the other side, the Antifederalists, or Democratic-Republicans, led by Jefferson, were the party of those supporting states' rights, a weak federal government, and agrarian—often slaveholding—interests. Once Jefferson defeated Adams, the Federalists would never elect another president, but the philosophical divide between the two parties would dominate American politics for decades.

Chapter Review

How well did the early American government under the Constitution uphold its spirit and ideals? How did issues not addressed or not clear within the document lead to controversy later on?

Chapter 7 Summary and Review

Convening a Congress, Inaugurating a President, Adopting a Bill of Rights

7.1 **Analyze the first federal elections and the adoption of the Bill of Rights.**

Summary

When Virginia and New Hampshire voted to ratify the Constitution in June 1788, it became the law of the land. By the spring of 1789, the members of the new Congress had been elected and George Washington had been unanimously elected president by the sixty-nine presidential electors. As the first president, Washington was well aware that every choice he made would set a precedent for future presidents. In the summer of 1789, the House of Representatives went to work on the Bill of Rights, sending twelve amendments to the states on September 25. Ten of these amendments were ratified and became the Bill of Rights. Collectively, these amendments placed clear limits on the power of the new federal government.

Review Question

1. Argument Development
   What concerns raised by the Antifederalists during the debate over ratification were addressed by the first ten amendments to the Constitution?

Creating an Economy: Alexander Hamilton and the U.S. Economic System

7.2 **Analyze the enduring argument begun by Hamilton's economic vision for the United States and the alternative vision of Jefferson and Madison.**

Summary

While the new republic faced a range of challenges when Washington took office, the most significant of them were economic. Under the Articles of Confederation, the federal government was unable to collect taxes, which meant that federal debts were not being paid and that the financial status of the United States was in question. Washington appointed Alexander Hamilton as his secretary of the treasury, placing him in charge of solving the financial crisis. In his report to Congress on the public credit of the United States, Hamilton argued that the federal government should assume all revolutionary debt and agree to pay all government promissory notes in full. Hamilton's plans faced significant opposition and were passed only after a deal in which the capital would be moved

to a site on the Potomac River. From this first debate, political factions emerged that would later solidify into parties and an age of bitter partisanship. When Hamilton introduced his second report to Congress for the approval of a Bank of the United States, it too was met with considerable opposition. Hamilton's last major report to Congress was his *Report on Manufactures*. In contrast to Jefferson's vision of an agrarian republic, Hamilton imagined a diverse economy, with the federal government playing an important role in the stimulation of manufacturing growth.

Review Questions

2. Contextualization
   Why was the resolution of the federal government's fiscal problems so critical to the success of the new nation?

3. Argument Development
   What larger political and regional divisions were reflected in the debates over debt assumption and the First Bank of the United States?

Setting the Pace: The Washington Administration

7.3 **Explain the precedents set by George Washington's presidential administration.**

Summary

Although economic issues were the top priority, Washington also faced many other challenges during his terms in office. Washington was deeply concerned about how to handle the frontier Indian tribes. Between 1790 and 1793, Washington mixed approaches, using military invasions and diplomacy. The American victory at the Battle of Fallen Timbers led to the signing of the Treaty of Greenville the following year. The treaty was significant, paving the way for white settlement of the Northwest Territory. Hamilton's tax on whiskey sparked an uprising in Kentucky and western Pennsylvania in 1793. In 1784, Washington led a federal army into the region to quash the rebellion. Washington's second term was dominated by the French Revolution. The revolution complicated U.S. relations with France and Britain. Domestic politics were also shaped by the revolution, with political factions developing around support for either France or Britain.

Review Questions

4. Argument Development
   Why did events in the western territory occupy so much of Washington's time and attention?

5. Contextualization

Why did so many Americans identify with the revolutionary cause in France? How did public reaction to the French Revolution contribute to the increasingly partisan nature of American politics in the 1790s?

The Birth of Political Parties: Adams and Jefferson

7.4 **Explain the growing split between the Federalist and Democratic-Republican factions, including how the French Revolution and the personal differences between Hamilton, Adams, and Jefferson affected American politics.**

Summary

In 1796, Federalist John Adams was elected president and Democratic-Republican Thomas Jefferson was elected vice president. Partisan division, particularly over U.S. relations with France, shaped the Adams presidency. In 1798 and 1799, following the XYZ Affair, France and the United States fought what became known as the Quasi-War. War hysteria led Congress to pass the Alien and Sedition Acts, the true design of which was to target the Federalists' political opponents. In response, Jefferson and Madison produced the Kentucky and Virginia Resolutions, respectively, which declared that states had the right to nullify federal laws, although their resolutions did not pass in the Congress. In 1799, Adams began negotiations that led to peace with France in 1800. The unpopularity of the Alien and Sedition Acts, as well as a split among the Federalists, contributed to Jefferson's victory over Adams in the presidential election of 1800.

Review Question

6. Contextualization

How are the Alien and Sedition Acts representative of American politics at the end of the 1700s? How might a supporter of the acts have defended them?

1. Preparing to Write: Plan Your Argument

Long Essay Question—Evaluate the extent to which there are differences between Hamilton's and Jefferson's respective visions for the government's role in the economy.

Hamilton's three economic reports might be a good place to start here. You can really just focus on the differences here because there are not many significant similarities between the two. Think of a thesis as a product of your inquiry. After studying this topic, is there an interesting angle you can take to make sense of it? From there you can write a clear, thoughtful thesis.

2. Preparing to Write: Plan Your Argument

Long Essay Question—Evaluate the extent to which there are differences between the federal response to internal unrest in the 1780s under the Articles of Confederation and in the 1790s under the Constitution.

You have the opportunity to discuss two significant events from these respective decades: Shays's Rebellion and the Whiskey Rebellion. There are other potentially fruitful topics, too, including the Alien and Sedition Acts. Once you decide on your events, use a simple Venn diagram to generate some thoughts on similarities and differences. Then you can outline your argument and write topic sentences. From there you can finish by writing your thesis statement.

Section I: Multiple-Choice Questions

Questions 3.1–3.2 refer to the excerpt below.

"The Disturbances in America give great trouble to all our Nations, as many strange stories have been told to us by the people of that country. The Six Nations who always loved the king, sent a number of their Chiefs and Warriors with their Superintendent to Canada last summer, where they engaged their allies to joyn with them in the defense of that country, and when it was invaded by the New England people they alone defeated them. ... We now Brother hope to see these bad children chastised, and that we may be enabled to tell the Indians who have always been faithfull and ready to assist the King, what his Majesty intends. ... We have only therefore to request that his Majesty will attend to this matter: it troubles our Nation & they can not sleep easie in their beds. Indeed it is very hard when we have let the Kings subjects have so much land for so little value, they should want to cheat us in this manner of the small spots we have left for our women and children to live on. We are tired out in making complaints & getting no redress."

—Mohawk Joseph Brant, "The Disturbances in America," 1776

3.1 Which of the following issues of the period was Brant concerned with in the excerpt?

  a. An expanding British colonial population
  b. Maintaining trade with France
  c. French defeat in the Seven Years' War
  d. British victory in the American Revolution

3.2 Brant's letter most directly reflected which of the following developments regarding American Indians during the eighteenth century?

  a. The use of war to maintain their autonomy
  b. A desire to integrate into British colonial society
  c. A need to develop warm relations with the American colonists
  d. The goal of maintaining a close alliance with the English

Questions 3.3–3.4 refer to the chart below.

Composition of State Assemblies in the 1780s					
State	**Farmers**	**Large Landowners**	**Artisan**	**Professional**	**Merchant**
Massachusetts	47	1	12	13	20
New York	37	8	10	18	19
Pennsylvania	37	2	22	15	20
South Carolina	14	32	3	15	13
Virginia	20	36	3	21	10

3.3 The chart most strongly supports which of the following arguments?

  a. Occupations in the North were becoming increasingly tied to manufacturing.
  b. State governments in the South were more democratic than those in the North.
  c. The spirit of the American Revolution meant that more women would be included in the political process.
  d. Plantation owners held a great deal of political power, which in part led to sectional division.

3.4 Which of the following depicts the most common development among state governments after the American Revolution?

  a. Their constitutions placed most of the power in the hands of the executive.
  b. Women had the right to vote in state elections.
  c. Residents had to own property to hold citizenship and vote.
  d. They outlawed slavery or at least put it on a road to extinction.

Questions 3.5–3.6 refer to the excerpt below.

"That there are important defects in the system of the Foederal [sic] Government is acknowledged by the Acts of all those States, which have concurred in the present Meeting; That the defects, upon a closer examination, may be found greater and more numerous, than even these acts imply, is at least so far probable, from the embarrassments which characterise [sic] the present State of our national affairs, foreign and domestic, as may reasonably be supposed to merit a deliberate and candid discussion, in some mode, which will unite the Sentiments and Councils of all the States. In the choice of the mode, your Commissioners are of opinion, that a Convention of Deputies from the different States, for the special and sole purpose of entering into this investigation, and digesting a plan for supplying such defects as may be discovered to exist, will be entitled to a preference from considerations, which will occur, without being particularized [sic]."

—"Proceedings of Commissioners to Remedy Defects of the Federal Government," 1786

3.5 In the document, "important defects in the system of the Foederal Government," refers most directly to

  a. threat of foreign invasion
  b. warfare with hostile Native American nations.
  c. internal unrest
  d. disputes between the states over the settlement of western lands

3.6 Which of the following is considered a major accomplishment by this federal government under the Articles of Confederation?

    a. An effective interstate system of interstate commerce

    b. A process for admitting new states

    c. The formation of a formidable standing army

    d. The establishment of a federal court system

Questions 3.7–3.9 refer to the excerpt below.

"That the General Assembly doth particularly protest against the palpable and alarming infractions of the Constitution, in the two late cases of the 'Alien and Sedition Acts' passed at the last session of Congress; the first of which exercises a power no where delegated to the federal government … and the other of which [is] … expressly and positively forbidden by one of the amendments thererto; a power, which more than any other, ought to produce universal alarm, because it is levelled against that right of freely examining public characters and measures, and of free communication among the people. …

That the good people of this commonwealth … solemnly appeal to the like dispositions of the other states, in confidence that they will concur with this commonwealth in declaring, as it does hereby declare, that the acts aforesaid, are unconstitutional."

                                        —Virginia Resolution, 1798

3.7 In signing the Alien and Sedition Acts and asserting executive power, President John Adams believed he was

    a. attempting to end the British impressment of sailors

    b. spurring debate about the need for a Bill of Rights

    c. putting the principles of the Constitution into practice

    d. quelling the forces that made up the Whiskey Rebellion

3.8 The Virginia Resolution most likely reflected which of the following debates in the 1790s?

    a. Economic policy

    b. The balance between liberty and order

    c. The role of Congress in foreign policy

    d. Internal improvements

3.9 Which of the following is an effect of the debates like the one represented in the excerpt?

    a. The formation of a political party system

    b. The Quasi-War with France

    c. A closer relationship with Britain

    d. A dominance of states over the federal government

Section II: Short-Answer Questions

Question 3.10 is based on the following two excerpts.

"The American revolutionary leaders do not fit our conventional image of revolutionaries—angry, passionate, reckless, maybe even bloodthirsty for the sake of a cause. … But if we measure the radicalism by the amount of social change that actually took place—by transformations in the relationships that bound people to each other—then the American Revolution was not conservative at all; on the contrary: it was as radical and as revolutionary as any in history. …

By the time the Revolution had run its course in the early nineteenth century, American society had been radically and thoroughly transformed. One class did not overthrow another; the poor did not supplant the rich. But social relationships—the way people were connected one to another—were changed, and decisively so. By the early years of the nineteenth century the Revolution had created a society fundamentally different from the colonial society of the eighteenth century. It was in fact a new society unlike any that had ever existed anywhere in the world. …

To focus, as we are today apt to do, on what the Revolution did not accomplish—highlighting and lamenting its failure to abolish slavery and change fundamentally the lot of women—is to miss the great significance of what it did accomplish; indeed the Revolution made possible the anti-slavery and women's rights movements of the nineteenth century and in fact all our current egalitarian thinking. The Revolution not only radically changed the personal and social relationships of people, including the position of women, but also destroyed aristocracy as it had been understood in the Western world for at least two millennia."

                       —Gordon S. Wood, *The Radicalism of the American Revolution*, 1991

"For more than two centuries historians have written about the American Revolution striving to capture the 'life and soul' of which Jefferson spoke. …

[W]e have not appreciated the lives and labors, the sacrifices and struggles, the glorious messiness, the hopes and fears of diverse groups that fought in the longest and most disruptive war in our history with visions of launching a new age filling their heads. Little is known, for example of Thomas Peters, an African-born slave who made his personal declaration of independence in early 1776, fought for the freedom of African Americans, led former slaves to Nova Scotia after the war, and completed a pilgrimage for unalienable rights by shepherding them back to Africa to participate in the founding of Sierra Leone. Why are the history books virtually silent on Dragging Canoe, the Cherokee warrior who made the American Revolution into a two-decade life-sapping fight for his people's life, liberty, and pursuit of happiness? We cannot capture the 'life and soul' of the Revolution without paying close attention to the wartime experiences and agendas for change that engrossed backcountry farmers, urban craftsmen, deep-blue mariners, female camp followers and food rioters—those ordinary people who did most of the protesting, most of the fighting, most of the dying, and most of the dreaming about how a victorious America might satisfy the yearnings of all its peoples."

                       —Gary B. Nash, *The Unknown American Revolution*, 2005

3.10 Using the excerpts above, answer (a), (b), and (c).

    a. Briefly explain ONE major difference between Wood's and Nash's historical interpretations of the American Revolution.

    b. Briefly explain how ONE specific historical event or development during the revolutionary period that is not mentioned directly in the excerpts could be used to support Wood's interpretation.

    c. Briefly explain how ONE specific historical event or development during the revolutionary period that is not mentioned directly in the excerpts could be used to support Nash's interpretation.

Section III: Long Essay Questions

Directions: Answer Question 3.11 **or** 3.12. (Suggested writing time: 40 minutes) In your response you should do the following.

- Respond to the prompt with a historically defensible thesis or claim that establishes a line of reasoning.

- Describe a broader historical context relevant to the prompt.

- Support an argument in response to the prompt using specific and relevant examples of evidence.

- Use historical reasoning (e.g., comparison, causation, continuity or change over time) to frame or structure an argument that addresses the prompt.

- Use evidence to corroborate, qualify, or modify an argument that addresses the prompt.

3.11 Evaluate the primary factors that led to Britain's economic and political parties in the American colonies following the Seven Years' War.

3.12 Evaluate the primary factors that led to George Washington's cautionary message about political parties and foreign alliances in his Farewell Address.

Section IV: Read on MyHistoryLab

Document-Based Question: Enlightenment Beliefs about the Role of Government

Part 4

Crafting a Nation, People, Land, and a National Identity 1800–1848

AP® KEY CONCEPTS

Key Concept 4.1

The United States began to develop a modern democracy and celebrated a new national culture, while Americans sought to define the nation's democratic ideals and change their society and institutions to match them.

Key Concept 4.2

Innovations in technology, agriculture, and commerce powerfully accelerated the American economy, precipitating profound changes to U.S. society and to national and religious identities.

Key Concept 4.3

The U.S. interest in increasing foreign trade and expanding its national borders shaped the nation's foreign policy and spurred government and private initiatives.

PART OUTLINE

Chapter 8

Creating a New People, Expanding the Country 1801–1823

The Conestoga wagon, pulled by a team of horses or oxen (as shown here), to transport white settlers west became a symbol of the changing United States after 1800 as explorers and then settlers moved ever farther toward the West, displacing the original inhabitants and building new communities.

Chapter Objective

Demonstrate an understanding of how the post-revolutionary generation created a new culture for the country while also expanding the land area of the United States.

 ## Learning Objectives

Jefferson and the Republican Ideal

8.1 Explain how Jefferson's republicanism shaped and reflected the nation's democratic culture.

The Ideal of Religious Freedom

8.2 Explain how Americans applied new individualist ideals in their religion and how the expansion of faith-based organizations mirrored, yet also challenged, Jeffersonian republicanism.

Beyond the Mississippi: The Louisiana Purchase and the Expedition of Lewis and Clark

8.3 Explain what effects the Louisiana Purchase and the westward expansion had on how various Americans saw themselves.

The War of 1812

8.4 Analyze the causes and impact of the War of 1812.

Expanding American Territory and Influence

8.5 Analyze how the United States acquired new territory and increased influence abroad.

On Inauguration Day, March 4, 1801, Thomas Jefferson had breakfast at his boardinghouse in Washington, D.C., and then walked up New Jersey Avenue to the unfinished Capitol building to take the oath of office as the nation's third president. He was sworn in by one of his political archenemies, the Federalist Chief Justice John Marshall. In his inaugural address, Jefferson acknowledged the bitterness of the 1800 presidential campaign but continued:

> But every difference of opinion is not a difference of principle. We have called by different names brethren of the same principle. We are all Republicans, we are all Federalists. If there be any among us who would wish to dissolve this Union or to change its republican form, let them stand undisturbed as monuments of the safety with which error of opinion may be tolerated where reason is left free to combat it.

Federalist ideas, which were at the core of the Constitution and the first two presidential administrations, were increasingly out of touch with the democratic tone of the new century. As the new president made clear, more trust and less fear as well as dynamic exchanges and significant freedom were to characterize Jeffersonian democracy and his emerging Democratic-Republican Party.

Republican ideals defined the politics and culture of Jeffersonian America. This chapter will examine these developments and their impact on the new United States. The same era that began with Jefferson's inauguration saw a rapid expansion and consolidation of American territory and power through the Louisiana Purchase, the War of 1812, and policies such as the Monroe Doctrine, but also new tensions over race and gender. Republican ideas also shaped a new American culture reflecting religious energy and diversity, new forms of literature and architecture, and new interactions at a local level throughout the United States.

Jefferson and the Republican Ideal

8.1 **Explain how Jefferson's republicanism shaped and reflected the nation's democratic culture.**

From the moment he took office, Jefferson set a new tone for the federal government. His inaugural address emphasized conciliation and national unity while his actions involved dramatic changes. Jefferson wanted to preside over a country in which social equality (among white male citizens) and individual freedom were the order of the day. The social hierarchies that had characterized the colonial era and the first years of the republic were, he thought, long out of date. He wanted a limited government that fostered the kind of freedom that was his ideal. Most of his countrymen, it seems, agreed.

Jefferson quickly sold the horses and coaches that John Adams had used. In place of formal state dinners, he held smaller dinner parties. What some called a "pell-mell" seating arrangement marked these gatherings at the White House. There was no assigned seating and no respect for the rank of the dignitaries who attended. The president simply sat down with whomever he found interesting and expected the other guests to do the same. A British diplomat described the new president as a host "with a most perfect disregard to ceremony both in his dress and manner" and vowed never to attend another White House dinner.

These changes in tone were not trivial. They represented what was quickly becoming the dominant ideology of the United States: a commitment to a Democratic-Republican government and also **republicanism** in personal styles and political beliefs (see Table 8-1). Americans valued equality not only in terms of representation in government but also in terms of how Americans treated others—at state dinners in the White House, at town meetings, and in taverns and family homes. They also valued a notion of freedom in which a nation of farmers could make their own decisions, independent of one another. American republicanism was a new way for citizens to relate to one another, emphasizing equality and independence far more than the class separation, deference, and dependence that had marked Great Britain, British North America, and the new United States.

Significant Dates

8.1

1800	Thomas Jefferson is elected president
1803	Louisiana Purchase
	U.S. Supreme Court's *Marbury v. Madison* decision
	Ohio is admitted to the Union
1804–1806	Lewis and Clark expedition
1807	*Chesapeake-Leopard* affair
	Congress passes Embargo Act
1808	James Madison is elected president
1812–1815	War of 1812
1812	American defeat at Detroit
1813	American victories on Great Lakes and Battle of the Thames
	Death of Tecumseh
1814	Jackson victory over Creeks at Battle of Horseshoe Bend
	The British burn Washington, D.C.
	Treaty of Ghent is signed (ratified 1815)
1815	U.S. victory at Battle of New Orleans
1816	James Monroe is elected president
1817	Rush-Bagot Treaty demilitarizes the Great Lakes between the United States and Canada
1818	Anglo-American Convention sets the border between the United States and Canada and includes an agreement for temporary joint ownership of the Oregon Territory
1819	Adams-Onís Treaty—Spain cedes Florida to the United States
1822	Plans for slave revolt in Charleston are led by Denmark Vesey
1823	Monroe Doctrine

8.2

8.3

8.4

8.5

republicanism

A complex, changing body of ideas, values, and assumptions that developed in the United States in the late 1790s and early 1800s around Thomas Jefferson's and James Madison's political organizing and their campaigns for the presidency.

Table 8-1 Comparison of the First Political Parties: Federalists and Democratic-Republicans

Federalists	Democratic-Republicans
Originally organized by supporters of the Constitution	Began as an informal protest movement led by Jefferson and Madison in response to Hamilton's economic plans
Although George Washington insisted he stood above party, he was usually considered to be a Federalist. The Federalists supported John Adams for president in the elections of 1796 and 1800	By the 1796 and 1800 elections, Democratic-Republicans formed a well-defined caucus within the Congress, though hardly a modern political party. Between 1800 and 1820s, it was the nation's majority party—the Democratic-Republican Party—sometimes called the Jeffersonian Republican or the Republican Party
The party wanted a strong national government, favored Hamilton's economic reforms, and generally supported stronger U.S. ties with Great Britain	The party sought a smaller federal government, wanted less federal involvement in economic matters, and generally favored France over Great Britain
After the 1800 election, the Federalists never again dominated the national government but remained strong in New England for another twenty years. They nominated their last presidential candidate in 1816	By the 1820s, it was the only remaining political party before splitting into the Democrats and the Whigs in 1828

There are many ironies in Jefferson's success. Jefferson, whose lack of religious orthodoxy was an issue in his campaigns, led the country during one of the great revivals of religion. Jefferson, the sophisticated aristocrat in his personal life, presided over White House events with a sense of informality that many officials found insulting. Jefferson, a slaveholder who had great misgivings about slavery, led the country during the time when slavery became stronger and more entrenched than ever as well as a source of bitter divisiveness between regions and groups of people. And Jefferson, the believer in an agrarian vision of the United States, presided over a growing commercial economy that saw an expansion of U.S. territory as well as the rise of cities, banks, and corporations, which would have pleased his old rival Alexander Hamilton. The apparent disconnect between Jefferson the political leader and Jefferson the person generated much criticism, but those ironies also reflected the dramatic changes afloat in the nation that no one leader could control.

Jefferson the Political Leader

Jefferson's changes in the government went far beyond symbolism. He shrank the federal bureaucracy while doubling the landmass of the United States. Jefferson thought the bureaucracy he had inherited from John Adams was "too complicated, too expensive" and vowed to cut it, though that government was hardly a large one. The largest federal office, the War Department, included the secretary of war, one accountant, fourteen clerks, and two messengers. The secretary of state had one chief clerk, six other clerks, and a messenger. The attorney general simply gave legal advice to the president and did not even have a clerk. Still, Jefferson thought this government was too big and cut it. In addition, having always feared the impact of a standing army, he cut the size of the army in the West and the size of the navy that patrolled the Atlantic Ocean. He founded the military academy at West Point only because he wanted to replace Federalist officers with a thoroughly professional (and Republican) officer corps. Jefferson's secretary of the treasury persuaded him to keep Hamilton's Bank of the United States, but Jefferson was never enthusiastic about the bank, and a Republican Congress refused to renew its charter in 1811, after he had left office.

Jefferson's commitment to a small government faced an immediate challenge when he took office. The so-called Barbary States of North Africa—Morocco, Algiers, Tunis, and Tripoli—had a long history of capturing European ships and enslaving their crews unless advance tribute or later bribes were paid. Britain had long paid the tributes, which had protected American ships traveling under a British flag, but with U.S. independence came trouble.

In 1784 and 1785, Morocco and Algiers captured American ships. Crews were enslaved. By the 1790s, the Washington and Adams administrations were paying huge tributes to avoid such trouble: by 1800, the tributes totaled $1.25 million, or 20 percent of the total federal budget. Although Jefferson had condemned what he claimed was Federalist interest in war making, he was also critical of the Adams administration for their payments to the North Africans.

In 1803, Jefferson ordered "the smallest force competent" to Tripoli. The USS *Philadelphia* ran aground in Tripoli's harbor and Tripoli's Pasha Yusuf Karamanli set ransom at $1.69 million. In February 1804, a second U.S. Navy squadron under a young Lieutenant Stephen Decatur successfully attacked Tripoli, making Decatur a national hero. A year later, a larger squadron shelled Tripoli, while a land force marched five hundred miles over desert from Egypt and took the strategic fort at Derne. The ensuing peace treaty did not satisfy everyone and did not resolve all of the issues, but all U.S. prisoners were freed, the United States no longer paid tributes, shipping continued safely, and the country celebrated an early victory.

While he kept the **tariff**—the tax on imported goods—Jefferson abolished all internal taxes. Beyond paying the added cost of the tariff on imported goods, if they used any, most Americans dealt with the federal government only through the post office during the Jefferson, Madison, and Monroe administrations. Washington, D.C., had fewer than ten thousand residents, most of whom lived in boardinghouses. A British diplomat described it as a capital city "like no other in the world" where one could get stuck in the mud on Pennsylvania Avenue, and "a carriage had to avoid tree stumps and grazing cows." To Jefferson, the capital city symbolized the way he thought the country should be managed, with states, not the federal government, having "principal care of our persons, our property, and our reputation."

One of Jefferson's early efforts to shrink the federal government sparked one of the most significant Supreme Court decisions in U.S. history. The new Jeffersonian majority in Congress repealed the Judiciary Act of 1801, which had expanded the number of federal judges and which John Adams had signed just before leaving office. Following Jefferson's views, Congress wanted fewer federal judges; it especially disliked the Federalist "**midnight judges**" that Adams had appointed in his last days in office, so named because of the hour at which the outgoing president appointed them. Congressional leaders and President Jefferson virtually dared the Supreme Court, particularly Chief Justice Marshall, a Federalist whom Adams had appointed, to declare Congress's actions unconstitutional. They promised that if the Court did so, Congress would reduce the Court's authority. But Marshall was a wily judge. He waited for the right case to make his decision. One of the many last-minute court appointments that Adams had made was to name William Marbury a justice of the peace for the District of Columbia. But Adams left office before Marbury's commission was delivered, and President Jefferson and his secretary of state, James Madison, refused to deliver it. Marbury sued, and in 1803, the Supreme Court, led by John Marshall, issued its decision in the case of *Marbury* v. *Madison*.

Marbury v. Madison was a complex decision with far-reaching consequences. Marshall began by saying that Jefferson had, indeed, been irresponsible in failing to deliver the commission, for even a president "cannot at his discretion sport away the vested rights of others." However, Marshall also said, the Court could do nothing because the clause in the Judiciary Act of 1789 giving the federal courts the right to issue writs requiring governmental action was unconstitutional because the Constitution did not give the judiciary such authority. The result of the ruling was threefold. First, Marbury did not get his job. Second, while the Court slapped Jefferson's wrist, it also gave him the legal victory in the case because he was not forced to appoint Marbury, and his party's overturning of the Judiciary Act of 1801 stood. Since Jefferson had won, there was nothing in the Court decision for him

tariff

A tax on imports into any nation.

Library of Congress Prints and Photographs Division [LC-DIG-ppmsca-15714]

During Jefferson's time in office, the nation's capital in Washington, D.C., was little more than a sleepy village along the shores of the Potomac River. Jefferson liked it that way, as a symbol of a weak federal government.

midnight judges

The name the Jeffersonian Democratic-Republicans gave to those judges appointed by the outgoing Federalist president John Adams at the end of his term.

Marbury v. Madison

Supreme Court decision of 1803 that created the precedent of judicial review by ruling part of the Judiciary Act of 1789 as unconstitutional.

8.1

8.2

8.3

8.4

8.5

judicial review

A power implied in the Constitution that gives federal courts the right to review and determine the constitutionality of acts passed by Congress and state legislatures.

to challenge. But third, Marshall also made a point of saying that the Court had the authority to declare an act of Congress unconstitutional. It was the first time the Court asserted this power of **judicial review**. The Court would not use this power to determine the constitutionality of an act of Congress again until 1857, long after Marshall was gone, but Marshall had dramatically expanded the authority of the federal courts while also ensuring that they would not be challenged by Jefferson or the Republican Congress.

Jefferson's Agrarian Ideal

In 1801, the occupations, opinions, and manners of most American voters were compatible with Jefferson's agrarian ideal of a nation of independent farmers, and they provided a solid foundation on which to build political consensus. The population of the United States when Jefferson took office was just over 5.3 million, almost 900,000 of whom were African slaves. Ninety percent of whites lived on farms.

However, far from being permanently attached to their isolated rural communities, many farmers moved often, seeking more and better land in Ohio, Kentucky, and Tennessee. Older farms were sold and resold regularly. A French observer, the Duc de La Rochefoucauld-Liancourt, visited the United States just before Jefferson's inauguration. He wondered whether American farmers had any of the French peasant's attachment to a particular piece of land, but when he asked the Americans, they said that such attachments represented a lack of pluck. So he wrote, "It is a country in flux ... that which is true today as regards its population, its establishments, its prices, its commerce will not be true six months from now."

For many in the Republic, all forms of authority were suspect. Republican virtue was to be found in equality, at least among white men. While voting restrictions related to race and gender continued, and even grew in the early 1800s, virtually all property qualifications for voting disappeared, and many people now wanted to vote. As a result, the number of voters, which had previously included about 20 percent of the white male population, expanded in most states to 70 and 80 percent. Compared with any earlier era, the white male electorate was large. It was also opinionated and individualistic.

Manners and Morals

European visitors were fascinated and appalled by the manners and morals of Americans. An Englishman, Charles William Janson, who lived in the United States from 1793 to 1806, called Americans "the only remaining republicans in the civilized world," but he also found them "in every respect uncongenial to English habits, and to the tone of an Englishman's constitution." Everyone in the United States, Janson said, from the poorest and least educated to the most elite, "consider themselves on an equal footing with the best educated people in the country."

The United States of the early 1800s was a violent place. Political arguments were often settled with fists. Urban riots were not unusual when crowds poured out of a tavern, theater, or factory. Fighting was as common in rural communities. Daniel Drake, who grew up in Kentucky and became one of the leading citizens of Cincinnati, described his childhood home in the early 1800s as a place where men fought with "no holds barred" using hands, feet, and teeth and "scratching, pulling hair, choking, gouging out each other's eyes, and biting off each other's noses."

Men of higher social standing often settled minor grudges with a duel. Jefferson's vice president, Aaron Burr, who never forgave his longtime political rival former treasury secretary, Alexander Hamilton, for his role in the final outcome of the 1800 election, later challenged him to a duel in response to further unkind comments that Hamilton made. Hamilton agreed as a point of honor, and Burr killed him in the resulting fight in 1804. Long before he became president in 1829, Andrew Jackson was shot in a duel. He carried that bullet in his chest for the rest of his life; his opponent was killed in the encounter.

One cause of the violence was the high level of alcohol consumption. An observer estimated that some workers were consuming a quart of hard liquor every day. One doctor complained that forty of the one hundred physicians in New York City were drunks. Charles

Janson reported his "horror" at "boys, whose dress indicated wealthy parents, intoxicated, shouting and swearing in the public streets."

The violence was not limited to whites alone. Violence between white Americans and Indians continued long after the Indian Wars in the East had ended. Individual Indians were easy marks for white attack. Similarly, slaves could do little to protect themselves against the violence that was always a part of the slave system. The beating, rape, and killing of slaves was seldom considered a matter of concern for anyone but those on the plantation.

Family life, too, was not exempt from violence. But while violence toward wives and children may have increased, it was also resisted as it had not been earlier. Divorce rates increased as women refused to stay in violent or unhappy marriages or remain legally connected to a man who had left them long before.

Jefferson the Individual

While Americans debated the many meanings of freedom and unfreedom in the democratic experiment of which they were a part, they also debated the personal life of their president and whether he was himself a good example of the ideals he espoused.

While Jefferson insisted on a simplified social scene at the White House, his life at Monticello was anything but simple. At Monticello, he entertained lavishly and served the finest food and wine, while continually expanding the house and the library. Slaves did all of the hard work and took care of the president's every need. The defender of republican equality in social relations lived an aristocratic private life.

The president's private life became national news soon after he took office. On September 1, 1802, the *Richmond Recorder*, edited by James Callendar, a former Jefferson ally-turned-enemy, carried a story that began, "It is well known that the man, whom it delighteth the people to honor, keeps, and for many years has kept, as his concubine, one of his slaves. Her name is SALLY." Thus did rumors of Thomas Jefferson's longtime relationship with his slave Sally Hemings become national news. Not everyone believed the story, and Jefferson remained silent, but his opponents used the story of his life with Sally Hemings and the birth of their children to smear the president. The Federalists made a major issue of the relationship when Jefferson ran for reelection in 1804. He still won easily, but the rumors persisted long after he died and Hemings's children were free. With the advent of DNA testing in the late 1990s, it has been established as highly likely that the children of Sally Hemings,

DeAgostini/SuperStock

Jefferson built a grand home, Monticello, for himself and his family, near Charlottesville, Virginia. Slave laborers expanded the house according to Jefferson's plans and attended to his personal needs.

8.1
8.2
8.3
8.4
8.5

Thinking Historically

Thomas Jefferson and Sally Hemings

As a young man, Jefferson married Martha Wayles Skelton, like himself a wealthy young Virginian. Martha Jefferson died at Monticello in 1782, and Jefferson never remarried. In 1787, a sixteen-year-old slave, Sally Hemings, who was the half-sister of Jefferson's wife, Martha, by her slave-owning father, became a servant in Jefferson's Paris home while he was ambassador to France. When Jefferson returned to the United States in 1789, Hemings could have stayed in France and been free by French law, but she returned with him. While much is not known about their relationship, Jefferson seems to have promised Hemings that he would free the children of their union. Hemings and many of her family lived at Monticello near the older children from Jefferson's marriage. Sally Hemings's last child was born there in 1808, and Hemings stayed at Jefferson's home until he died in 1826, when she went to live with her own free children.

In her book, The Hemingses of Monticello: An American Family (New York: W. W. Norton, 2008), historian Annette Gordon-Reed traces not only the story of Sally Hemings but also the story of the intertwined generations of the Jefferson and Hemings families. The story raises many questions for historians, including questions about the relevance of Jefferson's personal relationship with Sally Hemings in terms of judgments about his political career and as president.

Thinking Critically

1. **Argument Development**
   Was it possible for a slave woman and a powerful older free man who claimed ownership of her to form a truly consensual relationship in the early 1800s? How would you frame an argument either way?

2. **Analyzing Secondary Sources**
   What bearings might Jefferson's relationship with Sally Hemings have on his complex attitudes about the institution of slavery? What does an understanding of the Jefferson-Hemings family tell us about the nature of American slavery and society in the early 1800s?

four of whom survived into adulthood and were set free, were also the children of Thomas Jefferson. Although not without debate, this conclusion is the consensus of most historians who have studied Jefferson's life.

8.1 Quick Review

Jefferson called his election the "Revolution of 1800." Considering the changes in the government during his administration, do you agree with him? Why or why not?

The Ideal of Religious Freedom

8.2 Explain how Americans applied new individualist ideals in their religion and how the expansion of faith-based organizations mirrored, yet also challenged, Jeffersonian republicanism.

On New Year's Day near the end of his first year in the White House, Thomas Jefferson wrote to the members of the Danbury, Connecticut, Baptist Association:

> Believing with you that religion is a matter which lies solely between man and his God, that he owes account to none other for his faith or his worship, that the legislative powers of government reach actions only, and not opinions, I contemplate with sovereign reverence that act of the whole American people which declared that their legislature should "make no law respecting an establishment of religion, or prohibiting the free exercise thereof," thus building a wall of separation between Church and State.

wall of separation between church and state

A phrase coined by Thomas Jefferson to make clear his belief that the First Amendment to the Constitution guaranteed that governments should not interfere with the work of churches, and churches should not interfere with, or expect support from, government.

With the wide distribution of that letter, the "**wall of separation between church and state**" became part of the American lexicon. Some have pointed out that the "wall of separation" is merely a phrase coined by one president and not part of the Constitution or law of the land. They are right. But in 1802, Jefferson was expressing an aspect of the republican ideal. More and more Americans believed that two of the most important arenas of American life—politics and religion—should stay as far away from each other as possible. People who wanted to be treated equally with everyone else, no matter what their wealth or family; who wanted to be free to curse, drink, and fight without the law's intrusion; and who wanted to be left alone on their own farms also wanted to be able to pursue their religious beliefs as they chose.

In 1802, when Jefferson wrote his letter, Connecticut was one of four states that still had an official, state-supported church, a so-called **religious establishment**. Connecticut required all of its citizens, including its Baptists and nonbelievers, to pay taxes to support the state's Congregational churches, as did New Hampshire and Massachusetts. Maryland required support for the Episcopal Church. When it was adopted in 1791, the First Amendment to the U.S. Constitution, indeed all of the Bill of Rights amendments, applied only to the federal government. States could do as they pleased in these matters. Only after the Civil War was the reach of the Bill of Rights broadened to include restrictions on state and local governments. Long before the Revolution, all of the states had stopped requiring church attendance or prosecuting people for heresy, but the clergy in four states were still civil servants supported by the state government, and some other states had voting restrictions based on religious affiliation. Some of the governed, including Connecticut's Baptists and Maryland's Catholics, resented paying a tax that benefited other religious bodies but not their own. So in the 1802 letter, Jefferson was telling these Connecticut Baptists just what they wanted to hear. Not surprisingly, some of the Congregational leaders in Connecticut did not agree, but most of those leaders were Federalists and Jefferson had little interest in courting them.

religious establishment
The name given to a state church or to the creation of an "established church" that might play a role in, and expect support and loyalty from, all citizens.

The Separation of Church and State at the State Level

Jefferson, along with James Madison, had convinced the Virginia legislature to end public financial support for the Episcopal Church in that state in 1786, five years before Madison helped shepherd the First Amendment through Congress. Neither victory had been an easy one.

The fiercest battle over state support for specific churches, however, was fought in Connecticut, long after Jefferson wrote his 1802 letter. Timothy Dwight, who became president of Yale in 1795, was a firm Federalist who hated Jefferson's republicanism and who could not imagine good government or moral citizens without a state church. One of Dwight's students at Yale, Lyman Beecher, organized the Connecticut Society for the Suppression of Vice and the Promotion of Good Morals and published *The Connecticut Evangelical Magazine and Religious Intelligencer* in an effort to maintain the special status of the Congregationalist churches. But Beecher and his allies lost. In 1817, Oliver Wolcott, who opposed a state-supported church in Connecticut, defeated a Federalist for governor, and Connecticut would end its state support for all religious bodies. Beecher was heartbroken. Years later, however, he changed his mind:

> The injury done to the cause of Christ, as we then supposed, was irreparable. For several days I suffered what no tongue can tell for the best thing that ever happened to the State of Connecticut. ... By voluntary efforts, societies, missions, and revivals, they [clergy] exert a deeper influence than ever they could by queues, and shoe-buckles, and cocked hats, and gold-headed canes.

Religion in Connecticut, as Beecher noted, actually survived and flourished without state support, and not long afterward, Massachusetts, the last holdout, followed the same path to separate church and state. Jefferson's ideal ruled the day, with an impact he never could have imagined.

New Religious Expressions

Direct government support for churches disappeared in the early 1800s, but the importance of religion did not. The ideals of individual freedom in all areas of life generated an amazing growth in religious organizations and ideas in the same era.

deist

One who has a religious orientation that rejects divine revelation and holds that the workings of nature alone reveal God's design for the universe.

Second Great Awakening

A series of religious revivals in the first half of the 1800s characterized by great emotionalism in large public meetings.

Church attendance in America dropped during and after the Revolution. Many of the elite, like Jefferson, were **deists** who saw God as, at most, a distant force in human affairs; many working people ignored religious matters altogether. During Jefferson's presidency, however, Americans participated in an outpouring of Protestant evangelical Christianity—the beginning of the **Second Great Awakening**. This religious revival paralleled and, indeed, exceeded the Great Awakening of the 1740s that had transformed American Christianity. Although major developments of the Second Great Awakening occurred largely in the 1820s and 1830s, the movement began in the late 1790s and the early 1800s.

Cane Ridge and the Revivals of the Early 1800s

In 1796, a Presbyterian minister named James McGready moved from the Carolinas to Kentucky. Most of those who had moved across the Appalachian Mountains into Kentucky had left their religion at home. McGready described "Rogue's Harbor" in Logan County, Kentucky, as a place of horse thieves, murderers, robbers, counterfeiters, and runaways. They were the same people whom Daniel Drake had described as fighting with "no holds barred." McGready set out to make them good church going Christians. He was surprisingly successful. In 1799, he and other preachers held a church service at the Gaspar River Meeting House. John McGee, one of the others involved, remembered, "I left the pulpit and went through the audience shouting and exhorting with all possible ecstasy and energy, and the floor was soon covered with the slain." (Revivalist preachers often called those who experienced emotional conversion "the slain" because they were seen as having died to their old, sinful lives.)

The revival of 1799 led to more religious gatherings, and they grew so big that they needed to be held at outdoor campgrounds. In one of the largest religious gatherings before the Civil War, perhaps twenty thousand people—10 percent of the state's population—gathered at Cane Ridge in Bourbon County, Kentucky, for a five-day camp meeting in August 1801 that was led by Presbyterian and Methodist ministers. Preaching continued from dawn to midnight with little time for meals or rest. James Finley, who was himself converted to Christianity at the Cane Ridge Camp Meeting and went on to a long career as a frontier revivalist, described the days:

> I counted seven ministers all preaching at once, some on stumps, others in wagons, and one ... was standing on a tree trunk which had, in falling, lodged against another. Some of the people were singing, others praying, some crying.

Barton W. Stone, the pastor of the Cane Ridge Presbyterian Church that hosted the gathering, remembered, "Many things transpired there, which were so much like miracles, that if they were not, they had the same effect as miracles on infidels and unbelievers."

This popular illustration of an early camp meeting gives some sense of what went on at these events, though especially in the West, the crowds who attended were larger and more diverse than indicated here.

Methodists, Baptists, and Other Protestants

Although Cane Ridge was a joint Presbyterian-Methodist endeavor, it was the Methodists and Baptists who grew the most from the revival movement. Indeed, the revivals that began in the early 1800s made these two denominations the largest Protestant groups in the country.

Methodism had come to America through John Wesley (1703–1791), who founded the Methodist movement in England along with his brother, Charles, the hymn writer (1707–1788). John Wesley had also preached in Georgia. But it was the first American Methodist bishop, Francis Asbury (1745–1816), who established American Methodism. Asbury created a new form of Protestant ministry, the Methodist circuit riders, who moved from community to community preaching with great fervor and organizing churches at every stop.

John Wesley believed that it was in the power of every person to decide whether they wanted to experience salvation. His emphasis on the need for free individuals to make their own decisions appealed in freedom-loving Jeffersonian America. In addition, Wesley's experience of having his "heart strangely warmed" allowed a level of emotionalism in Methodism that was lacking in other denominations.

Baptists had been in North America for almost as long as the Puritans. They were the largest religious body in Rhode Island, where they founded Brown University. The Baptists of the Second Great Awakening, however, were a different breed from their earlier New England Baptist counterparts. Their religious events were more emotional, and they were more individualistic and determined to assert local authority.

Where Methodism was tightly organized from bishops to preachers to congregations, Baptists were decentralized, with each congregation retaining total control. While Methodists were largely united until the coming of the Civil War, Baptists tended to splinter into rival groups—Regular Baptists, Anti-Mission Baptists, Freewill Baptists, Church of God Baptists, Seventh-Day Baptists, Six-Principle Baptists, and Hard Shell Baptists. The model Methodist minister was the circuit rider; the typical Baptist minister was a farmer-preacher who grew up in a particular congregation and was selected to lead it while he continued to support himself by his own labor. Despite their differences, however, both the Methodist and the Baptist ministers were highly effective in changing the religious outlook of the country after 1800.

Faith in the Slave Quarters and Free Black Churches

White communities were not the only ones experiencing a revival of religion in the early 1800s. At revivals like Cane Ridge, blacks and whites, whether slaves or free people, mixed with surprising freedom. Revivals in some parts of the South, especially in the early 1800s, were seen as a kind of holiday, and many of the rules of daily life, including racial segregation, were suspended.

Many plantation owners organized religious services for slaves that focused on the virtues of submission and obedience. But slaves also practiced another form of worship—congregations that met, often at night, in secluded places. The scholar and activist W.E.B. Dubois (1868–1963) described the meetings of these clandestine congregations as occasions to speak of "the longing and disappointment and resentment of a stolen people" and about their deep passion for liberty.

Litt Young, a slave on a plantation near Vicksburg, Mississippi, remembered that the mistress of the plantation

> built a nice church with glass windows and a brass cupola for the blacks. A yellow man [a light-skinned African American] preached to us. She had him preach how we was to obey our master and missy if we want to go to heaven, but when she wasn't there, he come out with straight preachin' from the Bible.

Clara Young recalled her favorite preacher was a man named Matthew Ewing who, even though he could not read or write, "sure knowed his Bible." For these slaves, effective preaching involved knowing the Bible, either by memory or from the rare—and illegal—ability to read it, and an ability to preach with passion about freedom in the next life and quite possibly also in this life. Worship included singing, dancing, and a cathartic emotional release and renewal.

Any unsupervised meeting of slaves frightened whites. Denmark Vesey, a free black Sunday school teacher who saw himself as a latter-day Moses, ready to lead his people to freedom, led a slave revolt in South Carolina in 1822. In 1831, Nat Turner would lead the largest slave revolt before the Civil War. When Turner told the authorities that he knew he "was ordained for some great purpose in the hands of the Almighty," and that "the great day of judgment was at hand," he confirmed what they had been fearing about slave religion.

The longing for freedom usually took less violent paths, however. Slavery depended on hopelessness, and religion gave slaves hope that could lead to resistance. The songs of the slave quarters are often songs of freedom. Thus slaves sang:

> Steal away, steal away, steal away to Jesus!
> Steal away, steal away home, I ain't got long to stay here!

8.1

8.2

8.3

8.4

8.5

Sometimes these lyrics meant stealing away to the religious meeting, but they could also mean stealing away from slavery to flee North.

At the same time, northern free blacks began to form their own religious organizations. Richard Allen was born a slave in Delaware. He converted to Methodism and was able to purchase his freedom and begin preaching. Although Allen preached to white and black congregations, he "soon saw a large field open in seeking and instructing my African brethren, who had been a long forgotten people and few of them attended public worship."

Because white churches were not always welcoming, Allen became convinced that a racially integrated congregation was impossible. In response, he organized the Bethel Church in Philadelphia in 1794. Thus was born the African Methodist Episcopal Church, which by 1820 had four thousand members in Philadelphia and two thousand more in Baltimore. Other black Methodists founded the African Methodist Episcopal Zion Church in New York. African American Baptists also created their own congregations. Fears of religiously inspired slave rebellions, especially after Denmark Vesey's rebellion of 1822, led southern governments to block the growth of independent black churches, but in the North, free black churches thrived as their members exercised leadership, developed their own ideas, and worshipped among themselves.

American Catholic and Jewish Communities

In the early years of the Republic, there were few Roman Catholics or Jews in the original thirteen colonies. During the late 1700s and early 1800s, the largest number of Catholics in North America lived in New Orleans, which had become part of the United States only in 1803, and in Texas, New Mexico, and California, which were still either part of Mexico until the 1840s or in Mexico itself. Nearly all white immigrants to the British colonies had been at least nominally Protestant, except for Catholics who had been granted safe haven in Maryland. Religious freedom in the Jeffersonian era was tremendously important to those who were in the smallest minorities. The freedom to form their own religious organizations, free of government control and often free of full authority by their own senior leaders, was important to Catholics and Jews in Jeffersonian America.

In 1790, John Carroll was appointed the first Catholic bishop in America. He was based in Maryland, where Catholics, having lost their right to govern the colony, had again gained religious freedom after the Revolution (see Chapter 7). Carroll was later promoted to archbishop of Baltimore when the Vatican appointed bishops for Boston, New York, and Bardstown, Kentucky. Carroll worked hard to build Catholic strength and to fit into the democratic spirit of America. He established the first American Catholic college at Georgetown, Maryland (later part of the District of Columbia), and a Catholic seminary at Baltimore. In many places, Catholic laypeople created their own churches, appointed themselves trustees, and when possible, hired their own priests. Vatican responses to the radical secularism of the French Revolution led to pressure on Carroll to curtail this trend among the American laity and, instead, agree to the hierarchical appointment of priests, but throughout the early 1800s, American Catholicism had remarkably strong lay leadership.

At the time of the Revolution, most of the few American Jews lived in East Coast cities such as Newport, Philadelphia, and New York City. Between then and 1820, new congregations and synagogues were formed in Richmond, New Orleans, Cincinnati, and Baltimore. Jewish religious communities, like those of Catholics and Protestants, took on republican sentiments. In New York City, Congregation Shearith Israel adopted the words "Whereas in free states all power originates and is derived from the people" as the beginning words to their new congregational constitution. Something was in the air—including the religious air—in the America of the early 1800s.

8.2 Quick Review

How does this trend toward freer religious expression epitomize Jeffersonian republican values? How not?

Beyond the Mississippi: The Louisiana Purchase and the Expedition of Lewis and Clark

8.1
8.2
8.3
8.4
8.5

8.3 Explain what effects the Louisiana Purchase and the westward expansion had on how various Americans saw themselves.

Jefferson was a political philosopher committed to a small federal government and religious freedom, but he was also a pragmatic politician. One of the practical issues that he faced in leading a country of independent farmers was that those farmers living in western regions were not happy.

Geography shaped American politics at the beginning of Jefferson's term in office. Before the advent of railroads, farmers west of the Alleghenies found it very difficult to ship their goods over the mountains to the Atlantic coast or transport them down the Mississippi through New Orleans. These difficulties had helped fuel the Whiskey Rebellion and the short-lived effort to make Tennessee an independent nation during Washington's administration (see Chapter 7), and Jefferson worried that frustrated frontier farmers might still seek to form an independent country, as some of them advocated and as other nations like Spain would have liked to see happen. He was determined to do something about it.

French explorers and traders began to settle the banks of the Mississippi River in the 1600s, and French place names from Detroit to St. Louis to New Orleans reflected their continuing influence. However, at the close of the French and Indian War in 1763, France ceded all the land east of the Mississippi to Britain, which then ceded it to the United States, while at the same time, France ceded to Spain the area west of the Mississippi and the city of New Orleans. Throughout the Washington and Adams administrations and into Jefferson's, in spite of the provisions of the Pinckney Treaty, Spain periodically restricted non-Spanish vessels from sailing on the Mississippi and collected customs duties on all goods moving through New Orleans. That practice was detrimental because more than half of all the goods shipped out of the United States—and virtually all the goods produced by the western farmers—were shipped down the Mississippi River and through the port of New Orleans, not Atlantic ports. By 1800, Spain had become weaker, prompting Jefferson to write that Spanish control of the river and New Orleans "would hardly be felt by us."

However, Napoleon Bonaparte, who now ruled France, negotiated a secret treaty with Spain to return New Orleans and the entire Louisiana Territory to France. When word of the treaty reached the United States in 1802, it provoked a crisis. Jefferson believed that for France, then the strongest nation in Europe, to control American commerce was intolerable. The president told the American ambassador in Paris, "There is on the globe one single spot, the possessor of which is our natural and habitual enemy." That spot was New Orleans.

The Louisiana Purchase

The solution for securing the loyalty of Appalachian farmers and more secure commerce for the country, Jefferson thought, was to buy the city of New Orleans from France. Once the port was under American control, Jefferson was confident that he would have solved a long-term problem for his western constituents and won an important political victory. Jefferson dispatched two of his most trusted associates, James Monroe and Robert Livingston, to Paris to offer $6 million for the city. If they could not reach an accommodation with the French, Monroe was to proceed to London and try to make an alliance against France with Great Britain.

While Jefferson worried about control of New Orleans, Napoleon had worries of his own. Although he was victorious on the European continent, Napoleon needed money. In addition, French efforts to put down the slave uprising in Haiti had gone terribly. Militant slave resistance and yellow fever had killed twenty-four thousand French soldiers, and Haitian independence seemed inevitable. New Orleans and the Mississippi Valley, which supplied Haiti with food and raw materials, would become much less important to France

Louisiana Purchase

The 1803 U.S. purchase of the vast land holdings that France claimed along the west side of the Mississippi River beginning in New Orleans and extending through the heart of North America to the Canadian border.

if France no longer controlled the Haitian sugar and coffee plantations. So when the Americans offered $6 million for one city, Napoleon's government offered to sell the whole middle third of the present-day United States for $15 million.

Jefferson was thrilled with Napoleon's offer. He worried, however, that a strict reading of the Constitution did not authorize the federal government to make such a huge purchase of land; it certainly did not mention that authority in the powers granted to the national government. Nevertheless, the practical political benefits of the **Louisiana Purchase** overcame his constitutional doubts. Some Federalists in Congress opposed the purchase, fearing—correctly—that the influence of New England—the last Federalist region of the country—would be diminished in a vastly larger nation. But most Americans, even most Federalists, were enthusiastic. Congress acted quickly, and the treaty confirming the transfer of 828,000 square miles from nominal French control to the United States was easily ratified. The United States had solved the problem of New Orleans and secured control of both sides of the Mississippi River from the Great Lakes to the Gulf of Mexico, while almost doubling the nation's land area. How to incorporate this land into the United States, whether as states or territories, would be left for future administrations to determine.

The City of New Orleans

New Orleans was unusual for an American city when it became part of the United States in 1803. Many of its inhabitants spoke French or Spanish, but they now lived in a country where business was conducted in English. It was a Catholic city that was now part of an overwhelmingly Protestant country. Its citizens were a cosmopolitan mix with attitudes toward many things—including race and sexuality—that were different from those of most Americans.

Slavery in Spanish and French colonies varied widely. Some of the harshest slavery in the world was in the sugar plantations of French Haiti and in Spanish Cuba. But slaves in cities like Havana and pre-1803 New Orleans could maintain stable families, enjoy their own holidays, and earn money to buy goods for themselves and, sometimes, even their freedom. In New Orleans, slaves and free blacks could gather at Congo Square on Sundays to dance, play drums, and sing in their own languages under the watchful eye of whites but with a freedom of action unimaginable elsewhere in the United States. The music that they brought from Africa and developed in New Orleans was the foundation of American jazz.

There was also considerable racial mixing in New Orleans. Mixed-race people faced discrimination, but many black women nonetheless became long-term partners to white men. Such unions were an avenue of upward mobility for some black women, not only in New Orleans but also in many of the Spanish and French colonies in ways that were not true in British colonies or in the United States. That African women could maintain their own gardens, buy and sell goods, and be involved in intimate relationships with white men led to complex family negotiations. A libre (as free blacks were called) woman, Carlota d'Erneville, purchased her freedom in 1773 and the freedom of her son Carlos in 1775. She later became rich enough to own her own tavern and houses that she rented to others.

The New Orleans that Jefferson purchased in 1803 had a population of eight thousand with their own churches, dance halls, theater, newspapers, and police force. One-third of all people of African origin in the city were free compared with less than 2 percent in Kentucky or Tennessee and under 10 percent in the United States as a whole.

Many of the French-speaking women and men of New Orleans, black or white, slave or free, tended to refer to any citizens of the United States as "Kaintucks" or Kentuckians no matter where in the United States they came from. Kaintucks were the tough backwoods farmers and slaves who crewed flatboats. These large floating rafts, often fifteen feet wide by fifty to eighty feet long, carried up to one hundred tons of grain. For the Americans who came down the Mississippi on a flatboat, New Orleans was a city of pleasure that lured many to stay and create a new American population. Although the racial and cultural diversity of New Orleans frightened some Americans, its essential geographic location made it the prize of the Louisiana Purchase.

The Lewis and Clark Expedition

Jefferson wanted to assert American dominance in North America. In 1803, before he even knew the outcome of the Monroe-Livingston negotiations, he asked Congress to support a "scientific expedition" to study the people, lands, and animal and plant species of the North American continent across the Louisiana territory and on to the Pacific Ocean. While he wanted the scientific information, Jefferson was even more interested in a full report on Spanish and French military power in the region. The expedition was to be led by the president's private secretary, Meriwether Lewis, and an army officer, William Clark. Before Lewis and Clark could depart, word came of the Louisiana Purchase. Suddenly, the United States owned much of the land the expedition was authorized to explore, and Jefferson wanted to learn as much as possible about the new American lands and the places beyond them as well as make treaties with as many of the original inhabitants as possible. It was a daunting assignment that would become one of American history's most celebrated exploits.

Lewis and Clark and their **Corps of Discovery**—the team of soldiers, civilian woodsmen, boatmen, interpreters, and Clark's slave York—prepared for the trip during the winter of 1803–1804 in St. Louis on the west bank of the Mississippi River. The site was a Spanish/French trading post of about a thousand people, which was a gateway to the territory the United States had just acquired. French explorers were familiar with much of the land over which the expedition would travel, as was a British trader, Alexander Mackenzie, who had been the first European to cross North America in 1792–1793. Of course, the Indians living along the route knew their homelands well. Still, for Americans, this vast area was unknown. On May 14, 1804, the Corps of Discovery began their travel up the Missouri River into the heart of the Louisiana Territory. By the end of October, they reached an area close to the current U.S.-Canadian border in North Dakota. There, near a Mandan Indian village on the Missouri River, they made camp for the winter. The Mandans lived in earth lodges in settled villages. They had traded with the French for over a hundred years, had been decimated by European smallpox, and knew European ways, but the arrival of the Lewis and Clark expedition was their first contact with Americans. The Americans traded goods and celebrated feasts, including New Year's Day, with the Mandans, drinking, dancing, and playing the fiddle to the surprise of their hosts.

Critical to the success of the corps were French trapper Toussaint Charbonneau and his Shoshone partner, Sacagawea, who joined the expedition with their newborn child. Whether Sacagawea was the slave or the wife of Charbonneau is unclear, but she became an essential guide and an American legend. Sacagawea began as a cook and laundress for the corps while she carried her baby on her back but quickly used her knowledge of the countryside to find food and translate with some of the tribes they met. At the end of their journey, Lewis and Clark paid Charbonneau $500 for his services, but later they wondered whether they should have paid Sacagawea, too. According to unverified Shoshone tradition, Sacagawea lived to an old age, dying at the Wind River Indian Reservation in 1884.

As they tried to cross the Rocky Mountains in September of 1805, the corps moved beyond the rather inexact western boundary of the Louisiana Purchase into Oregon Country, which was claimed by Britain, Russia, and Spain, but not the United States. As instructed by Jefferson, they kept going, and almost starved. They had assumed that the Rocky Mountains were like the Appalachians. They crossed through a valley expecting to see downward slopes, but instead, Clarke noted in his journal, they faced higher mountains "in every direction as far as I could see." At Weippe Prairie in what is now Idaho, they stumbled into a party of Nez Perce Indians, by far the largest tribe in that part of the western Rockies, who brought them to a "large spacious lodge" and fed them. An Indian leader

8.1

8.2

8.3

8.4

8.5

Bettmann/Getty Images

The survival and success of the Lewis and Clark expedition was due to the friendly welcome the explorers received from native tribes whom they met along the way.

Corps of Discovery

The name given to the expedition led by Lewis and Clark in 1804–1806 that explored the Louisiana Purchase and the Oregon lands extending to the West Coast.

Map 8-1 Exploring the New Territory.

This map shows the size of the Louisiana Purchase in comparison with the original land of the United States and the routes of the Lewis and Clark, Pike, and Freeman expeditions through and beyond Louisiana.

known as Twisted Hair drew a map of the river system leading to the Columbia River and the Pacific coast and taught the Americans how to make dugout canoes out of pine. The food saved the explorers' lives, and the canoes saved the trip.

On November 24, 1805, the Corps of Discovery left their horses with Twisted Hair and, following the route he mapped for them, reached the Pacific Ocean. They built Fort Clatsop near present-day Astoria, Oregon, and wintered there until March 23, 1806, when they began the long, arduous journey home, reaching St. Louis on September 23, 1806 (see Map 8-1). Word spread quickly to the nation and to Jefferson at the White House that the party, whom many had given up for lost, had made it back.

While Lewis and Clark were exploring the northern parts of the Louisiana Purchase and the Oregon coast, Jefferson launched other expeditions. Zebulon Pike led an expedition that departed from St. Louis in the fall of 1805 to explore the Mississippi and Arkansas Rivers and much of the present-day state of Colorado. In 1806, Jefferson appointed a third expedition led by Thomas Freeman, an astronomer and surveyor, to track the Red River Valley in the southern portion of the new territory. The reports from these expeditions opened the way for other adventurers and traders, some of whom, like New York's John Jacob Astor, made a fortune in the fur trade. The result for the Mandans, Nez Perce, and other tribes was far too often disease, war, and the loss of lands and a way of life.

8.3 Quick Review

What key aspects of the Louisiana Purchase were of particular importance to the United States, and how would they change life for different groups of Americans?

American Voices

William Clark and Red Bear—Two Views of the Lewis and Clark Experience

The rescue of the Lewis and Clark expedition by the Nez Perce in 1805 was critical to their survival. But the explanation for why the Nez Perce were so friendly depends on who was describing the event. For William Clark, it was a response to his skill as a negotiator. For the Nez Perce, it was a response to a much earlier event.

From the Journals of Lewis and Clark	Red Bear
September 20—I Set out early and … proceeded on through a butifull Countrey for three miles to a Small Plain in which I found maney Indian lodges, at the distance of 1 mile from the lodges I met 3 boys, when they Saw me ran and hid themselves searched … found gave them Small pieces of ribin & Sent them forward to the village a man Came out to meet me with great Caution and Conducted me [us] to a large Spacious Lodge which he told me (by Signs) was the Lodge of his great Chief … great numbers of women gathered around me with much apparent Signs of fear, and … gave us a Small piece of Buffalow meat, Some dried Salmon beries & roots in different States, Some round and much like an onion which they call (Pas she co) quamash the Bread or Cake is called Pas-she-co Sweet, of this they make bread & Supe they also gave us the bread made of this root all of which we eate hartily, I gave them a fiew Small articles as preasents, and proceeded on with a Chief to his Village 2 miles in the Same Plain, where we were treated kindly in their way and continued with them all night. … They call themselves Cho punnish or Pierced Noses; their dialect appears very different from the (flat heads) Tushapaws (I have seen).	[*From an oral history recorded in 1926 with Red Bear's grandson*] Chief Red Bear first learned of white people through a girl of his band living on Tamonmo [the Salmon River]. When small she was stolen by the Blacklegs in the buffalo country, who sold her to some tribe farther toward the sunrise. In time she was bought by white people, probably in Canada, where she was well treated. It is a long story; how in time, carrying her little baby, she ran away and after several moons reached the friendly Selish, who cared for her and brought her in a dying condition to her own people at White Bird. Her baby had died on the way. She was called Watkuweis [Returned from a Faraway Country]. She told of the white people, how good they had been to her, and how well she liked them. When the first two white men, Lewis and Clark with their followers, came Watkuweis said to her people, "These are the people who helped me! Do them no hurt!" This was why the strange people had been received in friendship. There had been a prophecy about Red Bear and a new people, which was thus fulfilled in 1805. He met the strangers. They first have a smoke. If no smoke, then they must fight. Red Bear made presents of dressed buckskins, and they gave him beads and a few other articles. They afterwards found the white man's gifts to be cheap.

Source: Frederick E. Hoxie and Jay T. Nelson, editors, *Lewis & Clark and the Indian Country: The Native American Perspective* (Urbana: University of Illinois Press, 2007), pp. 136–141.

Thinking Critically

1. **Comparison**

   These two stories provide an ideal opportunity to compare different accounts of the same historical moment. How did Clark's and Red Bear's explanations differ? What circumstances might lead them to such different readings of the same interaction?

2. **Analyzing Primary Sources**

   What light do these documents shed on the assumptions white Americans often brought to their interactions with American Indians and Indians brought to white Americans?

The War of 1812

8.4   Analyze the causes and impact of the War of 1812.

Jefferson expanded the United States and ended the tension with the Barbary pirates, but he had been able to do little about the British and French navies that threatened the country as a result of conflicts between those two European powers. At the same time, the actions Jefferson took to protect the United States on the seas hurt the country economically. What had begun as an irritating concern to Jefferson escalated into the War of 1812 during the presidency of his successor James Madison.

8.1

8.2

8.3

8.4

8.5

That conflict, which continued from 1812 to 1815, deserves more attention than it often receives from historians. As a military matter, the war changed little but cost dearly. However, the war resolved issues that had limited U.S. development for decades, and its conclusion launched a new period of growth for the country. It was the last war ever fought between the United States and Great Britain. The two nations had been in conflict almost nonstop since 1775, but the end of this war brought real peace. It was also the last war in which Indian tribes were allied with one nation or against another. After the war, no tribe was ever again able to make an alliance with a foreign nation, and the U.S. government treated Native Americans less and less as citizens of sovereign nations and more as an "internal matter."

Renewed Tension between the United States and Great Britain

The tensions that led the United States and Great Britain to go to war in 1812 had existed since the battles of Lexington and Concord in 1775. Despite treaties, the two nations were never fully at peace, and each made alliances with Indian tribes to make trouble for the other.

For the British, troubles in North America were a sideshow to a world war with France that had begun in 1689 and continued, with brief pauses, until 1815. English colonists fought on the British side until the French and Indian War ended in 1763. In 1778, France had come to the aid—decisive aid—of the American colonists in the Revolution. With the coming of the French Revolution in 1789 and the rise of Napoleon in 1799, the war between Britain and France took on a deeper ideological tone. While earlier wars had primarily been territorial disputes, after their Revolution, the French saw themselves as the agents of democracy against a despotic coalition led by Britain. Especially after the rise of Napoleon, the British saw themselves as defenders of the free world against Napoleonic tyranny. In the United States, the emerging political parties were split, with the Federalist tilting toward Britain and the Democratic-Republican favoring France. By early 1806, Napoleon's armies controlled most of the European continent while the British Royal Navy controlled the oceans. For the United States, British control of the seas was a much larger threat than worries about who controlled the European continent.

To survive, Britain depended on its navy to protect the island nation from invasion and to dominate the oceans. But the Royal Navy was always short of sailors, and one of the reasons for the shortage was the tendency of British sailors to desert and join the crew of a U.S. merchant vessel where the working conditions were better and the pay up to five times higher. The British regularly stopped U.S. merchant vessels and occasionally warships on the high seas, in violation of international law, to search for their own sailors and, all too often, also to force any able-bodied seaman, British or American, into service.

This policy of seizing sailors, or impressment, was seen as vital to Britain, but it was a direct threat to American freedom and to the economic survival of the United States. Impressments had long infuriated Americans and, in fact, had helped spark the Revolution in 1776 (see Chapter 5). Between 1803 and 1812, three thousand to six thousand American citizens were pressed into service on British warships against their will, many of whom never returned. A major crisis erupted in June 1807 when the Royal Navy's HMS *Leopard* opened fire on the USS *Chesapeake* after its commander refused to let British officers board the ship to look for deserters. Three American sailors were killed in the fighting, and the British then took four sailors off the *Chesapeake* who were either deserters from their navy or Americans resisting impressments. President Jefferson wrote, "This country has never been in such a state of excitement since the battle of Lexington."

Jefferson and Congress, however, knew that the United States was too weak for a fight, in part because of the cutbacks Jefferson had authorized in the navy and army that Adams had previously built up. Congress initially passed a Non-Importation Act, hoping that boycotting British goods would be an effective strategy, but it failed to have an effect. Consequently, Jefferson urged the **Embargo Act**, which Congress passed in December 1807, preventing U.S. trade with any foreign ports to keep ships and sailors "out of harm's

Embargo Act

An act passed by Congress in 1807 prohibiting American ships from leaving for any foreign port.

way." The president was confident that the major impact would be on Britain, which he thought could not survive without American foodstuffs, and that the American people would be willing to suffer short-term loss to gain peace. He was wrong on both counts. British warehouses were full, the country was having a good harvest, other nations were willing to sell food, and the British could wait out the Americans. Most Americans were anxious to maintain the income that commerce provided. New England shipping was devastated, and farmers in all of the states lost money as cotton, grain, and tobacco piled up and could not be shipped. Smugglers became active, by land, across the border between New England and Canada, and by sea, eluding the small U.S. Navy that tried to enforce the embargo. The Massachusetts and Connecticut legislatures, following the precedent of Jefferson's own earlier Kentucky and Virginia Resolutions, declared the embargo illegal in their states, thus setting up talk of secession or civil war.

As a compromise that was meant to appease New England merchants, Congress replaced the embargo with the **Non-Intercourse Act** in 1809, just days before Jefferson left office. The new act authorized trade with everyone except Britain and France. (France had plundered U.S. ships for supplies during their war with Britain.)

During Madison's first term as president, tension continued to grow between the United States and Great Britain. In 1810, a further modification of the Non-Intercourse Act, known as Macon's Bill No. 2, created new tensions, especially between the United States and Britain. British impressments of U.S. sailors continued unabated while each new act continued to hurt commercial ties between the two countries.

Non-Intercourse Act

An act, passed by Congress in 1809, designed to modify the Embargo Act by limiting it to trade with Britain and France so as to extend U.S. commerce in the rest of the world.

Renewed Tension between Whites and Indians

While tensions mounted between the United States and Great Britain, warfare between the United States and Indian tribes broke out in the Ohio country. After the U.S. Army's victory at the Battle of Fallen Timbers and the subsequent Treaty of Greenville in 1795, the Old Northwest had been at peace. But a new generation of Indians was much less willing to live with what they saw as an unfair treaty. A new tribal alliance led by a charismatic religious figure named Tenskwatawa, or the Prophet, and his half-brother, the military leader Tecumseh, frightened white settlers and seriously challenged the small U.S. Army. Many assumed—correctly—that Tecumseh and Tenskwatawa were aided by the British.

After their losses from the Treaty of Greenville in 1795, many Shawnees came to believe that their sorry state was due to their having displeased Waashaa Monetoo, the Good Spirit, who, their traditions said, had re-created the world after its destruction by a flood. In the early 1800s, a spiritual leader, Tenskwatawa, told the tribes that their dependence on white culture was the source of the Good Spirit's unhappiness. After two hundred years of coexistence, tribes like the Shawnees had become dependent on European muskets, wore cotton clothing, cooked in European cookware, and even lived in European-style houses. Tenskwatawa promised that, if his people would renounce European ways and goods, they could renew their culture and drive whites out of their country. He created a new settlement at what is now West Lafayette, Indiana, called Prophetstown, where Shawnees and other tribes gathered for spiritual renewal.

While Tenskwatawa preached, Tecumseh prepared for war. Tenskwatawa was a religiously inspired leader, Tecumseh an inspired military tactician. White colonists had killed their father, Pukeshinwau, at the beginning of the American Revolution. The brothers had seen whites make and break treaty after treaty. Tecumseh traveled throughout the Ohio territory and sought help from British authorities in Canada. Tecumseh traveled as far south as Tennessee and Alabama to recruit Cherokees, Choctaws, and Creeks. In a meeting with Choctaw and Chickasaw leaders in the spring of 1811, Tecumseh (speaking in the Shawnee language) said:

> The whites are already a match for us all united, and too strong for any one tribe alone to resist; so that unless we support one another with our collective and united forces; unless every tribe unanimously combines to give check to the ambition and avarice of the whites, they will soon conquer us apart and disunited and we will be driven away from our native country and scattered as autumnal leaves before the wind.

Tecumseh (1768-1813) (oil on canvas), American School, (19th century)/Private Collection/Peter Newark American Pictures/The Bridgeman Art Library

Tenskwatawa (1775-1836) (colour litho), King, Charles Bird (1785-1862)/Private Collection/Peter Newark American Pictures/The Bridgeman Art Library

Two Shawnee leaders and half-brothers—Tecumseh, who led a diverse Indian military alliance, and Tenskwatawa, known as the Prophet—proposed a revival of Native American religion in opposition to white expansion.

8.1

8.2

8.3

8.4

8.5

American Voices

Tecumseh, Speech to the Governor of Indiana, 1810

Tecumseh met with William Henry Harrison, governor of Indiana Territory, in hopes of establishing a peace agreement in August 1810. Tecumseh spoke little or no English, but U.S. government interpreters were careful to transcribe the speech as accurately as possible. A year later, Harrison led the U.S. Army to attack the Shawnee encampment at Prophetstown and war followed.

Brother, I wish you to listen to me well. I wish to reply to you more explicitly as I think you do not clearly understand what I before said to you. I shall explain it again. …

You ought to know that after we agreed to bury the Tomahawk at Greenville we then found their new fathers in the Americans who told us they would treat us well, not like the British who gave us but a small piece of pork every day. I want now to remind you of the promises of the white people. You recollect that the time the Delawares lived near the white people (Americans) and satisfied with the promises of friendship and remained in security, yet one of their towns was surprised and the men, women, and children murdered.

The same promises were given to the Shawnees, flags were given to them and were told by the Americans that they were now children of the Americans. These flags will be as security for you; if the white people intend to do you harm hold up your flags and no harm will be done you. This was at length practiced and the consequence was that the person bearing the flag was murdered with others in their village. How my Brother after this conduct can you blame me for placing little confidence in the promises of our fathers the Americans?

Brother. Since the peace was made you have kill'd some of the Shawnee, Winnebagoes, Delawares, and Miamies and you have taken our lands from us, and I do not see how we can remain at peace with you if you continue to do so.

Source: There are slightly differing accounts of the speech. This account is from Logan Esarey, editor, *Messages and Letters of William Henry Harrison*, Vol. 1 (New York: Arno Press, 1975; reprint of 1922 edition), pp. 459–467, cited in Camilla Townsend, *American Indian History: A Documentary Reader* (Malden, MA: Wiley-Blackwell, 2009), pp. 96–99.

Thinking Critically

1. **Analyzing Primary Sources**
   Tecumseh provided specific evidence for his claim that the U.S. government could not be trusted by Native Americans. How might Harrison have responded? How might you, as an historian, respond?

2. **Argument Development**
   In your opinion, why was it so difficult for whites and Indians to live side by side in peace? What evidence does Tecumseh use to support his argument on the question?

Tecumseh was willing to negotiate with the United States, but his goal was an all-Indian alliance to drive all whites from the land south of Canada and from between the Alleghenies and the Mississippi.

Whites on the frontier were frightened. In September 1807, Thomas Kirker, the acting governor of the new state of Ohio, met with Tecumseh, and the two agreed to peace. But in November 1811, while Tecumseh was away seeking Cherokee allies, William Henry Harrison, governor of the Indiana Territory, attacked Prophetstown with one thousand U.S. troops. Harrison's troops burned the village to the ground, though the Prophet and most residents escaped. A year later, when the United States went to war with Great Britain, Tecumseh, strengthened by support from the British, who had never stopped stirring up Indian opposition to the United States, led his tribal confederation in an all-out war on the Americans. With the United States and Britain formally at war, the Shawnee alliance with Britain was a major threat to the Americans.

War and Its Consequences

War Hawks

Members of Congress, mostly from the South and West, who aggressively pushed for a war against Britain after their election in 1810.

As hostilities grew between the United States and Great Britain and its Indian allies, some in Congress, known as the **War Hawks**, saw a war with Britain as just what the country needed. Led by Henry Clay of Kentucky and Felix Grundy of Tennessee, they argued that war was key to territorial expansion. They were confident that if the United States went to war with Britain, French inhabitants of Canada would revolt, allowing the United States to seize Canada. The war hawks also wanted to attack the Spanish colonies in Florida and claim that territory for the United States. With Britain and Spain out of the picture, the country could then settle things once and for all on the Indian frontier. Elbridge Gerry of Massachusetts, eager to stop British disruptions to American trade in the Atlantic, told President Madison, "By war, we should be purified, as by fire."

8.1

8.2

8.3

8.4

8.5

Federalists, however, saw war as just one more step in a process by which the Democratic-Republicans had moved the country into an unnecessary, and commercially foolish, hostility with Britain. Earlier in his life, Madison had strongly opposed the United States going to war with anyone. In 1795, he had written, "War is, perhaps, the most to be dreaded, because it comprises and develops the germ of every other [enemy]." As a Jeffersonian advocate of small government, Madison in 1795 had worried that, with war, "the discretionary power of the Executive is extended; its influence in dealing out offices, honors, and emoluments is multiplied; and all the means of seducing the minds are added to those of subduing the force of the people." Yet in June 1812, when he was the executive, Madison asked Congress for a declaration of war with Britain. The war resolution passed by the smallest margin of any U.S. declaration of war—79–49 in the House and 19–13 in the Senate. The nation was far from unanimous in its commitment to war, and the war did not go well.

Madison was confident that the war would be quick and cost little in terms of money or American lives. He was terribly wrong. The attack on Canada was a disaster. Jefferson and Madison, with their commitment to a small government and modest taxes, had kept the army weak while many in Congress who voted for war had also voted against every military appropriation in the time leading up to the war. Far fewer of the people in Canada, English or French, wanted to become part of the United States than the Americans expected. In addition, the British army was strong and had been cultivating Indian alliances for a long time.

In July 1812, Detroit fell to British soldiers and Indians led by Tecumseh, and an American attack on British forts on the Niagara River failed. Far from taking Canada, the opening battles of the war had left the Northwest more open to attack by the British and Tecumseh's tribal alliance. Tecumseh is still remembered as a hero in Canada for his role in defending that country. Battles along the frontier were brutal. The Kentucky militia scalped British soldiers, and Indians scalped American settlers. Both sides complained of atrocities.

At first, the Royal Navy enforced a much tighter blockade on the Atlantic coast than Jefferson's embargo had ever accomplished, wrecking the U.S. economy. British landing parties attacked coastal towns at will. However, an American naval victory on Lake Erie by ships under the command of Oliver Hazard Perry gave the country a new hero. Tecumseh was killed in October 1813 when the U.S. Army won a significant victory over combined British and Indian forces at the Battle of the Thames in southern Canada. The combined victories brought some safety to the New York, Pennsylvania, and Ohio frontier, but all thought of conquering Canada disappeared.

By 1814, the war turned further against the United States. Napoleon's abdication in April 1814 freed the British for a full-scale fight. In August, British troops raided Washington and burned the Capitol and the White House. First Lady Dolley Madison collected state

In August 1814, only a short time after 1800 when the Capitol building and the White House had begun serving as the center of the American government, British troops burned both structures. The deserted husks of both buildings stood until the war ended and they could be rebuilt.

papers and the famous Gilbert Stuart painting of George Washington and fled just ahead of the British. However, on September 13, the British bombardment of Fort McHenry in Baltimore harbor failed to dislodge the American garrison. When Francis Scott Key, who was temporarily being held in British custody, saw that the American flag had not been struck in defeat, he was inspired to write "The Star-Spangled Banner." That same month, American forces also stopped a British invasion of New York. But stopping invasions was hardly winning the war.

On the Indian front, however, American forces were winning. Like the French and Indian War and the American Revolution, the War of 1812 was a disaster for Indians living east of the Mississippi. Tecumseh's death at the Battle of the Thames ended the fragile coalition he had built and opened all of Ohio and Indiana Territory to rapid white settlement. In the south, at the Battle of Horseshoe Bend in March 1814, Andrew Jackson defeated a Creek and Cherokee alliance, killing close to one thousand Indian fighters and two thousand more in subsequent battles, 15 percent of the tribes' total population. "My people are no more!" the Creek leader Red Eagle, or William Weatherford, said. In the Treaty of Fort Jackson, the Creeks were forced to give up almost twenty-five million acres in Georgia and Alabama, half of their total land.

An American peace delegation of Henry Clay, Albert Gallatin, and John Quincy Adams met with their British counterparts in Ghent, Belgium, to negotiate what would become the **Treaty of Ghent**. Despite its victories against the United States, Britain wanted to end its battles with the United States to conserve resources in case there was renewed conflict with France. Initially, the British asked for significant concessions, including a large protected zone for their Indian allies, but the American delegation stalled through much of 1814. Late in the year, the British agreed to a treaty that essentially returned all borders and issues to their status quo before the war began. It was a wise move for them. Napoleon, living in exile on the island of Elba off the Italian coast since his defeat in 1814, returned to power briefly in 1815. He again ruled France until his final defeat by British and German troops at the Battle of Waterloo in June 1815. If the British had lost at Waterloo, and the battle was a close call, it might have been because their best troops were in North America.

Even as the Ghent negotiations were taking place, Federalists in New England were taking actions against the war. Many New Englanders saw little value in the territorial expansion of the country and were convinced that new lands would only mean new Democratic-Republican representatives in Congress. The war had devastated the New England economy, which was dependent on international shipping. In protest, New England governors ordered their state militias to serve only within the borders of their own states. In December 1814, Federalist delegates from across New England convened the **Hartford Convention** in Hartford, Connecticut, to demand peace and consider New England's secession from the Union if peace did not come quickly. While a majority of the delegates ultimately opposed secession, the convention insisted on the right of nullification, the right of state governments to impede congressional actions within their own boundaries, and proposed amendments to the Constitution to protect New England's power. Delegates to the convention expected the Madison administration to give in to their demands, but when news arrived of Jackson's victory in New Orleans and then the peace treaty, the convention did more to discredit the Federalist Party than support their cause. Nevertheless, it signaled the level of hostility to what many came to call "Mr. Madison's War."

The war's final dramatic Battle of New Orleans was fought after the peace treaty was already signed but before news of it had reached Jackson or the opposing British army. The British planned to attack New Orleans so they could win control of the Mississippi River and cut U.S. trade on it. Major General Sir Edward Pakenham and his 8,000 troops were battle-hardened from years of fighting the French, but in New Orleans, they faced Jackson's 4,700 American troops, a collection of regular militia, Tennessee and Kentucky volunteers, and pirates and smugglers under the command of the infamous Jean Lafitte. On January 8, 1815, Pakenham's troops marched straight into a line of fire organized by Jackson's army. When, after hours of fighting, the British called for a truce, almost 700 British soldiers had been killed and 1,400 wounded. Of the Americans, 8 were killed and 13 wounded. It was one of the great victories of the war, and it made Jackson a hero and would help make him president. And, though it came

Treaty of Ghent

A treaty signed in December 1814 between the United States and Britain that ended the War of 1812.

Hartford Convention

A meeting of Federalist delegates from the New England states to protest the continuation of the War of 1812.

Map 8-2 Fighting the War of 1812.

Few parts of the United States were exempt from the fighting of the War of 1812. The British navy maintained a highly effective blockade of the nation's ports, bringing commerce to a stall and making it easy to attack and burn the capital in 1814. The American navy was more successful in battles on the Great Lakes. Armies also fought all along the Mississippi River from Tippecanoe in Indiana Territory to the final battle in New Orleans at the war's end.

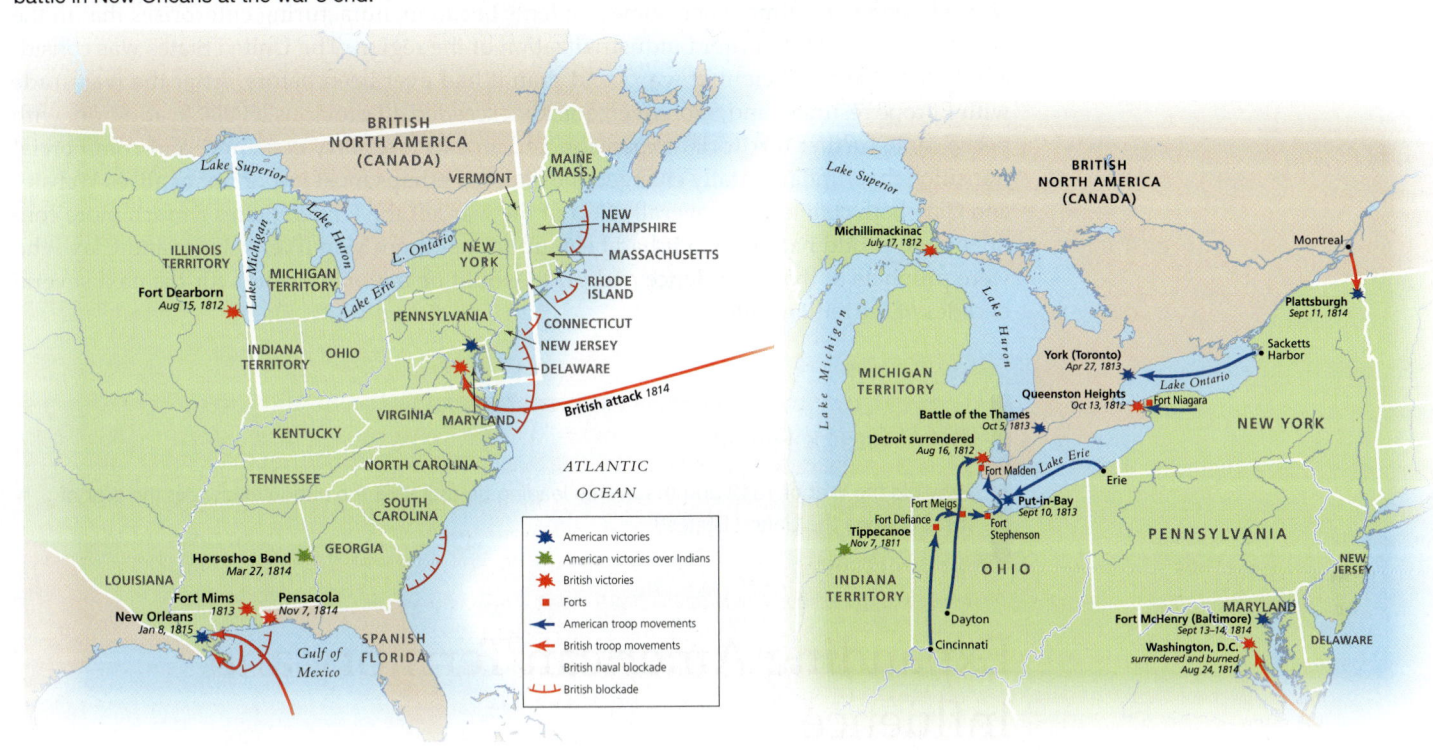

after the peace treaty, it helped convince the British that they should, indeed, honor the terms of the treaty—a treaty they might have reconsidered if they had taken New Orleans (see Map 8-2).

Far more Americans, Indians, and British soldiers and sailors died in the War of 1812 than anyone expected when the war began. Indian tribes from the Shawnees to the Creeks would never have significant power again. The United States was virtually bankrupt as a result of the war. Secretary of the Treasury George W. Campbell reported that the government needed to borrow $50 million in the fall of 1814 and resigned when he could not raise it, and the government, for the only time in history, defaulted on its debts.

Nevertheless, news of the Treaty of Ghent and of Jackson's victory in New Orleans was met with national celebrations. Henry Clay asked, "What is our present situation?" and answered his own question: "Respectability and character abroad—security and confidence at home." Daniel Webster, who as a representative from Massachusetts had opposed the war, now said:

> The peace brought about an entirely new and a most interesting state of things: it opened us to other prospects and suggested other duties. We ourselves were changed, and the whole world was changed.

It was an odd mood for a nation that had lost more battles than it won, had come close to bankruptcy, and had its new capital city lying in ashes. But Webster captured the national mood better than the statistics. The end of Britain's long war with France also brought an end to Britain's war with the United States, which had continued in various forms of conflict for forty years.

Almost immediately after the war ended, Britain and the United States negotiated a commercial treaty that gave the United States trading rights with Britain and much of Britain's empire. Two years later, in 1817, the Rush-Bagot Treaty guaranteed the disarmament of the Great Lakes, and the year after that another treaty, the Anglo-American Convention, resolved much of the border between the United States and Canada. These treaties were the beginning of long-lasting peace on the northern border of the United States. Indeed, after 1815, both Europe and America settled into a long period of relative peace and mutual prosperity.

In spite of all the complaints about the war, the years during which the region's ports were closed were a time when some residents began manufacturing enterprises that in the years ahead would fuel rapid industrialization of the region. The United States was considerably more self-sufficient at war's end than it had ever been before. After the war, trade with Europe resumed and, moreover, quickly exceeded all previous levels. In addition, with peace came further territorial expansion and an extraordinary economic and commercial transition that fundamentally changed the nation. Perhaps most important of all, as Webster and Clay both claimed, the overall effect of the war left the United States a much more confident and proud nation than it had been up to that time. Men like Webster and Clay who were prophets of that confidence and pride would be national leaders for the next several decades of the nation's life.

8.4 Quick Review

Why did the War of 1812 and the events leading up to it split the nation? How did the War of 1812 change the United States?

Expanding American Territory and Influence

8.5 Analyze how the United States acquired new territory and increased influence abroad.

In spite of wars and tensions, territorial expansion continued under Jefferson's handpicked successors, presidents James Madison (1809–1817) and James Monroe (1817–1825), as it had under Jefferson. During this twenty-four-year period, three men who were political allies from the same political party and the same state governed the nation, seeking many of the same goals. Rapid growth fundamentally changed the country. In 1799, Daniel Boone, who had created the first white settlements in Kentucky during the Revolution, moved with his family yet again, this time across the Mississippi River into Spanish-controlled Missouri. Other American settlers from Kentucky followed, seeking ever more land. They assumed that their rights as American citizens went with them and that, eventually, American sovereignty would follow. The Louisiana Purchase in 1803 confirmed Boone's assumptions.

Other Americans followed Boone's pattern in Florida, Texas, New Mexico, and California. Americans ventured far beyond the borders of the United States and expected, often demanded, that the American government protect them and eventually annex new lands to the Union. Many in the government agreed with the settlers, and successive governments, anxious to expand or consolidate regional control, approved.

During the War of 1812, the military victories of William Henry Harrison over the Shawnees in the Old Northwest finalized the opening of Ohio and the future states of Indiana and Illinois to white settlement. At the same time, Andrew Jackson's defeat of the Creeks and Cherokees in the Old Southwest opened up huge new tracts of land in what would become the states of Mississippi and Alabama. With the lands ceded by Britain in 1783 and the vast Louisiana Purchase now firmly under American control, the most obvious pieces of real estate left for further U.S. annexation after the War of 1812 were the territories known as West and East Florida, still controlled by Spain, and the Oregon Territory, which several European powers claimed.

8.1

8.2

8.3

8.4

8.5

Florida and Oregon

West Florida was more or less the southern third of what would eventually be Mississippi and Alabama while East Florida was what is today the state of Florida. To the United States, foreign control of those lands represented multiple threats. It gave Spain control of most access to the Gulf of Mexico, which was a threat to U.S. shipping. Slaves and others seeking to escape U.S. jurisdiction could easily escape south along a long, unguarded border and melt into the vast, unruly lands of Florida. Seminole Indians, already refugees from the growing white population north of Florida, often welcomed escaped slaves and created new communities that were united in their dislike of the Americans. Americans just north of the Florida border were hungry for more land. Many ignored international boundaries and crossed into Florida to farm and build settlements. These settlers in turn demanded U.S. protection from the Seminoles and Creeks, who had been displaced by the Treaty of Fort Jackson and were determined to defend their new land in Florida.

In 1817, Andrew Jackson, a military hero after his victories in 1814 and 1815, told President James Monroe and Secretary of State John Quincy Adams that he could seize Florida in sixty days. The president and Adams did not want a war with Spain but, in language that was deliberately vague, called on Jackson to attack the Seminoles who were harassing white settlers and gave him "full powers to conduct the war in the manner he may judge best." Given how Jackson had conducted the war against the Creeks, Monroe and Adams knew what their orders meant.

Jackson's army marched into Florida. Jackson's troops could not find many Seminoles, who were adept at disappearing into swamps and marshes, but they burned their villages and crops. They also seized Spanish forts and arrested a Scots trader named Alexander Arbuthnot and another British subject, Robert Armbrister, charged them with assisting the Seminoles, and after a quick trial executed both. When his troops did find Seminole and Creek leaders, Jackson simply executed them, including Hillis Hadjo, a Creek spiritual prophet who had been part of Tecumseh's movement.

The execution of Indians did not cause an uproar in the United States or Europe, but an American general executing British subjects in Spanish territory caused an international incident. Monroe and Adams, however, were skillful diplomats. They managed to both distance themselves from Jackson and use what Adams called "the Jackson Magic"—his immense popularity after his victories in the War of 1812—to bring pressure on Spain.

In fact, Spain did not care much about Florida but did have serious concerns about the independence movements in the Spanish colonies in Mexico and South America. The Spanish authorities wanted assurance that the United States would not aid or recognize these revolutions. Spain was also deeply worried about its control of the land from Texas to California. It was more than willing to trade Florida for assurances about Texas and the revolutions farther south. Monroe briefly considered making a bid for Texas, but he decided that it was more trouble than it was worth and agreed to the treaty.

Instead of pursuing a claim to Texas, Monroe and Adams decided to ask Spain for its support in the areas that Lewis and Clark had explored. Spain, Great Britain, and Russia all claimed the same territory along the Pacific coast known as Oregon. By the late 1700s, explorers from New Spain were making claims as far north as Alaska. At the same time, Russian fur traders and explorers had established permanent Russian settlements, complete with Orthodox churches, in Alaska and almost as far south as San Francisco. British sea captains, notably James Cook in the 1770s, had explored the Oregon coast. British explorers coming overland from Canada made land claims, among them the Hudson's Bay Company trading post at the mouth of the Columbia River, which represented the largest European settlement in the region. An earlier U.S. claim, based on Lewis and Clark's explorations in 1805, was weak by comparison, and there were no U.S. settlements in Oregon. Of course, the native peoples of the region had little use for any of the claims, though they traded with all the claimants. Nevertheless, the United States had an interest in Oregon. While some in Congress thought Oregon was far too distant and barren to be of interest, Adams—prompted by the merchant and fur trader John Jacob Astor—saw the value of an American presence at the mouth of the Columbia River, certainly for access to the fur trade there and, moreover, as a way to enter the Pacific trade with Asia.

8.1

8.2

8.3

8.4

8.5

Adams-Onís Treaty

An 1819 treaty between the United States and Spain that led to American acquisition of Florida and American rights in the Oregon Territory in return for a $5 million payment to Spain.

In the 1819 **Adams-Onís Treaty** with Spain, Spain not only ceded Florida to the United States but also agreed to transfer Spanish rights to the Oregon Territory to the United States. It was a significant accomplishment. The United States paid $5 million in Spanish debts, and the deal was done. All of Florida was now a U.S. territory. While the United States was negotiating with Spain, it was also negotiating with Great Britain about Oregon. In 1818, Adams negotiated the Anglo-American Convention in which Britain and the United States agreed to joint control of the Pacific Northwest for ten years and to resolve other issues in the future. The two treaties with Spain and Britain gave the United States as strong a claim to Oregon as either Britain or Russia, a claim it would not forget. Just before he ended his tenure as secretary of state, Adams agreed to an 1824 treaty with Russia that set the border of Alaska much farther north, leaving it to the United States and Britain to resolve questions about Oregon, which they finally did, though not until 1846 (see Map 8-3).

The Monroe Doctrine

Having taken Florida and asserted a claim to Oregon, the United States agreed—for the time being—to stay out of Spain's way in Texas and California. Nevertheless, the Monroe administration took further steps to consolidate U.S. power in the Americas. In 1822, despite earlier promises to Spain, the United States officially recognized the new independent states of Chile, Colombia, Mexico, and Peru. If Latin America was, in fact, going to be independent of Spain, then the United States meant to be both the region's benefactor and prime trade partner.

Map 8-3 Expanding Borders, 1817–1823.

During his term as secretary of state, John Quincy Adams negotiated a series of treaties that established the border between Maine and the Louisiana Territory and British Canada (the Rush-Bagot Treaty), gave the United States rights in the Oregon Territory and transferred Florida from Spain (the Adams-Onís Treaty), and created a joint U.S.-British ownership of Oregon (Convention of 1824). Only much later did the United States and Britain agree on the 49th parallel as the border between the United States and Canada (see Chapter 11).

Then in December 1823, President Monroe declared that, henceforth, the United States would not allow European intervention or the acquisition of any new territory by a European power in North and South America. Coming less than a decade after the United States had almost lost its independence in the War of 1812, it was a bold announcement. A complex set of international developments led Monroe and Secretary of State John Quincy Adams to formulate this stance, which became known as the **Monroe Doctrine**.

On the Pacific coast, Russian Tsar Alexander I was pressing Russian claims to Alaska and much of the Oregon Territory. In 1821, Alexander issued an imperial edict that claimed much of the Pacific coast and gave the Russian-American Company the right to trade there. The Russians threatened to confiscate American ships that traveled too far north, even though more American than Russian sailors were actually taking the sea lions and whales and trading with the Alaskan natives. Nevertheless, for the United States, Russian actions represented a dangerous European intrusion.

Halfway across the world, Greek patriots, borrowing language from the American Revolution, declared independence from the Ottoman Empire, and liberal constitutionalists briefly took power in Spain. The Greek and Spanish revolts were tricky for Monroe and Adams. Many Americans were sympathetic with the Greeks, but the administration also wanted good relationships with the Ottomans. American sentiment was on the side of a revolution in Spain, in spite of the many treaties with the Spanish government. These situations in Europe, though not the center of American concern, still had to be responded to carefully, given the strength of public opinion. Much more pressing, however, was the revolutionary activity in the Americas. Taking the wrong side in the revolutions of Latin America could hurt the United States politically and economically for a long time to come while little could be gained from interfering in Europe.

At that tense moment, British Foreign Secretary George Canning proposed a joint British-American declaration in which both nations would oppose European intervention in the Americas, including efforts to restore Spain's control, and that neither Great Britain nor the United States would have any territorial interests in the Americas. Canning's proposal was a problem for Monroe and Adams. They did not want Spain to reassert power in the Americas, and Britain's influence would be helpful in preventing it. But both the president and his secretary of state had their eyes on eventual U.S. takeover of parts of the Spanish Empire, from Texas to California and perhaps Cuba. Canning's hands-off agreement would jeopardize long-term American interests.

In the end, Monroe and Adams concluded that they would leave it to the Europeans to deal with Greece and Spain and essentially declared noninvolvement in the "internal affairs of Europe." On the other hand, they used President Monroe's December 2, 1823, message to Congress to say that any nation of the Americas that had assumed "free and independent conditions" would "henceforth not be considered as subjects of colonization by any European power." Many Europeans were amazed at what they saw as the arrogance of the new and still relatively weak United States. It was not clear that the country could enforce the new policy. But the Monroe Doctrine, which began as a simple diplomatic maneuver, became a bedrock of U.S. foreign policy. The independence of not only the United States but also all of the Americas from European control was, it seemed, this country's business. The new policy had no impact on Britain's long-standing control of Canada or Russia's dominance of Alaska or, indeed, on those colonies that Spain still claimed in Latin America. But it did announce that the United States would oppose any *new* colonies anywhere in the Americas. With the Monroe Doctrine, the U.S. government was again reflecting Jeffersonian

Monroe Doctrine

A declaration by President James Monroe in 1823 that the Western Hemisphere was to be closed off to further European colonization and that the United States would not allow European interference in the internal affairs of independent nations anywhere in the Americas.

Russian claims to Alaska dated back to the 1700s, but by the 1820s, the Russians were building up colonies, including their largest one in Sitka, Alaska. These outposts, complete with Russian Orthodox churches, fostered trade with indigenous Alaskans and provided fresh supplies for ships taking fish and sea lions off the coast.

8.1

8.2

8.3

8.4

8.5

pragmatism. It might be a small country of farmers, but the United States was claiming vast new influence in all of North and South America. It was a diplomatic move in an era of territorial and economic expansion, expansion that was unimagined when Thomas Jefferson took the oath of office in 1801.

8.5 Quick Review

How did the United States pursue its expansionist goals between 1815 and 1823?

Conclusion

When Thomas Jefferson became president of the United States in 1801, his election marked a victory for republican beliefs and his agrarian ideal—a nation of independent farmers rather than a nation run by any elites. In 1801, much of the country's population and economy was contained within the original thirteen states. Within the next twenty years, under his leadership and that of handpicked successors James Madison and James Monroe, the country's territorial claims would extend to the Pacific Ocean.

Religion played an increasing role in society, even as the last states ended their support for specific churches. Many Protestant groups made significant new gains among both white and black adherents with revivals in what came to be known as the Second Great Awakening. And Jeffersonian notions of egalitarianism permeated most aspects of American society.

The Louisiana Purchase virtually doubled the size of the United States and opened up trade along the Mississippi River and through New Orleans. Lewis and Clark led an expedition to explore the huge expanse of new U.S. territory, others explored different regions of the new lands, and diplomats pursued further territorial growth.

Tensions leading up to the War of 1812 began during Jefferson's term and came to a head under the administration of Madison. Ultimately, the inconclusive war did not change any borders but resolved issues that had limited U.S. development for decades, and launched a new period of growth for the country. Although the cost was high in terms of lives lost, money spent, and economies devastated, the end of the war left the United States more confident, proud, and self-sufficient than ever before. Subsequent treaties transferred Florida from Spain to the United States and gave the United States an important new claim to the Oregon Territory. Finally, the Monroe Doctrine limited any European claim in the Americas and announced to the world that the United States saw itself as the dominant player in all matters involving North or South America.

Chapter Review

What are the most significant differences between the United States in 1800 and the United States in 1823? Why would you argue that these differences are more important than others?

Chapter 8 Summary and Review

Jefferson and the Republican Ideal

8.1 Explain how Jefferson's republicanism shaped and reflected the nation's democratic culture.

Summary

Jefferson's style and tone reflected his commitment to republicanism. As president, he cut taxes except for the tariff, shrank the federal government, and cut the size of the army and navy. Democratic-Republican efforts to prevent the appointment of a Federalist judge led to the *Marbury v. Madison* decision, a Supreme Court ruling that established the Court's right to declare an act of Congress unconstitutional. In 1801, the occupations, opinions, and manners of most American voters were compatible with Jefferson's agrarian ideal of a nation of independent farmers. Over the course of the early 1800s, virtually all property qualifications for voting disappeared, a reflection of the national consensus that had emerged around republican ideals.

Review Questions

1. Argument Development
   Defend or refute the following statement: Thomas Jefferson, in both his policies and personal life, embodied the spirit of republicanism in the early 1800s. What evidence can you present to support your position? What evidence might support a different argument?

2. Comparison
   How did the political culture of the United States in the early decades of the 1800s differ from the political culture of the late 1700s? How would you explain these differences?

The Ideal of Religious Freedom

8.2 Explain how Americans applied new individualist ideals in their religion and how the expansion of faith-based organizations mirrored, yet also challenged, Jeffersonian republicanism.

Summary

By the early 1800s, more and more Americans were coming to the conclusion that the republican ideal required a strict separation of church and state. By 1833, state support for specific religious organizations had disappeared in the United States. Coming out of the Revolution, Americans had grown less and less religious. In the early 1800s, however, a religious revival known as the Second Great Awakening swept over the nation. The revivals of this period marked the emergence of Methodist and Baptist churches as major forces in American religious life.

African Americans, both free and enslaved, participated in the religious revival of this period by joining white congregations and by forming their own churches. While Catholics and Jews had always appreciated religious freedom in America, in the early 1800s they took on republican practices.

Review Questions

3. Argument Development
   When some historians have described the United States as being built on faith in "dynamic democracy" and "evangelical religion," what did they mean? Is this description an accurate interpretation of U.S. history in the years from 1800 to 1820?

4. Causation
   Why did African Americans, both slave and free, develop their own segregated religious institutions and gatherings over the course of the early 1800s? What needs might such churches and gatherings have met that white churches did not?

Beyond the Mississippi: The Louisiana Purchase and the Expedition of Lewis and Clark

8.3 Explain what effects the Louisiana Purchase and the westward expansion had on how various Americans saw themselves.

Summary

Economic and political concerns led Jefferson to seek the purchase of New Orleans from the French. When Napoleon offered to sell the entire Louisiana Territory, Jefferson jumped at the chance, despite his misgivings about whether or not he had constitutional authority to make the purchase. The purchase almost doubled the nation's land area. Perhaps more importantly, the United States obtained New Orleans, which meant it controlled both sides of the Mississippi River from the Great Lakes to the Gulf of Mexico. Jefferson commissioned Lewis and Clark to conduct an expedition whose mission was not only a scientific initiative but also an effort to help secure American dominance in North America. Sacagawea played a key role in the success of their Corps of Discovery. The expedition's reports opened the way for a generation of traders and explorers to head west.

Review Questions

5. Causation
   How did events in Europe and Haiti create the opportunity for the United States to acquire the Louisiana Territory?

6. Comparison

Compare and contrast race relations in New Orleans and the rest of the United States during the early 1800s. Why do you think New Orleans was so unique?

The War of 1812

8.4 Analyze the causes and impact of the War of 1812.

Summary

The tensions that had led the American people to war with Great Britain in 1775 never dissipated, and the two sides would go to war again in 1812. In spite of treaties, the United States and Great Britain were never fully at peace, especially with Britain's cultivation of Indian tribes in the West. The French Revolution and the Napoleonic Wars led to increased conflict between Britain and the United States. British naval and trade policies produced intense resentment in the United States. Efforts of the Jefferson administration to apply economic pressure on Britain failed. At the same time, new warfare between the United States and American Indian tribes broke out in the Ohio country. A new tribal alliance, supported by Britain, brought fear to white settlers and challenges to the small U.S. Army. In 1812, congressional war hawks pressured President Madison into asking Congress for a declaration of war. After three years of bloody fighting, the war ended with agreements that officially returned all matters to their prewar status, but Americans came out of the conflict with a new sense of pride and independence. As with the previous wars, the War of 1812 was a disaster for American Indians.

Review Questions

7. Causation

Trace the growing tensions between the United States and Britain from 1783 to the outbreak of war in 1812. What events were most crucial in propelling the two nations toward war?

8. Argument Development

Is it fair to describe the War of 1812 as an inconclusive war? Why or why not?

Expanding American Territory and Influence

8.5 Analyze how the United States acquired new territory and increased influence abroad.

Summary

After the War of 1812 came further territorial expansion. The era of Jefferson's successors, Presidents Madison and Monroe, was one of rapid growth that fundamentally changed the nation. In the Adams-Onís Treaty with Spain of 1819, Spain agreed to cede Florida to the United States and to also transfer Spanish rights to the Oregon Territory to the United States. In 1822, in spite of previous promises to Spain, the United States officially recognized the new independent republics of Chile, Colombia, Mexico, and Peru. In December 1823, President Monroe declared through the Monroe Doctrine that, henceforth, the United States would not tolerate European intervention in any of the affairs of the independent countries of North and South America.

Review Question

9. Argument Development

In what ways did the articulation of the Monroe Doctrine represent a turning point in American history? What light does the doctrine shed on the vision of America's future shared by the doctrine's supporters?

1. Preparing to Write: Organize Your Evidence

Long Essay Question—Evaluate the effects of republican values on American life in the period 1790 to 1823.

Create a three-column table and list specific political, social, and cultural manifestations of republicanism during this period. As you consider this question, what is bubbling up from your table? From here you can develop your thesis.

2. Preparing to Write: Plan Your Argument

Long Essay Question—Evaluate the extent continuity over time had in relations with American Indians during the period 1754–1815.

This prompt is interested in the fact that the new American government that began in 1789 might produce a change in Indian policy compared with British rule. You can discuss events as far back as the French and Indian War, and as far forward as the War of 1812. With this time frame in mind, design a time line and note what has changed on top and what has remained constant on the bottom. Use your findings to write an outline that provides a clear structure and addresses all parts of the question. From that outline, develop a thesis.

Chapter 9
New Industries, New Politics 1815–1828

This illustration, done in the early 1800s, shows the key role of slave labor in cotton production. Growing, processing, and shipping cotton was key to the economic development of the United States in the decades after the War of 1812.

Chapter Objective

Demonstrate an understanding of the changes in the U.S. economy brought about not only by the rapid expansion of cotton production but also by other commercial and financial developments, and the impact of these changes on U.S. political life.

∨ Learning Objectives

Creating the Cotton Economy

9.1 Explain the role of cotton in transforming the land and the lives of diverse people in the United States.

Commerce, Technology, and Transportation Create a Market Economy

9.2 Analyze the technological and financial changes that led to the emergence of a new market economy in the United States.

From the Era of Good Feelings to the Politics of Division

9.3 Explain the developments in the United States during the 1820s, including the shift of power toward the South and West that resulted from the changing economic and political situation.

The end of the War of 1812, Andrew Jackson's victory at New Orleans, the American takeover of Florida, and the Monroe Doctrine were all far from primary concerns of many Americans in the years after 1815. Something much closer to home—cotton—was transforming their lives. The rapid growth of cotton production changed the lives of more Americans, whether or not they were directly involved in cotton production, than any other development between 1800 and the Civil War. Cotton transformed the nation's physical, commercial, and political landscape.

Henry Bibb, a former slave, described what cotton meant to him and his fellow slaves on a Louisiana cotton plantation:

> The object of blowing the horn for them two hours before day, was, that they should get their bit to eat, before they went to the field, that they need not stop to eat but once during the day. ... I have often heard the sound of the slave driver's lash on the backs, of slaves, and their heart-rending shrieks. ... I have known the slaves to be so much fatigued from labor that they could scarcely get to their lodging places from the fields at night.

Slaves working on the new cotton plantations of the ever-expanding cotton-growing regions of the nation knew little respite from the fatiguing labor. They had to clear the land before they could plant, and once planted, the cotton plants needed almost constant care. The harvest was intensive, and much work was required afterward to prepare the harvest for market. Because of the value of the cotton crop and increasing demands for it, there was constant pressure to work harder and no end to the punishment for those who did not produce as expected.

While Bibb and thousands of other slaves cultivated the cotton, young women working in the mills, or textile factories like those in Lowell, Massachusetts, or Manchester, England, turned it into cloth to be sold around the world. An anonymous worker at one of the mills in Lowell described her life:

> Since I was between seven and eight years old, I have been employed almost without intermission in a factory, which is almost eighteen years. ... [T]he operatives were worked in the summer season, from five in the morning till seven in the evening. ... The time we are required to labor is altogether too long. It is more than our constitutions can bear. If any one doubts it, let them come into our mills of a summer's day, at four or five o'clock, in the afternoon, and see the drooping, weary persons moving about, as though their legs were hardly able to support their bodies.

North or South, for slaves in fields and workers in factories, cotton was wearying work. For some, cotton brought extraordinary wealth as "King Cotton" came to dominate the U.S. economy, but for others, drudgery permeated life. And for yet others—among them inventors, bankers, and ship captains and crews—cotton was at the center of their economic life. In one way or another, the rise and dominance of the cotton industry affected almost all Americans.

The transformation of the U.S. economy immediately after the War of 1812 involved many changes that made cotton dominant, including new inventions like cotton gins and steamboats, new institutions like corporations, and a different kind of bank—all of which worked together to expand the national economy. These changing economic and social structures also affected the political scene. The new cotton-based economy made slaves much more valuable and slave owners more anxious to defend slavery. At the same time, many northerners, including northerners in cotton industries, became more hostile to slaveholding, which led to deep national divisions.

Creating the Cotton Economy

9.1   **Explain the role of cotton in transforming the land and the lives of diverse people in the United States.**

Cotton's dominant role in the economy came about quickly. In 1800, a few southern plantations grew enough cotton to make cloth for their own use and ship a few bags to England, but the dominant plantation cash crops were rice, indigo, tobacco, and in southern

Louisiana, sugar. When an American ship entered Liverpool harbor in 1785 carrying a few bags of cotton, the cotton was confiscated. The Board of Trade in London explained that cotton "cannot be imported" from the United States, "it not being the produce of the American States." They simply could not imagine that any American state had actually produced such cotton, even when it did. And the American ship had no right to bring the cotton that came from the West Indies or the world's largest producers, India and Egypt, to England. But after 1800, cotton quickly outstripped every other American export and American cotton production outstripped all competitors. Cotton remained a major American industry until the 1930s (see Figure 9-1).

In 1790, the total U.S. cotton production was 1.5 million pounds. Ten years later, in 1800, production had grown to 36.5 million pounds, and in 1820, the number was 167.5 million tons. And it just kept growing. By 1802, the United States was the largest producer of cotton for the mills in Great Britain, a significant change in a very short time. By 1830, Britain imported 264 million pounds of cotton, 77 percent from the United States, and by 1840, 592 million pounds, 81 percent from the United States.

There were many reasons for the sudden dominance of the United States in worldwide cotton production after 1800. Certainly, cotton demand was growing from the 1790s onward, but cotton can be grown in many places. The invention of the cotton gin by Eli Whitney in the 1790s made U.S. cotton easy and cheap to produce. In addition, cotton planters in the United States had access to more and more land in the growing nation, an economic system that supported them, and perhaps most important, a virtually unlimited pool of very cheap labor because of American slavery.

Figure 9-1 Cotton Exports as a Percentage of All U.S. Exports, 1800–1860.

This graph illustrates the growing significance of cotton in the U.S. economy during the early 1800s. While all exports from the country were growing, cotton was quickly outstripping everything else, increasing from a tiny fraction in 1800 to one-third of all exports in the 1820 and to more than half by 1840.

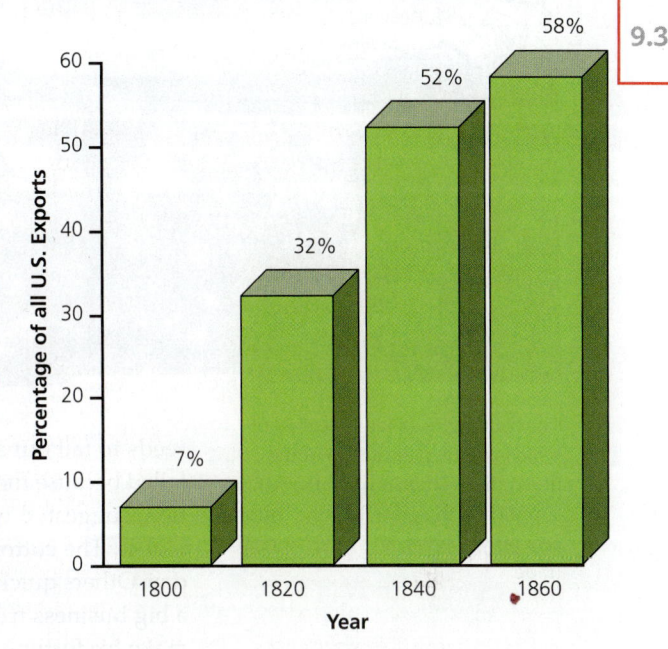

Demand and Technology

Two developments in the late 1790s set the stage for the rapid expansion of cotton production in the United States. First, during this period, many Europeans came to prefer cotton clothing to the wool or linen that had clothed them for generations. Cotton was cooler and more comfortable than wool, and it was getting cheaper. Most of Europe's cotton came from India via Great Britain's East India Company, but India could not produce enough cotton to meet Europe's growing demand.

The second development was a set of technological changes that launched the worldwide expansion of cotton. In England in 1733, John Kay invented a "flying shuttle" that made weaving cloth much faster and allowed a single weaver to handle a loom that previously required many weavers. In 1764, James Hargreaves invented the spinning jenny, which could run multiple spindles, each spinning cotton into thread. By 1800, a single jenny could be seen operating up to 120 spindles at once. In 1769, Richard Arkwright patented a "water frame" that used waterpower to drive the spinning process, a major step toward mass production, while James Watt's coal-powered steam engine, designed in 1763, added steam power to the English mills, expanding their size long before it provided the energy for railroads and ships.

Although developed in England, much of this technology was soon brought to the United States through transfers, legal or otherwise. British authorities knew that their new means of production were key to their industrial and political might. They provided patents for their inventors and kept their production process secret. However, in 1789, an Englishman, Samuel Slater, having been sworn to secrecy and apprenticed in Arkwright's textile business, sailed to New York to bring the industry to the United States. Slater ignored Arkwright's patents and re-created Arkwright's mechanical spinning in mills in Rhode Island. More technological transfers followed.

Despite the worldwide demand for cotton and England's growing industrial capacity for turning raw cotton into cloth, American farmers and plantation owners were skeptical that they could make money on it. Green-seed, or upland, cotton was the only kind that

BALING COTTON.

GINNING COTTON BY STEAM.

PICKING COTTON.

North Wind Picture Archives/Alamy Stock Photo

The cotton gin—a large version of which is shown at the top of the illustration—transformed the nation, supporting the growth of the cotton economy, slavery, and international trade.

cotton gin

Originally designed by Eli Whitney in 1793–1794, the cotton gin (*gin* is short for *engine*) allowed the inexpensive processing of cotton.

Black Belt

The cotton-growing region that was developed in the early 1800s, stretching from Georgia through Alabama, Mississippi, and Louisiana, named for its rich black soil.

would grow in the American South, except for a few places on the coast or coastal islands where a more profitable variety of long-stem cotton grew. But each ball of cotton produced on a green-seed cotton plant contained many of those green seeds. They had to be removed by hand before the cotton could be spun into threads. A slave, working hard all day, could clean about one pound of cotton, hardly enough to make a meaningful profit. Many people sought a mechanical way to clean cotton. Eli Whitney, a recent Yale graduate who had gone south to work as a tutor, lived on the Greene family plantation at Mulberry Grove in Georgia where he became interested in devising a machine to clean cotton. He gained fame, if not fortune, for his patent on the **cotton gin** (*gin* was short for *engine*).

Whitney decided to try pulling the picked cotton through a screen that would allow the seeds to fall out and the clean cotton fibers to be baled for shipment. When the first model failed because the wooden teeth were too brittle, Catherine Greene, the matron of the plantation, suggested wire (from her bird cage) and a brush to keep the seeds from clogging the works. The cotton gin that Whitney patented in 1794 could clean fifty pounds of cotton a day. Others quickly improved on Whitney's model, and manufacturing cotton gins became a big business from Natchez, Mississippi, to Bridgewater, Massachusetts. Whitney did not make his fortune from this invention; too many other people were improving it too quickly for him to maintain his original patent. However, he did become rich developing the idea of interchangeable parts and manufacturing rifles with such parts for the U.S. government. Interchangeable parts made everything from rifles to farm implements easier to repair since a replacement part could be counted on to work in the original gun or machine. Whitney did not invent the idea, but as the United States prepared for a possible war with France in the late 1790s, he won a government contract to manufacture ten thousand muskets and his Connecticut factory prospered for the rest of his life. Whitney's invention of the cotton gin transformed the nation. The United States now had an export crop that could make it prosperous. The cotton market led to the rapid development of new lands, especially the great plantations of Alabama, Mississippi, and Louisiana. In turn, the New England factory system that began in Rhode Island expanded to the great mill center of Lowell, Massachusetts, in 1823 and then to factories and factory towns all over the region. As the cotton market continued to grow, coastal and transatlantic shipping also expanded as more and more southern cotton was brought to the mills of New England and to the even larger mills of Manchester and Birmingham in England. New forms of banking and doing business were developed to serve the rapidly expanding market. And African slavery, which many had seen as a dying institution at the end of the Revolution, suddenly became both essential and wildly valuable to those who claimed ownership of other humans. This rather plain and simple product was a driving force for economics, technology, and politics in the period, and it seemed to have no limits.

The Land of Cotton

While some of the nation's first export cotton was grown along the Atlantic coast and especially on the Sea Islands off the coast of the Carolinas and Georgia, the greatest cotton production was on the plantations of the so-called **Black Belt** (named for its rich black soil), stretching from Georgia to Louisiana. The quality of the soil made it perfect for growing cotton.

Within this Black Belt area, only Georgia was one of the thirteen original states. The northern parts of Alabama and Mississippi were part of the land Britain ceded to the United

States at the end of the Revolution. The Louisiana Purchase added Louisiana. Andrew Jackson's defeat of the Creeks during the War of 1812 and the "Creek Cession" that he negotiated in 1816 opened much new land to white settlement, while the 1819 U.S. treaty with Spain placed the Gulf Coast of Mississippi and Alabama under U.S. control. Finally, in the 1820s and 1830s, Andrew Jackson, by then living in the White House, forced the Cherokees, Chickasaws, Choctaws, and Creeks off of their ancestral lands in Georgia, Alabama, and Mississippi, opening the land to white settlement and to cotton production (see Chapter 10).

White settlers—often single men, sometimes families—from Georgia, Tennessee, the Carolinas, and Europe, especially many Scots-Irish, poured in. They brought black slaves with them or acquired them through the rapidly growing overland slave trade of the early 1800s. A land rush that was known as "Alabama Fever" began in 1816 just as the War of 1812 ended. Alabama was admitted as a state in 1819 with a non-Indian population of 128,000, five times what it had been in 1810. Louisiana and Mississippi had been admitted in 1812 and 1817, respectively, and grew rapidly. More and more white planters and black slaves moved farther and farther west.

The federal government played a central role in the development of these lands. The first European settlers were illegal white squatters moving onto farms recently abandoned by Indians, but after the coming of peace in 1815, the federal government quickly began official surveys and legal sales of the land. Before the War of 1812, the largest sales of federal lands in one year had been 350,000 acres. In 1815, a million acres of newly acquired lands were sold at $2 per acre, and in 1818, 2.5 million acres were sold as the government acquired land from the Creeks and then from Spain and quickly made it available for sale. These sales helped the federal budget, and white settlement surged. The government spent some of the revenue from land sales on maintaining the army that protected the new lands. It also aided settlement by building a road from Columbia, South Carolina, to Columbus, Georgia, and then farther into the Black Belt region (see Map 9-1).

Map 9-1 The Expanding Cotton Belt.

The areas of greatest cotton production in the United States grew dramatically between 1807 and 1860 as cotton planters and the slaves who did the actual cotton production work moved into the area stretching from Georgia to Louisiana and into Texas.

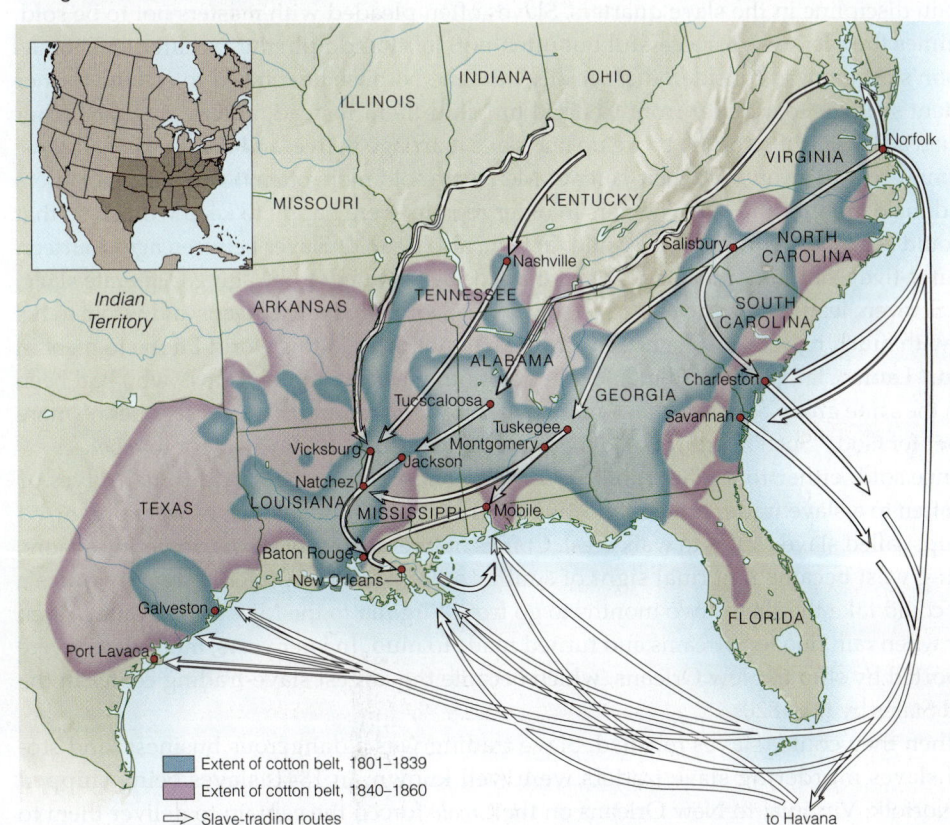

Legend:
- Extent of cotton belt, 1801–1839
- Extent of cotton belt, 1840–1860
- ⇨ Slave-trading routes

The new land was fertile. Planters who had grown three hundred pounds of cotton per acre in South Carolina could grow eight hundred to one thousand pounds an acre in the Black Belt. In 1801, 9 percent of the world's cotton came from the United States while 60 percent came from India. By 1820, the United States was exporting more cotton than India. By 1850, the American South was producing more than two-thirds of the world's cotton. The new technology, the new land, and the institution of slavery created great wealth for some; a poor, hard-earned living for others; and backbreaking, torturous misery for slaves.

The People Who Worked the Land—Cotton and the Transformation of Slavery

The white settlers who were able to buy large parcels of land in the rich new territory of what was known as the Old Southwest did not do most of the hard work of actually planting, hoeing, and picking the cotton that would be grown there. Other Americans did that work: African slaves, whose lives were transformed by the explosive growth of cotton production and whose value to their white owners increased even more than the value of the new land on which they labored.

Between 1800 and 1860, more than one million black Americans were forced to move from the homes they knew—and often from their families, too—to new homes in the interior cotton-growing lands of Georgia, Alabama, Mississippi, and Louisiana and later Arkansas and Texas. While slavery slowly disappeared in the North after 1800 and the slave population of Maryland, Virginia, and the Carolinas stabilized or declined, slavery exploded in the new land. In the sixty years before the Civil War, more slaves made the journey from coastal states to inland plantations than had made the terrible Middle Passage from Africa to North America in the previous two hundred years.

In some ways similar to the passage from Africa to North America, the journey from a settled community in Virginia, Maryland, or the Carolinas to the new interior plantations was a terrible ordeal. As more slaves were sold into the interior or sold from place to place within it, slaves on the coast lived in terror of being sold and losing all connections to family and birthplace. Slave owners used the threat of sale, or the sale of a perceived troublemaker, to maintain discipline in the slave quarters. Slaves often pleaded with masters not to be sold. Sometimes the pleas were successful but often not. Jeff Randolph, the executor of Thomas Jefferson's estate, was considered especially humane because he refused to sell the former president's slaves to a buyer from Georgia but sold them instead, at less profit, to other Virginians. The sale of a spouse broke up one slave marriage in five, and one-third of all slave children were sold away from their parents. Men were sold more often than women; planters wanted male muscle, and slave owners in older regions were happy to keep women so that they could bear more children who could, in turn, also be sold. Slaves between ages fourteen and thirty-five were sold much more often than the very young or the aging. A literate slave, Arena Screven, learned that he was to be sold from Georgia to New Orleans and wrote to his wife "with much regret" that he hoped "if we shall not meet in this world I hope to meet in heaven." Laura Clark, a slave, remembered her mother asking another slave, who had been sold in the same group as she, to "take care of my baby child ... and if I never sees her no more raise her for God." Such heartbreak led many slaves to despair, to run away, or to rebel.

Once sold, either to a plantation owner who had come east for additional slaves or more often to a slave trader whose job was brokering other humans, slaves were organized in groups called slave coffles to walk west. Coffles of twenty to fifty slaves, sometimes more, trudging west became a normal sight of southern life. Walking fifteen to twenty miles a day, it could take the slaves two months to go from Virginia to the Mississippi Valley, often longer when rain flooded streams and turned roads to mud. In later years, more slaves were transported by ship to New Orleans, which became the largest slave-trading center in the United States by the 1820s.

When they could, slaves rebelled. Slave trading was a dangerous business, and stories of slaves murdering slave traders were well known. In 1841, slaves being shipped from Norfolk, Virginia, to New Orleans on the *Creole* forced the captain to deliver them to the Bahamas, a British colony, where they found freedom because Britain had abolished slavery in 1833. More often, slaves simply ran away when they could, though many went home to family where they were recaptured and sold again.

Once slaves arrived at their destination, they often faced difficult and unfamiliar work. Work in cotton fields was back-breaking for men, women, and children. While tobacco and rice required more skill, cotton required long hours and hard work. Cotton was planted in the early spring and required constant attention and weeding throughout the grow-ing season. On most plantations, there was a strict gender divide: men plowed, and women and children hoed. Harvest began as early as August and lasted through September and October. Slaves worked the longest hours—from sunrise to sunset, and if there was a moon, much longer—to get the whole crop in before storms could hurt it. Prickly cotton pods cut their hands, and slaves who did not produce their quota were beaten at day's end. Finally, with the full crop in, there was a brief respite. But the winter was the time for the women to work the cotton gin and pack the cotton for market while men cleared more land and repaired buildings.

As this picture illustrates, slaves spent long hours in the fields surrounded by the cotton they were expected to cultivate and pick with no reward for their backbreaking labor.

Contrary to many images of the old South, most cot-ton was grown on relatively small farms. Many of those who first settled and began growing cotton on the new rich lands owned relatively small plots of land and one or a few slaves. These white owners worked in the fields with the slaves or, if the farm was larger, served as their overseers. Less than 1 percent of the pop-ulation owned the great plantations for which the South became known. In the largest plantations owned by the most wealthy planters, slaves worked in large gangs with certain slaves appointed as "drivers" to get the work done and poor whites employed as overseers to manage the whole labor force. It was on the large plantations, with constant pressure on the overseers to ensure profits, that slaves faced some of the worst conditions.

While the wealthy owners of large plantations were always a minority of the cotton producers, they set much of the cultural and political tone of the cotton-producing states. They created their own distinctive way of life and built grand mansions in a distinctive neo-classical style that was meant to showcase their newfound wealth.

Slaves established new communities within the slave quarters. Young slaves met new partners, children were born, and the rhythms of community life were reestablished, but always under threat of dissolution. New leaders emerged within the slave community, often preachers and deacons selected by other slaves. Although legally banned from learning to read or write, slaves sometime secretly did both and taught others to do so. As memories of Africa or the African American communities on the East Coast faded in later generations, a new culture was created in the slave communities, drawing on older traditions and adapt-ing to new contexts. Often with the permission of their owners, slaves grew their own food, made cloth for better clothing than their owners gave them, and even earned cash by selling surplus food and clothing to the free people in surrounding communities or to their own masters. While owners saw slaves exclusively as a source of muscle and work, many slaves and ex-slaves made it clear through their stories that for them family, community, faith, and the hope for freedom were the highest priority. Studies of the advertisements for runaway slaves also made it clear that slaves never stopped running away, no matter how far they might have to run. Similarly, small- and large-scale slave revolts never stopped.

Cotton in the North—Factories and the People Who Worked in Them

The technology that made cotton the core of the Industrial Revolution in the United States developed in England and North America during the 1700s. Just before the War of 1812,

9.1

9.2

9.3

American Voices

Charles Ball, *Fifty Years in Chains; or, The Life of an American Slave*, 1810–1860

Charles Ball was born a slave on a tobacco plantation in Maryland. He was sold to a slave trader and taken to Georgia. He never saw his home or family again. Half a century later, he escaped. His autobiography was popular among those who supported the end of slavery.

My master kept a store at a small village on the bank of the Patuxent River. … Whilst I was eating in the kitchen, I observed him talking earnestly, but low, to a stranger near the kitchen door. I soon after went out, and hitched my oxen to the cart, and was about to drive off, when several men came round about me, and amongst them the stranger whom I had seen speaking with my master. This man came up to me, and, seizing me by the collar, shook me violently, saying I was his property, and must go with him to Georgia. At the sound of these words, the thoughts of my wife and children rushed across my mind, and my heart beat away within me. I saw and knew that my case was hopeless, and that resistance was vain, as there were near twenty persons present, all of whom were ready to assist the man by whom I was kidnapped. I felt incapable of weeping or speaking, and in my despair I laughed loudly. My purchaser ordered me to cross my hands behind, which were quickly bound with a strong cord; and he then told me that we must set out that very day for the South. I asked if I could not be allowed to go see my wife and children, or if this could not be permitted, if they might have leave to come to see me; but was told that I would be able to get another wife in Georgia.

My new master, whose name I did not hear, took me that same day across the Patuxent, where I joined fifty-one other slaves. … A strong iron collar was closely fitted by means of a padlock round each of our necks. A chain of iron, about a hundred feet in length, was passed through the hasp of each padlock, except at the two ends, where the hasps of the padlock passed through a link of the chain. …

Our master ordered a pot of mush to be made for our supper; after dispatching which all lay down on the naked floor to sleep in our handcuffs and chains. The women, my fellow-slaves, lay on one side of the room; and the men who were chained with me, occupied the other. I slept but little this night, which I passed in thinking of my wife and little children whom I could not hope ever to see again. I also thought of my grandfather, and of the long nights I had passed with him, listening to his narratives of the scenes through which he had passed in Africa.

Source: Charles Ball, *Fifty Years in Chains; or, The Life of An American Slave* (New York: H. Dayton, 1860), pp. 28–31, 240–241, 280.

Thinking Critically

1. **Continuity and Change over Time**
   How does Ball's reflection on his fate and his grandfather's stories help us understand continuity and change in the experience of different generations of enslaved Americans?

2. **Analyzing Primary Sources**
   How does Ball's point of view as a former slave inform his understanding of the cotton economy that developed in this era?

Francis Cabot Lowell, an American who had spent two years working in and observing the British mills in Manchester, brought the technology he learned there to the United States. When he left Britain, customs agents searched his baggage to be sure he was not bringing with him drawings or plans from the British mills, which were a closely guarded national secret. But Lowell had been memorizing the plans. Like Slater, who had transferred British secrets about mechanical spinning to Rhode Island mills in 1789, Lowell was ready to build a British-style mill in Massachusetts. Lowell also brought with him a second, equally important idea—the multishareholder corporation that could raise more money than any one individual could provide and could offer less risk to investors.

In 1813, Lowell incorporated a new business with Patrick T. Jackson and Nathan Appleton: the Boston Manufacturing Company. Lowell and his mechanic, Paul Moody, re-created a British-style power loom in Massachusetts. With these steps, they established what would be the heart of American manufacturing for the next century: the multiowner corporation that produced cotton fabric in a large factory.

The partners built their first factory, or mill, at Waltham, Massachusetts, on the Charles River. After Lowell's death in 1817, they then created a new city in 1823: Lowell, Massachusetts, that housed an even larger complex, using the thirty-foot drop of the Merrimack River to power mills that could turn cotton into cloth for a domestic and international market at an astounding rate (Map 9-2). Similar large operations sprang up on New Hampshire rivers in Manchester, Dover, and Nashua and on other Massachusetts rivers in Chicopee, Holyoke, and Lawrence. Where Samuel Slater's mills in Rhode Island had been rather small, family affairs, the factories and towns that Lowell and his colleagues built

Map 9-2 Lowell, Massachusetts, in 1832.

The water-powered mills of the new company town of Lowell, Massachusetts, had to be very close to the rivers that surrounded the town, but the company also built boardinghouses for the workers in close proximity to the mills, making the trip to work and the supervision of the workers quite easy.

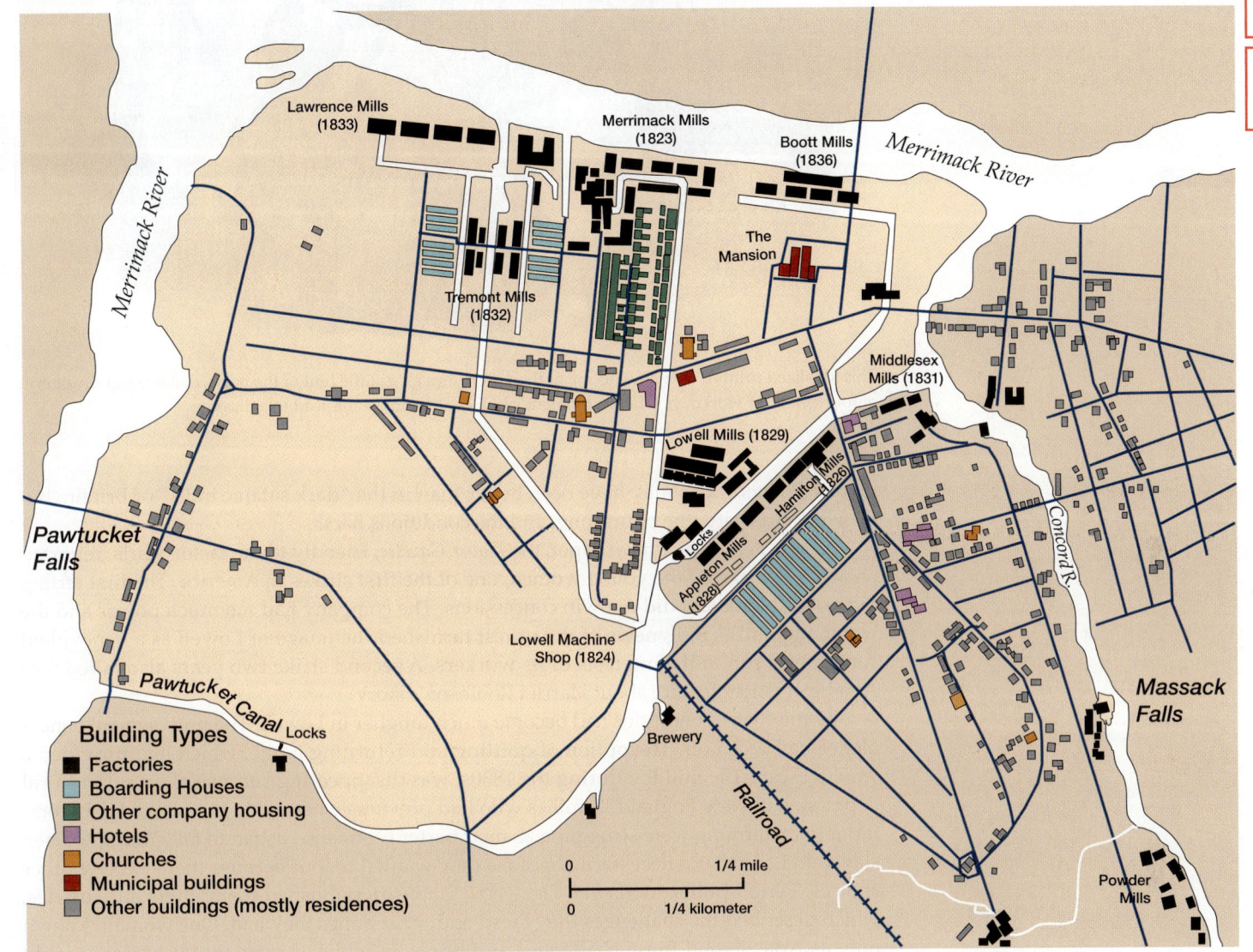

transformed the industry and the lives of the people involved in it. With the creation of Lowell as a new industrial city, the American Industrial Revolution was born.

The Boston Associates needed workers for their giant looms and mills. They turned first to young women from the farms where most New Englanders still lived. More men than women had been heading west for decades, and New England had a surplus of young women. Farm life was hard, young women were kept in subservient positions, and the independence and the potential to earn their own money appealed to many young women. To avoid the squalid conditions of the English factories, Lowell and his colleagues built clean, company boardinghouses for their female employees, complete with chaperones and opportunities for religious and educational activities. For the most part, they hired only single young women whose living conditions (and virtue) they could control.

The young women who worked in Lowell's mills in the early 1800s were known as "factory girls." Lowell was a show town, and its owners published the *Lowell Offering* to tell the world about the success of the venture and the good life the women who worked there enjoyed. But life at Lowell and the other mill towns was less rosy than the *Lowell Offering*

North Wind Picture Archives/Alamy Stock Photo

This idealized print of women working at their machines gives little hint of the noise, danger, and drudgery of fourteen-hour workdays where a moment's lack of attention could lead to a disaster.

reported. Conditions may have been better than in the "dark satanic mills" of Britain, but the work was hard, the hours long, and the conditions harsh.

A New Hampshire newspaper, the *Dover Gazette*, friendly to the factory girls, reported on an 1834 strike by the young women, one of the first strikes in America. The first strikes did not last long and did not win concessions. The company had too much power and the women too little. Still, news of the unrest tarnished the image of Lowell as a benevolent community run in the interests of its workers. A second strike two years also failed (see American Voices feature about Harriet Robinson's story).

By the 1840s, conditions had become much tougher in Lowell. The mill owners' benevolence had worn off. The option of quitting and returning home, which had provided a way to escape the mill life during the 1830s, was disappearing because of an agricultural depression in New England. Families who had previously been able to manage fairly comfortably by farming were struggling as their barter economies began to fail. Young women stayed in Lowell, not necessarily because they wanted to, but because they had few other choices. Period publications like *The Voice of Industry* published their letters and articles, which described the challenges they faced and what hopes they had. One woman, known only as Ada, shared these challenges and hopes in biblical terms that her peers would appreciate:

> "Do unto others, as ye would that they should do to you," is a great precept, given to us by our great Teacher. … What but the neglect of this great principle, has brought into the world all this confusion, this disorder, this isolated state of interest, between man and man; all this monopoly and competition in business?

As the Industrial Revolution expanded, Ada would not be the last one to ask that question.

New York and the International Cotton Trade

As significant as the mills of New England were in cotton production, most American cotton was shipped in its raw state to Manchester and Leeds in England. The permanent peace that had been established between the United States and Great Britain after the end of the War of 1812 made this trade easy. New York City became the center of the shipment of cotton across the Atlantic and, in the process, became the nation's largest city and commercial center, a position it has retained ever since.

New York City enjoyed several advantages that allowed it to play a dominant role in the nation's cotton economy, even though no cotton was grown within hundreds of miles

American Voices

Harriet H. Robinson

Harriet H. Robinson worked in the cotton mills at Lowell from 1835, when she was ten years old, to 1848. Her story, published half a century later, remains a classic story of what life was like for young women who took these jobs.

The working-hours of all the girls extended from five o'clock in the morning until seven in the evening, with one-half hour for breakfast and for dinner. …

One of the first strikes of cotton-factory operatives that ever took place in this country was that in Lowell, in October, 1836. When it was announced that the wages were to be cut down, great indignation was felt, and it was decided to strike, *en mass*. This was done. The mills were shut down, and the girls went in procession … and listened to "incendiary" speeches from early labor reformers.

When the day came on which the girls were to turn out, those in the upper rooms started first, and so many of them left that our mill was at once shut down. Then, when the girls in my room stood irresolute, uncertain what to do, asking each other, "Would you?" or "shall we turn out?" and not one of them having the courage to lead off, I, who began to think they would not go out, after all their talk, became impatient, and started on ahead, saying, with childish bravado, "I don't care what you do, I am going to turn out, whether anyone else does or not;" and I marched out, and was followed by the others.

As I looked back at the long line that followed me, I was more proud than I have ever been since at any success I may have achieved, and more proud than I shall ever be again until my own beloved State gives to its women citizens the right of suffrage.

Source: Harriet H. Robinson, *Loom and Spindle: Or Life among the Early Mill Girls* (Boston: T.Y. Crowell, 1898), pp. 31, 83–85.

Thinking Critically

1. **Analyzing Primary Sources**
   How did Robinson explain the factors that led to her decision to join the strike at her mill? How was her historical situation reflected in these factors?

2. **Contextualization**
   How did work in a textile factory change Robinson's outlook?

---

of the city. First, New York had an extraordinary deep-water harbor. Ships could dock directly in Manhattan and Brooklyn without needing to anchor offshore and unload goods to smaller boats. The port was also easily accessible by coastal vessels from southern ports. As the production of cotton expanded after 1815, most of the South's cotton was shipped north to New York and then reshipped either across the Atlantic to English ports or up Long Island Sound to Boston for the New England mills. Second, New York already had the infrastructure necessary to accommodate this level of shipping, including miles of docks and a community of merchants. Third, as an established port already, New York had experienced dockworkers and longshoremen (who handled cargo) to handle the hundreds of ships that did business there. The already large numbers of workers grew rapidly as New York (not counting Brooklyn, which was a separate city until 1898) grew six times its size between the American Revolution and 1820. In 1820, it mushroomed again from 125,000 residents, and to over 500,000 in 1850.

New York businesses sent agents (called "factors") to Charleston, South Carolina; Savannah, Georgia; Mobile, Alabama; and New Orleans to buy cotton for shipment to New York. In turn, the cotton was transferred from coastal ships to larger transatlantic ships that sailed to ports in England, racing each other to make the trip in the shortest amount of time.

On the return trip from England, these ships brought cash from the sale of cotton and all sorts of British and European goods—iron and steel tools from Sheffield, England, wine from France, and manufactured goods that the United States needed and that could often be bought in New York for less than it cost to make them elsewhere in America. While American manufacturers disliked this reality, merchants from across the country flocked to New York to stock up on cheap goods, enhancing the city's commerce..

In 1818, shipping across the Atlantic was improved when a Quaker businessman, Jeremiah Thompson, founded the Black Ball Line and established a fixed schedule of weekly departures of fast ships from New York to Liverpool, England. The Black Ball Line announced that it had "undertaken to establish a line of vessels between NEW YORK and LIVERPOOL, to sail from each place on a certain day in every month through the year," and printed the schedule. Until that time, commercial vessels waited to fill their holds with cargo, however long that took, before sailing. Now with the fixed schedule, passengers and goods could be sure of leaving on time, and factories in England could be sure of a steady flow of cotton to keep their mills operating.

The new ships were called packet ships because the line had a contract with the federal government to carry packets of U.S. mail. These packet ships became a regular feature of world commerce and New York's waterfront. Any packet ship captain who made the trip to Liverpool in under twenty-two days or the return trip to New York (which took longer because of less favorable winds) in under thirty-five days would be rewarded with a new coat and a dress for his wife, courtesy of Thompson. Competition with the Black Ball Line soon developed, and the passenger cabins became elegant as different lines competed for business. Shipwrights along New York's East River changed the construction of new ships so they could make the voyage even more quickly than the original schedule. But most important, the Black Ball Line's ships and its many competitors in the 1820s and 1830s ensured a steady supply of cotton for English mills and steady demand and profits to U.S. cotton growers. Jeremiah Thompson of the Black Ball Line made his fortune transporting slave-grown cotton, though as a Quaker, he opposed slavery itself.

New York was also the place in the United States to raise money, and the cotton economy required money and credit. From the time Alexander Hamilton established the first Bank of the United States in New York City in 1791, some New Yorkers grew rich financing commercial activities that were far away from the city itself. Many farmers had long needed to borrow money for seed and fertilizer to plant a crop. New corporations needed loans to build the factories for producing the cotton cloth. Without such financing, the Industrial Revolution would never have happened. Financial brokers had agreed to work together in New York in 1792, and the New York Stock Exchange was founded in 1817, to support this large-scale commerce by allowing investors to pool funds and create new industries as well as commercial enterprises that were larger than any one person, even a rich one, could fund alone.

New York was also home to many banks, investment houses, and insurance companies that helped finance the cotton industry. Nautilus Insurance Company wrote over three hundred life insurance policies on slaves, which protected the investments of plantation owners even if those policies did nothing for the slaves themselves. The investment house that became Brown Brothers, Harriman loaned millions of dollars to southern

The Five Points, Junction of Baxter, Worth and Park Streets, New York (hand-coloured engraving), Catlin, George (1796-1872) (after)/Museum of the City of New York, USA/Bridgeman Images

With the development of the trans-Atlantic cotton trade and the opening of the Erie Canal, New York City grew rapidly in its commercial success. However, especially in hard times, the city was also plagued with areas of squalid poverty. Many New Yorkers lived in the most difficult conditions, especially in the notorious crime-filled Five Points neighborhood of Lower Manhattan.

growers to finance the planting and shipping of cotton as well as the buying of slaves. At one point, the company owned three plantations and 346 slaves in Louisiana when owners defaulted on their loans. In general, however, New York financiers made their profits in trade and commerce and kept their distance from the institution of slavery and the risks of cotton growing.

The Panic of 1819

The economic boom that cotton produced was not a steady one. As more Americans invested in land or slaves to grow cotton or in the commercial activities that flowed from cotton, optimism led to overproduction and financial overextension. Suddenly in 1819, the growth came to a screeching if temporary halt. After four years of peace, Europe was growing more food, and a good harvest in 1818 meant less need for imported American grain. In addition, more raw cotton was being delivered to Liverpool than the mills could process, and new mills took time to build. The value of cotton fell from 32.5 cents a pound in October 1818 to 24 cents a pound in December. By early 1819, it was only 14 cents a pound. At that price, it was not profitable to grow cotton, to invest in land to plant more cotton, or to ship cotton either to New York or to Europe.

Unfortunately, the Bank of the United States decided to protect itself by limiting credit and calling in loans. State banks followed suit, and investors and farmers could not pay their debts. Small businesses failed, farms were foreclosed, and people across the country lost their jobs. Migration west came to a halt, at least for the time being, and the business cycle slowed dangerously. At the time, no one knew when or indeed if prosperity would return. A national economy was a new thing in the United States, and it was not well understood. In earlier eras, what happened to New England shipping had little impact farther south, and a crisis in southern tobacco never had much impact farther north. Farmers who lived by barter did not worry greatly about the outside world. By 1819, however, most Americans were living in a cash economy and the nation's economy was interconnected as never before. As a result, a widespread depression affected most Americans. The boom-and-bust cycle of this young industrial economy was new, and people were shocked and frightened. Eventually, the economy and the country recovered, but it took years and much hardship. The price of cotton and the value of the cotton industry eventually rebounded and grew beyond anything imagined before the panic, but the Panic of 1819 tempered the optimism of the next generation.

9.1 Quick Review

Why did cotton come to be known as King Cotton in the early 1800s?

Commerce, Technology, and Transportation Create a Market Economy

9.2 Analyze the technological and financial changes that led to the emergence of a new market economy in the United States.

While cotton was the prime factor in the growth of the U.S. economy after 1815, it was not the only one. North American wheat and corn had been feeding Britain and continental Europe long before North American cotton began to clothe them. Trees from North American forests provided wood for ships and buildings on both sides of the Atlantic. North American furs remained in demand as they had been before the American Revolution. And as more Americans moved farther into the interior, improvements in internal transportation became essential for the country's commercial development.

9.1

9.2

9.3

The Erie Canal

The Hudson River offered easy north-south connections between New Yorkers in Manhattan and Brooklyn and farmers along the river valley up to Albany and beyond, but the heartland of New York State, far to the west of the Hudson, was isolated. The Mohawk River had never been navigable, and rural roads were in terrible shape. The treaties with the Iroquois after the American Revolution opened up tens of thousands of acres, many of them rich lands that white farmers could settle, but these farmers faced terrible isolation and difficulty in selling their crops. Beginning in the 1790s, many New Yorkers wanted a way to ease transport across the state, but no easy approach seemed possible. Indeed, Americans throughout the rest of the growing country had similar needs—and a similar lack of know-how.

After Congress refused to fund a canal linking rural upstate New York with the Hudson Valley, former New York City mayor DeWitt Clinton ran for governor in 1816 with a promise to build a canal using state funds. The canal that Clinton proposed avoided the hard-to-navigate Mohawk River and Lake Ontario (using the lake would have lowered construction costs but risked diverting trade to Canada). Instead, he proposed a canal that would follow an old Mohawk Indian trading route (the governor knew his New York history) and run from the Hudson Valley directly to Buffalo on Lake Erie. Such a canal would give farmers along its route a link to markets and would connect all of New York State to the growing Ohio region and eventually to the Mississippi River. It would make New York City the commercial capital of the nation.

The plan called for an unimaginable engineering feat. Thomas Jefferson called it "madness." The canal needed a series of locks to raise and lower water to accommodate changes in elevation of 565 feet. The United States had few engineers, and no one really knew how to build such locks. The longest canal in the country at that time was only twenty-six miles, less than one-tenth of the projected plan. None of those problems discouraged Clinton or the canal's backers. When the anti-Clinton faction, led by Martin Van Buren, realized how much enthusiasm there was for the canal, they ended their opposition, and the project quickly moved through the state legislature.

At dawn on July 4, 1817, a gala ground-breaking celebration was held at Rome, New York, when the symbolic first shovel of dirt was dug to build the **Erie Canal** that would extend 363 miles between Albany and Buffalo and contain a total of eighty-three locks. Clinton was a wily politician. He made sure that many different contractors got a piece of

Erie Canal

Completed in 1825, the canal linked the Hudson River with the Great Lakes and gave farmers all along its route new ways to be part of a global economic system of trade.

The Erie Canal crossed rural New York State, connecting villages all along the way. Travelers needed to keep their heads down when traveling under bridges and wait as locks raised and lowered boats, but the canal boats provided transport at a speed unimagined before it was built.

the action digging the canal. He built political support by ensuring that up to three-quarters of the nine thousand men who did the actual digging were Dutch or English farmers and laborers from New York State and future Clinton voters. As soon as the section near Rome was completed, Clinton used the revenue it generated to cover the interest on the $7 million in bonds that had been floated to pay for the canal, reducing the cost to taxpayers.

Clinton found contractors willing to experiment with new approaches to construction. In one section, near the town of Lockport, locks needed to be constructed to raise and lower the boats over changing elevations. Contractors used gunpowder to blast out the rock, and horses hauled away the debris. By 1825, the canal, four feet deep and forty feet wide, was completed. Governor Clinton traveled from Buffalo across the state on the canal and then down the Hudson to mark the official opening by pouring water from Lake Erie into New York Harbor.

Many admired the engineering of the canal and many more enjoyed its economic impact. Goods and exports that had cost $100 a ton to ship from Lake Erie to New York City before the canal now shipped for $9, or even $3, a ton. Farmers in distant upstate New York and in Ohio could get their wheat to international markets through New York Harbor. Formerly isolated farm families could now send letters and even visit friends and relatives. They could also import goods that had earlier been unimaginable luxuries because they had been too heavy or perishable to transport. A newspaper in Batavia, New York, celebrated the arrival of "Oysters! Beautiful Oysters," from Long Island to a town where fresh seafood had never been available. Farmers and small-town residents now could not only eat seafood but also buy a clock for their wall, a mattress for their bed, or curtains for their home at a fraction of the price these goods had cost before the canal opened. By the 1830s, the Erie Canal carried more than twice the freight of the Mississippi River, and Rochester, Syracuse, and Buffalo boomed. Where cotton had made New York City the nation's commercial center, foodstuffs and other products from upstate New York and even western Pennsylvania and Ohio now cemented the city's role as the place where the nation's trade, commerce, and finance met. Other shorter canals were built in many other parts of the country, but none had the commercial impact of the Erie Canal.

Steamboats, Roads, Travel, and News

Erie Canal boats were pulled by horses walking along the bank. The packet ships that crossed the Atlantic were powered by sail as ships had been for thousands of years. But the invention of the steamboat revolutionized water transportation. In 1807, Robert Fulton built the first commercially successful steamboat, the *Clermont*, which significantly cut the travel time from New York to Albany. Within two decades, New York Harbor and adjacent areas had become a hive of steamboat activity for both freight and passengers, and many steamboat lines competed for the trade, none more successfully than the line Cornelius Vanderbilt owned.

Steamboats also transformed trade on the Mississippi River. In the early 1800s, farmers floated down the river on large riverboats with their goods and then sold the boats for lumber when they reached their destination and rode horses or walked home—often after some time spent enjoying the pleasures of New Orleans. Steamboats, however, could travel up the river against the current. In 1817, a steamer went from New Orleans to Louisville, Kentucky, in twenty-five days, an unheard-of speed. In less than a decade, the travel time had been cut to eight days as faster boats competed for the Mississippi River business and became a colorful part of America in the 1800s (see Map 9-3, p. 264).

Water transport was the fastest and easiest way to travel through and around the United States, but roads were also important. In 1802, Congress authorized the use of funds from the sale of government lands in Ohio to build a gravel road to the interior of the country. Beginning in 1811, at Cumberland, Maryland, the National Road was built across the Appalachian Mountains. When it reached its original terminus at Wheeling, Virginia (after the Civil War, West Virginia), in 1818, it not only had crossed the mountains but also had linked the Potomac River with the Ohio River, which flowed into the Mississippi, and from there to the Gulf of Mexico. Later, slowly, the National Road was extended across

9.1

9.2

9.3

9.1

9.2

9.3

Map 9-3 Canals and Roads in the United States.

Although the Erie Canal was without question the most important canal in the nation, a huge network of canals, dirt and gravel roads, and later, railroads connected inland areas to ocean ports and world markets.

Ohio, Indiana, and Illinois, connecting to the Mississippi River itself. While many, such as Jefferson's Secretary of the Treasury Albert Gallatin, argued for more federally financed construction, Presidents Jefferson, Madison, and Monroe—all three advocates of a small federal government—doubted whether the national government could finance such undertakings without an amendment to the Constitution. Those three were also Virginians, and Virginia, with a long coastline, benefited more from coastal shipping than from canals or roads. On occasion, they put their doubts aside and signed bills providing federal funding for specific projects, but none of those who lived in the White House between 1801 and 1825 were enthusiastic about federal support for a transportation infrastructure for the nation.

States built their own roads, like the Lancaster Turnpike across Pennsylvania, but travel by road was slow and expensive throughout the 1820s and 1830s. A stagecoach could travel six to eight miles an hour on a good road—eleven on the best road between New York and Philadelphia. Wagons could haul goods as far as the next river or canal. Tollbooths collected fees to pay for the roads, but on a poor road in the wilderness, it was easy to detour around the tollbooth. Until railroads arrived in the 1840s, proximity to a canal, river, or the Atlantic and Gulf coasts was essential for productive commerce in goods and services. People who lived near land or water routes for transport were able to get their goods to market, receive newspapers, and stay connected to an increasingly national economy and culture. Those who lived farther away from such transportation lived isolated lives—all the more isolated as others became more connected.

MARY POWELL.

Captain Anderson

DAILY LINE.—NEW YORK AND KINGSTON.

Steamships made for easy and fast travel up the Hudson River and along other rivers around the nation, but they were limited to water transport. Stagecoaches, which were much slower, were essential for travel over the country's poorly constructed roads until they were replaced on many routes by railroads.

With increased speed in travel, news also moved more quickly (see Table 9-1, p. 266). Packet ships from Liverpool brought European news, and as the ships cut trans-Atlantic travel time from fifty days in 1816 to forty-two days in the 1820s, that news traveled faster. Within the United States, by 1817, a man on a horse could bring news from New York to Philadelphia or Boston in two days. A steamboat traveling through Long Island Sound could also bring the news to coastal cities in Connecticut and to Boston in about the same amount of time. For southern coastal cities, the travel time was slower, and for inland towns, much slower. Newspapers sprang up across the country, and the federal government developed an extensive post office system (since the Constitution clearly sanctioned the post office and post roads) that helped Americans connect for personal and business matters. The packet ships, stagecoaches, and canal boats also depended on contracts with the federal post office to make their routes profitable. Commercial leaders and traders on the New York Stock Exchange were anxious to have the latest news, especially about crops, but also about European and American demand for goods. They supported the post office and newspapers as essential for the growing, unified market economy.

In 1837, Samuel F. B. Morse patented his invention of the telegraph. A year later, he sent the first telegram in the United States, and in 1844, he demonstrated the electronic telegraph's potential to transmit messages across greater distances with his famous message "What hath God wrought" from the U.S. Capitol in Washington to a depot in Baltimore. Morse was not the only inventor of the electronic telegraph. As an understanding of electricity grew, many in Europe and the United States were experimenting with electricity as a way to send messages. But Morse developed the system of using dots and dashes to transmit messages in "Morse code," and that system combined with his early patents enabled him to dominate the electronic telegraph market in the United States. Soon, more and more telegraph wires were reaching across the nation delivering messages, first between the big cities of the East Coast and, within two decades, across the continent. By 1861, the East and West Coasts were connected by telegraph, and the Pony Express, which had been

Table 9-1 Changes in Travel Times within the United States as a Result of the Revolution in Transportation

Route	1800	1830	1860
New York to Philadelphia	2 days	1 day	Less than 1 day
New York to South Carolina	More than 1 week	5 days	2 days
New York to Illinois	6 weeks	3 weeks	2 days
New York to New Orleans	4 weeks	2 weeks	6 days
New York to Florida	2 to 3 weeks	1 to 2 weeks	3 days
New York to Ohio	2 to 3 weeks	1 week	2 days

carrying messages, discontinued service. Messages that had taken days or weeks could now reach others almost instantly, an advantage that helped the Union victory in the Civil War. Western Union, the major telegraph service, continued to offer telegraph communication in the United States until after 2000.

Banks, Corporations, and Finance

In the early years of the Republic, many Americans harbored deep distrust of large business enterprises. The family farm was the business model with which most people were familiar, and other businesses were expected to be small, individual or family ventures. People might join together to finance a voyage or a project, but these efforts were short-term partnerships. At the time of the American Revolution, there were only seven American corporations, each chartered by colonial legislatures. State legislatures chartered forty more corporations in the 1780s and some three hundred in the 1790s, but gaining a corporate charter remained difficult. In general, such charters were given only to colleges or other nonprofit agencies to serve the public good. Commerce was considered as being for individual gain and therefore not worthy of a state charter.

Some of the first corporations were banks. Congress had chartered the Bank of North America, at Hamilton's urging in 1781. By 1815, the United States had two hundred state-chartered banks. Banks offered two essential services. First, they printed paper currency—banknotes—that were backed by the bank's gold and silver deposits (known as specie), making commercial transactions much easier than hauling actual gold and silver around. Second, banks also made loans and collected interest, making funds available to people who wanted to develop a new enterprise and making the banks themselves profitable investments. Soon, banks also began to issue bank notes not only on the specie they held but also on the loans in their portfolio. This development made banking more risky but expanded the amount of money in circulation and the credit available, essential elements in the growth of a commercial republic.

As commerce developed, however, larger commercial and industrial ventures, like the mills at Lowell, were too large and risky to be financed solely by individuals, even if those individuals could secure large bank loans. A new idea, that of a corporation as a free-standing commercial venture with multiple stockholders, took hold slowly. Two key elements in a corporation—limited liability for individual stockholders and the corporation's freedom from having its charter withdrawn or altered by the government—were new in the United States. Individually owned businesses came and went, but corporations with their many stockholders and secure charters eventually became a permanent and important feature of American economic life after 1815.

The Reality of the New Market Economy

In 1819, Washington Irving, already a well-known author, published *Rip Van Winkle*. The story has entertained generations of readers, but it also captured the changes in the United States in the first decades of independence. In the story, Rip, a lazy fellow living in New York's Catskill Mountains, takes a nap in the woods on a fine fall day. He awakes twenty years later and finds everything has changed in his home village. The picture on the sign over the inn was of someone named "General Washington" instead of King George III, but even more surprising, the whole town was different:

> The very village was altered; it was larger and more populous. There were rows of houses which he had never seen before, and those which had been his familiar haunts had disappeared. … The very character of the people seemed changed. There was a busy, bustling, disputatious tone about it, instead of the accustomed phlegm and drowsy tranquility.

Rip had been a passive subject of King George III. When he awoke, he was a citizen in an independent country that took politics, voting, and political parties very seriously. When he was asked whether he "was Federal or Democrat," Rip was at a loss. But Irving was saying something more about the decades after the Revolution—that "the very character of the people seemed changed." Where once rural America had moved to a relaxed, slow pace, the whole country was now a more unified commercial enterprise in which a "busy, bustling, disputatious tone" was the norm because people needed to work and work fast.

There were many real-life Rip Van Winkles who, while not necessarily having the benefit of a twenty-year nap, still came to live in an adult world utterly different from that of their youth. Ichabod Washburn was born in the small town of Kingston, Massachusetts, in 1798. His widowed mother supported the family with a loom in her home. When his mother could not feed her whole family, Washburn was "put out" to work as a harness maker and told that a boy should not ask too many questions about the world around him. Later, he found work in one of the factories that were springing up around New England and then founded his own business. Washburn & Moen Wire Manufactory became the largest wire maker in the country, sending its products all over the world and making Washburn a rich man. Not all Americans became as rich as Washburn, but many people in many parts of the land moved from isolated family businesses to work in large nationally and internationally connected industries. They went from a slow-paced world of barter to a cash economy based on trade, and they moved from rural isolation to participate in the exchange of information within a much larger world.

Before the American Revolution, most farmers lived in a barter economy in which most goods and services were simply traded. In that economy, life moved at a slow and

SAW-MILLS ON THE PENOBSCOT RIVER, AT OLDTOWN, MAINE.

The growing economy and the revolution in transportation only increased demand for the nation's raw materials such as lumber, which new machinery made easy to cut into standard-sized boards for shipment and use in building houses and ships.

predictable pace, and little money was transacted. By the 1820s, the barter economy had mostly disappeared. Farmers sold their goods on the world market and used the cash they received to purchase not only necessities but also, often, luxuries that their pre-Revolutionary forbearers never imagined.

To many Americans—not just to national leaders—distances seemed shorter, money more important, and politics more omnipresent after 1815 than even a few years before. Visitors to remote farm settlements in Illinois in the 1820s found that cloth coats and calico dresses purchased from a trader or a store were replacing homespun and buckskin. Once one family made the shift, everyone in the village felt pressure to earn enough money to keep up. As people worked harder and longer, public clocks—with an added hand that noted minutes, not just the passage of the hours—became more prominent. Chauncey Jerome's Connecticut clock company made a fortune manufacturing and shipping clocks to every part of the nation. As one 1840 traveler reported, "In every dell of Arkansas, and in cabins where there was not a chair to sit on, there was sure to be a Connecticut clock." Rip Van Winkle was not the only one waking up in a different time and in a money-conscious country.

> ### 9.2 Quick Review
>
> How did the U.S. economy benefit from faster and easier travel in the 1810s and 1820s? What else changed in people's lives with the advent of a market economy?

From the Era of Good Feelings to the Politics of Division

9.3 Explain the developments in the United States during the 1820s, including the shift of power toward the South and West that resulted from the changing economic and political situation.

Era of Good Feelings

The period from 1817 to 1823 in which the decline of the Federalists enabled the Democratic-Republicans to govern in a spirit of seemingly nonpartisan harmony.

James Monroe's two terms as president from 1817 to 1825 were known as the **Era of Good Feelings** because of the lack of rancor in his virtually unanimous election and reelection during a time when the Federalist Party almost disappeared. The period was quite a change from the days when John Adams and Thomas Jefferson contested the presidency and Federalists and Democratic-Republicans fought in the press and on the floor of Congress. But even during the Era of Good Feelings, all was not calm on the political front. The Supreme Court was rapidly expanding the reach of the federal government. Political tensions over the cotton economy, territorial expansion, and slavery exploded with surprising force in the 1820s. The good feelings were not destined to last.

The Supreme Court Defines Its Place

John Marshall served as chief justice of the U.S. Supreme Court from 1801 to 1835. Throughout his long tenure on the Court, Marshall was usually able to convince a majority of the justices to go along with his views. He used his position to define the role of the Court as arbiter of the Constitution, and he expanded the role and power of the federal government in many aspects of national life.

Early in his tenure, Marshall's 1803 *Marbury v. Madison* decision claimed a role for the Supreme Court in reviewing the constitutionality of acts of Congress. Marshall never again invoked that right, but in a series of subsequent decisions, he created the same right for the Court in relationship to state legislatures and state courts. Two 1819 decisions from the Marshall Court were especially important in expanding the role of the Supreme Court and the federal government.

In an appeal to the Supreme Court in the case of *Dartmouth College v. Woodward* (1819), the old Federalist Marshall reviewed a decision by lower courts that began when the

Democratic-Republican-dominated New Hampshire legislature revised the original charter of Dartmouth College, converting the school from a private to a state college. The Supreme Court ruled that state charters, including charters from colonial legislatures like Dartmouth's, were contracts and that contracts, once agreed to, were inviolable; thus, the legislature's actions were unconstitutional. The case was important not only because it asserted the right of the Supreme Court to review the actions of state legislatures as well as Congress but also because it asserted the inviolability of contracts. As a result, it became an important bedrock of the American economic system. After the Dartmouth College decision, the nation's growing businesses and industries were able to be certain that their contracts, once agreed to, could not be overturned by legislative action.

The other important 1819 decision was *McCulloch v. Maryland*. Congress had chartered the Second Bank of the United States at the end of the War of 1812 to stabilize the nation's finances. But the bank was not popular with many. In response to the opposition to the bank and to charges of irregularities in the bank's Maryland branch, the state of Maryland imposed a tax on the bank as a way to drive it out of business, or at least out of Maryland. In response, the bank brought suit in the federal courts and the case worked its way up to the Supreme Court. In the decision, written by Marshall, the Court took Alexander Hamilton's view that the "necessary and proper" clause of the Constitution meant that Congress had the right to charter a bank if it thought it was in the national interest, despite the Tenth Amendment's mandate that states should retain any power that was not specifically delegated to the national government in the Constitution. Marshall went further, saying that "the power to tax involves the power to destroy" while the "power to create" that Congress had invoked in the case of the bank "implies a power to preserve." With *McCulloch v. Maryland*, the Supreme Court declared that states could not interfere with the workings of the federal government and specifically could not tax any of its activities.

The Marshall Court continued to expand federal authority in subsequent cases. In *Gibbons v. Ogden* (1824), the Court ruled that the state of New York did not have a right to give Ogden, a partner of Robert Fulton, a monopoly to ferry service in New York Harbor since the harbor connected New York and New Jersey and thus involved interstate commerce, which only Congress could control. Later, in *Worcester v. Georgia* (1832), the Court ruled that the state of Georgia could not regulate private dealings by U.S. citizens within the territory controlled by the Cherokee tribe since Cherokees had sovereign rights, subject only to the authority of the federal government. In these and other decisions, the Court affirmed what came to be known as a "loose construction" of the Constitution, which as Marshall explained, enabled the Constitution "to be adapted to the various crises of human affairs" to preserve its relevance through time. Not everyone agreed with Marshall's perspective, and when he died in 1835, a Democratic-Republican paper did not mourn "the political doctrines" of a justice who sought "to strengthen government at the expense of the people." Nevertheless, many felt that both the Constitution and the rights of people were stronger for his efforts.

The Politics of Cotton and the Missouri Compromise of 1820

Although Missouri was too far north to be a cotton-growing state, its population also grew as a result of America's westward movement, and by 1819 Missouri applied to Congress to be admitted as a new state. A bill to authorize a state constitutional convention was introduced in Congress with little fanfare early in 1819. However, Congressman James Tallmadge, Jr., of New York introduced an amendment to the Missouri statehood bill to prohibit the introduction of new slaves into the state and gradually free those who were already there. Tallmadge's amendment created a huge crisis in which southern representatives and senators attacked it and its author.

In language that prefigured the heated debates of the next four decades, Georgia Representative Thomas W. Cobb told Tallmadge, "You have kindled a fire which all the waters of the ocean cannot put out, which seas of blood can only extinguish." Tallmadge responded in kind: "If a dissolution of the Union must take place, let it be so! If civil war, which gentlemen so much threaten, must come, I can only say, let it come." Threats of disunion were as old as the Constitutional Convention of 1787, but this language was harsher than Congress had heard in a long time. The reasons were clear.

When the Constitution was adopted, many from both the South and the North believed that slavery was dying; even its defenders tended to describe the institution as a sad though necessary evil. When George Washington and others of his generation freed their slaves, the economic impact was limited since slaves were not of great value. But that perspective was before cotton transformed the economics of slavery. A slave in the prime of life who might be sold for $400 or $500 in 1814 could be sold for $800–$1,100 in 1819, and though the price of slaves, as of land, decreased with the Panic of 1819, values in both cases recovered and then kept rising. Slaves had become valuable, whether as workers or as "products" to be sold. If Virginia and Carolina planters could not use all the slaves they owned, instead of freeing them, they could now sell them to cotton growers in Georgia, Mississippi, and Alabama at a substantial profit. Missouri had few slaves, but by 1820, slave owners were not about to allow an attack on the institution of slavery in which they had so much money invested. Although much of the debate about Missouri was spoken in the language of popular will and the sovereign right of (white) people there to decide their own policies, it took place as economic and racial realities were changing quickly.

In the North, hostility to slavery was growing. Many northerners, including many whose pre-Revolutionary parents and grandparents had owned slaves, now hated the whole idea of human slavery and disliked a constitutional system that protected it. Even before 1820, some people were starting to call themselves abolitionists—those committed to completely ending slavery. Many other northerners had more strategic objections to the constitutional protection of slavery. The three-fifths clause in the Constitution gave the slaveholding South seventeen more seats in the House of Representatives and, thus, seventeen more electoral votes in presidential elections than an allocation of representatives based on only free people would have done. As a result, four of the five U.S. presidents who had served by 1820 had come from Virginia. The nation was becoming divided between a commercial North and an agricultural South, and although neither region was purely for or against slavery, the fact that slavery gave the South a political edge came across to many northerners as being unfair.

The debates about Missouri, despite all the anger voiced by Tallmadge and Cobb, were not as vitriolic as future debates would be. There were not yet many radical abolitionists in the North, and few in the South who were yet saying that slavery was a positive good, which would become a common sentiment among some southern leaders in future decades. But already in 1819, neither side would back down, and Congress adjourned without doing anything about Missouri.

Before Congress reassembled in 1820, President Monroe and the Speaker of the House of Representatives, Henry Clay of Kentucky, designed a compromise to resolve the issue. While the North had a solid and growing majority in the House, the Senate was evenly divided between slave and free states. Since each state had two senators no matter what its population, eleven free states and eleven slave states meant a Senate that was split 22-22 on the issue of slavery. In addition, while Congress had debated what to do about Missouri, the region known as the District of Maine, within the Commonwealth of Massachusetts, was also petitioning for statehood with the blessing of the Massachusetts legislature. The compromise proposed that if Maine and Missouri were admitted at the same time, and if Missouri was allowed to be a slave state while Maine would be a free one, then the balance in the Senate would be maintained. The proposed compromise also restricted the spread of slavery: while Missouri would be admitted as a slave state, all other states north of the 36°30' north parallel, that is, the southern border of Missouri, would be admitted as free states. Although most northerners in the House and Senate voted against it, some supported the compromise, as did almost all of those from the South, and the **Missouri Compromise** passed Congress, allowing Missouri and Maine to be admitted to the Union. The crisis had been averted. The success would be the first of many such compromises for which Henry Clay would become known as the "great compromiser" over the next three decades. However, the need for this compromise signaled more clearly than ever before that slavery had become a divisive issue that would not go away (see Map 9-4).

Missouri Compromise

A compromise in Congress in 1820 that admitted Missouri to the Union as a slave state and Maine as a free state as well as prohibited slavery in the rest of the Louisiana Purchase territory above 36°30' north latitude.

Map 9-4 The Missouri Compromise Line.

This map shows the way the nation was divided in an equal number of free and slave states by the Missouri Compromise.

☐	Free states and territories
☐	Slave states and territories
☐	Open to slavery by Missouri Compromise
☐	Closed to slavery by Missouri Compromise
---	Missouri Compromise Line

RUSSIAN TERRITORY

BRITISH NORTH AMERICA

OREGON COUNTRY (US and Great Britain)

UNORGANIZED TERRITORY

Missouri R.

MICHIGAN TERRITORY

MICHIGAN TERRITORY

VERMONT

MAINE

NEW HAMPSHIRE

MASSACHUSETTS

NEW YORK

RHODE ISLAND

CONNECTICUT

PENNSYLVANIA

NEW JERSEY

Washington D.C.

DELAWARE

MARYLAND

Mississippi R.

ILLINOIS

INDIANA

OHIO

Ohio R.

St. Louis

VIRGINIA

SPANISH TERRITORY

Arkansas R.

MISSOURI

36° 30'

KENTUCKY

NORTH CAROLINA

TENNESSEE

SOUTH CAROLINA

Los Angeles

Santa Fé

ARKANSAS TERRITORY (1819–36)

Red R.

Natchez

GEORGIA

ALABAMA

ATLANTIC OCEAN

Rio Grande

Nacogdoches

San Antonio de Bejar

MISSISSIPPI

LOUISIANA

New Orleans

St. Augustine

FLORIDA TERRITORY

PACIFIC OCEAN

Gulf of Mexico

The Contested Election of 1824

As President Monroe came to the end of his second term, the political goodwill that had marked his tenure disappeared. In 1824, as the nation sought a new president, the United States experienced one of the most contested and confusing presidential elections in its history. For citizens of a nation that had elected James Monroe almost unanimously in 1816 and 1820, the ill will of 1824 was a surprise.

In one sense, the election of 1824 proceeded just as the writers of the Constitution—who hated the idea of political parties—envisioned: a contest in which members of the House, with each state's delegation having one vote, would decide on a president from among several of the nation's leading citizens who had been identified by the votes of the Electoral College. With the demise of the Federalists, the Democratic-Republican Party was the only party in the nation. It had been as that party's candidate that Monroe had been elected by an almost unanimous vote since the Federalists did not nominate a candidate in 1820 or any time after that. But in 1824, there were several different Democratic-Republicans, with radically different views, vying for the presidency.

By 1824, however, the usual process in which a party caucus within Congress would select a presidential nominee had broken down, and three members of Monroe's cabinet along with the speaker of the House of Representatives all sought the presidency. A fifth candidate from the same Democratic-Republican Party, Senator Andrew Jackson, the

Thinking Historically

The Missouri Compromise

When he heard about the Missouri Compromise, the aging Thomas Jefferson wrote to John Holmes, a Massachusetts congressman:

> I had for a long time ceased to read the newspapers or pay any attention to public affairs, confident they were in good hands, and content to be a passenger in our bark to the shore from which I am not distant. But this momentous question, like a fire bell in the night, awakened and filled me with terror. I considered it at once as the knell of the Union. It is hushed indeed for the moment. But this is a reprieve only, not a final sentence. A geographical line, coinciding with a marked principle, moral and political, once conceived and held up to the angry passions of men, will never be obliterated; and every new irritation will mark it deeper and deeper.

While Clay was being hailed as a national hero for crafting the compromise, Jefferson, perhaps, had a better sense of what lay ahead. The former president and slaveholder who also wrote passionately against slavery knew that, in the long term, no issue would so greatly divide the nation's citizens, and as he grew old, he saw the division become increasingly bitter.

Thinking Critically

1. **Contextualization**

   What might explain the widespread belief that the issue of slavery had been resolved with the passage of the Missouri Compromise? What would explain Jefferson's very different opinion?

2. **Argument Development**

   In hindsight, it is clear that Jefferson was correct and the Missouri Compromise was only a "reprieve." What evidence was available in 1820 to support Jefferson's point of view?

---

national war hero from Tennessee, also joined the race. In this type of contest, personal animosity and political intrigue were inevitable.

At first, many thought Secretary of the Treasury William H. Crawford of Georgia was the obvious choice. Crawford had stepped out of the way to support Monroe's election, and he and many of his supporters thought it was now his turn. The congressional caucus that traditionally nominated presidential candidates chose Crawford. However, in what was clearly a warning of trouble to come, less than a fourth of the members of Congress showed up to vote in the caucus. Others, in Congress and outside of it, would find other candidates.

Secretary of State John Quincy Adams of Massachusetts had a good claim to consideration. Many considered the office of secretary of state as the natural stepping-stone to the presidency. Monroe had been Madison's secretary of state as Madison had been Jefferson's, and Jefferson had been Washington's. In addition, Adams had served the nation well. He had acquired Florida for the United States, arranged treaties that opened vast new lands to settlement, and handled South American revolutions and potential European interference skillfully. As a former ambassador, senator, son of a former president, and favorite of the antislavery North, Adams had much going for him.

Secretary of War John C. Calhoun from South Carolina was another candidate. Calhoun had not yet become the fierce advocate of states' rights that he was later. In 1824, he was a nationalist. He advocated for a strong army and for federally supported roads, bridges, and canals connecting all parts of the nation. He also supported the Bank of the United States. Calhoun initially backed Adams, but when he became convinced that southern and border state electors would never support a New Englander, his own ambition was fired up and he campaigned actively.

Henry Clay of Kentucky, also a contender, was speaker of the House of Representatives and an ardent nationalist. Like Calhoun, he supported an expansive federal government that controlled the currency through a strong national bank and that built roads and bridges as well as supported commerce. From his political base in Kentucky, Clay hoped to be the first president from west of the Alleghenies. He was also shrewd enough to guess that with so many candidates in the race, the House of Representatives, which he controlled, might make the final decision.

Finally, there was Andrew Jackson of Tennessee. At first, Jackson seemed an unlikely candidate for president. Unlike any president after Washington, Jackson had never served in the cabinet or represented the nation abroad. Instead, he was the hero of the Battle of New Orleans. He had served briefly in the Senate, but his primary public role was as a military leader, and in the 1820s, the military was not always a popular institution. His wife, Rachel Jackson, strongly opposed his seeking the presidency. In 1822, however, the Tennessee legislature formally nominated Jackson as a candidate for president, primarily as a way to block the then frontrunner Crawford. At that point, Jackson probably supported Adams, in part, because Adams had supported Jackson's actions in Florida, while Crawford and Clay had not.

No one, including Jackson, counted on how popular he would be with the electorate. When a tavern keeper in Pennsylvania wrote, asking whether Jackson would indeed seek the presidency, the canny general, knowing that his response would be published, replied that it was his "undeviating rule neither to seek or decline public invitations to office." His response seemed the height of statesmanship to a country facing a divisive contest for the presidency.

The Constitution allows each state to decide how to choose presidential electors. By 1824, most states allowed voters to select electors pledged to a specific candidate, thus greatly democratizing the presidential selection process. That electorate had changed since the Constitution was adopted in 1789. Since 1808 when New Jersey retracted its decision to give women the right to vote, only men voted in all states. Property restrictions on voting, still common when Washington was elected, were long gone in most states, so nearly all white men could now vote, and in some northern states, so could free black men. In New York City, free blacks sometimes held the balance of power among various factions. Excluded from voting were women of all races, most blacks including all slaves, and Indians. Nevertheless, this broad male electorate made widespread popularity more important in selecting a president than it once had been. By 1824, the (white male) popular will was coalescing behind Jackson far more than anyone expected.

In a nation increasingly divided by sectional issues, a war hero had great appeal. In addition, a fierce opponent of banks like Jackson was popular with many people who were convinced—at least partially rightly—that the Bank of the United States had brought on the Panic of 1819. In places like Mississippi and Alabama where some people were growing rich on farmlands that Jackson had wrested from their Indian owners, he was a local hero. In a country where an elite's economic decisions had hurt many farmers and workers, a candidate who had been born in a log cabin and grown up poor, though he had become wealthy as an adult, had deep appeal. Popular appeal had not been a major factor in the elections of Madison and Monroe, but it was the factor in 1824.

In the 1824 election, Jackson won the popular vote. Calhoun, who had withdrawn from the campaign after deciding that Jackson was too popular to beat, was easily elected as vice president since the Twelfth Amendment, ratified in 1804 in the aftermath of the Jefferson-Burr fiasco, mandated that presidential electors cast separate ballots for presidential and vice presidential candidates. In addition to Pennsylvania, Jackson easily carried the Black Belt states of Georgia, Alabama, Mississippi, and Louisiana as well as most of the rest of the South, a region with extra electoral votes as a result of the three-fifths clause to the Constitution. Jackson defeated Adams in New Jersey, Crawford in North Carolina, and Clay in Indiana and Illinois. Adams carried New England, some of the mid-Atlantic region, and the Northwest. However, although Jackson won the most popular votes, no one had the 131 electoral votes needed for a majority:

Jackson	99 electoral votes
Adams	84 electoral votes
Crawford	41 electoral votes
Clay	37 electoral votes

Clay's prediction was right; the election had been tossed into the House of Representatives. Not since 1800 had the House of Representatives been called on to decide the outcome of a presidential contest.

9.1

9.2

9.3

Ironically, however, since the Constitution required the House to choose from among the top three candidates, Clay himself had been eliminated. Moreover, although his supporters had kept it hidden, Crawford had had a stroke and could not possibly assume the presidency. So the election came down to Jackson and Adams, and Adams was determined to fight for the office, despite ranking second in the popular and electoral votes. The Constitution mandated a process, and Adams wanted to follow it. Many of Adams's followers, and the supporters of other candidates, saw Jackson as a would-be American Napoleon who would undermine American democracy. Henry Clay—who was master of the House—agreed and was determined that Jackson should not be president. When the House met on February 9, 1825, Adams was elected president by a vote of thirteen states, with seven states for Jackson and four for Crawford.

On the evening of the vote, outgoing President Monroe held a party at the White House. Jackson approached Adams, and they greeted each other with considerable formality. Observers thought Jackson was "genial and gracious," while Adams was "stiff, rigid, cold as a statue." The two would not often meet again, but the interaction that night imprinted an image on the public that would follow them, to Jackson's benefit, for the next four years and beyond.

Whether Adams had made any secret agreement with Clay will never be known. But five days after the vote, Adams appointed Clay to be his secretary of state and thus his successor if the previous pattern held true. Jackson denounced both men for making a "corrupt bargain," resigned from the Senate, and returned to his home in Nashville to begin what was essentially a four-year campaign against Adams, Clay, and their administration in favor of his own election to the office that he and his followers believed he had won in 1824. The animosity of the campaign would make the next four years difficult for an administration led by two of the nation's most gifted political and diplomatic leaders.

The Adams-Clay Agenda

In his inaugural address in March 1825, Adams acknowledged that he came to the presidency "less possessed of your confidence in advance than any of my predecessors." Nevertheless, it was his goal to unify the nation and improve all parts of the country. He was the last president to believe that the "baneful weed of party strife" might be avoided, and he struggled—unsuccessfully—to avoid the creation of political parties and permanent national divisions.

Adams proposed a list of national improvements to be implemented by the federal government. Support for federally funded improvements such as roads, canals, and so on would be a hallmark of the Adams administration. An emerging political faction that supported strong federal actions agreed with the direction that the Adams administration was taking. Jackson and another emerging faction would strongly oppose this sort of activist federal government, advocating instead for states' rights.

Improvement, both personal and political, was a popular ambition in the 1820s. Adams worried about becoming a better person, and he swam naked in the Potomac every day to improve his body. But he also wanted to improve the country, and he saw the money freed from paying off the Revolutionary War debt and the income from sales of federal lands as the perfect opportunity for investing in the country. The General Survey, conducted by army engineers when John C. Calhoun was secretary of war, was the blueprint. Adams, with an eye to southern voters, proposed a second National Road to link Washington, D.C., to New Orleans. He proposed, and Congress approved, building the Chesapeake and Ohio Canal that would connect with the original National Road and link the Potomac with the Ohio and Mississippi Rivers. Postmaster General John McLean built post offices in rural areas and subsidized the stagecoach industry to carry the mail and connect the nation's far-flung people to one another. Adams also proposed a new national university to be based in Washington and a national observatory—a "lighthouse of the skies." All of these activities were designed to knit the nation together, advancing knowledge and making it easier to transport goods. In addition, the intent was to unite the nation in a single political entity and a market economy, especially after the divisions sparked by the debates around the Missouri Compromise (see Map 9-4, p. 271).

Secretary of State Clay was involved in all these efforts and described the program of internal improvements and protective tariffs as the "**American System**." In Clay's mind, the American System would reduce poverty by linking all Americans (all *white* Americans; Clay considered neither his own fifty slaves nor others' slaves to be Americans) in a prosperous commercial community. The system was American because it made the federal government an agent of economic development. Clay believed that the support of interstate commerce that he and Adams wanted to foster on a federal level would make a stronger and more united America, commercially, geographically, and socially. Ultimately, Clay wanted transportation and commerce to bridge traditional sectional divides and create a thriving commercial nation that was united by common national investments. Moreover, the system was potentially a way to protect the country by building an infrastructure that could serve military needs, allowing troops to move quickly from one part of the country to another when necessary. Finally, the American System would protect infant American industries through a strong tariff that would allow them to develop and thus reduce American dependence on cheaper foreign imports.

In one of his last acts as speaker in 1824, Clay led an effort to increase the average tariff from 20 percent to 35 percent. The new higher tariff made him a hero to New England mill owners and their workers whose jobs it protected. It was also popular in commercial centers like Cincinnati, Ohio, and Clay's hometown of Lexington, Kentucky, where new industries needed protection. But the improvements and tariffs of the American System were not popular in other parts of the country. A high tariff raised the cost of everything southern cotton planters had to buy but did nothing to raise the price of their cotton in the international market. They saw the tariff and the president's antislavery opinions as a sign of a federal government that was working against their economic interests, and many in the South hardened their opposition to Adams, Clay, and the American System.

As the 1828 presidential campaign built steam, Adams and Clay continued their pitch for the costs and benefits of the American System. Jackson, however, had another agenda: to replace Adams, the minority president, with the man who had rightfully won in 1824. Ironically, although Adams ardently wanted to avoid the "baneful weed of party strife," it was during his term that new American political parties were born.

The Jackson Victory of 1828 and the Rebirth of Political Parties

From the day he left Washington, D.C., in 1825, Jackson was running to become president in 1828. He believed that he and his supporters had been cheated, and he meant to be vindicated. Nevertheless, it took time for the campaign to take shape. It is easier to understand the birth of political parties in retrospect than it was at the time. Many Americans were glad to see the old Federalist Party gone and hated to see the Democratic-Republicans splinter. At first, the two factions in Congress were described simply as "Adams men" and "Jackson men." After the midterm congressional elections of 1826, the "Jackson men" controlled Congress. The "Adams men" then started to call themselves National Republicans who supported the national administration led by President Adams. This group, led by Henry Clay, would become the core of the new **Whig Party**, the party that advocated for a strong national government role in the economy, internal improvements such as roads and canals, and social reform movements in general. The "Jackson men" continued to call themselves Democratic-Republicans, emphasizing that they were the rightful winners of the last election and represented the democratic will of the people, which had been thwarted by Adams and Clay in the 1824 election. Soon, the Jacksonians dropped the "Republicans" in their name and were simply known as Democrats, forerunners of the **Democratic Party** that throughout the 1800s argued for the rights of the "common man" to be left alone by centralized government and economic interests.

Neither party was fully organized in the 1828 election and though each had newspapers that were strongly on their side, other hallmarks of national political parties like national nominating conventions came later. Nevertheless, from 1828 on, most Americans expected presidential elections to be hotly contested by two or more candidates representing their

American System

The program of government subsidies to improve roads and canals and to foster economic growth and protect domestic manufacturers from foreign competition.

Whig Party

Political party that began to take shape in support of the Adams-Clay American System and was first known as the National Republicans, but became the Whig Party in the 1830s in opposition to the Jacksonian Democrats.

Democratic Party

Political party that before the Civil War followed the ideas of Jefferson and Jackson and favored states' rights and a limited role for the federal government, especially in economic affairs (very different from the modern Democratic Party).

9.1

9.2

9.3

9.1

9.2

9.3

Bettmann/Getty Images

This stylized picture of Andrew Jackson speaking to a crowd suggests the enormous popularity that the former war hero had as he connected with diverse audiences of voters in a way no leader since George Washington had done.

respective political parties and running on specific promises. The era of electing a few wise men to select the best president was over forever.

The prime architect of Jackson's campaign and his political agenda, besides Jackson himself who delegated little, was Senator Martin Van Buren of New York. Van Buren was a strict constructionist of the Constitution who believed that the American System advocated by Adams and Clay violated the Constitution because it involved the federal government in many matters not specifically assigned to it by the Constitution. Although a New Yorker, Van Buren was closely allied with many in the South who liked Van Buren's commitment to a small federal government because they feared that if the federal government could involve itself in shaping the nation's economy, it could also interfere with slavery, a threat that terrified the slaveholding class.

The campaign of 1828 was as nasty as any in American history. Newspapers took on a larger role than ever before, endorsing candidates and spreading slander about the opposition. The National Republicans reminded voters of Jackson's temper and his many brawls and duels, which they said were unpresidential, as well as the times he may have exceeded his authority in attacking Indians or executing British subjects. In addition, they attacked his marriage to Rachel Jackson. More than thirty years earlier, the Jacksons had been married before Rachel's divorce from her first husband was final, so she was thus guilty of bigamy. The attack on their marriage infuriated Jackson and deeply hurt Rachel. When she died shortly after the election, Jackson never forgave his adversaries.

The campaign organized by Jackson and Van Buren was equally nasty. They reminded voters of the supposed "corrupt bargain" that had put Adams in the White House and claimed—with no proof—that Adams, as ambassador to Russia, had procured young American women for the Czar's pleasure. They portrayed Adams as cold and elitist and attacked his Unitarian beliefs as un-Christian compared with Jackson's devout Presbyterian faith. For the Democrats, the campaign was not about the American System but a choice "[b]etween J.Q. Adams, who can write, and Andy Jackson who can fight." The fighter won easily.

The popular vote nearly tripled between 1824 and 1828, and 57.5 percent of all eligible voters actually voted. All but two states, Delaware and South Carolina, chose presidential electors by popular vote for slates pledged to one candidate or another in 1828. Campaigning had risen to new heights, and more voters believed that their votes counted. Political parties organized a new get-out-the-vote effort, which for the first time included election materials such as buttons, mugs, posters, and slogans. In the end, Jackson won 647,286 votes—56 percent of the popular vote—and 178 electoral votes, and Adams won 508,064 popular votes and 83 electoral votes. (Four years earlier the popular vote had been 153,554 votes for Jackson to 108,740 votes for Adams.) There was no need for the House of Representatives to be involved. A new style of electioneering had emerged. And Andrew Jackson was president-elect.

9.3 Quick Review

How did the nation evolve from the Era of Good Feelings to the partisanship of the mid-to late 1820s? What were the most important factors in this transition and what were the results?

Conclusion

Although it would have seemed unimaginable even a few years earlier, after 1815, distances seemed shorter, money and material goods more important, and politics omnipresent to many Americans, not just national leaders. The new market economy changed economic matters and most routines of daily life for many Americans. Production of cotton and the accompanying commerce it generated changed the lives of nearly all of the country's residents and focused the attention of many Americans on productivity and hoped-for prosperity. Slavery expanded from the Atlantic coast as thousands of enslaved people were forced to move into the interior of the country where the Black Belt, stretching from Georgia through Alabama, Mississippi, and Louisiana, became the center of cotton production based on the backbreaking labor of slaves. At the same time, many white Americans, especially young women, went to work in highly regimented mills, spinning cotton into cloth. Other Americans transported cotton between states and across the Atlantic Ocean at speeds their forebearers could not have imagined. Bankers and corporate leaders arranged new forms of financing and business to manage the cotton economy. The new prominence of public clocks reflected the need for tight transportation schedules.

New York City emerged as a transportation and commercial hub connecting the United States to the international cotton trade. The Erie Canal also secured New York's place as a commercial center as it made transport between interior locations and coastal ports more efficient. Steamboats, canal boats, transatlantic packet ships, and stagecoaches traveled the routes in ever-faster circuits. Banks played an essential role in the market economy. Corporations with many shareholders deepened the stability of businesses and extended their ability to operate. However, the cotton market slumped in 1819, which caused an economic downturn and financial panic among Americans. Although the economy would eventually recover and thrive, the experience reflected a new and not fully understood national economy.

During Monroe's administration, the Supreme Court, led by Chief Justice John Marshall, reviewed a series of state legislative decisions and, as a result, expanded the power of the federal government. Despite general calm during the Era of Good Feelings of Monroe's two-term administration, political tensions over the cotton economy, territorial expansion, and slavery exploded with surprising force in the 1820s. When Missouri applied to become a state in 1819, the divisions over slavery intensified. Although the Missouri Compromise was meant to resolve the differences, the aging Thomas Jefferson said that it was "a reprieve only." The Era of Good Feelings gave way to divisive contests for the presidency in 1824—a victory for John Quincy Adams—and in 1828—a victory for Andrew Jackson—and the rebirth of political parties.

Chapter Review

How did the economic changes fostered by the growth of cotton production and the new national market economy in the United States affect national politics and governmental decisions? Why were economic and political trends so closely connected?

Chapter 9 Summary and Review

Creating the Cotton Economy

9.1 **Explain the role of cotton in transforming the land and the lives of diverse people of the United States.**

Summary

Two developments in the late 1790s set the stage for the rapid growth of the American cotton industry. First, demand increased when much of Europe came to prefer clothing made of cotton rather than of other fibers. Also, supply expanded through a series of technological innovations that revolutionized the production of cotton cloth, most notably the cotton gin. This development had a transformative economic effect on the American economy in the South as well as the North. And the new cotton economy fueled the expansion of slavery. While slavery slowly disappeared in the North after 1800 and the slave population of Maryland, Virginia, and the Carolinas stabilized or declined, the institution exploded in the Black Belt, territory that had been recently secured by the federal government. The production of cotton textiles in the North was at the core of the Industrial Revolution in the United States, and New York City played a key role in linking the United States to the international cotton trade. Lowell mills offered a new economic model, employing "factory girls" and establishing company housing. However, the work was difficult and got only more so over time. The overproduction of cotton as well as other economic factors led to the Panic of 1819, and the banks' reactionary responses only worsened the problem. Americans had not yet understood the nature of an increasingly industrial, interconnected economy, so this depression was especially surprising. The nation would feel hardships for quite some time before recovery.

Review Questions

1. Contextualization

How did the expansion of cotton production shape the development of slavery in the United States? In what ways did it make life harder for enslaved African Americans?

2. Causation

How did the expansion of cotton production shape the development of the commercial economy in the United States? What new opportunities and challenges did it create for northern workers?

Commerce, Technology, and Transportation Create a Market Economy

9.2 **Analyze the technological and financial changes that led to the emergence of a new market economy in the United States.**

Summary

With this new market economy came a need for a modern network of internal transportation. The Erie Canal linked the growing regions of upstate New York, western Pennsylvania, and Ohio to the eastern seaboard, particularly New York City. Steamboats revolutionized water transportation, producing dramatic changes in the role of the Mississippi River in commerce. Federal and state efforts to improve roads also contributed to better internal transportation. With increased speed in travel, news also moved much more quickly. As a result of a series of legislative actions and court decisions in the early 1800s, corporations became a permanent and important feature of American economic life after 1815. Some of the first and most important corporations were banks. They played an essential role in the market economy by printing paper currency and making loans. With this new market economy, Americans could feel the pace of life quickening and their lives changing.

Review Questions

3. Causation

How did the transportation revolution create new connections between Americans and alter old ones? How did it facilitate the movement and exchange of people, products, and ideas?

4. Argument Development

Defend or refute the following statement: The emergence of the market economy in the early 1800s would not have been possible without significant government involvement. What evidence can you provide to support your position?

From the Era of Good Feelings to the Politics of Division

9.3 **Explain the developments in the United States during the 1820s, including the shift of power toward the South and West that resulted from the changing economic and political situation.**

Summary

James Monroe's presidential administration that began in 1817 was known as the Era of Good Feelings because his election and reelection had lacked the rancor that had become customary every four years. However, the period was not without conflict. Debates about states' rights were settled by the Marshall Court in favor of the federal government. Slavery became a national issue with the 1819 Missouri statehood bill, and the controversy was eventually resolved by the Missouri Compromise of

1820—as least for the short term. The election of 1824 marked the end of the Era of Good Feelings. The election revealed deepening sectional divisions within the country. When no candidate received a majority of the electoral vote, the election was decided in the House of Representatives, where John Quincy Adams was declared the winner. Supporters of Andrew Jackson, who had won the popular vote, saw this decision as a "corrupt bargain" between Adams and Henry Clay, then speaker of the House of Representatives. President Adams and his newly appointed secretary of state, Henry Clay, argued that the federal government should play an active role in the promotion of economic growth and improvement. Jackson spent the years between his defeat in 1824 and the election of 1828 building a political organization capable of defeating Adams. The election of 1828 was a nasty affair, pitting Adams and the National Republicans against Jackson and the Democrats. Jackson's eventual victory was also a victory for a new kind of party politics.

Review Questions

5. Comparison
Why was the sectional divide over slavery deeper in 1820 than it had been in 1790?

6. Causation
To what extent did the economic policies of the Adams administration contribute to the emergence of new political parties? How was the growing sectional divide reflected in the new parties?

1. Preparing to Write: Organize Your Evidence

Long Essay Question—Evaluate the extent to which the market revolution contributed to social changes in the United States from 1800 to 1848.

Primary sources are an integral part of AP U.S. History, in part because they are well represented on practically every part of the exam. The Harriet H. Robinson excerpt in "American Voices" from Section 9.2 can be used as a good source of evidence in an essay for this question. How can content from this account of Robinson's help support your thesis? Paraphrase a key passage from Robinson and then explain how it supports your thesis.

2. Preparing to Write: Develop Your Thesis

Long Essay Question—Evaluate the extent to which there were different views on the American System as an economic policy from 1815 to 1828.

After you develop a list of differences, ask yourself the "So what?" question. Do your findings tell us anything about the state of American politics or the role of government at this time? What do the results of the popular vote tell us about the popularity of this agenda? By looking beyond the basic facts, you can elevate the quality of thought in your thesis and give yourself the opportunity for deeper analysis in the body.

Chapter 10
Democracy in the Age of Andrew Jackson 1828–1844

Art Resource, NY

Politics dominated the thinking of many Americans in the Age of Jackson. This painting titled *Stump Speaking* captures the scene as a large group of white men gathered to hear a political speaker.

Chapter Objective

Demonstrate an understanding of the changing definitions of democracy in the Age of Jackson and what Jacksonian democracy meant for different groups of Americans.

∨ Learning Objectives

Jacksonian Democracy, Jacksonian Government

10.1 Analyze Jackson's advocacy for Indian Removal, his opposition to the Bank of the United States, his support for a tariff, and the impact of these policies on other Americans.

Democratized Religion: The Second Great Awakening

10.2 Analyze the diversity of American religious experience and how the freedom of the era gave rise to diverse religious and philosophical expressions.

Democratized Education, Democratized Art: The Birth of the Common School, American Landscape Painting, and Photography

10.3 Explain the development of public education and art as a result of, and in response to, the cultural currents of the 1820s and 1830s.

Andrew Jackson's inauguration as president in March 1829 was a somber affair for Jackson himself, who was still mourning his wife Rachel's death the previous December. He did not make the traditional call on the outgoing president, blaming John Quincy Adams for attacks that he believed hastened Rachel's death, and he did not attend his own inaugural ball. For his supporters, however, Jackson's inauguration was a raucous celebration of democracy. When Jackson arrived at the White House, a festive crowd overran the place, stood on the furniture, broke china, and had to be lured outside with bowls of spiked punch. A Washington observer, Margaret Bayard Smith, complained about what she saw as the rabble that inundated the White House, describing their behavior as "scrambling, fighting, romping." Supreme Court Justice Joseph Story called it "the reign of King Mob." But order was restored, and Jackson's agenda began to emerge.

Jackson cared about a few big issues, and these shaped his agenda as president. During both of his campaigns for the presidency in 1824 and 1828, he had promised to acquire land for white settlement by forcing Indian tribes to move west of the Mississippi River. He also promised to undermine the Bank of the United States and the power of northern economic elites. He was opposed to Henry Clay's American System and wanted to keep taxes low and the role of the federal government modest. As he made clear, however, he would not tolerate challenges to federal authority by individuals or states. Jackson understood power and was committed to expanding the power of the presidency itself. As he proceeded with his agenda, he was often challenged, and his response was to fight back with all the resources he could find. He nearly always won.

The era during which Jackson led the country was known as the Age of Jackson. Jackson was the symbolic voice of a new generation and a specific class of American people. The first president born west of the Alleghenies, he was not connected to the Founding Fathers as all of his predecessors had been. He spoke for the economic and political interests of a broad spectrum of white America that was growing in influence in the country. Although it was not his doing, Jackson also presided over a nation in which the churches, the schools, and the arts expanded and changed significantly.

Significant Dates

1826	Charles B. Finney leads religious revivals in western New York
1828	Tariff of Abominations
	Jackson defeats Adams for president
1829	Andrew Jackson is inaugurated president
1830	Congress passes Indian Removal Act
	Nullification Crisis begins
	Joseph Smith founds the Church of Jesus Christ of the Latter-Day Saints
1832	Jackson vetoes recharter of Second Bank of the United States
	South Carolina legislature nullifies federal tariffs
	Black Hawk's War in Illinois
1833	Congress passes compromise tariff
	Nullification debate ends
1835	Treaty of New Echota
	Catharine Beecher publishes *Essay on the Education of Female Teachers*
1836	First *McGuffey's Reader* is published
	Second Creek War in Alabama
1837	Horace Mann elected secretary of the Massachusetts Board of Education
1838	Ralph Waldo Emerson "Divinity School Address"
1839	First daguerreotypes—forerunners of modern photography
1838–1839	Trail of Tears

Library of Congress Prints and Photographs Division [LC-USZC4-970]

This illustration of the crowd at the White House after Jackson's inauguration captures the mood of the day, even though the artist was not present and created it based on stories told by others.

Jacksonian Democracy, Jacksonian Government

10.1 Analyze Jackson's advocacy for Indian Removal, his opposition to the Bank of the United States, his support for a tariff, and the impact of these policies on other Americans.

Jackson knew what he wanted to accomplish as president. Before implementing any other policies, he planned a clean sweep of senior federal officeholders, some of whom had served under several presidents. Jefferson's successors—Madison, Monroe, and John Quincy Adams—had made few changes below the level of the Cabinet itself, partly because they were all from the same political party and partly because they did not see it as the president's role to make wholesale personnel changes. In a significant change of practice, Jackson replaced many officials, and in the process, created the suspicion that there had been corruption without evidence for it. Jackson believed in what came to be called the "**spoils system**," which was a patronage system in which a victorious political party rewards a candidate's supporters with government jobs. Jackson used the term "rotation in office," but his supporters believed "to the victor belongs the spoils." Suddenly with Jackson in office, experienced officials, including 25 customs collectors and 423 postmasters, were fired from what had been a small, stable federal bureaucracy. Services deteriorated, and the quality of some federal services like the postal service did not recover until civil service reform took hold in the 1880s.

Martin Van Buren, architect of Jackson's 1828 campaign for president, became secretary of state. But others of Jackson's cabinet officers were less talented, and Jackson often ignored them. Instead, he surrounded himself with informal advisors who came to be known as his "Kitchen Cabinet," longtime friends and advisors who worked closely with the president, particularly to accomplish his most cherished goals.

Jackson's Presidential Agenda

Jackson distrusted government at all levels but had unbounded trust in his own ability to govern. He meant not only to be an activist president—John Quincy Adams and other presidents had also pursued strong agendas—but also to make the presidency the center of the American government. He would not defer to Congress in ways that all of his predecessors had done. He vetoed more congressional bills than all of his predecessors combined and made it clear that Congress would have to reckon with him. As he had announced before the election, he was determined to force the Indians who lived in northern Georgia, Alabama, and Mississippi to move west to clear the land for white settlement. Although he supported a modified tariff, he meant to scale back the size of the federal government. He hated the Bank of the United States and was determined to destroy it. He saw its charter as an inappropriate use of federal authority and was convinced, probably rightly, that the bank had contributed to Adams's campaign. And perhaps most of all, Jackson was determined to preserve the Union at a time when southern leaders were insisting that each state had the right of **nullification**, the right to declare that specific federal legislation was null and void within its borders. Jackson was a slaveholder and a defender of slavery, but if slaveholders threatened national unity, they would have to deal with him.

In his two terms as president, Jackson realized most of his goals, despite fierce opposition. He established permanent precedents for presidential authority, precedents that later presidents from Lincoln to Franklin Roosevelt would cite. He was a hero to some and an evil genius to others. For most historians, he remains one of the most complex American leaders, expanding the roles of poor and working-class whites in the political process and of the presidency in American life while reducing the rights of Indians, slaves, federal employees, bankers, and indeed anyone who disagreed with him.

spoils system

A way of selecting people for government jobs based on the idea that "to the victor belongs the spoils."

nullification

A constitutional doctrine holding that a state has a legal right to declare a national law null and void within its borders.

The Indian Removal Act, the Trail of Tears, and the Settlement of Oklahoma

For some white Americans, "Indian Removal"—Jackson's policy of forcing the Cherokee Nation and other tribes to move to reservations in distant Oklahoma, or Indian Territory as it was called—was a great achievement. For the tribes caught in Jackson's web, the policy led to war within the tribes, terrible losses, resistance, resignation, and reinvention. Their white supporters, though passionate, were ineffective against Jackson.

Known as the **Five Civilized Tribes**, the Cherokees, Chickasaws, Choctaws, Creeks, and Seminoles had for generations lived in the region known as the Old Southwest—Georgia, Alabama, Mississippi—as well as in Arkansas and Florida. These tribes had traded and fought with Spanish, French, and English settlers and had sold or ceded much of their land, but based on treaties with the U.S. government, they still owned huge tracts of land in the heart of the cotton-growing South.

Far more than the Indians of the Northwest or the West, the Five Civilized Tribes had adopted many white ways and customs, intermarried with whites, and created a unique culture based on farming and trade. Of the five tribes, the Cherokees had the most sophisticated political, economic, and cultural institutions. Stretching over northwest Georgia, Alabama, Tennessee, and North Carolina, the Cherokees expected to be treated as a sovereign country. The Cherokees, who had supported the British during the Revolution, had signed a treaty with the new U.S. government in 1785 and never again waged war against the new nation. They supported Jackson in his battle with the Creeks and lived at peace with their neighbors, but that did them little good once Jackson determined his course of action.

The Cherokees took well to the European style of communication and farming. In 1821, a Cherokee warrior, Sequoyah, intrigued by what he called the "markings" of written English, invented an eighty-six-character alphabet that represented the syllables of spoken Cherokee. The new alphabet caught on quickly, not only in handwritten form but also in typeface for printing. The *Cherokee Phoenix*, published in both English and Cherokee, became an important means of communication. Sequoyah, who never learned English, created a similar alphabet for the Choctaw language. His achievement to invent a written language while being illiterate in all languages had never before been done. In addition, the Cherokees set up a large and effective trading network with other tribes and the white community. In 1827, they adopted a written constitution for the Cherokee Republic.

Beginning in the 1790s, Christian missionaries came to live among the Cherokees. The Cherokees welcomed them, though most never became Christians. Using Sequoyah's alphabet, the missionaries translated the Bible into Cherokee and later became some of the most heroic defenders of Cherokee rights.

Cherokees also cultivated cotton as their white neighbors did, and some owned African slaves. An 1825 census counted 13,563 Cherokees, 220 whites (some of whom were married to Cherokees), and 1,277 African slaves in the Cherokee Republic. Of all the American Indian tribes, the Cherokees were the model of assimilation that presidents from Washington to Jefferson claimed to want. But white settlers and President Jackson decided to ignore the assimilation. They wanted the land.

Georgia took the lead in seizing Indian land. In 1824, Governor George Troup announced that he was ending treaty rights for the Cherokee and Creek tribes. When President John Quincy Adams opposed him, citing the tribes' treaties with the U.S. government, Troup and his successor, John Forsyth, campaigned for Jackson in 1828. In December 1828, the Georgia legislature declared that, starting in June 1830, Georgia state laws would extend to all parts of the Cherokee Republic despite federal treaty agreements to the contrary. White Georgians then began moving onto Cherokee lands, and Jackson withdrew U.S. troops who had been protecting the Cherokees.

It was in this context that Jackson addressed Congress, advocating an **Indian Removal Act** to "protect" the Cherokees from Georgia laws. The president gave the tribes what seemed like a choice: "voluntarily" move west to new lands where their independence would be honored or choose to stay where they were. But if they chose to stay, they would

Five Civilized Tribes

The Cherokees, Chickasaws, Choctaws, Creeks, and Seminoles, who had established treaty agreements with the United States in the late 1700s or early 1800s, lived in peace with their neighbors and adopted more of the ways of the whites than most Native Americans.

Library of Congress Prints and Photographs Division [LC-USZC4-2566]

Sequoyah was intrigued with the way reading seemed to give whites power. He created an alphabet for the Cherokee language and, later, a similar one for the Choctaw language.

Indian Removal Act

Legislation passed by Congress in 1830 that provided funds for removing and resettling eastern Indians in the West. It granted the president the authority to use force if necessary and resulted in the involuntary transfer of thousands of Native Americans to new homes in Oklahoma.

be subject to the laws of Georgia, laws that said Indians could not vote, own property, testify against a white person in court, or obtain credit. It was not much of a choice, as Jackson himself said in private.

The land that the government offered to the tribes they were displacing was completely unfamiliar to them. Most people thought of it as simply a desert where farming would be impossible. Indian Territory, which eventually became the state of Oklahoma, was a portion of the Louisiana Purchase just north of Texas. The land was not empty, though the government tended to treat it that way. Some of the plains tribes—the Wichitas, Kiowas, Kiowa Apaches, and especially Osages—had lived there for generations. Some tribes from the Ohio-Illinois area—Shawnees, Delawares (Lenapes), Miamis, Kickapoos, Sacs, and Fox— had been relocated to that territory after defeats by the U.S. Army. In addition, there were a few white settlers and some slaves and former slaves seeking refuge in the region. Nevertheless, under Jackson's plan, the government was now offering a large part of the territory to the Cherokees and others of the Five Civilized Tribes (see Map 10-1).

Map 10-1 Indian Removal.

Indian Removal began with the forced relocation of the Sac (sometimes spelled Sauk) and Fox tribes from Illinois and Iowa. However, by far the largest relocation of tribes took place when the five Indian nations who were living in large territories in Georgia, Alabama, Florida, and Mississippi were forced far to the west to the newly created Indian Territory. (Note that Arkansas became a state in 1836 and Texas did so in 1845, but the map shows modern state boundaries to provide context.)

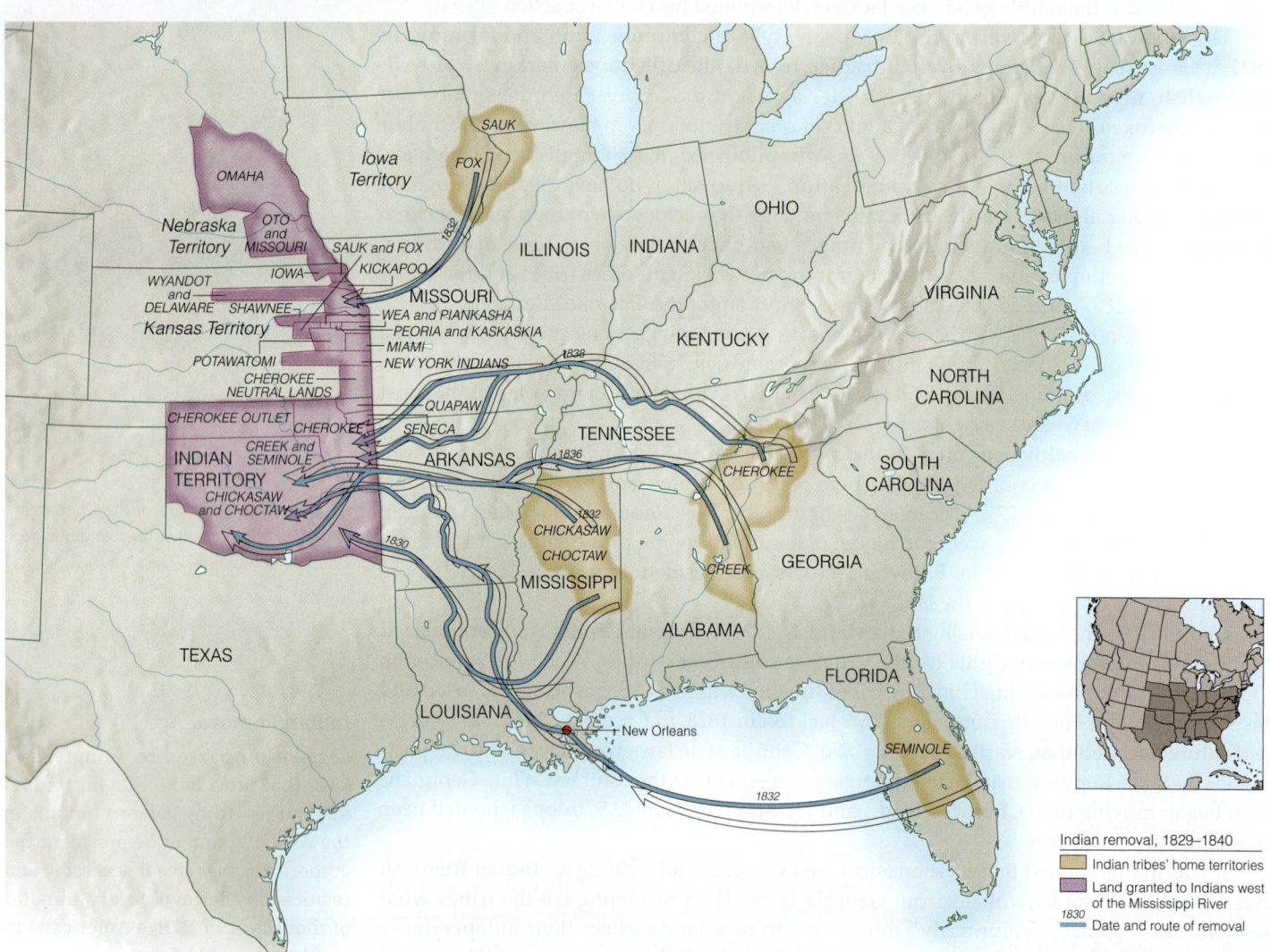

10.1

10.2

10.3

Cherokee, Creek, Chickasaw, Choctaw, and Seminole leaders had long feared just such a move, and many whites now rallied to their side. In Congress and the national press, Indian Removal became a major fight. Catharine Beecher, a reformer associated with many causes, organized women to defend Indian rights and flooded Congress with petitions. Missionaries campaigned against the bill so vigorously that Georgia sentenced two of them to prison at hard labor for refusing to abandon the Indians.

In the Senate, Theodore Frelinghuysen of New Jersey, long a supporter of Protestant missionaries, led the opposition to the Indian Removal Bill. Frelinghuysen insisted that the government was bound by its treaties and that, if need be, should use the U.S. Army to force Georgia to retract its claims to Indian lands. Henry Clay, who had not previously spoken in favor of Indian rights, joined the antiremoval forces. In the end, the removal bill passed the Senate 28-19, but passed the House by only a 102-98 vote. Among those voting no was Congressman Davy Crockett of Tennessee, who called the bill "oppression with a vengeance." But Jackson signed the law on May 28, 1830, making half a century of treaties void. The tribes would have to move. While all of the tribes resisted, the Cherokees went to U.S. courts to assert their claims to their lands. Initially, they won. In *Cherokee Nation v. Georgia* (1831) and *Worcester v. Georgia* (1832), the U.S. Supreme Court, under Chief Justice John Marshall, ruled that the Cherokees were a "domestic dependent nation" and could not be forced by the state of Georgia to give up land that treaty rights agreed to by the U.S. government had given them. Jackson simply ignored the Court. Jackson is supposed to have said, "John Marshall has made his decision, now let him enforce it." No one actually heard Jackson say that, but Jackson controlled the army and he was not about to enforce the Court's decision. No other president before or after ignored the Supreme Court in that way.

Indian Removal was a disaster for the Five Civilized Tribes. The government had seized their homes and offered in return land that was thousands of miles away and completely foreign to them. Moreover, the tribes were divided about how to respond. While most of the country was focused on the Cherokees, Jackson sent Secretary of War John Eaton to negotiate with the Choctaws. By excluding those he considered troublemakers and bribing others, Eaton got a small group of Choctaw leaders to agree to move, but a majority considered those who negotiated the removal treaty to be nonrepresentative and refused to abide by it. The federal troops enforced it anyway.

The French observer Alexis de Tocqueville, who became famous for his analysis of American life in the Jacksonian era, described the day the Choctaws crossed the Mississippi River on their way west:

> At the end of 1831, I stood on the left bank of the Mississippi. … It was then the depths of winter and the cold was exceptionally severe … the snow had frozen hard on the ground; the river was drifting with huge ice-floes. The Indians had brought their families with them and hauled along the wounded, the sick, newborn babies, and old men on the verge of death. They had neither tents nor wagons. … I saw them embark to cross the wide river and that solemn spectacle will never be erased from my memory. Not a sob or complaint could be heard … they stood silent. Their afflictions were of long standing and they considered them beyond remedy. Already the Indians had all embarked upon the boat which was to carry them; their dogs still remained upon the bank. When these animals finally saw they were being left behind forever, they raised all together a terrible howl and plunged into the icy Mississippi to swim after their masters.

Within the decade most members of the Cherokee, Chickasaw, and Creek tribes had made the same crossing. Only the Seminoles avoided their fate.

Alabama and Mississippi followed Georgia's lead and voted to end tribal rights for the Creeks. In March 1832, the Creeks surrendered all land east of the Mississippi, and most of them moved to Oklahoma. Those that took advantage of a promise that they could stay in the East as private citizens soon lost their lands. Some of the remaining Creeks began violent resistance to state and federal authorities, but the so-called Second Creek War of 1836–1837 ended quickly when Jackson's secretary of war ordered federal troops to expel all Creeks from lands east of the Mississippi. The Creeks who were deported after the Second Creek War suffered higher mortality rates than the Cherokees; perhaps half lived to see Oklahoma.

American Voices

Perspectives on Indian Removal, 1818–1830

Different Americans responded differently to President Jackson's plan for Indian Removal. While Jackson tried to justify his plan, groups of white women petitioned Congress to stop what they saw as an immoral process, and Cherokee women opposed the move even a decade earlier.

Andrew Jackson, *Message to Congress*, December 8, 1829

The condition and ulterior destiny of the Indian tribes within the limits of some of our States have become objects of much interest and importance. It has long been the policy of Government to introduce among them the arts of civilization, in the hope of gradually reclaiming them from a wandering life. This policy has, however, been coupled with another wholly incompatible with its success. Professing a desire to civilize and settle them, we have at the same time lost no opportunity to purchase their lands and thrust them farther into the wilderness. By this means they have not only been kept in a wandering state, but been led to look upon us as unjust and indifferent to their fate. …

Our ancestors found them the uncontrolled possessors of these vast regions. By persuasion and force they have been made to retire from river to river and from mountain to mountain, until some of the tribes have become extinct and others have left but remnants to preserve for awhile their once terrible names. …

Humanity and national honor demand that every effort should be made to avert so great a calamity. …

As a means of effecting this end I suggest for your consideration the propriety of setting apart an ample district west of the Mississippi, and without the limits of any State or Territory now formed, to be guaranteed to the Indian tribes as long as they shall occupy it, each tribe having a distinct control over the portion designated for its use.

Statements of Residents of *Steubenville*, Ohio, February 15, 1830

It is readily acknowledged, that the wise and venerated founders of our country's free institutions, have committed the powers of government to those whom nature and reason declare the best fitted to exercise them; and your memorialists would sincerely deprecate any presumptuous interference on the part of their own sex, with the ordinary political affairs of the country, as wholly unbecoming the character of American Females … yet all admit that *there are times* when duty and affection call on us to *advise* and *persuade*, as well as to cheer or to console. And if we approach the public representatives of our husbands and brothers, only in the humble character of suppliants in the cause of mercy and humanity, may we not hope that even the small voice of *female* sympathy will be heard? …

In spite of the *undoubted natural right*, which the Indians have, to the land of their forefathers, and in the face of solemn treaties, pledging the faith of the nation for their secure possession of those lands, it is intended, we are told, to force them from their native soil, and to compel them to seek new homes in a distant and dreary wilderness.

To you then, as the constitutional protectors of the Indians within our territory and as the peculiar guardians of our national character, and our country's welfare, we solemnly and earnestly appeal to save this remnant of a much injured people from annihilation, to shield our country from the curses denounced on the cruel and ungrateful, and to shelter the American character from lasting dishonor.

Cherokee Women's Petition, June 30, 1818

We have called a meeting among ourselves to consult on the different points now before the council, relating to our national affairs. We have heard with painful feelings that the bounds of the land we now possess are to be drawn into very narrow limits. The land was given to us by the Great Spirit above as our common right, to raise our children upon, & to make support for our rising generations. We therefore humbly petition our beloved children, the head men & warriors, to hold out to the last in support of our common right, as the Cherokee nation have been the first settlers of this land; we therefore claim the right to the soil.

We well remember that our country was formerly very extensive, but by repeated sales it has become circumscribed to the very narrow limits we have at present. Our Father the President advised us to become farmers, to manufacture our own clothes, & to have our children instructed. To this advice we have attended in everything as far as we were able. Now the thought of being compelled to remove [to] the other side of the Mississippi is dreadful to us, because it appears to us that we, by this removal, shall be brought to a savage state again, for we have, by the endeavor of our Father the President, become too much enlightened to throw aside the privileges of a civilized life.

We therefore unanimously join in our meeting to hold our country in common as hitherto.

Sources: Andrew Jackson, Annual Message to Congress, December 8, 1829, Messages and Papers of the Presidents, ed. J. D. Richardson, National Archives and Records Administration (1896), II, 456–459 (December 8, 1829); Ladies of Steubenville, Ohio, Petition against Indian Removal (February 15, 1830), Ellen Skinner, *Women and the National Experience: Sources in Women's History*, third edition (Boston: Prentice-Hall, 1996), pp. 142–143; "Petition of Nancy Ward and Other Cherokee Women to the United States Congress, 19\818," in Karen L. Kilcup, editor, *Native American Women's Writings, 1800–1924: An Anthology* (Malden, MA: Blackwell, 2000), pp. 29–30.

Thinking Critically

1. **Analyzing Primary Sources**

   Jackson is acting from the point of view of president of the United States. How might this point of view help us understand Jackson's policy of Indian Removal? How might opponents of Indian Removal have responded to this perspective?

2. **Contextualization**

   How might the fact that two petitions in opposition to Indian Removal were written by women have affected their reception? How did the women petitioners describe their place in society?

10.1

10.2

10.3

Among the Cherokees, a civil conflict broke out about how to respond to the demand that they move to Oklahoma. Principal Chief John Ross and most of the Cherokees were determined to fight for their lands. A minority, some of whom were among the rising middle class and slaveholders within the tribe, decided that a compromise was better than forced expulsion. John Ridge and Elias Boudinot, publisher of the *Cherokee Phoenix*, signed the Treaty of New Echota in December 1835, trading land in Georgia for new land in Oklahoma and $5 million. The U.S. Senate barely ratified the treaty after Daniel Webster and Henry Clay pointed out how fraudulent it was since the majority of the Cherokees opposed it.

After Ridge and Boudinot and their followers departed for Oklahoma, or Indian Territory as it was called, the U.S. Army put most of the remaining members of the tribe in detention camps. A few were able to flee into the wilderness and remained in their homelands but without their land. Others fought, but in the end, Chief Ross and General Winfield Scott negotiated a settlement to avoid further bloodshed. Even though Jackson had left office by then, his successor, Martin Van Buren, was determined to enforce his predecessor's policy. From the detention camps, soldiers forced twelve thousand Cherokee men, women, and children to march west in the fall and winter of 1838–1839. It was an especially cold winter and a terrible time to make a march of over a thousand miles into the unknown. The Cherokees never had enough food, blankets, or warm clothing, and as they moved in large groups, disease and exposure took a terrible toll. On what became known as the **Trail of Tears**, perhaps a quarter to a third of the marchers, including Ross's wife, died before they reached Oklahoma.

Seeing what was happening to other tribes, the Chickasaws moved west quickly on their own. The Seminoles of Florida Territory had no intention of moving, however. Although a minority of Seminoles agreed to move, most stayed in Florida, disappearing into the swamps and hiding places they knew well. When soldiers tried to force them to move, the Seminoles annihilated them. The Second Seminole War was not resolved until 1842. Fewer Seminoles than members of any other tribe ever moved to Oklahoma.

In the meantime, the Sac and Fox tribes, which had already been exiled to the Indian Territory as a result of earlier removals from the Old Northwest, were not too happy about life there. In April 1832, a chief named Black Hawk led one thousand to two thousand Sac and Fox people back east across the Mississippi, closer to their old homelands. The Sac and Fox Indians were moving mostly to escape from hostile Sioux groups on the Great Plains and Iowa Territory. The Illinois governor took the tribes' move into Illinois as an attack, called out the militia, and asked for federal troops. In Black Hawk's War, federal and state troops on the east side of the Mississippi and Sioux warriors on the west virtually annihilated the Fox and Sac tribes, to the delight of whites who were happy to see these tribes completely out of their way.

In fact, Jackson had meant to use the removal law for Georgia to force all Indians east of the Mississippi out of their lands. When the forced exile finally reached its goal by the

Trail of Tears

The forced march in 1838 of the Cherokee Indians from their homelands in Georgia to the Indian Territory in the West; thousands of Cherokees died along the way.

Cherokee men, women, and children, and their U.S. Army guards, rode or walked on the long march from their ancestral homes across a thousand miles to new territory in Oklahoma.

end of the 1830s, only the Iroquois in New York, a few Cherokees in North Carolina, tribes in the more remote areas of the upper Midwest, and scattered small communities remained legally east of the Mississippi, although others like the Seminoles simply melted into the woods and could not be found by the government. All in all, forty-six thousand Indians were forcibly removed during the Jackson administration, and subsequent administrations removed as many more.

The Cherokees and other tribes tend to disappear from the history books after the Trail of Tears. But the Cherokees, Choctaws, and Creeks were resilient people. Forced onto an inhospitable and alien land, they sought to reestablish their communities and culture. To a surprising degree, they succeeded. As the last Cherokees arrived in Indian Territory in 1839, the tribe adopted a new constitution and established Tahlequah as their capital. In 1844, they began publishing the *Cherokee Advocate* in both English and Cherokee. They also set up a school system with elementary schools as well as higher education institutes and seminaries to prepare teachers—European and Cherokee—for their schools. In the U.S. Civil War, parts of the tribe favored each side, and the divided tribe fought internally. But again they rebuilt after the war. Today, there are some 200,000 to 300,000 Cherokees, 70,000 of whom live within the Cherokee Nation in northeast Oklahoma and the rest are scattered around the country, making them the largest federally recognized tribe in the country.

Jacksonian Economics—The War on the Bank of the United States

In his campaign for president, Jackson pledged to do something about the Bank of the United States, which he and many others blamed for the Panic of 1819 and saw as an elitist threat to a democracy. The **Second Bank of the United States** was patterned on the first Bank of the United States, which had been a cornerstone of Alexander Hamilton's economic plans for the new nation (see Chapter 7). The first bank had been chartered in 1791 for a period of twenty years. In 1811, the Jeffersonian Republicans refused to extend its charter and it closed. Henceforth, it seemed, state banks would issue currency in the form of banknotes backed by gold or silver, federal funds would be deposited in state banks, and the federal government, like everyone else, would borrow money from these banks when needed. Then came the War of 1812.

As the War of 1812 threatened to bankrupt the country, some of the nation's richest men, led by John Jacob Astor, met with Treasury Secretary Albert Gallatin and offered to loan the nation the funds it needed if the Bank of the United States was rechartered. They believed that only a national bank could build long-term prosperity and ensure that their loan would be repaid. As a result, a charter for a Second Bank of the United States passed Congress in 1816. The Madison, Monroe, and John Quincy Adams administrations were strong advocates for a unified national market economy that could foster prosperity and stability, and they had used the bank to support that economy. Jackson wanted prosperity, but he disagreed about the government's role in the nation's economy.

The Second Bank of the United States was never without enemies. The Constitution never mentioned a bank, and strict constructionists—who thought the government should limit its role to things specifically included in the Constitution—always opposed it. The bank was also seen by many as a way to expand the power of the commercial elite based in New York and Philadelphia and, thus, was seen as an enemy by farmers whether they lived on small out-of-the-way farms in the still very rural country or on the burgeoning plantations of the cotton-growing South. In the opinion of many farmers, whether small- or large-scale, Jackson was the defender of their interests against threatening commercial elites. In the years since the Supreme Court's ruling on *McCulloch v. Maryland* that Congress had the right to charter a bank if it thought it was in the national interest, popular support for the bank had weakened (see Chapter 9). Many farmers did not believe "the national interest" that Congress saw was the same as their interests.

During his first months in office, Jackson did not say a lot about the bank, but in December 1829, he told Congress: "Both the constitutionality and the expediency of the law creating this bank are well questioned. … [I]t has failed in the great end of establishing a

Second Bank of the United States

A national bank chartered by Congress in 1816 with extensive regulatory powers over currency and credit.

uniform and sound currency." In spite of Jackson's challenge, the bank's charter ensured that it could continue for seven more years, but Jackson had fired a warning shot. Before long, he would do much more.

Many of Jackson's strongest supporters disagreed with him about the bank. The country was prospering, credit was solid, and the soundness of the currency, despite Jackson's words, seemed secure. The federal bank's policies of calling in loans may have helped start the Panic of 1819, but Nicholas Biddle, the bank's president, had done as much as anyone in the country to end the hard times after the Panic of 1819. Nevertheless, Jackson was a populist, intending to represent the common people politically. He told Biddle, "I do not dislike your bank any more than all banks," but the federal bank was the only one Jackson could do something about. His attack on the bank was as emotional as it was calculated.

In 1832, Jackson launched his campaign for reelection. For the first time, something resembling modern political parties played a role. Under Jackson's leadership, the Democratic-Republicans had become simply the Democrats. They easily nominated Jackson for a second term and his handpicked running mate, Secretary of State Martin Van Buren, for vice president. The opposition to Jackson, sometimes known as the National Republicans because they had supported a strong national government, now became known as the Whig Party. They nominated Henry Clay for president and John Sergeant of Pennsylvania as vice president. Unlike the Jacksonian Democrats, the Whig Party was committed to Alexander Hamilton's vision of a federal government that took an active role in shaping the economy, so they strongly supported the Second Bank of the United States. The Whig nominee, Henry Clay, urged Biddle to secure the bank's future as well as that of the pro-bank Whig Party. If Biddle was to request an extension of the bank's charter, even though the original charter would not expire for four years, Clay would promise to make the bank an issue in the campaign. Either Biddle would win the recharter fight immediately, or he would provide Clay a weapon with which to attack Jackson. Biddle, who was astute at counting votes in Congress, took Clay's advice and applied for a new charter. The charter bill passed both houses of Congress easily. But Jackson vetoed it. He told Martin Van Buren, who was now his running mate, "The bank, Mr. Van Buren, is trying to kill me, but I will kill it." In November 1832, Jackson defeated Clay 219 electoral votes to 49. Congress did not override the president's veto.

Biddle still tried to rally support in Congress. He made arguments, offered congressmen loans, and ensured that the bank's lead attorney was elected to Congress from Philadelphia. When Massachusetts senator Daniel Webster complained that his annual retainer from the bank had not been "refreshed as usual," Biddle promised quick action. Biddle also loosened credit across the country, ensuring short-term prosperity but provoking an eventual reckoning. He was desperate to save his bank.

Jackson then made his move. He ordered his treasury secretary to remove federal deposits from the bank and place them in twenty-three state banks that he selected—banks that were quickly called Jackson's "pet" banks by his opponents. The move was meant to destroy the Second Bank of the United States. But the law said that federal funds could be withdrawn only if there was clear evidence that the deposits were not secure. Even Jackson's handpicked auditors could find no such evidence. When Treasury Secretary McLane refused the president's order to move the funds, Jackson promoted him to secretary of state. When another treasury secretary also refused, Jackson fired him.

Finally, Jackson's third treasury secretary, Roger B. Taney, who also had doubts about the legality of removing federal funds, hit on a plan. He would not actually remove federal deposits from the bank, but he would do something just as effective to undermine the bank. Taney paid the government's bills with funds from the accounts in the Bank of the United States, but he stopped depositing new federal revenue in the bank. Instead, the government's income went to the state banks. It was a mortal blow. The federal government's accounts slowly shrunk to zero and the Second Bank of the United States was dead, though it took a few years to die.

Led by Clay, the Senate censured the president, saying he had "assumed upon himself authority and power not conferred by the Constitution and laws." But the censure did not hurt Jackson or save the bank. Biddle's politically motivated loans and payments sapped

Library of Congress [LC-USZ62-809] American cartoon print filing series, Prints and Photographs Division

By the time Jackson became president, political cartoons were becoming popular, including this one that shows Jackson using his order to withdraw government funds to topple the pillars of the bank as Nicholas Biddle, the bank's "devil president," and investors run.

support for the bank. The Second Bank of the United States became a wholly private bank and soon went bankrupt. The combination of inflation caused by Biddle's too-easy credit and the loss of a national bank that could stabilize the currency caused financial distress. By 1837—just after Jackson left office—the nation experienced another financial panic that many blamed on the closure of the federal bank, and when the crisis came, there was no national entity to help stabilize the economy. Nevertheless, efforts to revive the bank failed. For decades, all of the paper currency in circulation would be issued by state banks, some of less than solid credit. Only in 1863, during the Civil War, did the U.S. government again issue paper money, and not until the creation of the Federal Reserve Bank in 1913 did the nation again have a central bank to regulate the economy.

The Tariff, the Union, and the Nullification Crisis

The battle over the tariff began as a modest disagreement over federal tax policy. Before it ended, that battle was the greatest constitutional crisis the nation faced between the adoption of the Constitution in 1789 and the Civil War in 1861. To a degree, it was a personal battle between two proud and stubborn men, Andrew Jackson and John C. Calhoun. In another sense, it was a battle about the fundamental nature of the U.S. government.

ANDREW JACKSON VERSUS JOHN C. CALHOUN John C. Calhoun of South Carolina had been elected vice president when John Quincy Adams won the presidency in 1824, and he was reelected to that office in 1828 to serve with Jackson. Because separate ballots were cast for presidential and vice presidential candidates after the passage of the Twelfth

Amendment in 1804 and before the rise of party nominating conventions in 1832, no one thought it strange that two leaders as hostile to each other as Adams and Jackson would have the same vice president. As a congressman and as secretary of war under President James Monroe, Calhoun had been a nationalist who favored internal improvements as much as Henry Clay or John Quincy Adams. He sought a strong national government and had supported the Bank of the United States. Although his views differed from Jackson's on some issues, everyone expected Calhoun and Jackson, as proslavery southerners, to have a close partnership. It was not to be.

One of the first wedges between them was purely social. Jackson's secretary of war, John Eaton, had married the recently widowed Margaret O'Neale Timberlake, but rumors swirled that she was a widow only because her first husband, a naval officer, had committed suicide when he learned of her long adulterous relationship with Eaton. Jackson, who had been deeply hurt by attacks on his own marriage, defended the Eatons. Others in Washington, led by Mrs. Calhoun, snubbed Peggy Eaton. When Emily Donelson, Jackson's official White House hostess, joined with Mrs. Calhoun, Jackson temporarily banished her from the White House. He never forgave the Calhouns.

Another reason for the growing split between Jackson and Calhoun centered on the fact that Calhoun's political beliefs were changing. By 1828, Calhoun, who had previously advocated for a strong federal role in the life of the nation—far stronger than anything Jackson ever advocated—was becoming the nation's strongest defender of states' rights against federal authority. This new stance may have reflected an honest change of heart, but it also served a political purpose. Regardless, it guaranteed a clash with Jackson since no matter how much Jackson might have favored states' rights, he would not tolerate any challenge to his authority as president.

Many of the leaders in South Carolina, Calhoun's home state, were becoming very fearful of the federal government, and South Carolina was developing the strongest antifederal stance in the Union. The South Carolina Radicals, as they were called, dominated state government. They advocated the right of states to declare any federal law null and void or even to secede from the Union. The reason was clear: South Carolinians feared for the future of slavery more than people in any other state. Most residents of South Carolina—54 percent—were enslaved people of African descent. In some rice-growing regions of the state, that figure was closer to 90 percent. A wealthy but deeply fearful white elite governed these slaves and depended on their labor to generate continuing wealth. In 1827, a pamphlet called *The Crisis; or, Essays on the Usurpations of the Federal Government* argued that federal tariffs, calls for internal improvements, and support for other federal activities were all meant to enable the national government, if it chose, to abolish slavery. As word spread that Parliament was about to abolish slavery throughout the British Empire in the 1830s, the fear grew that Congress might try to do the same. Calhoun had to decide whether he was with his state's planter elite or against them. He might have dreamed about becoming president someday, but in the meantime, he would have to win elections in South Carolina. He made his choice.

NULLIFICATION AND THE FUTURE OF THE REPUBLIC   In 1828, Calhoun wrote a pamphlet arguing that a state could declare a tariff or any other federal law null and void. Calhoun claimed that since state-by-state conventions had ratified the Constitution, state conventions, not the Supreme Court, had the authority to decide what was constitutional. In his view, once a state convention declared a federal law void, other states would have to weigh in, and only a new amendment to the Constitution could force the law on the dissenting state. Calhoun did not advocate secession as many of the South Carolina Radicals did. Instead, he hoped nullification in response to a tariff or to restrictions on slavery would make secession unnecessary.

The tariff, not the issue of slavery, brought the issue of nullification to the fore. The tariff, or tax on imported goods, had been the major source of financing of the federal government since the Washington administration, and it had been an issue in the 1828 election in which Jackson defeated Adams. As Jackson's supporters prepared for that election, Jackson's chief advisor, Martin Van Buren, realized that, even though he and Jackson opposed a high tariff—in part, because they thought the federal government needed less money and, in part, because the tax raised the cost of foreign-made consumer products in the United States—the Adams-Clay tariff was popular in many parts of the country because it protected local industries from foreign competition and because many people liked the internal improvements that the tariff financed. Adams and Clay might want to fight the 1828 election on the issue of tariffs, but Van Buren did not.

When the Adams administration suggested a new tariff, Van Buren and his congressional allies decided to reshape it rather than oppose it. They knew they could not win New England in the next election, so they did not hesitate to modify the proposed tariff by reducing the protection for the cotton cloth produced by New England mill owners, thus allowing foreign-made cotton cloth to be sold more cheaply than might otherwise have been the case. They also raised tariffs to protect export of products like molasses, hemp, iron, and wool products, which were produced in the mid-Atlantic states, especially in Pennsylvania, to woo voters there by protecting their industries and jobs from foreign competition. The result was a tariff that raised the price of products that many Americans bought from foreign sources and that angered the cotton mill owners, who originally wanted the tariff but now saw the protection of their industry disappear. The new tariff also infuriated rural interests, especially southern plantation owners, who saw the cost of everything they needed go up while no protection was provided to the price of the goods—most of all, raw cotton—that they produced and sold on the international market. The 1828 tariff came to be known as the **Tariff of Abominations** because it was so uneven and obviously unfair in the industries and regions it protected, but it passed Congress and set the stage for a confusing presidential campaign and the crisis that followed.

Planters in South Carolina saw the tariff as a terrible hardship and an unfair use of federal power. To a degree, they were right. A tax on imports raised the cost of virtually everything the planters needed. Planters claimed that forty out of every one hundred bales of cotton they produced went to pay the tariff. This claim was an exaggeration, but the tariff may have raised the cost of living in South Carolina by 20 percent. In addition, planters worried that a tariff on imported goods might cause other nations to purchase less raw cotton either in retaliation or because, with Americans buying less from abroad, other nations might not have had the funds to purchase American-grown cotton. With their state's economy hurting, public opinion in South Carolina supported nullification of the tariff.

The issue of states' rights versus the rights of the federal government was argued on the floor of the U.S. Senate in January 1830. It was a debate that would be remembered for generations. South Carolina senator Robert Y. Hayne, a protégé of Calhoun's, claimed that the federal government "has invaded the State of South Carolina, is making war upon her citizens, and endeavoring to overthrow her principles and institutions." Everyone understood that Hayne was talking about the tariff and about the issue of slavery. He was determined to defend the right of South Carolina to nullify federal law and, if still dissatisfied, to secede from the Union if Congress ever made a move against slavery. Massachusetts senator Daniel Webster in his "Second Reply to Hayne" pleaded for a strong federal union that no state should be allowed to undermine. His closing line, "Liberty and Union, now and forever, one and inseparable," became part of American lore. Hayne congratulated Webster on winning the war of words, though Hayne never changed his mind.

At first, people wondered how the president would respond to the debate. Jackson had campaigned for reducing the federal role in people's lives, but he did not like to be crossed. He was not elected to see the government over which he

Tariff of Abominations

A revised federal tariff (or tax on imports) that lowered the tax on cotton products but raised it on many of the products made in the mid-Atlantic states.

Senator Daniel Webster of Massachusetts, no friend of Jackson, nevertheless became the most vocal opponent of nullification in the Senate. His 1828 speech calling for "Liberty and Union, now and forever, one and inseparable" was a well-remembered plea for a strong Union and federal government.

presided pushed aside. As a military man, he would not countenance mutiny. As a politician, he despised Calhoun's self-serving strategic maneuvering. To the surprise of some, Jackson, the president elected with virtually no support from New England, embraced Webster's speech. Four months after the Hayne-Webster debate, political leaders were asked to make toasts at a banquet. Looking directly at his vice president, Jackson, offered a simple toast, "Our Union: *It must be preserved.*" Calhoun responded, "The Union. Next to our liberty, the most dear. May we always remember that it can only be preserved by respecting the rights of the states." It marked the final break between the two men.

Nevertheless, as strongly as Jackson believed in asserting federal authority, he was still prepared to compromise about the tariff itself. The actual rate charged in the tariff mattered far less to Jackson than the principle that no state had a right to nullify federal law. A compromise seemed possible when Congress convened in 1831. Former president John Quincy Adams had been elected to the House of Representatives from Massachusetts (the only former president in history to return to Congress), and the congressional leaders asked him to write a new tariff to replace the Tariff of Abominations. Adams took the job seriously. He reduced the duty on goods not produced in the United States and therefore not in need of protection, but retained tariffs to protect growing U.S. industries, especially iron and cotton textiles. He also reduced the tariff on cheap woolens—which slaves wore—from 45 percent to 5 percent, a significant concession to the slave states.

Most of the South found Adams's tariff reasonable. Besides, much of the cotton-growing South was prospering, despite the tariff, because of other Jacksonian policies, especially from the new land that Indian Removal had made available for growing cotton. Other states were in no mood to press the nullification issue.

But South Carolina was different. Much of the state's farmland had been exhausted by decades of overuse, and its dependency on slave labor made its leaders more fearful of federal intervention in the institution of slavery than those of any other state. Led by Calhoun, the state's leaders believed that they had to win the right to nullify the tariff to establish the larger principle that states could nullify any law. For them, the Adams tariff was not enough. In November 1832, a South Carolina state convention declared that both the tariffs of 1828 and 1832 were unconstitutional and that "it shall not be lawful … to enforce payment of duties imposed by the said acts within the limits of this state" after February 1833. They also said that the state would secede if the federal government tried to force it to back down. The South Carolina legislature elected Robert Hayne, who had debated with Webster, as the governor to lead the state through these difficult times and elected Calhoun to replace Hayne in the Senate. Calhoun would essentially be South Carolina's ambassador to the federal government for the next two decades. Calhoun resigned as vice president in December 1832, a little more than two months before his term ended, and returned to the Senate as a member, a very belligerent member. The stage was set for a major confrontation.

In November 1832, the South Carolina legislature also raised a state militia of twenty-five thousand volunteers. Jackson responded with a proclamation, stating that the state's vote was "in direct violation of their duty as citizens of the United States." According to Jackson, they had no right to nullify federal law and certainly not to raise their own army and, he said, "Disunion by armed force is treason." He told a South Carolina congressman, "I will hang the first man of them I can get my hands on to the first tree I can find." He backed his words with action, reinforcing federal garrisons and sending armed revenue ships to Charleston Harbor. He also shifted the collection of customs duties in Charleston to warships offshore. When Governor Hayne told Senator Thomas Hart Benton of Missouri that he did not think Jackson would really hang anyone, Benton, who knew Jackson better, replied, "I tell you, Hayne, when Jackson begins to talk about hanging, they can begin to look out for ropes!" Jackson also lobbied to ensure no other southern state supported South Carolina and pushed Congress to keep the tariffs low.

In the end, no shots were fired. On March 1, 1833, Congress passed a compromise tariff that Henry Clay had crafted based on Adams's proposals and gave the president the authority to put down the rebellion. Wiser heads in South Carolina decided to compromise. The state convention reconvened and declared victory based on the new Clay tariff. For spite, they also nullified the congressional vote of new military authority, which they called the "Force Bill," but that action was now meaningless since South Carolina was no longer resisting federal authority.

Thinking Historically

The Nullification Crisis

The 1832 South Carolina convention that passed the Ordinance of Nullification said:

> Whereas the Congress of the United States, by various acts, purporting to be acts laying duties and imposts [taxes] on foreign imports, but in reality intended for the protection of domestic manufacturers, and giving the bounties to classes and individuals engaged in particular employments, at the expense and to the injury and oppression of other classes and individuals ... hath exceeded it just powers under the Constitution. ...
>
> We, therefore, the people of the State of South Carolina in Convention assembled, do declare and ordain. ... That the several acts and parts of acts of the Congress of the United States, purporting to be laws for the imposing of duties and imposts on the importation of foreign commodities ... are unauthorized by the Constitution of the United States, and violate the true meaning and intent thereof, and are null, void, and no law, nor binding upon this state, its officers or citizens.

This declaration was not the first of its kind. The Kentucky and Virginia resolves of 1798 and 1799, written by Thomas Jefferson and James Madison, had said the same thing about the Alien and Sedition Acts. The Hartford Convention said much the same thing in 1814 about the War of 1812. Yet unlike the response to earlier challenges, President Jackson declared the South Carolina ordinance "incompatible with the existence of the Union" and prepared for a military response.

Source: *Statues at Large of South Carolina*, Vol. I, pp. 329ff. (Columbia, SC: A. S. Johnston, 1836).

Thinking Critically

1. **Continuity and Change over Time**
   How similar or different was the South Carolina Ordinance of Nullification from either the Kentucky and Virginia resolves or the resolutions of the Hartford Convention? How do all three represent continuity or change in American thinking about the Constitution and the federal government?

2. **Argument Development**
   Defend or refute the following statement: "As the Nullification Crisis demonstrates, the ratification of the Constitution in 1788 was only a first, tentative step toward defining the relationship between the federal government and the states." What events and developments support your position?

Jackson won the nullification battle, but it was an incomplete victory. He made it clear, in words and actions, which Abraham Lincoln would use as precedent, that no state could nullify federal law and that the U.S. government would use force to assert its authority. He was treated as a hero in many parts of the country and even given an honorary degree by Harvard University. Even so, neither Calhoun nor the South Carolina legislature admitted defeat. In fact, that legislature passed a new law in 1834 requiring anyone holding state office to swear primary loyalty to South Carolina and only conditional loyalty to the federal government. This law effectively barred Unionists, those moderates who disagreed with nullification, perhaps a third of the state's voters, from state office for the next thirty years.

Alexis de Tocqueville was in the United States during the Nullification Crisis. He took a dim view of the compromise on the tariff and the decision of South Carolina to nullify the "Force Bill":

> Either I am mistaken or the federal government of the Unites States is daily losing its power . ... I think I have seen a more lively feeling of independence and a more evident affection for regional government developing in the individual states of the Union.

The outcome of this movement, Tocqueville said, was "hidden in the future and I do not claim the ability to lift the veil." But he remained worried for the future of the country.

10.1 Quick Review

Was Andrew Jackson's presidency democratic? Which of his actions and policies support your argument?

Democratized Religion: The Second Great Awakening

10.2 Analyze the diversity of American religious experience and how the freedom of the era gave rise to diverse religious and philosophical expressions.

Most Americans had strong opinions about Andrew Jackson. They might love him or hate him, but they paid attention to what he did. However, politics was far from the only interest of most people. Many things closer to home, and sometimes closer to their own souls, mattered more. For many Americans in the 1820s and 1830s, the growth of a more popular and individualistic democracy, economic changes and dislocations caused by the market revolution, greater opportunity to move to a new place or to move up—or down—on the social scale, and the growth of popular social movements led by ordinary citizens were far more important than President' Jackson's policies or opinions.

No popular movement was more powerful than the upsurge in religious activity that took place in Jacksonian America. Once again de Tocqueville understood the country well: "There is no country in the whole world in which the Christian religion retains a greater influence over the souls of men than in America." He described the Christianity he saw as "a democratic and republican religion." When de Tocqueville wrote these words in the early 1830s, the Second Great Awakening was in full swing. It had begun around 1800 (see Chapter 8) but gathered new strength in the Jacksonian Era. Not all Americans were Protestant Christians, and many of those who were Christians did not fit into traditional Protestantism. But for a large number of those who lived from the 1820s to the 1840s, religion of one kind or another was terribly important, even if formal membership in a specific religious congregation was not.

Charles G. Finney and New York's "Burned-Over District"

In 1821, Charles Grandison Finney, a twenty-nine-year-old lawyer in Adams, New York, not far from the Erie Canal, was struggling with the question of whether true religious belief was consistent with his legal career. He decided to leave his law practice, and began to preach in churches in upstate New York, eventually becoming one of the most influential preachers in the United States.

In July 1824, Finney was ordained a Presbyterian minister in spite of his lack of formal training. In 1826, the spirit of revivalism hit upstate New York, and in 1830, Finney led the largest religious revival ever seen in Rochester, New York. Six hundred people joined one of the town's three Presbyterian churches, and the other denominations were also strengthened.

Finney did not seek an emotional catharsis from his congregants but, like an attorney, argued his case logically using wit and wisdom. Nevertheless, in his preaching, the rigid religious orthodoxy that dominated Congregational and Presbyterian churches gave way to a more egalitarian spirit that fit with the era. Finney called people to change their lives, not necessarily to agree with specific creeds. Because of his preaching, hundreds, then thousands, took religion more seriously, joined churches, participated in reform movements, and changed New York and American society.

By the late 1830s, the area along the Erie Canal where Finney preached had become known as "the burned-over district" because of the fires of religious enthusiasm that rolled over the region. Finney was far from the only revivalist in New York. However, he gave the New York revivals a distinct tone—different not only from the emotionalism of frontier revivals but also from the staid life of many established churches. The Erie Canal also made communications easier and faster than before, so word of the revivals traveled fast.

Lyman Beecher and the Growth of Voluntary Societies

As a young minister, Lyman Beecher had been one of the staunchest defenders of state support for the Congregational churches in Connecticut (see Chapter 8). Once the Connecticut churches lost their government support, however, Beecher embraced the new situation and supported revivals and voluntary associations for moral reform as a far better approach than any state support for religion. Beecher described his goal as "a Bible for every family, a school for every district, and a pastor for every 1,000 souls."

As the Second Great Awakening grew, a series of voluntary societies or interdenominational organizations that Beecher helped launch also grew in influence. These societies were not owned by any one religious body but, rather, depended on the voluntary contributions of members of several different religious bodies. They represented a new form of cooperation in the service of a larger goal to change the culture of the United States. The American Bible Society distributed Bibles, the American Sunday School Union provided curriculum materials for church-based Sunday schools, and the American Education Society supported the education of ministers. In addition, the American Board of Commissioners for Foreign Missions sent missionaries around the world, including Adoniram Judson and his wife, Ann Hasseltine Judson, whose efforts in Burma became role models for generations of foreign missionaries seeking to convert the world to Christianity. Beecher included prominent members of the Congregational, Presbyterian, and Episcopal churches in the leadership of these societies. The mission of all these groups was moral reform—the creation of a sober, God-fearing, American public.

Lyman Beecher, one of the leaders of the Second Great Awakening, is shown here with his numerous children, including petitioner and educator Catharine (to the left of her father), Harriet Beecher Stowe (far right), and one of the most famous ministers of the next generation, Henry Ward Beecher (standing on the right).

In the early 1830s, Beecher became president of Lane Theological Seminary in Cincinnati to prepare future ministers, strengthen religious colleges, and place Protestant pastors in hundreds of midwestern churches. He also helped create the public school system of Ohio and supported schools and teachers across the Midwest.

The goal of all of this activity was to strengthen the moral sway of Congregational-Presbyterian Protestantism against the individualism of Jacksonian Democrats, Catholics, and other more individualistic Protestants. For Beecher, separation of church and state meant that specific denominations would not wield political power, but Protestant reformers would provide the leadership in a culture in which the churches, voluntary societies, and public schools would reinforce common beliefs and practices that would shape all aspects of American life.

Revivalism and Moral Reform Movements

Perhaps three-fourths of those converted by the revivals were women who then prayed and lobbied for their husbands and families to convert. Finney and his closest lieutenant, Theodore Dwight Weld, encouraged women to be active in their religious communities. Where New England churches had urged women to keep silent except at home, the new generation of revivalists welcomed them as prayer leaders and preachers. Speaking in "promiscuous assemblies" may have been familiar in Baptist and Methodist churches, but it was new in the more middle-class Presbyterian and Congregational churches. Women who became religious leaders in the revivals often also became leaders in their communities. The movement demanding women's rights that swept the United States in the 1840s sprang from the same areas of upstate New York that experienced major revivals in the 1820s and 1830s. The link was not surprising. Across the country, the Second Great Awakening led to crusades for political, moral, and social reforms among many Protestant groups and inspired the growth of utopian communities.

For Finney, conversion meant that one needed to show one's new faith in ethical behavior, and no ethical behavior was more important to him than opposing slavery. Upstate New York's churches sent revivalist preachers into the rest of the country to preach for the abolition of slavery. For the next thirty years, the Finney-Weld brand of revivalism spread across the country and helped inspire northerners to fight a war to end slavery.

The rights of women and opposition to slavery were not the only reform causes to spring from the revivalism of the Second Great Awakening. Other reformers, inspired by the same forces, began to advocate for changes in the way prisoners were treated. Too often, they said, overcrowded prisons were simply schools for crime, and the focus on punishment, whatever the original crime, did little to redeem or reclaim prisoners to reenter society. At first, reformers advocated the building of prisons in which each prisoner would be confined to a solitary cell where they would have time to reflect on their past, be taught new habits, and prepare to reenter society. But too often, the solitary confinement led to insanity rather than reform. In response, prison reformers built a new kind of prison in which each prisoner had a separate cell, with access to common dining quarters, workshops, and a chapel. In all of these spaces, the authorities sought to teach prisoners a new way of behaving as preparation for reclaiming them. In the 1830s, the New York state penitentiary at Auburn was redesigned to foster the new approach, and soon thereafter, a large new penitentiary at Sing Sing on the Hudson River was built with one thousand cells plus the common areas. Reformers hoped that the new, more humane approach would change lives and ultimately society. Other states quickly followed in adopting the new models.

Many mentally ill people were treated very much like prisoners before the reforms of the 1830s and 1840s, and they often found themselves in similar circumstances. Reformers quickly took up their cause. Perhaps no one equaled Dorothea Dix as a reformer in the treatment of the mentally ill. In 1843, Dix told the Massachusetts legislature that she was calling their attention "to the present state of Insane Persons confined within this Commonwealth, in cages, closets, cellars, stalls, pens! Chained, naked, beaten with rods, and lashed into obedience!" The result, beginning in Massachusetts, was that a system of state hospitals for the insane replaced the earlier prisons.

Other reforms also blossomed. Although the campaign against alcohol would reach its peak many decades later, it began during the Second Great Awakening. Lyman Beecher called for "the banishment of ardent spirits from the list of lawful objects of commerce." Many, including members of Congress, took the pledge to stop drinking. The U.S. Army stopped the old tradition of a ration of alcohol, and refusing to drink became a mark of religious observance. At the same time, the American Peace Society advocated an end to all wars. Schools were opened for those who were deaf and blind. Efforts were made to rescue prostitutes. Countless reforms designed to create a better, more humane, and sometimes more tightly controlled society emerged from the enthusiasm of the awakening.

This illustration from an anti-alcohol publication makes the claim that drunkenness was the cause of many problems in society, especially the abuse of women.

Utopian Religious Communities

The religious enthusiasm of the early 1800s also inspired untraditional ways of thinking about religious matters. The amount of space in a country as large as America allowed people to develop their own communities relatively undisturbed, and the American emphasis on liberty, even the liberty to be eccentric, made the United States fertile ground for radical experiments and utopian religious communities. Some of these religious experiments were short lived. Others lasted for generations. A few, most of all the Mormons, have continued to the present.

MOTHER ANN LEE AND THE SHAKERS The founder of the United Society of Believers in Christ's Second Appearing, or the Shakers, was Ann Lee—known as Mother Ann Lee—who gathered a few supporters in England and came to America in 1774. Lee was convinced that she was receiving a special revelation from God that human sexuality was the basis of all sin and celibacy was the only way to live a godly life.

Lee inspired Shaker communities in New York and New England. Shaker worship reflected Lee's spirituality and, according to observers, included "shaking and singing, hopping

10.1

10.2

10.3

American Voices

The Shaker Community, "'Tis the Gift to Be Simple," 1830s

The simplicity and joyfulness of the Shakers was noticed. Shaker furniture, now so popular, was not just a product. Mildred Barker, leader of a Shaker Community in Maine, who died in 1990, once reflected, "I almost expect to be remembered as a chair or a table." But Barker reminded those who came to interview her that behind all of the Shakers' physical artifacts, "There's the religion." The basic joy, humility, and playfulness of the Shaker faith continue to be remembered in this familiar hymn that dates to the 1830s:

> 'Tis the gift to be simple, 'tis the gift to be free;
> 'Tis the gift to come down where we ought to be;
> And when we find ourselves in the place just right,
> 'Twill be in the valley of love and delight.
> When true simplicity is gain'd,
> To bow and to bend we shan't be asham'd

> To turn, turn will be our delight,
> 'Till by turning, turning we come round right.

Source: Stephen J. Stein, *The Shaker Experience in America* (New Haven: Yale University Press, 1992), p. 191.

Thinking Critically

1. **Analyzing Primary Sources**

   What values and priorities are extolled in the hymn? What do these priorities tell you about the beliefs and the historical situation of the hymn's author?

2. **Comparison**

   Why might simplicity, certainty, and humility have been particularly appealing to 1830s Americans? At what other times in U.S. history might these virtues matter a lot?

In Shaker worship and community life, women and men were kept separate, but all participated in lively music and dance designed to shake sin out of their bodies.

Library of Congress Prints and Photographs Division [LC-USZ62-13659]

and turning, smoking and running, groaning and laughing." Shaker communities at New Lebanon, New Hampshire; Sabbath Day Lake, Maine; and elsewhere thrived, and the Shakers became one of the largest and most successful of the pre–Civil War communitarian movements.

Shaker theology placed Ann Lee on a par with Jesus and committed the society to the equal leadership of women with men. But Shakers were united by their community life more than by theology. They demanded celibacy, a requirement that limited the community's appeal and prevented increasing membership by means of childbirth. Instead, all new members had to be converts who were attracted to Shaker life. The revivals produced many such converts who sought a deeper spiritual life than they found in traditional churches. Shaker beliefs were reflected in their commitment to making things of beauty, and Shaker furniture remains a reminder of their beliefs. The things they created, whether furniture, houses, or art, were owned in common, not individually, a requirement that some found as difficult to accept as celibacy.

JOHN HUMPHREY NOYES AND THE ONEIDA COMMUNITY The Oneida Community also had its roots in the Second Great Awakening and flourished in Oneida, New York, between 1848 and 1879. Its founder and spiritual guide was John Humphrey Noyes, who was born in Vermont in 1811. As a student for the ministry, he became convinced that repentance from sin was not enough, that people should simply stop sinning, and that all Christians could achieve a state "in which all the affections of the heart are given to God, and in which there is no sin."

Gathering a small community in Putney, Vermont, he expanded his definition of Christian perfectionism to include what he called "complex marriage," an arrangement in which monogamy was replaced with many sexual companions. Noyes argued that sexual pleasure was a gift from God and that Christianity demanded the sharing of that gift without any exclusive or jealous reservations.

Vermont authorities, however, took a dim view of these sexual practices, and Noyes and his followers moved to Oneida, New York, where the community thrived for decades, supported ultimately by producing and selling silverware. Oneida eventually fell victim to Victorian morality and to its dependence on Noyes as its single charismatic leader. Between 1875 and 1879, Oneida was torn by debates as New York authorities began threatening arrests for Oneida's flouting of the state's marriage laws. Noyes fled to Canada and the community dissolved, although the silver business supported former members for generations.

ROBERT OWEN AND THE NEW HARMONY COMMUNITY   After making a fortune in London, Robert Owen founded a model factory town at New Lanark, Scotland, in which he sought to put the spirit of universal welfare into practice. In the early 1820s, Owen decided to relocate his utopian vision of a community designed to benefit all of it members and establish it in the United States.

In early 1825, nine hundred people arrived at New Harmony, Indiana, where Owen had purchased land. But New Harmony failed within a year. The community could not attract enough skilled workers to make it economically successful. There was tension between those who ran New Harmony and the rest of the community. As one disaffected resident recalled, the "aristocrats" quarreled, and the fields went to ruin. Owen lost most of his fortune, which he had invested in New Harmony, but returned to England to continue to advocate his version of social reform.

JOSEPH SMITH AND THE CHURCH OF JESUS CHRIST OF THE LATTER-DAY SAINTS   Joseph Smith (1805–1844) was as much a product of New York's burned-over district as Charles G. Finney. Smith was born in 1805 and moved with his family to a farm in Palmyra, New York, when he was the age of eleven. In 1827, word spread along the Erie Canal that Smith had found a treasure that would unlock the Indian history of the area. He had, he said, found golden plates and magical stones known as Urim and Thummim with which to read and translate what was written on the plates by an ancient prophet-historian named Mormon. He published the result, the *Book of Mormon*, in 1830. With that book, a uniquely American religious tradition was born, one that its followers believed represented a rebirth of true Christianity.

Smith, however, did much more than publish a new book; he organized a community. Within a month of the book's publication, the first Mormon community began to form near Palmyra, New York, with Smith as its leader. Some responded with hostility to his efforts, even tarring and feathering Smith at one point. But converts seeking religious truth poured in, a temple was built, and the community grew.

In response to the hostility, Smith and the Mormon community moved to Missouri and then, in the late 1830s, to Nauvoo, Illinois, which became the largest and fastest-growing city in Illinois because of Mormonism. The city's fifteen thousand residents became a virtually autonomous state, and their militia was recognized by state law. But Smith's political involvements and religious teaching, especially his suggestion that all members participate in marriages involving one husband and multiple wives, brought renewed hostility. On June 27, 1844, a mob killed Smith and his brother Hyrum.

With Smith's death, Brigham Young became the new leader of the Mormons in 1847 and led them on a cross-continent trek to the shores of the Great Salt Lake in what is now Utah. Salt Lake was then on the northern edge of the Republic of Mexico, which was soon to be annexed by the United States. There, far from any governmental authority, they set up settlements in a tight, church-regulated community. They also embraced Smith's revelation that a man could take as many wives as he could support.

But the Treaty of Guadalupe Hildago, which marked the end of the U.S. War with Mexico from 1846 to 1848, brought Salt Lake City and the Mormon community under the control of the U.S. government. For a while, the U.S. government left the Mormons alone, but in 1857, President James Buchanan replaced Young with a non-Mormon territorial governor, and the Mormon War broke out as federal authorities tried to enforce monogamy on the Mormons and the Mormons fought back. In one well-publicized incident, Mormons massacred a group of non-Mormon settlers. Only in 1890, after an intense time of prayer and a new revelation, did the Mormon leadership abandon plural marriage. Relations with the government improved, and Utah became a state in 1896. Of all the new religious

Pictorial Press Ltd/Alamy Stock Photo

Mormons, like those shown in this wagon train, crossed the plains and mountains to get to new homes in Utah.

communities spawned during the Second Great Awakening, the Church of Jesus Christ of the Latter-Day Saints has been by far the most successful.

Transcendentalism

In 1838, far from Salt Lake City or the revivals of New York, Ralph Waldo Emerson gave a speech at Harvard Divinity School in Cambridge, Massachusetts, that had as much impact as any revival sermon. Emerson had been ordained as a Unitarian minister but had resigned when he came to believe that the Lord's Supper and public prayer were barriers to direct experience of the divine. The focus on passionate direct experience of the world and of the divine would become the core of the Transcendentalist movement.

In the *Divinity School Address*, Emerson told an audience of future Unitarian ministers that too often in formal worship, "[t]he soul is not preached." And, he said, "The true preacher can be known by this, that he deals out to the people his life,—life passed through the fire of thought." Emerson's call to preach "throbs of desire and hope" rather than formal theology offended most of his audience and he was never invited back to the Divinity School, but the speech represented a new approach to religious life that was developing in America in the 1830s.

While Emerson continued to develop his ideas for another forty years, the Transcendentalist movement with which he is most associated blossomed in the 1830s. In 1836, a group that came to call themselves the Transcendental Club met at the Boston home of George Ripley, another Unitarian minister, to discuss ideas. In 1841, under Ripley's leadership, members of the Transcendental Club founded Brook Farm, a utopian community in West Roxbury, Massachusetts, where the residents sought to support themselves through manual labor. Women and men shared work equally, and an effort was made at true gender equity. But few of the residents of Brook Farm actually knew much about farming, the farm did not prosper, and the community disbanded in 1847. Nevertheless, Emerson's writings and the Transcendental movement he helped launch reflected an impatience with "old ways" and a desire for direct and immediate experience of the divine that continued to impact American religious life.

10.2 Quick Review

How did the increasing diversity of religion in America reflect other political and social changes in the nation?

Democratized Education, Democratized Art: The Birth of the Common School, American Landscape Painting, and Photography

10.3 Explain the development of public education and art as a result of, and in response to, the cultural currents of the 1820s and 1830s.

The years during which Andrew Jackson dominated American politics were also years in which the nation's public school system was radically transformed, though the transformation was mostly the work of Jackson's staunch opponents. Many of the most prominent education reformers were Whigs who did not share Jackson's vision for American society. They often sought to change the ways schools were organized and conducted for the same reasons they opposed Jackson politically. Schools, Whig educators believed, could build a new American culture more to their liking than the Jacksonian brand of individualistic democracy.

Many individuals contributed to what came to be known as the Common School Crusade. Catharine Beecher sought to empower women by opening the doors for them to become school teachers. Horace Mann, a Whig political leader, helped launch a new and more tightly organized school system in Massachusetts—a system that came to serve as a model for much of the nation. William Holmes McGuffey wrote a school book that became the text for American morality. The transformation of the nation's schools in this period was a key dynamic of the changing culture of the United States between the 1820s and the 1840s every bit as much as Jacksonian democracy transformed the nation's politics.

At the same time, a new generation of American artists sought to portray the country in a new light. While earlier artists had focused on portraits of heroic individuals or scenes in war or similar events, painters of this era wanted to show the beauty of the American land and the country's natural environment. Others mastered the technology of a new invention—the camera—and were able to record individuals and families in ways never before possible.

Women Become Teachers

In 1835, Catharine Beecher, daughter of the religious leader Lyman Beecher, was already well known for founding the Hartford Female Seminary to help educate women and for her petitions seeking to stop Jackson's Indian Removal. In her *Essay on the Education of Female Teachers* published in that year, Beecher argued that women were much better equipped than men to be teachers, and she wanted to educate them for the work. She saw teaching as an extension of motherhood and wrote, "Woman, whatever are her relations in life, is necessarily the guardian of the nursery, the companion of childhood, and the constant model of imitation. It is her hand that first stamps impressions on the immortal spirit, that must remain forever." At a time when most teachers were still men, Beecher argued not only that women made better teachers than men but also that including women as teachers would expand the supply of teachers for the country and open the door to a professional life for middle-class women who had few employment options.

Emma Willard had founded Troy Female Seminary in 1821 in upstate New York to prepare women to be teachers. Like Beecher, Willard had argued, "There are many females of ability, to whom the business of instructing children is highly acceptable." She also believed that women should get the same education as men and modeled the curriculum at Troy on what men studied at college, though she added courses on how to teach. In 1837, Mary Lyon founded Mount Holyoke Female Seminary in Massachusetts to give future female teachers a college education.

New Structures for Schooling

While Catharine Beecher and her colleagues were transforming the gender of the teaching profession, other reformers sought to transform the structure of schools. Horace Mann was

3LH/Superstock

Women, mostly very young women, taught school, most often in one-room schools like this one where children of all ages learned to read, write, count, and then advance through more complex assignments. Not all the schools were as comfortable as the one shown here and not all the children were as well behaved.

a rising star in the Massachusetts Whig Party in 1836, and he shepherded a bill through the legislature to create a state Board of Education. He then became the board's full-time, paid secretary—its only employee. Mann spent the next twelve years advocating tighter state standards for education, more money for schools and teacher salaries, and a better education for children. He became the best-known spokesperson for public education of his generation.

Mann described the schools of Massachusetts as "so many distinct, independent communities," which he meant to change by centralizing control of education at the state level. He also believed that it was the responsibility of all citizens to pay taxes to support quality schools. Like Beecher and Willard, Mann wanted educated teachers and created a system of state-sponsored teacher preparation schools, called "normal schools," that offered one year of state-funded preparation to any young woman or man who wanted to be a teacher. Mann's greatest concern, however, was the moral education of the state's citizens. He believed that there needed to be a public guardian of morality, and since the United States had no state church, that guardian had to be the public school.

While Mann was the best-known educational reformer, most Whigs came to advocate state systems of education, state support for teacher preparation, and state efforts to ensure a common morality. Mann and his allies could not understand why anyone would oppose them. Yet even in Massachusetts, there was opposition. Jacksonian Democrats in the legislature tried to abolish the Board of Education and the office of secretary. They saw the state control that Mann advocated as expensive, unnecessary, and an unwarranted interference by the state in local affairs, which would undermine local support for each town's school.

Roman Catholics were especially unhappy with the growing influence and cost of the public school system. Catholics saw the public schools as essentially a Protestant venture, something Protestants like Mann could never understand. Mann advocated teaching the Protestant Bible in school "without note or comment," leaving it to churches or parents to interpret it. But Catholics believed that the Bible should be read in light of the teachings of the church and not left to individual interpretation. They found anti-Catholic bias in many of the textbooks the public schools used. To pay taxes only to have their children read such material outraged them. Citing examples from textbooks that spoke of "deceitful Catholics," Catholics in New York City wrote that they could not "in conscience, and consistently with their sense of duty to God, and to their offspring" send them to the city's public schools and requested public funds so that they could operate their own schools. When such funds were denied, Catholics in New York and around the country started their own parochial system at their own expense.

The Nation's Textbook: *McGuffey's Reader*

In 1836, the small Cincinnati publishing house of Truman and Smith brought out a new textbook for schools. The first *McGuffey's Reader* became part of a series, the *McGuffey's Primer*, *McGuffey's Speller*, and the *First* through the *Sixth McGuffey's Eclectic Readers*. By

1920, when most school districts had turned to other materials, 122 million copies of the books had been sold.

The *McGuffey's Reader* offered lessons in reading and public speaking designed to create a unified, literate, and patriotic society. The *Readers* not only taught morality but also sought to create a common American pattern of speaking that would replace regional dialects. The texts included patriotic speeches by Patrick Henry and stories of George Washington as well as tales of the poor boy and his faithful dog or the poor boy who worked hard and made good. The contents also included ethical instruction—such as don't steal apples from someone else's tree—and instruction in how to speak and present oneself.

A story in the *Second Eclectic Reader*, "Henry, the Bootblack," begins with the story of Henry, "a kind good boy." Henry's "father was dead, and his mother was very poor. He had a little sister about two years old." One day, Henry found a pocketbook. He could have kept all the money in it, but he found the owner and returned it. The owner then gave him a dollar for doing so. Henry used the dollar to set himself up as a bootblack and he was "so polite that gentlemen soon began to notice him, and to let him black their boots." When Henry brought home his first fifty cents in earnings, his mother responded, "You are a dear, good boy, Henry. I did not know how I could earn enough to buy bread with, but now I think we can manage to get along quite well." This account is not the kind of success story that would appear later. Henry does not go on to own a factory or make a fortune. He is simply a dutiful child who makes his mother happy. The students who read the McGuffey texts were urged to do the same. They were also urged to learn the correct pronunciation and spelling for *support, boots, notice, money,* and other words in the story. McGuffey was teaching a common morality and a common American English.

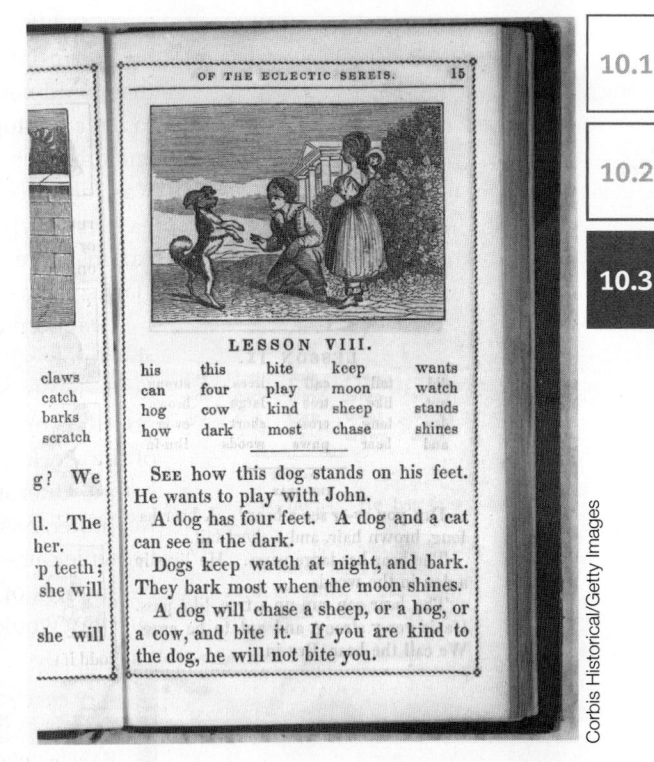

The *McGuffey's Readers* were filled with patriotic speeches and stories like the one shown here, designed to teach morality, in addition to instruction on common ways of pronouncing key terms.

American Artists: A Romance with the American Land

While Jacksonian Democrats and Whigs debated the kind of government the nation should have, both parties were united in a deep attachment to the United States as a new force in world history. And other Americans with much less political interest shared that attachment, including artists who sought to show other Americans—and the world—just how beautiful the United States was.

One group of such artists came to be called the **Hudson River School** of art because their primary focus was the beauty of New York's Hudson River Valley, though they also included scenes from the nearby mountains and farther afield into New England. The Hudson River School was not a formal association but rather a movement of independent artists who shared a sense of awe at the beauty of the landscape. They wanted to show nature and people living in rural settings, often through idealized pictures that included detail and accuracy along with a sense of light that has impressed later generations even as many later artists turned their backs on such representational forms of art.

The painter Thomas Cole is generally seen as the founder of the Hudson River School after he traveled up the Hudson River and into the Catskill Mountains in 1825. His paintings and those of many successors provided dramatic and colorful views of the region. In later years, other artists took the same approach to portray other parts of the nation, including the vast expanses of the American West or the grandeur of the Rocky Mountains. The romanticism and the deep love of the land portrayed by Hudson River artists can be found preserved in many museums today.

Hudson River School

In the 1820s and 1830s, a new generation of artists set out to show the rural American landscape to the nation and the world. Focusing mostly on New York's Hudson River Valley, they painted representational, but also idealized, pictures that showed the light, color, and natural beauty of the countryside.

American Photography

As the Hudson River artists took representational landscapes to a new height, the advent of photography began a process of representing people with far more accuracy than had ever before been possible. And Americans loved it. In 1839, the French inventor Louis Daguerre announced that he had found a chemical process to preserve images, the French government

10.1

10.2

10.3

provided the process as a gift to the world, and daguerreotypes—photos taken following Daguerre's process—quickly became enormously popular in the United States. Families that could never afford to hire an artist to do an oil painting of a loved one could arrange to have photographs taken. Daguerreotypes showed Americans scenes from European art and architecture and the world's landscapes never seen before, but the primary enthusiasm was for individual and family portraits. Thousands of families had family or individual daguerreotypes made to preserve their family memory. A daguerreotype of John Quincy Adams represents the first president ever to have been photographed, while William Henry Harrison was the first president to have his picture taken while in office.

Daguerreotypes, while considered a wonderful advance, still required a person to sit absolutely still and were hard to reproduce. By the 1850s, important advances were being made in photography. Tintypes, easier to take and easier to preserve, became the most popular form of photography. They contributed greatly to Americans' understanding of the world and preserved the horrors of the Civil War as no war had ever been shown before. Later in the 1800s, others would refine the process until in 1884 George Eastman of Rochester, New York, developed a much simpler process; by 1901, the mass-market Kodak Brownie camera meant that everyone could take pictures wherever they wanted. From the beginnings of American photography in 1839 and onward, American art and American memory would be preserved and transformed as never before.

10.3 Quick Review

Why might education be increasingly important in an expanding country? Why would Whig opponents of Andrew Jackson support a unified school system while Jacksonian Democrats distrusted such efforts? What themes in Jacksonian America did artists such as those of the Hudson River School or early daguerreotype photographers represent?

Conclusion

Andrew Jackson was like no other president before him. He had no connection to the Founding Fathers. Jackson was determined to make the presidency the center of American government, believing that since he had won the presidential elections, the government should be an expression of his agenda and of his party. In his two terms as president, Jackson realized his main goals, despite fierce opposition: an Indian Removal policy that forced thousands of Native Americans out of their ancestral homes in Illinois, Georgia, Mississippi, Alabama, and Florida and on to new lands in present-day Oklahoma; opposition to the Second Bank of the United States because he thought the federal government should have no role in banking, issuing paper currency, or expanding credit; and the Nullification Crisis in which Jackson successfully challenged South Carolina's efforts to declare federal taxes and federal law null and void in that state. Those actions would have long-lasting effects on the nation.

For many Americans in the decades between 1820 and 1850, the growth of a more popular democracy and popular social movements led by ordinary citizens were far more important than President Jackson's policies or opinions. A market revolution was transforming the physical, commercial, and political landscapes of the United States. The era was a dynamic period of social and religious revival and reform. It was the peak of the Second Great Awakening. Reform movements in the same era fostered greater rights for women, stronger opposition to slavery, reform in the treatment of prisoners and the insane, and radical transformation of the nation's public schools, whose teachers and morality-focused textbooks shaped American culture as significantly as any of the ventures of the Age of Jackson, as his years in the White House were called.

Chapter Review

Considering the political, economic, and social aspects of the "Age of Jackson," to what extent was the United States in that period different from the beginning of the 1800s?

Jacksonian Democracy, Jacksonian Government

10.1 Analyze Jackson's advocacy for Indian Removal, his opposition to the Bank of the United States, his support for a tariff, and the impact of these policies on other Americans.

Summary

For Andrew Jackson to represent the interests of common white Americans, he brought the executive powers of the presidency to the center of American government. This eventful presidency featured clashes over tariffs, nullification, the Bank of the United States, and Indian Removal. Although the Five Civilized Tribes, living in the Old Southwest, had adopted many white ways and customs, intermarried with whites, and created a unique culture based on settled farming and the production of goods, white settlers and President Jackson were determined to seize their land. Indian leaders rallied many whites to their side, but Indian Removal was approved by a narrow margin in Congress. It proved to be a disaster for the Five Civilized Tribes, as most members were forced to migrate west.

In terms of economics, Jackson blamed the Bank of the United States for the Panic of 1819 and saw it as an elitist threat to democracy and his supporters. Jackson waged war against the rechartered bank, a war that culminated in the bank's destruction. Another battle, over the issue of nullification, pitted Jackson against his first vice president, John C. Calhoun of South Carolina. The so-called Tariff of Abominations, passed in 1828, brought to the fore the issue of a state's right to declare any federal law null and void. Despite efforts at compromise, in 1832 the South Carolina legislature declared the tariffs of 1828 and 1832 unconstitutional and raised a state militia. Jackson responded with a proclamation denying South Carolina's right to nullify a federal law, and he prepared to send federal troops to the state. In the end, South Carolina backed down, but neither side admitted defeat. In his two terms, Jackson realized most of his goals, establishing permanent precedents for presidential authority in the process.

Review Questions

1. **Argument Development**
   What were Jackson's most important political priorities? What connections can you make between his policies and his vision of the presidency?

2. **Comparison**
   How did Jackson's vision of the presidency differ from that of his predecessors? In the process, how did Jackson change the presidency?

Democratized Religion: The Second Great Awakening

10.2 Analyze the diversity of American religious experience and how the freedom of the era gave rise to diverse religious and philosophical expressions.

Summary

The Second Great Awakening began in the 1790s and reached its height in the decades between 1820 and 1850. A fervent and emotional Protestantism was at the heart of the movement that came to have an enormous influence on the nation's culture and politics. The religious revivals, led by ministers like Charles G. Finney, attracted thousands, and by mid-century, religion returned to the center of American life. This "democratic and republican" form of Christianity had effects beyond religion. Women were encouraged to take more active roles in their religious communities. Inspired converts went on to be part of reform movements like women's rights, abolitionism, and a campaign against alcohol. This period also saw the emergence of numerous utopian religious communities while transcendentalism offered yet another alternative to traditional religion.

Review Questions

3. **Contextualization**
   Why do you think this surge of religious activity was taking place at this particular moment in history? How might changes in American life related to the economy and migrations help explain this surge?

4. **Causation**
   What might explain the close connection between calls for religious revival and campaigns for social reform in the 1830s and 1840s?

Democratized Education, Democratized Art: The Birth of the Common School, American Landscape Painting, and Photography

10.3 Explain the development of public education and art as a result of, and in response to, the cultural currents of the 1820s and 1830s.

Summary

American women began to argue that teaching was a natural fit with women's nature and aptitudes, and schools to train women to be teachers proliferated in the first half of the 1800s. Male reformers sought to transform the education system.

While Horace Mann led the fight for mandatory, standardized public education, his Jacksonian opponents saw public schools as undemocratic and unnecessary. Many Roman Catholics opposed public schools because they saw them as tools for the conversion of their children to Protestant values. The *McGuffey's Reader* became the standard reading and public speaking textbook in the United States. The *Readers* combined practical literacy training with ethical instruction. While painters from the Hudson River School began to capture the beauty of America's landscape in the Northeast, the newly invented photograph quickly became a regular part of American life.

Review Questions

5. Contextualization

Why did reformers like Catharine Beecher believe women had a natural aptitude for teaching? In what ways did Beecher see teaching as a natural extension of women's role in the home?

6. Argument Development

Is it fair to describe Mann's system of public education, as some of his opponents did, as nothing more than a vehicle for imposing mainstream Protestantism on all Americans? Why or why not?

1. Preparing to Write: Establish Context in Your Introduction

Long Essay Question—Explain the effects of a more democratic spirit in American society between 1800 and 1848.

It is important that you are clear on the central concepts you are asked to write about. The purpose of this question is to have students discuss the changes in American society during the first half of the century. Individuals felt more empowered and became more involved in politics, in religion, and in social reforms—what is meant by "the democratic spirit." With this in mind, create a three-column table and list evidence of the democratic spirit in politics, religion, and social reform. As you consider this question, what is bubbling up from your table? From here you can develop your thesis and then write a full four- to seven-sentence introduction that starts by establishing context.

2. Preparing to Write: Support Your Assertion

Long Essay Question—Evaluate the extent to which there were different views on the federal policies of American Indian Removal from 1800 to 1848.

For a Document-Based Question, you are given seven primary sources and asked to support your thesis with evidence from at least six of the sources. For four of the sources, you will need to explain the significance of at least one of the following: the author's point of view, the author's purpose, historical situation, or audience. Start by developing a thesis that answers all parts of this question. Study the three perspectives on American Indian Removal in "American Voices" from 10.1. Then identify a key passage from two of those perspectives and explain how each can be used as evidence to support the respective views you discuss in your thesis. In your discussion, explain the significance of the authors' points of view.

Chapter 11
Manifest Destiny: Expanding the Nation 1830–1853

Scotts Bluff National Monument

In this painting, *Emigrants at Kanesville* by William Henry Jackson, a backlog of wagons waits to be ferried across the Missouri River at Council Bluffs, Iowa.

Chapter Objective

Demonstrate an understanding of how the idea of Manifest Destiny and the policies of the Polk administration almost doubled the size of the United States in twelve years in spite of opposition from many people in the country.

⌄ Learning Objectives

Manifest Destiny—The Importance of an Idea

11.1 Explain what Manifest Destiny meant and how it led the United States to involvement in Texas, California, and Oregon.

The U.S. War with Mexico, 1846–1848

11.2 Analyze the causes, strategies, and outcomes of the U.S. war with Mexico.

West into the Pacific

11.3 Analyze the causes and outcomes of U.S. expansion in California and into the Pacific region, including establishing new relationships with Hawaii, China, and Japan.

Significant Dates

Manifest Destiny

The doctrine, first expressed in 1845, that the expansion of white Americans across the continent was inevitable and ordained by God and was a means to spread Protestant Christianity and Jacksonian Democracy to more people.

In the summer of 1845, the *Democratic Review*, a New York City paper edited by John L. O'Sullivan, urged the nation to annex the independent Republic of Texas: "It is time now for opposition to the annexation of Texas to cease," Sullivan wrote. Texas was a hot topic, and many newspapers were taking the same position. But the *Review* claimed that including Texas in the United States was an essential part of the "fulfillment of our manifest destiny to overspread the continent allotted by Providence for the free development of our yearly multiplying millions." *Manifest Destiny* quickly became a popular term and for many a core American belief. It was a mindset that justified the Louisiana Purchase of 1803 (though no one used the term then), and in the 1840s the hoped-for U.S. acquisition of the Oregon Territory along with the northern half of Mexico, including Texas and California, and a significant influence across the Pacific Ocean.

Manifest Destiny gave a new name to an old idea. Even before the American Revolution and in growing numbers in the 1790s, white Americans had crossed the Allegheny Mountains in spite of government prohibitions and had established colonies in Kentucky and in the Ohio River Valley. Soon after 1800, others were crossing into Florida and Missouri, both then under Spanish control. In both cases, the settlers were confident that the American army and American government would soon follow. While the first Americans to cross into Texas spoke of loyalty to the Republic of Mexico, by 1830, they too were soon seeking protection from the American government. In all these cases, many in the government were happy to oblige, seeing the movement of colonists as a first step in expanding the nation. Manifest Destiny became a way to describe the goal that appealed to many of long-term expansion for the nation. This chapter will explore the political, diplomatic, and military issues involved in turning the idea of Manifest Destiny into a geographic reality.

The acquisition of so much new territory in the 1830s and 1840s changed the lives of all those who lived in the United States. Citizens of the Republic of Mexico suddenly found themselves living in the United States because the border had moved, as did American Indians, whose lands were increasingly taken over. Migrants from around the world flocked to California to find their fortunes in the Gold Rush. The great expansion of these years transformed the country and shaped its future.

Manifest Destiny—The Importance of an Idea

11.1 Explain what Manifest Destiny meant and how it led the United States to involvement in Texas, California, and Oregon.

The idea that the United States had a "Manifest Destiny" to expand its territory to the Pacific coast led to more than simply acquiring land, though between 1845 and 1848, the United States almost doubled in size, from 1.8 million square miles to almost 3 million. Advocates of **Manifest Destiny** claimed that the United States should rule the heart of North America from the Atlantic Ocean to the Pacific and from a still-to-be-defined border with British Canada to an even more undefined border with the Republic of Mexico. For O'Sullivan and other supporters of Manifest Destiny, it was the nation's divinely appointed role to spread not only democracy—in its Jacksonian form—but also Protestant Christianity in place of the Catholicism of Mexico or the native beliefs of American Indians. The same year that O'Sullivan coined the term *Manifest Destiny*, Illinois Representative John Wentworth told Congress that he "did not believe the God of Heaven … designed that the original States should be the only abode of liberty on earth. On the contrary, he only designed them as the great center from which civilization, religion, and liberty should radiate and radiate until the whole continent shall bask in their blessing." That belief, that the United States was specially chosen by divine will to bring liberty and democracy to the planet—and especially North America—was a driving force in the push for new lands in the 1840s.

Many Americans supported Manifest Destiny for their own reasons. Land speculators and those promoting the extension of the nation's railroads wanted to exploit the vast lands in the West. Farmers dreamed of starting over in rich—and cheap—new lands. Workers believed that rapid national expansion would guarantee industrial profits and thus their jobs, or give them a chance to start over if necessary. Protestant leaders

11.1

11.2

11.3

At the mythical level, Manifest Destiny was seen as the spirit hovering over the westward movement of white settlers, leading them and urging them on whether they came by foot, covered wagon, or stagecoach.

and missionaries saw U.S. control of the new lands as an opportunity to ensure that a Protestant United States, not a Catholic Mexico, controlled the continent. Manifest Destiny also referred to a patriotic belief that the nation had a divine mission to become a world power.

Other Americans opposed the whole idea of a Manifest Destiny. While Jacksonian Democrats tended to support expansion, Whigs, led by Henry Clay, had grave reservations. Clay's goal was not necessarily a larger country but a better developed one with roads, canals, railroads, and industries knitting it together and ensuring its prosperity. Antislavery advocates opposed the acquisition of more land, especially Texas, since they were certain that new lands meant new slave states. However, some proslavery advocates, notably South Carolina senator John C. Calhoun, wanted Texas but worried that other incorporated lands, especially California and Oregon, might become free states peopled by darker-skinned citizens, which would shift power away from the white slaveholding regions.

Some Americans also saw the violence associated with expansion as simply wrong. Many residents of the lands from Texas to California did not want to become part of the United States at all. Antonio Maria Osio, a Mexican citizen in California before annexation, spoke for those who did not want to become U.S. residents when he described himself as "a *Californio* who loves his country and a Mexican on all four sides and in my heart." He opposed the annexation of California to the United States, and when it happened, he left, eventually settling in Baja California so that he could to remain a citizen of Mexico.

While many Americans debated Manifest Destiny in the Congress, the press, and the pulpits, other Americans, especially trappers and farmers, moved into the regions, just as a generation before the same types of people had expanded beyond the Mississippi. Regardless of whether the United States, Mexico, or Britain claimed the land, these frontiersmen and women were confident that, in time, their government would follow them. Most of all, they moved into Texas (see Map 11-1, p. 310).

Californio

Person of Spanish descent—and after 1821, citizen of Mexico—living in California.

Map 11-1 Trade Networks between Mexico, Texas, and the United States.

Mexico (and before it, Spain) had established settlements and trade networks throughout its sparsely populated northern territories. Texas trade ran south from San Antonio and Goliad in Texas to Monterrey and other trading centers in Mexico; it also ran east into the United States. Separate networks connected the heartland of Mexico with its settlements in Santa Fe and Taos in New Mexico, with Tucson in the future Arizona, and with the missions and presidios along the coast of California.

The Birth of the Texas Republic

The tensions between Americans living in Texas and the Mexican government had been building for a long time. When the United States purchased Louisiana from France in 1803, the western border of that territory was disputed. Spain insisted it was the Sabine River (the current border between Louisiana and Texas), but French officials hinted that the United States might claim territory farther west. Jefferson had wanted to include all of the land from modern-day Texas to the Rio Grande River in the definition of the Louisiana Purchase, but he was not prepared to fight Spain over it. In the Adams-Onís Treaty of 1819, Spain ceded Florida to the United States, along with Spanish claims to Oregon, in exchange for U.S. recognition of the Sabine River as the border between U.S. Louisiana and Spanish Texas. Even in 1819, some in Congress wanted more and criticized the treaty for that reason.

Soon after the Adams-Onís Treaty was signed, a revolutionary uprising began in Mexico. Like the people of the United States, most Mexican citizens wanted to be free of control by a European power. The Mexican Revolution against Spanish rule, which lasted from 1810 to 1821, was long and bloody and decimated the Mexican economy. In Texas, the Mexican population, people known as **Tejanos**, fell from 4,000 in 1800 to 2,500 in 1821. Comanche and Apache tribes dominated large parts of west Texas, and much of the desert was vacant of any human habitation. Nevertheless, after 1821, Mexico had won its independence. And all of present-day Texas was part of the Republic of Mexico.

With the establishment of the Republic of Mexico, two independent republics—the English-speaking, overwhelmingly Protestant United States in the north and the Spanish-speaking and mostly Catholic Republic of Mexico to the south—bordered each other at the Sabine River, with settlers from one living in the territory of the other.

Even before Mexican independence, the Spanish government had given Missouri merchant Moses Austin permission to start a colony in Texas, believing that more settlers—whatever their origin—would help stabilize a border area that was far from the population centers of either Mexico or the United States. In 1821, Moses's son Stephen F. Austin, along with Erasmo Seguín, a Tejano with liberal political views, rode into Texas to build the new settlement. A month later, Austin and his party learned that Mexico had won its independence. Austin then went to Mexico City where he met with Mexico's new leader, Agustín de Iturbide, and announced, "I make a tender of my services, my loyalty, and my fidelity to the Constitutional Emperor of Mexico." Austin's physical presence in Mexico City and willingness to make an oath of allegiance to the new nation impressed the new government. In April 1823, Austin received confirmation of his claims to a huge swath of land in Texas and his right to act as an *empresario*, or colonizing agent, for this land. He was the only American to get such rights.

At first, the new American colony grew slowly, but Austin continued to recruit settlers. The Mexican government, aware that it could do little to stop settlement and anxious for a buffer against Indian tribes and the United States, hoped that settlers in Texas would create a stable population of loyal citizens.

Few Europeans and even fewer Mexicans moved into Texas, but Americans came in large numbers. The Tejano community was overwhelmed by the newly arrived Americans. By 1830, twenty thousand American colonists had arrived and had brought two thousand slaves with them. The Americans generally ignored the requirement that they convert to Catholicism, though they did not build Protestant churches, and most absolutely refused to free their slaves in spite of the fact that Mexico had abolished slavery in 1829 and expected the residents of Texas to obey that decree. One American visitor to Texas, Amos Parker, wrote, "A person may travel all day; and day after day, and find Americans only." Those in the Tejano community were also divided. Many Tejanos profited from trade with the Americans and identified with their independent streak. Others clung to their connection to Mexico. Distance, difficult travel conditions, and an unstable government in Mexico City with more pressing concerns closer to home allowed an American community to develop in Texas that was officially governed by one set of laws but lived by its own rules (see Map 11-2).

The Mexican government's benign neglect of the American community in Texas ended in 1830 when the Mexican Congress closed Texas to further American immigration and the importation of slaves. Mexico also insisted that trade be routed through established ports in Mexico rather than directly between Texas and the United States. The government stationed more soldiers in Texas to enforce the new rules. Austin was stunned, and revolts broke out in the English-speaking colonies, a few of which drew Tejano support.

Tejanos

People of Spanish or Mexican descent born in Texas.

empresario

An agent who received a land grant from the Spanish or Mexican government in return for organizing settlements.

11.1

11.2

11.3

Map 11-2 Contested Boundaries between Texas and Mexico.

The borders of Texas were highly contested in the 1830s and 1840s. The Adams-Onís Treaty of 1819 had fixed the border between the two nations as the Sabine River—the border between modern Louisiana and Texas. Austin's land grant from the Mexican government allowed him to settle to the west of that line. Most people considered the Nueces River to be the western border of the Republic of Texas in the 1830s and 1840s, but at President Polk's insistence, the Rio Grande River became the border as a result of the Treaty of Guadalupe Hidalgo in 1848, which tripled the total size of Texas.

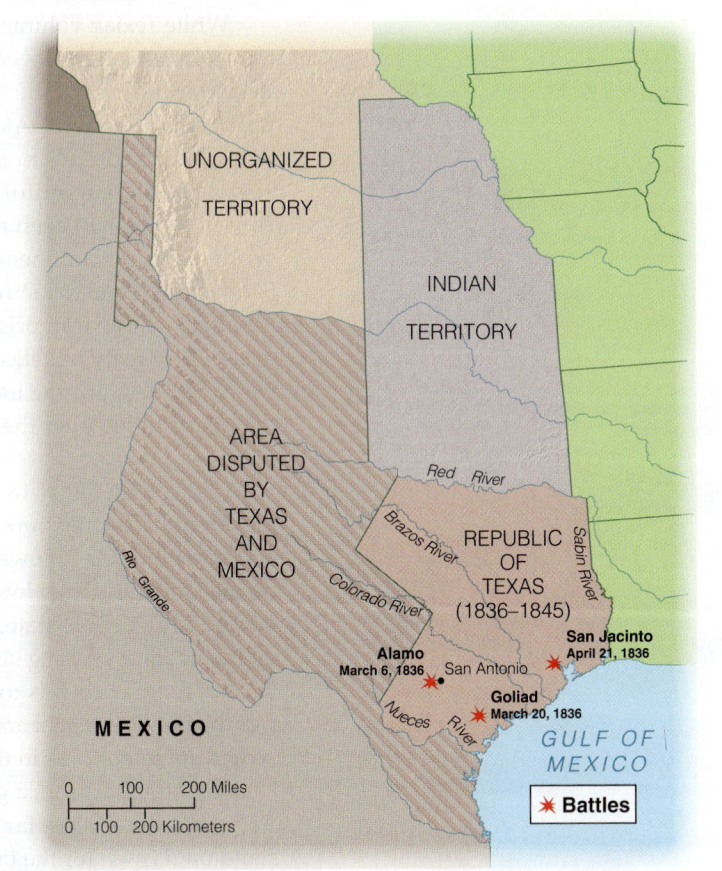

Alamo

A Franciscan mission at San Antonio, Texas, that was the site in 1836 of a siege and massacre of Texans by Mexican troops.

In 1832, Mexican troops defeated an American effort to take control of an army garrison, but in October, American colonists met at San Felipe and called for autonomy for Texas within the Republic of Mexico. In 1833, they organized an army under the command of Sam Houston and sent Austin to Mexico City to negotiate for them. Tejanos were not represented in these meetings, and most of the five thousand Tejanos probably opposed these actions. But by now, there were thirty thousand Americans in Texas, and the Tejanos were greatly outnumbered. Austin had little success in Mexico City. He was arrested in the fall of 1833. When he was released from jail in the summer of 1835, he wrote, "War is our only recourse. There is no other remedy." Most Americans in Texas seemed to agree.

Although revolt had been brewing since 1830, the campaign for the independence of Texas became a full-fledged war late in 1835 when American volunteers captured the **Alamo** fortress at San Antonio de Bexar from its Mexican garrison. In January and February 1836, James Bowie and William Travis took joint command of the Alamo, while another Texian (as the Americans in Texas were called) force remained in the town of Goliad under the command of James Fannin. Austin went to Washington, D.C., to try to secure American support for the insurrection while Sam Houston took command of a volunteer army based at the Texians' temporary capital of Washington-on-the-Brazos.

In response to these military actions, Mexican president Santa Anna ordered the Mexican army north. In March 1836, after a furious fight, the nearly two hundred defenders of the Alamo, including former Tennessee congressman Davy Crockett, adventurer James Bowie, and the garrison's commander William B. Travis, were killed, and the Alamo was captured by Santa Anna's army. It is estimated that six hundred Mexican soldiers were also killed in the assault. The defeat and grisly deaths of the Alamo's outnumbered defenders entered Texan—and American—legend. "Remember the Alamo!" became a rallying cry for the independence of Texas and later in the war with Mexico.

After his victory at the Alamo, Santa Anna marched his army to the second Texan garrison at Goliad, which surrendered in late March. Santa Anna ordered his soldiers to execute all of the Goliad troops and approximately 341 died on the spot, including the garrison's commander, James Fannin. For some, the phrase became "Remember the Alamo and Goliad."

While Texian volunteers fought against the Mexican army, political leaders in the American colony met in convention at Washington-on-the-Brazos and on March 2, 1836, declared the independence of the Republic of Texas and adopted a constitution. Having defeated the insurgent forces at the Alamo and at Goliad, Santa Anna had little use for the Texas declaration. He turned on Sam Houston's army, the only remaining defenders of the Republic of Texas. Houston, mindful of Santa Anna's strength, began a slow retreat. Then, after Santa Anna's troops had been marching for days with an increasingly thin supply line, Houston suddenly turned on them. On April 21, 1836, Houston defeated Santa Anna at the Battle of San Jacinto. Houston's troops showed no more mercy than Santa Anna had and executed hundreds of Mexican prisoners. The next day, Santa Anna himself was captured and forced to sign the Treaty of Velasco, promising to withdraw all Mexican troops from Texas, end the war, and recognize the independence of Texas. The Mexican Congress refused to recognize the treaty, but neither the Mexican government nor the Texians were in the mood for more fighting.

In the early fall of 1836, Sam Houston, the hero of the Battle of San Jacinto, was elected president of the new republic, defeating Austin, who became secretary of state. Both men, and most of their followers, did not want long-term independence but rather annexation by the United States. However, the United States was a reluctant partner. Texas would be a new and huge slave state, and many in Washington worried about the destabilizing impact on the nation of having such a powerful new slave state in the U.S. Senate. In addition, U.S. trade with Mexico was too important to trifle with. Even Andrew Jackson did not want to risk the political cost of annexing Texas, especially in 1836 when Martin Van Buren, his hand-picked successor, was in the midst of the presidential election. During his last months in the White House, Jackson, a good friend of Sam Houston, officially recognized the Republic of Texas, but that was as far as its neighbor to the north would go. The Texas Republic would stand on its own for the immediate future.

When Historians Disagree

The Legends of the Alamo

The story of the battle of the Alamo quickly became legendary. But the legends were different for different people. For most white Texans, then and now, the Alamo's defense was a self-sacrificing fight for liberty. But many Mexicans and Mexican Americans came to view the battle quite differently. The two historians cited below clearly represent these differences.

From William C. Davis, *Lone Star Rising: The Revolutionary Birth of the Texas Republic*, p. 213.

It was to be the stuff of legend, a virtual replay of the ancient tale of a desperate few selling their lives to buy precious time for the many, a story enacted as far back as Thermopylae if not beyond. Yet nowhere in the American saga would so many important elements be in play at the same time to ensure the creation of such a truly epic legend, the cornerstone of Texian [as Americans living in Texas were sometimes called] mythology and reality at one and the same time. Men who were already living semi-mythical heroes were here in the persons of Bowie and Crockett. Around them stood a small cadre of men seemingly willing to risk all in the defense of ideals of liberty and democracy. Arrayed against them were the myrmidons of absolutism led by a cynical incarnation of brutality. It was good and evil, the future and the past, freedom and slavery, all locked in mortal combat, an epic in the making that was ripe for begetting the cornerstones of Texian identity, and pride. It may have been a small event in the course of history, but it would loom paramount in defining Texas and its people now and forever.

From Rodolfo F. Acuna, *Occupied America: A History of Chicanos*, pp. 43–44.

Myths are common in history, and often become legends taken as truth. … [P]opular books have been written about Mexican cruelty at the Alamo and about the heroics of the doomed men, producing the Alamo myth, which justifies the Texas insurrection. … Those inside the Alamo were hardly legendary characters. William Barrett Travis had fled to Texas after killing a man and abandoning his wife and two children. James Bowie, an infamous brawler who made a fortune running slaves, had wandered into Texas searching for lost mines and more money. The aging Davy Crockett, a legend in his own time, fought for the sake of fighting. … Travis's stand had delayed Santa Anna's timetable by only four days, as the Mexicans took San Antonio on March 6, 1836. … Nevertheless, the Alamo battle and the Mexican victory at Goliad resulted in massive aid from the United States as volunteers, weapons, and money entered Texas. The cry of "Remember the Alamo" became a call to arms for Euro-Americans in both Texas and the United States.

Thinking Critically

1. **Analyzing Secondary Sources**
   Although both historians are discussing the same event, their interpretations could not be more different. How do you account for the differences?

2. **Argument Development**
   Why do you think different people want to remember this history so differently?

Distant California

While Texas was declaring its independence from Mexico, Alta California, as it was known to distinguish it from Baja California to the south, was a sleepy and distant outpost of the Republic of Mexico, and most people in Mexico and the United States were content to leave it that way. California had wonderful harbors, large and prosperous rancheros, and a string of missions, but it was a long way from the heart of either nation. In the 1830s, the population there included not only Mexicans, most of whom valued self-government in local matters and cared little for the authorities in Mexico City, but also a much smaller number of Americans. Neither group was thinking seriously about independence. A majority among the declining number of American Indians in California were doing their best to maintain their tribal ways and keep their distance from both Mexican and American settlers, though some of them were living under the supervision of the missions.

Although Spanish explorers had sailed the coast of California and claimed the lands in the 1500s, meaningful European settlements in California began only just before the American Revolution. In 1769, a Franciscan priest, Father Junípero Serra, was sent to Alta

California with instructions to found a chain of missions that would aid in converting the California Indians to Catholic Christianity, put them to work for the Spanish, and establish a stronger Spanish presence to protect against possible Russian expansion.

Father Serra and his Franciscan successors created a chain of missions stretching from San Diego to San Francisco. The Franciscan friars meant to save the Indian souls and bring them the gifts of Spanish culture, but they also worked them hard to ensure a good economic return for the missions, maintaining tight control and a tough discipline. One of the Franciscan friars noted, however, that the Indians "live well free but as soon as we reduce them to a Christian and community life … they fatten, sicken, and die." When Serra arrived in California, there were probably 300,000 Indians in the area, but by the time Spanish rule ended in 1821, that number had been reduced to 200,000. From the Spanish government's perspective, however, the missions were significant in asserting sovereignty as well as controlling the native people of California and managing the colony's cattle, grain, and trade.

The Franciscans administered the California missions until 1833 when the new Mexican government transferred ownership of the missions from church to state and eventually to private hands. Mexico's revolution was a rejection of Spanish royal authority and the role of the Catholic Church. Seizing the missions was a means to reduce the church's power. Missions were sold off or awarded to powerful ranchers.

As late as 1821, California's total Mexican population was about three thousand, though it grew to between ten thousand and fifteen thousand by 1846. The majority lived on large ranches spread along the coast. A few immigrants from the United States also moved to California in these years. Most of the Americans arriving before 1840 learned Spanish, converted to Catholicism, took on Mexican citizenship, and became part of the local culture of Alta California.

Beginning in the 1840s, however, a different group of immigrants from the United States began to arrive. These new immigrants were more interested in making California part of the United States than accepting the rule of Mexico. Even before the war with Mexico began, President Polk, well aware of the interests of the recent California immigrants, told Congress that California's harbors "would afford shelter for our navy, for our numerous whale ships, and other merchant vessels employed in the Pacific Ocean, and would in a short period become the marts of an extensive and profitable commerce with China, and other countries

North Wind Picture Archives / Alamy Stock Photo

An early illustration of a young Mexican American woman illustrates some of the comfort and confidence that the Californios had before their homes became part of the United States.

American Voices

Eulalia Perez, Memories of Mexican California, c. 1830s

11.1

11.2

11.3

Eulalia Perez was born about 1768 in Baja California. She and her husband first moved to the Alta California mission of San Diego and then to San Gabriel near Los Angeles, where the priests selected her as cook for the mission, a midwife, and eventually "keeper of the keys" or mayordoma—head of the mission household. Her account provides a rare glimpse of mission life in California before that area's acquisition by the United States.

When we arrived here, Father Jose Sanchez lodged me and my family temporarily in a small house until work could be found for me. ... He, as well as his companion Father Jose Maria Zalvidea, treated the Indians very well, and the two were much loved by the Spanish-speaking people and by the neophytes [Indians recently converted to Christianity] and other Indians. ...

In the morning the girls were let out. First they went to Father Zalvidea's Mass, for he spoke the Indian language; afterwards they went to the mess hut to have breakfast, which sometimes consisted of corn gruel with chocolate, and on holidays with sweets and bread. On other days, ordinarily they had boiled barley and beans and meat. After breakfast each girl began the task that had been assigned to her beforehand—sometimes it was at the looms, or unloading, or sewing, or whatever there was to be done. ...

The Indians were taught the various jobs for which they showed an aptitude. Others worked in the fields, or took care of the horses, cattle, etc. Still others were carters, oxherds, etc. ... The Indians also were taught to pray. A few of the more intelligent ones were taught to read and write. Father Zalvidea taught the Indians to

pray in their Indian tongue; some Indians learned music and played instruments and sang at Mass. The sextons and pages who helped with Mass were Indians of the mission.

The punishments that were meted out were the stocks and confinement. When the misdemeanor was serious, the delinquent was taken to the guard, where they tied him to a pipe or a post and gave him twenty-five or more lashes, depending on his crime. Sometimes they put them in the head-stocks; other times they passed a musket from one leg to the other and fastened it there, and also they tied their hands. That punishment, called "the Law of Bayone," was very painful. But Fathers Sanchez and Zalvidea were always very considerate with the Indians.

Source: Eulalia Perez, from an original manuscript in Spanish in the Bancroft Library, University of California, Berkeley, originally written in 1877 and published in Nancy F. Cott, et al., *Roots of Bitterness: Documents of the Social History of American Women* (Boston: Northeastern University Press, 1996), pp. 185–192.

Thinking Critically

1. **Analyzing Primary Sources**
   How would you characterize Perez's view of the mission system? How did she respond to its coercive elements? How might her own historical situation have shaped her views?

2. **Continuity and Change over Time**
   Perez's account of mission life was given long after the era she described. How might a careful look at her stories tell you what had developed in California that would let you decide approximately what era she was describing?

of the East." Polk's secretary of the navy George Bancroft anticipated the coming of war with Mexico and ordered Commodore John D. Sloat, commander of the U.S. Pacific squadron based in the then independent nation of Hawaii, to land in San Francisco if war came. At the same time, U.S. Army Captain John C. Frémont led what he claimed was a mapmaking expedition overland from St. Louis, arriving in Monterey, California, in late December 1845. Frémont told the Mexican authorities he was simply exploring. They had their doubts that he was just making maps—doubts that later turned out to be well founded—but allowed him to remain. Then in April 1846, a U.S. warship arrived at Monterey, with orders for Frémont and the U.S. counsel in California, Thomas Oliver Larkin, to stir up a pro-American revolt in California. The once distant outpost was quickly becoming an important focus of attention in the growing tensions between the United States and Mexico.

Manifest Destiny and American Presidential Politics

Jackson's creation of the Democratic Party as a vehicle to continue his political philosophy and support his handpicked successors was one of his most significant achievements. The twin pillars on which the party rested were, first, a small federal government that would not involve itself with things such as a federal bank or many internal improvements and, second, the idea of Manifest Destiny, epitomized in the removal of Indians from east of the Mississippi and the acquisition of new lands west of the river. America's founding generation disliked "party spirit." Martin Van Buren, who built the new Democratic Party that elected Jackson and who followed him as its candidate, had no such reservations. He thought it best "to deal with the subject of Political Parties in a sincerer and wiser spirit—to recognize their necessity [and] to give them the credit they deserve."

As part of their effort to build a strong political party, Jackson and Van Buren called the first national political convention to be held by a major party. The event was held in Baltimore in 1835, a year before the presidential election. (The small Anti-Masonic Party actually held the first national political convention, modeled on a religious revival in 1831, but it won only seven electoral votes in the 1832 election and faded from national prominence thereafter.) The Democrats borrowed the idea of a national convention as part of their preparation for the 1836 election, and their tight political organization allowed the Democrats to win most presidential contests until the Civil War when the party splintered. At the 1835 convention, Jackson stage-managed Van Buren's nomination as the party's candidate for what some said was basically a third term for Jackson. The outgoing president also managed to ensure the nomination of his hand-picked candidate for vice president, Richard Mentor Johnson of Kentucky, in spite of an effort by Virginia's delegates to derail his nomination.

The core principle of the emerging Whig Party was opposition to Jackson, though it also wanted a larger federal government that could manage internal improvements. The Whigs continued to support a Bank of the United States and distrusted territorial expansion. Whigs also disliked Van Buren's ideas of political parties and continued to distrust the growing sense of party spirit, or at least said that they did. Given this distrust, the Whigs were not well enough organized to have a national convention in preparation for the 1836 election, relying instead on state conventions. They reasoned that, even if the various states did not nominate the same candidate for president, they might use a number of popular candidates to gain enough electoral votes to throw the election into the House of Representatives where they were confident they could control the outcome. Having lost decisively with Henry Clay in 1832, most Whig leaders wanted a different candidate. One choice, popular in the North and West, was William Henry Harrison, who had won as many battles as Jackson during the War of 1812. Some states duly nominated Harrison, and Clay reluctantly supported him. Southern Whigs nominated Hugh Lawson White of Tennessee, who agreed with Jackson on many issues but had broken with him over what he saw as Jackson's abuse of power. Whigs in Massachusetts went their own way with Senator Daniel Webster. The Whig effort to appeal to diverse constituencies with different candidates failed. In November 1836, the Jackson magic stuck to Van Buren and he received 50.79 percent of the popular vote and 170 electoral votes against 124 votes scattered among the three Whig candidates.

Van Buren faced several challenges as he began to govern. He pledged to continue Jackson's policies and did so, in particular, presiding over the final removal of the Cherokees to Oklahoma and a long and bloody war against Seminoles in Florida. Given his difficulties with the Seminoles, Van Buren decided against removing the Iroquois from New York. He avoided a war with Britain when rebels in Canada recruited volunteers along the American side of the Great Lakes. In spite of his ties to the party of Manifest Destiny, he had no inclination to deal with Texas or Oregon.

In addition, issues of nullification and abolitionism continued, unresolved. Like Jackson, Van Buren opposed nullification or any effort to disrupt the Union. He also opposed abolitionism, which, despite his northern roots, he saw as an attack on the Union. Southerners supported Van Buren, and he repaid them by supporting a **gag rule** in Congress. The Constitution gave all citizens the right to "petition the government for a redress of grievances," and abolitionists had begun flooding the House and Senate with antislavery petitions. The gag rule was a promise by congressional leaders in the House of Representatives to ignore the abolitionist petitions. In the end, the gag rule only highlighted the divisions over slavery. As a member of the House, John Quincy Adams challenged the rule in every possible way. He saw it as a limitation on the constitutional rights of abolitionists, and they came to view him as "Old Man Eloquent." Through the 1830s and 1840s, Adams and a handful of like-minded Whigs began to introduce antislavery petitions at each session of Congress before the House adopted its rules, including the gag rule. Then, during sessions,

gag rule

A procedural rule passed in the House of Representatives that prevented discussion of antislavery petitions from 1836 to 1844.

he regularly interrupted other debates to ask the Speaker whether this or that petition ran afoul of the gag rule while knowing full well that it did but using the occasion to describe both the petition and the gag rule. Perhaps more effectively than if there had been no rule, Adams used these tactics to change public opinion on slavery, even if he could not get the votes he wanted from the House.

Most challenging for Van Buren's political fortunes, however, was the fact that some of the economic policies Jackson had advocated had their greatest impact during Van Buren's term and it was not a good one. Only two months after Van Buren's inauguration, the **Panic of 1837** hit the country. The initial cause of the panic was a sudden drying up of credit. Without the ability to borrow money, cotton brokers failed, banks failed, and the great New York mercantile house of Arthur Tappan and Company failed. In his hatred of banks and distrust of debt, Jackson had paid off the national debt—sending a great deal of U.S. currency to bond holders in Britain and reducing the currency available in the United States. Jackson also had closed the Second Bank of the United States, which had held the ability to expand credit when it was needed. In the absence of such a bank, no one was in a position to deal with the credit crisis that was at the core of the Panic of 1837. In addition, Jackson had issued a **Specie Circular** in 1836, requiring speculators to pay for federal land in silver or gold coinage, not banknotes. The Specie Circular reflected Jackson's distrust of banks, but once the economy began to decline in 1837, many Americans started to think that if the U.S. government would not trust banknotes, then they should not either. There was a run on banks, and few banks had sufficient reserves of silver and gold to redeem all of the banknotes they had issued. Banks failed, and credit became even scarcer, crippling the economy.

A second panic hit in 1839, this one the result of overspeculation in cotton and cotton-producing land. When British investments and international trade stalled, the value of cotton, land, and slaves all plummeted. The sale of public lands, and federal revenue from these sales, virtually stopped. Northern textile and shoe industries laid off thousands of workers. More banks closed. The panic lasted until 1843 and was arguably as severe as any economic downturn before the Great Depression of the 1930s.

Given his Jacksonian commitment to small government, there was little that Van Buren could or would do about the economy. His position enabled the Whigs in the 1840 election

Library of Congress Prints and Photographs Division[LC-US262-8844]

Soon after Jackson left office, the Panic of 1837, which many blamed on him, wracked the nation. In this political cartoon, the results of Jackson's economic policies are shown as drunkenness, women begging a rich banker for money, and long lines of the unemployed.

11.1

11.2

11.3

Panic of 1837

A major economic downturn brought on by temporary excesses in international trade and the inability of the United States to control the currency or make credit available after the closing of the Second Bank of the United States.

Specie Circular

A proclamation issued by President Andrew Jackson in 1836 stipulating that only gold or silver could be used as payment for public land.

to describe him as "cold and heartless." The Whigs had also learned from the Democrats. In 1840, they held a single national convention that unified them behind one candidate. For a second time, they pinned their hopes on the aging war hero William Henry Harrison, despite Clay's effort to secure the nomination for himself. They nominated John Tyler of Virginia, who had served as governor and senator, for vice president, an ill-fated choice. Tyler brought balance to the ticket—he was from the South while Harrison was from the North, and at age fifty, he was much younger than the sixty-eight-year-old Harrison. But Tyler was a Whig only because he found Jackson "high handed," not because he disagreed with most of his policies. The 1840 political campaign pitted Martin Van Buren, running for a second term, against "Tippecanoe and Tyler Too," a reference to Harrison's victory at the Battle of Tippecanoe in 1811. This time, the Whigs won with 52.8 percent of the popular votes and 234 electoral votes against only 60 for Van Buren. But the high expectations for the Whig presidency would not last long.

At his inauguration in March 1841, Harrison delivered a long address laying out the Whig agenda, the longest inaugural address in American presidential history. The day was cold and blustery, and Harrison did not wear a coat. He caught a bad cold that turned to pneumonia. A month later, President Harrison was dead and Tyler was president. This instance marked the first time a president had died in office, and Tyler made it clear that he was not just an "acting president" but that he had inherited the presidency for the full term. A worse disaster for the Whig Party was hard to imagine. The election of 1840 was the only time when the country elected Whig majorities in both houses of Congress along with a Whig president. After only a month into the new administration, "Tyler Too," who shared little of the Whig agenda beyond an intense dislike of Andrew Jackson and an interest in holding office, was president.

Before he became seriously ill, President Harrison had called a special session of Congress to deal with the economic crisis. When the Whig-dominated Congress convened, it re-created the Bank of the United States so that there could be federal control of the currency and credit, thus easing economic conditions that had been created when the bank had been abolished. President Tyler, a believer in small government every bit as much as Jackson or Van Buren, vetoed the bill. Congress then created a "fiscal corporation" that would have more limited powers. Tyler vetoed that, too. Tyler did sign the Land Act of 1841, which made it much easier for homesteaders to buy federal land or keep land on which they were squatters, and he signed the first federal Bankruptcy Act. But the Whigs were furious at Tyler. In September 1841, the entire cabinet except for Secretary of State Daniel Webster resigned in protest over the veto of the bank bills, and the Whig congressional caucus expelled Tyler from the party, marking the only time in U.S. history that a president was expelled from his own political party.

Expanding the size of the United States remained an issue throughout the Tyler presidency. Webster had refused to resign as secretary of state primarily because he was negotiating with Britain to resolve a dispute that came dangerously close to war over where to locate the border between Maine and Canada. The **Webster-Ashburton Treaty** of 1842 resolved the border with Canada as far west as Minnesota. Tyler supported Webster because he did not want problems with Britain when he turned to his real priority—Texas.

Tyler had two paramount goals—the annexation of Texas and his own reelection. He failed at the latter but not the former. In September 1843, Tyler began secret negotiations with Texas over annexation. In April 1844, Tyler's new secretary of state, john C. Calhoun, who was also a Whig only because of his hatred for Jackson over the nullification issue, presented a treaty to the Senate for the annexation of Texas. Calhoun justified the treaty in explicitly proslavery terms, insisting that if the United States did not annex Texas as a slave state, Britain would take it over and end slavery there, blocking the expansion of U.S. slavery. But the nation's leading Whig, Henry Clay, and former Democratic president Martin Van Buren both announced their opposition to annexation largely because of slavery. The Senate rejected the treaty by an overwhelming vote of 35 to 16.

Webster-Ashburton Treaty

The treaty signed by the United States and Britain in 1842 that settled a boundary dispute between the United States and Canada and provided for closer cooperation in suppressing the African slave trade.

11.1

11.2

11.3

The link between Texas and slavery doomed the presidential hopes of both Tyler and Calhoun since both were seen as using a political gimmick to gain their way. The Whigs nominated their old hero Henry Clay. Having been expelled by the Whigs, Tyler tried for the Democratic nomination, but the party spurned him. Jackson still dominated the Democratic Party. He would not allow Tyler to be their candidate, and Jackson was furious at Van Buren over Van Buren's opposition to the annexation of Texas. As a result, the Democrats ended up nominating Jackson's choice, a political unknown, James K. Polk of Tennessee, instead of their own former president Martin Van Buren.

James K. Polk was a true "dark horse" in American presidential politics. He had served as speaker of the house from 1835 to 1839 but had twice been defeated for governor of Tennessee. Few besides Jackson thought he would be president. His Whig opponent, Henry Clay, was one of the best-known political leaders in the United States. If Van Buren had been the Democratic nominee, the election would have been fought over Clay's support for federally financed internal improvements and his advocacy for the Bank of the United States, both of which Van Buren opposed. Polk's nomination changed everything. The Democratic Party platform called for "the reoccupation of Oregon and the reannexation of Texas." With Polk as their nominee, the Democrats planned to focus the election on Manifest Destiny, claiming that they were the party of national expansion while painting the Whigs as timid defenders of the status quo. This focus on Manifest Destiny, especially as it applied to Texas, assured Polk the support not only of Jackson but also of President Tyler and of Calhoun's proslavery partners who included both Whigs and Democrats in the South. Many Catholics also saw the Whigs as a Protestant party, while the Democrats courted Catholic voters, especially recent immigrants. Most of the country's Catholics voted Democratic, especially in Pennsylvania and New York. In the end, Polk won 170 electoral votes to 105 for Clay. Expansion in Oregon and Texas was going to be at the top of Polk's agenda.

Because the new president would not take office until March 4 (the practice from the country's beginning until passage of the Twentieth Amendment in 1933), Tyler still had four months to serve in office after the election. He did not waste them. When the Senate had rejected the annexation of Texas in 1844, it had rejected a treaty with the Republic of Texas. But the Constitution provided that while treaties had to be ratified by two-thirds of the Senate, a new state could be admitted by a majority vote in each house of Congress. Up to this point, all new states had been U.S. territories, not separate sovereign countries. There was no precedent for incorporating another country into the United States. Now Tyler, with Jackson's advice and Polk's support, tried a new approach: simply admit Texas as a state. The idea worked. Instead of a treaty with Texas, which required a two-thirds vote in the Senate that Tyler could not get, both houses of Congress passed a resolution admitting Texas as a state in February 1845, leaving it to the president to negotiate the Texas border with Mexico (see Map11-2, p. 311). Five senators, led by Missouri's Thomas Hart Benton, who had opposed annexation, now supported the statehood resolution based on a promise that President Polk would conduct the negotiations about the Texas border. Tyler did not feel bound by the promise. On March 1, 1845, with four days left in office, Tyler signed the resolution admitting Texas, sent envoys to Texas offering immediate statehood without any negotiations, and held a gala White House party to celebrate the admission of the new state to the union. Benton was furious, and most Whigs were equally distraught. Then on March 4, 1845, James K. Polk was inaugurated as president of a nation that considered Texas to be one of its states, even if Mexico did not agree.

54°40' or Fight—The United States and Oregon

While American political debates seemed fixated on Texas, Oregon was generally ignored by the press and in Congress. Since Lewis and Clark's return in 1806, only a few Americans had followed the route the expedition took or had settled in Oregon. The Canadian Hudson's Bay Company dominated the fur business in Oregon, and Indian tribes traded furs to the company for rifles and other goods. The lack of interest in Oregon began to change in July 1836 when some seventy people traveled through a pass in the Rocky Mountains into what is now Wyoming. Some of the group, including four

Protestant missionaries, traveled on to Oregon Territory and settled in the fertile farming areas of the Willamette Valley south of the Columbia River. Two of those missionaries, Marcus and Narcissa Whitman, also became first-rate publicists for Oregon's beauty (see Map 11-3).

The Whitmans' publicity of the beauties of Oregon was their own undoing. By 1847, Narcissa Whitman was describing "probably 80 or 100 wagons" that had passed their mission and more said to be on the way. She also noted that "[t]he poor Indians," who were supposed to be the focus of the Whitman Mission, "are amazed at the overwhelming numbers of Americans coming into the country. They seem not to know what to make of it." When a measles epidemic struck in 1847, the amazement turned to anger. The Whitmans provided medical care to Indian and white children, but many Cayuse still died. In November 1847, the Cayuse chief Tiloukaikt led a party that killed both Whitmans and burned the mission. In response, a white militia attacked the Cayuse. Two years later, Tiloukaikt was executed for the murder of the Whitmans. From the gallows he said, "Did not your missionaries teach us that Christ died to save his people? So we die to save our people." Disease and white raids so weakened the Cayuse that they could not continue as an independent nation, and they merged into the Nez Perce and Yakima tribes.

Map 11-3 Westward Trails.

Beginning at places like St. Louis or Independence, Missouri, or Council Bluffs, Iowa, a variety of trails were used by early American migrants seeking new homes in Oregon and in territory claimed by the Republic of Mexico from Texas to California.

American Voices

The Letters of Narcissa Whitman, 1836–1847

Narcissa Whitman and her physician husband, Marcus, were sent by the American Board of Commissioners for Foreign Missions to establish a mission to the Cayuse Indians near what is now Walla Walla, Washington, in 1836. The mission converted few Cayuse. But Narcissa's letters home and her husband's speaking tours encouraged white settlement in the territory, settlement that alienated Indians but led to a strong American presence. Although the letters were filled with descriptions of the hardships of the journey across the Rocky Mountains, Narcissa's praise of the beauty and fertility of the land made the greatest impact.

September 12. [1836] What a delightful place this is; what a contrast to the rough, barren sand plains, through which we had so recently passed. Here we find fruit of every description, apples, peaches, grapes, pears, plums, and fig trees in abundance; also cucumbers, melons, beans, peas, beets, cabbage, tomatoes and every kind of vegetable too numerous to be mentioned. Every part is very neat and tastefully arranged, with fine walks, lined on each side with strawberry vines. At the opposite end of the garden is a good summer house covered with grape vines.

Dec. 26th. [1836] … The rivers are barely skirted with timber. This is all the woodland we can see; beyond them, as far as the eye can reach, plains and mountains appear. On the east, a few rods from the house, is a range of small hills, covered with bunchgrass—a very excellent food for animals, and upon which they subsist during winter, even digging it from under the snow.

Source: www.pbs.org/weta/thewest/program/resources/archives/two/whitman1.htm#120536 www.pbs.org/weta/thewest/program/resources/archives/twowhitman2.htm#040447 *The Letters of Narcissa Whitman*, 1836–1847 (Fairfield, WA: Ye Galleon Press, 1986).

Thinking Critically

1. **Analyzing Primary Sources**
   On what aspects of the land did Narcissa Whitman focus? For what purpose or audience do you think she wrote as she did?

2. **Comparison**
   How might the Cayuse Indians' opinions have differed from Whitman's view that newcomers coming to Oregon were desirable?

The Oregon Territory was shared by the United States and Britain as it had been since the treaties negotiated by then Secretary of State John Quincy Adams between 1818 and 1824 created joint American-British governance of the territory (see Chapter 8). The Oregon Territory stretched along the Pacific coast from the northern border of Spanish-Mexican California to the southern border of what was then Russian America (now Alaska) and included the present U.S. states of Oregon, Washington, and Idaho as well as the Canadian province of British Columbia and the Yukon Territory. By the 1840s, both governments wanted to resolve the border and end the joint ownership of the territory.

In the Webster-Ashburton Treaty of 1842, the United States and Britain had already negotiated a U.S.-Canadian border at the 49th parallel from the Great Lakes west to the beginning of Oregon. Continuing that border west would split the Oregon Territory between the two countries. Tyler's ambassador in London proposed making the 49th parallel the boundary all the way to the Pacific but giving the British the southern tip of Vancouver Island, sliced by the 49th parallel, and giving both countries the right to navigate the Juan de Fuca Strait between Vancouver and the mainland. It seemed like a straightforward compromise. Polk, however, wanted more, or pretended to.

In his 1844 campaign, Polk promised to win all of Oregon up to the Alaskan border, or 54°40' in terms of latitude. But Polk needed his army for the war that he expected to have with Mexico and did not want to fight Britain, too. The coalition that elected him was divided about Oregon. Calhoun and the southern planters would have happily given all of Oregon to Britain. They did not want a war or even tension to interrupt the cotton trade with Britain that was making the South wealthy. In addition, from Calhoun's perspective, any future states carved out of the Oregon Territory would most likely be free states, tipping the balance in the Senate against southern interests. But Missouri's powerful senator Thomas Hart Benton was growing fond of Oregon in part because the trail to Oregon which began in Independence, Missouri, was adding wealth to his state. Polk had promised 54°40', and Benton meant to hold him to it. John Quincy Adams, now a power in the House of Representatives, agreed with Benton. Although he was opposed to annexing Texas because of slavery, Adams was still an American expansionist, he liked the Oregon region for all the reasons Calhoun disliked it, and he wanted Oregon in the Union.

11.1

11.2

11.3

The Whitman Mission in 1845 (colour litho), Jackson, William Henry (1843–1942) / Private Collection / Peter Newark American Pictures / Bridgeman Images

Whitman Mission. In 1836, Narcissa Whitman became the first white woman to cross the Rocky Mountains as she and her husband, Marcus Whitman, moved to Waiilapu, Oregon Territory—now southern Washington State—to start a mission to the Cayuse Indians. Their many letters describing the beauty of the Walla Walla Valley brought thousands of additional white settlers who in turn brought a tragic measles epidemic to the Cayuse who then destroyed the mission and killed the Whitmans in 1847.

The British government, led by Prime Minister Sir Robert Peel, also wanted a compromise that would support the Hudson's Bay Company but guarantee an uninterrupted flow of American cotton to British mills and avoid war with the United States. Peel also faced other issues that were more pressing than Oregon. But others in London wanted more of Oregon and insisted that the southern border of British Oregon should be the Columbia River, which created the so-called disputed triangle of land that both nations claimed.

The Peel and Polk administrations eventually compromised along the 49th parallel (the current border) in spring 1846 (see Map 11-4). The agreement was an obvious compromise, particularly for the United States, but it meant that the United States was free to pursue actions that Polk considered more important. As the Democratic *New York Herald* said, "We can now thrash Mexico into decency at our leisure."

11.1 Quick Review

Why was annexing Texas more controversial than dividing the Oregon Territory?

The U.S. War with Mexico, 1846–1848

11.2 **Analyze the causes, strategies, and outcomes of the U.S. war with Mexico.**

Two years before, Presidents Tyler and Polk had managed the U.S. annexation of Texas; Mexico had warned the United States that such a move would mean war because Mexico still claimed the territory. One week after Tyler signed the annexation legislation, the Mexican ambassador in Washington declared the move "an act of aggression," and Mexico severed diplomatic relations with the United States.

Although the vote to make Texas a state of the United States was passed and celebrated in Washington in March of 1845, Texas did not ratify the agreement until July 1845, and Congress did not ratify the Texas decision until December. Meanwhile, Mexican president José Joaquín Herrera, a political moderate, agreed to negotiate with the United States. He knew his country did not have the resources to fight a war, but he also knew that public opinion in his country would never accept the loss of Texas, particularly the larger area of

Texas going all the way to the Rio Grande that the United States now claimed. Polk sent former Louisiana congressman John Slidell to Mexico City to negotiate.

Fighting the War in Texas and Mexico, Responding to Resistance

Although there were tensions between Americans and the government of Mexico from Texas to California, the heart of the concerns in 1846 had to do with Texas. While both countries negotiated about whether the United States could annex Texas, another question loomed: just what constituted Texas? The Republic of Texas had never governed any land west of the Nueces River. Many in the United States and Mexico considered that river to be the western boundary of Texas. But Polk and many Texans claimed that the Rio Grande was the border, a claim that made Texas a much bigger state (see Map 11-2, p. 311). Herrera would never accept that claim. Moreover, Polk really wanted not only Texas as far as the Rio Grande but

Map 11-4 Disputed Triangle of Oregon Territory.

The border of the Oregon Territory became the subject of a complicated dispute between factions within the United States and within the British government regarding whether the border should be 54° 40´, the 49th parallel, or the Columbia River, leading to what was known as the "disputed triangle" that both nations claimed. The issue was resolved by compromise in 1846.

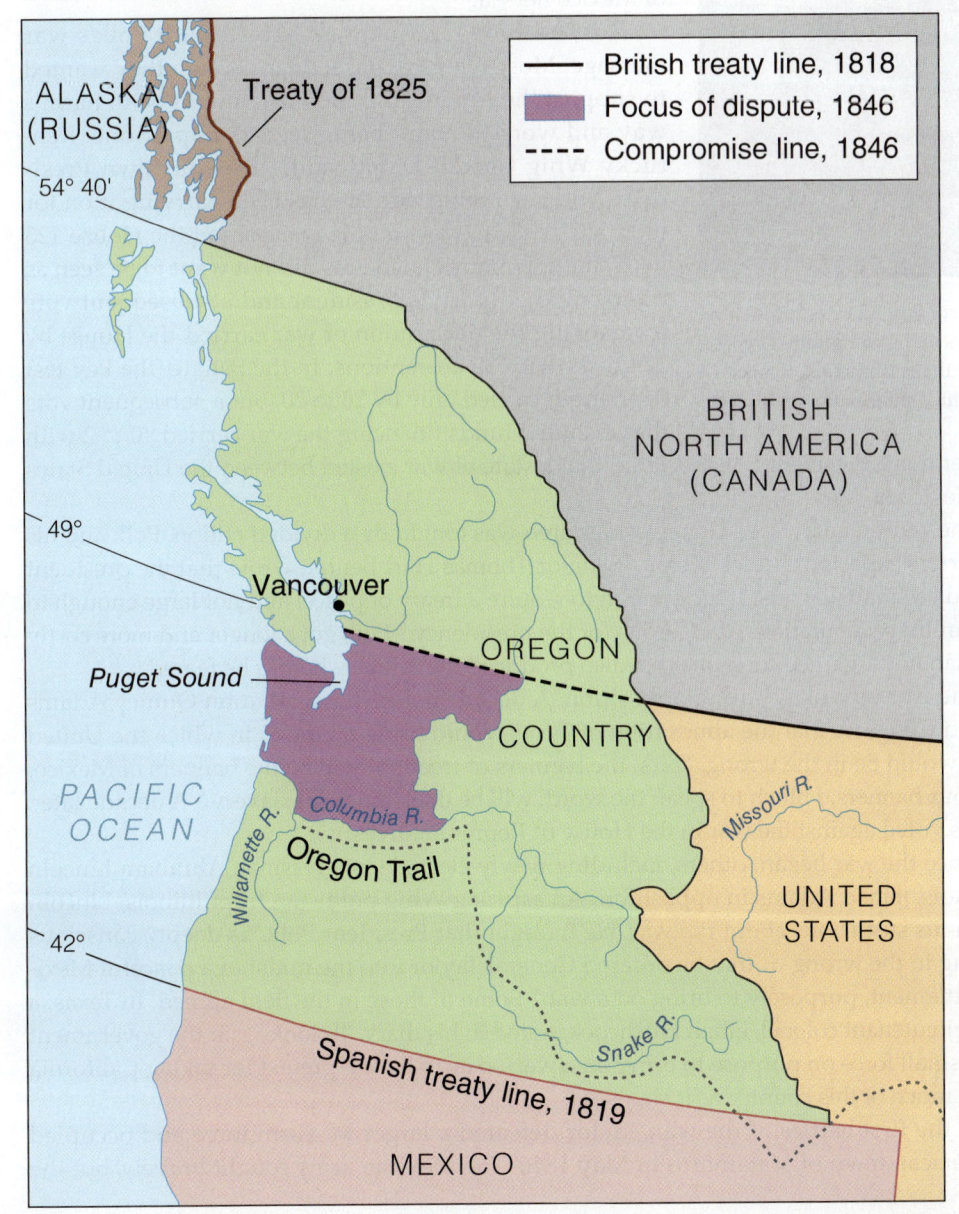

Bettmann/Getty Images

The artist Richard Caton Woodville's painting *War News from Mexico* captured the interest and, in some cases, surprise that came as news of the war reached people in most parts of the United States much more quickly than ever before, thanks primarily to the spread of telegraph lines that transmitted information faster than ever previously possible.

also New Mexico and California. He would purchase it if he could, but he also considered a war as a viable way to secure that land.

While the negotiations continued, Polk ordered General Zachary Taylor to cross the Sabine River into Texas in June 1845 and from there continue to "approach as near the boundary line, the Rio Grande, as prudence will dictate." Taylor was indeed a prudent general, and he initially moved only as far as the Nueces where he halted at Corpus Christi to train his four thousand troops. But his orders were clear: any Mexican movement across the Rio Grande would be considered an act of war. It took almost a year for Polk to get his war, but in April 1846, Taylor's army moved to the Rio Grande. When Mexican troops who had crossed the Rio Grande fought with some of Taylor's troops and eleven Americans were killed on April 25, 1846, Polk had his war. When Taylor reported that "hostilities may now be considered as commenced," Polk told the Congress that "Mexico … has invaded our territory and shed American blood upon the American soil. … War exists … by the act of Mexico herself."

Not everyone in Congress agreed with Polk's war message. Most Whigs opposed war, though they wanted to support the American troops who might be in harm's way and worried about being seen as unpatriotic. Kentucky Whig Garrett David said, "It is our own President who began this war. He has been carrying it on for months." The key vote on the war passed the House 123 to 67, though many Democrats did not want to be seen as opposing their party's president and a subsequent vote formalizing the declaration of war carried the House by 174 to 14 with 35 abstentions. In the Senate, the key test of strength carried only by 26 to 20, but a subsequent vote that included funds financing the war carried 40 to 2 with 3 abstentions. President Polk declared that a state of war existed between the United States and Mexico on May 13, 1846.

The war that a divided Congress declared was fought by a divided nation. Polk and his supporters expected a quick victory. Senator Thomas Hart Benton wrote that the president wanted "a small war, just large enough to require a treaty of peace, and not large enough to make military reputations, dangerous for the presidency." Polk got a longer and more costly war than he bargained for—one that also produced the military heroes he feared.

The war provoked strong opposition. A decade before it began, John Quincy Adams warned Congress that the annexation of Texas would bring on a war in which the United States would be in the wrong: "Sirs, the banners of freedom will be the banners of Mexico; and your banners, I blush to speak the word, will be the banners of slavery." A decade later, Adams voted against the war in the House of Representatives.

Once the war began, others, including newly elected Congressman Abraham Lincoln of Illinois, joined Adams in opposition. An aspiring Whig politician from Illinois, Lincoln voiced his suspicions about the war. He thought that President Polk "is deeply conscious of being in the wrong … that he ordered General Taylor into the midst of a peaceful Mexican settlement, purposely to bring on a war." Some of those in the field agreed. In Texas, a young lieutenant colonel, ethan Hitchcock, noted in his diary, "It looks as if the government sent a small force on purpose to bring on a war, so as to have a pretext for taking California and as much of this country as it chooses."

In the first battles of the war, Taylor defeated a larger Mexican force and occupied the Mexican town of Matamoros in May 1846. The Mexican army fought bravely, but the

Thinking Historically

Considering Henry David Thoreau

Henry David Thoreau (1817–1862) was a close friend of Ralph Waldo Emerson and a part of the circle of Transcendentalists. He generally divided his time between works that focused on the importance of nature—such as *Walden* (published 1854) and abolitionist tracts. In 1849, he published "On the Duty of Civil Disobedience." The essay, which reflected his opposition to the war with Mexico and his personal refusal to pay taxes to support it, has at least two themes: Thoreau's opposition to most, if not all, government, and his belief that civil disobedience—in this case breaking an immoral law—was the right thing to do. Thoreau's belief in refusing to obey an unjust law and a willingness to face the consequences has made him a model for others who advocated civil disobedience, including Martin Luther King, Jr. (1929–1968) in the United States and Mohandas Gandhi (1869–1948), who led the nonviolent protests that eventually won independence for India.

But Thoreau's arguments are complex and many who may agree with some of what he might say would reject other aspects of his essay. Thoreau begins by arguing:

I heartily accept the motto, "That government is best which governs least"; and I should like to see it acted up to more rapidly and systematically. Carried out, it finally amounts to this, which also I believe—"That government is best which governs not at all"; and when men are prepared for it, that will be the kind of government which they will have.

Having said this, Thoreau then moved on to his specific critique of the war with Mexico and his appeal for resistance:

How does it become a man to behave toward the American government today? I answer, that he cannot without disgrace be associated with it. … Under a government which imprisons unjustly, the true place for a just man is also a prison. The proper place today, the only place which Massachusetts has provided for her freer and less despondent spirits, is in

her prisons, to be put out and locked out of the State by her own act, as they have already put themselves out by their principles. It is there that the fugitive slave, and the Mexican prisoner on parole, and the Indian come to plead the wrongs of his race should find them; on that separate but more free and honorable ground, where the State places those who are not with her, but against her—the only house in a slave State in which a free man can abide with honor.

Finally, Thoreau said he was not willing to be like "the thousands who are in opinion opposed to slavery and to the war, who yet in effect do nothing." Thoreau wrote, "I meet this American government, or its representative the State government, directly, and face to face, once a year, no more, in the person of its tax-gatherer." This was the opportunity to resist what he considered to be an unjust and immoral war. He was arrested for not paying taxes and spent a night in the town jail in Concord before someone, to his frustration, paid the tax for him. But his willingness to face arrest for his convictions and the pamphlet that he wrote explaining his actions made Thoreau not only one of the most famous opponents of the war with Mexico but also a model of civil disobedience.

Source: Henry David Thoreau, *On the Duty of Civil Disobedience* (New York: Houghton Mifflin, 1893).

Thinking Critically

1. **Contextualization**
   What other developments in the 1840s would explain Thoreau's use of a fugitive slave, a Mexican prisoner, and an Indian as examples of those wronged by his government?

2. **Argument Development**
   What are the implications of his statement, "That government is best which governs not at all"? How might one develop a different argument for or against the U.S. war with Mexico?

Americans had superior technology—rifles that shot farther and better artillery. The U.S. Navy blockaded Mexican ports on the Gulf and Pacific coasts, so Mexico could not import supplies from abroad. Taylor's army moved slowly into Mexico, but heat and disease took a heavier toll than battles. One in eight U.S. soldiers died in a six-week encampment in the Mexican city of Camargo even though no battles took place there. If the troops, especially the volunteers, had learned to fill canteens upstream from where horses were washed, the death toll would have been far lower. Then in September 1846, Taylor defeated another larger Mexican force and captured the crucial Mexican town of Monterrey. With both armies now exhausted, Taylor allowed the Mexicans to withdraw peacefully and declared a truce, which infuriated Polk.

After the victory at Monterrey, Polk tried to open peace negotiations, but the Mexican government was not interested. This lack of interest came as a surprise because the United States had secretly helped the former Mexican dictator Santa Anna seize power in Mexico City, based on his promise to U.S. negotiators that he would conclude a peace treaty. But once in office, Santa Anna shifted his position and prepared to fight rather than bargain (see Map 11-5 , p. 326).

Map 11-5 Battles in the U.S. War with Mexico.

Once war was declared between the United States and Mexico, General Taylor led his armies into the disputed territory and farther south to battles in Monterrey and Buena Vista in northern Mexico, while General Kearney led forces across the continent to take control of Santa Fe, New Mexico, and then parts of California. The navy played a major role in the takeover of California and also blockaded Pacific and Gulf ports in Mexico while General Winfield Scott landed at Veracruz and soon thereafter won control of Mexico City itself.

Santa Anna marched north to engage Taylor, whom he knew was now short of troops. In February 1847, the two armies met at what Americans called the Battle of Buena Vista. It was the largest single engagement of the war, and it was a draw, which meant that Santa Anna had failed to defeat the Americans on Mexican soil. Taylor's army remained intact.

Many of Taylor's best troops had been moved farther south. As Polk realized he was in for a long fight, he also knew that Taylor could not march across the deserts to Mexico City. The distance was too long to supply an invading army. Polk also worried about making Taylor a war hero and political rival. So he turned to the experienced professional soldier Winfield Scott to plan an invasion of the Mexican heartland. In March 1847, Scott landed troops at the port of Veracruz. (It was the largest amphibious operation of U.S. troops before D-Day during World War II.) Scott's army then marched to Mexico City, taking the same invasion route that

Table 11-1 Major Battles of the U.S. War with Mexico

Battle	Date	Victor
Battle of Palo Alto	May 8, 1846	United States
Battle of Resaca de la Palma	May 9, 1846	United States
Battle of Monterrey	September 21–24, 1846	United States
Battle of San Pasqual	December 6, 1846	Mexico
Battle of Rio San Gabriel	January 8, 1847	United States
Battle of Buena Vista	February 22–23, 1847	United States
Battle of Sacramento Rier	February 27, 1847	United States
Battle of Veracruz	March 29, 1847	United States
Battle of Cerro Gordo	April 18, 1847	United States

11.1

11.2

11.3

Hernán Cortés had used against the Aztecs 328 years before (see Chapter 2). After hard fighting, Mexico City surrendered in September 1847. Polk, still worried about military heroes, then removed Scott from command in early 1848. The United States had lost 12,518 soldiers and spent almost $100 million in the war. (See Table 11-1 for a list of battles in the war.) Mexico had lost many more lives—soldiers and civilians—and its economy was devastated.

From New Mexico to Alta California and the Bear Flag Revolt

While the major focus of the fighting in the U.S. war with Mexico took place on the Texas border and in the heartland of Mexico, New Mexico and California were not exempt from battles, though they were of a smaller scale. The initial U.S. conquest of New Mexico was easy. In the summer of 1846, General Stephen Watts Kearny marched 850 miles from Fort Leavenworth, Kansas, to Santa Fe, the capital of New Mexico. The Mexican governor had already fled, and Kearny took silence and sullenness among the people to mean support or at least acceptance of the American takeover. He raised the U.S. flag in Santa Fe and promised that the government would respect the residents' property and religious freedom as well as protect them from Indian raids. Kearny appointed Charles Bent, an American already living in Taos, as territorial governor. Then in September 1846, a month after he had arrived, Kearny marched most of his troops off to secure the U.S. victory in California. Although a bloody rebellion against U.S. rule by Hispanics and Indians broke out later that year, and Bent himself was killed by the rebels, U.S. troops soon suppressed it, and most armed resistance to annexation ended in New Mexico.

Emboldened by U.S. victories elsewhere, a group of armed American immigrants in the inland California town of Sonoma arrested General Mariano Vallejo, the man they considered the symbol of Mexican authority in California, and jailed him at Fort Sutter near Sacramento. Vallejo had retired from active duty with the Mexican government and like many of his fellow Californios was quite friendly to a possible American takeover. But to the Americans, Vallejo symbolized Mexican authority. The rebels then organized what they called the **Bear Flag Revolt** by declaring California to be an independent Republic. They raised their flag in the town square in Sonoma. The flag displayed a large star next to a grizzly bear atop a bottom border stripe and the words "California Republic." To the Mexicans like Vallejo, the Bear Flag was a symbol that these new immigrants were the bears who came as a thief to take their cattle and their land. Soon after the Bear Flag was raised, Sloat's U.S. Navy squadron sailed into Monterey Bay and proclaimed U.S. conquest of California. The independent California Republic was a short-lived convenience. The rebels replaced the Bear Flag (now the state flag of California) with the Stars and Stripes.

Mexican citizens of California had a decidedly ambivalent attitude toward annexation by the United States, and many, including Vallejo, looked to the American democracy as an improvement over what they saw as a distant and incompetent Mexican government. Others opposed the American takeover and fought against the Bear Flag rebels and the

Bear Flag Revolt

A revolt led by recent American immigrants who temporarily declared California to be an independent Republic until U.S. forces took control of the territory.

American forces led by Navy Commodore Robert Stockton, who had replaced Sloat, and Captain Frémont. Those Californians saw themselves as citizens of the Republic of Mexico, even if sometimes disgruntled citizens, and saw the Americans as an invading army. In a series of skirmishes between 1846 and 1847, thirty-five of those fighting on the American side died in battle while an estimated eight Californios (those fighting for the Mexican cause) were killed. In 1847, the final skirmishes between Californio defenders under Andrés Pico and the American troops took place in southern California. As it became increasingly clear that no support could be expected from Mexico, Pico negotiated the terms of what he saw as an honorable surrender. In January 1847, Pico's troops marched into Los Angeles and disbanded. The American control of the region was complete. Later, the Californios suffered much greater losses in property and, indeed, their way of life.

Negotiating the Peace, Defining the Borders

In April 1847, Polk had sent Nicholas Trist, an experienced diplomat, to accompany Scott and negotiate a treaty with the Mexican government. After the fighting in Mexico City had ended, Trist began serious negotiations. With Mexico City, New Mexico, and California already in the hands of the U.S. Army, however, Polk decided that Trist was not being tough enough and recalled him. Instead of returning to Washington, Trist warned the Mexican authorities that he had been recalled and that his replacement would demand much more. Perhaps they might want to conclude a treaty quickly with him. The Mexicans were anxious to end the U.S. occupation of Mexico City and the country's key ports, and Trist was right: after the conquest of Mexico City, Polk wanted even more Mexican territory. On February 2, 1848, Trist and the Mexican commissioners signed the **Treaty of Guadalupe Hidalgo**. Trist told his wife that he had asked Mexico for the minimum that Polk would accept because he was ashamed of "the iniquity of the war, as an abuse of power on our part." But his minimum included all of Polk's original demands—all of Texas to the Rio Grande and land farther west to California as far south as San Diego. Mexico was paid $15 million, which went to its creditors. The treaty may have been for less land than Polk wanted, but it reshaped both the United States and Mexico.

A furious President Polk, realizing that he was stuck with the treaty that Trist had negotiated, submitted it to the Senate, which ratified it. But Polk refused to pay Trist for his services. (Trist was not paid until 1871.) The Whig-affiliated editor Horace Greeley wrote in his *New York Tribune*, "Let us have peace, no matter if the adjuncts are revolting." The

Treaty of Guadalupe Hidalgo

The treaty, signed in 1848, ended the U.S. war with Mexico and granted the United States control of all of Texas, New Mexico, and California.

U.S. General Winfield Scott led his troops into Mexico City to accept the official Mexican surrender in 1847. This popular picture shows the clean ending of the war but not the bloody battles that led to it.

abolitionist Frederick Douglass was harsher: "They have succeeded in robbing Mexico of her territory, and are rejoicing over their success under the hypocritical pretense of a regard for peace." Nevertheless, with the Treaty of Guadalupe Hidalgo, peace had come. The United States was much larger as a result of the war, now including ninety thousand new citizens who had been citizens of Mexico and even more Indians who preferred to stay independent of both countries. It was a different country from when Polk took office.

In 1853, one of Polk's successors, President Franklin Pierce, sent James Gadsden to Mexico City with instructions to buy a strip of land south of Arizona and New Mexico for a southern transcontinental railroad from New Orleans to El Paso and Los Angeles, which needed to be located south of the Rocky Mountains. Gadsden was also told to purchase as much additional land as possible, including perhaps all of Baja California. Mexican authorities suspected that the United States was after much more than a railroad route. In the end, Mexico sold only the minimum that the United States wanted. For $10 million, money its government badly needed, Mexico ceded thirty-nine thousand sparsely populated square miles to the United States. This area, known as the **Gadsden Purchase**, was the final extension of U.S. territory within what would be the contiguous forty-eight states (see Map 11-6).

11.1

11.2

11.3

Gadsden Purchase

The final acquisition of land in the continental United States was completed in 1853 when the United States paid Mexico $10 million for a strip of land in what is now southern New Mexico and Arizona.

Map 11-6 An Expanded Union.

With the treaty setting the Oregon border in 1846 and the Treaty of Guadalupe Hidalgo in 1848, the territory of the continental United States was almost set. The small Gadsden Purchase in 1853 made it easier to build a railroad south of the Rocky Mountains.

Territorial expansion in the 1800s
Date of territorial acquisition, e.g., 1850
Date of statehood, e.g. (1800)
Present-day state boundaries provided for orientation.

Original thirteen states 1783 — Louisiana Purchase 1803 — Florida Purchase 1819 — Texas Annexation 1845 — Mexican Cession 1848
Great Britain Cession 1783 — Acquired from Great Britain 1818 — Acquired from Great Britain 1842 — Oregon Country 1846 — Gadsen Purchase 1853

In his own eyes, Polk had an amazingly successful term. He had made the United States a continental nation. He had completed the job he had promised to do and did not seek a second term. For the election of 1848, Polk's Democrats nominated Lewis Cass of Michigan. The Whigs, having won once with a general and having lost three times with their hero Henry Clay, turned to a new war hero and nominated General Zachary Taylor, known as "Old Rough and Ready," and former congressman Millard Fillmore from New York as Taylor's running mate. While Taylor was as strong a nationalist as Jackson, he was also a slaveholder, and Cass, like Polk, was an expansionist. Northerners opposed to slavery could not stomach either of them and some created the Free Soil Party, which was committed to ensuring that all new territories would be free of slavery. The Free Soilers did not propose abolishing slavery where it already existed but opposed any extension of slavery into any new territories. Using that platform, they nominated former president Van Buren as their candidate. In the three-way race, Taylor won a solid victory. It was an ironic outcome for President Polk. The Whigs had opposed Polk throughout his term, especially on the issue of the war with Mexico, and the president feared creating military heroes throughout the war. In the end, a Whig war hero succeeded him. A little over a year into his term, on a hot July 4th of 1850, Taylor suddenly died and Vice President Fillmore ascended to the presidency. This time, however, unlike Tyler's accession with the death of Harrison, there were no major policy shifts when Fillmore took office.

> ### 11.2 Quick Review
>
> Considering U.S. actions in Texas and California, was the Mexican-American War a "land grab"? Why or why not?

West into the Pacific

11.3 Analyze the causes and outcomes of U.S. expansion in California and into the Pacific region, including establishing new relationships with Hawaii, China, and Japan.

Early in his term of office, President Polk had told Congress that he was interested in acquiring California's harbors from Mexico because, he said, these ports would shelter American ships and allow the Pacific Ocean to provide the basis for "an extensive and profitable commerce with China, and other countries of the East." He had no idea how quickly his dream would come true. Even before the negotiations with Mexico were complete, gold was discovered in California, and the resulting Gold Rush made the gold camps and the cities around harbors into thriving commercial centers. These same Pacific coast harbors quickly became home to American ships that had been dominating much of the Pacific Ocean for decades before Polk spoke. In the 1840s, American whaling ships led all other nations in the whale trade in the Pacific, and the U.S. Navy led the way to American negotiations for a role in trade with Hawaii and China. After the acquisition of California, the navy also established a trading relationship with Japan. After 1848, the profits of the Pacific trade poured into the United States through the newly acquired Pacific ports. The acquisition of Oregon and California not only expanded the United States to the Pacific coast but also allowed the nation to become a dominant player all across the Pacific Ocean.

The Gold Rush to California

Another 1848 development was perhaps even more important to California's history than the shift in political authority from Mexico to the United States. On January 24, 1848, while American and Mexican negotiators were still meeting in the Mexican town of Guadalupe Hidalgo, James Marshall, a carpenter at the fort and mill owned by Swiss native Johann Sutter on the American River in northern California, was deepening the channel going into the mill's water wheel when he noticed some odd material in the water. He reported, "Boys, I believe I have found a gold mine." His was the first discovery of gold, which would quickly lead to the **California Gold Rush**.

Sutter and Marshall tried to keep the discovery a secret, but word spread all too quickly. By May 1848, everyone in San Francisco seemed to know that gold had been discovered. And while communications were still slow, prospective miners from all over California—Indians, longtime Mexican residents, and American settlers—as well as immigrants from Oregon, Hawaii, Mexico, and as far away as Chile, Peru, Australia, France, and parts of China moved into the gold fields of the Sierra Nevada mountains. The rush was on. Two-thirds of the white men in Oregon came south to California. Recently discharged soldiers from the Mexican and American armies joined them there. In the earliest days, California Indians who knew the land best made excellent gold prospectors. Newcomers expressed surprise that in the first year of the Gold Rush, Miwok Indian women and men panned for gold alongside the newcomers from around the globe. The diversity in the fields did not last.

In August 1848, an article in the *New York Herald* included a brief mention that "gold, worth in value $30, was picked up in the bed of a stream of the Sacramento." President Polk, determined to show the value of the newly acquired territory, included a mention in his Annual Message to Congress. Ten million dollars in gold was produced in California in 1848, and within three years, the revenue had grown to $220 million. So much gold changed the economic calculations of the United States and much of the world from China to South America to Europe. Suddenly, there was a great deal of gold in circulation everywhere.

Thousands of people wanted to get rich quickly by coming to California to find the gold. California's non-Indian population was around seven thousand in 1845. It had grown to almost ninety-three thousand in the first U.S. Census of 1850. While the first prospectors had come from Mexico and South America as well as from the crews of Pacific whaling ships that had stopped in California harbors and from Hawaii and China, by 1849, the largest numbers were coming from the eastern United States and Europe. Getting to California from other parts of the United States or Europe could mean a long, slow, and expensive trip by ocean around the southern tip of South America. It could also involve a shorter sea voyage to Nicaragua, then an overland trek by pack mule across the isthmus, and another voyage from there up to San Francisco. Still for others, it could mean traveling overland, walking or on ox-drawn wagons across the continent. Sea travel around South America was certainly the most comfortable and perhaps safest, but it cost a lot, from $300 to $700, and it was slow, taking four to eight months. The trip via Nicaragua or Panama was almost as expensive, perhaps $600, and dangerous, but it was certainly the fastest, taking five to eight weeks. Coming by land across the continent was by far the cheapest, costing not more than $200, but it also took at least three months and had to be timed just right to avoid winter on the Rocky Mountains. The majority opted for the cheapest way. Small numbers of people had been coming west for decades, but in 1849–1850, many thousands of prospective Californians traveled along the Platte and Humboldt Rivers and then the Oregon and California Trails into the gold fields (see Map 11-3, p. 320).

The gold camps themselves were harsh places. Fortunes were made and lost, not only in the fields but also at gambling tables and through theft and intimidation. White Americans, some of them very recent Americans, resented the competition of miners from South America and elsewhere, especially those who came from China or who were Indians or Californios. Within a short time, most Chinese and Indian miners had been driven from the gold fields through violence and intimidation, though some Indians were retained to work for subsistence wages mining gold for others while the Chinese found other kinds of work, eventually building the western railroads and developing service industries for miners and others.

The incredible jump in California's immigrant population came at a terrible cost for the California Indians. Their population, already declining in the face of the missions, declined much more rapidly after the beginnings of the Gold Rush because of disease and outright murder, decreasing by almost 85 percent between 1848 and 1880 to twenty-three thousand. African slaves were rare both because slave owners knew it was all too easy for a slave to escape in California and because other miners hated all competition.

11.1

11.2

11.3

California Gold Rush

The rush to find gold that brought thousands of new residents to California and produced millions of dollars in new wealth for the region and the United States.

Few women were able to succeed as miners; indeed, far fewer women than men even came to California in the Gold Rush. Mining camps were overwhelmingly male communities. Some women who did come to California were forced or tricked into prostitution to pay for their passage from Europe, China, and Latin America.

The most freewheeling era of the gold camps was very short lived. By 1851, the chances of finding gold by simply looking in a stream bed, as Marshall and Sutter had done in 1848, or even finding gold with a pan had pretty much ended except in the more southerly Tuolumne and Merced gold regions. Some miners began using a "rocker" or "cradle" that washed dirt out more quickly. Soon enough, gold mining was transformed into large-scale hydraulic mining, which required large corporate investments and reduced most miners to hired labor. For hired laborers, though mining paid much better than most East Coast jobs, the possibility of making a fortune evaporated. Gold mining continued and fortunes were still made in the gold fields, but the Gold Rush was over.

Whaling in the Pacific Ocean

In February 1849, the owners of the whaling ship *Minerva* from New Bedford, Massachusetts, received a letter from its captain. He reported that, after hunting whales in the Pacific, he had stopped in San Francisco for supplies and to recruit more sailors, "but the excitement there in relation to the discovery of gold made it impossible to prevent the crew from running away. Three of the crew in attempting to swim ashore were drowned, and the ship's company soon became too much reduced to continue the whaling voyage." The *Minerva* thus joined dozens of other whaling ships abandoned in San Francisco harbor while their crews sought wealth in the California gold fields.

Some sailors no doubt found fortunes in the gold fields that had eluded them at sea, and some ship owners lost substantial sums when their ships were abandoned, but in general, the whaling industry remained a source of wealth to some Americans while supporting many others and contributing to the growth of the American economy. The golden age of the American whaling industry began after the War of 1812 and continued until the outbreak of the Civil War in 1861. During these years, hundreds of American ships moved from their earlier and safer whale hunts in the Atlantic to two-, three-, and four-year voyages to the Pacific Ocean. Whale oil, which burned brighter than any other fuel available at the time, was used for lamps across the globe. Whale products provided oil for the Industrial Revolution as well as the bone for the hoop dresses and corsets that were the height of women's fashion. Despite British efforts to launch their own whaling fleets, by the 1830s four-fifths of all the whaling ships in the world were American.

The owners and captains of most American whaling ships were mostly men of old New England English stock, many of them Quakers, but there were exceptions. A few African Americans, including Paul Cuffee and Absalom F. Boston, became captains, and Cuffee became a ship owner. The crews, white and black, came from almost every corner of the globe—Pacific Islanders, West Indians, South Americans, or Portuguese. Whaling was one of the few occupations in which blacks were paid the same as whites. Even a runaway slave could admit, as John Thompson did in 1840, "I am a fugitive slave from Maryland. … I thought I would go on a whaling voyage, as being a place where I stood least chance of being arrested by slave hunters." By some estimates, 10 percent of those who worked on whaling ships were black. Nevertheless, most sailors in the whaling business were white men, like Ishmael, the fictional narrator of Herman Melville's 1851 novel *Moby-Dick*, but whites on whaling ships served as part of racially diverse crews. When Melville described his fictional crew, it included Queequeg, Ishmael's best friend and a native of one of the Pacific islands where whaling ships landed; Tashitego, an American Indian; and Daggoo, a native of Africa. Real-life vessels were equally mixed.

Few women served on whaling ships. There were occasional stories of women who hid their gender and embarked with the crew, not easy in the close quarters of a small ship on a long voyage. Some captains also took along their wives and children, and some crew members said they appreciated having a woman on board who might know more medicine than the men and who could soothe an angry captain.

North Wind Picture Archives / Alamy Stock Photo

LAUNCH OF THE FLYING CLOUD.

Clipper ships like the famous *Flying Cloud* made the trip from New York to San Francisco in record speed—eighty-nine days in one case—while slower whaling ships traveling from New Bedford and other Atlantic ports into the Pacific often took two or three years. During the 1830s and 1840s, American sailing ships projected American influence into the world's oceans as never before.

Whaling ships also explored parts of the world unknown to previous generations of Americans. The first Americans to enter Japan were whaling sailors. Almost a decade before Commodore Perry's famous voyage to "open up" Japan in 1853–1854, the *Manhattan* entered Tokyo harbor in 1845 to return shipwrecked Japanese sailors. The *Superior* was the first whaling ship to enter the Arctic Ocean off the coast of Alaska in 1848. U.S. whaling ships explored much of the South Pacific, sailed off the coast of Australia, and explored Antarctica. As a result of the many whaling ships that anchored there, Honolulu and San Francisco became major American ports, rivaling New Bedford and Nantucket, and many a sailor had spent time in all four places.

The Navy and Diplomacy across the Pacific

American whaling ships had been sailing the Pacific since 1815, but the 1848 Treaty of Guadalupe Hidalgo added a string of Pacific ports, especially San Francisco, to the United States. The acquisition of those ports expanded U.S. interest in the Pacific and beyond. By 1851, Daniel Webster, who had become secretary of state again under President Fillmore, proclaimed that the United States should "command the oceans, both oceans, all the oceans."

Central to the "command" of the Pacific Ocean was securing U.S. influence in Hawaii. In 1778, the British explorer Captain James Cook was the first European to reach the Hawaiian Islands, but by the mid-1800s, the United States had a much larger presence in Hawaii. Many Protestant missionaries and merchants began arriving in Hawaii in the 1820s where they built churches, schools, and businesses. Missionaries, merchants, and whalers boosted the Hawaiian economy, but they also brought alcohol, gambling, prostitution, and disease, including venereal diseases that killed many Hawaiians and reduced the islanders' ability to maintain their independence.

On occasion, the United States did protect the native Hawaiians. An American missionary, William Richards, advised King Kamehameha II (r. 1819–1824) on ways to maneuver among the great powers and play the United States, Britain, and France against each other. In 1842, Secretary of State Daniel Webster added Hawaii to the protections of the Monroe Doctrine

A Japanese artist drew this version of Commodore Matthew Perry meeting with Japanese officials in Tokyo in 1854 as he delivered a letter from President Millard Fillmore to the Emperor of Japan, demanding that Japan open to trade with the United States.

Kanagawa Treaty

An 1854 agreement—the first between the United States and Japan—that opened two Japanese ports to American commerce, protected shipwrecked American sailors, and ended Japan's two hundred years of isolation.

and made it clear that the United States would not tolerate a British or French takeover. In 1851, Webster negotiated a secret treaty with King Kamehameha III that, in the event of war, Hawaii would become a U.S. protectorate. Webster's priority was securing trading rights and the use of Honolulu as a coaling station for U.S. steamships—merchant vessels and warships—on their way to China and Japan.

Just as the United States gained San Francisco and influence in Hawaii, Britain was forcing China to open to the West. China saw itself as the center of the world. Foreigners were barbarians who might be allowed to trade in a limited way through the port of Guang-zhou but would never be treated as equals. Despite the restrictions, American merchants wanted access to more trade with China, and American missionaries wanted access to its people. Both were mostly shut out. Losing patience with the Chinese, the British turned to violence. In the so-called Opium War (1839–1842), the British forced China to open its ports to British products, including opium from British India, and cede Hong Kong Island as a British colony. Following in the footsteps of the British, U.S. Ambassador Caleb Cushing negotiated the Treaty of Wang-hsia in 1844, which gained the United States the same trade rights as the British.

While Britain took the lead in China, the United States forced the even more isolated Empire of Japan to open to the West. The United States wanted Japan as another coaling station beyond Hawaii on the route to China and wanted to trade with Japan for its own sake. President Fillmore sent Commodore Mathew Perry to "open up" Japan and force what he called a "weak and semi-barbarous people" to deal with the United States. In July 1853, Perry led four large warships with nearly one thousand sailors into Tokyo Bay and began negotiations. He returned in March 1854 with an even larger fleet. Perry did everything he could to impress the Japanese, providing Japanese officials with champagne, Kentucky bourbon, and a history of the war with Mexico to let them know what happened to those who opposed the United States. In return, the Japanese grudgingly agreed to the **Kanagawa Treaty** that opened two relatively isolated ports to the United States. Only in 1858 did Japan open more ports and establish formal diplomatic relations with other countries. Britain quickly became a larger economic and military force in Japan than the United States. Nevertheless, the United States had established a solid presence in Japan and China by the late 1850s.

As a result of expansion in the 1840s, the nation's border was extended to the Pacific, and U.S. ships sailed everywhere on that ocean. The Pacific and every nation on its shores including China, Japan, and Russian Siberia were in much closer contact with the United States than they had been a short time before. After 1848, the United States was an emerging force in the world.

11.3 Quick Review

Was expansion to other nations (Hawaii, China, Japan) a logical extension of Manifest Destiny? How were U.S. intentions across the Pacific different from U.S. goals in North America?

Conclusion

In the 1830s and 1840s, the United States became a continental power whose territory spanned from the Atlantic to the Pacific Oceans. A strong belief in the Manifest Destiny of the United States justified the Louisiana Purchase of 1803 (though the term was not yet in use) and supported new acquisitions from Oregon to Texas to California. Manifest Destiny reflected the larger belief that the United States was specially chosen by divine will to bring liberty and democracy—usually in its Jacksonian form—to the planet.

While Americans debated Manifest Destiny, the financial Panic of 1837, brought on by a worldwide glut in trade and exacerbated by the closing of the Bank of the United States under Jackson, created economic uncertainty in the cotton-growing South and the industrial North. Nevertheless, the nation grew.

The Webster-Ashburton Treaty of 1842 ended the joint ownership of the Oregon Territory with Britain and set the northern boundary of the United States. The United States annexed Texas in 1845, and after a bloody war from 1846 to 1848, Mexico ceded to the United States much of what became the American West, including New Mexico, Arizona, and California. While many Americans, from politicians like John Quincy Adams to philosophers like Henry David Thoreau, opposed the war with Mexico, many other Americans celebrated the victory and the acquisition of so much new territory. The Gold Rush quickly accelerated the settlement of California with diverse people, and it produced enormous amounts of gold but decimated the American Indian population in the far west.

After 1848, new ports in California supported increased ventures across the Pacific. The United States established a relationship with Hawaii, increased its trade with China, and forced Japan to open itself up to the West. The intensification of American interest in Asia in the 1840s and 1850s reflected the desire of American policy makers to successfully compete with Europe for new markets and coincided with the realization of the long-standing desire among many Americans to create a continental nation that could become a world power on land and sea.

Chapter Review

How did U.S. belief in the idea of Manifest Destiny permanently alter the geographical, social, economic, and political complexion of the United States?

Chapter 11 Summary and Review

Manifest Destiny—The Importance of an Idea

11.1 **Explain what Manifest Destiny meant and how it led the United States to involvement in Texas, California, and Oregon.**

Summary

The term *Manifest Destiny* strongly implied that American rule over the heart of North America was part of a divine plan. For supporters of Manifest Destiny, American expansion was closely linked to the spread of Jacksonian democracy and Protestant Christianity. Many Americans, from farmers to missionaries, supported versions of Manifest Destiny for their own reasons. Opponents of Manifest Destiny, including most Whigs and almost all opponents of slavery, saw more problems than opportunities in expansion. Tensions between those Americans living in Texas and those in the Mexican government led to war and the establishment of the Republic of Texas. Andrew Jackson and Martin Van Buren worked hard to increase the strength of the Democratic Party. They used that strength to secure Van Buren's election to the presidency in 1836. Van Buren supported the efforts of southerners to prevent congressional debate about slavery. However, economic problems brought on in part by actions taken in the Jackson administration undermined Van Buren's presidency. Tensions were also growing between the two countries about California as the Mexican region began to attract American attention. Meanwhile, a treaty with Britain secured a sizable portion of the disputed Oregon Territory. Manifest Destiny began to play a larger role in presidential politics and Texas was finally admitted as a state in 1945.

Review Questions

1. Contextualization
   Why was the status of Texas such a divisive political issue in the 1830s and 1840s?

2. Continuity and Change over Time
   How did the meaning of the western frontier continue over time from the colonial era to the 1800s?

The U.S. War with Mexico, 1846–1848

11.2 **Analyze the causes, strategies, and outcomes of the U.S. war with Mexico.**

Summary

The desire of President Polk and his supporters to extend territory beyond Texas in the Southwest led to hostilities with Mexico. The specific event that triggered the U.S. war with Mexico was a dispute over the border between Texas and Mexico. In 1846, Polk responded to a clash between American and Mexican soldiers at the Rio Grande as a pretext for war. There was considerable opposition to the war, particularly among Whigs. Perhaps the most influential response to the war came from essayist Henry David Thoreau when he wrote *Civil Disobedience*. The war took longer and cost more in men and resources than American leaders had anticipated. The terms of the 1848 Treaty of Guadalupe Hidalgo added an enormous amount of new territory to the United States, and the Gadsden Purchase represented the final extension of U.S. territory in the contiguous forty-eight states.

Review Questions

3. Argument Development
   Was the United States justified in provoking war with Mexico to reach its foreign policy goals? Why or why not?

4. Contextualization
   What connections did opponents of the U.S. war with Mexico make between the war and slavery?

West into the Pacific

11.3 **Analyze the causes and outcomes of U.S. expansion into the Pacific region, including establishing new relationships with Hawaii, China, and Japan.**

Summary

U.S. victory in the war with Mexico meant a great presence in the West and beyond. The 1848 Gold Rush attracted thousands of prospectors from a variety of places, establishing California's diverse population from its early days of statehood. While the Gold Rush brought enormous wealth to some, the whaling industry made considerable contributions to the American economy in the mid-1800s. By 1835, four-fifths of all the whaling ships in the world were American. Whaling ships were crewed by sailors from almost every corner of the globe. The addition of Pacific ports after the U.S. war with Mexico fueled the expansion of the American merchant and whaling presence in the Pacific. Hawaii became an important part of the American economic network in the Pacific, and the U.S. government pushed for economic access to China and Japan.

Review Question

5. Argument Development
How would you explain the intensification of American interest in Asia in the 1840s and 1850s?

1. Preparing to Write: Organize Your Evidence

Long Essay Question—Explain the reasons why there was increased migration and settlement in the West between 1800 and 1848.

Social history questions like the one above can be a challenge because there is less concrete evidence available compared with evidence for other kinds of questions, but this content is important in helping us get a full picture of American life, so it deserves attention. For all questions, but especially social history questions, it helps to catalog evidence that can be included in an essay and be used to develop a thesis. Create a chart with the headings "Economic Opportunity," "Manifest Destiny," and "Religious Refuge." Then take notes on any evidence that helps you find reasons for migration, including the motivations of common people like Narcissa Whitman from the American Voices feature in Section 11.1. From there you can develop a thesis statement. Remember to address the Reasoning Skill in your thesis, which in this case is Causation.

2. Preparing to Write: Plan Your Argument

Long Essay Question—Evaluate the extent of change in American foreign policy from 1789 to 1848.

Draw a time line from 1789 to 1848. After reviewing important events related to this question, take notes on what is changing above the time line. Below the time line, take notes on what is remaining constant. Consider big events that act as markers along the way like Washington's Farewell Address and the War of 1812. After you take notes, write a thesis that addresses the question.

Section I: Multiple-Choice Questions

Questions 4.1–4.2 refer to the following image.

(Note that it is not important for you to be able to read the captions below the image.)

William Charles, "A Scene on the Frontier as Practiced by the HUMANE BRITISH and their WORTHY ALLIES," 1812.

4.1 The perspective of this image is most likely attributable to which of the following groups?

   a. Federalists

   b. Democratic-Republicans

   c. Whigs

   d. Free Soilers

4.2 The image reflects which of the following developments in the United States?

   a. Federal policies tried to control and relocate American Indian populations.

   b. An increasing number of migrants continued to move westward.

   c. An ambiguous relationship between the federal government and American Indian tribes contributed to problems regarding treaties.

   d. American Indian tribes made alliances with Europeans to maintain control of tribal land.

Questions 4.3–4.4 refer to the following excerpt.

"I thank you, Dear Sir, for the copy you have been so kind as to send me of the letter to your constituents on the Missouri question … but this momentous question, like a fire bell in the night, awakened and filled me with terror. I considered it at once as the knell of the Union. It is hushed indeed for the moment. But this is a reprieve only, not a final sentence. A geographical line, coinciding with a marked principle,

moral and political, once conceived and held up to the angry passions of men, will never be obliterated; and every new irritation will mark it deeper and deeper. … Of one thing I am certain, that as the passage of slaves from one state to another would not make a slave of a single human being who would not be so without it, … this certainly is the exclusive right of every state, which nothing in the constitution has taken from them and given to the general government."

—Letter from Thomas Jefferson to John Holmes, 1820

4.3 Which of the following issues of the period was Jefferson most likely concerned with in the excerpt?

   a. Abolitionist attempts to bring an immediate end to the institution of slavery

   b. The increased Northern reliance on cotton production for its textile industry

   c. Congressional attempts at compromise that only temporarily halted the growing tensions about slavery

   d. The South's increased reliance on the export of traditional agricultural staples and the subsequent growth of a distinctive Southern regional identity

4.4 Which of the following political doctrines most accurately identifies the author's political beliefs?

   a. States' rights

   b. Separation of powers

   c. Federalism

   d. Nullification

Questions 4.5–4.6 refer to the following excerpt.

"On a general survey, we behold cultivation extended, the arts flourishing, the face of the country improved, our people fully and profitably employed, … land raising slowly in value, but in a secure and salutary degree, a ready, though not extravagant market for all the surplus production of our industry; innumerable flocks and herds browsing …; our cities expanded, and whole villages springing up; our exports and imports increased and increasing; our tonnage, foreign and coastwise, swelling and fully occupied; the rivers of our interior animated by the perpetual thunder and lightning of countless steamboats; … Let us then adopt the measure before us, which will benefit all classes: the farmer, the professional man, the merchant, the manufacturer, the mechanic, and the cotton planter more than all. … Can we not all, whatever may be our favorite theories, unite on this neutral ground? … Our southern brethren believe that it is injurious to them, and ask its repeal. We believe that its abandonment will be prejudicial to them, and ruinous to every other section of the Union. However strong their convictions may be, they are not stronger than ours."

—Henry Clay, "In Defense of the American System," 1832

4.5 The excerpt best reflects which of the following topics of debate from the 1800s?

   a. Whether or not to allow slavery in the territories
   b. The role of government in funding internal improvements
   c. States' rights
   d. Westward migration

4.6 Which of the following political parties would most likely support the perspective from this excerpt?

   a. Federalists
   b. Democrats
   c. Whigs
   d. Free Soilers

Questions 4.7–4.8 refer to the following excerpt.

"He will by faith lead an active life. Faith will spur on his activities. Under an earnest faith in divine truth, how can he help being active and zealous? If he believes God's word, he will believe in the fearful peril of sinners, and in the awful doom that awaits them. How can he desist and abstain from labor for souls so long as he sees them stand on slippery places, with fiery billows rolling below? Will he not devote himself with untiring diligence to pluck whomsoever he can from the ruin of a lost sinner? … Faith secures sympathy with God. Confidence in any man ensures your sympathy with him. … Faith makes the Christian's life humane. It trains him to look on all as God's children and to love them and care for them as such. Seeing how much pity and forbearance God has towards his sinning creatures, he is drawn by his faith to exercise the same."

—Charles Finney, "Living by Faith," 1854

4.7 The passage above is representative of which of the following movements?

   a. Utopianism
   b. Revivalism
   c. Transcendentalism
   d. Nativism

4.8 Unlike the First Great Awakening, the Second Great Awakening resulted in

   a. the formation of new religions
   b. widespread social conflict
   c. a significant increase in religious formalities
   d. numerous social reforms

Questions 4.9–4.10 refer to the following image.

Library of Congress Prints and Photographs Division[LC-USZ62-8127]/Sarony & Co.,

DELIVERING OF THE AMERICAN PRESENTS AT YOKUHAMA

Delivering of the American Presents at Yokuhama, 1856.

4.9 Which of the following was a policy goal of the event depicted in the image?

   a. Create more economic ties with Asian countries
   b. Court Asian countries for an alliance against British imperialism
   c. Open Asian countries to American immigration
   d. Spread democratic ideals to Asian countries

4.10 Which of the following developments in part led to the event depicted in the image?

   a. Increased tension between North and South over the issue of slavery
   b. The annexation of western lands inspired by Manifest Destiny
   c. Increased migration from Asia to the United States
   d. The formation of social reform groups following the Second Great Awakening

---

Section II: Short-Answer Questions

Question 4.11 is based on the following two excerpts.

"Seeking the fundamental impulse behind Jacksonian Democracy, historians have variously pointed to free enterprise, manhood suffrage, the labor movement, and resistance to the market economy. But in its origins, Jacksonian Democracy (which contemporaries understood as a synonym for Jackson's Democratic Party) was not primarily about any of these, though it came to intersect with all of them in due course. In the first place it was about the extension of white supremacy across the North American continent. By his policy of Indian Removal, Jackson confirmed his support in the cotton states outside South Carolina and fixed the character of his political party.

Indian policy, not banking or the tariff was the number one issue in the national press during the early years of Jackson's presidency."

—Daniel Walker Howe, *What Hath God Wrought*, 2007

"In the saga of the Jackson presidency, one marked by both democratic triumphs and racist tragedies, we can see the American character in formation and in action. … A champion of extending freedom and democracy to even the poorest of whites, Jackson was an unrepentant slaveholder. A sentimental man who rescued an Indian orphan on the battlefield to raise in his home, Jackson was responsible for the removal of Indian tribes from their ancestral lands. An enemy

of Eastern financial elites and a relentless opponent of the Bank of the United States, which he believed to be a bastion of corruption, Jackson also promised to die, if necessary, to preserve the power and prestige of the central government."

—Jon Meacham, *American Lion*, 2008

Using the excerpts above, answer (a), (b), and (c).

a. Briefly explain ONE major difference between Walker Howe's and Meacham's historical interpretations of the Jackson presidency.

b. Briefly explain how ONE specific historical event or development during the 1800s that is not mentioned directly in the excerpts could be used to support Walker Howe's interpretation.

c. Briefly explain how ONE specific historical event or development during the 1800s that is not mentioned directly in the excerpts could be used to support Meacham's interpretation.

Question 4.12 is based on the image to the right.

4.12 Use the image and your knowledge of U.S. history to answer parts a, b, and c.

   a. Explain the point of view reflected in the image.
   b. Explain how ONE of the following themes is represented in the image:
      American and National Identity
      Politics and Power
      Migration and Settlement

c. Explain how the theme you identified in part b is illustrated in ONE specific American Indian event between 1800 and 1848.

Library of Congress Prints and Photographs Division[LC-USZC2-3313]

George Catlin, "Wi-jun-jon, Pigeon's Egg Head (The Light) Going to and Returning from Washington," 1837–1839.

Section III: Long Essay Question

Directions: Answer Question 4.13 **or** 4.14. (Suggested writing time: 40 minutes) In your response you should do the following.

• Respond to the prompt with a historically defensible thesis or claim that establishes a line of reasoning.

• Describe a broader historical context relevant to the prompt.

• Support an argument in response to the prompt using specific and relevant examples of evidence.

• Use historical reasoning (e.g., comparison, causation, continuity or change over time) to frame or structure an argument that addresses the prompt.

• Use evidence to corroborate, qualify, or modify an argument that addresses the prompt.

4.13 Evaluate the extent to which there were different views of states' rights in American politics from 1789 to 1835.

4.14 Evaluate the extent to which there were differences in the impact that the market revolution had on the North and the South from 1800 to 1848.

Section IV:

Read on MyHistoryLab

Document-Based Question: Common Man Democracy

Part 5
Expansion, Separation, and a New Union 1844–1877

Chronicle/Alamy Stock Photo

AP® KEY CONCEPTS

Key Concept 5.1

The United States became more connected with the world as it pursued an expansionist foreign policy in the Western Hemisphere and emerged as the destination for many migrants from other countries.

Key Concept 5.2

Intensified by expansion and deepening regional divisions, debates over slavery and other economic, cultural, and political issues led the nation into civil war.

Key Concept 5.3

The Union victory in the Civil War and the contested Reconstruction of the South settled the issues of slavery and secession, but left unresolved many questions about the power of the federal government and citizenship rights.

PART OUTLINE

Chapter 12

Living in a Nation of Changing Lands, Changing Faces, Changing Expectations 1831–1854

In the 1830s, 1840s, and 1850s, the United States became increasingly divided as immigrants and native-born Americans flocked to industrial cities of the North, while in the South, cotton-generated wealth created a life of ease for a few based on misery for the many.

VIEW IN RANDOLPH STREET, CHICAGO, ILLINOIS

Bettmann/Contributor/Getty Images

Chapter Objective

Demonstrate an understanding of how immigration, new debates over slavery, and an activist generation of women shaped the lives of Americans.

 Learning Objectives

The Changing Face of the American People in the 1840s and 1850s

12.1 Analyze how immigration from China, Ireland, and Germany, as well as the incorporation of Mexican citizens in the Southwest, changed the United States as a result of greater connections between the United States and the rest of the world.

Slavery in the United States, 1840S and 1850S

12.2 Explain how the lives of slaves, slaveholders, and abolitionists evolved in the decades before the Civil War.

New Strength for American Women

12.3 Describe how the women's rights movement developed in the United States in the 1830s and 1840s.

In 1848, as word of the discovery of gold in California traveled across the Pacific, a young man in Canton, the capital of Guangdong province in China, wrote, "Good many Americans speak of California. … They find gold very quickly, so I hear. … I think I shall go to California next summer." Halfway around the world in a thatched roof cottage in Ireland, a mother was facing the crisis caused by the rotting potato crop and a typhus epidemic that had claimed one of her daughters. She told her two remaining daughters, "There's a curse on ould [old] green Ireland and we'll get out of it." She saved enough money to send one girl, Tilly, to America and, as Tilly's sister remembered, "She came to Philadelphia and got a place for general housework at Mrs. Bent's." Tilly saved her money, sent for her sister, and eventually, they were able to bring the rest of their family from Ireland. Both sisters worked as housekeepers for decades before retiring comfortably after a lifetime of scrimping and saving. People in many nations were more aware of developments in the United States than previous generations had been, and the resulting wave of immigration that brought people of diverse ethnic backgrounds changed the face of the United States in the 1840s and 1850s. During the same years, many who had lived in the same places in the Southwest of what is now the United States for generations became U.S. citizens as a result of the Treaty of Guadalupe Hidalgo without moving at all.

In the 1830s and 1840s, slaves and abolitionists challenged the institution of slavery with a vehemence not seen before. Slaves rebelled and ran away. Abolitionists—white and black—were determined to end slavery, not just stop its expansion. In response, slaveholders became more defiant and defensive than ever before. When Abraham Lincoln looked at a nation that was "half slave and half free" and wondered if it could survive, he was not alone.

Women, who had struggled for rights since the Revolutionary Era, found new voice in the 1830s and 1840s. The Seneca Falls Women's Rights Convention of 1848 helped to launch a new political movement for women's rights, including the right to vote. While the right to vote was a key demand of the growing women's rights movement, other women also demanded a broader equality in all aspects of society, insisting that "whatever it is morally right for a man to do, it is morally right for a woman to do." This chapter takes a look at the changing nature of the country's racial and ethnic makeup and the thinking of its people, especially about slavery and women's rights, that took place during the 1840s and 1850s.

The Changing Face of the American People in the 1840s and 1850s

12.1 Analyze how immigration from China, Ireland, and Germany, as well as the incorporation of Mexican citizens in the Southwest, changed the United States as a result of greater connections between the United States and the rest of the world.

Immigration and the nation's expanding borders increased the population of the United States in the 1830s, 1840s, and 1850s. A nation of fewer than 13 million people in 1830 included 17 million people in 1840 and 23 million inhabitants in 1850. Births to native-born Americans accounted for the largest part of this increase, but many people also crossed oceans to come to the United States, especially from Ireland, Germany, and China. By 1860, the United States had about 1.5 million Irish-born inhabitants, about 1 million German-born inhabitants, and perhaps 35,000 Chinese-born inhabitants—a number that would grow dramatically in the next few years as more immigrants from China arrived, especially to build the railroads. Desperately poor people in Europe and Asia fled famines in their home countries. After failed revolutionary efforts in Germany and other parts of Europe that took place in 1848, participants fled to safety in the United States. The California Gold Rush and growing U.S. industrialization beckoned with new economic opportunities. Both the push of hunger and oppression and the pull of a better future that included religious, political, and economic freedoms brought many to the United States.

The extraordinary increase in the geographic area of the United States also incorporated many people who did not move at all. In 1840, the United States included 1.8 million square miles. Less than ten years later, the country included almost 3 million square miles. Some

Significant Dates

12.1
12.2
12.3

1831	William Lloyd Garrison launches *The Liberator*
	Nat Turner leads slave revolt in Virginia
1833	American Anti-Slavery Society is founded in Boston
1836	American Anti-Slavery Society launches campaign to send antislavery agents to every state of the union
1838	Sarah Grimké's *Letters on the Equality of the Sexes and the Condition of Women*
1843	Henry Highland Garnet's "Address to the Slaves of the United States of America"
1845– 1850	The Great Famine in Ireland
1847	Rebellion against American authorities in Taos, New Mexico
1848	Discovery of gold in California lures immigrants from around the world, including China
	Failures of Revolutions in Europe lead more people to immigrate to the United States
	Women's Rights Convention at Seneca Falls, New York
1849	Harriett Tubman escapes from slavery
1851	Sojourner Truth's "Ain't I a Woman?" speech
1854	William Lloyd Garrison burns a copy of the Constitution as "source and parent of the other atrocities" of slavery in the United States

12.1

12.2

12.3

of the land acquired through the war with Mexico was sparsely populated. However, many people—Mexican Americans in Texas, New Mexico, and California; Mormons in Utah; and the many tribes of Plains and Pueblo Indians—found themselves residing within the United States. As a result, the nature of the U.S. population shifted significantly in the late 1840s.

The United States of 1840 could accurately be described as including three major ethnic groups—Europeans mostly of English stock, Africans of different backgrounds, and American Indians of diverse tribes. Most of the Europeans and many of the Africans were Protestants. By 1850, the nation was much more ethnically diverse with many Asians (mostly Chinese), Irish, Germans, and Mexican Americans (of mixed European, African, and Indian ancestry). With the growth of these immigrant groups, the United States was also a more Catholic country, and with the coming of so many white immigrants, the percentage of African Americans in the population shrank even though their actual number grew. While the governing elite was still of European Protestant background, the people who made up the country were more diverse than ever before and were increasingly making their presence felt in ways that often made the native-born white Protestant population uncomfortable and angry.

Chinese Immigration across the Pacific

Many young people in China were fascinated by the stories from across the Pacific. Lee Chew described his neighbor's return to China from the "country of the American wizards," explaining that the man had earned enough in the United States to build a magnificent house and invite his fellow villagers, who lived mostly on rice, to a grand feast with roast pig, chicken, and duck. Soon after, Lee was on his way to California, which became known as *Gam Saan* (Gold Mountain) in Chinese communities on both sides of the Pacific.

Before 1840, only a few hundred Chinese lived in the United States, but in the 1840s and 1850s, Chinese immigrants came to California and also to the then-independent Kingdom of Hawaii because of a push from China and also a pull from the United States and Hawaii. Those years were hard in China, especially in Guangdong province where most immigrants originated. Under Chinese law, it was illegal for anyone to leave China, but in desperate times, thousands did anyway. California was one of many destinations. The Opium Wars that began in 1839 spawned great violence as British and Chinese forces battled and as violent feuds erupted within China. One Chinese migrant remembered the results of a revolt: "We were left with nothing, and in disillusion we went to Hong Kong to sell ourselves as contract laborers." The government of the Qing Dynasty in Beijing was not strong enough to suppress the civil wars or to prevent the British imposition of the opium trade on China.

In addition, the population of China had also grown from some 200 million in 1762 to 421 million in 1846. With this huge population, land became scarce, rents soared, and many peasants could not maintain their meager land holdings. For all its ancient expertise in rice cultivation, China simply did not have enough land to grow rice for 421 million people. Beginning in 1810, there were terrible famines in China, with some of the worst coming in the 1840s. In those decades, 45 million people may have starved to death. Poor people begged for admission to soup kitchens or simply died on the doorsteps of the rich. As one immigrant from Guangdong remembered, "Sometimes we went hungry for days. … We had only salt and water to eat with the rice." Under such conditions, a fresh start in a new place—temporary or permanent—was appealing and many immigrated to the United States as well as to many parts of Latin America.

Americans in Hawaii and California saw Chinese laborers as a key to solving a shortage of workers to toil on sugar plantations on Maui or to clear and cultivate land in California. Chinese peasant workers had long been known as *k'u-li*, literally "hard strength," and the Western term for Chinese laborers quickly came to be "coolie." A long-time presidential advisor, Aaron H. Palmer, reported to Congress that "[n]o people in all of the East are so well adapted for clearing wild lands and raising every species of agricultural product

… as the Chinese." At first, Chinese immigrants were warmly welcomed in California. An 1852 article in the *Daily Alta California* noted, "Scarcely a ship arrives that does not bring an increase to this worthy integer of our population." News took time to travel and the initial Chinese response to the Gold Rush was relatively small: 325 immigrants from China arrived in California in 1849 and 450 more in 1850. Then the numbers grew rapidly: 2,716 in 1851 and 20,026 in 1852. By 1870, Chinese immigrants represented 9 percent of the population of California (but 25 percent of the workforce since most Chinese immigrants were men of working age) and larger percentages in Oregon and Washington. The Chinese also made up 29 percent of the much smaller population of Idaho and 10 percent in Montana.

Nearly 95 percent of Chinese immigrants to California before 1870 were male. They tended to see their voyage across the Pacific—a harsh eight-week trip—as a temporary separation from their families in China. U.S. law dating from 1790 prohibited nonwhite immigrants from achieving citizenship, and most Chinese expected to return home after a few years. In the early years, most male Chinese immigrants joined other newcomers in the search for gold. Chinese gold miners could be seen all along the rivers of California in their blue cotton blouses and wide-brimmed hats, shoveling sand into pans or rockers. These men left wives, fiancées, children, and parents behind to find ways to support them.

Chinese culture dictated that a woman should stay with her family, especially her husband's parents, while the man found the means of support. Cultural practices such as these and the cost of travel made immigration difficult for women, though Hawaii was much more welcoming of families than was the United States. Of the few Chinese women who avoided the cultural prohibitions and came to California before 1870, many were forced to work as prostitutes, either lured into the work by false promises or forced into the work by the absence of other ways to survive. In 1870, nearly 2,157 of the 3,536 Chinese women in California reported their profession as "prostitute." Most prostitutes lived lives of virtual slavery and many died of exhaustion or venereal disease. Others managed to escape and find new lives either with the help of missionary societies such as the Presbyterian Home Mission or by gaining their freedom on their own. A few prospered, for example, Polly Bemis (Lalu Nathoy), who had been sold into prostitution but later married and operated her own ranch in Idaho.

As more Chinese men entered the gold fields, they encountered growing resistance from white miners. The cry "California for Americans" began in the gold fields and was picked up by political leaders of the state. In 1852, the California legislature adopted a foreign miners license tax of $3 per month, which was aimed specifically at the Chinese. It provided between a quarter and a half of state revenue before 1870. The tax, and the growing anti-Chinese sentiment that it represented, slowed but did not stop Chinese immigration. As the gold fields became less productive, many Chinese went to work building the railroads. Immediately after the Civil War, 12,000 Chinese laborers laid the tracks of the Central Pacific Railroad. Chinese workers also moved into agriculture, mining, fishing, and later into urban businesses. Men from China often found work at the least desirable jobs or jobs that other men considered to be "women's work." During the height of the Gold Rush, Wah Lee opened his "Wash'ng and Iron'ng" store in San Francisco. By 1860, there were 890 Chinese laundrymen in California and by 1870, 3,000. Chinese immigrants also took jobs as camp cooks or opened inexpensive restaurants. The ubiquitous Chinese laundries and restaurants were solely a Chinese American development that resulted from the exclusion of Chinese immigrants from most other kinds of work. Although many individual Chinese immigrants returned home after a few years, other Chinese immigrants stayed in the United States. Some stayed because they had no options. In a recently discovered letter, circa the 1870s, a husband wrote, "My Beloved Wife: It has been several autumns now since your dull husband left you for a far remote alien land. … Because I can get no gold, I am detained in this secluded corner of a strange land." Other Chinese immigrants chose to stay, creating permanent communities in the American West and surviving and thriving in spite of widespread hostility that continued for decades.

Art Resource, NY/Art Resource, NY

Miners of many nationalities competed for gold in the California gold fields, but the tensions, especially between miners of European and Chinese origin, were severe, and most Chinese miners were driven from the gold fields before long.

Irish and German Immigration of the 1840s and 1850s

The Irish who came to the United States as a result of the Great Famine of the late 1840s were not the first Irish to come to America, but they came from a part of Ireland different from their predecessors and for different reasons. Most Irish who had come before or immediately after the Revolution were Irish Protestants, mainly Presbyterians whose ancestors had emigrated to northern Ireland from Scotland. The Protestant Irish, who became known as Scots Irish, settled in all the colonies, but especially along the rural frontier from Pennsylvania to the Carolinas. After the American Revolution, and especially after the failure of an Irish rebellion of 1798 against the British, more Irish immigrants, both Catholic and Protestant, arrived.

Great Famine of 1845–1850

The potato blight in Ireland that caused mass starvation and immigration to the United States.

The roots of the **Great Famine of 1845–1850** go deep in Irish history—anchored in a rapidly growing population of poor people; in policies that made most people almost totally dependent on a single, easy-to-raise crop rather than a diversified agriculture; and in British policies that forced Irish Catholics to labor for Protestant landowners. But its immediate cause was a plant fungus of unknown sources that devastated potatoes. A potato disease, which had already affected parts of continental Europe, came to Ireland with surprising rapidity. August 1845 was unusually wet with heavy rains, and the early spread of the disease left potatoes blighted and mildewed and inedible. In 1846, the blight struck with full force, and up to 90 percent of the fall potato crop was lost. The result was widespread starvation. Potato crops continued to be blighted each year through 1850, and cholera struck in 1848 and 1849. Out of a total Irish population of approximately eight million, more than one million people died from disease or starvation in the five years of the Great Famine. During the decade that followed the start of the famine, over two million people left Ireland, most of them for the United States.

One observer described the suffering of the Great Famine:

> They died in their mountain glens, they died along the sea-coast, they died on the roads, and they died in the fields; they wandered into the towns, and died in the streets; they closed their cabin doors, and lay down upon their beds, and died of actual starvation in their own homes.

And when they could, they left. The cost of the trip to America was about three British pounds, about the same as the cost of a new cow or the annual rent on a farm. As the historian Cormac Ó Gráda noted, "In the hierarchy of suffering the poorest of the poor emigrated to the next world; those who emigrated to the New World had the resources to escape." Even when a family could scrape together enough funds to get only one family member off to America, there was a good chance that, if the rest could survive another winter or two, then they too would immigrate. In 1848, Irish immigrants to America sent 500,000 British pounds, a significant amount of money, back to Ireland to feed relatives and pay for their transport out of the country (see Map 12-1).

In the 1840s, the voyage from Ireland across the Atlantic was terrible. The ships, which took five to six weeks to make the crossing, became known as "coffin ships" because of the high death toll due to poor nutrition, unsanitary conditions, and overcrowding.

Once in the United States, the new Irish immigrants, overwhelmingly Catholic and poor, were seen as another race by many Protestant Americans who viewed Catholicism as a degrading religion and the Irish as an inferior race. Nevertheless, though many Irish immigrants lived in terrible poverty, they came at a good time to get a foothold in the American economy. Women immigrants got work as household domestic help for native-born middle-class Americans. Irish women and men also labored in the factories where their willingness to work hard made them prized employees, though not always welcome ones to the native-born Protestant factory workers. But the Irish took jobs that no one else wanted. In the 1840s, one observer wrote that "fewer and fewer [native-born women] were willing to hire out as household servants." In that situation, Irish men did the backbreaking work of building the nation's fastest-growing cities, most of all New York, which became the center of the country's Irish population. Irish immigrants also moved to Boston, Philadelphia, Chicago, and smaller cities from New Jersey to California. Few of the Irish moved to farms; it was too expensive to start a farm, and farming had little appeal to those who remembered the famine that had sparked their journey. After the Civil War, Irish laborers built the eastern end of the Transcontinental Railroad just as Chinese laborers built the western end.

Wherever the Irish Catholic immigrants settled, they created their own communities, including a Catholic church usually led by an Irish priest. By 1850, the Catholic Church had become the largest single denomination in the United States.

While Irish immigration was especially dramatic and rapid because of the famine, many other Europeans, including more than one million Germans, also came to the United States in the 1840s and 1850s. On average, German immigrants came with slightly more financial resources than the Irish, and many settled on farms or in cities in the Midwest. In new and growing cities such as Milwaukee, St. Louis, and Chicago, the majority of residents were foreign-born, mostly from Germany.

German immigrants often kept to themselves. And German-dominated immigrant farm towns and German neighborhoods were recognized and sometimes distrusted by the native-born elite. German immigrants introduced many traditions into American culture—including the Christmas tree and beer, both of which were relatively unknown in the United States until the Germans introduced them. One American observer described his surprise at visiting an isolated German community in the Southwest where people drank "coffee in tin cups," while listening to "a Beethoven symphony on the grand piano." In religion, the Germans were a diverse group.

Map 12-1 Depopulating Ireland.
The Great Famine led to a significant decline in the population of Ireland, especially in the western part, where some counties never recovered from the population loss of those years.

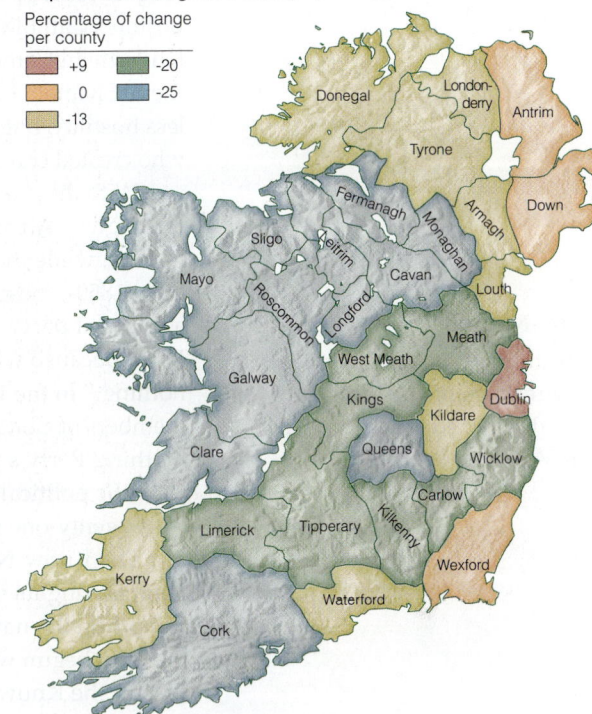

12.1

12.2

12.3

Many were Catholics, but there were also many different Protestants, including Lutherans, Calvinists, and the Amish.

The rapid growth of these new European groups also frightened many native-born Americans. The Irish were particularly vulnerable to prejudice because there was a long history of discrimination against the Irish, especially Irish Catholics, even before the Great Famine. In August 1834, a Protestant mob burned the convent and school of the Ursuline nuns in Boston. Boston's Catholic bishop Benedict Fenwick wrote, "No law or justice is to be expected in this land where Catholics are constantly calumniated and the strongest prejudices exist against them. Shame!" Perhaps because of their relative isolation, the Germans provoked somewhat less hostility, but many native-born Americans expressed their anger at German immigrants who created communities where English was not the primary language.

With the growth of the Irish Catholic and German populations in the late 1840s, the prejudice grew. An anti-immigrant group called the Native American Association was founded in 1837, while the semisecret Order of the Star-Spangled Banner was created in 1845. In the early 1850s, these and other similar anti-immigrant, anti-Catholic groups merged to become a political party—the so-called American Party—generally known as the **Know-Nothing Party** because when members were asked about the party, they were told to say "I know nothing." In the 1850s, the Know-Nothings elected eight governors, more than one hundred members of Congress, mayors in several major cities, and many state legislators. The Know-Nothing Party's platform was anti-Catholic and anti-immigrant, including plans to limit Catholic political power by banning immigrants from holding office and requiring them to wait twenty-one years to become citizens.

The Know-Nothing Party was important in elections in the 1850s, but it did not last long. During its short life, however, the American Party (its official name) had a significant impact on the nation's political system. It helped bring an end to the Second Party System that had begun with the emergence of the Democratic and Whig parties in the 1820s. In the North, the Know-Nothings took votes in approximately equal numbers from the Democrats and the Whigs, but in the South, they undermined the Whigs much more severely.

Know-Nothing Party

Anti-immigrant party formed from the wreckage of the Whig Party and some disaffected Northern Democrats in 1854.

American 'Know-Nothing' Party Cartoon, 1854 (engraving), American School, (19th century) / Private Collection/Peter Newark American Pictures/The Bridgeman Art Library

Native-born Americans, especially those in the Know-Nothing Party, reacted with fear and anger to the surge in immigration to the United States during the 1830s and 1840s. Some of the stereotypes included images of whiskey-drinking Irish and beer-drinking Germans in a country that was turning its back on its own hard-drinking ways.

12.1

12.2

12.3

Although both of the older parties condemned nativism, and some Whig leaders such as William H. Seward and David Wilmot led the attack, other Whigs quickly embraced the new party. The Democratic Party on the other hand was welcoming to immigrant voters and pro-immigrant in its policies. The internal party splits over immigration, when combined with the splits in both of the older parties as a result of growing tensions over slavery, badly divided the Democratic Party while the Whigs virtually disappeared in the 1850s. A new party, the Republicans, inherited both anti- and pro-immigrant Whigs as well as many anti-immigrant Democrats. But its organizing principle was antislavery, and Republicans tolerated many divergent views on immigration.

Moderate reformers like Horace Mann were horrified by the burning of the Ursuline convent in Boston and the political platform of the Know-Nothings but still sought to ensure that the public school system was used to make all future citizens, especially immigrants, into good "Americans" as they understood the term. Massachusetts governor Edward Everett told the state's school board to "save society not with the cannon and the rifle, but with the spelling book, the grammar, and the Bible." Nevertheless, despite hostility and their own poverty, Irish and German immigrants eventually gained political and economic power in the nation's major cities, usually as a powerful faction of a revitalized Democratic Party.

The Mexican Experience in the Southwest

In 1847, as immigrants to America were trying to fit in to the new culture, Father Antonio José Martinez was trying to keep peace in Taos, New Mexico, where Mexican and Pueblo Indian residents had rebelled against the new American authorities, killing the American-appointed governor, Charles Bent. Father Martinez tried to convince rebels that killing Americans was wrong and futile, while trying to convince the Americans to give due process to insurgents. He was not fully successful in either effort, but by the end of 1847, the rebellion had ended after the rebels were defeated by U.S. soldiers. Like the rebels he was seeking to defend, Father Martinez had suddenly become an American citizen, no longer a citizen of the Republic of Mexico, not because he moved, but because the American border had moved.

Under the Treaty of Guadalupe Hidalgo, territory that was home to Pueblo, Navajo, Comanche, Apache, Ute, and Cheyenne as well as Spanish settlements, some dating back almost three hundred years, was now part of the United States. While in the short run, the treaty had little impact on Native Americans, it almost immediately had a huge impact on people who were now Mexican Americans. The 1848 treaty gave every Mexican citizen within the new boundary of the United States the right to American citizenship or the right to keep Mexican citizenship. Mexico urged its citizens to move to Mexico, and some four thousand people from New Mexico and smaller groups from Texas, California, and Arizona did move south, back into Mexico. But most former Mexican citizens chose to stay in their homes and make new lives as citizens of the United States. Many within the Mexican community in California were initially optimistic about their new country. Indeed, quite a few of the Mexican leaders in California, men such as Mariano Vallejo and Juan Bandini, had been hoping for an American takeover of their territory even before the war with Mexico because they saw the United States as a vibrant democracy that could replace the distant and inept Mexican administration. When the constitutional convention met in Monterey in August 1849 to prepare California for statehood, eight of the forty-eight voting delegates were Californios (as former Mexican citizens were called). On most matters, they did not vote as a separate bloc, assuming that their interests and those of newer American residents were the same. The huge population surge of the Gold Rush, however, meant that the Californios quickly became a small minority in California. By the time that statehood came in 1850, they numbered only about thirteen thousand out of a non-Indian population of over one hundred thousand.

Ultimately, the sheer numbers of those newly arrived from the United States destroyed the economic base for the Californios. Looking back, Vallejo described the impact of statehood and the Gold Rush on California when, in spite of dreams he once had of being an equal citizen of the United States, "legal thieves, clothed in the robes of the law, took from us our lands and our houses, and without the least scruple, enthroned themselves in our homes like so many powerful kings."

The vehicle by which the "legal thieves" stole the land of the Californians was the U.S. Land Commission, set up specifically to challenge the Mexican land grants on which Vallejo's and his compatriots' fortunes rested. Although the Treaty of Guadalupe Hidalgo had promised that all residents of these lands "shall be maintained and protected in the free enjoyment of their liberty and property," the Land Commission treated every grant as invalid until documented and proven. The result was that many of the old families lost their land. Being of Mexican descent in California meant second-class citizenship for a long time to come.

Like their counterparts in California, the small Mexican or Tejano population in Texas did not fare well after Texas joined the United States. Juan Seguín, one of the heroes on the American side of the decisive battle of San Jacinto and mayor of San Antonio, eventually joined the exodus to Mexico. In San Antonio, the city with the largest Tejano population, the number of Tejanos elected to office, which had been high under the Republic of Texas, declined sharply. New migrants from the United States took over the political and economic control of the state.

The Mexican or Hispano elite in New Mexico fared better because American (non-Hispanic European) newcomers remained a minority in New Mexico until well after 1900—and became a minority again soon after 2000. While merchants from the United States had played a significant role in New Mexico since the 1820s when the Santa Fe Trail connected St. Louis with Santa Fe, the Hispano elite were a majority in the first American territorial assembly held in 1851, which published its proceedings in both Spanish and English. Despite the revolts in northern New Mexico after U.S. annexation, many in the territory made their peace with the new government, and some made fortunes in the new economy. Gertrudis Barcelo achieved both fame and fortune for her elegant saloon and gambling house in Santa Fe. Barcelo's saloon was a fixture for Santa Fe Trail traders from the 1820s to the 1850s and a business of sufficient success to allow her to make significant bequests to charity and leave three houses and other wealth to her heirs when she died in 1852. Barcelo was not alone in attending to her own interests whether the flag of Spain, Mexico, or the United States flew on the plaza near her establishment.

For many poor people in all parts of the Southwest, however, the transfer of authority from Mexico to the United States meant increased poverty and far less opportunity for justice in a court system that was operated in a strange language by people with deep racial and ethnic prejudices. Injustice to Mexican Americans was not limited to the legal system. Not surprisingly, the term *vigilante* (meaning people who take justice into their own hands rather than rely on lawful authorities) came from the **Committees of Vigilance** in the California mining camps. Vigilante groups made up of private citizens of non-Latino background delivered public whippings and lynched people they did not like, whether or not a crime had been committed. California mobs lynched at least 163 Mexicans between 1848 and 1860. In southern California, a white gang known as the El Monte boys used the hysteria around a short-lived Mexican rebellion to settle old scores and attack Mexican families regardless of whether they had been involved in the rebellion. Similar outrages happened across the West.

The Mexican American community fought back against legalized and extra-legal violence. Joaquin Murrieta became a California legend—feared in the white community, honored in the Mexican community—because of his vengeance on those who had stolen his gold claim, raped his wife, Rosa, and hung his brother. Murrieta stole horses and gold and killed those who had raped and murdered his loved ones before he, in turn, was discovered and killed by the California Rangers in 1853. Kangaroo courts (unauthorized and obviously biased courts) and lynchings were all too common as traditional community relationships were destroyed by distance and greed.

Committees of Vigilance

Also known as vigilantes, groups of people who took on extralegal means to assert law and order.

12.1 Quick Review

How did native-born Americans react to immigrants in the 1840s and 1850s? How did new immigrants react to their new surroundings?

Slavery in the United States, 1840s and 1850s

12.2 **Explain how the lives of slaves, slaveholders, and abolitionists evolved in the periods before the Civil War.**

The institution of slavery had existed in the United States from the nation's beginning, but slavery, which had never been a static institution, changed significantly yet again after 1820 (see Chapter 9). For enslaved people and those who claimed to own them, life in a slave society was a different experience at different points in history. Slavery was always harsh and dehumanizing, but it was harsh in different ways at different times.

After the end of the War of 1812, Southern planters experienced new economic benefits from slavery, benefits that grew with each decade as the world's cotton market exploded and slave labor made it possible and profitable for American slave-grown cotton to satisfy this market. Since most cotton was produced by slave labor, the new demand for cotton greatly increased the value of individual slaves. Thus, just as slavery was slowly dying out in the North—for both economic and ethical reasons—the new cotton economy of the South made slavery far more profitable than ever before. The result was an agriculture system that by the 1840s produced 60 percent of the world's cotton and made the South, and particularly some elite Southerners, extremely wealthy and prepared to offer new ethical rationales for slavery (see Map 12-2).

Map 12-2 Expanding Slavery.

In the thirty years before the Civil War, slavery became strongest in the cotton belt states of the Deep South. For an individual slave, the farther north one was, the better one's chances were to connect to the Underground Railroad, but slaves from every part of the South made their way North to freedom.

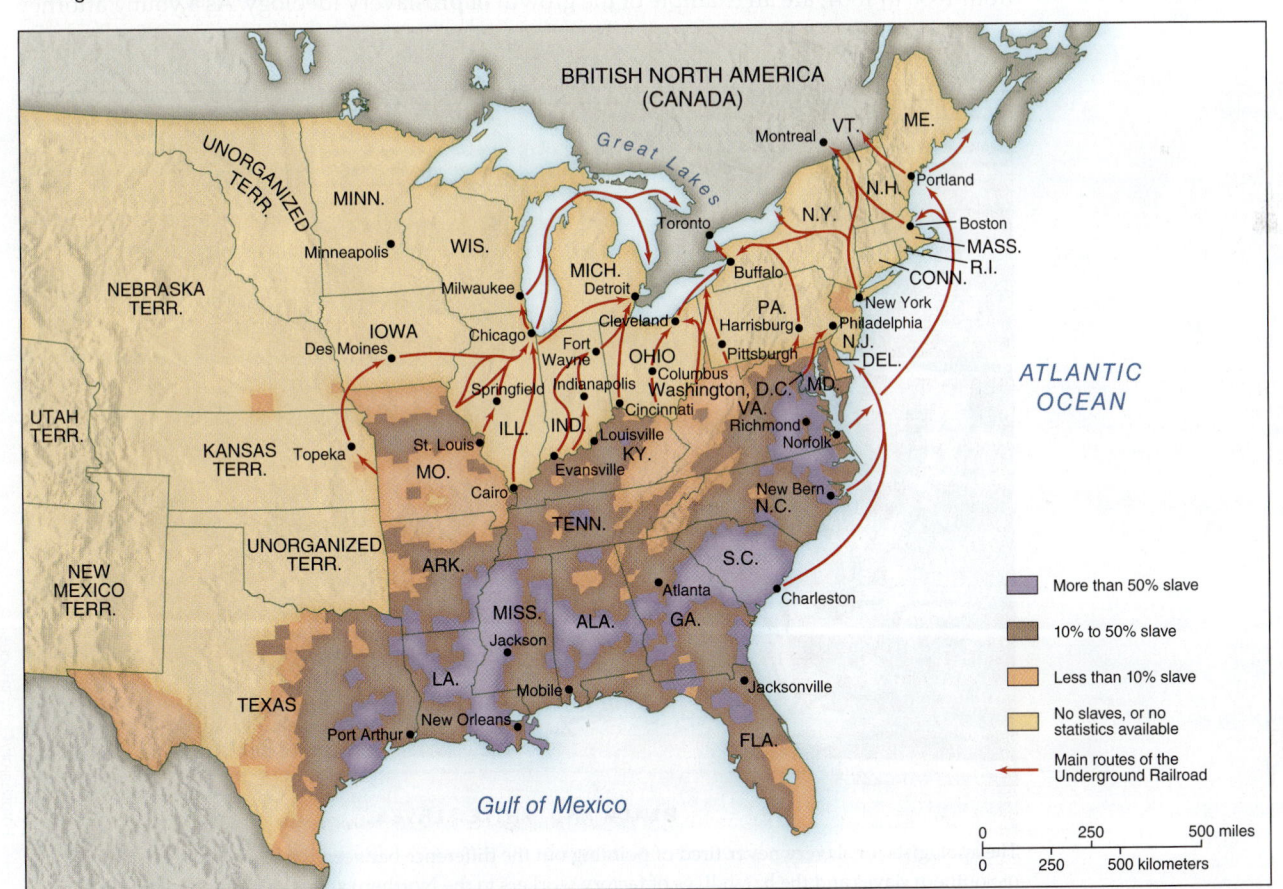

Slaves and Slave Masters

As cotton prices kept increasing from the 1830s to the 1850s, close to a million slaves were moved from the coast to new cotton states, where they had to learn the different and difficult work of tending cotton. Yet even as slavery was becoming more profitable, Northern public opinion was turning against it. More people were joining what had been a small group of abolitionists in viewing human bondage as a terrible wrong and a stain on the honor of a nation dedicated to human freedom. With slavery disappearing in the North, Northern abolitionists got an increasingly responsive hearing from their neighbors. Other Northerners who had fewer moral qualms about slavery saw slaves as competitors for scarce jobs, and they too joined the opposition to slavery. In 1840, antislavery forces created the Liberty Party and nominated James G. Birney for president, and in 1848, the short-lived antislavery Free Soil Party nominated former President Martin Van Buren as its candidate. Neither party campaigned for outright abolition, only for an end to extending slavery to new areas of the country. Nor did either party win any electoral votes, though Van Buren did win some 10 percent of the popular vote in 1848. Nevertheless, abolitionist rhetoric and political muscle were frightening an increasingly defensive slaveholding South.

At one time, most slaveholders, including those from the South who attended the Constitutional Convention, had defended slavery as a "necessary evil." Somehow, they argued, slavery had become an economic and social necessity that was, at best, unfortunate. However, after 1830, a new generation of slaveholders began to describe slavery as a positive good, an institution that Christianized "heathen" Africans while providing them with food, shelter, and an ordered life. These defenders of slavery developed the ideology of the racial inferiority of Africans, which, they insisted, meant that they needed to be kept in a subservient role. These defenders also contrasted slavery with work in Northern factories and noted that slaves, unlike factory workers, were not fired when work got slow or they grew old, but, rather, were provided for throughout their lives. Southern apologists also became increasingly angry with Northern critics of slavery.

The changing views of Roger B. Taney, who served as Chief Justice of the United States from 1836 to 1864, are an example of the growth of proslavery ideology. As a young attorney

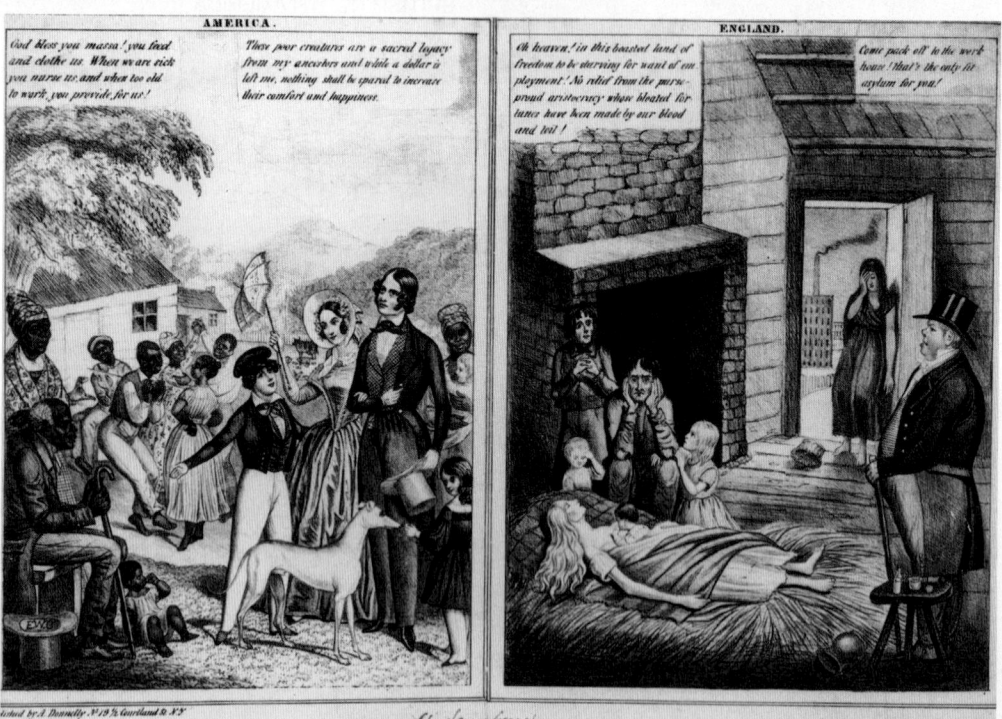

BLACK AND WHITE SLAVES.

The apologists for slavery never tired of pointing out the difference between the supposedly contented life of Southern slaves and the harsh lives of factory workers in the Northern states and Great Britain.

in Maryland in 1819, Taney defended a Methodist preacher, Jacob Gruber, who had been accused of inciting rebellion when he had warned it was inevitable that slaves would "rise up and kill your children, their oppressors." Taney asserted Gruber's legal right to free speech and said that slavery was "a blot on our national character, and every real lover of freedom, confidently hopes that it will be … wiped away."

In 1857, however, almost forty years after the Gruber trial and twenty years after Taney's appointment to lead the Supreme Court, he wrote the Court's *Dred Scott* decision (see Chapter 13) that said blacks were "altogether unfit to associate with the white race, either in social or political relations; and so far inferior, that they had no rights which the white man was bound to respect." The Chief Justice, like many other Southerners, had come to see slavery as simply the inevitable result of black inferiority.

As every able-bodied slave and every newborn slave child became more valuable from 1800 to the outbreak of the Civil War in 1861, any thought of abolishing slavery disappeared among slaveholders. After 1830, Southern states also made it more difficult to set any slaves free and for free blacks to stay in the South.

The growing value of individual slaves also led—ironically—to somewhat better treatment for them. A slave life was now of too much economic value to be lost easily. The same states that made it difficult to free slaves passed new laws against their murder or mistreatment. In many instances, the nutrition and medical care provided for slaves also improved.

A healthy, relatively well-fed slave could work harder than a sickly or starving slave. A pregnant slave could produce a valuable new slave who could, in time, also work or be sold. However, a slave who died of mistreatment was a lost investment. There is evidence that the actual treatment of slaves, while never approaching anything that could be called humane, did improve throughout the 1800s. Where multiple slave families had been crammed into cramped quarters, more plantation owners built—or had their slaves build—individual family cabins with board floors instead of dirt. More meat was added to slave

American Voices

Edmund Ruffin, *Slavery and Free Labor Described and Compared*, ca. 1860

Edmund Ruffin (1794–1865) was a Southern agronomist who in the 1850s turned to defending Southern slavery. He advocated secession of the Southern states after Lincoln's election and fought in the first battles of the Civil War. At the end of the Civil War, he committed suicide rather than live under what he called "Yankee rule."

The privilege of the English laborer to choose his employment and his master, even when such choice legally exists, does not prevent his service being truly slavery. For he has no choice but to toil incessantly for wages barely affording a scant and wretched support, or to starve—and no change of pursuit, or of service, can make that condition better. … [I]n comparison to the English pauper … the general condition of our negro slaves is one of comfort, ease and happiness. …

Until recent investigation and discussion had elicited more truth, it had been claimed by the people of the North and by all the opposers of slavery, and even was generally admitted by the people of the Southern States, that the free-labour States of New England were greatly superior to the old Southern States in obtaining the fruits of industry and capital. … Southern capital and industry were almost exclusively devoted to agriculture—northern capital was much more vested in commerce and manufactures, which are deemed much more profitable than agricultural investments. … It has

also been especially and loudly claimed, for and by the people of the New England States … that such difference was the necessary result of the blighting and demoralizing effects of negro slavery in the South, and of its absence in the North. …

Instead of our labors and investments in slave-labor being less profitable than northern operations, it is manifest that the slaveholding States are much richer than the free States, and to make this result the more striking, even if counting every slave as if free, and supposing the whole property to be divided among all the population, (slaves included,) still on this general average, the individual share of every one, bond or free, would be considerably larger than in the free States.

Source: Edmund Ruffin, "Slavery and Free Labor, Described and Compared," Library of Congress, American memory, From Slavery to Freedom: The African American Pamphlet Collection, 1824–1909, http://memory.loc.gov.

Thinking Critically

1. **Contextualization**
   How does Ruffin's account reflect his place and time?

2. **Analyzing Primary Sources**
   Who do you think was the intended audience for Ruffin's argument that slavery was a "positive good"?

Library of Congress Prints and Photographs Division|LC-DIG-ppm-sca-10964 |Mathew Brady

Slave quarters, like these shown on a South Carolina plantation, provided better living conditions than what was provided to previous generations of slaves, though hardly anything that could be called comfortable. The houses built close together also fostered a sense of community life that helped enslaved people survive.

diets, and slaves were allowed to grow their own vegetable gardens as well as hunt and fish to supplement their diet. Slave hours of work were controlled by custom and unspoken agreement; most slaves had Sunday as a day of rest, and except in harvest time, few were expected to work after dark. A new generation of slave children was allowed to play relatively freely. Former slave Harriet Jacobs wrote, "I was born a slave; but I never knew it till six years of happy childhood has passed away." For defenders of slavery such as Edmund Ruffin, such improvements in the lives of slaves became proof that slave life was better than the lives of some Northern or European workers and peasants.

The slave population of the United States grew from 1.5 million slaves in 1820 to 4 million slaves in 1860. After 1808, it was illegal and difficult to bring new slaves into the country, so much of this growth reflected reproduction among existing slaves. Many saw this growth as a sign of the new and better treatment that slaves were receiving. In the United States, slaves were surviving, reproducing, and providing significant profits to others.

Although some improvements in slave life occurred, there were limits to those developments. The slave cabins were hot and stuffy in summer and inflammable in winter. The meals were monotonous. The work for adults was backbreaking, being called out to work at 4:00 or 5:00 a.m., and then working in hot fields, hoeing or picking cotton, with little break until sunset. Slaves were whipped routinely for falling behind in their work or for infractions of the plantation rules. While some Southern reformers talked of honoring slave marriages, the separation of spouses continued without interruption. Slave women could not protect their own bodies. Harriet Jacobs also remembered that once she came of age, "[i]t was deemed a crime in her to wish to be virtuous." [a]nd she spent considerable time avoiding the constant advances of the owner of her plantation and the jealous anger of his wife. Many slave women were not so fortunate, and the rape of slave women by white men was a commonly acknowledged reality. Mary Boykin Chesnut, wife of a plantation owner, described the treatment of slave women as a "monstrous system," and noted that "[a]ny lady is ready to tell you who is the father of all the mulatto children in everybody's household but her own. Those, she seems to think, drop from the clouds." Even laws that were being passed against murdering a slave could be enforced only if there was a white witness because slaves were not allowed to testify in court. Most of all, no amount of reform or improvement could change the reality that slavery was still slavery.

In the midst of appalling conditions, slaves created lives for themselves and developed the psychological strength to withstand the horrors they faced. Historians have argued whether slave life was better on the small family farms that included only a few slaves or on large plantations with many. In reality, it probably depended on the conditions and the owner of an individual farm or plantation. Slaves on small farms worked alongside the owners and often shared the same meals. But if the owner was cruel, there was little respite from the suffering, and it was hard to maintain connections with other slaves. If the owner ran short of funds, and many did, it was all too easy to cut the food and clothing of the slaves or simply sell one member of a slave family away from the rest. Working conditions on a large plantation with several hundred slaves could be much harsher, but slaves had more opportunity to create a community and maintain a cultural identity of their own, including more of the African traditions of their ancestors. Often, the routines and expectations were more regularized on a larger plantation.

On large plantations, the work life of slaves was usually controlled by an overseer, often a poor white whom the plantation owner hired to get as much work—and profit— from the slaves as possible. Slaves and overseers had to develop a working relationship of sorts, however tense it might be. An overseer who was too lax would not produce the profits an owner expected; one who was too cruel could also be unproductive. The owner of one of Alabama's larger plantations, A. H. Arrington, wrote in his diary, "I have this day discharged my overseer, Mr. Brewer. I found so much dissatisfaction amongst the negroes that I placed under his charge that I could not feel satisfied to continue him in my employment." Such decisions were not uncommon. While overseers had total legal control over the slaves, slaves also knew that for any work to get done at all, an accommodation had to be reached between their white masters and themselves. Slaves knew how to make the most of what power they had. It was risky to complain about an overseer, but it was less risky to

American Voices

Susan Merritt, Memories of Slavery in the 1850s

In the late 1930s, Susan Merritt was interviewed near Marshall, Texas, not far from where she had once been a slave, by historians working for the Federal Writers' Project. She estimated herself to be eighty-seven years old but still remembered slavery all too well.

I couldn't tell how old I is, but does you think I'se ever forget them slave days? … I'se born right down in Rusk County [Texas], not a long way from Henderson, and Massa Andrew Watt am my owner. My pappy, Hob Rollins, he come from North Carolina and belonged to Dave Blakely and Mammy come from Mississippi. Mammy have eleven of us chillen, but four dies when they babies. Albert, Hob, John, Emma, Anna, Lula, and me lives to be grown and married.

Massa Watt lived in a big log house what set on a hill so you could see it round for miles, and us lived over in the field in little log huts, all huddled along together. They have homemade beds nailed to the wall and baling sack mattresses, and us call them bunks. Us never had no money but plenty clothes and grub, and wear the same clothes all the year 'round. Massa Watt made our shoes for winter hisself. … That man had everything.

The hands was woke with the bit bell. … They was in that field before day and stay till dusk dark. They work up till Saturday night and then washes their clothes, and sometimes they gets through and has time for the party and plays ring plays. …

When the hands come in from the field at dusk dark, they has to tote water from the spring and cook and eat; and be in bed when that old bell rings at nine o'clock. About dusk they calls the chillen and gives 'em a piece of corn pone about the size my hand and a tin cup milk and puts them to bed. But the growed folks et fat pork and greens and beans and such like and have plenty milk. Every Sunday Massa give 'em some flour and butter and a chicken. Lots … caught a good cowhiding for slippin' round and stealin' a chicken 'fore Sunday. Massa Watt didn't have no overseer. … He carry a long whip round the neck and I's seed him tie [slaves] to a tree and cowhide 'em till the blood run down onto the ground. …

Lots of times Massa Watt give us a pass to go over to George Petro's place or Dick Gregg's place. Massa Petro run a slave market and he have big, high scaffold with steps where he sells slaves. They was stripped off to the waist to show their strength.

Our white folks have a church and a place for us in the back. Sometimes at night us gather 'round the fireplace and pray and sing and cry, but us darn't 'low our white folks know it. Thank the Lord us can worship where we wants nowadays.

Source: Susan Merritt, interview, in Norman R. Yetman, editor, *Voices from Slavery: 100 Authentic Slave Narratives* (Mineola, NY: Dover Publications, 2000), pp. 224–226.

Thinking Critically

1. **Analyzing Primary Sources**
   How would you characterize Merritt's point of view in describing her master?

2. **Comparison**
   How might Merritt's life have compared with that of a Northern factory worker?

feign illness, even pregnancy, and more slaves did that. Some slaves feigned clumsiness and broke tools that then had to be repaired; others pretended laziness and attempted to slow the pace of work. Resistance took many ingenious forms, and it helped slaves survive.

Especially on larger plantations, slave families were also essential to the emotional, and often physical, survival of their members. While slaves were not allowed legally recognized marriages, many slave partnerships lasted for a long time while others were disrupted by the sale of one partner or the tensions that drive people apart in any circumstance. Slave parents, especially mothers, had a difficult task, loving children while also preparing them for the rigors of slavery. Many former slaves recalled parents being especially tough in ways that, as adults, they recognized as the most loving thing slave parents could do. After all, to allow a slave child to grow to adulthood without proper preparation for a world in which submission (at least outward signs of submission) was key to survival was to give that child a death sentence. Some slave mothers simply could not endure the thought of children they loved being raised to be slaves. One former slave told the story of a mother who, after seeing three children sold away from her, gave her fourth child "something out of a bottle" and soon it was dead: "'Couse didn't nobody tell on her or he'd [the owner] of beat her nearly to death."

Resisting Slavery

Enslaved people found many different ways to resist their enslavement, and passive resistance was not the only kind. Newspaper advertisements for runaway slaves give evidence that thousands and thousands of slaves tried to run away from the places where they were held. The actual number of runaway slaves was always hard to determine since those who ran did not want to be counted. At the time, the U.S. Census estimated one thousand runaways per year between 1850 and 1860. More recent scholars estimate between one thousand and five thousand per year between 1830 and 1860. While many runaways were caught, many tried again and again to find shelter in free states of the North or in Canada, Haiti, or England, and quite a few succeeded. And finally, in every generation, there were full-scale slave revolts, some small and some large, in which enslaved people attacked their oppressors and sought to claim their freedom.

RUNAWAY SLAVES In 1837, Joseph Taper and his family ran away from a Virginia plantation. It was a dangerous decision to do so. The chances of being caught were great and the punishments harsh—perhaps flogging, perhaps having the family separated and sold into the Deep South, farther from the opportunity for a second escape, perhaps being killed.

At first, the Tapers made their way to Pennsylvania where Joseph Taper found work. But when he read the offer of a reward for his return, the family moved farther north and eventually left the United States for Canada in 1839. Britain had abolished slavery in all its dominions in 1833, making it illegal for slave hunters to seek former slaves there. In November 1840, a year after their arrival in Canada, Joseph Taper wrote, "I am in a land of liberty, in good health. … My wife and self are sitting by a good comfortable fire happy, knowing that there are none to molest or make afraid."

As happy as the Taper story was, the long and dangerous journey north was frightening for any slave who sought to escape. Harriet Jacobs escaped from slavery by boat in 1843. She remembered that even after she was safely on the boat, "we were filled with constant apprehensions that the constables would come on board." But she was relieved when "the next morning I was on deck as soon as the day dawned … for the first time in our lives, on free soil." Nevertheless, though she had successfully escaped from slavery, Jacobs remembered the next days as difficult ones. She was lonely, having "left dear ties behind us; ties cruelly sundered by the demon Slavery."

The Taper and Jacobs stories are unusual. Most slaves who ran away were quickly caught. The route to freedom in the North was known as the **Underground Railroad**, a highly secret system of safe havens and supporters that guided slaves toward a new, free life. Through the 1800s, more and more slaves were aided by "conductors" who were either former slaves or free people, black and white, who hated slavery and were willing to take enormous risks to help new people on the road to freedom. Conductors on the

Underground Railroad

Support system set up by antislavery groups in the upper South and the North to assist fugitive slaves in escaping the South.

Underground Railroad knew the hidden paths and the safe houses where sympathetic owners were willing to hide runaway slaves as they journeyed ever farther north, either to cities in the United States or, increasingly, out of the United States to Canada. Both Taper and Jacobs were among the few slaves who were literate, which helped them elude the authorities and prosper. But they were not nearly so unusual in deciding to run away from slavery.

Advertisements that appeared in Southern newspapers offered considerable detail about runaway slaves. One 1850 issue of the *New Orleans Daily Picayune* reported the offer of rewards for Jack, Sam, Zip or Harry, Edward, Daniel, Henrietta, Mary Mackendish, William, and Tom. By 1860, some 50,000 slaves ran away every year out of a total slave population of 4 million who were held by 385,000 slave owners, which meant that 1 in 7 slaveholders could expect someone to run away each year.

Runaway slaves became abolitionists and some even national leaders. Henry Highland Garnet, whose writing inspired fear in the hearts of many slaveholders, was born a slave in Maryland. While he was a child, his family set out on the pretext of going to the funeral of a slave on a nearby plantation but went instead to the home of a Quaker Underground Railroad conductor in Delaware who started them on the road to freedom in New York City, where each member of the family took a new name in a ceremony of "baptism to Liberty."

Frederick Douglass was born a slave in Maryland around 1817. Douglass remembered visits from his mother who lived on another plantation twelve miles away and made the journey on foot at night before returning for the next day's work: "She was a field hand, and a whipping is the penalty for not being in the field at sunrise. … I do not recollect of ever seeing my mother by the light of day."

Douglass made his first attempt to run away in 1835 but was caught. He tried again three years later and succeeded in running away to freedom in New York in 1838. Though feeling terribly alone in New York, Douglass also felt exhilarated. He made contact with David Ruggles, secretary of the New York Committee of Vigilance, who befriended him. Ruggles contacted Anna Murray—a free black woman to whom Douglass was engaged—and Murray and Douglass were soon married in the Ruggles's parlor by Reverend James W. C. Pennington, himself a runaway slave, by then a Congregational minister. But given the number of slave catchers in New York, Ruggles urged the couple to go farther north to

By far the most famous conductor on the Underground Railroad, Harriet Tubman, shown here with a few of the perhaps three hundred people she led North out of slavery, ran away from slavery and then returned to the South again and again to lead others to freedom.

New Bedford, Massachusetts, because of the number of runaway slaves living there, many of whom worked on the docks or whaling ships that hired racially diverse crews. In New Bedford, Douglass met William Lloyd Garrison and his career as a leading abolitionist orator began.

Harriet Tubman became famous as a slave who not only ran away but also returned to the South and guided between two hundred and three hundred others along the Underground Railroad to freedom. By most reckonings, she was responsible for freeing more slaves than any other person in the institution's long history.

Tubman was born about 1820. Two of her older sisters were sold to a plantation farther south, and Tubman never shook her own fears of a similar fate. She almost died at the age of fourteen from a severe head injury when an overseer threw a two-pound weight at another slave but hit Tubman instead. In 1844, she married John Tubman, a free black who lived nearby. (Marriages of slaves and free blacks were uncommon, but not unknown.) The free husband thought his wife worried too much about being a slave. In 1849, Tubman made her way north to Philadelphia without her husband or other help and found work as a domestic. She recalled, "I was free; but there was no one to welcome me to the land of freedom." Everyone she knew and cared for was "down in the old cabin quarters, with the old folks and my brothers and sisters." For some among the slaves who made it to freedom, the pull of family was so great they returned to slavery. Tubman, however, decided that the best solution was to bring the rest of her family to freedom, which she did, though she never rejoined her free husband.

Having successfully brought most of her family north, Tubman developed a pattern that she would continue until the Civil War. She worked for a while, raised some money, and then made a trip south to free more slaves. Between 1850 and 1861, Tubman made trip after trip, helping slaves escape and taking them north. As the full impact of the 1850 Fugitive Slave Law took effect, she did not stop in Pennsylvania but accompanied each group to Canada. As Tubman's fame grew, it earned her the support of Northern abolitionists and the hatred of many slaveholders. The reward for her capture grew steadily, but she kept returning to free more people. Northern abolitionists supported her work, and in 1859, the Unitarian minister Thomas Wentworth Higginson took up a collection at the Massachusetts Anti-Slavery Society so that Tubman could "resume the practice of her profession!"

Thinking Historically

Understanding Advertisements for Runaway Slaves

On December 22, 1848, the following advertisement appeared in the *Baltimore Sun*:

FIFTY DOLLARS REWARD—Ran away from the subscriber, on the 10th inst [this month], a MAN named Celus, calls himself Celus Dorsey, about 23 years old, slender made, about 5 feet, 7 or 8 inches high, dark complexion, rather thick lip; he has a large scar on one of his hands from a burn. It is probable he is lurking about Baltimore. I will give the above reward if taken out of the State, and $30 if taken in the State, and secured so I get him again.

Historians have found hundreds of similar advertisements in newspapers in slaveholding states from the American Revolution to the middle of the Civil War. Each advertisement tells a small part of the story of someone who had the opportunity and the courage to

run away from slavery and the slaveholder's determination to see him or her returned.

Source: *Baltimore Sun*, December 22, 1848.

Thinking Critically

1. **Contextualization**
   Why might Hunt have thought that Dorsey was "lurking around Baltimore"? Was there something about a city, even in a slaveholding state, that might attract a slave?

2. **Argument Development**
   How would you frame your own interpretation of the reasons slaveholders were so willing to advertise about runaway slaves and let others know that enslaved people were running away so often?

12.1

12.2

12.3

REBELS AND SLAVE REVOLTS As much as they sought to catch runaway slaves, slaveholders most intensely feared the possibility of a slave revolt. Slave revolts were relatively rare, but they did happen. Historians have documented over two hundred slave revolts in the United States in the sixty years before the Civil War. Some were little more than small-scale events on a single plantation; others were much larger. On August 30, 1800, Gabriel Prosser led over one thousand slaves in a planned attack on Richmond, Virginia (see Chapter 7). In 1810, plans for a revolt were discovered in Lexington, Kentucky. In 1811, four hundred slaves revolted in New Orleans. And in 1815, a white man named George Boxley attempted to lead a slave revolt in Virginia.

In 1822, Denmark Vesey and his supporters planned to burn the military and financial center of Charleston, South Carolina, murder the white residents, and then seize the city's caches of weapons and gold. They would then set sail for a new life of freedom in Haiti. Vesey, who had purchased his own freedom, had been plotting his revolt for years. He led a Bible class in Charlestown for the African Methodist Episcopal Church, and he spoke of the biblical stories of moving from slavery to freedom with the passion of a latter-day Moses. He also spoke fluent French and was clearly influenced by the success of the Haitian slave revolt. No one really knows how close Vesey came to success before his plot was betrayed. Some estimated that his coconspirators numbered in the thousands, making it one of the largest slave revolts. In stories whispered behind closed doors, Vesey and his followers represented the ultimate terror to the white community.

In 1831, Nat Turner led a revolt that was more successful than Vesey's. Terror spread throughout the South when Turner's forces killed over sixty slave-owning whites before the revolt was defeated by state and federal troops. Over one hundred slaves were killed in the fighting or executed after capture. Turner himself was captured and interviewed by his white, court-appointed attorney, Thomas Gray, before he was executed. Gray's prejudices have led many to question the authenticity of *The Confessions*, but the book had a ring of truth about it. Gray, an attorney and planter in Virginia, accused Turner of "gloomy fanaticism" but reluctantly admired his "natural intelligence and quickness of apprehension." Gray subsequently published an account of the conversation as *The Confessions of Nat Turner*, and the book was picked up by the abolitionist press.

Turner reported having been a religious man from his earliest years. His prayers convinced him "that I was ordained for some great purpose in the hands of the Almighty," that the Almighty's purpose included freedom for American slaves, and that "the great day of judgment was at hand." When Gray asked Turner if in retrospect he considered the revolt a mistake, Turner replied, "Was not Christ crucified?" In the aftermath of the Turner revolt, Southern fears increased, and repressive laws were passed across the South. Turner's familiarity with the Bible and the conviction of Southern authorities that some of his ideas were the product of "Yankee peddlers" and the "incendiary publications" of abolitionist societies, led to new laws making it illegal to teach a slave to read and write so others like Turner would not be able to study the Bible or abolitionist publications. In the slave quarters, however, Turner became a legend, and stories of his exploits were told and retold.

A different kind of slave revolt took place at sea. From the 1500s on, there were times when slaves being transported from Africa to the Americas rebelled and attacked the crews of slave ships. But the rebellion aboard the slave ship *Amistad* in 1839 was different. Led by Cinque (Senbge Pieh), the fifty-three recently enslaved Africans on the *Amistad* took over the ship, killed the captain and some of the crew, and demanded that the surviving crewmembers sail the ship back to Africa. The sailors sailed west rather than east, and the ship was eventually intercepted by the U.S. Navy, which took the ship to port in New London, Connecticut, where Cinque and thirty-eight surviving Africans were indicted for murder and piracy.

Abolitionists quickly organized in support of the Mende-speaking *Amistad* Africans. Mende-speaking black sailors Charles

Pantheon/SuperStock

It was some time after the revolt before Nat Turner was captured. In spite of his capture, his actions had already sent fear through the slaveholding South.

Pratt and James Covey and linguists, including Thomas Hopkins Gallaudet, were able to translate the story of the terror of their enslavement and the stories of the free African societies from which they came. After a series of trials in state and federal courts, the case eventually went to the U.S. Supreme Court where former president John Quincy Adams defended the Mende and the Court ruled that the captives were indeed born free and had been kidnapped. In the winter of 1841–1842, thirty-five survivors sailed back to freedom in Africa. The *Amistad* case received support not only from abolitionists but also from colonizationists, who wanted to return former slaves to Africa—a step most abolitionists and most enslaved Africans opposed. Colonizationists sent missionaries along with the returning *Amistad* survivors; much later, Sarah Margru, one of the children enslaved on the *Amistad*, returned to study at Oberlin and become a missionary teacher in Africa. Some Northern blacks also called for slave uprisings. David Walker, who was born free in Ohio, published his *Appeal to the Colored Citizens of the World* in Boston in 1829. Walker's goal was "[t]o awaken in the breasts of my afflicted, degraded and slumbering brethren, a spirit of inquiry and investigation respecting our miseries and wretchedness in this Republican Land of Liberty!!!!!!" Walker asked white Americans, will God "let the oppressors rest comfortably and happy always?" But the primary audience for Walker's *Appeal* was African Americans to whom he said, "The whites want slaves, and want us for their slaves, but some of them will curse the day they ever saw us."

In his 1843 "Address to the Slaves of the United States of America," Henry Highland Garnet also did not mince words. He said to the slaves of the South,

> Brethren, arise, arise! Strike for your lives and liberties. Now is the day and the hour. … Let your motto be resistance! Resistance! RESISTANCE!

For Garnet and Walker, the time was long past for aiding individual escapes or agitating for a constitutional end to slavery; they were ready for direct action.

The Abolitionists

The Liberator

A newspaper dedicated to the anti-slavery cause launched by William Lloyd Garrison in 1831.

American Anti-Slavery Society

Founded in Boston in 1833, the society was dedicated to the abolition of slavery.

In the first issue of his newspaper ***The Liberator***, published in 1831, William Lloyd Garrison declared, "I am in earnest—I will not equivocate—I will not excuse—I will not retreat a single inch. – AND I WILL BE HEARD." Over the next thirty-five years until the passage of the Thirteenth Amendment ending slavery in the United States in 1865, Garrison never backed down. He was a loner who alienated most people who tried to work with him. Nevertheless, in 1833 he was one of the key members in launching the **American Anti-Slavery Society** in Boston, which, like *The Liberator*, was committed to the total abolition of slavery everywhere in the United States, and for a third of a century, he kept the issue of slavery in front of a white society that often did not want to hear about it. Garrison's role in the abolitionist movement can hardly be overstated.

A new journal, *The Liberator*, began publication in 1831 and was dedicated entirely to the complete abolition of slavery in all parts of the United States.

12.1

12.2

12.3

In the 1830s, Garrison was already a believer in the "free labor" doctrine that the Republican Party would adopt in the 1850s. He contrasted Northern free labor, which provided opportunities for anyone to gain the economic independence so important to freedom, and Southern slavery, which created a rigid hierarchy of wealthy elites, poor whites, and enslaved blacks.

Garrison was not a church member, but he modeled himself on an Old Testament prophet, and he saw the abuse that was heaped on him over many years as proof of his own righteousness. Other abolitionists, white and black, also were subject to considerable abuse. In 1835, Garrison was almost lynched in Boston. A year later, Theodore Dwight Weld, a spokesperson for the more religious wing of the abolitionist movement, was attacked by an antiabolition mob in Troy, New York, that dragged him from the church pulpit where he was speaking and stoned him. The resulting concussion ended Weld's public speaking though it did not stop his writing for the antislavery cause. A few years earlier, in 1833, Prudence Crandall admitted a black girl to the female academy that she led in Canterbury, Connecticut. When her white students revolted, Crandall made the school one for "colored scholars." Local politicians had Crandall arrested, while mobs pelted the school and the students. In spite of support from Garrison, Crandall was forced to close the school and leave town. In New York City, Lewis and Arthur Tappan, highly successful merchants, were also shunned for their abolitionist activity. And in Alton, Illinois, on the Mississippi River opposite the slaveholding state of Missouri, Elijah Lovejoy was killed by a mob in 1837 after he had set up a small printing press to publish antislavery literature. Antislavery activity was not for the faint of heart.

On the fourth of July in 1854, at a sunny afternoon picnic of the Massachusetts Anti-Slavery Society in Framingham, Massachusetts, Garrison burned a copy of the hated Fugitive Slave Act of 1850 that required all citizens to help return escaped slaves to those who claimed them. It was not a surprising action at an antislavery rally, but when the crowd roared its approval, Garrison also held up a copy of the U.S. Constitution—a sacred document to many—calling it "the source and parent of the other atrocities" because it protected slavery, and he set it on fire, too. And again the crowd roared its approval. For all his radicalism, Garrison was also a pacifist. He always insisted that his goal was "to accomplish the great work of national redemption through the agency of moral power," not force. While he argued that events like Nat Turner's bloody rebellion were inevitable, he could never condone violence, even the violence of the Civil War, to end slavery.

Garrison may have crusaded independently, but many other Americans, white and black, were joining forces as abolitionists in the 1830s and 1840s, and especially after the passage of the Fugitive Slave Act in 1850. But the roots of abolitionism go back at least to the 1820s and to efforts led by blacks and whites. In 1826, free blacks in Baltimore, Maryland—the city with the largest free black community in the United States—organized the Baltimore Society for the Protection of Free People of Color. As early as 1827, an African American Baptist minister, Nathaniel Paul, called on his congregation to "enter the field with a fixed determination to live and die in the holy cause" of abolition.

What came to be known as "Oberlin abolitionism" emerged from the revivals that a white minister, Charles Grandison Finney, led in upstate New York in the 1820s. In May 1836, the American Anti-Slavery Society began a campaign to evangelize the nation for abolitionism. What was needed, the society's leaders decided, were antislavery revivalists who modeled their activities on the work of religious revivalists. Funds would be raised to send out at least seventy organizers to preach the sin of slavery and the need for the repentance of abolitionism. Theodore Dwight Weld, who had begun his career working with Finney, was commissioned to choose the agents.

Weld turned to his old classmates from theology school, and eventually, thirty of the fifty-four students who had been part of Weld's class at Lane Seminary in the early 1830s became antislavery agents. They carried abolitionism to all the free states of the union.

In the 1840s and 1850s, 12 to 15 percent of all Americans were slaves and most Americans held some opinion about the issue of slavery. Some, including Edmund Ruffin, were defenders of slavery; others such as William Lloyd Garrison, David Walker, and Sarah Grimké were its opponents. Some Americans ran away from enslavement or bought copies of Garrison's paper or signed petitions or helped conduct runaways on the Underground Railroad, while other Americans joined antislavery mobs in places such as New York or Connecticut. But almost no Americans were completely free of economic ties to slavery or were able to ignore its impact on American culture and politics. Slaves produced cotton, which clothed most Americans and fueled the nation's economy. By the 1850s, the issue of slavery also dominated American politics. Whatever one's place in society and one's point of view, slavery was a central issue and topic of debate. It would not go away.

> ### 12.2 Quick Review
>
> In what different ways did enslaved people and their free allies, white and black, resist slavery and help individuals escape from it? How did apologists for slavery respond to the growing criticism that emerged in the 1830s and 1840s? What do the numbers of slaves who ran away say about slavery?

New Strength for American Women

12.3 Describe how the women's rights movement developed in the United States in the 1830s and 1840s.

On July 20, 1848, sixty-eight women and thirty-two men signed a **Declaration of Sentiments and Resolutions** at the end of their two-day meeting in Seneca Falls, New York. The document—which followed the form of the Declaration of Independence—is often viewed as the opening statement of the women's rights movement in the United States. This declaration stated,

> We hold these truths to be self-evident; that all men and women are created equal; that they are endowed by their Creator with certain inalienable rights; that among these are life, liberty, and the pursuit of happiness.

Then, just as Jefferson listed grievances against George III, those who gathered in upstate New York offered their grievances against the male-dominated culture in which they lived. Their document made history and achieved far more recognition than its authors ever imagined. But the Seneca Falls convention would likely not have happened without the work of others who began to question women's roles before the convention.

New Ideas about Women's Rights

The 1848 convention of women at Seneca Falls was not the first time women in the United States began to lobby for their rights. Although hardly a feminist in today's terms, Abigail Adams had reminded her husband, John, that the new government in 1776 should "remember the ladies." African American women along with white women were early voices for women's rights. Maria Stewart was born a slave in Connecticut in 1803. A friend of both David Walker and William Lloyd Garrison, in 1831 she wrote a pamphlet insisting, "Ye daughters of Africa ... Awake! Arise! [and] distinguish yourselves ... promote and respect ourselves ... improve our own talents." She continued that although "the great and mighty men of America ... the rich and powerful ones [may] kill, tyrannize, and oppress ... WE CLAIM OUR RIGHTS." Seven years later, in 1838, the abolitionist and feminist Sarah Grimké published *Letters on the Equality of the Sexes and the Condition of Women*, portions of which she first published in Garrison's *The Liberator* and which she originally addressed to the Boston Female Anti-Slavery Society, illustrating the very close ties that existed between the women's rights and abolitionist movements. In the 1838 book, Grimké argued that in the "condition of women in my own country," well-off women were "taught to regard marriage as the one thing needful, the only avenue to distinction," while "in those employments which are peculiar to women, their time is estimated at only half the value of that of men." Grimké also argued that men suffered from the assumption that they alone needed to

Declaration of Sentiments and Resolutions

The resolutions passed at the Woman's Rights Convention at Seneca Falls in 1848 calling for full equality, including the right to vote, for women.

support families while she believed they would ultimately find greater happiness in seeing women "as their equal" even if that view did not come easily to them.

Few women symbolized the strong links between feminism and abolitionism as did South Carolina sisters Sarah and Angelina Grimké. Born to a prosperous slaveholding family, both women broke with their family over slavery. By 1836, they had become the first female representatives of the American Anti-Slavery Society, based in New York City. They had also become ardent feminists. In 1838, Angelina married another abolitionist, Theodore Dwight Weld. For most of the rest of their lives, Weld and the two sisters lived together and campaigned to end slavery, racism, and sexism in society.

Sarah Grimké wrote *Letters on the Equality of the Sexes* after she and her sister were criticized for giving public lectures on the antislavery cause. The ministers and others who criticized them might have been sympathetic to the women's antislavery views, but they thought women had no place speaking in public to "promiscuous assemblies," that is, any group that included women and men. Sarah had no intention of backing down on her right to speak in public or her advocacy for abolitionism and women's rights. She began her *Letters*, "Here I plant myself. God created us equal." Then, focusing on women's rights, she continued:

> All history attests that man has subjected woman to his will, used her as a means to promote his selfish gratification, to minister to his sensual pleasures, to be instrumental in promoting his comfort; but never has he desired to elevate her to that rank she was created to fill. … To me it is perfectly clear that WHATEVER IT IS MORALLY RIGHT FOR A MAN TO DO, IT IS MORALLY RIGHT FOR A WOMAN TO DO … she is clothed by her Maker with the *same rights,* and … the *same duties.*

Grimké's *Letters* were in circulation a decade before the meeting at Seneca Falls, but that gathering brought the cause of women's rights to a much larger audience. Because it brought together such powerful women as Elizabeth Cady Stanton and Lucretia Mott—soon joined by others including Susan B. Anthony and Matilda Gage—Seneca Falls provided the foundation for a half-century-long campaign for women's rights and women's suffrage.

The Seneca Falls Convention Shapes a Movement

Elizabeth Cady Stanton and Lucretia Mott were the organizers of the **Seneca Falls Woman's Rights Convention**. Stanton and her family had come from Boston to rural Seneca Falls, New York, only the previous year, and they found life in Seneca Falls difficult and lonely.

In the summer of 1848, Lucretia Mott, already a well-known Quaker abolitionist and reformer, and her husband, James, were visiting Seneca Falls as part of a trip to the nearby Seneca Indian tribe and to former slaves now living across the border in Canada. Stanton poured out her frustration to Mott. Mott had similar grievances. Both women had long been active in the antislavery cause. Henry B. Stanton, Elizabeth's husband, was a well-known abolitionist, and he and Elizabeth had traveled widely in the service of the cause. Stanton and Mott had both attended the World Anti-Slavery Convention in London in 1840 with their husbands. At that gathering, all of the women were excluded from any speaking role. As they talked, Stanton and Mott decided, "then and there, to call a 'Woman's Rights Convention'" for the following week.

The 1848 Woman's Rights Convention at Seneca Falls generated far more attention—most of it negative—than the organizers expected. Stanton remembered, "All the journals from Maine to Texas seemed to strive with each other to see which could make our movement appear most ridiculous." Looking back on the hostility that the convention generated, Stanton said, "If I had had the slightest premonition of all that was to follow that convention, I fear I should not have had the courage to risk it."

Not all the responses were hostile, however. The abolitionist Frederick Douglass attended the Seneca Falls gathering and spoke in favor of, and signed, the declaration. Abolitionists were used to hostility, but much of the abolitionist press supported the Seneca Falls statement, launching an important alliance between abolitionists and advocates for women's rights. Looking back, Stanton wrote that "above all other causes of the 'Woman Suffrage Movement,' was the Anti-Slavery struggle in this country." Stanton, Mott, and

Seneca Falls Woman's Rights Convention

A significant convention demanding women's equality in legal rights, held in upstate New York in 1848.

Elizabeth Cady Stanton and Susan B. Anthony became lifelong friends soon after the Woman's Rights Convention at Seneca Falls and, in spite of occasional disagreements, worked together for almost half a century to fight for women's right to vote.

many like them were abolitionists first who then added women's rights to their concerns. Douglass and many male abolitionists were also among the strongest supporters of women's rights. And many of the most determined opponents of one movement also opposed the other.

Reports of the Seneca Falls Convention caught the attention of other women, and subsequent conventions were held across New York and in Massachusetts, Ohio, Indiana, and Pennsylvania. Among those who heard the news of the Seneca Falls convention were Susan B. Anthony and Matilda Joslyn Gage. Anthony was a teacher in Rochester, New York, and active in temperance and antislavery reforms. Gage gave birth to a son just before the Seneca Falls meeting and could not attend. Both of these women quickly became friends with Stanton and fellow leaders of the women's rights movement for over half a century. They also joined as editors of the first three volumes of *History of Woman Suffrage* published between 1881 and 1886. The gathering at Seneca Falls, the declaration that the convention issued, and the movement that followed became far more than the small band of organizers dared hope for when they gathered on those hot summer days.

A Growing Women's Rights Movement

Women continued to lead campaigns to open other doors to women. Some collaborated with the Seneca Falls leaders and some worked on their own. When Lucy Stone graduated from Oberlin College in 1847—Oberlin and Antioch were among the first American colleges to admit women as students—she was chosen as the commencement speaker but was told that a man would have to read her speech because it was not appropriate for women to speak to mixed audiences. In response, she refused to write one. In 1855, when she married Henry B. Blackwell, Stone insisted on keeping her own name, a huge break with tradition. Stone's Oberlin friend and sister-in-law Antoinette Brown Blackwell was the first woman ordained as a Protestant minister in 1851. In 1849, Elizabeth Blackwell, sister-in-law to both women, became the first woman awarded an M.D. degree.

Another reformer, Amelia Bloomer, who had participated in the Seneca Falls convention and served as a temperance lecturer, embraced a different kind of freedom for women when in 1851 she popularized a kind of trousers that women might wear instead of the cumbersome hoop skirts that were expected of all middle-class women.

Other women demanded other rights. One of the most important issues for many women was the right to control their own property. In nearly all the states before the 1830s, a married woman's husband controlled all of the couple's property. Women fought such rules, and after the Panic of 1837, in which many women saw their life savings disappear because of a husband's bankruptcy, their voices began to be heard. Mississippi was the first state to pass laws specifically allowing women to keep the property they brought into their marriages. The 1839 law said that property that women had before a marriage or inherited during a marriage—including slaves—could not be controlled by their husbands. Michigan passed a law in 1844 that protected a woman's property from a husband's creditors, and in the 1840s and 1850s, other states followed. In Texas and other states that had once belonged to Mexico, Spanish-era laws had long given women the rights to control their own property, and those rights were incorporated into the new American legal systems.

In the 1830s, other women formed antiprostitution societies to protect women from being forced into such work. Additional reformers of the 1830s became advocates for dietary reform, including Mary Gove Nichols, who along with Sylvester Graham (of Graham crackers) advocated a healthier diet free of alcohol, coffee, meat, sugar, and spices.

Advocates for the rights of women also had their differences with one another. Some of the most intense differences came over the issue of divorce. Frances (Fanny) Wright, who had been influenced by Robert Owen's ideas about an ideal community (see Chapter 10), represented an extreme view of the topic. Wright tried to create her own utopian community at Nashoba, Tennessee, where she advocated that the best way to end slavery and the racial prejudice that maintained it was to promote interracial unions that would produce a new breed of Americans. Even after the failure of Nashoba, Wright continued to argue that the institution of marriage was a barrier to women's equality. Other women, including Elizabeth Cady Stanton, argued that marriage was a simple legal contract, not a sacred institution, and that at least in the case of a husband who was a drunkard or abusive, divorce should be easy. Others disagreed, not only those hostile to women's rights but also leaders of the women's movement such as Antoinette Brown Blackwell.

The links between the women's rights and antislavery efforts, important as they were, were not without their tensions. Some African American women felt those tensions especially deeply. As early as 1832, the first female antislavery society in the United States was created by African American women in Salem, Massachusetts. White women soon followed with their own societies in a number of large cities, but black women were often reluctant to join the integrated societies in which white women nearly always claimed all of the leadership roles. At a women's rights convention in Akron, Ohio, in 1851, Sojourner Truth asked, "May I say a few words?" Truth was already a nationally recognized figure. She had been born a slave in New York State in 1799 but was freed by the New York Emancipation Act of 1827. She took the name Sojourner Truth and traveled across the nation demanding freedom for her fellow Americans of African origin. She told the convention:

> I have as much muscle as any man, and can do as much work as any man. I have plowed and reaped and husked and chopped and mowed, and can any man do more than that? I have heard much about the sexes being equal. I can carry as much as any man, and can eat as much too, if I can get it. I am as strong as any man. … But man is in a tight place, the poor slave is on him, woman is coming on him, he is surely between a hawk and a buzzard.

Versions of the speech published later added the famous refrain "And ain't I a woman?" In that speech, Truth linked the antislavery and women's rights campaigns, telling those who opposed that link that they would indeed be caught "between a hawk and a buzzard" if she had anything to do with it.

THE BLOOMER COSTUME.

The "bloomers" that Amelia Bloomer popularized were much more than a fashion statement. They essentially meant that women could wear pants, liberating them from the long hoop skirts that were virtually required wear for middle-class women and that made any sort of activity, from walking upstairs to physical activity out of doors, extremely difficult.

12.3 Quick Review

What did the women's and abolitionist movements have in common? How did the two movements build on each other?

Conclusion

In the decades leading up to the Civil War, the United States grew in area and in population. From 1830 to 1850, the number of people living in the United States almost doubled, from fewer than thirteen million to more than twenty-three million. Rising birth rates among native-born Americans fueled the largest proportion of this growth, but immigrants, particularly from China, Ireland, and Germany, contributed to this rise as did the new residents acquired after the war with Mexico. Immigrants flocked to America to escape hardships at home and to pursue economic opportunity and political and religious freedom on American soil as domestics, farmers, miners, railroad workers, builders, and factory laborers. In many cases, native-born Americans saw immigrants as a threat to their jobs and quality of life, bringing new tensions.

As the cultivation of cotton spread across the lower South, it transformed the Southern economy and the dynamics of slavery. The slave population increased from 1.5 million to 4 million between 1820 and 1860. By 1840, the American South was the leading producer of cotton in the world, and plantation owners, eager to exploit the rising demand for the crop, moved slaves into new cotton-growing regions to work in the fields from dawn to dusk. This new cotton economy made slavery in the South far more profitable than ever before. Under attack by Northern abolitionists, slave owners began to justify slavery as a "positive good," arguing that slaves were better off than Northern industrial workers. Slaves, through open revolt, escape, and other less dramatic means, resisted their enslavement. Abolitionists in the North—white and black—also resisted slavery, campaigning against the institution with renewed vehemence that heightened sectional tensions.

Women, who were also struggling for full rights as citizens, often in close alliances with abolitionists, launched a suffrage movement at Seneca Falls, New York, in 1848 and a campaign for full rights in all areas of society. Many women and some men saw a link between freedom from slavery and the emancipation of women, and they agitated tirelessly for both causes, even though others of both sexes renounced their efforts.

Chapter Review

Immigration (and sometimes the opposition to it), the growth of both antislavery and proslavery propaganda, and the campaign for equal rights for women all changed the United States in the 1840s and 1850s. What might the United States have looked like in the 1850s without these changes?

The Changing Face of the American People in the 1840s and 1850s

12.1 Analyze how immigration from China, Ireland, and Germany, as well as the incorporation of Mexican citizens in the Southwest, changed the United States as a result of greater connections between the United States and the rest of the world.

Summary

The mid-1800s saw the U.S. population expand considerably, while at the same time becoming increasingly diverse. Americans in Hawaii and California saw Chinese laborers as a key to solving a shortage of workers. Most Chinese immigrants were men, and most intended to return to China. As gold mines attracted more and more Chinese, a growing resistance emerged, first, from white miners and, later, from the California state government. Over time, the gold fields became less productive for Chinese workers, so many went to work building the railroads and doing less-desired jobs such as laundry. Meanwhile, Irish famine and German political discord led to a new wave of immigration in the late 1840s. Irish laborers played a key role in the construction and growth of America's cities. The rapid growth of America's Irish and German population frightened many native-born Americans, particularly because the Irish and some of the Germans had a strong Catholic heritage, because many immigrants were poor, and because important cultural differences among the Irish and Germans immigrants were unfamiliar. Soon the nativist Know-Nothing Party formed, which played an important role in the reorganization of the party system in the 1850s. In California, the Mexican community was deeply divided between a small elite who were initially sympathetic to the United States and a larger but marginalized number of poor people. The Californios, as this elite was called, soon found their hopes for power in the new California dashed. A similar fate befell the Tejano elite in Texas. The Mexican or Hispano elite that controlled New Mexico fared better than their counterparts, in large part because American newcomers remained a minority in New Mexico throughout the 1800s. For many poor people in the Southwest, the transfer of authority from Mexico to the United States meant increased poverty and far less opportunity for justice.

Review Questions

1. Causation

What forces seem to motivate the far-reaching nativist backlash immigrants in the 1800s? What do nativists fear Americans might lose with the influx of people with new beliefs and new traditions?

2. Continuity and Change over Time

How did life change for Hispanic elites living in California, Texas, and New Mexico after the absorption of those territories into the United States? What explains the changes you note?

Slavery in the United States, 1840s and 1850s

12.2 Explain how the lives of slaves, slaveholders, and abolitionists evolved in the decades before the Civil War.

Summary

Driven by an increasing demand for cotton, the institution of slavery changed significantly in the 1800s—for both the slaveholder and the slave. New lands, technological innovations, and the use of slave labor allowed the South to develop a kind of industrialized agriculture that produced 60 percent of the world's cotton. The growth of this cotton industry led to the transfer of slaves out of the upper South and into the lower South. This process proved enormously painful and disruptive for the slaves involved. As profits—and criticism from abolitionists—increased, slave owners began to dig in and defend the institution as a positive good, based in part on comparisons to the conditions of Northern workers and in part on arguments about black inferiority. The increasing value of slaves led to marginal improvements in their material conditions. Slaves did all they could to build families and communities within the confines of slavery. Most runaways were caught and punished, but some made it to the North. Some, most notably Frederick Douglass, were among the greatest abolitionist leaders. Harriet Tubman, another escaped slave, became one of the most successful conductors on the Underground Railroad. The most frightening outcome slaveholders could imagine was a slave revolt. In the aftermath of Nat Turner's 1831 revolt, Southern fears deepened, so states passed a series of repressive laws. White abolitionism intensified in the 1830s and 1840s as William Lloyd Garrison played a crucial role in shaping a movement that swelled, thanks to Evangelical Christians. As time passed, few Americans could say they were completely detached from the institution of slavery, and by the 1850s, the political issues surrounding it had taken center stage.

Review Questions

3. Contextualization

How did slaves build lives and communities of their own within the institution of slavery?

4. Causation

How would you explain the growth of antislavery sentiment in the North after 1830? What connections do you see between the rise of the abolitionist movement and the changing nature of the Southern defense of slavery?

New Strength for American Women

12.3 Describe how the women's rights movement developed in the United States in the 1830s and 1840s.

Summary

Decades before the Seneca Falls Women's Rights Convention, the Grimké sisters helped cement the link between abolitionism and feminism. The convention, spearheaded by Elizabeth Cady Stanton, turned out to be a seminal moment in the struggle for equal rights for women in the United States. Stanton, like many other advocates of women's rights, was influenced by her participation in the antislavery movement. While the convention attracted a great deal of negative response, it sparked similar actions by women in other places, including Susan B. Anthony. Sojourner Truth and other women sought to broaden the campaign for women's rights to include both white and African American women in their efforts.

Review Questions

5. Causation

What links were there between the abolitionist and women's rights movements of the 1840s and 1850s? How would you explain the connections you note?

6. Continuity and Change over Time

Why was the Seneca Falls convention such an important event in the history of the struggle for women's rights?

1. Preparing to Write: Develop Your Thesis

Long Essay Question—Evaluate the extent to which there were similarities in the experiences of Chinese and Irish immigrants from 1830 to 1860.

Start by creating a Venn diagram to record specific social, economic, and political developments related to the experiences of Chinese and Irish immigrants. Using that diagram, you can develop your thesis. What patterns do you notice emerging from your Venn diagram? Is there an interesting angle you can take that gets to the heart of this issue? Remember that in addition to answering the entire question—in this case similarities as well as differences—a thesis should be thoughtful, informed by deep content knowledge, and clear.

2. Preparing to Write: Establish Context in Your Introduction

Long Essay Question—Evaluate the extent of change in the politics of slavery from 1800 to 1860.

A good introduction will establish historical context before revealing the argument's thesis. One way to accomplish a good introduction here is by discussing the state of slavery before these interesting changes started to take hold. What was the "necessary evil" argument that was prominent among the Southerner planter elite in the late 1700s and early 1800s? Recounting that argument in three to five sentences will be a great way to establish context before you establish your essay's argument in the thesis.

Chapter 13
The Politics of Separation 1850–1861

Holy Bible
Thou shalt not deliver unto the master his servant which has escaped from his master unto thee. He shall dwell with thee. Even among you in that place which he shall choose in one of thy gates where it liketh him best. Thou shalt not oppress him. Deut XXIII 15,16

Effects of the Fugitive-Slave-Law.

Declaration of Independence
We hold that all men are created equal, that they are endowed by their Creator with certain unalienable rights, that among these are life, liberty and the pursuit of happiness.

Leaflets with pictures of the capture and reenslavement of free blacks, like this one, reflected the outrage many Northerners felt in response to enforcement of the Fugitive Slave Law.

Chapter Objective

Demonstrate an understanding of the growing split between the North and the South that led to secession and civil war.

 ## Learning Objectives

From Union to Disunion

13.1 Analyze the political jockeying in Congress and how reaction to the Fugitive Slave Act and the publication of *Uncle Tom's Cabin* changed the opinions of many Americans—in the South and the North—making a break between them hard to avoid.

Bleeding Kansas and *Dred Scott v. Sandford*

13.2 Analyze the causes and consequences of the battle over slavery in Kansas and of the Supreme Court's decision in the *Dred Scott* case, including the impact of those events on public opinion.

The Economy, the Panic of 1857, and the Lincoln-Douglas Debates

13.3 Explain how the economic crisis of 1857 and the growing political crises of the decade impacted one another and led the nation to divide.

From John Brown to the Secession of the South

13.4 Analyze the political impact of John Brown's raid, why Lincoln won the presidential election of 1860, and why the Southern states then voted to leave the Union.

Significant Dates

While thousands of Americans, along with Asians and Europeans, were pouring into California in search of gold, other Americans were attacking or defending slavery. These two seemingly separate issues came to a head in Congress in 1850. Because of its rapid Gold-Rush-inspired growth, President Taylor advocated statehood for California from the time that he took office in 1849, and that same year Californians adopted a state constitution and applied for statehood. It was only one year after the United States acquired California from Mexico. The territory far exceeded the minimum population threshold for statehood, but there was a problem. Contrary to some expectations, the U.S. war with Mexico had not produced another slave state for the Union after Texas. Admitting California as a free state would restore the balance in the Senate that had been the rule since the Missouri Compromise of 1820 and that the admission of Texas had disrupted in 1846, leading to fifteen slave states represented but only fourteen free states. Many in the North and South thought a balance was essential to maintaining the Union. But Southern senators, both Whig and Democrat, agreed that if California was admitted as a free state, then other free states might quickly follow, especially because there were virtually no slaves in either the Oregon or New Mexico territories which might logically soon be divided into states. The young senator from Mississippi, Jefferson Davis, warned his colleagues that "we are about permanently to destroy the balance of power between the sections." The South's ill and aging champion John C. Calhoun wrote in his diary, "As things now stand, the South cannot with safety remain in the Union." Much had happened to lead Davis and Calhoun to their conclusions. In the 1850s, more Southerners would come to believe that they could not remain in the Union, while in the North, hostility to the South and its "peculiar institution" of slavery would increase. A rising generation of Southerners, not only those who owned slaves but also many of their neighbors, began to believe that slavery was, indeed, a positive good and not merely a necessary evil. And many in the North were coming to believe that slavery was an absolute evil that was unacceptable in a democratic society. Although some in Congress tried again to enact the kinds of compromises that had held the country together since the adoption of the Constitution in 1789, those efforts no longer worked. The tensions that led Southern states to secede from the United States in 1861 are the focus of this chapter.

From Union to Disunion

13.1 Analyze the political jockeying in Congress and how reaction to the Fugitive Slave Act and the publication of *Uncle Tom's Cabin* changed the opinions of many Americans—in the South and the North—making a break between them hard to avoid.

The Congress that met in 1849 and 1850 and debated the admission of California was one of the most contentious ever seated. The same three men, Daniel Webster of Massachusetts, John C. Calhoun of South Carolina, and Henry Clay of Kentucky, who had dominated the Senate as young men in 1820, now, as old men, played the central role in 1850. The dramatic debates of 1850 would be the last time the three would appear on the Senate floor. A new generation of senators would also play crucial roles in the coming years: Stephen A. Douglas of Illinois (who would contest the presidency with Abraham Lincoln in 1860), William H. Seward of New York and Salmon P. Chase of Ohio (both of whom would seek the Republican nomination for president in 1860 and then serve in Lincoln's cabinet), and Jefferson Davis of Mississippi (who would be elected president of the Confederacy in 1861).

Proslavery senators like Calhoun and Davis were worried about California, but they were even more worried about abolitionism in the North, which had been growing since the 1840s. Throughout the 1840s and 1850s, there were many different kinds of abolitionists with differing levels of commitment to their cause, but Southerners tended to view all abolitionists as extremists. At the core of the movement were those known as the radical abolitionists for whom slavery was the greatest evil in the nation, an evil that needed to end immediately and completely. A larger group of Northerners were sympathetic with the radicals but not willing to move as quickly or do as much to oppose slavery. Many of these moderates fell into the free-soil category, willing to let slavery stay where it already existed but adamantly opposing any extension of slavery to new territories where it did not yet exist. Finally, there were others for whom ending slavery was perhaps a good thing but not the highest priority. People in all three of these groups were committed to "free labor," the belief that slavery undermined the value and dignity of hard work and that many white people were also marginalized in places where slave labor was predominant. The manufacturing economy that dominated in the North—an economy ironically often fueled by the industries that turned Southern slave-produced cotton into cloth—nevertheless depended on free workers who worked in the mills, factories, and ships of the industrialized North. In the 1850s, the commitment to free labor and against the spread of slavery, even among moderates who did not want to get involved in the more radical aspects of abolition, would lead voters in the new Republican Party to cheer for "Free Soil, Free Speech, Free Labor, and Free Men."

Many of the tensions that exploded in Congress in 1850 dated to the U.S. War with Mexico in the 1840s. In 1846, Democratic congressman David Wilmot of Pennsylvania proposed an amendment to a military appropriations bill, prohibiting slavery in any territory acquired from Mexico. This so-called **Wilmot Proviso** sprang from growing anger among Northern Democrats at what they saw as the pro-Southern tilt of the Polk administration. With support from Northern Whigs, the amendment passed the House but died in the Senate where Southern Senators were able to block all such measures in 1846 and 1847. A Boston newspaper said of the Proviso, "As if by magic, it brought to a head the great question that is about to divide the American people." By 1850, that question—the question of slavery's possible extension into any new territories—created divisions that cut across party lines, whether Democrat or Whig.

California, the Compromise of 1850, and the Fugitive Slave Act

A new Congress, elected just after the end of the War with Mexico, and a new president, war hero Zachary Taylor, tackled the complex question of California's statehood. Southerners tended to trust Taylor because he owned slaves and a Louisiana plantation, but forty years as an officer in the U.S. Army had led Taylor to value the Union. He hated the threat of secession. In 1849, Taylor proposed admitting not only California but also New Mexico as new states. California would certainly be a free state, but Taylor's proposal left the future status of New Mexico uncertain, though there were virtually no slaves there. By the time Congress convened in December 1849, much of the country was in an uproar, with many in the South threatening secession if two free states were admitted and many in the North willing to call their bluff.

In that charged situation, Senator Henry Clay of Kentucky, long known as the "Great Compromiser" for his role in crafting the Compromise of 1820, tried again. Clay offered a series of proposals that he hoped would pass Congress and avert a sectional crisis by defusing the sectional tensions. The first compromise would admit California as a state but organize New Mexico under a territorial government with no "restriction or condition on the subject of slavery," a plan that was a silent concession to what Stephen Douglas would later call "popular sovereignty"; the idea that voters in a territory or state should settle the issue of slavery there. In the meantime, as a territory, New Mexico would have no votes in the Senate, a key concern of slaveholders in Congress since they were certain—probably rightly—that New Mexico would opt to enter the Union as a free state. The second compromise Clay proposed would resolve the contested question of the Texas–New Mexico border by giving more land to New Mexico and giving Texas $10 million to pay off the debts of the former Republic of Texas. Since many Southerners held Republic of Texas bonds, this proposal had great appeal in the South. The third proposal abolished the slave trade, but

Wilmot Proviso

The amendment offered by Pennsylvania Democrat David Wilmot in 1846, which stipulated that "as an express and fundamental condition to the acquisition of any territory from the Republic of Mexico . . . neither slavery nor involuntary servitude shall ever exist in any part of said territory."

MPI/Getty Images

Henry Clay, John C. Calhoun, and Daniel Webster, three men who had dominated the Senate since 1820, debated for the last time in Congress as they tried to resolve the complex issues raised by the admission of California as a state.

not slavery itself, in the District of Columbia. Finally, to ensure Southern support, Clay proposed a fourth compromise: a law enhancing slaveholders' right to reclaim slaves who fled to the North and new federal agents to help them. The whole package may have seemed to Clay like a careful balance that would appeal to both sections. In fact, most members of Congress from each section disliked it, claiming that it did not go nearly far enough in the direction they wanted.

In the debate that followed Clay's proposals, John C. Calhoun warned that if California was admitted as a free state, Southerners could not remain in the Union. The threat of secession was clear. Three days later, Daniel Webster spoke in favor of the compromise. Webster began, "I wish to speak to-day, not as a Massachusetts man, nor as a Northern man, but as an American. . . . I speak to-day for the preservation of the Union." It was an impressive speech, but it virtually destroyed Webster's reputation in an increasingly abolitionist Massachusetts where many of his constituents were no longer willing to compromise with slaveholders or support those like Webster who did.

In the long hot summer of 1850, first Calhoun and then President Taylor both died in office. The new president, Millard Fillmore, from New York, favored compromise, perhaps more than Taylor had. In addition, a new generation of senators, of whom Stephen A. Douglas was the leader, managed to forge a final compromise close to Clay's proposal. In a series of separate resolutions, California was admitted as a free state; New Mexico and Utah were organized as territories with no votes in Congress, thus maintaining the balance in the Senate; the slave trade but not slavery was prohibited in the District of Columbia; and Texas happily accepted the $10 million in exchange for a less expansive border with New Mexico. Most fatefully, Congress also passed the **Fugitive Slave Act**, which was designed to please the South by giving slave owners the right not only to reclaim runaway slaves—a right guaranteed in the Constitution—but also to demand federal and local Northern help in the process.

There was great rejoicing in Washington in the fall of 1850 when the package passed. President Fillmore called it "a final settlement," but not everyone agreed. A convention of delegates from Southern states condemned the compromise and affirmed the right of seces-

Fugitive Slave Act

A law that was part of the Compromise of 1850. It created a new set of federal agents to help track runaway slaves and required authorities in the North to assist Southern slave catchers and return runaway slaves to their owners.

sion. In the North, Charles Francis Adams, son and grandson of antislavery presidents, called the compromise "the consummation of the iniquities of the most disgraceful session of Congress." Horace Mann, the former Massachusetts education leader who had succeeded John Quincy Adams in the congressional seat that was—because of Adams's long efforts—considered *the* abolitionist seat, said that the compromise meant the Declaration of Independence applied only to white men. For Northerners, the vigorous enforcement of the Fugitive Slave Act would soon become intolerable, and many Southern leaders became convinced that the abolitionists wanted to end slavery not only in the territories but also in the states where it was strong and that the only solution was to leave the Union. In 1850, no one knew what the next decade would hold, but the most perceptive among them thought the celebrations were premature.

Enforcing the Fugitive Slave Act

When Henry Clay proposed a new Fugitive Slave Act as part of the Compromise of 1850 and Stephen A. Douglas persuaded Congress to adopt it, and when Presidents Fillmore (1850–1853) and Franklin Pierce (1853–1857) vigorously enforced that law, none of them expected the firestorm that resulted. The core of the new law was not new. The Constitution said,

> No person held to service or labor (i.e., a slave) in one State under the laws thereof, escaping into another, shall in consequence of any law or regulation therein, be discharged from such service or labor, but shall be delivered up on claim of the party to whom such service or labor may be due.

Even though Northern states had passed "personal liberty laws" in the 1830s that made it harder to recapture a former slave, the Supreme Court in 1842 had affirmed that slaveholders had a constitutional right to capture slaves who had escaped to a free state. Given the number of runaway slaves, slave catching was a growth industry in the United States before 1850.

Nevertheless, the new Fugitive Slave Act went much further than any previous law. It created a new corps of federal agents to help capture runaway slaves. Court-appointed federal commissioners would determine whether a person claimed by a slave catcher was truly a slave or actually a free person. Commissioners were paid a double fee every time they found that a person was a fugitive slave as opposed to a free person, and there was no appeal from their decisions. Finally, the law provided for a $1,000 fine and up to a year in jail for anyone who helped a fugitive slave. Across the North, free blacks were worried, and many, knowing that it would be difficult to prove that they had been born free, moved to Canada before trouble arrived. But the slave catchers, now supported by federal agents, fanned out across the North, seeking escaped slaves, and in town after town, people saw the results. It was an ugly spectacle.

Anthony Burns escaped from slavery in Virginia, went to Boston, and found work in a clothing store. But his former owner discovered his whereabouts, and under the Fugitive Slave Act, a federal marshal arrested Burns on May 24, 1854. Bostonians were incensed. White and black abolitionists attacked the courthouse where Burns was held, and a federal marshal was killed in the melee. President Pierce ordered

CAUTION!!

COLORED PEOPLE

OF BOSTON, ONE & ALL,

You are hereby respectfully CAUTIONED and advised, to avoid conversing with the

Watchmen and Police Officers of Boston,

For since the recent ORDER OF THE MAYOR & ALDERMEN, they are empowered to act as

KIDNAPPERS

AND

Slave Catchers,

And they have already been actually employed in KIDNAPPING, CATCHING, AND KEEPING SLAVES. Therefore, if you value your LIBERTY, and the *Welfare of the Fugitives* among you, *Shun* them in every possible manner, as so many *HOUNDS* on the track of the most unfortunate of your race.

Keep a Sharp Look Out for KIDNAPPERS, and have TOP EYE open.

APRIL 24, 1851.

After enforcement of the Fugitive Slave Act became common, abolitionists posted warnings to African Americans that whether born free or escaping from slavery, they were no longer safe in Northern cities like Boston.

13.1

13.2

13.3

13.4

marines, cavalry, and artillery to Boston to ensure that the Fugitive Slave Act was enforced. On June 2, 1854, federal troops marched Burns in chains through the streets of Boston to a Coast Guard ship that was waiting in Boston Harbor to take him back to slavery in Virginia. Huge crowds watched the spectacle, church bells tolled, and flags flew upside down. Pierce had upheld the law, but he had lost the respect of many of the nation's citizens. Amos A. Lawrence, one of the richest men in Massachusetts and a conservative Whig, was a changed man after watching the Burns affair. He said that he and many of his friends "went to bed one night old fashioned, conservative, Compromise Union Whigs & waked up stark mad Abolitionists." Lawrence was far from alone. Happily for Burns, his Boston supporters eventually purchased his freedom. Nevertheless, the sight of this man being marched by U.S. troops back to slavery on the streets of Boston was indelible for many who saw and heard about it.

Similar incidents happened across the North. In Ohio, Margaret Garner, an escaped slave who had crossed the Ohio River from Kentucky, discovered slave catchers at her door, and she tried to kill her children rather than allow them to be returned to slavery. One of the children died. Garner was sold back to slavery in New Orleans. For Northerners, these sorts of events undermined the notion that they were living in free states. Many concluded that freedom could not exist in a nation that allowed the kind of support for slavery that the Fugitive Slave Act provided.

Southern defenders of slavery were coming to the conclusion that slave states and free states could not remain in the same country. Federal law had banned the international slave trade since 1808, but smugglers found ways to flout that ban and bring new slaves directly from Africa. Northerners likewise flouted the Fugitive Slave Act. When the best known of the Southern slave smugglers, Charles A. L. Lamar, was tried in federal court for smuggling slaves into the United States, a Southern newspaper asked, "What is the difference between a Yankee violating the fugitive slave law in the North and a Southern man violating . . . the law against the African slave trade in the South?" In the 1850s, the vigorous enforcement of some laws and the flouting of others angered many Americans, but they differed greatly on which laws they wanted enforced and which flouted.

Uncle Tom's Cabin

Anger at the Fugitive Slave Act also convinced Harriet Beecher Stowe, already an author, to do something for the antislavery cause. As the Fugitive Slave Act took effect, Stowe wrote "that the time is come when even a woman or a child who can speak a word for freedom and humanity is bound to speak." And speak she did. Novels had been written in the United States even before the American Revolution and had become a very popular form of literature in the 1840s. Nathaniel Hawthorne's *The Scarlet Letter*, published in 1850, and Herman Melville's *Moby Dick*, published in 1851, both became popular and profitable literary sensations in the United States and Britain. But nothing would equal the book that Harriet Beecher Stowe was about to publish in terms of readership or impact.

Although she was living in Brunswick, Maine, at the time, Stowe had spent many years in Cincinnati,

Bettmann/Getty Images

Selling 300,000 copies, *Uncle Tom's Cabin* was one of the bestselling books of the century and helped to galvanize Northern opinion against slavery.

Thinking Historically

Uncle Tom's Cabin

Early in Uncle Tom's Cabin, *Stowe described her heroine Eliza's decision to run away from a Kentucky plantation after hearing that her young son was about to be sold away from her:*

> It is impossible to conceive of a human creature more wholly desolate and forlorn than Eliza, when she turned her footsteps from Uncle Tom's cabin.
>
> Her husband's suffering and dangers, and the danger of her child, all blended in her mind, with a confused and stunning sense of the risk she was running, in leaving the only home she had ever known, and cutting loose from the protection of a friend whom she loved and revered. Then there was the parting from every familiar object. . . . But stronger than all was maternal love, wrought into a paroxysm of frenzy by the near approach of a fearful danger. Her boy was old enough to have walked by her side, and, in an indifferent case, she would only have led him by the hand; but now the bare thought of putting him out of her arms made her shudder, and she strained him to her bosom with a convulsive grasp, as she went rapidly forward. . . .
>
> If it were *your* Harry, mother, or your Willie, that were going to be torn from you by a brutal trader, tomorrow morning,—if you had seen the man, and heard that the papers were signed and delivered, and you had only from twelve o'clock till morning to make good your escape,—how fast could *you* walk?

For many Americans, Eliza's fear and determination made the reality of slavery come alive in ways that decades of antislavery publications and true-life stories had not. What a modern reader reads as melodrama, readers of the time found compelling.

Source: Harriet Beecher Stowe, *Uncle Tom's Cabin, or, Life among the Lowly* (Boston: J.P. Jewett, 1852).

Thinking Critically

1. **Analyzing Primary Sources**
   In the short passage about Eliza, how does Stowe transform the slavery question from an abstract political issue into a personal tragedy? Who is the audience for her question, "If it were *your* Harry, mother, or your Willie . . . how fast could *you* walk"?

2. **Continuity and Change over Time**
   How did other developments, like the debate about the Fugitive Slave Act, set the stage for the public reaction to the story of Eliza in *Uncle Tom's Cabin*? If the book had been published ten years earlier or ten years later, what would have been the impact?

Ohio, and had seen slavery in person. Cincinnati—a city that faced the Ohio River and from which one could see the slave state of Kentucky on the far shore—was itself home to many fugitives from slavery. She began writing what would become *Uncle Tom's Cabin*. It was first published in serial form in the *National Era* in 1851 and 1852 and then as a book. Within a year, 310,000 copies were in print, making it the bestselling book of the century, other than the Bible. What seems to modern readers to be an unrealistic and sentimental story of Uncle Tom, the ever-patient and kind slave, his evil owner Simon Legree, and heroic Eliza Harris, the slave mother who jumps on ice floes in the Ohio River to escape pursuing slave catchers, was not only a literary but also a political phenomenon in the 1850s and 1860s. If any one book brought home a picture of slavery to moderate or ambivalent Northerners, it was *Uncle Tom's Cabin*.

The book also enraged the South. *De Bow's Southern and Western Review*, one of the nation's largest proslavery publications, said the novel was "insulting to the South, because Mrs. Stowe wants the world to believe that all she has written is true!" In the turmoil of the 1850s, however, the book galvanized antislavery opinion not only in the North but also in England where it was credited with playing a role in keeping Britain neutral during the Civil War. The book angered both Southerners who rationalized slavery and Northerners, many of whom first saw the nature of slavery through its pages.

The Kansas-Nebraska Act of 1854

Developments in the early 1850s proved how wrong President Fillmore had been to think that the Compromise of 1850 was a "final settlement" of North–South tensions. The Fillmore administration's enforcement of the Fugitive Slave Act exacerbated antislavery

13.1

13.2

13.3

13.4

opinion across the North and probably cost Fillmore the Whig nomination for president in 1852. In the 1852 elections, the Whigs, deeply divided between North and South, voted on fifty-three ballots before finally nominating another war hero, General Winfield Scott. An almost equally divided Democratic Party nominated Franklin Pierce of New Hampshire, whom many in the South considered "as reliable as Calhoun himself" on the issue of slavery because, they thought, he would win the White House for them by sweeping the South. The Democrats' gamble paid off; Pierce won and enforced the Fugitive Slave Act as actively as Fillmore.

Despite the tense political atmosphere, Senator Stephen A. Douglas of Illinois hoped to get federal support for a transcontinental railroad from Chicago to the Pacific Coast. A railroad did not seem to be something that would immediately stir up the tensions swirling around slavery, but it soon did. As one step toward organizing the railroad, Douglas and Congressman William A. Richardson, a fellow Illinois Democrat, introduced bills into Congress in 1853 that would organize the remaining land in the Louisiana Purchase north of the Arkansas River, then called simply the Unorganized Territory, into what they called the Nebraska Territory—something they thought was essential to facilitate awarding a right-of-way for the railroad (see Map 13-1).

Map 13-1 The Compromise of 1850 and the Kansas-Nebraska Act.

The Compromise of 1850 admitted California as a free state and set the borders for the New Mexico and Utah Territories. Three years later, Senator Stephen A. Douglas proposed a plan for the Unorganized Territory between Minnesota and Oregon that eventually led to the Southern portion of it becoming the states of Kansas and Nebraska, but first set off a firestorm in Congress and the country about whether the territory might eventually become slave or free states. (Only much later did the northern portion of the then unorganized territory become the states of North and South Dakota.)

Southern senators feared an effort to create another free state out of Nebraska and blocked the bill. After several failed efforts at compromise, Douglas proposed to split Nebraska into two territories—Nebraska and Kansas—and allow each territory to decide whether to allow slavery. He called this approach "**popular sovereignty**"—letting each state or territory decide for itself whether to allow or ban slavery in its jurisdiction. Others had used the term before him, but Douglas became its most prominent proponent. The term sounded democratic—at least for white voters—but it explicitly repealed the Missouri Compromise of 1820, which banned slavery north of Missouri no matter what local residents said. The proposal to split the Nebraska Territory and allow popular sovereignty to overrule the Missouri Compromise got Douglas the support he needed from Southern senators, but it also raised "a hell of a storm," as Douglas knew it would. For many moderates, even for President Pierce, the Missouri Compromise had held the Union together for thirty-four years, almost half the nation's lifetime. Tampering with it seemed dangerous. Douglas was offering to repeal it to be able to organize the new territories that he thought were essential to his plans for a railroad. The risk was that repealing the Missouri Compromise could allow slavery, if the local voters supported it, in territory where it had been banned since 1820. While defenders of slavery were delighted, Northern abolitionists and moderates saw taking the plan as a step toward spreading slavery throughout the Union, something they found unacceptable.

Northern outrage was intense. Moderate free-soil advocates united with the radical abolitionists in opposition. Five state legislatures and hundreds of meetings and conventions sent petitions to Congress declaring, "This crime shall not be consummated." Whig senator William Pitt Fessenden of Maine called the Kansas-Nebraska bill "a terrible outrage." On the other hand, Southerners of both parties strongly supported the **Kansas-Nebraska Act**. In the end, the bill passed in 1854, Pierce signed it, and Douglas got his territory, but he also virtually destroyed the Whig Party.

The Congressional Elections of 1854 and the Birth of the Republican Party

The Kansas-Nebraska Act became the defining issue in the 1854 elections for Congress. Battles between antislavery and proslavery factions within Kansas dominated the national news for the next several years. In 1854, Northern Whigs, led by Senator William H. Seward of New York, along with members of the declining Free Soil Party came together to create the **Republican Party**. Many former Whigs and members of smaller parties campaigned for office as Republicans—members of a brand-new party—in the 1854 congressional elections, and the Republicans, not the Whigs, would nominate candidates for president in 1856 and 1860. Southern and proslavery Whigs tried to maintain their party for a few years, but what had been a major political party in the United States since it was organized to oppose Andrew Jackson disappeared during the 1850s.

In Illinois, a former one-term Whig congressman, Abraham Lincoln, was "aroused . . . as he had never been before" by the Kansas-Nebraska Act and began a campaign for a seat in the U.S. Senate that would allow him to oppose the act on the national stage. Stephen A. Douglas, in the middle of his own six-year term as the other senator from Illinois (since all states elect two senators for six-year terms at different times), opposed Lincoln, hoping instead for a fellow Democrat to join him in the Senate. Since U.S. senators were elected by state legislatures at that time, not by popular votes, the 1854 senatorial campaign was actually a race among candidates for the Illinois legislature, who would then elect the new U.S. senator. Everyone understood that, if the Democrats won a majority of the state legislature, they would elect a Democrat to join Douglas, but if the winning majority was from the emerging Republican Party, supported by the remnants of the Whig Party, they would, many expected, elect Lincoln.

In the fall of 1854, Lincoln and Douglas campaigned throughout the state to support the candidates they favored for the Illinois legislature. Lincoln was a moderate, far too

13.1

13.2

13.3

13.4

popular sovereignty

A solution to the slavery crisis suggested by Senator Lewis Cass of Michigan by which territorial residents, not Congress, would decide slavery's fate in any proposed new state.

Kansas-Nebraska Act

A law passed in 1854 creating the Kansas and Nebraska Territories but leaving the question of slavery open to local residents.

Republican Party

A new political party created in 1854 that was dedicated to stopping the spread of slavery in any place in the nation where it did not exist.

moderate for many abolitionists, and he remained a Whig throughout the 1854 campaign, choosing at that time not to join the new Republican Party; however, his opposition to the spread of slavery was growing stronger. He argued that while the Constitution protected slavery in the states where it existed, it "furnishes no more excuse for permitting slavery to go into our own free territory, than it would for reviving the African slave trade." When Douglas defended his long-standing policy of "popular sovereignty" and the "sacred right of self-government," Lincoln responded, "When the white man governs himself that is self-government; but when he governs himself and also governs another man . . . that is despotism." Lincoln said that he understood that ending slavery where it existed was difficult, but he also insisted that there could be no moral right for anyone to enslave any other person.

Lincoln's coalition won the majority of the Illinois legislature, but the coalition included former Democrats who would not vote for a Whig like Lincoln. In the end, Lincoln backed Lyman Trumbull, a former Democrat turned Republican, for the Senate rather than allow a Democrat to win. But during the 1854 campaign, Lincoln had established himself as a national actor on the political stage. The speeches that both Lincoln and Douglas made were a preview of the more formal debates that would take place between them four years later when Lincoln campaigned directly against Douglas in an effort to win his seat in the Senate.

Across the North, the 1854 election led to victories by anti-Kansas-Nebraska Act coalitions in state after state. Democrats lost control of most Northern state legislatures. The majority of the members of the Senate were not up for election in 1854, but the state of Wisconsin elected the first Republican to serve in that body. More significant changes came in the House of Representatives—the members of which are elected for two-year terms directly by the voters, not by state legislatures. Northern Democrats dropped from ninety-three to twenty-three seats in the House of Representatives while Southern Democrats held fifty-eight seats. But 150 members of Congress were now committed to stopping slavery in the territories, some as Whigs, some as Republicans, and some as members of minor parties. Since the formation of the Jacksonian Democrats and Whig opposition in the 1830s, leaders had changed party affiliations on occasion in response to strong issues, but never as often as they did in the 1850s as the old parties weakened. After 1854, voters—South and North—cared mostly about whether candidates were anti- or proslavery and whether they were moderate or radical in their views, not about their party. The Kansas-Nebraska Act had unified Northern political opinion against the spread of slavery as nothing before it had done. The new Republican Party spoke for that point of view. Unlike the Whigs or the Democrats, both of which included Northern and Southern members, the Republican Party represented only one section of the nation and one political perspective. The party had virtually no Southerners and no one who spoke for popular sovereignty or any other plan to allow the growth of slavery. When the new Congress assembled in late 1855, the House eventually elected as its new Speaker, Nathaniel P. Banks of Massachusetts, a former Know-Nothing who had recently switched his political allegiance to the Republican Party. A representative of a political party that had not existed two years earlier now held the gavel in the House of Representatives. The so-called **Second Party System**—which had existed since followers of Andrew Jackson had created the Democratic Party and opponents of Jackson had created the Whig Party—was a thing of the past. It was undermined first by the growth of the Know-Nothing anti-immigrant party and then by the growing sectional split that made it hard for any political group to include both Northern and Southern members.

Second Party System

A system that began when the followers and supporters of Andrew Jackson created the Democratic Party as a political party and Jackson's opponents organized the Whig Party in response.

> **13.1** Quick Review
>
> How did the escalation of hostility over slavery end the Second Party System and indicate the issue could not be settled peacefully?

Bleeding Kansas and *Dred Scott v. Sandford*

13.2 Analyze the causes and consequences of the battle over slavery in Kansas and of the Supreme Court's decision in the *Dred Scott* case, including the impact of those events on public opinion.

Despite the outcome of the 1854 elections, the Kansas-Nebraska Act was still the law of the land. The act essentially split the former unorganized territory in half (see Map 13-1, p. 376). The southern portion was the modern state of Kansas and the northern, called Nebraska, included the modern states of Nebraska, South Dakota, and North Dakota. As a result of the act, Kansas and Nebraska each had to decide whether to apply for admission to the Union as slave or free states. No one was sure when elections would be held or who would vote, though many wanted to control the outcome. While Nebraska stayed relatively calm, Kansas, with its proximity to the slave state of Missouri and its easy access to the free states of Illinois and Iowa, was easier for Southerners and Northerners to move to. It quickly became a dangerous and violent place.

Even before President Pierce appointed Andrew Reeder, a Pennsylvania Democrat, as territorial governor for Kansas, hundreds of proslavery "border ruffians" from Missouri and abolitionists from the North began pouring into the territory. The Missourians got there first and when the first elections were held for the territorial representative to Congress in November 1854, they won easily. They also gained a majority of the territorial legislature that was elected in March 1855. The proslavery faction could probably have won these early elections fairly, but the votes were accompanied by widespread cheating, fraudulent vote counting, votes by people who still resided in Missouri, and voter intimidation. The results of this election were challenged even as more antislavery voters began arriving in larger numbers and quickly came to outnumber the proslavery advocates.

In response to the first elections, the settlers who supported admitting Kansas as a free state called a convention in December 1855 in which they declared the territorial legislature elected in March to be illegitimate. They then held their own election, established their own legislature to meet at Topeka, adopted a state constitution (the Topeka Constitution), and elected their own governor. Thus by January 1856, Kansas had two legislatures and two governors as well as sent two different territorial representatives to Congress. For the most part, each faction voted in its own elections and boycotted the elections called by the other.

In 1856, U.S. troops under orders from President Pierce dispersed the Topeka legislature, and the "official" legislature called a convention to write a state constitution. A new federal governor, Robert Walker, finally began to establish order in the territory and convinced both sides that an honest election could be held. In the October 1857 elections—probably the most honest in the territory—in which both factions voted for the first time, the free-state faction won a sizeable majority. But while the free-state majority now controlled the legislature, the constitutional convention, which had been appointed by the previous proslavery legislature, continued to write a constitution. The situation in Kansas then got even more complicated.

In 1854 and 1855, thousands of "Missouri Ruffians," as their opponents called them, arrived in Kansas, well armed and determined to control the territory. Before long, equally well-armed abolitionists from the North began arriving in the territory. Given the presence of so many guns and such anger, it was not surprising that bloodshed quickly followed.

13.1

13.2

13.3

13.4

Lecompton Constitution

Proslavery state constitution drafted in 1857 by Kansas territorial delegates elected under questionable circumstances; it was decisively rejected by Congress.

Bleeding Kansas

Violence between pro- and antislavery forces in Kansas Territory after the passage of the Kansas-Nebraska Act in 1854 that led to significant bloodshed and national attention for Kansas.

The proslavery convention at Lecompton, Kansas, which wrote what came to be known as the **Lecompton Constitution,** finished its work in the fall of 1857, and a vote on the constitution was called for December. However, the convention decreed that the vote was on only the clause that would decide whether Kansas would be a slave or a free state. Free-state residents were convinced that the whole Lecompton document was a fatally flawed defense of slavery: even if voters made Kansas a free state, the Lecompton document said that slaves already in the territory would remain slaves. They boycotted the election, and the proslavery clause won by a vote of 6,226 to 569. Then the new legislature called for a vote on the whole constitution in January 1858. Proslavery residents boycotted this election, and the constitution was defeated by a vote of 10,226 to 162. Both votes were then sent forward to Congress to sort out.

After another long and bitter debate on Kansas in the late spring of 1858—this time with Douglas in opposition in the to admitting Kansas as a slave state because of the "trickery and juggling"—Congress called for a new vote in Kansas on the Lecompton Constitution. The legislation said that if the constitution passed, Kansas would gain immediate statehood, but if it did not, statehood would be delayed significantly. In August 1858, Kansas voters defeated the Lecompton Constitution and the offer of immediate statehood by a vote of 11,300 to 1,788. Kansas would remain a territory until 1861.

The four-year battle from 1854 to 1858 gave the territory the name of **Bleeding Kansas** and hardened public opinion in the North and South. The battle in Kansas was more than confusing; it was violent. Missouri "border ruffians" and Missouri militia intimidated and killed free-state voters. But the violence was not all on one side.

John Brown came to Kansas to "strike terror in the hearts of the proslavery people." Brown attacked a small proslavery community near Pottawatomie Creek and killed five settlers. The battles continued in 1856 and 1857. Missourians boarded steamboats on the Missouri River to search for antislavery immigrants. Both sides claimed their martyrs. In most parts of the territory, the U.S. Army slowly asserted control, but just before the final

SOUTHERN CHIVALRY — ARGUMENT versus CLUB'S.

Bettmann/Contributor/Getty Images

Congressman Preston Brooks of South Carolina was enraged by Massachusetts senator Charles Sumner's antislavery arguments during the debates about Kansas, which Brooks took as an attack on the honor of his family and the South. In May 1856, Brooks came into the Senate chamber and beat Sumner with a cane while he sat at his desk. Sumner never fully recovered from his injuries but remained in the Senate as a staunch Republican through the Civil War and Reconstruction until he died in 1874.

resolution in May 1858, proslavery guerrillas shot nine unarmed free-state farmers, and five of them died.

The violence was not limited to Kansas. In Washington, Congressman Preston Brooks of South Carolina, who believed that protecting the status of Kansas as a slave state was a "point of honor," badly beat Massachusetts senator Charles Sumner in the Senate chamber after Sumner delivered his "Crime against Kansas" speech favoring a free-state Kansas. In Brooklyn, New York, the nation's most famous preacher, Henry Ward Beecher, warned of the need to "stand firm," and collected funds for "Beecher's Bibles," which were Springfield rifles to be sent to Kansas. Even after the nation turned to other matters, few Americans forgot the intense emotions Kansas aroused.

The Supreme Court and Dred Scott

While the battle for Kansas transfixed the nation, a court case was making its way through the nation's judicial process. The case, **Dred Scott v. Sandford**, resulted in one of the most far-reaching decisions in the history of the Supreme Court. It began in state courts in St. Louis, Missouri, in 1846 when abolitionists urged Dred Scott, a slave, to sue for his freedom because his owner, an army surgeon, had taken him to Illinois and then on to Fort Snelling in what is now Minnesota (then simply the northern tip of the Louisiana Purchase where the Missouri Compromise banned slavery). After living for years in free territory, his lawyers claimed, Scott had won his freedom.

In a series of trials and appeals, Scott's case went back and forth. Scott lost the first time, but on retrial in state court in St. Louis, he won his freedom. The Missouri Supreme Court then overturned the decision on appeal in 1852 and returned Scott to slavery. Although the Missouri high court had previously found in favor of slaves who had lived in free territory, ideas were hardening across the South, and the court concluded that Missouri law governed the case even though Scott had been in federally controlled free territory for years. Scott's lawyers appealed to the federal courts, and when the district court in Missouri decided against Scott, his lawyers appealed to the U.S. Supreme Court where the case was heard in 1856.

The Supreme Court also decided against Scott. The justices could have based their ruling on fairly narrow grounds. Instead, the majority used the case to make a larger legal point. Considerable (though behind the scenes) pressure was apparently brought to bear on the justices. Chief Justice Roger Taney, however, did not need pressure to speak his mind. On March 6, 1857, he spoke for a majority of the Court. Taney made two key points. First, as a black man (presumably even a free black man), Taney said that Scott had no rights that the United States needed to honor. Taney said that black people "had no rights which a white man was bound to respect." When two dissenting justices noted that blacks had actually been voters in five of the states that had ratified the Constitution in 1789, Taney countered that they might, indeed, "have all the rights and privileges of the citizen of a State," but that they were "not entitled to the rights and privileges of a citizen in any other state." This opinion seemed to directly contradict Article IV, Section 2, of the Constitution, which said, "The citizens of each state shall be entitled to all privileges and immunities of citizens in the several states," but Taney ignored the clause and previous case law.

Second, Taney broadened the ruling. Scott had no standing to bring the case, the Chief Justice said, and even if he did have standing, he did not have a case. Fort Snelling was not actually free territory because the Missouri Compromise was unconstitutional. Congress did not have the right to bar slavery in any federal territories. Depriving slave owners of their slaves, he said, violated the Fifth Amendment, which said no one could be deprived of life, liberty, or property without due process of law, and slaves were the private property of their owners. He did not say anything about the lives or liberties of enslaved people. But he did say that Congress "could not authorize a territorial government to exercise" any power to prohibit slavery.

Dred Scott v. Sandford

A Supreme Court case brought by Dred Scott, a slave demanding his freedom based on his residence in free territories, though brought there as a slave.

Shown here are Dred Scott and his wife Harriet. After the Supreme Court's decision on the *Dred Scott* case, many Americans, North and South, concluded that slavery had to be banned everywhere or nowhere.

The Court not only returned Scott to slavery but also ruled that Congress could not prohibit slavery in any federal territory under any circumstances. Abolitionists soon purchased Scott and set him and his wife free. But the decision seemed to lock millions of their fellow African Americans either in slavery or in second-class status even if they were free. It also meant that all efforts to stop the spread of slavery into new territories were doomed.

The outcome thrilled Southern leaders. The proslavery *Constitutionalist* in Augusta, Georgia, editorialized that "Southern opinion upon the subject of Slavery . . . is now the supreme law of the land." At the same time, many Northern Democrats were also delighted, seeing the decision as "the funeral sermon" of the new Republican Party. Many moderate Northerners, however, were outraged. William Cullen Bryant, editor of the *New York Evening Post*, wrote that Taney's decision was a "willful perversion" of the Constitution. Republican leaders, especially Seward of New York and Lincoln of Illinois, attacked the decision as the result of a secret negotiation between the chief justice and President-elect James Buchanan. Lincoln also said that if the Taney policy stood, then the advocates of slavery would soon make it "lawful in *all* the States . . . *North* as well as *South*." He promised that, if a Republican was elected president in 1860, he would find a way to undo the decision. The lines between the pro- and antislavery camps were hardening, not only in Congress but also in the country as a whole.

13.2 Quick Review

Why was the *Dred Scott* case a significant turning point in public opinion—North and South—in the years leading up to the Civil War?

The Economy, the Panic of 1857, and the Lincoln-Douglas Debates

13.3 Explain how the economic crisis of 1857 and the growing political crises of the decade impacted one another and led the nation to divide.

Historians have long debated the degree to which economic issues, rather than arguments over slavery, caused the Civil War. The disagreements are nearly always ones of emphasis, but most agree that both issues—economic concerns and debates over the morality of slavery—were factors.

The growth of the cotton economy between 1815 and 1860 tied the nation together, creating common interests among Southern slave-owning producers of cotton, Northern mill owners, and owners of ships that transported cotton to Britain. Abolitionist senator Charles Sumner of Massachusetts despaired of a country dominated by the "lords of the lash and the lords of the loom."

Other economic forces, however, were dividing the country. The opening of the Erie Canal in 1825 created an east–west trade axis from New England through New York and into the Midwestern states of Ohio, Indiana, and Illinois with connections through the Great Lakes to Michigan, Wisconsin, and even Minnesota. This trade network rivaled and then exceeded the trade down the Mississippi River. In 1835, 95 percent of the trade in the Ohio Valley flowed south through New Orleans and only 5 percent through New York. But by 1850, more trade went from the Midwest to New York than to New Orleans. Midwesterners who before the mid-1830s saw their economic lives connected to the states that bordered the Mississippi were now much more connected to New York and New England and had little reason to care about the Southern states that had once been so important to them.

As the railroads were built, slowly in the 1820s and 1830s but much more rapidly in the 1840s and 1850s, they also followed the newer trade routes, linking the Midwest to the Northeast, while other rail networks linked the interior of the South to Charleston and New

13.1

13.2

13.3

13.4

Orleans. New settlement followed the trade routes. More and more of the growing population of the upper Midwest came from New York and New England, the most antislavery regions of the country. In the 1850s, the new Republican Party reflected the interests of this fast-growing swath of the nation that stretched from New England into all of the Ohio River Valley and beyond to Indiana, Illinois, and Iowa. Most people in the region tended to be opposed to slavery, even if few were serious abolitionists. In addition, the Republican Party also spoke for their economic interests. John Sherman (brother of Civil War general William Tecumseh Sherman) began his political career as a Whig, but by 1854, he was elected to Congress as a Republican from an Ohio district on the shores of Lake Erie. Sherman said that while the Republican Party was born with "the immediate purpose and aim" of stopping the spread of slavery into the territories, it also supported an increase in the tariff to strengthen American industries; a homestead bill to encourage settlement of the new territories by people who wanted to build small family farms and who had no intention, or money, to bring slaves with them; land grant colleges that would serve agriculture and industry; and a transcontinental railroad that would link California to the East Coast. It was a good summary of what would become the Republicans' economic program in the 1860s and 1870s, and it played well across the region.

However, neither the Republican economic program nor the Republicans' opposition to the spread of slavery was seen as a benefit in the South, especially the Deep South. The pre–Civil War South was not an economic backwater. Indeed, it was the most prosperous part of the nation in the 1850s, but the prosperity could not be separated from cotton growing and slavery. As much as Southern cotton served as the raw material for New England mills, far more of it was shipped across the Atlantic to the larger mills in England. And while the South was building railroads—often with slave labor—its rivers and extended coastline enabled water transport better in the South than in the North. The Southern planter elite

Bettmann/Contributor/Getty Images

As the price of Midwestern wheat and goods produced in Pennsylvania and Ohio fell rapidly in 1857, panic hit the nation's financial center of New York's Wall Street. Newsboys sold extra editions of newspapers with news brought by telegraph from around the country, and the papers were snapped up by fearful investors.

Panic of 1857

A banking crisis that caused a credit crunch in the North; it was less severe in the South, where high cotton prices spurred a quick recovery.

saw far less reason than most Northerners to support federal spending on canals or a federal tariff that protected Northern industries. Southern-leaning presidents from Polk in the 1840s to Pierce in the 1850s vetoed bills for internal improvement that most Northerners, regardless of political party, badly wanted.

The **Panic of 1857** exacerbated the economic split between the regions. It was much more severe in the North than in the South. Overproduction of Northern wheat helped precipitate the panic. When the Crimean War, which had pitted Britain and France against Russia, ended in 1856, European farmers resumed full-scale wheat production, and prices for American wheat fell sharply. But the English mills continued to need Southern cotton, and the price of cotton held steady. Moreover, in the iron- and coal-producing areas of the country, Pennsylvania and Ohio, demand for steel fell, people lost their jobs, banks failed, and panic ensued. Not surprisingly, the Republican platform of 1860 supported a tariff both to provide revenue for the government and to protect Northern industry. The platform solidified support for the Republicans, especially in Pennsylvania and New Jersey. It also showed how deeply these states were cut off from the interests of the South where the tariff raised the cost of manufactured goods but did nothing to keep the price of cotton high.

The Lincoln-Douglas Debates Define the Political Parties

On June 16, 1858, Abraham Lincoln spoke to the Republican State Convention in Springfield, Illinois, that had just nominated him as their candidate against Stephen A. Douglas for the U.S. Senate. Reflecting on the Fugitive Slave Act, the Kansas-Nebraska crisis, and the *Dred Scott* decision, Lincoln quoted the Bible—well known to all of the convention delegates—and told them: "A house divided against itself cannot stand." He continued:

> I believe this government cannot endure, permanently half *slave* and half *free*.
> I do not expect the Union to be *dissolved*—I do not expect the house to *fall*—but I *do* expect it will cease to be divided.
> It will become all one thing, or all the other.
> Either the *opponents* of slavery, will arrest the further spread of it, and place it where the public mind shall rest in the belief that it is in the course of ultimate extinction; or its *advocates* will push it forward, till it should become alike lawful in *all* the States, old as well as new—*North* as well as *South*.

He begged his fellow Republicans to be sure the outcome was what they wanted. "The result is not doubtful," he concluded. "We shall not fail—if we stand firm, we shall not fail." Some of the delegates who had just nominated Lincoln thought the speech was too radical and would hurt Lincoln in the fall elections, but by 1858 he was prepared to stand firm on his ideas.

Later that summer, on August 21, 1858, Democratic senator Stephan A. Douglas met Lincoln in Ottawa, Illinois, for the first of seven debates they held across Illinois in that election season. Douglas and Lincoln were campaigning indirectly for the Senate seat, hoping that legislative candidates they supported would be elected to the Illinois legislature, which would then elect them to the U.S. Senate. They were also seeking to define the philosophy of their respective political parties. Hundreds attended their debates, and newspapers in every part of the country took their words to thousands of Americans. The debates were long and closely argued. Each sometimes spoke for two hours at a time. The speeches and the responses were not sound bites, but carefully reasoned arguments that forced each leader to refine his views and the audience to follow them closely.

At the Ottawa debate, Douglas painted Lincoln and the Republican Party ("Black Republicans," Douglas called them) as allies of the radical abolitionists. He attacked Lincoln's "a house divided against itself" speech. "Why can it not exist divided into Free and Slave States?" Douglas asked. "Washington, Jefferson, Franklin, Madison, Hamilton, Jay, and the great men of that day, made this government divided into Free States and Slave States, and left each State perfectly free to do as it pleased on the subject of slavery."

Douglas also criticized Lincoln's attack on the *Dred Scott* decision. Douglas said that he agreed with the decision and told his audience that Lincoln's approach would fill Illinois with blacks who would "become citizens and voters, on an equality with yourselves." He warned that Lincoln was trying to "array all the Northern States in one body against the South, to excite a sectional war between the Free States and the Slave States." The Democrats, Douglas said, were the party of unity while Lincoln and the Republicans promised only civil war.

In response, Lincoln declared that he was no abolitionist and that he had "no prejudice against Southern people." He also said that he would not himself know how to quickly abolish slavery where it already existed and, indeed, would honor all of the South's "constitutional rights," to protect slavery. He would even support the Fugitive Slave Act if it "should not, in its stringency, be more likely to carry a free man into slavery." But the issue for him, Lincoln said, was the spread of slavery in the territories. Lincoln said that he had no interest in "perfect social and political equality with the negro." Douglas's efforts to say that he did were a "fantastic arrangement of words, by which a man can prove a horse-chestnut to be a chestnut horse." Lincoln also attacked Douglas's belief in "popular sovereignty": "When he invites any people, willing to have slavery, to establish it, he is blowing out the moral lights around us."

The Republicans lost the campaign for the legislature, and therefore Lincoln lost the senatorial election of 1858 to Douglas. But the 1858 debates helped shape the core philosophies of the nation's political parties. They also put in the spotlight two political rivals who would meet again in 1860.

13.3 Quick Review

How did the various expressions about slavery—written, spoken, and acted—deepen the already profound split in the Union?

From John Brown to the Secession of the South

13.4   **Analyze the political impact of John Brown's raid, why Lincoln won the presidential election of 1860, and why the Southern states then voted to leave the Union.**

The year 1859 was an off year in American electoral politics. Regardless, in August, not far north of the **Mason-Dixon Line**, which divided Pennsylvania from Maryland and thus free states from slave states, people in the small town of Chambersburg, Pennsylvania, suddenly turned their attention to the issue of slavery and abolition. One of the nation's best-known abolitionists, Frederick Douglass, who had escaped from slavery on a Maryland plantation when he was a young adult, gave a speech in the Franklin County town. Both the town's Democratic and Republican newspapers gave Douglass high marks as a speaker even though both said they disagreed with his views. But the speech was a cover for the real reason for Douglass being there. He had been summoned for a secret meeting with his old friend John Brown, who was a fugitive for his role in the violence in Kansas and who was living in Chambersburg under the name of Dr. Isaac Smith.

Mason-Dixon Line

A line surveyed by Charles Mason and Jeremiah Dixon between 1763 and 1767 that settled the border between the then colonies of Pennsylvania and Maryland and came to be seen as the dividing line between North and South.

John Brown at Harper's Ferry

Douglass knew that Brown harbored dreams of sparking a slave uprising across the South. Until he met with him that August day in 1859, however, he had no idea how close Brown was to implementing his ideas. Years later, Douglass recounted their meeting while the two went fishing at an old quarry: "The taking of Harper's Ferry, of which

13.1

13.2

13.3

13.4

Captain Brown had merely hinted before was now declared as his settled purpose." Douglass thought Brown's idea was crazy, would result in immediate defeat, and as "an attack upon the Federal government . . . would array the whole country against us." Brown was not persuaded. Douglass left Chambersburg dejected and fearful, perhaps doubly so because the former slave Shields Green who had accompanied Douglass to the meeting had decided to stay with Brown. As he told Douglass, "I b'leve I'll go wid de ole man."

All that summer, Brown had been planning for his raid. In the fall, he moved from Chambersburg to a farmhouse in Maryland not far from Harper's Ferry, where a lightly guarded federal arsenal stood at the junction of the Potomac and Shenandoah Rivers. Brown and his army of sixteen white and five black men began their attack on the evening of October 16, 1859. They were confident that the slaves of the region would rise up to join them. As they entered Harper's Ferry, they cut telegraph lines and took hostages, but they were also quickly attacked. They were encircled by angry townspeople, and within hours, federal troops under the command of Robert E. Lee arrived in Harper's Ferry. When Brown refused to surrender, the troops attacked, killing or capturing most of the rebels. Only a few escaped. Brown was wounded. He and the other captured fighters were tried on charges of insurrection and treason against the state of Virginia. The jury took less than an hour to find them all guilty, and they were sentenced to hang on December 2, 1859.

Brown used the six weeks between his arrest and execution effectively. His calm words and actions after the raid, much more than the raid itself, made him a hero in much of the North and a frightening figure in the South. At his trial, Brown told the court:

> Now, if it is deemed necessary that I should forfeit my life for the furtherance of the ends of justice, and mingle my blood further with the blood of my children and with the blood of millions in this slave country whose rights are disregarded by wicked, cruel, and unjust enactments, I say, let it be done.

While in prison, Brown also managed to conduct interviews and write letters that were widely circulated. He told a reporter from the *New York Herald*, "You may dispose of me very easily . . . but this question is still to be settled—this negro question I mean—the end of that is not yet."

Immediately after the October raid, virtually everyone—Democrats, Republicans, and even many abolitionists—condemned Brown as an insane fanatic. Soon, however, public opinion started to shift. In the North, Brown's words and actions began to galvanize a wide spectrum of public opinion. People who initially dismissed him as insane started, much to their own surprise, to be swayed by his condemnation of slavery and—even more surprising to themselves—to consider his claim that violence might be needed to end it.

Henry David Thoreau's "Plea for Captain John Brown" argued that Brown's violence could not be compared with the violence of slavery. The pacifist William Lloyd Garrison criticized the raid but came to view it as "a desperate self-sacrifice for the purpose of giving an earthquake shock to the slave system." Many Northerners concluded that Brown was a hero.

Northern sympathy for Brown sent a chill through the white South. With the emergence of the telegraph and faster printing presses, news traveled fast. Many Southerners became convinced that most Northerners were in league with radical abolitionists like Brown and with those slaves who harbored thoughts of revolt. Many in the South started to think that abolitionists really did want to promote a violent slave uprising. In response, much of the South quickly became an armed camp, and doubts about remaining in the Union grew.

Library of Congress Prints and Photographs Division [LC-DIG-pga-01629]

This famous painting of John Brown on his way to the gallows, stopping to kiss a slave child, shows Brown as the hero to the antislavery cause, which is the way that many in the North were beginning to see him.

American Voices

Lydia Maria Child and Governor Henry A. Wise, Letters Regarding John Brown, 1859

When she heard of John Brown's raid and trial, Lydia Maria Child, a Massachusetts abolitionist, defender of women's rights and the rights of American Indians, and popular children's author, deplored the violence of Brown's effort but offered to go to Virginia to support him while he recovered from his wounds and awaited execution. Virginia governor Henry A. Wise, known as a proslavery moderate, responded, offering Child protection in Virginia while also making it clear that he held her and her fellow abolitionists guilty of inspiring violence. Their correspondence was published in Garrison's Liberator.

Wayland, Mass., Oct. 26th, 1859.

Governor Wise! . . .

I and all my large circle of abolition acquaintances were taken by surprise when news came of Capt. Brown's recent attempt; nor do I know of a single person who would have approved of it had they been apprised of his intention. But I and thousands of others feel a natural impulse of sympathy for the brave and suffering man. Perhaps God, who sees the inmost of our souls, perceives some such sentiment in your heart also. He needs a mother or sister to dress his wounds, and speak soothingly to him. Will you allow me to perform that mission of humanity? . . .

I have been for years an uncompromising abolitionist, and I should scorn to deny it or apologize for it as much as John Brown himself would do. Believing in peace principles, I deeply regret the step that the old veteran has taken. . . . But . . . I will also say that if I believed our religion justified men in fighting for freedom, I should consider the enslaved everywhere as best entitled to that right. Such an avowal is a simple, frank expression of my sense of natural justice.

Yours, respectfully,

L. MARIA CHILD.

Richmond, Va., Oct. 29th, 1859.

Madam: . . . I will forward the letter for John Brown, a prisoner under our laws . . . for the crimes of murder, robbery and treason, which you ask me to transmit to him. . . .

You ask me, further, to allow you to perform the mission "of mother or sister, to dress his wounds and speak soothingly to

him." By this, of course, you mean to be allowed to visit him in his cell, and to minister to him in the offices of humanity. Why should you not be so allowed, Madam? Virginia and Massachusetts are involved in no civil war, and the Constitution "which unites them in one confederacy" guarantees to you privileges and immunities of a citizen of the United States in the State of Virginia. That Constitution I am sworn to support, and am, therefore, bound to protect your privileges and immunities as a citizen of Massachusetts coming into Virginia for any lawful and peaceful purpose.

Coming, as you propose, to minister to the captive in prison, you will be met, doubtless, by all our people, not only in a chivalrous, but in a Christian spirit . . . your mission being merciful and humane, will not only be allowed, but respected, if not welcomed. . . .

I could not permit an insult even to a woman in her walk of charity among us, though it be to one who whetted knives of butchery for our mothers, sisters, daughters and babes. We have no sympathy with your sentiments of sympathy with Brown. . . . His attempt was a natural consequence of your sympathy, and the errors of that sympathy ought to make you doubt its virtue from the defect on his conduct.

Respectfully,

HENRY A. WISE

Source: Anti-Slavery Tracts, No. 1. New Series (Boston: American Anti-Slavery Society, 1860).

Thinking Critically

1. **Analyzing Primary Sources**
   What might explain the authors' strenuous efforts to be polite to one another despite their very different points of view? What evidence do you find of hostility under the polite tone?

2. **Contextualization**
   What light do these letters shed on regional tensions in the years before the Civil War? What values and beliefs do the authors appear to share? On what points are they divided? What evidence from the words in the letters would you use to defend your conclusions?

The Election of 1860

The Republican Party that nominated Lincoln for the Senate in 1858 was still very new on a fast-changing political landscape. The first election that the new Republican Party contested had been in 1854. The Republicans, it seemed, were the party of the future. In contrast, the Democratic and the Whig parties were deeply divided with opposing members that included antislavery Northerners and proslavery Southerners. The Kansas situation was the death knell of the Whigs. They never again nominated a candidate for president.

By the 1856 presidential elections, the nation had three political parties, two of them new. The Democrats managed to continue as an uneasy coalition. The Republicans consolidated their strength in the North but were virtually nonexistent in the South. A third party, the American Party, known as the Know-Nothing Party, gained strength as anti-immigrant hysteria swept the country. The Democrats nominated James Buchanan from Pennsylvania

13.1

13.2

13.3

13.4

whose prime strength seemed to be an exceeding vagueness about slavery and who had been seeking the presidency since serving as Polk's secretary of state in the 1840s. The Republicans nominated war hero and adventurer John C. Frémont. And the Know-Nothings nominated former president Millard Fillmore. Fillmore carried only Maryland, where anti-immigrant feelings were especially strong, while Frémont carried a number of Northern states and Buchanan carried the South, plus Illinois, Indiana, and California, winning easily. If Buchanan entered the White House with any mandate in 1857, it was to avoid the issue of slavery. It was one the new president could not possibly fulfill, try though he did.

After 1856, the Know-Nothing Party faded rapidly. Opposition to immigration did not have staying power as a political issue, especially when new immigrants provided the swing votes in key states like New York. Most Know-Nothings became Republicans in an uneasy alliance with the pro-immigrant faction of the party led by people such as New York's senator and former governor William Seward. Republicans were also divided on just how far to go in embracing the abolitionists among them. As late as June 1859, Lincoln had begged Ohio senator Salmon P. Chase to be sure that the Ohio Republican Party's demand for "a repeal of the atrocious Fugitive Slave Law" not become an issue in the national Republican convention because "it will explode it." But after 1857, it was the Democrats' turn to divide as it became impossible for Northern moderates such as Douglas and Southern extremists such as Jefferson Davis to stay in the same political organization. Everyone knew that the elections of 1860 were going to involve tough political contests. No one knew they would lead to war.

While the Lincoln-Douglas debates of 1858 established Abraham Lincoln as a national political leader, it was by no means certain that he would be the Republican nominee for president in 1860. Lincoln himself had mixed feelings about a presidential nomination since he had hopes of a career in the U.S. Senate. The frontrunner for nomination was New York senator William Henry Seward, a former Whig and a founder of the Republican Party. But Seward also had many enemies, people who thought he was too radical or who just did not trust him. Many, including Lincoln, thought that if Seward did not get the nomination on the first ballot, his support would melt away. Two other prominent Republicans were also in the field—Governor Salmon Chase of Ohio, one of the party's staunchest opponents of slavery, and Judge Edward Bates of Missouri, the candidate of the more moderate Republicans. And then there was Lincoln, respected by everyone, an extraordinary speaker, and more moderate than either Seward or Chase.

Lincoln's convention manager, Judge David Davis, reported to Lincoln, "We are laboring to make you the second choice of all the Delegations we can, where we can't make you first choice." The strategy worked. While Seward took the lead on the first ballot, Lincoln—not Chase or Bates—came in second. By the third ballot, it was all over as delegates made Lincoln's nomination unanimous. Of course, being the nominee of a new political party did not guarantee victory. Seward, Chase, and Bates all campaigned hard for Lincoln, and after the election, he appointed all three to his cabinet as secretaries of state and treasury and attorney general. But in between the nomination and the victorious election, there was a hard-fought presidential campaign.

Given the tensions in the country in the summer of 1860, it is not surprising that traditional political parties splintered. A faction of the old Whig Party reemerged as the Constitutional Union Party. It nominated slaveholder John Bell of Tennessee for president and Edward Everett of Massachusetts for vice president on a vague platform of "the Constitution, the Union, and the Enforcement of the Laws" (presumably a reference to the Fugitive Slave Act). Some saw this small party as the best hope to hold the country together through new compromises. Others ridiculed them as the "Old Gentlemen's Party," since most of those who campaigned for Bell were well past age sixty.

The Democrats, who had elected the last two presidents, met in Charleston, South Carolina, in April 1860. They were deeply divided. Stephen A. Douglas was the frontrunner for the nomination, but although Douglas had once been popular in the South, most Southern political leaders considered him to be a traitor to their cause after his opposition to admitting Kansas as a slave state. Mississippi senator Jefferson Davis insisted on a platform that pledged the party to protect "the constitutional right of any citizen of the United States to take his slave property into the common territories." But Douglas's supporters could not stomach abandoning their candidate's long-held commitment to "popular sovereignty" and would not support a platform that opened all the territories to slavery regardless of what the voters said. After fifty-seven ballots, the convention could not agree on any nominee and adjourned to meet again in Baltimore in six weeks to try again.

When the Democrats convened again in Baltimore, however, the same splits were evident. One-third of the delegates—nearly all of the Southerners and a few proslavery Northerners—walked out of the convention. The remaining Democrats nominated Douglas and adopted a popular sovereignty platform. The delegates who had walked out of the convention organized their own convention and nominated John C. Breckinridge of Kentucky, who was Buchanan's vice president, adopting the platform advocated by Jefferson Davis. Southern Democrats understood that the split in the party would benefit the Republicans, but they were so angry with Douglas that they were willing to accept that result. Some also believed that a Republican victory would build support for their real goal, which was secession. A Democratic Party leader and former congressman, William Lowndes Yancey, told a crowd in Charleston that it was time for "a new revolution" and "an Independent Southern Republic."

The Republican ticket did not even appear on ballots in most of the South, and Republican candidates would have risked their lives campaigning in the region. Lincoln campaigned against Douglas in the North. Breckinridge campaigned against Bell in the South. No one had ever seen a presidential election quite like it. Despite the crazy split, the North, with its larger population, was going to settle the election. Douglas had a chance to win the election if he and the Northern Democrats could carry enough Northern states and some of the slave states known as "border states" where Northern influence was strongest and the attachment to slavery was weakest (see Map 13-2). Douglas claimed to be the only

Map 13-2 The Election of 1860.

This map, indicating the electoral vote of each state, illustrates the regional nature of the final vote in the 1860 presidential election. Lincoln carried all of the North as well as California and Oregon. Breckinridge, the Southern Democrat, carried all of the Deep South and beyond. Bell, the candidate who called for glossing over all the differences, carried the key border states of Virginia, Kentucky, and Tennessee, which Douglas had been counting on. In the end, Douglas carried only the slave state of Missouri and split the electoral votes of New Jersey with Lincoln.

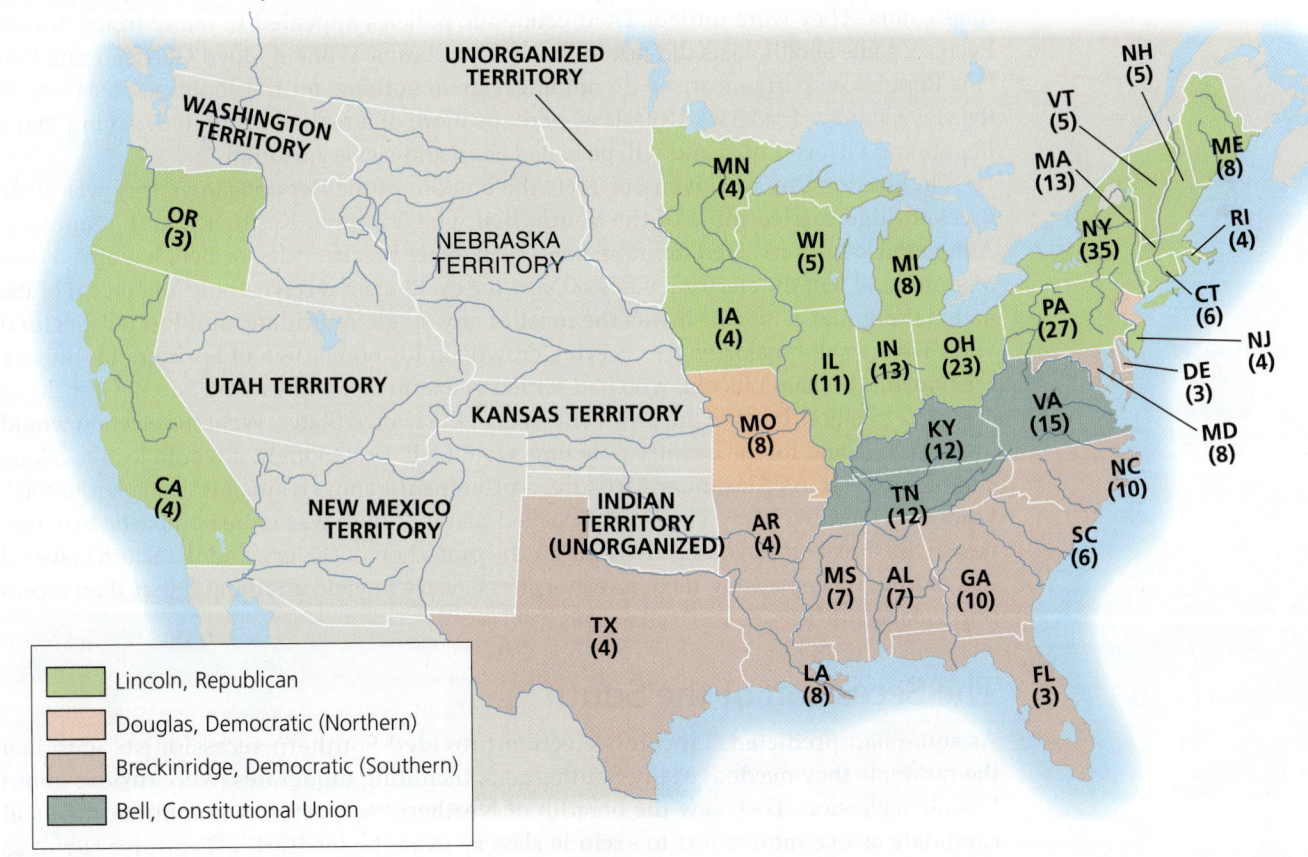

- Lincoln, Republican
- Douglas, Democratic (Northern)
- Breckinridge, Democratic (Southern)
- Bell, Constitutional Union

This political cartoon published during the 1860 presidential election depicts Lincoln and Douglas, on the left, fighting over much of the country while, in the center, Breckinridge tries to tear off the South and, on the right, Bell, with glue pot in hand, tries to put the whole thing back together.

candidate who could unite the nation. He continued to paint Lincoln as a radical and tried to frighten Northern voters by saying that Lincoln would bring blacks into the North as the social equals of whites who would also compete with whites for jobs.

The Republicans had a lot going for them. They were new. They attracted young, first-time voters. They were united. Their economic policies appealed to many in the North. Even so, some abolitionists did not trust the Republicans. William Lloyd Garrison said that "the Republican party means to do nothing, can do nothing, for the abolition of slavery in the slave states." Frederick Douglass, perhaps more of a realist, countered, saying that a Republican victory "must and will be hailed as an anti-slavery triumph."

On Election Day in November 1860, the breadth of the Republican victory was clear. Breckenridge carried most of the South. Bell won Virginia, Kentucky, and Tennessee. Although Douglas received far more votes than either Breckenridge or Bell, he carried only Missouri and half the electoral votes of New Jersey. Lincoln received only 40 percent of the national popular vote, but it was the most of any single candidate, and his 180 electoral votes were a solid majority. As cheering crowds in his hometown of Springfield, Illinois, celebrated, Abraham Lincoln, who had served one term in Congress and had never held an executive position, became the president-elect of the United States. What his election would mean for him and for the country only time would tell. Few thought it would lead to a long and bloody war. As Alexander McClure, a prominent Pennsylvania attorney, wrote forty years after the Civil War, "The North believed that the South was more bombastic than earnest in the threat of provoking civil war for the protection of slavery, and the South believed that Northern people were mere money-getters, ready to yield anything rather than accept fratricidal conflict."

The Secession of the South

As some had predicted, Lincoln's election provided Southern secessionists with just the rationale they needed. Many Southerners, including moderates, were furious about Lincoln's election. They saw the breadth of Northern support for a committed free-soil candidate as one more effort to exclude slavery from the territories. They also saw it as part of a larger pattern that included Northern failure to enforce the Fugitive Slave Act and

Northern support for John Brown. The *Charleston Courier* editorialized that Lincoln's election meant it was time for "a Southern Confederacy," something "desired by all true hearted Southerners."

The night after the election, a huge crowd of demonstrators in Charleston demanded action, and the South Carolina legislature called a special convention to consider secession. On December 20, 1860, the convention voted 169-0 in favor of dissolving "the union now subsisting between South Carolina and other states." Other states in the Deep South followed. In January 1861, Mississippi, Florida, Alabama, Georgia, and Louisiana all voted to leave the Union, followed by Texas on February 1. None of the other states after South Carolina were unanimous in their votes, but over 80 percent of the delegates in each of these states voted for secession, which was probably a fairly accurate reflection of the opinions of the white male population. Nevertheless, a minority in most Southern states, even in the Deep South, preferred to wait and see what Lincoln would actually do, but as Louisiana senator Judah P. Benjamin wrote, the "prudent and conservative men" of the South were not able "to stem the wild torrent of passion which is carrying everything before it."

The reality was, however, that the demands of these "prudent and conservative men" of the South were for things to which Lincoln would not agree. When Kentucky senator John Crittenden proposed the **Crittenden Compromise** to preserve the Union by extending the Missouri Compromise line to the Pacific and thus protect slavery in the New Mexico Territory and California, Lincoln refused to consider the compromise even though his close ally William Seward urged him to do so. As he had made clear in his various campaigns, he did not intend to abolish slavery where it existed, but he did not want to spread slavery any further. Lincoln had also come to believe that any effort at appeasement would do nothing to control slavery but would simply open the door for continuing demands. The pressing question in February and March 1861 was about the slave states that had not yet voted to secede, the so-called border states that were closer to the North, less militant in their defense of slavery, and perhaps most likely to stay with the Union: Maryland, Arkansas, North Carolina, Delaware, Missouri, and, most of all, the strategically placed states of Kentucky, Tennessee, and especially Virginia—the largest and most industrialized state in the South. Lincoln did not want to lose them, at least not all of them.

In the face of the secession crisis, the wait from November 1860 to the presidential inauguration in March 1861 seemed especially long. The outgoing Buchanan administration, never decisive, seemed more unsure of itself than ever. Rumors of a Southern invasion or an internal coup filled the capital. Many senators joined Seward and Crittenden in seeking a compromise that would avoid secession or war. Others in and out of Congress proposed all sorts of solutions, including even abolishing the office of president. The senators and representatives of the seven states that had voted to secede by February 1 packed their belongings, gave their farewell speeches, and left town to organize the government of the Confederate States of America—a project they accomplished with amazing speed at a six-day convention in Montgomery, Alabama, where they drafted a temporary constitution and selected a provisional president and vice president. In the meantime, the rest of the country seemed frozen.

Although the states of the Deep South voted to leave the Union, conventions in Virginia, Arkansas, and Missouri did not vote on secession. North Carolina and Tennessee did not even hold conventions. But leaders in all of these states warned that any violence by the federal government against those states that had voted to leave the Union would force them to depart also. Some in the North seemed happy to see part of the South depart. The *Chicago Tribune* said that if South Carolina wanted to leave, "let her go, and like a limb lopped from a healthy trunk wilt and rot where she falls." In New York, Horace Greeley's *Tribune* said, "If the Cotton States shall become satisfied that they can do better out of the Union than in it, we insist on letting them go." However, secession angered others in the North.

One resident of Illinois wrote to Congress, saying, "We elected Lincoln, and are just as willing, if necessity requires, to fight for him." A resident of Ohio wrote that Lincoln "must enforce the laws of the U.S. states against all rebellion, no matter what the consequences." Even Senator Seward's wife criticized her husband's efforts at compromise, telling him, "Compromise based on the idea that the preservation of the Union is more

13.1

13.2

13.3

13.4

Crittenden Compromise

A last-ditch effort at a compromise to amend the Constitution to protect slavery in states where it existed.

important than the liberty of nearly 4,000,000 human beings cannot be right." While it is likely that many Northern white voters would have been willing to preserve the Union at the cost of four million people remaining in slavery, a good portion of Northerners—though far from all—seemed to be ready to fight rather than let the Union be dissolved. In that tense and uncertain situation, after months of waiting, Lincoln made his way from Springfield to Washington.

Abraham Lincoln was inaugurated as the sixteenth president of the United States on March 4, 1861. His inaugural address broke little new ground. He said that he considered secession illegal and that he would assert federal authority, especially over forts and other federal installations in the South. He insisted that he had no interest in interfering with slavery in the states where it existed. And he promised to enforce the Fugitive Slave Act while also asserting that he wanted stronger protection against free people being kidnapped in the name of enforcing the law. In closing, he made a poetic plea that the Union must be preserved:

> We are not enemies, but friends. We must not be enemies. Though passion may have strained, it must not break our bonds of affection. The mystic chords of memory, stretching from every battle-field, and patriot grave, to every living heart and hearthstone, all over this broad land, will yet swell the chorus of the Union, when again touched, as surely they will be, by the better angels of our nature.

Northern response to the speech was mixed. Garrison's *Liberator* noted that Lincoln's insistence that free blacks needed protection from the Fugitive Slave Act represented the first time any president had spoken of citizenship rights for blacks—a direct contradiction of the *Dred Scott* decision. Other abolitionists were disappointed. Many moderates agreed with the Jersey City newspaper that said "it was hardly possible for Mr. Lincoln to speak with more mildness."

Confederate leaders did not see the speech as mild. Lincoln's refusal to recognize the right of secession and his claim on the federal property in the South seemed to them to be a prelude to war. Two days after the speech, the Confederate Congress authorized a call for 100,000 troops. Lincoln did not respond by making any similar call of his own. One of his advisors, Orville H. Browning, had written to the president that it was "very important that the traitors shall be the aggressors. . . . [T]hen the government will stand justified, before the entire country, in repelling that aggression." That policy was exactly the one Lincoln planned to follow.

Conflict seemed most likely to begin at Fort Sumter, a new federal installation guarding the harbor of Charleston, South Carolina. Sitting within view of the city where secession had begun, Fort Sumter was a dramatic symbol of federal authority in the heart of the Confederacy. The eighty-man garrison was commanded by Major Robert Anderson, a former slaveholder from Kentucky whose decades in the army had made him a devoted supporter of federal authority. Soon after their vote to secede from the Union in December 1860, South Carolina authorities demanded that outgoing President Buchanan remove the federal garrison and hand the fort over to them. In an uncharacteristic show of strength, Buchanan refused and tried to reinforce the fort in January 1861. South Carolina fired on the supply ship—but not the fort—and the ship turned back. By the time Lincoln came to office in March, Anderson was running low on supplies and knew he would have to either surrender or evacuate soon.

On April 6, after some hesitation, the new president announced that he was sending a supply ship with food and medicine, but not arms, to Fort Sumter. Jefferson Davis was not willing to allow the federal presence in what Davis now considered an independent country and ordered Pierre G. T. Beauregard, the officer in charge of Confederate troops in Charleston, to attack the fort. On April 12, 1861, at 4:30 a.m., shore batteries in Charleston began to shell Fort Sumter and continued to do so for the next day and a half. On April 13, out of food and ammunition, Major Anderson surrendered. Anderson and the defending troops were allowed to leave, and they sailed to New York where they were greeted as heroes, but the Confederates had control of the fort. The Confederates had won the battle, but they had fired on the American flag and started a war.

13.1

13.2

13.3

13.4

Library of Congress Prints and Photographs Division [LC-DIG-ppmsca-19520]

This popular illustration of the firing on Fort Sumter adds drama to the scene. Confederate guns did fire on the fort almost nonstop on April 12 and 13, and the fort's defenders, with very little ammunition, fired back on occasion before finally, out of food and ammunition, they surrendered on April 13.

President Lincoln declared that a state of insurrection existed and called on the state governors for seventy-five thousand volunteers while also ordering the expansion of the regular army and navy and recalling some troops from the West. The attack and Lincoln's response brought unity—even if temporary—to most of the North. Stephen A. Douglas, though seriously ill, came to the White House to promise his support and then returned to Illinois to tell Democrats and Republicans that they owed undivided loyalty to the Union.

As the president focused on preserving the Union, some African Americans and their supporters called the looming war "a White Man's war." Lincoln had made it clear, they said, that the fighting was to "save the Union," not necessarily to free the enslaved. Nevertheless, some abolitionists saw an opportunity. Senator Charles Sumner of Massachusetts reminded Lincoln that "under the war power the right had come to him to emancipate the slaves." The black-owned *Weekly Anglo-African* told readers that the slaves "have a clear and decided idea of what they want—Liberty." It would take time before the president or Northern public opinion would agree, but some supported the goal of emancipation from the first days of the war, especially slaves who followed the news closely.

Lincoln's call for federal troops united the South. Tennessee's governor announced that his state "will not furnish a single man for the purpose of coercion, but fifty thousand if necessary for the defense of our rights and those of our Southern brothers." Within days of the firing on Fort Sumter and Lincoln's call for troops, every border state had begun to consider secession and four—Virginia, North Carolina, Tennessee, and Arkansas—voted to join the Confederacy. The 88-55 vote to secede in Virginia was far from South Carolina's unanimity, and the western counties of Virginia later declared their loyalty to the Union. Representatives from that area took Virginia's seats in Congress until West Virginia could be organized as a separate state in 1863.

Missouri had its own civil war that started with mob violence in St. Louis where most German immigrants favored the Union cause while recent arrivals from the South supported the Confederacy. The Confederate government admitted Missouri as its twelfth state, but Union loyalists also organized their own state government. Two opposing Missouri state governments sent representatives to both Washington and Richmond while lawlessness reigned in most of the state throughout the war.

Kentucky declared neutrality. Since there was probably more proslavery and pro-Confederacy sentiment in Kentucky than in any other slave state that remained in the Union,

Lincoln courted the state carefully. If Kentucky seceded, the border between the United States and the Confederacy would be the Ohio River, dangerously far north. If Kentucky stayed in the Union, then Lincoln and his generals would have much easier access to multiple points of attack on the heartland of the Confederacy. Given its strategic importance, Lincoln was reported to have said that "he hoped to have God on his side, but he must have Kentucky." He got Kentucky. The state did not secede, and sentiment for preserving the Union was strong in that state, though Kentucky sent soldiers to both sides. Perhaps more than anywhere else, the Civil War in Kentucky was a war of brother against brother. Four of Henry Clay's grandsons fought for the Confederacy and three for the Union.

The other two border states also remained loyal to the Union: Delaware's northerly location and the few slaves there made the decision almost inevitable. Maryland's loyalty to the Union was assured by the influx of federal troops and Lincoln's arrest of some pro-Confederacy members of the state legislature. If Maryland had joined the Confederacy, Washington would have been cut off from the rest of the country, and Lincoln was not going to let that happen. Thus Maryland, Delaware, and Kentucky remained as slave states within the Union throughout the duration of the war while Virginia and Missouri were represented in both the Union and Confederate congresses. After Union victories in Louisiana and Arkansas, those states were also represented in the U.S. Congress by one set of people while others represented them in the Confederate Congress.

Despite Lincoln's success in retaining some of the border states, the loss of others, especially Virginia, was a severe blow to the Union. Over half of all those who fought in the Confederate Army came from border states, including several of the South's most prominent generals. On the day Virginia voted to secede, Robert E. Lee was offered command of the Union army but responded, "I cannot raise my hand against my birthplace, my home, my children." Lee resigned from the U.S. Army and eventually commanded the Confederate Army of Northern Virginia. Almost as important, Virginia included the Tredegar Iron Works in Richmond, the only factory in the South capable of making heavy shells and armor, and the federal arsenal at Harper's Ferry and the Gosport Navy Yard. All of these facilities were in Confederate hands by the end of April.

Even after the attack on Fort Sumter and the secession of the border states, many doubted that a real war would take place. People in the North were confident that the South would come to its senses, perhaps after an easy Union conquest of Richmond, Virginia. People in the South were confident that the North was not really up for a fight, certainly not a fight to end slavery where it had existed for over two hundred years and probably not a fight to save the Union either. Both sides were terribly wrong.

13.4 Quick Review

How did Lincoln's election impact the thinking of people in the South and, therefore, the course of U.S. history?

Conclusion

Throughout the 1850s, divisions between the North and the slaveholding South intensified. The burning question that continually threatened to divide the nation—would slavery be permitted to expand into new territories and states—could not be amicably decided.

Attempts by Southerners to defend the institution of slavery, and to ensure that slavery could expand into any new states in the West, were met by growing choruses of antislavery sentiment in the North. Once-moderate opponents of slavery hardened their positions as the decade unfolded. Abolitionism, whose adherents saw slavery as an evil that had to be destroyed, continued to grow in force, and many in the North, regardless of their opinions about racial equality, simply did not want the future of the country to be defined by slave labor. Slave labor anywhere undermined the "free labor" ideology of the North.

California's application for statehood endangered the balance of power in the Senate between the North and the South. In an effort to find a new middle ground, the Compromise of 1850, originally planned by the aging senator Henry Clay of Kentucky, admitted California to the Union as a free state but gave Southerners several incentives for resisting secession, including a new, strengthened Fugitive Slave Act. But the Fugitive Slave Act infuriated many in the North, and Northern reluctance to enforce the law infuriated many in the South, even people who themselves did not hold slaves.

Harriet Beecher Stowe's 1852 novel, *Uncle Tom's Cabin*, written in response to her own anger about the Fugitive Slave Act, brought the reality of the pain of slavery home to many in the North. It quickly became a best seller and inflamed public opinion, creating more opponents of slavery in the North and more anger in the South. When Congress passed the Kansas-Nebraska Act in 1854, the legislation allowed the spread of slavery, if supported by the "popular sovereignty" of voters in the territories, even where it had been banned by the Missouri Compromise of 1820. The result was not only national tension but also a civil war in Kansas so bloody that the territory came to be known as "Bleeding Kansas." In 1857, the Supreme Court's landmark decision in *Dred Scott v. Sandford* triggered further outrage in the North when the Court declared that African Americans "had no rights which a white man was bound to respect" and that the federal government had no authority to regulate the spread of slavery anywhere in the union. In that same year, the Panic of 1857, which hit the North far more than the South, illustrated how distinct the two regions had become in their economies. Later, Southerners were outraged by Northern sympathy for the radical actions of John Brown when he attacked the federal arsenal at Harper's Ferry, Virginia (now in West Virginia but then part of the state of Virginia), in 1859. All these events deepened sectional tensions and rivalries. A new political party, the Republican Party, emerged while the Whigs dissolved. Abraham Lincoln gained national prominence as he campaigned first for a U.S. Senate seat and then for the presidency. With Lincoln's election to the presidency in 1860, tensions came to a head: a majority of Southern states seceded from the Union and civil war, which many hoped and expected would be short, began.

Chapter Review

What areas of conflict between North and South led to the Civil War?
What do most historians consider to be the most important cause of the war?
Do you agree? Why? Based on what evidence?

From Union to Disunion

13.1 **Analyze the political jockeying in Congress and how reaction to the Fugitive Slave Act and the publication of *Uncle Tom's Cabin* changed the opinions of many Americans—in the South and the North—making a break between them hard to avoid.**

Summary

Many of the conflicts that wracked the Congress in 1850 had their roots in the U.S. war with Mexico. The admission of California as a free state threatened to start a process that would upset the careful balance of free and slave states in the Senate. Daniel Webster, John C. Calhoun, and Henry Clay all played key roles in the congressional debates over the issue. The Compromise of 1850 appeared to some to resolve the regional split, but it offered only a temporary reduction in tensions. The most provocative provision of the compromise was the Fugitive Slave Act, which galvanized antislavery opinion in the North. The 1852 publication of Harriet Beecher Stowe's book, *Uncle Tom's Cabin*, brought the reality of slavery home to many in the North, only intensifying antislavery feelings and furthering division. The Kansas-Nebraska Act of 1854 continued the slavery controversy as it angered the North even more, giving rise to the new Republican Party.

Review Questions

1. Contextualization
   What was at the root of the growing division between the North and South in the decades before the Civil War? How do the debates about the newly acquired territories shed light on this origin story?

2. Causation
   How did passage of the Kansas-Nebraska Act contribute to the rise of the Republican Party and the demise of the Whigs?

Bleeding Kansas and *Dred Scott v. Sandford*

13.2 **Analyze the causes and consequences of the battle over slavery in Kansas and of the Supreme Court's decision in the *Dred Scott* case, including the impact of those events on public opinion.**

Summary

Further political events in the 1850s did nothing to steady a country rocked over the issue of slavery. With popular sovereignty deciding the status of the Kansas and Nebraska territories, proslavery and eventually antislavery poured into Kansas. War broke out. The two sides would fight for four years in what would be called "Bleeding Kansas." Congress eventually intervened and called for a new vote and Kansas residents voted down a proslavery constitution. Kansas would have to wait until 1861 to achieve statehood. Meanwhile, the slave Dred Scott sued for his freedom on the basis that he and his master had lived in free territory for a number of years. After a long series of trials and appeals, Scott's case made it to the Supreme Court. In 1857, *Dred Scott v. Sandford* ruled against Scott. It turned out to be a decision that had sweeping consequences for the debate over slavery. The Court ruled that African Americans had no rights of citizenship, that the Missouri Compromise of 1820 was unconstitutional, and that Congress could not prohibit slavery in any federal territory under any circumstances. Republicans were outraged. The decision only intensified the political conflict over slavery, even as it denied the government the tools to reach further compromise.

Review Questions

3. Contextualization
   Why did both pro- and antislavery forces believe that victory in Kansas was critical to their cause?

4. Argument Development
   Defend or refute the following statement: The Supreme Court ruling in the *Dred Scott* case made a peaceful resolution of the conflict between the North and the South over slavery less likely.

The Economy, the Panic of 1857, and the Lincoln-Douglas Debates

13.3 **Explain how the economic crisis of 1857 and the growing political crises of the decade impacted one another and led the nation to divide.**

Summary

The growth of the Southern cotton economy and Northern industrialization, both of which expanded rapidly starting in the 1820s, tied the different regions of the country together more tightly than they had been before. At the same time, innovations in transportation and the growth of cities in the Midwest contributed to regional divergence. The Republican Party advocated an economic program designed to meet the needs of the fast-growing North. The Panic of 1857 exacerbated the split between the regions. The 1858 Lincoln-Douglas debates helped the Republican and Democratic parties define their respective philosophies in time for the presidential election two years later.

Review Question

5. Contextualization

How do the Lincoln-Douglas debates complicate our understanding of Lincoln's views on slavery and race?

From John Brown to the Secession of the South

13.4 Analyze the political impact of John Brown's raid, why Lincoln won the presidential election of 1860, and why the Southern states then voted to leave the Union.

Summary

John Brown's failed raid on Harper's Ferry in 1859 further polarized the nation on the issue. The Republicans emerged from the election of 1858 confident that they would be a force to be reckoned with in 1860.

Defying the odds, Lincoln won the 1860 Republican nomination for president, and given the tensions in the country in the summer of 1860, it is not surprising that traditional political parties splintered. A deeply divided Democratic Party could not agree on a nominee and ended up with two: Stephen Douglas for the Northern Democrats and John C. Breckinridge for the Southern Democrats. A remnant of the Whig Party, now calling itself the Constitutional Union Party, nominated John Bell. The Democratic split, combined with a number of other advantages, made Republican victory all but certain. Lincoln's election sparked a secession movement in the South. Last-ditch efforts to preserve the Union failed. Seven Southern states formed the Confederate States of America, and other states soon joined them. The Confederate attack on Fort Sumter led Lincoln to prepare for war as he called on states to supply seventy-five thousand volunteers. Despite Lincoln's efforts to prevent border states from leaving the Union, more left than stayed, which was a severe blow to the Union. As both sides prepared for hostilities, they were unsure what exactly was around history's corner, but few could imagine the war that was about to come.

Review Question

6. Argument Development

Defend or refute the following statement: "After Lincoln's election in November 1860, war between the North and the South was inevitable."

1. Preparing to Write: Support Your Assertion

Short-Answer Question—Answer (a), (b), and (c).

a. Briefly explain why ONE of the following had the greatest impact on the deepening sectional divide in the 1850s.

- The Fugitive Slave Act
- *Dred Scott v. Sandford*
- John Brown's raid at Harper's Ferry

b. Provide ONE example of an event or development that supports your explanation in (a).

c. Provide specific historical evidence that explains why ONE of the other (a), (b), or (c) options is less convincing as having the greatest impact on the deepening sectional divide in the 1850s.

Short-Answer Questions demand direct assertions and then specific evidence to support them. Try responding to each question above in three sentences. The first sentence should include a direction assertion, and the next two sentences should explain your assertion.

2. Preparing to Write: Organize Your Evidence

Document-Based Question—Evaluate the extent to which John Brown's raid at Harper's Ferry (1859) changed relations between the North and South.

After you develop a thesis that answers all parts of this question, study both sources from the "American Voices" in Section 13.4. How can the conflicting points of view illustrate just how far apart both sides were? Discuss the conflicting points of view in a way that supports your thesis. What other evidence can you point to that proves how the raid changed relations between the North and South? What evidence can you use to show how relations also stayed the same?

Chapter 14
And the War Came: The Civil War 1861–1865

This painting shows Union officer Brigadier General Francis Channing Barlow with captured Confederate officers in 1864 at the battlefield in Petersburg, Virginia.

Chapter Objective

Demonstrate an understanding of the strategies involved in fighting a civil war and the impact of the war on American life—in both the North and the South.

 Learning Objectives

From Fort Sumter to Antietam, 1861–1862

14.1 Explain how the early battles of the war shaped future events.

The Road to Emancipation

14.2 Analyze how the war influenced attitudes toward slavery in white and black communities, leading to the Emancipation Proclamation and to black soldiers in the Union army.

The Home Front—Shortages, Opposition, Riots, and Battles

14.3 Explain how the war's death toll and civilian shortages affected life—in both the North and the South—during the war.

From Gettysburg to Appomattox and Beyond

14.4 Analyze the strategies and costs of fighting a long and terrible war while looking at the resulting end of slavery in a unified nation.

Once Fort Sumter had been fired on, large patriotic rallies were held in both the North and the South. Of course, what it meant to be patriotic varied depending on where one lived. Calls for volunteers by Confederate and Union authorities were quickly oversubscribed. Young men did not want to miss out on the fun and glory of what everyone thought would be a short war and an easy victory. A Confederate volunteer from Mississippi wrote home in June 1861 that he was ready "to fight the Yankees—all fun and frolic." On the Union side, a New York volunteer wrote, "I and the rest of the boys are in fine spirits . . . feeling like larks."

Letters from new recruits also showed seriousness of purpose. A New Jersey soldier wrote that he joined the army because "[o]ur glorious institutions are likely to be destroyed," while a Midwestern recruit said that his service was "a duty I owe to my country and to my children to do what I can to preserve this government." Sentiment among soldiers in the Confederacy was equally patriotic. Mississippi's Lucius Lamar, who would achieve high rank in the Confederate army, said, "Thank God! We have a country at last to live for, to pray for, to fight for, and if necessary to die for." An enlisted man in the Confederate army gave a simple answer when he was asked after his capture why he, a nonslaveholder, fought for the South: "I'm fighting because you're down here." Soldiers were sent off in new uniforms with cheering parades. The war did not long remain so lighthearted.

This chapter traces life in the United States through the four years of the Civil War. The political battles as well as the army and navy engagements that were fought over those four long years determined the war's outcome. But the fighting also helped shape public opinion. No one, in the North or the South, was prepared for the terrible death toll of the war, and the fear of being killed or losing loved ones came to haunt almost everyone in the United States during the Civil War. Ideas were also changing throughout the nation as the war continued. Many in the North who started fighting a war to save the Union went through periods of wondering whether it might be better to just let the South go and then ended up fighting to end slavery. Many in the South—slaveholders and nonslaveholders alike—who started out fighting to preserve their independence from Northern influence slowly became resigned to a different fate even if they never stopped resenting the reality that the war created. And many who began the war as enslaved people, "owned" by other human beings according to the law, ended the war as free citizens, many of them veterans of the Union army that had won their freedom. The Civil War changed all of subsequent U.S. history, and its impact is important to understand.

From Fort Sumter to Antietam, 1861–1862

14.1   Explain how the early battles of the war shaped future events.

After Fort Sumter surrendered in mid-April, no further serious battles occurred for the next two months. Both governments raised and positioned their armies. The Confederates had only to fight a defensive war to protect their territory. They did not need to win victories in the North, only protect their lands to win what they wanted. The North, however, needed to defeat the Confederate army to reunite the nation. As the war began, the commander of the Union armies was the aging hero of the war with Mexico, General Winfield Scott. He proposed what came to be known as the Anaconda Plan to blockade the South by sea, take control of the Mississippi River, and slowly squeeze the Confederacy into submission—as an anaconda snake squeezes its victim. Scott wanted to end the war without a full-scale invasion of the South, which he thought would be too bloody and lead to generations of hatred no matter what the outcome. But many Northerners believed that the North needed to defeat the Confederates on Confederate turf.

Union generals wanted a lot of time to prepare supplies and train recruits. In Lincoln's opinion, his generals always wanted more time—until Grant took command much later in the war. When General Irvin McDowell, commander of the Union forces in 1861, complained that he had only green recruits, the president responded, "[Y]ou are green, it is true, but they are green, also; you are all green alike." For Lincoln, a quick attack on the Confederacy, especially if Richmond could be taken, would mean victory. No one was yet thinking of a long war.

Significant Dates

14.1

14.2

14.3

14.4

1861   Confederate States of America is organized

Abraham Lincoln is inaugurated

Fort Sumter surrenders

Slaves who come to Union army declared "contraband of war"

Confederates win First Battle of Bull Run

1862   *Monitor v. Merrimack* sea battle

Union army wins Battle of Shiloh, Tennessee

Union navy captures New Orleans

Second Battle of Bull Run, Confederate victory protects Richmond

Union victory at Antietam

1863   Emancipation Proclamation takes effect

Richmond Bread Riots

Fall of Vicksburg

Battle of Gettysburg, Union victory protects Washington, D.C.; Gettysburg address describes Union cause

New York City Draft Riots

1864   Battle of the Wilderness

Atlanta falls to Sherman's army, Sherman's March to the Sea

Farragut wins Mobile, Alabama

Lincoln is reelected

1865   Congress passes Thirteenth Amendment outlawing slavery

Lee surrenders at Appomattox Court House

Lincoln is assassinated

14.1

14.2

14.3

14.4

National Archives and Records Administration

Soldiers on both sides, like these Union soldiers in camp, spent most of the first months of the war either in training or sitting in camp and waiting. Note the one African American off to the side. This early in the war, African Americans were not yet in uniform, but that would soon change.

Early Inconclusive Battles

The first serious battle of the war took place on July 21, 1861 (see Map14-1). At Lincoln's prodding, McDowell, with eighteen thousand troops, finally advanced from Washington across the Potomac River into Virginia. The army was accompanied by Northern reporters, members of Congress, and others who thought it would be the one time they would see a battle. Confederate commander Pierre Beauregard was alerted to the Union army's movement by Confederate spies in Washington. The armies met at the small town of Manassas, Virginia, on Bull Run Creek. (Northerners called it the First Battle of Bull Run, Southerners the Battle of Manassas.) Union troops, tired from the long march from Washington, started to surround the Confederate forces, but the Confederates held their ground. In an afternoon charge, Confederates let out the scream that came to be known as the **rebel yell**. One Northerner said, "There is nothing like it on this side of the infernal region." The Union troops began to flee, merging with panic-stricken civilians who ran back to the relative safety of Washington, D.C.

The Battle of Manassas, or First Bull Run, was a clear Confederate victory. It gave the Confederates great, perhaps even dangerously high, levels of confidence. Confederate newspapers asked why their generals had not gone on to capture Washington, though in fact McDowell had done a good job of developing the defense of the capital. Northerners were despairing. Horace Greeley, who had done much to build support for the war, now wrote to Lincoln, "If it is best for the country and for mankind that we make peace with the rebels, and on their own terms, do not shrink even from that." Lincoln had no intention of taking that action, but the president now realized that it would take more than a few easy battles to win the war. Perhaps Mary Boykin Chesnut, the plantation wife who was deeply devoted to the Southern cause but never blind to reality, best understood the impact of the first battle when she wrote that she feared this early victory "lulls us into a fool's paradise of conceit."

Lincoln responded to the loss at Bull Run by calling for one million new volunteers. He fired several Union generals, including the unlucky McDowell, reorganized the army on the Maryland–Virginia line as the **Army of the Potomac**—which would remain the prime

rebel yell

A frightening yell that Confederate soldiers gave when entering battle. Many Northern troops commented on how unnerving it could be.

Army of the Potomac

The main Union army led by a series of generals until Ulysses S. Grant took command in 1863 and led it to the final victory in 1865.

Map 14-1 Major Civil War Battles, 1861–1862.

As this map shows, during the first two years of the war, the major battles took place in northern Virginia—where the Confederacy tried to defend its capital of Richmond and Union forces defended Washington, D.C.—and in the Mississippi River Valley.

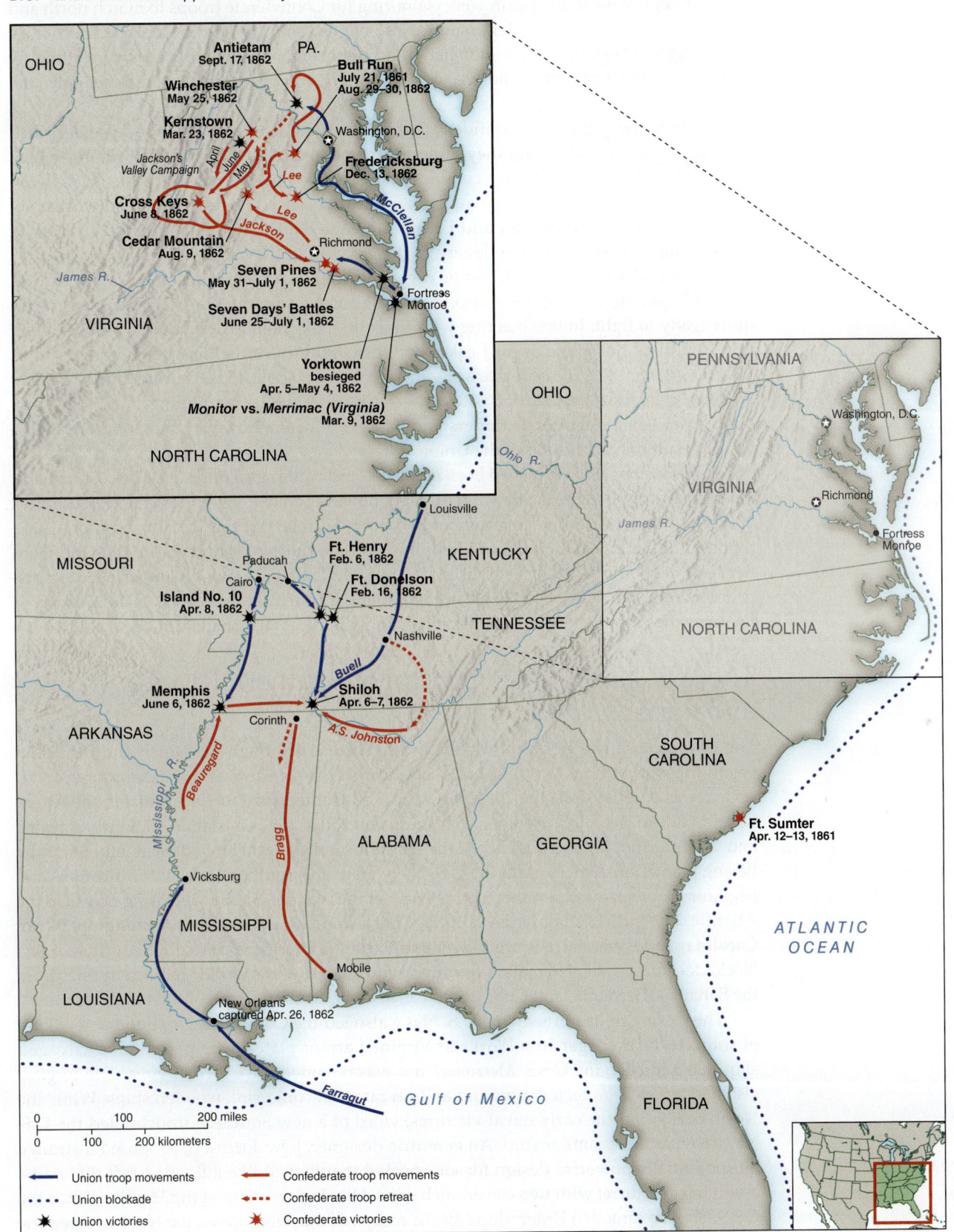

14.1

14.2

14.3

14.4

Union army throughout the war—and appointed George B. McClellan to command it. He tightened federal control in Washington and Maryland. In addition, he reorganized federal troops in the West as a separate army, with orders to proceed down the Mississippi River and try to divide the Confederacy. The country was in for a long war.

Although some in the South were clamoring for Confederate troops to march north and defeat the "damn Yankees," Jefferson Davis believed that the key to Confederate victory was doing what George Washington had done in the Revolution: simply survive. In time, he hoped, Northern opinion would tire of war and foreign governments would recognize the South.

Many in the South were confident that Britain would support them because of British need for Southern cotton. But they underestimated abolitionist opinion in Britain—which had abolished slavery in its own colonies in the 1830s—and the caution of the British government, which wanted to "keep quite clear of the conflict." Some owners and workers in the cotton mills in Manchester and Liverpool wanted a Confederate victory, but overall, British opinion was opposed to slavery. In the end, Britain stayed neutral.

General McClellan was a first-rate organizer, and he trained the Union army well. The Army of the Potomac became a strong fighting force. Nevertheless, McClellan was never quite ready to fight. In one meeting with Lincoln, the general made but one request, "Just don't let them hurry me, is all I ask." By October 1861, McClellan was in command of 120,000 soldiers. The Confederate army in Virginia was about 45,000 strong, but McClellan was sure it included at least 150,000 soldiers. Considering the possibilities for terrible loss of life, McClellan's caution is understandable. For Lincoln, however, that kind of caution would result only in the end of the Union.

By December 1861, there had been no major land battle since Bull Run. The cost of maintaining and supplying an army was still high, however, much higher than the expenditures of any previous peacetime government had been. Secretary of the Treasury Salmon Chase reported difficulty balancing the federal budget. The *London Times* reported "the independence of the South virtually established." Then McClellan got sick. In January 1862, a discouraged Lincoln said, "The people are impatient; Chase has no money. . . . The General of the Army has typhoid fever. The bottom is out of the tub. What shall I do?"

The U.S. Navy Takes Control of Southern Rivers and Ports

The Union cause was not as bleak as Lincoln feared. Although the North and the South began the war with more or less equal size armies, the North had a much stronger navy. As early as August 1861, the U.S. Navy attacked Confederate fortifications on the Atlantic and Gulf coasts. By November, the Union controlled the Sea Islands off South Carolina and Georgia and, not incidentally, some ten thousand slaves who had been left behind by fleeing plantation owners. With the U.S. Navy attacking Southern coastal fortifications and beginning a blockade of Southern ports early in the war, the South was losing access to the Atlantic. By April 1862, only the ports of Charleston, South Carolina; Wilmington, North Carolina; and Savannah, Georgia, were still open. From these ports, the South sent fast blockade-running ships to maintain contact with the rest of the world, getting supplies from the Bahamas, Bermuda, and Cuba as well as from Britain and France, but at high cost.

The closing of its ports by the U.S. Navy also led the Confederacy to build a new kind of ship. At the Tredegar Iron Works in Virginia, armor plates were placed on a salvaged ship that had been the U.S.S. *Merrimack* but was renamed the C.S.S. *Virginia*. The *Virginia* also had ten well-protected guns and an iron ram that could sink wooden ships. While the North celebrated the early naval victories, word of a new Southern ironclad led the U.S. Navy to plan for a similar ship. An eccentric designer, John Ericsson, proposed a strange but potentially powerful design for an ironclad that looked like a floating raft that had a revolving gun turret with two eleven-inch guns. His ship was named the *Monitor*. When the C.S.S. *Virginia* sank two Union ships off the mouth of the James River, the Navy ordered the *Monitor* to proceed south from the Brooklyn Navy Yard without even time for a test run. On March 9, 1862, the crew of the *Virginia* saw something they thought "was a raft" taking one

Bettmann/Contributor/Getty Images

The seagoing ironclad ships, the *Virginia* (formerly the *Merrimack*) and the *Monitor*, fought one battle in March 1862, but the Union Navy's smaller ironclad riverboats, like the one shown here, did more to turn the tide of the war as they attacked Confederate fortifications all along the Mississippi River and its tributaries.

of the Navy ships' boilers "to shore for repairs," but then the boiler started firing at them. After hours of firing and maneuvering, the *Virginia* returned to port, and each side declared victory. The two ships never fought again—the crew of the *Virginia* blew up their ship rather than let it fall into Northern hands when the Union army invaded Virginia in May 1862, and the *Monitor* sank in a gale. But naval warfare had changed forever as the two ships showed that ironclads could easily defeat a wooden-hulled navy. For the remainder of the Civil War, however, fast wooden ships continued as best they could to keep the Confederacy supplied with war material by outrunning the U.S. Navy, and the U.S. Navy blockaded most Southern commerce.

In early 1862, the U.S. Navy also won important battles on the Mississippi River. Cairo, Illinois, where the Ohio River flows into the Mississippi, was the southernmost city under Union control. South of Cairo, the Confederacy controlled the Mississippi as well as the Cumberland and Tennessee Rivers that flowed into it. The navy commander at Cairo was Andrew H. Foote, a sober abolitionist, while the army commander was the hard-drinking Ulysses S. Grant, who had given little thought to abolition before the war. Together, they attacked the South's rivers. On February 6, 1862, Union forces overwhelmed Confederate Fort Henry, and Union gunboats turned the Tennessee River into a Union thoroughfare. Grant became a hero. The Union controlled most of Kentucky and Tennessee. Southern optimism disappeared.

In April 1862, a fleet commanded by David G. Farragut got past a string of Confederate forts and took New Orleans, the largest city in the South, which remained in Union hands for the duration of the war. Farragut's ships moved up the Mississippi, capturing Baton Rouge and Natchez by the end of June. Only Vicksburg on high bluffs over the Mississippi River prevented complete Union control of the river, which would have cut the Confederacy in half.

The Beginning of a Long War

While the Union navy won battles, General Grant led 40,000 troops in an attack on Corinth, Mississippi. Corinth was where the South's major north-south and east-west rail lines crossed, and Grant meant to disrupt the network. Before Grant's forces got to Corinth, however, Southern forces attacked the Union army near Shiloh Church in Tennessee on

Army of Northern Virginia

The main Confederate army led for most of the war by Robert E. Lee, it fought in Virginia, Maryland, and Pennsylvania before surrendering at Appomattox Court House in April 1865.

Peninsular Campaign of 1862

In 1862, Union army General McClellan began a campaign to take Richmond, Virginia, and end the war. He attacked via a peninsula south of Richmond—hence the name—but never succeeded in his quest.

April 6. In two days of terrible fighting, Grant won, but at a high cost of killed or wounded troops—13,047 for the Union and 10,699 for the Confederates.

Shiloh undermined morale in both armies. A Confederate private wrote, "I never realized the 'pomp and circumstance' of the thing called glorious war until I saw this. . . . Men . . . lying in every conceivable position; the dead . . . with their eyes wide open, the wounded begging piteously for help." Union general William T. Sherman said, "The scenes on this field would have cured anybody of war." The cost of the Union victory at Shiloh convinced many that it would be a long and terrible war. Mary Boykin Chesnut wrote in her diary, "I have nothing to chronicle but disasters." Nevertheless, by May 1862, Union forces had won control of several Southern rivers and cities, disrupted the Southern rail system, and taken many prisoners. Grant, however, would spend the next year stalled at Vicksburg.

With Union victories in the west, Lincoln urged McClellan to attack the Confederate forces in the east. The Confederate **Army of Northern Virginia** was the South's elite force, assigned to protect the capital of Richmond, Virginia, and the essential supply sources nearby. McClellan landed troops on the Virginia coast to march up the peninsula—hence the name the **Peninsular Campaign of 1862**—to capture Richmond. With 135,000 troops, he seemed poised for victory. But McClellan moved slowly, with great caution, driving Lincoln to distraction.

In May and June 1862, Confederate general Stonewall Jackson defeated Northern forces in the Shenandoah Valley and kept Knoxville and much of east Tennessee in Confederate hands. It was an area filled with Northern sympathizers. But Jackson kept winning. Northern troops had to be diverted from the attack on Richmond to deal with Jackson, whose troops had captured badly needed food and medical supplies.

At the end of May, Union and Confederate forces fought a series of inconclusive engagements at the Chickahominy River only a few miles from Richmond. Jefferson Davis made Robert E. Lee commander of the Army of Northern Virginia, a move that almost turned the tide of war. Lee forced McClellan to pull back from Richmond to the James River. The costs

President Lincoln meeting with General McClellan at an army camp.

of the war were getting higher. General D. H. Hill, whose unit Lee had ordered to attack Union forces at Malvern Hill on July 1, said of the result, it "was not war—it was murder." Some twenty thousand Confederates had been killed or wounded, twice as many as in the Union army, but Lee kept up the pace.

At the end of August 1862, Union and Confederate armies met again at Manassas on Bull Run Creek where the South had won its first victory a year before. The Confederates, led by Lee and Jackson, again defeated the Union army, which pulled back into northern Virginia. At the beginning of the summer, Union soldiers could hear the church bells of Richmond. By the end of August, Richmond was safe, and the Confederate army was within twenty miles of Washington, D.C. It was a major reversal of fortunes.

By the fall of 1862, Lee and Jefferson Davis wanted a decisive win as badly as Lincoln had. The Confederate army planned to encircle Washington, D.C. As Lee's army marched north, McClellan attacked at Antietam Creek near Sharpsburg, Maryland, on September 17, 1862. The result was the single bloodiest day of the war with approximately twenty-three thousand soldiers killed or wounded—four times the number of U.S. soldiers killed or wounded on D-Day in World War II. Neither side could claim victory at Antietam, but neither side was defeated. The next day, Lee withdrew his army to the relative safety of the Shenandoah Valley in Virginia, but McClellan did not pursue Lee's retreating forces, which was the last straw for Lincoln. When a month later McClellan still had not moved and reported that he needed to rest his horses before any attack, Lincoln telegraphed, "Will you pardon me for asking what the horses of your army have done since the battle of Antietam that fatigue anything?" It was the end of the president's patience, and he relieved McClellan of command.

14.1 Quick Review

Did early Union army generals have reasons that made sense for being so reluctant to fight as hard as Lincoln wanted? Why was the navy so important to the North's ultimate victory?

The Road to Emancipation

14.2 Analyze how the war influenced attitudes toward slavery in white and black communities, leading to the Emancipation Proclamation and to black soldiers in the Union army.

Lincoln had long insisted that although he personally thought slavery evil, it was not the role of the national government to interfere with the settled institutions of states. For the last 150 years, historians and average citizens have debated just what Lincoln thought could be done about slavery. In February 1860 as a candidate for the Republican presidential nomination, Lincoln had given a speech at Cooper Union in New York. In his **Cooper Union address**, Lincoln argued that the Republicans had no interest in interfering with slavery where it existed but every intention of blocking the spread of slavery into new territories. He also attacked the *Dred Scott* decision, saying that the Court's ruling was based on ideas that had no "existence in the Constitution, even by implication." Soon after his election, he wrote to former congressman Alexander Stephens of Georgia, who was trying to convince his state not to secede:

> Do the people of the South really entertain fears that a Republican administration would, *directly, or indirectly*, interfere with their slaves, or with them, about their slaves? If they do, I wish to assure you, as once a friend, and still, I hope, not an enemy, that there is no cause for such fears.

In his March 1861 inaugural address, Lincoln said, "I have no purpose, directly or indirectly, to interfere with the institution of slavery in the States where it exists. I believe I have no lawful right to do so, and I have no inclination to do so." Even after the fighting began, Lincoln kept restating the same position.

Cooper Union address

While a candidate for the Republican presidential nomination, Lincoln had given a speech at Cooper Union in February 1860 in which he said that, while he had no interest in interfering with slavery where it existed, he would do everything he could to block the spread of slavery anywhere.

There is no way to know Lincoln's private thoughts. Clearly, he hated slavery. But if one believes most of what he said, at the beginning of the Civil War he had no inclination to do anything about slavery in the states where it already existed. But many in the South did not believe him. The *Richmond* [Virginia] *Enquirer* wrote, "No act of violence may ever be committed, no servile war waged, and yet [under a Republican administration] the ruin and degradation of Virginia will be fully and as fatally accomplished as though bloodshed and rapine ravished the land." And a member of Congress from Alabama said that the Republicans planned to "force the abolition of slavery" by constant pressure for state action and asked, "Do you not call this interference?" They were not about to take Lincoln at his word.

Once the Southern states began to secede, Lincoln's top priority was to hold the Union together with or without slavery. As late as August 1862, Lincoln wrote to Horace Greeley, knowing that his words would be published in the *New York Tribune*, insisting, "My paramount object in this struggle is to save the Union, and is not either to save or destroy slavery." He closed the letter noting that this was his *official* position but that he also intended "no modification of my oft-expressed *personal* wish that all men everywhere could be free." But his official position was evolving and, some historians would argue, so were his personal views.

contrabands

Also known as contraband of war, the name Union generals gave to former slaves who escaped to the Union lines and worked in support of Union troops.

colonization

A plan, popular in the 1830s and briefly considered by President Lincoln, to create colonies in Africa to which former slaves might return. It was never popular with slaves or former slaves themselves.

Contraband of War

While Lincoln's views were evolving, slaves and former slaves were clear on what they wanted from the war. Only a month into the Civil War, on May 23, 1861, three slaves found their way to the Union-held Fortress Monroe in Virginia and asked the fort's commander, General Benjamin F. Butler, for his protection. Butler put them to work. He also coined a term for escaped slaves who came behind Union lines: "contraband of war."

Since American law then defined slaves as private property, and since international law allowed belligerent nations to seize goods and property meant to help the other side wage war, there was logic to Butler's new term. If slaves were property that the Confederacy planned to use against the Union, then the Union had a right to seize that property. Throughout much of the war, slaves who fled to the Union army were known as **contrabands**. There were "contraband camps" and "contraband schools." Word of Butler's decision spread rapidly. More slaves started coming to Fortress Monroe, which some now called "freedom fort." Lincoln was not yet ready to set firm policy, but Butler's policy was "approved," and Fortress Monroe continued to be a haven for escaping slaves.

Nevertheless, federal authorities—including new officials appointed by Lincoln—continued to enforce the Fugitive Slave Act in the District of Columbia, and some generals returned slaves to their "rightful" owners. With no national policy to guide him, General John C. Frémont, the head of the U.S. Army in Missouri, announced that his troops would emancipate any slave belonging to a Confederate supporter. This announcement infuriated Lincoln because he believed that he—and not one of his generals—should decide an issue as weighty as emancipation.

Lincoln pressed for compensated emancipation in which the government would pay to free slaves in the areas loyal to the Union. Slaveholders in Kentucky, however, had no interest in giving up their slaves with or without payment, and the idea went nowhere. Lincoln also pursued the possibility of **colonization** in which freed slaves could leave the United States for Central America or Africa. No nation showed much interest in the project, and freed slaves showed even less interest. Lincoln continued to be more interested in keeping Kentucky loyal to the Union than in the fate of any slaves. A Northern reporter noted, "In all attempts to soothe southern wrath, the negro is thrown in as the offering."

Well into 1862, there was little cause for optimism for those who wanted the war to end slavery. Former slave and abolitionist leader Frederick Douglass wrote of his disappointment: "In dealing with the

In the summer of 1862, a group of former slaves, now officially contraband of war, waited for their next assignment. Before long, many such former slaves would be fighting as full-fledged soldiers in the Union army.

causes of our present troubles, we find in quarter high and low, the most painful evidences of dishonesty." For Douglass, the problem was obvious: "We have attempted to maintain our Union in utter defiance of the moral chemistry of the universe. . . . We have sought to bind the chains of slavery on the limbs of the black man, without thinking that at last we should find the other end of that hateful chain about our own necks." Regardless, in 1862, most of Northern white public opinion was not ready to agree with Douglass.

As the Union army marched deeper into the Confederacy, however, commanders realized that slaves could be of great value to them. Slaves knew the country, they knew hidden roadways, and they knew what white Southerners were thinking. George E. Stephens, one of the few black newspaper reporters accompanying Union troops, wrote that "when the Union soldier meets the negro in the enemy's country, he knows him as a friend." For many Union soldiers, meeting slaves firsthand began to change their minds. Future president James A. Garfield, commanding an Ohio unit in Tennessee, said that he found "the rank and file of the army steadily and surely becoming imbued with sympathy for the slaves and hatred for slavery."

With or without authorization, some blacks began to fight in the Union army. In Indian Territory (Oklahoma), blacks who lived with Creeks and Seminoles joined them in attacking other tribal members who had signed a treaty with the Confederates. Union officers in Kansas and on the coast of South Carolina began to recruit black troops. Secretary of War Edward M. Stanton approved the move, though he asked his officers to keep it quiet because it was "so much in advance of public opinion." But the government needed more soldiers, and many blacks wanted to fight—if the fighting was for their freedom.

Issuing the Emancipation Proclamation

President Lincoln also began to change his mind, or at least to change what he said in public. Lincoln was far too wise a politician to reveal all of his thinking. He had long said that although he thought slavery a terrible evil, the Constitution protected slavery where it already existed, and his only goal was stopping its spread into new territories. In 1861 and early 1862, his priority was securing the loyalty of Kentucky and other border states, which meant protecting slavery there. He understood that many Northerners feared free blacks almost as much as they disliked slavery. Public opinion would support a fight to save the Union, but not necessarily a fight to end slavery.

But by the spring of 1862, Northern opinion was changing. Treasury Secretary Salmon Chase wrote that Lincoln's "mind is not finally decided" but that he thought the president was moving to the belief that emancipation was becoming a "necessity." In 1862, Lincoln was not alone. Many Northern whites had come to believe that the slaveholding South was waging war against the United States because it wanted to defend the institution of slavery. Abolitionists were getting an audience where they had previously been shunned. Blacks were willing to fight in the Union army when many whites were not. And many slaves were fleeing to the Union lines. In July 1862, the Republican-dominated Congress declared that anyone convicted of assisting the rebellion against the U.S. government was liable to seizure and sale of all property and that all rebel-owned slaves who escaped to the Union army were "forever free of their servitude." Lincoln then began discussing emancipation with his cabinet in July. Secretary of State Seward among others urged caution until a Northern victory would make talk of emancipation look less like a desperate measure.

On September 22, 1862, Lincoln told his cabinet that he had promised God that if Lee's army was forced out of Maryland where they were then trying to encircle Washington, D.C., then he would act. The Battle of Antietam enabled him to do so. Senator Sumner had told him more than a year before that the South's rebellion gave the president war powers, including the right to seize property, even the kind of private property known as slaves. The proclamation that Lincoln was planning to issue was, he said, a matter of military strategy. It was also directed at building Northern support for the war, especially black and abolitionist support. His proposed emancipation would apply only to those areas of the country that were in a state of rebellion as of January 1, 1863. Lincoln hoped that, as a result, at least some areas would vote to shift sides and support the Union, and in an ironic twist, voters in Tennessee and southern Louisiana around New Orleans—both areas where the

14.1

14.2

14.3

14.4

Emancipation Proclamation

Decree announced by President Abraham Lincoln formally issued on January 1, 1863, freeing slaves in all Confederate states still in rebellion.

Peace Democrats

Also known as Copperheads, a large faction within the Democratic Party that advocated immediate peace with the Confederacy on terms that would allow it to leave the Union.

Union army was in control—did just that, thus exempting themselves from the impact of the proclamation.

The **Emancipation Proclamation** did not free a single slave when it was first issued. It did not apply in areas loyal to the Union, including slave states, and though it technically freed all of the slaves in the Confederate areas, the government had no power as of yet in areas that were not under Union control. However, the proclamation did resolve the issue of contraband slaves, made abolishing slavery a military goal, and fundamentally changed the Civil War.

Northern Democrats immediately attacked the proclamation. While the Democratic minority in Congress supported the war effort to save the Union, they opposed any widening of the war's goals. By 1862, some in Congress known as **Peace Democrats** advocated letting the Confederacy go rather than endure further bloodshed. In the November 1862 congressional elections, Peace Democrats attacked Republicans because, they said, the Emancipation Proclamation was widening the purpose of war and therefore making it longer and bloodier. The New York Democratic platform called the Emancipation Proclamation "a proposal for the butchery of women and children, for scenes of lust and rapine, and arson and murder." For governor, New York's Democrats nominated Horatio Seymour, who said that "the people of the South should be allowed to withdraw themselves from the government." Seymour won. In New Jersey, Joel Parker, a "war Democrat" who supported the war effort, was highly critical of the Emancipation Proclamation. Democrats gained control of the state legislatures in Illinois and Indiana. Northern Democrats opposed to emancipation also won thirty-four more seats in the House of Representatives. Since few Southerners remained in Congress, this number was not enough to win a majority, but it expanded the influence of those who wanted to challenge the president's new war goals.

The November 1862 Democratic gains seem to have hardened the views of Lincoln and his cabinet. Just after the election, Attorney General Edward Bates, usually one of the cabinet's more cautious members, ruled that free blacks had all the rights of citizens and that the *Dred Scott* decision held "no authority" except in the specific circumstances of the case. Bates's ruling did not include voting rights; free blacks were considered like women and children, who were citizens but could not vote. Nevertheless, they were now citizens.

On January 1, 1863, Lincoln signed the Emancipation Proclamation, declaring that all slaves in areas then in rebellion—about three million of the nation's four million slaves— "are and henceforth shall be free," and that the military should "recognize and maintain" their freedom. The proclamation also said that black soldiers and sailors could be organized in the "armed service" of the United States. There was no stirring rhetoric about human rights, only a claim of "military necessity," but the Civil War was now a war to end slavery.

While Northerners debated, slaves in the South voted with their feet. Slaves came to understand that their freedom was one of the issues the war would settle. By August 1862, Confederate troops had to be diverted from fighting to ensure that slaves did not escape, and a North Carolina resident wrote that "our Negroes are beginning to show that they understand the state of affairs, and insolence and insubordination are quite common."

Black Soldiers in the Union Army

In January 1863, just after Lincoln signed the Emancipation Proclamation, the *Weekly Anglo-African* said, "A century may elapse before another opportunity shall be afforded of reclaiming and holding our withheld rights." Blacks, both slave and free, joined the military in great numbers. More than 180,000 black soldiers—one-fifth of the nation's adult black male population under age forty-five and about 10 percent of the total Union force—eventually fought for the Union.

Former slaves quickly signed up for service. In the West, Grant encouraged full inclusion of blacks in the army. In Massachusetts, Governor John Andrew, with Lincoln's support, authorized the organization of what became the Fifty-fourth and Fifty-fifth Massachusetts regiments. Civil War regiments were typically organized by states, but the Fifty-fourth and Fifty-fifth, although they were Massachusetts regiments, recruited free blacks from across the North—though with white officers. In rural Franklin Country, Pennsylvania, not far

American Voices

Susie King Taylor, "Reminiscences of My Life in Camp," 1862

Susie King Taylor (1848–1912) published her autobiography long after the Civil War, but her memories of the war were vivid. After meeting up with the Union army, she opened a school for other newly freed slaves and later taught black troops to read and write while also serving as a nurse.

I WAS born under the slave law in Georgia, in 1848, and was brought up by my grandmother in Savannah. There were three of us with her, my younger sister and brother. My brother and I being the two eldest, we were sent to a friend of my grandmother, Mrs. Woodhouse, a widow, to learn to read and write. She was a free woman and lived on Bay Lane, between Habersham and Price streets, about half a mile from my house. We went every day about nine o'clock, with our books wrapped in paper to prevent the police or white persons from seeing them. We went in, one at a time, through the gate, into the yard to the L kitchen, which was the schoolroom. She had twenty-five or thirty children whom she taught, assisted by her daughter, Mary Jane. . . .

About this time I had been reading so much about the "Yankees" I was very anxious to see them. The whites would tell their colored people not to go to the Yankees, for they would harness them to carts and make them pull the carts around, in place of horses. I asked grandmother, one day, if this was true. She replied, "Certainly not!" that the white people did not want slaves to go over to the Yankees, and told them these things to frighten them. . . . I wanted to see these wonderful "Yankees" so

much, as I heard my parents say the Yankee was going to set all the slaves free. . . .

On April 1, 1862, about the time the Union soldiers were firing on Fort Pulaski, I was sent out into the country to my mother. I remember what a roar and din the guns made. They jarred the earth for miles. The fort was at last taken by them. Two days after the taking of Fort Pulaski, my uncle took his family of seven and myself to St. Catherine Island. We landed under the protection of the Union fleet, and remained there two weeks, when about thirty of us were taken aboard the gunboat P—, to be transferred to St. Simon's Island; and at last, to my unbounded joy, I saw the "Yankee."

Source: Susie King Taylor, *Reminiscences of My Life in Camp with the 33D United States Colored Troops Late 1st S.C. Volunteers* (Boston: Published by the Author, 1902), pp. 10–12.

Thinking Critically

1. **Analyzing Primary Sources**
   Based on this reading, what do you think were the most important steps the Taylor family took to deal with their historical situation in slavery and the search for freedom?

2. **Contextualization**
   What does this document tell you about the world of ideas for an enslaved African American as freedom approached? What might explain the importance attached to education? To the Union army?

---

from the Mason-Dixon Line, forty-five free black men signed up for the Fifty-fourth regiment and more joined the Fifty-fifth. Most free blacks who volunteered for service were from the lowest rungs of the economy, including Thomas Burgess, a carpenter; Joseph Christy, a woodcutter; and Hezekiah Watson and Thomas Cuff, quarrymen. The bounties paid to all soldiers for joining and the subsequent pay mattered to poor families—black or white. The opportunity to fight for freedom mattered even more to black soldiers.

In spring 1863, black soldiers in Louisiana rescued white troops who faced defeat, turning what could have been defeat into a victory. At Fort Wagner, South Carolina, the Fifty-fourth Massachusetts regiment lost half its number, including its white commander Robert Gould Shaw, after requesting the right to be first in the assault. After those encounters, many shared Secretary of War Stanton's view that these troops were "among the bravest of the brave in fighting for the Union." Their bravery convinced some, including Lincoln, that they were as deserving as any whites not only of their freedom but also of the right to vote and participate equally in the political process.

Black soldiers also demanded, and eventually got, equal treatment within the army. Officers were told that any soldier, whatever his rank, who mistreated freedmen would be dismissed. The Militia Act of 1862 set the pay of black soldiers at the level of military laborers on the assumption that their work would be behind the lines. As their role changed, black soldiers demanded equal pay. Soldiers in the Massachusetts Fifty-fourth and Fifty-fifth regiments refused to accept any pay until it was raised to that of white soldiers. In June 1864, Congress provided equal pay and enlistment bounties for blacks and whites. In the army, blacks also had equal rights in military courts and rights to testify in trials, something they could not do as civilians in most of the country. Finally, during the last months of the war, blacks were promoted to the officer ranks.

Library of Congress [LC-B817- 7861], Selected Civil War photographs, 1861-1865, Prints and Photographs Division

Even before, and especially after, the Emancipation Proclamation formalized their place in the Union army, thousands of African Americans joined the army to fight for the Union cause and for freedom.

The presence of black troops in the Union army enraged many in the Confederacy. In May 1863, the South refused to include black troops in prisoner of war exchanges since they had declared all such troops to be runaway slaves who should be returned to slavery. In response, and despite pressure, Lincoln suspended the exchange of all prisoners until early 1865 when the Confederacy agreed to resume exchanges. Black prisoners of war were treated more harshly than white prisoners. In April 1864, when the Union garrison at Fort Pillow, Tennessee, surrendered to Confederate general Nathan B. Forest, he ordered the massacre of black soldiers. Blacks who fought knew what danger they faced, and they fought anyway.

14.2 Quick Review

How did the fighting at the beginning of the Civil War change people's attitudes about the war in the North and the South?

The Home Front—Shortages, Opposition, Riots, and Battles

14.3 Explain how the war's death toll and civilian shortages affected life—in both the North and the South—during the war.

After the initial euphoria wore off, and as the reports of casualties began to circulate, support for the war dropped in both the North and the South. Even those supporting the war had second thoughts. It was not only the terrible toll from the battlefields, though nearly every family was touched by those losses, but also the war's effects on the home front, which had not been expected when it began.

Inflation and Bread Riots in the South

The war's heaviest toll was in the South. The Confederate government never succeeded in placing its financial house in order. Southern politicians had long objected to federal tariffs and other taxes. It was hard now that independence was claimed to turn to these taxes. Although there were modest tax increases, the Confederate government was always short of money. To finance the war, the Confederates issued war bonds. It was fair, many argued, for future generations to pay the cost of the war. But buying war bonds that paid 8 percent per year in interest when inflation was running at 12 percent per month was not a good investment. And even rich Southerners often did not have much cash to invest. Southern wealth was invested in land and slaves, and neither could be easily converted to cash, especially in wartime. So the Confederate government sought to solve its financial problems by simply printing more money—$20 million in May 1861, $100 million in August. Creating more currency, however, caused terrible inflation that undermined the sale of war bonds and drove the price of goods out of sight. In 1862, Southern workers saw their wages increase by about 55 percent while the cost of living increased by 300 percent. The price of salt, essential to preserving meat, rose from $2 a bag before the war to $60 by the fall of 1862. In addition, the disruption of southern transportation, especially after the loss of the rail terminals in Memphis in June 1862, meant that though one area might have ample supplies of food, other areas were literally starving.

Managing the home front in the South fell primarily to women. During the war, three out of four white men of military age—ultimately defined by the Confederate government as ages seventeen to fifty—served in the army, and one out of five of this age range was killed in the war. Margaret Junkin Preston of Lexington, Virginia, described a world in which there were "no men left." In New Bern, North Carolina, women wrote to the governor to say that of 250 whites remaining in their town, only 20 were male, and of these, 11 were old and 3 about to join the army. And in Carrollton, Alabama, a woman wrote to her governor in 1862 to say that the latest call for soldiers "almost literally depopulates the country of men." For white women, this situation meant taking on new roles, including managing slaves. In 1863, Lizzie Neblett of Texas wrote to her husband that she was "doing my best," as a manager and overseer, but by 1863, she realized that the news of the Emancipation Proclamation spreading in the slave quarter had changed everything: "I don't think we have one who will stay with us." Letters to distant husbands reflected how terribly their wives missed them and how these long separations were changing women's role in a society that had prided itself on male dominance and female fragility. As the *Montgomery Daily Advertiser* wrote in July 1864, "The surface of society, like a great ocean, is upheaved, and all the relations of life are disturbed and out of joint."

In spring 1863, food shortages led to bread riots across the South from Richmond, Virginia, to Mobile, Alabama. Women, often wives whose husbands were off fighting and who were trying desperately to sustain themselves and their children, attacked shops and warehouses.

By March 1863, the Army of Northern Virginia was subsisting on half rations, but the women of Richmond had far less. In April, a mob of over one thousand women shouting "Bread, Bread" and "Our children are starving," began looting shops in Richmond—first for bread and then for clothing. When President Davis threatened to shoot rioters, they disbursed, but the anger did not subside. The government tried to distribute food and to stop hoarding in warehouses. Nevertheless, as the war continued, it created streams of refugees, inflation, and starvation across the South. As many as 50,000 civilians died in the South during the war, in addition to the 260,000 Confederate war dead.

Bread riots by women in Richmond reflected the hardship of civilian life, especially in the South where food and supplies were in short supply throughout the war.

Taxes, Mourning, and Resistance in the North

Life was easier in the North. Most of the fighting took place on Southern soil, and the Northern economy was more stable (see Figure14-1). The North also

14.1

14.2

14.3

14.4

Figure 14-1 Comparison of Union and Confederate Resources.

At the start of the Civil War, the Union had significantly more industrial workers, factories, and miles of railroad tracks than the states of the Confederacy, as these three graphs show. All of these factors gave the Union a significant advantage in essential things such as the manufacture of war material and troop movements in a long war that was spread over most of the territory of the United States.

SOURCE: Inter-University Consortium for Political and Social Research, http://www.icpsr.umich.edu/icpsrweb/ICPSR/stud ies/2896?archive=ICPSR&q=historial+economic+data+united+states; Railroads and the Making of Modern America Digital History Project, University of Nebraska-Lincoln, http://railroads.unl.edu/shared/resources/1861_Railroad.kml.

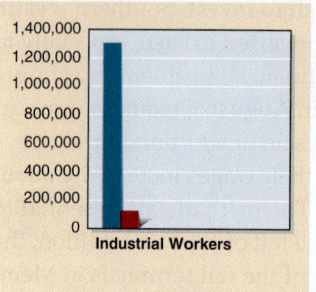
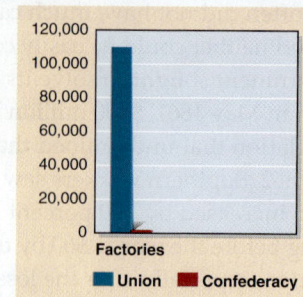
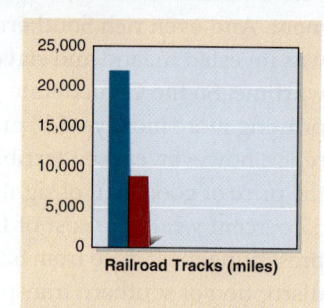

had an established Treasury Department and tax system when the war began, though revenue that had been sufficient for the 1850s was not even close to meeting the needs of a war economy. The financier Jay Cooke, one of the richest and most reviled bankers of his day, advised the Treasury Department and created new federal bonds in amounts that allowed not only banks but also individuals to buy war bonds. Cooke made a significant profit on these transactions, but the bonds kept the government solvent.

Congress also created the **Internal Revenue Service** and began a federal income tax in August 1861. Most people were exempt from the tax since income under $800 per year was not taxed, and only a minority made more than that. Finally, the federal government began issuing federal notes that were secured not by gold or silver but simply by the government's promise to redeem them. Congress not only authorized such banknotes, which came to be known as "**greenbacks**" for their green ink, but also declared that they were legal tender,

Internal Revenue Service

An agency created by Congress during the Civil War to collect federal taxes in support of the war effort.

greenbacks

Paper currency printed on order of Congress based on the federal government's promise to pay rather than backed by actual gold or silver as security.

In the decades leading up to the Civil War, the North became increasingly industrialized with many factories, as shown in the image on the left, while the South remained agrarian, as in the illustration on the right. The result was not only different economies and forms of wealth but also different images of what constituted the good society.

which meant that no one could refuse them as payment for goods or debts. The result was the creation of a solid monetary system that outlasted the war.

Although there was little fighting in the North, families saw sons march off to war and often received the terrible news that they were never coming home. Death on the scale of the Civil War had never been known before—and has not been known since—in the United States. After major battles, newspapers and telegraph offices posted casualty lists. Close comrades or hospital nurses caring for those who died wrote letters to their families, and the awful news changed life for those waiting at home.

In many parts of the North, as in the South, communities were virtually depopulated of military-aged men during the war, and women took on roles that they had never before considered. Although the prewar North had less rigidly defined gender roles than the South, changes were significant for many.

Many Northerners never supported the war effort, and their numbers increased after the Emancipation Proclamation. By 1863, as the death toll rose and the prospects of defeating the Confederacy dimmed, the peace faction within the Northern Democratic Party grew rapidly, though the party always included not only Peace Democrats but also War Democrats who supported the war to save the Union if not the Emancipation Proclamation. Peace Democrats came to be known as Copperheads, after Republicans had coined the term, comparing antiwar Democrats to venomous snakes. But by 1863, Peace Democrats proudly took up the term and continued to call for peace while hoping to make more gains in the state elections of 1863.

By 1863, Ohio congressman Clement L. Vallandigham had emerged as the leader of the Peace Democrats. For Vallandigham, the result of the war was "defeat, debt, taxation, sepulchers." Vallandigham strongly disapproved of the Emancipation Proclamation, declaring that the government should "look only to the welfare, peace, and safety of the white race." His words touched a nerve in Northern public opinion but did not win over a majority. In a May 1863 speech, he said that "King Lincoln" had widened the war from one to save the Union to one to free the slaves and must be stopped. General Ambrose Burnside, the Union military commander in Ohio, had issued an order that "declaring sympathy for the enemy" was against the law. Vallandigham was arrested and convicted. After briefly being jailed, he was exiled to the Confederacy. He met with Confederate officials in Richmond, and then made his way to Canada where, from exile, he ran as a Peace Democrat for governor of Ohio in November 1863. Although he lost the election, Vallandigham did win 40 percent of the votes.

New York City was a center of opposition to the war. Its large Irish Catholic population had little interest in fighting for the rights of African Americans. More free blacks, they thought, meant more competitors on the streets and docks of New York, and they did not like it after Lincoln issued the Emancipation Proclamation, New York's Catholic archbishop John Hughes wrote that "we Catholics . . . have not the slightest idea of carrying on a war that costs so much blood and treasure just to gratify a clique of Abolitionists."

While Northern support for the abolition of slavery was growing as the war progressed, especially among troops in the army, Northern opinion was divided, and many still had little interest in freeing slaves. As word of the Emancipation Proclamation spread in 1862, antiblack riots broke out in several cities, including Cincinnati where a strike by Irish dockworkers was defeated with the use of black strikebreakers. In Brooklyn, a mob attacked a tobacco factory where blacks were working.

As opposition grew in the North to the war itself, especially expanding the war goals to include emancipation, voluntary enlistment in the army declined. In July 1863, the government began to enforce a military draft, and the antiblack, anti-abolitionist, antiwar fervor broke into violence. In New York City on July 13, mobs attacked the draft offices and then turned on black neighborhoods, Republican newspapers, and government offices. Blacks were beaten, lynched, and shot. Before it was over, 105 people, most of them black, were killed. The **New York Draft Riot** was the worst riot in American history up to that time. Only the arrival of federal troops on July 15, fresh from the Battle of Gettysburg, ended the violence.

New York Draft Riot

A mostly Irish-immigrant protest against conscription in New York City that escalated into class and racial warfare.

Draft Riots in New York, 'The mob lynching a negro in Clarkson Street', 1863 (litho), American School, (19th century)/Private Collection/Peter Newark American Pictures/The Bridgeman Art Library

Those involved in the New York Draft Riot of July 1863 attacked Union draft officials, Republican newspapers and supporters, and, most of all, African Americans.

Warfare in the North and West

Although the Civil War was fought primarily in the South, battles took place in distant areas of the nation. A victory at Glorieta Pass near Santa Fe kept New Mexico in Union hands. In Missouri, bands loyal to each side fought battles throughout the war that spilled over into neighboring states and often were fueled by earlier disputes. William Clarke Quantrill, who had been among the Missouri "border ruffians" in the 1850s, led attacks on Union troops and sympathizers in Missouri, and in 1863, Quantrill led a band of 450 Southern sympathizers in a raid on Lawrence, Kansas. In retaliation for events in "Bleeding Kansas," Quantrill ordered, "Kill every male and burn every house." The band followed orders, killing 183 men and boys and burning 185 buildings in Lawrence, eluding capture by Union troops. Quantrill was eventually killed by Union soldiers, but many of his followers, including Jesse and Frank James, became famous outlaws and continued to terrorize parts of the West long after the war was over. Confederate agents also tried to arrange attacks on the Union from Canada and planned an uprising in Chicago during the Democratic convention of 1864, but nothing came of that effort.

Confederate and Union leaders both sought allies in Indian Territory. Cherokee, Creeks, and Seminoles were all divided between some who thought the Confederacy would offer better terms than the United States had done, and others who sided with the United States. Even without Confederate influence, some Northern tribes were angry at the U.S. government over the loss of supplies that had been diverted to the war effort and over Lincoln's withdrawal of troops that were protecting the tribes from expanding white settlements, as promised in various treaties. In Minnesota in August 1862, Santee Sioux under Little Crow killed hundreds of white settlers and U.S. troops but were soon defeated. Little Crow along with thirty-seven other Santee leaders were executed in the largest public hanging in U.S. history. Many from the tribe moved to Canada. In early 1863, the Shoshoni under Chief Bear Hunter, angry at the growing presence of white settlers and migrants in the tribe's region, attacked white settlements in the Utah and Idaho Territories. Union troops retaliated, massacring most of the Shoshoni warriors along with women and children in an attack on January 29, 1863. As Indian–white relationships degenerated during the war, Union troops were diverted from the war with the Confederacy to fight Indians. Indians suffered no matter which side they took, and most whites looked the other way.

> **14.3** Quick Review
>
> How did popular opposition to the war (especially where violent) and economic upheaval threaten the war effort in the North and in the South?

From Gettysburg to Appomattox and Beyond

14.4   **Analyze the strategies and costs of fighting a long and terrible war while looking at the resulting end of slavery in a unified nation.**

As both its proponents and opponents understood, the Emancipation Proclamation widened the purpose of the Civil War. Military tactics also changed in 1863. Early in the war, generals hoped for a short and limited war. McClellan was far from the only general, in the North or the South, who tried to avoid large losses of fighting troops. By the time the war entered its third year, however, military and civilian leaders on both sides had concluded that only a much more sustained offensive would end the war.

Lincoln relieved several cautious generals—McClellan, Hooker, and Meade—before he promoted Grant to overall command. Davis, on the other hand, promoted Lee to be the top military commander early in the war and kept him. In Grant and Lee, each president had selected a general who was willing to fight a large-scale offensive war and absorb large troop losses to win.

Gettysburg and the War in Pennsylvania and Virginia

In spring of 1863, Hooker, while he was still in command, marched Union troops into Virginia, and the two armies fought for seven days at Chancellorsville. When Stonewall Jackson led his troops around the end of the Union lines, Hooker lost his nerve and ordered a retreat. Chancellorsville was a major Confederate victory, though it came at the high cost of ten thousand Confederate dead and wounded and fourteen thousand Union losses. In the battle, Jackson was accidentally shot by his own troops and died a week later. Lincoln relieved Hooker of command and appointed General George Meade to replace Hooker. Meanwhile, Lee convinced Davis that the time had come to try again to invade the North, cut Washington, D.C., off from the rest of the country, and end the war.

June 1863 was the high point of Confederate confidence and Confederate advances. As Lee led the South's largest army through rural Pennsylvania, many in the North—not just the unfortunate inhabitants of the towns through which the army marched—grew fearful. If the Confederate army could control the Pennsylvania countryside, they could attack Philadelphia or Washington as a well-fed, well-organized army of conquest. The North could not continue the war if its capital and major cities were under rebel control.

Long before any battles took place, Pennsylvania residents knew one was coming. While people living in many parts of the South had already experienced two years of war, such fears were new north of the Mason-Dixon line. Philip Schaff, a theologian and historian teaching at Mercersburg Seminary in Pennsylvania, remembered that trying times did not bring out the best in frightened and confused people. They turned on their neighbors because of pro- or antiwar politics or over squabbles about what to hide and where to hide it.

When the rebel army did arrive, Mercersburg was luckier than some towns, at least for its white citizens. General Lee ordered that "no private property shall be injured or destroyed." Schaff described the first Confederate officer he met as "intelligent and courteous, but full of hatred for the Yankees." Not all the Confederates who followed were as polite.

Mercersburg had a large free black population, and they suffered far worse than whites. Schaff said that some of the troops went "on a regular slave-hunt, which presented the worst spectacle I ever saw in this war." When white households hid black friends, the invading troops "proclaimed, first, that they would burn down every house which harbored a fugitive slave." And they considered all blacks to be fugitive slaves. Schaff was terrified that his servant Eliza and her son would be found. They escaped, but other blacks in the town were caught and sold into slavery. For blacks and whites, southern Pennsylvania in 1863 was every bit as much a war zone as Virginia or the Mississippi River Valley had been in 1862.

Lincoln and Meade ordered the Army of the Potomac to stop Lee's advance at all cost. The Northern and Southern armies found each other near the town of Gettysburg, Pennsylvania. On July 1, Confederate forces drove Union troops out of the town and onto Cemetery Hill. The next morning, Lee ordered a major attack, but the Union army held its ground. After another major charge directly at the heart of the Union lines on July 3—known as Pickett's Charge for the officer commanding the lead unit—it became clear to Lee that, despite terrible losses, the Union forces, now reinforced, could not be dislodged. Of the fourteen thousand soldiers that Pickett led in the assault, only half returned. Confederate general Longstreet spoke of the Battle of Gettysburg as "hopeless slaughter . . . one of the saddest [days] of my life." In the three days at Gettysburg, fifty-one thousand soldiers were killed or wounded, twenty-three thousand from the North and twenty-eight thousand from the South. On July 4, Lee began a painful retreat back to Virginia. The Confederate army would never again be a major presence in the North. Lincoln, however, was furious that Meade, like McClellan, did not pursue the retreating Confederates.

While news was arriving in Washington that the Confederate forces had been turned back, word also came of a second Northern victory. Unable to defeat the Confederate garrison at Vicksburg in 1862, Grant surrounded the city and starved it. After holding on for a year, on July 4, 1863, the Confederate forces at Vicksburg finally surrendered. Watching the Union army march into Vicksburg, a local resident wrote, "What a contrast [these] stalwart, well-fed men . . . [were to] . . . the worn men in gray, who were being blindly dashed against this embodiment of modern power." The entire Mississippi River was now under Union control. The Confederacy had been cut in half. Lincoln made Grant general-in-chief of all Union armies. But it would be another hard year before there was another Northern victory like Gettysburg or Vicksburg and two years before the war ended.

In the days after the Battle of Gettysburg, bodies littered the battlefield. Photographs brought the high cost of war home to people, in the North and in the South.

The Terrible Cost of War

In early 1864, Grant took direct command in the East and marched into Virginia to attack Lee's army. He quickly stalled. In early May 1864 at the Battle of the Wilderness, Southern forces mounted a furious attack with high casualties. Neither side won the Battle of the Wilderness, but unlike his predecessors, Grant pursued the Confederate forces after the battle. At the end of May, Union forces took control of the crossroads town of Cold Harbor, Virginia, but Confederate forces attacked, and Grant ordered a counterattack. The armies fought along a line from Cold Harbor to the Chickahominy River. In this case, even Grant thought the cost too high. Wounded soldiers could not escape fires that roared through the thick undergrowth, and the suffering was terrible. He wrote in his *Memoirs* that this attack was the only one he wished he had never ordered. The Union lost 13,000 troops to the Confederate 2,500. In spite of the terrible losses, Grant still did not retreat.

In June 1864, Grant attacked Petersburg, then the second-largest city in Virginia, and settled down for a siege. Grant telegraphed Lincoln, "I propose to fight it out on this line if it takes all summer." It was what Lincoln wanted from a general. But while Grant was not retreating, he was not making much progress either. Some newspapers began to call Grant a "butcher." Others just wondered if the war would ever end.

At least three factors caused the Civil War's high death toll. Lee and Grant had shifted tactics from a limited war to a war of attrition. Each army meant to destroy the other, killing and wounding as many soldiers as possible. After 1863, there were no more limited engagements. Weapons were also deadlier than anything used in previous wars. Finally, medicine was still in its infancy. The wounded often died from infections that a few years later a new generation knew how to treat. Given all three factors, grieving became part of life, for troops and for families at home.

Thinking Historically

Abraham Lincoln, Gettysburg Address, 1863

After the victory at Gettysburg, which was accompanied by a terrible loss of life, the United States created a national cemetery on the site of the battle. In November 1863, a moving dedication ceremony was held. Edward Everett of Massachusetts was the main speaker, but President Lincoln was invited to give closing remarks. He used those short remarks to give one of the most memorable speeches of American history, insisting that the cause of freedom knew no bounds, asserting that compromises with slavery were a diversion from the ideals of the Declaration of Independence, and calling all Americans to "be dedicated here to the unfinished work which they who fought here have thus far so nobly advanced . . . that this nation, under God, shall have a new birth of freedom." Lincoln said:

> Four score and seven years ago our fathers brought forth on this continent, a new nation, conceived in Liberty, and dedicated to the proposition that all men are created equal.
>
> Now we are engaged in a great civil war, testing whether that nation, or any nation so conceived and so dedicated, can long endure. We are met on a great battle-field of that war. We have come to dedicate a portion of that field, as a final resting place for those who here gave their lives that that nation might live. It is altogether fitting and proper that we should do this.
>
> But, in a larger sense, we can not dedicate—we can not consecrate—we can not hallow—this ground. The brave men, living and dead, who struggled here, have consecrated it, far

above our poor power to add or detract. The world will little note, nor long remember what we say here, but it can never forget what they did here. It is for us the living, rather, to be dedicated here to the unfinished work which they who fought here have thus far so nobly advanced. It is rather for us to be here dedicated to the great task remaining before us—that from these honored dead we take increased devotion to that cause for which they gave the last full measure of devotion—that we here highly resolve that these dead shall not have died in vain—that this nation, under God, shall have a new birth of freedom—and that government of the people, by the people, for the people, shall not perish from the earth.

Source: *Lincoln Memorial* https://www.nps.gov

Thinking Critically

1. **Argument Development**
   Some historians say that the Gettysburg Address was Lincoln's effort to affirm that the Civil War was a war to forever end slavery. What would you quote from the speech to defend or critique that view?

2. **Continuity and Change over Time**
   How might the Gettysburg Address reflect—or not reflect— changes in Lincoln's thinking about the purpose of the Civil War from 1860 to 1863?

Before the Civil War, armies fought with muskets, which took time to load and were not that accurate. Most military authorities in prior wars agreed that the best way to attack was in a close-order formation in which a well-trained army marched forward shooting, reloading, and shooting again. If both sides had muskets, the inaccuracy and short range of the weapons reduced the danger to any one soldier. That strategy was what had been taught at West Point where most senior officers of both the North and the South had been trained.

But the close-order formation was a virtual death sentence to troops facing an army with rifles. The new rifles, developed in France and by the American James H. Burton at the federal armory at Harper's Ferry in the 1850s, increased the distance that a soldier could shoot fourfold, and the spin a rifle gave to a bullet meant that it did a lot more damage to the human body. By 1863, Union factories developed repeating rifles that made the firepower of these weapons much faster and more deadly. The accuracy of rifles also meant that opponents could identify officers and shoot them, a reason why so many generals were killed in the war and why generals, like Grant, began wearing privates' uniforms. The South never matched the North in weapons production, and many of its new weapons were either captured or came from blockade runners. The South's slow production of rifles was one reason it suffered more casualties than the North.

Artillery also became a key defensive weapon in the Civil War. New cannons that fired grapeshot and canister, rather than old-fashioned cannon balls, were like giant shotguns. Defending armies in the Civil War could shoot down row after row of attackers.

A Union cavalry officer described the results of these new weapons in combat. In July 1862, the morning after Confederate army units attacked Union placements at Malvern Hill, Virginia, he said, "Our eyes saw an appalling spectacle upon the slopes down to the woodlands half a mile away. Over five thousand dead and wounded men were on the ground . . . enough were alive and moving to give the field a singular crawling effect." That result is what the new weapons of war did to people.

Medicine, Nursing, and a New Role for Women

Many of those wounded in the Civil War died because of a lack of effective medical treatment. Indeed, more soldiers died of diseases during the war than died in combat. It was just after the war that European researchers Louis Pasteur and Joseph Lister developed modern bacteriology. No Civil War doctor, in the North or the South, knew that microbes in contaminated water or on hands or unsterilized instruments caused infection, or that mosquitoes could be as dangerous to troops as enemy bullets. Antiseptics did not exist. Medical education was primitive. No one knew that something as simple as having a doctor wash his hands might stop the spread of infection.

Military camps, where large numbers of men lived in close and often unsanitary quarters, were breeding grounds for disease. Many soldiers thought that it was better to avoid a physician than get close to one. Soldiers from both the North and the South agreed with the Alabama soldier who wrote that "I believe the Doctors kill more than they cour [cure]" and with the Massachusetts officer who said that the regimental surgeon was "a jackass."

To fill gaps in medical care, women began to nurse the wounded and the sick. Before the war, nursing had been almost exclusively men's work. But now the men were fighting, and the women were determined to aid the cause for which sons, husbands, and lovers were risking their lives. In the North, the U.S. Sanitary Commission became a powerful voluntary women's organization that was able to brush aside the army Medical Bureau and take on everything from raising money for medical supplies to providing nurses in field hospitals.

Sanitary Commission

Created by women in 1861 to improve the medical services and treatment for sick and wounded Union soldiers during the course of the war.

Elizabeth Blackwell, the first American woman M.D., began organizing the **Sanitary Commission** in 1861 and with widespread support, most of all from the troops whom its nurses aided, it flourished despite hostility from male army physicians. The reformer and social worker Dorothea Dix was named "Superintendent of Female Nurses." By the end of the war, Dix had organized three thousand Northern women volunteers to serve as army nurses in addition to others who were paid directly by the Sanitary Commission.

American Voices

Cornelia Hancock, "Letters of Cornelia Hancock," July 7, 1863

A young woman, Cornelia Hancock, from a Quaker family in New Jersey, was originally rejected for service by the Union army's Superintendent of Female Nurses, Dorothea Dix. On her own she made her way to the field hospital set up immediately after the Battle of Gettysburg and was quickly put to work.

Dear Cousin

I am very tired tonight; have been on the field all day—went to the 3rd Division 2nd Army Corps. I suppose there are about five hundred wounded belonging to it. . . . There are no words in the English language to express the sufferings I witnessed today. The men lie on the ground; their clothes have been cut off them to dress their wounds; they are half naked, have nothing but hardtack to eat only as Sanitary Commissions, Christian Associations, and so forth give them. I was the first woman who reached the 2nd Corps after the three days' fight at Gettysburg. I was in the Corps all day, not another woman within a half mile. . . . To give you some idea of the extent and numbers of the sounds, four surgeons, none of whom were idle fifteen minutes of time, were busy all day amputating legs and arms. I gave to every man that had a leg or arm off a gill of wine, to every wounded in the Third Division, one glass of lemonade, some bread and preserves and tobacco.

I feel very thankful that this was a successful battle; the spirit of the men is so high that many of the poor fellows said today, "What is an arm or leg to whipping Lee out of Penn." I would get on first rate if they would not ask me to write to their wives; *that* I cannot do without crying, which is not pleasant to either party. I do not mind the sight of blood, have seen limbs taken off and was not sick at all.

It is a very beautiful, rolling country here; under favorable circumstances I should think healthy, but now for five miles around, there is an awful smell of putrefaction. Women are needed here very badly, anyone who is willing to go to field hospitals.

Cornelia

Source: Henrietta Stratton Jaquette, editor, *South after Gettysburg, Letters of Cornelia Hancock, 1863–1868* (New York: Crowell, 1956), pp. 16–19; reprinted in Robert D. Marcus, David Burner, Anthony Marcus, *America Firsthand: Readings from Settlement to Reconstruction*, Sixth Edition, Volume One (Boston: Bedford/St. Martin's, 2004), p. 288.

Thinking Critically

1. **Analyzing Primary Sources**
   How does Hancock make the hospital come alive for those who are reading her letter? Who is her audience and how does her choice of audience make you trust (or distrust) her report?

2. **Contextualization**
   What assumptions about women of the Civil War era is Hancock challenging? What assumptions might she be reinforcing?

Still other women, most notably Clara Barton, who later helped create the American Red Cross, became free-agent nurses, helping wherever they could. Mary Ann Bickerdyke began serving as a nurse at Cairo, Illinois, and followed Grant's and Sherman's armies across the South. Mother Bickerdyke, as the troops called her, was the only woman Sherman authorized to serve in his advanced base hospitals.

Women in the South took up similar duties, often despite greater hostility. Southern culture, even more than Northern, treated middle-class white women as in need of constant protection. Moving into a hospital as a nurse was hardly protected work, and it brought women into close contact with male bodies, something previously thought improper. But the sick were there, and the women were determined to help. The *Confederate Baptist* offered religious sanction for this new role for women, saying that "they are most valuable auxiliaries." In spite of concerns about "delicacy," "modesty," and "refinement," women went to work as nurses in the South.

Sara Agnes Pryor, who had lived in comfort before the war, volunteered to help in Virginia hospitals. When she saw a nurse kneeling to hold the stump of an amputated arm she fainted and thought she was wholly "unfit for the work." But Pryor overcame her "fine-lady faintness" and became a serious professional. Mary Rutledge Fogg was from one of the South's grand families in Nashville, and she used her status to pressure Jefferson Davis to allow her to start military hospitals in Nashville, Memphis, and Knoxville after seeing "fifty brave soldiers" die "for the want of proper nurses." Phoebe Yates Levy Pember, a forty-year-old widow, was named matron of the Confederate hospital in Richmond where she and her sisters provided for the hundreds of wounded soldiers who streamed into the Confederate capital.

Women nurses, from both the North and the South, looked to their hero Florence Nightingale, the English woman who had virtually invented modern nursing while serving British troops in the 1853–1856 Crimean War. And, like Nightingale, the nurses of the Civil War

14.1

14.2

14.3

14.4

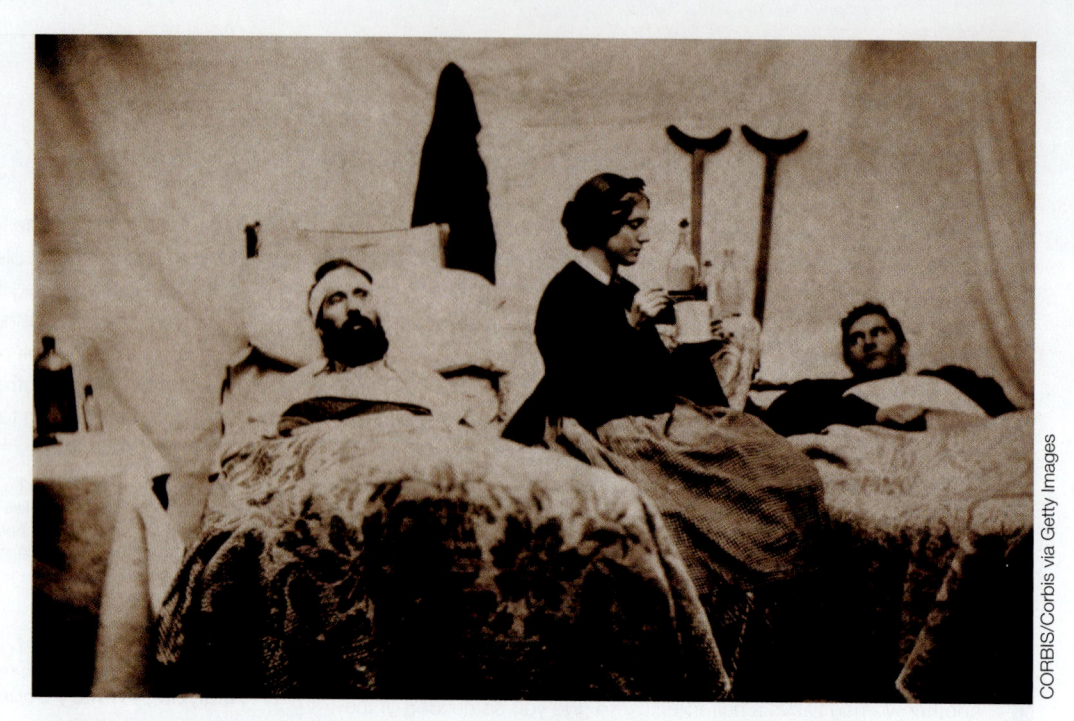

CORBIS/Corbis via Getty Images

Ann Bell, a young nurse with the U.S. Sanitary Commission, treats wounded Union soldiers.

sought to bring healing to wounded soldiers as well as comfort to the dying and those who were recovering.

Presidential Politics and Sherman's March to the Sea

While women like Pryor and Barton tried to comfort the wounded, soldiers fought, and Grant held his line in Virginia, it was not clear whether Lincoln could hold his office. Continuing losses, lack of progress at Petersburg, and hostility to emancipation all combined to strengthen the chances of the Copperhead antiwar Democrats in the 1864 presidential election. None were more aware of this situation than the leaders of the Confederacy. Lee knew he could not hold Petersburg forever, but he was confident that all he needed to do was hold the city until the November elections. If Grant made no progress, and casualties remained high, Lee and Davis thought that the Copperhead Democrats would win the election and make peace.

While the Democrats grew stronger, many Republicans were losing heart by 1864. Congressman Martin F. Conway, a Republican from Kansas who had once criticized Lincoln for pursuing the war too slowly, now urged the president, "For god's sake try and arrange [peace] with the South. . . . The war-spirit is gone." When in August 1864 the Democrats nominated General McClellan, whom Lincoln had fired for being too cautious, Lincoln expected to be a one-term president. His only hope, he wrote, was "to save the Union between the election and the inauguration" that would take place in March 1865. Then, the picture on the battlefield changed dramatically (see Map14-2).

When Grant had come east to fight in Virginia, he left his closest subordinate, William T. Sherman, in charge of the army in the west. Sherman began a march across the heart of the Confederacy. Just as the Mississippi River campaign had cut the Confederacy in half from north to south, Sherman aimed to cut it in half from west to east. Slowly, avoiding major confrontations and keeping a careful eye on his supply trains, Sherman led his army, moving from Tennessee across Mississippi, Alabama, and into Georgia. Sherman saw little value or glory in winning battles. He said that glory in war "is all moonshine; even success the most brilliant is over dead and mangled bodies, with the anguish and lamentation of distant families." Sherman just kept maneuvering and kept marching, fighting when necessary.

Confederate general John Bell Hood tried to stop Sherman before he reached Atlanta, an important railroad center. In August 1864, Sherman changed course, and the Confederate

Map 14-2 Major Civil War Battles, 1863–1865.

While armies fought in Pennsylvania, Maryland, and Virginia all through 1863, 1864, and 1865, a Union force led by William T. Sherman marched through the Confederate states from Tennessee to Georgia and the Carolinas.

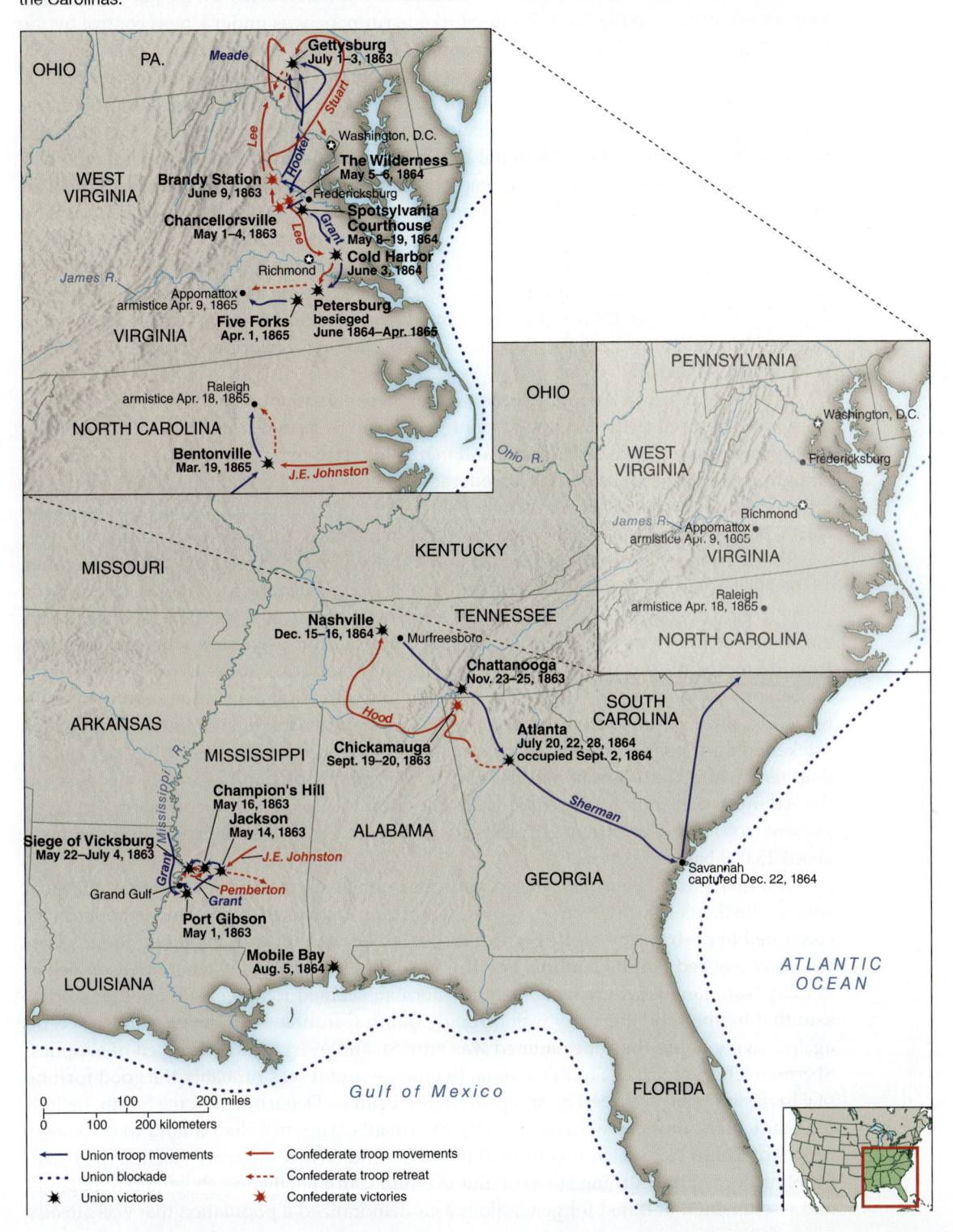

general thought Sherman was retreating, but Sherman won the next battle on August 30. The Confederates then evacuated Atlanta and burned most of the city. On September 1, Sherman led his troops into Atlanta. Mary Boykin Chesnut wrote in her diary, "Since Atlanta I have felt as if all were dead within me, forever. We are going to be wiped off the earth."

As Sherman was taking Atlanta, Admiral Farragut led a daring raid on Mobile Bay, Alabama. Confederate forts guarded the harbor and well-placed mines (known then as

14.1

14.2

14.3

14.4

torpedoes) blocked the entrance. When the lead ship in Farragut's fleet was sunk by an exploding mine, the fleet stopped. Farragut, in one of the war's immortal phrases ordered, "Damn the torpedoes! Full speed ahead." Farragut's fleet won control of Mobile's harbor. While Mobile, which was more inland, remained in Confederate hands, the port, which had been an essential base for Confederate blockade runners, was under Union control by the end of August 1864, adding one more link in the Union chain encircling the Confederacy.

Sherman's taking of Atlanta and Farragut's victory at Mobile Bay were important military victories, but they were also political victories for Lincoln and psychological victories for the North. Lincoln grew optimistic. Secretary of State Seward said, "Sherman and Farragut have knocked the bottom out of the" Democrats. Frederick Douglass, who had wanted a stronger abolitionist at the head of the 1864 Republican ticket, now said that "all hesitation ought to cease" regarding support for the president. Lincoln insisted that if he was reelected, the government must be based on "liberty and equality . . . an open field and a fair chance . . . in the race of life." Even the Democratic nominee McClellan shifted his tone, insisting that negotiations with the South be "on the basis of the Union," angering Copperhead/Peace Democrats who wanted peace on any terms. In November, Lincoln defeated McClellan by 2,220,846 popular votes to 1,809,445, ensuring Lincoln 212 electoral votes to McClellan's 21.

After the capture of Atlanta, no one was sure what Sherman would do next. His supply lines were stretched to the limit. In response, Sherman proposed to cut his army loose from supply lines entirely, live off the land, and march his sixty-two thousand toughened troops straight through the heart of the Confederacy. Lincoln and Grant agreed. There would be little armed resistance, Sherman argued, since the Confederate army was fighting in the North, not protecting the Confederate heartland, which they presumed was safe.

Sherman believed that "[w]ar is cruelty and you cannot refine it." On November 15, he started his "march to the sea," destroying every farm, factory, and railroad in his path. Troops destroyed all that the army could not eat or use. In Milledgeville, Georgia, then the state capital, Sherman's troops met Union prisoners who had escaped from the notorious Southern prison camp at Andersonville. Some Union prisoners at Andersonville had spent years with only the barest rations, and their uniforms had turned to shreds. Many died there. The sight of these emaciated soldiers wearing rags "sickened and infuriated" the Northern soldiers. Along the way, escaping slaves and Southern white Unionists joined the march. Sherman captured Savannah, Georgia, on the Atlantic coast in late December. His telegram to President Lincoln said, "I beg to present you, as a Christmas gift, the city of Savannah, with 150 heavy guns and . . . about 25,000 bales of cotton."

In January 1865, Sherman started north through Georgia and the Carolinas. His goal was to attack Lee's army from the south while Grant attacked from the north. Sherman continued to destroy any of the South's resources for waging war, including food. When the army reached South Carolina, one Union soldier said, "Here is where treason began and, by God, here is where it shall end!" Sherman seemed to agree, and another soldier said that by the time the army was through, South Carolina "will never want to secede again." Every house they encountered was burned, and every village stripped of supplies. Sherman left the coast of South Carolina to others—and it was probably the good fortune of Charleston to be occupied by troops from the Union's Department of the South, including many black units, who saved the city. Sherman's army marched inland to the state's capital of Columbia, which was burned to the ground. When the army reached the North Carolina border, the burning stopped. But in South Carolina, the march left a trail of anger and resentment that lasted for generations as it demoralized a population that was already losing faith in the war.

The Road to Appomattox and Peace

Before Sherman could finish his march through North Carolina and into Virginia, other events began turning in Grant's favor. As news of Lincoln's November reelection, the capture of Savannah, and the destruction in South Carolina began to sink in, many in the South

The first Union troops to arrive in Richmond on April 4, 1865, looked on a city in ruins.

began to lose hope. In early 1865, Lee even began recruiting black soldiers with the promise of freedom for them, though not the end of slavery for others. By March 1865, Lee knew his army could not stay at Petersburg.

The retreat of the remaining Army of Northern Virginia out of Petersburg left Richmond open to attack. On April 2, while Jefferson Davis sat in Sunday morning services in Richmond, a messenger gave him a telegram. Many in the congregation thought they knew what it meant when Davis slipped out. All Sunday afternoon, the leaders of the Confederate government moved out of Richmond, taking what records, gold, and materials they could and burning the rest. By evening, mobs had replaced the government. The next morning, the Union army marched into Richmond, not to burn the city but to put out the fires that the retreating Confederates had started. The day after that, President Lincoln, with only a small guard of sailors, came to Richmond, sat at Davis's old desk, and greeted former slaves who were shouting "Glory to God!" and "Bless the Lord!" When one former slave knelt at Lincoln's feet the president said, "Don't kneel to me. That is not right."

Davis fled south from Richmond to Danville where he announced that "nothing is now needed to render our triumph certain, but . . . our own unquenchable resolve." But resolve was melting. Lee's troops were weak from lack of food. He tried one last attack on April 9, and when that failed, sent word to Grant that he was ready to surrender. The two generals—Grant and Lee—met in Wilmer McLean's living room in Appomattox, Virginia, that afternoon. Grant remembered the encounter. "We soon fell into a conversation about old army times. . . . Our conversation grew so pleasant that I almost forgot the object of our meeting." But when Lee turned back to the matter at hand, Grant wrote out the terms of surrender. He allowed the

14.1

14.2

14.3

14.4

Table 14-1 Major Battles and Culmination of the Civil War

Battle	Significance
Fort Sumter Charleston, South Carolina April 12–13, 1861	The firing on the federal garrison by Confederate forces was the opening of the war.
Bull Run or First Manassas Fairfax and Prince William Counties, Virginia July 21, 1861	Union forces marching south from Washington, D.C., were met by Confederates at Bull Run Creek. Many Northerners expected a short skirmish and then a march to Richmond, but the Confederates turned the tide, and Union soldiers retreated back to Washington, D.C.
New Orleans, Louisiana April 23–28, 1862	U.S. Navy ships under David G. Farragut took New Orleans, the largest city in the South, which remained in Union hands for the duration of the war.
Second Battle of Bull Run or Second Manassas August 28–30, 1862	The battle was a major Confederate victory and ended Northern hopes for an easy attack on the Confederate capital.
Antietam or Sharpsburg Washington County, Maryland September 16–18, 1862	Lee marched into Maryland but was stopped in a fierce battle at Antietam. Lincoln was furious that McClellan did not pursue Lee on his retreat into Virginia.
Fredericksburg, Virginia December 13, 1862	Union general Ambrose Burnside led an attack on the town as a first step toward attacking the Confederate capital of Richmond but was defeated by a well-defended force commanded by Robert E. Lee. The U.S. Army lost thirteen thousand troops, mostly in ill-conceived direct attacks, while the Confederates lost five thousand. Northern morale sank.
Chancellorsville Spotsylvania County, Virginia April 30–May 6, 1863	A Union army led by General Joseph Hooker was defeated by a Confederate force, leading to a major incursion north of the Mason-Dixon line that threatened Washington, D.C.
Gettysburg, Pennsylvania July 1–3, 1863	The bloodiest battle of the war led to Lee's withdrawal back to Virginia, ending the threat to Washington, D.C.
Vicksburg, Mississippi May 18–July 4, 1863	Union troops commanded by Ulysses S. Grant finally took control of the Mississippi River from St. Louis to New Orleans and thus cut the Confederacy in half while securing easy access into the interior of the Confederacy.
Wilderness Spotsylvania County, Virginia May 5–7, 1864	Lincoln placed Grant in charge of all U.S. forces, and Grant led a bloody drive into Virginia. The first battle took place in deep woods (hence the Wilderness), and Grant—unlike previous Union generals—simply kept going.
Cold Harbor, Virginia May 31–June 12, 1864	Grant attacked the Confederate army and took horrible casualties. In his *Memoirs*, Grant wrote that this was the one attack he wished he had never ordered.
Atlanta, Georgia September 2, 1864	William T. Sherman led sixty-two thousand troops into Georgia, defeating Confederate forces and taking Atlanta. Sherman's army then began its "march to the sea," taking Savannah on December 21 before running north and attacking Confederate forces in South and North Carolina.
Mobile Bay, Alabama August 2–23, 1864	U.S. admiral David G. Farragut effectively ended the blockade running out of Mobile, which had deprived the South of badly needed supplies.
Appomattox Court House, Virginia April 9, 1865	Lee surrendered to Grant.

Confederate soldiers to keep their horses and mules with them to help in planting crops for the year ahead, and Lee noted that "this would have a happy effect."

Grant arranged for Lee's starving army to receive military rations. At 4:30 p.m., Grant telegraphed Secretary of War Stanton that "General Lee surrendered the Army of Northern Virginia this afternoon." The long and terrible war was essentially over (see Table 14-1). Years later, Grant remembered of a sense of sadness "at the downfall of a foe who had fought so long and valiantly, and had suffered so much for a cause, though that cause was, I believe, one of the worst for which a people ever fought."

Lee's surrender did not quite end the war. Jefferson Davis fled south, hoping to regroup his government, perhaps in Texas, until he was captured in Georgia on May 10. He was held in custody for two years at Fortress Monroe before being released on bail. Davis was indicted for treason, but the charges were never pressed, although he was barred from ever holding a federal office again. During the next two decades, he tried various business ventures and wrote his defense of the cause he had led. Isolated Confederate units carried on the fight in remote areas, especially Texas, until May. But after the April 9 surrender at Appomattox, almost everyone knew that the war was over. Washington, D.C., was draped with flags, people fired salutes, embraced, and sang. Soldiers on both sides found their weary way home. Those in the North were welcomed with grand parades; most of those in the South simply made it home.

Lincoln's Legacy

On January 31, 1865, even before Lee's surrender, the House of Representatives voted 119 to 56 to add a Thirteenth Amendment to the Constitution:

> Neither slavery nor involuntary servitude, except as a punishment for a crime whereof the party shall have been duly convicted, shall exist within the United States, or any place subject to their jurisdiction.

The floor of the House and visitors watching in the gallery erupted into cheers and applause. Many of those in the gallery were African Americans; people who had not been even admitted to the House gallery until 1864. The Senate and the states quickly followed, and the amendment became part of the Constitution on December 18, 1865. The war that began over slavery ended with its abolition in every part of the United States.

On March 4, 1865, Abraham Lincoln was inaugurated for a second term as president. Though the Confederacy still held Richmond and Lee had not yet surrendered, Lincoln, like many in the North, thought the end was finally in sight. He wanted to begin the healing process. In one of the shortest inaugural addresses on record, he reminded Americans that, at the start of the war, "[n]either party expected for the war, the magnitude, or the duration, which it has already attained. Neither anticipated that the *cause* of the conflict might cease with, or even before, the conflict itself should cease." And he reminded people that both sides "read the same Bible, and pray to the same God," though he added that it "may seem strange that any men should dare to ask a just God's assistance in wringing their bread from the sweat of other men's faces." But most of all he asked that we "judge not that we be not judged" and prayed that "this mighty scourge of war may speedily pass away" and that Americans be reunited "with malice toward none." Though he seemed to be amazingly free of malice after four terrible years of war, Lincoln was clear, as he had not been four years before, that with the end of the war, slavery was ending everywhere in the United States, and he would not make peace until that was won. Within a little over a month the Union had, indeed, won the war, and before the year was out, slavery ended.

After visiting Richmond, Virginia, on April 4 and 5 and receiving the news of Lee's surrender on April 9, President Lincoln began to grapple with what would come next. Among the most contentious issues were those related to defining the rights of newly freed slaves: Did they have the right to vote? Did they have other political rights? Did they have a right to some of the land they had worked for so long?

There were equally contentious arguments about the rights of the former Confederate states. Lincoln also called the question of whether the Confederate states had left the Union a "pernicious abstraction." He did not want to debate whether the states had really left the Union. The issue for him, he said, was much simpler: "We all agree that the seceded States, so called, are out of their proper practical relation with the Union; and that the sole object of the government, civil and military, in regard to those States is to again get them into that proper practical relation." In fact, the issue was not so simple. If the states had actually left the Union, then Congress could impose conditions on their readmission such as granting blacks the right to vote. If they had never left, then it was more difficult to impose such conditions.

No one really knew the answers or how to get answers. As Lincoln said in a speech on April 11, "Unlike a case of a war between independent nations, there is no authorized organ for us to treat with. No one man has authority to give up the rebellion for any other man. We simply must begin with, and mold from, disorganized and discordant elements."

As Lincoln began to give more attention to the postwar era in April 1865, some thought he had decided that guaranteeing former slaves the right to vote should be a key element in the integration of the Confederate states back into the Union, but he did not announce his policy. On the morning of April 14, he met with the cabinet to discuss what he was now calling "reconstruction." He directed Secretary of War Stanton to develop military districts and temporary military governments across the South to avoid anarchy and supervise a return to civilian rule. Those at the meeting remembered that Lincoln said the agenda had shifted

14.1

14.2

14.3

14.4

from the war to a new set of peacetime issues on which "we must soon begin to act." But Lincoln would not be the one doing the acting.

That same evening, the president and his wife attended a play at Ford's Theater. He was shot by John Wilkes Booth, who had become convinced that Lincoln was, indeed, going to give former slaves the right to vote. Early the next morning, Lincoln died. As April 1865 ended, the country was at peace but deeply in mourning, and no one knew what the future held.

14.4 Quick Review

How was the violence of the Civil War different from other wars in which the United States was involved? How was the outcome of the war similar to or different from what Lincoln and the U.S. government said it wanted when the war began?

Conclusion

When the Civil War began in 1861, people in both the North and the South hoped for and expected a short and limited war, but it was not to be. Four years of terrible violence would follow.

When the first calls for troops were issued, enthusiastic young men signed up for service in the Union and Confederate armies. But attitudes changed quickly. In the first significant battle of the war, at Bull Run Creek near Manassas, Virginia, in July 1861, tourists from Washington, D.C., accompanied Union forces to watch what they were sure would be an easy victory. But Confederate forces turned the tide and the Union army and their visitors were quickly driven back to the relative safety of the nation's capital.

In spite of early successes by the U.S. Navy in blockading many Southern ports and in opening up portions of the Mississippi River to Union forces, President Lincoln soon became convinced that the nation was in for a long and bloody war and began looking for a general who had the tenacity to lead troops to victory. But through 1861, 1862, and 1863, in spite of bloody battles—a second one at Bull Run in August 1862 followed by the bloodiest day of the war at Antietam, Maryland, that September; further battles at Fredericksburg, Virginia, in December; then Chancellorsville, Virginia, in April 1863; and Gettysburg, Pennsylvania, that July—the war seemed to have no conclusive end in sight. Many, in both the North and the South, began to lose hope.

In the North, Peace Democrats, soon called Copperheads, began to campaign for an end to the war and for letting the South go its own way. The New York Draft Riots of July 1863 illustrated the way many white immigrants in that city had little interest in fighting a war and, indeed, blamed local blacks—whom they attacked across the city—for causing their troubles. At the same time, in the South, starvation spread, and Southern cities, including the Confederate capital of Richmond, Virginia, were wracked with bread riots.

While others debated, however, black and white abolitionists knew exactly what they wanted from the war—an end to slavery everywhere in the United States. From the earliest days of the war, abolitionists had urged Lincoln to use his war powers to free all slaves, and some, like the former slave Frederick Douglass, insisted that the only terms on which the war could be won and the nation united was the complete abolition of the institution of slavery that had led to war in the first place. Finally, in the fall of 1862, after more than a year of caution, President Lincoln decided to act and on January 1, 1863, signed the Emancipation Proclamation, freeing all slaves in the rebellious states and calling on former slaves to enlist in the Union army. Former slaves who had been flocking to Union posts now joined the army and attained equality with white soldiers as well as a reputation for valor that impressed many.

Still the war itself continued. Women, from both the North and the South, became nurses—a previously all-male profession—to help the wounded and suffering soldiers. In 1863, after the Union army's victory at Vicksburg on the Mississippi River, Lincoln selected Ulysses S. Grant as the leader who had the determination to do what had to be done to win the war. Grant began attacks on Confederate forces in Virginia in an effort to both defeat the main body of the Confederate army and take the Confederate capital of Richmond. At the same time, William T. Sherman began a march across the South, from the Mississippi River to Atlanta, Georgia, and then a "march to the sea" that captured the port city of Savannah, Georgia, in December 1864. As 1865 began, Sherman's army turned north, marching through the Carolinas to attack Virginia from the south while Grant's army had new victories in Virginia. Finally on April 9, 1865, the main Confederate army commanded by Robert E. Lee surrendered to Grant. The Civil War was over. Days later, President Lincoln, who was just beginning to turn his attention to what might come next, was assassinated. The rebuilding of the country would be in other hands.

Chapter Review

The Civil War became a "war of attrition." How did that style of waging war contribute to the Union victory? How did debates about slavery play out?

Chapter 14 Summary and Review

From Fort Sumter to Antietam, 1861–1862

14.1 **Explain how the early battles of the war shaped future events.**

Summary

Once Fort Sumter had been fired on, large numbers of volunteers joined the army on both sides. The first significant battle of the war, the Battle of Manassas or Bull Run, was a clear-cut Confederate victory. After Bull Run, Lincoln prepared for a much larger and longer war than most had originally envisioned. The South pinned its hopes on a defensive strategy and the intervention of the British on the Southern side. The North was slow to bring its advantages in men and resources to bear on the fight. Union naval forces blockaded the South and took control of major river systems, undermining its economy and limiting its ability to move troops and supplies. The bloody battles of 1862, most notably Shiloh and Antietam, did not provide either side with a decisive breakthrough.

Review Question

1. Comparison
   Compare and contrast the strategies of the North and the South in the first two years of the war. How did each side's strategy reflect its strengths and weaknesses?

The Road to Emancipation

14.2 **Analyze how the war influenced attitudes toward slavery in both white and black communities, leading to the Emancipation Proclamation and to black soldiers in the Union army.**

Summary

During his presidential campaign and throughout the early years of the war, Lincoln insisted that he had no intent to interfere with slavery where it already existed. The realities of war, including large numbers of escaped slaves who sought the protection of the Union forces, complicated the issue. As the war dragged on, Lincoln began to change his mind. At the same time, antislavery sentiment in the North was strong. By September 1862, Lincoln was ready to move forward on emancipation. On January 1, 1863, the Emancipation Proclamation went into effect. The Emancipation Proclamation freed slaves in Confederate territories and allowed blacks to serve in the Northern military. More than 180,000 black soldiers eventually fought for the Union, most of them recently emancipated slaves but some longtime free blacks.

Review Question

2. Continuity and Change over Time
   How would you explain Lincoln's initial reluctance to link the war to emancipation? How do you explain Lincoln's evolving views in 1862?

The Home Front—Shortages, Opposition, Riots, and Battles

14.3 **Explain how the war's death toll and civilian shortages affected life— in both the North and the South— during the war.**

Summary

After the initial euphoria, public support for the war dropped in both the North and the South. The war's heaviest toll was in the South. The Confederate government found it difficult to raise the revenue necessary to pay for the war and attempted to solve its problems simply by printing more money, which brought on terrible inflation. In the spring of 1863, serious food shortages led to bread riots in cities and towns across the South. Managing home-front difficulties in the South fell primarily to women as they were forced to take on many new tasks, including the management of slaves. Life was not as chaotic for most civilians in the North, especially since almost all of the actual fighting took place on Southern soil. In addition, the Northern economy was much more stable than the South's, and the federal government had more and better options for raising money. Many in the North opposed the war effort, and their numbers increased after the Emancipation Proclamation. Anger over the war exploded in the New York City Draft Riots of 1863.

Review Questions

3. Comparison
   Compare and contrast perspectives on the Emancipation Proclamation in the North. How do you explain such deep division?

4. Causation
   How did Southern women contribute to the war effort? How did the war change the role of women in Southern society?

From Gettysburg to Appomattox and Beyond

14.4 Analyze the strategies and costs of fighting a long and terrible war while looking at the resulting end of slavery in a unified nation.

Summary

In 1863, military tactics underwent profound changes as the Union abandoned hopes of a short and limited war. The war became one of attrition. The Confederates enjoyed some success in the beginning of 1863, but the tide turned in July with Union victories at Gettysburg and Vicksburg. Despite heavy losses, the Union army, now under Grant's command, moved relentlessly south in 1864. The shift in strategy to a war of attrition, new military technology, and ineffective medical care all contributed to the horrific death tolls in 1863 and 1864. Women on both sides played a major role in delivering medical care to the troops. The capture of Atlanta and Mobile by the Union secured Lincoln's reelection in 1864. Sherman's "march to the sea" was meant to devastate the South's economy and undermine Southern morale. By early 1865, the South was all but defenseless, and Lee surrendered to Grant in April. Earlier in 1865, Congress had voted to add the Thirteenth Amendment to the Constitution, ending slavery, and it was later ratified. At the same time, Lincoln began to grapple with the difficult issues that arose over what he called "reconstruction." Just as he began to design a plan, Lincoln was assassinated, leaving the country with an even more uncertain future.

Review Questions

5. Argument Development

Defend or refute the following statement: "Grant's appointment as commander of Union forces meant the eventual defeat of the Confederacy was all but certain." What evidence can you produce to support your position?

6. Causation

Which factor contributed the most to the extraordinarily high death toll during the Civil War?

1. Preparing to Write: Develop Your Thesis

Long Essay Question—Evaluate the extent to which there were similarities in home-front opposition to the war for both the Union and Confederate governments from 1861 to 1865.

To write a strong essay, you will find it essential to plan before you begin writing. Start by taking an inventory of evidence you have on this double-sided subject. There was strong opposition in both the North and South, but why do you think Southern backlash was especially intense? Next, write a thesis and clear, direct topic sentences for each part of your argument's body.

2. Preparing to Write: Organize Your Evidence

Long Essay Question—Evaluate the extent to which the Emancipation Proclamation shaped the Union war effort from 1863 to 1865.

The Emancipation Proclamation is recognized by many historians as the most pivotal event of the war, and events of these proportions always have multiple effects. Begin by organizing your evidence to discuss these consequential outcomes. We know the cause of the war—union—has now been amended with the Emancipation Proclamation. Lincoln's Gettysburg Address can be a good primary source to discuss this change. Also, African American troops have a decisive impact on the battlefield. To add depth to your essay, remember that not all effects were positive for the Union. One section of your argument's body can be on the dissension and discord that the proclamation caused for Lincoln and the North. Once you have identified your evidence, you can write your thesis.

Chapter 15
Reconstruction
1865–1877

North Wind Picture Archives/Alamy Stock Photo

This popular picture, drawn by A. H. Ward for *Harper's Weekly* in November 1867, illustrated the prime meaning of Reconstruction for many African Americans, whether former slaves or former soldiers in the Union army. The end of slavery brought—for the moment—the right to vote.

Chapter Objective

Demonstrate an understanding of the development and decline of Reconstruction.

 ## Learning Objectives

Federal Reconstruction Policy

15.1 Explain the political development of federal Reconstruction policy—presidential and then congressional.

The Impact of Reconstruction

15.2 Explain the impact of Reconstruction on African American life in the South and the ways African Americans shaped Reconstruction policy.

Terror, Apathy, and the Creation of the Segregated South

15.3 Analyze the reasons Reconstruction ended and the impact of so-called Redemption.

Two months after Robert E. Lee's surrender, on June 19, 1865, a detachment of Union soldiers under the command of Major General Gordon Granger landed at Galveston, Texas. General Granger read a proclamation:

> The people of Texas are informed that in accordance with a Proclamation from the executive of the United States, all slaves are free. This involves an absolute equality of rights and rights of property between former masters and slaves, and the connection heretofore existing between them becomes that between employer and free laborer.

Slavery had ended in the United States.

Granger's order created jubilation, shock, and uncertainty across Texas. For those who had been enslaved, it was a day of freedom. They celebrated as others had done. Houston H. Holloway, a slave sold three times before his twentieth birthday, recalled the day emancipation came to Georgia: "I felt like a bird out of a cage. … The week passed off in a blaze of glory." Six weeks later, Holloway and his wife celebrated the birth of a new baby and "received my free born son into the world." For some former slaves, nothing mattered more than getting away from their old plantations. They moved short distances to be with friends and family or great distances to Louisiana, Indian Territory, or the North. For others, the news that they could now be wage-earning employees on the same plantations where they had previously worked without pay was the best option available. When emancipation came, it changed every aspect of life for all people of the United States.

After January 1863, the Emancipation Proclamation made the Union army an army of liberation for slaves. Word traveled quickly in slave communities, and many did not wait for the Union army to arrive. When Joseph Davis fled the plantation that he and his brother Jefferson Davis owned at Davis Bend on the Mississippi River in 1862, slaves took over the property and began running it themselves, much to the surprise of General Grant who arrived at Davis Bend with the Union army in 1863. In Mississippi, while the war was still far away, one slave responded to a planter's greeting "Howdy, Uncle" with an angry "Call me Mister." Other slaves either refused to work unless they were paid or simply left, often in search of family members, sometimes just because, for the first time in their lives, they could.

In the aftermath of the Civil War, women and men who had been considered the property of others found that they could buy property. They could refuse to work for people who only recently had coerced their labor. They could travel without the hated passes from white masters. Sometimes they were reunited with family members from whom they had long been separated. People for whom literacy had been illegal now learned to read and write. They became teachers, started their own schools, and opened colleges and universities. Slaves and free blacks who had never dreamed of voting became voters and officeholders, members of state legislatures, and members of the U.S. Congress. They passed laws creating a system of public education and dreamed of better days ahead. The story of Reconstruction, its high hopes and its violent and tragic ending, is the focus of this chapter.

Federal Reconstruction Policy

15.1 Explain the political development of federal Reconstruction policy—presidential and then congressional.

In December 1864, Senator Charles Sumner of Massachusetts thought Lincoln had agreed that former Confederate states must grant all citizens the same right to vote as whites (which meant the right of males to vote) to be readmitted to the Union. But while Lincoln had come to believe that blacks who fought in the Union army had won the right to vote, he also believed that the Constitution gave states the right to determine who voted and he did not yet seem ready, as far as anyone knew, to interfere.

When Lincoln died in April 1865, his own party was divided on the question of the vote for African Americans and on how best to handle the readmission of the Confederate states within the nation. With the war just ending, the majority of Republicans, in and out of Congress, were still moderates. Many had begun the Civil War with the intention only

Significant Dates

1865	Lincoln dies, Andrew Johnson becomes president
	Last battles of the Civil War in Cameron County, Texas
	President Johnson announces plans for Presidential Reconstruction
	"Juneteenth" Emancipation announced in Texas
	Thirteenth Amendment ratified
	Ku Klux Klan is formed in Tennessee
1866	Civil Rights Act is passed over Johnson's veto
1867	First Congressional Reconstruction Act is passed
1868	Both houses of Congress passes articles of impeachment against president Andrew Johnson
	Andrew Johnson is acquitted by one vote in the Senate
	Fourteenth Amendment is ratified
1869	Ulysses S. Grant is inaugurated as eighteenth president of the United States
1870	Fifteenth Amendment is ratified
	First Enforcement Act passed by Congress
	U.S. Department of Justice created to enforce Reconstruction laws
1871	Ku Klux Klan Act is passed by Congress
1872	U.S. Army troops seize Louisiana statehouse, return Republican legislature
1873	Massacre at Colfax, Louisiana
	Supreme Court decision in the *Slaughterhouse Cases* limits the reach of the Fourteenth Amendment
1874	Grant orders five thousand troops to New Orleans to return Republican governor
1875	Civil Rights Act of 1875
1876	*United States v. Cruikshank*
1877	Rutherford B. Hayes is inaugurated as president
	Slow ending of Reconstruction

15.1

15.2

15.3

Radical Republicans

A shifting group of Republican congressmen, who favored abolishing slavery and advocated full rights for former slaves in the South.

Freedmen's Bureau

Agency established by Congress in March 1865 to provide social, educational, and economic services as well as advice and protection to former slaves.

to save the Union but had come to believe that the end of the war had to mean the end of slavery. They were still not committed to voting rights or the award of land for newly freed African Americans. Other Republicans who were coming to be known as **Radical Republicans**—often called in Congress simply "the radicals"—were determined that the North's victory in the Civil War meant that the country should give formerly enslaved people not only their freedom but also the right to vote and to hold office and should provide land to those who had previously worked other people's land as their slaves.

A similar kind of split existed over the proper ways to readmit states to the Union. Lincoln and many other Republicans had argued throughout the war that the Southern states had never left the United States; after all, preserving the Union had been the initial reason that the North went to war in 1861. If the Southern states had never left, there was little to do at war's end but resume their place in the nation. Others, however, especially the Radical Republicans, argued that after four years of fighting against the Union, the states of the former Confederacy were effectively out of the country and could be readmitted only after some period in which the federal government reconstructed state governments to ensure that those who led the rebellion—traitors, as the radicals always called them— would not lead the new state governments and that the full civil rights of African Americans would be ensured. Compromise was not easy.

While Lincoln pondered the question of the vote, he also proposed establishing a federal Bureau of Freedmen, Refugees and Abandoned Lands in early 1865. The **Freedmen's Bureau**, as it came to be known, would last longer and do more than Lincoln ever imagined.

Lincoln placed great faith in the new government established in Louisiana after the Union victories there. The new legislature pledged loyalty to the Union, created a public school system, and ratified the Thirteenth Amendment abolishing slavery. It had not, however, granted former slaves the right to vote. Lincoln pondered the question of whether Louisiana could be brought into proper practical relation with the Union sooner by sustaining, or by discarding, her new state government. His own answer was clear: He believed that the Louisiana government could *eventually* extend the vote and would provide a model of transition back into the Union for other Confederate states. The more radical members of Congress did not want to give Louisiana full rights as a state until it had guaranteed

American Voices

Jourdon Anderson, Letter to Colonel P. H. Anderson, 1865

After Jourdon Anderson and his wife, Mandy, were freed from slavery on a Tennessee plantation belonging to Colonel P. H. Anderson, they moved north and settled in Dayton, Ohio. A year later, Colonel Anderson wrote to them asking them to return as employees. Jourdon Anderson responded:

As to my freedom, which you say I can have, there is nothing to be gained on that score, as I got my free-papers in 1864 from the Provost-Marshall-General of the Department at Nashville. Mandy says she would be afraid to go back without some proof that you are sincerely disposed to treat us fairly and justly—and we have concluded to test your sincerity by asking you to send us our wages for the time we served you. This will make us forget and forgive old scores, and rely on your justice and friendship in the future. I served you faithfully for thirty-two years and Mandy twenty years. At $25 a month for me, and $2 a week for Mandy, our earnings would amount to $11,680. Add to this the interest for the time our wages has been kept and deduct what you paid for our clothing and three doctors visits to me and pulling a tooth for Mandy, and the balance

will show what we are in justice entitled to. … If you fail to pay us for faithful labors in the past we can have little faith in your promises in the future.

Jourdon Anderson

P.S. –Say howdy to George Carter, and thank him for taking the pistol from you when you were shooting at me.

Source: John David Smith, *Black Voices from Reconstruction, 1865–1877* (Gainesville: University Press of Florida, 1997), pp. 43–44.

Thinking Critically

1. **Analyzing Primary Sources**
   What examples can you find in the document of Jourdon Anderson's sense of humor? How do you think Colonel Anderson responded to this letter? How did the point of view of the writer and reader of the letter differ?

2. **Continuity and Change Over Time**
   What internal evidence from the letter would you use to determine an approximate date for its writing?

that blacks would be given the right to vote. They blocked counting Louisiana's electoral votes in the 1864 election and the seating of the state's new senators. They would soon do more.

The post–Civil War era is often described as including three distinct time periods. The first period is referred to as **Presidential Reconstruction** in 1865–1866, when President Johnson sought to return states to their prewar status with only the institution of slavery being abolished. The next period is known as the more radical **Congressional Reconstruction** (sometimes Radical Reconstruction), which began when Congress began to challenge Johnson in 1867 and generally continued through the end of Grant's two terms in 1877. The last period, known as "**Redemption**" (by its defenders but not by those who lost rights in the process), began with the election of Rutherford B. Hayes in November 1876 and involved the withdrawal of federal troops from the South as well as the return of white-only governments. That last period culminated in the 1890s with the virtual disenfranchisement of all blacks in the South.

Although this chronology is too simplistic, it does provide a useful framework. The reality was that many factions battled from 1865 well into the 1880s and 1890s. Johnson was challenged from his first year in office. Congressional Reconstruction had many ups and downs. Grant generally agreed with the congressional radicals. Nevertheless, in every year between 1865 and 1877, those who sought a radical Reconstruction of the South met resistance, often very effective resistance in the South, and a growing inclination of Northerners to look the other way as they grew tired of the effort. Perhaps most important, the end of Reconstruction did not come all at once. It, too, was a long slow process, culminating only in the 1890s.

Library of Congress Prints and Photographs Division [LC-USZ62-22120]

This illustration from *Harper's Weekly* shows agents of the Freedmen's Bureau trying to settle a dispute between white and black Southerners. The Freedmen's Bureau took an active role in the lives of citizens in a way that the federal government had never done before, managing disputes, organizing schools, and ensuring political rights for recently enfranchised African Americans.

The Presidential Reconstruction of Andrew Johnson, 1865–1866

When Andrew Johnson became president on April 15, 1865, he had served as vice president for only six weeks. Even so, he came to the presidency with far more experience than Lincoln had in 1861. Like Lincoln, Johnson grew up in poverty, but he had risen in Tennessee politics from a city alderman to member of the state legislature, to Congress, to two terms as governor, to the U.S. Senate. When Tennessee seceded from the Union in 1861, Johnson—apart from any other senator from a Confederate state—stayed loyal to the Union and stayed in the Senate. He had long seen himself as a spokesman for the "honest yeomen" of Tennessee, and he hated what he called the state's "pampered, bloated … slaveocracy." During the Civil War, Johnson served with distinction as military governor of Tennessee where the Union army had taken control. When the Republicans met in 1864 to nominate Lincoln for a second term, incumbent vice president Hannibal Hamlin offered little to the ticket; his home state of Maine was sure to go Republican and he had played virtually no role in the war. The choice of Johnson as Lincoln's running mate—a border state senator and governor—might add essential votes. Although two previous vice presidents had succeeded to the presidency, no one expected it to happen again.

When Johnson became president after Lincoln died, many of those known as the Radical Republicans in Congress embraced him. In 1864, Johnson had said, "Treason must be made odious, and traitors must be punished and impoverished." And he repeated similar views to members of Congress who met with him right after Lincoln's assassination. Ohio senator Benjamin F. Wade said, "By the Gods, there will be no trouble now in running the government." Another was overheard saying, "I believe, that the Almighty continued Mr. Lincoln in office as long as he was useful, and then substituted a better man to finish the work."

When Johnson announced his plans for Reconstruction on May 29, 1865, there was widespread disappointment. Johnson supported the Thirteenth Amendment, already passed by Congress and ratified by several states, and insisted that support for the amendment be a condition for the readmission of any Confederate state to the Union. But Johnson refused to go beyond that. He made it clear that he had little interest in political rights for

Presidential Reconstruction

Name given to the immediate post–Civil War era, 1865–1866, when President Andrew Johnson took the lead to return full rights to the former Confederate states.

Congressional Reconstruction

Name given to the period 1867–1870 when the Republican-dominated Congress controlled Reconstruction-era policy. Sometimes it is also known as Radical Reconstruction.

Redemption

A term used by opponents of Reconstruction for the era in which the federal government ended its involvement in Southern affairs, and Southern whites took control of state governments and ended black political rights.

15.1

15.2

15.3

former slaves. In contrast to his earlier claims, Johnson declared a full amnesty and pardon for most of those who had taken part in the rebellion as long as they were willing to pledge loyalty to the Union and support the end of slavery. The amnesty included restoration of all land taken by the Union army. Only senior Confederate officials and individuals who owned more than $20,000 in taxable property had to seek individual presidential pardons.

At first glance, the policy seemed tough on the former slaveholders of the South—perhaps tougher than Lincoln would have been—and consistent with Johnson's pledge to keep slaveholders "out in the cold." But soon, Johnson began granting more and more presidential pardons to former slaveholders. Blacks, though now free, seemed destined to be excluded from most of the rights of citizenship in the Johnson plan. If former slaveholders were to be given back their land, what land would there be for former slaves? Illinois congressman Elihu B. Washburne said, "I have grounds to fear President Johnson may hold almost unconquerable prejudices against the African race."

While Republicans in Congress were disappointed, many Southern whites were delighted at the opportunity to create a "white man's government" if they accepted the end of slavery. Under Johnson's plan, former Confederate states were considered to be readmitted as soon as they ratified the Thirteenth Amendment. (Since most Republicans continued to insist that the rebellious states had never left the Union, there was no official way or time for them to be formally readmitted.) Once recognized, these state governments, dominated by many of the same people who had been in power before the Civil War, began passing laws strictly limiting black rights, most of all, the right to vote.

Hunting, fishing, and free grazing of livestock, which whites all assumed were their rights and which some slaves had enjoyed, were now declared illegal for blacks in a series of what were known as **Black Codes**, passed by states across the South, beginning with Mississippi's code passed in November 1865. One part of the Mississippi code said:

Black Codes

Laws passed by states and municipalities denying many rights of citizenship to free blacks and to control black labor, mobility, and employment.

> All freedmen, free negroes and mulattoes in the State, over the age of eighteen, found on the second Monday in January, 1866, or thereafter, with no lawful employment or business, or found unlawful assembling themselves together, either in the day or night time, and all white persons assembling with freedmen, Free negroes or mulattoes, or unusually associating … on terms of equality … shall be deemed vagrants.

In many states, Black Codes either made it illegal for an African American to own a gun or taxed guns at high rates. New urban police forces were designed to "keep good order and discipline amongst the negro population." Police patrols not only enforced the law but also often terrorized blacks, especially those who refused to sign long-term labor contracts with former slave masters. Any former slave who ran away from a labor contract could be either arrested and returned to the plantation holding that contract or sentenced to a chain gang to pay off the fine for running away. Arrests of unemployed blacks for vagrancy or other minor infractions resulted in long prison terms at forced labor that looked very much like slavery. African Americans in Louisiana noted how similar the incarceration and labor contracts were to slavery and how similar the new police were to the old slave patrols. They also asked "why men who but a few months since were in armed rebellion against the government should now have arms put in their hands." Johnson's policies made these oppressive developments almost inevitable.

Congressional Radical Reconstruction, 1867–1869

The new Congress that was elected with Lincoln in November 1864 did not assemble until December 1865—eight months after his death. This Congress had an overwhelming Republican majority, including many who had become disillusioned with Johnson by the time they met, especially as they saw what was happening in the states that had so recently been at war with the Union. The new president, they thought, was clearly siding with the former slaveholders rather than the former slaves.

Those in Congress most unhappy with Johnson, the Radical Republicans, were led by Charles Sumner in the Senate and Thaddeus Stevens in the House. Stevens told the House, "The whole fabric of southern society *must* be changed, and never can it be done if this opportunity is lost." For Stevens, the core values of the Republican Party remained "free labor" by "free men." But with Johnson moving quickly to recognize the new state governments in the old Confederacy and those governments passing rigid Black Codes, the moment seemed to be quickly slipping away. Johnson focused on the constitutional clause giving each state the right to set up its own government and arrangements for voting. Stevens and the radicals focused on a different part of the Constitution, the clause guaranteeing each state a republican form of government.

Most of the Republicans in Congress were not as radical as Stevens or Sumner. In 1865, a majority probably still had reservations about black voting rights. Even so, nearly all were disappointed at Johnson's easy amnesty of so many former Confederate leaders and the way Southern states were coming back into the Union with their old leaders in power. Johnson's version of Reconstruction resembled the antebellum South in far too many ways. In particular, the fact that fifty-eight members of the Confederate Congress, six Confederate cabinet officers, and the vice president of the Confederacy were all elected to Congress in 1865 and 1866 symbolized the failure of Johnson's policy to bring about meaningful change. However, the Constitution also gave Congress its own specific ways of asserting its authority.

THE LAST SPEECH ON IMPEACHMENT—THADDEUS STEVENS CLOSING THE DEBATE IN THE HOUSE, MARCH 2.—[SKETCHED BY T. R. DAVIS.]

Pennsylvania congressman Thaddeus Stevens speaking to Congress. Stevens led the action of the House of Representatives that wanted Reconstruction to mean a thorough reordering of Southern society in which former slaves would receive land and guaranteed voting rights from the federal government.

Soon after convening in December 1865, Congress created a Joint Committee on Reconstruction. Moderate senator William Pitt Fessenden of Maine was appointed chair, and most of the radicals, including Stevens, were excluded. Nevertheless, Congress challenged Presidential Reconstruction by refusing to seat the congressional delegates from the former Confederate states, even though Johnson considered those states to be fully restored to the Union. (Johnson's use of "restoration" rather than "reconstruction" irked many in Congress who wanted to see at least some change rather than restoring states to the place they had held in 1860.) The Constitution made each house of Congress sole judge of the qualifications of its members, and neither house was ready to seat former Confederate leaders. Senator Ben Wade demanded that no Southern state be given a vote in Congress until African Americans had the right to vote in that state. Others called for the creation of territorial governments in the former Confederate states, which would be under the control of Congress so that both voting rights and land redistribution could be assured. But Congress itself was divided, and action beyond rejecting the delegates from the South was hard to come by. Even legislation to give blacks in the District of Columbia the right to vote—something Congress clearly had authority to do—could not make it through both houses, especially after a December 1865 referendum of white voters in the District rejected black voting rights 6,951 to 35.

Early in 1866, Illinois senator Lyman Trumbull proposed two new pieces of legislation. Unlike the more Radical Republicans, Trumbull still maintained a good working relationship with Johnson and worried about the federal government exceeding its authority. But given developments in the South, Trumbull felt Congress had the authority—even the duty—to protect the rights of newly freed African Americans under the Thirteenth Amendment, which included language giving Congress the power to pass laws to enforce the amendment.

First, Trumbull proposed extending the life of the Freedmen's Bureau. Initially planned as a transition agency, the Freedmen's Bureau had become the key federal agency distributing food to former slaves, supporting the establishment of schools, and in some cases, even helping former slaves gain their own land. Trumbull became convinced that its work would take many years and proposed extending it to 1870. He also proposed giving it new authority to ensure that blacks had all "civil rights belonging to white persons" and giving bureau agents the authority to press charges against state officials who denied those rights.

Trumbull then proposed the far-reaching Civil Rights Act of 1866 that defined all persons born in the United States (except Indians) as citizens, permanently ending the *Dred Scott* distinctions between whites and blacks. Although the bill was silent on the issue of voting, given that many of the citizens it referred to—women and children, for example—could not vote, it explicitly guaranteed rights to make contracts, bring lawsuits, and have the equal benefit of the laws without regard to race. It also authorized federal authorities to prosecute violations in federal courts, a significant provision since Southern state courts were quickly reverting to their white-dominated ways.

Both of Trumbull's bills would have appeared radical a year or two earlier, but in 1866, they were seen as moderate proposals from a moderate senator, and everyone expected smooth sailing. Then, after they passed Congress easily, President Johnson vetoed both bills. He called the Freedmen's Bureau an "immense patronage" system that exceeded the constitutional authority of the federal government, and he characterized the Civil Rights Act as an unwarranted "concentration of all legislative powers in the national Government." In his veto of the Civil Rights Act, Johnson also went out of his way to say that giving blacks citizenship rights was wrong and that "the distinction of race and color is by the bill made to operate in favor of the colored and against the white race."

The vetoes ended congressional efforts to work with the president. Trumbull attacked the president. Senator William Pitt Fessenden, another moderate, predicted that Johnson would "veto every other bill we pass." Johnson was prepared to do just that. He wanted to court Northern Democrats and Southern whites in his bid for a second term. Congress passed both pieces of legislation over Johnson's vetoes and began to use a veto-proof two-thirds majority to pass similar legislation in spite of presidential opposition. The era of presidential-led Reconstruction was fast coming to an end.

After passing Trumbull's two major bills over the president's veto in the spring of 1866, Congress proposed another amendment to the U.S. Constitution. Amendments to the Constitution proposed in Congress are not subject to a presidential veto, although three-fourths of the state legislatures need to agree to them. So in 1866, Congress set out to put the civil rights law into the Constitution itself. Agreement to do so came quickly; however, agreement on the other provisions of the amendment came much more slowly. Congress was not yet ready to give black males the same voting rights as white males, but Sumner and some other radicals would never support an amendment that did not guarantee such rights. When their opposition was combined with the Democratic minority who did not want any new rights inscribed in the Constitution, crafting the amendment became difficult and led to months of wrangling. The compromise that emerged as the Fourteenth Amendment guaranteeing rights of citizenship to former slaves and others born or naturalized in the United States was nevertheless significant.

The key provision of the Fourteenth Amendment said:

> All persons born or naturalized in the United States, and subject to the jurisdiction thereof, are citizens of the United States and of the State wherein they reside. No State shall make or enforce any law which shall abridge the privileges or immunities of citizens of the United States; nor shall any State deprive any person of life, liberty, or property, without due process of law; nor deny to any person within its jurisdiction the equal protection of the laws.

Other clauses of the Fourteenth Amendment said that any state that limited the voting rights of male inhabitants of a state would have its representation in Congress reduced, that any person who had held federal office and then participated in rebellion against the government could not again hold office, and that Confederate debts were null and void as far as the federal government was concerned.

Congress passed the amendment in June 1866 and sent it to the states for ratification. Just as Johnson had refused to recognize a state as having returned to the Union until it ratified the Thirteenth Amendment, Congress now refused to seat the members of the House or Senate elected by a state until the state had ratified the Fourteenth Amendment. The amendment was popular in the North and many in the South were anxious to return to Congress, so approval from the required three-quarters of the states came quickly and the amendment was ratified in July 1868.

When Congress reconvened in December 1866, Johnson called for immediate restoration of the "now unrepresented States" to Congress, but Congress decided that the states of the former Confederacy needed to be governed directly from Washington until "some indefinite future time." Some said that Congress was raising the bar after earlier requiring only assent to the Fourteenth Amendment, but the majority in Congress were no longer in any mood to compromise.

In January 1867, Congress quickly passed a law—over presidential veto—giving black males in the District of Columbia the right to vote. They passed the Reconstruction Act of 1867, which declared all Southern state governments—already recognized by Johnson—to be inoperative and divided the former Confederate states into five military districts, ordering the military to oversee the writing of new constitutions that would guarantee universal male suffrage (see Map 15-1). Only after these new constitutions were in place, and after a state had ratified the Fourteenth Amendment, would Congress admit its representatives to Congress.

The president protested that the Reconstruction Act was "the death-knell of civil liberty." African Americans in the South, however, embraced the opportunity to participate in the political process. In addition to registering to vote and participating in constitution writing, blacks struck for higher pay in Charleston, Savannah, Mobile, Richmond, and New Orleans. Blacks in Richmond demanded integrated horse-drawn streetcars. Across the South, they created **Union Leagues**, which became a base for political action and mutual support. The leagues offered opportunities to gain experience in the political process or, as one former slave said, "We just went there, and we talked a little, made speeches on one question and another." Former slaves became political leaders. By 1867, James H. Jones, the former "body servant" to Jefferson Davis, was a featured speaker at Republican meetings across the South.

Union Leagues

In the South, a Republican Party organization led by African Americans, which became an important organizing device after 1865.

Map 15-1 Southern Military Districts.

Having lost all faith in President Johnson's leadership, the Congress in 1867 created five military districts to govern the states of the former Confederacy until new state constitutions that guaranteed the rights, including voting rights, of African Americans were put in place.

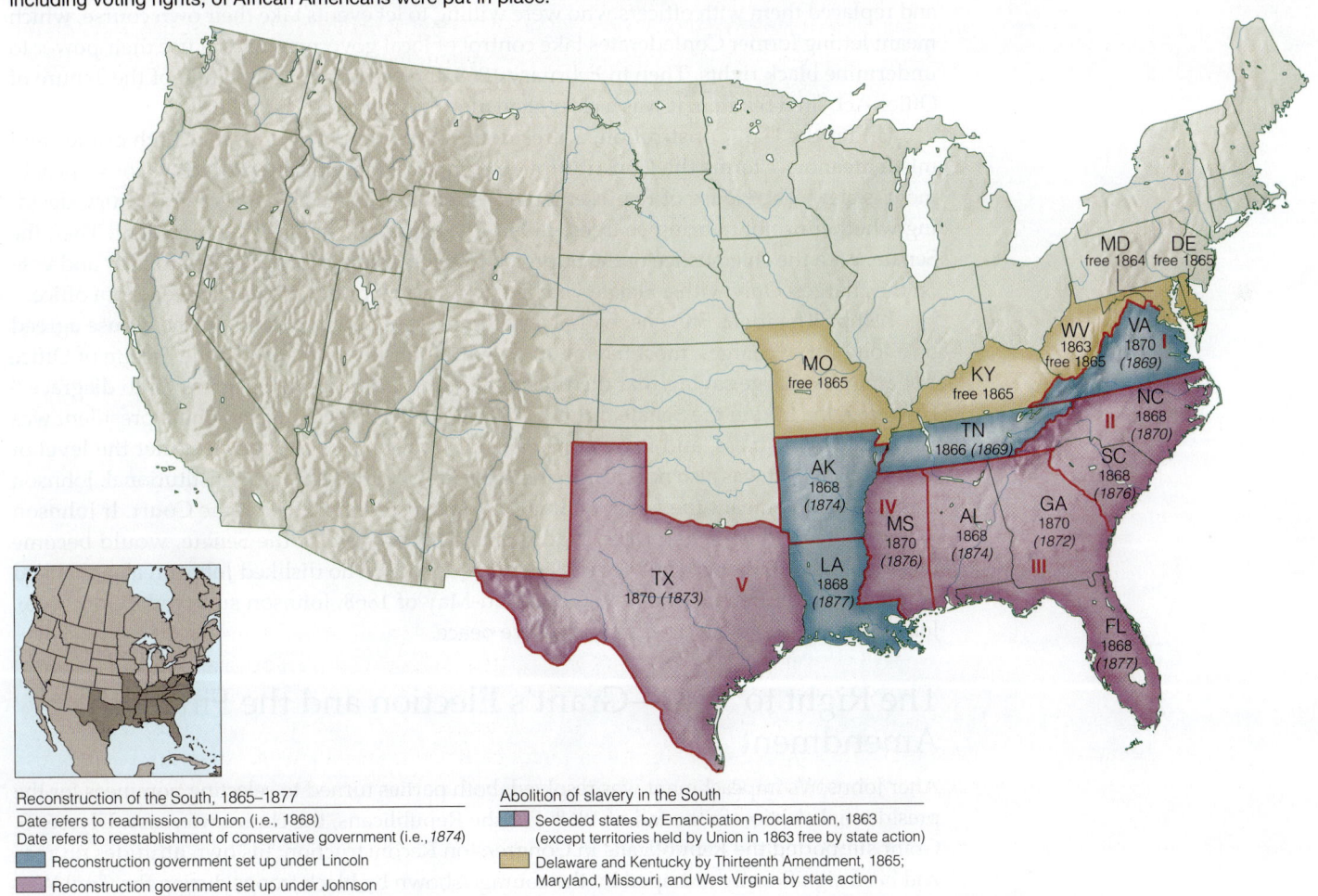

Reconstruction of the South, 1865–1877

Date refers to readmission to Union (i.e., 1868)
Date refers to reestablishment of conservative government (i.e., *1874*)

■ Reconstruction government set up under Lincoln
■ Reconstruction government set up under Johnson
□ Five military districts by Reconstruction Act, 1867

Abolition of slavery in the South

■ Seceded states by Emancipation Proclamation, 1863 (except territories held by Union in 1863 free by state action)

■ Delaware and Kentucky by Thirteenth Amendment, 1865; Maryland, Missouri, and West Virginia by state action

The Final Break—Johnson's Impeachment

By 1867, President Johnson had become virtually irrelevant to federal Reconstruction policy. Congress passed laws, the president vetoed them, and Congress passed them over the president's veto. But the Freedmen's Bureau was under the control of the president even if he vetoed the bill that kept it going. The creation of military districts in the South also gave the president significant powers as commander-in-chief, even though he had opposed creating them.

Some in Congress began to consider removing Johnson in early 1867, but the majority focused on passing laws that they hoped would keep Reconstruction moving in spite of the president. One law required all presidential orders to the military to pass through the army chief, General Grant, before going to commanders in the field. Grant was known to side with Congress, and this strategy seemed like an important safeguard. Congress also passed the Tenure of Office Act, which said that any person whose appointment required the Senate's consent, namely, members of the cabinet and ambassadors, could be replaced only when the Senate approved a successor. The goal of the act was to ensure that Secretary of War Stanton, who had been appointed by Lincoln and who took a tough stance on Reconstruction, stayed in office.

These congressional actions might have worked had Johnson been willing to play a passive role, but Johnson could be stubborn, proud, and self-focused. His loyal secretary of the navy, Gideon Welles, said, "He has no confidantes and seeks none." As a result, unlike Lincoln, Johnson was often out of touch with congressional thinking. These traits set the stage for an even more serious collision between the president and the Congress.

While Congress took charge of Reconstruction, Johnson became convinced that he had public opinion on his side and began to encourage opponents of Reconstruction, in the North and South. He also removed several of the tougher military commanders in the South and replaced them with officers who were willing to let events take their own course, which meant letting former Confederates take control of local governments and use their power to undermine black rights. Then in February 1868, the president, in violation of the Tenure of Office Act, fired Stanton. It was a clear challenge to congressional authority.

Under the U.S. Constitution, a president can be removed only for "high crimes and misdemeanors," terms the Constitution does not define. But the procedure for impeachment is clear. The House of Representatives is required to act as a sort of grand jury, deciding whether or not to bring charges, called impeachment, against the president. Then the Senate, with the chief justice of the Supreme Court presiding, acts as a jury to hear and vote on the charges. Only with a Senate vote to convict can a president be removed from office.

Led by Thaddeus Stevens, with every Republican voting positively, the House agreed on a long list of charges, most having to do with Johnson's violation of the Tenure of Office Act and one charge saying that the president had tried to bring Congress "into disgrace." However, the trial in the Senate did not go well for the radicals. Removing a president was very serious business, and it was unclear that Johnson's obstructionism met the level of a "high crime." It was also not clear that the Tenure of Office Act was constitutional. Johnson claimed that he meant the firing of Stanton to be tested in the Supreme Court. If Johnson were removed, then Senator Ben Wade, president pro tem of the Senate, would become president since there was no vice president, and many who disliked Johnson also disliked Wade. When the Senate finally voted in mid-May of 1868, Johnson survived by one vote. Johnson could serve out his term in relative peace.

The Right to Vote—Grant's Election and the Fifteenth Amendment

After Johnson's impeachment was resolved, both parties turned to selecting nominees for the presidential election in the fall of 1868. For the Republicans, the choice was easy. Ulysses S. Grant supported the Republicans in Congress on Reconstruction; his own attitudes on race had been significantly reshaped by the courage shown by black troops during the Civil War, and he was the nation's war hero. They nominated Speaker of the House Schuyler Colfax of

Indiana as his running mate. Grant ran on a cautious platform that nevertheless embraced extending voting rights to former slaves. His slogan was, "Let Us Have Peace."

Democrats were divided on issues of personality, on their opposition to Congressional Reconstruction, and on fiscal policies—whether to continue to authorize the printing of money, or "greenbacks," based on the federal promise to pay. After twenty-one ballots in which a number of candidates, including Andrew Johnson, failed to win the nomination, they chose former New York governor Horatio Seymour, who had flirted with supporting the Confederacy during the war and who had called participants in the New York Draft Riot "my friends." For vice president, they nominated a former Union general from Missouri, Francis Blair, who called for an end to Reconstruction, which he called the rule of "a semi-barbarous race of blacks."

While neither party articulated a fully developed economic policy, the lines between the parties were drawn on the issues of race. August Belmont, one of the nation's leading bankers, said that, in the 1868 election, financial matters paled in comparison with black voting rights. In November, Grant carried most of the North and the parts of the South under federal control, including North and South Carolina and Alabama. Seymour's home state of New York, along with New Jersey, Georgia, and Louisiana, favored Seymour. The state governments in Florida, Mississippi, and Texas had not yet been recognized, and those states did not vote. Grant won 53 percent of the popular vote but an overwhelming 73 percent of the electoral vote for an easy victory.

With Grant about to become president, Republicans in Congress moved quickly on voting rights. In February 1869, Congress passed the Fifteenth Amendment, which stated:

> The right of citizens of the United States to vote shall not be denied or abridged by the United States or by any State on account of race, color, or previous condition of servitude.

By February 1870, the required three-fourths of the states ratified the amendment and the right of former slaves, and other citizens, including the children of Chinese immigrants—who were citizens but had also been denied the right to vote—had been inscribed in the Constitution.

As powerful as the language of the Fifteenth Amendment is, it lacked some wording that many had wanted to include. The radicals had wanted the amendment to state that neither the right to vote nor the right to hold office could be abridged. But others feared that several Northern states, including California with its large Chinese population, might reject the amendment if the right of nonwhite people to hold office was included. Many also had wanted wording to prohibit the many tricks that some Southern governments were already using to limit the black vote, including literacy tests that could be manipulated to exclude whoever the test giver wanted excluded or tests related to property or education. Supporters of the amendment, however, worried that they would lose too much Northern

Harper's Weekly carried many illustrations of the changes happening in the South to Northern audiences. This issue of July 1868 showed the enthusiasm with which African Americans, many of whom had been slaves only a few years before, were taking to electoral politics.

support if they included such clauses. Massachusetts and Connecticut used literacy tests to limit voting by foreign-born citizens, while Pennsylvania and Rhode Island had property or tax qualifications for voting, and no one wanted to risk losing the support of those states. As a result, important safeguards were not included.

Most of all, many women, especially the most prominent leaders of the women's rights movement, were deeply angered by the Fifteenth Amendment. The amendment said that the right to vote could not be denied on the basis of race. But in 1869, every state in the Union denied the right to vote to women. Women like Susan B. Anthony, Elizabeth Cady Stanton, and Sojourner Truth had labored long and hard in support of abolition and the Union cause. They thought with the new campaign for voting rights, their rights might be included, and now they saw women's right to vote ignored. Frederick Douglass was an advocate of women's rights in addition to African American rights, but in 1869, he pre-cipitated a long and painful, though temporary, break with Anthony and Stanton over the Fifteenth Amendment. Douglass argued for one step at a time, guaranteeing black men the same rights as white men, and then guaranteeing women of all races the right to vote. Douglass said, "I hold that women, as well as men, have the right to vote, and my heart and my voice go with the movement to extend suffrage to women." These were not just words. In the decade before and after battles around the Fifteenth Amendment, Douglass actively campaigned for women's right to vote. But Douglass was willing to compromise to achieve his immediate goal.

The compromise that Douglass proposed brought a sharp rebuke from the former slave and abolitionist Sojourner Truth. In 1867, Truth gave her own passionate response to Douglass. She said that she, too, had been born a slave and rejoiced that "[t]hey have got their liberty—so much good luck to have slavery partly destroyed; not entirely. I want it root and branch destroyed." For Truth, root and branch meant the vote for all. Partial justice would not do, "and if colored men get their rights, and not colored women theirs, you see the colored men will be masters over the women, and it will be just as bad as it was before."

In spite of compromises and disappointments, many hailed the Fifteenth Amendment as completing the work of abolition. As late as 1868, free blacks could vote in only eight Northern states. In 1870, by law, black men could vote everywhere in the United States. William Lloyd Garrison celebrated "this wonderful, quite sudden transformation … from the auction-block to the ballot-box." While there was already clear evidence of the many steps—by law and by violence—that would be taken to deny most blacks the right to vote, in 1870, there was also grounds for very real optimism.

> ### 15.1 Quick Review
>
> Compare Presidential Reconstruction and Congressional Reconstruction. What are the most significant differences between the two?

The Impact of Reconstruction

15.2 Explain the impact of Reconstruction on African American life in the South and the ways African Americans shaped Reconstruction policy.

In the early years of Reconstruction, many of the South's former leaders returned to power. Only one Southern official was tried for treason and executed—Henry Wirz, commander of the infamous Andersonville prison where so many Union soldiers died. Jefferson Davis was imprisoned for two years but then was freed and retired to write his memoirs. Many other Confederate leaders received a pardon from Johnson and resumed leadership in their states. Within a year of announcing his plan to exclude wealthy political leaders of the Confederacy from the original amnesty, Johnson granted seven thousand individual pardons while doing nothing to help now free blacks gain political influence. The prewar status quo seemed to be returning in the Southern states. Then Congress took over Reconstruction, and everything changed. In state legislatures, local sheriff's offices, and school boards, former slaves, Northern abolitionists, and Southern Unionists took power under the banner of the Republican Party or local Union Leagues that were the basic Republican organizations in much of the South. A radical remaking of the South began in 1868 and continued in the 1870s.

Voting in the South

In January 1870, the Mississippi state legislature elected Hiram R. Revels to the U.S. Senate. Revels was the first African American ever elected to the Senate. The legislature that elected Revels included thirty-six blacks and seventy-three whites—hardly a black-dominated body but overwhelmingly one dominated by Republicans committed to black voting rights. He was elected, ironically, to fill Jefferson Davis's former seat, left vacant since Davis departed in 1861.

Revels was born free in Fayetteville, North Carolina, in 1827. Like many of the African American political leaders during Reconstruction, he was a minister in the African Methodist Episcopal Church, serving as a pastor in Baltimore, Maryland, when the Civil War began. Revels organized two all-black regiments and served as their chaplain. At the war's end, Revels went with his unit to Vicksburg, Mississippi, and then moved to Natchez. He was not initially a candidate for the Senate, but his lack of ambition for the post made him a perfect compromise candidate.

Senator Garrett Davis of Kentucky challenged the right of an African American to be seated in the Senate. But Revels's key defender, James Nye of Nevada, told his colleagues, "In 1861 from this hall departed two senators who were representing here the state of Mississippi; one of them who went defiantly was Jefferson Davis." For Nye, and eventually for a majority in the Senate, nothing was a more fitting symbol of the outcome of the Civil War than the seating of an African American in the place of the former president of the Confederacy. Forty-eight senators voted to seat Revels while only eight voted no.

Mississippi later sent Blanche K. Bruce to the Senate in 1874. Bruce was born a slave, but he attended Oberlin College and established himself as a planter in Mississippi in 1868. Unlike Revels, he worked his way up the political ladder, serving as the sergeant-at-arms of the Mississippi state senate, assessor and sheriff of Bolivar County, and a member of the Board of Levee Commissioners of the Mississippi River. Navigation on the Mississippi was a major concern of his during his U.S. Senate tenure, as was opposition to Chinese exclusion. Bruce was the last African American to serve in the Senate until Edward Brooke was elected from Massachusetts in 1966.

More African Americans were elected to the House. Twenty-two blacks served in Congress during Reconstruction, including thirteen who had been born slaves. Between 1871 and 1873, South Carolina had three African Americans in the House—Joseph H. Rainey, Robert B. Elliott, and Robert G. DeLarge. In the same sessions, Benjamin S. Turner represented Alabama; Josiah T. Walls, Florida; and Joseph Long, Georgia. Rainey served three terms in the House and played an important role in arguing for the first major bill for federal aid to education that was considered, although defeated, in Congress.

Often working through the Republican Party and local Union Leagues, African Americans not only won seats in Congress but also often took state and local offices where many important decisions affecting people's day-to-day lives were made. David Medlock, a former slave in Limestone County, Texas, used his extended family to gain the votes that made him a local leader and member of the state legislature in spite of the fact that he ran in a predominantly white district. Although only men—black and white—had the vote and held the offices, the fact that Reconstruction politics were local and often kin related meant that women, who often held kinship groups together,

THE FIRST COLORED SENATOR AND REPRESENTATIVES.
In the 41st and 42nd Congress of the United States.

Library of Congress Prints & Photographs Division [LC-DIG-ppmsca-17564]

Hiram Revels, the first African American senator (left), sits with six of the first blacks elected to the House of Representatives representing Alabama, Florida, South Carolina (three representatives), and Georgia.

15.1
15.2
15.3

American Voices

John Roy Lynch, The Work of Reconstruction, 1869

John Roy Lynch, born a slave, was elected as a Republican to the Mississippi legislature in 1869. He described what Reconstruction meant to those trying to create a new political system for the former Confederacy.

A state government had to be organized from top to bottom. A new judiciary had to be inaugurated. ... In addition to this, a new public school system had to be organized and established. There was not a public school building anywhere in the state except in a few of the larger towns, and they, with possibly a few exceptions, were greatly in need of repair. To erect the necessary schoolhouses and to reconstruct and repair those already in existence so as to afford educational facilities for both races was by no means an easy task. It necessitated a very large outlay of cash in the beginning which resulted in a material increase in the rate of taxation for the time being, but the constitution called for the establishment of the system and, of course, the work had to be done. It was not only done but also done creditably and as economically as circumstances and conditions at that time made possible. That system, though slightly changed, still stands as a creditable monument to the work of the first Republican state administration that was organized in the state of Mississippi under the Reconstruction Acts of the Congress. ...

A new code of laws also had to be adopted to take the place of the old one, and thus wipe out the black laws that had been passed by what was known as the Johnson legislature.

Source: John Hope Franklin, editor, *Reminiscences of an Active Life: The Autobiography of John Roy Lynch* (Chicago: University of Chicago Press, 1970).

Thinking Critically

1. **Causation**
   How did changing federal Reconstruction policy impact the work Lynch described? ?

2. **Analyzing Primary Sources**
   What light does the document shed on the historical situation faced by Republican governments during Reconstruction?

had significant influence. Often it was women who pushed the men to take the strongest political stands. As one observer remembered in the 1868 elections, if a black male did not have the courage to wear his Republican Party badge, "his wife would often take it from him and bravely wear it upon her own breast."

Legislatures in Alabama, Arkansas, Florida, Georgia, Louisiana, Mississippi, North Carolina, and Texas all had large African American minorities while, for a time in the late 1860s, South Carolina—the home to secession—actually had an African American majority in its state legislature. A Northern journalist, James S. Pike, no friend of Reconstruction, still reported from South Carolina that these black legislators, "with not more than a half dozen exceptions have been themselves slaves, and that their ancestors were slaves for generations," were making the laws of the state. It was "the spectacle of a society suddenly turned bottomside up," Pike said. Reconstruction state governments, with black and white leadership, expanded the right to vote, abolishing restrictions that had existed for black and poor white voters. In addition, newly formulated state constitutions created public school systems and internal improvements designed to bring the South into the modern world. It was a heady time, yet not an easy one.

Schools for Freedom

Northern whites who came to the South with the Union army were amazed by the thirst for literacy demonstrated by former slaves. Booker T. Washington, a well-known African American educator, remembered the immediate aftermath of emancipation: "Few people who were not right in the midst of the scenes can form any exact idea of the intense desire which the people of my race showed for education. It was a whole race trying to go to school."

John W. Alvord, who became the director of education for the Freedmen's Bureau, reported in 1866 that there were often black-initiated schools already in operation when he arrived to open schools. He wrote:

Throughout the entire South an effort is being made by the colored people to educate themselves. ... In the absence of other teaching they are determined to be self-taught; and everywhere some elementary text-book, or the fragment of one, may be seen in the hands of negroes.

Alvord was surprised by the commitment of the newly freed people to education and by their initiative in launching their own schools even before any federal or missionary teachers arrived.

Realizing that blacks saw the schoolhouse as "proof of their independence" surprised white observers. It did not surprise former slaves who had grown up in a world where literacy, for them, was a crime. As a slave child of seven or eight, Frederick Douglass had been taught the alphabet by a white woman, but the lessons did not last long. He remembered:

> Mr. Auld found out what was going on, and at once forbade Mrs. Auld to instruct me further, telling her, among other things, that it was unlawful, as well as unsafe, to teach a slave to read. …"It would forever unfit him to be a slave."

Nothing appealed more to young Douglass than being made unfit for slavery. Douglass found secret ways to continue his studies, and by the time he made his escape, Douglass had the literacy skills that would make him one of the great orators and writers of his day.

While the majority of teachers who went South to teach were white women, an African American, Charlotte Forten, began teaching in Port Royal, South Carolina, where she said, "The children are well-behaved and eager to learn. It will be a happiness to teach here." By 1870, several thousand teachers—whites and blacks, Northern immigrants, and veterans of the Confederate army—were teaching in schools for former slaves. Although a majority stayed for only a year or two, some found their life's work in these schools.

Many newly free African Americans welcomed Northern white teachers, but they also wanted African American teachers. The Freedmen's Bureau and Northern missionary groups helped in founding black colleges in the South, including Atlanta, Fisk, Hampton, and Tougaloo, which were specifically designed to train black teachers. As early as 1869, the bureau reported that of the three thousand teachers for the freedmen, the majority were now African American.

The Reconstruction Act of 1867 also fostered the growth of Southern schooling. It required states of the former Confederacy to call conventions to rewrite their state constitutions, and the new constitutions were expected to include support for public education. Later, even as state after state returned to white rule, the public school system remained. In *Black Reconstruction in America*, W. E. B. Du Bois, a renowned African American activist, wrote, "Public education for all at public expense was, in the South, a Negro idea."

The Reality of Sharecropping

For many newly freed slaves, another issue was as important as the vote or education—land. In Virginia, a freedman told a Union army officer that, if the army had a right to take away the master's slaves, then they "had the right to take master's land too." In Alabama, a state convention delegate insisted "the property which they hold was nearly all earned by the sweat of our brows." Those who had worked the land for no pay valued the promise of land ownership as essential to their economic freedom.

When Sherman's army arrived in Savannah, Georgia, in December 1864, the sixty thousand troops were accompanied by some twenty thousand former slaves. Sherman met with local blacks in Savannah. Garrison Frazier, a leader of that group, said what they wanted: freedom and land, "placing us where we could reap the fruit of our own labor." Four days later, Sherman's Special Field Order No. 15 provided for forty-acre parcels of land for black families, which was to be taken from the plantations of owners in active rebellion on the Sea Islands and coastal areas in Georgia and, later, in South Carolina (once his army got there). Sherman also offered army mules that were no longer needed. Thus, "forty acres and a mule" became the symbol of freedom to many, and by June 1865, forty thousand newly freed people were settled on "Sherman land" in the former Confederacy. As head of the Freedmen's Bureau, General

In the 1850s, Frederick Douglass, who had grown up in slavery, became one of the nation's best known abolitionist speakers. Even many who disagreed with, or were frightened by, his words admired his public speaking ability and his capacity to win many to the abolitionist cause.

A school operated by the Freedmen's Bureau in Richmond, Virginia, was shown in this September 1866 issue of *Frank Leslie's Illustrated Newspaper*.

Edisto Island, off the coast of South Carolina, was one of the first places where the government provided land and mules—and mule carts. Former slaves quickly used the opportunity to become independent farmers.

O. O. Howard expanded Sherman's original South Carolina plan, instructing his agents to "set aside" forty-acre tracts for individual freedmen. Blacks across the South quickly began farming their own plots. President Johnson wasted no time ending the redistribution of land after taking office. He ordered an end to the "forty acres and a mule" policy. He issued pardons to former plantation owners and ordered Howard to restore the land to them, which meant taking it away from those who were currently using it.

In October 1865, General Howard made a painful journey to Edisto Island in South Carolina to announce the president's order. A committee of freedmen responded:

> General, we want Homesteads … if the government having concluded to befriend its late enemies and to neglect to observe the principles of common faith between its self and us its allies in the war you said was over, now takes away from them all right to the soil they stand upon save such as they can get by again working for *your* late and their *all time* enemies. …You will see this is not the condition of really freemen.

Redistribution of land, it seemed, was not going to be part of Reconstruction.

In a few places, however, former slaves were able to purchase or win government land. Having spent their lives in unpaid labor, few slaves had any resources to buy land, even when it was being sold very cheaply in the aftermath of the war. In South Carolina, which had an exceptionally strong Reconstruction government, the legislature established a state land commission that, as Francis L. Cardozo, president of the local Union League said, "proposes to give the poor people the opportunity to become owners of the soil they cultivate." The commission provided grants of land to some fourteen thousand black families—perhaps one-seventh of the state's black population—in various parts of the state. They also created the town of Promised Land, which continues as a black-led community to the present. But South Carolina was the exception, and Reconstruction legislatures never accomplished as much in terms of land distribution as they did regarding the vote and education.

The primary economic opportunity open to slaves was to return to the plantations where they had worked in the past, but do so as paid employees. Neither former slaves nor former slave owners found the prospect encouraging. One Georgia planter complained that "[o]nce we had reliable labor controlled at will. Now … it is both uncertain and unreliable." When railroads or new enterprises offered jobs, blacks left the plantations to take other work.

During the Johnson-dominated Reconstruction, Southern landowners not only reclaimed their lands but also ensured that the passage of vagrancy laws made it a crime to be without a job, which meant former slaves had to take whatever was offered or be jailed. Some landowners agreed to hire only their own former slaves, making it extremely difficult for newly free people to bargain for wages or move to better opportunities in a system that white courts backed up with the threat of long prison sentences for unemployment.

Many in Washington were pleased to see blacks become wage earners, paid for raising the cotton, sugar, rice, and tobacco they had previously raised without pay as slaves. But former slaves did not like working for wages, especially the low wages that were offered They wanted land of their own, and if they could not get land—and in most parts of the South they could not—they wanted a share in the profits of their work.

Given the dissatisfaction that both white landowners and black workers felt, a new economic arrangement was born: **sharecropping**. Sharecropping meant just what the name implied. Instead of working for wages, former slaves worked as independent entrepreneurs who were guaranteed a share of the crop in return for their labor. At the same time, landowners, who provided the land, the seeds, and the loans to get through the year, also received a share of the crop.

As this agricultural economy developed after the Civil War, the owner of a large tract of land (almost always a former plantation owner who had the land returned by the Johnson administration) agreed to provide crude housing, a short-term loan for living expenses (known as the "furnish" and usually provided at the beginning of the growing season in March), seed, fertilizer, tools, and the right to grow cotton on a specified piece of land fifteen to forty acres in area. Landless tenants (almost always former slaves) agreed to work the land, plant, weed or "chop" the cotton through the growing season, and bring in a crop. Landowner and sharecropper would then split the profits after the harvest.

Once the harvest was done, just before Christmas at "the settle," the landowner would provide the sharecropper with a statement of accounts showing the value of the cotton harvest, the cost of the "furnish," purchases at the plantation store, and the difference or profit due to the sharecropper. Everyone knew that many planters cheated their often illiterate tenants. Asking for a detailed accounting meant risking one's home and perhaps one's life. Few took the risk, though many sharecroppers were privately furious when the end-of-year payments were finally made and, somehow, the results for those who had worked all year were so modest.

Sharecropping began on the sugar plantations of Louisiana and quickly spread to the rest of the agricultural South. With sharecropping, black workers had a significant new

Sharecropping

Labor system that evolved during and after Reconstruction whereby landowners furnished laborers with a house, farm animals, tools, and advanced credit in exchange for a share of the laborers' crop.

Charles Phelps Cushing/ClassicStock/Alamy Stock Photo.

Homes for sharecroppers were not much different from the cabins that had been built in the old slave quarters.

incentive to work since they retained a portion of the profit they created. Women and children, who had resisted work in the field for wages, now returned to the fields as families sought to make a living.

At first, landowners were far from enthusiastic about sharecropping. While it meant that they no longer needed to supervise employees, they did not like the sense of independence that sharecropping brought to former slaves. They also disliked the shift from having farm work done by gangs of laborers, as had been the case in slavery and wage-earning times, to having the work done by family units on smaller plots. One South Carolina planter complained about the black-led Union Leagues that fostered sharecropping, saying, "Their leaders counsel them not to work for wages at all, but to insist upon setting up for themselves." Nevertheless, by the early 1870s, sharecropping had become the primary means of agricultural organization in much of the South, especially the region's great cotton-growing heartland (see Map 15-2).

Before long, plantation owners found ways to manipulate sharecropping for their own ends. Owners developed a credit system whereby a plantation store sold everything from food to clothing on credit to the sharecroppers to be repaid when the crop was harvested. Many plantation owners made as much money with their stores as with their crops. With crops mortgaged before they were even planted, workers fell further and further into debt to the landowners. If sharecropping initially gave black families freedom that work for wages did not, it also tied them to the land in poverty for generations.

Map 15-2 Sharecropping Reshapes a Plantation.

These two maps show the changes in the living and work arrangements on the Barrow Plantation in Oglethorpe County, Georgia, between the last days of slavery in 1860 and the establishment of sharecropping in 1881. By the latter date, the old Slave Quarter had disappeared, replaced by dispersed cottages of the sharecropping families, each of whom worked a portion of the land.

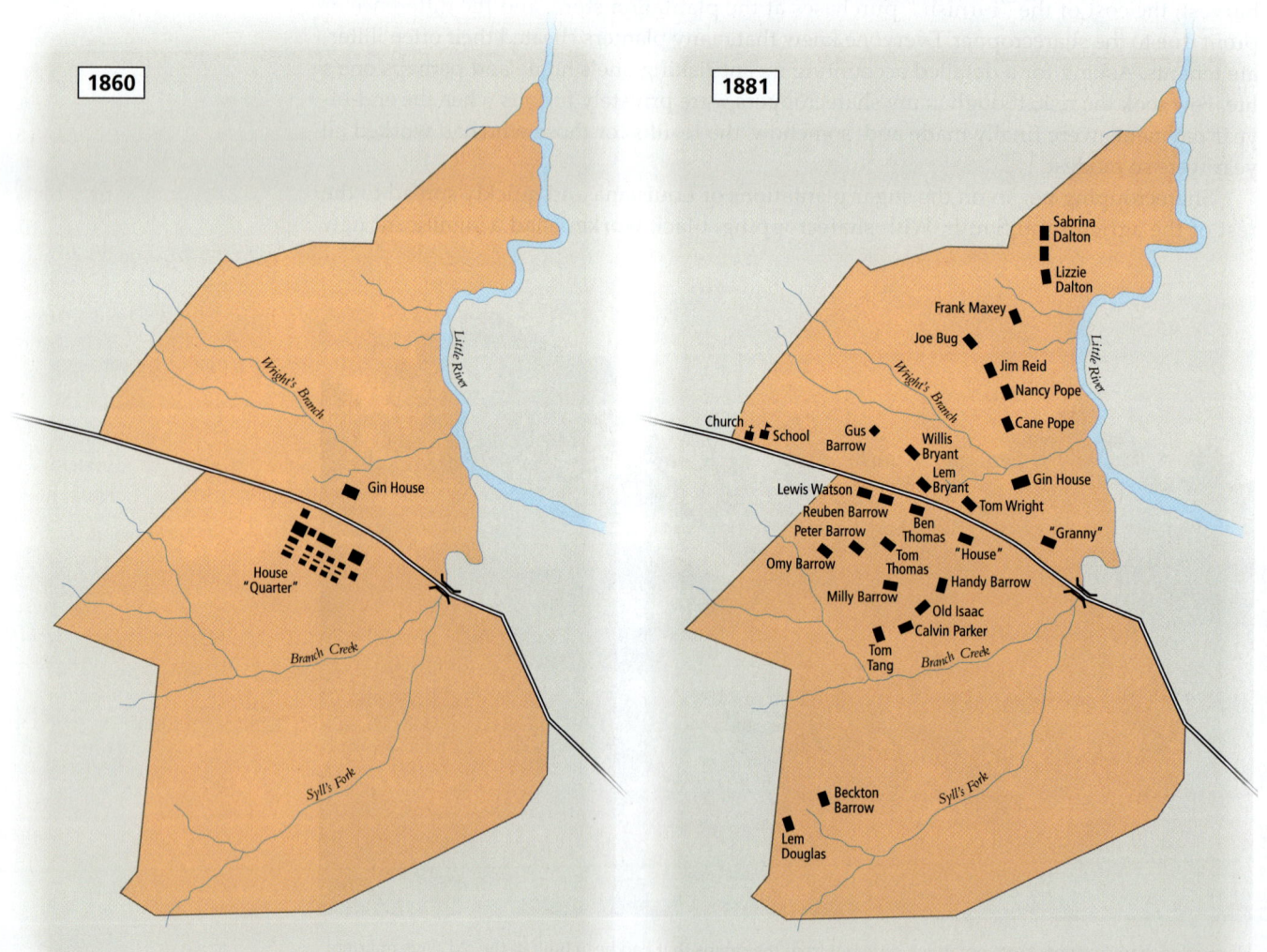

When Historians Disagree

Understanding Reconstruction

The greatest differences among those who study Reconstruction tend to be between historians who live at different times. In 1988, Eric Foner, a widely respected historian, wrote:

> *Revising interpretations of the past is intrinsic to the study of history. … Since the early 1960s, a profound alteration of the place of blacks within American society, newly uncovered evidence, and changing definitions of history itself have combined to transform our understanding of race relations, politics, and economic change during Reconstruction.*

Led by Columbia University historian William Dunning, and writing at a time when the United States was rigidly segregated by race, historians around 1900 concluded that Reconstruction was a terrible failure. One significant voice challenged the "Dunning School," African American scholar W. E. B. DuBois. Only much later did a new generation of historians reconsider Reconstruction, coming to conclusions almost the opposite of the "Dunning School."

William Archibald Dunning, *Reconstruction Political and Economic* (New York: Harper & Brothers, 1907), pp. xv, 11–12.

With the collapse of the Confederacy all the slaves became free, and the strange and unsettling tidings of emancipation were carried to the remotest corners of the land. As the full meaning of this news was grasped by the freedmen, great numbers of them abandoned their old homes, and, regardless of crops to be cultivated, stock to be cared for, or food to be provided, gave themselves up to testing their freedom. They wandered aimless but happy through the country … and were fascinated by the pursuit of the white man's culture in the schools which optimistic northern philanthropy was establishing wherever it was possible.

While the negro population, whose labor was so indispensable a factor in the productive system, was thus occupied, the returning Confederate soldiers and the rest of the white population devoted themselves with desperate energy to the procurement of what must sustain the life of both themselves and their former slaves.

W. E. B. DuBois, *Black Reconstruction in America, 1860–1880* (originally published 1934; republished New York: Oxford University Press, 2007), pp. 587, 590.

The chorus of agreement concerning the attempt to reconstruct and organize the South after the Civil War and emancipation is overwhelming. There is scarce a child in the street that cannot tell you that the whole effort was a hideous mistake and an unfortunate incident based on ignorance, revenge and the perverse determination to attempt the impossible. …

The chief witness in Reconstruction, the emancipated slave himself, has been almost barred from court. His written Reconstruction record has been largely destroyed and nearly always neglected. … The result is that most unfair caricatures of Negroes have been carefully preserved; but serious speeches, successful administration and upright character are almost universally ignored and forgotten. … In other words, every effort has been made to treat the Negro's part in Reconstruction with silence and contempt.

Eric Foner, *Reconstruction: America's Unfinished Revolution, 1863–1877* (New York: Harper & Row, 1988), pp. xxv–xxvi.

Although thwarted in their bid for land, blacks seized the opportunity created by the end of slavery to establish as much independence as possible in their working lives, consolidate their families and communities, and stake a claim to equal citizenship. Black participation in Southern public life after 1867 was the most radical development of the Reconstruction years, a massive experiment in interracial democracy without precedent in the history of this or any other country that abolished slavery in the nineteenth century. …

Racism was pervasive in mid-nineteenth-century America and at both the regional and national levels constituted a powerful barrier to change. Yet despite racism, a significant number of Southern whites were willing to link their political fortunes with those of blacks, and Northern Republicans came, for a time, to associate the fate of the former slaves with their party's raison d'être and the meaning of Union victory in the Civil War.

Thinking Critically

1. **Continuity and Change over Time**
   How much do you think the fact that Dunning wrote in 1907, DuBois in 1934, and Foner in 1988 explains the differences in their perspective? What else might explain the differences?

2. **Argument Development**
   Each of these three historians uses evidence to make their case. What evidence would you use to defend or refute one of them?

15.2 Quick Review

Consider the early impacts of Reconstruction up to 1877. What would you count among its successes or failures?

Terror, Apathy, and the Creation of the Segregated South

15.3 **Analyze the reasons Reconstruction ended and the impact of so-called Redemption.**

During the decade after the Civil War, slavery ended, and the Constitution was amended. Black males voted, held office, and served on juries, and black men, women, and children rode on integrated transit and attended school—occasionally even racially integrated schools. Some even managed to own their own land. However, few of the advances of the first decade of Reconstruction lasted.

The rise and decline of black rights was an uneven process. Blacks were organizing and gaining new rights while the Civil War was still being fought. Many whites resisted black political and economic progress throughout Congressional Reconstruction. Although the withdrawal of federal troops in 1877 greatly hastened the process of undoing the gains of Reconstruction—a process some white Southerners called "Redemption"—that, too, was uneven. In some areas, white-only government had been reestablished well before 1877, while in other areas, blacks maintained political rights well into the 1880s and 1890s. Nevertheless, eventually, the high hopes of Reconstruction ended virtually everywhere in the United States.

Opposition to Black Rights and the Roots of "Redemption"

Opponents of black rights were never completely excluded from power during Reconstruction. In September 1868, the white majority in the Georgia legislature voted to expel all twenty-seven African American representatives. Henry McNeal Turner, one of the twenty-seven, responded: "You may expel us, gentlemen, by your votes today; but while you do it, remember that there is a just God in Heaven." Two years later, in response to actions like the expulsion of the black legislators, President Grant reinstated military rule in Georgia. Black legislators returned to their seats and along with white allies ratified the Fifteenth Amendment.

Harassment of advocates of Reconstruction continued in all parts of the South. Charles Stearns, a Northerner who had gone south to support the work of Reconstruction, was elected as a judge in Columbia County, Georgia, by black and white voters. When he took office, however, he was met by a mob that dragged him out of the courthouse. He resigned. A Republican elected as a probate judge in Washington County, Alabama, was met by "about fifty or sixty men assembled all armed with revolvers," who kept him from taking office. When James Symes, an African American, was appointed district judge in McIntosh County, Georgia, the local lawyers simply refused to take any cases to court when he presided.

Grant and the Republican leaders in Congress were willing to use federal troops if necessary to support the rights of former slaves and their allies. In the South, the Republican Party—the party of Lincoln that had won the war—was the party of black rights and racial equality. Blacks, often organized in Union Leagues, were at the heart of the party, but there were also large numbers of white Republicans in the South, including both Southern born and immigrants from the North. Southern whites who supported Republican and multiracial efforts were called **scalawags**, and they were a diverse lot. Some had opposed secession from 1861. Others, like Confederate general James Longstreet or army veteran Albert R. Parsons, embraced the Republican Party only after the war. Some, like Parsons, strongly supported equal rights for blacks. For others, support for black rights was secondary, but they saw the party that controlled the White House, Congress, and many state legislatures as a place of personal opportunity.

Northern whites who came South were called **carpetbaggers** because, Southerners said, they could carry everything they owned in a single carpet suitcase. Resentful, Southerners claimed that carpetbaggers had come south to get rich. Carpetbaggers were on the whole

Scalawags

A disparaging term for Southern whites who supported the Southern Republican Party during Reconstruction.

Carpetbaggers

Term used by white Southerners for Northern transplants who came to the South to help with Reconstruction.

younger and less prosperous than the scalawags. Some carpetbaggers were no doubt opportunists, coming to make their fortune, while others were abolitionists, coming south to implement policies they had long advocated. Many were veterans of the Union army, and some, like Governor Adelbert Ames, the Republican governor of Mississippi, had first been ordered south by the army and had stayed on.

In the 1860s and 1870s, there were virtually no black Democrats in the South. The post–Civil War Democratic Party was the party of "white only" government. Southern Democrats organized at every political level from small towns to state legislatures and governors' offices. Their twofold goal was to ensure that, even if blacks were now free, they would have few rights and that whites committed to excluding blacks from power would dominate every aspect of society, politically, economically, and culturally. For these segregationist Democrats, African Americans of the Union Leagues, scalawags, and carpetbaggers were all their enemies.

Lucius Quintus Cincinnatus Lamar II of Mississippi, an example of the Southern Democratic Party leaders of his day, was from an old elite Southern family. He represented Mississippi in the U.S. Congress before the war and became a staunch secessionist. During the war, he was a general in the Confederate army. In the postwar period, he decided to enter politics again. Lamar wrote to a friend, "It does seem to me that if there ever was a time when the white people of this state … should rise & with one unanimous voice protest against the domination about to be piled upon them the present is that time." He proceeded to do everything he could to ensure white rule in Mississippi.

In November 1872, having long since secured a presidential pardon, Lamar won a seat in the U.S. Congress. He also helped organize the Democratic Party in Mississippi. In campaign speeches, Lamar attacked black voting rights. In Congress, he tried to ensure that the federal government did not enforce black rights. He helped defeat the Enforcement Act of 1875, which would have given President Grant more authority to implement the Fourteenth and Fifteenth Amendments in Mississippi. While he was engaged in partisan politics, Lamar also helped develop another political organization outside of the Democratic Party—hidden from view but essential to his political victory—the Ku Klux Klan.

The Rise of Violence and the Ku Klux Klan

The **Ku Klux Klan** was founded as a social club among Confederate veterans in Tennessee in 1866. It quickly turned into the largest of several secret and violent organizations bent on ensuring a reign of terror against Republican political leaders of either race and teachers in black schools and blacks in general. The Klan was committed to ending Reconstruction and returning the South to white rule. The Klan assassinated Arkansas's congressman James M. Hinds, members of the South Carolina legislature, and members of state constitutional conventions. It had only just begun its work.

Similar organizations grew across the South. In Louisiana, the Knights of the White Camellia played a similar role, as did the White Line organizations in Mississippi. Although leaders like Lamar maintained a public distance, they secretly kept close ties to these violent extralegal organizations. By political organizing and sheer violence and intimidation, they were confident that they could return the South to its prewar ways.

Even before the emergence of the KKK, African Americans and their white Republican allies faced violence. Just after the war's end in May 1866, a bloody riot in Memphis, Tennessee, resulted in the burning of black schools, churches, and over ninety black homes as well as the killing of at least forty-eight people, all but two of whom were black. A Memphis teacher was murdered, and others were told they would be killed if they did not leave the city immediately. The following fall, only thirteen of the forty teachers in the black schools of Memphis returned. A few weeks later, a similar riot in New Orleans, Louisiana, resulted in at least one hundred injuries as well as the killing of thirty-four blacks and three of their white supporters.

By the spring of 1873, what could only be described as a civil war was going on in Louisiana. Tension mounted after the November 1872 elections in which one group of voters elected a Republican governor and another group, a Democratic one. When a federal judge

Ku Klux Klan

One of several vigilante groups that terrorized black people in the South during the Reconstruction era, founded by Confederate veterans in 1866.

Klan members quickly adopted hoods and masks both to hide their identity and to frighten those who opposed them.

The Memphis riot was but one of many in which whites, enraged by new black rights, attacked homes, schools, and churches belonging to newly free blacks and any whites who supported them.

ruled in favor of the Republican slate, President Grant sent troops to New Orleans to oust the Democratic governor and install the Republican administration. But in the small town of Colfax, Louisiana, two sheriffs had also been elected, and federal troops were a long way off. On Easter Sunday, April 13, 1873, tensions reached a boiling point. Several dozen black families along with former slave and Union army veteran William Ward, the Republican sheriff, barricaded themselves inside the town and sent urgent telegrams to the governor in New Orleans, asking for the army to rescue them. Help was too late in coming. Two to three hundred whites marched on the town, led by the Democratic sheriff, Confederate veteran Christopher Columbus Nash. Nash and his army attacked the town and killed everyone they could find. At least sixty blacks, perhaps many more, were killed. The next day, witnesses saw bodies everywhere. Colfax was far from an isolated incident.

Some of the greatest violence was in Mississippi. At a July 4, 1874, Republican Party meeting in Vicksburg, armed whites shot and killed whites and blacks in attendance. Peter Crosby, the sheriff in Vicksburg, demanded federal intervention but did not get help. On September 1, 1875, at a Republican meeting in Yazoo City, Henry Dixon began shooting at the mixed-race gathering. Mississippi White Liners—the Mississippi version of the Klan—took over the town and forced its elected government to flee.

On Election Day in Mississippi in 1875, black voters arriving at the polls in Port Gibson were met by some eighty whites armed with Remington rifles, who started firing at them. One man was killed, six others wounded, and none voted. At Peytona, not a single Republican vote was cast. Democratic sentries on the Tombigbee River ensured that black voters could not cross the river to get to polling places. Governor Ames fled for his life before his term ended, while Democratic Party teams warned politically active Republicans, black and white, to leave the state before they were killed. The Democrats won statewide and Reconstruction ended in Mississippi with the 1875 elections.

Efforts to Defend Reconstruction

The antiblack, anti-Republican violence with which the South was slowly "redeemed" from Reconstruction met resistance at every step, sometimes very significant resistance. In March 1870, just as the Fifteenth Amendment was ratified, Congress also passed the first Enforcement Act, making the denial of the right to vote because of race through force, fraud, bribery, or intimidation a federal crime. In 1870, Congress had significant reasons not to trust states to protect African American voting rights. Two further Enforcement Acts gave the federal government the right to intervene when elections were unfair, and the Ku Klux Klan Act of April 1871 made conspiracies to deprive citizens of the right to vote a punishable federal offense. In June 1870, Congress also created the U.S. Department of Justice with a specific mandate to enforce Reconstruction. (Up until then, the U.S. attorney general had been a kind of in-house lawyer and legal advisor to the president and cabinet but with no agency to lead.) All of these acts represented a major expansion of federal power. Because of the new legislation, crimes against individuals could, for the first time, be prosecuted by the federal government, especially if state governments did not step in and do their duty.

President Grant used this legislation forcefully. In October 1871, the president proclaimed nine counties of South Carolina to be in a "condition of lawlessness" and sent federal troops to restore order and arrest several hundred Klan leaders, some of whom ended up in federal prison. In addition, perhaps two thousand Klan members left the state. Seven hundred leaders of the Klan were also arrested in Mississippi and more in North Carolina. By the end of 1872, the Klan, as an organization, had been destroyed.

Library of Congress Prints and Photographs Division [LC-USZ62-111152]

The Klan would rise again, but not for many decades. Nevertheless, despite its absence, violence against blacks and their white Republican allies continued in the 1870s. In the North, people were growing more and more willing to let the South settle its own affairs. When the Democrats nominated newspaper editor Horace Greeley for president in 1872, they adopted a platform attacking Republican corruption and calling for civil service reform while also promising a general amnesty for former Confederates and an end to federal intervention in the South. Grant was easily renominated by the Republicans and won the election handily, but Democrats gained power in Congress. As it turned out, Greeley died before the electoral votes were counted, which caused some confusion, but no one doubted that Grant had won the election. In his inaugural address at the beginning of his second term in March 1873, Grant told the nation, "The effects of the late civil strife have been to free the slave and make him a citizen. Yet he is not possessed of the civil rights which citizenship should carry with it. This is wrong, and should be corrected. To this correction I stand committed, so far as Executive influence can avail." Grant did his best, but it was not enough.

In 1875, Grant sent fellow Civil War general Philip Sheridan to Louisiana to investigate the political violence. Sheridan documented the killing of 2,141 blacks and the wounding of 2,115 more since the war had ended. All of these crimes remained unpunished. Another Civil War veteran, former slave Henry Adams, organized a committee of five hundred blacks to "look into affairs and see the true condition of our race." In northern Louisiana around the Red River area alone, the committee documented 683 murders, including the following notations:

> Sam Maybury, whipped to death, December 1865
> Henry West, badly whipped, November 1874
> George, a colored man, killed by white men 1873
> Nancy Brooks, badly whipped by a white man, 1873

In most cases, the list included the name of the victim and the unpunished killer. The reality that Sheridan and Adams documented would not change for a very long time.

A Changing National Mood and the End of Reconstruction

A number of factors led to the growing national weariness with federal intervention in the South. Southern Reconstruction governments were regularly accused of corruption, and some officeholders, black and white, certainly enriched themselves. P. B. S. Pinchback of Louisiana, the only black governor in the Reconstruction era, admitted that he made considerable profit for himself in his political career. South Carolina's white Republican governor, Robert K. Scott, speculated in state bonds, and North Carolina's governor, William Holden, was aware of "damnable rascality." In truth, the Reconstruction governments were probably no more corrupt than those that came before or after, but the charges tarnished Reconstruction.

The Grant administration also faced one corruption scandal after another. During Grant's first year in office, Jay Gould and James Fisk, the nation's leading bankers, tried to corner the nation's gold supply and thus control the economy, with possible support from administration insiders including Julia Grant, the president's wife. One after another, cabinet officers resigned after they were charged with taking bribes or other forms of corruption. In 1870, former Ohio governor Jacob Cox resigned as secretary of the interior to protest the administration's failure to implement civil service reform. In perhaps the biggest scandal, a congressional investigation uncovered the workings of the so-called Whiskey Ring, a group including elected officials, government employees, and whiskey makers who defrauded the U.S. Treasury of excise taxes on whiskey. Over two hundred distillers and revenue agents were indicted, and Grant's personal secretary, Orville E. Babcock, resigned. Grant directed the investigations to continue, saying, "Let no guilty man escape if it can be avoided," and he ordered the attorney general not to grant immunity to any suspects, but he was seriously tarnished by the widespread corruption.

The sheer size of the federal interventions in the South also undermined public support. In late 1874, White League militants ousted the Republican governor, William P. Kellogg, in Louisiana and took over the legislative hall. Since Louisiana was still under military

15.1

15.2

15.3

supervision, Grant ordered General Sheridan to restore order. With five thousand U.S. Army troops, Sheridan restored Kellogg to the governor's office and forcibly removed Democrats from the legislative hall. The spectacle of U.S. Army soldiers marching into a legislative chamber and removing people who claimed to have been elected created a huge backlash. Newspapers that had supported the Union cause now compared the White League to the founding fathers defending their freedom.

Debates in Congress reflected the change in Northern public opinion and the increasing swagger of Southern leaders. Joseph R. Hawley, a Connecticut Republican who called himself a "radical abolitionist," nevertheless argued that the "social, and educational, and moral reconstruction" of the South could "never come from any legislative halls." The Democrats in Congress praised "local self-government," while insisting that black and white Republicans in the South should stop depending "upon external aid." In that context, it was difficult for the federal administration or the U.S. Army officers in the South to get support.

The U.S. Supreme Court was not sympathetic to Reconstruction. In the *Slaughterhouse Cases* of 1873, the court severely restricted the reach of the Fourteenth Amendment. A group of butchers in New Orleans had challenged the right of the Louisiana legislature to grant a monopoly to one meatpacking company because, they said, it violated their Fourteenth Amendment rights to due process of law and citizenship rights. But the court ruled that the Fourteenth Amendment did not include such rights, making it much harder to bring other suits about state infringement of citizens' rights.

In March 1876, the court's decision in *United States v. Cruikshank* struck a further blow to Reconstruction. William J. "Bill" Cruikshank was a white participant in the attack on Colfax, Louisiana, in 1873. He was indicted on federal charges for violating the civil rights of blacks who were killed in the attack. But three years later, the Supreme Court ruled that the charges were unconstitutional. Chief Justice Morrison R. Waite wrote that protecting the rights of individual citizens was a state, not a federal, duty. *Cruikshank* took away one of the federal government's most important enforcement powers—the right to bring federal charges against those who attacked the rights of African Americans.

Finally, in 1883, the Court ruled that the Civil Rights Act of 1875 was unconstitutional because the Fourteenth Amendment gave Congress the right to outlaw only state government actions, not discrimination by individuals, which the Court left to the states to deal with. The legal foundation of Reconstruction seemed to be crumbling or, perhaps, the Court was simply following public opinion. Associate Justice Samuel Miller, a Grant appointee, wrote to a friend, describing what many Americans were also feeling: "I am losing interest in these matters."

As the country prepared for the 1876 presidential elections, the loss of interest in Reconstruction was evident. The Republicans nominated Ohio governor Rutherford B. Hayes, who was on good terms with all factions in the party and especially popular with some because of his crackdown on nascent labor unions in Ohio. The platform said surprisingly little about Reconstruction. The Democrats nominated New York governor Samuel Tilden, who had made a fortune as legal counsel for some of the country's richest bankers and railroads and gained fame for fighting corruption in government. Promising to continue the fight against corruption and foster prosperity, and never mentioning Reconstruction, Tilden was the strongest candidate the Democrats had nominated in some time.

The campaign was intense, especially in the South where violence and confusion reigned. In November, Tilden outpolled Hayes, winning the popular vote 4,286,808 to 4,034,142, but it was the electoral votes that counted. In three states, Florida, Louisiana, and South Carolina, Republican election boards discarded enough votes to declare Hayes the winner, which meant that he would also win the electoral count. Not surprisingly, the Democrats challenged these decisions.

The months between the election and the inauguration were as tense as any since the Jefferson–Adams contest of 1800. Some Democrats vowed "Tilden or War." Congress created an Electoral Commission of ten congressional representatives, five from each party plus five Supreme Court justices, to determine the outcome since the Constitution gave no guidance beyond saying that the votes "shall be counted" in the Senate. After intense negotiations, the Electoral Commission ruled 8 to 7 for Hayes. But the Constitution specified that a president could not be declared elected until the Senate actually counted the votes cast by the presidential electors from the various states. Democrats refused to convene the Senate to count that vote, thus making it impossible to resolve the crisis. Finally, on February 26, a group of Southern Democrats met with Ohio Republicans and negotiated a compromise. Hayes, who promised to treat the South with "kind consideration," agreed that, if he was made president, he would use his power to end Reconstruction, most of all by withdrawing the federal troops that were in the South protecting Republican governments. The Southern Democrats liked the offer and agreed to let the Senate meet and count the votes, including—following the Electoral Commission's recommendation—the votes of the Republican electors from Florida. On Inauguration Day, March 4, 1877, Hayes became president.

Southern Republicans who had supported Hayes were outraged. A former slave from South Carolina commented angrily, "To think that Hayes could go back on us when we had to wade through blood to help place him where he is now." Little could now be done, however. Hayes did not immediately remove federal troops from the South, but he made it clear that the troops who remained would not intervene in the South's internal matters as Grant had ordered. The changes in federal policy had been coming for some time, but after March 1877, there was little reason to expect any federal support for Reconstruction anywhere.

After 1877, the direction was clear. John C. Calhoun, an Arkansas planter and grandson of the South Carolina senator of the same name, told Congress that "left to ourselves," the white South could settle "all questions" about the region's political arrangements. And they did. Blacks, carpetbaggers, and scalawags were slowly excluded from offices. Many were forced to leave the South altogether if they wanted long lives. In addition, blacks were regularly excluded from voting, education budgets were slashed, and the regulation of sharecropping shifted further in favor of plantation owners. After 1877, white rule in the South was assured.

The Birth of the Segregated South

Disenfranchisement and segregation did not happen overnight. African Americans were still being elected to office in the 1880s and 1890s. George H. White of North Carolina, who was described as "the last of the Negro congressmen," bade a final farewell to the House of Representatives in 1901, saying: "This, Mr. Chairman, this is perhaps the Negroes' temporary farewell to the American Congress. But let me say, phoenix-like, he will rise up someday and come again." The absence of blacks from Congress lasted for twenty-eight years until Oscar De Priest was elected from Chicago. Only after another civil rights movement many decades later did African Americans reach the number of representatives in Congress that they had in the 1870s.

Various forms of what came to be called **Jim Crow segregation** developed at a rapid pace. (Jim Crow was a derogatory character in a minstrel show designed to denigrate blacks, but his name has been applied to the whole era of rigid racial segregation that was the rule in many parts of the United States from the 1870s to the 1960s.) Schools, public facilities, transportation, and almost every other aspect of life were segregated. In addition to losing political offices and the vote, blacks were marginalized economically so that sharecropping became virtually the only option for most. A vicious campaign of lynching backed up by long prison terms at hard labor for minor infractions controlled blacks through fear and intimidation. Perhaps the capstone of this segregation was the U.S. Supreme Court's 1896 *Plessy v. Ferguson* decision that "separate but equal" facilities were quite acceptable under the U.S. Constitution. By the time that decision was issued, the high hopes of Reconstruction were a dim memory and most Americans—white and black—were living in a very different world.

Jim Crow segregation

Segregation laws that became widespread in the South during the 1890s, named for a minstrel show character portrayed satirically by white actors in blackface.

15.3 Quick Review

Considering the events and trends of the later years of Reconstruction, or Redemption as it was called, who was most responsible for what happened?

Conclusion

After the Civil War, Americans grappled with what the future held for newly freed slaves and how best to return to the Union those states that had been in rebellion during the Civil War. The so-called Radical Republicans in Congress sought ways to protect the educational, political, and economic rights of the freedmen and women. Andrew Johnson, who became president upon Lincoln's death in April 1865, seemed indifferent to African American rights and soon alienated congressional radicals by restoring power to former rebels intent on limiting the freedoms of former slaves.

Congressional Republicans had their own plans, however, and eventually, the House of Representatives impeached Johnson for obstructing its plans to reconstruct the South. Although he was acquitted of "high crimes and misdemeanors," Congress passed a number of laws, including the 1866 Civil Rights Act over Johnson's veto and the Fourteenth and Fifteenth Amendments to the Constitution, designed to protect black rights as citizens and voters. Across the South, African Americans and whites committed to Reconstruction were elected to local and national office and began to reshape their states. In 1868, Ulysses S. Grant, a hero from the Civil War and the Republican nominee, was elected president. Grant was committed to the Reconstruction of the South in ways that would protect black rights, especially black voting rights.

After the war, African Americans pursued full citizenship rights, education, and economic independence. Terrorized by white supremacists and lacking money and credit, most African Americans never achieved either true equality or independence. At the same time, white veterans of the Confederate army were organizing to deny those rights, not only legally through the Democratic Party but also illegally through the Ku Klux Klan and other similar organizations. As time passed, and as public support for federal intervention in the affairs of the South eroded, the promise of Reconstruction's early days evaporated. By 1877, a new president, Rutherford B. Hayes, began to bring Reconstruction to an end, assuring white rule in the South and the disenfranchisement and "Jim Crow segregation" of African Americans for generations to come.

Chapter Review

Why might the historian Eric Foner call Reconstruction "America's Unfinished Revolution"?

Chapter 15 Summary and Review

Federal Reconstruction Policy

15.1 Explain the political development of federal Reconstruction policy—presidential and then congressional.

Summary

In the immediate aftermath of Lincoln's assassination, Andrew Johnson took the lead in Reconstruction. His goal was to return the Confederate states to their prewar status as quickly as possible, and he had no interest in the political rights of former slaves as long as slavery itself was ended. New state governments were quickly organized in the South and began passing laws limiting black rights. When a new, and overwhelmingly Republican, Congress was assembled in December 1865, it enacted a radical vision of Reconstruction that put it at odds with the president. Johnson vetoed the extension and expansion of the Freedmen's Bureau and the Civil Rights Act of 1866, but Congress overrode his vetoes. The Fourteenth Amendment put provisions of the civil rights law into the Constitution. The Reconstruction Act of 1867 divided the former Confederate states into five military districts, ordering the military to oversee the writing of new constitutions. Only after these new constitutions were in place, and after a state had ratified the Fourteenth Amendment, would Congress admit its representatives to Congress. Congressional efforts to prevent Johnson from undermining Reconstruction intensified the confrontation between Congress and the president and led to his impeachment and trial. After Grant was elected president in 1868, Congress moved quickly to pass the Fifteenth Amendment, guaranteeing blacks the right to vote. Supporters of women's rights were disappointed in the Fifteenth Amendment because their own voting rights had not been considered.

Review Questions

1. Continuity and Change over Time
   How would you explain the increasingly radical nature of Congressional Reconstruction? What factors pushed Congress toward more aggressive intervention in Southern society and politics?

2. Comparison
   Compare and contrast Presidential Reconstruction and Congressional Reconstruction. What were some of the ways that Congress forced the states of the former Confederacy to accept Reconstruction that Johnson opposed?

The Impact of Reconstruction

15.2 Explain the impact of Reconstruction on African American life in the South and the ways African Americans shaped Reconstruction policy.

Summary

During the era of Congressional Reconstruction, African Americans were elected to a variety of offices at the state and federal level. Reconstruction state governments expanded the right to vote, created public school systems, and promoted internal improvements designed to bring the South into the modern world. For many newly freed slaves, education was the highest priority. Along with education and the right to vote, former slaves sought land and the economic independence that comes with it. In the end, the federal government did not support the redistribution of land to former slaves, and a system of sharecropping emerged. While sharecropping was initially seen as a compromise between white and black economic desires, it quickly became a system through which whites could economically dominate blacks.

Review Questions

3. Contextualization
   Why did newly freed slaves place such a high priority on education?

4. Argument Development
   Defend or refute the following statement: By the end of the 1870s, from an economic perspective, most Southern blacks were almost as closely tied to the land and dependent on white landowners as they had been under slavery. What evidence can you produce to support your position?

Terror, Apathy, and the Creation of the Segregated South

15.3 Analyze the reasons Reconstruction ended and the impact of the so-called Redemption.

Summary

The first decade after the Civil War witnessed extraordinary changes, particularly in the lives of black Americans in the South, but few of these advances lasted long. The Republican Party in the South was made up of a coalition of blacks, Southern whites who supported Republican and multiracial efforts, and Northern white migrants to the South. In contrast, the Democratic Party was supported by the majority of white Southerners. Organizations like the Ku Klux Klan used political violence and terror to prevent blacks from using their rights or resisting attempts by whites to reimpose the prewar racial order. Among white Southerners, violent resistance to Reconstruction and to any role of blacks in government became common across the South in the 1870s. That violence played a central role in the "redemption" of Southern state governments by the Democrats. Under Grant, the federal government took a forceful role in resisting and punishing the violence. Nonetheless, Reconstruction suffered a series of setbacks in the 1870s as Northern whites lost interest in and commitment to the protection of the rights of Southern blacks. The Compromise of 1876, which resulted in the election of Rutherford B. Hayes, was the beginning of the end of Reconstruction. In the decades after 1876, discrimination and disenfranchisement increasingly led to the emergence of the segregated South.

Review Questions

5. Causation
What impact does white violence have on African American aspirations for political and economic equality in the South?

6. Argument Development
Reconstruction can be viewed as a period when multiple groups vied for political power in the Southern states. What year would you argue the white South began to have the most power? Defend your choice.

1. Preparing to Write: Develop Your Thesis

Long Essay Question—Evaluate the extent to which there were differing viewpoints within the women's rights movement on the Fourteenth and Fifteenth Amendments. Although this question is similar to a Comparison question, the language is different. "Evaluate the extent" questions are asking you to make a judgment on just how much there was a difference. Think of a continuum that runs from Compare on one side to Contrast on the other. In this case, where do the viewpoints fall? The center of gravity for this question is closer to Contrast. But is there anything to compare? To write a thesis with depth, include the central causes of the split.

2. Preparing to Write: Support Your Assertion

Short-Answer Question—Using the excerpts from Dunning and Foner in Section 15.2, answer parts (a), (b), and (c).

a. Briefly explain ONE major difference between Dunning's and Foner's interpretations about Reconstruction.

b. Briefly explain how someone supporting Dunning's interpretation could use ONE piece of evidence from the period between 1865 and 1877 not directly mentioned in the excerpt.

c. Briefly explain how someone supporting Foner's interpretation could use ONE piece of evidence from the period between 1865 and 1877 not directly mentioned in the excerpt.

For (b) and (c), identify the piece of evidence in the first sentence and explain the link. Then write an additional sentence or two to elaborate.

Part 5   AP® Practice Test

Section I: Multiple-Choice Questions

Questions 5.1–5.3 refer to the following excerpt.

"There are few things which present greater obstacles to the improvement and elevation of woman to her appropriate sphere of usefulness and duty, than the laws which have been enacted to destroy her independence, and crush her individuality; laws which, although they are framed for her government, she has had no voice in establishing, and which rob her of some of her essential rights. Woman has no political existence. With the single exception of presenting a petition to the legislative body, she is a cipher in the nation; or, if not actually so in representative governments, she is only counted, like the slaves of the South, to swell the number of law-makers who form decrees for her government, with little reference to her benefit, except so far as her good may promote their own."

—**Letter from Sara Grimké to Angelina Grimké, 1837**

5.1   Grimké's central arguments best reflect which of the following goals of the women's rights movement of the mid-1800s?

   a. Greater political equality for women
   b. More influence for women in the domestic sphere
   c. Better economic opportunities for women
   d. Increased awareness of slavery's evils

5.2   The women's movement of the 1800s expressed its ideals most publicly

   a. in *The Liberator*
   b. at the Hartford Convention
   c. in *Leaves of Grass*
   d. at the Seneca Falls Convention

5.3   Which of the following caused significant division with supporters of the women's rights movement?

   a. Emancipation Proclamation
   b. Thirteenth Amendment
   c. Fourteenth Amendment
   d. Fifteenth Amendment

Questions 5.4–5.6 refer to the following excerpt.

"The negro slaves of the South are the happiest, and, in some sense, the freest people in the world. The children and the aged and infirm work not at all, and yet have all the comforts and necessities of life provided for them. They enjoy liberty, because they are oppressed neither by care nor labor. The women do little hard work, and are protected from the despotism of their husbands by their masters. The negro men and stout boys work, on the average, in good weather, not more than nine hours a day. The balance of their time is spent in perfect abandon. Besides, they have their Sabbaths and holidays. White men, with so much of license and liberty, would die of ennui; but negroes luxuriate in corporeal and mental repose. … We do not know whether free laborers ever sleep. …

The free laborer must work or starve. He is more of a slave than the negro, because he works longer and harder for less allowance than the slave, and has no holiday, because the cares of life with him begin when its labors end. He has no liberty, and not a single right."

—**George Fitzhugh, *Cannibals All! Or, Slaves without Masters*, 1857**

5.4   Arguments like the ones in this excerpt were most likely a response to

   a. *The Scarlet Letter*
   b. the abolitionist movement
   c. Lincoln's presidential election
   d. Manifest Destiny

5.5   Fitzhugh's sentiments most directly reflected which of the following developments in the South during the 1800s?

   a. A shift to a "positive good" defense of slavery
   b. Attempts to write a constitutional amendment protecting slavery
   c. The support of radical activism like John Brown's raid at Harper's Ferry
   d. Speeches touting slavery as a "necessary evil"

5.6   Division over slavery was the leading factor in the creation of which political party?

   a. Know-Nothing   **c.** Republican
   b. Democratic   **d.** Whig

Questions 5.7–5.8 refer to the following excerpt.

"As both the North and the South mobilized for war, the relative strengths and weaknesses of the "free market" and the "slave labor" economic systems became increasingly clear—particularly in their ability to support and sustain a war economy. The Union's industrial and economic capacity soared during the war as the North continued its rapid industrialization to suppress the rebellion. In the South, a smaller industrial base, fewer rail lines, and an agricultural economy based upon slave labor made mobilization of resources more difficult. As the war dragged on, the Union's advantages in factories, railroads, and manpower put the Confederacy at a great disadvantage."

—**Benjamin T. Arrington, "Industry and Economy during the Civil War," 2011**

5.7   Before the war, the Southern economy was most directly connected to which industry in the North?

   a. Textiles   **c.** Lumber
   b. Agriculture   **d.** Banking

5.8   During the war the South was at a disadvantage economically, but which of the following was its greatest advantage?

   a. Naval fleet   **c.** Enlistment numbers
   b. Military leadership   **d.** Public support

Section II: Short-Answer Question

5.9   Use the image "Lincoln's Last Warning" to answer parts (a), (b), and (c).

   a. Briefly describe ONE point of view about Emancipation expressed in the image.

   b. Briefly explain ONE specific historical development that led to the action depicted in the image.

   c. Briefly explain ONE effect of the action depicted in the image.

"Now if you don't come down, I'll cut the Tree from under you." *Harper's Weekly*, "Lincoln's Last Warning," October 1862.

Section III: Long Essay Questions

Directions: Answer Question 5.10 **or** 5.11. (Suggested writing time: 40 minutes) In your response you should do the following.

- Respond to the prompt with a historically defensible thesis or claim that establishes a line of reasoning.
- Describe a broader historical context relevant to the prompt.
- Support an argument in response to the prompt using specific and relevant examples of evidence.
- Use historical reasoning (e.g., comparison, causation, continuity or change over time) to frame or structure an argument that addresses the prompt.

- Use evidence to corroborate, qualify, or modify an argument that addresses the prompt.

5.10 Evaluate the most significant difference between the outcomes of the Missouri Compromise (1820) and the Compromise of 1850.

5.11 Evaluate the most significant difference between the events that led to the nullification crisis (1832–1833) and the secession crisis (1860–1861).

Section IV:

Read on MyHistoryLab

Document-Based Question: Growing Sectional Divide

Part 6

Becoming an Industrial World Power—Costs, Benefits, and Responses 1865–1914

AP® KEY CONCEPTS

Key Concept 6.1

Technological advances, large-scale production methods, and the opening of new markets encouraged the rise of industrial capitalism in the United States.

Key Concept 6.2

The migrations that accompanied industrialization transformed both urban and rural areas of the United States and caused dramatic social and cultural changes.

Key Concept 6.3

The "Gilded Age" produced new cultural and intellectual movements, public reform efforts, and political debates over economic and social policies.

CONSTRUCTING A RAILROAD.

North Wind Picture Archives / Alamy Stock Photo

PART OUTLINE

Chapter 16
Conflict in the West
1865–1912

Library of Congress Prints and Photographs Division [LC-DIG-ppmsca-13514]

Buffalo Bill's Wild West Show created the image of the American West for many people, an image that was more fantasy than reality.

Chapter Objective

Demonstrate an understanding of the post–Civil War changes in the American West.

 ## Learning Objectives

The Tribes of the West and the U.S. Government

16.1 Explain western development from an American Indian perspective and the way Indian and white cultures shaped each other.

The Impact of the Transcontinental Railroad, 1869

16.2 Analyze the building of transcontinental railroads and its impact on the nation, especially the West.

The Transformation of the West

16.3 Analyze how indigenous people, ranchers, farmers, miners, outlaws, politicians, and mythmakers shaped the West and our understanding of its history.

In the midst of the Civil War, Abraham Lincoln met with fourteen western chiefs at the White House in March 1863. He urged them to adopt the "peaceful ways of the white people." Chief Lean Bear of the Cheyenne reminded the president that whites were responsible for most of the violence in the West. He did not mention the irony of Lincoln's statement coming in the midst of the bloodiest war in American history.

Subsequent presidents had similar, usually unproductive, meetings. President Grant tried hard to implement what came to be known as the Grant Peace Policy, but, though well intentioned, that policy ultimately depended on the U.S. Army to settle matters in the West, and the army in the field was often anything but peaceful. While both trade and warfare between white settlers and Indians east of the Mississippi River lasted for over two hundred years, the major battles between the western tribes and the U.S. Army lasted for less than thirty years. What began as a series of bloody skirmishes during the Civil War erupted into the Great Plains Wars in the 1870s and 1880s. By the 1890s, the armed conflict was all over as tribes were defeated and moved into ever-shrinking reservations.

At the same time, the transcontinental railroads made travel to and through the West much easier and faster than ever before and white ranchers, farmers, and miners built new settlements across the West. What began as vast cattle ranches were replaced within thirty years by smaller-scale farms, producing beef and wheat for national and world markets. Agricultural developments of the post–Civil War era depended on new technologies— most of all the development of railroads that brought supplies to isolated farmers and shipped their products—and on new economic and political arrangements. This chapter examines the resulting growth and the changing nature of the American West between 1865 and 1890.

The Tribes of the West and the U.S. Government

16.1 Explain western development from an American Indian perspective and the way Indian and white cultures shaped each other.

Native Americans fought on both sides in the Civil War and sometimes used the country's division to expand their territory, leading both the North and the South to divert troops from other battles. The Civil War also changed the lives of American Indians. For most whites, Indian matters existed only on the margin of their attention during the war. Once the Civil War ended, whites' relationships with Indians, especially on the Great Plains, took on greater significance. As many Americans, whites and some blacks, began to look for more land in the aftermath of the war, they ran directly into newly empowered Native Americans.

The Comanche Empire

For the Comanches, arguably the most powerful tribe on the western frontier in 1860, the Civil War was a great gift. The U.S. Army, the Texas Rangers, and other whites who had been harassing them for decades were called to fight against each other on distant battle-fields. The Comanches welcomed their absence.

In 1700, the Comanches were a small tribe who had recently moved into what is now the Southwest of the United States. They developed expertise using two European imports, rifles and horses, becoming the much-feared "Lords of the South Plains." The Comanches built a way of life based on hunting the buffalo, and like the buffalo, they traveled widely over the Great Plains hunting, trading, and fighting. They also made alliances (especially with the Utes), traded (with everyone), and fought bloody battles (especially with the Apaches and the Europeans) while they stole horses and supplies as well as kidnapped white settlers and members of other tribes. By the early 1800s, although they were without a permanent capital, borders, or bureaucracy, the Comanches ruled an empire that was equal in size and power to the United States or the Republic of Mexico.

Significant Dates

1858	John Butterfield opens overland stage route
1862	Congress passes the Homestead Act
1864	Navajo Long Walk to Bosque Redondo
1865	Civil War ends, units of U.S. Army return to patrol the West
	Chicago Union Stock Yards opens
1867	Chisholm Trail to Abilene, Kansas
	Medicine Lodge Creek Treaty between U.S. government and Comanches
1868	Treaty of Fort Laramie with Lakota Sioux
	Treaty of Bosque Redondo with the Navajos
1869	Transcontinental Railroad completed at Promontory Point, Utah
	President Grant announces new Grant Peace Policy for American Indians
1872	Modoc uprising in California
1873	Panic and Depression
1874	U.S. Army defeat of the Comanches
	Black Hills Gold Rush into Sioux territory in the Dakotas
1876	Battle of the Little Bighorn
1877	Nez Perce under Chief Joseph surrender to U.S. Army
1878	Billy the Kid and Lincoln County War in New Mexico
	El Fronterizo, Spanish-language newspaper, begins publication in Arizona Territory
1879	Beginnings of Carlisle Indian School
1881	Gunfight at the O.K. Corral
	Beginning of Great Dakota Land Boom
1882	Gustavus Swift creates new refrigerated rail car, allowing shipment of meat
	Opening of Anaconda Copper Mine in Montana

(continued)

16.1

16.2

16.3

Medicine Lodge Creek Treaty

An 1867 treaty between the Comanches and the U.S. Army in which the Comanches agreed to settle on a reservation.

Nevertheless, by the late 1850s, the Comanches seemed to be in decline. Working with Texas Rangers and with smaller tribes who had been Comanche victims, the U.S. Army began to gain the upper hand in Texas. In battles during 1858, over one hundred Comanche warriors, including chiefs, were killed, and a large number of women and children taken prisoner. Some Comanches were ready to seek peace. The Penateka Comanches, who had split from the larger tribe, gave up warfare and settled on a Texas reservation just before the Civil War.

The Civil War and, later, Reconstruction opened up new opportunities for the remaining Comanches. The war diverted troops from Texas to distant battlefields, and as early as 1863, Comanche raiding parties began to move back into parts of Texas they had left in the 1850s, stealing horses and cattle. When Texas joined the Confederacy, Comanches developed a brisk trade selling stolen Texas cattle to Union Army agents in New Mexico. With the coming of peace in 1865, the U.S. Army demilitarized any forces in Texas that had fought for the Confederacy in the Civil War, including the feared Texas Rangers. While U.S. Army troops were stationed in Houston, San Antonio, and along the border with Mexico, the area of west Texas, with several million cattle wandering on huge range lands, was only lightly protected. The Comanches saw their opportunity. They expanded their rich trade with prosperous New Mexicans who came to be known as the *comancheros* because of the trade.

From the mid-1860s into the early 1870s, great annual trading gatherings took place where *comancheros*, often backed by investors from the eastern United States, traded salt, hard bread, flour, sugar, tobacco, blankets, and knives as well as the ever-in-demand latest-issue revolvers and rifles in exchange for cattle that the Comanches had recently acquired in Texas. The Comanches also continued to trade in people—Mexican and Indian captives, especially women, who were in great demand as brides in New Mexico. While these trading gatherings integrated the Comanches into U.S. markets, the stolen cattle and the continued trade in humans were sources of serious tensions between the Comanches and the governments of the United States and the state of Texas.

To restore order to the Southwest and open up new land for white settlement, U.S. peace commissioners met with more than five thousand Comanches as well as Kiowas, Naishans, Cheyennes, and Arapahoes at Medicine Lodge Creek in Texas in October 1867. The U.S. delegation was led by William Tecumseh Sherman, head of the army of the West, a post he had also held during the Civil War. As a show of strength, the army team included five hundred well-armed soldiers in dress uniform. A newspaper reporter also at the meeting wrote that the Comanches arrived "with all their war paraphernalia, their horses striped with war paint, the riders bedecked with war bonnets and their faces painted red." They also knew a thing or two about a show of strength.

After elaborate opening ceremonies and the exchanges of gifts—including six thousand pounds of coffee, ten thousand pounds of bread, and three thousand pounds of tobacco from the government—the U.S. representatives made it clear they had come to Medicine Lodge Creek to end the Comanche status as a sovereign people. The government would help them become farmers on a reservation but would not tolerate a continuation of the old hunting, trading, and stealing ways. Sherman concluded, "You can no more stop this [change] than you can stop the sun or the moon. You must submit and do the best you can."

The Comanche chiefs were outraged by the government's demands. Several, including Paruasemena, the leader of the Penateka Comanches, expressed their anger in eloquent responses, but in the end, the chiefs signed a treaty, although it was one that left much open to interpretation. The **Medicine Lodge Creek Treaty** provided for a Comanche reservation and also gave them the right to hunt on open plains below the Arkansas River in Indian Territory (Oklahoma). The government representatives assumed that the Comanches would become farmers on the reservation while venturing out on occasional hunting trips to track the buffalo. The Comanches thought that the reservation would make a perfectly good winter campground, and they were more than happy to receive government rations, but they had no intention of becoming settled farmers. Along with hunting buffalo, the Comanches expected to continue hunting for Texas cattle and trading them to New Mexico buyers.

The radically different interpretations of the Medicine Lodge Creek Treaty between the Comanches and the U.S. government became clear the next spring when several thousand

Harper's Magazine, one of the most popular journals in the United States at the time, carried this illustration of the Comanche encampment and the Comanches and U.S. Army representatives determining an agreement at the 1867 Medicine Lodge Creek gathering.

Comanches, having spent the winter on the reservation, collected their government payments and began raiding cattle and horses in Texas, New Mexico, and Indian Territory. According to one report, 6,255 horses and 11,395 cattle were lost to Indian raids in Texas between 1866 and 1873.

After several unsuccessful peace efforts, the United States gave up on negotiations and ordered the army to attack and force the Comanches onto a permanent reservation. From 1871 to 1873, the army and the Comanches fought. While the army attacked, American buffalo hunters decimated the buffalo herds as industries found new uses for their hides. The buffalo had been at the heart of Comanche life, not only as food but also as a way to understand the universe, and their destruction undermined the Comanches.

During the fighting from 1871 to 1873, a new Comanche leader emerged. Quanah Parker was the son of a Comanche chief and Cynthia Ann Parker, a white Texan who had been captured by the Comanches. He became the fiercest opponent of compromise with whites. Then in 1874, Isa-tai, a young Comanche spiritual leader or shaman, became prominent, sharing a message heard many times among different Indian tribes—that if they would get rid of white ways and white people, the buffalo would return and life would be good again. In a great camp meeting in June 1874, several hundred Comanche warriors led by Isa-tai and Parker joined with Kiowas, Cheyennes, and Arapahoes to eliminate the white presence from the Great Plains, starting with the buffalo hunters.

The army counterattacked. On September 28, 1874, U.S. forces attacked Parker's main encampment, and though nearly all of the Indians fled, the army destroyed the camp, taking the horses and burning tents, blankets, and food. Faced with starvation, the Comanches began to surrender in small groups, coming to the army post at Fort Sill in Indian Territory over the course of the winter where they gave up their horses and rifles and moved to the reservations assigned to them. Isa-tai was discredited, but not Parker.

The winter of 1874–1875 was the low point of Comanche life, but it was not the end. Quanah Parker was only twenty-seven when he surrendered to federal authorities. Over the next four decades, he became principal chief of the Comanches and led them from warfare to farming and ranching. Parker was a tough negotiator with the federal Bureau of Indian Affairs for expanded land allotments. He had eight wives, built a fine ten-room house, and before he died he had his own telephone, owned a car, traveled by train, and went hunting

American Voices

Paruasemena (Ten Bears), Speech at Medicine Lodge Creek Treaty Meeting, 1867

Paruasemena was one of the Indian leaders to visit Lincoln at the White House in 1863. Four years later, the seventy-five-year-old leader spoke to the U.S. peace commission at Medicine Lodge Creek.

My people have never first drawn a bow or fired a gun against the whites. There has been trouble between us … my young men have danced the war dance. But it was not begun by us. It was you who sent out the first soldier. …

Two years ago I came upon this road, following the buffalo, that my wives and children might have their cheeks plump and their bodies warm. But the soldiers fired on us. … The blue-dressed soldiers and the Utes came out from the night … and for campfires they lit our lodges. Instead of hunting game they killed my braves, and the warriors of the tribe cut short their hair for the dead.

So it was in Texas. They made sorrow in our camps, and we went out like the buffalo bulls when the cows are attacked. When we found them we killed them, and their scalps hang in our lodges. The Comanches are not weak and blind, like the pups of a dog when seven sleeps old. They are strong and farsighted, like grown horses. We took their road and we went on it. The white women cried, and our women laughed.

But there are things which you have said to me which I do not like. … You have said that you want to put us on a reservation, to build us houses and make us medicine lodges. I do not want them. I was born under the prairie, where the wind blew free and there was nothing to break the light of the sun. I was born where there

were no enclosures and everything drew a free breath. I want to die there and not within walls. I know every stream and wood between the Rio Grande and the Arkansas. I have hunted and lived over that country. I live like my fathers before me and like them I lived happily.

When I was in Washington the Great Father told me that all the Comanche land was ours and that no one should hinder us in living upon it. So, why do you ask us to leave the rivers and the sun and the wind and live in houses? Do not ask us to give up the buffalo for the sheep. The young men have heard talk of this, and it has made them sad and angry. Do not speak of it more.

Source: Nathaniel G. Taylor et al. (1910), Papers Relating to Talks and Councils Held with the Indians in Dakota and Montana in the Years 1866–1869 (Washington, D.C.: Government Printing Office.) Original in the National Archives, Records of the Indian Division, Office of the Secretary of the Interior, Record Group 48.

Thinking Critically

1. **Analyzing Primary Sources**

   How did Paruasemena characterize the conflict between his people and the U.S. government? How do—or don't—his words shed light on the historical situation faced by American Indians in the western United States in the decades after the Civil War?

2. **Contextualization**

   What light does this document shed on the differences between white and Indian cultural values in the 1800s?

with President Theodore Roosevelt. The life Parker and his people lived as he grew older was radically different from the life he had lived as a youth, but he helped create the foundation for tribal survival in a new era.

The Navajos and the Apaches

The Navajos, or Diné as they prefer to be called, were as warlike as the Comanches and dominated large swaths of New Mexico, Colorado, and Kansas. The Union army ended their rule and that of the Mescalero Apaches, too. In August 1862, Union brigadier general James H. Carleton arrived in New Mexico in command of California volunteers, but when he learned that Confederates in the region had already been defeated, he ordered his troops to attack the Apaches and Navajos instead. In early 1863, the army invaded Apache lands and soon confined some four hundred Apaches at a new reservation at **Bosque Redondo** in central New Mexico. Carleton then appointed Kit Carson to lead the attack on the much larger Navajo tribe of some ten thousand people. Carson told the Navajos, "Go to Bosque Redondo, or we will pursue and destroy you. We will not make peace with you on any other terms." Carson kept his word, marching into Canyon de Chelly, the sacred Navajo heartland, attacking Navajo encampments as well as destroying orchards, crops, and livestock. By the spring of 1864, some six thousand Navajos had surrendered rather than die of starvation. U.S. troops pursued other resisters, and eventually eight thousand Navajos were forced on the "Long Walk," three hundred miles south to a strange way of life at Bosque Redondo.

The Bosque Redondo reservation was a complete failure. The Mescalero Apaches considered the Navajos to be their "inveterate enemies," and the two tribes had no interest

Bosque Redondo

A reservation in central New Mexico where the majority of the Navajos and Mescalero Apaches were confined during the Civil War.

Navajos under guard at Bosque Redondo, ca. 1864.

in cooperating. The arid land in the middle of New Mexico could not support thousands of families, even if they did turn to farming as the government asked them to do. The Comanches saw the confined reservation as an opportunity to attack old enemies.

After the Civil War, a congressional peace commission visited Bosque Redondo and realized that the government had created a disaster. A new Mescalero Apaches reservation in central New Mexico was established by executive order in 1873 and expanded in 1883. On June 1, 1868, the government signed a new treaty with the Navajos that allowed them to return to a reservation in their own homelands. Navajo leaders negotiated several expansions of their reservation between 1868 and 1886 so it covered a large part of New Mexico and Arizona up to the four corners area with Colorado and Utah. They also managed to avoid the division of the reservation into individual allotments that destroyed tribal ways for other tribes. The Navajo Nation kept their promise to stop raiding and re-created much of their old ways, living on lands they considered sacred and making a living by herding sheep, goats, and horses. The tribe grew from ten thousand in 1864 to thirty thousand in 1900, an unusual experience for American Indians.

The Modocs, the Nez Perce, and the Pacific Coast Tribes

Well before the Civil War, the rapid influx of white settlers who came to California with the Gold Rush was a catastrophe for the many small tribes that dotted the state. The California tribes had already been weakened by decades of Spanish and Mexican efforts to turn them into workers on the missions and the large rancheros of the state. The new American presence only made things worse. Federal commissioners negotiated treaties with 139 tribes to create small reservations, mostly in northern California, but Congress did not ratify the treaties and white settlers ignored them. In spite of the efforts of federal Indian agents to create reasonable safeguards for the Indians of California, settlers and miners ignored restrictions on Indian land if they thought they could find gold or plant a settlement. California Indians were starved and all too often simply murdered. In 1845, before the United States took control of California, there were some 150,000 Indians in California—down from probably 300,000 when the Spanish missionaries first arrived; just a decade after California became a state, only 25,000 remained.

In the fall of 1872, Kintpuash, a leader of the Modoc tribe in southern Oregon and northern California, led his people out of a reservation the Modocs had shared with the Klamaths and Snakes since signing a treaty in 1864. Kintpuash did not like reservation

Chief Joseph of the Nez Perce, who led the epic journey of his people.

Library of Congress Prints and Photographs Division [LC-USZ61-2085]

life, and the Modocs returned to their homelands on Lost River in California. The U.S. Army followed and attacked them, but the Modocs knew the territory, especially the great black lava fields that provided hiding to those who had grown up among them. The Modocs resisted, killing soldiers, settlers, and government negotiators. Orders came from Washington "that the name of Modoc should cease," because they had violated their treaty and killed federal negotiators. Eventually, the army won. Surviving Modocs were relocated in Indian Territory far from their homeland.

The Nez Perce, the tribe without whom Lewis and Clark would have perished, had long lived in Oregon and Idaho, but they were a deeply divided tribe. One group, known as the "progressives," signed a treaty in 1855 agreeing to live on a large reservation in Idaho. Another group, the so-called nonprogressives, refused. They lived independently in an area encompassing the Salmon River in Idaho and the Snake River in Oregon.

For some time, the nonprogressive Nez Perce were allowed to live in peace, but as white settlement grew in the Snake River's fertile Wallowa Valley, pressure came to force them and their leader, Chief Joseph, or Hin-mah-too-yah-lat-kekt, onto the Idaho Reservation. They resisted, but by 1877, the Nez Perce knew they could no longer live unmolested in the Wallowa Valley. They began a long retreat to preserve their independence, a retreat that turned into a well-chronicled but tragic journey. Initially, the Nez Perce moved east across the Bitterroot Mountains into Montana, hoping to find sanctuary with the Crow or Sioux. Then they turned north, hoping to cross into Canada. All along the way, the U.S. Army pursued them. Finally, when they were less than forty miles from Canada, the army caught up. A few escaped across the border, but the majority, led by Chief Joseph, surrendered. The chief said, "I am tired of fighting. Our chiefs are killed. … It is cold and we have no blankets. The little children are freezing to death. … My heart is sick and sad. From where the sun now stands, I will fight no more forever." Most of those who had made the long journey with Chief Joseph ended up on a reservation in Indian Territory, although some, eventually including Chief Joseph, were allowed to return to the Pacific Northwest but never to their ancestral lands (see Map 16-1).

The Lakota Sioux—From Fort Laramie to the Little Big Horn and Wounded Knee

The Sioux, by far the largest group in the northern Great Plains, also fought fierce battles with the U.S. Army. Teton and Santee Sioux had been embroiled with U.S. settlers and army troops through the 1860s, but the largest battles of the 1870s were with the powerful Lakota Sioux.

In December 1866, the Lakota attacked and killed U.S. troops. Rather than risk further fighting, the government sought peace with the Lakota as well as their Cheyenne and Arapaho allies. In the 1868 Treaty of Fort Laramie, the Lakota Sioux, led by Red Cloud, promised to avoid war, and the army agreed to abandon three provocatively placed forts. (An earlier Fort Laramie Treaty of 1851 was negotiated simply to keep peace between the tribes and give the U.S. Army and settlers rights-of-way across the plains to California and Oregon.) Although the 1868 Fort Laramie Treaty could be seen as a victory for the Sioux, one faction, led by Sitting Bull, derided the treaty, reservation life, and the government annuities that were promised, saying to those who signed, "You are fools to make yourselves slaves to a piece of fat bacon, some hard-tack, and a little sugar and coffee." Indeed, the treaty that Sitting Bull criticized did not protect the Lakota or the other tribes involved.

Less than a decade after the treaty was signed, when gold was discovered in the Black Hills and miners and settlers descended on the region, the government ordered the Lakota to leave winter camps and settle near the federal government's Indian agency headquarters. The Lakota resisted. The Great Sioux War of 1876–1877 had begun.

General George Armstrong Custer led a battalion of troops in an attack on the Sioux who were refusing to move. At the Little Bighorn River on June 25, 1876, Custer and his troops were surrounded by a much larger force of Sioux and Cheyennes. None of the army troops survived. It was perhaps the most famous Indian victory, but that success was soon followed by defeat. Less than a month after the Little Bighorn battle, General Philip

Map 16-1 The Plains Indian Wars.

As trails and then railroads brought more settlers, the great battles between the U.S. Army and the Plains Indians erupted all across the Great Plains.

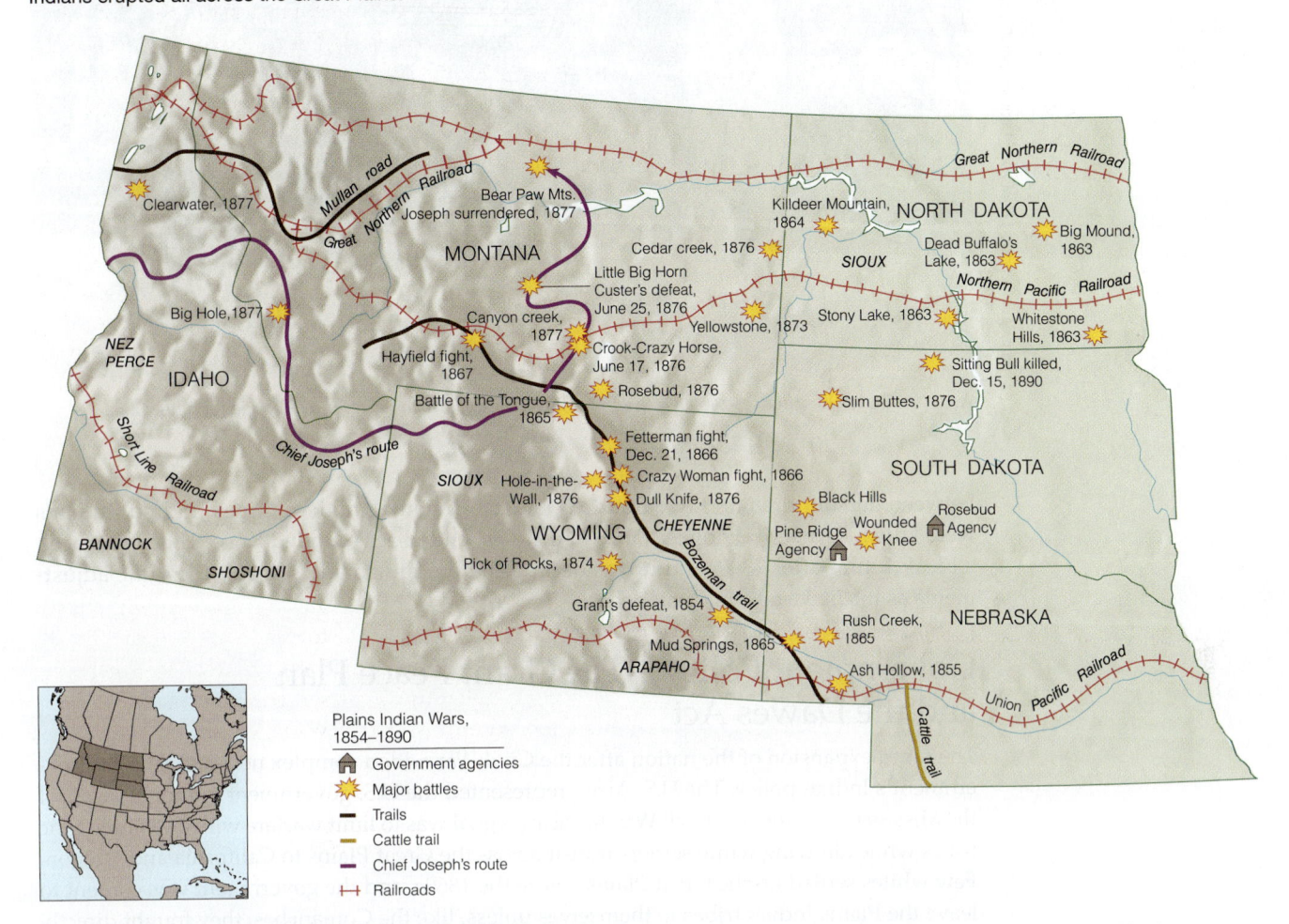

Plains Indian Wars,
1854–1890

- 🏠 Government agencies
- ✴ Major battles
- ▬ Trails
- ▬ Cattle trail
- ▬ Chief Joseph's route
- ⊢⊣ Railroads

Sheridan led a huge force that attacked and defeated the Sioux. The government then broke up the Great Sioux Reserve in the Black Hills of Dakota Territory, creating six much smaller reservations: Standing Rock, Cheyenne River, Lower Brule, Crow Creek, Pine Ridge, and Rosebud, while giving some of the best land, now declared "surplus," to white settlers and miners.

The defeats of 1876–1877, along with the destruction of the great buffalo herds, led to an era of depression, disease, and poverty for the Sioux. A little more than a decade later, in 1890, the religious phenomenon that had been seen among other tribes appeared among the Sioux. A spiritual leader, Wovoka, initiated the **Ghost Dance** movement, promising a return of the buffalo and the disappearance of white people if only the Sioux would take up the dance and return to their ancient ways, freeing themselves of dependence on white culture. The rise of the Ghost Dance frightened the white community, and the army was sent to Pine Ridge to investigate. A former Indian agent, Valentine McGillycuddy, appealed for calm, saying, "I should let the dance continue. … If the Seventh-Day Adventists prepare their ascension robes for the second coming of the Savior, the United States Army is not put in motion to prevent them. Why should not the Indians have the same privilege?"

McGillycuddy also warned that "[i]f the troops remain, trouble is sure to come." He was right. One band of Sioux under the leadership of Big Foot left the reservation while the Ghost Dance continued, and U.S. troops went after them. When Big Foot and his band were caught, they returned to Pine Ridge without a fight. The next day, however, Big Foot and his followers were asked to surrender themselves as prisoners. Ghost Dance leaders convinced them to make a stand. It was a fatal move. Gunfire erupted on the reservation and

Ghost Dance

Part of a religious awakening among the Lakota Sioux in 1890 in which they believed that if they returned to their traditional ways and ceremonies, the whites would be driven from their land.

Library of Congress Prints and Photographs Division [LC-US262-3726]

Artist Frederick Remington depicted the 1890 Ghost Dance, which represented a hope for a new age.

between one hundred and two hundred (some estimate as high as three hundred) Indians were killed. Armed Indian resistance in the West ended at Wounded Knee. The Sioux faced a bleak future after 1890, and it was decades before they made some of the same adjustments as the Navajos and Comanches.

Government Policy—The Grant Peace Plan and the Dawes Act

The rapid expansion of the nation after the Civil War added complex new issues to the government's Indian policy. The U.S. Army represented the U.S. government to Indians west of the Mississippi. Before the Civil War, the army's goal was to limit warfare with and among the tribes while allowing white settlers transit across the Great Plains to California and Oregon. Few whites settled on the Great Plains before the 1860s, and the government was content to leave the Plains Indian tribes to themselves unless, like the Comanches, they fought directly with the army. The first Treaty of Fort Laramie in 1851 did not limit Indian land use except to try to keep the peace by keeping tribes apart from one another. No reservations were established for tribes living west of the Mississippi before the Civil War. Rather, in exchange for gifts, the army asked the tribes to avoid conflict with one another, with military forts, and with the transit routes for the mail and for settlers. Asking for anything more was beyond the limits of what the 270 soldiers at Fort Laramie could reasonably ask in a meeting attended by perhaps 10,000 American Indians, including the Sioux, Arapaho, Cheyenne, Assinboins, Shoshones, Arikaras, Hidatsas, Mandans, and Crows.

After the Civil War, the pressure for space for white settlement greatly intensified and U.S. Army units were now available for service in the West. Among these units were segregated African American units that came to be known as Buffalo Soldiers because their white commanders thought their hair was like that of the buffalo. Even though most military units were demobilized after the war, there were more than sufficient numbers of soldiers—white and black—to provide a formidable fighting force in the West.

In 1862, a Republican Congress had passed, and President Lincoln had signed, the **Homestead Act**, fulfilling a major Republican campaign promise to make more federal land available for white settlement. The act provided 160 acres of federal land to a family that would settle and maintain the land for five years. The act, however, did not specify where the land would come from. Many of the initial homestead settlements were in Iowa, Kansas, Minnesota, and Nebraska, all on lands that had been prime buffalo-hunting locations for various tribes. Unlike before the Civil War when most whites had moved across the Great Plains and kept going to the West Coast under the protection of U.S. Army, after the Civil War, whites were coming to the plains to stay and larger army forces were coming with

Homestead Act

Law passed by Congress in 1862 providing 160 acres of land free to anyone who would live on the plot and farm it for five years.

16.1

16.2

16.3

them. In addition to farming, the discovery of mineral wealth in places like the Black Hills of the Dakotas brought more whites and further racial conflict.

Immediately after the war, the same Congress that was taking control of Reconstruction also created its own Indian peace policy and assigned the army to implement it. The battles with the Lakota Sioux led to the creation of the Indian Peace Commission to negotiate treaties with the Plains tribes. The congressional commission developed the idea of tribal reserves or reservations, large tracts of land that would, they hoped, be set aside for the Indians, protecting the tribes from encroaching white settlers while ensuring their eventual assimilation into white culture. It was same policy that had been used in negotiating with tribes that originally lived east of the Mississippi but with one big difference. The majority of eastern tribes had been forced onto reservations in the West, specifically, in Oklahoma or Indian Territory. There was no place farther west to push the western tribes, so the government tried to move them onto as limited an amount of land as possible. At the same time, of course, confining the tribes on reservations would ensure that most of the land of the West could be opened for white development. Tribes like the Sioux, Nez Perce, and Comanches resented the confinement of reservation life and often wandered far beyond their assigned bounds.

When Ulysses S. Grant became president in 1869, he initiated a new Indian Peace Policy that became known as **Grant's Peace Policy**. Grant's thinking was shaped by the terrible bloodshed he had seen in the Civil War and by his identification with the emancipation of

Grant's Peace Policy

A new effort by President Grant to end the Plains Indian Wars by creating a series of reservations on which tribes could maintain their traditional ways.

American Voices

Charles W. Allen, Report from Wounded Knee, 1890

Charles W. Allen, a white newspaper editor who had spent most of his life among the Sioux, reported the event he saw at the Pine Ridge Reservation on December 29, 1890.

Presently all the Indian men began coming in bunches of from two to a dozen or more, stringing leisurely along then taking their seats in a circle on the grass before the commander and his staff. … Then General Forsyth addressed in a firm but conciliatory manner. … [H]e told them that for the time being they were prisoners, and as such they were to give up their arms peaceably. … He then told them to go back to their lodges, bring all their firearms, and turn them over to him. The Indians departed for their camp in a reluctant, obviously sulky mood. …

After what seemed an unreasonable length of time the Indians came strolling back pretty much as they had come to the first meeting, except that they seemed purposely to adopt a more independent swagger in approaching the council field. Many of them were painted hideously and conspicuously grim of visage. … Quite a number of their wives had accompanied the braves to this meeting, robed in long blankets reaching almost to the ground, and each took a position immediately behind her husband. … The women who stood close behind their men concealed, under each blanket, a repeating rifle and well filled cartridge belt. …

Chief Big Foot had been escorted from his tent, and urged his followers to maintain peace and comply with the general's orders. … I also observed a Hotchkiss gun that had been placed in commanding position on a small knoll at the north edge of the camp, not far from the site on which the Catholic church now commemorates the tragedy. …

Gen. Forsyth ordered a detail of dismounted troops under Capt. Wallace to close in and surround them at a distance of about twenty paces. … During this procedure, which was very interesting,

an Indian ghost dance master, arrayed in full paraphernalia, began to make medicine, holding his hands up to the sun and calling upon the Messiah to visit his wrath upon the soldiers. He would take up hands full of dirt and scatter it, then hold up his hands as if momentarily expecting the earth to open and swallow up the troops. It was evident that he was getting the Indians worked up and he finally told them to be brave and that bullets would not hit them if the soldiers did shoot at them. The commander was told of what he was saying, and he ordered him to sit down, which order he finally complied with after he had walked clear around the circle as though he owned the earth. … They had proceeded to disarm but some eight or ten of these, when the brave who had been inciting them jumped up and said something and fired at the soldier who was standing guard over the arms that had been secured. The first gun had no sooner been fired than it was followed by hundreds of others and the battle was on. The fighting continued for about a half hour, and then was continued in skirmish for another hour.

Source: Charles W. Allen, *From Fort Laramie to Wounded Knee: In the West That Was*, edited with an introduction by Richard E. Jensen (originally published 1938, republished Lincoln: University of Nebraska Press, 1997), pp. 192–202.

Thinking Critically

1. **Argument Development**
   In Allen's story, who was responsible for the fighting at Wounded Knee? Do you find this account to be a credible version of what happened at Wounded Knee? Why or why not?

2. **Continuity and Change over Time**
   Why might historians call Wounded Knee the end of an era in American history? Do you see it as a moment of unique historical change or part of a longer pattern?

slaves. He wanted to end the corruption that he saw in the Indian Bureau, and he wanted to treat the Indians with dignity. His goal was peace. At the same time, Grant wanted room for white settlement and was certainly not planning to keep whites out of the vast tracts of western land that the Indians used for hunting. In his first annual message to Congress in December 1869, Grant said there was no turning back the clock, that the past "cannot be undone, and the question must be met as we now find it." Meeting the question, he believed, meant assimilating Indians into white society, or as the president asked, "Can not the Indian be made a useful and productive member of society by proper teaching and treatment?" Since most of the Indians did not want to become "useful and productive members" of white society, Grant's policy may have been doomed from the beginning, but he tried to find a human solution to the clash that was taking place in the American West.

When Grant announced his Peace Policy he said,

> The building of rail-roads and the access thereby given to all the agricultural and mineral regions of the country is rapidly bringing civilized settlements into contact with all the tribes of Indians. … I see no remedy for this except in placing all the Indians on large reservations … and giving them absolute protection there.

Grant then appointed a member of the Seneca tribe, Ely S. Parker, as the first Native American Commissioner of Indian Affairs, the first nonwhite to hold a high government position. Grant also turned to Christian missionaries, not the army or the Indian Office, to take the lead in managing reservation affairs. He declared the reservations off-limits to the army, even troops that were chasing Indians with whom they had been in battle.

The missionaries, people like the Quaker Lawrie Tatum who was appointed to lead the Comanche and Kiowa reservation, tried to make the peace policy work. But government supplies were slow in coming and often of shoddy workmanship. Many Indians resisted the confinement of reservation life. The army was frustrated by the rule that they could not follow Indians into the reservations. General Sheridan condemned the Peace Policy, saying, "If a white man commits murder or robs, we hang him or send him to the penitentiary; if an Indian does the same, we have been in the habit of giving him more blankets." The Indians, seeing through the references to peace, considered the whites as thieves who were stealing their land.

Although the Indian Peace Policy remained in force, the army simply ignored it. Sherman's defeat of the Comanches in 1874–1875 was in violation of the policy that army units could not enter reservations, but the general was praised, not reprimanded. Within a year after Custer's 1876 defeat, the army had subdued nearly all of the Sioux. Crazy Horse, one of the Sioux who was at the Little Big Horn the day Custer died, became an army scout and was killed at an army post in September 1877. Sitting Bull was arrested in 1881 after returning from exile in Canada. He toured briefly with Buffalo Bill Cody's Wild West Show in the 1880s and then retired to the Standing Rock reservation where, as the Ghost Dance movement grew, he was killed in a standoff with other Sioux sent by the army to arrest him. But the Grant Peace Policy had unofficially died long before the old chief met his end.

Within a decade of the last major Indian wars in the 1870s and the settlement of most western Indians on reservations, the U.S. government again began to change policy. By the 1880s, reformers in and out of government were concluding that the assimilation of Indians into white society—a goal many shared—would not happen as long as they maintained their ancient ways on reservations. If the key to Indian survival was for them to become independent farmers who attended churches and schools just as whites did, then why, reformers asked, should they live on reservations? Why not give them all the benefits of the Homestead Act and allow Indians, like whites, to gain free title to their own 160-acre farm and American citizenship?

In response to these arguments, Congress passed the General Allotment Act, known as the **Dawes Act** for its prime sponsor Massachusetts senator Henry L. Dawes, in 1887. The Dawes Act divided the reservations into 160-acre tracts to be assigned to each family. After a twenty-five-year waiting period, Indian families could sell the land like their white neighbors. Indians who took possession of a homestead also became U.S. citizens. At first glance, the Dawes Act might seem like an enlightened piece of legislation and at least some of its sponsors certainly believed that it was.

The Dawes Act had other far more negative provisions, however. Indian culture was tribal and communal, and hunting was a major activity, but the Dawes Act pushed Indians to be

Dawes Act

An 1887 law terminating tribal ownership of most reservation land and allocating some parcels to individual Indians while the remainder was opened for white settlement.

farmers and to join an individualistic culture that many found to be quite alien. Beyond that, the most immediate impact of the act was that, after each family on a reservation was allotted its 160 acres, all "surplus" land could then be sold by the government to white families. Later, after the twenty-five-year waiting period, Indian families sometimes sold their land, giving them a profit but alienating them from their tribe. A few tribes, the Navajos and the Senecas, were able to avoid implementation of the Dawes Act and retain communal ownership of their reservations. But for many, the act was an economic and cultural disaster.

In 1881, 155 million acres were set aside as reservations belonging to Indian tribes. As a result of the Dawes Act, Indians controlled only 78 million acres by 1900. While the Dawes Act broke up tribal lands, other federal perspectives undercut Indian culture. Few white authorities believed that the First Amendment protections of religious freedom applied to Indian religion, especially because Indian religion and Indian warfare were often linked. It was not until 1978 that Congress declared traditional Indian religions to have First Amendment rights.

Sending Indian young people to special schools was also seen by officials as one of the surest ways of implementing Grant's promise to "favor any course towards them which tends to their civilization and ultimate citizenship." In 1875, the army ordered seventy-two Indian prisoners—among them, Cheyenne, Arapahos, Kiowas, Comanches, and Caddos—moved from Fort Sill in Indian Territory to a new federal prison in St. Augustine, Florida. Lieutenant Richard Henry Pratt, a Civil War veteran who was put in charge of the prisoners, decided to create a model Indian school. He hired Sarah Mather from Mt. Holyoke College, and the two began to teach the prisoners American-style dress, the English language, and Protestant Christianity. The isolation of the prisoner-students made the process easier. Soaring Eagle, a Cheyenne warrior, said, "It is good to go to church. … When I go home, I hope to sit down and sing God's hymns." Of course, Soaring Eagle and the other prisoners knew that the only chance they had to actually go home was to comply with the school's policies.

Pratt and Mather's experiment drew widespread praise. They were authorized to expand their efforts and open the **Carlisle Indian School** in old army barracks in Carlisle, Pennsylvania. Twenty-five Indian boarding schools, eventually both Catholic and Protestant, were built on the Carlisle model between 1879 and 1902. Using federal tax dollars, these schools taught religion, western customs, and values to their Indian students.

Indian students resisted the goal of the boarding schools, though such resistance was harshly punished. Francis La Flesche, an Omaha who attended a Presbyterian mission school in the 1860s, reported that he and his friends spoke English during the day, but at night when the missionaries were gone, they continued to tell each other the Omaha stories and speak the Omaha language.

Carlisle Indian School

A boarding school for Native American children opened in Carlisle, Pennsylvania to teach white ways and separate Indian children from tribal culture.

16.1 Quick Review

How did actions after the Civil War—in particular, reassigning U.S. Army units to the West and offering land for white settlement through the Homestead Act—irrevocably change life for Indians in the West?

The Impact of the Transcontinental Railroad, 1869

16.2 Analyze the building of transcontinental railroads and its impact on the nation, especially the West.

When he proposed his Indian Peace Policy in December 1869, Grant said that it was needed because "[t]he building of rail-roads … is rapidly bringing civilized settlements into contact with all the tribes of Indians." Only seven months earlier at Promontory Point, Utah, Leland Stanford, governor of California and president of the Central Pacific Railroad, and T. C. Durant, vice president of the Union Pacific Railroad, had driven the last spike—made of California gold—to connect the first rail line that spanned the North American continent.

16.1

16.2

16.3

16.1

16.2

16.3

transcontinental railroad

The transcontinental railroad was the first to span the whole United States, allowing travel from the East to the West. With it, the Union Pacific rail line from California connected to the Central Pacific line out of Chicago and points East.

CENTRAL PACIFIC RAILROAD—CHINESE LABORERS AT WORK.

Corbis Historical/Getty images

Chinese crews, working in the isolated mountains of California, had to blast tunnels and build bridges to complete the rail line.

Library of Congress Prints and Photographs Division [LC-USZ62-57524]

When crews building the Union Pacific Railroad and the Central Pacific Railroad met at Promontory Summit, Utah, in May 1869, the nation celebrated the completion of the first transcontinental railroad.

The dream of a **transcontinental railroad** gained widespread support in the 1850s. An army survey in 1853 offered four possible routes across the country variously ending in Portland, San Francisco, Los Angeles, or San Diego. More debate focused on where the routes should begin. Illinois senator Stephen A. Douglas wanted them to start in Chicago, while Mississippi senator Jefferson Davis wanted them to begin in Memphis or New Orleans. It had been Douglas's dream of a route starting in Chicago that originally led him to propose the Kansas-Nebraska Act. But before the issue of the best transcontinental rail route could be settled, the Civil War had intervened. Once the war began in 1861, the departure of Southerners from Congress meant that a more northerly route became the obvious choice of the remaining members. The Pacific Railroad Act passed easily in 1862. The California-based Central Pacific started building east from San Francisco and Sacramento, while the Union Pacific started building west across the Great Plains from terminals in Kansas, Nebraska, and Missouri, all of which were already connected to the East Coast by existing rail lines. The federal government provided a four-hundred-foot right of way, federal loans, and major land grants to the two railroads. The right of way was a grant of the federal lands along the whole length of the railroads and constituted a government subsidy without which the transcontinental railroad could not have been built. Construction moved very slowly during the war—workers and supplies were needed elsewhere—but the coming of peace in 1865 brought a rush to complete the work.

The hard physical labor of actually laying track was done mostly by Irish workers on the Union Pacific and by Chinese laborers on the California-based Central Pacific. Those starting in the east were sometimes able to lay track at the rate of four rails per minute, covering five hundred miles and reaching Cheyenne, Wyoming, by November 1867. Those starting in California had the far more difficult task of crossing the Sierra Nevada Mountains. They had to build snow sheds and blast through solid rock to make their way. Finally, in the spring of 1869, the lines connected, and the nation was knit together as never before.

The first rail connection across the continent was only the beginning. By the early 1890s, four major lines reached across the country, connecting to a large network of midwestern and eastern rail lines. The major cities within California, Oregon, and Washington were connected by their own lines. All of the country's large cities, and most of the medium-sized ones, were connected by rail. A city without a rail link was doomed to wither since the railroads made it possible for farmers to get their products to market much faster and cheaper than ever before while also making nonfarm goods available to isolated rural people, *if* they lived near a rail line. The new markets that were opened as a result of the railroads changed the country as much as the movement of people, especially settlers, that was facilitated by the rail lines. In a few decades after the Civil War, vast tracts of western lands that had been home to Indian tribes and buffalo became home to white settlers from the East Coast and Europe who produced wheat and corn, mined silver and gold, and managed livestock and who shipped all of those products to world markets via the railroads—sometimes creating new prosperity and sometimes shipping so much that prices collapsed and markets fell. All of this development happened at great cost, of course, to the Indians whose land it had been, but often also to settlers who lived isolated and marginalized lives and who increasingly blamed the large railroad corporations for their plight.

Technological changes helped extend the railroads. George Westinghouse's invention of an air brake system in 1873 made trains safer and the rides smoother as it became possible to stop all of the cars of a train at once rather than needing to coordinate the work of a brakeman on each car. Eli Janney invented a safer system for coupling and decoupling railway cars, saving the lives of innumerable railway workers. Safer construction of tracks and bridges, the replacement of iron rails with steel, and new improved locomotive production all improved speed and safety. Whereas travel to the California Gold Rush in 1849 took six to eight weeks or more, by the 1870s, a person could travel across the United States in ten days and, if one could afford it, do so in the comfort of a Pullman sleeping car.

The railroads linked communities with a speed that created a new sense of time. When a traveler moved by horse or wagon, the exact time of day did not matter that much. Trains, however, needed to follow a schedule if passengers and freight were to depart and arrive on time and collisions were to be avoided. Schedules, particularly coordinating trains over great distances, required something no one had considered before—standardized time. Although some objected, like the Cincinnati editor who asked why his city should shift its clocks "so as to harmonize with an imaginary line through Pittsburgh," the clear majority of the country readily agreed to the plan. On Sunday, November 18, 1883, known as the "Day of Two Noons," all but the most isolated American communities adjusted their clocks to place them in one of the four time zones into which the nation was being divided—time zones that still regulate daily life today.

What had once been isolated regional economies quickly became part of a national commercial network because of railroads. The cost of moving food and other goods dropped dramatically. People followed the same time schedule. The railroads that crossed the continent ended at docks where ocean-going steamships carried food, lumber, and other materials from the United States to Europe or to Asia and South America. Within three decades of acquiring the West Coast, the United States was connected to a Pacific market of international trade and commerce that would create work for many—from lumberjacks in Oregon and Washington to miners in Idaho or the Dakotas to wheat farmers across the Midwest—creating wealth for a few and linking the nation's economy to the rise and fall of world markets. After 1890, a glut of wheat in Argentina could impact the life of a farmer in Nebraska, and a drop in the value of silver in Japan could hurt a miner in Idaho. Even though the United States was not quite yet a major world power, it was connected to the world as never before (see Map 16-2).

Map 16-2 Connecting the Nation.

Rail lines and cattle trails connected far-flung parts of the West. Gold and silver mines, cattle ranches, and wheat farmers were suddenly part of a worldwide market.

16.1

16.2

16.3

16.2 Quick Review

How did railroads improve transportation and communication in ways that other innovations such as canals and steamboats could not?

The Transformation of the West

16.3 Analyze how indigenous people, ranchers, farmers, miners, outlaws, politicians, and mythmakers shaped the West and our understanding of its history.

The defeat of the Indian tribes and the Homestead Act, along with extraordinary changes in time, speed, and transportation brought on by the railroads, transformed the American West. Land that had been part of Mexico in the 1840s and that people from the East Coast only wanted to get across in the 1850s became the site of vast new ranches, settled farms, and rapidly expanding towns. By the 1880s and 1890s, a new region was becoming part of the nation's cultural, economic, and political networks.

Of course, not all of the new settlers in the American West got along with each other. Cattle ranchers depended on vast wide-open spaces to feed and move their herds. Farmers seeking to establish 160-acre homesteads depended on barbed wire to fence off their land, and keep cattle in or out. Older residents of what had been the northern parts of Mexico had relied on sometimes vague property lines and depended on communal grazing lands, while the newly arriving Americans wanted precise lines and built fences across the land that had once been held in common. Settlers seeking to establish farms or build towns depended on law and order, while others—outlaws and gunfighters—thought that the best way to make one's fortune was to take it from others. As these groups battled for control, they soon came to create political organization if not always social order.

Cowboys, Cattle, the Open Range, and Barbed Wire

White families seeking to make their fortune, or at least a living, raising cattle moved into southwest Texas in the 1850s, expanding throughout the West by the 1860s and 1870s. Allowing the cattle to graze the vast open areas enabled herders to manage far greater numbers at much less cost than if they had to confine them to pens or small farms and then pay for their feed. Texas Longhorn cattle, the result of interbreeding cattle of Spanish origin and Anglo-American stock, seemed especially perfect for the region. They could survive on easy-to-find grass on the wide plains, did not need additional feed, and were resistant to Texas fever, the tick-borne disease that killed other cattle. Farther north in Kansas, Nebraska, and the Dakotas, other cattle ranchers also discovered that cattle thrived on the bunchgrasses of the northern prairies, which dried out by mid-summer but retained their protein and fed cattle well, even when they had to find it through the snow.

By the time the Civil War called most of the cattlemen off to distant battlefields and left the cattle to fend for themselves, there were probably five million cattle in west Texas. Although the Comanches took their share of the abandoned cattle, many remained by the end of the war, and some herds grew substantially, having been allowed to breed without being slaughtered for food for several years.

In the summer of 1865, returning veterans reconnected with families and sought to reestablish the herds on which their families depended. Lee Moore remembered helping his veteran father reassemble a herd in southwest Texas: "We didn't call it roundup in those days. We called it cow-hunts and every man on this cow-hunt was a cattle owner just home from the war and went out to see what they had left and to brand up."

Most of those trying to reassemble herds in 1865 could not be called ranchers. They did not own or maintain ranches, as such. Rather, they allowed their cattle to graze freely on the open Texas, land officially owned by the federal government, though contested by various Indian tribes. They identified their cattle by branding them when they were young.

16.1

16.2

16.3

Unbranded cattle—known as mavericks—were free for the taking. The few who did own ranches managed vast operations, like the huge King Ranch where Richard King owned 84,000 acres at the end of the Civil War, eventually expanding to 1,270,000 acres. The King Ranch was one of several huge ranches in Texas and New Mexico, but much of the cattle raising in the 1860s and 1870s was a much more informal affair that depended on public lands and respect for cattle brands rather than private lands.

Several developments account for the huge increase in cattle ranching in the decades after the Civil War. Americans started to eat a lot of beef, and in prosperous times, they could afford to do so. Cookbooks reported new ways to prepare beef while telling readers that pork, which had fed much of the nation in earlier times, was unwholesome and hard to digest. Hiram Latham, a publicist for the Union Pacific Railroad, wrote a pamphlet, *Trans-Missouri Stock Raising*, in 1871 that declared the only way to support the nation's manufacturing workers was to ensure they had a large supply of clothing and cheap food, food that needed to include a healthy amount of beef (see Map 16-3).

In spite of the ease of raising cattle, particularly in Texas, Colorado, Wyoming, or Montana, it was a long distance from those areas to the mouths of most Americans, whether on the Pacific Coast or in the Midwest or on the Atlantic Coast. In 1867, Joseph G. McCoy founded Abilene, Kansas, one of the nation's first cattle towns, to facilitate the loading of cattle onto transcontinental trains that would speed the beef to consumers. Jesse Chisholm began herding cattle along what came to be known as the Chisholm Trail from Texas, across Indian Territory, to Abilene to connect with those railroad lines. In 1867, some thirty thousand cattle made their way along the Chisholm Trail, and over the next twenty years, two million more followed.

Map 16-3 Cattle Trails and Rail Lines.

Cattle were driven north from Texas and parts of Kansas and Nebraska to rail lines where they could be moved to world markets.

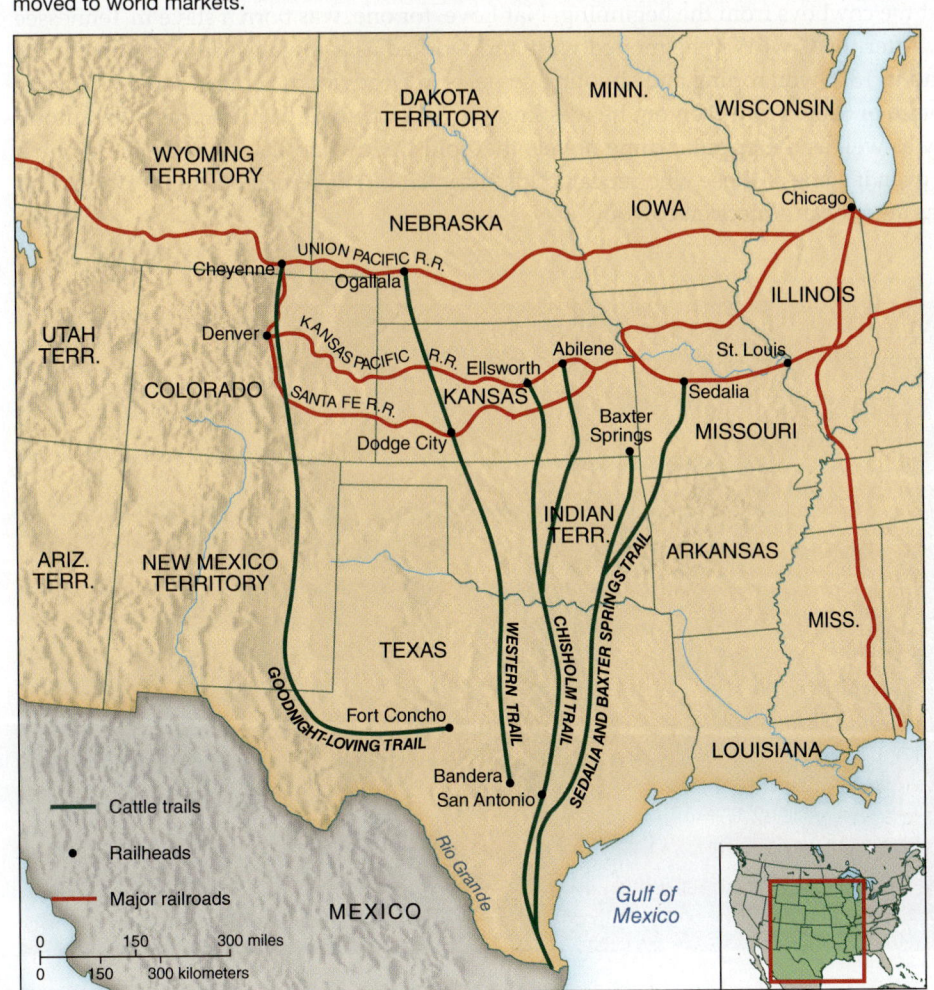

Not surprisingly, Abilene and other towns at the end of the drive became wild places when the cattle drive reached town. Cowboys, young single men who had spent many months following the herds, were ready for a party when they got to town. The infamous Longbranch Saloon and the Dodge House Hotel, both in Dodge City, Kansas, hosted many celebrating cowboys. These environments offered some of the only economic opportunities for women in the cattle industry, and those opportunities were less than reputable. Prostitution was often the only way to survive and, sometimes, a route to independence. A Wichita newspaper reported on the "ten bawdy houses" in Newton, Kansas, in 1871: "Here you may see young girls not over sixteen drinking whisky, smoking cigars, cursing and swearing." Most prostitutes in the cattle towns were very young, between fourteen and twenty-three, and from the eastern United States, Europe, and even Indian Territory. Few stayed in the business for very long.

As the demands for beef increased and cowboys brought more cattle into the railroad towns, developments in rail transport made the cattle industry more profitable. In 1882, Gustavus Swift created a new fleet of refrigerated railroad cars. Beef spoiled or took on an odd and unappetizing look in earlier refrigerator cars when it was packed in ice. Swift kept the ice separate and above the beef so the beef stayed cold without touching ice. A few Chicago packinghouses—Swift, Armour, Morris, and Hammond—along with smaller ones in Kansas City, Omaha, and Fort Worth, came to dominate the nation's meatpacking industry. By 1900, 82 percent of the nation's cattle were killed and packed in such places. The Chicago's Union Stock Yards, first opened in 1865, became the hub for feeding the world.

As the beef industry became more centralized in the 1870s and 1880s, it continued to depend on the muscle of cowboys who cared for cattle, kept track of them when they drifted away, and handled the roundups and cattle drives. The greatest era of the cowboys of the American West was between the Civil War and 1900. The cowboys who did the work of the cattle industry were mostly poor, mostly young, and of many different backgrounds.

In spite of the lonely days and only rare occasions to celebrate, romantic legends surrounded the cowboys from the beginning. Nat Love, for one, was born a slave in Tennessee in 1854. After the Civil War, he moved west and worked as a cowboy. He was good at the work and in 1876 won roping and shooting contests in Deadwood, South Dakota, that gave him a prize of $200. From then on, he was known as Deadwood Dick and his own autobiography as well as the popular dime novels that told Deadwood Dick stories made him a legend, even if some of those who repeated his story left out the crucial fact that Deadwood Dick was an African American cowboy.

North Wind Picture Archives/Alamy Stock Photo

Most of a cowboy's life was hard, lonely work.

16.1

16.2

16.3

In the 1860s, many of the cowboys in Texas were white Confederate veterans, and those in Kansas or Montana were Union veterans. Still, there were a relatively large number of African Americans and American Indians among them. Cattle companies, especially in Texas, soon began replacing the Anglo cowboys with those of Mexican descent whom they could pay substantially less. In 1883, white cowboys in Texas struck for higher wages, but the Panhandle Cattleman's Association quickly broke the strike and found new sources of labor among poor single men of all races who wanted any job or who thought the work might be glamorous.

As the cattle business came to be controlled by larger ranches and corporations in the 1880s and 1890s, cowboys became less independent and more like hired workers in other industries, liable to be assigned to fence building one day and cattle branding the next. Nevertheless, herding cattle over great distances required skill, especially using a rope to lasso and understanding the behavior of herds. The most successful cattle producers knew that they had to provide for their staff. Cowboys had originally carried their own food, but cattle owners began to supply the food from specially constructed wagons, accompanied by a cook, who provided the meals on the range. The first rancher to carry food and bedding for the roundups and trail drives was Charles Goodnight, and in his honor, the wagons came to be known as "Chuck Wagons."

Although the cattle industry prospered, it also experienced significant changes and downturns. Branding cattle—using a hot iron to create a scar on the left flank of a calf that was easy to identify—was key to identifying cattle that roamed over very large areas of range, perhaps a hundred miles or more. While branding continued, by the 1880s, cattle owners began using barbed wire fences to set off their ranges. Barbed wire fences kept herds in more contained areas and protected the best grass. Of course, protecting the grass meant identifying who had the rights to certain areas, which brought cattle ranchers into conflict with each other and with the federal government since most of the western ranges were federal lands. The conflict often turned violent, perhaps most dramatically in the Johnson County War of 1892 when the Wyoming Stock Growers Association hired gunfighters to force smaller ranchers out of the state.

Success also depended on the price of beef staying high and a ready supply of cattle, both of which were problematic. The winters of 1880–1881, 1884–1885, and 1886–1887 were all unusually harsh. Cattle died for lack of food, or they drifted in front of a storm until they piled up against a barbed wire fence and died. In addition, economic recessions in the 1870s and again in the late 1880s led Americans to eat less beef. By the mid-1880s, the market for the twenty million cattle in the American West was declining. After a recovery, another depression in the 1890s made it hard to predict what the value of cattle would be in any given year.

By the end of the 1890s, the era of open ranges, roundups, and huge cattle drives was coming to an end. Growing demand for high-quality beef and new knowledge about the best feed enabled the cattle industry to shift to smaller-scale ranches where a rancher could maintain a few hundred cattle, ensure that they were well fed and cared for, and bring them to market at the best moment.

The male world of the cowboys was replaced by ranch families. Men still did most of the work with the cattle, while wives and daughters tended houses and gardens doing the "inside work." But in isolated communities, rigid gender lines were hard to maintain. A woman who lived on a Wyoming ranch in 1899 wrote, "The heavy work of the ranch naturally falls to men, but I think most ranch women will bear me out in saying that unless the women … be always ready to do anything that comes along … the ranch is not a success." Cowboys still worked on these ranches and urban Americans still ate beef, but the world of beef production and life on the plains was quite different from what it had been only a short time before.

Latino Resistance in the Southwest

Mary A. Fulgenzi, a long time resident of San Miguel County in New Mexico Territory, recalled the time in the late 1880s when tensions in her county exploded:

> In the early days of Las Vegas the wealthier people wanted to take possession of most of the lands. They fenced in any land they fancied, whether it belonged to them or not. The poor people also needed land to graze their stock and felt that they should have their share, for, according to the land grant, lands not allocated to individuals were to be used by the community in general.

Throughout much of the West, the battle between those who wanted to fence and control the land and those who wanted free grazing land for their herds was one of the great divides. The emergence of cheap barbed wire changed the face of the West. The specific details about contained and open grazing were different in different places and for different groups of people, but across the West there were clashes between those who wanted to fence off private property and those who wanted open prairies.

At the heart of the battle in San Miguel County, New Mexico, were two different views of the nature of land ownership. The majority of Mexicanos—as people of Mexican descent in New Mexico preferred to be called at the time—saw themselves as *las masas de los hombres pobres* (the masses of the poor). Their assumption was that any land that was not specifically part of the home or the irrigated farmland of one family was held in common—open grazing land that all could use. By the 1880s, however, Anglo-Americans with very different views of land ownership were arriving, especially after the Atchison, Topeka, and Santa Fe Railroad opened a line in 1879. Representatives of investors from the East Coast of the United States and from Britain, who could not imagine any alternative to private ownership of land, began buying up land and fencing off their property to create their own cattle ranches.

For some longtime residents, the fences were threatening their way of life, and the remedy was simple: get rid of the fences. When the ranchers did not comply with requests to take down their fences, a secret organization called the White Caps cut the fences, destroyed the posts, and opened the range again. In response to widespread fence cutting, the territorial governor requested federal troops. In spite of federal troops, most citizens of San Miguel County were sympathetic with the fence cutters. By the summer of 1890, San Miguel County's dissidents were running for political office and soon controlled the balance of power between Republicans and Democrats in the territorial legislature. What had started as an outlaw movement had become part of the political process.

Latino resistance took different forms elsewhere in the Southwest. In New Mexico, which retained a Mexicano majority well into the 1900s, it was possible for resistance to move into the political process and prevail. In Texas, where racial tensions were especially sharp and where the white majority grew rapidly, older Latino communities had fewer options. Police power rested with the Texas Rangers, who were seen by the Latino community as simply the force of the Anglo community. While the Rangers saw their opponents as outlaws, many in the Mexican American community saw those who challenged the Rangers as heroes. Perhaps most famous was the case of Gregorio Cortez (1875–1916) who came to Texas from the Mexican city of Matamoros. Cortez shot the sheriff of Manor, Texas, in 1901

Thinking Historically

Cutting Fences in New Mexico

Las Gorras Blancas, or the White Caps, cut fences in an effort to retain the traditional communal grazing lands in San Miguel County, New Mexico. In March 1890, they announced their reasons by posting Nuestra Platforma, a platform announcing their goals, which said:

Our purpose is to protect the rights and interests of the people in general; especially those of the helpless classes.

We want the Las Vegas Grant settled to the benefit of all concerned, and this we hold is the entire community within the grant.

We want no "land grabbers" or obstructionists of any sort to interfere.

We will watch them. ...

Be fair and just and we are with you, do otherwise and take the consequences.

The White Caps, 1,500 Strong and Growing Daily

Source: Robert J. Rosenbaum, *Mexicano Resistance in the Southwest* (Dallas: Southern Methodist University Press, 1998), p. 166.

Thinking Critically

1. **Comparison**

   How do the "rights and interests" described in this platform fit with the ideas about the "rights and interests" of private property that many new arrivals brought with them to New Mexico?

2. **Contextualization**

   How does a Mexican American perspective change or complicate the traditional story of the history of the West in the post–Civil War era?

when he tried to arrest Cortez for a crime he did not commit. After a long manhunt by the Texas Rangers, Cortez was arrested and sentenced to life in prison, but eventually pardoned by the governor of Texas. For generations, Latino songs and ballads—known as *corridos*—celebrated Cortez's story within the Mexican American community.

Mexican American resistance also took other forms. Carlos Velasco emigrated from Sonora to Tucson, Arizona, and in 1878 launched *El Fronterizo*, one of many Spanish-language newspapers in the Southwest. The paper continued to be published until 1914, successfully supporting the election of Mexican Americans to local office and promoting Mexican customs, pride, and links across the international border.

Farmers and Farm Towns

As the cattle industry was transitioning into a more settled ranching industry, farmers were also arriving on the Great Plains in numbers never before thought possible on the arid grasslands. Large numbers of them were responding to massive advertising by the railroads, who also owned much of the western lands; indeed historians have questioned how many people would have moved west in the late 1800s if not for the advertisements of the railroad companies. New techniques of farming enabled these farmers to cultivate areas where only buffalo herds had roamed just a short time before.

Those who began creating new lives, new homesteads, and businesses in the West came from widely varying backgrounds. They included people of different faiths, Americans from eastern regions of the United States, immigrants from Europe and Mexico, former slaves, and Indians, among others.

Joseph Fish, a Mormon, lived upstream from Salt Lake City in the village of Parowan, Utah, where he worked as a miller and a tanner as well as farmed, exchanged work with neighbors, pulled sagebrush, built fences, and harvested wheat and oats to make his living.

Gro and Ole Svendsen moved from Norway to Emmet County, Iowa, in 1863. Ole cut and sawed timber and harvested wheat. Gro made and sold butter and taught her children in Norwegian and English. Drops in agricultural prices and grasshoppers undermined their profits, but they carried on.

For others, the challenges were too great. In the 1880s, a group of Ukrainian Jews created a utopian community in South Dakota, but the transition to the plains of South Dakota was too difficult and the community failed. Many other settlers and homesteaders also failed, and wagons traveling west to Kansas emblazoned with "Kansas or bust" met other returning wagons that said "Busted by gosh." But people kept coming.

Thomas Johnson, a former slave from Kentucky, joined over three hundred former slaves, known as Exodusters, in settling Nicodemus, Kansas, a town that was attracting people across the post-Reconstruction South with advertisements that said, "All Colored People that want to GO TO KANSAS, on September 5, 1877, Can do so for $5.00." Initially, there was not much to this town. The wife of the first pastor said that she "began to cry" when she first saw it, but people stayed on, eventually building it up.

Mariano G. Samaniego moved north from the Mexican state of Sonora in the 1850s to Tucson, Arizona. He did not establish a homestead but opened a clothing store. Later, he earned a college degree from Saint Louis University and then expanded his business, supplying the Union army during the Civil War. By the 1880s, Samaniego shifted his focus to cattle ranching and was known as a respected leader of the Mexican community in Arizona.

Steven Arrow and Big Eagle took advantage of the Homestead Act and acquired their own homesteads in South Dakota, separate from the reservation land. They were an exception to the American Indian experience, but a Sioux Falls merchant said of the Sioux Homesteaders that they "gave more indication of civilization and industry and a show of living like white people than the same number of Norwegian families located a few miles below."

Fifteen percent of homestead claims were filed by single women. Married women could not file their own claim, being already part of a household. Elinore Pruitt Stewart wrote,

> [A]ny woman who can stand her own company, can see the beauty of the sunset, loves growing things, and is willing to put in as much time at careful labor as she does over washtubs … will have independence, plenty to eat all the time and a home of her own in the end.

16.1

16.2

16.3

Texas State Library and Archives Commission

Because of his success in eluding the feared Texas Rangers for months, Gregorio Cortez was a hero to many in the Mexican American community, even as he was seen as just an outlaw by many Anglos. His exploits were celebrated in song and story for generations.

George Barnard/Everett Collection Historical/Alamy Stock Photo

Women were part of the westward movement, sometimes as part of families, occasionally alone. Given European American assumptions about the proper role of women in dress and household maintenance in the 1800s, the move West often involved personal and social challenges reflected in their faces and stories.

The move by farm families into the West was relatively steady. The Homestead Act of 1862 made 160-acre tracts available to those who settled, and Congress later allowed larger homesteads in the more barren lands. The railroads advertised for farmers to settle on their lands. James J. Hill arranged for the settlement of over 200,000 farmers on lands the Great Northern Railroad owned in Montana alone. People who had moved west wrote to friends and families and invited them to join them. Some farm families moved often in search of better prospects. Other families put down deep multigenerational roots, providing stability to their communities.

Farms and homesteads dotted Minnesota, Nebraska, Kansas, and northwestern Iowa in the 1860s as well as California, Oregon, and Washington territory. Stagecoach and wagon transport companies maintained links between rail centers and the isolated farms and towns that were not on a rail line. Throughout the 1870s and 1880s, settlements continued to increase. Between 1881 and 1885, sixty-seven thousand new settlers claimed homesteads in North and South Dakota in the "Great Dakota Land Boom." In 1889, homesteaders rushed into Oklahoma when the federal government declared a large swath of the former Indian Territory to be separate from any tribal reservation and opened it to white settlement.

As farmers and small-town businesses filled the land, Indians felt the pressure on their reservations. Some sold land under the provisions of the Dawes Act, while the government sold off other previously tribal lands. In addition, cattle ranchers were forced to confine herds that had previously roamed freely. Long-standing Mexican communities in west Texas, New Mexico, Arizona, and California lost economic and political power to newcomers who had little respect for the rights of the older inhabitants of the region. Even so, the number of new farmers kept growing. In 1850, there were 1.5 million farms in the United States, just 119,000 of them west of the Mississippi River. By 1910, there were 6.4 million farms in the nation, and a very large number of them west of the Mississippi.

Successfully growing crops in these new areas required discovering which ones thrived best. While corn grew well in the eastern United States, the hot temperatures and the lack of water made it hard to grow in much of the West. Mennonite settlers brought Russian hard winter wheat with them, and in Kansas and the surrounding "Golden Belt," this wheat became the staple crop by the 1880s. In other areas, spring wheat did better while, in the high plains, sorghum crops resisted drought well. Experimentation, luck, and watching what worked for the neighbors all were essential to the success of farming in areas never before farmed.

Farming was not for the poorest people. It cost money to start a farm, even the most modest homestead. An 1862 farm publication estimated that the cost of starting a farm was $968. Homesteaders had to cover expenses in getting a family to a new place as well as in breaking the sod, clearing forest, building fences, buying farm implements, purchasing livestock and seed, and building a house. Nevertheless, there were thousands, eventually hundreds of thousands, of American families who saved or borrowed funds and began the farms that fed much of the world and settled much of the North American continent.

Mining and Miners

The Gold Rush to California was the first rush to seek wealth in the minerals of the West, but it was far from the only one. As early as 1859, Henry Comstock found silver along the Carson River in Nevada, and thousands of California miners rushed east into Nevada to seek new opportunities for wealth. Comstock himself sold his claim, but corporate interests made fortunes in Nevada. In 1874, thousands of miners, many fresh from the now played-out California goldfields and the Nevada silver mines, made their way to the Black Hills of South Dakota. The land was part of the Sioux reservation, but neither the U.S. Army nor the Sioux were able to stop many of the more than fifteen thousand prospectors who had come for gold. Some of them got rich, many of them died in the effort, and all of them helped launch some of the most intense of the Plains Indian Wars.

Mining and the quest for mineral wealth continued to lead to fortunes and to death in the West. In 1882, a poor Irish immigrant, Marcus Daly, persuaded California investors to back his claim to a silver mine near Butte, Montana. Very little silver was ever found at the Anaconda mine, but it turned out to be one of the richest deposits of copper in the world, making millions for Daley, his backers, and the Anaconda Copper Company. Others found mining wealth in gold, silver, copper, coal, and lead mines in Idaho, Montana, Colorado, and as far away as Arizona and Alaska. The mineral wealth of the West seemed endless, and many from around the world sought to find it, though only a very few gained any real wealth.

Seemingly overnight, new towns emerged wherever there was mining for copper, silver, and gold, including Carson City, Nevada; Deadwood, South Dakota; and Anaconda, Montana. Like the cattle towns, these overwhelmingly male mining towns made up of transients could be violent places where the smallest disagreement could erupt into violence. In addition, ethnic rivalries often divided the miners. As in California's gold fields, Chinese miners were soon driven out of most mining operations, in spite of the fact that Chinese immigrants were 10 percent of Montana's population and 25 percent of Idaho's in the 1870s. When not driven out, the Chinese were forced to take low-level jobs working water cannons or doing laundry for other miners. Miners of European origin also drove Mexican American miners out of the fields.

Mining was male work and typically did not lead to a settled life. In 1860, the mining camps of Virginia City and Gold Hill, Nevada, reported a population of 2,300 men and 30 women. The towns also reflected the transient nature of the population. In 1879 Leadville, Colorado, had 4 banks, 4 churches, and 120 saloons, plus a fair share of brothels. While some mining towns later became important commercial centers, many soon became empty ghost towns once the mining played out.

Creede, Colorado, was a typical western mining town with quickly built buildings and a transient, virtually all-male population.

While prospectors sought wealth from their discoveries, most of the money in mining was made by large corporations like the Anaconda Copper Company that could afford expensive mining equipment to extract deeply buried ore. Work in the mines was dangerous. Jobs were often divided by ethnicity, with Chinese and Latino miners given the least-skilled and lowest-paying jobs and miners from Europe getting the better-paying positions. Nevertheless, with little attention to safety, all of the miners faced explosions, floods, cave-ins, and asphyxiation from poisonous gasses. Only the emergence of new unions among the miners began to address the dangers, if not the ethnic divides, in the 1890s (see Chapter 18).

16.1

16.2

16.3

Outlaws, Gunfighters, and Mythmakers—Legends of the Old West

The West of the late 1800s could be a very violent place. Contrary to Hollywood images, cowboys and Indians tended to keep their distance from each other rather than fight. It was the army that fought the Indian wars, not the cowboys. But there was plenty of violence among whites. Ranch owners and land developers hired professional gunfighters to eliminate people they saw as troublemakers. Angry people on the margins, or those pushed to the margins of society, struck back violently, cutting fences in New Mexico or becoming outlaws and counting on the vast distances and easy anonymity of the West to protect them. Cowboys in town at the end of a long and dull cattle ride shot each other. Much of the violence was local and personal, some was between people wanting very different development in the region, especially between cattle ranchers and farmers, and some was also a carryover from the Civil War.

In Tombstone, Arizona, the local elite hired Wyatt Earp and his brothers, Virgil, Morgan, and Warren, along with Doc Holliday to make the town safe enough to encourage investors from California and the East Coast. The local elite and the Earp brothers all had strong Union Army and Republican Party connections. They were bothered by an outlaw group, ex-Confederate cattle rustlers led by the Clanton brothers and McLaury families. On October 26, 1881, at the O.K. Corral, the two sides met. Both Clanton brothers and one of the McLaurys were killed, and Tombstone became a more respectable place.

Another crime wave took place in Missouri, Kansas, Oklahoma, and Arkansas. During the Civil War, Confederate raiders led by William Quantrill and including Jesse and Frank James terrorized Union supporters in Missouri and Kansas (see Chapter 14). Quantrill was killed before the war ended, but the James brothers continued a long reign as postwar outlaws, starting with a bank robbery at Liberty, Missouri, on February 13, 1866, and continuing in the new and lucrative arena of train robberies well into the 1880s. Many robbers like the James brothers received quiet support from farm families who would never attempt illegal behavior but who hated the railroads and the large commercial ranchers and privately cheered when those commercial ventures suffered losses at the hands of outlaws, however violent and self-serving they might be.

In New Mexico, the so-called Lincoln County War of 1878 pitted two groups of ranchers seeking to dominate the county. Both hired outlaws, one of whom was a young teenager named Henry McCarty who changed his name to William Bonney (a famous pirate) and who came to be known as "the Kid." After the Lincoln County War ended, the hired outlaws drifted away. After trying unsuccessfully to find honest work, and after being promised a pardon but then having it revoked by New Mexico's governor, "the Kid" turned to cattle rustling and robbery until he was shot by Lincoln County sheriff Pat Garrett. Billy the Kid, who was twenty-one when he died, had killed ten people in his short and violent life. His legend grew far beyond his life as a whole publishing industry came to thrive on the retelling and expansion of his exploits.

Stories of gunfighters like Billy the Kid and Wyatt Earp became legends of the American West, but the person who did the most to create the legend of the Wild West was a former army scout named William Cody who created his highly successful Buffalo Bill's Wild West Show in the 1880s. According to his autobiography, Cody was born in Iowa in 1846, but his family soon moved to Kansas where his father was killed by the "border ruffians" from Missouri in the battles of "Bleeding Kansas." Cody took a job herding cattle to support his family when he was eleven years old. During the Civil War, he was part of a local militia that protected the territory from attacks by Quantrill and the James brothers. Later, he hunted buffalo and served as a scout. On one occasion, Cody scouted for a party that included James Gordon Bennett of the *New York Herald*, one of the nation's great publicists. Bennett fictionalized Cody as the hero of one of the popular dime novels of the time, *Buffalo Bill: The King of the Border Men*, which gave Cody the chance to launch his "Wild West, Rocky Mountain, and Prairie Exhibition."

Buffalo Bill's Wild West Show was everything eastern crowds wanted it to be. It included scenes from Indian battles, Indian dancing, stagecoach robberies, and always the shooting prowess of Annie Oakley, who epitomized the "good" frontier woman of wholesome character who could outshoot any man. In the 1880s, Sitting Bull himself traveled with the show, giving it an "authentic" aura for many who were anxious to see the leader who had defeated Custer in 1876.

The Wild West show was a long way from any true representation of the West. Although the Indians performed amazing feats of horseback riding, they nearly always ended up fulfilling stereotypical images in the minds of their white audiences. Similarly, while the true cowboys were an ethnically diverse lot—white, Mexican, Indian, and African American—all of Cody's cowboys were white. The U.S. Army units in the show were also white, in spite of the active role of African American Buffalo Soldiers in the West. Annie Oakley, who was an amazing shot with a rifle, lived in Ohio and never traveled farther west except on tour with the show. Indians almost never had the battles with the cowboys that Cody portrayed; Indians fought with the army, and cowboys avoided those battles. However, Indians facing desperate poverty on the reservations found work in the shows, which brought needed income, and they were allowed to dance traditional dances in the shows that were banned by federal authorities on the reservations.

Cody's shows were performed all across the United States and in Europe, twice before Queen Victoria, and one of his riders performed in Outer Mongolia. Prince Albert I of Monaco came to Cody, Wyoming, to hunt with Buffalo Bill. When the show declined in popularity, Cody reinvented himself once again as an advisor to the new Hollywood studios—as did Wyatt Earp—on "realistic" ways to portray the old West in the new medium that was sweeping the nation. In the process, an image of the Wild West was formed that still persists.

Annie Oakley (1860–1926) won fame for her shooting ability and often traveled with Buffalo Bill's Wild West show.

Becoming States

Before 1890, much of the West was organized into territories that were directly controlled by the federal government rather than as states that sent senators and representatives to Congress and voted in presidential elections. California was admitted in 1850, just after the war with Mexico and the discovery of gold. Minnesota was admitted in 1858 and Oregon in 1859. Kansas became a state in 1861, Nevada in 1864, Nebraska in 1867, and Colorado in 1876. More than a decade later, in 1889 and 1890, six new western states were all admitted almost at once—the former territories of North Dakota, South Dakota, Montana, Washington, Idaho, and Wyoming. Utah was admitted in 1896, Oklahoma in 1907, and New Mexico and Arizona in 1912. Several unique issues account for the time lags.

In some cases, local elites prospered by controlling the federal appointments and federal funds in their territory while bypassing the democratic processes that statehood brought. Many in Congress also liked, and profited from, these arrangements. The federal government owned much of the land in western states, and until the Indian wars came to an end, the U.S. Army was the chief protector of western citizens. The U.S. Geological Survey and the U.S. Army Corps of Engineers mapped and shaped the land of the West. Through the territorial stages and beyond, the federal government was a more important part of life in the West than in the East.

Some of the states posed unique issues. Long before it was admitted as a state, the territorial legislature in Wyoming granted the 1,200 women in the territory the right to vote. When Wyoming became a state in 1890, it also became the first state to grant women the right to vote, while their sisters elsewhere could not. Three years later, the state of Colorado granted women the right to vote. After that, campaigns for women's votes stalled. A commitment to women's rights was not universal in the West, but it was more popular there than elsewhere (see Map 16-4, p. 484).

A more complicated issue arose in Utah and delayed statehood for years. The area around the Great Salt Lake had been settled by Mormon families in 1846 and 1847 when it was still part of Mexico (see Chapter 10). After the region became part of the United States in 1848, the federal government initially left the Mormons on their own, and Brigham Young served as territorial governor as well as spiritual leader. However, in the late 1850s, President Buchanan forced Young out of office and appointed a non-Mormon governor.

The issue for Buchanan was the Mormon commitment to plural marriage. Mormon men—but not Mormon women—were encouraged to take more than one spouse. The

Map 16-4 Early States Granting Women Suffrage.

Before 1920, a number of states, especially in the West, granted women the right to vote as indicated on this map.

1916, **Helena, MT.** Jeanette Rankin is elected the first woman to the U.S. House of Representatives.

1908, **Salem, OR.** *Miller v. State of Oregon* U.S. Supreme Court upholds Oregon's 10-hour workday for women.

1894, **Denver, CO.** First U.S. women elected to State House of Representatives.

1848, **Seneca Falls, NY.** Women gather for convention to organize women's rights.

1848, **Albany, NY.** Model married women's property act passed granting married women legal right to own property in their own name.

1889, **Chicago, IL.** Jane Addams establishes Hull House.

1916, **Brooklyn, NY.** Margaret Sanger opens first U.S. birth control clinic.

1932, **Little Rock, AR.** Hattie Wyatt Caraway is the first woman elected to the U.S. Senate.

1892, **Memphis, TN.** Journalist Ida B. Wells launches an anti-lynching campaign.

1839, **Jackson, MS.** First married women's property act passed granting married women ownership over limited property.

PERCENTAGE OF WOMEN IN THE WORKFORCE, 1900

- ☐ Less than 10%
- ☐ 10–20%
- ☐ 20–30%
- ☐ More than 40%

(1918) Date women's suffrage legislation was passed

* States that never ratified the Nineteenth Amendment in 1920

majority of Mormon men had only one wife, but a significant number had two, and Brigham Young himself had twenty-seven wives and fifty-six children. As with more traditional families, some extended Mormon families succeeded quite well while others were torn. When questioned, the majority of Mormon women, including women whose husbands had other wives, defended their arrangement.

Plural marriage horrified people in the rest of the United States. While Presidents Lincoln and Johnson had been too preoccupied with war and Reconstruction to worry much about the Mormons, Presidents Grant, Hayes, Garfield, and Arthur all promised to deal with the "Mormon Question." As early as 1862, Congress passed the Morrill Anti-Bigamy Act, making it a federal crime to take multiple wives, but Utah was far away and Mormon juries were not about to convict anyone accused of that crime.

In spite of all of the controversy and hostility generated by the issue of plural marriage, the Mormon community prospered. By the 1860s, there were enough people living in Utah Territory to qualify for statehood. By 1870, the population stood at eighty-seven thousand. Unlike other parts of the West, where white men far outnumbered white women, Utah had a balanced gender ratio. Women and men prospered in a community of strict morality and hard work, including work for women outside of the household. Women ran their own industries, cooperative stores, as well as relief societies and charities.

The rest of the United States remained dissatisfied with Utah's practices, however, and eventually, the Mormon leadership decided that statehood was more important than maintaining plural marriage. In 1890, the Mormon Church announced the end of plural marriage, and although there were those who continued to practice it, the majority of members went along with the decision. With that key issue resolved, Utah was admitted as a state in 1896. One of the first moves by the new state legislature was to give women the right to vote and hold office, making Utah the third state, after Wyoming and Colorado, to do so.

Issues of race delayed the admission of the last three western states. Oklahoma had been established as Indian Territory when Andrew Jackson's Indian removal policies forced some northern tribes and the five southeastern tribes to move there. By the late 1800s, the tribes had put down roots, developed new communities, and were thriving. Other western tribes had also been forced to settle in Indian Territory. Nevertheless, the Dawes Act and other federal policies opened much of the western part of the territory to white settlement. In 1905, representatives of the tribes proposed establishing two separate states: Sequoyah in the eastern portion would be made up of the Indian Reservations, and Oklahoma in the western portion would be made up of the white areas. Indiana senator Albert J. Beveridge, chair of the Senate Committee on Territories, wanted to have just one territory dominated by "Americans," by which he did not mean Indians, and President Theodore Roosevelt agreed. Oklahoma was admitted in 1907 as a single state.

The Territory of New Mexico initially included all of Arizona and New Mexico. The population quickly reached the level required for statehood, indeed, enough for Arizona and New Mexico to be separate states as many residents advocated. However, unlike the other areas acquired from Mexico, especially Texas and California, the majority of the people living in New Mexico Territory were of Mexican descent. For many years, Congress was not prepared to admit two self-governing states with Mexican American majorities, in spite of the fact that those populations were now U.S. citizens. In 1902, Senator Beveridge proposed uniting them again and admitting them as a single state since that strategy would ensure a larger "American" (or non-Mexican) population, but that proposal failed. Finally in 1912, President William Howard Taft signed legislation admitting New Mexico and Arizona as the forty-seventh and forty-eighth states of the Union.

Well before New Mexico and Arizona became states, the political, economic, and cultural shape of the vast region known as the West was settled. The original inhabitants who had fought with each other and with whites and had hunted buffalo across the plains or lived comfortably on the rich resources of the Pacific Coast were moved to distant reservations where they were alternatively ignored and challenged by federal authorities while building new cultures for themselves. By 1900, much of the West was divided into settled communities of farms, large and small, and growing towns connected by railroads. There was still plenty of desolate empty country to be found, but the West of the 1800s was a receding memory (see Table 16-1).

Table 16-1 Growing Population in the West

	1860	1890
Montana	N/A	142,924
Idaho	N/A	88,548
Wyoming	N/A	62,555
Colorado	34,277	413,249
New Mexico	93,516	160,282
Arizona	N/A	88,243
Utah	40,273	210,779
Nevada	6,857	47,355
Washington	11,594	357,232
Oregon	52,465	317,704
California	379,994	1,213,398

SOURCE: Data from United States Resident Population by State, U.S. Censuses of Population and Housing. http://lwd.dol.state.nj.us/labor/lpa/census/1990/poptrd1.htm

16.3   Quick Review

What were the major concerns involved in admitting new states in the West? How were these issues similar to or different from those involved in admitting states in the East?

Conclusion

The American West changed dramatically between 1865 and 1890. The end of the Civil War marked the beginning of a violent era in the West as units of the U.S. Army fought Native Americans, trying to force them to give up their traditional hunting and nomadic ways and to settle on reservations. By the 1890s, conflict between whites and Indian tribes was over as tribes were defeated and forced to move into ever-shrinking reservations. While the impacts of white settlement and the Civil War on American Indians varied from tribe to tribe, in the long run, they were a disaster.

After the Civil War, white ranchers, farmers, and miners were encouraged to move west by railroad advertising and the offers of free federal land, and they built new settlements across the West. What began as great cattle ranches were replaced by smaller farms producing beef and wheat for national and world markets. The agricultural developments of the post–Civil War era depended on new technologies—most importantly, railroads that brought settlers and then supplies to isolated farmers and shipped their products to world markets. What had once been isolated regional economies quickly became part of a national and international commercial network because of railroads, and the United States was connected to the world as never before. As more and more people settled the West, access to vast regions for grazing cattle became limited and tensions began to mount. Still, the West was largely rural, and disputes were often settled by hiring outlaws rather than by more traditional means. Farmers came to the West for many reasons, including the desire for land, the search for better economic opportunities than were available in the East, and a longing for adventure. Although most farmers established homesteads in hopes of establishing permanent roots, mining towns sprang up around impermanent mines, and they were often violent places. The story of the West that was told to people on the East Coast and in Europe was as much the product of the fertile imagination of entertainers like "Buffalo Bill" Cody as it was any western reality, but it is a story that has stuck in the popular imagination for a long time.

Once a distant frontier, by 1890, the American West was becoming part of the nation's cultural, economic, and political networks, and by 1912, the last of the western territories had become states.

Chapter Review

How do the typical depictions of the American West in the late 1800s differ from the realities of life in the region?

Chapter 16 Summary and Review

The Tribes of the West and the U.S. Government

16.1 Explain western development from an American Indian perspective and the way Indian and white cultures shaped each other.

Summary

The impact of the Civil War on American Indians varied from tribe to tribe. For the Comanches, arguably the most powerful tribe on the western frontier in 1860, the Civil War was a great gift. The diversion of troops to distant battlefields gave the Comanches the opportunity to move back into parts of Texas they had been forced out of in earlier decades. For a time, the Comanches became major players in the regional trade in cattle, weapons, and human beings. By the mid-1870s, however, the Comanches had been forced onto reservations, defeated by a sustained military effort and the depletion of the buffalo herds. During the Civil War, the Apaches and the Navajos faced a relentless assault by U.S. forces. Over time, the Navajos were able to negotiate a reservation system with the U.S. government that allowed them to keep their way of life alive. An influx of settlers and miners from the 1850s onward put northwest tribes like the Modocs and Nez Perce under ever-increasing pressure. Efforts to resist white encroachment were met with violence, and by the end of the 1870s, both the Modocs and Nez Perce had been decimated. Years of fighting between the Lakota Sioux and the U.S. Army led to the Treaty of Fort Laramie of 1868. The United States, however, failed to live up to the treaty, and in 1876, a new round of warfare began. Once defeated, the Sioux were forced onto reservations. Rapid expansion after the Civil War complicated governmental Indian policy. The 1887 Dawes Act replaced the reservation system with the allotment of land to individual families. In the long run, it proved to be a disaster for Indian peoples.

Review Questions

1. Argument Development
   Why did the U.S. government come to believe that it needed new approaches to Indian policy in the 1870s and 1880s? Whose interests did the new policies serve?

2. Contextualization
   What does the Ghost Dance phenomenon tell us about the state of the Sioux in 1890?

The Impact of the Transcontinental Railroad, 1869

16.2 Analyze the building of transcontinental railroads and its impact on the nation, especially the West.

Summary

The dream of a transcontinental railroad gained widespread support in the 1850s. A variety of routes were explored, but the coming of the Civil War ensured that a northerly one was chosen. With federal subsidies, two companies employing immigrant labor laid down rail—one from the east and one from the west—until they met at Promontory Point, Utah, in 1869, completing the nation's first transcontinental railroad. By the early 1890s, there were four major lines across the country connecting to a large network of midwestern and eastern rail lines. Railroads became the essential economic link between American cities. Technological changes helped extend the railroads and cut down travel time significantly. The railroads made a crucial contribution to the emergence of a national economy, connecting regional economies and facilitating American overseas commerce by moving American products quickly and efficiently to American ports.

Review Question

3. Causation
   What factors might explain the widespread support for a transcontinental railroad in the 1850s and 1860s?

The Transformation of the West

16.3 Analyze how indigenous people, ranchers, farmers, miners, outlaws, politicians, and mythmakers shaped the West and our understanding of its history.

Summary

The Homestead Act and the railroads brought about extraordinary changes to the West and, in the process, to America itself. More land was now open for white settlement, made easier by the defeat of the Indian tribes. Once a distant frontier, by the end of the 1800s, the region had become part of the nation's cultural, economic, and political networks. Intensified settlement brought with it new conflicts as cattle ranchers, farmers, miners, and other interest groups battled for control of the land and of the governments of the new states and territories.

Review Questions

4. Continuity and Change over Time
   How did the business of cattle ranching change over time during the second half of the 1800s?

5. Causation
   What factors helped bring about the culture of violence that was so prevalent throughout the West in the late 1800s?

1. Preparing to Write: Organize Your Evidence

Document-Based Question—Evaluate the extent of change in the development of American Indian culture and tribal identify from 1860 to 1890.

Understanding the first part of this prompt is critical. "Evaluate the extent" means that you're to give a judgment about how much change there has been regarding the subject of the prompt. What's implied here is that there might be very little change. Or in some cases there could be both change and continuity. Such is the case with this question. Draw a time line from 1860 to 1890. Above it, keep track of the important changes taking place and what remains constant below. It is very important to focus on why these changes are happening. "Why?" is an implied question in every prompt. As you plan, use one of the American Indian accounts to integrate into your essay. Write a short paragraph that uses that account as evidence to prove a larger point. In that discussion, include the significance of the source's point of view, purpose, historical situation, or audience.

2. Preparing to Write: Establish Context in Your Introduction.

Long Essay Question—Discuss how railroads led to the growth of communities of commercial activity in the West during the period 1860–1900.

Write a four- to seven-sentence introduction that establishes context in the beginning and ends with a strong thesis. One way to establish context here is to describe the scattered economy of the West to set up your discussion of the railroad's deep impact.

Chapter 17

The Gilded Age: Building a Technological and Industrial Giant and a New Social Order 1876–1913

Science and Society/SuperStock

If anything symbolized the new industrial might that began to characterize the United States in the Gilded Age, it was the production of steel at one of Andrew Carnegie's plants.

Chapter Objective

Understand how the United States became an industrial giant, at what cost, and with what impact on its diverse peoples and cultures.

 ## Learning Objectives

Technology Changes the Nation

17.1 Explain the inventions of the late 1800s and early 1900s and their impact.

Corporations and Monopolies

17.2 Analyze the role of the new giant corporations in American life.

Lives of the Middle Class in the Gilded Age

17.3 Analyze daily life, popular ideas, and political direction for the middle class during the Gilded Age.

Immigration

17.4 Explain the reasons immigrants came to the United States in such large numbers during the Gilded Age and what their experience was.

17.1

Significant Dates

On May 10, 1876, Ulysses S. Grant, then in his eighth year as president, traveled to Philadelphia to open the Centennial International Exhibition of Industry. The event celebrated the 100th anniversary of the signing of the Declaration of Independence with a massive show of the nation's progress in science, technology, and industry. The exhibition covered 285 acres on the banks of Philadelphia's Schuylkill River and included pavilions from each state and from many foreign countries. Among them, Colorado and Kansas displayed corn twenty-feet high, and Germany displayed a giant artillery piece from the Krupp works. Alexander Graham Bell demonstrated his new telephone to an appreciative audience that included the Emperor of Brazil. Between the pavilions were refreshment stands selling popcorn, waffles, soda water, root beer, and German *lager bier* as well as a fountain built by the Sons of Temperance, which was serving ice water. The event represented a cross section of the nation in 1876, both as it was and as it wanted to be. The focus was on great mechanical achievements, symbolized by the giant Corliss steam engine that provided power for all the exhibits in Machinery Hall and that seemed to be without vibration or noise (because its boiler was outside the building) as well as by the many mowers, reapers, sewing machines, typewriters, and fans for ventilating mines, plus the Pullman sleeping cars. Most of all, the fair told the world that the United States had arrived as a manufacturing and technological giant.

The exhibition was a fitting opening to an era in which business, manufacturing, and technology would dominate the nation's political, economic, and cultural life, bringing prosperity and power that was previously unimagined. It would also bring clashes between those who benefited and those who did not, which nearly tore the nation apart. This chapter explores how the nation came to be that giant, at what cost to its people and the world, and with what results.

Technology Changes the Nation

17.1   **Explain the inventions of the late 1800s and early 1900s and their impact.**

Alexander Graham Bell saw himself as a teacher more than an inventor. While teaching deaf students at Boston University, Bell sought new ways to help deaf people hear. In July 1874, he discovered that if a person spoke into a vibrating set of reeds, it created a fluctuating current that could, at the other end of an electronic wire, be turned back into the same sound through another set of tuned reeds. He patented his new invention in March 1876 and demonstrated it first by calling his assistant, Thomas Watson, from the next room. Later, he showed it at the Massachusetts Institute of Technology and then at the 1876 World's Fair. While Bell returned to teaching, others organized the Bell Telephone Company. By 1880, there were 30,000 telephone subscribers. By 1900, the number had grown to 1.3 million, and by 1920, to 13 million. In four decades, Bell's experiment had become a necessity of modern life. For most Americans, the telephone replaced the telegraph, developed by Samuel F. B. Morse from earlier inventions in 1835. By the 1840s, telegraphs were relaying messages and news in Morse code, consisting of dot and dash signals, over miles of telegraph wires—215,000 miles of wires by 1900. But the telephone could transmit a human voice and quickly made the telegraph outdated.

Before Bell gained fame for his telephone, Thomas Edison was already on his way to being known as the greatest inventor of the era. Edison was born in Milan, Ohio, in 1847, the same year as Bell. At sixteen, with little formal schooling, he became a telegraph transmitter. Several people in the telegraph industry were trying to design what they called a "diplex," a way to send two messages—one in each direction—on the same telegraph wire at the same time. In 1873, Edison produced both a diplex and a quadruplex that could send two messages simultaneously each way on a single wire, greatly increasing the value of every telegraph line in the nation and securing Edison's fame and fortune. While he was toying with that invention, Edison had also invented the Edison Universal Stock Printer in 1871, a greatly improved version of the stock ticker tape machine.

In 1876, Edison established an independent research laboratory at Menlo Park, New Jersey. The many employees there were made to understand that they worked only at Edison's direction and he got all of the credit. Eventually, he had one thousand patents to his name, thus becoming the most productive American inventor of all time. He tinkered with ways to record a human voice and music. On April 18, 1878, he demonstrated his new phonograph at the National Academy of Sciences in Washington, D.C., and, later that night, at a midnight show at the White House.

Edison's most important invention was the electric lightbulb. In the 1870s, large meeting halls were lit by arc lamps, and gas lights were popular in many places. The rest of the nation—city as well as country—depended on kerosene lamps or candles when the sun went down. The electric lightbulb changed the country. Edison was able to assemble a consortium of financiers, led by J. Pierpont Morgan, to support his research. After toying with different options, the Edison labs created a bulb that lit a room for sixteen hours on November 17, 1879. Almost immediately, everyone wanted electric lights, and Edison wanted everyone to have them. He made London, Paris, and New York the priority cities because he knew that what happened in those places would quickly be reported elsewhere. Within two years, all three cities had buildings lit by electric lights. On September 4, 1882, Edison pulled the switch that lit a number of buildings in southern Manhattan, including the House of Morgan, the New York Stock Exchange, and the headquarters of the *New York Times* and *New York Herald*.

The inventions just kept coming. George Westinghouse and Nikola Tesla found that alternating current was a much more efficient way to transmit electricity than the direct current that Edison used. Edison was initially skeptical, but by the 1890s, alternating current produced at generating plants from New York to California was powering much of the nation. Frank J. Sprague introduced the first electric streetcars in Richmond, Virginia, in 1888, and these cars, which were cheaper and cleaner and safer than horse-drawn or steam cars, caught on quickly.

In 1892, the General Edison Electric Company merged with a rival to create General Electric, the company that produced lightbulbs and, eventually, all things electric. By 1896, using film developed by George Eastman of Rochester, New York, Edison moved from small-scale to large-screen moving pictures, and in 1902, the Victor Talking Machine Company began mass-producing recording disks and players. The country was radically

1893	Panic of 1893—Major U.S. depression
1896	Edison demonstrates first moving pictures
1901	U.S. Steel becomes the largest corporation in history
1902	Victor Talking Machine Company begins mass-producing recording disks
1903	Wright Brothers make first flight at Kitty Hawk, North Carolina
1913	Henry Ford's moving assembly line begins operation at Highland Park, Michigan

17.1

17.2

17.3

17.4

Sueddeutsche Zeitung Photo / Alamy Stock Photo

Thomas Edison with two models of his most famous invention, the lightbulb.

different because of Edison's work and that of other prolific inventors who gave the country elevators invented by Elisha G. Otis, machine tools from Pratt and Whitney, steam boilers from Babcock and Wilcox, newspaper linotype compositors, and typewriters. A total of 440,000 patents issued between 1860 and 1890 transformed modern life.

In the 1890s, a number of independent manufacturers began experimenting with gasoline-powered vehicles, putting a gasoline engine on bicycles or carriages, which led to automobiles. Although by 1899 only 2,500 automobiles were produced per year, many were predicting that the new vehicles would replace horse-drawn carriages. They were right. By 1916, 1 million automobiles were produced in the United States, which created massive change as work with horses declined and a new set of jobs in the automobile industry began and as more and more Americans experienced the freedom that an automobile gave them.

The key to the vastly expanded production of automobiles was not the vehicle itself, which was relatively simple, given other inventions that already existed. Rather, expanded production was possible only after a way was found to produce large numbers of cars at low cost. The genius who revolutionized the *production* of automobiles was Henry Ford, a former machinist, who built his first automobile in 1896. His invention of the assembly line made possible the mass production of cars at reasonable costs. Ford took the idea of interchangeable parts, first developed for guns by Eli Whitney, and applied it to cars. Then he created a process whereby those parts could be assembled in a routinized fashion that greatly speeded production, thus lowering cost significantly.

Ford opened a plant for the production of the Model T Ford in Highland Park, Michigan, in 1910 and added a moving assembly line in 1913. Each worker was assigned one small task to be repeated over and over. As Ford described it, "Every piece of work in the shop moves. There is no lifting or trucking of anything other than materials." Worker after worker did his assigned task over and over again. At the end of the process, a fully assembled Model T emerged from the assembly line. Ford paid his workers well. He had to. They found the work mind numbing, but valued the pay—high enough that they, too, could afford their own Model T. He transformed an industry, bringing the cost of an automobile to within the reach of many Americans and spawning new industries from highway construction to automobile repairs. The success of the automobile dramatically expanded the nation's need for oil, now refined into gasoline to power the rapidly growing numbers of vehicles (see Table 17-1).

While Ford, Walter Chrysler, and the founders of General Motors were creating the automobile industry in Detroit, Michigan, other inventors were tinkering with additional ways to advance transportation. Wilbur and Orville Wright, two bicycle makers from Dayton, Ohio, were determined to develop a flying machine. On December 17, 1903, on a deserted beach at Kitty Hawk, North Carolina, their machine took off. By 1908, Orville Wright had a contract with the Army Signal Corps to conduct test flights at Fort Myer, Virginia. The Wright brothers conducted test flights around the country, including Los Angeles and Chicago. Air travel did not transform the lives of most Americans as quickly as the automobile because it remained inefficient and dangerous for some time. Nevertheless, watching people actually leave the ground on machines confirmed for many that, in the realm of technology, anything was possible.

Table 17-1 Factory Sales of Passenger Cars per Year

Year	Numbers of Vehicles Sold
1900	4,100
1905	24,200
1910	181,100
1915	895,000
1920	1,905,500

Although the real impact of flight on American people and culture came only later, the automobile, the electric lightbulb, the telephone, and a number of related inventions were immediate. By or soon after 1900, American workers were paid more because of developments such as the efficiencies in production that resulted from Henry Ford's assembly line, they enjoyed longer days because of electric lights, and they had far greater chance for movement and privacy because of the automobile. For those who could afford the inventions, the standard of living was beyond anything their parents or grandparents could have imagined. For those who could not, the sense of being left behind was greater than ever. And for many who worked on the production lines that made such goods, the sense of alienation was increasingly more intense. Without question, technology brought a revolution in the American way of life between the 1870s and 1900. At what benefit and cost is still a subject of great debate.

17.1
17.2
17.3
17.4

17.1 Quick Review

How did the inventions of the late 1800s and early 1900s better connect the nation? How did they change people's lives—for good and for ill?

Corporations and Monopolies

17.2 Analyze the role of the new giant corporations in American life.

The kinds of inventions that were appearing in the 1880s and 1890s, like the earlier railroads and telegraph systems, could not be produced by a family business. Electric generation required huge investments. Telephones were useful only if they connected large numbers of people. Most of the country's earliest corporations had been for public benefit— building universities and hospitals—or for temporary partnerships for specific ventures. New corporate structures emerged during the Jacksonian era in response to larger, more expensive ventures to process cotton and manufacture other materials. After the Civil War, corporate structures achieved a level of size and power undreamed of by earlier generations. Managing the investments involved in the great new industries required a new kind of financing and new "middle management" jobs. In the absence of a federal bank—nothing had replaced the Bank of the United States that Jackson had abolished in the 1830s (see Chapter 10)—private bankers played an increasingly important role. Post–Civil War corporations and banks made a few Americans extremely wealthy—richer than any American ever had been before. The outsized wealth of the era, sometimes lavishly spent, inspired the humorist Mark Twain to name this post–Civil War era the "**Gilded Age**," a reference to gilding a lily, coating a flower or other items with gold. In grand parties in New York and at summer "cottages" or mansions in Newport, Rhode Island, or elsewhere, the newly rich showed off their wealth to the delight of some and the disgust of others. While the economic changes also created a new middle class, other Americans felt moved further and further to the margins as the gap between rich and poor grew.

Gilded Age

Term applied to America in the late 1800s that refers to the shallow display and worship of wealth characteristic of the period.

Financing and Controlling the Railroads—Jay Cooke, Cornelius Vanderbilt, and Others

At the end of the Civil War, the most powerful banker in the United States was Jay Cooke, who saved the Union's finances during the war (see Chapter 14). In the early 1870s, however, he almost wrecked the nation's economy.

Cooke financed the Northern Pacific Railroad (see Chapter 16), telling European investors that a rail line from Duluth, Minnesota, to the Pacific coast would connect the world's breadbasket to shipping across the Pacific. He insisted, "There is nothing on the American continent equal to it. … There is no end to the possibilities of wealth here." The promise of

Panic of 1873

A major economic downturn—launched when the country's leading financier, Jay Cooke, went bankrupt—during which thousands lost their jobs and from which the country took years to recover.

wealth was enticing, and investment poured in. However, there were too many railroads, and few were making profits. At the same time, the end of the seemingly faraway Franco-Prussian War (1870–1871) caused world grain prices to drop precipitously as European countries produced more of their own wheat. The result was further reduced profit on the rail lines that hauled American wheat. A government investigation into the Union Pacific Railroad's shaky finances during this period undermined public confidence in rail investments. As a result, Cooke could neither sell new railroad bonds nor meet obligations on the old ones. On September 18, 1873, Jay Cooke and Company declared bankruptcy and closed its doors.

The news that the nation's most leading banker could not meet his obligations launched what was known as the **Panic of 1873**. *The Nation* magazine described Wall Street: "Great crowds of men rushed to and fro trying to get rid of their property, almost begging people to take it from them at any price." The Stock Exchange closed for ten days. Banks collapsed. Railroad construction stopped. By 1874, 500,000 people had lost their jobs, and breadlines were seen in New York and wherever railroad construction and the demand for steel rails, wooden ties, or products that moved by rail had been boosting the economy. The depression of 1873 demonstrated the boom-and-bust cycle of the new economy and the degree to which railroads and banking connected all parts of the nation's financial structure.

As the economy recovered after 1873, the man who profited most was already very rich—Cornelius Vanderbilt. After Robert Fulton invented the steamboat in 1807, Vanderbilt created a steamboat empire, first in New York Harbor, and then around the world. After 1815, Vanderbilt's steamers began to travel to Boston, New Orleans, and—during the California Gold Rush—to Nicaragua to meet other steamers that took gold seekers up the coast to California. Controlling the transit to California was far more profitable than seeking gold there. His style of doing business was illustrated on one occasion when Vanderbilt told competitors, "Gentlemen: You have undertaken to cheat me. I won't sue you, for the law takes too long. I will ruin you." During the Civil War, Vanderbilt kept his ships moving between New York and Union-held New Orleans and beyond to South America in spite of Confederate efforts to stop them.

After the Civil War, Vanderbilt shifted from steamships to railroads. Vanderbilt did not build railroads; he bought them and made them profitable. He also launched a managerial revolution. The corporations that Vanderbilt led involved levels of managers reporting to powerful central offices. The new bureaucracies could ensure safety: trains that ran on schedule were less likely to collide, and trains that ran on well-laid tracks were less likely to derail. They also created great new wealth even as they reduced the role of any one individual.

In 1863, Vanderbilt bought a major interest in the New York & Harlem Railroad, a small line that ran to the heart of Manhattan. He improved its tracks, cars, and service and purchased the connecting Hudson River Railroad. Then in 1867, he forced the directors of the state's largest railroad, the New York Central, to sell to him or be shut out of New York City. His New York Central Railroad empire made Cornelius Vanderbilt the richest man in America when he died in 1877.

Others became rich simply by extracting wealth from companies. In the 1860s and 1870s, Daniel Drew, along with Jay Gould and Jim Fisk, came to be known as corporate pirates. As a young man, Drew herded cattle from farms to slaughterhouses. He once claimed to have perfected a technique of feeding salt to his cattle and then, just before reaching the slaughterhouses, giving them all the water they wanted so they would arrive looking plump and, thus, fetch a good price. In later life, he did the same thing with stocks: buying companies, issuing stock far beyond the company's value—called watering the stock in honor of his experience with cattle—and then leaving the company almost bankrupt while he walked away with the profit from the stock sales.

In 1869, speculators led by Gould and Fisk teamed up to corner the nation's gold supply (see Chapter 15). First, they convinced President Grant to appoint Daniel Butterfield to the key treasury post overseeing the nation's gold supply. They then bribed Butterfield to join in their conspiracy. As they kept buying and hoarding gold, the price kept going up and up because of the demand they were creating. Grant discovered, or at least guessed, what Butterfield and the trio were up to, and he ordered the government to sell up to $4 million in gold, bringing the price back down. The trio sold their gold just before Grant issued his order. Although they no longer controlled the gold supply, they emerged very well-off. Many others who had invested in gold were ruined, and what became known as "Black Friday" created a significant drag on the nation's economy. Henry Adams, grandson and great-grandson of presidents, who was just beginning his own career as one of the nation's major intellectuals, wrote:

> For the first time since the creation of these enormous corporate bodies, one of them has shown its power for mischief, and has proved itself able to override and trample on law, custom, decency, and every restraint known to society, without scruple, and as yet without check.

It would be another thirty years before there were effective checks on the corporate gamblers.

New Industries: Rockefeller's Oil, Carnegie's Steel, and Morgan's Banking

Before the 1800s were over, however, a new generation of corporate leaders exceeded the most optimistic hopes of the Vanderbilts and their generation. Among them was John D. Rockefeller, who, though he did not discover any oil nor invent new ways to refine oil into kerosene or gasoline, did discover new ways to make money from oil, amassing more money than anyone had previously imagined possible. Mark Hanna, a childhood friend who later became President McKinley's closest advisor, remembered that John D. was "sane in every respect save one—he was money mad!"

John D. Rockefeller (1839–1937) created the Standard Oil Company, which came to have monopoly control of the sales of oil in the United States, making Rockefeller an extraordinarily rich man as he drove competitors out of business.

When Rockefeller was twenty years old, he heard news that got as much national attention as John Brown's raid on Harper's Ferry that same year. On August 28, 1859, Edwin Drake struck oil while drilling a well near Titusville, Pennsylvania. "Rock oil," as the oil that came from the ground was called (as opposed to whale oil and oil refined from coal), was in great demand. Before the invention of electric lights in 1879, kerosene lights were the brightest and most popular form of illumination, and kerosene was refined from oil. They were significantly brighter than candles and safer than gas lights. With kerosene lights, families could read in the evening, and the mills could start earlier and operate later. In addition, the machinery that the country was using, from railway engines to factory presses and looms, needed to be lubricated with oil to avoid seizing up. However, the oil had been scarce and expensive. Drake's oil well significantly changed the potential supply of oil.

A rush ensued to sink oil wells in western Pennsylvania. Rockefeller, however, did not like the dirt or the risk of drilling in which some struck it rich while others with a dry well or two went bankrupt. (He also did not like the risk of fighting as a soldier and quickly paid the $300 for a substitute to fight for him in the Union army.) He focused instead on refining the oil that others produced. With two partners, Rockefeller built a refinery in Cleveland where he could take advantage of nearby supplies of crude oil and get his products to market by using Great Lakes shipping and the rail lines between the East Coast and Chicago that ran through Cleveland.

Rockefeller dominated the Cleveland refining market. He kept his products better and his prices lower than any of the competition. He quickly bought out his partners, one of whom later commented, "John had abiding faith in two things: the Baptist creed and oil." Rockefeller also had great faith in his own ability to strike a good bargain and manage his business, cutting costs in every possible way. He brought in a new partner, Henry M. Flagler, who was as religious and as cost conscious as himself. Rockefeller's Cleveland refinery was soon shipping more oil than any other in the region, which gave him great influence with the railroads. Jay Gould offered a rebate to Rockefeller if he would ship on the Erie system, and Rockefeller accepted but then convinced the Erie's primary competition, the Lake Shore Railroad, to give an even better one. When word of the secret rebates leaked out, other oil producers complained, but Rockefeller and Flagler had already made enough money to buy them out.

In 1870, the Rockefeller–Flagler partnership became the Standard Oil Company, and the two set out to gain control of the nation's oil business. They bargained with oil producers to keep costs low. They bought up every rival refining company they could, leaving producers with little option but to sell their oil to Standard Oil at whatever price Standard Oil was willing to pay. When a company would not sell to them, they went into direct competition, cutting prices, until the competitor either sold to Standard Oil or went out of business. They created the Standard Oil Trust, a separate corporation, to buy up virtually every other refinery in the nation. While competition kept prices low, Rockefeller thought competition was a terrible waste of effort and a drain on his profits, and he meant to end it. By the 1880s, companies under the control of Standard Oil refined nine out of ten barrels of oil produced in the United States. This control over oil production came to be known as **horizontal integration** or, in cases like Standard Oil where nearly all of the industry was integrated, a horizontal monopoly. Standard Oil kept growing. Rockefeller produced his own tank cars and leased them to the railroads, making it difficult for competitors to transport oil. When pipelines started replacing oil tank cars, Standard Oil bought the pipelines. In the 1890s, tired of haggling with oil producers, Standard Oil simply started buying oil wells and became the largest producer and refiner of oil in the nation. In the 1890s, the United States had no meaningful antimonopoly laws in force, and Rockefeller's tireless work had made him the master of oil from its production to its refining to its sales.

Just as Edison's lightbulb was starting to reduce demand for kerosene, Henry Ford's automobiles created a huge new demand for gasoline, refined from the same crude oil as kerosene. Automobiles would dwarf all previous markets for Standard Oil's products. In addition, the world's navies were also turning from sail to oil-powered steamships. After 1900, everyone knew that with the development of these gas- and oil-powered vehicles, Standard Oil's greatest days were still ahead (see Map 17-1).

horizontal integration

The merger of competitors in the same industry.

Map 17-1   The Nation's Industrial Heartland.

The giant corporations of the Gilded Age tended to concentrate in the Northeast of the United States. The factories of the region attracted immigrants from around the world and within the United States while also concentrating wealth and increasing the country's transportation networks.

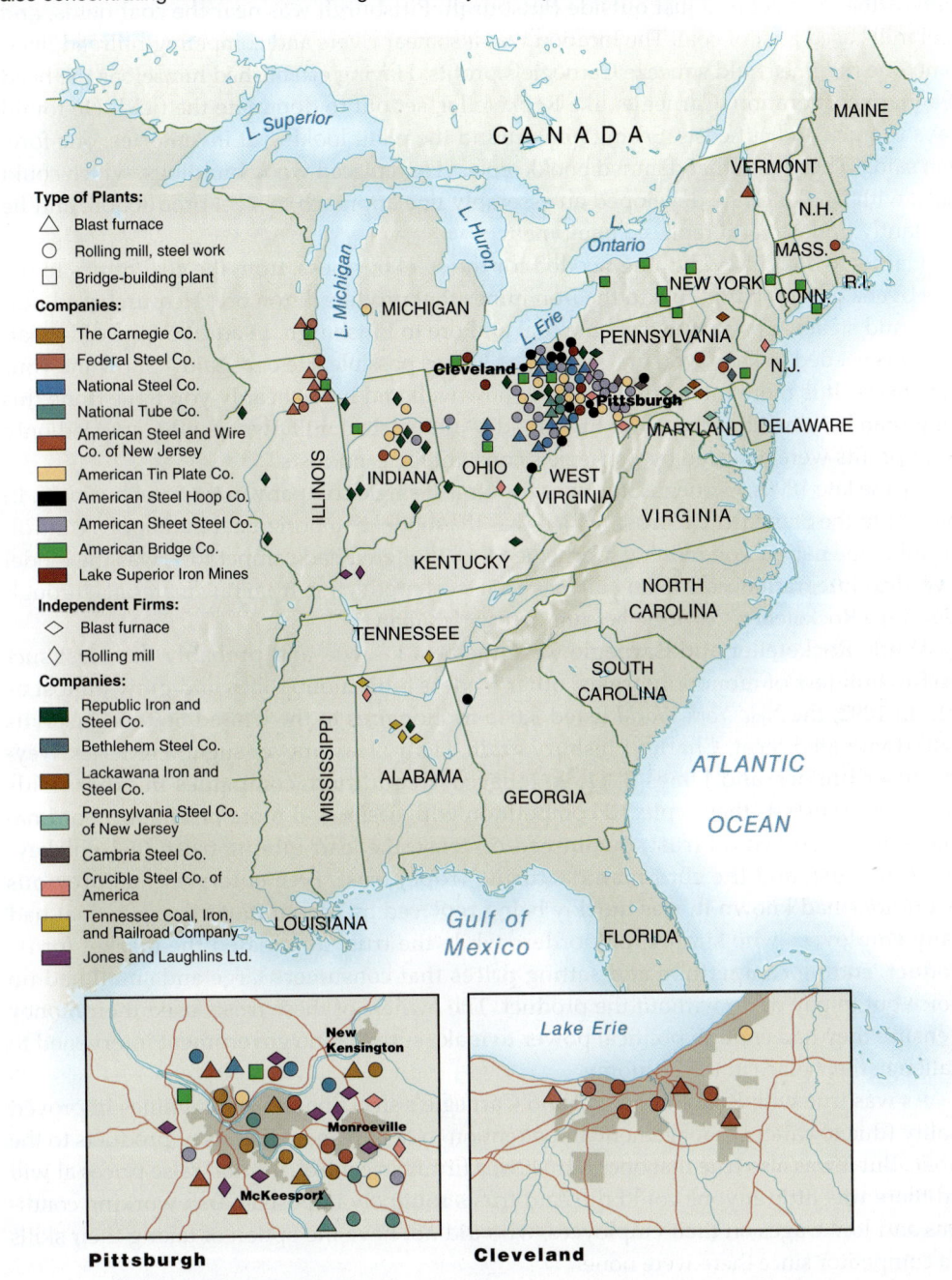

Andrew Carnegie was only a little older than Rockefeller. In 1848, when he was twelve years old, his family came to the United States from his native Scotland after his father, a successful linen weaver, was thrown out of work by the mechanization of the industry. Carnegie's first job was in a textile mill in Allegheny, Pennsylvania, where he earned $1.20 per week. He soon moved to higher-paying jobs and eventually became the personal assistant to the division superintendent of the Pennsylvania Railroad, a position in which he quickly learned the inner workings of American industry.

Like Rockefeller, Carnegie paid someone to serve as his substitute in the Union army—a practice that was entirely legal, though ethically questionable, during the Civil War. In 1863, he decided to leave salaried work because he was confident he could make more money by

17.1

17.2

17.3

17.4

vertical integration

The consolidation of numerous production functions, from the extraction of the raw materials to the distribution and marketing of the finished products, under the direction of one firm.

investing, and he valued his independence. He advised others that the key to success was "Put all your eggs in one basket and then watch that basket." Carnegie's basket was steel, which he quickly realized was coming to dominate American commerce.

In the early 1870s, Carnegie persuaded several investors to join him in opening a new state-of-the-art steel mill just outside Pittsburgh. Pittsburgh was near the coal fields, and steel mills used a lot of coal. The location was also near rivers and competing railroad lines, so no one rail line could squeeze Carnegie's profits. Having established himself as the head of a giant corporation, Carnegie, like Rockefeller, set out to dominate the field. He found ways to track and cut costs. Seeing him around the plant looking at inventories, one foreman said, "There goes that damned bookkeeper." He replaced wood buildings, which could burn, with iron ones; he developed an assembly line approach to steel production; and he constantly updated and replaced equipment.

Carnegie bought everything needed for the steel business, from the coal mines to the coke ovens that prepared fuel to the iron mines that produced iron ore. He purchased railroads and steamships to transport the coal and ore to Pittsburgh. In addition, he did whatever was needed to keep workers' salaries as low as possible. He once said, "Show me your cost sheets. It is more interesting to know how well and how cheaply you have done this thing than how much money you have made." Other steel mill owners who worried only about profits were defeated by Carnegie's constant focus on costs.

By the late 1890s, Carnegie Steel was the largest single company in the steel business. In contrast to the Standard Oil Trust, which was the model of a horizontal monopoly, controlling all of the nation's oil refining, Carnegie Steel, though it had competitors, was the model of **vertical integration**, controlling all means of steel production from raw materials through sales. Like Rockefeller, Carnegie became a very rich man.

While Rockefeller and Carnegie were the best known, and probably the most successful, builders of monopoly trusts, other leaders built monopolies and grew almost as rich. In 1892, the *New York World* listed 3,045 millionaires in the United States. Gustavus Swift dominated meat, Charles Pillsbury grain, Henry Havemeyer sugar, Frederick Weyerhaeuser lumber, and James B. Duke tobacco. In addition, companies in other fields established trusts as they replaced competition with easier and more profitable coordination—the cottonseed oil trust, the linseed oil trust, the lead-mining trust, the whiskey-distilling trust, and the cord-manufacturing (rope) trust. Free enterprise, as previous generations had known it, was quickly being replaced by corporations or trusts that had many employees who simply took orders while the trust dominated the market for its product, ending competition and setting prices that consumers large and small had no choice but to pay or do without the product. The owners of these trusts used their money to ensure they had enough political power to make sure that no government intervened to challenge their place in the economy.

As was true with Rockefeller's oil and Carnegie's steel, the trusts sometimes improved quality (due to careful management and attention to detail) and cut costs of products to the public. But it was also true that once a trust was firmly in control, it could raise prices at will and there was little anyone could do. And trusts routinely imposed harsh working conditions and low wages on their employees, who did not have the option of taking their skills to a competitor since there were none.

While Rockefeller and Carnegie were amassing their fortunes, another American was amassing the greatest economic power that the country had ever seen. Although never as personally wealthy as Rockefeller or Carnegie, John Pierpont Morgan was the banker that everyone else, including the richest industrialists and often the U.S. government, looked to. Like Rockefeller and Carnegie, Morgan was born in the 1830s, and like them, he paid for a substitute rather than let the Civil War divert him from banking. In the financial chaos of the Civil War, Morgan launched J.P. Morgan & Company. During the war, Morgan made great profits. He once sold reconditioned army rifles back to the federal government at a considerable profit. Working with European banks, Morgan helped finance the transcontinental railroad in the United States and the Suez Canal in the Middle East (both of which were completed in 1869). Using his skill and formidable resources, Morgan helped pick up the pieces of the American economy after the collapse of Jay Cooke and Company in 1873.

In 1877, after Cornelius Vanderbilt died, Morgan helped Vanderbilt's son, William, sell off some shares of the New York Central Railroad. In return, Morgan got a $3 million fee but also, more valuable to him, a seat on the board of directors of the New York Central. He helped others with similar sales and gained seats for himself on other equally powerful boards. As a result, Morgan knew more about American industries than any other banker. In particular, he knew that the railroads were overbuilt and he was determined to reduce the competition among them.

In the late 1880s, two of the largest railroads, the New York Central and the Pennsylvania Railroad, ran competing lines from Philadelphia to Pittsburgh and from New York to Chicago. Morgan decided to be a very forceful peacemaker. He invited—or summoned—the principal directors of each railroad to his yacht, the *Corsair*, and then ordered the captain to sail up and down the Hudson until finally, in exhaustion, they agreed to a settlement. The result of the agreement—some called it collusion—was better organization and higher profits for both lines, especially for stockholders and directors like Morgan himself, who also always collected a hefty fee for his services, but at considerable cost to shippers who had benefited from the cutthroat competition and who now saw that disappear.

The Panic of 1893 showed Morgan's power as much as prosperity did. In May 1893, the National Cordage Company, known as the rope trust, which was producing far more rope than the market demanded and issuing far too many promissory notes, went bankrupt, launching a major drop in stock prices among related businesses. In an economy as

American Voices

Andrew Carnegie, "Wealth," 1889

In "The Gospel of Wealth," Carnegie justified his vast fortune (he would be the richest person in America by 1901) and explained his late-in-life generosity that would lead to Carnegie libraries and the creation of the Carnegie Corporation of New York in 1911.

The price which society pays for the law of competition, like the price it pays for cheap comforts and luxuries, is also great; but the advantage of this law are also greater still, for it is to this law that we owe our wonderful material development, which brings improved conditions in its train. ... The question then arises ... What is the proper mode of administering wealth after the laws upon which civilization is founded have thrown it into the hands of the few? ...

There are but three modes in which surplus wealth can be disposed of. It can be left to the families of the decedents; or it can be bequeathed for public purposes; or, finally, it can be administered during their lives by its possessors. ... Why should men leave great fortunes to their children? . ... Observation teaches that, generally speaking, it is not well for the children that they should be so burdened. Neither is it well for the state. ...

As to the second mode, that of leaving wealth at death for public uses, it may be said that this is only a means for the disposal of wealth, provided a man is content to wait until he is dead before it becomes of much good in the world. ... Besides this, it may fairly be said that no man is to be extolled for doing what he cannot help doing. ...

There remains, then, only one mode of using great fortunes. ... This, then, is held to be the duty of the man of Wealth: First, to set an example of modest, unostentatious living, shunning display or extravagance; to provide moderately for the legitimate wants of those dependent upon him; and after doing so to consider all surplus revenues which come to him simply as trust funds, which he is called upon to administer, and strictly bound as a matter of duty to administer in the manner which, in his judgment, is best calculated to produce the most beneficial results for the community—the man of wealth thus becoming the mere agent and trustee for his poorer brethren, bringing to their service his superior wisdom, experience and ability to administer, doing for them better than they would or could do for themselves. ...

Such, in my opinion, is the true Gospel concerning Wealth, obedience to which is destined some day to solve the problem of the Rich and the Poor, and to bring "Peace on earth, among men of Good-Will."

Source: Andrew Carnegie, "Wealth," *North American Review*, Vol. 148, No. 391 (June 1889).

Thinking Critically

1. **Analyzing Primary Sources**
   Thinking like an historian, what is the purpose of this document? Is it a critique of how other wealthy people use their money? Is it a defense of great wealth in a society? Is his acceptance of economic inequality as necessary an acceptable conclusion?

2. **Argument Development**
   Defend or refute the following statement: "Andrew Carnegie's views on wealth were nothing more than a thinly veiled effort to justify exploitation and social injustice." Use evidence from the document and the description of Carnegie Steel above.

deeply interconnected as the U.S. economy had become, a drop in one area meant a drop in many others. In the course of the ensuing depression, the Philadelphia and Reading, Northern Pacific, Union Pacific, and Santa Fe Railroads as well as a host of other businesses all followed into bankruptcy.

The 1893 panic hit rich and poor. In the fall of 1893, a Methodist minister from Lincoln, Nebraska, told the story of "an honest Methodist farmer" who sold his year's harvest for $31 and "with this he paid his taxes and half his grocery bill, and went home without dinner because there was not a nickel left in his pocket." A lot of honest Methodist, Baptist, and Presbyterian farmers were in the same boat, as well as factory workers and members of the rising middle class who lost their jobs and their hopes in the 1893 depression.

The U.S. government also found itself vulnerable. As European investors watched the collapse of the U.S. economy, they started withdrawing gold held in U.S. banks. At the beginning of 1895, the federal government's gold supply, kept in vaults in New York City, was $100 million. By the end of January, it was down to $50 million and falling quickly as investors withdrew their gold. In early February, Morgan traveled from New York to Washington, D.C., in his private rail car to offer help. President Grover Cleveland, a Democrat, did not want the political embarrassment of being rescued by—or being seen under the control of—J. P. Morgan. However, by the time the two met, Morgan informed Cleveland (since Morgan always had the most up-to-date financial information) that there was but $9 million in gold still available and that a $10 million draft was on its way. The banker told the president, "You can't meet it. It will be over before three o'clock."

Morgan also had a solution to offer. He reminded the president and the treasury secretary of a long-forgotten piece of Civil War legislation that said, "The Secretary of the Treasury may purchase coin with any of the bonds or notes of the United States, authorized by law, at such rates and upon such terms as he may deem most advantageous to the public interest." He then offered $65 million in gold in return for thirty-year government bonds. The president asked Morgan whether he could promise that the deal—which not only provided gold but also put the full faith and credit of the House of Morgan behind the credit of the United States—would end the rush on the treasury and Morgan said, "Yes sir, I will guarantee it."

The deal worked. European bankers who had lost faith in the U.S. government still had faith in Morgan. They bought the bonds and stopped demanding payments in gold. The government had been protected from going the way of National Cordage and the Reading Railroad. The publisher Joseph Pulitzer called the deal an "excellent arrangement for the bankers," but "[f]or the nation it means a scandalous surrender of credit and a shameful waste of substance." Morgan not only made a fortune on the deal but also saved the U.S. economy. In the absence of any federal bank, the House of Morgan essentially served that role until the Federal Reserve Bank was created in 1916.

No Morgan project was as great, however, as the one he launched in 1900. It began with the kind of competition that Morgan always hated. Illinois Steel, which Morgan had helped finance, was making a direct run at Carnegie Steel for control of the market. Charles Schwab, one of Carnegie's partners, organized a holiday dinner with Morgan to see whether they could work out a deal to end the competition. Carnegie had talked of retiring, and his wife was anxious for him to enjoy life and devote himself full-time to his charities. Carnegie was asked his price and, after a night's sleep, offered to sell Carnegie Steel for $480 million. Morgan agreed and later shook Carnegie's hand, saying, "Mr. Carnegie, I want to congratulate you on being the richest man in the world." Morgan, Schwab, and Elbert Gary, the head of Illinois Steel, then negotiated with Rockefeller, whom Morgan disliked personally, to buy out Rockefeller's ownership of iron deposits in the Mesabi Range and the ore boats that went with them. In March 1901, Morgan announced the creation of the U.S. Steel Corporation, bringing together Carnegie's formidable assets, Illinois Steel, the Rockefeller iron mines, and other assets worth a total of $1.4 billion, the largest corporation ever seen at the time. The giant monopoly corporation was now the dominating fixture of the U.S. economy.

When Historians Disagree

Were They Robber Barons or Benefactors?

17.1

17.2

17.3

17.4

The two books cited here represent fundamentally different assessments of the financial titans of the late 1800s, which some historians have called "robber barons" but others see as essential players in creating the wealth that made the United States the most powerful nation in the world after 1900. Both authors are nuanced in their work, but the perspectives represent important differences.

Sean Dennis Cashman, *America in the Gilded Age: From the Death of Lincoln to the Rise of Theodore Roosevelt*, Third Edition. New York: New York University Press, 1993, pp. 30–38.

The way the railroads were established and fortunes made from their operation has colored most interpretations of the Gilded Age according to which sharp practice became standard practice in commerce and politics. Whereas English historian Thomas Carlyle called the entrepreneurs of the Industrial Revolution "captains of industry," they were known more commonly in America as robber barons. …

The House of Morgan had a uniform policy to all the insolvent companies it penetrated. It dried out the old stock, issued new bonds at a lower rate of interest, and insisted on consolidation or collusion with rivals. …

The plan for organizing the United States Steel Corporation was announced on March 3, 1901, through an advertisement posted by Morgan. …

John Brisbane Walker, editor of *Cosmopolitan Magazine*, wrote in the April 1901 issue how "the world, on the 3rd day of March, 1901, ceased to be ruled by. … so-called statesmen. True, there were marionettes still figuring in Congress and as kings. But they were in place simply to carry out the orders of the world's real rulers— those who control the concentrated portion of the money supply."

H.W. Brands, *American Colossus: The Triumph of Capitalism, 1865–1900*. New York: Doubleday, 2010, pp. 6, 542–545.

During the decades after the Civil War, Morgan and his fellow capitalists effected a stunning transformation in American life. They turned a society rooted in the soil into one based in cities. They lifted the standard of living of ordinary people to a plane associated, not long before in America and for decades after elsewhere, with aristocracy. They drew legions of souls from foreign countries to American shores. They established the basis for the projection of American economic and military power to the farthest corner of the planet. …

The capitalist revolution was in many ways the best thing ever to befall the ordinary people of America. The country's population grew from forty million in 1870 to seventy-six million in 1900, with the two-thirds of that growth derived from natural increase reflecting the healthful, hopeful conditions among those already in America, and the one-third from immigration the belief of the newcomers that they might share the natives' health and hope. Infant mortality declined by a third; life expectancy increased by a seventh (to nearly fifty years for whites; blacks died about a decade sooner). The nation's total output tripled in real terms; average per capita income nearly doubled.

Thinking Critically

1. **Analyzing Secondary Sources**
   What evidence would persuade you that the corporate leaders of the Gilded Age were "robber barons"? What would convince you that "[t]he capitalist revolution was in many ways the best thing ever to befall the ordinary people of America"?

2. **Contextualization**
   How would one's position in society—then or now—impact one's view of the corporate leaders of the Gilded Age?

17.2 Quick Review

How did the businessmen of the Gilded Age and their tactics revolutionize American industry? Whom do you think had the greatest impact?

Lives of the Middle Class in the Gilded Age

17.3 Analyze daily life, popular ideas, and political direction for the middle class during the Gilded Age.

During the Gilded Age, what came to be known as the middle class and middle-class values emerged in the United States. More Americans than ever before achieved a level of comfort and social respectability that, while it was a long way from the wealth of the Rockefellers,

17.1

17.2

17.3

17.4

Carnegies, and Morgans, was also a long way from the poverty of most of rural America or those who worked in steel mills, on the railroads, or in the refineries. As Americans moved from farms to towns, some of the urban residents became comfortable professionals and managers and, in the process, created a set of norms for "middle-class respectability" that had not been known before.

Middle-Class Life and Expectations

John Lewis came to the United States from Great Britain before the Civil War and got a job in the wholesale grocery business in New York City. By the 1870s, Lewis was the proprietor of his own store and a solid member of America's emerging urban middle class. Lewis wrote to his brother in England describing his life. For the Christmas of 1875, Lewis took the train to visit relatives in Philadelphia. In addition to the feasting, which greatly impressed Lewis, he also noted the Christmas tree decorations:

> As *large* and fine a tree as can be accommodated being procured and set up, it is covered with every conceivable shape into which coloured and gilt paper and card can be cut and … little pictures, glass balls, chains, garlands &c, anything to make a gay and imposing display.

Lewis also noted that the enjoyment of the trees seemed to be a prime adult occupation while the children wanted candy. He noted, "The candy stores are among the gayest and most prosperous, and the consumption of their wares by women and children all the year round is enormous."

In maintaining his own store, traveling easily from city to city, celebrating holidays, Lewis symbolized the emerging middle-class culture of the late 1800s. Before the Civil War, Christmas celebrations among American Protestants were limited affairs, but after the war, the fondness for that holiday grew rapidly. More people owned homes, decorated them, and traveled to visit relatives than in any previous generation.

Middle-class women enjoyed many of the same pleasures as John Lewis but with a definite gender twist. While working-class women, especially immigrant women and women of color, entered the workforce in increasing numbers in the 1870s and thereafter, the notion of "separate spheres" for women and men stayed strong, especially among the rising middle class. When an 1873 U.S. Supreme Court decision said, "The paramount destiny and mission of women are to fulfill the noble and benign offices of wife and mother," the Court was talking about middle-class women. Urged on by the courts, churches, and the media, middle-class women were told that the home was a sanctuary from the outside world and that it was their duty to provide for their children and their weary menfolk, keeping homes pious and pure.

Some women's response was an enthusiastic embrace of the ideas of home economics developed by women like Ellen Swallow Richards, the first woman to teach at MIT. Middle-class housewives were led to be thoughtful consumers of newly available products. Ready-to-wear garments became popular after 1890, and by 1910, women were shopping for clothing for their families in department stores or the Sears Roebuck catalog. Canned goods made food preparation easier, and the refrigerated rail cars brought not only meat but also vegetables to stores. Traveling salesmen, often Jewish peddlers, brought the products of the Fuller Brush or Singer Sewing Machine Company as well as pots and pans, clothing, and some art to even the most isolated households. Gilded Age women became consumers and fueled economic development with their consumption.

Advertising expert Emily Fogg Mead described the 1890s as a time when Americans, women and men, had "the ability to want and choose" as never before. She assured merchants that, while earlier generations may have had religious or democratic scruples about massive consumption, "the next generation has no conscientious misgivings." The result was a new kind of market economy in the United States in which freedom was often defined as the freedom to consume. As a result, while one set of industrial giants transformed American production, another set—big retail operations such as Sears and Roebuck, Woolworths, Wanamaker's of Philadelphia, and Marshall Field and Company of Chicago—created a consumer revolution for the rising middle class. These stores had dozens of departments that sold everything from ready-made clothing to food to household items large and small. In 1890, 32,000 pianos were sold in the United States. By 1904, that number was 374,000. A piano in the home was one sure sign that a family had arrived at middle-class status.

While some led the consumer revolution, other middle-class women chose different directions for their lives. From the 1870s through the 1920s, between 40 and 60 percent of the young women who graduated from college—clearly a marker of a middle-class woman in those years—did not marry. This development was in a society where 90 percent of all American women—the vast majority not college graduates—did get married. But the Gilded Age was a time when a woman with a certain amount of means could carve out freedoms unknown to any previous generation. Middle-class women became college professors, followed the model of Jane Addams into settlement house work, moved to cities and took on clerical jobs, and found ways to support themselves financially and depend on other women for emotional support. Many single women were accused of being lesbians by those who found such independence frightening, and certainly a new generation of women and men had more freedom to pursue private intimate relationships than any before. Lesbian or not, women sought to create new lives outside the bounds that had always limited their gender, and the prosperity of the era made this possible for them.

Those in the rising urban middle class were redesigning not only their private homes but also their expectations, particularly for city buildings and services that supported their emerging tastes and desires. The architect Daniel Burnham, the leading voice of what came to be known as the City Beautiful movement, designed public buildings in a classical style that showed a permanence and beauty that this emerging class expected. City Beautiful planned major revitalization efforts in Washington, D.C., Cleveland, San Francisco, and Chicago, designing buildings such as the grand new Boston Public Library, based on the model of a Renaissance palazzo; the new building for the Library of Congress, which was completed in 1897; and the new New York Stock Exchange that opened in 1903.

The architect Louis Sullivan, Burnham's professional rival, sought a much simpler and, he said, more American style of architecture that reflected the energy of a culture that constructed buildings soaring to heights previously unimagined. Sullivan hated classical Renaissance style and preferred more simple lines. Frederick Law Olmsted designed major new park systems, including Central Park in New York, Boston's chain of connected parks around the city known as the Emerald Necklace, and the Mall in Washington, D.C., all of which spoke to the commitment to beauty and permanence for a new and growing class of people who had the time and inclination to use such public spaces for leisure and uplifting pastimes.

Architect David Burnham's City Beautiful movement made its debut in 1893 at the World's Columbian Exposition, Chicago, Illinois. In this photograph, the Palace of Mechanic Arts and lagoon showcase the classical style that characterized the movement.

17.1

17.2

17.3

17.4

While architects designed new buildings and park systems, other urban planners found ways to make cities more livable or to help the middle class escape what they found difficult. These planners found ways to bring pure water into city neighborhoods, greatly improving the lives—and health—of city dwellers. Cholera and other waterborne diseases had long been a fact of city life. Once a cholera epidemic began to spread, wealth and class did little to protect people from it. Cities, like small towns, tended to depend on well water and on small, individual cisterns that collected rain water for their water supply. However, in growing urban areas, stagnant cisterns were a breeding ground for disease, and wells easily became contaminated. Beginning in 1842, New York started building a reservoir for water to be piped into the city from rural areas to provide a healthier water supply. As New York grew, a large new system—the New Croton Aqueduct—was built from 1885 to 1893 to bring water to all of the city's neighborhoods. Other cities followed the same pattern. Water, which had been a source of disease, became one of the healthiest aspects of urban life.

Even as city life improved, many in the middle class wanted to put some distance between themselves and the cities. Railroads, which had initially connected cities over long distances, began to build shorter lines that would allow people who worked in cities to live in suburbs—a new development in American life during the Gilded Age. They commuted between their homes in semirural settings and their work in the commercial centers of urban America.

The railroads also facilitated another attribute of middle-class life, the summer vacation, and later, the automobile expanded opportunity. Previous generations of farmers or factory workers may have enjoyed a day off and farmers lived by seasonal cycles, but the new middle class began to take actual vacations—a week or two in which they left work and home to see and enjoy another part of the country. One of the first resort guide books was written by William H. H. Murray in 1869, advocating vacations in New York's Adirondack Mountains. The federal government created Yellowstone as the first national park in Montana and Wyoming territories in 1872, not only to preserve nature but also to enhance the enjoyment of those who could get there. Resort towns like Saratoga Springs, New York, areas like the Dells or Great Lakes sailing ports in Wisconsin, and Pacific beach resorts in California all used their unique beauty to cater to a new class of people and boost their economy in the process. Earlier Methodist Camp Grounds from Martha's Vineyard, Massachusetts, to the Great Smoky Mountains of North Carolina also became vacation resorts.

Cities also quickly took to adding electric lights that kept cities alive at night, electric elevators that allowed much taller buildings to be built, and electric trolleys that made it easier to get from one part of a city to another, as they also developed water, sewer, and public health systems that made them much healthier places. The cities of the Gilded Age were cleaner, brighter, and faster paced than anything known in the United States before that time, and people living in them lived longer and more comfortable lives.

Gilded Age Religion

The Gilded Age saw new levels of religious activity among white middle-class Protestants. Most of the middle class were, indeed, both white and Protestant, and they viewed themselves as living in a "Christian America," by which they meant a Protestant Christian one. Between 1860 and 1900, the major Protestant denominations—the Methodists, Baptists, Presbyterians, Congregationalists, and Episcopalians—tripled their membership from five million to sixteen million. Americans not only joined Protestant churches but also participated in nondenominational religious organizations, including the YMCA as well as Bible, mission, and social reform societies. The theology that was being preached changed with the times, becoming more individualistic and more optimistic. And no one represented the changes as much as the great revivalist of the era, Dwight L. Moody.

Like many Americans of his generation—the same generation as Rockefeller, Carnegie, and Morgan—Moody grew up on a farm but moved to a city. When the Civil War began, Moody gave up his shoe business to work full-time for the YMCA. He led a Sunday school for poor immigrant children and supported the YMCA's social service missions. By 1875, Moody had an international reputation. He launched the Northfield and Mount Hermon

North Wind Picture Archives/Alamy Stock Photo

Electric lights, electronic trolleys, and fast-moving trains not only speeded transportation but also created a new kind of energized nightlife in cities such as New York.

schools as well as a new Bible training school in Chicago in 1886 that eventually became the Moody Bible Institute.

Another prominent minister, Lyman Abbott, described Moody's preaching in 1899, saying, "As he stood on the platform, he looked like a business man; he dressed like a business man; he took the meeting in hand as a business man would." If other businessmen were dominating the culture and the economy, a preacher who stressed an individualized gospel and a love of home and who acted like a businessman could be a success. Moody did not shout. He gave a simple message focused on the need for conversion and the love of God. The preacher was deeply critical of both sides in the growing debates that pitted liberal biblical scholarship against those who insisted the Bible was the literal truth. He wondered whether both sides could stop arguing and just "get on with the practical work of the kingdom."

Ira D. Sankey's music was as important as the preaching at Moody's revivals. Some of the most popular hymns that Sankey led were written by Fanny J. Crosby, who wrote over eight thousand of them. The hymns, like the popular *Pass Me Not, O Gentle Saviour*, reflect an individualistic faith in which the focus is on divine comfort and love far more than on sin, divine judgment, or great social change. Protestant Americans sang these hymns during Sunday morning services and at home around a piano—which those of the emerging middle class could now afford.

Electoral Politics

Between 1876 and 1896, electoral politics reflected the interests of the era. While groups within the major parties and new political parties like the Populists (see Chapter 18) protested against the poverty and corruption that was part of the Gilded Age, the major parties, Republicans and Democrats alike, reflected the ideas and aspirations of the middle and upper classes. In a nation where a few were growing exorbitantly wealthy and a larger number were moving into new comforts, the leaders of the political parties had no interest in challenging the status quo.

In the 1870s and 1880s, the Republican Party was the political voice of most corporate leaders and most Protestants outside of the South. But the party was split between the heirs of the antislavery wing of the party—**Stalwarts** they called themselves—and others who believed that it was time to forget about the goals of Reconstruction and simply embrace

17.1

17.2

17.3

17.4

Stalwarts

A faction of the Republican Party in the 1870s and 1880s who wanted the party to stay true to its earlier support for Reconstruction in the South and who were less connected to the emerging big-business interests than others.

17.1

17.2

17.3

17.4

Mugwumps

A reform faction of the Republican Party who supported Cleveland, the Democratic nominee, over the Republican Blaine in the 1884 election.

the nation's growing prosperity. The party was also split along lines of personal animosity, none deeper than the hatred between Roscoe Conkling, Stalwart leader of the New York delegation in the Congress, and James G. Blaine, a congressman from Maine since 1862 who had quickly risen over many more senior members to be Speaker of the House. Blaine was among those ready to focus on the future; to embrace the economy that Rockefeller, Carnegie, and Morgan were creating; and to forget about reform efforts, whether in the form of the now-fading Reconstruction goals or the needs of the urban poor. Blaine was a man of great charm and eloquence, but perhaps too smooth and a participant in some of the worst corruption of the Grant administration.

After the tensions of the 1876 Hayes-Tilden election (see Chapter 15), the Republicans did not want to renominate President Hayes and turned instead to another Civil War veteran and compromise candidate from Ohio, James A. Garfield, who defeated the Democrats' Union war hero Winfield Scott Hancock in the November 1880 election. Unlike many in either political party, Garfield was committed to civil service reform—ending the use of government jobs to reward political favorites—and to uniting Stalwarts and their opponents. His running mate was the New York customs collector Chester A. Arthur, better known for his ability to find government jobs for friends than for any reform agenda. Three months after the inauguration, Garfield was shot by a disgruntled office seeker, and although he seemed to be healing from his wounds, he died on September 19, 1881. Arthur became the president and, as some said, served a less undistinguished term than expected.

In 1884, Blaine was determined to stop Arthur's renomination. He tried hard to convince yet another war hero, William T. Sherman, to run for president, but Sherman's unequivocal response was, "If nominated I will not run, if elected I will not serve." Eventually, the Republicans gave Blaine his turn as their candidate.

Governor Grover Cleveland was the Democratic nominee. Cleveland had fought corruption when he was mayor of Buffalo, New York, a reputation that propelled him to the governor's office in 1882 and only two years later to the White House. Given Cleveland's reputation for honesty and Blaine's for corruption, a number of longtime Republicans campaigned for the Democrats. These party crossovers became known as **Mugwumps**, a word they claimed came from an Indian word for "big chief" but that their opponents said meant someone whose mug was on one side of a fence while their "wump" was on the other.

In the midst of the 1884 campaign, a preacher from Buffalo revealed that Cleveland had fathered a child with a young widow, Maria Halpin, and then paid child support. Cleveland supporters said that Halpin had many boyfriends and that Cleveland was only protecting the others, some of whom were married. The nominee ordered his campaign to "[t]ell the truth." While the nation faced serious economic choices, the campaigns fell to chanting "Blaine, Blaine, James G. Blaine, continental liar from the state of Maine," against "Ma, Ma, where's my *Pa*?" Just before the election, another preacher who supported Blaine castigated the Democrats as the "party of rum, Romanism, and rebellion," a phrase that may have cost the Republicans key Catholic votes in New York State where Cleveland won by only 1,100 votes, which gave him a majority in the Electoral College.

Cleveland was not significantly different from the Republicans who served before him, though he did take a strong stand against the annexation of Hawaii and other expansionist efforts that Republicans had been pursuing. But as African Americans in the South suffered from ever-increasing segregation and inequality, white and black farmers faced poverty, and workers began efforts to organize unions to end starvation wages, Cleveland, like the Republicans, tended to ignore their needs or, when pushed, sided with the corporations and their owners (see Chapter 18).

In a close race, Cleveland was defeated for reelection in 1888 by the Republican nominee, Civil War general, and presidential grandson Benjamin Harrison, whose main campaign issues were Cleveland's veto of a pension bill for Civil War veterans and Cleveland's return of Civil War banners to Southern states. A tactic called "waving the bloody shirt"—reminding everyone in the North that Republicans had won the Civil War while Democrats represented the states of the Confederacy—seemed to win elections for Republicans. Yet four years later, Cleveland, in a return match, defeated Harrison and served a second term from 1893 to 1897—the only president in history to serve nonconsecutive terms. It was

United States Senate

While political leaders like Hayes, Garfield, and Cleveland vied for the presidency, many reformers were coming to the conclusion that the business trusts led by people such as Rockefeller, Carnegie, and Morgan really controlled the country. This political cartoon from 1889 showed who many thought actually ran the Senate and the country.

Cleveland's bad luck to begin his second term just as the Panic of 1893 began, and while his negotiations with J. P. Morgan may have avoided even worse disaster, the economic crisis of 1893 hurt many Americans. The political stability of the 1870s and 1880s seemed to be coming to an end in the 1890s.

Global Connections

American influence around the world grew dramatically during the Gilded Age. Americans had been sending missionaries to foreign countries since the early 1800s, but far greater numbers went abroad in the 1880s and 1890s. Dwight L. Moody called on young converts to consider careers as foreign missionaries, and some of them launched the China Inland Mission to convert China. Another Moody convert, John R. Mott, organized the Student Volunteer Movement that eventually sent over five thousand missionaries to India, Africa, China, Japan, and the Middle East (the Movement later became the World Student Christian Federation). Individual churches and religious bodies sent their own preachers, teachers, and medical missionaries to all parts of the globe. Missionaries brought western values, a respect for human rights—especially women's rights. However, they also brought American commercialism interests, and missionaries were quickly followed by merchants and industrialists, though missionaries sometimes led the protests against the commercialization of international relations. Returning missionaries became the voice of the world for many, describing people and cultures unfamiliar to American audiences.

Missionaries were far from the only Americans to visit other parts of the globe during the Gilded Age. As the United States grew in population and industrial production, it became a player of growing importance in world markets, second only to Great Britain. After the Panic of 1873, many worried that the rapid growth in U.S. industrial productivity could become a problem rather than a boon. If the country produced more and more and depended only on domestic markets, then prices and income were doomed to keep falling. The only solution, some argued, was to find foreign markets, lots of foreign markets, to be sure that American products were sold all over the world, bringing new income to American producers. Exporting goods was nothing new to the United States (from 1815 on, the export of cotton was the largest single driver of the nation's economy), but after 1870, many U.S. business leaders intensified the range and scope of exporting efforts. The total value of U.S. exports jumped from $234 million in 1865 to $1.5 billion in 1900, and the country was transformed from a debtor to a creditor nation.

The United States had long been interested in Cuba. Southern senators regularly suggested making the island a slave state before the Civil War, and in 1854, the American ambassadors to Europe's leading powers issued the so-called Ostend Manifesto, demanding that Spain sell Cuba to the United States. After the Civil War, Cuba was no longer of value as a slave state, but interest in the island never disappeared. When a rebellion against Spanish rule broke out in Cuba in 1868, perhaps 100,000 Cubans died and the island's economy was devastated. U.S. merchants took advantage of the situation and bought sugar plantations, mines, and ranches in Cuba while U.S. diplomats forged an agreement with Spain for free and open trade between the island and the United States. By 1890, the United States was the dominant economic force on the island, and trade with Cuba was important for the U.S. economy.

The United States also had long-standing interests in Mexico. During the Civil War, Napoleon III had sent French troops to Mexico, installing Austrian archduke Maximilian and his wife, Carlotta, as rulers of the country. Secretary of State Seward warned the French that their meddling was an "act of hostility," and U.S. general Philip Sheridan informed Mexican revolutionaries that he had placed a substantial supply of weapons at the border and would look the other way if they disappeared. The supply vanished, and Maximilian was overthrown by a new government led by reform-minded Benito Juárez. Maximilian was executed by a revolutionary firing squad in June 1867. Later, Porfirio Díaz, who did not share Juárez's reform agenda, claimed dictatorial power in Mexico. Díaz was anxious to expand U.S. investment in Mexico, and Americans bought railroads, mines, and oil exploration companies. By 1900, Americans had some $500 million invested in Mexico, enough to make the country a major trading partner and, indeed, to give American businesses significant influence in the Mexican economy and political life. Some feared Mexico was becoming almost an economic satellite of the United States.

U.S. commercial interests extended far beyond the Americas. In the 1870s, Belgium's King Leopold II created a private colony around the Congo River in Africa. It was a brutal affair. Residents of the Congo were pressed into slave labor on the vast rubber plantations that were meeting growing demands for rubber, and they were making Leopold very rich. Anxious to gain a new market, some businessmen persuaded President Arthur to recognize King Leopold's rule as the legitimate government of the Congo in 1884; however, Arthur's successor, Grover Cleveland, reduced U.S. involvement in light of the violent conditions.

In Europe, the growth of U.S. exports almost provoked a trade war between the United States and Europe's leading economic powers, including Britain, Germany, and France. Bad harvests in Europe starting in 1879 led to significant demand for American food, lifting the U.S. economy out of the last vestiges of the Panic of 1873. But European governments became nervous about their growing dependence on U.S. food and claimed that U.S. pork and beef was not safe, leading to a huge fall-off in exports. The *New York Herald* urged "avenging the American hog" with a boycott of French wine and German sugar, but an eventual compromise led meat exports to double.

In Asia, a U.S. Navy squadron sailed to Korea in 1867 but was sent away. But the U.S. Navy kept trying, as it had with Japan and China, and in 1882, Korea agreed to open itself to U.S. markets. The two governments signed the Treaty of Chemulpo after which Korean officers studied at the U.S. Military Academy at West Point and the Brooklyn Navy Yard. While Korea remained a relatively small trading partner, the determination to open a country known as the "Hermit Kingdom" was typical of the era. From Korea to Latin America, the Congo, and Europe, the United States emerged from the Gilded Age as a trading partner not only in familiar countries but also in parts of the world previous generations had barely heard about.

17.3 Quick Review

How did the expansion of industry contribute to changes in noneconomic arenas during the Gilded Age?

Immigration

17.4 **Explain the reasons immigrants came to the United States in such large numbers during the Gilded Age and what their experience was.**

In the seventy-five years between 1815 and 1890, fifteen million people immigrated to the United States, the great majority from northern Europe—Britain, Ireland, Germany, Scandinavia, Switzerland, and Holland. In the next twenty-five years, from 1890 until the start of World War I in 1914, fifteen million additional immigrants came to the United States, and those immigrants came from new places—80 percent of them from Italy, Greece, Russia, the Empire of Austria-Hungary, Romania, and the Ottoman Empire, and others from Japan, China, and Korea, as well as Mexico and other parts of Latin America. With their arrival, they changed the makeup of the nation. What all these immigrants had in common was a "push-pull" experience in which various factors pushed them to leave their home countries and, at the same time, other factors pulled them to try a new life in the United States.

The Push from around the World

When Sadie Frowne described the desperate poverty of Poland or when the Lithuanian, Antanas Kaztauskis, expressed his family's fear that he was about to be drafted into the Russian army, they were relating reasons that pushed hundreds of thousands of people to move not only from southern and eastern Europe—Italy, Greece, Poland, Russia—but also from China, Japan, and Korea to start new lives in the United States. Most of those who emigrated from those countries to the United States between 1890 and World War I did so in part because something, often grinding poverty and fear of persecution, pushed them to get out of the places where they and their families had lived for many generations (see Map 17-2 and Figure 17-1, p. 510).

Map 17-2 Immigration to the United States.

Between 1820 and 1914, but especially between 1880 and 1914, immigrants transformed the United States. This map shows where they came from.

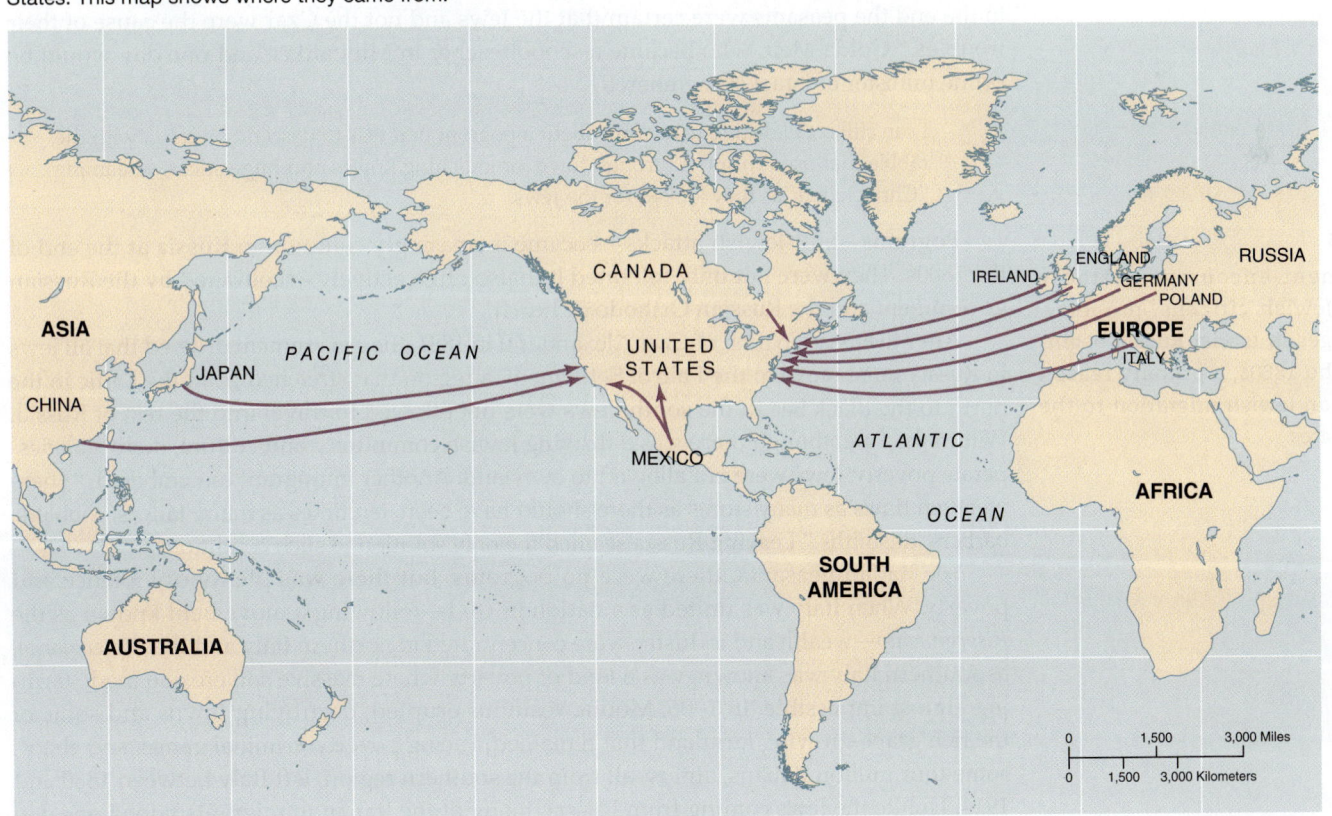

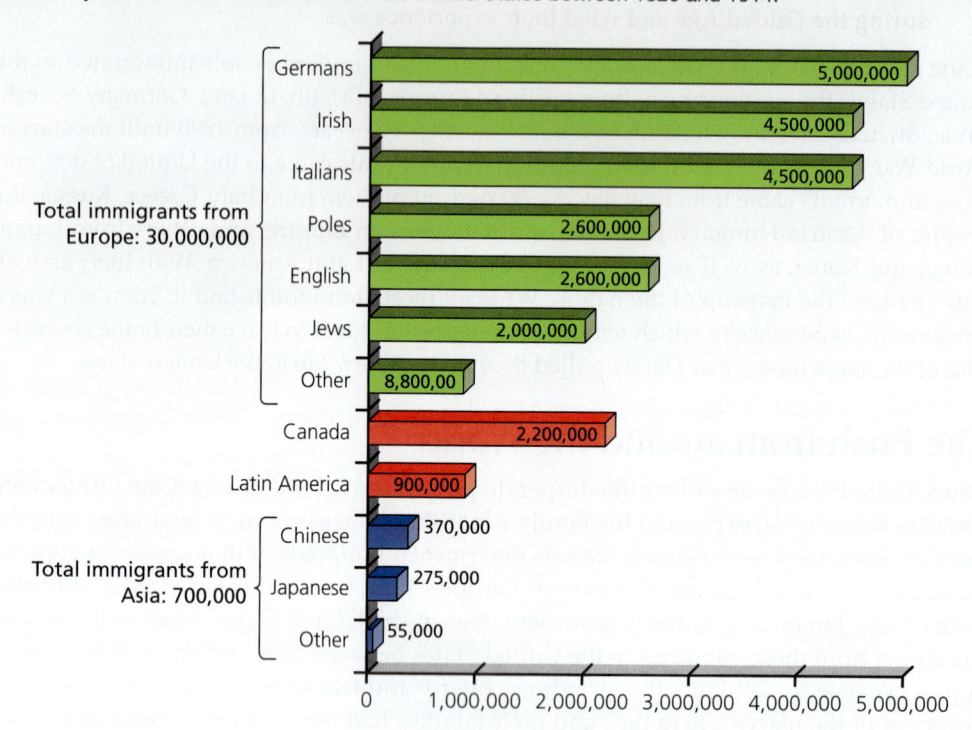

Figure 17-1 A Specific Look at Immigrants to the United States.

The United States has always been a nation of immigrants. This figure shows the numbers of immigrants from many different nations who came to the United States between 1820 and 1914.

Nowhere was the push to leave greater than in Russia and Russian-dominated parts of eastern Europe including the Ukraine, Lithuania, and Poland. Abraham Cahan, who came to the United States from Russia as a young man, explained what drove him: "The government itself had set off the pogroms in order to save the throne from a revolutionary upheaval. By making the Jews the scapegoats, it had confused the common people so that in the end the peasants were certain that the Jews and not the Czar were the cause of their troubles." Golda Meir, who became a schoolteacher in Milwaukee and one day would be prime minister of Israel, remembered,

> I can still recall distinctly hearing about a pogrom that was to descend on us … with the rabble that used to surge through town, brandishing knives and huge sticks, screaming "Christ killers" as they looked for the Jews.

Pogroms—anti-Jewish attacks—became increasingly common in Russia at the end of the 1800s. They were not only tolerated but also often actively encouraged by the Russian government and the Russian Orthodox Church.

After the assassination of Czar Alexander II in 1881, the government ordered that all Jews in Russia must move to the Pale of Settlement, a region that stretched from the Baltic in the north to the Black Sea in the south. Jews were not allowed to travel into the rest of Russia. Within the Pale, though there was a thriving Jewish community and culture, there was desperate poverty. Jews were not allowed to own land. Another immigrant remembered, "There were ten times as many stores as there should have been, ten times as many tailors, cobblers, barbers, tinsmiths." Leaving Russia seemed the only solution to such conditions.

For Italian peasants, there were no pogroms, but there was plenty of violence and poverty. When Italy was united as a nation in 1871—following a movement known as the *Risorgimento*—wealth and industry were concentrated in northern Italy and the *Mezzogiorno*, as southern Italy was known, was a land of poverty where massive soil erosion made farming almost impossible. In 1906, Mount Vesuvius erupted, destroying towns and some of the rich grape-growing farmland that remained. Facing poverty, criminal gangs, and chaos, some four million Italians, almost all from the southern region, left Italy between 1880 and 1914. Unlike the Jews coming from Russia, many of the Italian immigrants hoped one day

Pogroms

Government-encouraged attacks against Jewish citizens, property, and villages in tsarist Russia beginning in the 1880s, a primary reason for Russian Jewish migration to the United States.

American Voices

Sadie Frowne, A Polish Sweatshop Girl, 1906

Sadie Frowne's account of her move from a small village in Russia to become a garment worker in New York City's Lower East Side is one example of the experience of thousands of immigrants.

My mother … kept a little grocer's shop in the little village where we lived at first. That was in Poland, somewhere on the frontier. … She had a wagon in which she used to drive about the country, selling her groceries, and sometimes she worked in the fields with my father.

When I was a little more than ten years of age my father died. …

Mother wrote to Aunt Fanny, who lived in New York, and told her how hard it was to live in Poland, and Aunt Fanny advised her to come and bring me … She said we should both come at once, and she went around among our relatives in New York and took up a subscription for our passage.

We came by steerage on a steamship in a very dark place that smelt dreadfully. There were hundreds of other people packed in with us, men, women and children, and almost all of them were sick. It took us twelve days to cross the sea, and we thought we should die, but at last the voyage was over and we came up and saw the beautiful bay and the big woman with the spikes on her head and the lamp that is lighted at night in her hand (Goddess of Liberty) …

So I went to work in Allen Street (Manhattan) in what they call a sweatshop, making skirts by machine. I was new at the work and the foreman scolded me a great deal …

Some of the women blame me very much because I spend so much money on clothes … Those who blame me are the old country people who have old-fashioned notions, but the people who have been here a long time know better. A girl who does not dress well is stuck in a corner, even if she is pretty, and Aunt Fanny says that I do just right to put on plenty of style.

Source: Sadie Frowne, "A Polish Sweatshop Girl," in Hamilton Holt, editor, *The Life Stories of Undistinguished Americans as Told by Themselves* (originally 1906, republished New York: Routledge, 2000), pp. 21–28.

Thinking Critically

1. **Analyzing Primary Sources**
   What evidence in the document would you use to describe the historical situation that led Sadie Frowne's mother to decide to move to America?

2. **Contextualization**
   What elements of the author's story might make it typical of immigrant stories of the period? What elements would allow a historian to guess the approximate date of Frowne's immigration to America?

---

to return home after making some money, and perhaps one in four did return. Those who came, whether temporarily or permanently, settled in major American cities and took on some of the hardest work at the bottom ranks of the American economy.

Russian Jews and southern Italian Catholics were far from alone. All across Europe, the population was growing faster than the land could support. Immigration provided a way out. Political upheaval in many places led to violence. Turkish violence against the Christian minority, especially the massacres of 1894, 1895, and 1896, led many Armenians to leave for America. Roman Catholics in Orthodox areas like Lithuania and Orthodox believers facing persecution in Catholic or Muslim countries wanted to move.

Chinese immigrants had been coming to the West Coast since the Gold Rush of 1848, but poverty and continued political turmoil kept them coming, though the numbers were slowed significantly after 1882 when Congress passed the **Chinese Exclusion Act**. Until 1882, immigration had been a relatively easy matter for the Chinese. If one could afford the passage, one simply booked it and then walked off the ship in San Francisco. However, many in California and other parts of the West were threatened by the Chinese who by their sheer numbers increased the competition for jobs or mining claims, even if most Chinese immigrants did the low-paid work no one else wanted. After a string of anti-immigrant petitions led Congress to change the law—the first time an entire nationality was barred from the country—only Chinese who could prove to the satisfaction of new immigration agents that they were either returning citizens or that they brought with them educational, economic, or diplomatic skills were allowed into the United States. Japanese immigrants, however, began to arrive, especially after 1885 when the emperor ended a ban on emigration and increased taxes to build up the government, causing many farmers to lose their fields.

In addition, about 300,000 French-Canadians moved from Quebec into the United States between 1860 and 1900, especially into New England and New York. Remote villages in Mexico experienced almost constant revolutionary violence in the late 1800s and early

Chinese Exclusion Act

Federal legislation that suspended Chinese immigration, limited the civil rights of resident Chinese, and forbade their naturalization.

17.1

17.2

17.3

17.4

This Italian woman with her children at Ellis Island, the main Atlantic coast port of entry for immigrants, represented the way many families came to the United States. A father would come first and, later, after making some money, send for his wife and children, who followed on their own.

Library of Congress Prints and Photographs Division [LC-USZ62-67910]

1900s as regime followed regime. As a result, many Mexicans moved across the Rio Grande into the United States to find jobs on farms, mines, or fields in Texas and California, greatly expanding an earlier Mexican American community that had been in the United States since the changing border made them Americans in the 1840s. Eventually, some four million Italians, two million Russian Jews (one-third of all of the Jews in Russia), and nine million other immigrants from almost every other part of the planet came to the United States in the thirty-year period before 1920.

The Pull from an Industrializing United States

While there was good reason to leave Russia or Italy or Japan or Mexico in the late 1800s, there were also reasons to want to come to the United States. The pull of opportunity was as important as the push of poverty and oppression. Although stories of the wealth to be found in the United States often led to terrible disappointment, the conditions in the United States were often still significantly better than what immigrants had left behind.

Prospective immigrants learned about jobs and opportunities from many sources. In a small village in Lithuania, Antanas Kaztauskis heard a man who lived in his village talk about the success of his son who was working in the stockyards in Chicago and who had sent his father a Lithuanian-language newspaper from Chicago where the old man read of the rights of "life, liberty, and the getting of happiness."

American employers, often short of workers during economic boom times, advertised for help, even publishing a guidebook, *Where to Emigrate and Why*, in 1869. Steamship companies advertised for passengers, who could now, they claimed, take advantage of quicker travel times—fourteen days in 1867 and perhaps six days by 1900—all in safer and healthier conditions.

In Japan, farmers heard that a plantation laborer in the Kingdom of Hawaii could earn six times more than in Japan. It might be possible in a few years of working in Hawaii or the United States to save enough to return home, buy new land, and make a fresh start in Japan. Many Japanese women saw the opportunity to start a new life as a "picture bride" for a Japanese immigrant who was already in Hawaii or the United States. In a culture in which arranged marriages were the norm and in which women were encouraged to become educated and make their own way in the world, the idea of women, traveling to a new land, starting a new life with a new husband, did not seem so strange. Riyo Orite, said of her experience, "I was engaged at the age of sixteen and didn't meet Orite until I was almost eighteen. I had seen him only in a picture at first … Being young, I was unromantic. I just believed that girls should get married. … [P]eople around me praised the match."

Mexicans who returned after spending time in the United States came back to families and friends with "shoes and good suits of clothes." Others who moved north wrote to family and friends, "Come! Come! Come over, it is good here!" Jesus Garza remembered, "As I had heard a lot about the United States it was my dream to come here." And many did come.

The Reality—Jobs, Cities, and Americanization

When immigrants arrived in the United States, they did not always find what they had been expecting or hoping for. Italian immigrants often summed up their experience:

> Back in the old country, the young and naïve immigrants had been told that the streets of America were paved with gold. But when they got here, they discovered three important things: First, the streets weren't paved in gold; second, they weren't paved at all; and third, they were expected to pave them.

Few immigrants were quite as naïve as the story implies, but Italian immigrants liked the image.

New York was the prime point of entry for immigrants from Europe. In 1892, the federal government built a new immigration center on Ellis Island in the harbor, which replaced the old one at Castle Garden at the tip of Manhattan. Ellis Island combined quarantine, customs, and reception. Twelve million people came through Ellis Island before it closed in 1954. It could be an intimidating experience as clerks asked a battery of questions, trying to be sure that no physically or mentally ill people or troublemakers were allowed into the country. They did not make life easy for anyone. Nevertheless, only about 2 percent of those who arrived at Ellis Island were actually turned away because they either carried disease or seemed unlikely to be able to support themselves.

During this process at Ellis Island, the clerks often gave immigrants a new anglicized name. A Russian named Cooperstein became Cooper, a Finn named Huttama became Hanson, or a Greek named Kiriacopoulis became Campbell. In one case, a German Jew became so confused with all the questions he was being asked that he forgot his own name. When he responded to the clerk's question about his name with "Ich vergesse" ("I forget"), the clerk registered him as Ferguson.

Steamships from Europe also docked in Boston or Philadelphia where the government established similar centers. Immigrants from Canada and Mexico were sometimes processed at border crossing points or simply walked across the long borders between the countries. In the Southwest, people had long traveled back and forth across the Rio Grande, and they did not stop doing so.

Most Asian immigrants came through the Port of San Francisco. In 1910, the federal government created a processing center on Angel Island in San Francisco Bay that was designed to be a kind of West Coast Ellis Island. Over the next thirty years, 175,000 immigrants entered the United States through Angel Island, the vast majority of them Chinese. Similar but smaller stations were created in other ports, especially Seattle. Although Angel Island might have been designed as a counterpart to Ellis Island, it was a very different place. At both islands, immigrants faced frightening medical inspections and batteries of questions from federal immigration agents. But while most of those coming through Ellis Island left within a day, many on Angel Island were kept for weeks or months. From the time of the passage of the Chinese Exclusion Act in 1882 until changes in U.S. policy in 1943, only Chinese immigrants who could prove that they were returning U.S. citizens or the children of U.S. citizens were allowed into the country. The Chinese immigrant population was essentially frozen at its 1882 levels. However, the destruction of all federal records in the earthquake and fire in San Francisco in April 1906 meant that if someone claimed to be a U.S. citizen, it was hard to disprove the claim. So-called paper sons came to the United States with high hopes that they could answer the required questions and gain admission to the

AP Images

Arrival at Angel Island in San Francisco might mean long waits in confining conditions for Asian immigrants like these Japanese women.

melting pot

An often popular idea that somehow immigrants from other countries should quickly lose their culture and language and "melt" into being just like other Americans.

country. Some succeeded. Others were deported. As a result, Angel Island became a place of constant tension. Paul Chow, whose parents had come through Angel Island, remembered the fear the place evoked in his family. "Whenever my mother would mention it, she'd say, 'Angel Island, shhh,'" he said. "I thought it was all one word 'Angelislandshh.'"

Although the phrase "**melting pot**" became a popular way to describe the immigrant experience, the reality was different. The term *melting pot* came from a play by Israel Zangwill, produced in New York in 1908, in which the hero wants to forget the pain of his life as a Jew in czarist Russia and announces that he is happy to be in America, "God's Crucible," where he can be part of "the great Melting-Pot where all the races of Europe are melting and reforming." In fact, many of those who arrived had no interest in "melting" into a common American culture and were not always welcome in the larger culture but were, instead, creating a richly diverse nation of far more ethnic and cultural variety than had ever been seen before.

For Jews arriving in New York, the next step after leaving Castle Garden or Ellis Island was often the Lower East Side of Manhattan, the heart of the Jewish community. To be in the Lower East Side in the 1880s and 1890s was, as Rose Cohen said, as though "we were still in our village in Russia." There was little actual cultural melting going on, especially for women who sometimes stayed home while learning little English. But the children of these immigrants—or immigrants like Sadie Frowne who came as young people—adapted quickly. While one found friends in immigrant communities like the Lower East Side, living conditions were hard in some of those most crowded blocks in the country. The *American Magazine* described Lower East Side tenement housing in 1888:

> They are great prison-like structures of brick, with narrow doors and windows, cramped passages and steep rickety stairs. … The narrow court-yard … in the middle is a damp foul-smelling place, supposed to do duty as an airshaft. … In the hot summer months … these fire-escape balconies are used as sleeping-rooms by the poor wretches who are fortunate enough to have windows opening upon them.

Bathrooms were at the end of the hall and were shared by multiple apartments.

Most apartments were packed with people as families crowded into tiny rooms and took in boarders who would help pay the rent. One 1908 survey found that 50 percent of families slept three or four persons to a room and another 25 percent had five or more persons per room.

Jewish immigrants found work where they could. Jewish peddlers sold nearly everything—fruit, vegetables, fish, clothing, and kitchen utensils—filling streets like Delancey Street with pushcart after pushcart, all selling something different and trying to convince passers-by to purchase. Other Jewish peddlers fanned out into the most remote parts of the country from suburbs to rural Maine or the backwoods of Appalachia, bringing goods—and inadvertently customs—to areas where a non-Christian had never been seen.

Hester Street in New York's Lower East Side was the heart of the city's immigrant community.

Even more Jewish immigrants found work in the garment industry. Many Russian Jews had survived as tailors (the Singer sewing machine was a major export from the United States to Russia). In America, skill with a needle meant a job. The demand for uniforms for the Union army led to the establishment of standard sizes for clothing, first for men and later for women, and this change allowed the development of mass-produced rather than individualized clothing. Because of the development of standard sizes, the garment trade was able to shift from made-to-order work for the elite to mass production of clothing for everyone. Men's suits and pants, women's dresses and shirtwaists, as blouses were called, were produced in the thousands, making the clothing business a major industry.

At first, garment work was done at home as families or small groups took in piece work and returned the finished products. Later, larger factories, known as **sweatshops**, brought together hundreds of workers who were expected to sew at a fast pace for long hours to ensure that they kept their jobs and the owners made a decent profit. Whether working at home or in sweatshops, child labor was common in the garment industry, and large numbers of very young children labored long hours to help support their families. One could walk for blocks in southern Manhattan and see nothing but such work going on from early morning to late evening. In spite—or perhaps because—of the harsh living and working conditions, New York's Jewish community grew strong. Russian Jews had no intention of returning to Russia where pogroms and poverty reigned. They established synagogues, foreign-language newspapers provided news, and some three hundred Hebrew schools maintained their language and culture.

Italian immigrants also created their own neighborhoods. In Chicago, Taylor Street became the heart of Little Italy. In Milwaukee, the Third Ward on the east side was the heart of the Italian community where some twenty Italian grocery stores existed on Brady Street alone. In Boston, the North End and East Boston housed Italian communities. And in New York, many Italian immigrants, like Russian Jewish immigrants, moved to the Lower East Side of Manhattan.

Since most Italian immigrants came from the rural poverty of southern Italy, they had few marketable skills when they got to the United States. Like Russian Jews, some became pushcart owners, selling fruits and vegetables. Others opened restaurants. More than a few became the laborers who built the cities where they lived: New York, Chicago, Milwaukee,

sweatshops

Small, poorly ventilated shops or apartments crammed with workers, often family members, who pieced together garments.

17.1

17.2

17.3

17.4

Lewis Hine's photograph of garment workers sewing by hand in a small New York City sweatshop in 1908.

and Boston all have water and sewer lines dug by Italian laborers. Italian immigrants were sought as workers in coal mines and steel mills. Coal mine operators hired very young boys, known as breaker boys, to work in the mines because they could often fit through narrow tunnels more easily than full-grown men and were less likely to go on strike. Gender roles were, perhaps, more rigidly defined in the Italian immigrant communities than elsewhere. Italian families tried every way they could to encourage married women to stay at home and to depend on the men to earn a living for the family.

For the 900,000 French Canadians who immigrated to the United States between 1840 and 1930, the move meant escape from rural poverty and a chance for a new start, especially in the mills of New England. Like every ethnic group that went to work in the mills, immigrants from French-speaking Canada went to work at a very young age and child labor was common. Although some states, especially in the North, required children under age fifteen who worked in factories to attend school for at least three months per year and limited their workday to ten hours, these laws were enforced quite inconsistently. More than most immigrant groups, those coming from Quebec tended to bring their priests (nearly all French Canadians were Catholic), doctors, lawyers, and grocers with them, all of whom were sure that life might be better—or at least marginally more prosperous—in rapidly industrializing New York and New England than in the isolated farms of Quebec.

Like the Italians and the French Canadians, Mexican immigrants often moved back and forth between the United States and home communities, but in their case, that move meant crossing only a river rather than an ocean. Nevertheless, more and more immigrants from Mexico eventually made permanent homes in the United States, creating the *barrios*, which were often extensions of Mexican communities that had long stretched along the border from Texas to California.

Mexican American communities, like those of European immigrants, often reflected quite different home regions. One immigrant remembered, "We came to know families from Chihuahua, Sonora, Jalisco, and Durango. Some had come to the United States even before the revolution, living in Texas before migrating to California." The barrio was also home in other ways. Immigrants from Mexico could find familiar food, including tamales, frijoles, tortillas, and menudo. They could see traditional clothing, enjoy traditional holidays and festivals, and feel much less like strangers in someone else's land.

For all Catholic immigrants, the Catholic Church was an essential link with their faith and their past. At the end of the U.S. Civil War, there were forty-two dioceses and three thousand Catholic churches in the United States. By 1900, there were seventy dioceses and ten thousand churches, many serving specific ethnic communities. The Italian parish, the Polish parish, the Mexican parish, and the German parish might be in very close proximity, but they served their own group, often offering parochial schools and classes in a home language, which was important to parents coping with children growing up in an English-speaking society.

Those who entered the United States from Asia found different kinds of work in their own ethnic communities. Chinese immigrants such as Lee Chew found work when they could:

> When I got to San Francisco ... [a] man got me work as a house servant in an American family, and my start was the same as that of almost all the Chinese in this country. The Chinese laundryman does not learn his trade in China; there are no laundries in China. ... All Chinese laundrymen here were taught in the first place by American women just as I was taught.

For the Japanese in Hawaii (an independent country until 1898), housing and work were found on the sugar plantations, which were new to them. Hawaiian companies encouraged whole families to immigrate, believing that "dependable married men" made better workers, and women, children, and men were given jobs in the fields. Japanese communities were able to establish themselves with their own traditions; religious practices, including Buddhist temples; Japanese-language schools for children; and festivals, including the Emperor's Birthday, when work ceased in spite of the frustration of the plantation owners. In time, Japanese, Portuguese, Chinese, and native Hawaiian workers got to know one another, exchanged food, and developed real if tenuous friendships.

17.4 Quick Review

Which were more important in bringing immigrants to the United States in the late 1800s and early 1900s—the push factors or the pull factors? Give evidence for your answer and other evidence to show that the other cause was less significant.

Conclusion

The well-named Gilded Age was a time of great extremes. In the decades after the Civil War, Americans built bigger corporations, cities, and buildings than ever before. Some made huge fortunes and lived a life of lavish spending. Other Americans created a new middle class with its own new culture and values. Still others, especially immigrants living in tightly packed urban communities, lived on the edge of poverty while also creating new cultures with their own values and norms. All of them created a vastly different nation than any previous generation had known.

During the Gilded Age, America emerged as an industrial giant. Technological innovation and vast reserves of coal, oil, steel, and timber, along with expanding railroad networks, fueled a growing economy. New forms of corporate ownership and banking developed to manage large-scale industrial operations. A new middle class also emerged in the Gilded Age. Made up mostly of the families of men who managed or serviced the large new corporations, the middle class created its own new lifestyle that changed gender roles and that also included more time for leisure, education, and consumption than had been possible for all but a small elite in past generations. City services—from a healthy supply of water to new high-rise buildings with elevators to giant department stores—catered to the needs of this growing middle class. Rail and trolley lines facilitated the growth of suburbs in which private homes replaced apartments, and many in the middle class enjoyed a mix of urban and rural amenities.

The rapidly expanding new industries needed workers, and the call for workers exerted a pull on people living in far distant places, including Russia, Italy, China, and Japan. At the same time, developments in these and other countries were creating a push that led many to want to leave. Whether it was the anti-Jewish pogroms in Russia or the grinding poverty of Italy or the civil wars that wracked China, the chance for a better life was appealing, and the United States experienced a massive era of immigration between 1880 and 1914. Once in the United States, immigrants were not always welcomed. Many native-born Americans distrusted what they saw as foreign cultures. But the jobs—though low level and low pay—were there and immigrants began working in the factories and in the booming urban sweatshops that were clothing the country and the world.

As a result of all of these changes, by 1900, the United States was a very different place from what it had been only a few short decades earlier.

Chapter Review

What were the biggest differences in the United States in 1900 as a result of the events, trends, and innovations of the Gilded Age?

Technology Changes the Nation

17.1 Explain the inventions of the late 1800s and early 1900s and their impact.

Summary

The late 1800s was an age of industrial innovation as new forms of technology transformed day-to-day life. In many cases, new technologies gave rise to new industries as inventors and their financial backers formed companies to market their inventions and develop new applications for their use. In the case of the automobile industry, the creation of a mass market depended on innovations in both technology and methods of production. While there was a constant flow of meaningful inventions during this period, the automobile, electric lightbulb, and telephone emerged as the ones that had the deepest, most immediate effects on American society.

Review Question

1. Causation

What are the factors that gave rise to this flurry of inventions in the late 1800s?

Corporations and Monopolies

17.2 Analyze the role of the new giant corporations in American life.

Summary

The development and application of the most important new technologies of the late 1800s required resources on a scale that only large organizations could provide. It is not a coincidence that the period saw the rise of new forms of industrial corporations, business structures, and industrial financing. These new institutions controlled more wealth and wielded more power than any previous business organization. Industrialists and financiers won unheard-of fortunes by consolidating their control over entire industries, using monopoly power to eliminate competition and increase profits. Men like Vanderbilt, Rockefeller, Carnegie, and Morgan became familiar giants of the new industrial age. Speculators played a major role in the expansion of American industry and commerce, sometimes with disastrous consequences for the public at large as the period saw two major panics. By the turn of the century, the giant monopoly corporation was the dominating fixture of the U.S. economy.

Review Questions

2. Continuity and Change over Time

How did American manufacturing evolve from the early 1800s to the early 1900s? At the same time, how did it stay the same?

3. Argument Development

What does J. P. Morgan's involvement in the Panic of 1893 and in its resolution tell us about the relative power of American industry compared with that of the U.S. government at the turn of the century?

Lives of the Middle Class in the Gilded Age

17.3 Analyze daily life, popular ideas, and political direction for the middle class during the Gilded Age.

Summary

The same era that saw the rise of the super wealthy saw the emergence of a new middle class whose values would come to dominate American culture. The rising class of professionals and managers demanded new levels of material comfort and expected to live in cities that mirrored the value they placed on cleanliness and orderliness. Middle-class women found themselves playing an integral role in the new industrial economy, whether in the workforce or managing the household. Many white middle-class Protestants saw their own religious views and social values as the essence of American culture. In the 1870s and 1880s, most Protestants outside of the South and the nation's corporate leaders supported the Republican Party, and the era saw the election of a string of largely undistinguished Republican presidents. Meanwhile, the booming American economy was making new connections with the rest of the world.

Review Question

4. Causation

What connections can you make between the growth of American business and changes in American religious life in the late 1800s?

Immigration

17.4 **Explain the reasons immigrants came to the United States in such large numbers during the Gilded Age and what their experience was.**

Summary

Between 1890 and 1914, fifteen million immigrants arrived in the United States. Unlike previous immigrants who came largely from northern Europe, most of the new arrivals were from southern and eastern Europe, Asia, and Mexico. A variety of forces, including poverty and fear of persecution, pushed immigrants to leave their countries of origin. At the same time, the pull of opportunity was equally important in bringing new immigrants to America.

Review Questions

5. **Causation**
   What factors explain the migration of large numbers of eastern European Jews to the United States at the turn of the century?

6. **Argument Development**
   What did immigrants hope to find in America? How did their expectations compare with reality?

1. Preparing to Write: Support Your Assertion

Short-Answer Question—Answer (a), (b), and (c).
Using the excerpts from "When Historians Disagree" in 17.2, answer (a), (b), and (c).

a. Briefly explain ONE major difference between Cashman's and Brand's historical interpretations of the financial titans from the late 1800s.
b. Briefly explain how ONE specific historical event or development during the age that is not mentioned directly in the excerpts could be used to support Cashman's interpretation.
c. Briefly explain how ONE specific historical event or development during the age that is not mentioned directly in the excerpts could be used to support Brand's interpretation.

Respond to each question above in three sentences. For (a), make your assertion about a major difference in the first sentence, and then explain that difference in the next two. For (b) and (c), identify the specific historical event or development in the first sentence, and then explain that choice in the next two.

2. Preparing to Write: Plan Your Argument

Long Essay Question—Evaluate the extent to which there are similarities in immigration during the mid-1800s and immigration during the late 1800s/early 1900s.

Consider planning your argument using the push and pull factors. What is similar and different about the push factors? An outline for this comparison can set up the first part of your argument's body. An outline of similarities and differences of the pull factors can set up the second part. From here you can develop a thesis. As you look at your push and pull outlines, what bubbles up? What is interesting about the comparison that can serve as a basis for your thesis?

Chapter 18

Responses to Industrialism, Responses to Change 1877–1914

Everett Collection/SuperStock

Drivers and mules with young laborers in a West Virginia coal mine in a 1908 photo by Lewis Hine.

Chapter Objective

Demonstrate an understanding of how the rapid industrialization after the Civil War impacted the lives of diverse people and the rise of distinct resistance movements.

 Learning Objectives

Conflict in the New South

18.1 Analyze how the combined impact of industrialism and the end of Reconstruction created the unique character of the New South.

The Politics of Conflict—From Populist Movement to Populist Party

18.2 Analyze how agrarian unrest and protest came to have a significant impact on American politics.

Worker Protest and the Rise of Organized Labor

18.3 Explain the tensions in industrial America that led to major labor strife between the 1870s and 1914.

When he accepted the nomination of the relatively new Socialist Party for president in the 1912 presidential elections, Eugene V. Debs said:

> The world's workers have always been and still are the world's slaves. They have … produced all the world's wealth and supported all the world's governments. They have conquered all things but their own freedom.

It was the goal of the Socialist Party, Debs said, to win that freedom. Debs had an expansive goal for his political organization—a party for women and men, blacks and whites, struggling farmers as well as factory and railroad workers. When the presidential election was held in November, Debs won some 900,000 votes, or 6 percent of the total. Although that percentage was small, it reflected nonetheless unusual support for a nontraditional candidate.

In a nation in the midst of rapid social change, Debs sought to speak for those being hurt by the changes. Although he failed to rally as many as he hoped to his political banner, his campaign reflected the deep tensions in the United States in the late 1800s and early 1900s. In the face of extraordinary technological and industrial change, and extraordinary wealth controlled by a few, many were angry. This chapter traces the reasons so many Americans were angry in the years between 1877 and 1914 and the results of that anger in reshaping the political and cultural life of the nation. Chapter 19 traces the ways that yet other Americans began to tackle the problems of this era.

Conflict in the New South

18.1 **Analyze how the combined impact of industrialism and the end of Reconstruction created the unique character of the New South.**

In 1886, the young editor of the *Atlanta Constitution*, Henry Grady, was invited to New York City to speak at the prestigious New England Society of New York, one of the city's most elite groups. Coming twenty years after the end of the Civil War, the invitation was quite an honor for a Southern newspaper editor. The society, like Grady, was ready for a fresh start regarding the nation's regional differences. Grady was in New York to tell his audience that a **New South** had been born. It had been born, Grady said, out of the defeat of the South's "brave armies" in the late war and the ending of slavery. A new day had begun. But it had begun under leaders who were proud of their past and wanted to be clear that "[t]he South has nothing for which to apologize. … The South has nothing to take back."

The New South meant several things to Grady. First, Grady was saying that the South was done apologizing for the Civil War, for slavery, and for the increasingly rigid social, political, and economic segregation that was developing in place of slavery. On race relations, Grady said, the South wanted to be left alone. Grady was also announcing that the South had come of age economically. It was building railroads and industrializing at an impressive pace, and Southerners wanted to be fully integrated into the economic prosperity of the rest of the nation. On the economic front, the New South that Grady was discussing was indeed different from the Old South.

Economic Development and Economic Optimism

The pre–Civil War South had been dominated by agriculture. In the New South, sawmills, factories, mines, and railroads were being built, and old wooden buildings were being replaced with new brick ones in many towns. Optimism was growing, though not everyone was celebrating. The decline in the price of cotton was devastating farmers, and for most African Americans, segregation and exclusion made life almost unbearable. Nevertheless, for a fortunate subset of white Southerners, the years between 1875 and 1900 were a time for optimism.

Before the Civil War, the South had far fewer miles of railroad track than the North. Catching up on railroad construction was a key element in defining the New South. The new railroads brought all sorts of change. The investment in building railroads—much of it

Significant Dates

1877	Great Railroad Strike
1882	Agricultural Wheel farmers' organization is launched
1886	Haymarket bombing
	Henry Grady announces the "New South"
	Charles W. Macune elected president of the Farmers' Alliance, beginning its rapid growth
1890	New Mississippi state constitution effectively excludes blacks from voting
	Farmers' Alliance establishes headquarters in Washington, D.C.
	United Mine Workers of America is founded in Columbus, Ohio
1891	The People's Party (Populists) is launched
1892	Homestead strike
1893	American Railway Union is organized
1894	Coxey's Army marches on Washington, D.C.
	Pullman strike
1896	U.S. Supreme Court's *Plessy v. Ferguson* decision
	William Jennings Bryan runs for president on Democratic and Populist Party tickets
1905	Industrial Workers of the World is organized
	Niagara Movement is organized
1909	National Association for the Advancement of Colored People is launched
1911	Triangle Shirtwaist Fire
1912	Bread and Roses strike in Lawrence, Massachusetts
1914	Colorado miners' strike

18.1

18.2

18.3

New South

An ideology developed by some elite Southerners that declared an end to the nostalgia for slavery and plantation life and a beginning for the economic development of the South while protecting the growing racial segregation of the region from any Northern interference.

Northern or European money—brought work to many Southerners, not only those who did the actual work of laying track but also those supporting them. As one Mississippi resident noted, "The women and children were busy producing vegetable crops, chickens, eggs, milk and butter, and the men were butchering and delivering fresh meat and other supplies to the men working on the railroad." Once the new lines were in place, there were also jobs working on the railroads. The work was dangerous and injuries were common, but the pay was better than anything many Southerners had seen.

The rail lines provided Southerners with important new connections to the outside world (see Maps 18-1A and 18-1B). A generation earlier, rail lines had connected many parts of the North, but when the rail lines finally reached an isolated town like Harrison, Arkansas, in February 1900, the local newspaper announced, "Harrison Is a Rail-road Town at Last." Henry Hammond, an astute observer of Southern life, pointed out that country people "who formerly were satisfied with their weekly paper, who went to town annually or semiannually, in some instances not more than two or three times during a long life, can now go quickly, safely, pleasantly and cheaply several times a day." Farms were connected to towns and towns to cities beyond the imaginings of people's parents and grandparents.

The railroads that brought people to town also brought goods from around the world while shipping goods that the South produced to world markets. Country stores sold manufactured goods that made life easier and fertilizer that made the land more productive.

In many small towns, stores also sold goods on credit, making them virtually banks. In this capacity, stores also accepted fields planted in cotton as collateral for loans, as cotton remained the prime cash crop of the South.

In addition to cotton, new industries were growing in the South in the 1880s. Sawmills and turpentine camps produced lumber and turpentine that was shipped around the world. Phosphate mining expanded but was then eclipsed by coal mining as new markets demanded coal. Tobacco, which the South had shipped to the world since the 1600s, became a growth industry. Using effective advertising and marketing skills, Julian Carr shipped his Bull Durham tobacco bags worldwide, and Washington Duke and his son James shipped prerolled cigarettes that quickly became the most popular way to enjoy "clean, quick, and potent" tobacco. Iron and steel were produced at the South's fastest-growing city of Birmingham. The South's textile production, which had involved 10,000 people in 1870 (as it had in 1850), employed almost 100,000 by 1900. Finally, a new product, Coca-Cola, developed by Asa G. Candler in 1889, became highly popular and, eventually, a drink of choice for many on every continent.

Nostalgia and Celebration of the "Lost Cause"

The rapid changes in the South made some uneasy. The movement of Southerners—white and black—in search of jobs and economic opportunities created a sense of dislocation. C. L. Pettigrew of North Carolina, like many others, remembered a slower pace and complained about "that striving, rough and eager crowd." Others mourned to see "the white-columned porticos of the favorite colonial architecture now maundering in decay," as ambitious young people moved to opportunities elsewhere.

A Texas veteran wrote to the legislature, asking them to be sure that "the sons of Confederates and the public generally" remember the "Lost Cause." Another ex-Confederate, Wade Hampton, insisted, "I believe now, as always, that the South was right." For veterans like Hampton and others and for Southern widows of those who had died in the war, the memory of the "Lost Cause" as a glorious time and a righteous fight made the pain of a sometimes lonely and often economically challenging present more bearable.

Southern writers produced romantic stories of the "Lost Cause" of the Civil War and the days of slavery that preceded it. Thomas Nelson Page, of a prominent Virginia family, created the "plantation school" of writing, recounting tales of a chivalrous past. Page also started the tradition of the

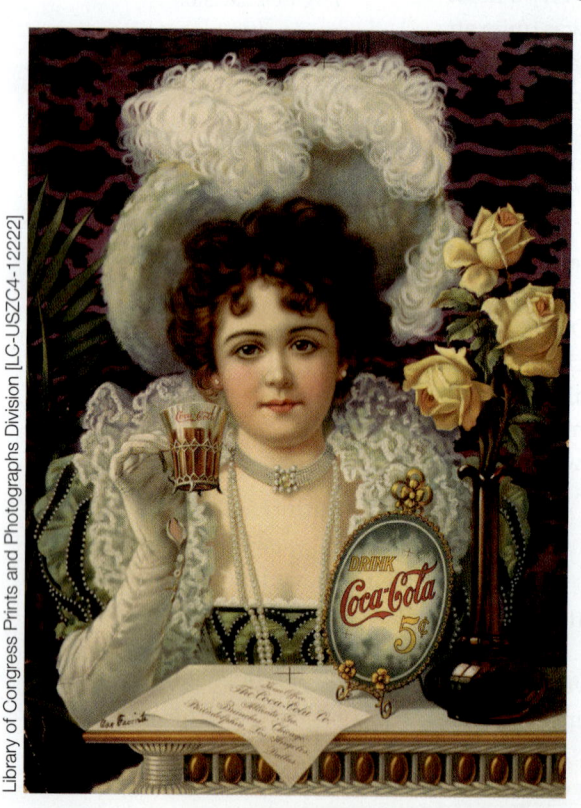

Library of Congress Prints and Photographs Division [LC-USZC4-12222]

This ad from the 1890s introduces the new drink Coca-Cola, which was one of the many new industries that emerged in the South.

Map 18-1A and 18-1B Expanding Southern Railroads, 1859–1899.

Map 1A at top illustrates the extent of railroad lines in 1859 on the eve of the Civil War. Map 1B illustrates the expansion of rail lines by 1899.

18.1

18.2

18.3

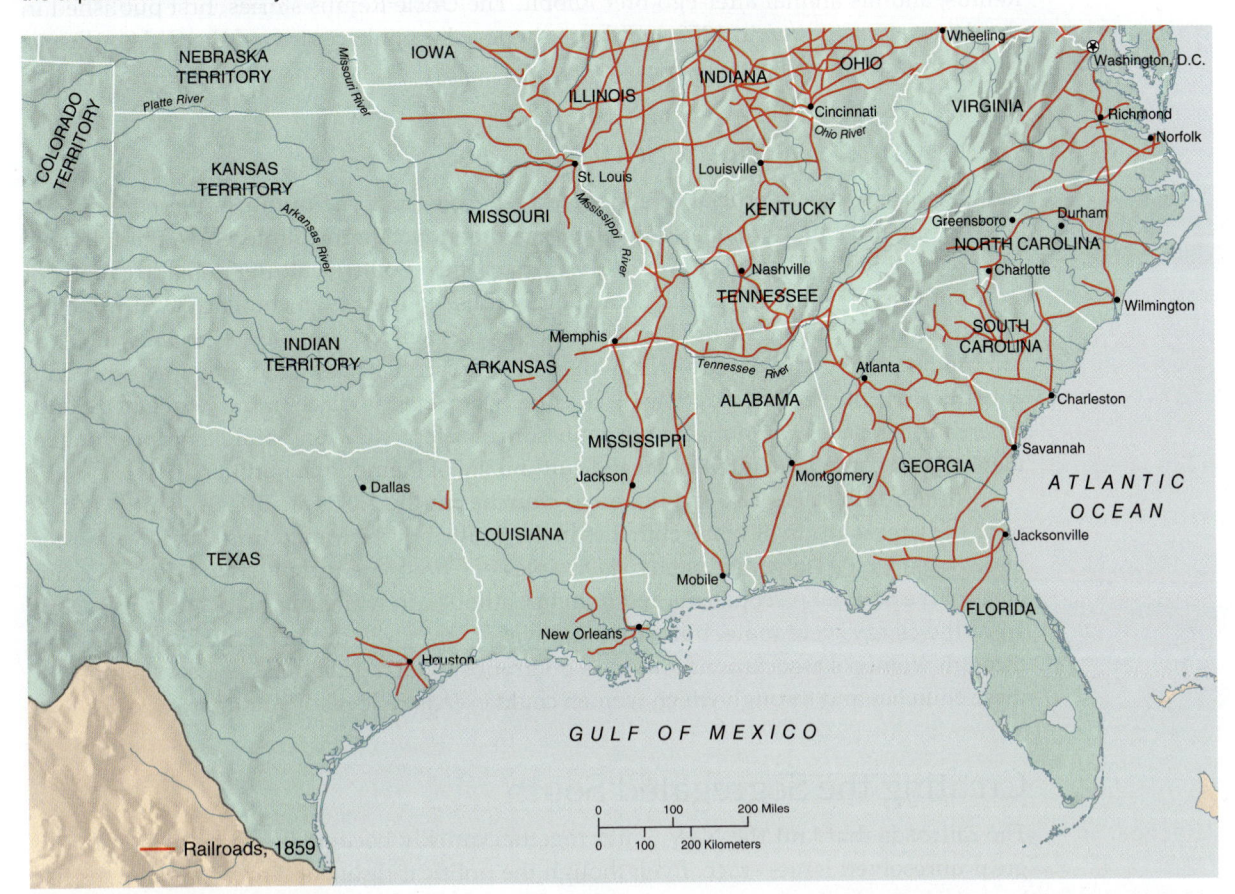

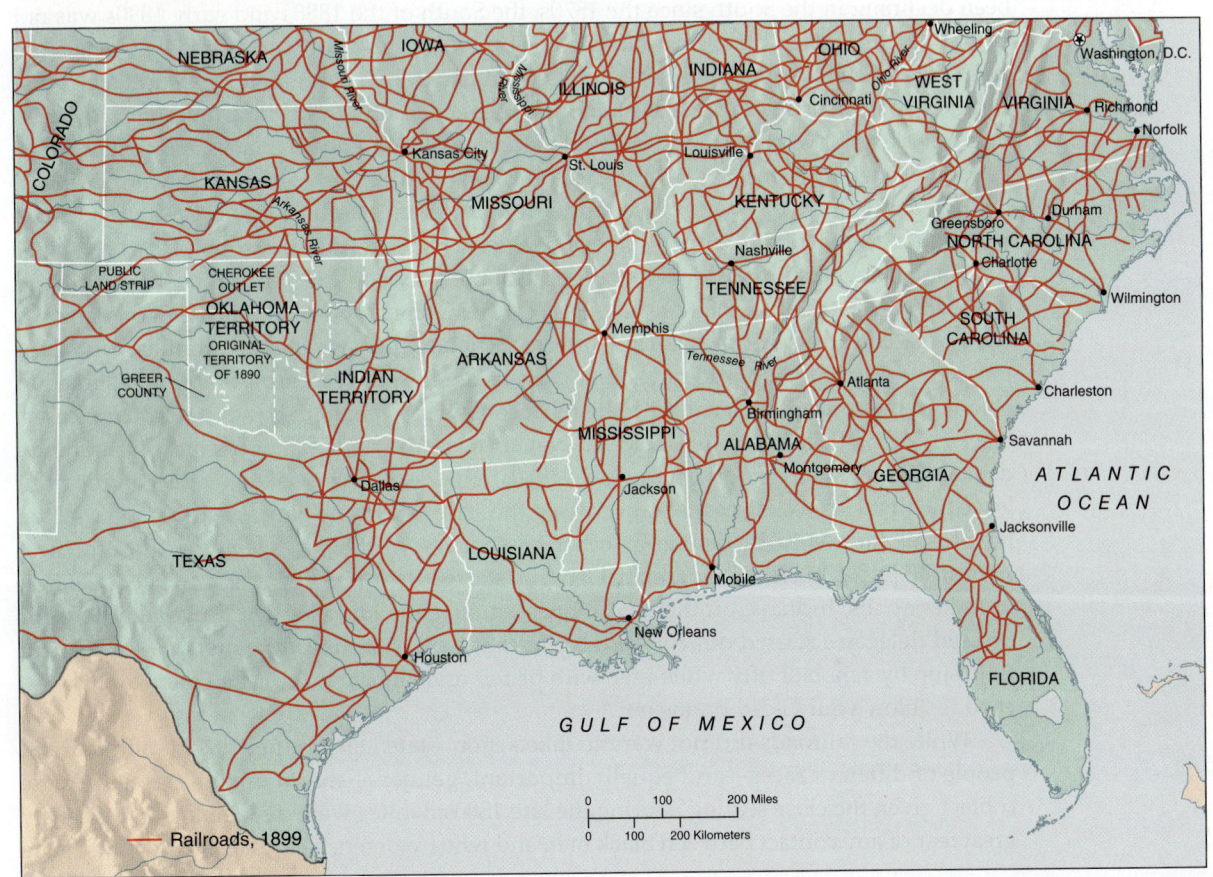

wise and loyal slave, who, Page told his white readers, longed for the days before the war when everyone had a secure place in a well-ordered society. The most famous author of the plantation school, Joel Chandler Harris, created the fictional elderly black man Uncle Remus, and his animal alter-ego Brer Rabbit. The Uncle Remus stories, first published in the *Atlanta Constitution* in 1879 and then as a popular book, portrayed the Old South as a romantic and happy place.

Religion in the New South

Religion also played a crucial role in the post-Reconstruction South. Southerners did not actually attend church in greater numbers than their Northern counterparts, but religious imagery and biblical language were a strong part of the South's culture. With the coming of freedom, Southern blacks quickly joined or established their own churches. By 1890, there were 1.3 million black Baptists in the South. Northern black churches, especially the African Methodist Episcopal and African Methodist Episcopal Zion denominations, also built churches for Southern blacks. The black church became the place in the segregated South where former slaves could meet with a measure of safety, share and build a new communal identity, and control the intellectual and cultural life of their own institution.

White Southerners also gravitated to churches in the 1880s and 1890s. Baptist bodies were the largest group of white churches in the South, but the Methodists claimed almost as many members. Also strong were the Disciples of Christ, the Presbyterians, and in certain areas of the South, Episcopalians and Roman Catholics. In white and black churches, nearly all of the clergy were male, but women played a large role in the churches, particularly through women's associations and mission groups, which provided necessary support to these churches and through which women could exercise a level of autonomy.

Creating the Segregated South

The railroads that knit the New South together quickly became the focus of the South's great unresolved issue—race. Even though the political rights of African Americans had been declining in the South since the 1870s, the South of the 1880s and early 1890s was not the rigidly segregated place it would become by 1900. Churches were segregated by custom and choice. Schools, hospitals, and hotels were generally segregated by law. Blacks were confined to the balcony in most theaters, and the races did not mix in restaurants. However, in many places of work, at many political gatherings, and in travel, blacks and whites could be found together in the South of the late 1800s. The railroads were certainly not going to build separate lines or even run separate trains, and most railroads saw all talk of racial segregation as potentially troublesome and expensive. Nevertheless, trouble was brewing.

As passenger railroads developed in the South between 1865 and 1880, they generally offered two classes of service—a first-class car for women and men who did not smoke or chew tobacco and a second-class car—often a section of the baggage car—for men who used tobacco or people too poor to buy a first-class ticket. In some cases, blacks were assumed to belong in the second-class car with the tobacco-using white men; however, in many cases, blacks rode first class without incident. Nevertheless, a trip that might start without incident could quickly turn ugly. In the early 1880s, a black man was asked by the conductor to leave the first-class car after the train crossed the state line from Tennessee to Georgia. When he refused, he was badly beaten by other passengers. In 1889, a delegation from the first African Baptist Church of Savannah, Georgia, started their journey to a church convention in Indianapolis, Indiana, on the East Tennessee, Virginia and Georgia Railroad. The well-dressed delegates started out comfortably in first class, but they were met at a subsequent train stop by a mob of fifty white men with pistols and clubs who attacked them and threatened to "blow your G-d-d brains out."

While the railroads did not want to take action, state legislatures did. In railroad cars, people of different races—and equally important, genders—might mix in especially close contact given the close seating. During the late 1800s, whites were developing an especially great fear of any contact between black men and white women. Tennessee was the first state to respond, enacting a law saying, "All railroad companies shall furnish separate cars, or portions of cars cut off by partition wall, which all colored passengers who pay first-class rates of fare may have the privilege to enter and occupy." The law seemed to imply that it was up to blacks whether they wanted to be segregated or not, but that was not the way the arrangement worked. Across the South, trains were rigidly segregated a decade before the 1896 U.S. Supreme Court's 7-to-1 decision in *Plessy v. Ferguson* declared that "separate but equal" transportation—and, by implication, other matters—did not violate the equal protection clause of the Fourteenth Amendment to the U.S. Constitution.

The Politics of Exclusion

The end of the racially integrated governments of the Reconstruction era and the almost complete exclusion of African Americans from the political life of the South took place in two distinct stages between the 1870s and 1900. These stages are often merged in the popular mind as if they happened all at once, though they did not.

The first step in ending Reconstruction took place in the 1860s and 1870s (see Chapter 15). Black legislators and white legislators who supported them (almost all of whom were Republicans) were defeated by white Democratic segregationists at different times in different states, nearly always in elections marked by violence and voter intimidation. Virginia was the first to shift from a Republican to a Democratic legislature in 1869. Conservative Democrats soon also won large majorities in other states—North Carolina in 1870, Georgia in 1871, Texas in 1873, Alabama and Arkansas in 1874, and South Carolina and Mississippi in 1876. Finally, contested elections in Louisiana and Florida were awarded to the Democrats in 1877 as part of the same compromise that put Hayes in the White House. The limits on federal troop involvement that the newly inaugurated Hayes ordered in 1877 were thus the culmination, not the cause of the end of Reconstruction.

However, the defeat of Reconstruction was not the end of the story. While every Southern state had a conservative Democratic legislature and governor after 1877, quite a few blacks still voted and some were still elected and appointed to public offices in the South for another decade. Black voters could provide the margin of victory in close contests. Most state legislatures had at least a few African American representatives, and many federally appointed officials from postmasters to census officials were black. In 1891, as the Arkansas legislature was debating railroad segregation, it was a black legislator, John Gray Lucas, who objected. It was also a black delegate to Mississippi's 1895 state constitutional convention, Thomas E. Miller, who told the majority that they needed to remember, "It was your love of power and your arrogance which brought Reconstruction on you."

In most cases, the black officeholders remaining were too few in number to have an impact. Nevertheless, some whites objected, especially when the presence of black officeholders challenged racial and gender conventions such as when a black male postmaster would help a white woman who visited the post office. When the Republicans won the White House and Congress in 1888, some white Southerners feared a repeat of Reconstruction, perhaps even the appointment of federal election officials who would monitor Southern election procedures. At the same time, a new generation of Southern whites were tired of the Klan-style violence that accompanied elections. An 1889 article in the Jackson, Mississippi, *Clarion-Ledger* said, "The old men of the present generation can't afford to die and leave the election to their children and grandchildren, with shot guns in their hands, a lie in their mouths and perjury on their lips in order to defeat the negroes." The solution to the election violence that the newspaper wanted was not to hold fair and race-neutral elections but, rather, to establish legal means to exclude all blacks from all political participation.

A conductor evicts a well-dressed black man from a first-class coach. Enforcing segregation on the railroad coach was seen by many white Southerners as somehow essential to protecting white women.

Bettmann/Getty Images

18.1

18.2

18.3

Fears of black political involvement grew in the 1890s when the Populist movement disrupted Southern politics. It was one thing for a handful of blacks in the state legislature to raise questions about a bill before the white majority voted for whatever it wanted. It was a different matter if the white Democratic majority was split between Populist and traditional Democratic factions and the black representatives had the tie-breaking votes or if, as happened in North Carolina, a Populist-Republican ticket, with black support, could actually win the majority of seats in a state legislature. In 1896, South Carolina's arch-segregationist governor Ben Tillman warned of an "unholy alliance between the independents and the negroes."

For many Southern whites, the solution was a new set of laws that would ensure "white supremacy" forever. Political leaders called new state constitutional conventions to ensure that they secured absolute power. Blacks and their white allies had been marginalized by the violence and the voting that ended Reconstruction, but the new state constitutions of the 1890s moved from marginalization to complete exclusion. When the work of these new constitutional conventions was done, extremely few black voters and no black officeholders remained anywhere in what came to be known as the "solid South," which meant solidly white and Democratic.

Mississippi rewrote its state constitution in 1890, creating obstacles that would stop virtually all blacks from voting. The most obvious restrictions—a literacy test or a poll tax or a property qualification for voters—would also exclude many poor whites who were themselves illiterate and who could not meet a property qualification or pay a poll tax. So Mississippi's delegates created a complex set of limitations on voting and office. To be able to vote, the new constitution said, a person had to have lived in the state for at least two years and in the election district for at least one; a sharecropper who moved for a better chance at life thus lost the right to participate in elections at least for a time. Other states instituted "grandfather clauses" that said anyone whose grandfather had been a voter was exempt from other restrictions, a privilege no descendent of slaves could claim. Those intending to vote in Mississippi and elsewhere could not do so if they had been convicted of petty crimes such as arson, bigamy, or petty theft, crimes that blacks were routinely charged with. Ironically, conviction for murder, rape, or grand larceny did not exclude one from voting. The Mississippi convention did require a modest poll tax. Finally, the convention adopted a requirement that every voter be able to understand and interpret the state constitution. White state-appointed registrars would decide whose interpretation was "reasonable." An editorial in the Jackson, Mississippi, *Clarion-Ledger* described the new system: "[I]f every negro in Mississippi was a graduate of Harvard … he would not be as well fitted to exercise the right of suffrage as the Anglo-Saxon farm laborer." Once the new Mississippi Constitution took effect, it had its intended impact. As other Southern states observed what was happening in Mississippi, they too adopted the approach.

After the U.S. Supreme Court declared poll taxes and literacy tests to be constitutional in their 1898 ruling in *Williams v. Mississippi*, there was little chance that any Southern state would fail to enact Mississippi-style voting tests. In 1908, Texas became the last state of the former Confederacy to add a poll tax, and across the region, that tax was usually one of several mechanisms that ended black voting.

Then, as though all of the new laws were not enough, new forms of violence toward African Americans emerged in the late 1800s. Where the Klan and other groups had terrorized black communities during Reconstruction, blacks now found themselves being arrested for vague terms like "vagrancy," and serving long sentences when they could not pay a fine. The ultimate horror of lynching became widespread. Individual African Americans, typically young men, were singled out, often accused with little or no evidence of raping a white woman, and hung in a public spectacle. The issue was rarely an actual rape but, more often, a young black man's failure to observe the customs of stepping out of the way for a white person to pass, a black man's challenging the payment of a landowner at the sharecroppers settle, or a black man asserting his political rights. Most of all, long jail terms and lynching were ways to strike terror into the black community while asserting and celebrating white dominance. In 1900, the New South was fast becoming a region governed exclusively by white voters and white elected officials and would remain so until the black civil rights movement of the 1950s, 1960s, and 1970s transformed the region and the nation.

African American Responses

As the rigid segregation of "separate but equal," which everyone knew meant separate and very unequal, settled on the South and, indeed, much of the country, especially after 1896, African Americans debated how to respond to a legal system that excluded them from voting while seldom prosecuting the all-too-frequent violence against them. In addition, they considered their response to being barred from access to quality schooling and to any but the most menial jobs as well as to being restricted from entering rail cars, hotels, or theaters that served whites. They also argued against cultural expectations responses to cultural expectations that they "give way," allowing whites to pass in front of them in stores and on sidewalks, that they call all whites by their last names while they were called by their first names by whites, and that they live with the oppressive knowledge that even the slightest challenge to segregation could be met with not only ostracism but also unimaginable violence, from long prison terms to lynching.

Ida B. Wells-Barnett became the most effective national spokesperson for the antilynching crusade.

Ida B. Wells-Barnett (1862–1931) was one of the African Americans who challenged lynching. Between 1889 and 1918, 386 lynchings took place in Georgia, 373 in Mississippi, and similar numbers in several other states. Wells-Barnett argued that the rape charge, which was often the excuse for lynching a black man, was a "thread-bare lie" and a cover for punishing any black who challenged the rules of segregation. In response to her writing, a white mob destroyed her printing press at her *Memphis Free Press*, but throughout her life, she continued to write, publish, and organize legal challenges to segregation and especially the violence of lynchings.

In the face of the harsh reality of segregation and exclusion, Booker T. Washington (1856–1915), perhaps the nation's best-known African American leader, argued that it was time to adjust to segregation rather than challenge the laws and customs excluding blacks. Washington urged blacks to create an economic foundation for themselves, offering what came to be known as the **Atlanta Compromise**—that African Americans would accept segregation in return for being able to develop economically. In the midst of the harsh realities of the 1890s, Washington's course of action seemed the only realistic option.

Atlanta Compromise

An 1895 proposal from Booker T. Washington that African Americans remain separate from whites while focusing on economic self-help.

Not all African Americans agreed with Washington, and a young African American scholar, W. E. B. Du Bois (1868–1963), became his harshest critic. Du Bois criticized compromises and wrote that "the problem of the twentieth century is the problem of the color line." He described the kind of "double consciousness" or "twoness" that African Americans were forced to develop in a country that proclaimed liberty but excluded them by law and custom.

In 1905, Du Bois joined other African American leaders meeting at Niagara Falls— in a hotel on the Canadian side because no hotel on the American side would give them rooms—to begin a campaign for "every single right that belongs to a free-born American, political, civil, and social" without compromise. The **Niagara Movement** that emerged from the conference fought for an end to segregation and for full equality for African Americans. Four years later, in February 1909, Du Bois, others from the Niagara Movement, and additional African American leaders, including Ida B. Wells-Barnett, Mary McLeod Bethune, and Mary Church Terrell, joined with white reformers, including Jane Addams, John Dewey, Clarence Darrow, and Lincoln Steffens. They created the **National Association for the Advancement of Colored People** (the NAACP) to fight for full enforcement of the Fourteenth and Fifteenth Amendments; bring public exposure and legal challenges to the mostly unpunished wave of lynchings that were happening in all parts of the country; and begin what would be a long, slow legal process of court challenges to the "separate but equal" laws that provided the legal foundation for black exclusion.

Niagara Movement

African American group organized in 1905 to promote racial integration, civil and political rights, and equal access to economic opportunity; the movement later helped organize the NAACP.

National Association for the Advancement of Colored People (NAACP)

An interracial organization founded in 1910 dedicated to restoring African American political and social rights.

18.1

18.2

18.3

Thinking Historically

Debating Booker T. Washington's "Cast Down Your Buckets Where You Are" Speech

On September 18, 1895, Booker T. Washington spoke to a mostly white audience at the Cotton States and International Exposition in Atlanta, Georgia, explaining just what he meant by the Atlanta Compromise. Washington said:

> To those of my race ... I would say: "Cast down your bucket where you are"—cast it down in making friends in every manly way with the people of all races with whom we are surrounded. Cast it down in agriculture, mechanics, in commerce, in domestic service, and in the professions. ... In all things that are purely social we can be as separate as the fingers, yet one as the hand in all things essential to mutual progress. ... The wisest among my race understand that the agitation of questions of social equality is the extremist folly, and that progress in the enjoyment of all the privileges that will come to us must be the result of severe and constant struggle rather than of artificial forcing. No race that has anything to contribute to the markets of the world is long in any degree ostracized. It is important and right that all privileges of the law be ours, but it is vastly more important that we be prepared for the exercise of these privileges. The opportunity to earn a dollar in a factory just now is worth infinitely more than the opportunity to spend a dollar in an opera-house.

Washington's speech was greeted with great applause in the white community, but eight years later in 1903, W. E. B. Du Bois published *The Souls of Black Folk*, an unsparing critique in which he said:

> Mr. Washington represents in Negro thought the old attitude of adjustment and submission. ... Mr. Washington distinctly asks that black people give up, at least for the present, three things—
>
> First, political power,
>
> Second, insistence on civil rights,
>
> Third, higher education of Negro youth—
>
> And concentrate all their energies on industrial education, the accumulation of wealth, and the conciliation of the South. This policy has been courageously and insistently advocated for

over fifteen years, and has been triumphant for perhaps ten years. As a result of this tender of the palm-branch, what has been the return? In these years there have occurred:

> 1. The disfranchisement of the Negro.
> 2. The legal creation of a distinct status of civil inferiority for the Negro.
> 3. The steady withdrawal of aid from institutions for the higher training of the Negro.

These movements are not, to be sure, direct results of Mr. Washington's teachings, but his propaganda has, without a shadow of doubt, helped their speedier accomplishment. The question then comes: Is it possible, and probable, that nine millions of men can make effective progress in economic lines if they are deprived of political rights, made a servile caste, and allowed only the most meager chance for developing their exceptional men?

While privately Washington provided funds for court challenges of segregation and challenged lynching, the division between him and Du Bois were stark. Washington had been born in slavery and lived and worked in Alabama in the heart of a segregated world. Du Bois, a generation younger, was raised in the North and had much less patience with any form of accommodation. The two leaders outlined differences that remained in the African American community for decades.

Source: Booker T. Washington, *Up from Slavery: An Autobiography* (New York: Doubleday-Page, 1901); W. E. B. Du Bois, *The Souls of Black Folk* (Chicago: A.C. McClurg, 1903).

Thinking Critically

1. **Comparison**
   What do you see as the starkest differences between Washington and Du Bois?

2. **Contextualization**
   How did the location in which Washington and Du Bois were each born and in which each lived as an adult impact their writing? What evidence from these documents would you give to support your argument?

18.1 Quick Review

Support why or why not "New South" is an appropriate name for the society that emerged after Reconstruction. Consider the economics, politics, and social aspects of the region in formulating your answer.

The Politics of Conflict—From Populist Movement to Populist Party

18.2 Analyze how agrarian unrest and protest came to have a significant impact on American politics.

In the 1870s and 1880s, American farmers were living very difficult lives. The work was backbreaking. They had no time for much of an education and far too little time for family or community life. The economic cycles seemed structured against them. While new forms of mechanization allowed them to increase production significantly, the increased production often resulted in lower prices for their products so that they seemed to be no better off while struggling to pay for the new machinery. The rapid increase in agricultural production, facilitated by new fertilizers and new mechanization, significantly increased farm output across the country. In just six years, from 1899 to 1905, American food production increased by almost 40 percent. For consumers, this new level of output meant far greater choice and lower prices. For farmers, it meant only a vicious cycle in which the more they produced, the less they were paid for it. In addition to dealing with that dynamic, other situations such as a glut of wheat in Russia or overproduction of cotton in Egypt or some other issue left them in a pattern of debt. Even in good times, it seemed that the railroads and middlemen in New York or New Orleans or London or Paris took the profits that they produced. Perhaps most galling to many farmers was the sense that the rapid changes happening in the rest of the country seemed to be leaving them behind. It is not accidental that the derogatory word "hayseed" entered the nation's vocabulary at this time. Urban America saw itself as up to date and modern, but the very consumers who benefited from increased farm production saw farmers, living in isolated rural areas, as backward and out of date. Moreover, the new technologies that enabled rapid communication let these farmers know just what others in the country thought of them. Jefferson's agrarian ideal seemed like part of a very dim past.

The Farmers' Alliance and Other Farm Groups

By the beginning of the 1880s, many farmers were deeply in debt to the banks on which they depended for their mortgages and for loans to obtain equipment and supplies for the planting year. Railroads that might give a break to John D. Rockefeller's Standard Oil kept raising the rates to haul farm products to market. By the time farmers paid off their loans and paid to get the wheat, corn, and other farm products to market, they had little, if any, money left. Eventually, farmers started to do something to change their circumstances. Nelson Dunning of the Farmers' Alliance wrote, "Nothing could withstand their power, if the farmers of America would organize," particularly, as he believed, in ways the Standard Oil Company had done. In the Farmers' Alliance and eventually in their own political party, farmers, who had indeed been observing what the Rockefellers and Carnegies were doing, tried to create their own power base.

The earliest nationwide farmer organization was the Patrons of Husbandry, also known as "**the Grange**." Farmers gathered in Grange Halls to celebrate their work and foster a sense of community, but they also organized to deal with the chronic debt and the sense that the nation's financial arrangements were stacked against them. Especially in the South, local Grange chapters organized cooperative buying and selling through their own cotton gins and warehouses, knowing that they would get better prices for their crops and better rates from the railroads if they banded together. The national leadership of the Grange focused on lobbying for agricultural colleges, attracting more people to farming, encouraging crop diversity, and promoting a richer home life for farm families.

Farmers also started additional organizations. In 1882, Arkansas farmers launched the **Agricultural Wheel**. By 1885, the Agricultural Wheel had 1,105 local chapters in four states. The Wheel became a tough organization that excluded any but working farmers. The organization used its size to negotiate price reductions with manufacturers of farm implements. In an effort to make improvements in mechanization more widely available at more

the Grange

The Grange, or the Patrons of Husbandry, a national organization of farmers formed after the Civil War to promote the rights and dignity of farmers.

Agricultural Wheel

An organization of farmers, begun in Arkansas in 1882. More militant than the Grange, it sought to advance farmers' economic status.

The Grange, the first national farmers' organization, painted an idealized picture of farming. Later, farmers' organizations were less idealistic and more militant.

reasonable prices, the Agricultural Wheel got up to 50 percent reductions on the prices of wagons, buggies, reapers, and mowers, while organizing its own warehouses to hold crops until prices met expectations and so address the chronic problem of overproduction wrecking the price farmers were paid for their work.

A number of similar organizations coordinated similar efforts, but the largest by far was the **Farmers' Alliance**, which began as the Texas Alliance in Lampasas County, Texas, in the 1870s. After Charles W. Macune was elected president of the Texas organization in 1886, the Alliance grew rapidly. Macune had trained as a pharmacist and a physician before he settled in Milam County, Texas, in 1879 where he practiced medicine while farming on the side. His rural medical practice gave him a sense of the isolation and the lack of economic clout ranchers and farmers faced.

Under Macune's leadership, the Farmers' Alliance began organizing the farmers (including ranchers) of Texas, and eventually the nation, to use the best of corporate practices. The Alliance sought to get a better financial deal for farmers through the negotiating power of a large organization demanding lower prices for the things they bought and higher prices for the products they sold.

The Texas Farmers' Alliance grew from 38,000 members in 1886 to 225,000 members in 1889—almost half of all the eligible farmers in Texas. In 1887, the Alliance merged with the

Farmers' Alliance

A broad mass movement in the rural South and West during the late 1800s, encompassing several organizations and demanding economic and political reforms; it helped create the Populist Party.

Library of Congress Prints and Photographs Division/Strobridge & Co. Lith, [LC-DIG-pga-04170]

Arkansas-based Agricultural Wheel and continued to grow, with local units stretching from North Carolina to California and from Texas to the Dakotas. In 1890, Macune moved to a national headquarters in Washington, D.C., and the Alliance had over 1 million members.

Under Macune's leadership, the Farmers' Alliance steered clear of direct political involvement. The goal of the Alliance was simple: farmers would combine their power to equal the power of other businesses. They were not opposed to monopolies; they wanted to be one. The Washington office published the *National Economist*, mailed to farmers across the country, while sponsoring lecturers, organizers, and corresponding secretaries to spread Alliance ideas. The organization sought to overcome rural isolation and lack of educational opportunities through lending libraries, schools, conferences, and social occasions for farm families. Most of all, the Alliance sought to open a "new era" of prosperity for farmers through tough negotiations on their behalf.

Macune believed that whites and blacks had different economic interests and insisted that the Farmers' Alliance should include only white farmers. When the Agricultural Wheel joined the Alliance, it dropped its black members. In response to Macune's segregationist policy, African American farmers created their own **Colored Farmers' National Alliance and Cooperative Union**, which had 1.2 million members by 1890. Given the political and social disenfranchisement that black farmers faced, they organized primarily through black churches. In many communities, the black Baptist Church and the Colored Farmers' Alliance had virtually the same membership. Lacking the resources to publish their own materials or hire lecturers or organizers, the black organization never had the clout of the white alliance, even though it had as many or more members.

While the Farmers' Alliance was racially segregated, it welcomed women as members and leaders, as did the Colored Farmers' Alliance. Fully a quarter of the members of the Colored Farmers' Alliance were women. In contrast to the Grange, which had special positions for women, the Farmers' Alliance opened all positions to both women and men. Annie L. Diggs of Kansas was one of the senior editors of the National Reform Press Association, the white Alliance's publishing house. Mary E. Lease of Kansas was the most famous of the Alliance's many speakers, while Marion Todd of Illinois was considered to be the most effective theoretician for the movement. Bettie Munn Gay, who had turned a highly mortgaged Texas farm into a successful cotton-growing operation, became one of the leaders in the Texas Alliance. Women and men within the Alliance debated women's suffrage and occasionally argued over the prohibition of alcohol. But they were united in a commitment to improve the life of farm families, economically as well as intellectually and culturally, ending the terrible isolation that farm families experienced.

Colored Farmers' National Alliance and Cooperative Union

An organization of Southern black farmers formed in Texas in 1886 in response to the Southern Farmers' Alliance, which did not accept black people as members. It also helped launch the Populist Party.

Defining a National Agenda

While Macune focused the Farmers' Alliance on cooperative economic efforts and stayed out of electoral politics, others wanted direct political involvement. In California, the president of the state Farmers' Alliance, Marion Cannon, became convinced after long battles with the Southern Pacific Railroad that only public ownership of the railroads would allow farmers to get a fair deal. Alliance lecturer Marion Todd published *Railways of Europe and America* in 1893 in which she argued for managing railways in ways similar to how the government managed post offices. Some in the Alliance wanted a federal commission to limit the power of the railroads, but Cannon and Todd were convinced that the railroads were too big to be tamed and that a government takeover was the only answer.

Even Macune came to advocate for what he called the **subtreasury system**. He wanted to have a unit created within the U.S. Department of the Treasury that would provide low-interest loans to farmers. These loans would be secured by cotton, wheat, and other staple crops. The subtreasury would protect its investment and support farmers through a federal system of warehouses and grain elevators in one thousand counties across the country. In this system, the government would ensure minimum prices for crops and hold warehoused crops until they sold at those prices, thus ensuring that the dramatic increases in the nation's agricultural production did not harm farmers by undermining what they were paid. If speculators could use the telegraph to make money buying and selling crop futures,

subtreasury system

A proposal for a unit of the U.S. Treasury Department (or "subtreasury") to own warehouses that would store farmers' crops until prices rose.

American Voices

Mary E. Lease, Women in the Farmers' Alliance, 1891

Mary E. Lease, a well-known speaker for the Farmers' Alliance, rose to national fame telling Kansas farmers to "raise less corn and more hell." In 1891, she gave a speech to the National Council of Women of the United States in which she said:

It must be evident to every intelligent man and woman to-day that there is something radically wrong in the affairs of this Nation. …

My friends, the lash of the slave-driver's whip is no longer heard in this country, but the lash of necessity is driving thousands to unrequited toil. Conscienceless capital is robbing manhood of its prime, mothers of their motherhood, and sorrowful children of sunshine and of joy. Look around you! What do you behold to-day? A land which less than four hundred years ago we received fresh from the hands of God, a continent of unparalleled fertility … and yet, in this land of plenty and unlimited resources, the cry of humanity is going up from every corner of this Nation. The plaint of motherhood, the moans of starving children! Capital buys and sells to-day the very heart-beats of humanity. …

Oh, yes; we can point to the rivers bridged, to the transcontinental railway connecting ocean with ocean, to wonderful churches and cathedrals; he can point to the most wonderful system of agriculture that ever brought joy to a hungry world; he can jostle his rags against the silken garments his toil has secured; he can walk shelterless and sad by the side of the home he has helped to build; he can wipe the sweat from his weary face, and reflect that the twenty thousand of American millionaires who own one billion five hundred million dollars, gathered from the toils and tears of sixty-four millions of American people, have it in their power to name their Governors and our legislators and representatives and Congressmen,—and they *do* name them, and they *have* named them for the last quarter of a century, and they have it in their power to fix the price of labor, to fix the price for every ton of coal.

Source: Mary E. Lease, "Speech to the National Council of Women of the United States, Assembled in Washington, D.C., February 24, 1891."

Thinking Critically

1. **Analyzing Primary Sources**
   What evidence does Mary Lease provide in her speech to explain her point of view supporting the "necessity of the formation of the Farmers' Alliance"?

2. **Contextualization**
   What evidence in the document tells the reader the era in which it was written and the intended audience?

why couldn't farmers, with the right government support, use the same technical arrangements to ensure their own profits?

While the Alliance took up the subtreasury idea, the leadership of the Democratic Party resisted, as did virtually all Republicans, and the subtreasury was never created. As a result, many within the Alliance began to question the value of staying out of politics.

More than public ownership of railroads or the subtreasury idea, the political issue that engaged U.S. farmers was federal fiscal policy. When the government limited the supply of currency, farmers had a very difficult time paying their debts, getting loans, or getting the price they wanted for their crops. When the government made more funds available, the resulting inflation made it easier to pay debts (because the debt amounted to less in current dollars) and made it easier to sell the products of the farms. Although easing the supply of money improved the situation of farmers, one policy made it difficult to do: the nation's adherence to the gold standard, requiring that every dollar in circulation be backed by a dollar's worth of gold in a bank vault.

During the Civil War, the federal government had temporarily dropped the gold standard. Instead, it created federal banknotes, known as "greenbacks" because of their color, essentially printing dollars based not on gold but on the "full faith and credit" of the government's promise to pay. The government also allowed the additional use of silver as backing for currency during the war. Both of these policies eased the supply of money significantly, but they also fueled inflation since, with more dollars available, any dollar was worth less. Farmers liked inflation, but investors and bankers hated it. After the Civil War, the nation's bankers demanded a return to the gold standard by gradually withdrawing greenbacks from circulation as the government paid down its Civil War debt and then in 1873 "demonetizing" silver so only gold, and not silver, could be used for coins or backing for dollars in circulation. These policies were effective in curbing inflation, but they led to an extremely tight money supply, tight credit, and challenging times for farmers. The tight money of the 1880s was thus a direct result of federal policy, and the Farmers' Alliance as well as the other farmer organizations were determined to change the policy. Some advocated expanding the number of greenbacks, others supported the coinage of more silver, and some called for both, but all agreed that something needed to be done.

Populism Becomes a Political Party

The rapid growth of the Farmers' Alliance in the 1880s brought many state leaders into the organization who advocated direct political involvement. Leonidas L. Polk of North Carolina was the strongest of all these leaders. A Confederate hero, Polk made his fortune in real estate development when the Carolina Central Railroad crossed his old family plantation in 1873. He was active in the Methodist Church and in the Grange. He also helped ensure the end of Reconstruction in his state while helping re-create the Democratic Party there. Polk lobbied for the creation of a state Department of Agriculture, became its first commissioner in 1877, and in 1886, published his own newspaper, *Progressive Farmer*. In 1888, he brought the state organization he led into the Farmers' Alliance, and within the year, forty-two thousand North Carolina farmers were members of the national organization.

Other states had similar leaders. South Carolina's Benjamin R. Tillman had served in a militia that kept blacks and Republicans out of politics. He became active in the state Grange in the 1880s and became convinced that "the yoke of the credit system" was keeping farmers down. He convened a large meeting of white farmers in 1886, lobbied for a state agricultural college, and created a twenty-thousand-member South Carolina Alliance that remained independent of the national organization. Georgia's Tom Watson was a lawyer and "friend and follower" of the Farmers' Alliance, though as a nonfarmer he could not join. Nevertheless, he was elected to Congress as a Farmers' Alliance candidate in 1890, expanding the movement of the Alliance into politics.

As the price of cotton fell to the lowest level in thirty years in 1891—and the farm economy continued to worsen throughout the 1890s—Watson, Tillman, Polk, and others rallied for a change. They saw that the Knights of Labor and the Women's Christian Temperance Union (see later in this chapter and Chapter 21 for more about these organizations) had recently launched a new political organization, the **People's Party** (or Populist Party), at a convention in Cincinnati in 1891 that was advocating for many of the reforms to currency and regulation of railroads that the Alliance wanted. If the Farmers' Alliance was to merge with the People's Party, they could win elections and have their voices heard in state capitals, in Congress, and perhaps even in the White House.

Macune continued to oppose political involvement, preferring farmer-controlled cooperative economic development. Polk led those who said yes to political involvement and specifically to joining the People's Party. Everyone knew that the 1892 convention of the Farmers' Alliance would decide the issue. Polk won. The Alliance joined the Populists. Macune retired from the Alliance and spent the next thirty years practicing medicine and law while preaching in Methodist churches in rural Texas.

The People's (or Populist) Party grew dramatically. The Colored Farmers' Alliance and smaller groups like the Farmers' Mutual Benefit Association also joined. The widespread assumption was that when the People's Party, now a multiracial coalition of farmers, labor, and women's groups, held their national convention in Omaha, Nebraska, in July 1892, they would nominate Leonidas Polk for president. The Omaha Convention adopted a platform that called for inflation of the money supply (to help farmers pay their debts), government regulation of railroads, and election reform. However, just a month before the convention met, Polk suddenly died. The People's Party nominated James B. Weaver of Iowa, a former Union general, and James G. Field, a former Confederate from Virginia, as his running mate. Polk's charisma did not adhere to the new nominees. Nevertheless, Weaver won over a million votes in the 1892 presidential election that ultimately returned Cleveland to the White House. Not since the late 1850s, when the Republican Party had come out of nowhere, had the nation witnessed anything like the phenomenal growth of the Populists, as the members of the People's Party quickly came to be known. Populist candidates won the governor's office in Colorado and Kansas in the 1892 elections. Populists elected Marion Cannon to Congress from southern California as well as congressmen from Colorado, Kansas, Nebraska, and North Carolina. They elected eight representatives to

People's Party

Usually known as the **Populist Party**, a major third party of the 1890s formed to fight for the rights of working people.

18.1

18.2

18.3

18.1

18.2

18.3

the California state legislature, a group that held the balance between the Democrats and Republicans and almost succeeded in electing California's U.S. senator.

Two years later, Populist candidates won over 1.5 million votes, electing seven to the U.S. House, six to the U.S. Senate, and many to state legislatures. In a partnership with Republicans, Populists won control of the North Carolina legislature—the only time since Reconstruction when the Democrats had lost control of a state—and sent Marion Butler to the U.S. Senate. In 1894, Populist candidates won 41 percent of the vote for statewide offices in Colorado, 39 percent in Washington State, 39 percent in Kansas, and 36 percent in Texas. Populists were elected to Congress from Alabama, Kansas, Nebraska, and North Carolina. The Populists, it seemed, were gaining power.

As the Populists approached the 1896 presidential elections, the Republican and Democratic Parties were keeping a worried eye on them and, at the same time, borrowing parts of their message. No one borrowed more from the Populists than the young former congressman from Nebraska, William Jennings Bryan. Bryan was a Democrat, not a Populist, but his views on many issues, most of all his advocacy for the unlimited coinage of silver, were the same as those of the Populists and anathema to leaders of the Democratic Party, including President Cleveland who was not seeking reelection but who wanted a successor more like himself. Nevertheless, Bryan worked tirelessly for the Democratic nomination, courting as many "silver" delegates to the party's 1896 convention in Chicago as possible.

When the Democrats finally met in early July, the debate on the platform was intense, pitting those who wanted to hold to the gold standard against the "free silver" Democrats who agreed with the Populists. Bryan spoke to the convention, electrifying the gathering as he concluded:

> If they dare to come out in the open field and defend the gold standard as a good thing, we shall fight them to the uttermost, having behind us the producing masses of the nation and the world. Having behind us the commercial interests and the laboring interests and all the toiling masses, we shall answer their demands for a gold standard by saying to them, you shall not press down upon the brow of labor this crown of thorns. You shall not crucify mankind upon a cross of gold.

After the cheering stopped, the Democrats adopted a silver platform and nominated Bryan for president. The Populists were torn about what to do since Bryan's views seemed so close to their own, and with him, they might actually win the White House. The Populist Convention that met in July ultimately nominated Bryan as their candidate for president. By joining forces with the Democrats, they were confident of victory.

The Republicans nominated William McKinley, a genial congressman from Ohio, and the last Civil War veteran to run for president. In the fall campaign, managed by Marcus Alonzo Hanna, a wealthy supporter who was emerging as something close to a modern professional political advisor, the Republicans equated a vote for Bryan with a rebellion against the nation. They linked the Republican ticket with the flag, patriotism, and economic caution. They called McKinley the "advance agent of prosperity" and some, like a young Theodore Roosevelt, described the Democrats and Populists as "plotting a social revolution and the subversion of the American Republic." In the contest, the notions of patriotism, economic caution, and northeast regional distrust of the South and West won. A comfortable majority elected McKinley, though the results show how deeply divided the country had become (see Map 18-2).

The Populists never recovered from their loss in 1896. Those who had supported Bryan and the alliance with the Democratic Party blamed those who did not. Populists who had not wanted to compromise blamed those who had "sold out" and supported a Democrat. African Americans, whose votes had been essential to Populist victories in many close contests, were deeply disillusioned at how quickly Populist leaders like Tom Watson turned into arch segregationists after 1897.

Map 18-2 The Election of 1896.

This map of the electoral votes in the 1896 presidential election shows how deeply divided the country was. States where farming was dominant voted overwhelmingly for Bryan.

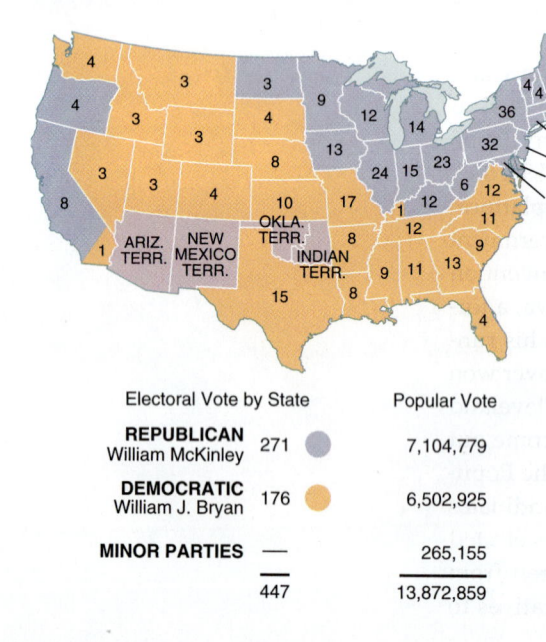

Electoral Vote by State		Popular Vote
REPUBLICAN William McKinley	271	7,104,779
DEMOCRATIC William J. Bryan	176	6,502,925
MINOR PARTIES	—	265,155
	447	13,872,859

The Populist Party continued for a short time, but the enthusiasm and confidence were destroyed by the divisions over the 1896 election. In 1900 and 1904, the party nominated Tom Watson who, having courted black voters in the 1890s, now campaigned on a platform of white supremacy even while he maintained the Populist economic program. The Democrats renominated Bryan in 1900, but he did poorly without Populist support and in the face of prosperity and McKinley's considerable popularity. The new Socialist Party, emerging from Northern labor unions, began to contest presidential elections, taking many of the Populists' labor union supporters. A moment and a movement had passed. In the early 1900s, national interest turned elsewhere, although many elements of the Populist platform were adopted and became the basis for a later progressive movement championed by both Republicans and Democrats after 1900. The farmers of the South and West, who had organized themselves so successfully and had bridged theretofore uncrossed gender barriers, were never able to resolve their racial divisions. Never again would they have the same level of political power.

18.2   Quick Review

Was politics the best way for the farmers to address their grievances? Why or why not? What might have been a more effective strategy?

Worker Protest and the Rise of Organized Labor

18.3   **Explain the tensions in industrial America that led to major labor strife between the 1870s and 1914.**

The Great Railroad Strike of 1877 began spontaneously in Baltimore, Maryland, and Martinsburg, West Virginia, on July 16 and 17, 1877, after the management of several railroads announced a wage cut. At Camden Junction, two miles from Baltimore, a fireman simply refused to keep the train moving. Soon others joined, and before long, all traffic on the Baltimore & Ohio Railroad had come to a halt. The management then fired the strikers. In response, others joined the strike, and by July 19, rail workers prevented all freight from leaving Pittsburgh. Now mostly forgotten, the strike inspired some Americans, frightened others, and for decades shaped people's responses to the country's rapid growth and industrialization.

The strike was marked by widespread violence. A large crowd of strikers and their supporters in Baltimore attacked state militia troops who then fired on the crowd, killing eleven people. In Pittsburgh, a huge crowd hurled insults and rocks at a militia unit who then started shooting, killing twenty. The crowd vented its fury on the Pennsylvania Railroad, burning everything in sight. By July 22, some 39 Pennsylvania Railroad buildings, 104 engines, and more than 1,200 freight cars had been destroyed. As news of the violence spread, strikes took place all along the major rail lines from New York and New Jersey to Indiana and Illinois. Black and white workers went out on strike together. In St. Louis, Missouri, a weeklong general strike led workers to take control of the city. Workers went on strike as far away as Kansas City and San Francisco.

Women played a crucial role, and the *Baltimore Sun* reported about the "very active part taken by the women, who are the wives and mothers of the firemen. They look famished and wild, and declare for starvation rather than have their people work for the reduced wages."

In response to a plea from the railroad management, President Hayes declared that a state of insurrection existed and called out federal troops who, armed with rapid-fire

Twisted track and the wheels of burned-out rail cars show some of the $10 million in damage caused by the 1877 railroad strike.

Gatling guns, put an end to the strike. Former president Grant criticized his successor, noting the irony that he himself had been criticized for sending the army to protect black voting rights but, "[n]ow, however, there is no hesitation about exhausting the whole power of the government to suppress a strike on the slightest intimation that danger threatens." But in the eyes of the new president, attacks on black voters and attacks on the property of the railroad companies were two different things.

Others drew their own lessons from the 1877 uprising. E. L. Godkin, editor of *The Nation*, called for doubling the size of the U.S. Army to guard against future violence, but instead, something new was created, the National Guard, made up of part-time soldiers who could be called out when needed. After 1877, states created National Guard units and built massive National Guard armories, stern stone buildings where arms might be stored in case of a new insurrection. These National Guard armories can still be seen in many cities—a monument to the 1877 rail strike. The strikes also inspired the rise of labor unions, which sought to help workers organize to demand new rights rather than just vent their fury. These unions sometimes led to additional uprisings, but in addition, they brought about changes in how corporations did business.

The Knights of Labor

Knights of Labor

Labor union that included skilled and unskilled workers irrespective of race or gender; founded in 1869.

Founded by tailors in Philadelphia in 1869, the **Knights of Labor** quickly emerged to become the country's largest and most powerful labor union after the 1877 strike. The Knights welcomed white and black workers, immigrants as well as the native-born, and skilled and unskilled workers. Terence V. Powderly was the head, or Grand Master Workman, of the Knights of Labor in the 1870s and 1880s. Powderly believed that isolated workers and small local unions were doomed to defeat when facing railroads and other large corporations, and he wanted his union to have the same organizational power as the largest corporations.

Under Powderly's leadership, the Knights tried to avoid violence. The Knights believed that workers and owners had more in common than their differences and hoped that eventually many workers could become independent owners rather than part of a permanent labor force. The union campaigned for government support of agricultural cooperatives, an eight-hour workday, equal pay for women, and government ownership of railroads and banks. Powderly took the commitment to racial integration seriously. At their October 1886 convention in Richmond, Virginia, Powderly caused quite a stir in the local community by inviting an African American delegate, Francis Ferrell, to introduce him to the meeting. In 1883, they organized a successful strike against the Western Union Telegraph Company and, in 1885, were strong enough to win a strike against several railroads that agreed to restore lost wages and hire back all striking workers. For Powderly, the success of the 1885 strike showed what a strong union could do. By 1886, the Knights had 700,000 members. In an even larger railroad strike that began in Marshall, Texas, in 1886, some 9,000 workers stopped freight on lines in Texas, Missouri, Arkansas, and Kansas. Strikes, it seemed, were becoming a national phenomenon, and the Knights were in the forefront. However, while national leaders of the Knights urged peaceful negotiations, in the 1886 strike, strikers pushed rail cars off tracks and set fires to railroad buildings. To avoid further violence, the Knights called off the strike while claiming a victory that was not really theirs.

The railroad strike of 1886 showed the power of a union to bring the trains, and thus the country, to a halt. It also demonstrated the split between many members of the Knights who harbored deep hatred for industrial owners and union leadership that still sought conciliation. While the Knights remained strong and were an essential element in the Populist political campaigns of the 1890s, the split between the rank and file and the leadership of the Knights was never fully healed. In time, other unions, some more moderate, some more radical, would replace the Knights.

The American Federation of Labor

While the Knights of Labor attempted to organize all workers, those in some of the more skilled trades created their own separate unions. In 1886, many of these small elite unions came together to create the **American Federation of Labor** (A.F. of L.) with fifty thousand members. Samuel Gompers of the Cigar Makers Union was elected as its president and, except for one year, served as president of the A. F. of L. until his death in 1924, by which time the union had grown to three million members, by far the strongest labor union in the United States.

American Federation of Labor
Labor organization formed in 1886 as a federation of smaller elite craft unions.

Under Gompers's leadership, the A.F. of L. continued to organize workers in separate craft unions with membership in each union restricted to workers in a specific trade such as cigar makers, plumbers, or iron molders. Gompers carefully avoided larger issues, preferring to negotiate specifically for immediate ends—increased wages, job security, an eight-hour day, benefits, and the right of the union to bargain collectively for workers. Early in its history, the A.F. of L passed a resolution calling on states to ban work by children under age fourteen, and under Gompers's leadership, they were successful in getting New York State to ban child labor, at least in cigar making. Union members wanted to protect their own children from harsh working conditions. They also wanted to avoid the competition of young workers who might be less likely to support a strike. Nevertheless, in spite of the A.F. of L. leadership, in 1900, there were more child laborers than ever before in the United States, especially working in mines, in agriculture, and as newsboys, messengers, and bootblacks where union organizing was most difficult. As a general rule, Gompers said, "We fight only for immediate objects ... that can be realized in a few years." He was happy to leave political ideology and more far-reaching social change to others. If the growth in the A. F. of L.'s membership is a measure, it was a successful strategy.

Haymarket, 1886

On May 4, 1886, many of the tensions in the United States exploded at Chicago's Haymarket Square. Between forty thousand and sixty thousand of Chicago's workers went on strike on Saturday, May 1, chanting their demands for an eight-hour workday, "eight hours for work, eight hours for rest, eight hours for what we will." The A. F. of L. supported the strike. So did socialists and anarchists in Chicago's diverse immigrant communities.

Socialism and anarchism, though quite different political philosophies, were both very strong in Chicago. Socialists believed that the workers should own the means of production and that private ownership of factories, businesses, and lands should be abolished in favor of ownership by all, which often meant government ownership. Anarchists deeply distrusted any government—including a Socialist government—and disdained elections as fraudulent exercises in futility. In place of government, anarchists wanted small, local, voluntary organizations. They believed that by abolishing higher authorities, a new era of peace and freedom would come. Nevertheless, for two anarchist leaders, Albert Parsons and

August Spies, the eight-hour movement was an opportunity to bring skilled and unskilled workers together as a step toward their larger goal.

As the strike continued on Monday, May 3, Spies issued a call for a mass meeting to be held the following night at Haymarket Square and asked Albert Parsons to join him. Perhaps three thousand people showed up at the Haymarket rally. But just as the rally was ending and Parsons himself was enjoying a beer at a nearby tavern, a police contingent marched into the rally to end it. Someone—no one ever found out who—threw a bomb into the middle of the police ranks, killing one police officer. Six more officers soon died of their wounds.

As news of the Haymarket bomb spread, newspapers blamed anarchists and Socialists for the violence. Eventually, Albert Parsons, August Spies, and six others were tried and convicted for being part of "a general conspiracy to annihilate the police force and destroy property," even though none of them could possibly have thrown the actual bomb. Appeals and a nationwide campaign for clemency ensued. Samuel Gompers, who certainly disagreed with anarchists, nevertheless said that Parsons, Spies, and the others had been "fighting for labor from different sides of the house." In spite of all the appeals, four, including Parsons and Spies, were hung on November 11, 1887.

Haymarket—as the strike, rally, bombing, and executions all came to be called—was a pivotal moment in American labor history. For some, the trial and executions were a validation of the rule of law. For others, the trial and execution of men who never threw the bomb and did not have any known links to whoever did provided proof that justice was not possible for those who protested in Gilded Age America. Lucy Parsons, Albert's widow, spent the rest of her long life speaking and writing about their cause. Emma Goldman, a young girl at the time, traced her own career as a lifelong radical organizer to the stories of the Haymarket martyrs, as the four executed leaders came to be called.

Haymarket

The name given to the strike, rally, and bombing that took place around Haymarket Square in Chicago in May 1886 as well as to the subsequent executions of four leaders of the incident.

Homestead Strike, 1892

While the 1886 strike for an eight-hour day was a national event, other strikes followed, none more important than the 1892 Homestead Strike at Andrew Carnegie's plant at Homestead, Pennsylvania. By the 1890s, Carnegie owned a dozen plants in western Pennsylvania and northern West Virginia. Workers at these huge mills turned out a quarter of the nation's steel supply and earned $40 million per year in profits for Carnegie. Carnegie wanted to be seen as a friend to working people, but profits still came first. In 1892, when workers at Carnegie's Homestead Steel Mill went on strike, Carnegie left his top lieutenant, Henry Clay Frick, in charge while he remained at his castle in Scotland. Frick decided that the time had come to break the twenty-four-thousand-member Amalgamated Association of Iron, Steel, and Tin Workers.

In June 1892, when it came time to negotiate a new contract, Frick offered only a cut in salary. When the union rejected the offer, Frick closed the plant, fired all of the workers, and built an eight-foot fence around it. He then hired new nonunion workers and three hundred Pinkerton agents to protect them. The Pinkerton agency had been created to support the North during the Civil War (Allan Pinkerton himself protected President Lincoln at difficult moments before the advent of the Secret Service), but in the 1880s and 1890s, the Pinkerton agency turned into a quasi-police force for industrial owners who were caught in conflict with unions. The Homestead workers fought back.

On July 6 when two barges of Pinkerton detectives came down the river to the plant, strikers who had been patrolling the area rushed the pier. No one knows who shot first, but both sides kept shooting. Eventually, between five and nine steelworkers and between three and ten Pinkerton agents were killed. Pennsylvania's governor sent eight thousand militia troops to Homestead to keep the peace, and Frick brought in new workers who began operating the mill. Union leaders were arrested but were acquitted (it was hard to find an antiunion jury in the region). Public opinion generally blamed Carnegie and Frick for the bloodshed. Nevertheless, Frick had won his battle. He had defeated the union and reopened the mills with nonunion workers. Unlike Andrew Carnegie, he did not care about public opinion. Carnegie also blamed Frick for the troubles, and the two never spoke again, but Carnegie also did not reinstate the union.

Coxey's Army, 1893–1894

In 1893, a grand world's fair, the Columbian Exposition, opened in Chicago. Like earlier fairs, this one displayed the nation's technological marvels and industrial success, including four hundred buildings lit with ten thousand electric lights. While the fair was a booming success, the nation's economy was collapsing in the Panic of 1893. J. P. Morgan rescued the country's gold reserves (see Chapter 17) but did not end the terrible unemployment. By the end of the year, one-fifth of those who had been working before the panic were out of a job. Many were desperate, and the contrast between the desperation and the fair's glitter was obvious.

An Ohio businessman, Jacob Coxey, was dazzled when he attended the Chicago fair, but deeply touched by the poverty and desperation he saw among unemployed in the city. Back in his hometown of Massillon, Ohio, near Akron, Coxey announced a plan to put the unemployed to work building roads. Coxey argued that America needed to improve its mostly dirt roads and also end unemployment. The solution was clear to him. Congress should appropriate $500 million in government bonds and offer every man who wanted to work $1.50 per day for an eight-hour day fixing the country's highways. (Coxey assumed that the key was putting men, not necessarily women, to work.) And, Coxey insisted, if Congress did not act, the unemployed should march to Washington and demand action.

Although only about one hundred marchers assembled at the beginning of the march, by the time the march got to Homestead, Pennsylvania, site of the Carnegie strike, it had grown to six hundred. All along the way, people gave them food and shelter. Coxey marched into Washington, D.C., on schedule on May 1, 1894. The *New York Times* called the march a "Battle between Law and Anarchy." Federal troops were put on alert. By mid-May, some eight hundred Coxeyites were in the District of Columbia, a number that grew to twelve hundred in August. But Congress, dominated as it was by the corporate interests, did not pass Coxey's legislation or do anything else to aid the unemployed. In August, police scattered **Coxey's Army**, as they were called by the press. Coxey returned to Ohio where he lived to the age of ninety-seven and died in 1951, still advocating federally financed highway improvement and pleased to see his goals partially fulfilled by the New Deal's employment programs in the 1930s.

Coxey's Army

A protest march of unemployed workers, led by businessman Jacob Coxey, demanding a public works highway program and guaranteed jobs during the depression of the 1890s.

Coxey's Army with their supporters marched through towns from Ohio to Washington, D.C., on their way to make their demands of Congress.

The American Railway Union, the Pullman Strike of 1894, and the Socialist Party

The American Railway Union was created in 1893 and led by Eugene V. Debs, who would go on to play an important role in American labor and political life for the next several decades. Debs was born in 1855 in Terre Haute, Indiana, and left school at age fifteen to take a job on the railroads. In 1875, he joined the Brotherhood of Locomotive Firemen but soon came to believe that having different unions for engineers, firemen, brakemen, and the workers who maintained the tracks was a recipe for defeat. His response was to help organize one union for everyone who worked on the railroads.

Almost immediately after its founding, the American Railway Union won a strike against the Great Northern Railroad in 1894. It looked like a new force was emerging. But then Debs found himself pulled into a strike he did not want, and the early successes of the American Railway Union turned to failure when the new union was involved in another strike at the Pullman Palace Car Company.

George Pullman did not operate a railway; he made railway cars—the very best railway cars anywhere in the United States. Pullman cars were elegant sleeping cars that cost four times as much as other railway cars and that allowed travelers who could afford the accommodations to cross the country in comfort. Having designed and manufactured the cars, Pullman leased the cars and their staff to various rail lines that attached them to regular trains. Both Pullman and the lines profited handsomely from the exchange.

To keep his employees out of industrial strife, Pullman built his own town, Pullman, Illinois, twelve miles outside of Chicago. In Pullman, 8,000 workers and their families lived in 1,400 houses that they rented from the company. They were provided with schools, an athletic club, free lectures, a local theater, and health care. The housing at Pullman was substantially better than housing available to most other industrial workers, but the rents were high and the rules strict. Pullman did not allow alcohol, and he had "spotters" who kept an eye on the behavior and home life of his employees.

Facing the Panic of 1893, Pullman laid off some workers and cut wages for the rest. He did not, however, reduce rents in Pullman since he also expected the town to pay its own way. The Pullman Company paid its standard dividends to its shareholders. In response, the workers went on strike. Ninety percent of the residents of Pullman did not show up for work. They called on Debs and the American Railway Union for support.

Federal troops, on orders from President Cleveland, escorted trains and destroyed the union in the aftermath of the Pullman Strike.

Debs told the Pullman workers that the midst of a depression was a terrible time to call a strike and urged them to postpone. They refused and Debs felt bound to support them. The American Railway Union refused to handle any train that had a Pullman car attached. By June, rail traffic through Chicago had stopped. The union took special care to keep the mail trains running so there would be no reason for federal intervention, but the federal government intervened anyway.

The Cleveland administration obtained an injunction ordering the strikers back to work, and when they refused, Cleveland ordered fourteen thousand federal troops to Chicago to end the strike. When the army arrived in Chicago, there was a riot and thirty-four people were killed. Federal authorities not only ended the strike but also arrested Debs and disbanded the union.

The strike and the jail term transformed Debs. He went to jail a charismatic labor leader. He came out convinced that the American economic system was permanently stacked against workers and their unions and that the only way to bring about change was political. He supported the Populist movement in the 1896 election but then founded the **Socialist Party** in the United States. The Socialists advocated government ownership of the nation's major industries and a mandate for higher salaries for workers. In the national elections of 1904 through 1920—except 1916—Debs ran for president as the party's candidate, winning hundreds of thousands of votes and giving himself a platform to advocate for a completely different economic system.

Miners and Their Unions

The steel that was transforming America required two key ingredients, iron ore and coal to fuel the smelting process that turned iron into steel. Coal also heated most of the nation's cities, and coal-fired generators produced much of the nation's electricity. Coal and iron ore had to be mined from deep in the earth, as did gold and silver, still the most valued forms of exchange. Lead pipes provided water to most houses. Bringing these resources to the industrial process required the backbreaking and dangerous work of miners. As the United States industrialized, the need for mines and miners grew exponentially. However, since every dollar paid to a miner increased the cost of finished products, or reduced the profits of those who owned the manufacturing process, mine owners were determined to keep the pay of miners as low as possible and recruited new immigrants who found themselves with few options.

Even before the Great Railway Strike of 1877, the country's coal miners had been an angry lot. Coal had been mined in Pennsylvania's Schuylkill Valley for generations, but in the 1860s and 1870s, miners had to dig deeper than ever, using pumps to lower the water table and machinery to ventilate the mines. Those deep mines were dangerous. The pumps could fail or a new stream could break through and drown miners. Tunnels could collapse. Methane or other dangerous gasses could collect and kill miners before they knew what was happening. And of course, the very properties that made coal valuable made fire an ever-present danger.

In the aftermath of the Panic of 1873, the mine owners cut pay, and in response, the miner's union called a strike. By January 1875, Pennsylvania coal production stopped. Since cities were heated with coal, midwinter seemed like a good time to win a strike, but the mine owners had stockpiled coal and the cities stayed warm while miners starved. By July 1875, the strike was defeated and the miners went back to work, at the reduced wages.

The failure of the 1875 strike produced a secret organization among the Irish immigrant coal miners in Pennsylvania, the Molly Maguires, who attacked and sometimes murdered foremen, superintendents, and even a mine owner. The mine owners hired the Pinkerton detective agency, which had played an important role in the Homestead Strike. A Pinkerton agent infiltrated the Mollys, and eventually ten men were convicted of murder based on their involvement in the Molly Maguires and were executed in June 1877.

In the 1880s and 1890s, new efforts were made to create a new and stronger union among the coal miners of Pennsylvania, Ohio, Virginia, and West Virginia that was focused not on violence against owners but on victories for the workers. The **United Mine Workers of America** was founded in Columbus, Ohio, in 1890. The new union's charter called for ensuring that the miners received a fair share of the wealth they created, "fully compatible with the dangers of

Socialist Party

A new political party that was organized after the defeat of the railroad strikes in the 1890s. It nominated candidates for president in 1904 and many following elections, and although they lost, it won some lesser offices.

United Mine Workers of America

A new union organized in 1890 to bring together mine workers in the eastern half of the United States in one organization that eventually became a national union.

our calling." The United Mine Workers of America was open to all races and religions to avoid the divisions that had undermined earlier unions. During an 1894 coal strike in Alabama, the *Chicago Tribune* reported, "For the first time in this district, no distinction as to color was made. Negroes marched in companies sandwiched between the white men. A negro and a white miner carried a banner." It was an all too rare moment in American labor history.

Under the leadership of a former Knights of Labor member, John Mitchell, who knew how to call a strike and when to call for arbitration, the United Mine Workers won a 10 percent raise in 1900 and then in 1903 won another raise along with recognition for the union and guarantees of fair weighing of the coal (since miners were paid by the weight of the coal they dug and often felt that they were cheated). By the early 1900s, the mine workers of the eastern part of the country were better paid and living in better conditions than had been thought possible even a few years earlier, although it had been a hard road for them to get there.

Mining developed later in the West than in the East (see Chapter 16) but expanded rapidly. In 1883, gold was discovered in the Coeur d'Alene region of Idaho, the narrow northern part of the state. Before long, the gold was played out but deposits of silver, lead, and coal were found. The lead and coal, however, were buried much deeper than silver and gold, and western miners found themselves working deep underground in dangerous conditions as employees of large corporations that were financed by eastern stockholders. Several unions merged in 1891 to create the Miners' Union of the Coeur d'Alenes. When the price for silver and lead fell on national markets in 1892, the Miners' Union went on strike to protest a cut in wages from $3.50 a week to $3.00 a week, for a seven-day week of ten-hour days.

As in Pennsylvania, the mine owners hired the Pinkerton agency to infiltrate the union and pitched battle broke out between unionized miners and nonunion workers. The governor of Idaho called for federal troops to end "a state of insurrection and rebellion." In April 1899, striking miners used dynamite to blow up the Bunker Hill Mine in the Coeur d'Alene region after the mine superintendent fired all union workers. The governor of Idaho, Frank Steunenberg, who had been elected with union support in 1896, called for federal troops to restore order. When Steunenberg was assassinated in 1905, the Western Federation of Miners was blamed, but none of its leaders were convicted. The struggles in the West continued, and some of the union leaders, especially the charismatic William D. (Big Bill) Haywood, became national labor leaders.

The Industrial Workers of the World

On June 27, 1905, over two hundred delegates gathered in Chicago to found a new union, the **Industrial Workers of the World** (IWW, or the **Wobblies**). The IWW's founders wanted to create "one big union" of all workers no matter what their trade or skill. Western Federation of Miners leader Big Bill Haywood opened the convention saying they were there to build "a working class movement that shall have for its purpose the emancipation of the working class." Eugene V. Debs expressed the hope that the time had come to "begin the work of forming a great economic or revolutionary organization of the working class." Mother Jones, Lucy Parsons, and other labor leaders joined in launching the IWW.

The convention adopted a constitution that began, "By organizing industrially we are forming the structure of the new society within the shell of the old." This mission was very different from the incremental goals of the American Federation of Labor. For the IWW, contract negotiations and strikes were only a step "within the shell of the old" to help launch the new world.

In the early 1900s, workers were not embarrassed to sing about their dreams, and the IWW *Song Book* described them in songs, including one that mocked the idea that the poor should hope that "[y]ou'll get pie in the sky when you die" instead of taking action now. Another IWW song promised that "[i]f the workers took a notion," they could bring the current economy to a halt.

The IWW was attacked by the press, the corporate world, and the government. It was also torn by ideological splits, personality tensions, and factional divisions. But for fifteen years, the IWW was a major force in labor organizing around the country and included some of the country's most charismatic labor leaders among its members.

Industrial Workers of the World (Wobblies)

Popularly known as Wobblies, organized in 1905 to bring together the nation's workers in "one big union" to fight for a radically different economic system that favored workers over owners.

American Voices

Mother Jones, "Victory at Arnot," 1897

Mother Jones became a union organizer and traveled the country supporting mine workers, other unions, and later the Socialist Party and the Industrial Workers of the World. Her approach was illustrated in an incident that most likely took place during the United Mine Workers strike of 1897.

In Arnot, Pennsylvania, a strike had been going on four or five months. The men were becoming discouraged. ... Sunday afternoon I held a meeting. ... "You've got to take the pledge," I said. "Rise and pledge to stick to your brothers and the union till the strike's won!"

The men shuffled their feet but the women rose, their babies in their arms, and pledged themselves to see that no one went to work in the morning. ...

Then the company tried to bring in scabs [nonunion workers]. I told the men to stay home with the children for a change and let the women attend to the scabs. I organized an army of women housekeepers. On a given day they were to bring their mops and brooms and "the army" would charge the scabs up at the mines. ... I selected as leader an Irish woman who had a most picturesque appearance. She had slept late and her husband had told her to hurry up and get into the army. She had grabbed a red petticoat and slipped it over a thick cotton night gown. She wore a black stocking and a white one. She had tied a little fringed shawl over her wild red hair. Her face was red and her eyes were mad. I looked at her and felt that she could raise a rumpus.

I said, "You lead the army up to the Drip Mouth. Take that tin dishpan you have with you and your hammer, and when the scabs and the mules come up, begin to hammer and howl. Then all of you hammer and howl and be ready to chase the scabs with your mops and brooms. Don't be afraid of anyone."

Up the mountain side, yelling and hollering, she led the women, and when the mules came up with the scabs and the coal, she began beating on the dishpan and hollering and all the army joined in with her. The sheriff tapped her on the shoulder.

"My dear lady," said he, "remember the mules. Don't frighten them."

She took the old tin pan, and she hit him with it and she hollered, "To hell with you and the mules!"

From that day on the women kept continual watch of the mines to see that the company did not bring in scabs. Every day women with brooms or mops in one hand and babies in the other arm wrapped in little blankets, went to the mines and watched that no one went in. And all night long they kept watch. They were heroic women. In the long years to come the nation will pay them high tribute for they were fighting for the advancement of a great country. ...

The last of February the company put up a notice that all demands were conceded ... before I left, the union held a victory meeting. ... The women came for miles in a raging snow storm for that meeting, little children trailing on their skirts, and babies under their shawls. Many of the miners had walked miles. It was one night of real joy and a great celebration.

Source: Mary Harris Jones, *The Autobiography of Mother Jones* (Chicago: Charles H. Kerr, 1990), pp. 30–39.

Thinking Critically

1. **Causation**

   If you were writing a history of the Arnot strike, what would you say might have led the women to be willing to follow Mother Jones?

2. **Comparison**

   Compare the strategy used by Mother Jones with that used by workers during the Homestead Strike. Do you think the different strategies help explain the differences in outcome?

The Garment Industry and the Triangle Shirtwaist Fire of 1911

The garment industry, one of the nation's largest, employed mostly women. Between 1900 and 1910, New York City became the nation's center in the manufacture of ready-to-wear clothing. Led by innovative owners, much of the work moved from the small sweatshops of the Lower East Side to larger factories in the new high-rise buildings of ten and twelve stories in southern Manhattan. Max Blanck and Isaac Harris operated their factory, the Triangle Shirtwaist Company, in Greenwich Village. There, over five hundred workers, most of them young Jewish and Italian women, assembled the popular shirtwaists (as women's blouses were called) that were sold in department stores across the country where more middle-class women bought them.

In New York City alone, over forty thousand people worked in the garment trades in the early 1900s. Although divided by language—Yiddish, Italian, English, and a host of other languages—the garment workers joined together to protest low salaries. The International Ladies' Garment Workers Union (ILGWU) had a tough organizer, Clara Lemlich, who had emigrated from Russia in 1903 and who led women in a number of strikes. During some of the strikes, factories hired replacement nonunion workers while police arrested strikers or thugs beat them up. Women from New York's social elite, including Anne Morgan, daughter of J. P. Morgan, sometimes joined the picket lines and they, too, were sometimes arrested or beaten.

In the late fall of 1909, as the ILGWU considered a general strike in the garment industry, many, including A. F. of L. president Samuel Gompers, urged caution. But Clara Lemlich said, "I have no further patience for talk. … I move that we go on a general strike." Workers cheered and the strike began. Factories all over Manhattan were picketed that fall. The garment industry owners organized their own association and refused to give in to the strikers' demands.

Striking garment workers got help from the national leadership of the A.F. of L. and from the Western Federation of Miners whose leader, Big Bill Haywood, sent word that "the Western miners are hearty admirers of your courage and fighting qualities." They also got support from society women like Morgan and from African American women who were being recruited as strikebreakers but who refused, though they asked the union to "exercise a proper consideration of the claims and demands of the men and women of color who desire to enter the various trades." The long strike ended in exhaustion for both sides in early 1911 when the union and the owners agreed to a compromise.

On Saturday March 25, 1911, only a month after the strike ended, a fire started under one of the cutting room tables at the Triangle Shirtwaist Factory. Perhaps a cigarette butt had been tossed in the bin of cotton scrap and dust, which exploded in a massive fire. Workers tried to put the fire out with buckets of water they kept on each floor, but it spread too rapidly. The fire started on the eighth floor and quickly filled the cutting room with smoke. Flames spread up airshafts to the ninth and tenth floors. Workers ran for exits, some of which had been blocked by the owners who, fearful of theft, insisted that all workers use only one exit. New York's firefighters arrived, but none had ladders that could reach to the eighth or higher floors. Some workers were quickly consumed by flames. More than 50 jumped from the windows, and 20 were killed when a flimsy fire escape on the outside of the building collapsed. In the end, 146 workers, most of them young women, were killed in the **Triangle Shirtwaist Factory Fire**, the deadliest industrial catastrophe in Manhattan for decades. Eventually, the Triangle Shirtwaist Fire led to new industrial regulations and important labor reforms. At the time, however, when devastated husbands, parents, friends, and relatives lined up at the makeshift morgue on Twenty-Sixth Street to try to identify the bodies, only the terrible loss seemed real.

Triangle Shirtwaist Factory Fire

A fire in the Triangle Shirtwaist Factory in New York City in 1911 that killed 146 workers and that later led to new factory inspection and safety laws.

Everett Collection Historical/Alamy Stock Photo

Victims of the Triangle Shirtwaist Fire fell from the eighth and ninth stories to their death on the sidewalk below.

Bread and Roses: The Lawrence Strike of 1912

A few months after the Triangle Fire, on New Year's Day 1912, a new Massachusetts law limited the workweek to fifty-four hours, a cut from the fifty-six-hour norm in the mills of Lawrence. The management of the mill companies complied with the law and cut wages accordingly. They saw little reason to worry about any protest. The workers of Lawrence spoke forty-five different languages and were divided into different crafts; fewer than one in ten were union members. Cutting their pay seemed both prudent and low risk. But when the pay cuts appeared in the pay envelopes, workers immediately started to walk off the job. An estimated fourteen thousand workers were on strike by the end of the first day. In response to the strikers' spontaneous action, the IWW, then at the height of its influence, sent some of its top organizers to Lawrence. They planned smaller meetings by language groups and coordinated large rallies on the Lawrence Common (as the town's central park was called). To get around a city ordinance that banned gatherings in front of any of the mills, the strikers devised a new tactic—a moving picket line in which strikers did not stop but kept walking in a continuous line around the mill.

When IWW leaders were accused of putting women in the front lines, the IWW's Elizabeth Gurley Flynn responded, "The IWW has been accused of putting the women in the front. The truth is, the IWW does not keep them in the back, and they go to the front." At some point in the strike, when women, with their babies in their arms, marched through the streets of Lawrence with signs reading, "We Want Bread and Roses, Too" the strike was given a new name. The public generally supported the strikers, and the mill owners eventually agreed to an increase in salary and no discrimination against strikers. The **Bread and Roses strike** was a success, probably the greatest success in the IWW's short history.

Library of Congress Prints and Photographs Division [LC-DIG-ggbain-04507]

The IWW supported strikes all over the country, like this one by women from the Ladies Tailors union on the picket line during the "Uprising of the 20,000" garment workers strike.

Ludlow, Colorado, 1914

In the mountains of southern Colorado, brutal working conditions persisted in the coal mines that were owned by John D. Rockefeller. On September 15, 1913, delegates from the mining camps gathered at Trinidad, Colorado, and voted for a strike demanding recognition for their union, a 10 percent increase in wages, an eight-hour day, the right to elect those who would weigh the coal, free choice of stores and doctors (rather than only company stores and doctors), and enforcement of Colorado mining laws. Mother Jones told the miners, "Don't be afraid, boys. … Fear is the greatest curse we have." Within a week, 80 to 90 percent of the miners were on strike.

The strike lasted fourteen months. It was long and bloody. The coal companies evicted the striking miners from their company-owned housing and the union arranged tent camps. Violence erupted between the coal company's guards and strikers, and by the end of the first month, more than twenty people had been killed. Worse violence followed.

On April 20, 1914, militia troops recruited by the coal company took up positions around the miners' camp at Ludlow, Colorado, and the nervous inhabitants then took up their own positions. No one knew who fired the first shot, but one shot quickly led to several hours of murderous fighting. Tents burst into flame, possibly from a bullet striking something explosive. Over thirty people were killed, including several women and eleven children found under one of the tents where they had huddled for safety. The **Ludlow Massacre** became a rallying cry for labor, and the loss of life, especially of children, permanently tarnished and troubled the Rockefeller family. President Woodrow Wilson sent U.S. Army troops to restore order and the United Mine Workers Union declared that ending the strike was "doing the best thing possible for the men on strike who have suffered so long in order that justice might be done." Further justice would take much longer.

Bread and Roses strike

A spontaneous strike of workers in the mills of Lawrence, Massachusetts, in 1912.

Ludlow Massacre

Violence during a coal strike in Ludlow, Colorado, in 1914 in which at least thirty people, including eleven children, were killed.

18.3 Quick Review

Why or why not was the violence that accompanied many strikes inevitable?

Conclusion

The rapid industrialization of the United States after the Civil War created new disparities and violent tensions in the United States.

Combined with the country's growing indifference to the original goals of Reconstruction, the New South movement successfully limited the advancement of African Americans through legal exclusions that denied civil rights and economic opportunities to African Americans for many decades to come. Even as the South was opening up to the world with the introduction of new railroad lines and the diversification of its economy, power and prosperity came only to some. Those who were excluded fought back, particularly African Americans, who challenged segregation, violence, and their economic exclusion.

Farmers, white and black, also challenged their economic exclusion from the prosperity of Gilded Age America. Through the Grange, the Farmers' Alliance, and later the Populist Party, farmers sought economic might equal to the giant corporations and political access at the highest levels. In 1896, the Populist Party supported the Democratic nominee, William Jennings Bryan, who campaigned on a platform of "free silver" as a way to increase inflation that would reduce the costs and debts felt by many farmers.

Industrial workers also organized to fight for their rights. New Unions—the Knights of Labor, the American Federation of Labor, the United Mine Workers of America, and the Industrial Workers of the World—sought to protect workers' rights. The nation was wracked by strikes, from the Railroad Strike of 1877 to the Miners' Strike in Pueblo, Colorado, in 1914 as well as tragedies including the Triangle Shirtwaist Fire of 1912. Basic union demands—for higher pay, safer conditions, and shorter workdays—were only partially met, and it would be another two decades, during the Great Depression and New Deal era, before industrial workers could get much of what they had been asking for from 1877 onward.

Chapter Review

How did some of the disenfranchised (workers, blacks, farmers, etc.) attempt to make their voices heard in the late 1800s and early 1900s? Why were their tactics different? How successful were various groups?

Conflict in the New South

18.1 **Analyze how the combined impact of industrialism and the end of Reconstruction created the unique character of the New South.**

Summary

The end of Reconstruction brought about a new era in the American South. While cotton remained the prime cash crop, new industries and an expanded railroad network heralded the arrival of a "New South." Southern religion and nostalgia for the "Lost Cause" and the pre–Civil War era contributed to the emergence of a distinctive Southern culture. Railroads became a focal point of racial tension as segregation grew more rigid in the 1890s. The persistence of black participation in politics in the decade following Reconstruction angered many Southern whites, and state and local governments took steps in the 1880s and 1890s to further disfranchise blacks. In the 1890s, the enforcement of white supremacy became an avowed goal of Southern state governments. Black resistance to the increased racial rigidity of the South took a number of forms.

Review Questions

1. Continuity and Change over Time
   What was new about the New South?

2. Argument Development
   Of Washington's or Du Bois's plans for African Americans at the turn of the century, which was better? Why?

The Politics of Conflict—From Populist Movement to Populist Party

18.2 **Analyze how agrarian unrest and protest came to have a significant impact on American politics.**

Summary

In the face of a difficult and rapidly changing economic landscape, farmers banded together to advance their common interests in the late 1800s. The earliest nationwide farmer organization was the Patrons of Husbandry, known as "the Grange." The Grange worked to create a sense of community in rural areas, and its members organized to deal with the financial problems that beset many farmers. Begun in Texas in the 1870s, the Farmers' Alliance was the most powerful farmers' organization in the late 1800s. It segregationist policies led to the formation of the Colored Farmers' National Alliance. While some participants in farmers' organizations wanted to stay out of electoral politics, others saw politics as the key to real change and developed a national political agenda centered on making changes to federal fiscal policy. Farmers' organizations, the Knights of Labor, and the Women's Christian Temperance Union joined forces in the populist People's Party. The People's Party (or Populist Party) had a strong showing in the election of 1892 and seemed to gather strength in the years leading up to the election of 1896. When William Jennings Bryan won the Democratic nomination after adopting Populist policies like "free silver," the People's Party officially made Bryan their nominee, too. The victory of Republican William McKinley in 1896 fatally wounded the Populists, leaving them a divided force with diminishing influence.

Review Questions

3. Causation
   What factors contributed to the rise of farmers' organizations in the late 1800s?

4. Argument Development
   What is the legacy of the People's Party?

Worker Protest and the Rise of Organized Labor

18.3 **Explain the tensions in industrial America that led to major labor strife between the 1870s and 1914.**

Summary

Some of the same forces that gave rise to farmers' organizations gave rise to new workers' organizations in the second half of the 1800s. The Great Railroad Strike of 1877 galvanized the labor movement and helped make the Knights of Labor the largest and most powerful labor union of the 1880s. The Knights welcomed white and black workers, immigrants as well as the native-born, and skilled and unskilled workers. In contrast, Samuel Gompers' American Federation of Labor concentrated on skilled workers, organizing them into separate craft unions. Unlike the Knights who dealt with general social and economic issues, the A.F. of L. focused on immediate workplace-related issues. The death of six policemen in Chicago's Haymarket Square in 1886 and the subsequent trial exposed public fault lines about the rapidly growing labor movement. For the next fifty years, battles between labor and management were contentious and sometimes violent.

Review Questions

5. Contextualization

What role did government play in the labor disputes of the late 1800s?

6. Argument Development

By 1915, to what extent were unions successful in bringing about improved wages and working conditions for America's laborers?

1. Preparing to Write: Plan Your Argument

Long Essay Question—Evaluate the extent to which there was continuity in African American political and economic power in the South from 1865 to 1900.

As you plan your argument, consider the gains for African Americans in the early years of Reconstruction—at least politically. Then look at the state of the South at the end of the century. You will remember that whatever gains had been made were mostly rolled back. Why? What happened in between? What was the role of the federal government and how did that change? Sharecropping and Booker T. Washington would be good content to include in your section on economics.

2. Preparing to Write: Organize Your Evidence

Long Essay Question—Evaluate the extent to which there was change in the labor movement from 1877 to 1914.

Draw a time line from 1877 to 1914. Above it, keep track of the important changes taking place, and below, record what remains constant. As you organize evidence, consider why these changes are happening. There are a number of strikes during the period. What role do they play in the changes? Based on the results of what you have mapped out, develop a thesis that answers all parts of this question.

Chapter 19
Progressive Movements, Progressive Politics 1879–1917

No one individual symbolized the Progressive movement as much as Theodore Roosevelt. As an advocate of the outdoor life, a "trustbuster," and a conservationist, he captured the hearts of many Americans in the early 1900s.

Chapter Objective

Demonstrate an understanding of the many ideas that were labeled progressive and the impact of those ideas on life in the United States.

 Learning Objectives

The Revolt of the Intellectuals

19.1   Explain the role of muckraking journalists and intellectuals in shaping a progressive agenda.

The Transformation of the Cities

19.2   Analyze the changes in urban life that inspired progressive reforms and the impact of those reforms on cities.

Religious Responses to the Gilded Age

19.3   Explain the main currents of religiously based reform movements during the Progressive Era.

Progressive Politics on the National Stage

19.4   Analyze the three "progressive presidents" and their administrations.

single tax movement

Proposed by Henry George in 1879, the single tax—a 100 percent tax on any increase in the value of real estate—was designed to keep property values low and therefore limit the accumulation of wealth while spreading opportunity more broadly in the society.

Theodore Roosevelt had been president for less than four months in December 1901 when he sent his first annual message to Congress. The new president said that, in light of the "tremendous and highly complex industrial development" in the country, the "old laws, and the old customs which … were once quite sufficient to regulate the accumulation and distribution of wealth … are no longer sufficient." He asked Congress for new laws and new presidential authority to meet the new situation. Roosevelt was ready to act.

Roosevelt rejected the radicalism of Democrats like William Jennings Bryan or Socialists like Eugene V. Debs. He insisted that "it cannot too often be pointed out that to strike with ignorant violence at the interest of one set of men almost inevitably endangers the interests of all." He was full of praise for the corporate leaders who had created great wealth. Nevertheless, he asserted, "There is a wide-spread conviction in the minds of the American people that the great corporations known as trusts are in certain of their features and tendencies hurtful to the general welfare." And since the "conditions are now wholly different," therefore "wholly different action is called for." As Roosevelt defined those "wholly different" actions in the weeks and months that followed, it became clear that he was charting a new course in American politics. He was no radical, but he was not a McKinley Republican either. He was determined to address the anger that fueled strikes—though certainly not to adopt the economic changes advocated by many strikers. In addition, he was committed to changing urban and industrial conditions and conserving the country's natural resources.

As a result of his efforts, Roosevelt and the two presidents who followed him, William Howard Taft and Woodrow Wilson, came to be known as the progressive presidents. Presidential politics, however, were far from the only aspect of the larger Progressive movement that dominated American life between 1890 and 1917 and, indeed, led to the electoral success of Roosevelt and his successors. This chapter seeks to understand the many ideas that were labeled progressive and the impact of those ideas on life in the United States.

The Revolt of the Intellectuals

19.1 Explain the role of muckraking journalists and intellectuals in shaping a progressive agenda.

Long before Theodore Roosevelt became president, numerous people in the United States were thinking about how best to respond to the extraordinary changes brought about by immigration, urbanization, and the rapid industrialization of the country. Upper-class reformers, newspaper reporters, ministers, writers, and college professors proposed new ways of ordering economic and political life. New ideas, and those who envisioned them, began to shape the future of the country.

Utopian Idealists

Henry George, a young journalist in California, was deeply troubled by the railway strike of 1877. Two years later, he published *Progress and Poverty*, which quickly became a bestseller. George understood that there were benefits from industrialization, but the result, he said, was that "[f]rom all parts of the civilized world come complaints … of want and suffering and anxiety among the working classes."

As a solution, George proposed a 100 percent tax on any increase in the value of land or any rents on land. He argued, "We already take some rent in taxation. We have only to make some change in our modes of taxation to take it all." George said that his proposal would reduce the value and cost of land, thus allowing workers to turn to farming if they wished, which would create a labor shortage that would inevitably raise wages and improve conditions in factories. While many economists argued with George's logic, the **single tax movement** became a political force, and single tax clubs sprang up everywhere. In 1886, New York's Central Labor Union persuaded George to run for mayor of the city. Although George lost, his campaign led to a permanent reform coalition in New York.

In 1888, ten years after George's book, Edward Bellamy, a journalist from Massachusetts, published *Looking Backward*. The book described a new perfect society in which class and class warfare had disappeared in a country of prosperous citizens who enjoyed their lives free of poverty or wealth and also free of lawyers and politics.

In contrast to Bellamy's hopeful work, Ignatius Donnelly wrote *Caesar's Column* in 1891, a book that described a country rigidly divided between a large working class living brutal lives and a small, comfortable elite. In Donnelly's fictional story, a few Americans were able to escape from their world and start a happy new community organized around the platforms of the Greenback Party, the Knights of Labor, and the Farmers' Alliance.

George, Bellamy, and Donnelly and other authors like them were often unrealistic. Their images of a new perfect society seemed romantic and their economic proposals unworkable even in their own day. Nevertheless, in a country groping its way to a different economic order, all of them gave ideas, energy, and optimism to other reformers.

Library of Congress Prints and Photographs Division, George Grantham Bain Collection [LC-B2-6197-13]

Henry George's proposal for a 100 percent tax on any increase in the value of land made him a very popular reform leader in the 1870s and 1880s and a serious candidate for mayor of New York City in 1886. Although many saw the plan as impractical, George's plan was a forerunner of other progressive reforms that were implemented a few years later.

The Professors

John Dewey is best remembered for his educational ideas, but his goal was a wider philosophical response to industrialism. Dewey was born in 1859 in a small town in Vermont, studied philosophy at Johns Hopkins University, and taught at the University of Michigan. In 1894, Dewey was invited to the new University of Chicago. Dewey accepted the offer with enthusiasm. Chicago in the 1890s was the center of social reform in which Dewey and his wife, Alice Chapman Dewey, were deeply interested. When it came time to make the move, however, Dewey had a hard time getting to Chicago.

When Dewey set out for Chicago in July 1894, most of the nation's rail lines were shut down because of the Pullman strike. He found transit on a Michigan Central train that did not use Pullman cars. Traveling in the midst of a nationwide strike was informative to the young philosophy professor. He spoke with one of the American Railway Union organizers and wrote to his wife that "my nerves were more thrilled than they had been for years." He wondered "if I had better resign my job teaching & follow him round till I got into life." Dewey was considerably less impressed by another passenger who was "voluble on the outrage" of the strike because it was preventing him from getting home for dinner. For Dewey, the focus was on higher considerations.

Young intellectuals like Dewey were then challenging the dominant economic theory of the time, **Social Darwinism**. The foremost American exponent of Social Darwinism, the economist William Graham Sumner, opposed what he called "the absurd effort to make the world over." For Sumner, Charles Darwin's description of biological evolution showed that the fittest of each species survive and thus shape the future. So, Sumner argued, in the social order, the fittest were rightfully the owners and the dominant class of society. Those less fit are condemned by their natural "un-fitness" to be laborers and employees. Any interference with the system, Sumner argued, would destabilize the economy and weaken the nation. Herbert Spencer, a British writer who proposed similar ideas, also had a large following in the United States, especially among the wealthy.

Dewey saw the ideas of Spencer and Sumner as easy but unethical justifications for privilege. Instead, Dewey believed that wise people could and should intervene in the economy to make it more just. His thinking was shared by a generation of philosophers, including William James, Charles S. Peirce, and future Supreme Court justice Oliver Wendell Holmes, who in the 1880s and 1890s doubted all ideological certainties and did not want to see Social Darwinism become the dominant mind-set in society.

Another young scholar, Richard Ely at Johns Hopkins University, also attacked the Social Darwinists. Ely had visited the town of Pullman before the strike, but workers would not talk to him, fearing that he was a spy. He called the town's culture "benevolent, well-wishing feudalism." As a counter to Social Darwinism, Ely was developing an economic theory that allowed for—indeed, called for—government to intervene directly in the economic affairs of the country.

Social Darwinism

The application of Charles Darwin's theory of biological evolution to society, holding that the fittest and the wealthiest should thrive and lead, the weak and the poor "deserve" their fate, and government action is unable to alter this "natural" process.

While Dewey focused on philosophy and Ely on economics, Albion Small was helping to build the new academic discipline of sociology. For Small, sociologists did not simply study society; they meant to reform it. In 1896, Small sought to help define his field when he wrote in the new *American Journal of Sociology* that "action, not speculation, is the supreme teacher." Dewey, Ely, and Small were all part of a generation of academics who shared the goal of changing society.

The Muckraking Journalists

Although newspapers had been important in the United States since well before the American Revolution, newspapers changed significantly in the late 1800s. When Joseph Pulitzer bought the *New York Evening World* in 1887, he made it the largest circulation paper in the country with several innovations—banner headlines, comic strips, and investigative journalism. The *World* did an exposé of the speculative adventures of the managers of the Equitable Life Assurance Society, which the paper said were "gambling with the people's money." Public anger over this news of the insurance industry's excesses led to the election of a reforming Republican, Charles Evans Hughes, as governor of New York in 1906 and to new regulations on the insurance industry. The huge response to the exposé also made the *World* a very successful paper.

Almost a decade later, William Randolph Hearst, who had used the Pulitzer formula for his *San Francisco Examiner*'s exposés of the Southern Pacific Railroad, purchased the *New York Morning Journal* to compete directly with Pulitzer. Hearst hired some of the country's best reporters, Edward Markham, Ambrose Bierce, and Winifred Black, and published his own exposés of New York City corruption. Many other newspapers began to imitate Pulitzer and Hearst.

The trend toward investigative journalism that exposed misconduct of important people or organizations was emerging even before Pulitzer and Hearst took advantage of it. Henry Demarest Lloyd, who wrote for Chicago newspapers, became one of the first of the so-called **muckraking journalists**. The term *muckraking* referred to the job of raking through filth. Muckraking journalists saw it as their duty to expose the filth of corruption. Not everyone liked the new investigative journalism, and those who objected included more than just those being investigated. President Theodore Roosevelt thought the journalists described problems but failed to offer solutions. It was Roosevelt who coined the term *muckrakers*. He said the journalists were simply raking up the muck from the bottom of society's pond, and the name muckraker stuck. For many, however, it became a term of respect.

muckraking journalists

Journalism exposing economic, social, and political evils, so named by Theodore Roosevelt for its "raking the muck" from the bottom of American society.

Early in his career, Lloyd covered the 1877 railroad strike. He wrote that if something did not happen to improve the lot of the country's workers, "the country will drift into a convulsion as much greater than the convulsion that wrecked the Roman Empire." Lloyd's 1881 exposé of Standard Oil Company and his 1894 book, *Wealth against Commonwealth*, denounced the monopolies as a threat to the welfare of everyday people.

Hearst also launched *Cosmopolitan* magazine as a vehicle for investigative journalism. In 1893, S. S. McClure launched *McClure's Magazine*, which until 1926 was the leader in the investigative field. Investigative journalists—writing with the conviction that if people knew more of what was wrong in society, they would act to change it—played a key role in the Progressive movement.

The January 1903 issue of *McClure's* included articles by Ida M. Tarbell as part of her continuing analysis of John D. Rockefeller and the Standard Oil Company, later published as *The History of the Standard Oil Company* in 1904; Ray Stannard Baker's report of visiting striking coal miners and their families; and the report by Lincoln Steffens on "The Shame of Minneapolis" about the trial of the infamous four-term mayor of Minneapolis who got rich from payments from opium joints, unlicensed saloons known as "blind pigs," and "disorderly houses" of prostitution. Issue after issue of *McClure's*, *Cosmopolitan*, and daily newspapers were creating a new public consciousness that was forcing cities to clean up corruption, compelling sometimes reluctant legislators to enact new restrictions on monopolies, and helping political reformers gain office.

19.1

19.2

19.3

19.4

Lebracht Music and Arts Photo Library/Alamy Stock Photo

The Jungle, by muckraking journalist Upton Sinclair, exposed the inhumane and unhealthy conditions of meat processing in Chicago. One result was typical of progressive legislation designed to improve people's lives, the Pure Food and Drug Act, which regulated the meatpacking industry.

In 1906, a young reporter named Upton Sinclair took a job in Chicago's slaughterhouses to report, from the inside, on the meatpacking industry. He found a world where workers suffered terrible injury, animals suffered inhumane treatment, and unsanitary conditions poisoned the meat consumed by Americans. When Sinclair's exposé, *The Jungle*, was published in 1906, the public response was immediate. Consumption of meat fell precipitously, and within months, Congress passed the Federal Meat Inspection Act and the Pure Food and Drug Act, regulating the meat industry as well as the food and drug industries. While Sinclair's main goal had been to draw attention to inhumane working conditions, the primary result of his efforts was sanitary regulation of meatpacking plants. As Sinclair reflected years later, "I aimed at the public's heart and by accident I hit it in the stomach." Nevertheless, the passage of reform legislation within months of Sinclair's book showed the power of such reporting and raised journalism to new heights as a respectable profession.

19.1   Quick Review

How did ideas and different authors help launch the Progressive movement? Which ideas seemed to make the greatest difference?

The Transformation of the Cities

19.2 **Analyze the changes in urban life that inspired progressive reforms and the impact of those reforms on cities.**

The United States grew from a little under 40 million people in 1870 to just over 75 million people in 1900 (for comparison, the 2010 census showed the United States at over 300 million people). Perhaps one-third of the growth between 1870 and 1910 was due to immigration and two-thirds to a high birthrate. While the population almost doubled, it also became concentrated in cities, which became much larger and more densely populated in 1900 than they had been in 1870. In 1870, the United States had only seven cities with over 250,000 people and none yet held a million people. Thirty years later, three cities had passed the 1 million mark—New York with 3.4 million, Chicago with 1.7 million, and Philadelphia with 1.3 million. There were also dozens of large cities scattered among most of the states and territories of the union. Americans were adjusting to urban life, and the adjustment was not always easy.

The Rise of Machine Politics and the Progressive Response

As cities grew, a new kind of urban politics took root in the United States, shaped by the fact that cities were the major points of entry for new immigrants to the nation. Many immigrants desperately needed services, especially help with a job. Some took quickly to city political life, finding in politics a way to gain social respectability and financial security.

Nowhere was the mix of urban growth, immigration, and the need for new services greater than in New York City. In New York, a new kind of political organization, the political machine, was created. In political machines, constituents supported a candidate in return for anticipated favors, which would be repaid when that candidate was elected. New York's Democratic political machine was known as **Tammany Hall**, named for the building where it first met. Tammany effectively ruled New York for most of the years from the 1850s to the 1930s. Many other urban political machines were often associated with Irish political leaders, but Tammany predated the Irish influence. In fact, gaining access to Tammany was part of the Irish rise to power in New York City.

The most famous, or infamous, of early Tammany bosses was William M. (Boss) Tweed, who led Tammany in the 1860s and 1870s. Tweed was a Protestant of English background. After holding the office of alderman (city council member) and then being elected to Congress, Tweed turned to where he saw the real power—in Tammany.

Tammany Hall

Dating from well before the Civil War, New York City's Democratic Party organization, which evolved into a powerful political machine after 1860, using patronage and bribes to maintain control of the city administration.

Political cartoons like this one showing a corrupt political boss handing out special privileges and demanding votes in return did much to turn public opinion against machine rule in politics.

19.1

19.2

19.3

19.4

In 1863 at the age of forty, Tweed became the chief of Tammany. He made sure one of his close allies, Abraham Oakley, was elected mayor while he stayed in the background and kept control of the political process. Tweed became immensely wealthy as he and his Tammany associates benefited from—some said stole from—development projects like the Tweed Courthouse in lower Manhattan (now the home of the city's school department) and Riverside Park, built over the New York Central Railroad tracks—beautiful municipal improvements that provided jobs but cost many times what they should have, with large kickbacks going to the chosen developers and to Tweed himself.

Tweed and the New York political bosses who came after him robbed the city shamelessly, by one estimate taking $45 million (one billion in current dollars). At the same time, the political machine made sure that the city's poor—or more specifically, those among the city's poor who supported them on election day—got jobs when they needed them. When necessary, Tammany created more jobs than the city needed to be sure that every loyal voter got one, even if that meant that the city had twenty inspectors for its four water pumps and Central and Riverside parks were kept immaculate by an impressively large number of park workers. Tammany and other political machines could also be counted on for more direct aid when it was needed—a handout to tide a family over a rough spot, a basket of food for the holidays, or someone to show up at court and indicate to the judge or district attorney when charges should be dropped.

Tweed's corruption was attacked by the cartoonist Thomas Nast and eventually provoked a public backlash. Tweed was arrested, convicted of theft, and died in jail in 1878. Some of his collaborators fled the country. But Tammany survived, and the new leader, John (Honest John) Kelly was the first of a long line of Irish politicians to direct Tammany. Kelly avoided the kind of theft that led to Tweed's downfall. But he did ensure that a tightly organized political machine maintained close links to immigrant communities and Catholic parishes, as well as local and district bosses. Kelly controlled the city's forty thousand jobs and made sure that loyal Tammany supporters—those who remembered to vote the Tammany ticket on election day—got those jobs.

One of Tammany's district leaders, George Washington Plunkitt, was also a state senator. In 1905, Plunkitt described how New York politics worked. He said that reformers failed to draw "the distinction between honest graft and dishonest graft. There's all the difference in the world between the two." Plunkitt would have nothing to do with "dishonest graft—blackmailin' gamblers, saloon-keepers, disorderly people, etc." But there was another way, he said; "There's honest graft, and I'm an example of how it works. I might sum up the whole thing by sayin': 'I seen my opportunities and I took 'em.'" He explained, "Well, I'm tipped off, say, that they're going to lay out a new park at a certain place. … I go to that place, and I buy up all the land I can in the neighborhood … ain't it perfectly honest to charge a good price and make a profit on my investment and foresight?" It was an arrangement that Plunkitt saw no reason to hide. Reformers might not have liked it, but that was how cities worked in Plunkitt's day.

New York was far from alone in the rise of machine politics that was often Irish dominated. Most large cities had something similar. Politics in Boston was played at the neighborhood level, where a number of legendary figures—Patrick J. Kennedy in East Boston, John F. (Honey Fitz) Fitzgerald in the North End, P. J. Maguire and later James Michael Curley in Roxbury, and most powerful of all Martin Lomasney in the West End—each ruled their neighborhood. In 1905, Fitzgerald won election as mayor. He served two terms and was succeeded by his arch-rival, James M. Curley, who dominated Boston politics for the next half century. Fitzgerald's favorite daughter, Rose, married Patrick Kennedy's son Joseph, and their son, John Fitzgerald Kennedy, became the first Irish Catholic elected president.

While the political machines met real needs for their poor and working-class constituents (and along the way made a few of their leaders wealthy), the closed-door deals, the graft—"honest" or "dishonest"—and the political favoritism dismayed many. The political machines greatly increased the cost of municipal government. They also shut many out of office, especially the children and grandchildren of the native-born elite who thought it was their duty and destiny to rule. A new generation of political reformers began challenging the political machines, making municipal reform an important element in the progressive agenda and, for some, a means to return to political power that had been in their families for generations.

19.1

19.2

19.3

19.4

The Progressive Challenge to City and State Government

Progressive reformers believed that the country's political and economic systems could be fixed if honest people of good will put their minds to it. They had little interest in radical reforms like socialism and little sympathy for the old-line politicians like Boston's Martin Lomasney. They were what they said they were, reformers, trying to reform current structures of government.

In their campaigns for efficient urban management, progressive reformers sometimes came across as cold and heartless to residents who preferred the face-to-face dealings of old-style political bosses. Moreover, in their desire to cut costs, some reformers attacked services that others thought essential. Progressive reform was also seen—sometimes accurately—as an effort by an older Protestant and native-born elite to reclaim power from more recent immigrant groups, especially the Irish, who had built up their own political organizations.

Nevertheless, candidates committed to cleaning up urban corruption and providing more efficient urban services came to power in a number of cities. Progressive reform cut across the political parties. Republicans and Democrats alike included both reformers and those who resisted reform.

Grover Cleveland was elected mayor of Buffalo, New York, as a Democrat in 1881 with a promise to clean up the municipal corruption. Cleveland established a reputation

American Voices

Lincoln Steffens, "Boston—1915," 1908

Lincoln Steffens, one of the leading "muckraking" journalists, was invited to support a reform effort that was launched in Boston in 1908 and called "Boston 1915" by local businessmen. Boston taught Steffens some important lessons about not only the role of political machines but also the place of reformers like himself in the life of the urban poor.

My sponsor, E. A. Filene, called together a group of earnest, representative men, some of them reformers, not all ... I [asked them], Who was the worst, the most impossible, man in Boston?

"Martin Lomasney," they said, all in quick agreement. A politician he was ... and the next morning early I took my little dog, Mickey Sweeney, and went over in the bad wards where Martin Lomasney was the boss. ...

"Who do you want?" he demanded.

"Martin Lomasney."

"That's me," he said. "Who are you?"

I told him. "Sure," he said. "I've read your stuff. What do you want?" ...

"The reformers sent me to you," ... "I asked them who was the worst man in town, and they named you. So I've come to get the low-down on things, and—will you give it to me?" ...

"You must want something," Martin grumbled at me. ...

"Yes," I said. "Police graft. What do you do about the petty crooks?"

He was cross, or he pretended to be. "What do you mean by petty crooks?"

"Oh, you know, the dips, the burglars and thieves, the regular professional crooks that we honest grafters call criminals."

"And what do you mean by what I do about them?"

"Well, you go to the front for them, don't you? See the district attorney or a judge or the cops—you get them off, don't you?"

"Yes, I do," he said, dropping his feet and facing me with three fingers thrust under my nose. "Three times."

I laughed. "Ah, now, don't you sometimes do it four times?"

He was defying me. "Seven times? Martin, don't you even get 'em off seventy times seven times?"

"Yes, I do," he burst. "I never quit some of 'em, not the way you do."

"Of course," I said. "You stick, but tell me, how do you justify it to yourself, saving these hopeless crooks over and over and over again when you know they'll come back and do it over and over and over again!"

I did not expect him to answer this question. It was more of an exclamation on my part, but he did answer it; inarticulate people can sometimes express themselves.

"I think," said Martin Lomasney, "there's got to be in every ward somebody that any bloke can come to—no matter what he's done—and get help. Help, you understand; none of your law and your justice, but help."

That hit me hard, and we got no further that day. ... They provided help and counsel and a hiding-place in emergencies for friendless men, women, and children who were in dire need, who were in guilty need, with the mob of justice after them. And, as I sat there and thought I saw that if we were to build up in Boston an organization to replace the political machine and so win the town the loyalty that now went to the boss and his party, we must provide for that service.

Source: Lincoln Steffens, *The Autobiography of Lincoln Steffens* (New York: Literary Guild, 1931), pp. 612–618.

Thinking Critically

1. **Causation**

   What issues in urban life led to the rise of men like Martin Lomasney? How might Steffens or his sponsors have answered Lomasney's question about providing for those in need?

2. **Analyzing Primary Sources**

   How did Lomasney justify his politics? What does his point of view suggest about the challenges faced by the reformers who hoped to supplant him?

for honesty, especially after he rejected a street-cleaning contract approved by the city council as a "bare-faced, impudent, and shameless scheme." Cleveland's honesty led to his election as a reform governor of New York and, only two years later, to the White House.

Hazen S. Pingree was elected mayor of Detroit, Michigan, as a Republican reformer. Born in Maine in 1840, Pingree served in the Union army and then moved to Detroit where he went to work in a shoe factory. By the 1880s, he owned one of the largest shoe manufacturers in the Midwest. In 1889, Republican business leaders, determined to oust Detroit's Democratic machine, sought out Pingree, who quickly took to politics, was a tough campaigner, and became a popular mayor. Pingree challenged the awarding of city contracts for the schools, ferries, toll roads, and street and sewer services. When the private City Railway Company wanted a long-term contract, Pingree forced them to cut fares from five cents to three cents, a significant benefit to Detroit's citizens.

When the depression of 1893 put 25,000 of Detroit's 250,000 people out of work, Pingree, who did not want to increase municipal spending, convinced owners of vacant lots to allow the city to use them, provided seeds and farm implements to the unemployed, and urged people all over the city to start their own potato patches and vegetable plots. In time, he became known as "Potato Patch Pingree" for his efforts.

Samuel M. Jones, known as "Golden Rule Jones," served as mayor of Toledo, Ohio, from 1897 until 1904. Jones started work as a day laborer, but eventually started his own oil company. When Jones sold the company to Standard Oil, he emerged a rich man. Reform-minded business leaders nominated Jones for mayor in Toledo in an effort to dislodge a corrupt machine. Jones spent municipal funds freely, opening kindergartens, building parks, and instituting an eight-hour day for city workers. He also called on voters to renounce political parties, believing that a nonpartisan approach to politics would work best. The Republican Party, unhappy with Jones's free-spending ways, refused to renominate him, but he was elected as an independent and continued to serve as a popular mayor until his death. His successor in office, Brand Whitlock, continued his policies through four terms until President Woodrow Wilson appointed Whitlock as U.S. ambassador to Belgium on the eve of World War I. Between them, Jones and Whitlock gave Toledo a national reputation for good government and effective public services when many cities were still mired in corruption and inefficiency. Other cities were also known for their progressive mayors, including San Francisco's James D. Phelan, 1897–1902, and Cleveland's Tom Lofton Johnson, 1899–1909.

Grover Cleveland and Hazen S. Pingree both moved from the mayor's office to become governor of their states. The move was not merely upward political mobility. Many progressive reformers became convinced that legislation at the state level was essential to limit the power of corporations or corrupt urban machines. Other state reforms became core progressive issues, especially proposals for **initiative**, **referendum**, and **recall**, measures aimed at limiting the power of political elites by giving voters the chance to change government policy. South Dakota in the 1890s, Oregon in 1902, and then other states, especially in the West, began adopting these measures. Initiative laws allowed voters to put new laws on the ballot through a petition process while a referendum allowed a similar process to review legislation already in force in a state. Finally, recall petitions and votes allowed voters to remove public officials—legislators, mayors, and governors—from office before their terms ended. Never as popular east of the Mississippi as in the West, initiative, referendum, and recall were typical progressive measures, based on the same assumption that drove muckraking journalists: the belief that an educated and informed public would do the right thing once the right information was in hand.

Governors and legislatures also adopted other reforms in the Progressive Era. Workers who were injured on the job had been left on their own or blamed for accidents, but progressives passed workers' compensation laws. Some passed limits on the length of the workday, especially for women and children, or banned child labor altogether, and tried to regulate the safety of working conditions for everyone.

Reform came to New York City by a different route. Seth Low, the president of Columbia University, was elected mayor of New York as an anti-Tammany candidate in 1901. He fought graft and instituted civil service reform, but Low was not popular, especially in

initiative

Procedure by which citizens can introduce a subject for legislation, usually through a petition signed by a specific number of voters.

referendum

Submission of a law, proposed or already in effect, to a direct popular vote for approval or rejection.

recall

The process of removing an official from office by popular vote, usually after using petitions to call for such a vote.

19.1

19.2

19.3

19.4

This young Pittsburgh miner lost his leg in a mine accident. Referring to people like this worker helped progressives pass workers' compensation laws.

communities that depended on Tammany, and he was defeated for reelection two years later. At that point, New York was back in Tammany hands, and Tammany's boss, Charles Murphy, was the most powerful politician in the state although he held no office. After state elections in 1910, however, Murphy launched his own reform efforts. He selected two Tammany loyalists who were among the youngest and newest in the legislature, thirty-three-year-old Robert F. Wagner in the Senate and thirty-eight-year-old Alfred E. Smith in the House, to be the party leaders. Wagner and Smith were known as the "Tammany Twins." In their long political careers, they were also among the most important reformers in American history.

After the Triangle Factory Fire in 1911 (see Chapter 18), Murphy knew they had to do something or lose the support of families who had lost daughters and sons in the fire. Murphy directed Wagner and Smith to sponsor the creation of the New York Factory Investigating Commission, which the legislature approved within three months. Where Tammany-controlled police officers had harassed striking garment workers only months before, the Tammany-created Factory Investigating Commission hired some of the same strikers to investigate conditions in the city's garment industries, where they found unsafe and unworkable fire escapes and locked exits. A social worker, Frances Perkins, who had witnessed the Triangle Fire, was one of many to volunteer her services to the Factory Investigating Commission. Perkins also wrote much of the legislation that came from the commission's work. In the next two years, Wagner and Smith, working closely with Perkins, pushed thirty-six measures through the New York legislature, including those requiring sprinklers in high-rise buildings, fire drills in large shops, unlocked exits, and a reorganization of the state Department of Labor to enforce the new regulations.

Later, these New Yorkers would bring progressive legislation to a national stage. Frances Perkins served as the head of the state's Department of Labor and then from 1933 to 1945 as the U.S. Secretary of Labor, the first woman to serve in a presidential cabinet. Robert Wagner went to Washington as a U.S. senator; there, he sponsored legislation creating the Social Security system and legislation guaranteeing unemployment insurance and workers' compensation. In addition, he sponsored the Wagner Act, which gave labor unions the right to bargain effectively—the most important piece of labor legislation enacted in the United States in the

1900s. Al Smith served as a progressive governor of New York in the 1920s and as the Democratic nominee for U.S. president in 1928, the first Catholic nominated by a major party. Progressive reform had influenced one of the most powerful political machines, Tammany, and in turn, Tammany had cultivated powerfully effective legislators who generated historic reforms.

Progressive Education

In 1899, John Dewey wrote *The School and Society*, describing what he thought a progressive approach to education should be, one that he had tried to create with his wife, Alice Chapman Dewey, and Ella Flagg Young, a Chicago teacher leader (who would later be superintendent of schools in Chicago, the first woman to lead a big-city system). Together, they opened the Laboratory School at the University of Chicago in 1896, a child-centered approach. For Dewey and others, the focus was not on structure at all but on the child. These child-centered progressives wanted to shift the emphasis in schools from the curriculum to the needs of the child. Progressive education meant many different things to different people, and Dewey represented only one aspect of it. Other educators who also called themselves progressives argued bitterly with him. For some, progressive education meant reorganizing schools to be more businesslike, with centralized administrations and bureaucratic top-down modes of decision making. Progressive teachers wanted to restructure schools to give themselves more voice and more influence while also earning better pay and teaching smaller classes. For yet others, the goal was to make education scientific, including the use of standardized testing to improve schools. Certainly, in the field of education, there were many movements that called themselves progressive, and no one definition fit all of them.

Jane Addams and the Settlement House Movement

In 1913, when Jane Addams had been living at Hull House on Halsted Street in Chicago for more than twenty years, she summed up her belief about the role of the settlement house and all efforts to improve society. "We have learned to say," she wrote, "that the good must

Jane Addams (1860–1935) spent all of her adult life at Hull House in Chicago, living among the city's poor. She not only provided social services but also learned much from her neighbors.

19.1

19.2

19.3

19.4

be extended to all of society before it can be held secure by any one person or any one class; but we have not yet learned to add to that statement, that unless all men and all classes contribute to a good, we cannot even be sure it is worth having." While many progressives might have agreed that society must find a way to extend the good things of life to all citizens, far fewer would have agreed with Addams that all citizens needed to play a role in defining what "good" looked like. Nevertheless, at Hull House, social reformers met those they were trying to help in face-to-face encounters, and all involved learned from one another.

Addams was born to a comfortable life in 1860 (her father was a friend of Abraham Lincoln's) and moved to Chicago in 1889 when she and her friend Ellen Starr opened Hull House. Chicago's Hull House, though not the first American settlement house, became the model for most others. Addams said she was at Hull House to be a part of the community, not to offer help from above. She knew that she was living there as much to learn as to help her economically poorer neighbors.

Hull House and similar settlement houses in other cities organized badly needed social services in poor urban neighborhoods. Lillian Wald and Mary Brewster founded the Henry Street Settlement and the Henry Street Visiting Nurse Services in New York City's Lower

American Voices

Jane Addams, *Twenty Years at Hull House*, 1910

Jane Addams lived at Hull House for forty-five years, serving successive generations of Chicago's poor. She described her decision to begin such a life.

The next January [1889] found Miss [Ellen] Starr and myself in Chicago, searching for a neighborhood in which we might put our plans into execution. In our eagerness to win friends for the new undertaking, we utilized every opportunity to set forth the meaning of the Settlement as it had been embodied in Toynbee Hall, although in those days we made no appeal for money, meaning to start with our own slender resources. ...

In those early days we were often asked why we had come to live on Halsted Street when we could afford to live somewhere else. I remember one man who used to shake his head and say it was "the strangest thing he had met in his experience," but who was finally convinced that it was "not strange but natural." In time it came to seem natural to all of us that the Settlement should be there. If it is natural to feed the hungry and care for the sick, it is certainly natural to give pleasure to the young, comfort to the aged, and to minister to the deep-seated craving for social intercourse that all men feel. Whoever does it is rewarded by something, which, if not gratitude, is at least spontaneous and vital and lacks that irksome sense of obligation with which a substantial benefit is too often acknowledged. ...

From the first it seemed understood that we were ready to perform the humblest neighborhood services. We were asked to wash the newborn babies, and to prepare the dead for burial, to nurse the sick, and to "mind the children." ...

But in spite of some untoward experiences, we were constantly impressed with the uniform kindness and courtesy we received. Perhaps these first days laid the simple human foundations which are certainly essential for continuous living among the poor: first, genuine preference for residence in an industrial quarter to any other part of the city, because it is interesting, and makes the human appeal; and second, the conviction in the words of Canon Barnett, that the things which make men alike are finer and better than the things that keep them apart, and that these basic likenesses, if they are properly accentuated, easily transcend the less essential differences of race, language, creed, and tradition.

Perhaps even in those first days we made a beginning toward that object which was afterward stated in our charter: "To provide a center for a higher civic and social life; to institute and maintain educational and philanthropic enterprises, and to investigate and improve the conditions in the industrial districts of Chicago."

Source: Jane Addams, *Twenty Years at Hull House* (originally published 1910).

Thinking Critically

1. **Analyzing Primary Sources**
   Why did Jane Addams believe that her preference for living among the poor was a central part of her mission? Was this preference essential to the purpose of her mission as described in her charter?

2. **Contextualization**
   How did Addams see her relationship with the people she served? What aspects of the Progressive movement were reflected in her views? Might other progressives of the same era have had a different view?

East Side. Others did the same. Visiting nurses based in settlement houses visited the tenement apartments of the poor and brought medical help.

Under Addams's leadership, Hull House did more than provide services to the poor. It also took the side of the poor in labor and legal disputes. When Addams realized that young women strikers were in danger of losing their company housing, Hull House launched a cooperative women's boardinghouse. Such direct support for strikers did not endear Addams to some of Chicago's most powerful leaders, who were willing to tolerate, even support, social services but were hostile to her involvement in a strike. Nevertheless, such efforts solidified her base within the communities that mattered the most to her.

19.2 Quick Review

Why did progressive reformers deem political reforms, school reforms, and assistance for the working class necessary to improve life in American cities?

Religious Responses to the Gilded Age

19.3 Explain the main currents of religiously based reform movements during the Progressive Era.

In the late 1800s, reform movements seeking to improve the lives of working people, bring an end to municipal corruption, and build a just economic order often took on the language and style of evangelical religion. Both reform movements and religious revivals emphasized personal and social transformation. Both wanted changes in people's hearts and were unafraid to use government to bring about changes in behavior. Many reformers were themselves Protestants, and reform efforts were often rooted in the ideas and individualistic ethos of Protestant Christianity.

Temperance and the Woman's Christian Temperance Union

Certainly, no political renewal movement was more rooted in Protestant Christianity than the women's campaign against alcohol that began in the 1870s (see Map 19-1, p. 562). Early in the 1800s, many Protestant ministers began to oppose excessive drinking, and some Protestants took a strong stand against all liquor. Still, most Americans continued to drink alcohol. The Panic of 1873, however, led a group of midwestern women to start a new temperance movement. Many women seemed to reach the same conclusion at about the same time: liquor was consuming their husbands' wages while leading the men to arrive home drunk and ready to abuse wives and children. The answer to this problem, and the key to defending their homes and families, they said, was a campaign against "Demon Rum."

In Hillsboro, Ohio, women began to meet to pray and then to take their prayers into the local saloons or, if banned, to stand outside and pray. Through the depression winter of 1873–1874, Ohio women claimed credit for closing some three thousand saloons. The following fall, in November 1874, two hundred women from seventeen states met in Cleveland and formed the **Woman's Christian Temperance Union** (WCTU). They were determined to make temperance—abstinence from liquor—the key moral and political issue of the decade. In the process, the WCTU empowered a generation of women who had been taught that ladylike behavior meant quietly taking care of home and family and leaving politics to men.

Woman's Christian Temperance Union

National organization formed after the Civil War dedicated to prohibiting the sale and distribution of alcohol.

19.1

19.2

19.3

19.4

Map 19-1 Prohibition in the States.

The power of the Woman's Christian Temperance Union is shown in the number of states that, starting with Kansas in 1881, prohibited the sale of alcohol outright and those many more that passed local option laws giving cities and towns the right to ban alcohol.

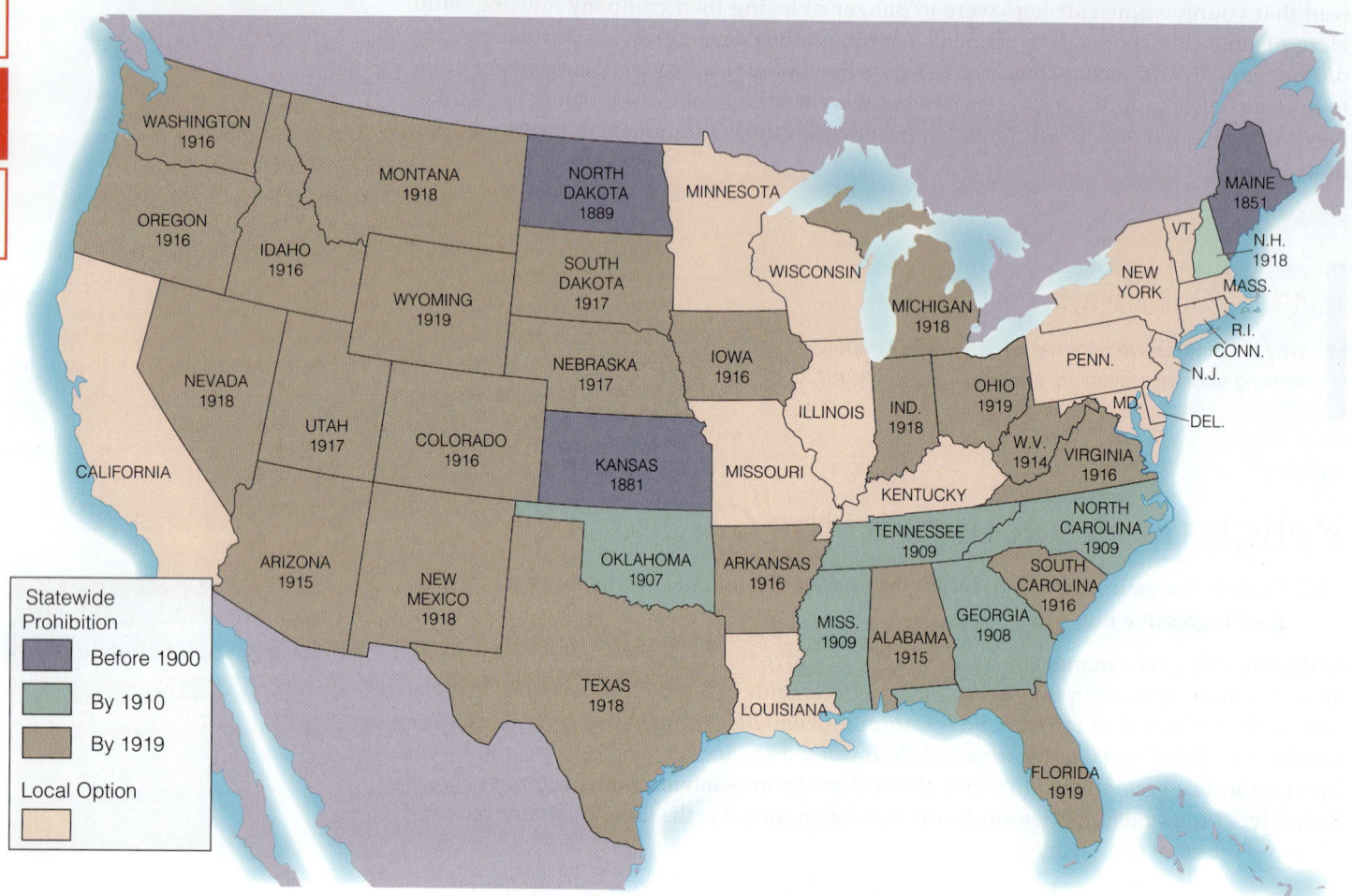

Frances Willard (1839–1898) led the Woman's Christian Temperance Union from 1879 to 1898, making it a powerful force in the United States.

When the WCTU began, Frances E. Willard, dean of women and professor at Northwestern University in Chicago, was too busy with her academic duties to pay much attention. Soon thereafter, however, she left Northwestern to become a full-time organizer for the WCTU. Five years later in 1879, Willard became its second president, and she led the WCTU for the next twenty-four years until her death in 1898, becoming probably the most prominent woman in the United States at the time.

Under Willard's leadership, the WCTU broadened its goals while never losing sight of ending the use of alcohol. Willard was convinced that "much of the evil by which the country is cursed," especially the evil of drink, is the fault of "the men in power whose duty is to make and administer the laws." She took the organization into the political arena, demanding for women the right to vote so they could vote on matters affecting drink and the home. She coined the phrase "home protection" to describe the WCTU's agenda. If drink was destroying families, she argued, then women needed the right to defend their families. If the WCTU was going to pursue its mission of saving homes and reconstructing the nation, then, Willard insisted, "[w]e must show power."

By the time Willard died, the WCTU had almost 200,000 members, a twelve-story national headquarters in Chicago, and a powerful national presence.

Others took the temperance cause in very different directions. Carry Nation, from Kiowa, Kansas, was married to a man who was a hopeless drunk. After he died, Nation moved and married a nondrinker. In response to what she believed was a call from God, Nation went back to Kiowa and smashed up the local saloon, breaking bottles, mirrors, and pictures. She followed up with "hatchetations" of other saloons and became a national symbol of one version of the temperance movement.

Whether in the direct action of Carry Nation or the more organized approach of Frances Willard, the temperance movement changed the United States. It laid a solid foundation not only for the Eighteenth Amendment that in 1919 banned the manufacture and sale of liquor but also for the Nineteenth Amendment that a few months later in 1920 gave women the right to vote. The temperance crusade also demonstrated the power of organized religion, both in churches led by clergy and in extradenominational organizations often led by women. The United States in the late 1800s was still an overwhelmingly Protestant country, and a movement that could tap the Protestant religious fervor of the nation's majority could go far.

The Social Gospel

In 1897, Charles M. Sheldon, a young Congregationalist pastor in Topeka, Kansas, published a novel, *In His Steps*, which eventually sold fifteen million copies. *In His Steps* told of a fictionalized minister who asks his congregation, "What would be the result, if in this city every church member should begin to do as Jesus would do? … What would Jesus do in the matter of wealth?" In the novel, the question "What would Jesus do?" transformed the town. Similarly, *In His Steps* also struck a chord in the country. Sheldon's question, "What would Jesus do?" led many Protestants to embrace reform movements.

Other religious leaders began to talk of what they called the **Social Gospel**, which was based on the idea that improving society was both the right thing for religious people to do and, indeed, God's will. There were many Social Gospel preachers, but one of the most prominent was Walter Rauschenbusch whose 1917 book *A Theology for the Social Gospel* broadened the definition of sin from a focus on individual flaws to include oppressive social institutions. George D. Herron was a pastor whose most famous sermon, "The Message of Jesus to Men of Wealth," claimed simply that "a rich Christian is a contradiction of terms." Josiah Strong edited a Social Gospel magazine, *The Gospel of the Kingdom*, and published a book, *Our Country*, pleading for missionary work within American cities and around the world. In every city, local city mission societies carried out their own Social Gospel mission.

Social Gospel

Application of religious ethics to industrial conditions and thereby alleviating poverty, slums, and labor exploitation.

Even more than his writing, the photographs that Jacob Riis made, like this one, showed middle-class America the poverty in which "the other half" lived.

Thinking Historically

How the Other Half Lives

Jacob A. Riis, an immigrant from Denmark working as a newspaper police reporter, published *How the Other Half Lives* in 1890. In that book, Riis sought to describe the housing conditions of New York's poor through text and photographs.

> The death of a child in a tenement was registered at the Bureau of Vital Statistics as "plainly due to suffocation in the foul air of an unventilated apartment." ... Another was the case of a hard-working family of man and wife, young people from the old country, who took poison together in a Crosby Street tenement because they were "tired." There was no other explanation, and none was needed when I stood in the room in which they had lived. It was an attic with sloping ceiling and a single window so far out on the roof that it seemed not to belong to the place at all. With scarcely room enough to turn around in they had been compelled to pay five dollars and a half a month in advance. There were four such rooms in the attic, and together they brought in as much as many a handsome little cottage in a pleasant part of Brooklyn.

Riis said, "[T]he proprietors frequently urged the filthy habits of the tenants as an excuse for the condition of their property, utterly losing sight of the fact that it was the tolerance of those habits which was the real evil, and that for this they themselves were alone responsible." In pinning responsibility for poverty and misery directly on those who profited from it, Riis created considerable hostility toward himself and great publicity for the book.

Later, Riis described the difficulty he had in getting the *How the Other Half Lives* published:

> For more than a year I had knocked at the doors of the various magazine editors with my pictures, proposing to tell them how the other half lived, but no one wanted to know. ... [I]n the church one might, at all events, tell the truth unhindered. So I thought; but there were cautious souls there too.

Eventually, Riis met Dr. Schauffler, the manager of the City Mission Society, and Dr. Josiah Strong, the author of *Our Country*. They were impressed with the photos and arranged for Riis to tell the stories within *How the Other Half Lives* to a group at the Broadway Tabernacle, a Congregational church associated with Schauffler and Strong. Riis continues the account:

> One of the editors of *Scribner's Magazine* saw my pictures and heard their story in his church, and came to talk the matter over with me. As a result of that talk I wrote an article that appeared in the Christmas *Scribner's*, 1889, under the title "How the Other Half Lives," and made an instant impression. ... It could not have been long after I wrote "How the Other Half Lives" that he [Theodore Roosevelt, then Police Commissioner of New York City] came to the *Evening Sun* office one day looking for me. I was out, and he left his card, merely writing on the back of it that he had read my book and had "come to help." ... There is very little ease where Theodore Roosevelt leads, as we all found out. ... Mr. Roosevelt was a member of the Health Board, and sometimes it was the tenements we went inspecting when the tenants slept. He was after the facts, and learned speedily to get them as he could. When as Governor, he wanted to know just how the Factory Law was being executed, he came down from Albany and spent a whole day with me personally investigating tenements in which sweating [sweatshop manufacturing done at home] was carried on.

Source: Jacob A. Riis, *The Making of an American* (New York: Macmillan, 1901), pp. 191–225.

Thinking Critically

1. **Contextualization**
   How do you think real estate owners responded to his pictures and his explanations of conditions?

2. **Comparison**
   Compare and contrast the contributions of Riis, Roosevelt, and Addams to the Progressive movement. What common beliefs, approaches, and goals did they share? What differences might they have had? How did all of them differ from union organizers or socialists like Eugene Debs or Mother Jones?

While the Social Gospel was a Protestant movement, social issues also swept Catholic America. Cardinal James Gibbons, the longtime archbishop of Baltimore and nominal leader of American Catholics, defended the American labor movement and the role of Catholics in it to a wary Vatican. Gibbons argued that the rise of monopolies with their "heartless avarice" demanded action.

Not all religious communities shared in the Social Gospel movement, however. Many first-generation Jewish immigrants put all of their religious energy into secular political reform and labor movements. Some rabbis, in turn, worried that the focus on secular politics would undermine the spiritual world of the immigrants. Parish priests in Italian, German, and Czech parishes in Chicago tangled with the anarchists and union radicals whom they saw as taking people away from the faith. Some Catholics focused on private devotional activities or large street festivals often devoted to the Virgin Mary, seeing their faith as a refuge from the larger society rather than a way to change society. They valued the ministry of individuals like Frances Xavier Cabrini—Mother Cabrini—sent to the United States by an Italian bishop in 1889 to serve the needs of the Italian immigrants but who, unlike Cardinal Gibbons, avoided labor organizing and politics. Religious people, like others, had widely differing ideas about how to live well in the new urban and industrial society of the United States.

19.3 Quick Review

How were religiously inspired progressives similar to or different from other progressive reformers?

Progressive Politics on the National Stage

19.4 Analyze the three "progressive presidents" and their administrations.

A significant turning point in American politics came early in the morning of September 14, 1901, when President William McKinley died in Buffalo, New York. He had been visiting the Pan American Exposition when he was shot by a lone anarchist, Leon Czolgosz, on September 6. The president survived the bullet but died of the infection that followed. McKinley was the third American president to be assassinated after Abraham Lincoln in 1865 and James A. Garfield in 1881. The fact that his assailant described himself as an anarchist led to a strong backlash against the anarchist movement, just regaining its political standing after the widespread hostility engendered by the Haymarket violence of 1886 (see Chapter 18).

Vice President Theodore Roosevelt, who had been on a camping trip with his family in New York's Adirondack Mountains when McKinley was shot, arrived in Buffalo to take the oath of office. Sitting on the train bringing McKinley's body from Buffalo to Washington, D.C., was Ohio senator Mark Hanna, who had helped McKinley select Roosevelt as vice president. Hanna understood what the transition meant for many like him who constituted the old guard of the Republican Party. "Now look!" Hanna muttered. "That damned cowboy is President of the United States!"

There was a reason that some referred to the new president as a cowboy. Theodore Roosevelt had already had an extraordinary career in and out of politics when he ascended to the presidency. Born to a wealthy New York family whose roots went back to Dutch New York, he grew up as a sometimes awkward and sickly child. He compensated by lifting weights and learning to box. He attended Harvard College and was elected to the New York State Assembly at twenty-three, a year after his marriage to Alice Hathaway Lee. When his wife died, Roosevelt abandoned politics for a cowboy life in the Dakotas. He soon returned to New York, married Edith Kermit Carow, and started on his rapid political ascent. He was appointed U.S. civil service commissioner at age thirty-one, police commissioner of New York at thirty-seven, and assistant secretary of the navy at thirty-nine. During the Spanish-American War, Roosevelt took command of a unit in Cuba known as the Rough Riders, making himself a war hero. He was elected governor of New York when he had just turned forty and was already plotting his own campaign for the presidency.

Roosevelt's hopes for the presidency were almost derailed by his differences with the old guard in the New York Republican Party. As governor, Roosevelt wanted to end corruption, tax the street railways, and provide for industrial safety as well as workers' compensation for those injured on the job. He had advocated for the inspection of tenement housing since being shown their conditions by Jacob Riis. But not everyone in New York, Democrats or Republicans, liked those new ideas.

The boss of the Republican Party in New York, state senator Tom Platt, supported Roosevelt for governor in November 1898 because his war hero popularity and anticorruption image seemed the only way to win the election and maintain Republican power. But once Platt discovered that Roosevelt actually meant what he said, the boss decided he needed to get rid of the governor before he wrecked the Republican machine. Platt planned to sideline Roosevelt by getting him the nomination as McKinley's running mate for 1900. Roosevelt did not want the nomination. In 1900, no sitting vice president had been elected president since Martin Van Buren succeeded Andrew Jackson more than half a century earlier. Even so, the nomination was hard to reject without seeming disloyal to the party. McKinley and Roosevelt won the election, and state politics in New York returned to normal. Then, only months into McKinley's second term, the president was dead and the reforming politician from New York was the president of the United States. At the age of forty-two, he was also the youngest president ever.

Teddy Roosevelt—Progressive President

Taking the oath of office, the new president promised "to carry out absolutely unbroken" the former president's policies. One observer responded, "[Y]es, the same way one carries out the trash." That comment represented an accurate view of the new president. After a brief period of mourning, very brief for him personally, the White House and the country started to experience Roosevelt's considerable reforming energy, which New Yorkers had known for some time.

THE TRUSTBUSTER AND THE SQUARE DEAL Roosevelt soon outlined his departure from McKinley and his determination to limit the power of industrial corporations. TR (as he came to be known to everyone) told Congress that "there are real and grave evils" that come from the power of the great corporations, and the federal government needed to assume the authority to supervise and limit that power.

Only a month before Roosevelt spoke to Congress, James J. Hill, owner of the Great Northern Railroad, and E. H. Harriman, who controlled the Union Pacific Railroad, met with representatives of J. Pierpont Morgan, who controlled the Northern Pacific Railroad. These three lines were competitors across the northern plains. The competition among them kept prices low and helped farmers and industries who wanted to ship their products. As had been the case with steel less than a year before, such competition struck Morgan as terribly inefficient and a drain on profits. Hill, Harriman, and Morgan solved their problem by creating a new entity, the Northern Securities Company Limited, to which they then sold all of their railroads. In place of competition, the transcontinental railroad routes would now be one happy family.

Roosevelt did not mention Northern Securities in his December speech, and some industrialists hoped that his speech was mere rhetoric. Then in February 1902, the attorney general announced that, at the president's request, he was filing suit under the 1890 **Sherman Antitrust Act** to break up Northern Securities. To the new president, the Northern Securities Company was too big and too powerful, and the lack of competition on the rails meant that the new trust could charge virtually any rates it wanted to haul freight and passengers.

Roosevelt's actions were not the first time that the Progressive movement led the federal government to take action. In response to the assassination of President Garfield by a disappointed office seeker in 1881, Congress passed the **Pendleton Civil Service Reform Act** of 1883, which sought to replace political patronage with merit in the selection of government employees. Chester A. Arthur, the vice president who became president when Garfield died, strongly supported the act and lost the backing of the bosses in his own party for doing so. The act created the Civil Service Commission whose job was to give federal employees a measure of protection from losing their jobs over their political ideas while keeping federal civil servants—not elected officials—from actively fundraising or campaigning. In addition, in response to public pressure about the power of monopolies, Congress had passed the Sherman Antitrust Act in 1890, which its sponsor, Senator John Sherman of Ohio, said was to outlaw any business practices that would unfairly raise costs for the consumer.

The Pendleton Act, however, covered only about 10 percent of federal employees when it was passed and none at the state or local level. The Sherman Act had been a virtual dead letter after a series of court cases reduced its scope soon after it was passed. Suddenly, with

Sherman Antitrust Act

The first federal antitrust measure, passed in 1890; sought to promote economic competition by prohibiting business combinations in restraint of trade or commerce.

Pendleton Civil Service Reform Act

A law of 1883 that reformed the spoils system by prohibiting government workers from making political contributions and by creating the Civil Service Commission to oversee their appointment on the basis of merit rather than politics.

the Northern Securities suit, a new administration was bringing the Sherman Act back to life and warning of further progressive initiatives to follow.

Soon after the suit was announced, J. P. Morgan visited the White House for a private meeting with the president and the attorney general. Morgan told the president, "If we have done anything wrong, send your man to my man and they can fix it up." Roosevelt, who saw things quite differently, said, "That can't be done," and Attorney General Philander Chase Knox added, "We don't want to fix it up, we want to stop it." Morgan then asked if the government was now going to attack his other interests, especially U.S. Steel, and Roosevelt responded, "Certainly not—unless we find out that in any case they have done something that we regard as wrong." After Morgan left, Roosevelt told Knox he found it quite revealing that Morgan could deal with him only as "a big rival operator" with whom to make a deal. But there would be no deal.

The Northern Securities case took two years to move through the federal courts, but in March 1904, the U.S. Supreme Court affirmed Roosevelt's interpretation of the Sherman Act. The majority opinion said that "[n]o scheme or device could … more effectively and certainly suppress free competition" and ordered the Northern Security trust broken up into competing lines. From then on, Roosevelt would be known as the "trustbuster," and he liked the title.

Roosevelt kept up the pressure for change. In a series of speeches in the summer of 1902, he told audiences, "The great corporations which we have grown to speak of rather loosely as trusts are the creatures of the State, and the State not only has the right to control them, but it is in duty bound to control them wherever need of such control is shown." His natural inclination to expand the government's power to supervise corporations was supported by many in Congress and by muckraking publications like *McClure's*, which Roosevelt may have disliked, but which nonetheless provided him with new ammunition with every issue. Roosevelt wanted a new cabinet-level Department of Commerce with investigative authority, a ban on secret deals between railroads and specific companies (of the sort that launched Rockefeller's oil empire), and additional funds for the Department of Justice to expedite antitrust cases. Ironically, once Roosevelt had won his Northern Securities victory and gained the tools that Congress gave him, he did not pursue many other antitrust cases. The Taft and Wilson administrations would use the new tools more than Roosevelt himself. The president had made his point. As was often the case during his seven years in office, having done so, he moved on to other issues.

CONSERVATION IN NATURE   As a child, Theodore Roosevelt was a birdwatcher and developed an intense love of nature. Years later, he walked into a cabinet meeting and asked, "Gentlemen, do you know what has happened this morning?" The members of the cabinet waited for important news. Roosevelt told them, "Just now I saw a chestnut-sided warbler— and this is only February!" The birds did not usually appear in Washington on their return from Central America until much later in the spring.

While Roosevelt loved nature, watched birds, and as president saved thousands of acres of land from development, he was also an avid hunter who loved to shoot bear, cougar, or just about anything in the wilderness. However, on one bear hunt in 1902, Roosevelt refused to shoot a bear that had been captured and tied to a tree so the president could have the honor of the shot. He was happy to kill many other bears on real hunts, but attacking a tied-up bear was unsportsmanlike. His refusal made national news and sparked a new craze, fostered by the Steiff and Ideal toy companies—a new toy known as a Teddy Bear in honor of the president who would not shoot one.

Just before he became vice president, Roosevelt published *The Strenuous Life* in which he argued that Americans were getting far too little time to replenish their bodies and souls in the great outdoors. But the strenuous life in nature that he advocated was possible only if the wilderness and the wildlife were preserved for future generations to enjoy. Once he became president, Roosevelt combined all of this considerable enthusiasm for nature with his political skill to become perhaps the most conservation-minded of any president.

Although a keenly passionate advocate, Roosevelt was not, however, the first president to care about conservation. Harrison, Cleveland, and McKinley all set aside federal lands for

19.1

19.2

19.3

19.4

permanent parks, and both Yellowstone and the Grand Canyon were federal reserves before Roosevelt took office. But from Roosevelt's perspective, too few animals were protected, too little land had been put aside, and too little was being done to protect the environment.

Even though his attack on the trusts got most of the headlines, a short line in TR's December 1901 message to Congress said, "The preservation of our forests is an imperative business necessity." People like his friend Gifford Pinchot and members of the Audubon and Sierra clubs cheered. Western senators were furious at an attack on the prime source of wealth in their states. Again, some hoped that it was a mere rhetorical flourish. They soon learned differently. When Roosevelt came to the presidency in 1901, 43 million acres of land were included in U.S. forest reserves. When he left office in 1909, that number had increased more than fourfold to 194 million acres.

Roosevelt also professionalized the protection of nature. He wrote that the "Nation as a whole should earnestly desire and strive to leave to the next generation the National honor unstained and the National resources unexhausted," and only new conservation efforts would preserve either honor or resources. He appointed a former Rough Rider, David E. Warford, as a federal forest ranger with authority to protect the 4.15 million acres of federal land in Arizona and Colorado. He nominated Gifford Pinchot, who shared the president's commitment, to be head of the Division of Forestry and, later, head of the U.S. Forest Service in the Department of the Interior and gave him "an absolutely free hand."

Between 1906 and 1908, Roosevelt used—or misused, his critics said—authority given to him by the Antiquities Act of 1906 to declare a 295-acre stand of giant redwood trees just north of San Francisco as Muir Woods National Monument; 800,000 acres in Arizona as the Grand Canyon National Monument; and 2,500 acres, later expanded to 26,000 acres, as the Pinnacles National Monument in California. He also set aside the Natural Bridges National Monument in Utah and a dozen other similar monuments, ensuring that the land would never pass into private hands (see Map 19-2).

Map 19-2 Major National Parks.

While the federal government claimed ownership of much of the land in the West, no president matched Theodore Roosevelt in setting aside large tracts of that land as national parks and forests so it would be preserved for future generations rather than be sold or developed.

19.1

19.2

19.3

19.4

The president's continued expansion of the amount of land protected by the federal government provoked resistance in Congress. In early 1907, Senator Charles W. Fulton, a Republican from Oregon, attached an amendment to the Department of Agriculture's appropriations bill that said that no further forest reserves or expansions of reserves could be created within six western states without an act of Congress. When the bill reached the president, he had ten days to sign it or risk having no funds to operate the Department of Agriculture. Roosevelt quickly approved a total of twenty-one new forest reserves in the six states—Medicine Bow Forest in Colorado, Priest River Forest in Idaho and Washington, Toiyabe Forest in Nevada, Blue Mountain in Oregon, and Olympic and Rainier forests in Washington. When the paperwork creating these new forests was done, Roosevelt then signed the agriculture bill with Fulton's amendment, saying that no *additional* forests would be created.

Roosevelt and African Americans

One of Roosevelt's first moves as president was to invite Booker T. Washington, the country's best-known African American, to the White House for a meeting and then, in October 1901, for dinner with the president and his family. No African American had ever before eaten a meal as a guest at the White House. Roosevelt was making a very public statement about race relations in the United States. He was also taking a first step toward securing a full term as elected president for himself. Booker T. Washington controlled a block of delegates to the Republican nominating conventions, since even though blacks could not vote in the segregated South of Roosevelt's day, they could and did win election as delegates to national Republican nominating conventions.

Although neither Roosevelt nor Washington discussed the dinner in public, the press made a great deal of the evening. While some reports were positive, papers like the *Memphis Scimitar* called the dinner "[t]he most damnable outrage which has ever been perpetrated by any citizen of the United States."

For the rest of his seven years in the White House, Roosevelt had a decidedly mixed record on African American concerns. He did not mention black disenfranchisement or lynching in his first presidential message to Congress. However, in his 1906 annual message to Congress, he said, "The members of the white race … should understand that every lynching represents by just so much a loosening of the bands of civilization." They were important words, though with too little follow-up. In symbolic ways—the White House dinner and speeches on lynching—Roosevelt did more to support African Americans than several of his predecessors or successors. In comparison with the energy he gave to other issues he considered important, however, his track record was certainly lackluster.

Roosevelt's Continuing Popularity

Roosevelt's obvious joy at life and enjoyment of the presidency was infectious. People loved having a young and enthusiastic chief executive. A friend once said of Roosevelt that he "wanted to be the bride at every wedding and the corpse at every funeral."

Roosevelt's large family brought life and vitality to the previously staid White House. Alice, daughter of his first marriage, was a young adult who flirted with and charmed everyone she met, including Ohio congressman Nicholas Longworth whom she married in a White House wedding. She would continue to charm Washington society for the next three-quarters of a century. The president and Edith's younger children—Ted, Kermit, Ethel, Archie, and Quentin—played at the White House, chasing rabbits on the White House grounds, marching with the White House police, and riding bicycles on the lawn and occasionally down the stairs.

In 1904, the Republicans easily nominated Roosevelt for a full term. Having lost with Bryan in 1896 and 1900, Democrats were looking for a fresh face and nominated Alton B. Parker, chief justice of the New York Court of Appeals. It was not a close contest. Parker was a colorless candidate, but it is unlikely that any Democrat could have won.

Republicans were the country's major party and Roosevelt's energy carried the day. He won by a landslide.

After his reelection, Roosevelt's popularity only grew, and he and everyone knew that he could easily win a third term or, as his daughter Alice kept saying, "a second elected term" if he was a candidate in 1908. Nevertheless, he had promised himself and the country in 1904 that he would not seek a third term, saying as he claimed victory in November 1904, "The wise custom which limits the President to two terms regards the substance and not the form." As 1908 approached, the president was tempted to break the pledge but did not. Roosevelt's goal in 1908 was to find a candidate who would carry on the policies that he had championed. He thought he had found just the right candidate in Secretary of War William Howard Taft.

Taft Wins, Taft Loses—The Elections of 1908 and 1912

Secretary Taft had served as a federal district court judge in Ohio before becoming governor general of the Philippines and then secretary of war. He would have loved an appointment to the Supreme Court, one he finally won in 1921 when Warren Harding appointed him. But in 1908, Roosevelt had picked Taft as the successor most likely to continue his programs, and once Roosevelt had made up his mind, there was little that Taft or anyone else could do to stop him.

Having failed miserably with the conservative Alton Parker in the 1904 election, the Democrats returned to William Jennings Bryan for a third try for the White House. The Socialist Party was also growing in strength and their candidate, Eugene V. Debs, made a respectable showing. But the election was never really in doubt, and Taft won easily on the promise to continue Roosevelt's progressivism.

TAFT'S ADMINISTRATION, TAFT'S POLICIES Not surprisingly, given their very different personalities, tensions between the outgoing and the incoming president began even before Taft's inauguration. Roosevelt expected Taft to keep most of the existing cabinet; Taft wanted some of his own people. Most disappointing to the conservationist Roosevelt, Taft replaced Secretary of the Interior James R. Garfield, an ardent conservationist, with Richard A. Ballinger, a Seattle lawyer and former reform mayor, who was more interested in exploiting public lands than conserving them. Nevertheless, Taft kept Gifford Pinchot on at the U.S. Forest Service, and Roosevelt sailed for Africa soon after the inauguration to pursue a big-game hunt, confident that the country was in good hands.

Taft kept a key Roosevelt-Taft pledge and called Congress into special session in early 1909 to lower the nation's tariff rates. Ida Tarbell, one of the best-known muckraking journalists, insisted that the poor could not afford warm clothing because of the high tariff charged on imported wool, and many economists felt that overly high tariffs were protecting industries that no longer needed protection. Income and inheritance taxes seemed more equitable ways to pay for the government. But not everyone in Congress agreed, especially Rhode Island senator Nelson Aldrich and House Speaker Joe Cannon.

New York representative Sereno Payne proposed reducing the tariff rates and substituting an income tax. But when the bill reached the Senate, Aldrich dropped the income tax and revised the tariffs up—significantly. Aldrich acknowledged that the Republican platform had promised to revise the tariff, but he asked, "Where did we ever make the statement that we would revise the tariff downward?" Everyone knew that the downward revision had been the promise, but it was not the outcome. Even most moderate Republicans criticized the Payne-Aldrich tariff, but Taft signed the bill. When Congress later passed bills to lower the tariff on cotton, wool, steel, and iron, Taft vetoed them. In the process, he built an alliance with the conservative Aldrich wing of the party, losing the support of many Roosevelt progressives.

While Roosevelt was in Africa, word came to him in January 1910 that Taft had fired Pinchot. Pinchot wrote to the former president, "We have fallen back down the hill you led us up." The tariff might be abstract to Roosevelt, but conservation was the issue nearest and

A widely distributed cartoon showed former President Roosevelt's disappointment with his hand-picked, but ensnarled, successor, President Taft.

dearest to him, and Pinchot was the agent TR had counted on to keep the movement alive in the new administration.

On many fronts, Taft kept his pledge to carry out Roosevelt's policies, in some cases with more vigor than TR had ever shown. It was Taft, not Roosevelt, who decreed an eight-hour workday for government employees and who advocated the Sixteenth Amendment to the Constitution, passed in 1913, to ensure that federal income taxes could be collected. In addition, Taft was a far tougher trustbuster than Roosevelt, breaking up John D. Rockefeller's Standard Oil Company and bringing more antitrust suits in his four years than Roosevelt did in seven.

THE UNIQUE ELECTION OF 1912 Roosevelt was not alone in his estrangement from the Taft administration. Critics abounded, and Senator Robert La Follette of Wisconsin was hinting broadly that he might challenge Taft for the Republican presidential nomination in 1912. La Follette was a different kind of progressive from Roosevelt. He advocated a more open nominating process for candidates and an income tax to limit the power of the very rich. He wanted to destroy the monopolies that Roosevelt wanted only to regulate. La Follette was also appalled by concessions to the white South, believing that if African Americans "had been fairly treated," then they would have been able to take the places now denied them as farmers and businessmen.

As Roosevelt waited, La Follette campaigned for the nomination. Then in February 1912, La Follette gave a speech in Philadelphia in which, either exhausted or drunk, he went on for over two hours, repeating himself again and again. He lost not only his audience but also the nomination with that speech. A week later, seven Republican governors asked Roosevelt to run. TR announced, "My hat is in the ring" and wrote, "I will accept the nomination for President if it is tendered to me." He also set out to be sure that the 1912 nomination was, in fact, so tendered.

Through the spring, Taft and Roosevelt fought it out—Taft always reluctantly, Roosevelt with his usual exuberance. In the South, Taft used the party machinery to control the delegates. Roosevelt defended his challenge, saying, "If that be revolution, make the most of it." Taft responded, "This wrenches my soul. … I do not want to fight Theodore Roosevelt, but sometimes a man in a corner fights. I am going to fight."

Taft won in the states where delegates were controlled by caucuses while Roosevelt won nearly all of the states that held primary elections, including Pennsylvania, California, Minnesota, Nebraska, Maryland, South Dakota, and even Taft's home state of Ohio. After seeing the primary returns, Idaho senator William E. Borah declared, "There can be but one result, and that is the nomination of Mr. Roosevelt," and Nebraska's senator George Norris happily said, "Taft is out of the race."

Taft, however, was not out of the race. He still controlled the party machinery. When delegates were contested—and 254 convention seats were contested—the Republican National Committee decided who should vote at the convention. The committee awarded 235 of the contested delegates to Taft and only 19 to Roosevelt, sealing the nomination for Taft.

Two months after the Republican convention, in early August 1912, a new Progressive Party held its convention in the same hall. The fourteen thousand delegates were mostly middle-class reformers—social workers, teachers, and owners of small businesses. It was the first major political convention to include female delegates, and there were many. Also attending were a few American delegates from border states and New England, none from the Deep South where Taft controlled the party. Few of the farmers and laborers representing past Populist Party conventions were there. The platform included support for the rights of labor unions, conservation, women's suffrage, the eight-hour workday, workplace safety, as well as unemployment and old-age insurance. In a doomed effort to court white Southern votes, the platform was silent on the rights of African Americans. By acclamation, the convention nominated Theodore Roosevelt for president and California governor Hiram Johnson for vice president. In the first convention speech by a woman, Jane Addams seconded Roosevelt's nomination. Roosevelt, saying that he felt "as fit as a Bull Moose," happily accepted the nomination. A convention like no other launched a presidential election like no other.

Many Democrats saw the Republican split as the chance for a Democratic presidency. Champ Clark of Missouri, the Speaker of the House, was the frontrunner. He was popular within the party but was a dull speaker. Oscar Underwood of Alabama was more conservative but perhaps a better speaker than Clark. Others hoped to be kingmakers. Charles Murphy, the boss of Tammany, controlled the New York delegation while William Jennings Bryan controlled many other delegates. Finally, the governor of New Jersey, Woodrow Wilson, campaigned for the nomination.

Wilson had held elected office for only two years. He was an expert on constitutional law with a Ph.D. from Johns Hopkins, who had served as the president of Princeton University from 1902 to 1910. He had sought to transform Princeton from a country club for rich boys to a serious academic institution. He battled with faculty, alumni, and trustees and showed little aptitude for compromise.

In 1910, just as Wilson saw some of his most cherished goals defeated at Princeton, the political bosses who ran the Democratic Party in New Jersey were looking for an appealing candidate for governor. They offered Wilson the nomination, and he surprised even his supporters by being a magnetic candidate, winning easily. Then, to the surprise of the bosses, Wilson kept his word that he would be independent, broke with those who had put him in the governor's office, and refused to follow their lead in patronage. He governed as a progressive, getting the state to adopt workers' compensation, a commission to regulate public utilities, and more open election laws, winning great popularity as well as the undying hatred of political bosses. Wilson entered the Democratic nominating convention as a strong candidate but not the leader. While Clark led on the first ballots, Wilson kept gaining; on the forty-sixth ballot, exhausted delegates gave Wilson their party's nomination.

With the nominations of Roosevelt, Taft, and Wilson—a former, the current, and a future president—the 1912 election was unique. In addition, a fourth candidate, Eugene V. Debs, was once again the candidate of the Socialist Party, and by 1912, the Socialists were a force to be reckoned with. In local elections the year before, Socialist candidates had been elected as mayor in fifty-six cities and towns, and one of the party's candidates, Victor Berger, was elected to Congress from Wisconsin. The Socialist Party, always highly factionalized, enthusiastically nominated Debs as their standard bearer for a fourth time. Some Socialists worried that Roosevelt's Progressive Party would steal their platform, but while the Progressive Party called for governmental oversight of the monopolies, the Socialists called for government ownership of all large-scale industries—especially the railroads. Like the Progressives, the Socialist platform also called for shorter working hours, workers' compensation, electoral reform, and giving women the right to vote. However, unlike the Progressives, it also called for ensuring blacks the right to vote.

Wilson wrote to a friend that "Roosevelt's strength is altogether incalculable. The contest is between him and me, not between Taft and me." He was right. It was difficult for Wilson, who was running as a progressive Democrat, to differentiate himself from Roosevelt's Progressive Party. If the contest was to be one of personal popularity, no one was more popular than Teddy Roosevelt. Boston attorney Louis D. Brandeis suggested a way forward to Wilson. While Roosevelt spoke of the New Nationalism and governmental controls over the monopoly trusts, Brandeis suggested Wilson should speak of a **New Freedom** that would give people the greatest freedom by simply breaking up the great trusts and fostering competition at every level. Four years later, Brandeis would receive his reward when Wilson appointed him as the first Jew to serve on the U.S. Supreme Court.

In the fall campaign, Wilson called Roosevelt a "self-appointed divinity" who wanted to control the trusts and people's lives. Wilson, in contrast, wanted freedom from trusts and from government regulation. "Ours is a program of liberty," he said, "theirs is a program of regulation." Roosevelt struck back, saying that Wilson's approach was "simply the laissez-faire doctrine of … three-quarters of a century ago." Taft morosely stayed on the sidelines. Debs went after them all.

While Roosevelt was speaking in Milwaukee, Wisconsin, in October, a would-be assassin shot him at close range. The bullet lodged in Roosevelt's chest, but a heavy coat and the text of a long speech that was in the coat pocket prevented a serious injury. Roosevelt, with typical pluck, went ahead with an hour-long speech before allowing himself to be taken to a hospital. His chances of victory improved as stories of his courage spread. In the end, however, the deep division within the Republican ranks, their failure to crack the Democrats' hold on the "solid South," and Wilson's use of Brandeis's antitrust rhetoric all ensured the outcome. Wilson won the popular vote with over a million votes more than Roosevelt, who defeated Taft by another half-million. Debs came in fourth with just over 900,000 votes (see Map 19-3).

Woodrow Wilson's New Freedom

Woodrow Wilson planned four major initiatives for his administration—conservation, access to raw materials, banking and finance, and the tariff and taxes. He announced that he would call the new Democratic-majority Congress into a special session in April 1913, a month after his inauguration and months ahead of when it would normally meet.

While Wilson spoke to the importance of conservation in his inaugural address, and while he did push the creation of the National Park Service, his commitment to conservation did not come close to Roosevelt's. Wilsonian progressivism focused elsewhere.

19.1

19.2

19.3

19.4

New Freedom

Woodrow Wilson's 1912 program for government intervention in the economy to restore competition by curtailing the business monopolies, thereby providing opportunities for individual achievement.

Map 19-3 The Election of 1912.

This map shows the breadth of Woodrow Wilson's electoral victory after Roosevelt and Taft split the Republican vote and Debs failed to carry a single state as the Socialist Party candidate.

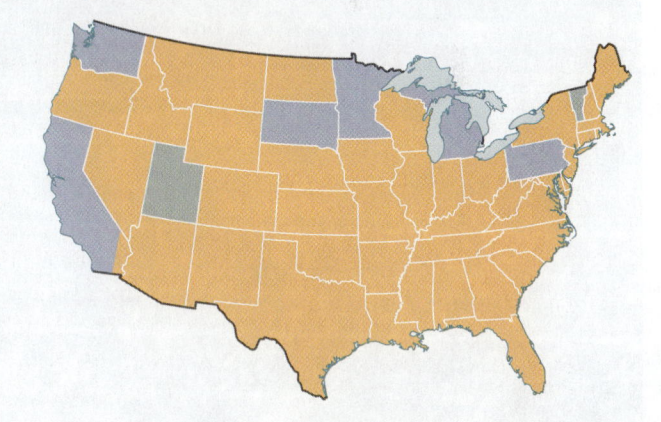

	Electoral Vote	Popular Vote
WOODROW WILSON (Democrat)	435	6,296,547
Theodore Roosevelt (Progressive)	88	4,118,571
William Taft (Republican)	8	3,486,720
Eugene Debs (Socialist)	–	900,672

Only a month after the inauguration, Wilson broke a custom followed by every president since Jefferson and gave a speech in person to a joint session of Congress. Widely televised presidential addresses to Congress are now such a normal feature of American life that is it easy to forget that no president from Jefferson to Taft ever spoke directly to Congress. Nevertheless, Wilson did, and he continued to do so throughout his two terms in office.

Wilson's first congressional victory was the passage of the Underwood-Simmons tariff, which the new president signed in October 1913. Cleveland, McKinley, Roosevelt, and Taft all failed to get tariff reductions through Congress, mostly because of the power that lobbyists had with the Senate. But Wilson managed to embarrass several senators with a very public investigation of the role of lobbyists. He also met privately with several Democratic senators to hear their concerns and shore up their support. In the end, Wilson got a new tariff that reduced the tax on goods imported into the United States by at least 10 percent across the board, more on some things. The new law also used the power given in the new Sixteenth Amendment to introduce the first federal income tax since the Civil War, starting at 1 percent on incomes above $4,000 (considerably more than most Americans made in 1913).

Wilson then turned to reform of the nation's banking system. Since Andrew Jackson closed the Bank of the United States in the 1830s, the federal government's role in the nation's banking system had been very limited. In the financial panics of 1893 and 1907, J. P. Morgan had acted as the nation's banker, ensuring that the nation's credit system stayed intact. While Morgan's interventions were essential to protect the government and the nation's largest banks, they did little to help farmers or proprietors of small businesses or to allow the government to control the supply of money, a role that Bryan and his followers had been demanding for a long time.

Library of Congress Prints and Photographs Division [LC-DIG-hec-11546]

Woodrow Wilson broke a precedent going back to Thomas Jefferson and began the modern practice of presidential speeches to a joint session of Congress.

Working closely with Virginia senator Carter Glass, Wilson was able to create the Federal Reserve System in a matter of months. Following the advice of Brandeis that "concessions to big business interests must in the end prove futile," the president spent no time with representatives of business but, instead, built a coalition of the many factions within the Democratic Party and of progressive Republicans. The final bill passed the House 287 to 85, and the Senate, after a desperate last-minute attempt to derail the bill by Frank A. Vanderlip of the National City Bank of New York, passed the bill 54 to 34. Before the end of his first year in office, Wilson and the Congress had created the Federal Reserve, which remains the core of the nation's banking system today.

During the presidential campaign, Wilson had differentiated himself from Roosevelt with his claim that he was the real "trustbuster." In office, he supported his attorney general, James McReynolds, in attacking the American Telephone and Telegraph Company, United States Steel, and the New Haven Railroad, all companies in which J. P. Morgan had an interest. Then he went to Congress and asked for more authority. The Clayton Anti-Trust Act, signed in October 1914, outlawed interlocking directorates (under which the same individuals might serve on the boards of directors of supposedly competing companies), and defined unfair trade practices, including the kind of collusion over prices that had allowed John D. Rockefeller to create the Standard Oil monopoly. Perhaps most important, the Clayton Act exempted labor unions and farmer cooperatives from the definition of a "combination in restraint of trade," a charge that had been used in federal court cases against unions since Eugene Debs was sent to jail in the 1890s. Although the bill did not give unions everything they wanted, Samuel Gompers declared it to be the "Magna Carta" of labor union organizing. Separate legislation also strengthened the investigative powers of the Interstate Commerce Commission and created a new **Federal Trade Commission** with a specific, if somewhat vague, mandate to limit the growth and power of monopolies.

Federal Trade Commission
Government agency established in 1914 to provide regulatory oversight of business activity.

While Wilson delivered quickly on some of his reformist campaign pledges, he deeply disappointed other followers. When the House passed legislation outlawing child labor in February 1915, Wilson did nothing and the bill died in the Senate. Only much later in his presidency did he support child labor legislation, and only much later, in the New Deal of the 1930s, did the federal government take on child labor in an effective way. He also disappointed farmers, a key Democratic constituency, when he quietly allowed a plan for rural credits to help farmers with mortgages to die in congressional conference committee.

African Americans were greatly disappointed with Wilson. Booker T. Washington had a long-standing link to the Republican Party, but during the 1912 campaign, younger blacks, including African Episcopal Zion bishop Alexander Walters and W. E. B. Du Bois, endorsed Wilson. It was a significant departure from the African American–Republican Party alliance that had existed since Reconstruction. Perhaps, these leaders argued, this Virginia-born and Georgia-reared intellectual could finally break the hold of segregationists on the Democratic Party. During the campaign, Wilson was happy to receive their support, but once in office, Wilson spoke only vaguely of a federal commission to investigate race relations in the United States and allowed his cabinet to set policy that did not support the African American cause.

Citing what they said was white anger at "racial mingling," especially in Southern post offices, Post Master General Albert S. Burleson and Secretary of the Treasury William Gibbs McAdoo ordered the segregation of offices, restrooms, and eating facilities at the Post Office, Treasury Department, and Bureau of Printing and Engraving. Federal employees who had long worked in racially integrated settings were now segregated by race. The Democratic majority in Congress allowed segregationist senators like James K. Vardaman of Mississippi to block black appointments to federal jobs that previous Republican presidents had provided.

The black press attacked Wilson for the segregation policy and the lack of federal appointments. Wilson's most pointed confrontation about his racial policies was with the African American editor William Monroe Trotter of Boston. In November 1913, Trotter met with the president to lay out a long list of specific concerns about segregation in the federal service and the lack of African Americans being hired in the government. Wilson responded blandly, saying, "Now, mistakes have probably been made, but those mistakes can be corrected." A year later, Trotter led another delegation to the White House and received another round of bland vagueness. Trotter lost his temper, saying, "We are here as full-fledged American citizens" and reminded Wilson of the support he had received from African Americans. Wilson in turn lost his temper, telling Trotter, "You are an American citizen … but you are the only American citizen that has ever come into this office who has talked to me with [such] a tone." The president insisted that Trotter be excluded from any future meeting, but there would be few future meetings with African Americans with or without Trotter during Wilson's presidency.

Wilson's reputation in the African American community was further tarnished when in early 1915 he allowed one of the first full-length motion pictures, D. W. Griffith's *Birth of a Nation*, to be shown at the White House. The National Association for the Advancement of Colored People was actively protesting the film, which, though a masterpiece of cinematography, was also a glorification of the Ku Klux Klan. Wilson did not endorse the film, but the president also refused to announce his nonendorsement. Later, Wilson signed a letter prepared by his personal secretary saying that "the President was entirely unaware of the character of the play before it was presented and has at no time expressed his approbation of it." Nevertheless, the film incident, along with the segregation of the federal workforce, seriously undermined Wilson's reputation among African Americans.

When Wilson became president, his agenda focused exclusively on domestic policy. In his first year in office, with the Underwood Tariff, the Clayton Anti-Trust Act, as well as the creation of the Federal Reserve System and the Federal Trade Commission, he had extraordinary success. A little more than a year after the inauguration, however, a political assassination in the far-off town of Sarajevo, Bosnia, began a chain of events that would change the president's and the nation's focus in succeeding years. After 1914, international matters, far more than his domestic agenda, dominated his administration. Indeed, the assassination in the Austrian Empire in June 1914 can be seen as the ending of the Progressive Era. In the new era, discussed in the next chapter, international matters are central.

19.4 Quick Review

What were the main similarities and the main differences between the three "progressive presidents"?

Conclusion

Between 1870 and 1900, America's population almost doubled, from forty million in 1870 to seventy-five million in 1900, with immigration responsible, perhaps, for one-third of this growth. More Americans also moved into cities, drawn there by jobs in America's rapidly expanding industrial economy. A new urgency to focus on the challenges of immigration, urbanization, and industrialization took hold. By 1900, a rising cohort of Americans—including intellectuals, social reformers, and political leaders—argued that new ideas and new levels of activism would be needed for the changing country.

Muckraking journalists such as Ida Tarbell, Upton Sinclair, and Lincoln Steffens sought to convince other Americans to heed the call to solve a wide range of problems related to the health and well-being of Americans. Some reformers attempted to limit the excesses of industrialists and the financial markets; others focused their attentions on the urban poor, the nation's education system, preservation of the natural world, electoral reforms, decent wages for the laboring classes, industrial safety and sanitation, or—in one of the strongest movements—ending the use of alcohol by Americans.

Beginning at the city and state level, progressive reformers sought elected office and sought to use their offices to implement many progressive reforms in the conduct of elections and in the protection of individuals through such things as pure food and drug laws. Theodore Roosevelt, who gained the presidency after the assassination of William McKinley in 1901, successfully brought progressivism to the White House. He expanded the powers of the presidency to control giant corporations, protect the nation's natural resources, and bring a new vitality to electoral politics. The two presidents who followed him, William Howard Taft and Woodrow Wilson, shared some of Roosevelt's reformist tendencies and furthered the goals of progressivism, changing, in particular, the relationship between business and government in the decades leading up to World War I.

Chapter Review

How progressive was the "Progressive Era"? Include the work of individuals, government policy, and philosophy in your answer.

The Revolt of the Intellectuals

19.1 Explain the role of muckraking journalists and intellectuals in shaping a progressive agenda.

Summary

Responding to the rapid industrialization and urban growth of the late 1800s, progressives promoted new ways of ordering economic and political life. Utopian idealists offered visions of a transformed society. Academics like John Dewey challenged Social Darwinism and proposed new models of social and economic change rooted in rigorous intellectual analysis. Investigative journalism developed first in the nation's newspapers and then became a powerful force in magazines and books. Soon muckrakers like Ida Tarbell and Upton Sinclair played key roles in exposing and publicizing social and economic ills. Americans became conscious of corporate greed, the plight of the poor, and government corruption.

Review Question

1. **Comparison**
   Contrast the views of William Graham Sumner and John Dewey about social and economic inequality.
   What assumptions underlie each author's position?

The Transformation of the Cities

19.2 Analyze the changes in urban life that inspired progressive reforms and the impact of those reforms on cities.

Summary

Between 1870 and 1900, the urban population of the United States almost doubled. Immigration and a high birthrate combined to dramatically increase the size of America's largest cities. As cities grew, political machines gained control of city governments. Political machines such as Tammany Hall provided services to the urban poor, especially immigrants, in exchange for political loyalty. Secure in their power, the machine bosses used their positions to enrich themselves and their supporters. The destruction of the machines was a key political goal of the progressives. Progressives did not promote political revolution. Instead, they argued for reforms, including increased government openness, responsiveness, and efficiency, as well as an end to political corruption. The diversity of opinions among progressive educators reflected the diversity of opinion within the Progressive movement as a whole. Some

progressives like Jane Addams took direct action to improve the lives of the urban poor.

Review Questions

2. **Contextualization**
   Why did many poor and immigrant residents of American cities support political machines? How might such machines have looked from their point of view?

3. **Argument Development**
   In what ways was Jane Addams's Hull House typical of the Progressive movement? In what ways did it depart from other progressive initiatives?

Religious Responses to the Gilded Age

19.3 Explain the main currents of religiously based reform movements during the Progressive Era.

Summary

Protestant religious revival was an important element in the Progressive movement. The temperance movement embodied the connection between social reform and religious revival. The Woman's Christian Temperance Union took a leading role in the fight against alcohol. The WCTU reflected the importance of women in both progressive reform and religious revival. Proponents of the Social Gospel movement believed that reform was the duty of every Christian and that it was God's will that religious people work for social improvement. A new commitment to social issues was not limited to Protestants, and some American Catholic leaders were also active.

Review Question

4. **Contextualization**
   What does the prominence of the Woman's Christian Temperance Union tell us about the relationship between social reform and religious revival in the late 1800s?

Progressive Politics on the National Stage

19.4 Analyze the three "progressive presidents" and their administrations.

Summary

The assassination of William McKinley elevated Vice President Theodore Roosevelt, a progressive, to the presidency. Roosevelt's use of the Sherman Antitrust Act against Northern

Securities earned him a reputation as a "trustbuster." In addition to taking steps to limit corporate power and to increase the role of government in business oversight, Roosevelt was a champion of wilderness conservation. Roosevelt's record was not impressive, however, when it came to the concerns of African Americans. His decision not to run for a third term paved the way for the election of Roosevelt's handpicked successor, William Taft. Taft's tendency to favor the conservative wing of the Republican Party angered Roosevelt and led to a showdown between the two men in the election of 1912. Roosevelt's decision to run on a third-party ticket split the Republican vote and contributed to the election of Democrat Woodrow Wilson. Once in office, Wilson concentrated on reform of the banking system and on the expansion of the federal government's regulatory powers.

Review Questions

5. Comparison
Compare and contrast the policies of Roosevelt and Wilson. What aspects of the progressive agenda did each emphasize?

6. Causation
How did the progressive presidents discussed in this section transform the role of the presidency?

1. Preparing to Write: Support Your Assertion

Long Essay Question—Evaluate the extent to which there were different social and economic beliefs between Social Darwinists and Progressives.

As you will recall, when a prompt asks you to evaluate the extent of anything, imagine a continuum running from "Not at all" to "Totally." Then you are to pick a point along the continuum that reflects the historical reality. In the case of this prompt, there is more to discuss regarding the differences, and it is natural that your essay reflects that. Of course, you will have specific evidence of their respective visions, but your paragraph should not be merely a laundry list of evidence. After developing a thesis, write a paragraph of support that addresses either trusts or economic inequality. Choose evidence wisely, and then most of your paragraph should feature analysis, explaining to the reader how the two visions contrast.

2. Preparing to Write: Support Your Assertion

Short-Answer Question—Use Map 19-2 in Section 19.4 to answer parts (a), (b), and (c).

a. Briefly explain ONE specific historical cause that contributed to the emergence of the developments depicted in the map.

b. Briefly explain ONE effect of these developments depicted in the map.

c. Identify ONE other specific conservation policy from 1879 to 1917 and explain how it is consistent with the developments depicted in the map.

Section I: Multiple Choice Questions

Questions 6.1–6.3 refer to the following excerpt.

"Oh, yes; he can point to the rivers bridged, to the transcontinental railway connecting ocean with ocean, to wonderful churches and cathedrals; he can point to the most wonderful system of agriculture that ever brought joy to a hungry world; he can jostle his rags against the silken garments his toil has secured; he can walk shelterless and sad by the side of the home he has helped to build; he can wipe the sweat from his weary face, and reflect that the twenty thousand of American millionaires who own one billion five hundred million dollars, gathered from the toils and tears of sixty-four millions of American people, have it in their power to name their Governors and our legislators and representatives and Congressmen, — and they do name them, and they have named them for the last quarter of a century, and they have it in their power to fix the price of labor, to fix the price for every ton of coal."

—Mary E. Lease, *Speech to the National Council of Women of the United States*, 1891

6.1 What was the root cause of farmers' problems in the late 1800s?

a. New tenant farmers increasing competition

b. Competition from overseas

c. Overproduction of agricultural products

d. The increased movement of people from rural to urban areas

6.2 Which of the following was a target of agrarian discontent in the late 1800s?

a. Immigrants for competing with farmers for fertile land

b. The duty of the U.S. military to protect settlers from Indian attacks on the plains

c. Railroads for exploiting farmers' need for transport

d. The federal government for closing of the frontier to new settlement

6.3 Based on the excerpt, which part of the Populist platform would have likely been most important to Mary Lease?

a. Government ownership of transportation

b. Direct election of senators

c. Free and unlimited coinage of silver

d. A graduated income tax

Questions 6.4–6.6 refer to the following excerpt.

"But there are things which you have said to me which I do not like. They were not sweet like sugar, but bitter like gourds. You have said that you want to put us on a reservation, to build us houses and make us medicine lodges. I do not want them. I was born under the prairie, where the wind blew free and there was nothing to break the light of the sun. I was born where there were no enclosures and everything drew a free breath. I want to die there and not within walls … I live like my fathers before me and like them I lived happily.

When I was in Washington the Great Father told me that all the Comanche land was ours and that no one should hinder us in living upon it. So, why do you ask us to leave the rivers and the sun and the wind and live in houses? Do not ask us to give up the buffalo for the sheep. The young men have heard talk of this, and it has made them sad and angry. Do not speak of it more."

—Paruasemena (Ten Bears), Speech at Medicine Lodge Creek Treaty Meeting, 1867

6.4 One difference in interpretation between the U.S. government representatives and the Comanches regarding the Medicine Lodge Treaty was the Comanche belief that they would

a. become farmers on the reservation while occasionally hunting buffalo

b. be forced to adopt the culture of European Americans by sending their children to boarding schools

c. have no more disagreements with European Americans over land issues, since the Indian territory would be their property

d. still hunt across the Great Plains as they had before the treaty

6.5 The Comanches eventually surrendered and moved onto reservations primarily as a result of

a. U.S. military campaigns

b. their desire to hunt buffalo there

c. their inability to adapt to American culture

d. U.S. government promises that the Comanches would retain tribal sovereignty

6.6 In response to calls to reform government policy toward American Indians, Congress passed legislation that

a. forced Indians to begin assimilating into white society

b. reinstated treaties that had been violated by the U.S. government

c. provided restitution to tribes for mistreatment by the military

d. returned large tracts of Indian land to the individual tribes

Questions 6.7–6.8 refer to the following excerpt.

"The railroad network, in turn, had grown swiftly primarily because of the near desperate requirements for efficient transportation created by the movement of population westward after 1815. Except for the Atlantic seaboard between Boston and Washington, the construction of the American railroads was stimulated almost wholly by the demand for better transportation to move crops, to bring farmers supplies, and to open up new territories to commercial agriculture.

By greatly expanding the scope of the agrarian economy, the railroads quickened the growth of the older commercial centers, such as New York, Philadelphia, Cincinnati, Cleveland, and St. Louis, and helped create new cities like Chicago, Indianapolis, Atlanta, Kansas City, Dallas, and the Twin Cities. This rapid urban expansion intensified the demand for the products of the older consumer goods industries—particularly those which processed the crops of the farmer and planter into food, stimulants, and clothing.

At the same time, railroad construction developed the first large market in this country for producers' goods. ... More than this, the railroad, with their huge capital outlay, their fixed operating costs, the large size of their labor and management force, and the technical complexity of their operations, pioneered in the new ways of oligopolistic competition and large-scale, professionalized, bureaucratized management."

—**Alfred D. Chandler, Jr., "The Beginnings of 'Big Business' in American Industry," Business History Review, Volume 33, Issue 1 April 1959, 1–31, pp. 10–11**

6.7 Which of the following made it possible for construction of the nation's railroad network?

　　a. Loans from European and Asian banks and investors

　　b. Deep discounts for supplies provided by trusts

　　c. Labor supplied by the U.S. military

　　d. Government subsidies and land grants to finance construction

6.8 The existence of the "large market in this country for producers' goods," eventually led to the rise of

　　a. municipal machine politics

　　b. the standard of living for Americans

　　c. political conflict about tariff and currency issues

　　d. the disappearance of the middle class

Questions 6.9–6.11 refer to the following cartoon.

THROWING DOWN THE LADDER BY WHICH THEY ROSE.

Cartoon by Thomas Nast, 1870

6.9 The cartoonist is criticizing

　　a. Chinese immigrants for trying to come to the United States

　　b. efforts to Americanize immigrants

　　c. nativists whose people were once excluded themselves

　　d. restrictive U.S. immigration policies

6.10 Which of the following was a great source of assistance for immigrants in large cities?

　　a. Political machines

　　b. American Protective Association

　　c. Social Darwinists

　　d. Temperance associations

6.11 Which of the following was a major factor in the increased numbers of immigrants in the second half of 1800s?

　　a. America's widespread toleration of immigrants

　　b. New Congressional legislation lifting immigration restrictions

　　c. Laws in various countries that outlawed unpopular political parties

　　d. A desire to escape poverty

Section II: Short-Answer Questions

6.12 Answer (a), (b), and (c).

    a. Briefly explain ONE important similarity between the railroads built in the East during the first half of the 1800s and in the West during the second half of the 1800s.

    b. Briefly explain ONE important difference between the railroads built in the East during the first half of the 1800s and in the West during the second half of the 1800s.

    c. Briefly explain ONE factor that accounts for the difference that you indicated in (b).

Question 6.13 refers to the following cartoon.

Cartoon, 1873

6.13 Using the image, answer parts (a), (b), and (c).

    a. Briefly describe ONE point of view about corporate power expressed in the image.

    b. Briefly explain ONE specific historical development that led to the point of view expressed in this image.

    c. Briefly explain ONE way in which the point of view expressed in the image was challenged in the period 1865 to 1900.

Section III: Long Essay Questions

Directions: Answer Question 6.14 **or** 6.15. (Suggested writing time: 40 minutes) In your response you should do the following.

- Respond to the prompt with a historically defensible thesis or claim that establishes a line of reasoning.

- Describe a broader historical context relevant to the prompt.

- Support an argument in response to the prompt using specific and relevant examples of evidence.

- Use historical reasoning (e.g., comparison, causation, continuity or change over time) to frame or structure an argument that addresses the prompt.

- Use evidence to corroborate, qualify, or modify an argument that addresses the prompt.

6.14 Explain the effects of trusts on the U.S. economy from 1865 to 1914.

6.15 Evaluate the extent to which there were differing goals between the Social Gospel movement of the late-1800s and the reform movements from the mid-1800s.

Section IV:

Read on MyHistoryLab

Document-Based Question: Uses of Land in the West

Part 7
War, Prosperity, and Depression 1890–1945

AP® KEY CONCEPTS

Key Concept 7.1

Growth expanded opportunity, while economic instability led to new efforts to reform U.S. society and its economic system.

Key Concept 7.2

Innovations in communications and technology contributed to the growth of mass culture while significant changes occurred in internal and international migration patterns.

Key Concept 7.3

Participation in a series of global conflicts propelled the United States into a position of international power while renewing domestic debates over the nation's proper role in the world.

PART OUTLINE

Chapter 20

Foreign Policy and War in a Progressive Era 1890–1919

The British luxury liner *Lusitania*, shown here in New York Harbor during its maiden voyage, was sunk by a German submarine with the loss of over 1,100 lives in May 1915, an event that did much to galvanize American public opinion against Germany and bring the United States into World War I.

Chapter Objective

Demonstrate an understanding of the ways in which the United States engaged with the world and the impact of that engagement on the people of the United States.

 ## Learning Objectives

Continuing Expansion
20.1 Explain continued U.S. expansion, particularly U.S. acquisition of what would much later be the forty-ninth and fiftieth states.

The Splendid Little War … with Spain—Cuba, Puerto Rico, and the Philippines, 1898
20.2 Analyze the causes and consequences of the U.S. war with Spain in 1898.

Foreign Policy, Foreign Adventures, 1900–1914
20.3 Explain developments in U.S. policy in Panama, Asia, and Mexico between the war with Spain and World War I.

The United States and the Great War
20.4 Analyze the causes and consequences of U.S. involvement in World War I.

In 1914, Europe went to war. President Woodrow Wilson was determined to stay out of the conflict and campaigned for reelection in 1916 with the slogan, "He kept us out of war." Although Wilson would not continue to keep the nation out of the European war, the man he defeated in the 1912 presidential election, former president Theodore Roosevelt, was ready to go to war much sooner than Wilson. As president, Roosevelt liked to summarize his foreign policy with the proverb, "Speak softly and carry a big stick." When Europe began what was then called the Great War, the former president was speaking less and less softly and arguing that the United States should prepare for war and that Wilson's neutrality was a sign of personal and national weakness.

Roosevelt talked of an activist approach to foreign policy as he did with everything else in his presidency, but surprisingly, other than his very active involvement in the acquisition of the Panama Canal Zone, Roosevelt was cautious in international relations. When he became president in 1901, the United States had already acquired Alaska, Hawaii, and other islands in the Pacific. Many Americans wanted more land, or at least greater influence around the world. In fact, Roosevelt reduced U.S. involvement in the Philippines, negotiated an end to war between Russia and Japan, brokered an agreement to soften Japan's sense of insult at California's anti-Japanese measures, and sought successfully to keep peace with the world. Many of Roosevelt's strongest political supporters, progressive senators like Robert La Follette and reformers like Jane Addams, adamantly opposed U.S. endeavors abroad and U.S. involvement in World War I. Nevertheless, although foreign policy is always shaped by many people and many forces, presidents Roosevelt and Wilson, as well as Roosevelt's predecessor McKinley, were certainly the dominant figures in U.S. international relations between 1898 and 1920, though each approached the topic quite differently. Their story, and the world they and so many others shaped, is the subject of this chapter.

Continuing Expansion

20.1 **Explain continued U.S. expansion, particularly U.S. acquisition of what would much later be the forty-ninth and fiftieth states.**

The geographical expansion of the United States that had continued from the time it declared independence persisted throughout the Progressive Era, but after 1901, the focus was more on influence and less on the acquisition of new territory. Admiral Alfred Thayer Mahan of the U.S. Navy persuasively laid the foundation for continued expansion in his book, *The Influence of Sea Power upon History*, published in 1890. Few books were ever as influential in the development of U.S. foreign policy. Mahan argued that all great nations in history had great navies that could control the world's oceans and, specifically, that the U.S. Navy needed to be large enough to be a significant player in the Pacific. He worried that the U.S. Navy was too small and that the lack of U.S. control of Pacific islands limited the nation's reach. The popularity of his book accelerated developments already under way, and within a decade, the U.S. Navy had been expanded to the third largest in the world while the United States had annexed Hawaii and Puerto Rico in 1898 and had assumed control of Samoa, the Philippine Islands, and Cuba.

Not surprisingly, some have called the late 1800s the age of **U.S. imperialism**. Whether that term correctly describes U.S. expansion in this era continues to be debated. Certainly, thinking in the United States was influenced by the ways British, French, and German imperialists were seeking new colonies in Africa and the Middle East. Many Americans did not want their country to be left behind. Some people in the United States agreed with those Europeans who insisted that the white race was destined to rule the world's people. Immigrants or the children of immigrants sometimes wanted the United States to intervene in their old homelands to protect the rights of compatriots. Even so, a surprisingly diverse array of Americans did not want their country involved in anything beyond its borders. Expansion beyond North America was never without controversy, even as the United States became involved around the globe.

20.1
20.2
20.3
20.4

Significant Dates

1890	U.S. Navy Admiral Alfred Thayer Mahan publishes *The Influence of Sea Power upon History*
1893	United States supports overthrow of Hawaiian government, but Cleveland administration blocks U.S. annexation of the islands
1898	Hawaii is annexed by United States
	U.S. war with Spain leads to American control of Cuba, Puerto Rico, and Philippine Islands
1904	U.S. support for revolution in Panama is followed by Panama Canal Treaty
1907–1908	Gentlemen's Agreement with Japan limiting Japanese immigration to United States
1912	Alaska—acquired from Russia in 1867—is granted territorial status
1914–1917	U.S. intervention in Mexico
1914	World War I (known then as the Great War) begins in Europe
1915	British liner *Lusitania* is sunk with loss of American lives
1917	United States enters World War I on side of Britain and France
1918	World War I ends
1919	Treaty of Versailles is negotiated, including League of Nations, then rejected by U.S. Senate

U.S. imperialism

A term used to describe the U.S. acquisition of Hawaii, Puerto Rico, and the Philippine Islands in 1898.

Alaska

Long before Mahan argued for greater U.S. control of the oceans, the United States assumed ownership of the huge Russian territory known as Russian America, or Alaska. In the 1740s, Vitus Bering, a Danish captain serving the Russian navy, explored the Arctic Oceans between Asia and North America. Soon thereafter, Russia had joined Britain, France, and Spain in claiming a part of North America. A Russian governor moved to Sitka, Alaska, in 1799 to administer Russian communities that dotted the coast of what is today Alaska, Canada, Washington, Oregon, and northern California. Control and management of the vast Russian territory was vested in the private Russian American Company. Russians fished and traded in sea otter skins, providing support for the colony and modest returns to Russia itself.

The value of Alaska to the Russian company or government was never great. Tensions with native residents ran deep. Russians exploited Native Alaskans while Western diseases took a heavy toll of the native population. In response, Native Alaskans massacred Russian communities at Sitka and Nulato. By 1860, the government was unhappy with the Russian American Company and worried about defending the long Alaskan coast from the British Navy.

American settlers in Washington Territory were learning about the rich fishing, whaling, and fur trapping that was possible in Alaska. Secretary of State Seward envisioned its value and coordinated negotiations to purchase it from Russia. The negotiators agreed on a price of $7.2 million, and on October 18, 1867, the Russian flag was hauled down at Sitka and the Stars and Stripes rose in its place. Congress balked at appropriating the funds for the purchase and critics called the whole transfer "Seward's Folly," but the nation had gained valuable new territory. Fishing, mining, the fur trade, and indeed the sale of ice to Californians made Alaska a good investment. However, Aleuts, Sitkas, Kolosh, and other Alaskan tribes found that they had only substituted one overlord for another. U.S. troops, miners, and settlers fought with Alaskan tribes as they had with native peoples farther south.

Having purchased Alaska, the U.S. government was slow to do much with it. Only in 1884 did Congress create any official government for what they called the District of Alaska. Soon thereafter, gold was discovered, and the Klondike Gold Rush of the late 1880s expanded the American population of Alaska as did 1898 legislation that extended the provisions of the 1862 Homestead Act to Alaska. Finally, in 1912, President Taft signed legislation giving Alaska full territorial status, and the elected legislature first met at Juneau the following year.

Hawaii

Although the United States was already a major influence in Hawaii long before Mahan argued for a wider Pacific influence for the nation, it was in Mahan's time that the United States annexed Hawaii. While the American Revolution was being fought, a British explorer, James Cook, landed on a chain of islands that he named the Sandwich Islands, which came to be known as Hawaii. Before Cook's arrival in 1778, there had been no recorded contact between the native Hawaiians and Europeans. The Polynesian people whom Cook encountered were governed by a stable if loose feudal monarchy. Unfortunately, like other native peoples, they had no immunity to Western diseases, and the contact initiated by Cook took a terrible toll.

Hawaii's strategic location halfway between California and Japan and its harbors that were perfect for American whaling vessels greatly interested American and European merchants and U.S. Navy officers. By the early 1800s, Hawaiian harbors were filled with U.S. Navy ships and private whaling vessels, and Americans mixed with Hawaiians on a regular basis. In 1820, a group of New England missionaries and three American-educated Hawaiians arrived to convert Hawaiians to Christianity and interest them in American culture.

U.S. control of California with its large Pacific harbors in 1848 and the completion of the Transcontinental Railroad in 1869 expanded U.S. commercial and military interest in

ArtPix / Alamy Stock Photo

Hawaii's Queen Liliuokalani was overthrown in an uprising led by American planters. A century later, the U.S. government apologized to native Hawaiians for this illegal act.

the kingdom of Hawaii. Trans-Pacific steamship lines that began at the Pacific docks where the railroad ended sought fueling stations on their way to Asia, and Hawaii's Pearl Harbor was the perfect stopping place. At the same time, American-owned sugar plantations had become a major economic force in Hawaii. Native Hawaiians, who were now a minority within their own country and controlled perhaps 15 percent of the land and 2 percent of the capital, did not want further U.S. influence in their country, but the Hawaiian government agreed that it would not grant special trading rights or naval bases to any other country in return for a promise that Hawaii could ship a steady supply of sugar duty-free to the United States. Hawaii's King Kalakaua visited the United States in 1874 to formalize the agreement.

By the 1880s, American economic power in Hawaii was overwhelming, but the islands remained independent. When King Kalakaua died, his sister, Queen Liliuokalani, succeeded him. She sought to regain "Hawaii for the Hawaiians" and reduce the economic and political power of the United States. Most of the American planters on the island did not like the queen's moves and formed the Annexation Club. In 1893, the annexation group overthrew her and seized power. The U.S. minister in Hawaii, John L. Stevens, cabled Washington, "The Hawaiian pear is now fully ripe and this is the golden hour for the United States to pluck it." The U.S. Navy landed sailors "to preserve order," thus securing the queen's overthrow. Hawaii would have been annexed to the United States if the recently inaugurated Democratic president Grover Cleveland had not sensed that there was something unseemly about the whole affair and ended negotiations with the rebels. Cleveland announced his firm opposition to annexation.

Under Cleveland, the United States might have supported Liliuokalani's restoration had she not insisted that she would execute all of the rebels. That action was too much for Cleveland, and his administration ignored Hawaii, which continued as an independent nation under the control of the American planters who had overthrown the queen's government.

20.1

20.2

20.3

20.4

Map 20-1 The United States in the World, 1900.

By 1900, the United States had claimed many islands in the South Pacific and had strong involvement with other Pacific islands as well as Latin American countries.

When William McKinley was elected president in 1896, he demonstrated none of Cleveland's resistance to U.S. acquisition of Hawaii as the next step in the nation's "Manifest Destiny." McKinley said, "We need Hawaii as much … as in its day we needed California." In June 1897, McKinley proposed a treaty of annexation, to which the planter government agreed. McKinley realized that anti-imperialists in the Senate could block the two-thirds vote required to approve the treaty, so the president used the same strategy that John Tyler had used half a century earlier for Texas. He asked both houses of Congress to annex the territory by joint resolution, which required only a majority vote. By June 1898, to the protests of native Hawaiians and the cheers of the planters, Hawaii became a permanent territory of the United States. In that same year, the United States annexed tiny Midway and Wake islands and, a year later, agreed to divide Samoa with Germany. Across the Pacific, Mahan's dream of stations for the growing navy was a reality (see Map 20-1, p. 588).

20.1 Quick Review

How did worry about other nations, as well as domestic events and developments in the United States, contribute to the nation's interest in acquiring Alaska and Hawaii as new territories?

The Splendid Little War … with Spain—Cuba, Puerto Rico, and the Philippines, 1898

20.2   Analyze the causes and consequences of the U.S. war with Spain in 1898.

The U.S. war with Spain in 1898 (often called the Spanish-American War) followed decades of U.S. expansionism—much of it expansion into territory that had previously been part of Spain's once-vast empire in the Americas. Beginning with Columbus, Spain had exercised political control of all of Latin America, except for Brazil, for a long time, and it had ruled the Philippine Islands for almost as long. As a result of successful independence movements, all that was left of the Spanish empire in the 1890s was the Philippines and a collection of Caribbean islands. Many in Spain wanted to retain those outposts for their own value and as symbols of Spain's past glory. Nevertheless, as a result of a short war—which future secretary of state John Hay called "a splendid little war"—Spain lost the last of its holdings. The United States gained long-term influence in both Cuba and the Philippine Islands, and made Puerto Rico a permanent U.S. territory.

Tensions in Cuba

The U.S. war with Spain started in Cuba. The United States had long been interested in Cuba. Well before the Civil War, Southern senators had suggested that the United States ought to acquire Cuba as a slave state to offset the growing number of Northern free states. In 1854, the American ambassadors to Europe's leading powers issued the so-called Ostend Manifesto, demanding that Spain sell Cuba to the United States, but it did not happen. After the U.S. Civil War, Cuba was no longer of value as a slave state, but U.S. interest in the island never disappeared, and American investors were active there. By the 1890s, almost 90 percent of Cuban exports came to the United States, and American investors owned much of the best farmland on the island.

Cubans wanted to throw off Spanish rule and win independence. An 1890 agreement with Spain had reduced the tariff on sugar, launching a boom in the Cuban economy, but a new U.S. tariff in 1894, strongly influenced by lobbying from the Sugar Trust in the United States, significantly raised the tariff on imported sugar. The increased cost of Cuban sugar in the United States reduced the sales of Cuban sugar and devastated the Cuban economy. Cuban revolutionaries led by José Martí, who had been living in exile in New York City, saw the resulting Cuban depression as the ideal moment to gain independence. Martí returned to Cuba in 1895, and his revolutionary forces began burning cane fields, killing Spanish soldiers, and making Spanish rule more costly. Spanish authorities responded by creating concentration camps where they held Cubans in controlled enclaves that separated them from the rebels. Many in these camps suffered from malnutrition and disease.

When William McKinley was inaugurated as U.S. president in 1897, he made it clear that he wanted Spain out of Cuba. American public opinion was on the side of the rebels. New York newspaper editors William Randolph Hearst and Joseph Pulitzer engaged in what was called "yellow journalism" (named for a popular cartoon character of the day known as the "Yellow Kid"), publishing sensationalized accounts of Spanish atrocities in Cuba. They sent well-known artists like Frederic Remington, and writers like Richard Harding Davis, to Cuba to report on Spanish actions to increase circulation for their publications.

While many Americans saw the Cuban revolution of the 1890s as a simple question of good Cubans against bad Spaniards, American business leaders with investments in Cuba also worried that a revolutionary victory would threaten their investments. Martí, while grateful for American support, worried about long-term American influence, insisting that "[t]o change masters is not to be free."

The Spanish government in Madrid did not want a war with the United States, and they worried—correctly, it would turn out—that the government, and indeed the Spanish monarchy, could not survive the overthrow of the last bastion of Spain's empire in the Americas.

A large number of the troops who fought in Cuba, including those commanded by Theodore Roosevelt in his assault on San Juan Hill, were African American soldiers like these from the Ninth Cavalry.

As U.S. public opinion became more belligerent, so did public opinion in Spain. Spanish people rallied to their flag, and in one town a mob attacked the U.S. consulate.

War in Cuba, Puerto Rico, and the Philippine Islands

In February 1898, over two hundred American sailors were killed when the battleship USS *Maine* blew up in Havana Harbor. The explosion may well have been the result of a bad boiler; however, Americans blamed Spain, and "Remember the *Maine*" became a rallying cry. McKinley managed to get Congress to declare war without ever asking for it.

The U.S. invasion of Cuba was not well managed. American troops arrived wearing wool uniforms—hardly the right material for a hot Caribbean summer. Even though Theodore Roosevelt gained fame for leading mostly African American troops (shown as white in subsequent pictures) in a rapid assault on San Juan Hill, the battles in Cuba were generally slow and difficult. In four months of fighting, 345 Americans were killed in action while 5,000 died from disease.

Since the United States was at war with Spain, McKinley also approved the orders that had been issued by Assistant Secretary of the Navy Roosevelt (issued just before he resigned that position to fight in Cuba) to Admiral George Dewey to sail the U.S. fleet to the Spanish-owned Philippine Islands. The six warships under Dewey's command quickly sank the Spanish fleet at the Battle of Manila Bay on May 1, 1898, giving the United States control of a Pacific territory much larger than Cuba. The American Pacific fleet also captured the Spanish garrison on Guam Island and took control of the uninhabited atoll of Wake Island.

Finally, the United States decided to take the last Spanish outpost in the Caribbean, Puerto Rico. Once control of Cuba seemed assured in July 1898, McKinley ordered General Nelson A. Miles to Puerto Rico. He wanted to be sure the troops arrived before peace talks began with Spain. In 1898, some Puerto Ricans welcomed the U.S. overthrow of Spanish authority, and the indigenous independence movement in Puerto Rico was not as strong as that in Cuba.

By August 1898, Spain was ready to ask for peace. Much to McKinley's displeasure, the congressional resolution authorizing the war had included the Teller Amendment, named for Senator Henry Teller of Colorado, which said the United States could not permanently annex Cuba. If the United States could not annex Cuba, Puerto Rico seemed like the next best permanent U.S. territory in the Caribbean. In the case of the Philippines, which had not been an initial focus of the war, McKinley felt that he could "see but one plain path of duty—the acceptance of the archipelago." In the Treaty of Paris of December 1898, Spain ceded control of Cuba, Puerto Rico, and the Philippines to the United States for a payment of $20 million. Afterward, the United States promised eventual independence for Cuba. Suddenly, the United States was a world power, joining the nations of Europe with its own far-flung empire. What to do with that empire would be a subject of considerable debate in the future.

The Anti-Imperialists

When the U.S. war with Spain ended, that debate about empire began in earnest in the United States. In spite of the Teller Amendment, President McKinley did everything possible to maximize U.S. involvement in Cuba, including ensuring that the U.S. Navy would have a perpetual base at Guantanamo Bay. The United States was going to keep Puerto Rico, but what about the distant Philippines? The war had begun and ended in the Caribbean over issues of Spanish control of Cuba; however, as part of the war, the United States also found itself in control of a chain of seven thousand islands with seven million people living thousands of miles away from the United States.

President McKinley told a group of visiting Episcopal clergy that he had lost sleep and had prayed long and hard about what to do with the islands and that the answer had come to him: "[T]here was nothing left for us to do but to take them all, and to educate the Filipinos, and uplift and civilize and Christianize them." The United States could not give them back to Spain or another country and, he insisted, "they were unfit for self-government."

Nearly all Filipinos were already Christian since Catholic Spain had ruled the islands for nearly four hundred years, but McKinley meant Protestant Christianity. The Constitution might prohibit the government's direct involvement with the religious beliefs of the Filipinos, but allowing missionaries was easy.

A greater difficulty with the president's plan was the fact that many Filipinos did not want to be annexed by the United States. A revolt against Spain had been under way long before Commodore Dewey sank the Spanish fleet in Manila Bay. In addition, Dewey had encouraged Emilio Aguinaldo, leader of the Filipino insurrection, to establish an interim government for the islands. Aguinaldo expected U.S. recognition of Philippine independence, and even after it became clear that this was not President McKinley's plan, Aguinaldo hoped for either the defeat of McKinley's treaty in the Senate or a victory in the 1900 presidential elections by William Jennings Bryan, who strongly opposed annexation of the Philippines. When the Senate ratified the treaty with Spain and Bryan lost the election, Aguinaldo led a revolt against the United States. What the U.S. government called the "Philippine Insurrection," Aguinaldo called a war for independence.

Between 1898 and 1902, and beyond, the U.S. Army engaged in a brutal battle with Filipino insurgents. Many more American soldiers were killed in the postwar insurgency in the Philippine Islands than were killed in the war with Spain. Thousands of Filipinos were killed—perhaps 20,000 in combat and 200,000 from war-related causes—and many more left homeless.

Within the United States, broad-based opposition to the war in the Philippines was organized by the Anti-Imperialist League, founded in Boston in June 1898. The league included unlikely allies. Andrew Carnegie offered to buy the islands from the United States to secure their independence and wrote to one member of McKinley's cabinet, "You seem to have finished your work of civilizing the Filipinos; it is thought that about 8,000 of them have been completely civilized and sent to Heaven; I hope you like it." Charles Francis Adams (descendant of two presidents), former abolitionist Thomas Wentworth Higginson, reformers including Jane Addams and Henry Demarest Lloyd, labor leaders including Samuel Gompers, rival Democrats William Jennings Bryan and Grover Cleveland, and university presidents like Harvard's Charles W. Eliot and Stanford's David Starr Jordan all opposed the annexation.

The nation's best-known authors, Mark Twain and William Dean Howells, turned biting humor on McKinley's efforts. Twain said that the U.S. efforts in the Philippines meant that the United States had become "yet another Civilized Power, with its banner of the Prince of Peace in one hand and its loot-basket and its butcher-knife in the other." Booker T. Washington said, "Until our nation has settled the Indian and the Negro problems, I do not think we have a right to assume more social problems."

Most anti-imperialists insisted that the Constitution did not allow for the United States to acquire any territories that it did not plan to eventually admit as states and that **"the Constitution follows the flag"**—meaning all of the civil and political rights guaranteed in the Constitution also applied to other people under U.S. control. The advocates of territorial

Library of Congress Prints and Photographs Division [LC-DIG-ds-00353]

After liberating the Philippine Islands from Spain, the United States quickly found itself at war with the Filipino people who wanted independence and, as this picture shows, took many of the people of the island prisoner.

"the Constitution follows the flag"

An argument that the rights of U.S. citizens should be extended to any people living in a territory conquered by the United States.

expansion did not agree, and in May 1901, the U.S. Supreme Court in a series of 5–4 decisions in the Insular Cases declared that the Philippines and Puerto Rico were territories, not future states, and that therefore those residing there were "subjects," not "citizens." It was a bitter moment for the anti-imperialists.

While Roosevelt had been one of the staunchest advocates of going to war in 1898 and of keeping control of the Philippine Islands after the war, by the time he became president in 1901, the U.S. effort was increasingly unpopular and he had other priorities. In 1901, the army captured Aguinaldo. William Howard Taft, who had been governor general of the Philippines, was welcomed home, and a truce settled on the islands, though U.S. troops remained until the Japanese invasion at the start of World War II. U.S. attention turned elsewhere.

> **20.2** Quick Review
>
> Was the U.S. war with Spain a triumph for the United States?

Foreign Policy, Foreign Adventures, 1900–1914

20.3 Explain developments in U.S. policy in Panama, Asia, and Mexico between the U.S. war with Spain and World War I.

When Theodore Roosevelt became president in September 1901, he inherited two major foreign policy issues from McKinley—the ongoing war in the Philippines, which he quickly put behind him, and the question of a Central American canal connecting the Atlantic and Pacific Oceans, which he embraced with Rooseveltian enthusiasm. Roosevelt considered the Central American canal one of his proudest achievements.

A Canal in Panama

Ever since the California Gold Rush of 1848, there had been talk of building a canal across Central America that would allow shorter travel by ship from the Atlantic to the Pacific Oceans, but the hurdles were significant. The narrow point of land between North and South America was hot and damp, and mosquito-borne diseases made working there a death sentence. The land was also mountainous, and for any canal to be built, engineers had to design a series of locks to raise and lower ships. Nevertheless, in 1850, the United States and Britain negotiated the Clayton-Bulwer Treaty, stating that any canal would be a joint venture though neither controlled the territory. Fifty years later, few in the United States still wanted a joint venture with Britain, and in November 1901, Secretary of State John Hay and the British ambassador to the United States, Lord Pauncefote, concluded a treaty that gave the United States the exclusive right to build an interocean waterway in Central America. McKinley had created an Isthmian Canal Commission that recommended building a canal in Nicaragua, but Roosevelt preferred a shorter route through Panama.

The canal was not the first time Roosevelt involved the United States in Latin America. In 1902, shortly after he came to office, the government of Venezuela held back on debt payments to European banks. Britain, Italy, and Germany sent ships to Venezuela, but Roosevelt, citing the Monroe Doctrine, pressured them to withdraw. A year later when the Dominican Republic seemed set to follow the same route as Venezuela, Roosevelt sent U.S. forces to the island and took control of its customs operation, dividing the revenue between the country and the European creditors, an involvement in the finances of the Dominican Republic that lasted until 1941. Then in 1904, he formalized U.S. action in the

Dominican Republic, announcing the "**Roosevelt Corollary**" to the Monroe Doctrine, stating that the United States had a right to intervene in any nation in the Americas that could not manage its own affairs.

Roosevelt's greatest interest in Latin America, however, remained constant. He wanted a canal, and he wanted it built in the territory of Panama, which then belonged to Colombia. Even though the government of Colombia did not agree, many in the province of Panama saw the situation differently. Panama was a frontier province of Colombia, distant enough that it could take fifteen days for messages from Panama City to reach the national government in Bogotá. Many in Panama were ready to declare independence. There is no evidence that Roosevelt actively urged a revolution, but he certainly did nothing to discourage one either. In November 1903, when Panama revolted against Colombian rule, Roosevelt sent orders to U.S. Navy ships standing by on both the Pacific and Atlantic coasts of Panama to "prevent landing of any armed force with hostile intent, either government or insurgent." Since the insurgents were already in Panama and the only forces that wanted to land were from the Colombian government, the impact of the order was clear. Describing the independence movement in Panama, Roosevelt told the U.S. Congress that the people of Panama had risen up against Colombia, "literally as one man." Senator Edward Carmack retorted, "Yes, and the one man was Roosevelt."

Once Panama declared independence, the United States quickly—with "indecent haste," one critic said—recognized the independent Panamanian government and then proposed the canal to them. Three months later in February 1904, both nations ratified a treaty giving the United States the right to a canal zone ten miles wide, which "the United States would possess … [as] if it were the sovereign of the territory," while the new government in Panama City got the $10 million that had originally been offered to Colombia. Roosevelt got the route he wanted, if not the goodwill of Latin America.

Late in his term, Roosevelt visited Panama. Ever the energetic enthusiast, he climbed up to the driver's seat of the biggest steam shovel digging the canal, spoke with some of the nineteen thousand West Indian laborers who were doing the backbreaking work (and who died at an astounding rate—eighty-five just in the month of the president's visit), met

Roosevelt Corollary

President Theodore Roosevelt's policy asserting U.S. authority to intervene in the affairs of Latin American nations; an expansion of the Monroe Doctrine.

20.1

20.2

20.3

20.4

Glasshouse Images/Alamy Stock Photo

Digging the Panama Canal was a massive engineering project that included the use of miles of temporary rail lines, steam shovels, as well as hand tools and the labor of thousands of mostly West Indian workers who did the actual work of building the canal.

20.1

20.2

20.3

20.4

with authorities of the new government, and envisioned ships passing through the canal and towns rising on the banks of what was still, at that point, a muck-filled ditch. The canal did not open until 1914, long after Roosevelt had left office. With or without Roosevelt, the United States would most likely have built a canal between the oceans at some point. Nevertheless, the route and the speed were a result of Roosevelt's efforts.

The United States, Russia, Japan, and China

Across the world, Russia had long been expanding its territory. Russian Cossacks had asserted control of Asian Siberia for Russia in the 1600s and then looked west to North America and south in Asia. All Russian expansion came to an abrupt halt in early 1904, however. Japan, which had emerged as a modern military and diplomatic power, was determined to stop Russia from acquiring influence in Manchuria and Korea. The Japanese fleet under Admiral Heihachiro Togo attacked and destroyed a Russian fleet anchored at Port Arthur. To America, the war seemed far away, and the United States quickly declared neutrality. A year later in May 1905, another Russian fleet was destroyed. The Japanese navy sank twenty-two Russian ships, killed some four thousand Russian sailors, and captured several more ships along with the Russian commander Admiral Rozhdestvenski. Nevertheless, no peace treaty emerged, and Japanese resources were spent.

The Japanese government sent a secret message to Roosevelt, asking if he would "directly and entirely of his own motion and initiative ... invite the two belligerents to come together." Roosevelt loved the idea of playing mediator and proposed arbitration to the tsar. Russia agreed, and the announcement of the peace conference won Roosevelt worldwide praise.

Once Roosevelt got representatives of both countries to Portsmouth, New Hampshire, in August 1905, they argued about borders, money, and a postwar plan. But eventually, Roosevelt's arm-twisting led to a peace agreement. The war ended, and Roosevelt was praised by the Russian tsar and the Japanese emperor. A year later, Roosevelt was rewarded with the Nobel Peace Prize.

While the czarist government was grateful for Roosevelt's role in ending the war, Russian immigrants to the United States had their own grievances against the tsar's rule. When hundreds of Russian Jews were killed in pogroms between 1903 and 1906, Jewish immigrants in the United States pressured the U.S. government to do something about the situation, and President Roosevelt and Secretary of State John Hay issued a formal protest. The Russian ambassador responded to the protest saying that it was "unbecoming for Americans to criticize" Russia in light of American lynching of African Americans and the bad treatment of Chinese immigrants.

Japan, too, though appreciative of Roosevelt's efforts to mediate with Russia, was not pleased by San Francisco's segregation of Japanese students. California was the port of entry for immigrants from Japan and China. It was also the place where anti-Asian feelings ran strongest. In October 1906, in the aftermath of the city's great earthquake, as they reorganized and reopened the city's schools, the San Francisco School Board adopted a policy of racial segregation for Chinese, Korean, and Japanese children. The government of China protested but was too weak to do more. In Japan, however, anger at the insult led to calls for war. Roosevelt tried to convince Californians to rescind the segregation order while encouraging the government of Japan to ignore the insult, but failed at doing both. However, in 1907 and 1908, he successfully negotiated the **Gentlemen's Agreement** by which the United States agreed not to pass any formal limit on Japanese immigration and the Japanese government agreed to limit the emigration of laborers to the United States. For Japan, it was important not to face anything as insulting as the Chinese Exclusion Act of 1882 had been. For Californians, Roosevelt had accomplished the goal of establishing a limit on Japanese immigration. At the same time, Roosevelt used Japan's threat of war to ask Congress to appropriate funds to expand the U.S. Navy and then sent the **Great White Fleet**—sixteen battleships painted gleaming white rather than navy gray—around the world with a dramatic stop at Tokyo Bay. The 1908 tensions with Japan had receded, though they were hardly ended.

Gentlemen's Agreement

A diplomatic agreement in 1907 between Japan and the United States curtailing, but not abolishing, Japanese immigration.

Great White Fleet

A U.S. Navy fleet sent around the world from December 1907 to February 1909 by President Theodore Roosevelt to show American strength and to promote goodwill.

In China, anger was also rising against the United States. The Society of Righteous and Harmonious Fists (called Boxers by foreigners), a secret society consisting of local farmers, peasants, and other victims of disastrous floods and opium addiction, led the Boxer Rebellion in 1901, attacking all foreigners, including American businessmen and missionaries, whom they blamed for their plight. Although the Boxer Rebellion was quickly quashed by an international force, Chinese citizens, carrying anti-American posters and singing anti-American songs, organized a massive boycott of U.S. goods in 1905.

Woodrow Wilson's Asian Policy

While he was president, Theodore Roosevelt insisted that the long-standing Open Door Policy allowing the United States and Britain free trade with China be continued in spite of Japan's desire to dominate all Asian markets. President Taft had less lofty goals for America's role in the world, and though he was wary of political ties, he strongly encouraged American investment wherever there was an opportunity, leading critics to call his policy **dollar diplomacy**. Late in Taft's term, J. P. Morgan negotiated a large international loan to China to support the building of new rail lines there. Upon becoming president, Woodrow Wilson found himself immediately involved with Asian matters and specifically the Morgan loan. Wilson's new secretary of state, William Jennings Bryan, had deep reservations about the loan. Within two weeks of the inauguration, Wilson announced that the government of the United States opposed the loan because its terms undermined "the administrative independence of China." China did not get the loan. Unfortunately, it also did not get the railroads that the loan was supposed to finance, something that weakened the country in its future dealings with Japan.

Tensions with Japan that had been brewing since Roosevelt's time continued. Just as Wilson assumed office, the California legislature adopted a law that no one "ineligible for citizenship" could buy land in California. Since Japanese immigrants could not become citizens, everyone knew at whom the law was directed. Secretary Bryan made two trips to California to try and get the law rescinded, but failed. Japan's government reacted angrily, as it had with school segregation in 1906, and again a war seemed possible. Wilson and Bryan did everything they could to defuse the situation. The leaders in Tokyo also did not want a war, but in Japan, feelings of deep anti-American animosity were furthered by California's continuing determination to marginalize Japanese immigrants.

Wilson and Bryan also tried to end U.S. control of the Philippines. They convinced Congress to pass legislation granting eventual independence to the islands, but Republican opponents succeeded in deleting any specific deadline. Only after World War II did the United States recognize the independence of the Philippines, though it had been promised in 1916.

Mexico and Latin America

The most difficult foreign policy issue for Wilson in his first term involved Mexico. In February 1913, just before Wilson's inauguration, Mexican army general Victoriano Huerta led a military coup against the elected moderate, President Francisco Madero, who was killed in the bloody overthrow. Many American investors wanted the U.S. government to support the new Huerta administration, but Wilson announced, "We can have no sympathy with those who seek the power of government to advance their own personal interests or ambitions." Wilson and Bryan believed that the coup was part of a battle between British and American oil companies, and they wanted none of it.

Wilson desperately wanted to let Mexico work out its own future. As he told the journalist Ray Stannard Baker, he "felt shame as an American over the first Mexican war" of 1848. He continued that it was "his resolution that while he was president there should be no such predatory war." He also believed that a people had the right "to do as they damned pleased with their own affairs." Baker added that the president did, indeed, use the word *damned*.

In spite of the president's intentions, Americans had major investments in Mexico, and thousands of American citizens worked in Mexico as teachers, nurses, and construction

dollar diplomacy
The U.S. policy urged by President Taft of using private investment in other nations to promote American diplomatic goals and business interests.

workers. Wilson could not ignore the country, and he sent envoys to try to persuade Huerta to resign, but failed. He spoke passionately about "the self-restraint of a really great nation." When a revolution against Huerta led by Venustiano Carranza and Francisco "Pancho" Villa broke out, Wilson recognized it. In April 1914, when Wilson got word that a large shipment of European arms for Huerta's government was on its way to the Mexican port of Veracruz, Wilson ordered the navy to land at the port and stop the arms. The arms were stopped, but to Wilson's surprise, Mexico did not welcome the intervention, Mexican forces fought the U.S. Marines, and seventeen Americans were killed. Not only Huerta but also Carranza condemned what they called a U.S. invasion. The end result was good for Carranza. Without the new arms, Huerta resigned and went into exile, and Carranza rode into Mexico City as the victor. Argentina, Brazil, and Chile agreed to negotiate a solution, and the Americans withdrew from Veracruz.

Unfortunately, a new civil war began in Mexico when Villa split with Carranza. In March 1916, Villa, who was now leading a full-scale revolt, led several hundred troops in an attack on the U.S. border town of Columbus, New Mexico. They wanted arms that were stored at nearby U.S. Army Fort Furlong, but more important, the wily Villa wanted to create an international incident. He did not get the arms, but he did get the incident.

Wilson notified Carranza of his intention to respect Mexican sovereignty, but also ordered the U.S. Army, under General John J. Pershing, to enter Mexico and find Villa. Carranza had much to benefit from eliminating Villa and stayed out of the battle. Some ten thousand U.S. troops under Pershing's command were well equipped with motor vehicles and airplanes, but they never found Villa, though they engaged in some bloody battles as they chased him through northern Mexico for months. Eventually, in early 1917, as Wilson became more concerned with the war in Europe, the U.S. forces withdrew without success, and Villa survived until he was assassinated in 1923.

The United States intervened in several other Latin American matters during Wilson's administration (see Map 20-2). Bryan offered an apology to Colombia for the U.S. role in the revolution that had separated Panama and negotiated a $25 million payment to Colombia. Roosevelt was furious at an obvious slap at his administration, and his friend Henry Cabot

Library of Congress Prints and Photographs Division [LC-DIG-ggbain-15609]

Mexican revolutionary Pancho Villa not only clashed with others in Mexico but also conducted a long-running battle with U.S. forces.

Map 20-2 U.S. Intervention in the Caribbean and Latin America.

Between 1865 and 1933, but especially under the administrations of McKinley and the "progressive presidents"—Roosevelt, Taft, and Wilson—the United States intervened regularly in the nations of the Caribbean and Latin America.

Lodge blocked authorization of the funds in the Senate. The United States sent Marines to end unrest in Nicaragua, the Dominican Republic, and Haiti; they stayed in Haiti until 1934. For all of their talk of nonintervention, Wilson and Bryan seemed quite willing to intervene in the Americas.

20.3 Quick Review

How would you summarize the similarities and differences in McKinley's, Roosevelt's, Taft's, and Wilson's foreign policy? Give specific examples of ways they differed.

20.1

20.2

20.3

20.4

The United States and the Great War

20.4 Analyze the causes and consequences of U.S. involvement in World War I.

Just after the November 1912 election, while he was still living in Princeton, President-Elect Wilson told one of his former faculty colleagues, "It would be an irony of fate if my administration had to deal chiefly with foreign problems, for all my preparation has been in domestic matters." It was an irony that would come to pass with a vengeance.

War in Europe

On June 28, 1914, the Austrian archduke Franz Ferdinand, heir apparent to the throne of the Austro-Hungarian Empire, and his wife, Sophie, were assassinated in the town of Sarajevo by a Serbian nationalist who wanted independence for Serbia. Nothing could have seemed as far removed from the United States as the murder of members of a central European royal family. However, within a very short time, the impact of the assassination was felt everywhere in the world.

In the summer of 1914, Europe was at peace. Even so, independence movements within the Austro-Hungarian and Ottoman Empires, particularly in Balkan states (including Serbia), were challenging the empires (see Map 20-3). In addition, a newly united Germany was angry at being shut out of the colonies in Africa and Asia by the speed with which the British and French had moved. An arms race had developed among the continent's greatest powers, and in their quest for security, European nations had developed a complex series of defensive alliances. Germany, Austria-Hungary, and the Turkish Ottoman Empire were known as the Central Powers. Russia, France, and Great Britain were known simply as the Allies. All of these factors quickly led Europe to tumble into all-out war when Austria set out to punish Serbia and Russia came to the aid of the Serbians. By August, Europe was engulfed in what was called the Great War. (The term World War I was coined only after the outbreak of another great war in 1939, one that quickly came to be known as World War II.)

At the beginning of the war, many Europeans were caught up in patriotic fervor. Young men signed up promptly and marched off proudly. Both sides expected an easy victory. The German army attacked France by moving through neutral Belgium. It was a move that cost Germany dearly in public support, but it allowed the German army to get within thirty miles of Paris early in the war. Then an allied counteroffensive drove the Germans back, and by November 1914, both sides were dug in for the long trench warfare that would not move very much—though every small move cost thousands of soldiers their lives—until March 1918. The long years of trench warfare were ghastly. In 1916 at the Battle of the Somme, sixty thousand British soldiers were killed in a single day. In a yearlong battle for the town of Verdun, a million soldiers were killed. New forms of artillery, tanks, and flamethrowers, along with the introduction of poisonous mustard gas, caused what seemed like never-ending waves of death while life in the trenches involved living for months with mud, rats, and rotten food. Despite these costs, the battle lines did not change significantly. Wilson called it "this vast gruesome contest of systematized destruction."

The United States saw all of these developments as a distant tragedy. A young American mining engineer, Herbert Hoover, organized the Commission for Belgian Relief, which along with the American Red Cross, sent aid to people caught in the path of war. Hoover gained international fame as the "Napoleon of mercy" for his efforts. However, most Americans preferred not to get involved and agreed with U.S. ambassador to London Walter Hines Page, who said, "I thank Heaven for many things—first the Atlantic Ocean." President Wilson declared neutrality. He wanted to stay out of the war, and he understood that any European war would stir up deep tensions in a nation made up of immigrants from every one of the nations at war. Neutrality, however, would not be easy.

The warfare on land and on the oceans around Europe cut into U.S. trade, hurting wheat farmers and cotton growers who could not get their goods to European markets. Britain began to place large orders for farm products and for munitions while using its powerful navy to maintain a blockade of the Central Powers. War-torn Britain needed money to buy these things, but when J. P. Morgan began to float large loans, Secretary of State Bryan

Map 20-3 Europe and the Middle East before and during World War I.

This map shows the areas dominated by the Austro-Hungarian and Ottoman Empires, both of which would disappear at the end of World War I.

imposed a ban on loans to belligerents, seeking the "true spirit" of strict neutrality. Bryan's ban hurt U.S. commerce, and Britain and France claimed it was prejudicial toward them, so Bryan and Wilson announced that "commercial credit" could be extended to the Allies. No one understood the difference between "commercial credit" and loans, but the distinction allowed the European allied powers to get the goods they wanted, U.S. farmers and manufacturers to profit, and everyone to pretend that neutrality was still maintained.

The Wilson administration had to steer a difficult course while facing considerable internal pressures. Former president Roosevelt urged massive buildup of the army and navy as well as a military draft, all in the name of preparedness for an eventual war on the side of the British and French. From Roosevelt's perspective, Wilson was dangerously passive.

In contrast, progressive senator Robert La Follette of Wisconsin and other politicians, especially those from states with large German populations, led a peace movement, fearing that Wilson was edging toward war. Jane Addams led a large woman's movement for

Library of Congress Prints and Photographs Division

Especially before the United States entered World War I, songs like "I Didn't Raise My Boy to Be a Soldier" were popular among many who did not want to see young American men caught up in the fighting.

peace. Many union leaders saw the war as a battle between European capitalists in which the working class should not be involved. Anarchists and socialists condemned the war. Between 1914 and 1916, in spite of Roosevelt's best efforts to build support for preparedness and war, most Americans in and out of office favored keeping far distant from Europe's problems.

Of the many diplomatic tensions that the war in Europe created, by far the greatest had to do with the German use of a new kind of sea power—the submarine, or U-boat. Britain's navy ruled the waves, but German U-boats could glide under the waves and strike at ships bringing supplies to Britain and France. On February 4, 1915, the German Admiralty announced that the waters around Britain were a "war zone" and its submarines would freely attack any ship bringing supplies to Britain. Wilson and Bryan sent a formal diplomatic note that sinking ships without warning was "an act so unprecedented in naval warfare" that the United States would hold them to "a strict accountability for such acts." No one defined what "strict accountability" meant. Somehow, submarine warfare—having a ship struck by a torpedo seemingly out of nowhere—terrified people far more than direct ship-to-ship combat. Submarine warfare also threatened the profitable U.S. trade with Britain. For Wilson, it raised the issue of basic rights of U.S. citizens, as neutrals, to travel freely. On the last point, the president and his secretary of state differed strongly. Bryan asked "whether an American citizen can, by putting his business above his regard for his country, assume for his own advantage unnecessary risk and thus involve his country in international complications." For Wilson, the freedom of neutrals to travel was "in the interests of mankind," and protecting the rights of neutrals under international law was a national duty.

In March 1915, a submarine sank a small British passenger ship, the *Falaba*, and an American citizen was killed. Then on May 7, 1915, a submarine sank the British liner *Lusitania*, the grandest and fastest ocean liner then in service. The *Lusitania* sank in eighteen minutes and 1,198 people were killed, including 127 American citizens. The United States demanded an apology from Germany. When Bryan suggested also issuing a formal warning to American citizens not to travel on ships belonging to countries that were at war, Wilson refused.

In response to the American note, the German government sent secret orders to its submarine captains to avoid large passenger liners, but their official word to the United States was evasive. Wilson promised that if Germany would give up submarine warfare, he would also press Britain to end the blockade of goods flowing to Germany and Austria, but he also prepared a second note to Germany saying that the sinking of the *Lusitania* involved "principles of humanity."

Bryan argued for protesting the British blockade and for linking the second note to a policy that would bar passenger ships from carrying munitions (the *Lusitania* may well have been carrying munitions in addition to passengers). Wilson thought that Bryan's plan would undermine the needed message of protest. Bryan resigned rather than sign the second *Lusitania* note. He told the president that he was risking war by creating a situation where a foolish move by the German government could drag the United States into a war and that he could do more for peace by building public opinion outside the administration than within. Bryan's departure was a sad parting between two people who had come to like and admire each other but who deeply believed in different courses of action. Robert Lansing became acting secretary and signed the note. Congress debated but did not pass a law barring Americans from travel on belligerent ships. Sinkings and diplomatic notes continued, as did American domestic politics and new developments in Woodrow Wilson's personal life.

In the summer of 1914, as Europe began to move toward war, Ellen Wilson, the president's wife of thirty years whose warmth offset Wilson's sometimes dour personality, became desperately ill. Her kidneys were failing, and through the summer, the president read diplomatic cables while sitting by his wife's bedside. She died at the White House at the beginning of August. The president wrote, "I never understood before what a broken heart meant." Less than a year later, Wilson met a vivacious forty-two-year-old widow named Edith Bolling Galt and quickly fell in love. Although some in the cabinet worried about how the public would respond to a new marriage so quickly after the loss of his first wife, the two were married in December 1915. The nation had a new First Lady who would support Wilson and have a significant role in policy as war and illness later sapped his energy.

While Wilson was seeking to maintain neutrality and dealing with his personal life, 1916 was also an election year. After Ellen's death, he had seriously considered not running, but his new personal life and his desire to see the diplomatic crisis through led him to declare his candidacy for a second term. The Republican Party was reunited and nominated Supreme Court Justice Charles Evans Hughes. Hughes had served two terms as governor of New York, but he had also been on the Supreme Court since 1910 and thus sat out the Roosevelt-Taft split. Roosevelt called him "the bearded iceberg," but campaigned strongly for the ticket as did Taft. It was a very close contest, but in the end, Wilson carried California by four thousand votes and, with it, the Electoral College.

A month after the election, Wilson tried to broker a peace between Europe's warring powers. He asked both sides for their demands. Germany indicated that it was willing to discuss peace, but a new British government led by Prime Minister Lloyd George said it had no interest in American mediation. Then in December, Lloyd George indicated willingness to talk while the Germans backed off. In the midst of this diplomacy, the German government made two fateful mistakes. On January 31, 1917, it announced to the United States that it was resuming "the full employment of all the weapons … at its disposal." At the same time, German foreign minister Arthur Zimmermann sent a secret cable to the German embassy in Mexico with an offer to the Carranza government—long estranged from Wilson and the United States—that if it would attack the United States, Germany would see to the restoration of the territory from Texas to California that had been taken from Mexico in 1848.

The British government managed to intercept and decode the Zimmermann telegram and release it to the public, turning much of American public opinion against Germany. Wilson was more concerned with unrestricted submarine warfare than any interference from Carranza. He broke diplomatic relations with Germany. He then asked Congress for authority to arm merchant ships, but La Follette and other Republican progressives blocked the bill in the Senate. Wilson called them "a little group of willful men" and claimed the authority to arm the ships on executive authority. At the same time, other Americans, including former president Roosevelt, were pressing Wilson to do more for Britain. As early as January 1915, Roosevelt, although out of office, wrote to British foreign minister Sir Edward Grey, calling Wilson's lack of greater support for the British "very obstinate." In the end, when war came, it brought Roosevelt political and personal tragedy. Wilson would accept neither his advice to help Britain nor his offer of service, and in July 1918, Roosevelt's beloved son Quentin was killed in combat in France.

From the German perspective, an immediate attack on supplies going to Britain and France was the only way to win the war. If they could block food and munitions from getting to the Allies, then the Germans believed they could win the war before the United States could organize itself to do much harm. In March, U-boats sank three U.S. merchant ships with the loss of fifteen American lives. As Bryan had warned, Wilson's hard line meant that Germany had the initiative. The president felt he had run out of options. On April 2, 1917, Wilson appeared before a joint session of Congress and asked for a declaration of war against Germany.

The War at Home—Support and Opposition

Not everyone was convinced by Wilson's eloquence. In the Senate, Wisconsin's La Follette and George Norris of Nebraska led the opposition to a declaration of war. Norris, a Republican long part of the Progressive movement, said, "We have loaned many hundreds of millions of dollars to the Allies in this controversy." And he saw the war as simply a way to defend those loans, insisting, "We are going into war upon the command of gold." He would have none of it. When the vote came, six senators, three Republicans and three Democrats, opposed the war. In the House, fifty representatives

American Voices

Woodrow Wilson, War Message, 1917

Wilson had spoken directly to Congress many times before. Nevertheless, when he decided that the United States needed to go to war on the side of Britain and France, the words took on new importance.

Gentlemen of the Congress:

On the 3d of February last I officially laid before you the extraordinary announcement of the Imperial German Government that on and after the 1st day of February it was its purpose to put aside all restraints of law or of humanity and use its submarines to sink every vessel that sought to approach either the ports of Great Britain and Ireland or the western coasts of Europe. ... Vessels of every kind, whatever their flag, their character, their cargo, their destination, their errand, have been ruthlessly sent to the bottom without warning and without thought of help or mercy for those on board, the vessels of friendly neutrals along with those of belligerents. ...

With a profound sense of the solemn and even tragical character of the step I am taking and of the grave responsibilities which it involves, but in unhesitating obedience to what I deem my constitutional duty, I advise that the Congress declare the recent course of the Imperial German Government to be in fact nothing less than war against the Government and people of the United States; that it formally accept the status of belligerent which has thus been thrust upon it. ...

What this will involve is clear. It will involve the utmost practicable cooperation in counsel and action with the governments now at war with Germany. ... It will involve the organization and mobilization of all the material resources of the country to supply the materials of war. ... It will involve the immediate addition to the armed forces of the United States already provided for by law in case of war at least 500,000 men, who should, in my opinion, be chosen upon the principle of universal liability to service. ... It will involve also, of course, the granting of adequate credits to the Government, sustained, I hope, so far as they can equitably be sustained by the present generation, by well conceived taxation. ...

The world must be made safe for democracy. Its peace must be planted upon the tested foundations of political liberty. We have no selfish ends to serve. We desire no conquest, no dominion. We seek no indemnities for ourselves, no material compensation for the sacrifices we shall freely make. We are but one of the champions of the rights of mankind.

Source: Woodrow Wilson, *War Messages*, 65th Cong., 1st Sess., Senate Doc. No. 5, Serial No. 7264, Washington, D.C., 1917; April 2, 1917.

Thinking Critically

1. **Analyzing Primary Sources**
   In analyzing Wilson's argument for war, what are the key reasons he used to persuade his audience (U.S. Congress)? What reasons would antiwar people in Congress use to oppose war?

2. **Contextualization**
   How did Wilson justify American military intervention on moral and ethical grounds? What does the speech tell you about Wilson's vision of America's place in the world?

---

voted no on the war resolution. The most dramatic vote came from Jeannette Rankin of Montana. Rankin was the only woman in the House, elected at a time when women in most states still did not have the vote. She was under intense pressure to vote for the war from some suffragists, who planned to demand votes for patriotic women as a war measure, but in the roll call Rankin answered, "I want to stand by my country, but I cannot vote for war. I vote no." (In 1941, after a long absence, Rankin would be on the floor of Congress again and would be the single vote of no against U.S. entry into World War II.) Once the United States was formally at war, the previous antiwar constituency split between those including Bryan, who believed that once the United States had made the decision to go to war everyone should support the war effort, and others—from Jane Addams to Eugene V. Debs to Emma Goldman—who continued to oppose the war no matter what the president asked or how the Congress voted. Despite the opposition, once the United States was formally at war in the spring of 1917, the Wilson administration set out to do everything possible to assure the support of every citizen. In his war speech, Wilson had said, "If there should be disloyalty, it will be dealt with with a firm hand of stern repression." He meant it.

To build support for the war, Wilson created the **Committee on Public Information** (CPI) and appointed the respected progressive journalist George Creel as its head. No one could challenge Creel's progressive credentials as a muckraker, supporter of women's rights, and political reformer. Creel rejected crude propaganda, insisting that "[a] free people cannot be told what to think. They must be given the facts and permitted to do their

Committee on Public Information

Government agency during World War I that sought to shape public opinion in support of the war effort through newspapers, pamphlets, speeches, films, and other media.

own thinking." Creel also insisted that he and the Wilson administration would be the ones to decide what "facts" to give people and, more seriously, what alternative "facts" should be blocked.

Creel announced, "It was a fight for the minds of men, for the 'conquest of their convictions,' and the battle-line ran through every home in the country." Under his leadership, the CPI hired other muckraking journalists, including Ray Stannard Baker and Ida Tarbell, and published seventy-five million pamphlets supporting the U.S. war effort. They recruited seventy-five thousand "Four Minute Men," volunteers who were ready to speak at a moment's notice in favor of the war effort and against Germany at any theater or neighborhood meeting. He worked with the still-new movie studios to create films like *The Kaiser: Beast of Berlin*. Creel's CPI launched a special "War Americanization Plan" to encourage foreign-born immigrants, especially those who had come to the United States from the Central Powers, to buy Liberty Bonds and otherwise assert their American patriotism. He also hired Charles Dana Gibson, famous for creating the nation's model of feminine beauty in the "Gibson Girl," to produce prowar posters that would glorify the American war effort and call on all Americans to purchase war bonds and tend home vegetable gardens—or victory gardens—as well as for young men to serve in the army. The government also launched "war study courses" to encourage patriotism and loyalty among public school students. Creel was confident enough of his efforts that he opposed more blatant limitations on civil liberties. After the war, he wrote, "Better far to have the desired compulsions proceed from within than to apply them from without."

Herbert Hoover, who had gained fame organizing support for people in war-ravaged Belgium, became the head of the U.S. Food Administration and urged Americans to support the war by eating less and conserving more so that food could be sent to the troops or the Allies. Like Creel, Hoover believed that voluntary compliance was most effective, so he rejected rationing in favor of what he described as mobilizing "the spirit of self-denial and self-sacrifice in this country." People got the widely touted message, "FOOD WILL WIN THE WAR—DON'T WASTE IT." The federal government also created the Fuel Administration and the War Industries Board and took direct control of the nation's railroads. Most of the new agencies were led by business executives, and the criticism of business leaders that had characterized Wilson's first term virtually disappeared as the nation's corporate elite became essential supporters of the war effort.

While Creel led the "fight for the minds" of the American people and Hoover tried to change their eating habits, other self-styled patriots had their own agendas. The nongovernmental American Protective League (APL), which eventually grew to 250,000 members, included some who had opposed German immigrants or domestic political radicals and who saw the war as a time to further their agenda. APL members, without government authority, opened mail and listened in on telephone calls, looking for spies and traitors. Fearing such animosity, many German Americans were careful to demonstrate their loyalty. The Deutsches Haus of Indianapolis became the Athenaeum of Indiana; sauerkraut became liberty cabbage; and German-language classes, schools, and newspapers were closed. On occasion, the split between those who supported and those who opposed U.S. involvement in the war turned violent. A few months after the United States entered the war, during the hot summer of 1917, some two thousand members of the APL along with the sheriff of Bisbee, Arizona, raided a mass meeting of the Industrial Workers of the World—the large and radical union that strongly opposed the war—and rounded up over a thousand IWW members and supporters, a third of whom were Mexican American, leaving them out on the desert without food or water for two days before letting them escape to New Mexico. A German American, Robert Prager, was lynched by a mob in Collinsville, Illinois. An IWW organizer, Frank Little, was lynched in Butte, Montana, after he told striking copper miners that they were battling an "imperialist, capitalist war." An editorial in the *Washington Post* said of the violence, "In spite of excesses such as lynching, it is a healthful and wholesome awakening in the interior of the country."

In 1917 and 1918, Congress passed several acts to control the country's responses to the war, including the Espionage Act of 1917 and the Sedition Act of 1918, giving the government vast new powers to limit free speech and the press that had not been seen in the United

Library of Congress Prints and Photographs Division|LC-USZC4-1281

The U.S. government and private organizations like the Red Cross used advertising that had been effective in other sectors of American life to recruit Americans to support the war effort, as in this poster of a young woman summoning Americans to service.

20.1

20.2

20.3

20.4

20.1

20.2

20.3

20.4

Sedition Act

Broad law restricting criticism of America's involvement in World War I or its government, flag, military, taxes, or officials.

States since the Alien and Sedition Acts of the John Adams administration. The **Sedition Act** of 1918 made illegal "uttering, printing, writing, or publishing any disloyal, profane, scurrilous, or abusive language about the government of the United States ... or the military or naval forces of the United States." Postmaster General Albert Burleson banned from the U.S. mail anything that he thought violated the act. Attorney General Thomas W. Gregory and his successor A. Mitchell Palmer prosecuted violators or left it to local U.S. attorneys to do so.

In spite of government policies and the efforts of many in organizations like the APL to force all Americans to support the war, dissenters continued to speak out. Jane Addams, leader of the Women's Peace Party as well as Chicago's Hull House, spoke to the City Club of Chicago just after war had been declared, saying, "That the United States has entered the war has not changed my views of the invalidity of war as a method of settlement of social problems a particle, and I can see no reason why one should not say what one believes in time of war as in time of peace." Her words were greeted only by silence from the club women. The National Federation of Settlements, which Addams had helped to found, said, "It has been very painful to many of us who hold Miss Addams in deep affection and wholly respect her, to find that we cannot think or act in unison with her."

Jane Addams continued to oppose the war and seek international mediation to end it. She not only wanted the United States out of the war but also wanted to end the war wherever it was fought. At the same time, Addams, ever the practical settlement house leader, sought to ensure that there was "bread in time of war," no matter who needed to eat. She happily cooperated with the U.S. government's Food Administration though she objected to its slogan, "Food Will Win the War." Nevertheless, Addams urged residents of Chicago to plant vegetable gardens and consume less so that more could be sent to those in greatest need.

While Addams was snubbed for her antiwar stance, others paid a much higher price. Radical leaders were watched carefully for "unpatriotic" words and actions. Over a hundred IWW and Socialist Party leaders were arrested and jailed on charges of violating the Sedition Act. In June 1918, Eugene V. Debs told a huge rally in Canton, Ohio, "I realize that, in speaking to you this afternoon, there are certain limitations placed upon the right of free speech." But Debs also made it clear that he was equally as opposed to the leadership of Germany as to that of the Allies for, he said, all sides were using working people to fight their battles. So he continued, "The master class has always declared the wars; the subject class has always fought the battles." In particular, he added, "[T]he working class who make the supreme sacrifices, the working class who freely shed their blood and furnish the corpses, have never yet had a voice in either declaring war or making peace. It is the ruling class that invariably does both." Debs was arrested for the speech and sentenced to ten years in prison under the **Espionage Act** of 1917.

Espionage Act

Law whose vague prohibition against obstructing the nation's war effort was used to stop dissent and criticism during World War I.

War and Victory

Many of those who supported U.S. entry into the war assumed that the country would limit its role to patrolling the oceans and providing material to the Allies. But once Wilson led the nation to war, he wanted full-scale involvement just as he had told the Congress. He was determined to defeat Germany and to win a place for himself at the table of the peace negotiations that he knew must come at the war's end.

General John J. Pershing, fresh from the failed effort to find Villa in Mexico, became the commander of the American Expeditionary Forces (AEF) in large part because he had kept silent when others were criticizing Wilson's lack of early preparation for war. Wilson refused an offer by former president Roosevelt to raise his own all-volunteer unit. Pershing's orders were to work closely with the British and French while protecting the separate identity of the American forces.

Deciding to send troops to fight in Europe was one thing. Actually getting an army raised and across the ocean was quite another. Over significant opposition, Congress passed a military draft, and draft boards across the country began processing the not-always-willing recruits. Training camps were set up. Regardless, it took time to raise and train an army. It also took both time and ships to get them across the Atlantic, and the United States was short on both. Since the Civil War, the U.S. Merchant Marine, needed to transport troops and supplies, had shrunk even as the navy had grown, and German attacks had reduced Britain's shipping capacity significantly.

On July 4, 1917, a token force of "doughboys," as the American troops were called, paraded in France to enthusiastic acclaim. But it would be many months before large numbers of U.S. troops arrived in France and an even longer time before Pershing thought they were ready to fight.

While the United States was raising, training, and transporting its army, the Allies came close to losing the war. The German government knew that it needed to win quickly before Americans arrived in force. In the long run, the United States had more people, and thus more potential soldiers, than any of the combatants except Russia. Knowing that the Americans were coming, the British and French launched a major offensive in the summer of 1917. As with previous efforts, the offensive was turned back, and the terrible losses led to mutinies throughout the French army. The Allied armies seemed to be losing the will to fight.

On Germany's eastern front, the Bolshevik Revolution in Russia in November 1917 led to a new government that wanted nothing to do with the war. The Bolsheviks signed the Treaty of Brest-Litovsk, which ended the war between Germany and Russia on German terms, the most important term of all being that Germany could now focus exclusively on the western front and attack France in the spring of 1918.

The treaty did not come in time to save Germany, however. By 1918, 850,000 fresh U.S. troops had arrived, and they quickly went into combat, while the German troops were exhausted by four years of war. For the German soldiers, the fact that they were facing so many well-armed fresh troops undermined morale as much as any specific American victories, though those victories were not without importance. At Château-Thierry in June of 1918, U.S. forces helped stop a German offensive toward Paris. By that fall, the Americans were part of an Allied effort that had driven the German army out of France and back inside Germany. The end was becoming clear. An armistice was signed, and on November 11, 1918, at 11:00 a.m., the guns of Europe fell silent.

Peace Talks, and the Failure of the Treaty of Versailles

No one knows exactly how many were killed and wounded in World War I or how many more died of disease and exposure. By some estimates, as many as sixty-five million men fought, of whom eight million were killed. In Europe, hardly a family escaped losing

Niday Picture Library/Alamy Stock Photo

This picture of men with an ambulance bogged down in mud is a more accurate portrait of the experience of those who fought in World War I than the romanticized posters that the government distributed.

Thinking Historically

Limiting Free Speech

Once the United States voted to go to war, most Americans supported the war effort, but a sizeable minority did not, and their claim to opposition under the free speech clause of the U.S. Constitution caused great tension. Many years later, Miriam E. Tefft, whose family supported the war, still remembered the fear when she was fifteen years old and "the tragic hysteria which was World War I broke out in the copper mining camp of Bisbee, Arizona, where I lived and the citizens took over the law." In Bisbee the IWW was leading a miner's strike but since the union was also opposed to U.S. involvement in the war, the two issues—the right of the miners to strike and loyalty or opposition to the war effort—merged. "You could almost smell fear," Tefft remembers. "Men didn't look at each other in the face. Everyone was under suspicion. Loyalties were divided. One could sense an undercurrent of outrage seething." Then on July 12, 1917, Tefft recalled seeing

> that the deputies and armed citizens were keeping the strikers in line as they were herded into the ball park behind the high board fence. The men had evidently been taken completely by surprise; some were still in their nightshirts, many in long underwear; some apparently hadn't been given time to put on their shoes. "Where are they taking them?" people asked. A few days later the answer came. "The loads of strikers had been shipped to New Mexico, where they were turned out into the desert near Columbus."

Many other Americans were arrested and sent to jail under the Espionage Act. Charles Schenck mailed pamphlets urging people to resist the military draft and was convicted and sent to prison. Speaking to farmers in North Dakota, Kate Richards O'Hare said, "Any person who enlists in the army of the United States of America will be used for fertilizer," and a federal judge sentenced her to five years in prison. Perhaps the most famous American to oppose the war, Eugene V. Debs, was sentenced to ten years in prison for his speech in Canton, Ohio.

Schenck, O'Hare, Debs, and others appealed that their basic rights under the Constitution were being undermined. Some were eloquent in their testimony. O'Hare told the judge who sentenced her,

> I am dangerous to the war profiteers of this country who rob the people on the one hand and rob and debase the Government on the other. … You can convince the people that I am dangerous to these men; but no jury and no judge can convince them that I am a dangerous woman to the best interests of the United States.

Debs, in perhaps his best-known statement, told the judge who was sentencing him:

> Your Honor, years ago I recognized my kinship with all living beings, and I made up my mind that I was not one but better than the meanest on earth. I said then, and I say now, that while there is a lower class, I am in it, while there is a criminal element I am of it, and while there is a soul in prison I am not free.

Despite the eloquence, no courts overturned the Espionage Act convictions. The U.S. Supreme Court upheld enforcement of the Espionage Act. In the case of Charles Schenck, *Schenck v. United States*, Justice Oliver Wendell Holmes wrote that Congress could limit free speech if the words "are used in such circumstances as are of such a nature as to create a clear and present danger." In *Debs v. United States*, the court upheld Debs's conviction even though he had not urged violation of the draft laws. And later, when foreign-born opponents of the war were deported, the court upheld those rulings also.

Finally, in the case of the IWW miners in Bisbee, Arizona, Tefft concluded,

> It was anticlimax when President Wilson, breathing fire and brimstone, sent a commission to investigate. The commission was headed by Felix Frankfurter [later appointed to the U.S. Supreme Court]. They found the government was helpless to punish anyone. No law could be found against kidnapping people en masse and dumping them in another state.

Many Americans who did not agree with Debs or Addams were still appalled by the Wilson administration's attacks on free speech and the court's decisions. Samuel Gompers, president of the American Federation of Labor, supported the war, but condemned the attacks on other unionists, including on members of the IWW. Even Theodore Roosevelt criticized the president for the excessive force of the Espionage and Sedition Acts, which he called "sheer treason to the United States," and dared Wilson to send him to jail because it "would make my voice carry farther." A group of liberals in New York City created the National Civil Liberties Bureau in 1917, an organization that under the leadership of a young social worker, Roger Baldwin, became the American Civil Liberties Union in 1920 and has continued to defend free speech in the decades since. After Wilson had left office, his successor, Warren Harding, pardoned Debs, who had served some two years in federal prison. The country moved on, but the laws remained on the books.

Source: Miriam E. Tefft, interview dated February 2, 1982, from arizona.edu/bisbee/docs2/rec_teff.php; The Trial of Kate Richards O'Hare for Disloyalty, Bismarck, North Dakota, 1917, reprinted in Robert Marcus and Anthony Marcus, editors, *On Trial: American History through Court Proceedings and Hearings*, Vol. 2 (St. James, NY: Brandywine Press, 1998), pp. 96–104; William A. Pelz, editor, *The Eugene V. Debs Reader* (Chicago: Institute of Working Class History, 2000).

Thinking Critically

1. **Contextualization**

   What larger fears and tensions within American society were revealed by the multifaceted efforts to suppress dissent during World War I? When else in American history have such fears and tensions been seen in the United States?

2. **Comparison**

   To what degree does Tefft's description of the era as one of "wartime hysteria" account for the decisions? How might those who were arrested have described the situation? How might those who arrested them or supported the arrest of antiwar speakers have described it?

someone, and for a generation young women outnumbered young men by significant numbers. Ships were sunk, villages and towns destroyed, national economies wrecked. While some, including Wilson, wanted to use the end of the war to secure "a just and lasting peace," others wanted vengeance, and still others wanted to forget all about war and simply have a good time in a life that they knew could be cut all too short. Amid all these conflicting political and emotional cross-currents, leaders of the victorious nations met in Paris at the beginning of 1919 to write a peace treaty.

Woodrow Wilson, who had broken precedent early in his term by speaking directly to Congress, broke precedent again when the war ended. He sailed for Paris to personally lead the American delegation at the Paris peace talks. No American president had ever left the United States while in office (Theodore Roosevelt had been careful to stay only on U.S.-owned land in his 1906 trip to the Panama Canal Zone, which was considered to be U.S. territory) and some even wondered whether it was constitutional for a sitting president to leave the country. Wilson waved the concerns aside. Modern communications would allow him to remain in close touch with Washington while he was across the Atlantic. The British, French, and Italian prime ministers were all going to be present, and Wilson had no intention of handing the American role off to anyone else.

When the president and Mrs. Wilson arrived in Brest, France, on December 13, 1918, they were greeted as heroes, and they continued to be honored as they toured France, Britain, and Italy. A banner on the Champs-Élysées in Paris announced, "Honor to Wilson the Just," and an American newspaper reporter wrote, "No one ever had such cheers." It must have been a satisfying moment for the war-weary president. For Wilson, one ominous cloud over the negotiations was the fact that Republicans had made substantial gains in the congressional elections of November 1918 in spite of his impassioned appeal to the voters to keep the

Schenck v. United States

The first of several decisions by the U.S. Supreme Court upholding the Sedition and Espionage Acts.

20.1

20.2

20.3

20.4

American Voices

Mathew Chopin, "Advancing Over the Top and Carrying Wounded Comrade Under Shell-Fire," 1918

U.S. soldiers began arriving in France in the summer of 1918 and were quickly moved to the front lines. While presidents and generals planned, those doing the actual fighting—recent arrivals to war from farms and crowded city neighborhoods—told their own stories of fighting, fear, bravery, and sorrow, including this one recorded here.

At early dawn we continued advancing "over the top" through clouds of gas and smoke—under rain of machine gun bullets, shrapnel and steel. The Huns [as most Americans called the Germans during the war] were shelling heavily the edge of the roadside. It was freezing cold; we were out of water and had just a small ration of salmon and hard-tack. Completely exhausted and thirsting for a drink, I remember grabbing a canteen from a passing artillery caisson to soothe my parched lips, when the explosion of a shell sent over deadly gas, getting four of our men. We got down in a valley for a while during a machine gun barrage and then up again, firing away at the enemy as fast as our automatics could work. …

So many of our men were getting wounded and as the litter-bearer was killed while going out under fire for wounded, my sergeant sent me with another man to replace him. It was a dangerous situation going over rounds of Hell, as we had to go up and get them under machine gun and rifle fire. … We began picking up the wounded as fast as they came and bandaging

those in need of first aid. It was a heartrending sight that weakened the strongest, for everywhere were wounded and lifeless forms—some all torn to pieces, their limbs and heads entirely severed from their bodies! I remember making a trip about a mile under heavy gun fire to get a wounded stretcher-bearer whose partner had been killed. He was a game little Yank, yet a pitiful sight, with his side all ripped open by shrapnel. As I laid him gently on the stretcher, I still remember his last uttered words, "Oh God, if I could only live to die at home!"

Source: Mathew Chopin, *Through the Valley of Death*, 1919, from www.geocities.com/louisiana_doughboy/index.htm and cited in P. Scott Corbett and Ronald C. Naugle, *Life, Liberty, and the Pursuit of Happiness: Documents in American History, Volume II, 1861 to Present* (Boston: McGraw Hill, 2004), pp. 108–109.

Thinking Critically

1. **Analyzing Primary Sources**
   What impression of World War I do you get from Chopin's point of view as an average soldier rather than a leader or civilian?

2. **Contextualization**
   What light does Chopin's account shed on the impact of new military technology on the fighting during World War I?

National Portrait Gallery,Smithsonian Institution/Art Resource, NY

The peace talks at Versailles brought together a wide range of world leaders but were dominated by the leaders of Great Britain, France, and the United States.

Fourteen Points

The proposed points outlining peace offered by President Woodrow Wilson in 1918 as the United States entered World War I; the treaty agreed to at the Versailles peace conference did not, however, include all fourteen.

Democrats in charge while he negotiated a treaty. Then, while he was in France in January 1919, Wilson received a telegram that his arch-rival Theodore Roosevelt had died. A reporter said he thought he saw a look of pity and then a smile of triumph on the president's face, though Wilson was far too diplomatic to say anything.

When the Paris peace talks convened at the old royal palace of Versailles, Wilson thought he was in a very strong bargaining position given the role of U.S. resources and troops in bringing the war to a successful conclusion for the Allies. His counterparts thought differently. Georges Clémenceau, the tough seventy-seven-year-old French premier, wanted vengeance for France's terrible losses, and British prime minister David Lloyd George, though more moderate than Clemenceau, harbored nothing like Wilson's generous spirit. France and Britain had lost ten to twenty times as many soldiers as the United States, most of the battles had been fought in France, and neither leader nor their followers were in any mood to be generous. The losers—Germany, Austria, and the Ottoman Empire—were excluded from the conference. The new Communist government of Russia, which had signed its own separate treaty with Germany in early 1918, was also excluded from the peace conference. Indeed, Wilson sent troops to try and support the overthrow of the Communist government, which would lead to long-term tension between Russia and the United States.

Since 1916, Wilson had been telling his fellow Americans what he wanted from a peace conference. He insisted that the traditional U.S. isolationism could not continue and that the nation must be willing to "become a partner in any feasible association of nations to maintain the peace." In October, just before the presidential election, he told an audience in Omaha, Nebraska, "[W]e are part of the world." And in January 1917, he told the Senate that the United States wanted "peace without victory." His goal was to avoid future wars based on the "covenant" of a new international organization that would ensure that "no such catastrophe shall ever overwhelm us again."

In January 1918, as the United States was entering the war, Wilson outlined what came to be known as his **Fourteen Points**. The president said that America insisted on "open covenants of peace, openly arrived at." The commitment to openness was a mix of Wilsonian idealism and a reaction to the release by the new Russian leader, V. I. Lenin, of secret agreements that had been negotiated by the czarist government, Britain, and France. Although he did not use the word *self-determination*, Wilson condemned old-style European imperialism and, indeed, any wars fought for territory. He insisted that the many diverse nationalities living within the Austro-Hungarian and Ottoman Turkish Empires should have "an absolutely unmolested opportunity of autonomous development" (see Map 20-4). Most of all, he called for a "general association of nations" to preserve peace.

Wilson stayed at the peace conference for six months except for one two-week return trip to the United States. He did not have as much success as he expected. He was not well staffed. He found himself in painful meetings with the three European premiers who had different goals from his and who, especially Clemenceau, obviously did not respect him.

The treaty that emerged from the peace conference was, perhaps inevitably, a disappointment to everyone. Wilson got his League of Nations, which would include not just the Allies—as Clemenceau initially wanted—but would be open to every nation of the world. The league's covenant included Article X in which member nations agreed to "respect and preserve as against external aggression the political integrity and existing political independence of all Members of the League." However, though the league now existed, Wilson had also paid a high price to get it.

Clemenceau compromised on his initial goal of dividing Germany into several smaller nation-states, but he won on achieving strict limits to German military power, temporary occupation of the Rhineland, and a "war guilt" clause, which meant that

Map 20-4 A Changing Middle East.

While the major impact of the Treaty of Versailles was within Europe, the peace conference also created several new Middle Eastern nations, including Syria, Iraq, and Trans-Jordan—later Jordan and Israel—out of the former Ottoman Empire.

20.1

20.2

20.3

20.4

Germany should pay most of the war's cost. Most of the world's non-European peoples were bitterly disappointed with the treaty. Middle Eastern and African colonies that had belonged to the defeated Central Powers expected to be granted their independence by the peace conference. Instead, they became "mandates" assigned to various victorious powers that were supposed to grant them independence at some unspecified future date. Japan, which had played only a modest role in the war, won the right to continue its control over Shandong province in China, leading a young Mao Zedong to call the treaty "really shameless." Protests erupted in India, Egypt, Korea, and China over other provisions in the treaty.

African American leaders also protested the failure of the Treaty of Versailles to respect the right of citizens of former German colonies in Africa or mention racial discrimination in the final treaty. W. E. B. Du Bois tried to organize a Pan-African conference in Paris to protest the treaty's failings, but the British government would not give passports to Africans from British colonies who wanted to attend, and the U.S. State Department refused permission to American delegates, including Madame C. J. Walker, the first African American woman millionaire, and journalists Ida Wells-Barnett and William Monroe Trotter. Du Bois made it to the meeting only by signing up as a cook on a freighter bound for France.

During the peace negotiations, several new nations were created within Europe—Yugoslavia, Romania, and Czechoslovakia—that were supposed to recognize the hopes for independence by ethnic groups who had been dominated by the old, tottering Austro-Hungarian and Ottoman Empires, but the mapping of those boundaries set off its own ethnic tensions, especially for people who suddenly became an ethnic minority in a new country (see Map 20-5 page 610).

Map 20-5 Europe in 1919.

The Treaty of Versailles created a number of new nations in Eastern Europe out of what had once been the Austro-Hungarian and Ottoman Empires, plus several new nations in the Middle East that had also been part of the Ottoman Empire.

Changes in European
boundaries after World War I

- Areas lost by Russian Empire (now Soviet Union)
- Areas lost by Austro-Hungarian Empire
- Areas lost by German Empire
- Areas lost by Bulgaria

Wilson convinced himself that he had gotten as good a treaty as he could—which was perhaps true given the other actors at the peace conference—and he invested his greatest hopes in the idea that the League of Nations could resolve any remaining issues. He signed the treaty at Versailles in June 1919 and sailed for home. On July 10, Wilson personally spoke to the U.S. Senate, asking them to ratify the treaty. He reminded his audience of the nation's high ideals in going to war and the fact that "in the settlement of the peace we have sought no special reparation for ourselves." The key to the whole treaty and, indeed, to future peace, Wilson continued, was that the League of Nations was "the only hope of mankind." So he begged the Senate to ratify the treaty immediately without any amendments, asking, "Shall we or any other free peoples hesitate to accept this great duty? Dare we reject it and break the heart of the world?" The Senate, which had final authority to approve any treaty, would take eight months to give Wilson his answer.

Wilson was greeted as a hero when he arrived home in the United States, and public opinion seemed to be on his side, but there were problems lurking for the Versailles Treaty. The battle over the treaty has often been portrayed, as it was by Wilson, as one between his internationalism and an older isolationist view of America; however, the issues were more complex. Wilson had made the treaty needlessly partisan by campaigning vigorously, but unsuccessfully, for a Democratic victory in the 1918 elections and then failing to take any Republican leaders with him to Paris. He had also lost many of his strongest supporters who were disillusioned by the attack on civil liberties that he had allowed during the war and the compromises he had made at Paris. Some senators, such as California's Hiram Johnson and Idaho's William Borah, opposed any binding promise to intervene in other nation's affairs. Borah said that he wanted "not isolation but freedom to do as our own people think wise and just."

The greatest threat to the treaty came from Massachusetts Republican senator Henry Cabot Lodge, chair of the Senate Foreign Relations Committee, who hated the treaty and hated Wilson even more. Lodge objected to the treaty, he said, because it gave an international organization "the power to send American soldiers and sailors everywhere"—a power, Lodge insisted, "which ought never to be taken from the American people or impaired in the slightest degree." Some thought Lodge was less concerned about the league than about the insult to people like himself who had been excluded from the treaty-making process and about his personal animosity toward the president. Nevertheless, Lodge insisted that the issues were beyond party, that the United States "is the world's best hope but if you fetter her in the interests and quarrels of other nations, if you tangle her in the intrigues of Europe, you will destroy her power for good and endanger her very existence."

As he had done at Princeton and in New Jersey state politics when he faced opposition, Wilson appealed over the heads of his immediate opponents to a wider audience, in this case, the whole nation. In the fall of 1919, Wilson began a ten-thousand-mile tour of the country, giving forty speeches in twenty-one days to enthusiastic audiences, asking them to tell their senators to support the treaty. The public response was gratifying but did not move votes in the Senate. The trip also broke the president's already fragile health. On September 25 at Pueblo, Colorado, after a speech in which he said that with the treaty he had negotiated, "international law is revolutionized by putting morals into it," and promising that his beloved league would "lead us, and through us the world, out into pastures of quietness and peace such as the world never dreamed of before," he collapsed and admitted that he could not go on. After he returned to the White House, Wilson suffered a life-threatening infection and a massive stroke that left him partially paralyzed. The medical conditions may also have clouded his judgment and made him more stubborn.

The Senate Foreign Relations Committee recommended approval of the treaty but with fourteen reservations, including one insisting that the U.S. military could not be sent to defend Article X without specific congressional approval. Wilson adamantly refused to consider the reservations. In a final vote on November 18 and 19, 1919, the Senate first came to a tie vote for the treaty with reservations—far short of the two-thirds majority needed to approve a treaty. Then on a second vote in which they considered the treaty without reservations, the Senate defeated the entire treaty by a vote of 55 to 39. The League of Nations would be launched in Geneva, Switzerland, but without the participation of the United States. Wilson's grand vision for a world at peace with the United States as a leader was dead. Many argued that the president's refusal to compromise had been among the forces that killed it. Colonel House, who had once been Wilson's closest confidant, wrote that he had once thought that Senator Lodge was the worst enemy of the treaty, but before the debates and votes were over, he had decided that the worst enemy had actually been Wilson himself.

Topical Press Agency/Getty Images

At the end of World War I, most Americans desperately wanted peace. Thousands of Americans responded positively to Woodrow Wilson's promise that the League of Nations would mean that World War I was "the war to end all wars" and that the league was the best vehicle to bring long-term peace to the world. Unfortunately for the Wilsonian dream, this outpouring of support was never enough to secure the needed votes in the U.S. Senate.

With the end of World War I, Europe had a dramatically different map and the United States had a dramatically different political situation. People who had fervently gone to war in 1917 were tired and cynical by 1919. The cost of the war in lives, money, and liberties led many to question the government and the role of business leaders who had been most enthusiastic about going to war. By 1920, many in the nation were ready to forget high-sounding idealism, progressive or otherwise. It was, perhaps, time for more joy or, at least, the election of a more genial and less idealistic president.

20.4   Quick Review

How did U.S. participation in World War I shape Wilson's presidency? The country?

Conclusion

During the Progressive Era, the United States began to extend its power and influence farther across the globe. The three American leaders known as the "progressive presidents"— Theodore Roosevelt, Taft, and Wilson—as well as Roosevelt's predecessor McKinley all spent much of their administrations dealing with foreign policy. In what some have called "the age of U.S. imperialism," the United States took control of vast new territories. Alaska, which had previously been purchased from Russia, now became an official U.S. territory.

Hawaii was annexed after an American-led revolt on the island, and the Canal Zone was acquired by treaty after complex negotiations with Panama and Colombia. While Cuba and the Philippine Islands eventually attained independence, U.S. influence continued there for a long time, and Puerto Rico remains part of the United States.

The increased involvement of the United States in international affairs between 1898 and 1918, and its expanded territorial reach, made the United States a major world power. Consequently, diplomatic tensions began to mount, especially between the United States and Latin America, where construction of the American-controlled Panama Canal and military interventions in Mexico, Nicaragua, the Dominican Republic, and Haiti created resentment. Although the United States had successfully brokered a peace agreement between Russia and Japan in 1905, further U.S. involvement in Asia coupled with anti-Asian legislation in California embittered the Japanese. Many within the United States also opposed American involvement in the affairs of the rest of the world, especially after the 1898 war with Spain and the continued U.S. occupation of the Philippine Islands.

After the assassination of Archduke Franz Ferdinand in 1914, the Central Powers (Germany, Austria-Hungary, and the Ottoman Empire) went to war against the Allies (Russia, France, and Great Britain). Americans were divided about the conflict and looked to President Wilson to maintain U.S. neutrality. However, American policy changed when German U-boats sank U.S. merchant ships and then a British ocean liner, which killed 127 American citizens. The publication of a secret German cable to Mexico—known as the Zimmermann telegram—in which Germany promised the return of Texas to Mexico if Mexico would attack the United States, turned more of American public opinion against Germany. In 1917, when Germany expanded its submarine attacks, the United States entered the war.

Many in the United States supported the war once it came in 1917, and Wilson and the government-sponsored Committee on Public Information (CPI) created pamphlets, posters, and films describing the war as a fight to save democracy. Support for U.S. involvement in the war was not universal, however, and a large and vocal peace movement emerged. But the Wilson administration pressed for laws to silence dissent, giving the government unprecedented power to restrict free speech. The Supreme Court upheld these laws, and many antiwar protesters were prosecuted and jailed.

By 1918, the Allies, with support from American troops, had defeated the Central Powers and an armistice was signed. At the Paris peace talks, President Wilson hoped to secure a lasting peace and favored treaty provisions that called for a League of Nations. Republican opposition to the league blocked U.S. adoption of the treaty, and the League of Nations was launched without American involvement.

Chapter Review

How was U.S. foreign policy between 1898 and 1918 different from that of the pre–Civil War period?

Continuing Expansion

20.1 **Explain continued U.S. expansion, particularly U.S. acquisition of what would much later be the forty-ninth and fiftieth states.**

Summary

The geographical expansion of the United States that had continued from the time it declared independence persisted throughout the Progressive Era but transformed to involve the acquisition of overseas territories and took place in the context of intensified European imperialist activity. In 1867, the United States acquired Alaska from Russia and gave it territorial status in 1912. Hawaii's strategic location led to a steady increase in the American presence on the islands over the course of the 1800s. By the 1880s, American economic power in Hawaii was overwhelming, and in the 1890s, a coup by American planters led to annexation. The expansion of U.S. naval power went hand in hand with the acquisition of overseas territories.

Review Question

1. Causation
   Consider the new U.S. possessions in the late 1800s and early 1900s. How did Alfred Thayer Mahan's *The Influence of Sea Power upon History* shape American foreign policy in this period?

The Splendid Little War … with Spain—Cuba, Puerto Rico, and the Philippines, 1898

20.2 **Analyze the causes and consequences of the U.S. war with Spain in 1898.**

Summary

The 1898 U.S. war with Spain came at the end of a long period of American expansion into territory that had once been controlled by that country. Spanish efforts to suppress a revolutionary uprising in Cuba led to tensions between the United States and Spain. Finally, the destruction of the U.S. battleship *Maine* gave President William McKinley the excuse he needed to go to war. The United States' victory resulted in control of Puerto Rico, Guam, and the Philippines. U.S. efforts to supplant the government formed by the leaders of the Filipino insurrection against Spain led to a long and bloody occupation. Events in Cuba and the Philippines prompted a group of prominent Americans to form the Anti-Imperialist League.

Review Questions

2. Contextualization
   How does the context of renewed European colonization help explain calls for American imperialism?

3. Argument Development
   Defend or refute the following statement: The United States went to war with Spain to seize control of parts of the Spanish Empire, not to defend the rights of the Cuban people.

Foreign Policy, Foreign Adventures, 1900–1914

20.3 **Explain developments in U.S. policy in Panama, Asia, and Mexico between the war with Spain and World War I.**

Summary

When Theodore Roosevelt became president in 1901, he inherited two major foreign policy issues: the war in the Philippines and the question of a Central American canal to link the Pacific and Atlantic Oceans. The construction of such a canal in Panama was one of Roosevelt's proudest achievements. Roosevelt carried out an interventionist foreign policy in Latin America. The Roosevelt Corollary to the Monroe Doctrine stated that the United States had the right to intervene in any nation in the Americas that could not manage its own affairs. American influence was also reflected in Roosevelt's successful negotiation of a peace treaty between Pacific rivals Japan and Russia. Tensions with Japan over anti-Asian immigration legislation led to the 1907 Gentleman's Agreement and the expansion of the U.S. Navy. Although President Wilson took steps to pull back from intervention in Asia, the United States was heavily involved in Mexico and a number of other Latin American countries during his presidency.

Review Questions

4. Comparison
   Compare and contrast Wilson's foreign policy in Asia with his actions in Mexico and Latin America. How would you explain the differences?

5. Contextualization
   What does this expansionist period suggest about U.S. power and confidence at the turn of the century?

The United States and the Great War

20.4 Analyze the causes and consequences of U.S. involvement in World War I.

Summary

The Great War broke out in Europe in 1914, and by the presidential election of 1916, there was considerable external pressure on the United States to intervene. Most Americans, however, wanted to stay neutral. German submarine warfare led to increasing tensions between Germany and the United States. The Zimmermann telegram and the German decision to pursue unrestricted submarine warfare led Wilson to ask Congress for a declaration of war in 1917. Once America entered the war, the Wilson administration did everything in its power to suppress dissent and build public support for the war. Propaganda played an important role in Wilson's wartime domestic policy, and Congress took aggressive steps to abridge individual liberties during the war. Some Americans took advantage of wartime conditions to attack immigrants and workers' organizations. Despite initial difficulties, American troops helped turn the tide of the war and ultimately achieve Allied victory. The peace talks that followed the war were undermined by the Allies' conflicting agendas. The refusal of Congress to ratify the treaty was the end of Wilson's dream of American leadership in the League of Nations.

Review Questions

6. Argument Development
   Summarize the U.S. government's plan at home to help the war effort.

7. Continuity and Change over Time
   What was Wilson's vision for the U.S. role in the world following the Great War, and how was that vision a departure from previous periods?

1. Preparing to Write: Plan Your Argument

Long Essay Question—Evaluate the extent to which the Spanish-American War (1898) changed U.S. foreign policy.

For this question category, you actually do not need to discuss the Spanish-American War unless something in the war plays a role in your response. You will be making a judgment. Is this U.S. involvement in Cuba and the period that follows no different from American expansion westward during the 1800s? Or is something markedly different? Consider what is driving U.S. intervention in 1898 and the early 1900s and whether or not it is similar to what was driving westward expansion.

2. Preparing to Write: Develop Your Thesis

Long Essay Question—Evaluate the extent to which there were differing views on intervention abroad between the years 1898 and 1919.

This question has a little twist because the debate about the annexation of Hawaii and the Philippines was different from the debates in 1917 and 1919. In fact, Henry Cabot Lodge was on the side of intervention in the first set of debates and then was the leading opponent to a permanent American role in the world in 1919. So what is different about the nature of intervention in these respective debates? Answering this question will help you develop a thoughtful thesis.

Chapter 21

A Unique, Prosperous, and Discontented Time 1919–1929

Sueddeutsche Zeitung Photo/Alamy Stock Photo

The 1920s were known as the Jazz Age not only because of the decade's most popular music but also because jazz music provided the background to an era in which many Americans wanted to forget the past and have fun dancing, drinking, and riding in increasingly popular automobiles.

Chapter Objective

Demonstrate an understanding of the unique aspects of a decade in U.S. history that lasted from 1919 to 1929.

Learning Objectives

The Prelude—The Red Summer of 1919

21.1 Explain how events at the end of World War I shaped the decade that followed.

The 1920s—The Exuberance of Prosperity

21.2 Analyze how Prohibition and other developments of the 1920s reshaped American culture and led to a decade that some considered an especially prosperous and fun-filled time.

The 1920s—The Conflicts about American Ideals

21.3 Explain the elements of discrimination, hardship, and fundamentalism that also shaped American life in the 1920s.

Harding, Coolidge, and Hoover—National Politics and Policies in the 1920s

21.4 Analyze the political and policy developments of the decade.

The eleven years that were framed by the end of World War I in November 1918 and the stock market crash of October 1929 were unique in many ways. Almost as soon as the era ended, journalists and historians began talking about the "Jazz Age" or simply "the 1920s." As troops returned to the United States from Europe after World War I and as national leaders debated the Treaty of Versailles, many Americans wanted to forget about the rest of the world and its troubles. They expected the resulting peace to usher in a time of pleasure and plenty.

For some white middle-class Americans, the twenties were, indeed, a time of great prosperity and a time to enjoy the freedom of the Jazz Age. And more Americans entered the middle class than ever before. Income inequality that had been so severe in the Gilded Age declined, and more people saw their income increase. The gap between the rich and the middle class narrowed. The 1920s were the decade in which—for the first time—more Americans lived in cities and towns than on remote farms, and urban life often meant a move into the middle class with the freedom and anonymity that urban life brought. American identity shifted as urban middle-class Americans came to see themselves as the national norm. However, for others, including poor urban residents of whom many lived in ethnically isolated neighborhoods, many white farmers in the Midwest and South, Southern black sharecroppers, and American Indians living on isolated reservations, the twenties were not prosperous at all, and to them, the sense of being left out hurt. The rise of the new middle class did not close the gender gap in salaries, though women who were married to men of the rising middle class certainly benefited from increased family income. For many recent immigrants and for residents of small towns and rural areas, the 1920s were a decade when they felt especially marginalized, when it was clear that sophisticated urban dwellers looked down on them and their cultural and religious values and their resentment took many forms. Understanding the differing experiences of those who lived through this decade is the focus of this chapter.

The Prelude—The Red Summer of 1919

21.1   Explain how events at the end of World War I shaped the decade that followed.

When the guns of World War I fell silent on November 11, 1918, the world celebrated. While the United States had been spared much of the war's cost, many Americans were not sure what to make of the postwar world. Some Americans had talked of socialism, even communism, since the strikes of the 1870s, but most did not follow their lead. In the aftermath of World War I, Communists had seized control of Russia. Some Americans celebrated the new Russian government, but many more feared it and wondered whether there might be links between America's homegrown radicals and Russia. For African Americans who had fought in the war, had risked their lives for democracy, and had seen different cultures, the idea of returning to a United States with rigid segregation generated new anger. Other African Americans who had moved north to take wartime jobs had no intention of returning to the segregated South.

With the coming of peace, American workers wanted a part of the new postwar prosperity. The American Federation of Labor had promised no strikes during the war, and with the coming of peace, many workers tried to gain back the money they had lost from stagnant wages in an era of wartime inflation. Before the year was over, one out of every five workers in the United States had been on strike at some point. In January 1919, thirty-five thousand shipyard workers went on strike in Seattle, Washington, and a month later, sixty thousand workers in other industries joined them when the city's Central Labor Council voted for a general strike. The weeklong Seattle General Strike, when virtually no one in the city went to work, stands as the largest citywide strike in U.S. history, and it frightened many.

The Seattle strike was the largest but hardly the only strike in 1919. Textile workers in Lawrence, Massachusetts, the scene of the 1912 Bread and Roses strike (see Chapter 18), engaged in a short and successful strike to demand a forty-eight-hour workweek in January 1919. In September, the police force of Boston, Massachusetts, who had not received a raise

Significant Dates

1919	Palmer raids and Red Summer
	Major strikes in many industries
	Chicago race riot
1920	Eighteenth Amendment creating Prohibition takes effect
	Nineteenth Amendment giving women the right to vote takes effect
	Congress again defeats Treaty of Versailles
	Charles Ponzi's scheme collapses
	Warren Harding is elected U.S. president
	First radio broadcast as Station KDKA reports election returns
1921	Margaret Sanger founds American Birth Control League
	Washington Conference agrees to limit growth of world's navies
1923	Warren Harding dies
	Calvin Coolidge becomes president
1924	Calvin Coolidge defeats John W. Davis for president
1925	*The Great Gatsby* is published
	Scopes trial in Dayton, Tennessee
1927	Babe Ruth hits sixty home runs
	Sacco and Vanzetti are executed
	Kellogg-Briand Pact outlawing war is negotiated
1928	Herbert Hoover defeats Al Smith for president
	Mickey Mouse is born

21.1

21.2

21.3

21.4

since 1913, went on strike. Without a police force in Boston, mobs looted stores and bars. The police commissioner created a temporary voluntary force, and Massachusetts governor Calvin Coolidge gained national fame when he fired all of the striking police officers, saying, "There is no right to strike against the public safety by anybody, anywhere, any time."

While people debated the right of public employees to strike, steel workers went out on strike in September 1919 after the chairman of U.S. Steel, Judge Elbert Gary, refused to meet with union representatives. A month later, coal miners walked off the job, just as the nation's demand for coal for winter heat was beginning.

Strikes were not the only signs of political chaos in 1919. In April, bombs arrived in the mail of Postmaster General Albert Burleson, Attorney General A. Mitchell Palmer, several members of the U.S. Senate, Seattle's antistrike mayor Hanson, and federal immigration authorities and judges. Not one of them was injured, but no one ever discovered who sent the bombs. What evidence there was pointed to anarchists more than members of the Communist Party—which anarchists would never join—but the bomb-induced fear led to the prosecution of many, including anarchists, Communists, Socialists, and union members. On May Day, an international Socialist holiday in honor of the Haymarket events (see Chapter 18), riots erupted in several cities, including Cleveland, Ohio, where one Socialist was killed and forty others were injured in a parade. A few days later, a protester in Washington, D.C., was shot and killed when he refused to stand for the national anthem. The crowd applauded. The American Legion, a new organization of returning soldiers, promised to uphold Americanism and attack radicals. In Centralia, Washington, IWW members killed four parading legion members, and the legion lynched an IWW organizer.

At the same time, the worldwide influenza pandemic that began in 1918 came to the United States. During 1919, half a million Americans died of the flu, many more than had died in the war. The influenza virus did not discriminate between young and old or rich and poor. Although its source was microbes, not radicals, the influenza epidemic contributed to the sense that something was terribly wrong in the postwar world.

Some Americans claimed that the chaos of 1919 proved there was a link between U.S. labor unions, Socialists, and the Bolshevik Communist regime in Russia. Communism seemed to be spreading with a revolt in Hungary and uprisings in the old capitals of Vienna and Berlin. Maybe, some said, it was coming to the United States. Seattle mayor Ole Hanson toured the country, proclaiming that he had put down a Bolshevik uprising in his city. The *Los Angeles Times* told people that they needed to wake up to the Bolshevik menace, while former president William Howard Taft said that the Bolsheviks were "crusaders, pushing their propaganda in every country, seeking to rouse the lawless, the discontented, the poor, the lazy, and the shiftless to a millennium of plunder and class hatred." The Senate ordered an investigation of Russian Bolshevik influence in the United States. Attorney General Palmer claimed that he had evidence of Communist influence in the country. Palmer's proof was a witness who had heard one striker say, "The IWW was not as bad as it was supposed to be." It was hardly overwhelming proof of an international conspiracy. Inflation and stagnant wages seemed to have more to do with the strikes and protests than international intrigue.

Nevertheless, within months of the armistice, the country became a very tense place. People were frightened and the federal government responded. The Wilson administration not only asked Congress to extend the wartime Lever Fuel Act that had prohibited the obstruction of coal distribution during the war but also asked for a peacetime sedition law to continue some of the wartime restrictions on civil liberties. Using the Lever Act, Attorney General Palmer persuaded a federal judge

Library of Congress Prints and Photographs Division [LC-DIG-ds-01290]

The influenza epidemic of 1918 killed far more Americans than World War I—more than 500,000. Police and public officials, like these members of the St. Louis Red Cross Motor Corps, wore masks to protect themselves. Images such as this one, and the disease itself, helped spread fear around the country.

to issue an injunction against the coal strike. Palmer also ordered an all-out effort to find dangerous radicals and appointed a young Justice Department staffer, J. Edgar Hoover, later the first director of the Federal Bureau of Investigation, to lead it. By the end of November, the so-called **Palmer Raids** had led to many arrests, and 249 of those arrested who had not been born in the United States were ordered deported, among them, the well-known radical Emma Goldman, who told federal authorities:

> Ever since I have been in this country—and I have lived here practically all my life—it has been dinned into my ears that under the institutions of this alleged Democracy one is entitled to think and feel as he pleases. What becomes of this sacred guarantee of freedom of thought and conscience when persons are being persecuted and driven out for the very motives and purposes for which the pioneers who built up this country laid down their lives?

Palmer Raids

A series of raids by U.S. government agents in 1919 and 1920 to find, arrest, and sometimes deport people considered to be dangerous radicals.

Goldman and the other deportees left New York on the liner *Buford*, bound for exile in Russia, accompanied by an impressive number of guards. At the same time, Congress expelled its one Socialist member, the strongly anti-Communist representative Victor Berger from Milwaukee, who had opposed the war and remarked that all the American people had gotten out of it was flu and inflation. Milwaukee was not represented in Congress until 1921. The November arrests and deportations were not the end of the hysteria. On January 2 and 3, 1920, Justice Department agents led by J. Edgar Hoover arrested between five thousand and ten thousand suspected radicals in thirty-three cities. This second round of Palmer Raids destroyed the tiny U.S. Communist Party and caught many others. The size and scope of the raids and the lack of evidence of a widespread conspiracy undercut public support for Palmer. By the spring of 1920, more Americans were starting to question the raids. Maybe there were not as many Bolsheviks in the country as Palmer thought.

Fears about Communists and labor unions were not the only concerns to rock the country in 1919. The city of Chicago had been on edge for weeks in the hot summer of 1919. While nearly five thousand public employees—from garbage collectors and street sweepers to city hall clerks—were on strike, someone put up signs in Chicago's black community that said, "We will get you July 4." Somehow, the fear of Communists and the fear of expanded rights for African Americans merged as such fears often did. One newspaper asked, "Have the Blacks Turned Red?" Chicago's black residents, some with little interest in radical politics but fearing an immediate assault, armed themselves. Then on July 27, a black boy swimming in Lake Michigan drifted across the line that supposedly separated the races on Chicago's lakefront beaches. A white mob beat the boy to death while a policeman ignored them. Blacks attacked the policeman and the white mob.

In the days that followed, armed whites attacked Chicago's black community, and blacks fought back. An injured black military veteran confronted a white crowd, yelling, "This is a fine reception to give a man just home from the war." The crowd beat him to death. When a group of whites drove a truck armed with a machine gun into a black neighborhood, blacks killed them. When the riot ended five days later, twenty-three blacks and fifteen whites had been killed and over five hundred people had been injured. Unlike previous race riots in other cities, which had been almost exclusively white attacks on blacks, Chicago's blacks fought back. The black-owned *Chicago Defender* noted that "the youngest generation of black men are not content to move along the line of least resistance as did their sires."

While the Chicago race riot was by far the worst, it was not the only one that summer. In Charleston, South Carolina, a brawl between white sailors and local blacks left two blacks dead and several white sailors injured. In Longview, Texas, a white mob beat up a black schoolteacher for distributing the *Chicago Defender*. In the nation's capital, blacks retaliated. After the *Washington Post* published a series of stories about black crime, especially rape, a riot between white soldiers and black residents left six dead and hundreds injured.

Thirty-six blacks were lynched in 1917. In 1919, seventy-six lynchings were recorded, including some of veterans recently home from World War I. In one Mississippi lynching, the Jackson newspapers announced plans in advance. In September, in Omaha, Nebraska, a mob attacked the jail where a black prisoner was being held, beat up the mayor who tried to stop them, and then lynched the prisoner, William Brown. Only U.S. Army troops under General Leonard Wood brought order to Omaha. As the African American writer James Weldon Johnson looked at the racial violence and the fear of Communists that were roiling the country, often being mixed, he called the season the "Red Summer" of 1919. That Red Summer was a strange and violent start to a decade of prosperity and discontent that followed.

21.1 Quick Review

To what extent did America's growing involvement in the world contribute to domestic events in 1919?

The 1920s—The Exuberance of Prosperity

21.2 Analyze how Prohibition and other developments of the 1920s reshaped American culture and led to a decade that some considered an especially prosperous and fun-filled time.

On May 11, 1921, when Prohibition had been in effect for a little over a year, the *New York Times* reported that an attractive twenty-four-year-old legal stenographer from West 156th Street in Manhattan, Claire Fiance, had been arrested when a detective stopped her to ask about a suspicious-looking package she was carrying and, "with a bright smile and a shake of her bobbed hair," Fiance replied that she was carrying a bottle of whiskey (a violation of the law that prohibited the transportation of alcohol). Fiance's arrest, and those of many more women like her, was a symbol of two of the most important shifts that took place in the 1920s—shifts in many Americans' attitudes toward the consumption of alcohol and toward the appropriate role of women.

During the course of the 1920 presidential campaign, the Republican nominee, Warren G. Harding, coined a new word that described the nation's mood. He said, "America's present need is not heroics but healing; not nostrums but normalcy." **Harding's normalcy** was less a return to some previously "normal" era than a plea to give the reforming spirit of the previous decades a rest. People were as tired of Roosevelt-era reforms as they were of Wilson's internationalism. Many wanted to enjoy themselves, take part in the growing national prosperity, and keep the reformers and the government out of their lives. There was nothing very normal about the era—especially in terms of a national law that banned alcohol, or in terms of the changing roles of women or the new technologies that changed the culture—but it seemed to summarize what many Americans wanted for themselves and their country.

Harding's normalcy

A word coined by Warren G. Harding while he was the 1920 Republican presidential candidate to convey what he thought the country wanted—a new kind of "normal," free from war, international entanglements, and reform efforts.

Prohibition—The Campaign for Moral Conformity

Just at the time when many sought "normalcy," the greatest reform experiment in the nation's history—the prohibition of alcohol—took effect. Even though Prohibition seemed like a reform more typical of the Progressive Era, the way Prohibition was implemented was typical of the 1920s. Indeed, Prohibition—and resistance to it—defined the 1920s for many.

Americans had long been fond of alcohol. But some Americans had also long worried about the nation's drinking habits. In the 1830s, the army ended the traditional whiskey ration for the troops. By the 1850s, school children learned to read from *McGuffey's Readers* that included stories about the "scene of desolation" that liquor created. Some religious groups concluded that drinking and Protestant Christianity were incompatible. The Woman's Christian Temperance Union (WCTU) became the primary voice of temperance reform in Protestant America in the 1880s (see Chapter 19).

While the WCTU sought to persuade people to give up drink, a new organization, the Anti-Saloon League, sought to banish alcohol by law in the 1910s. The male-dominated league had a solid financial base, greatly helped by John D. Rockefeller, and relied on professional experts to organize campaigns, lobby legislators, and attack opponents. In political campaigns, the Anti-Saloon League supported "dry" (supporting Prohibition) candidates of any party and attacked any politician it considered either "wet" (opposing Prohibition) or insufficiently dry. As elected officials saw colleagues elected or defeated because of the league's political acumen, they started to support Prohibition whatever their personal feelings or drinking habits.

The campaign to prohibit alcohol can be understood as no small part of a larger effort by native-born white Protestants, especially those living on farms and small towns, to retake control of a national culture that they saw increasingly under the sway of recent immigrants. As native-born Protestant America became more and more hostile to drink, many immigrants did not appreciate the campaign for moral conformity—or rather, for conformity to a moral code about the drinking of alcohol with which they did not agree.

The Protestant evangelist Charles Stelzle, though a Prohibition leader, was more understanding of the role of the neighborhood saloon than many of his compatriots. While many prohibitionists described saloons as dens of iniquity, Stelzle remembered growing up on New York's Lower East Side where "the working men … held their christening parties, their weddings, their dances, their rehearsals for their singing societies, and all other social functions" in the neighborhood tavern. Saloons were often where ethnic groups could maintain language and tradition. In the evening, Germans could have their beer, Italians their wine, and Irish their whiskey, while enjoying the company of others like themselves. For people who gathered over a drink, Prohibition was an attack on the freedom and acceptance they had come to America to find.

Anti-Saloon League leader William Anderson condemned immigrant resistance to Prohibition. The Board of Temperance, Prohibition, and Public Morals of the Methodist Church said, "If it is true that foreign-born laborers are rebellious against the country because of Prohibition, it may be said that the country is not being run for their benefit. If they do not like the way things are being done let them go back to Europe." As a result of statements like that, many recent immigrants experienced Prohibition as an attack on themselves and their cultures, and some of Prohibition's strongest advocates did little to discourage such an assumption.

With the coming of World War I, the Anti-Saloon League made support for Prohibition a test of patriotism. The league had successfully inserted a clause into the Lever Food and Fuel Control Act banning the use of grain for hard liquor, while giving the president authority to regulate wine and beer production. Wilson was no fan of Prohibition, but it was hard for him to reject a call for national sacrifice in support of the war. In December 1917, Congress—with intensive lobbying by the Anti-Saloon League—passed the Eighteenth Amendment to the U.S. Constitution prohibiting the manufacture, transport, and sale of liquor. The league worked quickly to ensure that the required three-quarters of the state legislatures acted and, in January 1919, Nebraska became the thirty-sixth state to ratify, putting the amendment over the line. In October 1919, Congress passed the Volstead Act, sponsored by Minnesota representative Andrew J. Volstead, banning not only hard liquor (which many even among the amendment's supporters thought was its purpose) but also wine and beer—anything with more than one-half of 1 percent alcohol. Violating the law carried as much as a $1,000 fine. The U.S. Treasury was given authority for enforcement. Like the Eighteenth Amendment, the Volstead Act did not ban the possession of alcohol, only its manufacture, transportation, and sale—a loophole that made enforcement extremely difficult. The act also allowed doctors to prescribe whiskey for medical needs and drugstores to dispense it, and it allowed sacramental wine for religious purposes and industrial use of alcohol—all loopholes that would be exploited in the 1920s.

When Prohibition took effect on January 16, 1920, Americans observed the day in widely different ways. Liquor stores sold out. People who could afford to do so filled their basements with bottles (since possession remained legal), and that night, saloons, hotels, and private clubs gave one last grand party. Assistant Secretary of the Navy Franklin D. Roosevelt drank champagne with former Harvard classmates at the Metropolitan Club in Washington.

21.1

21.2

21.3

21.4

21.1

21.2

21.3

21.4

Library of Congress Prints and Photographs Division [LC-USZ62-123257]

With the coming of Prohibition, federal agents and local police regularly raided establishments that served alcohol, pouring it into sewers. In spite of many such raids, alcohol consumption was hardly slowed by the Eighteenth Amendment or the Volstead Act as illegal production and sales filled the gap.

Other Americans held very different celebrations. The best-known evangelist of the day, Billy Sunday, told worshipers in Norfolk, Virginia, "The reign of tears is over. ...The slums will soon be only a memory. We will turn our prisons into factories and our jails into storehouses and corncribs. Men will walk upright now, women will smile, and children will laugh. Hell will be forever for rent." In fact, Prohibition unleashed a crime wave not only because illegal liquor produced great profits, emboldening criminals to new levels of creativity and violence, but also because so many average Americans were willing to disobey the law.

A Scandalous Age—Bootleg, Ponzi, and Teapot Dome

As Prohibition began in 1920, a Chicago gangster known as "Big Jim" Colosimo owned saloons and brothels across the city. Colosimo's nephew and business manager, Johnny Torrio, had moved from Brooklyn to Chicago to work for him in 1909, and both men had become millionaires. Prohibition meant they had to change some of their ways, but they certainly planned to continue, expecting increased profits. One day, Torrio asked Colosimo to meet a load of whiskey that Torrio was having delivered to one of their cafés. Colosimo showed up on schedule and, as he walked through the dining room, someone emerged from the cloakroom and shot him. Colosimo died instantly. While no evidence was ever found that Torrio or his new bodyguard from Brooklyn, Al Capone, was involved in the murder, Torrio—aided by Capone—quickly took control of the liquor business in Chicago. The Colosimo murder was only the start of the violence to come with Prohibition—all across the country. Organized crime had existed long before Prohibition, but once Prohibition took effect, criminals from Los Angeles to Boston took control of the now-illegal liquor business, expanding their operations and criminal networks beyond anything seen before, often violently.

The single most violent incident in Prohibition came near its end. By 1929, Capone had consolidated his control of illegal liquor in Chicago. He also controlled much of the police force, the elected political leadership, and the courts of Chicago and had his own squad of gunmen and rumrunners to bring illegal alcohol to the city, especially from Canada. When an upstart gangster, "Bugs" Moran, tried to take part of his business away, Capone responded. On February 14, 1929, five men, two dressed as police officers, arrived at Moran's headquarters. They lined up the seven men there against a wall, shot and killed them, and calmly drove off. That bloody St. Valentine's Day massacre provided a fitting capstone to a bloody decade wherein gangsters killed each other and innocent bystanders. Many other people were killed in drunken brawls in the illegal saloons, or speakeasies, that proliferated or by drinking improperly made bootleg liquor that poisoned them.

Capone's influence with politicians and police made him safe from arrest in Chicago, but after 1929, the newly elected president Herbert Hoover demanded that the U.S. Treasury Department do something to uphold the law, even in Chicago, and Capone was eventually arrested and imprisoned for income tax evasion in 1931. The liquor trade continued unabated.

While Prohibition-related crimes made the headlines in the 1920s, they were not the only criminal enterprise to flourish in a decade that many experienced as particularly lawless. In 1919, Charles Ponzi, an Italian immigrant, opened a new investment firm in Boston, announcing an extraordinarily high rate of return because of the skill he claimed in international trade. In fact, he simply paid old investors with money provided by new investors. Other than using the profits to live a very high life, Ponzi did not invest at all. The scheme made Ponzi rich and famous, but newspapers and bank investigators started asking questions and Ponzi's world collapsed in August 1920. He was arrested and eventually deported from the United States. Investors lost all their money. The Ponzi scheme was neither the first nor the last time that someone tried to get rich by catering to the greed of others, but it became the term used to describe that kind of fraud.

Perhaps the largest criminal enterprise of the 1920s was conducted within the federal government itself. In 1909, the government set aside three large oil reserves, two in California at Elk Hills and Buena Vista and one in Wyoming at Teapot Dome. They were managed by the Navy Department until the Harding administration came into office in 1921.

Harding, a most genial president, hated to say no to anyone, especially old friends whom he met for poker games and illegal drinking throughout his administration. When Harding's secretary of the interior, Albert B. Fall, asked to have the oil reserves transferred from the Navy Department to the Department of the Interior, Harding agreed. Fall's long-standing ties to the oil industry might have helped him manage the national assets.

In 1922, officials in the U.S. Navy were growing nervous about the growth of Japan's navy and wanted some of the reserve oil transferred to Pearl Harbor. To meet the U.S. navy's needs, Fall secretly leased the reserves to oil companies owned by his friends Harry F. Sinclair and Edward Doheny for very low rates. The two pumped oil from the reserves, paying a royalty, in oil, to the navy. The navy got the oil it needed in Hawaii. Sinclair and Doheny made a considerable profit. After a congressional investigation led by Montana senators Burton K. Wheeler and Thomas Walsh began in 1924, it was discovered that Sinclair had made a gift of $260,000 to Fall while Doheny had lent the secretary $100,000 with no interest or deadline for payment. A great deal of additional money seems to have changed hands behind the scenes as Sinclair and Doheny stole not only from the government but also from their own companies. Once Congress began to unearth the trail of oil and money, what became known as the **Teapot Dome** scandal kept spreading. Eventually, the U.S. Supreme Court declared both leases "illegal and fraudulent," Fall was found guilty of accepting a bribe and spent a year in prison, and the Harding administration was tagged as one of the most corrupt in history.

Teapot Dome
The name given to a major scandal of the Harding presidency in which U.S. Navy oil reserves, including those at Teapot Dome, Wyoming, were used to enrich the secretary of the interior and his friends.

While the Teapot Dome scandal was the largest of the Harding scandals, there were plenty of others. Harding's appointee as head of the Veterans' Bureau, Charles R. Forbes, managed to lose some $200 million in two years, buying new goods at a high price from friends and selling goods on hand as cheap surplus. The arrangement made money for his friends but cost the government a fortune. Similar scandals involved the Alien Property Custodian office, which was supposed to manage German assets in the United States, and the Prohibition Enforcement Division of the Treasury Department, which, it was said, would ignore violations as long as the right amount of money was left in a fishbowl in a New York City hotel room. With senior-level officials of the U.S. government behaving in such a manner, it was no surprise that regular citizens viewed obedience to the law as optional.

The Vote for Women

In August 1920, just months after the Prohibition amendment had been ratified, the U.S. Constitution was amended again to say, "The right of citizens of the United States to vote shall not be denied or abridged by the United States or by any State on account of sex." The Nineteenth Amendment took effect in time for women in every part of the United States to vote in the presidential election of November 1920. Women's suffrage and the new roles for women that evolved in the 1920s helped shape that decade as much or more than Prohibition or any other development.

The women most associated with the two amendments—Susan B. Anthony and Elizabeth Cady Stanton, leaders in the long-lasting women's suffrage movement, and Frances Willard of the Woman's Christian Temperance Union—all died before the campaigns they led achieved their goals. It was Carrie Chapman Catt's privilege to preside over the victory of voting rights, being an active member of both the Woman's Christian Temperance Union and the National American Woman Suffrage Association. As World War I began in Europe, Catt was active in the Women's Peace Party but left it after the United States entered the war.

While other women such as Jane Addams and Jeanette Rankin continued to oppose the war, Catt supported the war and then demanded a suffrage amendment as a "war measure."

The Northeastern Federation of Colored Women's Clubs extracted a promise from a sometimes reluctant Catt not to agree to any compromise language in the constitutional amendment that could leave enforcement to the states. They knew all too well what Southern state legislatures would do with the votes of African American women. Sadly, after the war, Catt did all too little to support voting rights for African American women, in the South or the North.

In spite of differences about the war itself, women found ways to work together. Jeannette Rankin introduced the "Anthony Amendment," the woman's suffrage amendment, to the House of Representatives on January 10, 1918. The amendment passed the House 274 to 136. The Senate moved more slowly, but under Catt's leadership, the National American Woman Suffrage Association helped defeat four anti-suffrage senators in November 1918, and the amendment was approved and sent on to the states in June 1919. The first states ratified quickly, but opposition remained strong. Nevertheless, a little more than a year after Congress proposed the amendment, the Tennessee legislature gave the amendment the required thirty-sixth state. The final vote in the Tennessee Senate was 49 to 47 and the amendment carried only because a twenty-four-year-old senator, Harry Thomas Burn, changed his vote at the last minute after a passionate plea from his mother. That plea, and many others like them, worked, and on August 26, 1920, the secretary of state announced that the amendment had been ratified.

In November 1920, more than twenty-six million women across the country voted in the presidential election. One of them, Charlotte Woodward, at ninety-one, was the only surviving signer of the Seneca Falls Declaration of 1848. It had been seventy-two years since Elizabeth Cady Stanton and her allies proclaimed their right to vote.

Thinking Historically
Understanding Different Perspectives on Women's Rights

Very soon after women gained the vote, the National American Woman Suffrage Association became the League of Women Voters. The newly organized league—initially an all-white organization—committed itself to nonpartisan education and helping women join parties and vote wisely.

Other women viewed the right to vote as merely a first step and pushed for a much more militant approach to women's rights. Alice Paul led the National Woman's Party that adopted a Declaration of Principles in 1923, which in part, insisted:

In short—that woman shall no longer be in any form of subjection to man in law or in custom, but shall in every way be on an equal plane in rights, as she has always been and will continue to be in responsibilities and obligations.

In their quest for these rights, the Woman's Party began a long fight for an Equal Rights Amendment to the U.S. Constitution.

Opposition to women's suffrage did not disappear in 1920. One anti-suffrage group, the National Association Opposed to Woman Suffrage, wrote that they "fought the grant of the ballot because they foresaw that it was the logical boundary line between the old institution-of-marriage ideal of the Family as the unit of society and the Feminist revolt against nature." A new contest had just begun.

During the 1920s, voting was almost impossible for African American women or men in much of the country. African American women also faced other pressing issues. Charlotte Hawkins Brown (1883–1961) of the National Colored Woman's Club spoke to a conference of mostly white women that was meeting in Memphis, Tennessee, in 1920:

We have begun to feel that you are not, after all, interested in us. … We feel that so far as lynching is concerned that, if the white woman would take hold of the situation that lynching would be stopped, mob violence stamped out and yet the guilty would have justice meted out by due course of law and would be punished accordingly.

Source: Ellen Skinner, editor, *Women and the National Experience: Sources in Women's History* (Boston: Prentice Hall, 2011); Mari Jo Buhl, Teresa Murphy, and Jane Gerhard, *Women and the Making of America* (Upper Saddle River, NJ: Pearson/Prentice Hall, 2008).

Thinking Critically

1. **Causation**
   What debates about women's role did the Nineteenth Amendment spawn?

2. **Comparison**
   Compare and contrast the responses to the passage of the Nineteenth Amendment by different women. How would you explain the differences?

Bettman/Getty Images

Many women in the 1920s asserted new freedoms not only in dress and style but also in claiming the right to hold a job, though too often the jobs that were available were at the bottom of the economic ladder, in places such as the typing pool.

A Revolution in Culture—Manners, Morals, and Automobiles

Gaining the right to vote and Prohibition both played a part in fostering a new lifestyle for a generation of young women who came to be known as "flappers." Flappers cut their hair short and dressed in ways that exposed more skin—on their necks, arms, and legs—than any previous generation. Some flappers embraced their own sexual freedom, objecting to the older rules about sexuality, and many chose to drink or smoke. Certainly, the flappers of the 1920s were not the first women to rebel against the sexual double standard that made women guardians of morality. But in the 1920s, having won the right to vote, the activism of many women changed drastically.

Flappers were determined to have equal freedom as men to do as they pleased in work and in their social lives. The emergence of the flappers was one—but only one—aspect of that new activism. Pre-Prohibition saloons and bars had been male preserves. No respectable woman would enter one. However, the illegal speakeasies that replaced the old bars in the 1920s—often in the same location—catered not only to men but also to women, and not just flappers. As Elmer Davis, a thoughtful observer of his times, said of Prohibition, "The old days when father spent his evenings at Cassidy's bar with the rest of the boys are gone, and probably gone forever; Cassidy may still be in business at the old stand and father may still go down there of evenings, but since Prohibition mother goes down with him."

It was not only young middle-class women—flappers—who challenged their status in the United States in the 1920s. The voices of those advocating for women had become stronger, and elected officials began to listen to the newly expanded electorate. In 1921, Congress passed the Sheppard-Towner Act providing federal funds for prenatal and infant care. In 1922, Congress passed the Cable Act, protecting the citizenship rights of American women who married noncitizens. By 1923, three women, all Republicans, were serving in the House of Representatives. Women became active in both political parties and ran for office in all parts of the country. In New Mexico, a descendant of one of the old Spanish landholding families, Adelina Otero Warren, who had been honored for her leadership when New Mexico ratified the Nineteenth Amendment, ran for Congress in 1922, winning the Republican nomination but losing the final election. Had Warren won her close race, she would have been the first Latina in Congress.

American Voices

Ellen Wells Page, A Flapper's Appeal, 1922

Middle- and upper-class young women known as flappers were the symbols of the revolution in morals that took place after World War I. One self-described flapper appealed for understanding of her generation.

If one judges by appearances, I suppose I am a flapper. I am within the age limit. I wear bobbed hair, the badge of flapperhood. (And, oh, what a comfort it is!) I powder my nose. I wear fringed skirts and bright-colored sweaters, and scarfs, and waists [blouses] with Peter Pan collars, and low-heeled "finale hopper" shoes. I *adore* to dance. I spend a large amount of time in automobiles. I attend hops, and proms, and ball-games, and crew races, and other affairs at men's colleges. But none the less some of the most thoroughbred superflappers might blush to claim sistership or even remote relationship with such as I. I don't use rouge, or lipstick, or pluck my eyebrows. I don't smoke (I've tried it, and don't like it), or drink. …

I want to beg all you parents, and grandparents, and friends, and teachers, and preachers—you who constitute the "older generation"—to overlook our shortcomings, at least for the present, and to appreciate our virtues. …

We are the Younger Generation. The war tore away our spiritual foundations and challenged our faith. We are struggling to regain our equilibrium. The times have made us older and more experienced than you were at our age.

Source: Ellen Welles Page, "A Flapper's Appeal to Parents," *Outlook*, December 6, 1922.

Thinking Critically

1. **Analyzing Primary Sources**
   How did Page define the attributes of "flapperhood"? Who do you think her intended audience was?

2. **Contextualization**
   What does Page say is the explanation of the flapper phenomenon? How important was the context of the 1920s to this explanation?

In 1921, Margaret Sanger, who became a birth control advocate while working as a visiting nurse in New York City, organized a birth control conference for physicians and researchers in New York City and later the same year founded the American Birth Control League. In 1923, she opened a physician-run birth control clinic since, by law, only physicians, not nurses like Sanger, were allowed to dispense birth control information in the 1920s. She organized several international conferences on birth control in the 1920s. In the 1930s, she tested federal laws against the importation of foreign-made contraceptives and won. In 1942, the American Birth Control League became Planned Parenthood with Sanger as honorary chair. Planned Parenthood also supported the research that led to the first birth control pill, approved by the U.S. Food and Drug Administration in 1960.

While responses to Prohibition and women's issues were changing the culture, technological changes of the 1920s also reshaped the ways Americans thought about culture and morality. For many Americans, urban and rural, the radio and motion pictures brought news of national and international events and shaped a more unified and fast-changing national culture. The relatively low-cost automobile made it possible for more Americans to travel while giving younger Americans a degree of privacy unheard of by previous generations—especially once enclosed sedans replaced open cars in the mid-1920s. Washing machines, refrigerators, vacuum cleaners, and toasters reshaped traditional housework for women. In addition, new forms of financing allowed people to buy all of these goods on installment plans, dramatically increasing consumer debt while making the new inventions available to more people.

When the nation's first radio station, KDKA in Pittsburgh, began operating, broadcasting the election returns in the Harding-Cox presidential contest in November 1920, it ushered in a new era in news and entertainment. Within a very short period of time, hundreds of stations were reporting news; playing records; covering religious services, sports events, and political campaigns; and broadcasting live concerts (once they had figured out how to manage acoustical control). In 1927, Congress passed the Radio Act, which created a plan to license radio stations and regulate the wavelengths at which they broadcast. A decade after KDKA started its first broadcast, half of all American households owned a radio.

Although automobiles had already been introduced, they became increasingly common during the 1920s. Fords, Chryslers, Chevrolets, Cadillacs, Lexingtons, Maxwells, and Hudsons showed up in front of American homes. During that decade, the number of cars registered in the United States tripled from 9 million to 26.5 million.

Margaret Sanger, the nation's best-known proponent of birth control from the 1920s to the 1950s.

Auto-related industries such as steel, paint, textile, and tire production along with highway construction boomed in the 1920s. Auto dealerships, gas stations, repair shops, roadside restaurants, and hotels grew. Congress provided funds for the federal Bureau of Public Roads in 1921, and metropolitan areas expanded as distances became easier to traverse. New York City built the Bronx River Parkway, connecting large parts of the city, and Los Angeles opened new highways into the heretofore farming country of the San Fernando Valley.

Americans moved to cities in the 1920s but also to suburbs, which expanded dramatically as the automobile and growing roadways allowed people to spread farther than the train and streetcar tracks had during the first wave of suburbanization in the 1880s. The pace of suburbanization was quickened when General Motors purchased a number of streetcar companies and tore up the tracks, replacing the service with General Motors buses. The nation's trolley system slowly withered, replaced with buses that could move more freely but that later added to growing traffic congestion.

Like the automobile, silent motion pictures had been invented well before World War I, but became an important part of the culture of the 1920s. By the end of the decade, an average of 100 million Americans, out of a total population of 123 million, attended a movie every week. Movies offered fun, escape, and entertainment. For people in small towns and rural areas, movies brought the larger world into their community. After 1927, motion picture technology enabled the addition of sound and voice, and "talkies" became popular. Whether people watched the comedies of Charlie Chaplin, the cartoons of Walt Disney's Mickey Mouse (created in 1928), the religious enthusiasm of *The King of Kings*, or the sexually suggestive acting of Clara Bow and Rudolph Valentino, movies gave them new ways of looking at the world. Not insignificantly, movie theaters were air-conditioned well before most other buildings, making a summer evening at the movies especially appealing.

Movies, newspapers, and magazines such as *Time* (started in 1923) created an age of new heroes. Heroes seemed to be emerging all the time, including "Babe" Ruth of the New York Yankees, who hit sixty home runs in 1927 in the increasingly popular game of baseball, or boxers like Jack Dempsey and Gene Tunney, whose matches generated over a million dollars in revenue, or Gertrude Ederle, the first woman to swim the English Channel in 1926, or the decade's most celebrated hero, Charles A. Lindbergh, who flew solo across the Atlantic in his airplane the *Spirit of St. Louis* in 1927 and was welcomed home with what was becoming a New York institution, a ticker-tape parade down Fifth Avenue.

In addition, a new form of self-defined, sophisticated culture took hold. When *The New Yorker* appeared in 1925, its editor, Harold Ross, said that it was "not edited for the old lady in Dubuque" but, rather, was "a reflection in word and picture of metropolitan life." Part of *The New Yorker*'s success was the guidance it gave to members—or aspiring members—of New York's "smart set" on how to navigate the city's nightlife—which nightclubs, speakeasies, cafes, and hotel lounges provided the best entertainment, the grandest design, and (though it didn't overtly say so) the best drinks.

During the 1920s, New York also became a center of gay and lesbian life, sometimes hidden but sometimes quite open. In 1927, Gene Harwood, then nineteen, was one of hundreds of gay men and lesbians who moved to New York City. An older gay friend told Hardwood about the freedom he would find there in contrast to his small-town home and he embraced it. Clubs in Greenwich Village became known as gathering places for gay men or lesbians, sometimes together, sometimes separately. Eva Kotchever, a Polish Jewish émigré also known as Even Addams, presided over a tearoom on MacDougal Street that announced, "Men are admitted but not welcome," but men also had plenty of places to gather. Farther north in Manhattan, Harlem had become the center of the city's African American community and a place where the clubs and nightlife were as welcoming to homosexuals as they were to straight people. The artist Edouard Roditi described Harlem as "Much more! Much more!" welcoming to gay men than even Greenwich Village.

Library of Congress Prints and Photographs Division|LC-USZ62-54357|

Listening to the radio became possible for many in the 1920s, uniting the culture in shared information and shared tastes as never before.

21.1

21.2

21.3

21.4

The U.S. writers of the 1920s spoke to a generation disillusioned with the idealism of past decades as well as the business and moneymaking that characterized so much of 1920s bourgeoisie culture. Many lived abroad and were dubbed the "Lost Generation" by Gertrude Stein, who herself lived most of her life in Paris. Among them were Ernest Hemingway and other writers as different as T. S. Eliot and John Dos Passos. Sinclair Lewis published *Main Street* in 1920 and *Babbitt* in 1922, both of which looked at the stifling conformity and hypocrisy of small-town America. F. Scott Fitzgerald dropped out of Princeton, where he had spent most of his college career at parties, and then described that culture he knew so well in *This Side of Paradise* in 1920 and *The Great Gatsby* in 1925. In their literature and their assumptions, the social and artistic elite who lived between the end of World War I in 1918 and the coming of the Great Depression in 1929 lived at a unique, prosperous, and discontented moment in American history and literature.

The Harlem Renaissance and Marcus Garvey

In 1920 as in 1820, 90 percent of African Americans lived in the South. A significant majority of these African Americans were sharecroppers, living on someone else's land and dependent on an economic and an educational system that kept them impoverished. However, by 1920, some blacks had begun to move away from rural poverty and segregation in the rural South to new opportunities in Southern cities and in the larger industrial cities of the North. Although the height of the **Great Migration**—the great movement of African Americans from the rural South to the urban North—took place in the 1940s and 1950s (see Chapter 24), it had its beginnings during and immediately after World War I. (See Map 21-1.) The result

Great Migration

The mass movement of African Americans from the rural South to the urban North, spurred especially by new job opportunities that began during World War I and the 1920s.

Map 21-1 People Moving in the 1920s.

Many Americans chose to, or were forced to, move during the 1920s. Cities and suburbs grew rapidly. Throughout the era, African Americans moved from the South to Northern cities such as Chicago, Detroit, and New York. In some areas, the farmers' depression meant either giving up on cultivated land and starting over to farm another region or becoming a city worker.

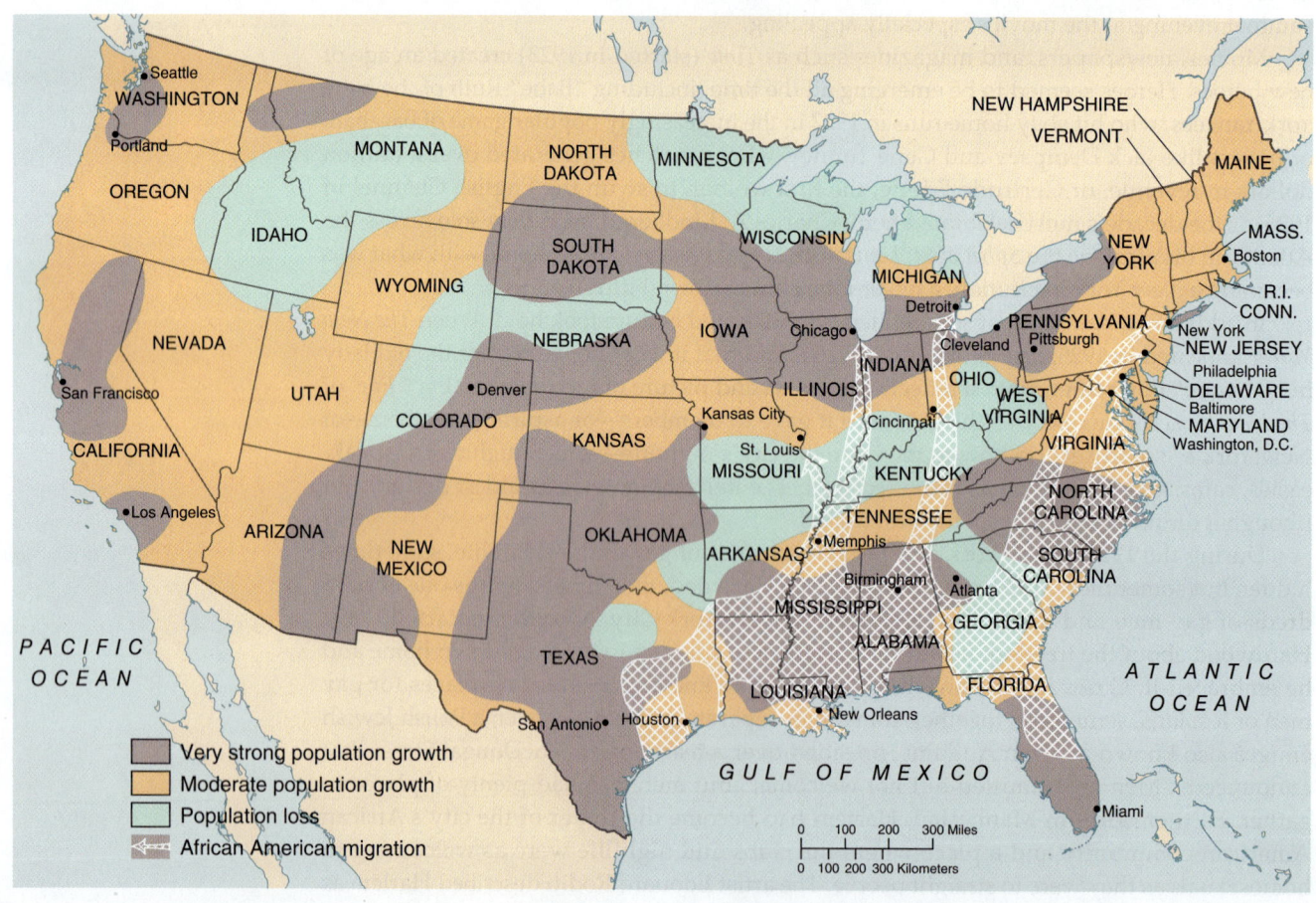

Legend:
- Very strong population growth
- Moderate population growth
- Population loss
- African American migration

0   100   200   300 Miles
0 100 200 300 Kilometers

was a population shift, a cultural flowering, and the development of something new in the United States—a small but powerful black middle class.

World War I created new opportunities for African Americans. As work expanded, factories in the North needed more workers. The Illinois Central Railroad, which ran straight from the heart of the cotton-growing Mississippi Delta to job-rich Chicago, enabled those who wanted to move north to get there. The nation's most widely read black newspaper, the *Chicago Defender*, announced "The Great Northern Drive" in May 1917. The newspaper called on Southern blacks to make "The Flight Out of Egypt," commissioned songs like "Bound for the Promised Land," and negotiated special group rates with the Illinois Central. The paper told sharecroppers about jobs available in the stockyards and meatpacking houses in Chicago that paid salaries unimagined in a sharecroppers' shack in Mississippi or Alabama.

Black music reflected the emotions of those who moved north. The blues, music born out of gospel, ragtime, and jazz, began on back porches, small-town bars and dance halls, and prison cells in the Mississippi Delta early in the 1900s. At first, blues musicians sang of hard lives in the South. John Hurt sang, "Avalon [Mississippi] my home town, always on my mind," and Bill Broonzy sang, "Anywhere in Mississippi is my native home." But in the 1920s, the blues moved north. Those who had sung about life in Mississippi began to sing, "I'm going to Detroit, get myself a good job. Tired of stayin' round here with the starvation mob."

Some 50,000 African Americans moved to Chicago during World War I and another 100,000 in the ten years that followed. Chicago's black population grew from 44,000 in 1910 to 109,000 in 1920 to 234,000 in 1930. During and after World War II, many more blacks would follow. In addition to Chicago, African Americans moved to Detroit, Gary (Indiana), Los Angeles, Milwaukee, Newark, New York City, Oakland (California), Philadelphia, Syracuse (New York), and other cities that offered jobs and a modicum of freedom.

Cotton planters did everything possible to stop the northern migration. The *Chicago Defender* was branded as dangerously subversive. Plantation owners opposed anything more than rudimentary education for blacks so they would have few skills to take north. In Greenville, Mississippi, the town's leading white citizen, LeRoy Percy, opposed the Klan because he feared that their brand of terror would lead to "an exodus within a year" of the black people who were essential to the economy. African Americans kept moving anyway.

The novelist Richard Wright described the experience of many of the early migrants in his novel *Native Son* and his autobiography *Black Boy*. Wright was born to a sharecropper family in Natchez, Mississippi. He left the rural South for Memphis and then in 1927 for Chicago to experience, he said, "the warmth of other suns." It was not an easy move. Wright remembered, "I had fled a known terror, and perhaps I could cope with this unknown terror."

The North to which the Southern immigrants came was not always a welcoming place. After World War I, some whites sought to reclaim the industrial jobs they had held before the war at the same time that wartime demand for workers ebbed. Salaries were much higher in the North, but so were rents. Living conditions in increasingly segregated and rapidly growing urban neighborhoods made for tightly packed homes. Race riots in Chicago and St. Louis in 1919 made it very clear just how unwelcoming the North could be.

African Americans had long lived in cities such as New York, Philadelphia, and Providence since before the American Revolution. Free black communities had also emerged before the Civil War in places such as Cincinnati, Cleveland, and Pittsburgh. Nevertheless, in 1910, at least 90 percent of African Americans lived in the South, mostly the rural South, and only a tiny percentage of Northern blacks were professionals, mostly preachers or teachers in African American churches and schools. Most Northern black men were janitors, porters, servants, or waiters while black women were cooks, laundresses, maids, or servants. Still, there was often conflict between longtime urban blacks and the newcomers from the South who started arriving in large numbers after 1917. Each found the social and economic position of the other threatening.

21.1

21.2

21.3

21.4

21.1

21.2

21.3

21.4

American Voices

Alain Locke, *Voices of the Harlem Renaissance*, 1925

When Alain Locke edited The New Negro: Voices of the Harlem Renaissance *in 1925, the word* Negro *was the preferred term of respect for most Americans of African descent— just as the term* African American *would be in future decades. Locke's goal was to define something new in African American culture.*

From Alain Locke's "Foreword"—

This volume aims to document the New Negro culturally and socially,—to register the transformations of the inner and outer life of the Negro in America that have so significantly taken place. … Negro life is not only establishing new contacts and founding new centers, it is finding a new soul. There is a fresh spiritual and cultural focusing. We have, as the heralding sign, an unusual outburst of creative expression. There is a renewed race-spirit that consciously and proudly sets itself apart.

From James Weldon Johnson's essay in *The New Negro*, "Harlem: The Culture Capital"—

In the make-up of New York, Harlem is not merely a Negro colony or community, it is a city within a city, the greatest Negro city in the world. It is not a slum or a fringe. … It has its

own churches, social and civic centers, shops, theaters and other places of amusement. And it contains more Negroes to the square mile than any other spot on earth. …

I believe that the Negro's advantages and opportunities are greater in Harlem than in any other place in the country, and that Harlem will become the intellectual, the cultural and the financial center for Negroes of the United States, and will exert a vital influence upon all Negro peoples.

Source: Alain Locke, editor, *The New Negro: Voices of the Harlem Renaissance*, New Introduction by Arnold Rampersad (originally 1925, new edition New York: Simon & Schuster, 1992).

Thinking Critically

1. **Analyzing Primary Sources**
   According to the point of view of the authors, what made Harlem different from other African American communities? What did Locke and Johnson see as the hallmarks of the "Negro" or "Harlem" Renaissance?

2. **Contextualization**
   How would you describe the historical situation in which Locke and Johnson wrote regarding black lives in the South and the North?

Harlem Renaissance

A new African American cultural awareness that flourished in literature, art, and music in the 1920s.

Michael Ochs Archives/Getty Images

Marcus Garvey, pictured third from the left with some of his followers, used lavish uniforms and parades to foster pride and self-confidence in his mostly poor, African American supporters.

Nevertheless, in spite of fear, pain, and segregation, something very important started happening in the expanding black communities of the urban North in the 1920s, most of all in New York City's Harlem (see Map 21-2). Alain Locke's 1925 book, *The New Negro*, was his effort to define the **Harlem Renaissance** as an era in which the African American was "moving forward under the control largely of his own objectives." Locke became known as the "dean" of the New Negro movement, an artistic and intellectual flowering of an assertive new cultural identity. The acknowledged capital of this new movement was New York City's Harlem, and during the 1920s, the "Harlem Renaissance" defined elite black culture.

While the intellectual and cultural leaders of Harlem celebrated their Renaissance, other African Americans, especially those on the lowest rungs of the economy, looked to the charismatic Marcus Garvey (1887–1940) to foster racial pride and self-determination. Garvey established the Universal Negro Improvement and Conservation Association and African Communities League (UNIA) in Jamaica in August 1914.

For poor blacks, especially those seeking to adjust to life in Northern cities, Garvey's message rejecting integration with white America and focusing on self-help, self-determination, and African nationalism struck a powerful chord. At the beginning of 1918, the New York branch of the UNIA had about 1,500 members. By 1920, Garvey claimed a membership of 2 to 4 million in thirty branches across the country.

In the early 1920s, Garvey outlined an independent path for blacks, "not to hate other people," but to take responsibility for their own fate. "We are organized," he said, "for the absolute

Map 21-2 Harlem in the 1920s.

Before World War I, only a few blocks of New York City's Harlem neighborhood had an African American majority. By the end of the 1920s, nearly all of Harlem, from Central Park to the Harlem River, was an African American community, and for many—including the voices of the Harlem Renaissance and the followers of Marcus Garvey—it was the capital of black America.

21.1

21.2

21.3

21.4

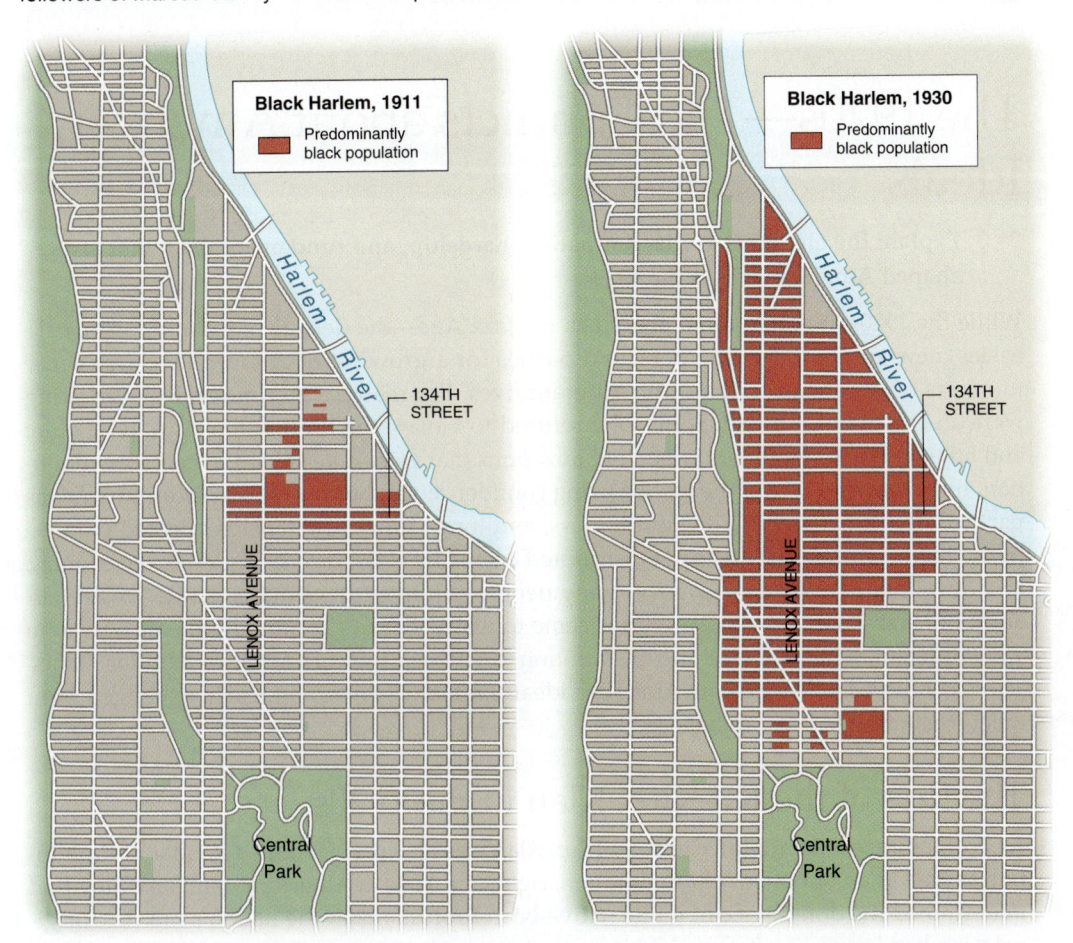

purpose of bettering our condition, industrially, commercially, socially, religiously and politically."

Garvey was at the height of his popularity in the early 1920s. In 1919, the UNIA purchased a large auditorium in Harlem, and in August 1920, twenty-five thousand delegates from Africa, the Caribbean, and the United States adopted the Negro Declaration of Rights. A UNIA parade in Harlem included UNIA men of the African Legion in uniform and a delegation of two hundred women of the Black Cross Nurses marching in a show of strength and pride.

Garvey created a shipping company, the Black Star Line in 1920, to carry passengers and freight between the United States, the islands of the Caribbean, and Africa. The shipping line was the crown jewel of Garvey's economic development plan, but it was also Garvey's downfall. Selling stock at $5 per share, Garvey eventually collected over $750,000, perhaps much more. But whether through mismanagement or corruption, or both, the line floundered.

The Black Star Line was attacked by blacks as well as whites. In December 1920, W. E. B. Du Bois published an indictment of the Black Star Line. The finances of the Black Star Line collapsed and with it the rest of Garvey's U.S.-based efforts. He was arrested for fraud, convicted, and sentenced to five years in federal prison in 1923 and began serving his term in the Atlanta Federal Penitentiary in February 1925. In November 1927, President Calvin Coolidge commuted Garvey's sentence but had him deported to Jamaica. Garvey continued to build the UNIA in Jamaica and traveled through much of the world. But his influence, though significant, declined in the United States.

21.2 Quick Review

How did changes in American culture reflect the postwar desire for fun and leisure? What were other causes of cultural change in the 1920s?

The 1920s—The Conflicts about American Ideals

21.3 **Explain the elements of discrimination, hardship, and fundamentalism that also shaped American life in the 1920s.**

While the 1920s are often remembered as the Jazz Age—the decade of Prohibition, speakeasies, new automobiles, flappers, and parties for a growing urban middle class—large numbers of Americans lived quite different lives. For many, the crime and the drinking were an evil to be shunned. Some who refused to violate the Prohibition laws lived quiet and law-abiding lives; others joined organizations that were determined to enforce Prohibition, not always by lawful means. Growing confidence and hope among African Americans particularly threatened white Southerners, and long-simmering tensions heated dangerously. The new prosperity was not distributed evenly by class, race, or region of the country, and despite the relative prosperity, many people still lived lives of desperate poverty. In addition, many native-born Americans came to distrust and fear immigrants or those who were different, while the teaching of evolution threatened the very fabric of faith for others. These conflicts challenged core American ideals on many levels, and reactions ranged from quiet frustration to vocal defiance.

The Rise of the Ku Klux Klan in the 1920s

As Prohibition came into force, the Ku Klux Klan was also revived as a defender of Prohibition as well as an opponent of immigration, rights for African Americans, and anything that undermined the dominance of white native-born Protestants in the nation's life. The original Klan had been one of several white terrorist organizations that opposed Reconstruction after the Civil War. Because of prosecution by the Grant administration, the Reconstruction-era Klan virtually disappeared in the 1870s. In 1915, a Georgian, William Joseph Simmons, inspired by nostalgia for a bygone era, re-created the Klan. During its first few years, Simmons's Klan was an insignificant organization of a few hundred members. Then, in the early 1920s, a Texas dentist, Hiram Wesley Evans, pushed Simmons aside and turned the Klan into a hugely successful hate organization aimed at African Americans, immigrants, Catholics, Jews, and anyone who challenged the Prohibition laws. Under Evans's leadership, the Klan increased from a few hundred to as many as five million members, including a female auxiliary that became the separate Women of the Ku Klux Klan (WKKK). As the Klan struck fear into many, it enriched a few leaders who controlled access to everything from membership dues to Klan robes and paraphernalia, which had to be ordered directly from the national headquarters.

The Klan slogan was, "One flag, one school, one Bible." It advocated for strict enforcement of Prohibition and—ironically, some thought—a cabinet-level

The men and women of the Ku Klux Klan staged massive rallies and demonstrations in all parts of the nation throughout the 1920s, including this one in Washington, D.C., in 1925.

Department of Education that would ensure that all American children were taught Klan-defined patriotism, or "100% Americanism." It gave flags and Bibles to public schools while demanding the firing of Catholic and Jewish teachers. The Klan sought to require every student to attend public schools and succeeded in Oregon, though the law was overturned by the U.S. Supreme Court.

Most people understood that the Klan also had another agenda: maintaining rigid racial segregation and, by using terror if need be, keeping African Americans from asserting their rights. If a black man was accused of flirting with a white woman, he might expect a whipping or worse from robed Klan visitors. If the Klan discovered an interracial couple, they attacked them. If a black did not want to sell land at a price offered by a Klan member, he or she might expect a lashing until agreeing to sell. In 1920, Nathan Taylor, an African American attorney in Mississippi who previously had been protected by white attorneys, was abducted by the Klan and taken out to the middle of the Mississippi River and warned that, one way or another, he was to leave the state. Preferring to leave alive, Taylor moved to Chicago.

The Klan, often with the Women of the Klan in the lead, launched boycotts of stores owned by blacks, Catholics, or Jews. Klan publications condemned the "foreign influence" of the Catholic Church and reprinted articles from Henry Ford's fiercely anti-Semitic *Dearborn Independent*. The Klan's Constitution defined a goal

> to unite white male persons, native-born Gentile citizens of the United States of America, who owe no allegiance of any nature to any foreign government, nation, institution, sect, ruler, person, or people … to shield the sanctity of the home and the chastity of womanhood; to maintain forever white supremacy.

The Klan provided entertainment in isolated small towns where there was not much to do. A hundred thousand people attended a Klan rally on July 4, 1923, in Kokomo, Indiana, which featured music and food. Almost as many attended a speech by Imperial Wizard Evans at Ku Klux Klan Day at the Texas State Fair in Dallas that fall. The Klan was especially strong in the Midwest and the South, but there was Klan activity from Maine to California.

A number of groups, from the Catholic Knights of Columbus to the African American press to the new and specifically anti-Klan American Unity League (AUL), began to challenge the Klan. Where the Klan spoke of "pure Americanism," the AUL spoke of "true Americanism." In some places, pitched battles erupted between Klan members and their opponents, but one of the most effective anti-Klan tactics was simply to find and publicize lists of members in the secret organization, asking, "Is Your Neighbor a Kluxer?" Opposition to the Klan, battles among its leaders, and exposure of internal corruption all weakened the organization, and by 1930, the Klan, which had once had perhaps five million members, had dropped to fifty thousand. Although it did not disappear, the Klan as a power in American life was a phenomenon of the 1920s.

Eugenics and IQ Tests—The Science of Discrimination

It was not only the Klan that sought to marginalize African Americans, Asians, Catholics, and Jews in the United States in the 1920s. The eugenics movement used ideas from evolutionary biology, derived loosely (inaccurately and simplistically, many said) from Charles Darwin, to "prove" that some ethnic groups were more highly evolved than others. The **eugenics** movement was begun in England in the 1880s by Francis Galton, who concluded that the social elite—people like himself—were significantly higher on the evolutionary scale than England's working class, who in turn were more evolved than society's poor and criminal element. Eugenics quickly became popular in the United States. Eugenics gave a scientific patina to efforts to limit the immigration of ethnic groups from southern and eastern Europe and from Asia. Southern segregationists quickly latched on to eugenics as a "scientific" justification for racial segregation.

Margaret Sanger, the advocate for family planning and birth control, was a lifelong advocate of eugenics, particularly its focus on preventing inherited traits and weaknesses, which had been a long-used approach to agricultural breeding. The eugenics movement

eugenics

A movement that claimed scientific basis to apply Darwinian theory to the "natural selection" of the "fittest" human beings to reproduce and improve the human race.

applied this knowledge to human concerns, including various efforts to limit possibilities for those with disabilities such as deafness or limited intelligence—the "unfit"—to procreate.

Henry Goddard, a prominent American psychologist and eugenicist established an intelligence-testing program on Ellis Island in 1913, which was used to "sort" the thousands of immigrants entering the country, helping to create some of the notions about higher or lower intelligence in various ethnic groups. The Carnegie Institute for Experimental Evolution, based at Cold Spring Harbor in New York, conducted tests and kept records to "prove" that heredity divided the able from the "feeble minded," and in 1916, a New York attorney published *The Passing of the Great Race* in which he argued that the so-called Nordic race of northern Europeans was being overrun by less able southern Europeans and non-Europeans.

Efforts to predict intelligence and ability grew as a result of the development of scientific intelligence testing that began with the army during World War I. By the 1920s, educators led by Stanford University's Lewis M. Terman and Columbia University's Edward L. Thorndike believed that "[W]hatever exists at all exists in some amount," and that by measuring the amount of intelligence in a given child—through the newly popular IQ (or Intelligence Quotient) test—educators could assign him or her a "mental age" and sort the more advanced for college and the rest for menial jobs. These tests actually measured the kind of culturally specific knowledge that children of native-born Protestant and northern European families learned at home, so test takers from those backgrounds tended to score considerably higher than the children of southern Europeans, who still scored higher than eastern European Jews. Those of African and Asian descent tended to score the lowest on the IQ tests. Such "science" reinforced immigration restriction and racial segregation in the 1920s.

In 1927, the U.S. Supreme Court endorsed the eugenics movement when it ruled in an 8–1 decision that the state of Virginia could force the sterilization of a twenty-one-year-old young woman, Carrie Buck, the daughter and granddaughter of hardscrabble white farmers who had seen their prospects dim in the aftermath of the Civil War. The state of Virginia had identified Carrie as an "imbecile," though others said she was merely poor and therefore had limited opportunity for a good education. In a decision written by the respected jurist Oliver Wendell Holmes, the Court said that "[t]hree generations of imbeciles are enough," and Virginia was free to proceed with the surgery, which it did in October 1927, in spite of Buck's objections.

Interest in eugenics faded in the 1930s, especially as Adolf Hitler embraced the idea in *Mein Kampf* and used it as the basis of his anti-Semitic and anti-Slavic efforts to achieve a "pure" race and eliminate any they considered "unfit." IQ tests remained popular much longer, being used well after World War II to sort and track students in school. In the 1920s, however, eugenics and IQ testing reinforced popular opinion about who might be fit or unfit in the United States and were embraced widely.

Immigration Restriction, 1924

While groups like the Anti-Saloon League and the Klan were often hostile to African Americans, Catholics, and Jews, they found allies in Congress who were also trying to end further immigration into the country. In 1924, the opponents of immigration, who included union members worried about too many new workers, followers of the eugenics movement who disliked all people who were not from northern Europe, and white supremacists fearing any forms of difference, banded together and succeeded spectacularly when Congress cut off virtually all immigration from southern and eastern Europe, Africa, and Asia. In addition to anti-immigrant groups like the Klan, labor unions and some African American organizations feared that a never-ending stream of new immigrants could depress wages or take jobs. Cultural elitists, supported by the eugenics movement, worried that the traditional Anglo-American culture was being diluted. Hostility to new immigrants was not new. In the 1840s, the Know-Nothing Party attempted to limit Irish immigration. In 1882, Congress excluded Chinese immigrants. The largest movement to limit immigration to the United States, however, was led by the Immigration Restriction League (IRL), which was founded in 1894 but achieved its greatest successes in the 1920s.

In 1917, on the eve of U.S. entry into World War I, Congress passed a literacy test for new immigrants over President Wilson's veto. Similar legislation had also been vetoed by presidents Cleveland and Taft, but by 1917, the anti-immigrant vote in Congress was strong. More immigrants than expected were, in fact, literate and the literacy test did not significantly reduce the number of immigrants. Wilbur Carr of the U.S. Consular Service warned that Poland's Jewish ghettos were about to empty into the United States after World War I, fueling new fears of a new "horde" of immigrants from war-torn Europe. In response, Congress passed an emergency Immigration Restriction Act in 1921, for the first time setting quotas for the numbers of immigrants who could enter the United States.

Tougher anti-immigrant legislation followed in 1924. Congressman Albert Johnson of Washington State, chair of the House Committee on Immigration, wrote the new legislation. Johnson hated radical organizations like the IWW and was convinced (incorrectly) that most of its members were immigrants. He was also strongly anti-Japanese and a member of the Asiatic Exclusion League. In addition, he was influenced by the "scientists" who argued that eugenics and IQ tests proved that Asians as well as southern and eastern Europeans were inferior people to "Nordic" stock.

In setting the quota for immigrants, Johnson decided not to refer to the 1910 census, which had been the basis of the 1921 restriction but which was taken well after large numbers of Russian, Italian, and other southern European immigrants had arrived in the United States. Instead, he referred to the 1890 census, taken just before that wave of immigration, to set new quotas. Using the 1890 census, and limiting the percentage of immigrants allowed into the country to 2 percent of that number, Johnson cut the total number of immigrants allowed into the United States per year from 357,803 to 161,184. The proposed law also tilted the ethnic makeup of the new arrivals against ethnic groups that had arrived in large numbers between 1890 and 1910. Italy was cut from 42,057 immigrants per year to 3,912; Poland from 21,076 to 5,156; and Russia from 5,638 to 474. Yugoslavia, created out of the pre–World War I Austro-Hungarian Empire, was cut from 6,426 to 851 immigrants. Russian Jews, Italians, and Slavic immigrants were reduced to a trickle. In contrast, German immigration was only cut from 67,607 to 51,299 and Britain's from 77,342 to 62,458. Under the Johnson formula, Japan should have been allowed 240 immigrants, but Johnson insisted that the bill ban all Japanese immigration to the United States.

Urban representatives led by New York's Fiorello LaGuardia protested. The American Jewish Committee criticized the bill. It did no good. The restrictions passed the House and Senate by wide margins, and President Coolidge, who had told Congress that "America must be kept American," signed the bill. Although some modifications were made, from 1924 until the 1965, immigration to the United States from southern and eastern Europe and all of Asia and Africa was severely limited.

The 1924 legislation, however, did not impact all immigration. It did not stop Irish immigration since large numbers of Irish immigrants had come to the United States before 1890, which under Johnson's formula kept the quota high. It also had no impact on immigration from North and South America, since the bill allowed unlimited immigration from Canada and Mexico. Approximately 500,000 Mexican workers came to the United States during the 1920s. They were required to pay a tax on entering the United States and after 1929 to obtain a visa, but they filled agricultural jobs in the West previously held by Japanese immigrants; railroad, mining, smelting, and agricultural jobs; and industrial jobs in Chicago, Illinois; Detroit, Michigan; and Gary, Indiana. The Mexican community in Los Angeles, a city founded by Mexican immigrants, grew rapidly, outpacing San Antonio, Texas, as the largest center of Mexican immigrants to the United States and becoming one of the largest Mexican communities in the world during the 1920s. Northern cities, especially Chicago and Milwaukee, developed large and vibrant Mexican American neighborhoods built on the jobs offered in steel mills, the spiritual support of Spanish-speaking Catholic parishes, and the development of local Mexican American social, artistic, and sports organizations.

While allowed into the United States by the immigration legislation, new immigrants from Mexico did not have it easy. As with other immigrant groups, families who had been in the United States for generations did not always welcome those of the same ethnicity who came later, seeing them as competitors for jobs. School systems from Texas to California

21.1

21.2

21.3

21.4

21.1

21.2

21.3

21.4

used IQ tests to place most Mexican American students in vocational classes or, in the case of Santa Ana, California, to simply declare that because of their "special needs," all Mexican American youth needed to be in separate schools. In spite of hostility, the Mexican American community thrived. Workers formed their own Mexican unions, especially in agribusiness. They created their own newspapers such as *La Prensa* in San Antonio or *La Opinion* in Los Angeles. Women's organizations such as *La Sociedad de Madres Mexicanas* raised funds to defend Mexicans who faced legal difficulty. *Carpas*, or tent theaters, provided entertainment, often with plays given by traveling troupes from Mexico.

The 1924 immigration restrictions created deep tensions between the United States and some other countries, most of all China and Japan. The government of Japan, which had sought to work with several American administrations to construct "Gentlemen's Agreements" limiting immigration, was incensed at the disrespect in the ban of even the 240 immigrants per year that the quota would have allowed. Coming on the heels of previous insults like the 1906 segregation of Japanese students in the San Francisco public schools, the 1924 legislation contributed to deep-seated anti-American feelings in Japan. Other governments, including those of Italy and Romania, objected to the legislation. Nevertheless, the United States was in an isolationist mood after the end of World War I, and the protests did not stop the closing of America's previously very open gates. Members of Congress responded to foreign protests by saying that "the nation's immigration laws should be made for Americans and not to please foreigners" and "No foreign government has the right to tell the United States who we shall or shall not admit."

Just as the United States was closing its doors, the trial of two recent immigrants polarized the nation. Nicola Sacco and Bartolomeo Vanzetti, both Italian immigrants, were arrested on May 5, 1920, for robbery and the murder of a paymaster and guard of a shoe factory. They were tried in the midst of the antiradical, anti-immigrant hysteria sweeping the country and were convicted in July 1921. After a long series of appeals, reviews, and massive public protests, during which Sacco and Vanzetti maintained their innocence, their conviction was upheld and they were executed in Boston at Charlestown Prison on August 23, 1927.

The case of Sacco and Vanzetti took on enormous symbolic importance during the 1920s. Opponents of immigration and of political radicalism generally assumed that they were guilty simply because they were immigrants and anarchists. For others, winning freedom for Sacco and Vanzetti could be, depending on one's view, a blow struck for the cause of anarchism, or for the rights of immigrants, or simply for the right to a fair trial. For observers during the 1920s, the Sacco and Vanzetti case symbolized how much a nation made up of immigrants had turned against those immigrants who arrived most recently.

Nicola Sacco and Bartolomeo Vanzetti's trial symbolized the widespread fear of immigrants held by some and the hopes for justice held by other Americans. Vanzetti defined the way he wanted to be remembered. In May 1927, he told a journalist who visited him in the Dedham jail, "If it had not been for these things, I might have lived out my life talking at street corners to scorning men. ... Never in our full life could we hope to do such work for tolerance, for justice, for man's understanding of man as now we do by accident."

The Farmers' Depression

For many farmers, World War I had brought prosperity as the prices for wheat, cotton, and other agricultural products went up significantly. With new money to be found in every bushel or bale, farmers extended production between 1914 and 1918. Farmers enjoyed amenities as never before. In the early 1920s, one farm wife wrote about the "running water in the house! What a constant cause of thankfulness! What a joy to use all I need and want!" No more would she have a long hot walk to the spring for a pail of water to soothe a thirsty child or to wash a diaper because "the water from that same spring is in our pressure-tank." The improvement was a long way from the isolation and poverty that had been a norm in rural life in previous generations.

Farmers kept expanding the areas they cultivated. The rich lands of the Delta in northwest Mississippi were still more than 60 percent wilderness

21.1

21.2

21.3

21.4

in 1914. Bears were seen in cornfields and wolves attacked livestock. But in the war years, the world needed more cotton than ever, and planters cleared land as fast as they could. By the war's end, much of the Mississippi Delta was in cotton production and land sold for up to $1,000 an acre. Agricultural centers like Greenville, Mississippi, "The Queen City of the Delta," had fifteen thousand people with paved streets and factories in 1920. Some twenty railroad trains stopped every day, and agents in Greenville sold cotton directly to buyers in New York, Chicago, and New Orleans as well as the European cotton markets at Liverpool, England. Prosperity, it seemed, had finally arrived in the Delta.

Similarly, in the arid cattle country of southern Kansas and the panhandle region of Oklahoma, grassland that had never been plowed was being turned into farmland as fast as developers and settlers could break the sod with a plow and set up windmills to bring water from deep below. Driven by the insatiable wartime need for wheat and encouraged by the Union Pacific Railroad, which brought settlers, plows, and windmills, settlers filed fifty-three thousand new homestead claims in the Great Plains in 1914 alone. "Plant more wheat to win the war," the government said, and farmers were happy to mix patriotism and profit.

Then, the war ended. Europe began planting its own wheat again. Disbanded armies did not need uniforms. By 1920 and 1921, most of the world was caught up in an economic downturn that drastically reduced the demand for everything, especially wheat and cotton. The general economy started to recover in 1922 and 1923, but the farm economy did not. Even with its new prosperity, the United States could not consume all of the wheat and cotton and meat produced on the nation's farms. For many farmers, the Great Depression of the 1930s began in 1920 or 1921.

Not all farmers were impacted in the same way. Due to the new popularity of ice cream and increased use of milk in American diets, dairy farmers prospered. Vegetable farmers sold celery, spinach, and carrots to city people who had discovered vitamins. But those producing the staple crops—wheat, cotton, and corn—did not prosper. In 1921, cotton, which had brought a dollar a pound only a year before, sold for only twenty cents a pound—if a buyer could be found. Wheat prices also fell drastically. However, the price of the fertilizer farmers needed for their crops and the coal they needed to heat their homes kept rising.

Desperate to maintain their incomes, farmers did what seemed logical: they worked harder. If the price for a bushel or bale dropped, the only thing to do was to produce more. What was logical on an individual basis was disastrous on a national one. The more the farmers produced, the more the oversupply led prices to fall. There seemed to be no way to break the pattern.

Senators and representatives from the farm states were desperate for help, and Congress passed the McNary-Haugen bills under which the federal government would set a minimum price for farm products and buy them when the price fell to that level. The government would then store the goods until prices rose. But President Coolidge vetoed the bills as unsound government intervention in free markets. Midwestern progressives complained, but they did not have the votes to override the veto.

In 1927, nature seemed to turn against rural America. It rained a lot that spring. Farmers generally like spring rains, but in 1927, there was too much rain. One of the most intense storms in history came on Good Friday, April 15, 1927. In New Orleans, 14.96 inches of rain fell in less than a day. The Mississippi River flooded from Illinois to Louisiana (see Map 21-3, p. 638). Engineers had been building levees to contain the Mississippi and its tributaries for decades, and by the 1920s, levees were everywhere. Behind the levees, farmers had cleared and planted thousands of acres of land. Cities and towns had grown up. However, prosperity, even survival, depended on the levees holding. That April in 1927, they did not hold. The flood of 1927 covered an area 150 miles long and 50 miles wide along the Mississippi River with water, some of it 20 feet deep, and made two hundred thousand people homeless, perhaps even three times that number. Secretary of Commerce Herbert Hoover directed the rescue efforts, and the Red Cross provided aid across a stricken country. Many criticized rehabilitation efforts that spent an average of $20 per flood victim as too little too late.

Map 21-3 The Mississippi River Flood.

This map gives some sense of the huge territory that was impacted when the Mississippi River flooded in 1927.

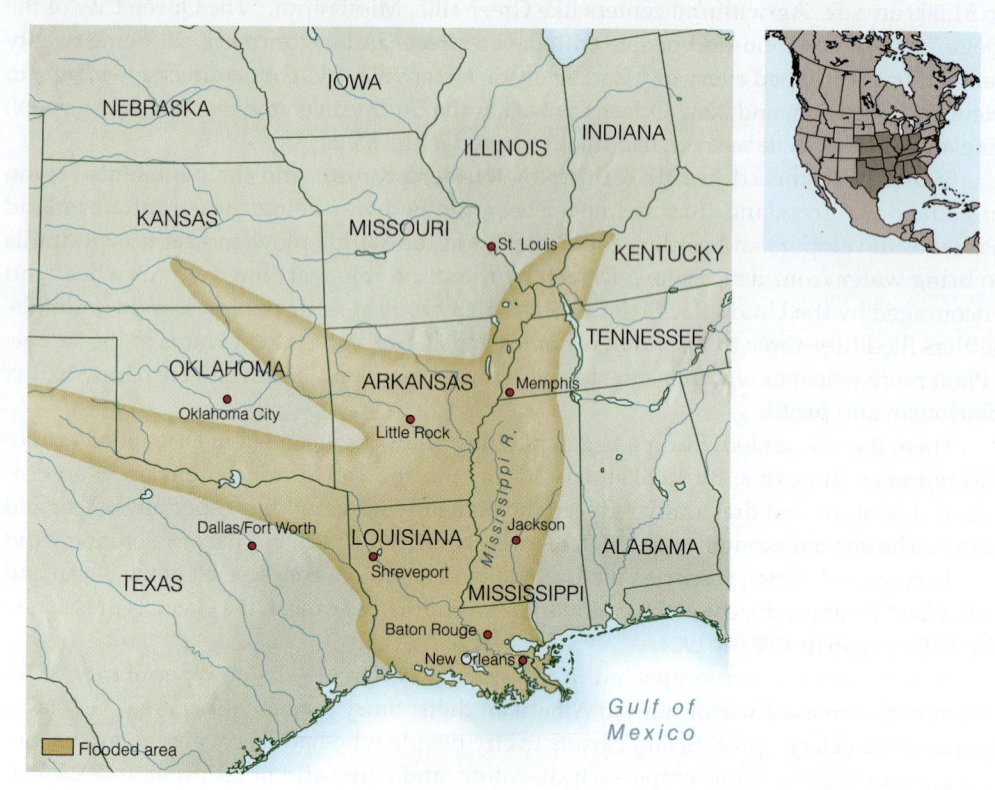

Crops planted later that year were beset by disease and an early frost. Pellagra, the result of poor diet, afflicted fifty thousand people in the Mississippi Delta. Farmers gave up on the land. Sharecroppers simply moved away. More blacks moved north, and more farmers—black, white, and Latino—moved to town. However, the generally prosperous nation quickly forgot the flood and the devastation.

The Scopes Trial

The general prosperity of the 1920s drove many social changes. High schools began to spring up in small towns and scattered rural communities, offering educational opportunities that had been limited to big cities before 1920. In 1890, a total of 200,000 American youth were enrolled in high school. Thirty years later, that number was 2 million—a tenfold increase. The rapid increase of secondary schooling had significant benefits for those able to attend (more often whites than African Americans or Mexican Americans). Indeed, many economists today see the increased years of schooling available to many Americans as the greatest driver of growing prosperity.

With the growth of high schools, some Americans started to worry about just what was being taught in them, in particular in biology classes. High school biology classes were greatly influenced by the 1859 publication of Charles Darwin's *Origin of Species*, which described the evolution of plant and animal life, including the emergence of human beings, as a result of natural selection—a process by which random biological changes in individuals within a species that are beneficial for survival become passed on to subsequent generations—or what some called "survival of the fittest."

The book immediately raised theological questions. Most scientists embraced Darwin's work and many saw no conflict between the new biology and traditional religious teachings. Harvard's Asa Gray wrote a popular high school botany textbook in the late 1800s that presented evolution as showing that all life was "part of one system," showing "One Mind."

After 1900, however, a new generation of scientists stopped talking about One Mind. George William Hunter's textbook, *A Civic Biology*, simply said, "Species have been modified during a long course of descent, chiefly through natural selection."

Popular religion was also evolving. Before 1900, most Protestants, liberal or conservative, assumed that the Bible was an accurate historical record, but that assumption was challenged by German-inspired "higher criticism" of the Bible that sought to understand the Bible in terms of the social context in which it was written. In reaction, a new movement known as fundamentalism began within American Protestantism in the early 1900s. Fundamentalist ministers called for a literal reading of the Bible and rejected any other interpretation of the "unchanged word of God." Fundamentalism represented a new militant form of Protestantism and a much more pessimistic view of modern society. The changes in scientific thinking and the increasing influence of fundamentalism came into a dramatic collision in the trial of a local high school biology teacher, John Thomas Scopes, in the small town of Dayton, Tennessee, in 1925. Scopes, as required by Tennessee regulations, used *A Civic Biology* in his classes. In following the mandated state curriculum, he also violated a Tennessee law against the teaching of evolution.

Between 1922 and 1925, a number of states, under pressure from fundamentalists, outlawed the teaching of evolution. Tennessee was one of them. The American Civil Liberties Union (ACLU), however, saw these new laws as an assault on free speech. They sought a test case and in defending Scopes they found one.

Clarence Darrow, the best-known lawyer in the country, volunteered to join the ACLU team. Former presidential candidate William Jennings Bryan volunteered for the prosecution. Every major newspaper in the country covered the trial. Most people thought Darrow got the better of Bryan in the arguments, but on the facts, Scopes was clearly guilty. Scopes admitted he had violated the law, and he was found guilty and fined $100, though the Tennessee Supreme Court threw the case out on a technicality.

Cautious textbook publishers changed their books. In future editions, *A Civic Biology* stopped calling Darwin "the grand old man of biology" and instead simply said that he was a "leading biologist." Evolution, which in the earlier editions had been a "wonderful discovery" now became merely Darwin's "interpretation of the way in which all life changes." Only in the late 1950s would a full discussion of evolution return to high school textbooks.

CSU Archives/Everett Collection Inc/Alamy Stock Photo

Although they had long been on the same side of political battles, the nation's leading attorney, Clarence Darrow, and three-time presidential candidate William Jennings Bryan, represented opposite sides in the trial of Tennessee biology teacher John T. Scopes that captured national attention.

21.1

21.2

21.3

21.4

21.3 Quick Review

To what extent were the racism, anti-immigration efforts, and fundamentalism of the 1920s the result of changes throughout the United States?

Harding, Coolidge, and Hoover—National Politics and Policies in the 1920s

21.4 Analyze the political and policy developments of the decade.

Three Republican presidents led the United States during the 1920s. The election of Warren Harding in November 1920 was almost a foregone conclusion given the general disenchantment with Woodrow Wilson's policies, the war, and the League of Nations. A politician who promised to return the nation to "normalcy" was just what people wanted. Harding and his running mate, massachusetts governor Calvin Coolidge, defeated the Democratic nominee, Ohio governor James Cox, and his running mate, the young Franklin Roosevelt, by sixteen million to nine million popular votes. In what was his last race, the Socialist Party candidate, Eugene V. Debs, polled close to a million votes while still in prison for violating the World War I sedition laws. Late in 1921, Harding commuted his sentence, and Debs was freed.

Although Harding was remembered mostly for his campaign speech insisting that "America's present need is not heroics, but healing; not nostrums but normalcy; not revolution, but restoration"—and for the scandals of his administration—he also made some very strong appointments. Three months after coming to office, he appointed former president William Howard Taft to the job Taft had always wanted, chief justice of the Supreme Court, where Taft served until 1930. Charles Evans Hughes, the 1916 Republican presidential candidate, became secretary of state. Knowing that there was no chance of U.S. participation in the League of Nations but wanting to foster peace in the postwar world, Hughes called the **Washington Conference** in 1921 to try to end the competition among the United States, Britain, and Japan to build up their navies. To the surprise of many, the result of the conference, the **Five Powers Treaty** of February 1922, slowed the worldwide navy buildup and established limits on battleships, battle cruisers, and aircraft carriers in a ratio of 5 each for the United States and Britain, 3 each for Japan, and 1.75 each for France and Italy. No limits were set for other types of ships. In 1922, Hughes also ended the long-standing U.S. occupation of the Dominican Republic.

Harding also appointed Andrew Mellon, one of the wealthiest people in the United States, to serve as secretary of the treasury. Mellon, who served through the Harding, Coolidge, and Hoover administrations, ensured that there was a close and comfortable relationship between government and business. He cut government spending, cut taxes, and retired half of the World War I debt while in office. He was often hailed as "the greatest secretary of the treasury ever," until the coming of the Great Depression raised serious questions about his policies. Herbert Hoover, perhaps the most liberal member of the cabinet, served as secretary of commerce for Harding and Coolidge, encouraging cooperation between businesses to stabilize industrial production and the economy. Hoover's liberalism involved the creation of a more activist government than some of his colleagues wanted to see. He supported stronger law enforcement, new highways to streamline commerce, and the work of the Bureau of Foreign and Domestic Commerce to support trade. He tried to limit overproduction through voluntary means. But his focus was on partnerships with business, not government control of markets.

Harding died suddenly in August 1923, probably the result of a heart attack. His wife's refusal to allow an autopsy led to rumors that he was poisoned or committed suicide, though there was never any evidence for either. His death came just as the Teapot Dome scandal was about to come to light. He was reported to have asked Herbert Hoover "what a President should do whose friends had betrayed him." Harding was deeply mourned,

Washington Conference

A conference called by the United States in 1921 that led to the adoption of the Five Powers Treaty in 1922 in an ultimately ineffective effort to limit the growth of the world's navies and thus preserve peace.

Five Powers Treaty

An agreement by the United States, England, Japan, France, and Italy to limit the number of battleships in their navies as an effort to stop the worldwide growth of armaments.

but as the scandals of his administration surfaced, his reputation was tarnished before the year was out.

Fortunately for the Republican Party, Harding's vice president, the stern and distant Calvin Coolidge, had no connection to the scandals and quickly took steps to investigate them. News of Harding's death reached the vice president while he was vacationing with his father in a rustic Vermont farmhouse. Since the house had no electricity, Colonel John Coolidge administered the presidential oath of office to his son by the light of a kerosene lamp—a reassuring image that perfectly fit the tone of austerity and adherence to old-time values that the new president wanted to set. More important to Coolidge's success, the economic downturn of 1921 had eased, and by 1923, many Americans were experiencing an economic boom, known as the "Coolidge prosperity." To no one's surprise, Coolidge, a man of so few words he came to be known as "silent Cal," was nominated for a full term by the Republican Party in the summer of 1924. He summed up his economic and political philosophy, saying, "After all, the chief business of the American people is business. They are profoundly concerned with production, buying, selling, investing and prospering in the world." And a majority of voters were.

This cartoon from the 1920s shows President Calvin Coolidge and his secretary of the treasury Andrew Mellon speeding toward economic growth while the cartoonist notes the worry that the brakes may not hold up against runaway spending and financial overconfidence.

The Democratic Party was deeply divided between a southern and western wing that was primarily white, Protestant, rural, and supportive of Prohibition and a northern wing that, though also very white, included many Catholics and Jews, and was highly urban as well as strongly anti-Prohibition. The Klan was a force at the Democratic nominating convention in the 1920s where their opposition to a Catholic candidate who wanted to repeal Prohibition made itself felt. The two leading contenders for the 1924 nomination were former treasury secretary William G. McAdoo, who favored Prohibition and was supported by the southern and western wing of the party, and New York governor Al Smith, a Catholic and a staunch opponent of Prohibition. They battled for 103 ballots before the delegates turned to the West Virginia lawyer and former congressman John Davis in an exhausted compromise. Others, disgusted with both parties, rebuilt the old Progressive Party of 1912 and nominated Wisconsin's popular progressive senator Robert La Follette for president.

Coolidge's victory in the 1924 elections was as decisive as Harding's had been in 1920. Coolidge won 54 percent of the total with only 28.8 percent for the Democrats' John Davis and 16.6 percent for the Progressives' La Follette. Except for Wisconsin, which went for La Follette, Coolidge carried every state outside of the then solidly Democratic South.

The Coolidge administration took some important steps in foreign policy. Just before he took office as Coolidge's vice president, Charles G. Dawes negotiated the so-called Dawes Plan to help ameliorate the German financial crisis brought on by the huge reparations payments to Britain and France. In 1925, Coolidge appointed Frank Kellogg as secretary of state. Two years later in 1927, French foreign minister Aristide Briand proposed a joint U.S.-French alliance, but Kellogg turned the conversation to a multilateral treaty. **The Kellogg-Briand Pact** outlawing war was signed in Paris in August 1928, and eventually, sixty-two nations were signatories to the much acclaimed agreement. Unfortunately, there was no enforcement mechanism to the Kellogg-Briand Pact. While passive at home, U.S. government under Coolidge also enthusiastically encouraged engagement with Latin America, maintaining military force in some countries and doubling investment in others. After coming to office in 1929, Hoover tried to improve relations with Latin America, removing American troops from Nicaragua and Haiti. In addition, while not officially recognizing the government of the new Soviet Union, the Coolidge and Hoover administrations encouraged

The Kellogg-Briand Pact

A 1928 international treaty that denounced aggression and war but lacked provisions for enforcement.

Fotosearch/Getty Images

business investment and the Soviet government welcomed it, especially the mass production of automobiles that they called "Fordism."

The 1928 presidential election that brought Hoover to office was very different than the previous two. The tone of the contest was angrier. When Calvin Coolidge announced that he would not seek another term as president, the Republicans nominated Hoover. The Democrats, tired of their losses in 1920 and 1924, decided that Al Smith's charisma and enthusiastic support in the North would make him a winner. After all, many asked, didn't the South vote for the Democratic nominee no matter who he was?

On many issues, Hoover and Smith were not far apart. Hoover was more liberal than Coolidge and privately worried that the Coolidge prosperity was a balloon that would surely pop. He said that he looked forward to the day when "poverty will be banished from this nation," though he saw business success, not government intervention, as the key to accomplishing that goal. Coolidge once called him "that damn Bolshevik." Smith was also a friend to big business. Once nominated, Smith chose John J. Raskob of General Motors to run his campaign and included several leading industrialists in his inner circle.

Nevertheless, there were two huge differences between the candidates. Hoover was a "dry" who favored continuing Prohibition, and Smith was a "wet" committed to ending it. Hoover called Prohibition "a great social and economic experiment, noble in motive and far-reaching in purpose." Smith told the convention that nominated him that "there should be fundamental changes in the present provisions for national prohibition." With many people becoming disillusioned with Prohibition, on that issue alone Smith might have had the edge.

However, another issue influenced the race. Hoover, a Quaker, was a Protestant. Smith was a Catholic. Many Catholic voters in places such as Boston, Chicago, New York, and San Francisco rallied to Smith with an enthusiasm they had never shown for any previous presidential candidate. Meanwhile, in much of the nation's Protestant heartland, Smith's Catholicism was the only issue of the campaign. The candidate himself thought he had addressed it, but as he campaigned in the Midwest and South, Smith could see burning crosses on the hillsides and his rallies were met by Klan members. At one rally in Oklahoma, Smith eyed the crowd and commented to a reporter, "I don't know those people out there. I don't speak their language." On election day in November 1928, Hoover won, carrying states in the South that had not voted Republican since the end of Reconstruction and even Smith's home state of New York. Smith won 40 percent of the vote and carried Massachusetts, Rhode Island, and parts of the South, but Hoover's 58 percent of the vote and 444 electoral votes guaranteed that he could enter the White House with a solid mandate. The stock market responded to Hoover's election by reaching greater heights than ever before. The new president kept his reservations about the stock market bubble to himself. The nation seemed confident in their new president, the economy, and the way society had been moving for the last ten years. It would be Hoover's bad luck that none of this confidence would last through his first year in office.

21.4 Quick Review

How were the elections of 1920, 1924, and 1928 similar? How were they different?

Conclusion

The 1920s marked a period of significant social and political change in the United States. This period, known as the Jazz Age, began at the conclusion of World War I in 1918 and ended with the stock market crash in 1929. For many Americans, especially those in the middle and upper classes, the 1920s were a time of prosperity. For other Americans, however, the 1920s were harsh.

In the so-called Red Summer of 1919, there was violence in much of the country. Striking workers wanted their salaries adjusted to reflect the inflation generated by the war. Strikes were common in 1919, and they were often violent confrontations between wage earners and business elites. Fear of communism and opposition to organized labor were often linked. Racial tensions also boiled over in that summer, and race riots took place in cities around the country.

In January 1920 when the Eighteenth Amendment to the Constitution outlawed the "manufacture, sale, or transportation" of any alcoholic beverage, the resulting era of Prohibition set off a wave of opposition. Bootleggers found ways to manufacture and sell alcohol in defiance of the Eighteenth Amendment, and average citizens found ways to drink alcohol as they flouted the law.

Women gained the right to vote when the Nineteenth Amendment was passed in 1920. With their newly gained power, some younger women declared themselves to be "flappers," flouting social conventions, and many women began reforms around prenatal care and birth control as well as other issues relevant to them. The economic growth of the 1920s sustained a new mass culture focused on materialism and consumerism and was characterized by the automobile, the radio, and the movies. African Americans began moving from the rural South to the urban North. The result was a flowering of black culture in music, novels, and poetry, centered in New York City's Harlem, while Marcus Garvey led his fellow black followers in a hopeful business effort.

For many other Americans, the 1920s were a difficult time. The Ku Klux Klan opposed African American rights and immigration of non-Protestant whites to the United States. In 1924, legislation drastically reduced immigration to the United States. White farmers in the Midwest and South also suffered greatly as crop prices plummeted. Other Americans turned to a new kind of religious fundamentalism, challenging such things as the teaching of evolution in the public schools.

Three Republican presidents—Warren G. Harding, Calvin Coolidge, and Herbert C. Hoover—presided over a prosperous and relatively content nation during the 1920s, and while they differed among themselves, all three supported the growth of a business-oriented culture and saw business success as the key to prosperity for all. In spite of the failure of the United States to endorse the League of Nations, all three presidents sought an activist foreign policy and treaties to limit the potential for future wars.

Chapter Review

Why are the 1920s a unique era in American history?

The Prelude—The Red Summer of 1919

21.1 Explain how events at the end of World War I shaped the decade that followed.

Summary

The period that immediately followed World War I proved to be chaotic, marked by uncertainty and fear in a number of areas in American life. The difficult transition from a wartime to a peacetime economy brought on large-scale strikes while an influenza pandemic killed half a million Americans. Much of the public associated labor unrest with Russia's new Communist regime, which fueled Attorney General Alexander Palmer's anti-Communist crusade that targeted immigrants and labor leaders. In Chicago and a number of other American cities, racial tensions sparked major riots.

Review Question

1. Contextualization
   Considering World War I was a largely successful endeavor for the United States, how do you explain the anger and violence that marked 1919?

The 1920s—The Exuberance of Prosperity

21.2 Analyze how Prohibition and other developments of the 1920s reshaped American culture and led to a decade that some considered an especially prosperous and fun-filled time.

Summary

The passage and implementation of Prohibition reflected a shift from the Progressive Era to the social issues of the 1920s. Enforcement of Prohibition was weak, and the law was widely flouted. Moreover, Prohibition proved a boon to organized crime. Under Prohibition, the sense that obedience to the law was optional was reinforced by the corruption within the Harding administration. The culture of the 1920s was epitomized by the flapper, the adventurous "new woman" who frequented speakeasies and rejected the sexual double standard. The automobile industry was both the engine of the American economy and a major cultural force in its own right, while radio, movies, and magazines offered a popular culture for Americans on a scale that had not been seen before. Meanwhile, urban neighborhoods such as Greenwich Village offered gathering places for gay men and lesbians. The 1920s were a rich period for literature as writers provided commentary on what they saw as a world marked by lost ideals. In part due to the Great Migration, the period also saw the emergence of jazz and the blues in a cultural explosion called the Harlem Renaissance. Marcus Garvey's African nationalism struck a chord with many African Americans, particularly those near the bottom of the economic ladder.

Review Question

2. Comparison
   Contrast the domestic ideal of womanhood of the late 1800s with the "new woman" epitomized by the flappers of the 1920s. What was new about the "new woman"?

The 1920s—The Conflicts about American Ideals

21.3 Explain the elements of discrimination, hardship, and fundamentalism that also shaped American life in the 1920s.

Summary

The Jazz Age culture prompted a backlash, particularly in rural America. The 1920s Ku Klux Klan presented itself as the defender of "100 percent Americanism" against immigrants, minorities, and non-Protestants. Some of the same sentiments that were behind the new Klan inspired a wide-reaching eugenics movement. Congress responded to anti-immigrant sentiment in 1924 by passing legislation that heavily favored those from Nordic countries and limited immigrants from almost every other racial group. Immigrants from the Americas were not affected by the new quotas, and large numbers of Mexican workers settled in many parts of the country. While much of America prospered during the 1920s, rural America did not; the Depression began for farmers long before 1929. The Scopes trial became a major event of the decade as it illustrated the cultural divide between rural and urban America.

Review Questions

3. Continuity and Change over Time
   How did the function of the Ku Klux Klan change by the 1920s compared with its early years? In what way was the Klan consistent during this period?

4. Argument Development
   What did it mean to be "American" for those in positions of power during the 1920s? Who counted and who didn't?

Harding, Coolidge, and Hoover—National Politics and Policies in the 1920s

21.4 Analyze the political and policy developments of the decade.

Summary

The Republican Party dominated national politics in the 1920s as Harding, Coolidge, and Hoover all ran on probusiness platforms. For much of the decade, America experienced an economic boom. Also during the 1920s, the United States led efforts to tamp down possibilities for future global conflict. The contest between Hoover and Democrat Al Smith that brought Hoover to the White House highlighted some of the cultural divide of the 1920s. While prosperity continued in the early days of Hoover's administration, he worried that it would be short lived.

Review Question

5. Causation

What accounts for the Republican dominance of national politics in the 1920s? Does the long period of reform from the preceding period have anything to do with it?

1. Preparing to Write: Organize Your Evidence

Long Essay Question—Explain the reasons why a social backlash occurred in the United States between 1919 and 1929.

Create a three-column table for the topics "Chaos of 1919," "The New Woman," and "Immigration." For each topic, record evidence that proves the great impact each had on the United States. Then identify the nature of the backlash for each. What did these changes mean to many Americans? How can their reactions be seen as an attempt to stabilize what they saw as a rapidly changing nation? As you answer these questions, include specific evidence such as the Palmer Raids. Using all this information, develop your thesis.

2. Preparing to Write: Support Your Assertion

Document-Based Question—Discuss how the Great Migration helped give rise to art and literature that centered around African American identity.

To answer this question, you will need to devote a section of your essay to the nature of this new African American art and literature. Start by developing a thesis, and then craft a topic sentence for this section. In your support, use two or three pieces of evidence that would support your topic sentence and thesis. Also integrate two primary sources: the Alain Locke excerpt in 21.2 and song lyrics from the same section. Explain how each is evidence for your argument. In your explanation, include discussion of the authors' points of view.

Chapter 22
Living in Hard Times 1929–1939

Library of Congress Prints and Photographs Division [LC-USZ62-91536]

During the Great Depression, lines of unemployed, impoverished workers seeking food and shelter could be seen in cities and towns across the United States.

Chapter Objective

Demonstrate an understanding of the causes and consequences of the Great Depression.

 Learning Objectives

The Coming of the Great Depression

22.1 Explain the coming of the Great Depression and the initial response to it.

The New Deal

22.2 Explain the goals and results of the New Deal and the responses on the part of diverse Americans.

The Deep Roots of War—The United States, Europe, and Asia

22.3 Analyze the international impact of the Depression, German and Japanese military expansion, and the initial U.S. response.

In late October 1929, the value of shares sold on the New York Stock Exchange collapsed. Prices kept dropping for the next three years in a dizzying decline in which paper wealth simply evaporated. For most Americans, the stock market crash seemed irrelevant at first, but the impact spread far and wide. And in 1930, an international trade war accelerated, dramatically cutting exports and devastating an economy already suffering from overproduction. For industrial workers, who rarely owned stock, the value of shares in the enterprises where they worked was not important, but the subsequent drop in industrial jobs as production and sales of automobiles, radios, appliances, and clothing dried up was all too real. For many farmers, the Depression began with the drop in agricultural prices in 1920 (see Chapter 21) and did not end until World War II began. For other farmers, especially those who had plowed the plains and created the wheat farms of Oklahoma and Kansas, the drop in wheat prices was something to worry about, but the full impact of the Depression came later with the terrible dust storms of the 1930s.

If the 1920s was a decade of optimism, the 1930s was a decade of fear for the majority of Americans. As one person who lived through it remembered, "[E]veryone was emotionally affected. We developed a fear of the future that was very difficult to overcome. … [T]here was this constant dread." This chapter traces the many causes of the Great Depression and its impact in the United States and the world.

The Coming of the Great Depression

22.1   **Explain the coming of the Great Depression and the initial response to it.**

The Great Depression was a worldwide crisis. People lost their jobs in Japan. In Chile, mineral exports, the mainstay of its economy, collapsed, leading to joblessness, and the government, which lost tax income, could do little. In Germany, already suffering from a precarious economy, industries went bankrupt and millions of workers were laid off. Industrial production collapsed in Great Britain, leading to hunger marches by the unemployed. Jobs disappeared in Canada. And in the United States, the combined impact of the stock market crash (which had an impact worldwide), the continuing farm depression, and the rapid decline in industrial production as the demand for goods disappeared led to national paralysis.

The Great Crash: October 1929

Speculative booms and busts had occurred regularly (and continue) as people's enthusiasm allowed prices to rise far beyond value, prompting an inevitable crash. In the 1600s, Dutch investors were caught up in speculation in tulip bulbs. In the 1720s, English investors lost fortunes in what came to be known as the Great South Sea Bubble. In the mid-1920s, many Americans began to buy Florida real estate that later became worthless.

The Great Crash of 1929 was a prime example of this phenomenon. The U.S. economy did well in the 1920s and it would have been strange if the value of stocks had not gone up. Stocks, after all, are merely partial ownership in a company, so a share of stock purchased on the New York Stock Exchange for a company (U.S. Steel or General Electric, for example) is a share in the ownership of that company. If the company makes a sufficient profit, dividends are paid to shareholders. If a company increases in value, the value of each share increases. However, if a company does poorly, or a lot of people start to worry that a company *will* do poorly, shares decrease in value. The stock market is—in theory—a place where people who want to sell a share of stock meet people who want to buy one and agree on a price; the price of the most recent sale of stock is then listed as the current value of the stock.

Between 1924 and 1928, stock prices generally rose, with some modest downturns. Toward the end of 1928, especially after Herbert Hoover's election victory in November, the stock market started going up much faster. Many people—including President-elect Hoover, as he later wrote in his memoirs—were worried that the prices were showing all the hallmarks of a speculative boom, going up too fast. Still, people continued to buy stocks. The Radio Corporation of America, known on the stock market simply as "Radio," was a relatively new company that had never paid a dividend. Radio sold for $85 a share at the beginning of 1928, and the price rose to $420 a share by the end of the year. (Stock prices are reported simply as whole numbers, so Radio sold for 85 and 420.) Other companies followed the same course: DuPont began the year at 310, ending at 525; department store giant Montgomery Ward began at 117, ending at 440. At the height of the market in September 1929, still without distributing a single dividend, Radio was selling for 505.

As people saw the chance to make money, they also borrowed money to buy stocks, a process called buying on margin. If a person could invest $85 in Radio and a year later have a stock worth $420, why not borrow enough to buy ten shares for $850 and fairly quickly reap $4,200? And brokers were more than happy to lend the money. Buyers put up 25 percent to 50 percent of the value of a stock but could easily borrow the rest. Early in the 1920s, perhaps a billion dollars of loans were provided to cover stock purchases; by the end of 1928, those loans reached six billion dollars.

In the spring of 1929, the outgoing president, Calvin Coolidge, reported that the economy was "absolutely sound," and stocks were "cheap at current prices." The more cautious Hoover, who understood economics better than his predecessor, believed that the "growing tide of speculation" was not merely a problem but was, indeed, a "crime," yet he worried that his saying so might cause a devastating loss in confidence. By September 1929, a respected economist, Roger Babson, warned, "Sooner or later a crash is coming and it may be terrific." Factories will shut down, he predicted, and "men will be thrown out of work." The speech precipitated a drop in stock prices, but the so-called Babson Break lasted for only one day. Most economists thought Babson was wrong.

Stock prices kept going up through the spring of 1929, and then in the summer they skyrocketed. From the beginning of June to the end of August, Westinghouse stock went from 151 to 286, General Electric from 268 to 391, and U.S. Steel from 165 to 258. At the sight of those kinds of profits, most investors simply forgot about the warnings.

The market reached its high point on the day after Labor Day in 1929. There was a small downturn in September, and by October, everyone started to worry. Then in late October, speculation turned to panic as stock prices just kept falling. Tuesday, October 29, known as Black Tuesday, was the worst single day in the history of the stock exchange. Crowds formed all up and down Wall Street. Contrary to latter-day myths, there were no suicidal leaps from windows, though a few speculators did die by their own hand on that and the following days. Most quietly watched their life savings disappear as prices continued to fall.

In the months and years that followed, stock prices continued to plunge. On November 11, 1929, the Dow Jones Industrial Average closed at 224—a drop by half from 452 in September. Prices kept falling through 1930, 1931, and 1932. By July 1932, the *New York Times* reported the Dow Jones Industrial Average as 58—a little more than a tenth of what it had been only three years earlier. Value, it seemed, had simply disappeared from American businesses.

The loans that had enabled many to buy stock "on margins" made things worse. When the value of a stock fell to the actual percentage the buyer had invested, 50 percent or 25 percent, the stockbroker who had arranged the loan would notify the owner that he or she had to produce more money to pay off the loan or else the stock would be taken over by the broker and sold to recoup the loan. Since many investors had put all their savings into the stock market, they had no funds to cover such "calls" and were wiped out. Even if the market later rallied, they had no investment left. In addition, the brokers often were not able to sell the stock in time to protect the loan either, so brokers lost money, too.

This picture reflects some of the chaos on New York's Wall Street on October 29, 1929, as stock values crashed and people saw their life savings disappear.

Speculation and the subsequent crash of the American stock market was but one of multiple causes of the economic catastrophe. Many economists have argued that overproduction in industry and agriculture as well as counterproductive international competition were far more significant. The basic underpinnings of the American economy, including banking, manufacturing, farming, and international trade, were also surprisingly fragile. When the economy came apart, it came apart thoroughly. Perhaps as many as half of Americans—farmers, farmworkers, and sharecroppers; American Indians living on reservations; factory workers; widows; and the elderly—had been living on the edge of poverty throughout the boom. In 1930, before even the initial impact of the Depression, 60 percent of American families had a total income of less than $2,000 per year, which was then considered the poverty line.

In early 1932, U.S. Army troops and local police attacked the Bonus Marchers camp within sight of the U.S. Capitol Building. The attack on former soldiers who had come to Washington from all parts of the United States seeking pensions from Congress infuriated many and further undermined Hoover's reputation.

The Hoover Years, 1929–1933

Herbert Hoover had been president for only seven months when the stock market crashed. Given his background, Hoover seemed the ideal president for such a moment of crisis. As a trained engineer who had helped feed a starving Europe during World War I and had served as secretary of commerce, he understood economics, and he was far more flexible than Coolidge. Hoover called for voluntary action—asking business leaders to keep wages and prices up, asking bankers to pool resources to help weaker banks, and encouraging farmers to form cooperatives and keep excess crops off the market. He cut taxes and supported federal public works such as construction of dams, bridges, and hospitals to stimulate the economy. In 1932, he reluctantly agreed with a Democratic Congress to create the Reconstruction Finance Corporation to provide funds to keep banks and railroads from bankruptcy as well as the Emergency Relief and Construction Act to lend money to states for relief and public projects.

As the economy worsened, however, Hoover's call for voluntary solutions seemed weak. Farmers were reluctant to cut back on their crops if their neighbors would simply fill the gap. Bankers were too worried about staying solvent to bail out other banks. The Reconstruction Finance Corporation never invested enough to save all the banks that needed saving. Hoover tried but failed to negotiate a reduction in the reparations that were wrecking the German economy and thus undermining U.S. trade with Europe. Then in 1930, Congress passed the Smoot-Hawley Tariff, a disastrous move that was designed to protect American industries by raising the cost of imported goods, but resulted in a trade war as other nations also raised their tariffs in return, leading to a huge decrease in international trade with devastating results since many industries that had long sold on a world market saw their business disappear. Despite the dire circumstances, Hoover, though no orthodox conservative, could not bring himself to support further government intervention and debt.

Perhaps it was simply Hoover's bad luck to preside over the beginning of the Depression. People would have blamed him no matter what he did. When he tried to restore confidence by announcing that "[t]he fundamental business of the country, that is production and distribution of commodities, is on a sound and prosperous basis," things just kept getting worse and people lost confidence in him. When homeless families built communities of shacks, they called them **Hoovervilles**. When out-of-work veterans marched to Washington as the "**Bonus Army**" to demand a pension, he ordered the army to disperse them and people called him heartless. When he had lost his bid for reelection and tried to get the incoming administration to cooperate on a plan for the banking crisis in early 1933, Roosevelt ignored him. Hoover's was an unhappy presidency in an unhappy time.

Hoovervilles

Shantytowns, sarcastically named after President Hoover, in which unemployed and homeless people lived in makeshift shacks, tents, and boxes. Hoovervilles cropped up in many cities in 1930 and 1931.

Bonus Army

A protest movement of World War I veterans in 1932 demanding early payment of service bonuses not due until 1945 to help them through the Great Depression and to provide a stimulus for the economy.

22.1 Quick Review

How did the fragile economy of the 1920s create a dire situation for the American people? What actions did the Hoover administration take or fail to take?

The New Deal

22.2 Explain the goals and results of the New Deal and the responses on the part of diverse Americans.

In the desperate situation that the United States faced in 1932, probably the most desperate economic moment in American history, most thought that whoever won the 1932 Democratic nomination would win the election. After all, the crisis had occurred under the leadership of a Republican president. Among the Democrats, Al Smith entered the race again along with Speaker of the House of Representatives John Nance Garner, former cabinet member Newton Baker, and New York governor Franklin Delano Roosevelt. Roosevelt won the nomination on the fourth ballot and, breaking precedent, flew to the Democratic National Convention in Chicago to accept the nomination in person on July 2, 1932, where he promised a "**New Deal** for the American people," coining the phrase by which his administration would be known. He selected Garner to be his running mate. Promising few specifics, other than an end to Prohibition, Roosevelt (FDR as he came to be called) defeated Hoover by a landslide in the November election, carrying 57 percent of the vote and 472 electoral votes.

In the long months between the election in November and the inauguration on March 4, 1933, the U.S. economy kept getting worse. (The date of the inauguration was later changed by the Twentieth Amendment to the Constitution so that every president after Roosevelt was inaugurated on January 20 after a much shorter wait.) The number of unemployed workers and evicted farmers kept growing. In addition, the banking system, the heart of the nation's economic structure, faltered, and more banks closed.

Banks that had given loans to buy stocks now held worthless paper since the loans could never be repaid. Banks that had given loans to farmers now owned worthless farmland or were blocked from foreclosure by angry farmers. As more banks failed, people began to take their money out of the remaining banks. A "run on a bank," as a large number of withdrawals all at once was known, could put any bank out of business because no bank simply kept deposits in its vaults but, rather, invested the money. In 1930, 1,352 banks closed; in 1931, 2,294 more went out of business; and in 1932, another 1,453 failed. In November 1932, Nevada's governor proclaimed a "bank holiday," temporarily closing all banking before more banks got into trouble. Iowa followed in January 1933, then Michigan, Maryland, Oklahoma, Indiana, Ohio, Arkansas, and Arizona in February. Sixteen more states closed banks at the beginning of March, and finally, on March 4, Illinois and New York—home to the nation's largest banks in Chicago and New York City—declared a bank holiday. On that day at noon, with most banks closed and most economic activity in the country at a standstill, Franklin Roosevelt was inaugurated as president. Two days after taking office, FDR made the bank holiday national, temporarily closing all banks. But he did much more.

The Brain Trust and the First One Hundred Days

At his inauguration, the new president told the nation that it must not "shrink from honestly facing conditions in our country today." He was blunt about those conditions, saying:

> Only a foolish optimist can deny the dark realities of the moment. Yet our distress comes from no failure of substance. ... Plenty is at our doorstep, but a generous use of it languishes in the very sight of the supply. Primarily this is because the rulers of the exchange of mankind's goods have failed, through their own stubbornness and their own incompetence, have admitted their failure, and abdicated.

But in that same address, he also insisted on his "firm belief that the only thing we have to fear is fear itself—nameless, unreasoning, unjustified terror which paralyzes needed

New Deal

A term for the programs and legislation developed during Franklin Roosevelt's administration aimed at ending the Great Depression.

American Voices

Letter to Eleanor Roosevelt, April 20, 1935

In her first year as the nation's First Lady, Eleanor Roosevelt received more than 300,000 letters, many of which put a human face on the needs of those living through the Great Depression.

Dear Mrs. Roosevelt,

I am a thirteen year old girl and live on a farm with my mother and Step-Father we are very poor people I have lived here for five years and have wished each year for a radio but as the years go by our circumstances get worse and worse. I am wondering if I would be asking to much of you to help me obtain one. As we live in the country we wold have to have a Battery Radio. We live five miles from town, and we are poor and we have no money for boughten amusements. There is not a radio around in the country and I get terribly lonesome in summer.

Sincerely yours, M.N.C.

Source: Robert Cohen, editor, *Dear Mrs. Roosevelt: Letters from Children of the Great Depression* (Chapel Hill, University of North Carolina Press, 2002), p. 183.

Thinking Critically

1. **Contextualization**
   What does this letter tell you about the hopes and dreams [point of view] of a child living through the Depression?

2. **Analyzing Primary Source**
   What does this letter tell you about the historical situation in which Eleanor Roosevelt found herself and the public persona that she projected in response?

22.1

22.2

22.3

---

efforts to convert retreat into advance." Given the nation's situation, many could think of quite a few things to fear, but Roosevelt made it clear that he was ready to act to address the crisis, and that alone gave people optimism—for a time.

Roosevelt had a magnetic, optimistic personality. He used radio, still a new medium, to connect with the American people through frequent **fireside chats** and press conferences. Roosevelt had been paralyzed by polio in the early 1920s, but few Americans knew that he could not walk without help, and the media kept his secret. Radio carried the president's voice and kept his disability out of sight. Another well-kept secret was the deep strain in Roosevelt's marriage. While Franklin and Eleanor Roosevelt's personal life was often tense, as a public couple, they were extraordinary. The new First Lady was often the eyes and ears of the administration, visiting desperate farmers and industrial workers, travel- ing down mine shafts to coal mines, speaking to audiences around the country, and bring- ing the nation's problems back to the White House. People responded to her on a personal level. Together, Eleanor and Franklin Roosevelt projected hope to a nation that wanted desper- ately to believe even as a great fear continued throughout the 1930s.

The new president knew that although people were willing to give the new adminis- tration a chance, their patience was short. Banks could close for a few days, but if people could not get their money, pay their bills, keep their mortgages up-to-date, a worse crisis would follow. Roosevelt's economic team moved to reopen the banks. They ignored a proposal by Wisconsin senator Robert La Follette, Jr., to nationalize the banks. Using a plan that had been drafted by officials in the outgo- ing Hoover administration, they convinced Congress to pass an Emergency Banking Act on March 9 that allowed those banks deemed safe to open, and permanently liquidated the weakest. After one week in office, President

fireside chats

Speeches broadcast nationally over the radio in which President Franklin Roosevelt explained complex issues and programs in plain language.

Eleanor Roosevelt could travel many places where her husband could not go. Her visits to migrant camps, African American sharecroppers, or in this case a coal mine highlighted the needs of many people and gave many faith in her husband's administration.

Roosevelt gave his first fireside chat, assuring people that "it is safer to keep your money in a reopened bank than it is to keep it under the mattress." The run on the banks stopped, and the newly federally approved banks remained solvent.

Three months later, Congress passed the Glass-Steagall Act, which created the Federal Deposit Insurance Corporation to guarantee bank deposits. Given the role banks had played in the stock market speculation of 1928 and 1929, the Glass-Steagall Act also separated commercial banks and investment banks; the former could take deposits and make loans, with government guarantees, and the latter could invest in the stock market, at their own risk.

Early in 1932, while he was still a candidate for the presidency, Roosevelt created what he called his "Brain Trust." The original core group—Raymond Moley, a political scientist; Rexford Tugwell, an economist; and Adolf Berle, a legal financial expert, were all professors at Columbia University. Others joined or departed from the group. Although they argued with each other, the members of the Brain Trust all agreed that a lack of purchasing power was a key cause of the Depression and that a way had to be found to raise farm income and industrial wages so more Americans could buy more of what the nation could produce, thus putting more Americans back to work. They, like FDR, disliked what they called "the dole" and preferred jobs, any jobs, to welfare.

When Roosevelt came to office in 1933, the Brain Trust guided much of his policy. Some members of the official cabinet represented the older, more cautious Democratic Party establishment. However, others in the cabinet were closer to the Brain Trust, especially farm editor and inventor Henry Wallace, who became secretary of agriculture; Chicago reformer Harold Ickes, who became secretary of the interior; and Roosevelt's longtime New York State ally, Frances Perkins, who became secretary of labor and the first woman in a president's cabinet.

first one hundred days

The first one hundred days of the Roosevelt administration, beginning with his inauguration on March 4, 1933, in which the Democratic Congress passed several important pieces of legislation designed to put Americans back to work and undercut the effect of the Great Depression.

In what became known as the **first one hundred days**, Congress passed a steady stream of new legislation (see Table 22-1, p. 654). On March 13, Congress passed the Economy Act, giving the president broad powers to cut government spending. It also amended the Volstead Act to legalize beer while the country waited for the repeal of Prohibition, a repeal that the president urged forward. While the Economy Act cut federal costs—and did nothing to stimulate the economy—the amended Volstead Act not only allowed people to drink beer legally but also brought millions of dollars of new tax money into the treasury. Before the end of March, Congress established the Civilian Conservation Corps, probably the most popular New Deal agency, through which hundreds of thousands of unemployed young men worked in rural camps planting forests, pruning trees, building parks, and shoring up the nation's wildlands, thus giving many of the unemployed jobs and income to spur the economy. In April 1933, FDR took the country off of the gold standard, replacing currency backed by gold with currency backed by the government's promise to pay. The change put badly needed money into circulation since the supply of dollars was no longer limited by the amount of gold in government or bank vaults.

In May, the president signed the Federal Emergency Relief Act, which provided direct government grants to those without incomes (Hoover had provided loans). He also signed the Agricultural Adjustment Act, which sought to shore up farm prices with a not-always-popular program to plow under 10.5 million acres of cotton and slaughter 6 million piglets. Many, including Agriculture Secretary Henry Wallace, were heartsick at the destruction of food in a nation with many hungry people, but one-third of the nation's workers were in agriculture, and the Brain Trust believed that raising farm prices and therefore farmers' incomes by ending the surplus of agricultural products was the highest national priority. Before the end of May, Congress also created the Tennessee Valley Authority (TVA) to build dams on the Tennessee River that would control floods, bring electricity to rural areas that were without it, and provide jobs (see Map 22-1).

In June, Congress also passed the National Employment System Act, the Home Owners Refinance Act, the Farm Credit Act, the Railroad Coordination Act, and perhaps most significant, the National Industrial Recovery Act. The last

The Civilian Conservation Corps was a very popular New Deal program that eventually put hundreds of thousands of young men to work—and gave them and their families an income—as they planted trees and built outdoor facilities around the country.

Map 22-1 The Range of the TVA.

The TVA, or Tennessee Valley Authority, built dams that controlled flooding and brought electric power to thousands of Americans living in one of the most poverty-stricken parts of the nation along the length of the Tennessee River.

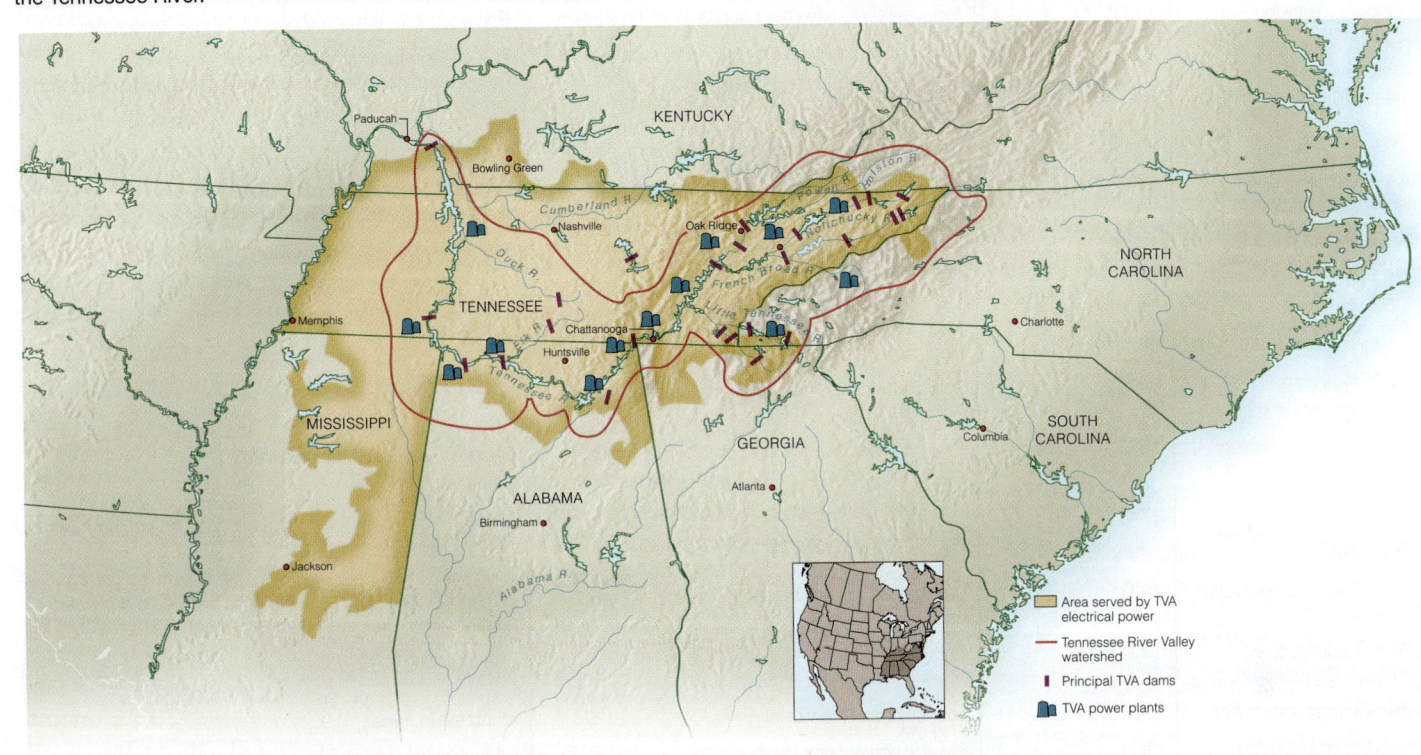

Area served by TVA electrical power

Tennessee River Valley watershed

Principal TVA dams

TVA power plants

act established two of the best-known New Deal agencies, the Public Works Administration (PWA)—committed to large-scale construction projects across the country—and the National Recovery Administration (NRA) with a mandate to create a voluntary national network of businesses to maintain wages and prices. In one hundred days, the United States had a quite different federal government than it had ever seen before. Government policies and new regulatory agencies expanded the reach and the bureaucracy of the federal government far beyond anything ever seen before. And the nation never returned to the older, much smaller, and less activist government that had been the rule from Washington to Hoover. The National Recovery Administration set minimum wages and prices, outlawed child labor, and guaranteed labor the right to organize. The NRA was later declared unconstitutional, but from 1933 to 1935, the NRA, with its "We Do Our Part" signs in store windows across the nation, was a prime symbol of the New Deal.

The Indian New Deal

The New Deal was a time of extraordinary change for many Americans, including American Indians. Like other New Deal initiatives, the changes began during the Hoover years. In 1928, Lewis Meriam led a study of federal Indian policy. Meriam's team conducted the first large-scale examination of the impact of the 1887 Dawes Act (see Chapter 16).

In his report, *The Problem of Indian Administration*, Meriam was blunt, writing, "The work of the government directed toward the education and advancement of the Indian … is largely ineffective." Meriam called for moving the education of Indian children to their home and tribal context.

Roosevelt appointed social worker John Collier as commissioner of Indian affairs. Collier came to office determined to right past wrongs, and by June 1934, he had convinced Congress to pass the Wheeler-Howard Act, also known as the Indian Reorganization Act. Two years later, Congress extended the same rights to native Alaskans. This law was the

Table 22-1 Major New Deal Laws and Agencies

Agency/Law	Year Launched or Passed	Purpose	What Happened?
Emergency Banking Act	1933*	Initial action to save the nation's banking system	Replaced later the same year by Glass-Steagall Act
FDIC—Federal Deposit Insurance Corporation, created by Glass-Steagall Act	1933*	FDIC—to guarantee bank deposits, restore consumer confidence in banks Glass-Steagall Act—to separate commercial and investment banking; banks with guaranteed deposits could not speculate in stock market	FDIC still operating, guaranteeing bank deposits Glass-Steagall separation of commercial and investment banking repealed in 1999
AAA—Agricultural Adjustment Administration	1933*	Subsidize farmers to restrict production and boost farm prices	Declared unconstitutional in 1936; replaced with farm subsidies in 1938, which still continue
Home Owners Loan Corporation and Farm Credit Administration	1933*	Provide home and farm loans to refinance mortgages	Temporary emergency measures
TVA—Tennessee Valley Authority	1933*	Build dams to stop flooding and generate electricity	Still operating
FERA—Federal Emergency Relief Administration	1933*	Provide funds for state and local relief agencies	Temporary emergency measure
NRA—National Recovery Administration	1933*	Protect prices, wages, and employment with codes for business (a major New Deal agency)	Declared unconstitutional in 1935
PWA—Public Works Administration (authorized by the NRA)	1933*	Stimulate economy by building schools, hospitals, dams, etc.	Continued until 1943 when replaced by wartime construction
CCC—Civilian Conservation Corps	1933*	Employ young men to plant forests, build roads, etc.	Continued until 1943, employing 2.5 million men, when wartime jobs eliminated unemployment
SEC—Securities and Exchange Commission	1934	Regulate the stock market	Still operating
Indian Reorganization Act	1934	Launch Indian New Deal	Much still in force
FHA—Federal Housing Administration	1934	Provide home loans	Still operating
WPA—Works Progress Administration	1935	Provide large-scale construction jobs building schools, parks, post offices	Continued until 1943 when replaced by wartime construction
Social Security Administration	1935	Support retirement pensions through payroll tax	Still operating
National Labor Relations Board created by Wagner Act	1935	Provide new rights for union organizing and free union elections	Partially repealed by Taft-Hartley Act in 1947
NYA—National Youth Administration	1935	Provide jobs and support to students (officially part of the WPA)	Closed in 1943; federal work study component still operating
Fair Labor Standards Act	1938	Ensure minimum wage and maximum hours	Still operating with wage raises from time to time

*Indicates a program enacted during of first one hundred days of Roosevelt's administration.

Indian New Deal

A series of policy changes, including the Indian Reorganization Act of 1934, that transformed government Indian policy and strengthened Indian tribal government of the reservations.

beginning of what came to be known as the **Indian New Deal**. Under the Indian Reorganization Act, the government recognized the legal rights of Indian tribes (not done since 1887), including tribal right to hold reservation lands. Tribes adopted constitutions and formed governments. Tribes, not the federal government, were given the right to decide on tribal membership—not an easy issue after generations of relationships between whites and Indians. For most tribes, the Indian New Deal was a fresh start.

African Americans, the Depression, and FDR's "Black Cabinet"

The Great Depression hit African Americans especially hard. Many who had moved to northern cities were still on the bottom of the economic ladder and were often among the first to lose their jobs. As businesses failed and the need for goods and services declined, African American jobs declined precipitously. In 1934, a government survey estimated that 17 percent of whites but 38 percent of blacks were out of work.

Racism was alive and well throughout the United States in the 1930s, but the most rigid segregation was in the seventeen states of the South. And segregation warped federal policy. Not more than 4 percent of African Americans were able to vote in the 1930s, and the members of Congress from the South—all of them elected almost exclusively by the region's white voters—were some of the New Deal's strongest supporters though at the same time determined to ensure that the New Deal did not impact racial segregation. Theodore Bilbo was a senator from Mississippi throughout the New Deal. One observer described him as someone whose commitment to "New Deal liberalism ... never wavered, so long as the rights of the people of his state were not infringed." This commitment referred to the rights of the white voters of Mississippi. Bilbo was a member of the Ku Klux Klan and an ardent racist. Although Bilbo and his Southern colleagues were racist, the New Deal was not. But New Deal legislation would never have gotten through Congress without racist support, and the price of that support was often the exclusion of benefits to African Americans.

In spite of the efforts of some in Congress, most New Deal agencies were designed to help both blacks and whites, but in some cases, discrimination was built into the policies, and in other cases, policies that should have been fair were implemented by people who were not. The NRA, which set minimum wages for jobs, set low minimum salaries in laundry services, tobacco production, and other fields where there were large numbers of black workers. Agricultural Adjustment Administration (AAA) payments often helped landlords but were not passed on, as they should have been, to help tenant farmers or sharecroppers. In the Civilian Conservation Corps (CCC), which provided jobs for unemployed young people—originally only males—some 200,000 African American young men did get jobs and work experience, but the CCC maintained rigidly segregated camps. The federal Home Owners Loan Corporation was designed to give loans to blacks and whites, but local officials of the Federal Housing Authority often decided that blacks were a poor risk and so denied loans to them.

Nevertheless, many African Americans made significant gains during the Great Depression, and in spite of its failures, they saw the Roosevelt administration and the Democratic Party as their friends. They also fought hard for more inclusion. Recognizing that AAA payments were being withheld, African American sharecroppers organized the Southern Tenant Farmers Union to demand payments. African American voters began to shift political allegiance from the "Party of Lincoln" to the Democratic Party because of New Deal policies and especially Eleanor Roosevelt's active support as she visited black communities, advocated for black civil rights, and courted African American voters. Blacks began to win elections to state legislatures. In 1928, Chicago's Oscar DePriest was elected to the U.S. Congress, the first black since Reconstruction. Black votes helped defeat candidates who opposed antilynching bills.

Early in his administration, Roosevelt created what came to be known as the **Black Cabinet**, a shifting and informal group. Roosevelt's (white) secretary of the interior Harold L. Ickes, former president of the Chicago branch of the NAACP, and Eleanor Roosevelt enlarged the size and power of the Black Cabinet. Robert L. Vann, editor of the *Pittsburgh Courier*, served as special assistant to the attorney general, and William H. Hastie, dean of the Law School at Howard University, served as a legal advisor to the Department of the Interior. Robert C. Weaver (who in the 1960s would be the first African American in the cabinet) advised the Department of the Interior.

Perhaps the most prominent member of the Black Cabinet was Mary McLeod Bethune. Bethune was head of a school for girls in Daytona, Florida, that became Bethune-Cookman College. During the 1920s, Bethune became president of the National Association of Colored Women, which advocated for a federal antilynching bill and for support for black women in attending training programs and college. Frustrated by what she saw as the conservatism of the NACW, she launched the more aggressive National Council of Negro Women in 1935.

At Eleanor Roosevelt's urging, Bethune was appointed as the director of the Negro Division of the National Youth Administration (NYA), where she channeled

Black Cabinet

An informal network of high-level African American officials and advisors to the Roosevelt administration who worked together to influence government policy.

Mary McLeod Bethune was a leader in FDR's Black Cabinet and, through her friendship with Eleanor Roosevelt, an influential voice across the administration, but she was also an influential educator and organizer in her own right.

some of the NYA's considerable resources toward creating jobs for African American youth. Bethune used her position and her friendship with Eleanor Roosevelt to organize a Federal Council of Negro Affairs to ensure that blacks in and out of the administration spoke with one voice. When Secretary of War Henry L. Stimson called a conference on women and the war effort in 1941, and failed to invite black women, she wrote to him, "We are not humiliated. We are incensed." Bethune was not going to be ignored. And she was heard.

The Dust Bowl and the "Okie" Experience

Unlike the many farmers who faced troubles in the 1920s, wheat farmers of Kansas, Oklahoma, and the Texas panhandle often prospered during that decade because even when the price of wheat fell they could always plow more land and plant more wheat. As the Depression worsened, however, the Plains farmers faced a unique crisis.

Eventually, the ever-expanding production of wheat caught up with the farmers. The wheat harvest in the fall of 1931 was the most bountiful in history. Farmers had been planting more land, and it was exceedingly fertile. The result was that far more wheat was produced that fall than could possibly be consumed. Europe, like the United States, was in a depression and tariff restrictions made American wheat expensive in the rest of the world. Wheat exports and wheat consumption were down. The price paid for wheat fell so low in 1931 that farmers lost money on every bushel produced. Many vowed not to plant in 1932, and probably a third of the Great Plains farmers faced foreclosures for debt or back taxes.

Then a different disaster struck. Starting late in 1932 and continuing in 1933, 1934, and 1935, farms across the Great Plains simply blew away. Year after year, the dust storms continued, but the worst storm came on Sunday, April 14, 1935, known to those who lived through it as Black Sunday. The day began sunny and windless. Then in the afternoon, the wind picked up, and what looked like a purple or black wall started blowing in from the northwest. Jeanne Clark remembered that she had been outside playing when she heard a panicked call from her mother to come inside. Before she could get to the house, the storm hit. "It was like I was caught in a whirlpool," Clark said. "All of a sudden it got completely dark. I couldn't see a thing." That one storm took 300,000 tons of soil from the Great Plains and deposited it hundreds of miles away—twice as much soil as had been dug out of the Panama Canal. Clark remembered the terrible coughing that followed. A doctor said she had "dust pneumonia" and might not survive. Clark did survive, but others, mostly children and old people, died from the dust storms. Before the end of the 1930s, more than 250,000 people—two-thirds of the Plains population—simply left what had become known as the **Dust Bowl** (see Map 22-2).

The Dust Bowl was an environmental catastrophe of human making. After 1910, scores of white settlers with high hopes had come to the Great Plains and built farms in the "last frontier." Since the land was so dry, the government doubled the homestead allotment to 320 acres. The weather could be terribly hot in the summer and cold in the winter, but the soil was rich. A few old-timers and ranchers said, "God didn't create this land around here to be plowed up." But farmers plowed and grew crops on land that had previously grown only grass.

In the 1930s, however, there was a prolonged drought, and the wells had to be dug deeper to find any water. The soil started to dry up, and then the wind, which always blows hard on the Plains, started to carry the soil away. Cattle suffocated from the dust. People rubbed Vaseline in their nostrils to protect them, and the Red Cross gave out respirator masks at school. People stuffed wet towels and sheets into cracks in doors or windows only to see their houses filled with dust anyway.

As the New Deal administration began to grapple with the Dust Bowl crisis, agricultural agents arrived in the region in 1934 offering up to $16 a head for the remaining cattle, which were either shot on the spot or shipped to a slaughterhouse in Amarillo, Texas. The government offered payments averaging $498 for a promise not to raise a wheat crop the following year. The CCC tried to build demonstration projects to reclaim the land. The reclamation projects did not work. Farming was now impossible for many and unprofitable

Dust Bowl

An area of the Great Plains, centered in Oklahoma, where dust storms from 1932–1935 blew away most of the topsoil, making life there impossible for farm families.

Map 22-2 The Dust Bowl.

Overplanting and plowing of soil with too little water led to massive dust storms that destroyed agricultural communities in states from Texas to North Dakota. Route 66, the highway from Chicago to Los Angeles, became the route by which many Dust Bowl refugees sought a new life in California agriculture.

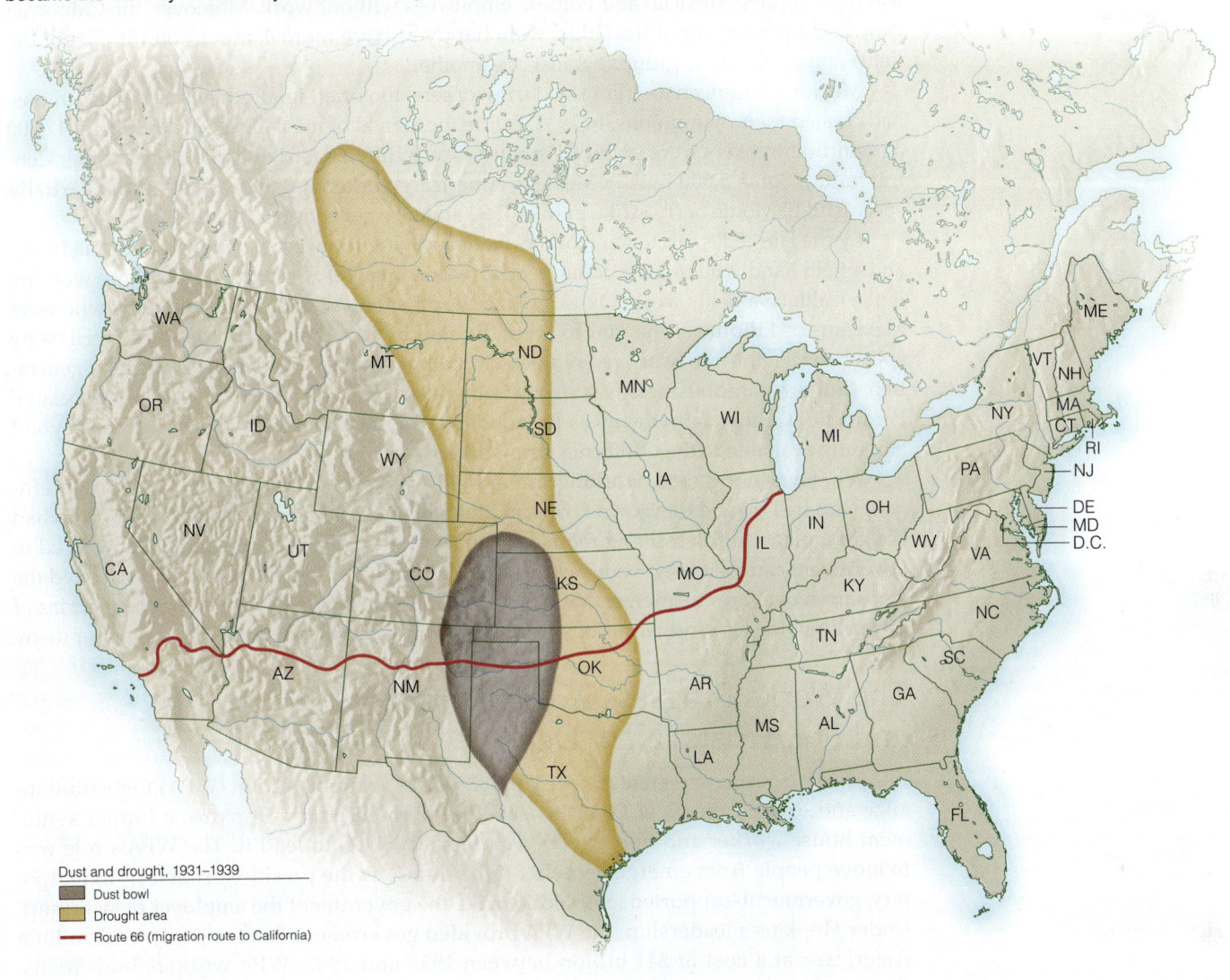

Dust and drought, 1931–1939

- Dust bowl
- Drought area
- Route 66 (migration route to California)

for most. The $498 paid off old debts, but hope of a more bountiful year in 1935 or 1936 seemed remote. Farmers and townspeople began departing in 1934, and before long, a region and a way of life—one that was less than a generation old—simply disappeared.

Most people who left the Dust Bowl moved to California. In the midst of a national Depression, they became migrant farmworkers—hired hands on the farms of California's Central Valley where they were given the derogatory name of "Okies" (on the assumption that they were all from Oklahoma). For many Californians, the "Okies" were desperately poor intruders in a state whose own economy was suffering terribly. Photographers working for the Farm Security Administration (FSA) took their pictures; Carey McWilliams, a young California lawyer, wrote *Factories in the Fields* describing their plight, and one of the country's best-known writers, John Steinbeck, immortalized their experience in *The Grapes of Wrath*. Tom Joad, the hero of Steinbeck's novel, defined what it meant to be an Okie: "Okie use' a mean you was from Oklahoma. Now it … means you're scum. Don't mean nothing itself, it's the way they say it." Nevertheless, for the characters in Steinbeck's novel and for thousands of real-life migrants, it was also a term of pride and of grim determination.

Longtime residents of California's Central Valley feared the Okies. Mexican and Filipino agricultural workers worried, for good reason, that white Dust Bowl refugees would take their jobs. A preference for those who were native-born led many California farmers to give jobs to whites, including recent arrivals from the Dust Bowl during the Great Depression, leaving longtime Mexican and Filipino employees without work. Moreover, the California growers, a powerful political bloc, were happy to have more competition for jobs in the fields and to pit ethnic groups against one another.

Mexican American and Filipino farmworkers, too often ignored by traditional unions, had created their own unions. In 1933, before the arrival of most Dust Bowl refugees, 47,500 agricultural workers were involved in thirty-seven different strikes in California's rich Central Valley. Some 5,000 mostly Mexican American workers were involved in the partially successful El Monte berry strike in June 1933 and a larger cotton strike that fall.

By the late 1930s, up to ten workers were applying for every job in the California fields, and a field hand who made a dollar per day was doing well. Probably half of those working in the California fields were "Okies," while the other half were longtime workers who were Mexicans or Filipinos. The unions were divided by ideological differences as well as by splits between the newly arrived refugees and those who had been in the fields for a generation. California agribusiness was strong and got stronger during the 1930s. The Associated Farmers of California, which was founded in 1934, had resources and power far beyond anything available to the California farmworkers.

Whatever one's race, working in the field was terribly hard work. Dust Bowl refugees who had owned their own farms and had viewed the future with optimism, who had bought a piano for their living room and a new Model T Ford for the family, now lived in government camps if they were lucky, and under bridges if they were not, and followed the crops from one farm to another. Most of the Dust Bowl refugees survived on the margins of society until the new industrial jobs created by World War II ended the Depression for them.

The Works Progress Administration and the Artists' New Deal

In April 1935, Congress created the Works Progress Administration (WPA) to institutionalize and expand the New Deal. Roosevelt appointed Harry Hopkins, a former settlement house worker and one of FDR's closest advisors, to lead it. The WPA's role was to move people from emergency relief ("the dole," as the president called it) to temporary, government-supported jobs and to make the government the employer of last resort. Under Hopkins's leadership, the WPA provided government-funded jobs for 8.5 million Americans at a cost of $11 billion between 1935 and 1942. WPA workers built roads, theaters, and public buildings, and in some cases, they planned communities in every state of the Union as well as planted forests, laid out new parks, and changed the face of the countryside. Providing WPA jobs also provided opportunities for Roosevelt's political allies—usually Democrats, but in some cases, also Republicans, including New York City's mayor Fiorello La Guardia—to win political favors by handing out the coveted jobs to political supporters.

At the urging of Eleanor Roosevelt, Hopkins included jobs for artists in the WPA. In response to one critic of the artists program, Hopkins said, "Hell, they've got to eat just like other people." In 1935 and 1936, WPA artists painted murals in post offices; provided music through symphony orchestras, jazz groups, Appalachian banjo pickers, and Texas fiddlers; staged theater productions of everything from Shakespeare to new, cutting-edge works; wrote guidebooks to every part of the United States; and recorded the oral histories of former slaves, among many other projects. Besides ensuring that many artists were able to eat and practice their craft, the WPA art programs left a lasting cultural legacy, though not one without criticism.

Other federal agencies also hired artists. Rexford Tugwell, one of the most influential members of the Brain Trust, charged the Farm Security Administration with creating a "Pictorial Sourcebook of American Agricultural History." Between 1935 and 1939, a team of photographers, including several who later became famous for their work—Dorothea

Lange, Walker Evans, and Ben Shahn—roamed the country, creating a picture of often-hidden rural poverty.

Organized Labor, the Committee for Industrial Organization, and the Factory Floor

In its early years, many labor union leaders were not sure they trusted the New Deal. However, although the primary purpose of the National Industrial Recovery Act of June 1933 was to stabilize prices, at Roosevelt's insistence it also included a clause protecting collective bargaining through unions. The National Labor Relations Act of 1935 (the Wagner Act), sponsored by New York senator Robert Wagner, expanded the rights of union members, outlawing "unfair labor practices" as well as giving workers the right to join a union without getting fired, rights to collective bargaining, and the right to strike. For the next decade, unions could be relatively sure that the federal government would not intervene in a strike on the side of management, as it had done repeatedly in the past. The Wagner Act did not create any unions, but it did provide a new context; labor organizers took the next steps on their own.

In 1935, when the Wagner Act was passed, only about 10 percent of American workers were union members, mostly in the skilled craft unions of the American Federation of Labor (A.F. of L.). Within the A.F. of L. some of its leaders, John L. Lewis of the United Mine Workers of America, Sidney Hillman of the Amalgamated Clothing Workers, and David Dubinsky of the International Ladies' Garment Workers Union, pushed the A.F. of L. to organize the unorganized. Lewis and his colleagues wanted industrial unions that would organize a union of all the workers in an industry such as steel or automobiles or textiles, as opposed to the craft unions, which focused on a single trade—carpenters, plumbers, or electricians. But the leadership of the A.F. of L. would have none of it. They meant to protect their current members.

Lewis, Hillman, and Dubinsky created a Committee for Industrial Organization within the A.F. of L. When other union leaders within the A.F. of L. continued to resist their efforts, the Committee for Industrial Organization became the **Congress of Industrial Organizations** (CIO), a separate union and a competitor to the A.F. of L.

John L. Lewis, founding president of the CIO, could be tough, arbitrary, arrogant, and self-absorbed. He also was able to speak to workers as no one had since Eugene Debs and Mother Jones. Lewis believed that by the 1930s a "mighty surge of human sentiment" was about to change industrial America.

Sometimes the "mighty surge" got ahead of those who were trying to lead it. Across the country, workers, even many who had not yet joined a union, launched a new kind of strike—the sit-down strike. Instead of walking off the job and onto the picket lines, CIO-inspired workers simply stopped work and sat down where they were. In doing so, they guaranteed that they could not be replaced by nonunion workers, and they were hard to attack without harming the machinery they were guarding. They were also much more comfortable inside the plant than outside, especially on cold winter days. It turned out to be a brilliant tactic.

One of the first sit-down strikes took place in Akron, Ohio, at the Firestone Tire Plant on January 29, 1936. After the workers sat down where they were and the noise of the assembly

Photographer Dorothea Lange was one of the many artists who were given employment by the New Deal but who also used their positions to tell the nation of the need for many New Deal programs such as, in this case, the work of the Farm Security Administration in helping rural families.

Congress of Industrial Organizations (CIO)

A new labor union that sought to organize industrial workers by industry, such as all automobile workers, rather than by individual skill or job.

Striking workers at a General Motors factory in Flint, Michigan, sit on car seats in front of unfinished automobiles. The sit-down strike created a new form of labor union organizing.

line stopped, one worker said of the silence, "It's like the end of the world." The Firestone workers stayed where they were for three days and won.

The CIO reported a surge of telephone calls like this one: "We've sat down! Send someone over to organize us!" From September 1936, through the following spring, 485,000 workers engaged in sit-down strikes. The CIO grew to 2 million members in six months.

For most assembly line workers fortunate enough to have jobs in the 1930s, the primary complaint was not salary. As one Chevrolet worker told an NRA investigator in 1934, "Of course, we make enough to live on while we are working, but we don't work enough time." Workers on assembly lines were angry because when there was no work they had no income. They also complained about constant speed-ups on the assembly lines when they were working. In an assembly line industry, the pace of the line ruled everything. At Flint's Fisher Body plant, a worker said, "I ain't got no kick on wages, but I just don't like to be drove."

On December 30, 1936, workers in two General Motors units in Flint, Michigan, stopped the line and sat down where they were. The Flint Sit-Down Strike had begun. By January 4, 1937, workers were sitting in at GM plants in Atlanta, Georgia; Anderson, Indiana; Cleveland, Ohio; Kansas City, Missouri; and Norwood, Ohio. It was the beginning of a long, cold winter.

On January 11, the GM management turned the heat off even though it was sixteen degrees outside. Police blocked a delivery of food. A group of about thirty strikers went to the main gate and broke through a police lock to get to supporters outside. The company called the Flint police, who fired tear gas. Strikers responded by throwing door hinges, bottles, and stones at the police. The United Auto Workers union (UAW) called it "the Battle of the Running Bulls." The wind blew the tear gas back on the police. The gas and the continuing hail of missiles from the plant infuriated them, and they began shooting at strikers and picketers. Amazingly, no one was killed. The young wife of one striker, Genora Johnson, who was herself on the picket line, remembered, "I did not know fear. I knew only surprise, anguish, and anger."

Everyone—strikers and GM management—wondered about the ability of the strikers to continue. Most of those engaged in the sit-in were not yet union members, and few of them had ever been involved in a strike before, much less a protracted sit-in. But one remembered, "It was like war. The guys with me became my buddies."

Negotiations began in mid-January and on February 11 a settlement was reached. General Motors recognized the UAW's right to represent its members, something the company had sworn never to do. It promised to negotiate in good faith on future contracts and that there would be no punishment of workers because of the sit-down. The union ended the strike. The *United Automobile Workers Journal* said of the settlement, "The greatest strike in American history has been victoriously concluded." One striker said it more modestly: "Even if we got not one damn thing out of it other than that, we at least had a right to open our mouths without fear."

Opponents of the New Deal

Not everyone celebrated the union's victory over General Motors or other direct or indirect results of the New Deal. In July 1934, the du Pont brothers, Pierre, Irénée, and Lammot, invited a number of business and political leaders, including the 1928 Democratic nominee Al Smith, to New York to discuss "the dangers to investors" in the New Deal. The du Ponts, who owned a major share of General Motors, had many reasons to dislike the Roosevelt administration. They and their guests created the **American Liberty League** to oppose the New Deal.

Irénée du Pont said that the family had "followed the President in the belief that he was sincere," but thought that "the so-called New Deal" was nothing more or less than the socialistic doctrine. Al Smith, once Roosevelt's mentor, told those at a Liberty League dinner that he would probably "take a walk" (not participate) during the next presidential election and accused Roosevelt of handing the government over to dreamy professors and bleeding-heart social workers. A league publication said that the New Deal stirred up the "dragon teeth of class warfare." Other members of the American Liberty League included John J. Raskob, a former Democratic Party chair, who had been an executive at General Motors and the DuPont corporation; John W. Davis, the 1924 Democratic presidential nominee; Alfred P. Sloan of General Motors; and Sewell Avery of Montgomery Ward. (Herbert Hoover declined to join, derogatorily calling the League the "Wall Street model of human liberty.")

The National Association of Manufacturers also became a tough opponent of the New Deal. The association was created before 1900 to coordinate business opposition to labor unions. With the advent of the New Deal, leaders of the organization sought to "serve the purposes of business salvation," and by 1937, were spending $1.5 million a year on radio programs, motion pictures, billboards, direct mail, and speakers, attacking the New Deal.

While conservative critics of the New Deal said that it was driving the country toward socialism, Roosevelt worried much more about other critics—those who thought the New Deal was not socialistic enough. The Communist Party was always unhappy with Roosevelt. Communists dismissed the New Deal as mere "bourgeois democracy." Communists created unemployment councils, led rent strikes, and defended union members and civil rights workers. Although the party was small, it was not without influence in the 1930s. Many non-Communists also wanted to push the country further than Roosevelt wanted to go. Socialists as well as many midwestern progressives talked of a third-party challenge in 1936.

A sixty-six-year-old Californian, Dr. Francis Townsend, proposed a federal pension of $200 per month to any person over sixty years of age who would retire from work, leaving a job open for someone younger. The idea spread like wildfire. A number of candidates were elected to Congress in 1934 with Townsend's support. In addition, there were some five thousand Townsend Clubs around the country, and twenty-five million people signed Townsend petitions to Congress.

While Townsend's ideas were gaining political traction, the muckraking author Upton Sinclair announced that he would seek the Democratic nomination for governor of California in 1934 based on a pledge to "End Poverty in California" (EPIC). Like the Townsend movement, the EPIC campaign took off among voters who were impatient with the New Deal. Sinclair won the nomination, received widespread support—though not from Roosevelt, who saw EPIC as an effort to confiscate private property—and helped shape the national dialogue, even though he lost the election.

More influential than Townsend or Sinclair was the "radio priest" Charles Coughlin, pastor of a small Catholic parish in Detroit where auto workers formed the core of his congregation. A local radio station broadcast his Sunday sermons, and after 1930 Columbia Broadcasting System carried him nationally (which prompted the anti-Catholic Klan to burn a cross on his lawn). As the Depression worsened, Coughlin's sermons became more political. He relentlessly attacked Hoover and the nation's bankers, and he described himself as the voice of "the little people, the average man [who] was suffering." Given the size of his radio audience, Roosevelt was delighted that Coughlin supported his 1932 campaign.

After the election, the two met at the White House, but Coughlin later turned on the New Deal. He accused FDR of having "out-Hoovered Hoover" and talked of organizing his own political party. His sermons took on an increasingly anti-Semitic and isolationist tone, and some thought he was starting to sound like the new German chancellor Adolf Hitler.

American Liberty League

Launched in 1934, the group was one of the largest and most well funded of several organizations opposed to the New Deal, which it considered socialistic.

22.1

22.2

22.3

In Roosevelt's mind, however, the greatest challenge came from Louisiana's grass-roots populist senator Huey P. Long. Long was a product of the pine woods region of Louisiana where poverty, the Baptist church, and political independence flourished. Long's forebearers had supported the Union cause during the Civil War and Eugene V. Debs during the early 1900s. In 1928, as Al Smith was going down to defeat, Long was elected governor of Louisiana after a campaign attacking big corporations, especially Standard Oil, while promising opportunity for the poor. "Every man a king, but no one wears a crown," was his campaign slogan. He raised taxes on oil and gas production, built new highways, schools, and hospitals, provided free textbooks, and grew very popular and very powerful. Some said that Louisiana under Long was a virtual dictatorship. He was elected to the U.S. Senate in 1930. In Washington, he showed disdain for Democrats as well as Republicans, called the president "Frank," much to FDR's displeasure, and said that all he cared about was "what the boys at the forks of the creek think of me." There were a lot of boys and girls at the forks of a lot of creeks who thought a lot of Long. FDR considered him a dangerous demagogue.

In 1934, Long launched what he called the Share Our Wealth Society. Long promised a onetime grant of $5,000 per family and a guaranteed income of $2,500 (twice the 1934 national average) as well as educational subsidies for the young and pensions for the elderly (specifically designed to attract Townsend support), all to be paid for by seizing the wealth of the few. When people said his numbers did not add up, that there was not enough wealth to seize even if people wanted to, Long responded that his followers needed to "be prepared for the slurs and snickers of some high ups." But, he insisted, "Let no one tell you that it is difficult to redistribute the wealth of this land. It is simple."

Neither the conservative opposition nor Communists and Socialists worried Roosevelt, but Townsend, Coughlin, and Long did. The president worried about a dictatorship emerging in the United States, just as dictatorships had emerged as a result of the Depression in Italy and Germany. Democratic chairman James Farley commissioned a poll that showed that a third-party ticket led by Long could lead to Roosevelt's defeat in 1936 and perhaps even a Long victory, if not in 1936 then by 1940. There was plenty to worry about. "Long plans to be a candidate of the Hitler type for the presidency in 1936," Roosevelt said. The president reshaped his political agenda to take control of the national dialogue.

The Continuing Depression and the Expanding New Deal, 1935–1939

During Roosevelt's first one hundred days, indeed during his first two years, the New Deal consisted of a series of experiments, some contradictory, some well thought out, but all designed to stem the worst of the Depression and begin a new course—to keep people from starving, to put them back to work, and to get more money into circulation. All of this federal action made a difference, but it did not end the Depression. In 1935, there was a shift in focus; some called it the "Second New Deal." It was not a radical change, but it did involve greater attention to long-term financial security for more Americans.

Before accepting the job as FDR's secretary of labor, Frances Perkins had insisted that the president promise to back pensions for the aging and unemployment insurance. In an early meeting, Roosevelt told Perkins, "I will authorize you to try, and if you succeed, that's fine." It was all the authorization she needed. Perkins had witnessed the tragic Triangle Shirtwaist Fire in New York in 1911. She had also led the investigation that followed and helped craft some of the health and safety legislation that emerged from it. The growth and popularity of the Townsend movement gave Perkins more political clout than she might otherwise have had. If a plan could be devised that was financially viable (unlike the Townsend plan), then 1934 and 1935 was the time to get it passed.

Roosevelt worried about amassing too much power in the federal government. He insisted that the states play the lead role in unemployment insurance, though he was willing to have a federal role. But he was adamant that "[a]ll the power shouldn't be in the

Franklin Roosevelt signed the Social Security Act in 1935, one of the most long-lasting New Deal initiatives. Frances Perkins, the secretary of labor and its prime architect, stood behind him.

hands of the federal government. Look—just think what would happen if all the power was concentrated here, and Huey Long became president!" Treasury Secretary Henry Morgenthau was determined that any plan be fiscally viable. But many in the administration thought Townsend had a point: the country did need to encourage older Americans to retire and leave their jobs to younger people but not be impoverished as a result. And Perkins was determined to get a bill through Congress.

On January 17, 1935, FDR announced plans for a Social Security program that would protect some twenty-six million citizens with "security against the hazards and vicissitudes of life." The proposed bill included a federal tax on employees and employers to fund the retirement system, a federal tax to help support a state-administered unemployment insurance system, and emergency grants to fund the immediate relief of the indigent elderly, Aid to Dependent Children, and modest support for public health. Since the Constitution clearly gave the government the right to tax, there was no room for a constitutional challenge to the legislation as long as Social Security was a tax. Congress passed the Social Security Act seven months later on August 14, 1935. The proposed **Social Security Act** included a federal tax on employees and employers to fund the retirement system. In January 1940, the fifth anniversary of Roosevelt's speech about the program, Ida M. Fuller, a seventy-six-year-old woman living in Vermont, received the first Social Security check.

As Roosevelt prepared for the reelection battle of 1936, he also toughened his rhetoric. In his 1933 inaugural address, FDR had criticized "the rulers of the exchange of mankind's goods." In 1936, however, he spoke of his "old enemies," the bankers and profiteers, and condemned their "greed" and "autocracy." He said of business leaders, "They are unanimous in their hate for me—and I welcome their hatred."

Roosevelt attacked business leaders every chance he got during 1935 and 1936, but he did not actually *do* very much to hurt them. Nevertheless, his rhetoric stole the thunder from Coughlin's and Long's new legislation, especially Social Security, and undermined Townsend's organization. Roosevelt's support for the Wagner Act also created great loyalty among labor unions. As a result, Roosevelt amassed great political capital going into the 1936 presidential election.

Huey Long was assassinated in September 1935. After his death, his Share Our Wealth clubs became the Union Party, which nominated William Lemke, a congressman from

Social Security Act

Legislation that established a system of federal old-age pensions in effect to the present day.

American Voices

Frances Perkins, "The Roots of Social Security," Reflecting on 1935

Long after she left office, FDR's secretary of labor Frances Perkins looked back on the work she did.

[T]he real roots of the Social Security Act were in the Great Depression of 1929. Nothing else would have bumped the American people into a social security system except something so shocking, so terrifying, as that Depression. ...

In the spring of 1932, Franklin Roosevelt ... made a speech which was full of pleasant hyperbole of one sort or another—flattery to various Governors—but at one point he began to discuss the great problems now facing this country, and he spoke about unemployment. Then he said, "I am for unemployment insurance but not for the dole."

Until we heard those words come over the wires, I wasn't sure he was going to say he was for unemployment insurance. I was afraid he was going to say he was against the dole, and nothing else. ... It created a great interest and a great enthusiasm among the voters, which he was not slow to catch on to. He had that kind of a mind, you know; he could feel the public pulse, and he cared about the public pulse. ...

At any rate, we worked all summer. ... It was a terribly hot summer and everybody worked hard all the time and finally we actually did bring forth a report ... that recommended unemployment insurance and old-age insurance but omitted health insurance just because the experts couldn't get through with health insurance in time to make a report on it. ...

Senator Wagner put it up—a bill which he called a model bill—and held public hearings in the Senate, which attracted a great deal of attention from the Senators. We had a number of senatorial committees which we asked to look into this or that. We got advice. All these actions were for the purpose, not so much of advice as of propaganda—that is, of education of the public. ... The result was a bill that finally was presented to Congress and, as you know, was debated very briefly. ... And finally, we did get the basic bill passed.

Source: Frances Perkins, "The Roots of Social Security," speech delivered at Social Security Administration Headquarters, Baltimore, Maryland, October 23, 1962, downloaded from www.ssa.gov/history/perkins5.html, January 9, 2013.

Thinking Critically

1. **Analyzing Primary Sources**
   From Perkins's point of view, what role did Roosevelt play in the development and passage of Social Security? What role did she and her team play?

2. **Argument Development**
   Do you agree with Perkins that, without the Great Depression, Social Security would never have been enacted? Why or why not? What evidence would you use to support your argument?

North Dakota, for president. The Republicans nominated the liberal Kansas governor Alf Landon. In spite of polls, including one by the *Literary Digest* that predicted a Landon win, Roosevelt won a stunning electoral victory in November 1936. He carried forty-six of the nation's forty-eight states and a huge plurality of the popular vote.

As he began his second term in January 1937, the president said, "I see one-third of a nation, ill-housed, ill-clad, ill-nourished." It was not only a call to action but also an admission that in four years the New Deal had not accomplished all that he had hoped for. Perhaps worst of all, the generalized fear that the president had acknowledged in his first inaugural address had abated but had not disappeared, and for many, confidence had not returned.

In spite of his extraordinary election victory and the high hopes for more permanent reform it engendered, Roosevelt accomplished far less in his second term than in the first. The sense of national crisis was not as great in 1937, and Roosevelt's own missteps got in the way.

One of FDR's greatest frustrations was the fact that a conservative U.S. Supreme Court kept undermining his efforts. Late in his first term, the Court declared the NRA and then the AAA unconstitutional, as well as state minimum wage laws. Court challenges to Social Security and the Wagner Act were working their way through the lower courts. He was not sure what would come next and he feared what the Supreme Court might do to the rest of the New Deal. In early February 1937 after his reelection, Roosevelt offered a plan that would allow him to appoint one additional Supreme Court justice for every member who was over the age of seventy—which in 1937 would mean six new justices—and similar numbers in the lower courts. The Constitution never mentions a number of justices for the Court, and the number had fluctuated between five and ten.

FDR's proposal was constitutional but politically unwise. FDR claimed that the goal was to speed judicial review. Everyone knew that, in fact, there was only one goal: to stop the Court from overturning the New Deal.

To many in Congress, not only conservatives, the Court-packing bill was a step toward dictatorship. For some Southern senators, it would open up the way to civil rights legislation, which they always feared might someday emerge from the White House. Montana senator Burton Wheeler, an old progressive who usually sided with the president, led the assault, claiming that the bill "cut down those guarantees of liberty written by the blood of your forefathers." The legislation was defeated by the friends of the New Deal before its enemies got a chance to join in the debate.

Ironically, while Congress defeated Roosevelt's plan to expand—or "pack"—the Supreme Court, the justices, perhaps reading the 1936 election returns, shifted ground. Chief Justice Charles Evans Hughes and Associate Justice Owen Roberts, who had both voted against the New Deal, changed their minds, first on a minimum wage law and then on the all-important Wagner Labor Relations Act, which the Court found to be constitutional. The changes in the Hughes and Robert votes were dubbed "the switch in time that saved nine." After 1937, although no new justices were added, the Court stopped declaring New Deal legislation unconstitutional.

Nevertheless, with the defeat of Roosevelt's Court plan, the momentum behind the New Deal slowed. Divisions in Congress engendered by the Court plan never healed. Unemployment actually rose in 1937 and 1938 in the "Depression within a Depression," which most likely occurred due to Roosevelt's effort to balance the federal budget by cutting back on the federal spending that was keeping the economy moving. Congress did pass a bill to resurrect parts of the old AAA now that the Court seemed more open to it. A Fair Labor Standards Act that prohibited child labor and set an hourly minimum wage and a forty-hour workweek also passed. However, Congress defeated a plan to expand the Tennessee Valley Authority to other regions of the country and a reorganization plan for the executive branch of the government that FDR wanted. When the president signed the Fair Labor Standards Act in June 1938, he was heard to say, "That's that." The New Deal, it seemed, had come to an end even if the Depression that launched it would run on for another year or more.

The New Deal did not end the Great Depression. The economy rebounded only as the United States prepared for World War II and government spending in preparation for war far outpaced anything that had been spent to "prime the pump" during the 1930s. Nevertheless, the New Deal changed the country. The Glass-Steagall Act and the Federal Deposit Insurance Corporation stabilized the nation's banking system, and the CCC and other agencies put people to work who desperately wanted—needed—jobs. Franklin and Eleanor Roosevelt's optimism gave people hope, and the president's commitment helped keep democratic institutions alive at a time when they were under assault not only in Europe and Asia but also in the United States. The federal government has never shrunk to its pre–New Deal size when the Post Office was the largest government agency. Social Security and federal regulatory agencies play a continuing role in the economy and in people's lives. Including women and African Americans in more than token positions within any administration is now the norm. The New Deal also inspired a new conservative movement and philosophy as opponents of the New Deal, especially business leaders, began to attack the new government intervention in the economy. While historians will long debate the value and the impact of the New Deal, all agree that the United States was a very different place in 1939 than it had been in 1929.

22.1

22.2

22.3

22.2 Quick Review

Was the New Deal the best response to the Great Depression of the 1930s? What parts of the New Deal were most effective? What merit do you find in the arguments of those who opposed the New Deal?

When Historians Disagree

What Was the Impact of the New Deal?

From the 1930s to the present, politicians, economists, and historians have argued about the causes of the Great Depression and about the value of the New Deal programs that were aimed at ending it. The debate remains fierce because so many of the issues—the value of government intervention and the role of government in managing the economy—are as relevant today as they were then.

Amity Shlaes, *The Forgotten Man: A New History of the Great Depression* (New York: HarperCollins, 2007), pp. 7–9.

Both Hoover and Roosevelt misstepped in a number of ways. Hoover ordered wages up when they wanted to go down. He allowed a disastrous tariff, Smoot-Hawley, to become law when he should have had the sense to block it. He raised taxes when neither citizens individually nor the economy as a whole could afford the change. …

Roosevelt's errors had a different quality but were equally devastating. He created regulatory, aid, and relief agencies based on the premise that recovery could be achieved only through a large military-style effort. Some of these were useful—the financial institutions he established upon entering office. Some were inspiring—the Civilian Conservation Corps, for example, which created parks, bridges, and roads. … Other new institutions, such as the National Recovery Administration, did damage …

Where the private sector could help to bring the economy back—in the arena of utilities, for example—Roosevelt and his New Dealers often suppressed it. The creation of the Tennessee Valley Authority snuffed out a growing—and potentially successful—effort to light up the South. …

One of the most famous Roosevelt phrases in history … was Roosevelt's boast that he would promulgate "bold, persistent experimentation." But Roosevelt's commitment to experimentation itself created fear. … Both the taxes and the strikes were the result of Roosevelt policy; the strikes had been made possible by the Wagner Act the year before. … The trouble, however, was not merely the new policies that were implemented but also the threat of additional, unknown, policies. Fear froze the economy, but that uncertainty itself might have a cost was something the young experimenters simply did not consider.

… From 1929 to 1940, from Hoover to Roosevelt, government intervention helped make the Depression Great.

Anthony J. Badger, *FDR: The First Hundred Days* (New York: Hill & Wang, 2008), pp. xv–xvi, 172–174.

For Amity Shlaes, writing in 2007, Calvin Coolidge and Andrew Mellon were the heroes of interwar America; the villains were Herbert Hoover and Franklin Roosevelt, who both failed because of their penchant for government intervention and their lack of faith in the marketplace. …

The desperate plight of ordinary Americans exposes the wishful thinking that lies behind the criticisms of the economic historians and the lamentations of the right. … How long would the unemployed who had lost their faith in the beneficence and competence of American businessmen remain fatalistic? It is simply unrealistic to think that the government could stand back and concentrate on cutting spending and securing a controlled international reflation alone. The desperate need of ordinary Americans meant that Roosevelt and Congress did not have the luxury of such a hands-off policy. … The key point about the New Deal in the summer of 1933 was that it gave immediate assistance in cash and kind to those on relief. The farm programs may not have solved the problem of over production but they stopped the foreclosures and put money into the hands of southern and Midwestern farmers later that year … Roosevelt gave indispensable assistance to many Americans in the summer of 1933. He instigated a regulatory regime for financial institutions that prevented a repeat of the Great Crash. He made a start on a massive program of investment in the physical infrastructure of the United States. What he had not found in 1933 was the magic key to economic recovery. But in the Hundred Days Roosevelt demonstrated that a democracy need not be paralyzed in the face of economic catastrophe.

Thinking Critically

1. **Analyzing Secondary Sources**
   According to Shlaes, the New Deal made the Great Depression worse. According to Badger, the same exact programs met immediate needs and saved American democracy. How could two historians have such different interpretations of the same events and programs?

2. **Argument Development**
   Given what you know, which historian do you think is more correct and why?

The Deep Roots of War—The United States, Europe, and Asia

22.3 Analyze the international impact of the Depression, German and Japanese military expansion, and the initial U.S. response.

While the United States emerged from World War I relatively unscathed, much of Europe was devastated, and the Treaty of Versailles caused significant lingering pain and anger, most of all among the defeated Germans. When a worldwide depression came, suffering, fear, and resentment all planted the seeds of another greater conflict.

In Europe, some of the earliest signs of the postwar ill will appeared in Italy. In 1922, the leader of the ultranationalist Italian Fascist Party, Benito Mussolini, became prime minister. "Il Duce" (the leader), as he called himself, ruled Italy with an iron fist for more than twenty years. Mussolini's dream was to restore Italy's ancient glory by building prosperity and reestablishing the ancient Roman Empire, especially in North Africa, starting with Ethiopia. Mussolini and the Fascists dismissed liberal democracy, hated traditional politics and politicians, and as one Italian newspaper reported, expressed "contempt for every norm of established government."

For Germany, the 1920s were a terrible decade. The German Weimar Republic governed a defeated country. Hyperinflation between 1921 and 1924 made German currency virtually worthless. Shifting government coalitions were not able to create stability, especially in the face of the country's need to pay some $33 billion in reparations—payments that Britain and France used to pay their own $10 billion debt to the United States. In the late 1920s, as the worldwide depression worsened, the German economy collapsed under the load of debt payments and inflation. Banks closed in Germany and Austria. President Hoover described the German bank crisis of 1931 as "a gigantic explosion which shook the foundations of the world's economic, political, and social structure." Anger in Germany brought a new German political party to power.

Adolf Hitler's Nazi (or National Socialist) Party grew from a group of street thugs in the 1920s, known as Brown Shirts, to a formidable group leading to Hitler's election in January 1933 as German chancellor, with 44 percent of the vote, just before Roosevelt became president. Hitler promised that a greatly expanded German nation would provide *Lebensraum* (living space) for people of German nationality by pushing other peoples, Slavs and Jews, out of the way to make room for the "master race."

A month after coming in to office, on February 27, 1933, the Nazi Party issued a decree ending free speech and assembly in Germany. They arrested Communist deputies in the German Parliament, giving themselves a solid majority there. Hitler took the title *der Fuhrer,*

Kristallnacht, November 9, 1938, was a Nazi Party–inspired attack on Jewish businesses and synagogues across Germany. It was the beginning of worse to come for Jews in Nazi-controlled countries.

World History Archive/Newscom

the leader. Later that year, just as the United States was implementing the prolabor New Deal, the Nazi government outlawed trade unions and other political parties. They authorized a new police force, the *Geheime Staatspolizei* or Gestapo, to enforce Nazi authority. In 1935, as the U.S. Congress was passing the Social Security Act and the Wagner Act, the Nazi Parliament passed the Nuremberg Decrees, which took away the citizenship of German Jews, excluded Jews from most professions and the military, and made the marriage of a Jew and non-Jew illegal. In November 1938, in a well-orchestrated attack across Germany known as *Kristallnacht* (or "Crystal Night," for all the broken glass), crowds attacked Jewish stores, homes, and synagogues while the government arrested some twenty thousand Jews. The Nazi government then ordered an "atonement fine" on Jews to pay for the cost of *Kristallnacht*, closed Jewish stores, and a short time later, confiscated all Jewish property. Before long, Germany's Jews, and then those in Austria, Czechoslovakia, Poland, and other territories under German control, were being forced to wear yellow stars to identify them. They were packed into tightly controlled urban ghettos, and within two years, the first of them were being transported to slave labor and death camps.

While the German government was attacking its Jewish citizens, Hitler also renounced the clause in the Treaty of Versailles calling for German disarmament and began to build a new army. A year later, in March 1936, Hitler's army marched into the German Rhineland, which under the terms of the Treaty of Versailles was supposed to be kept free of troops. Two years later, in March 1938, Hitler announced that the independent country of Austria was to be known as the German province of Ostmark, and German troops marched into Austria. On March 14, 1938, Hitler rode in triumph through Vienna, welcomed as a hero by many.

Hitler did not stop there. Since the Sudeten region of Czechoslovakia had a large German population (though still a minority), Hitler claimed that they had the right under the Treaty of Versailles—which he otherwise ignored—to self-determination and should be incorporated into Germany. After a summer of negotiations and with British agreement, Hitler annexed the Sudeten region. The following spring, in March 1939, Hitler sent the German army into the rest of Czechoslovakia and made a triumphant journey to Prague.

As Nazi power grew in Germany and fascism continued its hold on Italy, the two countries formalized their Rome-Berlin Axis by treaty in November 1936. A few months earlier, in July 1936, another Fascist, Spanish general Francisco Franco, commander of the Spanish army garrison in Morocco, led an attack on the left-leaning and democratically elected Republican government of Spain. Spain was engulfed in a bloody civil war. The governments of Germany and Italy sent planes and troops to aid Franco. The Communist government of Russia and Western governments sent modest aid to the Republicans. But by early 1939, the Fascists had won. Spain joined Italy and Germany, forming a powerful Fascist bloc.

While Fascists were consolidating their power in central Europe, militarists in Japan were also growing in power. Japanese militarism had a strong anti-American strain as various American policies—from the exclusion of Japanese children from San Francisco schools in 1906 to the exclusion of all Japanese immigrants as a result of the 1924 immigration law—sparked continuing anger even as people in the United States forgot those incidents.

In the 1910s and 1920s, as Japanese power grew, Japan declared a goal of "Asia for Asians," which meant Japanese domination of the whole of the western rim of the Pacific Ocean to replace Britain, France, and the United States as dominant powers. Many Asians resented U.S. control of the Philippine Islands, British involvement in China and Burma, Dutch control of the oil-rich East Indies, and French control of Indochina (modern Vietnam, Laos, and Cambodia). Except in China, where Japanese advances were deeply resented, the Japanese conquests were often welcomed in the rest of Asia.

By the 1930s, Japan faced the same worldwide depression conditions as other industrialized countries. Japan saw its economic salvation in expansion. The island nation could not provide enough food for its people and lacked key natural resources such as iron and oil. If the Europeans could have Asian colonies, its leaders asked, why not Japan? In September 1932, Japan used an explosion at a Japanese-owned railway in China as an excuse to send troops into China, and they installed a puppet government in the Chinese province of Manchuria. Then in July 1937, Japanese troops captured Shanghai, the largest city in China, and the Chinese capital of Nanking. The Rape of Nanking, as the Japanese attack was called, was a brutal assault. As many as 300,000 Chinese were killed as the Japanese army raped, beheaded, machine-gunned, and bayoneted civilians. The Chinese government led by Chiang Kai-shek retreated and set up a new capital in the inland city of Chungking. Japan renamed the expanded territory in Manchuria as the Japanese province of Manchukuo. A half a million Japanese moved into the territory to farm and govern the subjected Chinese population. At the same time, Chiang's Kuomintang Party (the Nationalists) was locked in a bitter civil war with the Chinese Community Party led by Mao Zedong.

In the face of so much worldwide violence and aggression, the governments of Great Britain, France, and the United States did virtually nothing while the League of Nations proved to be a meaningless barrier to aggression. The government of France ordered the construction of the supposedly "impregnable" Maginot Line (named for war minister André Maginot) along the border with Germany but did little more. When Hitler's troops, in violation of the Versailles Treaty, marched into the Rhineland in 1936, Hitler wrote privately that "[i]f the French had then marched into the Rhineland, we would have had to withdraw with our tails between our legs." But France did not act.

The desire for peace was equally strong in Britain, driven by still-recent memories of the bloodbath of World War I. If 420,000 British soldiers could die at the single and inconclusive Battle of the Somme in 1916, the next generation was determined to avoid war. In 1933, students at Oxford University voted: "This house will in no circumstance fight for its King and its Country." In 1935, several thousand young people in Britain joined the Peace Pledge Union, opposing any British military planning. When Mussolini invaded Ethiopia in 1935, Britain, which then controlled the Suez Canal, could have cut off the Italian troops by closing the canal but did not do so. In spite of pleas from Ethiopia, the League of Nations did nothing.

As late as September 1938, at a conference in Munich, Germany, British prime minister Neville Chamberlain agreed to allow Hitler's claim to the Sudetenland in exchange for a promise of peace. Chamberlain was greeted with large crowds in London when he returned, promising "peace in our time." In the British Parliament, however, Chamberlain was criticized by Winston Churchill who called the Munich agreement "a total and unmitigated defeat." However, in 1938, Chamberlain, not Churchill, set British policy.

As France and Britain did nothing to stop the Fascists, most people in the United States were even more determined to keep their distance from any conflict. During the 1920s and 1930s, a significant majority of Americans wanted nothing to do with Europe's or Asia's problems. In 1935, George Earle, the governor of Pennsylvania, said, "If the world is to become a wilderness of waste, hatred, and bitterness, let us all the more earnestly protect and preserve our own oasis of liberty." Minnesota senator Thomas Schall said more succinctly, "To hell with Europe and the rest of those nations!" While isolationism was strongest in the Midwest, many people everywhere agreed. In April 1935, 50,000 World War I veterans marched for peace and laid wreaths on the graves of three members of Congress who had voted against U.S. entry into World War I. Days later, 175,000 college students staged a strike for peace.

There were many reasons for the **isolationism** that was rampant in the United States in the 1930s. Most Americans had concluded that the many thousand American soldiers killed in the Great War had died for no reason. Wilson's dream of a generation of peace sustained by the League of Nations was clearly a failure, and Europeans were once again at each other's throats. Writers like John Dos Passos, Ernest Hemingway, and e.e. cummings all wrote novels about the meaninglessness of World War I, and as Dos Passos said, "Rejection of Europe is what America is all about." In the mid-1930s, a Senate Special Committee known as the Nye Committee, chaired by North Dakota's Gerald Nye, concluded that big business had led the United States into the World War. In 1935, when President Roosevelt sought U.S. entry to the World Court, the Senate rejected the plan. Americans simply wanted nothing to do with the troubles of other nations.

In Congress, the isolationist and peace sentiment led to the passage of a number of neutrality laws designed to keep the United States out of war. A 1935 law required an embargo of arms to all belligerents in any war while

isolationism

A belief that the United States should keep clear of nearly all involvement with the rest of the world, stay neutral and out of any foreign wars.

Mothers with baby carriages march for peace outside the Woolworth building in New York City, 1939.

(in a direct slap at Woodrow Wilson's policies) declaring that any American who traveled on a belligerent ship did so at his or her own risk. In 1936, Congress added a proviso that prohibited loans or credit to any nation at war, and in 1937, Congress explicitly extended the arms embargo to Spain.

Not every American shared the isolationist sentiments of the majority. In 1936 and 1937, several thousand young Americans, mostly from various left-leaning movements, volunteered to fight in Spain on the side of the Republican government. Volunteers named themselves the Abraham Lincoln Brigade and joined an ill-trained and ill-equipped but courageous force that fought against the Fascists. In one battle near Madrid, 120 Americans died and another 175 were wounded. By the beginning of 1939, when the last Republican units were defeated, President Roosevelt himself concluded that neutrality in Spain had been a "grave mistake … as events will very likely prove."

While the Abraham Lincoln Brigade fought and President Roosevelt began to believe that the United States would eventually have to fight fascism in Europe, most people in the country and the Congress continued to believe that they could stay out of all entanglements. When Congress passed the 1937 Neutrality Act, they toughened the prohibition on selling arms to any side and made it illegal for Americans to travel on a belligerent ship. The law also declared that nonmilitary material—food, clothing, and so on—could be sold to a nation at war only on a "cash and carry" basis, insisting that there be no loans to belligerents and that all goods bought in the United States had to be taken out of the country in non-U.S. ships.

The neutrality legislation attempted to keep the United States out of a European war, but violence in Asia was growing. When Japan had attacked Manchuria in 1931, President Hoover's secretary of state, Henry L. Stimson, proclaimed the "Stimson Doctrine": that the United States would never officially recognize the new regime in Manchukuo or any other arrangement imposed on China by force. The unstated part of the doctrine was that the United States also would not do anything much to enforce its policy. American public opinion was solidly on the side of China. The novelist Pearl Buck, author of *The Good Earth* published in 1931, and Henry Luce, the owner of the Time-Life publications, were both children of missionaries to China and between them did a lot to build public sympathy for China. In the fall of 1937, a Gallup poll showed that 59 percent of Americans favored China compared with 1 percent who favored Japan in the quest for control of Manchuria. But almost no one wanted to do more than offer sympathy to the Chinese.

In December 1937, Japanese pilots sank the U.S. gunboat *Panay* in Nanking, China. While Americans were angry, they were not angry enough to challenge Japan. After the *Panay* was sunk, Texas congressman Maury Maverick said, "We should learn that it is about time for us to mind our own business," and a poll showed that most Americans agreed with him. While Americans wanted to stay out of war, American scrap iron and American oil continued to be shipped to Japan, strengthening that country's military. Since there was no formal war between Japan and China, the Neutrality Act did not apply, and most of the battles in Manchuria were fueled with American petroleum and bombs made of American metal. Indeed, through the late 1930s and into 1940 and 1941, Roosevelt and his cabinet feared not only American isolationists but also the wrath of Japan. If they were to cut off oil shipments—they did eventually cut metal shipments—they worried that Japan would quickly attack the Dutch colonies in Asia, which were the only other potential source of oil for Japan. To keep the peace, the United States kept the oil flowing.

In the face of the Nazi attacks in Germany and then Austria and Czechoslovakia, many Jews tried to leave Europe. But leaving was not easy, and the strict quotas of the 1924 legislation made immigration to the United States very difficult. In the 1930s, the American Jewish Congress protested loudly against both the Nazi attacks and American immigration policy. The group urged boycotts of German goods and staged a mock trial of Hitler. Roosevelt felt blocked by the immigration laws, though he did combine the German and Austrian quotas, allowing some additional Jewish immigration in 1936 and 1937. Britain also allowed modest immigration but resolutely opposed further expansion of the Jewish population of Palestine, then governed by Britain under a League of Nations mandate. Nazi laws limited the amount of money a departing Jew could take to about $4, an amount that made a potential immigrant a pauper and therefore ineligible for admission to the United States.

22.1

22.2

22.3

After *Kristallnacht*, the November 1938 attack on Jews, New York senator Robert Wagner and House members Edith Nourse Rogers of Massachusetts and Emmanuel Celler of New York proposed legislation that would create an expanded quota for racial and religious refugees. However, as with China, most Americans offered sympathy but little more, and Congress followed public opinion, voting the proposal down. A 1939 poll showed that 85 percent of Protestants, 84 percent of Catholics, and even 25.8 percent of Jews opposed opening the United States to Jewish refugees from Europe.

As the Nazi attacks on Jews escalated, European Jews became desperate to leave. In May 1939, the German ship *St. Louis* arrived in Havana with 930 Jewish refugees. The Cuban government refused temporary visas. The captain of the *St. Louis* then sailed up the U.S. coast, well within sight of Miami and other American cities, while negotiators tried desperately to get the U.S. State Department to allow the refugees to land. But the State Department would not agree and a Coast Guard cutter was ordered to intercept any *St. Louis* passengers who tried to go ashore. Finally, in June, the *St. Louis* returned to Europe. Before the war ended, perhaps a quarter or more of the passengers had died in concentration camps. Most Americans were sympathetic to the plight of Jews, but anti-Semitism was also strong in America.

Charles Lindbergh, the aviation hero of the 1920s, became an avid opponent of any revision of the neutrality laws or any support for Jewish refugees. Lindbergh became a popular speaker at rallies of the America First Committee, which had been organized in the fall of 1940 to keep the United States out of war in Europe. Father Charles Coughlin began calling it the "Jew-Deal." For Lindbergh, Coughlin, and a significant American following, Nazism was appealing. Others, probably the majority of the supporters of the America First Committee, simply did not want any part of a war that the United States could avoid. Nevertheless, isolationism mixed with old hatreds kept the United States from providing the support for Europe's Jews that they so badly needed.

While Americans tried to ignore developments in Europe and Asia in the late 1930s, Hitler was on the move. He understood that the faster he acted the greater his chances of success. Once Hitler invaded the rest of Czechoslovakia, Prime Minister Chamberlain, who had agreed to an earlier compromise, announced that Britain was committed to the defense of Poland and that if Hitler's forces attacked that country, his forces would be met with armed resistance.

In April 1939, Mussolini invaded Albania. Hitler made feints toward Poland. Then in August, Hitler stunned the world by signing a nonaggression pact with Joseph Stalin, the dictator of the Soviet Union (as Communist Russia was known). The erstwhile enemies—Germany and the Soviet Union, each with radically different economic systems and ideologies—now agreed to the partition of Poland. Everyone knew what was coming next. In the State Department, one official said that the feeling in the world was like "sitting in a house where somebody is dying upstairs." Very early in the morning on September 1, 1939, President Roosevelt received a call: "Mr. President," the U.S. ambassador in France said, "several German divisions are deep in Polish territory. … There are reports of bombers over the city of Warsaw." The president replied, "It has come at last. God help us all!"

Britain and France followed through on their promise to declare war. World War II had begun in Europe. On September 3, Roosevelt gave a radio fireside chat in which he said that the United States would remain neutral, but "[e]ven a neutral cannot be asked to close his mind or close his conscience." The country's mind was certainly not neutral. Eighty-four percent of Americans supported Britain and France, only 2 percent Germany. But a very large majority also wanted to stay out of the war no matter how much sympathy they might have for one side. After September 1939, more Americans, led by the president, were starting to have grave doubts that staying out of the battle was going to be possible.

22.3 Quick Review

Considering how the United States was drawn into World War I, why might so many Americans have favored isolationism in the years leading up to World War II?

Conclusion

The stock market crash of 1929 was a dramatic and symbolic end to the prosperity of the 1920s, but it was not the first sign that something was very wrong with the U.S. economy. In addition to the stock market crash, overproduction of industrial goods and agricultural products resulted in a glut on the market. There were too many goods and prices fell. But with many people unemployed, consumption also dropped dramatically, leading to more industrial layoffs and to the collapse of farm prices.

President Herbert Hoover responded to the nation's economic woes with new policies that nevertheless failed to alleviate the crisis or restore confidence among Americans. In 1932, he was defeated for reelection by Franklin Roosevelt, who began to try to stabilize the nation's economy and its banking system, extend relief to the impoverished, and create jobs for the unemployed. Roosevelt, with the backing of the Democrats in Congress, passed nine separate pieces of legislation in his first one hundred days as president. Dubbed the "New Deal," his agenda and policies provided important help for some Americans but did little for others.

The New Deal did not end the Depression, but it did provide much needed social welfare, create jobs, shore up the banking system, improve working conditions, and install protective barriers against future economic downturns. It dramatically—and permanently—changed the size of the federal government and the government's role in people's lives. Roosevelt faced powerful conservative opponents (who believed that the New Deal was socialism) and liberal opponents (who believed that the New Deal was not progressive enough). Despite such opposition, Roosevelt was popular and was reelected in a landslide in 1936.

By the end of the 1930s, the violence in Europe and Asia was demanding more and more attention. Fascists Adolf Hitler and Benito Mussolini had seized power in Germany and in Italy and had begun to threaten all of Europe. Similarly, Japan had begun a campaign of imperialist expansion in Asia. Most of this behavior initially went unchecked. Not until 1939, when Germany invaded Poland, did Britain and France declare war. Most Americans desperately wanted to stay out of Europe's and Asia's problems despite any sympathy they may have felt for the people in those situations. Some, including FDR, began to doubt that it would be possible.

Chapter Review

How did the Great Depression affect the United States both in the 1930s and for the future? What were the *most* significant effects? Explain why.

Chapter 22 Summary and Review

The Coming of the Great Depression

22.1 **Explain the coming of the Great Depression and the initial response to it.**

Summary

The speculative boom that culminated in the stock market crash of 1929 was one of the many factors that triggered the Great Depression, but it was not its underlying cause. The prosperity of the 1920s masked the fundamental weaknesses of the U.S. economy. Poverty was widespread in many communities throughout the 1920s, particularly in rural America. As the impact of the Depression deepened, farmers lost their land, the nation's banking system began to collapse, and millions of Americans lost their jobs. Herbert Hoover's initial response to the Depression was to call for voluntary actions by the financial and business community and to take limited government action to ameliorate the Depression's effects. Hoover's actions proved ineffective, and the American people lost confidence in his leadership.

Review Question

1. Contextualization
   Why did President Hoover find it so difficult to craft an adequate response to the Great Depression?

The New Deal

22.2 **Explain the goals and results of the New Deal and the responses on the part of diverse Americans.**

Summary

In the months between Franklin D. Roosevelt's election and his inauguration, the economic situation grew steadily worse. The whirlwind of activity that took place during Roosevelt's first one hundred days in office began with steps to stabilize the nation's banking system. Under Roosevelt's New Deal, program after program was created to provide relief to the destitute, jobs to the able-bodied, and stability to the economy. The New Deal affected different groups in American society in different ways. Federal policy toward Native Americans was fundamentally reformed. African Americans were hit especially hard by the Depression, a situation that was made worse by the difficulties they faced gaining access to New Deal jobs and resources. Nonetheless, they made important advances in the 1930s. Farmers on the Great Plains faced the combined impact of economic and environmental disaster. Organized labor made dramatic gains as unions gained government support and protection for their activities. The New Deal was not embraced by everyone, and Roosevelt had powerful opponents on both the left and the right. As the election of 1936 approached, Roosevelt responded to his critics and to the continuing grip of the Depression with an expansion of the New Deal. Roosevelt accomplished far less in his second term than his first, and the political momentum behind the New Deal lost steam. While the New Deal did not end the Great Depression, it did bring stability and optimism to a nation that desperately needed both. At the same time, the role of government was forever changed.

Review Questions

2. Causation
   What factors contributed to the growth of organized labor in the 1930s?

3. Argument Development
   In your opinion, what were the most important accomplishments of the New Deal? What were its greatest failures?

The Deep Roots of War—The United States, Europe, and Asia

22.3 **Analyze the international impact of the Depression, German and Japanese military expansion, and the initial U.S. response.**

Summary

The Treaty of Versailles did little to ease tensions and mistrust between European nations. Some of the earliest signs of postwar ill will appeared in Italy, where the leader of the ultranationalist Italian Fascist Party, Benito Mussolini, took power. In Germany, hard times hit in the early 1920s and then again at the end of the decade. It was against this backdrop of economic and political crisis that Adolf Hitler and the Nazis rose to power. Once in power, Hitler quickly moved to consolidate his dictatorship and to begin an assault on Germany's Jews. He then began a process of remilitarization and expansionist aggression that took Europe to the brink of a second world war. While Fascists were consolidating their power in central Europe, militarists in Japan were also growing in power. In the response to depression, Japan began a campaign of imperialist expansion in China and elsewhere. For much of the 1930s, the United States and Europe's democracies did little or nothing to inhibit the growth of Fascist power in Europe and Asia. The invasion of Poland by Germany and the Soviet Union in 1939 proved to be the last straw, and it led France and Britain to declare war on Germany. Despite what was happening abroad, however, the vast majority of Americans wanted to stay out of the war.

Review Questions

4. Causation

What connection can you make between economic events and the rise of Fascist parties to power in Germany, Italy, and Japan?

5. Contextualization

Why were so many Americans committed to isolationism?

1. Preparing to Write: Perspective in the Conclusion

Long Essay Question—Evaluate the extent to which government policies from 1918 to 1932 led to the Great Depression.

The rubrics for both the Long Essay Question and the Document-Based Question require students to "demonstrate a complex understanding of the historical development that is the focus of the prompt." As the rubric shows, there are a number of ways a student can demonstrate a complex understanding. Although the student may have already been awarded this point earlier in the essay, the conclusion is a good place to get

a larger perspective by demonstrating complexity. To quote the rubrics again, one way to accomplish this complexity is to explain "relevant and insightful connections within and across periods." What happens next with government policies? How can you tie in the New Deal's drastically different approach? Start by identifying the difference in the first sentence of your conclusion, and then explain how it developed in the next two to three sentences.

2. Preparing to Write: Support Your Assertion

Document-Based Question—Evaluate the extent to which there were similarities in the effects that economic downturns had on rural Americans in the 1880s and the 1930s.

A section of your essay will need to address the experiences of rural Americans in the 1930s. Start by developing a thesis, and then craft a topic sentence for this section. In your support, use two or three pieces of evidence that would support your topic sentence and thesis. Also integrate the young girl's letter from "American Voices" in Section 22.2. Use the sentiments expressed in the letter as evidence to support your argument. In your explanation, include discussion of the author's audience and why that is significant.

Chapter 23
Living in a World at War 1939–1945

Library of Congress Prints & Photographs Division [LC-USW33-018433-C]

World War II started out with disaster for the United States after Japan attacked the U.S. Navy base at Pearl Harbor, sinking much of the Pacific fleet. It would be a long time before the tide turned.

Chapter Objective

Demonstrate an understanding of many aspects of World War II—the critical role of individual men and women who served in different ways, military tactics, mobilization of U.S. society and the U.S. economy, and the war's impact on diverse American lives.

⌄ Learning Objectives

Preparedness and Isolation, 1939–1941

23.1 Explain support for and opposition to the U.S. support for Britain and the nation's growing tensions with Japan.

Mass Mobilization in a Society at War

23.2 Analyze the war's impact and the contributions of widely diverse groups of Americans who fought, supported the war effort at home, or otherwise lived through the war years.

Industrial Strength, Industrial Prosperity

23.3 Analyze U.S. industrial strength and productivity and its impact on the outcome of the war and on American society.

Winning a World War—North Africa, Europe, Asia, the Pacific, 1943–1945

23.4 Explain the course of the war leading to victory in Europe and then the Pacific.

Significant Dates

On the morning of December 7, 1941, 350 Japanese airplanes attacked the sleeping port of Pearl Harbor, Hawaii, where much of the Pacific fleet was anchored and where planes were lined up in close formation (to protect them against sabotage on the ground). In a few short hours, 2,500 soldiers and sailors were killed, 150 U.S. airplanes destroyed, and 5 battleships as well as many others vessels were sunk. It was a devastating loss.

The next day, Franklin Roosevelt addressed Congress, speaking of the attack as "a date which will live in infamy." He asked for a declaration of war against Japan. Hitler and Mussolini then declared war on the United States. The long wait was over. With the direct attack on the United States at Pearl Harbor, most isolationists and antiwar voices rallied to the president and the war effort. Every citizen would be touched by the war whether by serving in the military, working in war-related industries, or using ration stamps to buy food. It had been a long wait during the two years in which Roosevelt increased support for Britain, negotiated fitfully with Japan, and inched toward war. This chapter traces the story of preparation between 1939 and 1941 and the nation's full-scale involvement in World War II from December 1941 to the war's end in August 1945.

Preparedness and Isolation, 1939–1941

23.1   Explain support for and opposition to the U.S. support for Britain and the nation's growing tensions with Japan.

When Germany attacked Poland in September 1939, Britain and France declared war on Germany as they had promised to do. Europe was at war. Neither Japan nor the United States intervened. After the rapid German defeat of Poland that fall, the winter of 1939–1940 was known as the "Phony War" since there was so little fighting. Poland disappeared, split between Nazi Germany and the Soviet Union. Britain and France waited for an attack they knew would come—and the war did not stay phony.

The Battle of Britain

At the beginning of 1940, Hitler hinted at peace initiatives, then in April invaded Denmark and Norway and quickly defeated both. On May 10, Germany unleashed its *Blitzkrieg* (lightning war) on Holland, Belgium, and Luxembourg, bombing Rotterdam into rubble and sending in airborne and ground troops. All three countries surrendered.

On May 14, 1,800 German tanks crossed the border into France, overran the Maginot Line (see Chapter 22), which turned out to be useless, and turned toward Paris. Italy joined Germany, declaring war on France on June 10. It was a short war and an easy victory for Germany. On June 22, 1940, France surrendered. For the next several years, Germany directly governed northern France, including Paris, while a puppet government, led by the aging French World War I hero Marshal Philippe Pétain, governed the southern part of France known as Vichy France from a capital in the town of Vichy. By the summer of 1940, Hitler was the master of Europe (see Map 23-1).

Only Great Britain stood against Germany. As the German forces rushed toward Paris, they attempted to cut off a retreat by French and British armies. But 338,000 British, French, and Allied troops were evacuated from the beaches of Dunkirk, leaving nearly all equipment behind. In a radio broadcast, the new British prime minister Winston Churchill promised, "We shall go on to the end," but he added, Britain would hold out "until in God's good time, the new world, with all its power and might, [shall] step forth to the rescue and the liberation of the old." It was a rescue that Churchill and Roosevelt tried hard to assure over the next eighteen months.

After the defeat of France, Hermann Goering, Nazi air chief, announced, "The Fuhrer has ordered me to crush Britain with my Luftwaffe," and he tried hard. Bombers attacked British coastal fortifications, airfields, and then in September 1940, began the terror bombing of London. The "Blitz," as the British called it, eventually killed thousands of residents of Britain's capital—six thousand in October alone. Edward R. Murrow, the voice of the Columbia Broadcasting System (CBS), gave Americans nightly reports that "London is

Map 23-1 Nazi Europe, 1941.

This map shows the extent of Nazi control of Europe. When one adds Vichy France and its territory in North Africa, it is clear that Hitler basically controlled the continent between Great Britain and the Soviet Union (Russia).

Legend:
- Axis states and annexed areas
- Axis allies
- Axis occupied
- Sudetenland
- France's unoccupied territory until 1942

burning." The small British air force fought back. Churchill begged Roosevelt for more help. Roosevelt set about finding ways to provide it.

Moving toward Lend-Lease Legislation

Every step that Roosevelt took brought hostility from neutrality advocates. Senior officers within the U.S. military worried that sending arms to Britain would undermine U.S. defenses. Secretary of War Henry H. Woodring was committed to a "fortress America" strategy, arming this country and ignoring the rest of the world. No one opposed Roosevelt's support for Britain more than Charles Lindbergh, a hero from his 1920s flight across the Atlantic. In October 1939, Lindbergh said, "An ocean is a formidable barrier, even for modern aircraft." The U.S. ambassador in London, Joseph P. Kennedy, predicted that Britain would quickly fall.

23.1

23.2

23.3

23.4

America First Committee

Committee launched in 1940 that argued for American neutrality and for staying out of World War II.

destroyers-for-bases

An agreement between the United States and Great Britain to exchange obsolete navy destroyers for British bases.

arsenal of democracy

A phrase coined by Franklin Roosevelt for the materials needed by Britain in its fight with Nazi Germany.

four freedoms

Freedoms announced by President Roosevelt in December 1940 that became a rallying point for the causes the United States would fight for.

Republican leaders in Congress opposed any intervention, and they had a lot of public support. In July 1940, students at Yale University, supported by midwestern business leaders, formed the **America First Committee**. Most America First supporters saw the new war as an extension of the last one, simply an intra-European battle for power and colonies. Some sympathized with the Nazis or hated Jews. Many Republicans distrusted Roosevelt.

Roosevelt argued with the isolationists in Congress, ignored his ambassador in London as someone whom he thought "has been an appeaser and always will be an appeaser," and thought Lindbergh was a Nazi. He promoted military officers who supported his efforts and sidelined others. In 1940, FDR replaced isolationist Secretary of War Woodring with longtime internationalist Republican Henry L. Stimson, who had been secretary of war in Taft's administration and secretary of state for President Hoover. Roosevelt also added Frank Knox, another Republican internationalist, as secretary of the navy.

In the fall of 1940, FDR concluded a "**destroyers-for-bases**" deal, which circumvented congressional restrictions on selling ships to Britain by "trading" obsolete ships to Britain in exchange for ninety-nine-year leases on a string of British navy bases. He pressured the navy to declare ships obsolete and defended the deal as a way to strengthen America's defenses. However, he also worried that he had exceeded his constitutional authority, and his opponents worried even more.

As war raged in Europe, the November 1940 presidential election loomed. Roosevelt broke precedent going back to George Washington and sought a third term. The Democrats, after some grumbling, mostly by supporters of Vice President John Garner, nominated Roosevelt. The Republicans, wanting to avoid having an isolationist candidate, nominated a corporate attorney and utility company executive, Wendell Willkie, an ardent opponent of the New Deal who did not disagree with Roosevelt greatly on foreign policy, though he did denounce the destroyers-for-bases deal as "the most arbitrary and dictatorial action ever taken by any president."

In the middle of the campaign, Roosevelt asked Congress to institute a military draft so the country could have a trained army ready in case of war. Many opposed the draft, but when a reporter told Willkie that "if you want to win the election you will come out against the proposed draft," Willkie responded, "I would rather not win the election than do that." The draft became law on September 16 and, with Willkie's stance and the appointment of Stimson and Knox to the cabinet, the issue of isolationism was neutralized until late in the campaign.

Just before the election, polls showed that a majority of prospective voters preferred Willkie unless war was coming, in which case they wanted Roosevelt's steady hand. On Election Day, they chose the steady hand, and FDR won a third term.

Only a month after the election, Roosevelt received an urgent message from Churchill spelling out just how desperate things were for Britain and making clear that "the moment approaches when we shall no longer be able to pay cash for shipping and other supplies." In a fireside chat just after Christmas in 1940, Roosevelt said, "If Great Britain goes down … all the Americas, would be living at the point of a gun." There is only one alternative, he told his radio audience: "We must be the great **arsenal of democracy**." A week later, FDR proposed Lend-Lease legislation that would "loan" or lease war materials to the British for the duration of the war. The president insisted, "We cannot, and we will not, tell them that they must surrender, merely because of present inability to pay for the weapons which we know they must have."

In the same speech, Roosevelt also described larger purposes for American action, which was, he said, to secure **four freedoms**:

> Freedom of speech and expression
> Freedom of every person to worship God in his own way
> Freedom from want
> Freedom from fear

Roosevelt's "four freedoms" were very popular. Lend-Lease was much less popular. Isolationists like Montana senator Burton Wheeler said that the plan "will plough under every fourth American boy." Newspapers like the *Chicago Tribune*, the *New York Daily News*,

23.1

23.2

23.3

23.4

Figure 23-1 Unemployment Rate and Gross National Product.

After 1940, the nation's unemployment rate went from almost 15 percent to less than 2 percent for most of the war while gross national product more than doubled from $100 billion to $200 billion.

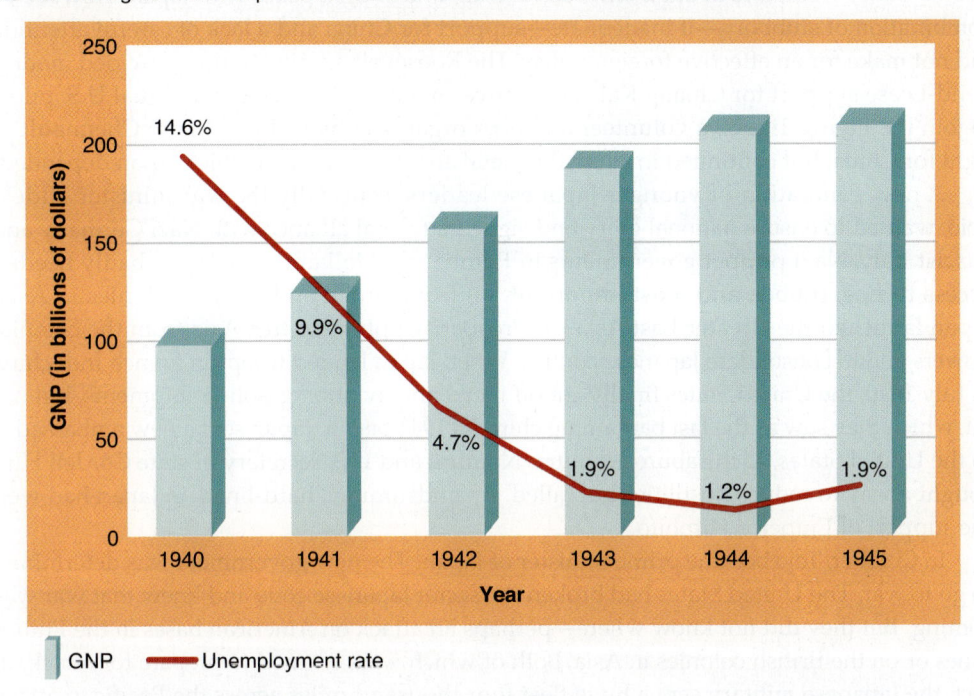

and the *Washington Times-Herald* editorialized against the plan. Nevertheless, the Congress that had passed so many neutrality acts in the 1930s approved the **Lend-Lease Act** by a 60 to 31 vote in the Senate and a 317 to 71 vote in the House. Britain would get the aid that Churchill wanted.

The military preparation in 1940 and 1941 ended the Great Depression. Spending $7 billion on Lend-Lease efforts and an additional $13.7 billion on the expansion of the U.S. military (up from $2.2 billion in 1940) provided a huge stimulus to the economy, far larger than any stimulus tried during the New Deal. Nearly a million young men were drafted by early 1941, and new jobs opened everywhere, virtually ending unemployment. New or redesigned federal agencies brought business leaders into the government to manage the conversion to a war-oriented economy (see Figure 23-1).

While the United States geared up to serve as the "arsenal of democracy," Hitler suddenly attacked his erstwhile ally Russia in June 1941. While there was no love lost in the United States for Communist Russia, most Americans knew that if the Nazis defeated Russia, it would mean disaster. Missouri senator Harry S. Truman said he would not mind it if both sides lost, but he also said, "I don't want to see Hitler victorious under any circumstances." The United States extended Lend-Lease aid to the Russians.

Lend-Lease aid to Britain brought the United States close to war with Germany. German U-boats sank ships carrying goods to Britain at five times the rate that new ships could be built. The United States began patrolling the western Atlantic, guarding ships as far as Greenland before turning them over to the British navy for escort to Britain.

In August, Roosevelt and Churchill met in Newfoundland, planned ways to work together, and issued the **Atlantic Charter**, which included a somewhat vague commitment to national self-determination for other countries, nonaggression, and "the establishment of a wider and permanent system of general security"—planting the seeds of what became the United Nations. Meanwhile, patrolling U.S. Navy ships ran into conflict with German submarines. In October 1941, a U-boat attacked the U.S. destroyer *Kearny*, killing 11 sailors, the first U.S. casualties of the war. Roosevelt said, "America has been attacked." Later that month, a submarine sank the USS *Reuben James*, killing 115 sailors. War did not seem far off.

Lend-Lease Act

Legislation passed in 1941 for a program through which the United States "loaned" or leased military equipment to Britain and other World War II allies for the duration of the war.

Atlantic Charter

Statement of common principles and war aims developed by President Franklin Roosevelt and British prime minister Winston Churchill at a meeting in August 1941.

Growing Tensions with Japan

While the United States focused on Europe, tensions were also building in the Pacific. The United States wanted to avoid a "two-ocean war" and sought peace with Japan. However, a combination of stubborn—if inadequate—support for China and a lack of careful attention did not make for an effective foreign policy. The Roosevelt administration provided modest Lend-Lease support for Chiang Kai-shek's government and allowed individual U.S. pilots to join the Flying Tigers, a volunteer air corps organized by Colonel Claire Chennault to fight for China, but continued to allow the metal and oil exports on which Japan depended.

A new generation of younger Japanese leaders, especially the war minister Hideki Tojo, wanted to ensure national glory and signed a formal alliance with Nazi Germany and Fascist Italy. Nazi puppet governments in France and Holland gave Japan badly needed access to rice, rubber, and most important, oil from Dutch and French colonies in Asia. Japan launched the Greater East Asia Co-Prosperity Sphere to free Asia from the colonial powers and to consolidate Japanese control. When Japan landed troops in French Indochina in July 1940, the United States finally cut off metal and aviation gasoline shipments, but not oil, which they saw as the last bargaining chip. As 1941 began, Japan sent a new ambassador to the United States, Kichisaburo Nomura. Nomura and U.S. secretary of state Cordell Hull sought a way to reduce hostilities but failed. By midsummer, hard-liners in Japan had won the support of Emperor Hirohito.

In October, Tojo became prime minister of Japan. The new government was determined to go to war. The United States had broken the secret Japanese code and knew that war was coming. But they did not know where—perhaps an attack on American bases in the Philippines or on the British colonies in Asia, both of which were warned to prepare for attack. In fact, the Japanese military sent a huge fleet four thousand miles across the Pacific to attack the United States itself at Pearl Harbor.

Japanese admiral Takijiro Onishi warned that a direct attack on U.S. soil would make the Americans "insanely mad." He said that while Japan would have the advantage in a short war, in a longer war, the U.S. industrial capacity and its large supply of oil—the fuel of modern war—meant that Japan would have a very hard time of it. But Japan's leaders were confident of a quick victory.

When Japan did attack on December 7, the location was a greater surprise than the fact of the attack itself. But Japan's attack on Hawaii solidified American public opinion. Even the staunchest opponents of preparedness, including Charles Lindbergh, now supported going to war.

> **23.1** Quick Review
>
> How did the United States move from an isolationist stance to one supporting the war effort? How did the attitudes of the government and the people differ?

Mass Mobilization in a Society at War

23.2 Analyze the war's impact and the contribution of widely diverse groups of Americans who fought, supported the war effort at home, or otherwise lived through the war years.

For the people of the United States, the attack of December 7, 1941, changed everything. Before the war ended in 1945, 16 million Americans served in the armed forces, and 405,399 died in combat. All Americans had their lives changed by the war. At the beginning of the war, half of white Americans and 90 percent of black Americans lived in poverty. The war provided a job for everyone, and wartime jobs vastly expanded the size of the nation's middle class and lifted a lot of people out of poverty. The Great Depression was over. Americans moved around a lot during the war. The military brought rural and urban Americans

"above and beyond the call of duty"

DORIE MILLER
Received the Navy Cross
at Pearl Harbor, May 27, 1942

Dorie Miller, a kitchen attendant at Pearl Harbor, was able to pull the captain of a battleship to safety and then use a machine gun to shoot at attacking Japanese planes. Although Miller was proclaimed a hero, the navy continued to limit African Americans to non-combat roles throughout the war.

together in units that faced the same fears and hopes. Far less often, it brought people of different races together since the military of World War II remained segregated not only by race but also by gender. New prosperity and new knowledge, but also terrible losses and fears, became central to people's lives.

Early Battles, Early Losses, 1941–1942

In the spring of 1941, a secret conversation in Washington between British and American officials (known by the code name ABC-1 or American-British Conversation Number 1) resulted in an agreement that, in the event of a two-front war, which everyone hoped to avoid, the United States would focus first on joining Britain to defeat Germany. As U.S. Army chief George C. Marshall explained, "Collapse in the Atlantic would be fatal; collapse in the Far East would be serious but not fatal."

Within hours of the December 7 attack on Pearl Harbor, Japan also attacked U.S. bases in the Philippine Islands, the Aleutian Islands off Alaska, as well as Guam and Wake Island in the mid-Pacific. Within days, Japanese pilots and troops were in the British colonies of Malaysia and Burma, French Indochina, the Dutch East Indies, and independent Thailand. To some, the Japanese were liberators, freeing them from the hated European and American colonial authorities. The Japanese had been preparing well and were a superb fighting force. British Hong Kong and American Guam and Wake Island surrendered within a week. In February 1942, Singapore surrendered to the Japanese with eighty-five thousand crack British troops now prisoners of war. American and British navy forces lost the battle of Java Sea and the Dutch East Indies with their rich oil fields fell to Japan.

In April and May 1942, after holding out for months against impossible odds, the last U.S. troops on the islands of Bataan and Corregidor in the Philippines surrendered. Ben Steele, a young rancher from Montana who had volunteered for service, remembered that during the ninety-nine-day defense of Bataan, the Americans constantly faced starvation. After news spread that the commander in the Philippines, General Douglas MacArthur, had left for Australia, Steele and the others knew that "[o]nly two things can happen to us now, we're going to be dead or we're going to be prisoners of war."

After surrendering, the American and Filipino troops from Bataan were forced to march sixty-six miles to a railroad junction where they were transported to prison camps. The march came to be known as the Bataan Death March. The Japanese captors were overwhelmed by the numbers and had been taught to hate Americans. If a prisoner fell, he was kicked, and if he did not move, he was killed with a bayonet. If prisoners, desperately thirsty in the hot sun, moved off the line to get water, they were shot. The surviving defenders of Bataan and Corregidor spent more than three years as Japanese prisoners. By the middle of 1942, Japan controlled the western Pacific from the far north to Australia, which remained in British hands.

Three days after the United States declared war on Japan, Hitler and Mussolini declared war on the United States. It was an odd move on their part. Germany, Italy, and Japan were allies—based on treaties they had signed with each other in 1936 and 1937—but if Germany and Italy had held back in declaring war on the United States, FDR would have been under great pressure to focus the war only on Japan, leaving Britain still isolated. German and Italian declarations of war allowed FDR to keep the focus on the Atlantic, which he believed was essential. The three nations at war with the United States—Germany, Italy, and Japan— were known as the Axis as opposed to the Allied forces of the United States, Great Britain, and the Soviet Union, joined by exiled French troops who called themselves the Free French and forces from China and a number of other nations that allied with them.

Even though the primary American focus was on Europe, U.S. and British forces won a partial victory in the Pacific in the Battle of the Coral Sea in May 1942 when they stopped a Japanese advance to Port Moresby, Papua New Guinea. Then in June 1942, the Japanese attacked U.S. forces on Midway Island. But U.S. intelligence officers broke the Japanese code and knew that the attack was coming. In addition, U.S. pilots were learning new maneuvers that allowed direct attacks on Japanese ships. The Japanese lost four of their six aircraft carriers and all of their planes and pilots involved in the battle. U.S. forces also captured a Japanese Zero airplane, then the most modern in the war, and used it to build the U.S.

23.1

23.2

23.3

23.4

Navy's new Hellcat plane, which could out maneuver the Zero. The Hellcats began arriving in the Pacific in 1943.

Despite the successes, winning the war in 1942 was far from a sure thing. Germany and Japan both had very strong hands. German submarine commander Karl Donitz began sinking American coastal shipping vessels in January 1942. New York and other coastal cities refused to turn their lights off, and the submarines used the bright city lights to target shipping. In three months, the Germans sunk 216 ships, half of them tankers with essential oil for Britain. Burned-out ships littered the American beaches.

In the summer of 1942, German forces were besieging the Soviet Union while their planes bombed Britain. The German submarine fleet shifted from the U.S. coast to Atlantic convoys, hitting them especially hard in midocean where little help was possible. In July 1942, a convoy of thirty-four Allied ships headed for the Russian ports of Murmansk and Archangel was attacked in the Norwegian Sea, and twenty-three of the thirty-four ships were sunk. German admiral Donitz was confident—and the Americans, British, and Russians fearful—that the Allied forces simply could not continue in the face of such losses.

Japan controlled the whole of the western Pacific (see Map 23-2). In August 1942, U.S. forces invaded the tactically important island of Guadalcanal in the Solomon Islands and

Map 23-2 Japanese Power in the Pacific.

In the early months of World War II, Japan extended its reach through much more of the Pacific region from the Aleutian Islands off Alaska to Borneo and New Guinea in the South Pacific.

renamed its airfield Henderson Field. A counterinvasion by Japan came close to success. The reporter John Hersey, staying with the troops on the island, told readers:

> The uniforms, the bravado, the air of wearing a knife in the teeth—these were just camouflage. The truth was all over their faces. These were just American boys. They did not want that valley or any part of its jungle. They were ex-grocery clerks, ex-highway laborers, ex-bank clerks, ex-schoolboys. … [T]hey had joined the Marines to see the world, or to get away from a guilt, or most likely to escape the draft, not knowingly to kill or be killed.

But there they were. With navy support, the Marines on Guadalcanal held their position. The Japanese forces were beaten back until, in February 1943, in a move they seldom made during the war, the Japanese abandoned Guadalcanal.

Men in the Military—Volunteers and Draftees

As the war began, young men quickly found themselves in uniform. Women were not drafted, but as the war progressed, more women also enlisted in the military while more of their sisters worked in war industries, moving into positions of men who went off to fight. Sixteen million men had registered for the draft when the war began, more did so soon after, and others volunteered in anticipation of an expanding draft. The draft was administered by the **Selective Service System** through 6,443 local draft boards that decided who was eligible for various deferments—for married men, for those with children, and for those in crucial war work—which were granted less and less often.

Lloyd Kilmer was working as a bellhop at a hotel in Rochester, Minnesota, when he heard the news of Pearl Harbor. Six months later, Kilmer enlisted in the Army Air Corps and flew combat missions over Europe until he was shot down in June 1944. U.S. troops liberated his prisoner-of-war camp in April 1945. Growing up in the immigrant neighborhood of East Boston, Massachusetts, during the Depression, Al Fossett ascribed his success on the high school track team to pretending that he was running after something to eat. When war came, he served as a gunner on planes that flew supplies from British India to beleaguered Chinese forces and, for the first time he could remember, he had enough to eat. Woodrow W. Crockett was born in Texarkana, Arkansas, and joined the army as a private in 1940. In 1942, he was assigned to the Tuskegee Airmen, an African American unit that achieved considerable distinction. He flew 149 combat missions during the U.S. invasion of Italy and received the Distinguished Flying Cross. Tyrone Power kept his homosexual identity a secret and enlisted as a private in the Marines in 1942, but later became a pilot and was promoted to first lieutenant. He was one of the first to fly supplies into the island of Iwo Jima under artillery fire from the island's Japanese defenders. Only after the war did he achieve fame as an actor.

Induction into the military meant a physical and a psychological examination, both fairly perfunctory because the need for more men in the military made doctors reluctant to reject anyone. The psychological examination, successfully added to the military screening at the urging of a number of leading psychiatrists, was designed to keep homosexuals out of the military. It seldom worked if someone wanted to keep their sexual orientation a secret. Robert Fleischer remembered a psychiatrist asking, "Do you like girls?" He responded yes since, as he said, he did *like* girls; he just wasn't attracted to them. Once in the military, some gay men faced taunts and in some cases dishonorable discharge if their sexuality became public—often because they were seen in gay bars or letters to lovers were found. Others were protected by comrades or superior officers. Robert Gervais recalled a friend in the Pacific Fleet who never hid his sexual orientation but was also respected "as the best torpedo officer in the 7th Fleet." Gervais remembered, "Our captain put the word out that if heard any gossip about his torpedo officer, they would hear from him! He later personally decorated him (silver medal) with the entire crew standing at attention."

Most of those who served were white males like Kilmer, Fossett, and Fleischer, though most were straight. The Great Depression shaped their childhood, and they liked the food and security of the army even when they were frightened. Only a minority were enthusiastic about serving, while most were willing to do a job they believed needed to be done out of

Selective Service System

Federal agency that coordinated military conscription (the draft) beginning in World War II.

loyalty to their country and the belief that the war was a fight for the survival of freedom. In the process, they met a greater diversity of people than any previous generation of Americans and saw more of the world and its people.

Deferments, Alternative Service, and War Work

Not everyone served in the military. The Selective Service allowed local draft boards considerable discretion. Throughout most of the South, draft boards, which were nearly all white, showed a deep aversion to putting black men in uniform and giving them guns, with the result that they had to dip much deeper into the pool of white men, offering whites few deferments. Congress allowed young men to complete college so that, as one draft board member reported, "fathers in their middle thirties were being inducted from their stores, garages, and other businesses," while they saw younger single men sitting in classrooms. A November 1942 law, the Tydings Amendment, exempted agricultural workers from the draft. Men in key war industries and some who would not fight for religious reasons were also sometimes exempted.

Other Americans found themselves in new jobs they had never before imagined. Charles Briscoe's family left the Dust Bowl for California where he learned sheet metal work. In 1940, he took a job at Boeing Aircraft in Wichita, Kansas, building the super-secret B-29 long-range bomber. Briscoe remembered, "We knew the B-017s and B-24s didn't have the range to get to Japan. We had to have the B-29 to win the war and get the men home from over there." At fourteen, Ed Powers was too young for the military, but he joined his father—who was too old to serve—in patrolling their hometown to be sure that everyone was honoring the blackout to avoid a German bombing.

Joseph Bullock was among the forty-three thousand conscientious objectors (COs) who, in the words of Selective Service regulations, "by reason of religious training and belief, is conscientiously opposed to participation in war in any form." The largest number of COs, as they were called, some twenty-five thousand, served as noncombatants in the military, providing first aid to troops under extraordinarily dangerous conditions or behind-the-lines logistical support. Those who for religious reasons could not support the war effort in any form were allowed to work in a program called Civilian Public Service (CPS). Bullock and the twelve thousand CPS men worked on forestry projects planting trees and building roads or staffed mental hospitals. They received no pay, had to cover their own expenses, and did not receive veteran benefits at the end of the war. A final group of some six thousand refused out of conscience to have anything to do with the Selective Service System, and these men were sent to federal prison. Some of them, like David Dellinger, became lifelong antiwar activists. In some areas, COs were treated with respect; in others, they met deep hostility. Harry Van Dyck remembered being told, "You goddamn COs should all be shot." After the war, Bullock was told that he could not teach Sunday School because his wartime service made him an inappropriate role model for Christian children.

When 40 percent of the twenty-one-year-olds who signed up for the first draft registration in late 1940 then got married, the head of the Selective Service announced that he would consider that recent marriages "might have been for the purpose of evading the draft." When the draft was expanded to include married men, most fathers were still exempted, leading one young couple to name their new child "Weatherstrip" because he kept his father out of the draft. However, as the need grew, fathers were also drafted, and by 1945, nearly a million fathers were in the service.

Women in Military Service

Early in the war there was some talk of conscripting women, if not for the military then for wartime industrial work. In the end, however, the United States, unlike Great Britain or the Soviet Union, left it up to individual women to decide whether they wanted to serve.

Each of the branches of the military enlisted women in special noncombat units that freed men for combat: the U.S. Army established the Women's Auxiliary Army Corps, or WAACs (later the *Auxiliary* was dropped, and they became the WACs); the U.S. Navy

Universal Images Group/Superstock

Young women begin their service as WACs during World War II.

created the Women Accepted for Voluntary Emergency Service, or WAVES; the Army Air Corps set up the Women's Auxiliary Service Pilots, or WASPs; the Coast Guard launched the Women's Reserve of the Coast Guard, nicknamed the SPARS; and the Marines organized an unnamed women's branch. Some 350,000 women (compared with over 15 million men) served in uniform during World War II. Claudine "Scottie" Scott remembered her freshman year at the University of Kansas in the fall of 1940 as "a fun and exciting time," but by the following year, the world had become a much more serious place. Scott volunteered for the WAVES and was assigned to the Joint Chiefs of Staff to deliver the "log of fighting going on all over the world" to the White House every day. She was at the White House and saw President Roosevelt on the day of the Allied invasion of Europe in 1944, but her focus was on the fate of her boyfriend, who was part of the invading force. He was wounded but returned home, and they were married in the Veterans Hospital in Richmond, Virginia.

Martha Settle grew up in Norristown, Pennsylvania. As an African American, she experienced racism within the War Manpower Commission. She applied, and was selected by Mary McLeod Bethune, for one of the few officer slots allowed to African American WACs. Margaret Ray grew up in Indiana and was recruited into a small elite unit of WASPs within the Army Air Force that handled domestic military flying so men could be freed up to fly overseas. "Here I was, this farm girl," Ray remembered, "and it was so exciting." Mary Louise Roberts became a nurse with the army. She commanded a field operating room for troops during the landings in Casablanca, North Africa, in 1943 and on Anzio beach in Italy in 1944. Some worried about lesbians in all-women units in the military, but concerns about lesbian interaction were not nearly as strong as those about gay male interaction.

Rosie the Riveter and Her Friends

Just before the attack on Pearl Harbor, twelve million women in the United States held jobs—a dramatic increase from the depths of the Depression. Middle-class white women tended to be teachers, nurses, social workers, or secretaries. In the course of the war, more than six million more women entered the workforce. Some two million women

Library of Congress Prints and Photographs Division [LC-USW33-028626-C]

Women working at the Douglas Aircraft Plant in Long Beach, California. Gender diversity was common as women often constituted half of the labor force in the industrial plants. Racial diversity was less common.

American Voices

Kathy O'Grady, "What Did You Do in the War, Grandma?"

In 1995, Kathy O'Grady interviewed her grandmother Katherine O'Grady ,who remembered the war and her work in war-related industries.

In 1939 I lived in East Providence [Rhode Island … I worked at Gibson's, a soda fountain at the bus stop on Westminster Street. … Servicemen from all over used to come in. I made $15 for a forty-eight-hour week. I bought my own clothes, paid my own expenses, … If you had a five-dollar bill then you were very wealthy.

I met my husband while I was working at Gibson's. …

After my husband went into the Seabee's I quit my job at Gibson's and went to work in a woolen mill, Lister's, which before the war was just a normal routine job. When the war started they needed wool very badly so this was considered a service job. In other words, it was important. At the mill the government used to send out all the Purple Heart soldiers to talk to us and tell us that we couldn't take time off, and pushed all this patriotism on us. … I think I got $27 a week, so it did pay more. The soldiers needed woolen blankets. At the time all servicemen were issued their clothing, their blanket, their bedroll, the whole bit. The blankets that came home

after war had traveled all over the world. … We were very proud of [our work], because it meant that we were doing our part. …

After the war things changed because women found out they could go out and they could survive. They could really do it on their own. That's where I think women's lib really started.

Source: An Oral History of Rhode Island Women during World War II, downloaded from www.stg.brown.edu/projects/WWII_Women/; downloaded July 30, 2012.

Thinking Critically

1. **Causation**
   In what ways did Katherine O'Grady think wartime changed her life? Might other factors have caused her sense that "after the war things changed"?

2. **Analyzing Primary Sources**
   What clues, if any, does the document provide about the long-term impact of the war on the place of women in American society? Do you agree with O'Grady's point of view?

went to work in previously all-male defense plants where they sometimes made up half of the workforce. Women also constituted a quarter of the workers in the converted auto industry that was producing tanks and trucks. On the West Coast, 500,000 women worked in the aircraft industry and 225,000 in shipbuilding. They made more money than most women had ever made. They took on hard jobs that before the war people thought only men could handle or from which tradition, law, and all-male unions had excluded them. But even during wartime, women were often relegated to the lower rungs of the industrial order while men took on the highest-skilled, highest-paying jobs. Drilling rivets was high-skill and high-pay work, and in spite of the "Rosie the Riveter" name and public relations posters, far more women worked in routine production jobs than among the elite riveters.

Women working in industrial plants had to develop a new fashion style that provided room for safe movement, including pants, which made movement much easier than a skirt, and short hair, which was essential around dangerous machinery. In addition, they had to develop a tough attitude in the face of catcalls and wolf whistles. Delana Jensen made 155-millimeter howitzers for the army. She was hired when the plant was still not sure whether women could handle the work, but within months, she was training men. It was exacting work and "had to be perfect … within 1/1,000th of an inch." She liked the denim coveralls and remembered, "We were living in a special time and place. There was an energy in the air and in the people. We were wanted and needed and important to the war effort."

Marginalization in a Democracy—The March on Washington and the War at Home

In 1940, African Americans and Latinos continued to be excluded from the new prosperity. In 1940, the Brotherhood of Sleeping Car Porters, perhaps the most powerful black-led organization in the United States at the time, asked the government to prevent discrimination in the expanding armed forces. A. Philip Randolph, long time president of the Brotherhood of Sleeping Car Porters, and Walter White, the executive secretary of the National Association for the Advancement of Colored People (NAACP), met with President Roosevelt and were convinced that they had a friend in the federal government.

The rapidly expanding war industries were less friendly. When the president of North American Aviation announced, "We will not employ Negroes," he spoke for many whites in management and on the shop floors of the companies. Then in late 1940, the War Department announced its policy "not to intermingle colored and white enlisted personnel in the same regimental organization." Randolph felt betrayed, and he meant to do something about it.

Randolph proposed a massive march on Washington, initially thinking that 10,000 blacks would come to Washington, D.C., to demand that the government protect their economic rights. As word spread, Randolph raised the number to 50,000 and then to 100,000. He insisted that this event would be an all-black march. "There are some things Negroes must do alone," he said. The march was called for July 1, 1941.

As it became clear that the march might be a powerful and embarrassing event, many people within the administration began to panic. They challenged Randolph's patriotism— How could he do such a thing with war imminent? What will they think in Berlin? Randolph's response was, "Oh, perhaps no more than they already think of America's racial policy." Friends within the administration tried to persuade Randolph to postpone the march, but he persisted. The only grounds on which the march could be called off, he said, would be a government order "with teeth in it" that would truly protect the economic rights of African Americans in the new industries. Randolph won.

On June 25, 1941, Roosevelt signed Executive Order 8802 "to provide for the full and equitable participation of all workers in defense industries, without discrimination because of race, creed, color, or national origin." The order created the **Fair Employment Practices Committee** (later Commission) to enforce the policy. It was the order "with teeth in it." The march was called off. Some called Executive Order 8802 an economic Emancipation Proclamation. Executive Order 8802 was enforced unevenly but sufficiently enough to make a real difference. Sybil Lewis was a maid in Oklahoma being paid $3.50 a week before the war. She was hired at Lockheed Aircraft in Los Angeles at $48 per week. She was paired with a white woman from Arkansas, and though they certainly had their differences, Lewis remembered that they learned "to relate to each other in ways that we never experienced before." Not all encounters were as positive.

White workers went on strike at a Western Electric factory in Baltimore, Maryland, demanding segregated restrooms. In a factory in Mobile, Alabama, shipyard workers rioted over the promotion of a black welder. Riots also took place in Detroit and New York City in 1943. Twenty-five blacks and nine whites were killed in a June riot in Detroit, and six blacks were killed in another riot in New York's Harlem. As news of these clashes spread, army bases around the world also exploded as segregated white and black units clashed in England and in the United States.

Latinos also faced exclusion and violence. The most obvious symbol of Mexican American resistance to white culture were gangs known as *pachucos*, or zoot-suiters, for the exaggerated clothing—a long suit coat with baggy pants that came in at the ankles—that symbolized their defiance of social norms. During wartime frugality when most people were channeling money and resources toward the war effort, the zoot suits also seemed an unpatriotic extravagance. In June 1943, white servicemen in boot camps in the Los Angeles area took out their own frustration by attacking zoot-suiters. Police looked the other way. The **zoot suit riots** spread elsewhere until FDR intervened, ordering the military to take actions to stop the violence, at least partly because he had been courting Mexico as a wartime ally and did not want domestic events to rupture the relationship, though First Lady Eleanor Roosevelt was more blunt, writing of the riots that "[i]t is a racial protest."

In spite of riots and discrimination, and they were very real, World War II also gave African Americans, Latinos, and American Indians new opportunities. New wartime jobs meant important new economic opportunities for those who had been most marginalized in the United States. Because of the wartime labor shortages and federal enforcement efforts, many who had previously been excluded got jobs in industries previously closed to them. Others became more politically active, and more would do so once the war ended,

Fair Employment Practices Committee

Federal agency established in 1941 to curb racial discrimination in war production jobs and government employment.

zoot suit riots

Race riots in June 1943, primarily centered in Los Angeles, in which American military personnel attacked Latinos.

Bettmann/Getty Images

While some Latinos faced hostile rioters in places like Los Angeles, others, like these Mexican American soldiers, served in the U.S. military and believed that the war was the beginning of their successful civil rights movement.

beginning an era of civil rights activism that would continue long after the war itself.

Japanese Internment

In an era when many Americans sacrificed much, including their lives, other Americans, especially Japanese Americans, saw their most basic freedoms undermined by wartime hysteria. The immigration legislation of 1924 had prohibited immigration from Japan. As a result, the Japanese population in the mainland United States had not grown since then and comprised some 120,000 people of Japanese descent split between some 40,000 *Issei*, or first-generation immigrants who had arrived before 1924 and were by law "aliens ineligible for citizenship," and twice as many younger *Nisei*, or American-born Japanese who were American citizens. A majority of the Issei were over the age of fifty by 1941, while many Nisei were under eighteen and largely quite Americanized. The small Japanese Issei and Nisei community remained relatively isolated. Most supported themselves by small truck farms or nurseries, providing fruits, vegetables, and garden supplies all along the Pacific coast.

In the immediate aftermath of the Pearl Harbor attack, there was little overt hostility toward Japanese Americans. The usually conservative *Los Angeles Times* editorialized that the Japanese were "good Americans, born and educated as such." Speaking of the Nisei, General John L. DeWitt, head of the U.S. Army on the West Coast said, "An American citizen, after all, is an American citizen." In addition, U.S. attorney general Francis Biddle wrote that he was determined "to avoid mass internment and the persecution of aliens that had characterized the First World War." All would quickly change their minds.

While there were 120,000 people of Japanese ancestry living on the U.S. mainland in 1941, there were 200,000 Japanese living in Hawaii, almost half of the population of the islands. After the attack on Pearl Harbor, the federal government declared a state of martial law and suspended basic rights in Hawaii. Several hundred Japanese were arrested as suspected spies and saboteurs. But the entire economy of Hawaii would have collapsed if the whole Japanese community had been interned, and there would have been no place to put them and no one to guard them.

The situation for the Japanese on the West Coast was very different. Their treatment dramatically contrasted with not only the situation in Hawaii but also the way that Germans and Italians in the United States were treated. Unlike during World War I, the German and Italian communities were not subjected to mass discrimination during World War II, even though the United States was at war with Germany and Italy. There were arrests of individuals suspected of activities supporting the country's enemies, and non-citizens from Germany and Italy were labeled "enemy aliens" when the war began, but FDR ordered the attorney general to cancel the designation in the fall of 1942—just before Election Day.

When some accused Japanese Americans of spying, FBI Director J. Edgar Hoover said that such charges were utterly without foundation. Nevertheless, leaders of the California Grower-Shipper Vegetable Association, representing large-scale agriculture, did not like the competition of the small Japanese American truck farms, and one association leader declared, "We might as well be honest. … It's a question of whether the white man lives on the Pacific Coast or the brown man." Respected journalists, including Walter Lippmann and Westbrook Pegler, pushed for removal. Pegler wrote, "The Japanese in California should be under armed guard to the last man and woman right now, and to

23.1

23.2

23.3

23.4

hell with habeas corpus until the danger is over." By early 1942, General DeWitt, who had first said, "An American citizen is an American citizen," was saying, "The Japanese race is an enemy race and … the racial strains are undiluted." A few, very few, white voices, like the tiny Committee on American Principles and Fair Play, defended the rights of Japanese Americans. With public opinion running so strongly in favor of removal, President Roosevelt signed Executive Order 9066 on February 19, 1942, ordering the War Department to create "military areas … from which any and all persons may be excluded." The order did not specify which areas or which persons were to be excluded, but the result was that people of Japanese ancestry were ordered out of most of the three West Coast states.

Initially, Japanese families were allowed to move to the Midwest or the East. The rest of the country, like Hawaii, was not covered by the internment order. Some fifteen thousand people voluntarily moved before General DeWitt ordered an end to such moves in late March. After that, people of Japanese ancestry were ordered to report to "assembly centers," including the Santa Anita racetrack in Southern California and the Tanforan Racetrack in San Bruno near San Francisco.

Yamato Ichihashi, a Stanford professor, described Santa Anita as "mentally and morally depressive." Families who had lived in their own homes, managed their own businesses, and, in some cases like Ichihashi, had been involved in rich professional lives, were suddenly in armed camps, living in stables that had recently held horses, and kept behind barbed wire under the watch of armed guards. The instructions were to bring only what they could carry—no pets and no cameras.

Forced out of their homes and into the temporary relocation centers, some 100,000 Issei and Nisei were then moved a second time to ten relocation camps scattered through sparsely inhabited regions of the West (see Map 23-3). The first to open was at Manzanar on a dried-up lake bed between the coastal mountains and the higher Sierra Nevada range. In this desert location, summer temperatures were often above one hundred degrees while the winter was freezing. Each family had a twenty-by-twenty-foot uninsulated cabin.

For most of the internees, the next three years were a time of enforced idleness while the rest of the country worked harder than ever. Some young men volunteered to join the all-Japanese units fighting in Europe and served with distinction while their families waited

---

Map 23-3 Internment Camps.

Japanese internment camps were located in isolated areas in many parts of the United States.

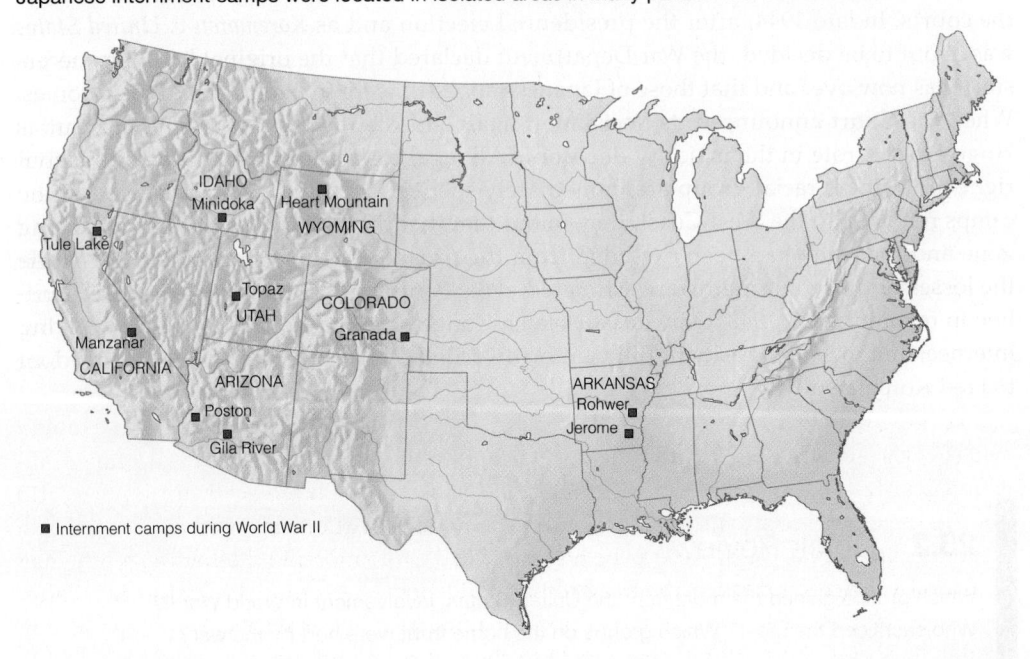

■ Internment camps during World War II

National Archives and Records Administration

Photographer Dorothea Lange, who had taken iconic images during the Great Depression, captured the pride and tragedy of this Japanese family waiting to be taken from their homes to a relocation center.

for them in the camps. Other young men, offended at being asked to forswear allegiance to an emperor they had never cared about, refused any form of service and were held as virtual prisoners at Tule Lake, California.

Some challenged the process of internment. Gordon Hirabayashi remembered hearing of the order to report to the camps and thinking, "I was confronted with a dilemma: Do I stay out of trouble and succumb to the status of second-class citizen, or do I continue to live like other Americans and thus disobey the law?" He disobeyed the law and challenged it in court. The U.S. Supreme Court threw out Hirabayashi's challenge and he served time in a prison camp. Although Justice Frank Murphy supported the Court's unanimous decision to allow internment, he noted that the **Japanese internment** was the first time in history that the federal government had "sustained a substantial restriction on the personal liberty of citizens of the United States based upon the accident of race or ancestry," while noting the parallels with what Nazi Germany was doing to Jews.

Japanese internment

A federal government policy implemented by executive order through which Japanese Americans were forced to enter internment camps.

A second set of cases known as *Korematsu v. United States* then began to move through the courts. In late 1944, after the presidential election and as *Korematsu v. United States* was about to be decided, the War Department declared that the original "military necessity" was now over and that those of Japanese ancestry were free to return to their homes. When the Court announced its decision, it again sidestepped the specific issue, but as Hugo Black wrote in the majority decision, "All legal restrictions which curtail the civil rights of a single racial group are immediately suspect." As those who had lived in the camps returned to the West Coast, they found that their homes and businesses were long gone and that they had been excluded from the prosperity of wartime America. While the losses of those interned were estimated at $400 million, Congress provided $37 million in reparations in 1948. Only decades later, Congress voted $20,000 for each surviving internee, and in 1998, President Bill Clinton awarded the Presidential Medal of Freedom to Fred Korematsu.

23.2 Quick Review

Which groups gained the most from the United States' involvement in World War II? Who sacrificed the most? Which groups on the home front were hurt by the war?

Industrial Strength, Industrial Prosperity

23.3 Analyze U.S. industrial strength and productivity and its impact on the outcome of the war and on American society.

America's wartime ally, Soviet dictator Joseph Stalin, understood the key role the United States would play in World War II. Even though the Soviet Union supplied far more soldiers (and suffered almost twenty times as many battlefield deaths), Stalin said, "The most important things in this war are machines. … The United States … is a country of machines." It was an accurate analysis.

A month after the United States entered the war, Roosevelt told Congress, "It will not be sufficient for us … to produce a slightly superior supply of munitions to that of Germany, Japan, and Italy." The president said the United States needed to provide "crushing superiority of equipment in any theater of the world war." Roosevelt insisted that the United States produce 60,000 airplanes in 1942 and 125,000 more in 1943, plus 120,000 tanks, 55,000 antiaircraft guns, and 16 million tons of merchant shipping. Few thought it could be done, but the goals were met.

Wartime Production

Several factors led to the extraordinary U.S. output in the machinery of war in 1942 and 1943. Compared with the rest of the world, the United States was a manufacturing giant, and the United States had huge supplies of iron ore, coal, and oil. In 1937, while perhaps half of all U.S. manufacturing plants were idle because of the Great Depression, the United States still produced 4.8 million automobiles while Germany produced 331,000 and Japan only 26,000. It did not take long, once the country put itself on a war footing, for the unemployed to go to work, the plants to start up, and those already in operation to shift from peace time to war-focused production. The War Production Board, the government agency charged with ensuring the production of war materials, prohibited the manufacture of automobiles for private use. On February 10, 1942, auto workers in Detroit held a little ceremony for the last cars coming down the line and then began rebuilding the machinery to make tanks and trucks. Aircraft plants, especially the giant Boeing and Lockheed plants on the West Coast, and Ford's Willow Run aircraft plant near Detroit started to turn out planes. Shipyards went to three shifts.

The United States also had an attitude toward manufacturing that greatly helped its success. German armaments minister Albert Speer told Hitler that he was worried because it was the Americans, not the Germans, who "knew how to act with organizationally simple methods and therefore achieved great results" while Germany was stuck with an "outmoded, tradition-bound, and arthritic organizational system." At the beginning of the war, Germany made 425 different kinds of aircraft, 151 kinds of trucks, and 150 different motorcycles all to exacting precision standards. The Americans made far fewer models, accepted lower standards, and got things done—a high-volume output that far surpassed allies or enemies.

Perhaps the best example of American industrial productivity was the Liberty ship, the workhorse of the merchant marine that kept Britain, Russia, and later U.S. forces in the Pacific supplied throughout the war. The Liberty ships were all built to the same standard: 440 feet long with a cargo hold that could contain 330 freight cars, 440 tanks, or 3.4 million C-rations. When the first Liberty ship, the *Patrick Henry*, was christened on December 30, 1941, just after the Pearl Harbor attack, it had taken 355 days—just shy of a year—to build. Six months later, in June 1942, it took 105 days to build a Liberty ship, and in November 1942, working around the clock, workers built the *Robert E. Peary* in less than 5 days. One engineer called the Liberty ships the "Model T of the seas," and President Roosevelt called them ugly ducklings, but they did the job.

Henry Kaiser created a huge new industrial facility in Richmond, on San Francisco Bay, where tens of thousands of workers of different races and from every part of the country, many of whom had never worked in any industry before, built these ships. The highly specific jobs of mass-produced shipbuilding in which each worker repeated one small task over and over again took much less skill than had the jobs of elite shipbuilding workers in the past, but new workers loved the opportunities the yards provided, and the finished ships just kept coming.

The huge increase in American industrial activity was not without its problems. Early in 1942, the government took several steps to control inflation and costs. The Office of Price Administration announced a General Maximum Price Regulation in April that made the prices of goods and services in March 1942 permanent until the end of the war. Known as "General Max," the regulation did help control costs and inflation. The National War Labor Board negotiated a settlement between union and management at Bethlehem, Republic, Youngstown, and Inland Steel Companies that limited wage increases to cost of living. Known as the "Little Steel agreement" (the U.S. Steel Company was "Big Steel"), the agreement became a norm throughout American industries. Although there had been several strikes in the months just before the war, most of organized labor took a "no strike pledge" for the duration of the war in return for a government policy that required industries to maintain labor contracts and union membership.

Wartime Prosperity

In spite of restrictions on wage increases, more Americans were employed and earned more money than ever before in their lives or the nation's history during World War II. Wartime rationing limited some goods. People needed ration stamps to purchase their monthly allotment of meat, coffee, tires, and gasoline, and new cars were simply not available. Housing was very hard to find, and many lived in cramped quarters, while extended families often moved in together. Nevertheless, Americans who could remember the Great Depression found themselves with previously undreamed-of opportunity. Laura Briggs, a young farm woman from Idaho, remembered, "We and most other farmers went from a tarpaper shack to a new frame house with indoor plumbing ... [and] a hot water heater. ... It was just so modern we couldn't stand it." A shipyard worker in Portsmouth, Virginia, said, "I felt like something had come down from heaven. I went from forty cents an hour to ... two seventy-five an hour. ... [T]he war completely turned my life around." By December 1944, Macy's department stores reported the highest volume of sales in their history.

National leaders worried about a combination of prosperity and complacency. One Pentagon officer said that Americans "have never been bombed. ... They have little appreciation of the horrors of war." In December 1943, FDR told his cabinet that he sometimes thought, "One of the best things that could happen, would be to have a few German bombs fall here to wake us up." But other than isolated and utterly unsuccessful enemy efforts to fire on the Oregon coast and New York's Long Island, the continental United States was never bombed or shot at, which was a dramatically different experience from that of Britain or Russia or, of course, Italy, Germany, and Japan. Letters home from those doing the fighting were censored, and even if they had not been, many soldiers did not want to discuss the horrors of war.

Sometimes complacency had a high cost. When two inmates escaped from Auschwitz and brought stories of the Holocaust to the United States, many simply refused to believe that such things were possible. In the summer of 1943, given detailed reports of the Nazi death camps, Supreme Court Justice Felix Frankfurter simply responded, "I am unable to believe you." It was simply too horrible to contemplate. The degree to which traditional anti-Semitism played a role in some people's responses to the news about Nazi death camps, the degree to which people such as Frankfurter simply could not believe what they were hearing, and the extent to which other urgencies of the war led people to focus elsewhere has been debated ever since the war. For whatever reason—or probably many reasons—few Americans took the stories of the emerging Holocaust seriously until the end of the war demonstrated their awful truth.

Initially, the administration wanted to raise taxes to pay most of the war's cost immediately, but in the end, taxes covered about 45 percent, while loans covered the rest. Nevertheless, taxes increased significantly during the war. The Revenue Act of 1942 raised $7 billion in new taxes. In 1939, only four million of the richest Americans paid income tax. The 1942 law brought thirteen million new taxpayers into the system. The government also began payroll tax withholding in 1943, requiring employers to deduct taxes and pay them directly to the government before issuing paychecks. The rapid increases in wages and job opportunities, coupled with continued appeals to patriotism, limited objections to the new and higher levels of taxation.

The government also borrowed money. Low-cost Series E bonds were sold, allowing many Americans to save some of what they were earning and contribute to the war effort. Larger loans were also forthcoming. Commercial banks increased their holdings in U.S. government debt from $1 billion in 1941 to $24 billion in 1945. In spite of all the borrowing and spending, the United States emerged from the war as the one remaining economic powerhouse in the world as the economies of all the other economic leaders suffered much more from the war.

> **23.3** Quick Review
>
> How was the American experience during World War II different from that of people in Europe and Asia?

Winning a World War—North Africa, Europe, Asia, the Pacific, 1943–1945

23.4 **Explain the course of the war leading to victory in Europe and then the Pacific.**

While many Americans prospered during World War II, for those in the military, especially those in combat, World War II was a combination of long waits, boredom, and occasional moments of sheer terror, pain, and heroism.

The War in Europe, 1943–1945

In late 1942, the Russians insisted that it was time for their western allies to open a second front and attack Germany and German-occupied France directly to take the pressure off of Russia. But Churchill, remembering the terrible British losses of World War I, would not agree. Instead, Britain and America kept bombing Germany, and Allied troops landed at Oran, Algeria, in November 1942 to attack German forces in North Africa, a huge diversion as far as Stalin was concerned, but victories there lifted spirits among the Allies.

In January 1943, Roosevelt went to Casablanca in North Africa to meet with Churchill, becoming the first president since Wilson to travel outside of the Western Hemisphere and the first since Lincoln to visit U.S. troops in the field. They agreed that they would continue to bomb Germany; that after North Africa, they would invade Italy, not the coast of France; and that while the United States would continue to supply Britain and Russia, a third of new forces and supplies would go to the Pacific. At a press conference at the end of the meeting, FDR also said that the Allies would accept only unconditional surrender from Germany, Italy, and Japan; there would be no intermediate peace negotiations. Then, in February 1943, the Russian army and the Russian winter defeated the Nazi troops at Stalingrad, and the tide of war began to change. The Russian army, known as the Red Army, went on the offensive. The German *Wehrmacht*—the military machine that had been undefeated in Europe since 1939—started retreating.

In the summer of 1943, American and British units began the attack on what was known as "fortress Europe"—the Nazi-controlled territory at the heart of the continent. On July 10, 1943, U.S., Canadian, and British forces, having sent coded messages that lured the Germans and Italians into defensive positions on the northern part of Sicily, instead landed on the south coast of the island. U.S. forces under General George Patton made rapid progress

23.1

23.2

23.3

23.4

across the island, taking Palermo on the north coast on July 22. The effort was bolstered by welcoming crowds who helped them and shouted "Down with Mussolini." Italy's King Victor Emmanuel III dismissed Mussolini and had him arrested, but German units in Italy continued to fight. Allied forces continued a long, slow, and bitter battle up the Italian peninsula, attacking Salerno in September 1943, sustaining a long battle around Monte Cassino, making a fresh landing on the beaches at Anzio outside of Rome in January 1944, and finally taking control of Rome itself in June 1944. (See Map 23-4.)

While the Red Army rolled west from Russia into Poland and eventually Germany, and while American and British forces won battles in North Africa and Italy, American pilots joined their British counterparts in what became round-the-clock bombing of Germany. The British had begun bombing German military targets, first in France and then, as the planes got better, in the Ruhr Valley of Germany itself. Precision bombing in real wartime conditions was exceedingly difficult, so the British simply tried to destroy the morale of the German civilians, especially industrial workers, by bombing wherever they could—what some called terror bombing. When the Americans joined the war, they initially found the terror bombing to be abhorrent, but they worked out a compromise: the British would bomb at night, bombing wherever they could, and the Americans, with more sophisticated equipment, could bomb specified targets during the day. The first U.S. bombers began their attacks in August 1942, and by January 1943, hundreds of U.S. bombers were hitting industrial targets like the German city of Bremen. The losses of pilots and crews were staggering. Six hundred Americans were killed in the summer of 1943, 16 percent of those who flew missions. One pilot remembered his terror when being attacked by German Messerschmitt 109s:

> The plane shook with the chatter of our guns. ... As other planes were hit, we had to fly through their debris. ... When a plane blew up, we saw their parts all over the sky. We smashed into some of the pieces. One plane hit a body which tumbled out of a plane ahead. A crewman went out the front hatch of a plane and hit the tail assembly of his own plane. No chute. His body turned over and over like a bean bag tossed into air.

And still the crews kept flying.

In November 1943, President Roosevelt left the United States for a second time, flying to Cairo, Egypt, for a third meeting with Prime Minister Churchill and then on to Tehran, Iran, for his first meeting with Stalin, which Churchill and the nominal Chinese leader Chiang Kai-shek also attended. FDR was intrigued to meet Stalin in person. At Cairo, FDR also tried to persuade Churchill that Britain must renounce its colonies in India, Burma, Malaya, and Hong Kong and promise them independence after the war as the United States was doing with the Philippine Islands. Churchill was a great wartime leader in Britain, but he was equally a lifelong British imperialist, and he was not about to be persuaded.

Tehran Conference

Meeting in Tehran, Iran, in late November 1943 between Roosevelt, Stalin, Churchill, and Chiang Kai-shek. The four leaders coordinated wartime strategy, including an eventual invasion of the French coast by the United States and Britain and later Soviet involvement in the war against Japan.

Operation Overlord

U.S. and British invasion of France in June 1944 during World War II.

At the **Tehran Conference**, Stalin kept up the pressure for the United States and Britain to invade France as quickly as possible and promised to join the war against Japan once the war in Europe was won. The conference was also a test of the personal chemistry between Stalin and FDR. Although the U.S. president was confident of his own skill in persuading people, he confessed, "I couldn't get any personal connection with Stalin." U.S. ambassador to Russia Averell Harriman described Stalin as someone of "high intelligence," with a "fantastic grasp of detail" and "shrewdness." Stalin, Harriman said, was "better informed than Roosevelt, more realistic than Churchill, in some ways the most effective of the war leaders. At the same time he was, of course, a murderous tyrant." Stalin wanted an absolute promise that the United States and Britain would start the invasion of Germany—code-named **Operation Overlord**—in the spring of 1944. And he wanted to make sure that others knew, as he had told Josef Tito, who was leading a Communist uprising behind German lines in Yugoslavia, "whoever occupies a territory also imposes his own social system."

The Red Army, Stalin assured everyone, would not pull back from the lands it was seizing from Germany. Operation Overlord was set for May 1, 1944. In the meantime, U.S. and British planes kept bombing Germany and German-occupied France—six thousand bombing runs during one week alone in February 1944—to make it difficult for German forces to prepare for an invasion that they knew was coming. Although Roosevelt had become

Map 23-4 The War in Europe and North Africa.

Early in the war, Nazi forces had attacked France and then the Soviet Union, but as the tide of war turned, Soviet forces moved across much of eastern Europe and into Germany itself while U.S. and British forces attacked Nazi forces in North Africa, Italy, and finally France and Germany.

World War II in Europe

- Axis powers
- Areas under Axis control, May 1941
- Allied powers
- Neutral
- → Axis forces
- → Allied forces: U.S.S.R.
- → Allied forces: U.S. and British
- ✴ Major battles

23.1

23.2

23.3

23.4

convinced as early as 1942 that the Nazis were killing Jews, the planes did not bomb the Nazi death camps or the rail lines to Auschwitz. U.S. planners simply could not bring themselves to believe that anything like the scale of the Holocaust was happening in spite of the fact that by 1944 they had clear evidence of the reality. Questions remain about why, with so many bombs being dropped, some better effort was not made to stop the trains going to those camps.

Everyone agreed that the Americans would lead the invasion of Western Europe. Roosevelt passed over several other army officers and appointed General Dwight D. Eisenhower to lead the attack. Born in Texas and raised in Abilene, Kansas, Eisenhower, better known as Ike to everyone, had spent his entire career in the peacetime army. He had been promoted to the rank of colonel months before the United States entered the war in 1941. Ike had a unique ability to get people to work together and do so with good cheer, skills that would be needed in the utmost to coordinate the American, British, and French forces involved in the invasion of Europe.

The buildup in Britain in 1943 and early 1944 was huge, with 150,000 U.S. soldiers arriving every month. The British called these American troops "overpaid, oversexed, and over here," but welcomed them not only for what they were about to do for the liberation of Europe but also for the supplies of cocoa, canned meat, candy bars, tobacco, and even toilet paper they brought. Finally, with the tides right and a break predicted in the weather, Eisenhower decided that June 6 was the time to go—and so the day became known as **D-Day**, 1944.

D-Day

June 6, 1944, the day of the first paratroop drops and amphibious landings on the coast of Normandy, France, in the first stage of Operation Overlord during World War II.

One young soldier, Elliott Johnson, remembered, "On the morning of June 6, we took off. I can remember the morning. Who could sleep? … I was on an LST, a landing ship tank." An armada of 6,483 vessels of all sorts of descriptions made the brief seasickness-inducing trip across the English Channel to land on several beaches in Normandy, code-named Utah, Omaha, Gold, Juno, and Sword, under intense German shelling and rifle fire. Units of the U.S. 82nd and 101st Airborne divisions parachuted behind the German lines to break communications between the Germans on the beach and their commanders. In the confusion of the invasion, most Allied troops were also cut off from their commanders and had to make their own decisions.

Troops landing on Omaha beach on D-Day had to use grappling irons to reach the tops of the cliffs facing them, suffering large losses. Once they got off the beaches and over the cliffs, British and U.S. troops got stuck on hedgerows, long lines of tightly planted bushes five to ten feet wide that farmers in Normandy had used instead of fences and that now provided far better protection for German troops than planners had estimated. Slowly the troops broke past the initial defenses. General Omar Bradley reflected that this "thin wet line of khaki that dragged itself ashore" held its ground and then started moving inland. Johnson remembered the odd scenes of battle: "Now on my way down the road I saw, on my right, these dead German boys. On my left, going across the field, is a French peasant leading a cow, cradling its head in his arms, protecting it with his body as much as possible. He had come back to get his cow, leading it away from all the noise and death." Johnson and the rest kept moving.

American forces moved quickly to take control of the French towns of Brest, Lorient, and St. Nazaire and then moved on to Paris, which they liberated on August 25, 1944. A tank force under the command of General Patton headed straight for the Rhine River and Germany itself. German troops fought hard, but they were outnumbered as more troops came across the Channel. By November, the Allied forces were at the Rhine River and the border of Germany.

In December, Hitler ordered one last desperate *Blitzkrieg* and eight German divisions roared out of the

National Archives and Records Administration

An iconic picture of some of the first American troops wading ashore on the beaches of Normandy, France, on D-Day, June 6, 1944, to complete the conquest of Nazi Germany.

Ardennes forest to surround American troops in a bulge in the Allied line near the village of Bastogne, Belgium. When the Germans called on the surrounded American forces to surrender, their commander, General Anthony C. McAuliffe, responded with one word, "Nuts!" When the German officer who received the message didn't understand it, a translator explained that it meant "Go to Hell!" With the help of tanks ordered north from Paris, the Allied forces defeated the Germans in the so-called Battle of the Bulge, and U.S. forces began moving into Germany.

As Americans moved across Germany, they discovered the full reality of the Nazi death camps. Russian units liberated the first camps early in 1945, and then in April, U.S. forces liberated Buchenwald with twenty thousand prisoners. U.S. soldiers described the horror of the smell and seeing the bodies stacked up in piles. Just before the army arrived, prisoners seized control of Buchenwald, thinking, correctly, that the Nazi guards might well try to kill all of them to hide the evidence of what had been going on. U.S. forces later liberated Dora-Mittelbau, Flossenburg, Dachau, and Mauthausen camps, while British and Soviet forces liberated others. In many of the camps, the liberating armies found prisoners on the brink of starvation and weakened by disease. They also found piles of corpses, human bones, cremation ovens, and ample other evidence of the horrors that had actually taken place. The Nazis had systematically killed six million Jews and another six million people—gypsies, homosexuals, people with disabilities, and others they considered inferior humans.

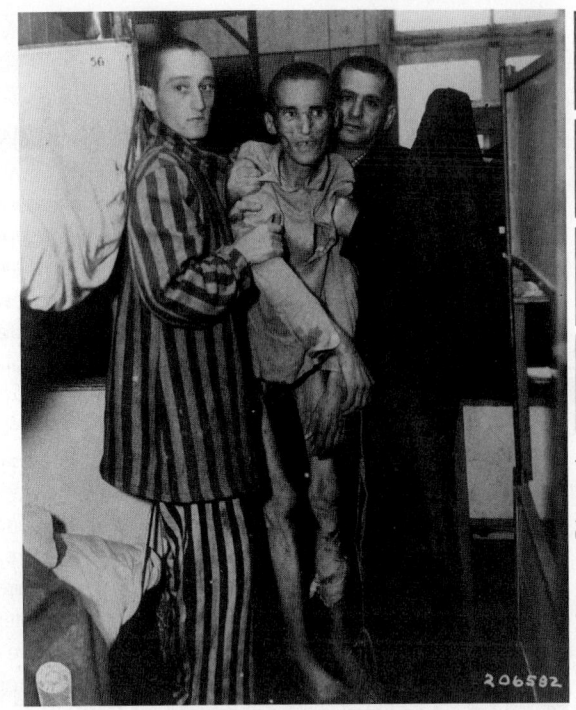

As U.S. forces discovered the full extent of Nazi death camps, Americans came face-to-face with the terrible reality. This twenty-three-year-old Czech victim of the Nazi camp at Flossenburg, Germany, was found by the 97th Division of U.S. Army.

Allied troops kept moving east and Red Army troops moved west. While armies marched, the bombing of Germany continued, including a controversial joint U.S.–British bombing of the city of Dresden, Germany, in February 1945 in which the resulting firestorm killed perhaps twenty-five thousand people. The Russians were soon within miles of Berlin itself. U.S. troops finally crossed the Rhine River in March and the Elbe River in April while the Russian army attacked Berlin. On April 30, in a Berlin bunker fifty-five feet underground, with Russian troops directly above, Hitler shot himself. A week later, Admiral Donitz, who had replaced him, ordered all German units to cease operation. The war in Europe was over.

Roosevelt's Death, Truman's Leadership

Just days before the war in Europe ended, on April 12, 1945, President Franklin D. Roosevelt died. Roosevelt had led the United States longer than any president ever had or ever would. And suddenly, he was gone. In the last year of his life, Roosevelt's health was terrible. His blood pressure was dangerously high, his hands shook, and he found it hard to stand even with his leg braces. Few of those closest to him were surprised when he died on a short vacation at Warm Springs, Georgia. Nevertheless, the news was devastating. Months earlier, in November 1944, Roosevelt had been elected to a fourth term in office after a campaign in which he said that he wanted to see the war through to the end. His Republican opponent was the reformist young governor of New York State, Thomas E. Dewey, but more Americans wanted continuity in a time of war. Roosevelt defeated Dewey by a comfortable margin, winning 53 percent of the popular vote and 432 electoral votes to Dewey's 99.

The November 1944 election had brought one important change, however. In 1940, Roosevelt had turned to his trusted confidante, Agriculture Secretary Henry A. Wallace, to serve as vice president. By 1944, many in the Democratic Party, worried that Roosevelt might not live out the next term, thought Wallace was too liberal, and convinced Roosevelt and the nominating convention to find another candidate. The compromise candidate was Missouri senator Harry S. Truman. Truman had served in the army in World War I, tried unsuccessfully to open a clothing store in Kansas City, and then worked his way up in the Democratic political machine of his hometown. He was elected to the Senate in 1934 and strongly supported the New Deal. In his second Senate term, he led a committee looking into war profiteering. He had been vice president for less than three months, had seldom

23.1
23.2
23.3
23.4

American Voices

Alvin Kernan, *A Bluejacket's Odyssey in World War II*

Alvin Kernan went on to a successful academic career at Princeton and Yale, but in 1940, he was a seventeen-year-old living in southern Wyoming with no prospects who joined the navy and served in the Pacific from Pearl Harbor to the Japanese surrender.

[On the morning of December 7, 1941] The captain came on the public address system to announce that Pearl Harbor had been bombed and that we were now at war with the Japanese.

I didn't worry about being killed, but I did wonder how long I was going to have to stay in the navy now. … Each sailor was given postcards to send home: two with the printed message "I am well and will write soon," and another two with "I am wounded and will write details as soon as possible." We joked that there should be a third message, "I am dead." … Death lived on an aircraft carrier operating in wartime conditions. … [A] thoughtless step backward on the flight and hanger decks where the planes were turning up led to decapitation and gory dismemberment by a propeller. Planes went out on patrol and were never heard from again.

[In October 1942] A little after 0900, the public address system broke the quiet of the ship with an announcement from the bridge,

"Enemy aircraft at fifty miles and closing." … As I started back across the flight deck, the guns began firing again as a single diver-bomber made a run on us. I lay flat on the deck, covering as much of my body as possible with my tin hat, trying to work my way into it, and thinking for the first time that I was likely to die, and resenting it, feeling that at nineteen I really hadn't had a chance to do most of the things people do and vowing to do them if I survived. From that moment to this, life has seemed a gift—overtime, in a way—and all the more enjoyable for it.

Source: Alvin Kernan, *Crossing the Line: A Bluejacket's Odyssey in World War II* (New Haven: Yale University Press, 2007).

Thinking Critically

1. **Analyzing Primary Sources**
   While every story is unique, how representative do you think Kernan's point of view is?

2. **Contextualization**
   What light does Kernan's story shed on the experience of living through World War II?

met with FDR, and did not know many of the highest-level government secrets, including the development of the atomic bomb, when, on the afternoon of April 12, 1945, he stood in the White House cabinet room and took the oath of office as president of the United States. It would be Truman, not Roosevelt, who would lead the nation in the final months of the war and the crucial years after it.

The War in the Pacific, 1943–1945

While the war in Europe was over in April 1945, the war in the Pacific was far from over, and U.S. troops were preparing for what they knew would be a horrific invasion of Japan itself. After the successful seizure of control of Guadalcanal in the Solomon Islands in February 1943, commanders made the decision to skip some Japanese-held islands, leaving their troops isolated, and instead "**island-hop**" toward their main objective, Japan itself. The defeats of 1942 seemed further behind. American factories produced machine guns, ships, and airplanes at an extraordinary rate, far faster than Japan could match.

The war in the Pacific was brutal. The Japanese lived by a code that prohibited surrender. The Imperial Japanese Army's Field Service Code said, "Never give up a position but rather die," and there were no instructions for surrender. The Japanese troops knew that the Americans would always have more food, more armaments, and more backup, but they were confident that their loyalty and fighting spirit was enough to make up for all of that.

Bombers based on Midway and Henderson Field on Guadalcanal or on aircraft carriers supported U.S. troops who were landing and fighting on sweltering beaches. They attacked Tarawa and Makin islands in the Gilbert Islands in November 1943 and then turned them into bases for further movement. In the first six months of 1944, U.S. Marines took Kwajalein, Eniwetok, Truk, and Saipan. On Saipan, more than a thousand Japanese civilians and soldiers jumped to their deaths from rocky cliffs rather than surrender. In air battles during June, U.S. forces, flying new and much better planes, virtually decimated the Japanese air force. U.S. submarines cut off the shipment of oil from Indonesia to Japan. U.S. commanders did not stage a landing on an island until navy ships had bombarded an island for some time while planes dropped bomb after bomb. Once an island was secure, the Seabees

island-hop

U.S. military leadership's decision to skip some Japanese-held islands in the Pacific and "hop" from strategic island to strategic island to get closer to Japan itself with minimal fighting and maximum speed.

H. Armstrong Roberts/ClassicStock/Alamy Stock Photo

U.S. troops fought on sandy beaches and in thick jungles and terrible heat to take control of one Japanese-held island after another across the Pacific.

(the navy term for uniformed construction workers) moved in and with amazing speed built airfields, shelters, and bases.

In June 1944, the United States began a campaign to retake the Philippine Islands. In October, the American and Japanese navies engaged in one of the largest sea battles in history, involving 282 ships and over 200,000 sailors off of Leyte Island. The U.S. fleet was victorious in spite of the continuing strength of the Japanese navy and the use of suicide *kamikaze* planes, basically planes that were used as bombs.

General MacArthur, who had left Corregidor under cover of darkness in early 1942, waded ashore facing carefully located cameras on October 20, 1944, and announced, "People of the Philippines, I have returned. ... The hour of your redemption is here." In spite of MacArthur's heroics, the Japanese were able to reinforce Luzon, the main island of the Philippines, and major battles during the first three months of 1945 took place before the United States secured control of its former colony. Manila, the city that young servicemen had considered a paradise in 1941, was now a city of rubble.

In some of the fiercest fighting of the war, U.S. Marines seized Iwo Jima island in February and March 1945, moving ever closer to Japan. The attacks on Iwo Jima and those on some of the earlier islands were aided by Navajo code talkers who relayed messages in the Navajo language—a code the Japanese were never able to break. Iwo Jima was tiny, only 4.5 miles by 2.5 miles, but U.S. control of its airfield and radar meant that U.S. bombers going to Japan had a much shorter flight.

After a long navy bombardment, Marines landed on the beach at Iwo Jima on February 19 and sank into the volcanic sand. In spite of the bombardment, the Japanese forces on the island were still strong, and fierce hand-to-hand combat followed the landing. The Japanese refused to surrender, and many died at the hands of new U.S. flamethrowers that literally incinerated them. Associated Press photographer Joe Rosenthal took his famous photo of the Marines raising the flag on Iwo Jima's Mount Suribachi on February 23, but the fighting went on for another month. Of the twenty-one thousand Japanese defending the island, over twenty thousand died in combat.

Map 23-5 The War in the Pacific.

Early in the war, Japan controlled a huge area around the western Pacific, and only a long series of sea and island battles turned the tide.

The battle for Okinawa in April to June 1945 was equally brutal; some 70,000 Japanese troops and 100,000 Okinawan civilians as well as almost 8,000 Americans died there. By June 1945, with the war in Europe over and after intense fighting in the Pacific, the U.S. forces in the Pacific were close to a landing on Japan itself. But it never happened.

The Atomic Era Begins

Manhattan Project
The effort, using the code name Manhattan Engineer District, to develop an atomic bomb during World War II.

While armies and navies clashed, a small team of U.S. scientists had begun work in 1942 on a top-secret venture, code-named the **Manhattan Project**. Enrico Fermi won the Nobel Prize for Physics in 1938 and used the prize money to leave Fascist Italy for New York. In March

1939, Fermi warned that recent research, including his own, in atomic physics pointed to the potential development of a new form of weapon. When Fermi went to the U.S. Navy Department, a receptionist announced, "There's a wop outside." The officers who received him were not much more interested. But some of the world's best-known physicists, many of whom were Jewish refugees from Nazi Germany (eleven German Jewish refugees would eventually win the Nobel Prize), were determined that the U.S. government needed to act before the Nazis. A group drafted a letter to President Roosevelt, which was signed by their most well-known and respected member, Albert Einstein, and delivered in the fall of 1941. After considering the letter and the report on Nazi research, Roosevelt said simply, "This requires action." And action, top-secret action, it got.

The Manhattan Project began under a stadium at the University of Chicago, where the first chain reaction was achieved in December 1942. Then, under the scientific direction of physicist J. Robert Oppenheimer and the military oversight of General Leslie Groves, the work moved to the isolated town of Los Alamos, New Mexico, where it was easier to keep it secret. The scientists bent all of their efforts to beating Germany in the development of "the bomb," which they now knew they could build. Ironically, partway through the war, Germany suspended further research on atomic warfare because of the cost and because Hitler considered atomic physics to be "Jewish physics." However, the Americans did not know that and kept going. In Oak Ridge, Tennessee, TVA dams provided the power for the extraction of U-235 (a form of uranium), and at Hanford, Washington, other New Deal dams, the Bonneville and Grand Coulee, drove the plants that squeezed plutonium out of uranium. With those ingredients, the engineers at Los Alamos could build their bomb.

Over $2 billion was spent on the project and 150,000 people were involved, though only a tiny percentage had any idea of what they were working on. The Danish physicist Niels Bohr, who had once said that the United States could not produce an atomic bomb "unless you turn the United States into one huge factory," reviewed the work in 1945 and said, "You have done just that." They had. On July 16, 1945, Oppenheimer and his team tested the first bomb in the Nevada desert. That evening, they sent a top-secret telegram to

National Archives and Records Administration

Navajo code talkers like these fought on Pacific islands, but by communicating in the native Navajo language, they were able to establish a means of communication that the Japanese, expert at breaking American coded messages, were never able to understand.

23.1

23.2

23.3

23.4

akg-images/Newscom

This picture of Nagasaki gives some sense of the total devastation caused by a single atomic bomb on what had previously been a large urban area.

President Truman: "Operated on this morning. Diagnosis not yet complete but results seem satisfactory and already exceed expectations." Truman, who had been briefed in April, understood fully.

While people in the postwar era have debated the morality of using something of the power of the atomic bomb, few in the administration seem to have had any doubts about it. By 1945, the war had hardened everyone and come to a point where the actors would use any weapon they could.

As scientists developed the atom bomb, regular bombs were doing their work on Japan. Boeing B-29s were dropping tons of explosives on Japanese cities. The firebombing of Tokyo

Thinking Historically

The Decision to Drop the Atomic Bomb

President Harry Truman was clear: "The final decision of where and when to use the atomic bomb was up to me. ... Let there be no doubt about it. I regarded the bomb as a military weapon and never had any doubt that it should be used." None of the president's inner circle seem to have had any doubts about dropping the atomic bomb on a major city in Japan either, and few beyond that circle knew anything about the top-secret project until news of the bombing of Hiroshima reached the world on August 6, 1945. For soldiers and sailors facing the invasion of Japan, word of the bomb's use was seen only as a blessing. The then twenty-year-old sailor Alvin Kernan remembered, "Each of us felt, further, that those two bombs had saved our lives—not life in general, but our own felt, breathing life. No one who was not there will ever understand how fatalistically we viewed the invasion of Japan. ... [E]ach of us felt that survival was unlikely."

Some, however, did argue for a different course of action. U.S. Army Chief of Staff General George C. Marshall worried about the "opprobrium which might follow from an ill-considered employment of such force." Some senior military leaders had moral qualms about the killing of so many civilians if the bomb was dropped on a Japanese city.

Some of the physicists who helped develop the bomb also argued for a different course of action. Leo Szilard and James Franck, key researchers on the Manhattan Project, recommended that instead of dropping the bomb on a city, it first be used on a "desert or a barren island" to show Japan what might be coming, and they later organized a petition signed by sixty-eight Manhattan Project scientists, raising questions about the arms race they feared would come. They said that once the first atomic bomb was dropped, a new arms race "will be on in earnest not later than the morning after our first demonstration of the existence of nuclear weapons," and they argued for putting international controls of nuclear weapons in place.

So why did Truman ignore these recommendations and order that an atomic bomb be dropped on Hiroshima and three days later on Nagasaki? Could he have opted for the idea of a demonstration explosion first? Was the bombing of Nagasaki necessary before the Japanese government even had time to consider the implications of the bombing of Hiroshima? At the time, and for the rest of his life, Truman insisted that he had

made the decisions himself and never—then or later—had any doubts about them. Still, historians debate the reasons for his action. Because the United States had access to many Japanese secret cables, Truman knew that the country was under enormous pressure to end the war but nevertheless still had resources to keep fighting. Early in the war, President Roosevelt and the other Allied leaders had agreed that only unconditional surrender by Germany and Japan would be acceptable, and in July 1945, Truman, Churchill, and Stalin reaffirmed that only the "unconditional surrender of all Japanese armed forces" would end the war and that the only "alternative is prompt and utter destruction of Japan." Truman also knew that the Soviet Union had promised to join the war against Japan once the war in Europe was over, and some have argued that Truman was determined to show Stalin the full extent of American power by defeating Japan first. U.S. military leaders estimated that the United States might lose 200,000 soldiers and sailors in the planned November invasion of Japan, and Truman certainly wanted to avoid that death toll. Some have also seen the bombing as revenge for the bombing of Pearl Harbor in 1941. Certainly, four years of terrible warfare had hardened everyone. Documents, most finally declassified in the 1990s, lead different historians to many different conclusions about why President Truman made the specific decisions he did. There probably will not be a final answer.

Source: Based on The Atomic Bomb and the End of World War II A Collection of Primary Sources National Security Archive Electronic Briefing Book No. 162 Edited by William Burr - 202/994-7000 Posted - August 5, 2005. See http://www.gwu.edu/~nsarchiv/NSAEBB/NSAEBB162/index.htm downloaded January 10, 2013.

Thinking Critically

1. **Contextualization**

   Given the situation Truman faced in the spring of 1945, what options, including the use of atomic weapons, did Truman have for bringing the war with Japan to a conclusion? In that context, would you argue for a different decision?

2. **Argument Development**

   In your opinion, why did Truman decide to use atomic weapons on Japan? What evidence can you produce to support your position? What evidence must you consider even if it would point in a different direction?

in February and March 1945 killed almost a million people and left eight million homeless, far more than either atomic bomb. Still, there was something unique in the use of a single bomb, harnessing the power used in the sun, for warfare.

On August 6, 1945, Air Force colonel Paul Tibbets piloted a B-29 named the *Enola Gay* that took off from recently captured Tinian Island. The plane carried a single bomb that was dropped on Hiroshima, killing 40,000 people instantly and an additional 100,000 from burns and radiation. Three days later another atomic bomb was dropped on Nagasaki. Japanese leaders debated what to do. Some diehard Japanese militarists wanted to keep fighting no matter what and saw the "peace faction" as traitors. Finally, Emperor Hirohito, who had been silent through so much of the war, said, "I swallow my own tears, and give my sanctions to the proposal to accept the Allied proclamation." On August 15, Japanese radio carried a voice never heard in Japan before, that of the Emperor, who told his people that the unthinkable had come about; Japan had surrendered. World War II was over.

As word spread of the Japanese surrender, huge crowds celebrated from San Francisco to New York City. Similar crowds celebrated in London, Paris, Moscow, and Beijing. Most people breathed a huge sigh of relief. The most terrible war in modern history was over. Few knew what the postwar world would look like.

On September 2, the U.S. battleship *Missouri* sailed into Tokyo Bay. A Japanese delegation came on board to sign the instruments of surrender while an advance unit of U.S. sailors and Marines landed to begin the occupation of Japan. It was a short, somber ceremony. A new era had begun.

23.4 Quick Review

What was the key to U.S. success in World War II?

Conclusion

By the end of 1939, Europe was once again at war. After the German invasion of Poland, Great Britain and France had declared war on Germany. By June 1940, France was also invaded and it surrendered. Now Britain stood alone against fascism. At the same time, tensions mounted between the United States and Japan. Even those Americans who suspected that a war was coming hoped to avoid a war with Germany and Japan at the same time.

British prime minister Winston Churchill asked the United States for assistance in resisting Germany. Through a series of complex maneuvers, Roosevelt managed to provide some military aid to Britain but was hampered by neutrality legislation and by public opinion. Full-scale U.S. involvement in World War II came only with the Japanese attack on Pearl Harbor in December 1941.

During the war, 16 million Americans served in the armed forces, including 350,000 women. As the country shifted from peacetime to wartime industrial production, jobs were plentiful and Americans experienced unprecedented prosperity. Even during this time of rapid industrial expansion, racial and ethnic discrimination continued. African Americans and Latinos, though many served in the military or found jobs in war-related industries, were often marginalized. Ethnic hostility on the home front also resulted in the internment of 100,000 Japanese Americans living on the West Coast. During the course of the war, the Soviet Union (Russia), which had originally been allied with Germany, was then attacked by Germany. After fierce fighting in the Russian winter, Russian forces began to counterattack against Germany from the east while British and American forces attacked from the west—first in North Africa and Italy and later directly into France and Germany. After years of fighting, Nazi Germany was eventually forced to surrender, in April 1945, just after Roosevelt died in office. After the German surrender, the United States, under the leadership of Harry S. Truman, focused on the war in the Pacific, and in August 1945,

Truman made the controversial decision to drop two atomic bombs on the Japanese cities of Hiroshima and Nagasaki, which led to Japan's surrender, bringing World War II to a close. Because of American wartime prosperity and the lack of fighting on American soil and because of the engagement of American troops and the use of American technology around the world, the United States emerged from World War II as the most stable and powerful nation in the world. In September 1945, the world entered a new era as it had only a few times in history.

Chapter Review

Why was World War II a life-altering event on both personal and national levels? How did the war shape the place of the United States in the world?

Chapter 23 Summary and Review

Preparedness and Isolation, 1939–1941

23.1 **Explain support for and opposition to the U.S. support for Britain and the nation's growing tensions with Japan.**

Summary

With Britain isolated and under intense military pressure from Germany, Roosevelt sought ways to circumvent neutrality legislation and aid Britain. Despite fierce opposition from American isolationists, Roosevelt steadily increased American assistance to Britain at the same time that he worked to convince the American public that America's national interests depended on Britain's survival. While the United States focused on Europe, tensions were also building in the Pacific. American policy makers tried to use economic sanctions to curtail Japanese expansion in Asia. In response, the Japanese launched a surprise attack on Pearl Harbor, Hawaii, on December 7, 1941. Within days, the United States was at war with both Japan and Germany.

Review Question

1. Contextualization
   Why did so many Americans oppose U.S. involvement in the war in Europe, and how did Roosevelt navigate public opinion to aid Britain?

Mass Mobilization in a Society at War

23.2 **Analyze the war's impact and the contributions of widely diverse groups of Americans who fought, supported the war effort at home, or otherwise lived through the war years.**

Summary

The Axis nations had the upper hand in the early phases of the war, making the final outcome quite unclear. As part of the effort to mobilize for war, millions of young American men were drafted into the military, and although women were not drafted, some 350,000 women volunteered for service. Six million more entered the workforce, with 2 million working in defense plants. Discrimination in war industries and in the armed services sparked protests by African Americans and other minorities. With a heightened fear of sabotage, martial law was declared in Hawaii while 120,000 Japanese Americans on the Pacific Coast were forced to live in internment camps. Only after the war was over did the federal government admit wrongdoing and pay reparations.

Review Questions

2. Comparison
   Compare and contrast the roles of young men and young women in the war effort.

3. Argument Development
   How do you explain the widespread discrimination and racial turmoil on the home front while the United States is fighting a war to preserve fundamental freedoms and democratic institutions?

Industrial Strength, Industrial Prosperity

23.3 **Analyze U.S. industrial strength and productivity and its impact on the outcome of the war and on American society.**

Summary

American industrial might played an essential role in securing Allied victory. Federal agencies helped oversee the transition from peacetime to wartime production and took steps to control wages and prices. American companies retooled to produce war materials, and the power of American scale dwarfed the output of any other nation. Despite rationing and restrictions on wage increases, wages for the war economy brought unprecedented prosperity to millions of ordinary Americans, funded by a combination of taxes, bonds, and loans.

Review Questions

4. Causation
   What factors contributed to the extraordinary U.S. military production during World War II?

5. Continuity and Change over Time
   How did the federal government expand its powers during World War II, and how is that expansion part of a longer story of government growth going back to the Progressive era?

Winning a World War—North Africa, Europe, Asia, the Pacific, 1943–1945

23.4 **Explain the course of the war leading to victory in Europe and then the Pacific.**

Summary

The year 1943 proved to be the turning point of the war. After the Soviet victory at Stalingrad, the Soviets went on the offensive, pushing forward toward Germany from the east. Allied victories in North Africa led to the invasion of Italy. Once much of Italy and North Africa were secure, Allied bombing raids on Germany intensified. On June 6, 1944, the Allied invasion of France began. By early 1945, American and British troops were moving into Germany from the west. As the Allies closed in from both directions, they discovered the full reality of the Nazi death camps, confirming speculation of the worst crimes imaginable. When Roosevelt died in April 1945, Vice President Harry Truman became president, and Germany surrendered weeks later. The Allies then turned their attention to the Pacific. The campaign of "island hopping" was slow and bloody, and many feared that the final invasion of Japan would cost some 200,000 American lives. It was against this backdrop that President Truman decided to use atomic weapons against Japan. Shortly after the bombing of Hiroshima and Nagasaki, Japan surrendered.

Review Questions

6. Comparison
How did the fighting in Europe during World War II differ from that in World War I? How would you explain these differences?

7. Argument Development
What is the turning point of World War II that gives the Allies the upper hand?

1. Preparing to Write: Support Your Assertion

Short-Answer Question—Answer (a), (b), and (c).
a. Briefly explain ONE important similarity between U.S. mobilization of American society during World War I and World War II.
b. Briefly explain ONE important difference between U.S. mobilization of American society during World War I and World War II.
c. Briefly explain ONE factor that accounts for the difference that you indicated in (b).

For each response, identify your assertion in the first sentence, and then support that assertion in the next two. Consider what happened between the wars to help explain why the federal government was more active in World War II.

2. Preparing to Write: Support Your Assertion

Long Essay Question—Evaluate the extent to which Axis actions shaped Americans' view of World War II as a fight for democratic values.

Presumably, a section of this essay will discuss the German and Japanese atrocities. Start by developing a thesis, and then write a topic sentence for this particular section. In your support, use two or three pieces of relevant evidence, including the Bataan Death March. In a sentence or less, explain the event. Then turn to what the focus of your writing will need to be: analysis. In a few sentences, explain the effects that such stories had on the troops and Americans at home.

Section I: Multiple-Choice Questions

Questions 7.1–7.2 refer to the following image.

Political cartoon, late 1800s.

7.1 What is the purpose of this political cartoon from the late 1800s?

    a. It advocates American expansionism in the world.

    b. It illustrates a critical view of American expansionism.

    c. It is propaganda produced by the U.S. government.

    d. It is a political message fueled by the Red Scare.

7.2 The offerings on the menu were largely the result of which of the following?

    a. Allied victory in World War I

    b. Conflict between Mexico and the United States

    c. American adherence to the Roosevelt Corollary

    d. American victory in the Spanish-American War

Questions 7.3–7.5 refer to the following excerpt.

"XIV. A general association of nations must be formed under specific covenants for the purpose of affording mutual guarantees of political independence and territorial integrity to great and small states alike.

In regard to these essential rectifications of wrong and assertions of right we feel ourselves to be intimate partners of all the governments and peoples associated together against the Imperialists. We cannot be separated in interest or divided in purpose. We stand together until the end."

Woodrow Wilson, "Speech on the Fourteen Points," 1918

7.3 Why were President Woodrow Wilson's Fourteen Points created?

    a. To help resolve the Spanish-American War

    b. To expand American influence globally

    c. To punish Germany for its role in World War I

    d. To resolve World War I and promote peace

7.4 The Fourteenth Point was included in the Treaty of Versailles of 1919. Despite President Wilson's support, the U.S. Senate did not approve the treaty because of this point. What was the most important reason for the Senate's opposition to this point?

    a. They did not want the United States to interact with former enemies such as Germany.

    b. They wanted America to become more active in the international community.

    c. They thought it would cause the United States to become entangled in future conflicts.

    d. They believed the treaty did not provide enough American leadership globally.

7.5 Which of the following reflects President Wilson's chief purpose for pushing an international organization after World War I?

    a. To end colonialism and help colonies achieve independence

    b. To create an organization where all nations could discuss and work out issues

    c. To strengthen the effort to make large and small nations more equal

    d. To reduce the influence of communism and socialism

Questions 7.6–7.7 refer to the following excerpt.

"JOHN BARLEYCORN LURES MAN TO DEATH

EL PASO, Tex., Jan. 6—Liquor smuggling across the international boundary here claimed its fifth victim in pistol battles when Henry Renfro, a Colored man, was killed.

Renfro was killed when he was caught between a volley of rifle and pistol shots from police officers and smugglers, near the Mexican line.

Renfro, according to Claude Smith, captain of detectives, had offered to guide Captain Smith and another officer to a place where he said smugglers would cross during the night. Arriving near this place the officers said Renfro turned on them, drew a gun and opened fire, while at the same time other shots were fired at the police officers.

It had not been determined as yet whether a bullet from a police gun or from the opposing side killed Renfro."

The Cleveland Advocate, 1920

7.6   The event detailed in the newspaper article best exemplifies problems created from which Progressive Era reform?

   a. Prohibition

   b. Women's suffrage

   c. Labor reform

   d. Socialism

7.7   Progressive causes like the one that related to this excerpt were typically led by

   a. middle-class women

   b. older African Americans

   c. Social Darwinists

   d. new immigrants

Questions 7.8–7.9 refer to the following image.

Culver Allen

7.8   This political cartoon from 1919 best illustrates the American fear of

   a. modernists

   b. Fascists

   c. suffragettes

   d. Communists

7.9   The cartoon best reflects which of the following beliefs?

   a. The U.S. government was harboring radicals during the early 1920s.

   b. A new international ideology was threatening America's core values.

   c. The Russians were threatening to invade America and overthrow the government.

   d. The U.S. government was smothering the rights of those with radical beliefs.

Questions 7.10–7.11 refer to the following excerpt.

"Harlem is indeed the great Mecca for the sight-seer, the pleasure-seeker, the curious, the adventurous, the enterprising, the ambitious and the talented of the whole Negro world; for the lure of it has reached down to every island of the Carib Sea and has penetrated even into Africa.

In the make-up of New York, Harlem is not merely a Negro colony or community, it is a city within a city, the greatest Negro city in the world. It is not a slum or a fringe, it is located in the heart of Manhattan and occupies one of the most beautiful and healthful sections of the city. It is not a 'quarter' of dilapidated tenements, but is made up of new-law apartments and handsome dwellings, with well-paved and well-lighted streets. It has its own churches, social and civic centers, shops, theaters and other places of amusement. And it contains more Negroes to the square mile than any other spot on earth. …

I believe that the Negro's advantages and opportunities are greater in Harlem than in any other place in the country, and that Harlem will become the intellectual, the cultural and the financial center for Negroes of the United States, and will exert a vital influence upon all Negro peoples."

—James Weldon Johnson, "Harlem: The Culture Capital," 1925

7.10   Which of the following migrations contributed to the growing population of Harlem during the early 1900s?

   a. Immigration from Eastern Europe

   b. The Great Migration

   c. The Dust Bowl migrations

   d. Refugee movements from Africa

7.11   Which of the following occupations did leading figures from Harlem use to "exert a vital influence"?

   a. Senators

   b. Poets

   c. Realtors

   d. Architects

Questions 7.12–7.13 refer to the following excerpt.

"I've always said, and I still think we have to admit, that no matter how much fine reasoning there was about the old-age insurance system and the unemployment insurance prospects—no matter how many people were studying it, or how many committees had ideas on the subject, or how many college professors had written theses on the subject—and there were an awful lot of them—the real roots of the Social Security Act were in the great depression of 1929. Nothing else would have bumped the American people into a social security system except something so shocking, so terrifying, as that depression. …

In the spring of 1932, Franklin Roosevelt had gone out to Utah to the Conference of Governors. … He made a speech which was full of pleasant hyperbole of one sort or another—flattery to various Governors—but at one point he began to discuss the great problems now facing this country, and he spoke about unemployment. Then he said, 'I am for unemployment insurance but not for the dole.'"

Former Secretary of Labor Frances Perkins, "The Roots of Social Security," 1962

7.12 Who was President Roosevelt's most likely audience when he said, "I am for unemployment insurance but not for the dole"?

 a. Liberal critics
 b. The elderly
 c. Conservative critics
 d. Cabinet members

7.13 The Social Security Act is an example of the New Deal's attempt to

 a. shift costs to citizens
 b. build a more inclusive America
 c. return power to state governments
 d. reform America's economic system

Questions 7.14–7.15 refer to the following excerpt.

"Americans could not see that future clearly in 1945, but they could look back over the war they had just waged. They might have reflected with some discomfort on how slowly they had awakened to the menace of Hitlerism in the isolationist 1930s; on how callously they had barred the door to those seeking to flee from Hitler's Europe; on how heedlessly they had provoked Japan into a probably avoidable war in a region where few American interests were at stake; on how they had largely fought with America's money and machines and with Russia's men, had fought in Europe only late in the day, against a foe mortally weakened by three years of brutal warfare in the east, had fought in the Pacific with a bestiality they did not care to admit; on how they had profaned their constitution by interning tens of thousands of citizens largely because of their race; on how they had denied most black Americans a chance to fight for their country; on how they had sullied their nation's moral standards with terror bombing in the closing months of the war; on how their leaders' stubborn insistence on unconditional surrender had led to the incineration of hundreds of thousands of already defeated Japanese, first by fire raids, then by nuclear blast."

—David M. Kennedy, *Freedom from Fear*, 1999

7.14 What historical developments were highlighted in this passage?

 a. The obstacles that the American people had to overcome in World War II
 b. The problems that Americans would have to deal with during the Cold War
 c. The mistakes the American people and government made during World War II
 d. The sacrifices that the American people made during World War II

7.15 Which event does the author refer to when he states that "they had profaned their constitution by interning tens of thousands of citizens largely because of their race?"

 a. Nativism toward immigrants
 b. Internment of German Americans
 c. Slavery in America before the Civil War
 d. Internment of Japanese Americans

Section II: Short-Answer Questions

Question 7.16 refers to the following graph.

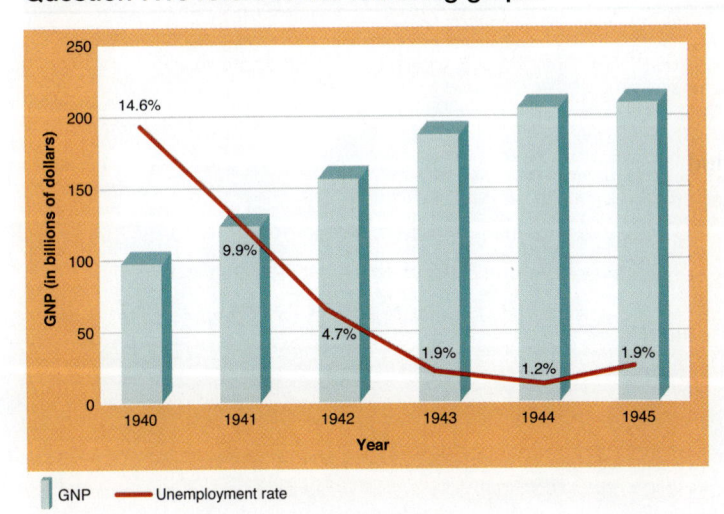

7.16 Answer (a), (b), and (c).

 a. Briefly explain ONE specific historical event or development that accounts for the state of the U.S. economy in 1940.
 b. Briefly explain ONE specific historical event or development that accounts for the changes in the U.S. economy beginning in 1941.
 c. Briefly explain ONE specific historic effect of the changes in the U.S. economy beginning in 1941.

Question 7.17 is based on the following image.

7.17   Using the World War II image to the left, answer (a), (b), and (c).

   a. Briefly describe one perspective about mass mobilization depicted in the image.

   b. Briefly explain ONE specific historical effect of the mass mobilization effort during the period 1940–1945.

   c. Briefly describe ONE other example of mass mobilization during the period from 1940 to 1945.

Section III: Long Essay Questions

Directions: Answer Question **7.18 or** 7.19. (Suggested writing time: 40 minutes) In your response you should do the following.

- Respond to the prompt with a historically defensible thesis or claim that establishes a line of reasoning.

- Describe a broader historical context relevant to the prompt.

- Support an argument in response to the prompt using specific and relevant examples of evidence.

- Use historical reasoning (e.g., comparison, causation, continuity or change over time) to frame or structure an argument that addresses the prompt.

- Use evidence to corroborate, qualify, or modify an argument that addresses the prompt.

7.18   Evaluate the extent to which immigration fostered change in definitions of American identity from 1865 to 1925.

7.19   Evaluate the extent to which international events fostered change in United States foreign policy from 1890 to 1945.

Section IV

Read on MyHistoryLab

Document-Based Question: Foreign Policy in the Progressive Period

Part 8

Fears, Joys, and Limits 1945–1980

Library of Congress Prints and Photographs Division|LC-DIG-ppmsca-04297

Chapter 24
The World the War Created 1945–1952

Library of Congress Prints and Photographs Division [LC-USZ62-47325]

Members of 11th Airborne Division kneel on the ground as they watch the mushroom cloud of a 1951 atomic bomb test in Nevada. Threat of the new weapon hung over the world during the Cold War.

Chapter Objective
Demonstrate an understanding of the post–World War II world that emerged in the United States.

 ## Learning Objectives

The United States in 1945
24.1 Describe the new technology, living patterns, and political arrangements in the United States that resulted from World War II.

The Cold War Begins
24.2 Analyze the coming of the Cold War, tensions with the Soviet Union, and McCarthyism at home.

Politics, 1948 and 1952
24.3 Explain political developments that led to the elections of Truman and then Eisenhower as Cold War–era presidents.

On August 6, 1945, the White House released a statement from President Harry Truman:

> Sixteen hours ago an American airplane dropped one bomb on Hiroshima. … It is an atomic bomb. It is a harnessing of the basic power of the universe. The force from which the sun draws its power has been loosed against those who brought war to the Far East.

Thus began the atomic age, a new and previously unimagined era. The bomb brought World War II to a quick end, but it also launched the United States and the world into an uncharted arena. For people living in the United States in 1945, that announcement was but one of many extraordinary changes that year.

In early May 1945, less than a month after Roosevelt's death on April 12, Nazi Germany surrendered. In June, the United Nations, a new international organization designed to preserve peace, held its first meeting. Then came the news of the atomic bombing of Hiroshima on August 6 and Nagasaki on August 9. Japan surrendered on August 14. World War II was over.

During the two-day holiday that followed, Americans celebrated the coming of peace. Few had any sense of what peace would mean. People wanted to get on with their lives, even if it was hard to imagine what the new "normal" might look like. A navy petty officer and his wife, walking hand in hand through the celebrations in Seattle on August 14, told a reporter their plans: "Raise babies and keep house!" Many returning from the war followed these plans, but they did so in a world much more complex than could be imagined on that idyllic August evening. This chapter traces the experience of those Americans who built a new world in the aftermath of World War II, describing not only their hopes and fears but also their surprises and disappointments as the postwar world took shape between 1945 and 1952.

The United States in 1945

24.1 Describe the new technology, living patterns, and political arrangements in the United States that resulted from World War II.

Those who had been fighting in Europe or Asia wanted to get home as fast as they could, certainly faster than was possible given difficulties in transporting troops and managing war-ravaged Germany and Japan. For some women working in wartime production, it was time to welcome a long-absent husband or boyfriend, quit work, and raise a family. Other women very much wanted to continue working. For some who had moved because of the war, it was time to go home. Others who had moved wanted to stay in their new locations and have families join them or create new families. The war began a significant movement of people within the United States. For many African Americans, it was a move from the South to the North. For many others, it was a move to the warm climates of the Pacific Coast and other parts of the Sun Belt stretching from Texas to the West Coast. For industrial leaders, peacetime conversion meant new profits that would come from fulfilling pent-up demands for goods that had been unavailable during the war and, later, from the development of a new consumer culture in which prosperity and easy credit facilitated consumption on a scale never seen before. A general sense of well-being also came from harnessing new discoveries related to medicines and emerging technologies. For government leaders, negotiating uneasy postwar international arrangements made the postwar era extremely difficult. The World War II alliance between the United States and the Union of Soviet Socialist Republics (USSR), commonly called the Soviet Union, turned into a new Cold War, creating surprising new tensions for leaders and for all citizens.

Science, Technology, Consumer Culture, and the Bomb

If the nuclear physicists who designed and built the atomic bomb were in the vanguard of wartime scientific breakthroughs, biologists and medical researchers were not far behind. During World War II, the wonder drugs—penicillin and streptomycin—combated infections and resulted in a dramatic reduction in battlefield deaths. Soon after the war, medical scientists and pharmaceutical companies marketed other new antibiotics. The National Institutes of Health, which had begun as a tiny government agency in the 1930s, now led the nation's war on disease.

By 1956, 80 percent of prescribed drugs had been invented after the beginning of World War II. Vaccines ended traditional childhood diseases such as whooping cough, diphtheria, mumps, and measles. In 1955, a vaccine was found for the feared scourge of polio. For those having a hard time keeping pace with modern life, physicians offered tranquilizers, sales of which boomed. People were growing taller and living longer thanks to advances in medicine, nutrition, and hygiene. In 1940, the average American's life span was 62.9 years, but by 1960, it had reached 69.7. Science, it seemed, was offering the key to life itself.

For consumers, science and technology offered tangible improvements that changed daily life. In 1945, consumers were being introduced to freezers, dishwashers, automatic transmissions, and ballpoint pens, and they were buying all of them with an enthusiasm not seen before. Office workers were beginning to use electric typewriters. Other technologies that had been developed before World War II—from washing machines to electric ranges to electric trains—were suddenly available after wartime production restrictions were lifted. Pent-up consumer demand and industrial availability combined quickly. What had been impossible to find during the war was now in every store. Just before the war, 44 percent of American families owned a mechanical refrigerator. By 1950, 80 percent owned one.

No automobiles for private use had been produced in the United States between 1942 and 1945. But by 1947, new models were replacing the old vehicles from the 1930s. Sales of passenger cars jumped to 6.7 million per year in 1950 and to 7.9 million in 1955. General Motors, which then sold about half of all cars in America, became the first corporation to earn $1 billion in a single year. Advertising by General Motors, Ford, and Chrysler convinced people to trade in 4.5 million old cars per year in the 1950s for large, sleek new models with automatic transmissions, air conditioning, and picturesque tail fins. By 1960, 80 percent of all American families owned a car, and 15 percent owned two or more cars.

While most households had radios in 1945, only a very few had televisions (black-and-white, of course). Television was developed by a number of inventors, notably Philo T. Farnsworth in the early 1930s, and was introduced at the 1939 New York World's Fair. But television production stopped during World War II while factories made radar equipment. The number of television sets in American homes exploded after the war. In 1946, eight thousand homes owned a set; by 1950, five million; and by 1960, forty-five million—or 90 percent of all American homes. In 1945, half of the nation's farm homes, where twenty-five million people lived, still did not have electricity to plug in a TV, but that, too, would change very quickly.

All of the consumer spending that the consumption of these items generated fueled a gigantic period of economic growth. Factories were converting from building machines of war to automobiles, televisions, refrigerators, and coffeepots, and new factories were being built. For the most part, wartime jobs turned into peacetime jobs with little downturn. Wartime savings had built up since many people could find little to buy during the war itself, and they provided the funds to jump-start the new economy of consumerism, but the postwar generation was also offered a steady stream of credit, starting with installment payments and, later, store and bank credit cards. In 1955, *Life* magazine reported a "revolution in consumer purchasing [where] instead of saving for years to afford major purchases, customers buy on credit and enjoy the goods while they pay for them."

Hanging over all of the advances, however, was the atomic bomb. As Americans learned more about the bomb, they realized that it could end all of their improved health and new-found prosperity. Few Americans had questioned the morality of using the atomic bomb in 1945; indeed, only a tiny handful even knew that the weapon existed before its use. The few physicists who had developed the bomb understood what it meant, however. Very soon, many more came to understand the sobering reality of "the mushroom cloud" that a nuclear explosion unleashed. "The bomb" might be a new form of protection, since only the United States had it, but it was also a new threat (see Chapter 23).

Some scientists proposed the voluntary sharing of atomic technology to avoid an arms race, but President Truman decided that the safest course was for the United States to retain

24.1

24.2

24.3

sole knowledge of nuclear secrets. However, in 1949, to the great surprise of many, the Soviet Union successfully tested its own atomic bomb. By that time, the wartime ally had become a potential enemy. Suddenly, with the Russian test, the idea that the United States was protected by its unique control of the bomb vanished. Before long, other nations joined the "atomic club." Great Britain, the closest U.S. ally, exploded its own bomb in 1952, France followed in 1960, and others were not far behind, but fear of the Russian bomb is what hung over Americans.

Officials and scientists within the Truman administration debated the development of an even more powerful weapon. The atomic bomb depended on nuclear fission (the splitting of an atom), but scientists knew that, theoretically, an even more powerful explosion could arise from nuclear fusion (the merging of atoms) to create a thermonuclear explosion—a hydrogen bomb. While virtually no one involved opposed the development of the atomic bomb during World War II, many senior scientists opposed the "super bomb." Albert Einstein, whose scientific work formed the basis for nuclear science, said that with such a super bomb, "general annihilation beckons." J. Robert Oppenheimer, who led the development of the first atomic bomb at Los Alamos, New Mexico, in 1944, opposed the larger bomb on moral and practical grounds. Others disagreed. When President Truman asked his advisory panel, "Can the Russians do it?" even those who opposed development of the hydrogen bomb had to answer yes. The president responded, "In that case, we have no choice. We'll go ahead."

The science and the engineering involved were daunting. When many of those who had built the first atomic bombs declined to participate in the new project, a fresh team, led by Hungarian refugees Edward Teller and John von Neumann, moved ahead. The first U.S. test of a thermonuclear bomb took place on November 1, 1952, at Eniwetok Atoll in the Pacific. The predictions about the Russian capabilities also became true: the first Russian hydrogen bomb was exploded in Siberia in August 1953, little more than nine months after the first U.S. test.

The bombs that the United States and Russia exploded were powerful beyond imagination. The United States' test sent a fireball five miles into the sky and produced a mushroom cloud twenty-seven miles high and eight miles wide. Eniwetok Island disappeared, replaced by a large hole in the ocean floor. The Soviet bomb was similar. Soviet premier Georgi Malenkov told the world that "the United States no longer has a monopoly on the hydrogen bomb." The possibility of "mutually assured destruction" influenced international diplomacy and daily life. Children practiced hiding under school desks in case of nuclear attack (though critics wondered what good that would do in the face of a bomb that could vaporize a city). Families built bomb shelters in their basements. The bomb was as much a part of daily life in the 1950s as televisions, refrigerators, new automobiles, and healthier lives.

Returning Veterans, the Baby Boom, and Suburban Homes

In August 1945, as World War II ended, twelve million American men were in the military, two-thirds of those between the ages of eighteen and thirty-four. They had been through a brutal war, and now they wanted to get home and get on with their lives. Those waiting at home were equally anxious to get the troops back. It took time to organize the military governance of Germany and Japan and to arrange the transport of troops. By fall, members of Congress started to get warning letters: "No boats, no votes." Demobilization moved at a rapid pace. In less than a year, three-quarters of those in the military had been mustered out, leaving an active military of three million. Congress voted to cut that number to one million in another year.

Coming home from the war was joyous but also difficult. Soldiers and sailors, desperately tired of the killing, the dying, and the boredom of war, sometimes had a hard time adjusting to a world where life had gone on without them and in which civilians could never comprehend the horrors they had experienced. Married couples who had been apart, sometimes for three or four years, especially those who had married just before a husband shipped out, found adjustments difficult. The divorce rate skyrocketed in the late 1940s.

24.1

24.2

24.3

GI Bill of Rights

Legislation in June 1944 that eased the return of veterans into American society by providing educational and employment benefits.

baby boomers

The name given to the generation of children born to the families of returning World War II veterans between 1945 and 1960.

The government offered generous benefits to returning servicemen (and the few servicewomen) to help with the adjustment. The **GI Bill of Rights** provided $20 per week for up to a year for those seeking new jobs. (The maximum payment of $1,040 for a full year was very close to the average American salary of $1,074 in 1945.) The G.I. Bill also offered college tuition for returning veterans, allowing a whole generation of young men to be the first in their families to attend college and prepare for middle-class occupations. In addition, the Veterans Administration made loans available for veterans to buy a house. Only later would some note that since the draft often passed over African Americans and Latinos and excluded women, the GI Bill constituted a kind of affirmative action for white men. But in 1945, most Americans thought that these men had richly earned any favors they got.

Perhaps the greatest goal of returning veterans and the spouses and fiancées who met them was indeed to "Raise babies and keep house!" They did both with amazing speed. Many veterans married very quickly, and the new couples started to have babies. In May 1946, nine months after the end of the war, 233,452 babies were born in the United States, up from 206,387 earlier that February. In June, the number of babies was 242,302, and in October, 339,499. A total of 3.4 million babies were born in the United States in 1946, 20 percent more than were born in 1945, a birthrate unmatched in the United States in decades, though it kept climbing after that.

The speed with which returning veterans chose to marry and have children came as quite a surprise. Nothing similar had followed World War I, even though "normalcy" had been a theme of the 1920s. Nevertheless, Americans across the spectrum of class and race started having children. The population soared, and a generation known as the **baby boomers** became a demographic bulge whose sheer size affected many aspects of American life throughout boomer life spans (see Figure 24-1).

For white middle-class Americans, a new home located in a suburban neighborhood offered the chance to build a safe and modern life. Just as these new families were getting started, Abraham Levitt and his sons, William and Alfred, bought four thousand acres of potato farms in the town of Hempstead, Long Island, outside of New York City. On this huge parcel of land, the Levitts built Levittown, the largest private housing project in American history. Their plan was simple: clear the land, lay out curving roads or lanes (never streets), pour concrete slabs every sixty feet along these roadways, drop off a set

Figure 24-1 Number of Births for the United States from 1929 to 1980

With the end of World War II, the birthrate in the United States spiked as never before. Soldiers returning from the war married quickly, and the new families produced a generation that came to be known as the baby boom, a bulge in the population that has continued to have outsized influence in the country.

SOURCE: National Center for Health Statistics, Technical Appendix from Vital Statistics of the United States: 2003 (NCHS: Hyattsville, MD). www.cdc.gov/nchs/data/statab/natfinal2003.annvol1_01.pdf; accessed October 26, 2017.

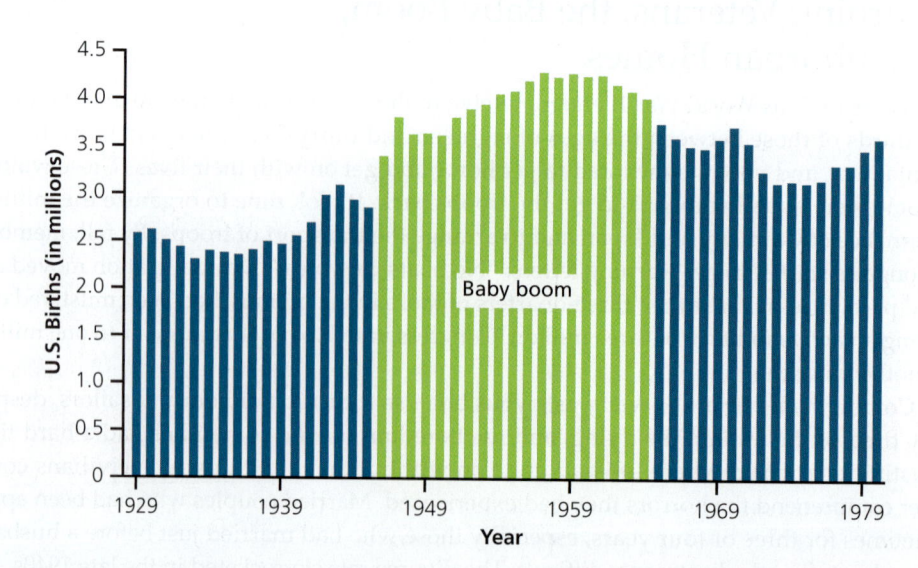

of construction materials at each slab—composition rock-board and plywood—then send in construction crews armed with new power tools—saws, routers, and nailers—each of whom was assigned a specific step in the construction process. At the peak of production, thirty houses were built each day. Each had a twelve-by-sixteen-foot living room, one bathroom, two bedrooms, and a fireplace. Levittown eventually included 17,400 houses that were home to 82,000 people.

Occupants moved into the first houses in Levittown in October 1947. At first, houses were sold only to veterans but soon were sold also to other families. Modest down payments and Veterans Administration and Federal Housing Authority loans brought the price of $7,990 to $9,500 within the range of many middle-class and aspiring middle-class families. Long Island's Levittown was so successful that the Levitts built two more planned communities, one in Pennsylvania near Philadelphia and the other in New Jersey—all called Levittown. Other developers—Del Webb in Phoenix, Joseph Kelly in Boston, and Louis H. Boyar and Fritz B. Burns in Los Angeles—created similar developments that sold at an astounding pace. Between 1945 and 1960, ten times as many houses were constructed in suburbs as in older central cities, and 95 percent of these houses were detached single-family homes. Mass production, which had come to automobiles in the earliest 1900s, came to housing after 1945. By 1959, the Census Bureau was reporting new housing starts as a monthly key to the nation's economic well-being.

Architectural and social critics disliked suburban developments. The nation's best-known critic, Lewis Mumford, described suburbs as

> a multitude of uniform, unidentifiable houses, lined up inflexibly, at uniform distances, on uniform roads, in a treeless communal waste, inhabited by people of the same class, the same income, the same age group, witnessing the same television performances, eating the same tasteless pre-fabricated foods, from the same freezers, conforming in every outward and inward respect to a common mold.

For veterans and their families and those who followed after them in the 1950s, however, the new suburbs were a dream come true. Immediately after the war, a desperate housing shortage led many to double up with parents or other relatives. Half a million veterans lived in army Quonset huts or other temporary buildings. Chicago sold 250 old trolley cars as temporary homes. A home of one's own, previously often a reality only for the upper-middle class and the rich, now became a new norm. The first issue of the community newspaper in Levittown noted that "our lives are held closely together because most of us are within the same age bracket, in similar income groups, live in almost identical houses, and have common problems." The residents also made their own contribution to the baby boom to such a degree that the community became known as "Fertility Valley" and "the Rabbit Hutch."

As many in the postwar generation moved to suburbia, Americans also moved from the East to the West. Between 1940 and 1950—the years of the war and the immediate postwar era—the Sun Belt grew rapidly. Texas grew by 20 percent, Nevada by 45 percent, and Arizona and California by over 50 percent (see Map 24-1, p. 718). Soldiers and sailors coming through California on the way to the Pacific liked what they saw and vowed to return.

Not all young Americans could or wanted to participate in the rush either to the suburbs or to the West, however. African Americans, Latinos, and Asians were excluded from most suburban developments. Levittown specifically excluded people of color from

Harold M. Lambert/Archive Photos/Getty Images

With the end of World War II, Americans embraced a new image of domestic bliss in a suburban home filled with children and a stay-at-home mom.

Hulton Archive/Archive Photos/Getty Images

A house in a subdivision like Levittown, New York, was a key part of the American dream for many in the 1940s and 1950s, though it was often a dream limited to white families.

24.1

24.2

24.3

Map 24-1 Americans on the Move.

Many Americans moved around a lot during and after World War II, and many settled in communities distant from where they had been children. While African Americans moved from the South to the North in large numbers, accounting for much of the population growth in states like New York and Illinois, white Americans moved from the East to the West, especially to California, which grew by 53 percent between 1940 and 1950.

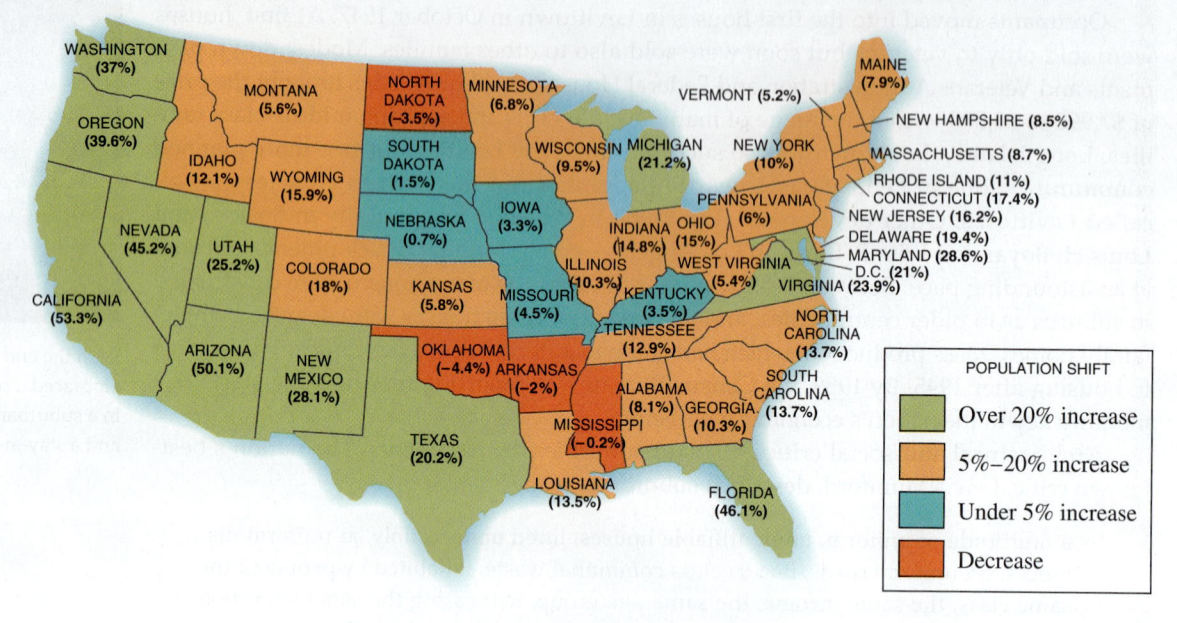

POPULATION SHIFT

- Over 20% increase
- 5%–20% increase
- Under 5% increase
- Decrease

its subdivisions for the first twenty years of the community's existence. William Levitt believed that if blacks were allowed to move in to Levittown, the whites would leave. He commented, "We can solve a housing problem, or we can try to solve a racial problem. But we cannot combine the two." As late as 1960, not a single African American lived among the eighty-two thousand residents of Levittown, New York.

Post–World War II suburbanization was a white affair that greatly exacerbated housing segregation in the United States. Most older cities had their Irish, Italian, and Jewish neighborhoods as well as neighborhoods for African Americans and for Latinos. However, the growth of suburbs created even more ethnic segregation as nonwhites were left behind in core urban communities with a declining tax base, declining services, and declining opportunities.

Race may have been the most obvious divide, but it was not the only divide to appear in suburbia. In 1959, social critic Vance Packard wrote *The Status Seekers* in which, like Mumford, he deplored the "mass produced suburbia." Packard also worried that the new developments had created one-class communities: "There is no need to rub elbows with fellow Americans who are of a different class," he wrote. Gay men and lesbians of any race were generally excluded from suburbia unless they chose to live deeply closeted lives. One lesbian wrote, "It has never been easy to be a lesbian in this country, but the 1950s was surely the worst decade in which to love your own sex." Others simply preferred to stay in older urban neighborhoods or small towns. Women who worked, especially those who remained single or were divorced, often found the conformity of suburbia difficult. From the GI Bill to the federal tax code, the government, intentionally or not, fostered the "traditional family" in which men—especially returning veterans who were given college scholarships and Veterans Administration loans—earned most of the money and were eligible for more credit often denied to women. For the poets and playwrights who became the "beat generation" of the 1950s who celebrated nonconformity, suburbia was unthinkable. There was virtually no way to get around in most suburbs without a car, and for those who needed public transportation, cities remained essential. Nevertheless, starting in 1945, great numbers of American men and women moved to the suburbs and embraced life there.

Thinking Historically

Observations on Levittown and Other Suburbs

In June 1958, a sociologist, Herbert J. Gans, and his wife were among the first twenty-five families to move into the new Levittown development just outside Philadelphia. Unlike many others who wrote about suburbia, Gans noted more positive than negative observations.

One Levittown resident told Gans:

We didn't know before we moved here that we would entertain more, go out less. Not that we were boozehounds before, though. Not that we can't afford to go out; we just don't want to. We have a new house and want to keep it up nice; this is not work but enjoyment. I've never been more content. … Working in the yard is just like fishing, so relaxing. I have more pep here.

Even if outside critics did not like what they saw in suburbia, Gans found that most of those who actually lived in Levittown liked it a lot.

A major exception was found among adolescents. Gans interviewed one girl who complained, "After school hours, you walk into an entirely different world. Everyone goes his own separate way, to start his homework, take a nap, or watch TV. This is the life of a vegetable, not a human being." As a result of the isolation, a car became as important to adolescents as it was to adults. One

high school senior took a job to buy a car and told Gans, "I had no choice, it was either going to work or cracking up. … I'll start living. I can get out of Levittown. … In plain words, a boy shouldn't live here if he is between the ages of 14–17."

While he expected to find more boredom and depression among the sometimes-isolated residents of Levittown, he did not. Gans worried about the impact of suburbanization on older cities. But in the end, he concluded, "I should like to emphasize once more that whatever its imperfections, Levittown is a good place to live."

Source: Herbert J. Gans, *The Levittowners: Ways of Life and Politics in a New Suburban Community* (New York: Vintage Books, 1967).

Thinking Critically

1. **Causation**
   How did Gans explain the dissatisfaction adolescents may have felt with suburban living?

2. **Comparison**
   How do you explain the gap between the negative view of many social critics and the sense of contentment that Gans found among so many suburban residents?

The Great Migration—African Americans Move North

While white Americans moved to the suburbs, a new generation of African Americans moved from the South to the North. The Great Migration of African Americans to the North began during World War I, continued through the 1920s, and slowed during the Depression years of the 1930s (see Chapter 21). During and after World War II, the rate of migration exploded. By 1960, half of the nation's African Americans lived in Northern cities—a huge change from the time when more than 90 percent of all blacks lived in the rural South. While the pull of Northern industrial jobs and the push of Southern segregation and violence remained constant from the 1920s to the 1950s, another factor accelerated the pace of movement in the late 1940s; the sharecropping system, around which the economic lives of many Southern blacks had been organized from the 1880s to the 1940s, began to disappear.

On October 2, 1944, as the tide of war was turning, a crowd gathered at the Hopson cotton plantation outside of Clarksdale, Mississippi, on Highway 49 to look at a new machine that had nothing to do with the war. Howell Hopson was conducting the first public demonstration of a new International Harvester cotton-picking machine. He described the scene: "An estimated 2,500 to 3,000 people swarmed over the plantation on that one day, 800 to 1,000 automobiles leaving their tracks and scars throughout the property."

The machine that the visitors had come to see changed the face of the South, and changed the lives of the nation's African Americans. The bright red picker looked like a tractor with a large metal basket on the top. As it drove down a row of cotton, the spindles mounted on the front rotated and stripped the cotton off the plants and then suctioned the cotton up to a basket. The picker could pick a thousand pounds of cotton in an hour; a good worker, only twenty pounds. Hopson said it cost $5.26 for a machine to pick a bale of cotton. A sharecropper cost $39.41 per bale. He wrote, "The introduction of the cotton harvester may have been comparable to the unveiling of Eli Whitney's first hand-operated cotton gin."

Hopson was thinking of the machine's impact on his profits. But like Whitney's invention a century and a half earlier, the machine's largest impact was on men and women of African descent. Whitney's cotton gin made slavery profitable. International Harvester's

As more and more African Americans moved from the rural South to the urban North, they created their own community institutions and black-owned and black-servicing business, especially beauty shops and barbershops, like this one in Harlem.

cotton-picking machine made sharecropping obsolete. A wave of 1.5 million African Americans had moved North between 1910 and 1940, but 5 million followed between 1940 and 1960. (See Figure 24-2 to get an idea of this migration.)

As people whose lives were centered in the communities, churches, and culture of the rigidly segregated South moved North, they now lived in quite different communities with changing norms. Racial discrimination, generally seen as a Southern issue until World War II, became a national one. Nevertheless, opportunities in the North were better than those offered by sharecropping, and the newcomers created their own jobs and a new urban culture.

Housing in the North was even more segregated than in the South. While the Federal Housing Authority dropped explicit racial rules by the 1940s, its handbook still said, "If a neighborhood is to retain stability, it is necessary that all properties shall continue to be occupied by the same social class." In reality, that wording meant, "Don't give mortgages to black families in white neighborhoods." The white rush to segregated suburbs opened up new urban housing for blacks. Unscrupulous real estate agents made large profits while engaging in blockbusting in older neighborhoods, convincing frightened white homeowners to sell quickly and cheaply. From Boston to Los Angeles, whole city blocks went on the market at the same time, transferring the majority of homes from white to black hands in short order. Changes in the racial makeup of urban neighborhoods happened at the same time as cash-strapped cities cut back on municipal services and many banks dramatically reduced the availability of mortgages and loans for home improvements. The creation of the white suburbs and the vastly expanded urban black ghettos went hand in hand in the 1950s.

Moving from the South to an unfamiliar North could be painful for African Americans. In *The Last Train North*, Clifton Taulbert described the longing for things left behind:

> There were no Chinaberry trees. No pecan trees. … Never again would I pick dew berries or hear the familiar laughter from the field truck. This was my world now, this strange new family and their cramped quarters over the tiny grocery store they grandly called the "confectionary."

Nevertheless, they kept coming through the 1940s and 1950s. As a migrant from Tennessee to Milwaukee said, "Every train, every bus, they were coming."

Figure 24-2 Share of African American population living in the southern United States, 1910–1970.

As the figure shows, the successive waves of the Great Migration had an extraordinary impact on where African Americans lived in the United States. From the first census in 1790 to 1910, close to 90 percent or more of people of African lineage lived in the South. Then large numbers of them started moving to the North so that by 1970, almost half of all African Americans in the United States lived in the North or West. Interestingly, since 1970, there has been a slight movement of return to the South, though in no way in numbers sufficient to counter the impact of the Great Migration.

SOURCES: Campbell Gibson and Kay Jung, "Historical Census Statistics on Population Totals by Race, 1790 to 1990, and by Hispanic Origin, 1970–1900, for the United States, Regions, Division, and States," Working Paper No. 56 (Washington, DC: U.S. Census Bureau, September, 2002), http://mapmaker.rutgers.edu/REFERENCE/Hist_Pop_stats.pdf; "Profile of General Population and Housing Characteristics: 2010, 2010 Census Summary File 1," U.S. Census Bureau, http://factfinder.census.gov/faces/nav/jsf/pages/index.xhtml; "Profile of General Population and Housing Characteristics: 2000, 2000 Census Summary File 1," U.S. Census Bureau, http://factfinder.census.gov/faces/nav/jsf/pages/index.xhtml.

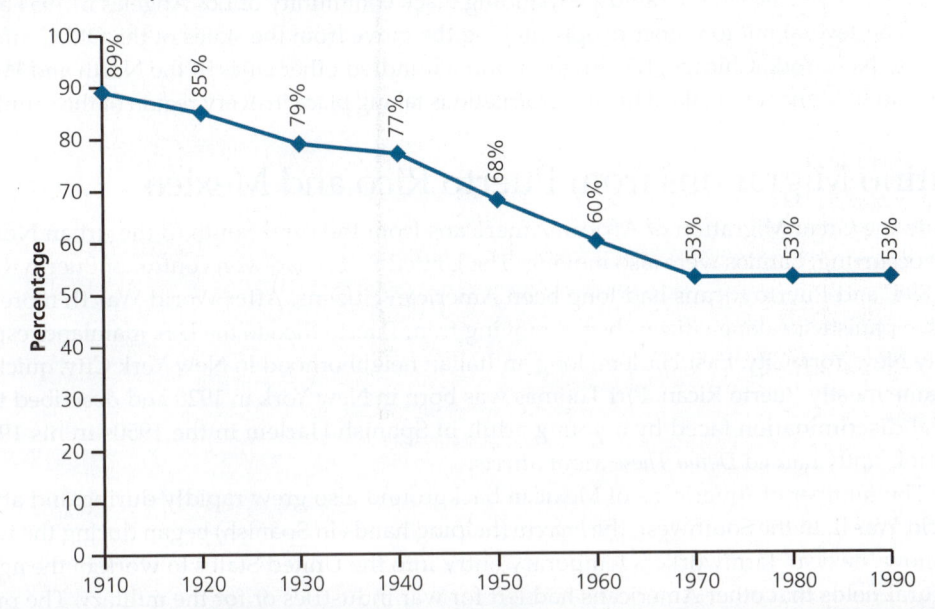

As they had in the 1920s, African American artists embraced urban life and the new growing black communities of the North, few more enthusiastically than musicians like Charlie Parker and Miles Davis, shown here performing in New York City in the 1940s.

Many who arrived were disillusioned. When Harvey Clark, who originally hailed from Mississippi, tried to move his family from a crowded apartment in South Chicago to a larger one just across the city line in Cicero, he was greeted by a mob and a police chief who told him to "[g]et out of Cicero." The chief told the agent who arranged the apartment, "Don't come back in town, or you'll get a bullet through you." The white mayor of Dearborn, Michigan, told Alabama's *Montgomery Advertiser* that "Negroes can't get in here. Every time we hear of a Negro moving in, we respond quicker than you do to a fire." As Detroit became a majority-black city, its suburb of Dearborn remained 99 percent white.

Black migrants also found new freedoms and opportunities in the North. Ida Mae Brandon Gladney, who had never been able to vote in Mississippi, cast her first vote for Franklin Roosevelt in Chicago in 1940. (The black vote in Chicago carried the state of Illinois for Roosevelt in that election.) Robert Joseph Pershing Foster, a physician in Louisiana, established a new practice in the rapidly expanding black community of Los Angeles in 1954 and 1955. The several million other people making the move from the states of the Old Confederacy to New York, Chicago, Los Angeles, and a hundred other cities in the North and West each had his or her own tale of the transformations taking place in every region of the country.

Latino Migrations from Puerto Rico and Mexico

While the Great Migration of African Americans from the rural South to the urban North was occurring, Latinos were also moving. The United States had won control of Puerto Rico in 1898, and Puerto Ricans had long been American citizens. After World War II, more of these Spanish-speaking citizens began moving from Puerto Rico to the U.S. mainland, especially New York City. East Harlem, long an Italian neighborhood in New York City, quickly became mostly Puerto Rican. Piri Thomas was born in New York in 1928 and described the racial discrimination faced by a young adult in Spanish Harlem in the 1950s in his 1967 memoir aptly named *Down These Mean Streets*.

The number of Americans of Mexican background also grew rapidly during and after World War II. In the Southwest, the *bracero* (helping hands in Spanish) began during the war to allow Mexican farmworkers temporary entry into the United States to work in the agricultural fields that other Americans had left for war industries or for the military. The program was expanded after the war, and between 1948 and 1964, almost five million braceros were brought to the United States. Although they were expected to return to Mexico when the work was done, not all did, and they, along with others who sought a hard-to-get visa or who walked across the hot deserts and the border, expanded the country's Mexican American population, creating a large group, some of whom remained under constant threat of deportation.

In Southern California, growth led to new militancy in the Mexican American community. In Santa Ana, Mexican American parents hired an attorney and sued the Board of Education over school segregation. In 1946, the courts issued a permanent injunction against this segregation, and later a federal grand jury considered an indictment against the Santa Ana board.

In Los Angeles, with the largest Mexican American population, the Community Service Organization began to fight for political rights in 1947 and was successful in electing Edward Roybal to the Los Angeles City Council in 1949, the first time since 1881 that someone of Mexican descent had served on that body since the days when Los Angeles was part of Mexico. In 1962, Roybal was elected to the U.S. Congress. Other Mexican American organizations sprang up across the Southwest, supporting a successful mine workers strike in New Mexico in 1950–1952 and building a solid base before the civil rights movements of the later 1950s while also supporting a small but growing middle-class Latino community in California and Texas.

The United Nations and the New Economic Order

Even before World War II ended, a series of international gatherings reshaped the political and economic climate of the coming postwar world.

THE INTERNATIONAL MONETARY FUND AND THE WORLD BANK In 1944, leaders in the United States and Britain were determined not to repeat the mistakes of the Treaty of Versailles. Among those mistakes, they believed, were the huge reparations imposed on the defeated Germany and the failure of the victors to ensure robust economic activity after the war.

In early 1944, Roosevelt's secretary of the treasury Henry M. Morgenthau invited Great Britain and the Soviet Union to join the United States in establishing a postwar economic system. Both agreed. Morgenthau then invited representatives of more than forty wartime allies to meet at the Mount Washington Hotel in Bretton Woods, New Hampshire, in July 1944.

The resulting Bretton Woods agreement created an International Monetary Fund (IMF) for "promoting international monetary cooperation." The purpose of the IMF was to maintain exchange rates between different currencies so people could buy and sell in different countries without fear that values would fluctuate wildly (as happened in the 1930s), to provide loans to a nation that was having problems balancing payments, and to provide technical assistance to banks. The U.S. dollar was made the base on which all other currencies were calculated (and it remained so until 1971).

The Bretton Woods delegates also created the International Bank for Reconstruction Development (better known as the World Bank) to get the world on stable economic footing as quickly as possible after the devastation of the war. The World Bank was designed to support economic recovery in war-torn Europe and to reduce world poverty, especially in Latin America, Africa, and parts of Asia that did not have the economic foundation for recovery. The first loans from the World Bank were made to war-torn France in 1947, and loans were soon extended around the world.

THE UNITED NATIONS When Franklin Roosevelt and Winston Churchill agreed to an Atlantic Charter in August 1941, they called for the "establishment of a wider and permanent system of general security" (see Chapter 23). By 1944, Roosevelt was ready to get more specific. He proposed an international body that would include every nation but in which the most powerful ones—in his proposal, the United States, Britain, the Soviet Union, and China—would serve as the "Four Policemen." As he told reporters in the summer of 1944, if some aggressor "started to run amok," these policemen would be needed to "stop them before they got started." By 1944, the wartime alliance was calling itself the **United Nations**, and Roosevelt wanted to keep the name.

The United States invited representatives from "the four policemen" to meet at a mansion known as Dumbarton Oaks in Washington, D.C. In seven weeks, from August to October 1944, Edward R. Stettinius, U.S. undersecretary of state; Andrei Gromyko, Soviet ambassador to the United States; and Sir Alexander Cadogan, permanent undersecretary in the British Foreign Office, consulting with V.K. Wellington Koo, the Chinese ambassador to London—with whom Gromyko refused to meet directly—erected the basic structure of the United Nations (UN). They agreed that the core of the new organization would be a Security Council made up of five permanent members (France was added as a fifth member) plus other delegates serving on a rotating basis. The Security Council would have the real power within the UN. A majority vote of the Security Council would be sufficient to authorize military force to stop aggression. Everyone also agreed that each of the core members of the Security Council should have a veto over any such actions; the United States, Britain, and the Soviet Union were not about to allow sanctions of which they did not approve.

The planners also proposed a UN General Assembly that would permit all of the nations of the world to debate issues but that, unlike the Security Council, could not enforce its resolutions. In addition, they agreed that there should be a secretary with a staff. Finally, they agreed that the new body should convene for the first time the following spring in San Francisco, California.

Roosevelt, mindful of Woodrow Wilson's failure to take Republicans to Versailles, appointed a bipartisan delegation to go to San Francisco, including Republican Arthur Vandenberg of Michigan, one of the most respected members of the Senate. Vandenberg's support would be crucial, and Roosevelt knew it.

Two weeks before the San Francisco meeting was to begin, Franklin D. Roosevelt died. Moments after taking the oath of office, Harry S. Truman made his first presidential

United Nations

An international organization launched at the end of World War II with leadership from the United States, the Soviet Union, Great Britain, and China.

American Voices

United Nations Universal Declaration of Human Rights, 1948

Three years after the United Nations was created, a UN Commission on Human Rights, chaired by former First Lady Eleanor Roosevelt, proposed a Universal Declaration of Human Rights. By 1948, the Cold War between the United States and the Soviet Union was fully under way, and few expected the Commission on Human Rights to accomplish much. But Eleanor Roosevelt was able to calm the waters enough to get the document approved. While the Universal Declaration of Human Rights had no enforcement mechanism, it set a new standard of international behavior against which every nation could be measured.

PREAMBLE

Whereas recognition of the inherent dignity and of the equal and inalienable rights of all members of the human family is the foundation of freedom, justice and peace in the world,

Whereas disregard and contempt for human rights have resulted in barbarous acts which have outraged the conscience of mankind, and the advent of a world in which human beings shall enjoy freedom of speech and belief and freedom from fear and want has been proclaimed as the highest aspiration of the common people,

Whereas it is essential, if man is not to be compelled to have recourse, as a last resort, to rebellion against tyranny and oppression, that human rights should be protected by the rule of law,

Whereas it is essential to promote the development of friendly relations between nations,

Whereas the peoples of the United Nations have in the Charter reaffirmed their faith in fundamental human rights, in the dignity

and worth of the human person and in the equal rights of men and women and have determined to promote social progress and better standards of life in larger freedom,

Whereas Member States have pledged themselves to achieve, in co-operation with the United Nations, the promotion of universal respect for and observance of human rights and fundamental freedoms,

Whereas a common understanding of these rights and freedoms is of the greatest importance for the full realization of this pledge,

Now, Therefore THE GENERAL ASSEMBLY proclaims THIS UNIVERSAL DECLARATION OF HUMAN RIGHTS as a common standard of achievement for all peoples and all nations.

The document then includes a total of thirty articles that elaborate the points in detail.

Source: Universal Declaration of Human Rights. General Assembly resolution 217 A www.un.org/en/documents/index.shtml, downloaded May 19, 2011.

Thinking Critically

1. **Contextualization**
   How did the Universal Declaration of Human Rights reflect failures that led to World War II?

2. **Analyzing Primary Sources**
   What do you think was Eleanor Roosevelt's purpose in framing this document? What difference could such a document make in the future?

decision: the conference would go ahead as scheduled on April 25. Some thought the San Francisco conference would simply be a celebration of work already done, but new tensions, especially between the United States and the Soviet Union, almost scuttled the conference. Nevertheless, most Americans wanted the United Nations to be successful, and public opinion influenced the delegates, especially Vandenberg. On June 25, 1945, the delegates unanimously approved the UN Charter. On July 28, the U.S. Senate ratified the charter by a vote of 89 to 2. The United Nations was launched.

24.1 Quick Review

What would you argue were the most significant postwar changes domestically and internationally? How did the context of the war and postwar developments shape each change?

The Cold War Begins

24.2 Analyze the coming of the Cold War, tensions with the Soviet Union, and McCarthyism at home.

In 1945, most people in the United States admired the Soviet Union, even if American leaders had already become wary of Stalin and his government. After meeting Stalin for the

SPUTNIK / Alamy Stock Photo

This picture of American and Soviet soldiers in Germany soon after the Nazi surrender illustrates the friendship between the people of the two nations that developed during World War II but that ended very soon after the war was over.

first time at Tehran in late 1943, Roosevelt said, "I 'got along fine' with Marshall Stalin." Privately, however, he confided his doubts.

The two nations were allies in World War II. American wartime propaganda talked positively about "our valiant allies." The Soviet people had withstood a murderous onslaught by Nazi forces and a terrible siege at Stalingrad. The Soviet army had done most of the fighting against Nazi Germany in World War II. Few Americans knew much about Stalin's policies within Russia, including the deadly purges of political enemies or the mass starvation that resulted from efforts toward collectivist Russian agriculture in the 1930s. Yet within a year after World War II ended, the Soviet Union and the United States were engaged in a **Cold War** that lasted forty years, until the dissolution of the Soviet Union in the late 1980s. What happened to turn former allies against each other? And why did it happen so quickly? Historians still disagree on the answers, but the main events of the Cold War are clear.

The Hardening of Positions: Containment, the Truman Doctrine, the Marshall Plan, and the Berlin Airlift

From the beginning of their wartime alliance, the United States and the Soviet Union had very different goals in World War II. The Soviets wanted a permanent buffer zone between themselves and Germany, and they wanted to ensure that they obtained absolute control over the countries of Eastern Europe. Having suffered so much from the war, the Soviets were also determined to take all of the machinery, munitions, and art they could from Germany. The United States wanted a rapid post-Nazi German recovery. In 1942, Roosevelt told Soviet foreign minister V. M. Molotov that "there might be a proper time" to address the differences in war goals between the two nations, but in the midst of the war, FDR said, "the present was not the moment."

Within weeks of taking the oath of office, President Truman became convinced that the Soviets were violating promises they had made to Roosevelt and needed to be stopped. When he met with Foreign Minister Molotov for the first time, he was ready to show how tough an American president could be. When Molotov began the conversation with diplomatic chitchat, Truman immediately accused the Soviets of breaking promises they had

Cold War

The political and economic confrontation between the Soviet Union and the United States that dominated world affairs from 1946 to 1989.

made to FDR at the Yalta meeting. As Truman continued his tirade, Molotov responded, "I have never been talked to like that in my life," to which Truman responded, "Carry out your agreements and you won't get talked to like that." It was not an auspicious start to a new relationship. Truman later told friends, "I gave him the one-two, right to the jaw." Molotov and Stalin quickly concluded that Truman was reversing Roosevelt's policies, especially when Truman cut aid to the Soviet Union, claiming that, with the war in Europe over, they no longer needed it. But Stalin did not back down. Indeed, almost immediately after the Truman-Molotov meeting, Stalin asserted Communist control over the new governments of Poland, Romania, and Bulgaria.

In spite of Truman's tough tone with Molotov in April 1945, Truman knew that he had a weak hand in dealing with the Soviets. He sent one of Roosevelt's most trusted advisors to Moscow to try to build a better relationship, and then in July for the first—and only—time, he met face-to-face with Stalin in Potsdam, just outside the newly conquered Berlin. Truman and Stalin seemed to get on, and after the Potsdam meeting, Truman wrote, "I can deal with Stalin." The Americans agreed that Stalin had the right to dismantle factories in eastern Germany and move them to Russia and could arrange the government of Poland as he chose.

There were many reasons for these concessions. Most important, when the fighting in Europe ended, the Soviet army was in Eastern Europe and the American army was not. Truman knew that the American people had no stomach for maintaining an army in Europe after the war. Until the last day of the Potsdam meeting, Truman was not sure that the atomic bomb would work. Finally, with war still raging in the Pacific, Truman wanted the Soviets to keep their promise to attack Japan once the war in Europe was over.

In the year that followed the end of the war, however, both sides hardened their positions. In February and March 1946, new tensions flared. In a speech on February 9, Stalin said that the only key to future world peace was for "monopoly capitalism" to be replaced by communism around the world. Supreme Court Justice William Douglas called Stalin's speech a "Declaration of World War III."

A week later, George Kennan, a senior diplomat in the American embassy in Moscow, sent what came to be known as the "Long Telegram" to the U.S. State Department. This widely distributed document called the Soviet government an "Oriental despotism" in which Communist ideology was merely a "fig-leaf" covering tyranny at home and rapid expansion abroad. Kennan told his State Department superiors that the Soviet Union was "a political force committed fanatically to the belief that with the United States there can be no permanent modus vivendi [accommodation between disputing parties], that it is desirable and necessary that the internal harmony of our society be destroyed, the international authority of our state be broken." He suggested that the United States should adopt a policy of **containment**, acknowledging Soviet influence where it existed but taking all necessary steps to ensure that the influence did not spread into new areas of the globe. Containment of Soviet communism would come to define U.S. foreign policy for a long time under both Democratic and Republican administrations.

containment

The policy of resisting further expansion of the Soviet bloc through diplomacy and, if necessary, military action, developed in 1947–1948.

Two weeks later, Winston Churchill, no longer in office but still a revered war hero, gave a speech as Truman's guest at Westminster College in Missouri in which he said:

> From Stettin in the Baltic to Trieste in the Adriatic, an iron curtain has descended across the continent. From what I have seen of our Russian friends and allies during the war, I am convinced that there is nothing they admire so much as strength, and there is nothing for which they have less respect than weakness, especially military weakness.

iron curtain

A phrase coined by former British prime minister Winston Churchill in 1946 when describing the post–World War II division of Europe into two hostile segments.

The image of an **"iron curtain"** dividing Europe became one of the central images of the Cold War. The call for military strength to counter Soviet strength became the foundation of a massive arms race on both sides of the iron curtain.

Although Democratic and Republican leaders generally supported an anti-Soviet policy, not everyone in the United States agreed that a Cold War with the Soviet Union was inevitable. Three senators issued a statement saying, "Mr. Churchill's proposal would cut the throat of the Big Three, without which the war could not have been won and without which the peace cannot be saved." Former vice president Henry Wallace, by then secretary of commerce, insisted that it was important for the United States to "allay any reasonable Russian grounds for fear, suspicion, and distrust." Privately, Truman called these critics of Churchill's speech "the American Crackpots Association."

As 1946 came to an end, more Americans were coming to the conclusion that Stalin was an evil dictator and the Soviet Union could not be trusted. Truman decided that his administration needed to speak with a single voice and dropped Wallace and Secretary of State James Byrnes from the cabinet, replacing the latter with George Marshall, who was U.S. chief of staff during the war. A year later Truman also sponsored a reorganization of the nation's military forces in which the previously separate cabinet-level War and Navy departments were merged into a single Department of Defense that was responsible for all military matters. Truman was quickly concluding that the end of World War II did not mean the end of the need for U.S. military strength.

Meanwhile, in early 1947, Greece was in the midst of a civil war between its government and Communist forces, and Turkey was resisting Soviet demands for greater control of access to the eastern Mediterranean and the Middle East. Great Britain, which had been providing support for both governments, said it could no longer afford to do so. Truman, Marshall, and Marshall's deputy, Dean Acheson, agreed that the United States needed to step in to take Britain's place in supporting resistance to communism in the region. If the containment policy meant anything, it certainly meant stopping Soviet moves into places like Greece and Turkey. The **Truman Doctrine** made it clear that containing communism would be at the bedrock of U.S. foreign policy. Needing the support of a reluctant Congress, Truman appeared in person and said, "I believe that it must be the policy of the United States to support free peoples who are resisting attempted subjugation by armed minorities or by outside pressures."

In June, the administration announced plans for massive economic aid to Western Europe. The winter of 1946–1947 had been the worst in years. By spring, Europe was running dangerously low on coal and food. People were cold, hungry, and desperate. Secretary of State Marshall used a Harvard commencement speech to tell the world:

> Our policy is directed not against any country or doctrine, but against hunger, poverty, desperation, and chaos. … We know that in this trying period, between a war that is over and a peace that is not yet secure, the destitute and oppressed of the earth look chiefly to us for sustenance and support until they can again face life with self-confidence and self-reliance.

The speech was partly true. The humanitarian goals, a campaign against hunger, poverty, and desperation, were real. But the **Marshall Plan**, as it came to be called, was also directed against one country and its doctrine. People in the United States and in the Soviet Union knew that the goal of the Marshall Plan was to stop Soviet expansion in Western Europe. Congress funded $13.34 billion in U.S. aid for Europe between 1948 and 1952. People were fed, economies recovered, and western capitalist democracies were established.

Stalin saw the Truman Doctrine and the Marshall Plan as a direct assault. Some Americans, notably the now-out-of-office Henry Wallace, also thought it was a needless provocation. The Soviets quickly solidified the power of a pro-Soviet regime in Hungary and arranged a pro-Soviet coup in Czechoslovakia in February 1948. Then in June 1948, the Soviet Union closed off American, British, and French access to Berlin. Before World War II ended, the Soviet Union, Britain, the United States, and France had agreed that each of them would assume military authority not only in a different quadrant of Germany but also within a different quadrant in the city of Berlin, even though Berlin itself was deep inside the Soviet quadrant. The result was a divided Germany and a divided Berlin, a precarious situation especially for the former capital city (see Map 24-2, p. 728).

The Soviets saw Berlin as a useful pressure point in the Cold War. By closing off western access to the city, they could challenge the Truman Doctrine and the Marshall Plan. When they blocked all rail and highway access to Berlin in the spring of 1948, Truman decided to support the city with an airlift. In the days and weeks that followed, the **Berlin Airlift** sent hundreds of U.S. airplanes every day to Tempelhof Airport in the western sector of Berlin. The city was well supplied, and West Berlin withstood the siege. Eventually in May 1949,

Truman Doctrine

President Harry Truman's statement in 1947 that the United States should assist other nations that were facing external Communist pressure or internal revolution.

Marshall Plan

The European Recovery Program (1949), which provided U.S. economic assistance to European nations in large part to keep them out of the Soviet Union's sphere of influence.

Berlin Airlift

In 1948 and 1949, food and supplies delivered by air into Berlin to keep the city attached to Western Europe.

Map 24-2 A Divided Germany.

With the end of World War II, American, British, French, and Soviet forces each controlled a portion of Germany and a portion of the German capital city of Berlin as well as, temporarily, Austria. The arrangement would soon lead to a new crisis.

Occupation of Germany and Austria, 1946–1949

- Land annexed by Poland
- Land annexed by U.S.S.R.
- Iron Curtain

Virtually nonstop flights brought vital supplies to the city of Berlin and sustained it during its isolation from June 1948 until May 1949.

the Soviet Union relented and reestablished access to Berlin. Nevertheless, by the beginning of 1949, the iron curtain that Churchill had described was more firmly in place than ever, and the Cold War, which had been developing since 1945, was a reality.

1949—The Soviet Atom Bomb and the Fall of China

Just as the crisis in Berlin was coming to an end, the U.S. Senate ratified American membership in the North Atlantic Treaty Organization (NATO) by an 82 to 13 vote in July 1949. Fearing a Soviet invasion of Western Europe, twelve nations, led by the United States and Britain, created the NATO alliance, in which each member agreed to treat an attack on any one from any source—though only one source was feared—as an attack on all. There would be no repeat of Nazi Germany's attacks on the nations of Europe, one after another. The NATO treaty was the first time in history that the United States agreed to such a peacetime partnership.

In 1955, when the Federal Republic of Germany, or West Germany, was created out of the merged British, French, and U.S. occupation zones and admitted to NATO, the Soviet Union formed the Warsaw Pact—a military alliance in Eastern Europe specifically designed to counter NATO with the same guarantees of mutual assistance for its members, all of whom were under tight control by the Soviet Union. NATO and the Warsaw Pact would be more powerful entities in the coming decades than the United Nations (see Map 24-3, p. 730).

Two further events in the fall of 1949 sped the growth of Cold War sentiment in the United States. First, in August, the Russians exploded their own atomic bomb. Soon after this development, the government of the U.S. wartime ally Chiang Kai-shek was defeated by Chinese Communists. The creation of the Communist People's Republic of China under the leadership of Mao Zedong and the flight of Chiang's government to the island of Taiwan was a huge blow to American pride even though the United States continued to recognize the Taiwan-based government as the official voice of China until the 1970s. Chiang's government had been an important symbol to Americans since the Japanese invasion of China in the 1930s, and the United States had spent almost $3 billion to help Chiang since the end of World War II. Americans had tended to ignore the corruption and inefficiency of Chiang's Nationalist government. An internal U.S. State Department paper written in August 1949

24.1

24.2

24.3

Map 24-3 A Divided Europe.

As the Cold War escalated, countries within NATO and those within the Warsaw Pact, with few neutral nations, made up the new Europe.

- Members of NATO (1949)
- Members of Warsaw Pact (1955)
- Nonaligned counties
- $ Participants in the Marshall Plan, 1947–1952
- Year first atomic device was tested by that country

U.S loan of $3.5 billion, 1946

Berlin blockade, 1948–1949

Communist coup, 1948
USSR invasion, 1968

Anti-Communist revolution failed, 1956

Joined NATO, 1955

Withdrew forces from NATO, 1966

Zones of occupation ended, 1955

Tito–Stalin Schism, 1948

Joined NATO, 1982

Withdrew from Warsaw Pact, 1968

Truman Doctrine, 1947
joined NATO, 1952

just before the fall of Chiang's government said, "The unfortunate but inescapable fact is that the ominous result of the civil war in China was beyond the control of the government of the United States." However, many Americans—in Congress, in the media, and around the country—were convinced that the United States had somehow "lost China" and that the Truman administration was at fault. It was a sour time in a country that was not used to losses.

The Cold War at Home—Joseph McCarthy and a New Red Scare

As Americans tried to make sense of the Cold War, the Soviet manufacture of an atomic bomb, and the Communist takeover in China, some looked for internal enemies to blame, and some in Congress sought political gain by fomenting a new Red Scare similar to the one that had followed World War I (see Chapter 21).

On January 21, 1950, Alger Hiss, a former State Department official who had been with FDR at Yalta and who helped organize the United Nations, was accused of having been a spy for the Soviets in the 1930s. One week later, Klaus Fuchs, an atomic scientist, was arrested in London and accused of turning over nuclear secrets to the Soviets. Fuchs implicated several Americans, including David Greenglass; Greenglass's sister, Ethel Rosenberg; and her husband, Julius Rosenberg. And little more than a week after the arrest of Fuchs, Wisconsin senator Joseph McCarthy gave a speech in Wheeling, West Virginia, in which he claimed to have a list of active Communist Party members who worked for the federal government. People began to suspect Communist infiltration everywhere. The nation was in for five years of fear and suspicion.

Although the Communist Party in the United States was tiny, during the Great Depression, thousands of Americans had considered communism as an alternative to the nation's battered economic system. During World War II, the Soviet Union was America's close ally in the fight against Nazi Germany. Before 1945, no one could have anticipated that helping the Soviets would be such a serious crime later in the decade.

Like many State Department officials, Alger Hiss was from the highest social stratum, making him an ideal choice for those who wanted to whip up class resentment as well as anticommunism. When Hiss was accused of passing state secrets to the Soviets, he insisted on testifying under oath in front of Congress, a move that opened Hiss to a charge of libel, and even though he was never convicted of espionage, he was eventually convicted of lying under oath to Congress and served three years in prison. More recently available documents show that Hiss had probably been a Communist in the 1930s, but when politicians like Republican representative Karl Mundt of South Dakota said that the conviction proved that the United States "had been run by New Dealers, Fair Dealers, Misdealers and Hiss dealers," they were lumping into the same category an awful lot of other people who had never even flirted with communism. Mundt's comment did prove that deep resentment of the New Deal and of the eastern elite was alive and well and could easily be linked with fears of the growing international influence of communism in the late 1940s.

In 1951, Greenglass and the Rosenbergs were charged with being Soviet spies and with passing on atomic secrets to the Soviets. Greenglass worked at the top-secret Manhattan Project, Julius Rosenberg was a wartime engineer, and both had access to highly secret data. They were also Jewish, and even though Americans were horrified by the Holocaust, anti-Semitism was alive and well in the United States in the 1950s. Just as Hiss suffered for his East Coast elite status, Greenglass and the Rosenbergs suffered for being Jewish. In the end, Greenglass served a long prison term. Ethel and Julius Rosenberg, who always maintained their innocence, were executed in 1953, the only Americans ever executed under the 1917 Espionage Act. (In the 1990s, when Soviet archives were opened and when another one of the accused coconspirators, Morton Sobell, admitted that he had, indeed, been a spy, it seemed clear that at least Julius, if not Ethel, had been a Soviet spy.) It was also clear that in the atmosphere of 1950 and 1951, it was virtually impossible for them to get a fair trial.

Senator Joseph McCarthy was not the first elected official to try to make political gains by stirring up the fear of communism, but he stole the leadership from all the others. He had been searching for a new political issue on which to build his reelec-

CSU Archives/Everett Collection/Newscom

Senator Joseph McCarthy lectured widely on the Communist menace. Although he gave few details, he successfully created great fear. In this image, he exhibits a photograph that he claims is evidence of Communist infiltration during a Senate investigation in 1954.

tion campaign in Wisconsin, and in February 1950, he thought he had found it when he heard the national reaction to a speech in which he said, "I have here in my hand a list of 205—a list of names that were made known to the Secretary of State as being members of the Communist Party who nevertheless are still working and shaping policy in the State Department."

McCarthy was far more interested in his own fame than in actually finding Communists. His Senate colleagues knew him as a pathological liar who had lied about his military service (he said he had flown thirty combat missions when he had flown none; his limp was not from shrapnel, as he claimed, but from a fall), and he embarrassed them. He drank heavily, fanned the flames of homophobia, and attacked both Republicans and Democrats whom he thought were "soft on communism." Nevertheless, few were willing to challenge McCarthy while the country was caught up in the fear of communism.

McCarthy said, "The government is full of Communists" who had "lost" China. For those who believed that only Communist agents in America could have led to the growth of Communist influence around the world, McCarthy was the perfect voice. In June 1951, he described what he called "a conspiracy, a conspiracy on a scale so immense as to dwarf any previous such venture in the history of man." McCarthy never did name the names on his list, and the numbers kept shifting in different speeches, but he ruined careers and frightened many into silence. His popularity seemed to protect him. In May 1950, a Gallup poll showed that 84 percent of Americans knew who McCarthy was and 39 percent believed that his attacks were good for the country. Few political leaders were willing to challenge him. However, in June 1950, Maine's Republican senator Margaret Chase Smith and six colleagues issued a "Declaration of Conscience," saying that McCarthy was using the Senate as a "publicity platform for irresponsible sensationalism." Still he continued for four more years.

When he became president in 1953, Eisenhower did not challenge McCarthy directly, but helped those who wanted to undermine him. In 1954, Edward R. Murrow, perhaps the most respected journalist in the country, did an exposé on McCarthy on his *See It Now* program on CBS television. Both the Senate declaration and the CBS program hurt McCarthy's reputation, but it was only when McCarthy decided to probe for Communists in the U.S. Army that he met his match. As the army's attorney Joseph Welch grilled him, McCarthy accused a young attorney on Welch's team of being a Communist because he was a member of the left-leaning National Lawyers Guild. Welch exploded, "Until this moment Senator, I think I never really gauged your cruelty or your recklessness." The hearing room burst into applause. After that, on December 2, 1954, the Senate voted to condemn McCarthy by a vote of 67 to 22. He continued to serve out his term until his death in 1957, but he was no longer a force in national politics.

McCarthy was hardly the only leader of the Red Scare of the late 1940s and early 1950s. J. Edgar Hoover, who had been head of the Federal Bureau of Investigation (FBI) since 1924 and a participant in the government's attack on radicals after World War I, cultivated a reputation as the nation's top crime fighter, especially after FBI agents killed John Dillinger, "Public Enemy Number One," during Prohibition. But Hoover also cultivated a role as a leading anti-Communist, seeking to expose what he claimed was Communist influence in the government, universities, religious groups, and later, civil rights organizations. He collected files on hundreds of Americans, from members of Congress to union officials. Although President Truman complained about Hoover, insisting, "We want no Gestapo or Secret Police," he did not stop Hoover.

Others in Congress realized that the search for Communists could lead to electoral success. The **House Committee on Un-American Activities (HUAC)** became their forum. One of its members, John Rankin, a Democrat from Mississippi, linked communism, Jews, and civil rights workers, saying of the Civil Rights Movement, "This is part of the communistic program, laid down by Stalin approximately thirty years ago. Remember communism is Yiddish. I understand that every member of the Politburo around Stalin is either Yiddish or married to one, and that includes Stalin himself." A young Republican Representative from California, Richard M. Nixon, used HUAC to investigate Hiss, look for Communists in government, and extend the search into the entertainment industry and education.

House Committee on Un-American Activities (HUAC)

Congressional committee (1938–1975) that investigated suspected Nazi and Communist sympathizers.

While some in the entertainment world quickly cooperated with HUAC, many fought back. Judy Garland, one of the nation's most popular stars since her childhood role in the *Wizard of Oz*, pleaded, "Before every free conscience in America is subpoenaed, please speak up!" Frank Sinatra asked, "Once they get the movies throttled … how long will it be before we're told what we can say and cannot say into the radio microphone? If you make a pitch on a nationwide radio network for a square deal for the underdog, will they call you a Commie? … Are they going to scare us into silence?" Undeterred, HUAC continued with its hearings. Many witnesses refused to testify on the Fifth Amendment grounds that they could not be compelled to testify against themselves. Ten actors, known as the Hollywood Ten, took the more difficult route of claiming that the hearings threatened their First Amendment rights of free speech. The ten and others were blacklisted and had their careers ruined, in spite of efforts by the Committee for the First Amendment led by Humphrey Bogart, Lauren Bacall, Katharine Hepburn, and Danny Kaye to protect them.

24.1

24.2

24.3

Thinking Historically

Looking at the Art of the Postwar Nation

In his book, the *Unfinished City: New York and the Metropolitan Idea*, historian Thomas Bender wrote, "Intellectual historians have failed to grasp the variety of artistic and critical work that characterized the 1940s, partly because concerns of the Cold War era gave precedence to certain ideological themes and political trends." Bender argued that it was also important to pay attention to the "remarkable creativity and critical discourse in the fields of painting and sculpture, photography, architecture, music, and dance."

As Bender observed, while many focused on the Cold War, others were using the arts to ask different questions about American life and the threat of nuclear disaster. Often, artists were pointing to the confusions—some said pointlessness—of contemporary thinking as much or more than they were making overt statements about political ideology.

James Agee, himself a very well-known author, was the film critic for the *Nation* magazine in the late 1940s. In a 1948 review he wrote:

> Several of the best people in Hollywood grew, noticeably, during their years away at war; the man who grew most impressively, I thought, as an artist, as a man, in intelligence, and in an ability to put through fine work against difficult odds, was [film director] John Huston. … His first movie since the war has been a long time coming, but it was certainly worth waiting for. *The Treasure of the Sierra Madre* is … about as near to folk art as a highly conscious artist can get. … I doubt we shall ever see a film more masculine in style; or a truer movie understanding of character and of men.

As a generation of young men returned from the fighting of the war and took up their day-to-day lives in the civilian workforce, some worried that perhaps they had left their masculinity behind on the battlefields. Artists, like the film director John Huston, addressed these fears. While the films of the late 1940s and early 1950s were, like all films, meant to entertain, they also helped

The abstract artist Jackson Pollock painted *Convergence* in 1952. Like most abstract art, the complex work leaves it to the beholder to make meaning of the lines and colors the artist has depicted.

some in the audience think through some of their greatest hopes and fears.

Source: Thomas Bender, *Unfinished City: New York and the Metropolitan Idea* (New York: New York University Press, 2002), pp. 135–136; James Agee, "The Treasure of the Sierra Madre," *The Nation*, January 31, 1948.

Thinking Critically

1. **Analyzing Secondary Sources**
   What is Bender's purpose, as an historian, when he asks us to focus on the "remarkable creativity and critical discourse in the fields of painting and sculpture, photography, architecture, music, and dance" in understanding the immediate postwar years? In your opinion, what can a period's art tell us about people's concerns? What sort of ideas might one see in an abstract painting or a film about masculinity?

2. **Argument Development**
   How would you explain the emergence of abstract art in the era of the atomic bomb after World War II in place of the much more realistic paintings of the 1930s?

Many labor unions purged Communist members. Aspiring new leaders used the accusation of Communist influence to push aside older leaders. The United Electrical Workers union was replaced by a new union—the International Brotherhood of Electrical Workers—because the United Electrical was considered to be Communist and was expelled by the American Federation of Labor. Civil rights organizations, including the Urban League, the Congress of Racial Equality, and the National Association for the Advancement of Colored People (NAACP), purged Communist members. Many school districts and twenty-one states required loyalty oaths from teachers. In 1948, the University of Washington fired three professors when they refused to answer questions about the Communist Party. Some thirty-one professors were ultimately fired from the University of California under similar circumstances. And the American Federation of Teachers, the leading union of elementary and secondary teachers, voted that Communists should not be allowed to be members or teach in the nation's schools.

Not everyone was caught up in the Red Scare hysteria. Philip Murray, president of the Congress of Industrial Organizations, one of the nation's largest unions, wrote to President Truman in 1947 to protest that government policy did not ensure due process for accused employees. Secretary of the Treasury John Snyder protested the government's Loyalty Review Board in 1948.

George Kennan, who had played an important role in launching the Cold War, added a somber note in his *Memoirs*: "What the phenomenon of McCarthyism did ... was to implant in my consciousness a lasting doubt as to the adequacy of our political system. ... I could never recapture after these experiences of the 1940s and 1950s, quite the same faith in the American system of government and in traditional American outlooks that I had, despite all the discouragements of official life, before that time." Not everyone shared Kennan's pessimism, but many felt that American democracy itself had been wounded by the Red Scare.

War in Korea

On June 25, 1950, to the surprise of U.S. leaders, the army of North Korea attacked South Korea. Korea was a part of the world to which U.S. planners had paid very little attention. But it was the place where the Cold War turned very hot.

With the Japanese defeat in 1945, the victorious allies determined to honor Korean hopes for independence. U.S. military authorities used the same formula as they had for Germany: a divided military occupation that was meant to be temporary. Military planners agreed that the Soviet army would occupy Korea north of the 38th parallel (North Korea) and that U.S. forces would occupy the southern half of the peninsula, including the old capital of Seoul (South Korea), until a permanent plan for national unification could be achieved. It would be a long wait.

The United States backed a new government led by the seventy-five-year-old Syngman Rhee, who was conservative, charming, fiercely independent, as well as corrupt and dictatorial. The Soviets backed an even more dictatorial thirty-one-year-old Communist, Kim Il-Sung. Both Rhee and Kim were committed to Korean unification, but on very different terms. Between the end of World War II and 1950, constant clashes between the two governments cost the lives of perhaps 100,000 Koreans.

At the same time, the Truman administration, worried that the United States was spread too thin, and seeing Korea as of only marginal significance, withdrew the U.S. military, leaving Rhee's government on its own. A year later in 1950, in a speech he later regretted, Secretary of State Dean Acheson described the U.S. "defensive perimeter" in Asia in a way that did not include either Korea or Taiwan. Stalin and the North Korean dictator Kim Il-Sung assumed that the United States was not prepared to defend South Korea. Kim pressed Stalin to approve an attack and Stalin agreed, though he warned Kim, "[I]f you get kicked in the teeth, I shall not lift a finger." It was all the permission Kim needed. On June 25, 100,000 North Korean troops, supported by tanks, artillery, and planes, invaded the South.

The Communist leaders had misread U.S. intentions. Truman viewed the Korean invasion through the prism of British and French inaction in the face of Nazism. He was determined to maintain the Truman Doctrine of containment of communism anywhere in the world.

Secretary Acheson appealed to the United Nations Security Council for UN action to stop the North Koreans. It was a propitious moment to do so. In 1949, the Soviet delegate to the United Nations, Jacob Malik, had started boycotting the Security Council because that body continued to give the Nationalist Chinese government of Chiang Kai-shek the UN vote even though the Communist government ruled mainland China. The protest meant that the Soviet Union could not veto Security Council resolutions, and Acheson got a unanimous vote in favor of UN action. The Korean War was called a UN police action, although nearly all of the fighting was done by U.S. and Korean troops.

Public opinion polls showed solid support for American action, and people as diverse as Republican governor of New York Thomas Dewey and liberal Henry Wallace (both of whom had run against Truman in the 1948 presidential election) supported Truman. Congress appropriated $10 billion.

Truman ordered General Douglas MacArthur, then commander of U.S. troops occupying Japan, to take command in Korea, and troops were rushed to Korea. Meanwhile, the North Koreans kept coming. By September, three months after the war began, U.S. and South Korean forces controlled only a small section of southeast Korea around the port of Pusan, known as the Pusan perimeter. Slowly, however, the U.S. forces were built up and supplies brought into Korea. American planes bombed North Korean troops heavily. The bombing wreaked havoc on Communist supply lines and destroyed rice fields. Perhaps half the invading North Korean army were killed or wounded in the first two months of the war, and most of the North Korean tanks were disabled. Two to three million Korean civilians, 10 percent of the prewar population of Korea, died either from bombing or from starvation because of lost rice crops.

In September 1950, under MacArthur's command, the U.S. and UN forces made a surprise amphibious landing at Inchon, on the west coast of Korea close to the 38th parallel. The Communist forces were cut off from their supplies and captured or forced to retreat. The tide of war suddenly turned, and in less than a month, the Americans advanced from the small perimeter to retake South Korea (see Map 24-4, p. 736).

For MacArthur, the initial victory was only the beginning. He insisted, and Truman agreed, that the moment had come to unify the whole Korean peninsula under Syngman Rhee. The UN, with the Soviets still boycotting, agreed and MacArthur's forces began moving north, closer to the Chinese border at the Yalu River. MacArthur was confident that he could win the war and be home by December. When Truman asked about the chance of a Chinese intervention, MacArthur responded, "Very little." He was wrong.

By late November, as MacArthur's army continued north, a huge Chinese army attacked them. "The Chinese have come in with both feet," Truman said. This time it was the Americans that had long, drawn-out supply lines. They were ill-prepared for the freezing cold of a Korean winter. The Chinese wore warm padded clothing, had fought for years in similar territory, and were adept at terrifying hand-to-hand night fighting when American planes and troops could not see them. The fighting in November and December 1950 was brutal. Soldiers were killed as they slept or froze in the winter cold. The retreats were frightful. The U.S. Army Seventh Infantry Division lost five thousand troops, one-third of its force, in a three-day retreat over mountainous roads as the

24.1

24.2

24.3

Bettmann/Getty Images

U.S. troops bogged down in the snow and cold of Korea found the war far more difficult to fight than had been expected.

24.1

24.2

24.3

Map 24-4 The Korean War.

At the beginning and end of the Korean War, the peninsula was divided into two nations at the 38th parallel. However, between 1950 and 1953, the dividing line moved many times as indicated.

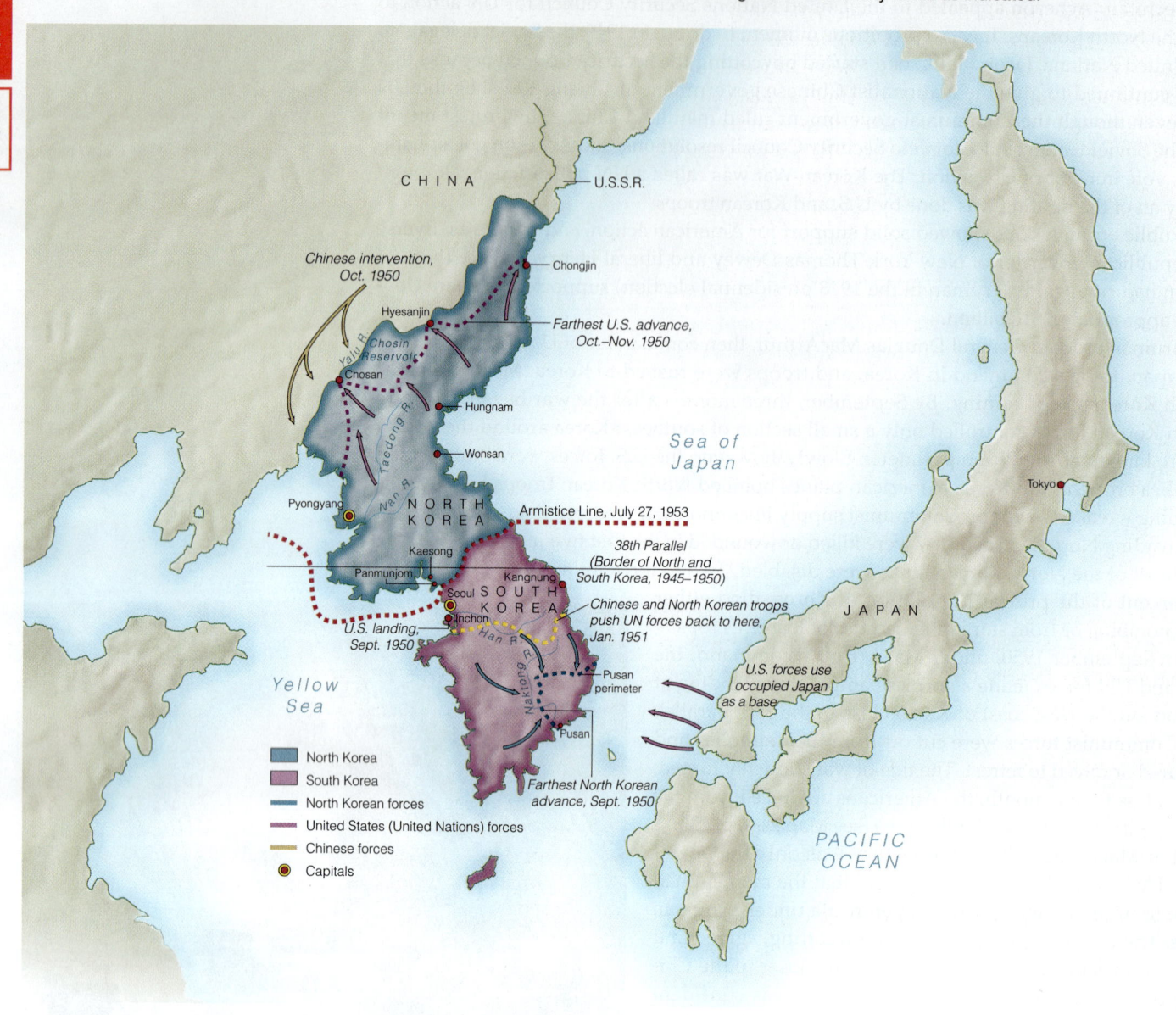

Chinese attacked from every angle. By January 1951, the line dividing the two armies was well south of the 38th parallel. The war settled into a bloody stalemate.

For Truman, the defeats in Korea at the end of 1950 were a diplomatic and a political disaster. Republicans now saw him as weak. Some urged the use of atomic weapons on China. General MacArthur, whom Truman despised, had strong Republican support. (MacArthur's fellow senior officers had their own opinions. When General Eisenhower was asked if he had met MacArthur, he responded, "Not only have I met him. … I studied dramatics under him.") In early 1951, MacArthur bypassed Truman and tried to get congressional support for a wider war. Truman had had enough. With support from the Joint Chiefs of Staff, he fired MacArthur, who had been a hero to many. Army Chief of Staff General Omar Bradley was more concerned with Europe and fearful of a land war in Asia. Bradley said Korea was the "wrong war, at the wrong place, at the wrong time, and with the wrong enemy." The new commander in Korea, General Matthew Ridgway, stabilized the defense lines and arranged better support and supplies for the troops.

The Chinese and American governments became resigned to a partial victory. Neither wanted a larger war, no matter what the two Korean governments thought. Battles for places the American troops called "Heartbreak Ridge," or "No-Name Ridge," described how those on the ground thought about what they were doing. Armistice negotiations began in the summer of 1951, but stalled over the fact that many Chinese and North Korean prisoners did not want to be returned home. It would take two more years, and the election of a new U.S. president, before the final armistice was signed in July 1953. More than 36,000 Americans were killed in the war, many times more Korean and Chinese troops, and probably three million Korean civilians. The final armistice line was not far from where the prewar line had been near Panmunjom. Well over sixty years later, Korea is still a tense and divided place.

> **24.2**   Quick Review
>
> How did changing attitudes toward, and experiences with, the Soviet Union between 1945 and 1949 contribute to major changes in U.S. foreign policy?

Politics, 1948 and 1952

24.3   Explain political developments that led to the elections of Truman and then Eisenhower as Cold War–era presidents.

When Harry Truman became president in April 1945, few Americans knew much about him. Many expected Truman to merely serve out the term to which Roosevelt had been elected. Truman decided otherwise, but he had a lot of time and a lot of responsibility to manage before any thought of reelection loomed.

Riding a Tiger—Truman's First Term

As war and foreign policy dominated Truman's first months in office, Truman said he felt like he was riding a tiger. The liberal wing of the Democratic Party included New Deal activists such as Secretary of Commerce Henry Wallace and Secretary of the Interior Harold Ickes, who never trusted Truman, viewing him as a product of Missouri machine politics who had been forced on FDR by the conservative wing of the party. Truman reciprocated the distrust. Looking ahead to the postwar world, Truman told Clark Clifford, one of his key advisors, "I don't want any experiments. The American people have been through a lot of experiments, and they want a rest from experiments." But Truman was not proposing any sort of Warren Harding "normalcy."

On September 6, 1945, just four days after the Japanese surrender, Truman proposed legislation that would implement FDR's Economic Bill of Rights, expanding the federal role in public housing, public utilities, job creation, and national health, increasing the minimum wage, offering Social Security benefits to more people, while also making the Fair Employment Practices Commission permanent. It was a sweeping agenda, delighting liberals and dismaying conservatives. Southern segregationists filibustered the fair employment bill that would have continued FDR's executive order, ensuring that employers with federal contracts could not discriminate among employees on the basis of race, and kept it from reaching a vote. Other bills were watered down by Congress. Congress turned Truman's effort to launch a national system of health insurance into the Hill-Burton Act that benefited doctors and hospitals and private medical insurers, but did not guarantee health insurance.

While there was Democratic as well as Republican opposition to Truman's domestic agenda, the president's single most powerful opponent was Ohio senator Robert Taft, the son of the former president, known to many as "Mr. Republican." Taft not only opposed Truman's agenda but also pushed legislation that reduced taxes, forcing cuts in government programs, and persuaded Congress in 1947, over Truman's veto, to pass the Taft-Hartley

Act, which lifted many of the protections organized labor had enjoyed since the passage of the Wagner Act in the 1930s.

Taft was not alone. The Republican Party was strong. Just as after World War I, many Americans simply wanted to be left alone. In the 1946 midterm elections, Republicans took control of both houses of Congress. But Harry Truman was a fighter, more of a fighter than some expected. His goal was to win a full term in his own right and elect a Democratic Congress in 1948, goals many thought unrealistic in 1946.

The 1948 Election—A Four-Way Contest

In planning his campaign for 1948, Truman sought to maintain and expand the New Deal coalition that had elected Roosevelt four times. He wanted to have a large plurality among white blue-collar workers, immigrant groups, farmers, and poor people. He made special efforts to court African Americans and Jews. In 1946, he appointed a President's Committee on Civil Rights and its report, released in October 1947, led him to propose an antilynching law, a permanent fair employment commission, and laws against poll taxes and discrimination in transportation. When the Republican Congress failed to pass these and other legislation, Truman called them "the do-nothing Congress." Under pressure from civil rights leaders, Truman overruled the objections of some of the nation's highest-ranking military officers and ordered the desegregation of the nation's armed forces in 1948. It would take several years before the last segregated regiments were phased out, but the process was under way for a dramatic change from the segregated military of World War II.

Truman also favored the establishment of an independent state of Israel. On this issue, there was deep disagreement within the administration. Secretary of State Marshall threatened to resign if the United States gave support to Israel, and most leaders of the State, Army, and Navy departments opposed recognizing the new nation. They feared that the United States would permanently alienate the Arab world, jeopardize the smooth flow of oil to the United States and Europe, and create a situation that would remain tense and untenable. The White House staff tended to support creation of a Jewish state in the Middle East. Truman's own reading about the Holocaust and Middle Eastern history led him to support Israel. He got— and occasionally resented—considerable pressure from American Zionists. Thirty-three state legislatures passed resolutions favoring the establishment of a Jewish state. Truman responded to one anxious State Department official, saying, "I have to answer to hundreds of thousands who are anxious for the success of Zionism. I do not have hundreds of thousands of Arabs among my constituents." On May 14, as the last British forces left Palestine, Zionists proclaimed the independent state of Israel. At Truman's direction, the United States immediately recognized the new government. To the surprise of many, Israel was able to defend itself successfully against an Arab attack and secure its borders and its existence.

Truman's policies from fair employment to his support for Israel also had an impact on American voters. While many African Americans were moving into the Democratic Party and most Jewish voters were prepared to support Truman, especially after his May 1948 decisions, the road to nomination and election that year was not easy. Many New Dealers in the Democratic Party still hoped for a more liberal or a more popular candidate.

When it became clear that Truman would win the nomination—and invite Senate leader Alben Barkley to be his running mate—Henry Wallace, former vice president and commerce secretary, bolted and set up the Progressive Party to defeat Truman, end the Cold War, and return the country to what he saw as the Roosevelt legacy.

Then, when Truman supported a platform plank supporting civil rights, introduced by Minnesota senator Hubert Humphrey at the Democratic convention, thirty-five delegates from Alabama and Mississippi walked out of the convention waving Confederate flags and proceeded to nominate South Carolina's governor and future senator J. Strom Thurmond to run against Truman. These "Dixiecrats" were a serious threat to a party that always counted on the "solid South" to ensure national electoral victories.

The Republicans, sensing that this was their year, especially with the divisions in the Democratic ranks, nominated Governor Thomas E. Dewey of New York, the 1944 standard bearer, with California governor Earl Warren as his running mate. The team seemed to have everything going for it and ran a cautious campaign designed to avoid mistakes. Unfortunately for the Republicans, they were too cautious and Dewey was too stiff. Alice Longworth, Theodore Roosevelt's daughter, called him "the little man on the wedding cake." The Wallace campaign never took off and gained little support, though it may have denied Truman the majority in a few crucial states, especially New York. The Thurmond campaign got virtually no support outside of the Deep South, though it did carry the electoral votes of four states—Alabama, Louisiana, Mississippi, and South Carolina. Truman waged a very tough and spirited campaign against the "do-nothing Congress" and the "Wall Street reactionaries." As he campaigned, people started yelling, "Give 'em hell, Harry!" He had solid support from organized labor and farmers and held most of the New Deal coalition together. Still, the Republicans, led by Dewey, were confident of victory. But when the votes were counted, Truman won, receiving 24,179,345 votes to Dewey's 21,991,291, and 303 electoral votes to Dewey's 189. Thurmond won 39 electoral votes. Wallace won none.

Many were confident of a Republican victory in the 1948 election, including the editors of the *Chicago Tribune*, who published this erroneous early edition over which the eventual winner, Harry S. Truman, delighted to gloat.

As he began his new term in January 1949, Truman called his agenda the **Fair Deal**. The Truman Fair Deal included repeal of the Taft-Hartley Act, support for family farmers, a more progressive income tax, federal aid to education, an increase in the minimum wage, national medical insurance as well as another try at broadening Social Security, and expanded civil rights. In his inaugural address, Truman also called for more U.S. technical assistance to developing countries. Technical assistance became known as Point Four because it was the fourth point in Truman's speech.

Even though the Democrats controlled both houses of Congress in 1949, virtually none of the Fair Deal legislation passed. Southern Democrats made sure there was no movement on civil rights, organized labor did not have enough support to overturn the Taft-Hartley Act, urban representatives saw little value in spending federal tax money on farmers, and the American Medical Association made sure that there was no national system of medical insurance such as most Western European countries adopted after World War II. Point Four foreign aid passed, but the appropriations were small and the resulting technical assistance generally insignificant. Much of Truman's second term was focused on the war in Korea—which the Congress was willing to fund—and the ongoing Red Scare, which Truman did little to oppose.

Fair Deal

The name President Harry Truman gave to his policies to continue and extend many of the New Deal's domestic policies.

A War Hero Becomes President

In a belated slap at Franklin Roosevelt, the Republican Congress passed the Twenty-Second Amendment to the Constitution in 1947, which prohibited a president from serving more than two terms. A majority of states ratified the amendment. The amendment did not apply to the sitting president, and Truman considered seeking a third term. When he was defeated in the first primaries by Estes Kefauver, a crusading senator from Tennessee, however, Truman decided that two terms was enough and dropped out of the race. In spite of his spirited come-from-behind race in 1948 and his later reputation as a tough decision maker, Truman was not a widely popular president.

The most popular person in the United States in the early 1950s was Dwight David Eisenhower, known to everyone as Ike. Born in 1890 and raised in Abilene, Kansas, by pacifist parents, Eisenhower had attended West Point, seeing it as a free education for a career in engineering. Instead, he became a long-term officer in the peacetime army between the wars, moving slowly through the ranks. He was still a colonel when World War II began but was then promoted rapidly and commanded the Allied force that defeated Nazi Germany. He probably could have had the presidential nomination of either party in 1948 but opted to become president of Columbia University and then commander of NATO forces in Europe in 1951. He managed to convey a disinterested, "above the fray" persona. Some who knew him better saw another side. General George Patton said, "Ike wants to be President so badly you can taste it."

24.1

24.2

24.3

Although Eisenhower had served as a senior military commander under Democrats—Roosevelt and Truman—and was an internationalist on foreign policy matters, he was a fiscal conservative, and the New Deal and Fair Deal programs offended his sense of the proper role of the federal government. If he was going to run, it would be as a Republican. Liberals within the Republican Party, including the 1944 and 1948 standard bearer Thomas Dewey and Massachusetts senator Henry Cabot Lodge, were desperate to find an internationalist candidate who could stop the Republican front-runner, Senator Taft, an isolationist in foreign policy and a conservative on domestic issues. They courted Eisenhower, who remained coy. However, primary voters preferred Ike to Taft: Ike defeated Taft 46,661 to 35,838 in the March New Hampshire primary even though he was still at NATO headquarters in Europe and did not campaign. After that primary, the momentum was hard to stop and Eisenhower was nominated by the Republicans in the summer of 1952—a bitter loss for Taft and his supporters.

Eisenhower asked California senator Richard M. Nixon to be his running mate. Although the two were not close, and never were, Nixon brought balance to the ticket. Nixon was thirty-eight; Ike was sixty-two. Nixon had made his name with his search for Communists when he was a member of the House Committee on Un-American Activities. He was from the West Coast, while Ike's strongest support was in the East.

Ike almost dumped Nixon at one point in the campaign because of charges that Nixon had a private campaign fund donated by wealthy Californians. Nixon gave what became known as his "Checkers" television speech for its maudlin promise to keep the family dog, named Checkers, even though the dog had been a gift. The speech was a success, and Nixon stayed on the ticket. For the rest of his career, even after his own presidency, Nixon celebrated the day of the speech. The Democrats nominated Illinois governor Adlai Stevenson. Like Eisenhower, Stevenson was a strong Cold Warrior and an internationalist who had been one of the founders of the United Nations. He had a reputation as an honest politician in a state where Democrats were often corrupt. He was more conservative than Truman on domestic issues, especially race, and he selected Alabama senator John Sparkman as his running mate, in part to ensure that there would be no Dixiecrat walkout in 1952. Stevenson was also very popular with many liberals, mostly because of his intelligence and wit. One said that his speeches were "simply gems of wisdom and wit and sense." Unfortunately for Stevenson, this skill mattered more to the party's intellectual elite than to many in the black urban working class that had been key to the election of Roosevelt and Truman.

The campaign was the first in which television played a major role. The Republicans made effective use of TV spots that carried brief comments by Ike along with his famous smile. Ike promised a nation that was desperately tired of the war, "I shall go to Korea." Many hoped that meant he would find a way to end the war, though it was unclear what he would actually do there. In November, Ike won 55 percent of the vote and carried the Electoral College 442 to 89, winning even Florida, Tennessee, Texas, and Virginia, states that had voted Democratic for decades. The Republicans won small majorities in Congress.

Eisenhower fulfilled his campaign promise and went to Korea two weeks after the election. It was a grueling seventy-three-hour trip in 1952. Wearing an army uniform with no insignia, Eisenhower visited troops and met with Syngman Rhee. He made it clear that there was "no panacea" to ending a long, dreary war. Early in his term, however, Ike was able to conclude the peace treaty that had eluded Truman. Korea remained divided, but the conflict ended.

Eisenhower intended to create what he called "Modern Republicanism." He kept the United States active in the UN and NATO. Under Ike, there would be no return to 1920s-style isolationism. He was determined to balance the federal budget and not likely to launch major new programs, but not roll back the major New Deal initiatives either. He once said, "Should any political party attempt to abolish social security, unemployment insurance, and eliminate labor laws and farm programs, you would not hear of that party again in our political history." He dismissed the conservative wing of the Republican Party, saying of the conservative California senator William Knowland, "In his case, there seems to be no final answer to the question, 'How stupid can you get?'"

With Eisenhower's election, a new Republican administration was prepared to maintain many of the New Deal's domestic policies and Truman's Cold War internationalism. Individuals changed, but surprisingly little policy changed after the inauguration.

Nevertheless, as the Great Depression and World War II receded and a new generation grew up with no memory of that difficult past, and as many Americans experienced unprecedented prosperity, the culture began to change. The 1950s were staid to some, surprisingly novel to others, and full of surprises for most.

24.1

24.2

24.3

24.3 Quick Review

Aside from their political parties, how different were Truman and Eisenhower as candidates and as presidents?

Conclusion

The experience of World War II had a profound effect on American society in the decades that followed. The federal government offered generous benefits to returning veterans, allowing a whole generation of young men to attend college, to buy homes, and to live comfortable middle-class lives. Men and women, anxious to leave the war behind, married quickly and had children, a lot of children. With the baby boom, the population soared.

In the postwar era, the living patterns of Americans changed drastically. Many middle-class white Americans left the cities for homes in newly created suburban communities. Many also moved farther west in the United States, leading to explosive growth in the Sun Belt. At the same time, the rate of migration of Southern blacks to the urban centers of the North exploded. Many black migrants moved into city centers because they were excluded from suburban developments. Latinos from Puerto Rico and Mexico also moved to cities, notably New York and Los Angeles. Consumers, who had more money and easier credit than ever, purchased goods produced by American manufacturers and achieved new levels of economic security and affluence, buying automobiles, televisions, and electric appliances in the postwar economy.

The end of World War II also brought on new attempts at international cooperation. In an effort to create political and economic stability and a lasting peace, the United Nations, the International Monetary Fund, and the World Bank were ushered into being.

While enjoying the remarkable prosperity of the postwar era, Americans worried about the Soviet Union—a World War II ally that quickly became a new enemy as the Soviets sought to spread communism and Soviet power around the world. The containment of communism became the bedrock of U.S. foreign policy in the Truman administration. By 1952, both the United States and the Soviet Union possessed hydrogen bombs, and the possibility of "mutually assured destruction" set off a Cold War between the two countries that would last forty years. In Europe, the Cold War was institutionalized in the western-led North Atlantic Treaty Organization and the Soviet-led Warsaw Pact. Within the United States itself, a new Red Scare was fueled by the fiery rhetoric of Senator Joseph McCarthy and others. Americans began to suspect Communist infiltration everywhere, and many personal and professional lives were ruined by accusations of treason, espionage, and Communist Party membership that often had little basis in reality.

In 1950, the American policy of containment was tested when North Korea attacked South Korea. The United States, with support from the United Nations, took up the defense of South Korea. After fierce fighting, the outcome of the war was ambiguous. With the election of a new president, Dwight Eisenhower, in November 1952, the United States and China signed an armistice that left Korea divided much as it had been since the end of World War II, and Americans settled into what many hoped would be a new era of peace and prosperity even as they continued to fear the Soviet Union and the mushroom cloud of atomic destruction.

Chapter Review

How did the actions of the United States after World War II reflect its new position as a world superpower?

Chapter 24 Summary and Review

The United States in 1945

24.1 **Describe the new technology, living patterns, and political arrangements in the United States that resulted from World War II.**

Summary

The transition from war to peace brought new challenges and new opportunities. Government investment in science continued after the war was over and led to important breakthroughs in medicine and technology. New technology found its way into homes in the form of new consumer products. Pent-up consumer demand created huge markets for American manufacturers. The negative side of scientific advance was reflected in the nuclear arms race between the United States and the Soviet Union. Aided by the GI Bill, returning veterans rushed to start new lives and new families. The 1950s saw building and baby booms. The West and Southwest were the fastest-growing regions in the country. While white Americans moved to the suburbs, African Americans moved from the South to the North, pushed by segregation and discrimination and pulled by the promise of better economic opportunities. The same decades saw significant Latino migration to the United States from Mexico and Puerto Rico. New international organizations helped establish the importance of the United States in the global political and economic order.

Review Questions

1. Causation
   How did advances in science and technology change everyday life for Americans in the 1950s?

2. Comparison
   Compare and contrast the migration of African Americans and Latinos in the 1950s. What similarities and differences do you note?

The Cold War Begins

24.2 **Analyze the coming of the Cold War, tensions with the Soviet Union, and McCarthyism at home.**

Summary

Even before World War II was over, tensions emerged between the United States and the Soviet Union over war goals and the shape of the postwar world. Many in the U.S. government became convinced that the Soviets were bent on rapid expansion. In the immediate aftermath of the war, tensions focused on the fate of Eastern Europe. The Truman Doctrine established containment as the foundation of U.S. foreign policy. The Marshall Plan strengthened the relationship between the United States and Western Europe, but it also contributed to the deterioration of relations with the Soviet Union. The creation of NATO, the Communist victory in the Chinese civil war, and the Soviet acquisition of atomic weapons all contributed to the hardening of Cold War divisions. The advent of the Cold War led to anti-Communist hysteria, which was manifested in the McCarthy hearings as well as the hearings of the House Committee on Un-American Activities. A brutal war in Korea brought the Cold War—and U.S. commitment—to Asia.

Review Questions

3. Comparison
   Compare and contrast the Red Scares that followed World War I and World War II. What similarities and differences do you note?

4. Argument Development
   What were the various forms that the new "containment" policy took in Europe and Asia, and what form did the reorganization of the military take?

Politics, 1948 and 1952

24.3 **Explain political developments that led to the elections of Truman and then Eisenhower as Cold War–era presidents.**

Summary

Truman's first months in office were dominated by war and foreign policy. His efforts to continue and expand Roosevelt's New Deal were blocked by Republicans and conservative Democrats. In the 1948 election, Truman tried to keep the New Deal coalition together and to run against the "do-nothing" Congress. The election turned into a four-man race, featuring Truman, Wallace, Dewey, and Thurmond. Despite winning reelection, Truman failed to get most of his Fair Deal agenda passed by Congress. During his eight years in office, Eisenhower established his own brand of Republican politics: carrying out interventionist approaches abroad and maintaining the status quo at home by keeping new initiatives to a minimum while leaving his Democratic predecessors' programs in place.

Review Question

5. Argument Development

Why do you think Truman is viewed favorably by many historians today but was not so popular with Americans in 1952?

1. Preparing to Write: Establish Context in Your Introduction

Long Essay Question—Evaluate the extent to which events from 1945 to 1952 changed the relationship between the United States and the Soviet Union.

Before you get to your thesis, it helps to discuss the historical context beforehand. For this question, start your introduction by discussing the enormous transition from World War II to peace and the new role for the United States. What had each side just gone through and what did each want in the postwar world?

2. Preparing to Write: Plan Your Argument

Long Essay Question—Evaluate the extent of continuity in causes and outcomes of the Great Migration from 1917 to 1952.

Start by designing a time line from 1917 to 1952. Above the time line, note what is changing, and below, note what is staying relatively constant. Most "Change and Continuity" questions tend to offer ample opportunity for students to discuss changes, but this one might be an opportunity to focus more on what is staying relatively constant: motivations to migrate and discrimination in the North. From here you can design a rough thesis and outline of your argument.

Chapter 25
Complacency and Change 1952–1965

Burt Glinn/Magnum Photos

Only the arrival of federal troops assured the integration of Little Rock High School in 1957.

Chapter Objective

Demonstrate an understanding of how different aspects of the 1950s, from the seeming complacency of Eisenhower's time to the growing Civil Rights Movement, reshaped the United States.

∨ Learning Objectives

Eisenhower's America, America's World

25.1 Explain the continuation of the Cold War under a new Republican administration.

A Culture on the Move

25.2 Explain the impact of cultural and technological changes on the country.

Race and Civil Rights

25.3 Analyze the growth and impact of the Civil Rights Movement between 1954 and 1965.

Dwight Eisenhower was the U.S. Supreme Commander in Europe when Harry Truman became president in the spring of 1945. In that role, he worked for Truman as he had for Roosevelt. But when Eisenhower decided to enter the Republican race for the White House and attacked Truman and the Democrats during the campaign, the relationship between the two men was deeply strained. Between Eisenhower's election victory in November 1952 and inauguration in 1953, the outgoing Truman administration had little to do with the new one. Nevertheless, once in office, Eisenhower made surprisingly few changes to Truman's policies. The Republican Eisenhower ended the war in Korea, mostly with a veiled threat to use atomic weapons, and surprisingly, solidified core New Deal policies and the Cold War.

Eisenhower's was a reassuring presence, and many considered his eight years in office to be a time of complacency and stability in national life. However, the era was also one of extraordinary change. New technology, most of all television, changed the culture. Dissent from the dominant complacency was found in many places, most of all among the young and the more than 10 percent of Americans who were of African origin. The modern Civil Rights Movement began in the 1950s. The perceived stability and the many real changes of the 1950s are the focus of this chapter.

Eisenhower's America, America's World

25.1 **Explain the continuation of the Cold War under a new Republican administration.**

The successful test of a U.S. hydrogen bomb in November 1952, followed only months later by the successful test of a similar bomb by the Soviet Union (Union of Soviet Socialist Republics, or U.S.S.R.) in August 1953, meant that Eisenhower and every subsequent president would govern in a world that was quite different from that of any of their predecessors. While alliances like the U.S.-led NATO and the Soviet-led Warsaw Pact might position ground forces, the reality was that each of the superpowers had the capacity to destroy the other in a single stroke, and probably, for the first time in history, to destroy all life on earth. The Cold War between the United States and the Soviet Union was a daunting reality for every person on the planet in the 1950s and for a long time thereafter.

Foreign Policy in a World of Hydrogen Bombs

Early in his first term, Eisenhower lamented, "We are in an armaments race. Where will it lead us? At worst, to atomic warfare. At best to robbing every people and nation on earth of the fruits of their own toil." Eisenhower tried to defuse the situation. In December 1953, he proposed an "Atoms for Peace" plan to the United Nations by which the United States, the Soviet Union, and the United Kingdom would turn over some of their nuclear material to an international agency for peaceful use. However, little came of the plan. The distrust between the two superpowers was too great. Influential political leaders in the United States would not support a reduction in defense spending because they worried about the Soviets and because military spending—a total of more than $350 billion during Eisenhower's two terms—was key to defense industries and jobs in almost every congressional district in the country. So the United States and the Soviets continued to build. The United States tested 203 nuclear weapons in the Pacific and at Nevada test sites, exposing some 200,000 civilians and soldiers to radiation and even more people to the radioactive fallout. The Soviets conducted at least as many tests if not more.

Along with his secretary of state John Foster Dulles, Eisenhower tried to craft a foreign policy that kept the financial costs of the Cold War to a minimum, protected U.S. influences in key corners of the globe, and avoided war. This foreign policy comprised two key elements. The first was a policy of **massive retaliation**, announced by Dulles in January 1954. The United States was not prepared to take on the cost of keeping troops in every corner of the globe, especially after the war in Korea. Rather, the United States would try to protect the non-Communist world with programs like the Marshall Plan and the Berlin airlift where possible, but with the promise that if the Soviets tried to expand their

Although he was often dealing with complex matters affecting life-and-death issues behind the scenes, Eisenhower maintained a public image of a genial, above-the-fray leader whose famous smile gave many people confidence that events were in good hands.

massive retaliation

A policy adopted by the Eisenhower administration to limit the costs of the Cold War. Rather than keep a large military presence, the administration used the threat of using the hydrogen bomb if the Soviet Union expanded its grasp to new territory.

Central Intelligence Agency (CIA)

Established by President Truman and expanded by President Eisenhower, the CIA was the nation's spy agency charged with keeping tabs on developments in other countries and with engaging in secret missions to advance American interests.

sphere of influence, if they were to invade European or other countries allied with the West, then, said Dulles, the United States was prepared "to retaliate, instantly, by means and at a place of our choosing." Some called the policy "brinkmanship" since the United States was ready to go to the brink of destruction if the Soviets moved outside their sphere of influence, and the Soviets were being put on notice that the United States was prepared to use its H-bombs and use them quickly. The Soviets might have had a larger army and navy, but the United States had plenty of bombs and Polaris submarines, as well as Atlas and Minuteman rockets that could hit the Soviet Union any time and any place. From a force of 1,500 nuclear weapons, the U.S. stockpile increased to 6,000. Relying on those weapons, the United States reduced the size of the military and overall military expenditures, kept taxes relatively low, and avoided inflation yet still ensured U.S. power around the globe.

The second element in Eisenhower's foreign policy depended on secret activities organized by the **Central Intelligence Agency (CIA)**. During World War II, the United States developed the capacity to spy on and disrupt the Axis countries through the Office of Strategic Services. At the end of the war, President Truman disbanded that office. Two years later, he received congressional authorization to re-create it, as the CIA, to spy and conduct covert operations in foreign countries that the United States feared might become Communist.

A number of nations did not want to be part of either the Soviet or U.S. sphere of influence, much to the frustration of some U.S. government officials who saw the world divided between the two superpowers. Often calling themselves the "Third World"—in contrast to the first and second worlds of the United States and the Soviet Union—these nations, especially those emerging from colonial rule in Asia, Africa, and the Middle East, maintained their distance even as they sought benefits from their role as a fulcrum in world politics. (See Map 25-1 for the Cold War–era division of the world into three large groupings—U.S. and allies, U.S.S.R. and allies, and the "Third World.")

In 1953, the Indian diplomat V. K. Krishna Menon told the United Nations that these nations represented a non-aligned movement, and in 1961, the leaders of India, Indonesia, Egypt, Ghana, and Yugoslavia created a formal organization of the Non-Aligned Movement. Josip Broz Tito had successfully led the still-Socialist Yugoslavia out of the Soviet sphere while India and Ghana were former British colonies and Indonesia had been Dutch. All felt strongly the need to maintain their independence, even if some Americans thought this was a cover for strong Soviet influence within them.

In the summer of 1953, the CIA organized a coup against the elected prime minister of Iran, Muhammad Mussadegh, who had nationalized oil interests belonging to British companies and who some feared might have Communist sympathies. With the covert help of the CIA, he was overthrown and replaced with the pro-Western Muhammad Reza Shah Pahlevi, who ruled the country for more than twenty years before being displaced by an anti-U.S. Islamic revolution in the late 1970s.

Then in June 1954, the CIA helped overthrow the democratically elected government of Jacobo Árbenz Guzmán in Guatemala. Árbenz was promoting land reform by expropriating land owned by the U.S.-based United Fruit Company. Although the Árbenz administration had compensated United Fruit for the land, the company was angry and the U.S. government feared a Communist movement until CIA operatives, working with local insurgents, drove Árbenz from office. Neither action received much publicity in the United States, but the not-very-secret U.S. involvement built up significant anti-U.S. sentiment in the Middle East and Latin America. Later, in 1958, the CIA tried unsuccessfully to overthrow the government of Indonesia. In 1959, it played a role in installing a new pro-Western government in Laos. While Eisenhower knew of those actions, he may not have known about plans to assassinate the popular elected leader of the Congo, Patrice Lumumba (who was killed by dissidents before the CIA reached him), and the new leader of Cuba, Fidel Castro.

The Eisenhower administration also found itself caught up in other world crises that could not easily be handled by massive retaliation or CIA intervention. After World War II, France sought to reclaim control of its former colonies in Indochina, but many there wanted independence. In September 1945, with initial support from the United States, Ho Chi Minh proclaimed Vietnamese independence using words familiar to the Americans: "We hold these truths to be self-evident, that all men are created equal." But the French were determined to reclaim Vietnam. They installed Bao Dai, the former emperor of Annam, a part of Vietnam, as the leader in Vietnam. Ho Chi Minh's forces attacked the French. The United States, fearing a Communist government under Ho and more worried about alienating France in Cold War Europe than events in Asia, sided with the French. By late 1953, the French were isolated in a fortified area, Dien Bien Phu, and facing defeat. Some, including Vice President Nixon, urged U.S. intervention, even the use of nuclear weapons. Eisenhower responded, "You boys must be crazy. We can't use those awful things against Asians for the second time in less than ten years. My God." There was no U.S. intervention at that time.

When the French were defeated in 1954, an international conference temporarily divided Vietnam into North Vietnam, to be led by Ho Chi Minh, and South Vietnam, to be led by Bao Dai and a pro-Western nationalist Ngo Dinh Diem. Elections to unify the country were scheduled for 1956. When Diem refused to participate in the 1956 elections, knowing that Ho, a national hero, would win, the United States did not intervene. The United States relied on the South East Asian Treaty Organization (SEATO), a much weaker version of NATO that it had helped to create in 1955, to keep Communists out of Southeast Asia, but the organization had little effect.

The next crisis also occurred in Asia. Chiang Kai-shek's Nationalist government had been defeated on the Chinese mainland in 1949 and was ensconced on heavily fortified off-shore islands, the largest of which was Taiwan, then known as Formosa. In 1954, the Communist government of China began shelling two tiny Nationalist-held islands, Quemoy and Matsu, just off the Chinese coast. Eisenhower wanted to protect Chiang's government, but Quemoy and Matsu were small islands that were much closer to mainland China than to Taiwan. Having seen the war in Korea, Eisenhower was determined not to fight Communist China over Quemoy and Matsu. Eventually, both sides tired of the conflict and the islands remained under Nationalist rule. Nevertheless, the incident pointed to larger possible threats.

Challenges to Maintaining Peace

In July 1955, Eisenhower met in Geneva with the new Soviet leader, Nikita Khrushchev, and leaders of Britain and France. The summit meeting, whose purpose was to reduce international tensions, produced a treaty recognizing the independence of Austria, which had been jointly occupied by the four powers after World War II, much like Germany had been. Although the summit did not accomplish all that Eisenhower wished, many were optimistic about a new spirit of coexistence.

In February 1956, Khrushchev surprised the world with a speech—originally a "secret speech" to Soviet leaders only, but word spread quickly—in which he said that Stalin had been a tyrant who had inflicted purges, show trials, forced labor, terror, and mass executions on his people. Khrushchev declared it was time to begin the de-Stalinization of the Soviet Union. The speech was a relief to those who saw the beginning of a new era in Russia, though devastating to die-hard Communists. It did not, however, reduce American fear of Soviet intentions around the world.

Despite these advances, conflicts continued. In October, hostilities flared in the Middle East. Gamal Abdel Nasser, the Arab nationalist ruler of Egypt, like many leaders who were not aligned with either the United States or the Soviet Union and who sought to use the Cold War to their own advantage, sought funding from both the United States and the Soviet Union to build the Aswan High Dam on the upper Nile River to irrigate new areas of Egypt, provide electricity, and promote industrialization. His flirtation with both sides angered both countries, and in 1956, Dulles canceled the U.S. loan. Nasser responded by

Map 25-1 A World Divided.

As the Cold War continued in the 1950s, the world was divided into two major spheres of influence: the West led by the United States, which included the members of NATO and other allies, and the East (see page 749) led by the Soviet Union, which included the members of the Warsaw Pact and other allied nations. Both competed for influence in the remaining neutral nations, especially in Africa.

Military alliances in the 1950s
- U.S. allies
- U.S. allies/NATO members
- U.S.S.R. allies
- U.S.S.R. allies/ Warsaw Pact members
- Neutral nation

taking control of the Suez Canal, the essential waterway between the Mediterranean and the Red Sea that was owned by a British and French canal company and crucial to the flow of oil to Europe. Nasser said he wanted the revenue from the canal to build his dam, but his actions angered and frightened the British and French.

On October 29, with British and French backing, Israel attacked Egypt. Eisenhower was outraged. He sponsored a UN resolution demanding an Israeli withdrawal. It was an ironic

moment with the United States and the Soviet Union united in opposition to Britain, France, and Israel. When the British and French ignored the UN and bombed Egypt, Nasser sank ships and blocked the canal. The United States condemned the British action and threatened to send troops to Egypt. The British never expected the United States to take a hard line. British prime minister Anthony Eden and Ike were wartime friends, but the president was furious. A cease fire was arranged, and the canal was reopened under Egyptian management. The Soviet Union and the United States looked good to Arab countries. Israel remained strong. Only Britain and France suffered. Eden resigned as prime minister, and neither Britain nor France was again a major influence in the Middle East.

In October 1956, in the midst of the Suez crisis, discontent with Soviet rule boiled over in Hungary. Khrushchev's denunciation of Stalin had raised hopes for a more liberal policy in Eastern Europe. The Soviet government granted some concessions to the Hungarians, but when they pressed for more independence, Khrushchev sent 200,000 troops and 4,000 tanks to Budapest to end the uprising and maintain Soviet dominance. Some 40,000 Hungarians were killed and another 150,000 fled the country, seeking asylum in the West. Some called for American intervention; after all, Eisenhower had talked about the liberation of "captive peoples," but the old general understood the military reality that Hungary was surrounded by other Communist nations. Most Americans seemed satisfied to label the uprising as more proof of Soviet tyranny and leave it at that.

While the Suez crisis and the Hungarian uprising were taking place, the United States was in the midst of a presidential election. The Democrats again nominated Adlai Stevenson. Although Eisenhower had a serious heart attack in 1955 and was hospitalized for six weeks, he had recovered fully. The Republicans again nominated their highly popular president and his not-very-popular running mate. The Democrats ran anti-Nixon television ads that they thought might be more effective than any attack on Eisenhower. Eisenhower was well liked, the country was at peace, and prosperity was evident. Eisenhower won 57 percent of the popular votes, but the outcome rested on Eisenhower's personal popularity; the Democrats carried both houses of Congress.

Neither the country nor the president expected any major change of course in the next four years. However, new developments on the international front presented not only new crises but also an opportunity unimagined when Ike's second term began.

A Small Satellite and a Big Impact

Sputnik

The world's first space satellite, launched by the Soviet Union in 1957.

On October 4, 1957, the Soviet Union launched *Sputnik*, a space satellite. Although *Sputnik* was small, about the size of a large beach ball, and weighed only 184 pounds, it was the first orbiting satellite ever launched into space. A month later, a much larger *Sputnik II* was launched, which carried a dog, Laika, as well as scientific and medical instruments. While the Soviet Union celebrated, Americans panicked. Critics said the Soviets were winning the "space race." Democratic senator Henry Jackson of Washington State talked of the "shame and danger" of the moment. G. Mennen Williams, Michigan's Democratic governor, wrote of *Sputnik*, "It's a Commie sky. And Uncle Sam's asleep."

Because of U.S. spy flights over the Soviet Union, Eisenhower knew that although the Soviets might launch a satellite, the United States was far ahead in missile development.

ITAR-TASS Photo Agency/Alamy Stock Photo

Sputnik I, the first space satellite.

However, he could not say so without admitting to the spying, which he did not want to do. It was a difficult moment for an administration that worried as much about national security as they did about a race to space. Nevertheless, two important results came from *Sputnik* and the fears that the satellite induced—a new government space agency and improved education.

In 1958, the administration proposed the creation of the **National Aeronautics and Space Administration (NASA)** and before long, NASA scientists and engineers had launched the first U.S. satellite and soon closed the gap with the Soviet Union. Later NASA-led efforts resulted in human flight in space, a moon landing, a string of satellites that could be used for telecommunications (and spying), and a space shuttle that could bring cargo and replacement crews to orbiting space stations. For all of the fears of 1957 and 1958, the United States had far greater resources than the Soviets to devote to these efforts once the determination was made to do so.

Sputnik also had a major impact on American education. Many saw the Soviet advances in space as the result of superior Soviet education. Eisenhower proposed the **National Defense Education Act (NDEA)**, which was passed by Congress in September 1958. After many failed efforts to get federal aid for the nation's schools, funding was approved because of *Sputnik*. The NDEA provided funds to improve science education, provided scholarships, and created an education division within the National Science Foundation.

Although fear of the Soviets led to new science curriculum materials, the 1950s had already seen considerable advances in education. In 1940, less than half (49 percent) of the nation's seventeen-year-olds graduated from high school. By 1950, 57.4 percent of seventeen-year-olds completed high school; in 1960, 63.4 percent; and in 1970, 75.6 percent graduated. Before 1950, more girls than boys had finished high school, but more males than females went to college. For a time after that, graduation and college attendance ratios began to even out, though imbalance would return later. Although white graduation rates remained far ahead of those for African American and Latino students, many more students of color attended and graduated from high school in the 1950s than ever before. Given the perceived national need, federal programs began to encourage more females to study in the sciences. At the college level, the GI Bill had generated a rapid increase in college attendance for military veterans, overwhelmingly white men, but as the decade went on, more students of all races and genders attended college. College faculty in the sciences benefited from grants for military research, though some worried about the impact of these grants. Even before *Sputnik* was launched, a *Time* magazine article asked, "Is the military about to take over U.S. science lock, stock, and barrel, calling the tune for U.S. universities and signing up the best scientists for work fundamentally aimed at military results?"

In spite of "mutually assured destruction" and the space race with the Soviets, Eisenhower, who had seen more of war than most Americans, desperately wanted to find a path to lasting peace. Although the July 1955 summit conference at Geneva had been disappointing in terms of any concrete results, the **"Spirit of Geneva"** represented a commitment to coexistence by both the United States and the Soviet Union that was something on which Eisenhower wanted to build, especially in his last years in office. On October 31, 1958, the United States announced that it was suspending nuclear testing in the atmosphere. The Soviets also suspended their testing. By 1958, atmospheric nuclear testing was found to be a health risk to millions around the world as well as an unnecessary military provocation, and the cessation was important.

When a new crisis arose over Berlin in early 1959, Eisenhower and Khrushchev managed to avoid escalation. Each of the two leaders agreed to invite the other to visit his respective country in the next year. Khrushchev's tour of the United States in September 1959 was a major success in spite of Khrushchev's ill-timed boast that "[w]e will bury you." The two leaders agreed to another summit in Paris in May 1960. Progress seemed to be in the air.

On May 1, 1960, the progress stopped. A U-2 reconnaissance plane—the type that had been providing the kind of information about Soviet military capability that Eisenhower had kept secret—was shot down by a Soviet rocket as it flew 1,300 miles inside Russia. Khrushchev announced that the Soviets not only had the wreckage of the U-2—and it was no weather plane as the United States initially said—but also had captured the pilot, Francis

25.1

25.2

25.3

National Aeronautics and Space Administration (NASA)

A new government agency created in 1958 in response to *Sputnik* and specifically charged with fostering American space efforts; eventually led to the first manned moon landing and the space shuttle.

National Defense Education Act (NDEA)

Federal aid to improve education, especially science and math education, approved by Congress in 1958.

Spirit of Geneva

A perspective fostered by Eisenhower and Khrushchev that their personal engagement with each other might put limits on the worst aspects of the Cold War.

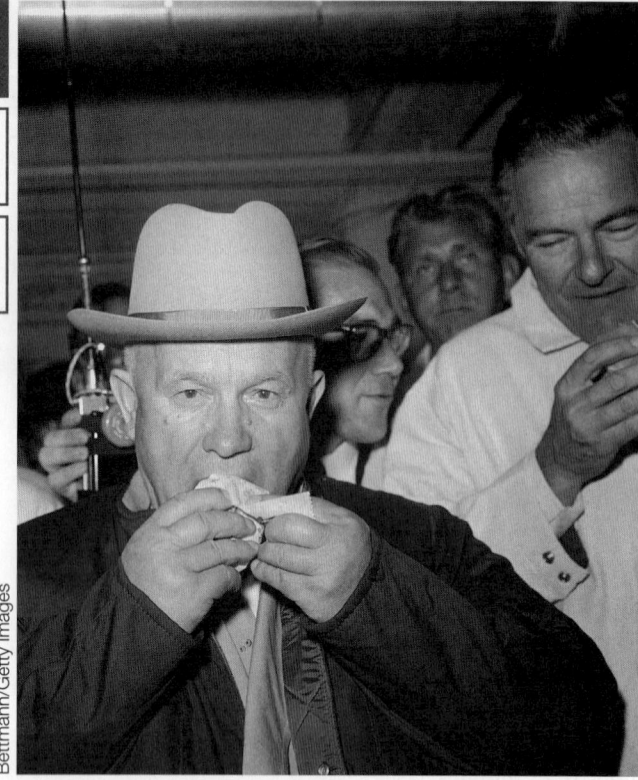

During the goodwill that emerged between the United States and the Soviet Union in 1958 and 1959, Soviet premier Nikita Khrushchev visited the United States and was a hit on tours such as this one of an Iowa farm.

Gary Powers, alive and had found both the poison needle with which he was supposed to kill himself rather than risk capture and a pistol with a silencer that he had been supplied. "Why the silencer?" Khrushchev asked, and then answered, "To blow men's brains out! The men who supplied him with the silence gun pray in church and call us godless atheists!"

The U-2 incident dominated the Paris summit. Khrushchev insisted that Eisenhower condemn the U-2 flights and punish those responsible, which Eisenhower could not do, though he did agree to suspend the flights. Khrushchev withdrew the invitation for Eisenhower to visit the Soviet Union. There would be little talk of friendly coexistence in the next two years.

From Oldest to Youngest—The Transition to the Next President

While the administration dealt with the U-2 incident, the United States was in the midst of the 1960 presidential election. Eisenhower's popularity was high, and if the Constitution had allowed it and he had wanted it, he could easily have won a third term. But the Constitution had been changed and Eisenhower at the age of seventy, the oldest serving president, had no interest in a third term.

The Republican Party nominated Vice President Richard Nixon as their presidential candidate. The Democratic race was contested between several candidates, including Senators Lyndon B. Johnson of Texas, Hubert Humphrey of Minnesota, Stuart Symington of Missouri, and John F. Kennedy of Massachusetts. Many remembered the defeat of Al Smith in 1928—the last time a major party had nominated a Catholic—and wondered if Kennedy, a Catholic, could be successful. Liberals also worried about Kennedy. Eleanor Roosevelt remembered how slow he had been to attack McCarthy and how little he had done for civil rights. She preferred Adlai Stevenson. But Kennedy had extraordinary personal charisma, charming most everyone he met, as well as virtually unlimited campaign funds because of the wealth of his father, Joseph P. Kennedy, and could far outspend his opponents. Under the leadership of his brother Robert Kennedy, he had a superb campaign team. He won the Democratic nomination on the first ballot, asked Lyndon Johnson to be his running mate, and entered the general election as a strong candidate.

Nixon, having been vice president for two terms, was the better known. For the first time in American politics, the two candidates held a series of television debates. Those who listened to the debates on radio thought Nixon had won due to the clarity of his argument. For the much larger television audience, however, Nixon seemed tired and haggard while Kennedy who arrived from California well rested and with a tan seemed at the height of new youthful vigor. In response to Kennedy's charisma, *Newsweek* reported that there were "jumpers" who leapt to see him, "runners" who chased his car, and others who simply screamed themselves hoarse. People applauded politely for Nixon.

Although Eisenhower despised the Kennedys, whom he saw as rich, ambitious, and unprincipled, his lack of enthusiasm for his vice president was hard to hide. When a reporter asked Ike to name a major Nixon contribution to the administration, he replied, "If you give me a week, I might think of one." Although he immediately recanted, the damage was done.

During the competitive campaign, Kennedy accused Eisenhower of allowing a "missile gap" to develop between the United States and the Soviet Union and promised that, if elected, the United States would expand its defenses and its missions in space. He also addressed his Catholicism in a well-received speech to Protestant clergy in Houston, Texas. Late in the campaign, when Martin Luther King, Jr., was arrested in Georgia, Nixon tried to intervene quietly, but Kennedy made a very public call to King's wife, Coretta, and Bobby Kennedy made a successful request for King's release. Many blacks, key voters in some

In the first ever televised presidential debate, John Kennedy managed to project charm and confidence to the viewers.

states, decided to vote Democratic that fall. On election day, with the highest turnout since World War II, Kennedy won by one of the smallest margins in history—49.7 percent to Nixon's 49.6 percent—though he won in the Electoral College 303 to 219.

On inauguration day, January 20, 1961, the youngest person ever elected president replaced the oldest serving president. The general who had commanded all Allied troops in Europe in World War II was replaced by a man who had commanded a small PT (Patrol Torpedo) boat in the Pacific and who became a hero when his PT-109 was sunk. The new president made much of the leadership change, telling the nation, "Let the word go forth from this time and place, to friend and foe alike, that the torch has been passed to a new generation of Americans."

25.1 Quick Review

How did Eisenhower continue fighting the Cold War while trying to reduce tension?

A Culture on the Move

25.2 **Explain the impact of cultural and technological changes on the country.**

During and after the 1950s, many looked on that era as one of complacency at home and trouble abroad. By 1960, however, the United States was a very different place at home from what it had been in 1950. During the 1950s, the nation became much more prosperous. In 1960, the average family income of $5,620 was 30 percent higher than it had been in 1950, and 62 percent of homes were owner occupied—up from 55 percent in 1950 and 44 percent in 1940. After the end of the Korean War in 1953, the decade was one of relative peace for the United States despite conflicts elsewhere. But the decade of the 1950s was also, as the writer Morris Dickstein noted, "a fertile period, a seedbed of ideas that would burgeon and live in the more activist, less reflective climate that followed."

The Growing Impact of Television

In 1948, Wayne Coy, a member of the Federal Communications Commission, which regulated television and radio, said, "Make no mistake about it, television is here to stay. It is a new force unloosed in the land. I believe it is an irresistible force." From 104 commercial stations broadcasting to 5 million homes in 1950, television expanded to almost 600 stations received in 45,750,000 homes in 1960—almost 80 percent of all of U.S. homes.

Some of the early television programs were impressive. *Playhouse 90*, the *Goodyear Television Playhouse*, and the *Kraft Television Theater* brought serious drama to the television screen. Talented young actors, including Grace Kelly, Paul Newman, Joanne Woodward, and Eva Marie Saint, were seen by wide audiences. The *ABC Concert* carried the Chicago Symphony Orchestra around the country.

Television news, though generally limited to a fifteen-minute program, included the *Camel News Caravan* with John Cameron Swayze and the CBS *Television News with Douglas Edwards*. These programs brought current events into living rooms as never before. Beginning with Truman's 1949 inauguration and Eisenhower's 1952 campaign commercials, television changed politics; people felt a new intimacy with candidates and leaders. Edward R. Murrow's *See It Now* programs brought investigative journalism to television, including coverage of Senator McCarthy's hearings.

Lighter entertainment was very successful, too. Radio had been available to many since the 1930s, and some programs, like Jack Benny's comedy routines, shifted from radio to television with little change. The long-running *I Love Lucy* show with Lucille Ball and Desi Arnaz was the most popular show on television. Other comedies, especially *The Adventures of Ozzie and Harriet*, *Father Knows Best*, and *Leave It to Beaver*, used humor to reaffirm the white, middle-class, suburban lifestyle in which the wise, sometimes befuddled father supported the family while the passive (if sometimes conniving) mother stayed home to happily manage the house.

A middle-class, white family sitting at home and watching *The Lone Ranger* on television epitomized the 1950s for some.

American Voices

Newton N. Minow, Television and the Public Interest, 1961

25.1

25.2

25.3

As he began his presidency, John F. Kennedy appointed attorney and longtime Democratic Party activist Newton N. Minow to chair the Federal Communications Commission (FCC). In May 1961, only a few months into his tenure at the FCC, Minow gave this controversial speech to the National Association of Broadcasters, declaring that television was "a vast wasteland." While many in the television industry strongly disagreed, many critics thought Minow was on target.

Your industry possesses the most powerful voice in America. ...

When television is good, nothing—not the theater, not the magazines or newspapers—nothing is better.

But when television is bad, nothing is worse. I invite each of you to sit down in front of your television set when your station goes on the air and stay there, for a day, without a book, without a magazine, without a newspaper, without a profit and loss sheet or a rating book to distract you. Keep your eyes glued to that set until the station signs off. I can assure you that what you will observe is a vast wasteland.

You will see a procession of game shows, formula comedies about totally unbelievable families, blood and thunder, mayhem, violence, sadism, murder, western bad men, western good men, private eyes, gangsters, more violence, and cartoons. And endlessly, commercials—many screaming, cajoling, and offending. And most of all, boredom.

Source: Speech delivered May 9, 1961, National Association of Broadcasters, Washington, DC; downloaded from www.americanrhetoric.com/speeches/newtonminow.htm, May 11, 2011.

Thinking Critically

1. **Analyzing Primary Sources**
   What evidence did Minow use to express his point of view about a "vast wasteland" in television programming? What evidence might a broadcaster use to express a different point of view and counter the claim?

2. **Contextualization**
   In what ways, if any, does Minow's speech shed light on the nature of the growing discontent with mainstream 1950s culture?

On *The Ed Sullivan Show*, the poker-faced Ed Sullivan introduced Elvis Presley (who Sullivan insisted be shown only from the waist up) and, later, The Beatles to American audiences. Daytime soap operas (their original sponsors were soap companies) moved from radio to television, and *Guiding Light*, *Love of Life*, and *Search for Tomorrow* provided a dash of scandal to daytime viewers. Families gathered to eat TV dinners (first marketed in 1954) on TV trays, rather than around a dining room table, to watch *Gunsmoke*, featuring a stronger and more silent Marshal Dillon than had been possible on radio, plus *Maverick* and *Have Gun—Will Travel*, as well as detective stories, including *Dragnet*, *77 Sunset Strip*, and *Perry Mason*. Children's cartoons took over Saturday mornings. Reruns of old movies were shown in the late evening.

While some of the first programs had a single sponsor—such as the *Goodyear Television Playhouse*, the *Kraft Television Theater*, and the *Camel News Caravan*, broadcasters quickly discovered that they could make higher profits with multiple advertisers, and thirty-second commercials urged Americans (always seen as white and middle class) to "see the USA in your Chevrolet," or "move up to Chrysler," and handle their indigestion with "Speedy" Alka Seltzer.

Television was rocked by a series of scandals in the late 1950s. The most popular quiz show, *The $64,000 Question*, turned out to be rigged. Charles Van Doren, a major winner on the show, had been given answers in advance. As commercial stations focused on advertising revenue, they became increasingly cautious. One advertiser reminded the station owners, "A program that displeases any substantial segment of the population is a misuse of the advertising dollar." Since showing Americans in all of their diversity could displease some, television became bland. Even President Eisenhower said, "If a citizen has to be bored to death, it is cheaper and more comfortable to sit at home and look at television than it is to go outside and pay a dollar for a ticket." It was hardly a ringing endorsement of the new medium. The Kennedy administration would not be any more positive in its appraisal.

The Impact of the Automobile

Automobiles had been invented before 1900, had been mass-produced in the 1910s, and had had a significant impact by the 1920s (see Chapter 21). Nevertheless, the automobile, like the TV, came to dominate American culture in the 1950s as never before.

Interstate Highway System

A national system of superhighways that Congress approved at the urging of President Eisenhower in 1956 to improve car and truck travel across the United States.

Once wartime shortages ended, the sales of private automobiles grew rapidly. By 1960, 80 percent of American families owned an automobile (the same percentage as owned televisions). The total number of cars registered at the end of the decade was seventy-four million, almost double the thirty-nine million registered in 1950. In addition, the cars were becoming larger, faster, more powerful, and much flashier. In an era of cheap gasoline, the symbolism of power, sexiness, and speed was far more important than fuel efficiency.

Automobiles needed support services and infrastructure, most of all, highways. By the early 1950s, the American Road Builders Association was able to successfully lobby for the creation of the Highway Trust Fund in which all revenue generated from automobiles, especially the tax on gasoline, could be used only to build highways with the result that, in the United States, funding for road building was ample, though funds for mass transit were more scarce. European countries used similar gas tax funds not only for roads but also for mass transit, schools, and hospitals.

President Eisenhower, who remembered a miserable cross-country journey he had made as a young army officer on the nation's ill-maintained highways of the 1920s, adopted a plan that had been put together during the Truman administration and proposed the Interstate Highway Act, which became law in 1956. The act created the **Interstate Highway System**, a numbered network of forty-one thousand miles of roads that connected the country east and west, north and south, including Interstate 5 running through California, Oregon, and Washington; Interstate 95, which ran from Florida to Maine; I10, which followed the nation's southern border from Santa Monica, California, to Jacksonville, Florida; I90 from Seattle, Washington, to Boston, Massachusetts; plus feeder highways for which the federal government paid 90 percent of the cost (see Map 25-2). These highways made travel by car, truck, or bus much easier and cheaper than ever before. At the same time, urban, suburban, and rural sprawl was exacerbated. Suburban houses sprang up and tight-knit urban communities went into decline. Shopping malls replaced Main Street. Mass transit declined. In Los Angeles, what had once been the largest electric interurban railway in the world with 1,100 miles of track was replaced with a system of highways using buses produced by General Motors with tires from Firestone Rubber.

New industries sprang up to service the automobile and the highway. Fast-food restaurants allowed busy drivers to pick up a meal and keep moving. Medical, legal, and insurance services for the victims of traffic accidents grew. Motels became a new place to stay, replacing grand downtown hotels that had catered to those who traveled by train or ship. Kemmons Wilson and Wallace E. Johnson opened the first "Holiday Inn" in Memphis, Tennessee, in 1952, and by 1960, there were sixty thousand motels, many belonging to chains like Holiday Inn or Howard Johnson, catering to people who valued cleanliness, comfort, and the convenience of being able to drive directly to the door of a room.

Between 1920 and 1950, gasoline service stations offering fuel and automobile services, some in a grand style, became the most widely built new commercial structure in the United States. With their signs advertising Mobil, Shell, and Esso (later Exxon), they made it possible to keep cars fueled and on the move. The gasoline these stations pumped also had an impact on U.S. foreign policy as American political leaders understood the nation's love affair with the automobile and the need to maintain a steady supply of cheap gasoline, much of it from the Middle East and Latin America, if they were to stay in office.

Critics worried about the impact of the automobile on American culture. In *The City in History*, Lewis Mumford complained that the automobile "annihilates the city whenever it collides with it." For Mumford, it was the city not suburban sprawl that created community. Raymond Tucker, mayor of St. Louis, also noted, "The plain fact of the matter is that we just cannot build enough lanes of highways to move all of our people by private automobile and create enough parking space to store the cars without completely paving over our cities." Nevertheless, in the 1950s, more Americans agreed with New York's master highway builder Robert Moses, who designed a series of bridges in and around New York as well as the Brooklyn Queens Expressway, the Cross Bronx Expressway, and the Long Island Expressway, and who kept advocating for more roads even as some protested.

Map 25-2 The Interstate Highway System.

The current Interstate Highway System, shown in this map, is surprisingly close to the original plan approved by the federal government in 1956 for a system of superhighways linking all parts of the forty-eight contiguous states.

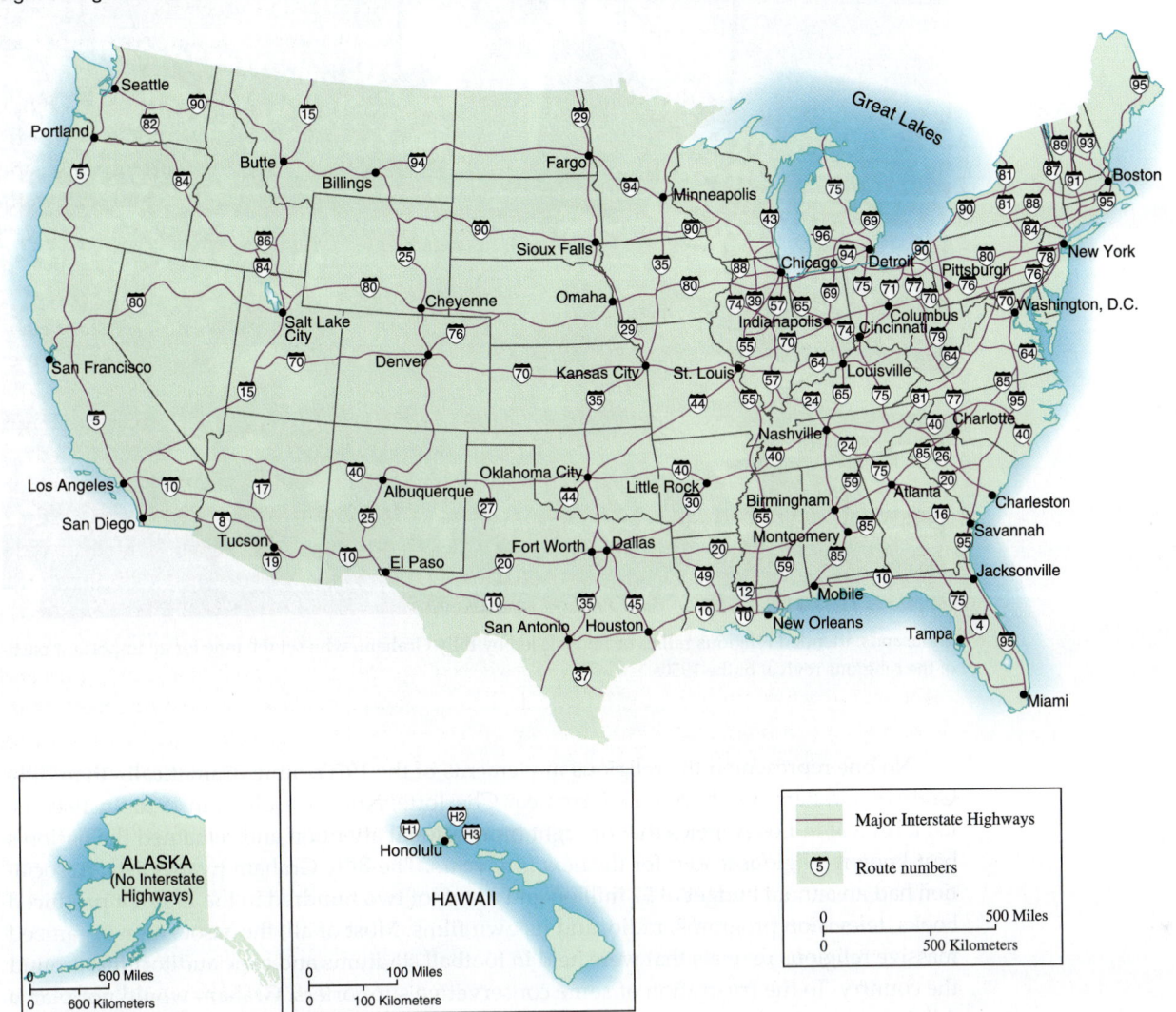

The Boom of Religion

In the 1950s, Americans drove to church and watched religious programs on television in numbers never seen before. The religious boom of the 1950s was both a cultural and a spiritual phenomenon.

For most of the nation's history, a little over one-third of the people were involved in religious activities. However, in the 1950s, that number grew to over two-thirds, and on some Sunday mornings, more than half of all of the people in the country were in church. After World War II, Americans became active in religious organizations in numbers never seen before, and their participation kept rising for the next fifteen years. Visitors from other countries were stunned by the American embrace of religion. In no other country was there a similar upsurge, certainly not in war-weary Europe. Americans identified with religious communities, built new churches at an astounding rate, especially in the new suburbs, and enjoyed songs like "I Believe," "It's No Secret What God Can Do," and "Vaya con Dios," as popular secular music. Historians continue to ask what accounted for this upsurge in religious activity. The roots of something as elusive as religious faith and as hard to discover as social conformity may be impossible to find, but the signs of the times that pointed to a more religious culture were numerous.

Thousands attended religious rallies or revivals led by Billy Graham, who set the tone for an important part of the religious revival of the 1950s.

No one represented the religious movements of the 1950s more dramatically than Billy Graham. Graham was born on a farm near Charlotte, North Carolina, in 1918. In 1949, he led a revival in Los Angeles that brought him national attention and remained the nation's best-known religious leader for the next fifty years. The Billy Graham Evangelistic Association had an annual budget of $2 million and a staff of two hundred in the 1950s. It produced books, television programs, radio, and its own films. Most of all, the association organized massive religious revivals that were held in football stadiums and civic auditoriums around the country. To the frustration of some conservative supporters, Graham would not plan a religious crusade, as he called a revival, without the support of the local council of churches, which included liberal as well as conservative clergy. Graham also refused to hold racially segregated revivals, even in the Deep South.

Graham was immensely successful in bringing out thousands of people night after night. At the end of each event, individuals were invited to come forward and make a personal confession of faith to counselors who were waiting for them, as the audience sang, "Just as I Am Without One Plea." Although he was a Baptist, Graham did not worry about religious denominations and urged the converted to attend any church that appealed to them. Graham's success was such that he also became a religious advisor to several U.S. presidents.

While Graham was by far the best-known and most successful revivalist of the 1950s, many others, black and white and increasingly Latino evangelists, conducted their own religious revivals in churches, tents, and fields across the United States. Oral Roberts, a Pentecostal Holiness revivalist and faith healer, built up his own media empire, which rivaled Graham's. Less emotional versions of religion, including the sermons of the Presbyterian minister Peter Marshall, published in 1949 as *Mr. Jones Meet the Master*, also attracted a wide audience.

A Protestant minister, Norman Vincent Peale, took the quest for peace of mind to a wide audience through his books, *Guide to Confident Living* published in 1948 and *The Power of Positive Thinking* published in 1952, which broke all previous records for the sales of a religious book. Peale's message was "believe in yourself" and develop "a humble but reasonable confidence." Religious groups known as the "mainstream" of American Protestantism—Methodists, Baptists, Presbyterians, Congregationalists, and Episcopalians—flourished in memberships and gained influence in the 1950s. Reinhold Niebuhr's book, *Moral Man and Immoral Society*, challenged religious people to find ways to make ethical decisions in a complex world. Both Reinhold Niebuhr and the German-born theologian Paul Tillich appeared on the cover of *Time* magazine.

In the 1950s, American Catholics were still a minority but were more numerous than any single Protestant denomination. As white Catholics moved to new suburban communities, Catholic bishops created new parishes where none had been. Some Catholic prelates such as New York's Francis Cardinal Spellman continued to keep their distance from Protestants, but others such as Boston's Richard Cardinal Cushing found ways to reach out to non-Catholics while building Catholic churches and parochial schools at a furious rate. The walls of distrust were still high in the 1950s: parish priests warned young people not to date a Protestant, and many Protestants still saw Catholicism as inherently foreign and undemocratic. Nevertheless, many of those who sat in the pews of Catholic and Protestant churches were ready to ignore the old divides.

Monsignor Fulton J. Sheen became a popular preacher not only at Catholic religious gatherings (never called revivals) but also on television. He brought Catholic teachings into the mainstream of American culture, and his book *Peace of Soul*, published in 1949, anticipated some of the positive-thinking themes in Peale's work. Sheen restated traditional Catholic beliefs in ways that appealed to a wide audience, Catholic and non-Catholic.

While 66 percent of Americans identified themselves as Protestant and 26 percent as Catholic, only 3 percent were Jews, but Jews also participated in the religious upsurge of the 1950s. Before World War II, secularism and assimilation seemed to go hand in hand among many Jewish immigrants. Although a growing awareness of the Holocaust brought despair and cynicism to some, it brought a renewed interest in their faith to others. A new generation of leaders like Rabbi Abraham Joshua Heschel spoke of the need to link modern thinking with traditional Jewish practices and inner piety. Many American Jews wanted to rediscover their faith. The children of parents who had argued over politics now argued over theology. Attendance at synagogues reached peaks never seen before. The Orthodox, Conservative, and Reform branches of Judaism all grew.

African American communities also had their own revivals of religion, usually quite separately from white communities. The National Baptist Convention, the African Methodist Episcopal, and the African Methodist Episcopal Zion churches, the nation's three largest African American religious bodies, all grew during the 1950s. Black Pentecostalism flourished in Northern cities as it long had in the rural South. The Church of God in Christ, founded in the 1890s, saw its largest growth in the 1950s and by 1965 had 420,000 members in 4,150 churches. The United House of Prayer for All People, led by "Sweet Daddy" Grace, promised grace in return for strict obedience to the church's teaching. In addition, Elijah Muhammad built up the **Nation of Islam** from the small Detroit Temple Number One, to a Muslim-oriented community of perhaps 100,000 members.

A much smaller number of Americans also looked beyond the bounds of the traditional Western faiths. The inspiration of Mohandas Gandhi in India led some to look at Hinduism. From the teachings of the Vedanta Society or the California-based Self-Realization Fellowship, some people turned to yoga or transcendental meditation. Others were attracted to the Bahá'í movement, an offshoot of Shiite Islam in Iran that sought to synthesize the teachings of all world religions. Buddhism remained small in the United States in the 1950s, mostly limited to communities of Asian immigrants, though in the 1960s that status would change quickly as much more diverse groups of people embraced Buddhist teachings to one degree or another.

As Americans became more actively engaged in their religious communities, political leaders sought to catch up. In the midst of the Cold War, they saw American religious sentiment as an important counter to atheistic communism. In 1954, Congress voted to add the phrase "one nation under God" to the Pledge of Allegiance to the Flag. A year later, Congress added the words "In God We Trust" to American paper currency. While some believers and

Nation of Islam

A religious and political organization founded by Elijah Muhammad that mixed Muslim religious teachings with a campaign for African American separatism, pride, and self-determination.

25.1

25.2

25.3

nonbelievers found this public religiosity offensive, most Americans embraced the sort of civic religion embedded in the new pledge and coins with enthusiasm. President Eisenhower said, "Our government makes no sense unless it is founded on a deeply felt religious faith—and I don't care what it is."

Dissent

Although the 1950s have been described as a time of conformity, not everyone conformed. Born in Brooklyn, New York, in 1897, Dorothy Day joined the Socialist Party and later the IWW as a young woman, opposed U.S. entry into World War I, and was arrested for picketing the White House as she demanded the vote for women. In the 1920s, she lived a bohemian life with poets and Communists in New York's Greenwich Village. Then in 1927, she experienced a dramatic conversion to Catholicism, left the man with whom she was living, and was baptized along with her new baby. Then in the 1930s, along with the Catholic mystic Peter Maurin, Day founded the Catholic Worker Movement and its related newspaper, *The Catholic Worker*, which she edited until her death in 1980. Day embraced voluntary poverty, set up the St. Joseph's House of Hospitality in New York to provide food and clothing to those in need, and protested the buildup of nuclear arms and the wars in Korea and later Vietnam. The Catholic Worker Movement sometimes made church officials uncomfortable but represented a religious voice of dissent in the 1950s and beyond.

A Protestant from the rural South, Myles Horton had much in common with Dorothy Day. Horton studied with Reinhold Niebuhr and later Jane Addams, joined the Socialist Party, picketed for the International Ladies' Garment Workers' Union, and participated in endless seminars and late-night discussions. In 1931, he moved back to Tennessee where he opened the Highlander Folk School "to work with people from the bottom, who could change society from the bottom." In the 1930s and 1940s, Highlander trained grassroots leadership for the labor movement, and in the 1950s and 1960s, for the Civil Rights Movement.

These groundbreaking dissidents, however, seemed tame to many compared with the influence of rock 'n' roll, and no rock 'n' roll figure got more attention, or worried more people in the 1950s, than Elvis Presley. Presley grew up poor in Mississippi and Tennessee, learning to sing and play a guitar in his Assembly of God congregation. Music producer Sam Phillips knew that although many young white Americans loved black music, even the best of black entertainers could not break through the culture's rigid color barrier. "If I could find a white man with a Negro sound," Phillips said, "I could make a billion dollars." With Elvis, he came close.

With Phillips handling the marketing, Elvis Presley became a star. The music in "Hound Dog" and "Heartbreak Hotel" represented a new amalgam of rhythm and blues, jazz, and pop as well as the earlier rock 'n' roll of groups like Bill Haley and the Comets whose "Rock Around the Clock" sold sixteen million records.

Elvis sold more than his music. His alienated look and his gyrating sexuality connected with young audiences who loved what he represented. Critics were appalled. One said that his performances were "strip-teases with clothes on … not only suggestive but downright obscene." Exactly that sultry suggestiveness is just what made him so popular to a generation tired of conformity. When Elvis appeared on *The Ed Sullivan Show*, fifty-four million people watched, the largest television audience in history.

Elvis was the top musical star, leading many other musicians such as black rock 'n' roll artists Chuck Berry, Chubby Checker, and Fats Domino as well as traditional pop music and jazz greats, but it was the new rock 'n' roll that defined the era. Leonard Bernstein, one of the great composers of the 1950s to 1980s, once described Elvis Presley as "the greatest cultural force in the twentieth century."

Even in science, more overt attention to human sexuality challenged traditional norms in the 1950s. Alfred Kinsey, the Indiana University researcher whose book *Sexual Behavior in the Human Male* had produced an outcry in 1948, published *Sexual Behavior in the Human Female* in 1953, which though long and full of dry scientific data, sold 250,000 copies. While Kinsey insisted that he was simply reporting, not making value judgments, findings like

25.1

25.2

25.3

Elvis Presley's music and performance style captivated fans and frightened more cautious observers, but transformed rock 'n' roll music in American culture.

the fact that 37 percent of all men and 13 percent of women had at least one homosexual experience or the fact that 50 percent of married men and 26 percent of married women had committed adultery, shocked Americans and simultaneously created an "everybody's doing it" mentality.

Hugh Hefner played into that mentality when he first published *Playboy* magazine in December 1953, which represented pure hedonistic pleasure … for men. *Playboy* linked sexuality with upward mobility and defined the good life as enjoying sex, liquor, smoking, and consumer products, without restraint. When Hefner published the first issue, with Marilyn Monroe as the centerfold, he was deeply in debt but sold enough copies that he could issue another, and by 1960, *Playboy* sold over a million copies a month.

Novelists joined in the celebration of sexuality. Grace Metalious, who had never written a book before, published *Peyton Place* in 1956, a novel that detailed scandalous affairs in a suburban context. Vladimir Nabokov, a respected writer, published *Lolita*, about the life of a young sex-addicted woman and a sex-obsessed middle-age man. In 1958, Grove Press published an unexpurgated edition of D. H. Lawrence's *Lady Chatterley's Lover*, unavailable previously in the United States. Whatever else Americans were doing in the privacy of their homes, larger numbers of them were clearly reading much more sexually explicit material in the 1950s than in any previous generation.

Within this context of breaking from traditional cultural norms, other artists explored their own alienation in a conformist society. In J. D. Salinger's novel, *The Catcher in the Rye*, the book's teenage hero, Holden Caulfield, saw adults as "phonies" who kept up pretenses that did not fit reality. Novelists like Ralph Ellison, Flannery O'Connor, Saul Bellow, Bernard Malamud, James Baldwin, John Updike, Mary McCarthy, and Philip Roth explored America's racism and the quiet desperation of many. In the late 1950s, poets and political radicals like Allen Ginsberg and Jack Kerouac took dissent to new levels. The "beat generation" challenged not only cultural pretentions of Eisenhower's America but also the artistic pretentions of its major critics. In Ginsberg's 1956 poem, "Howl," he complained—poetically—about the mind-numbing conformity of the era. It was Ginsberg's good luck that police in San Francisco seized

25.1

25.2

25.3

Howl and Other Poems as obscene and forced a trial that brought Ginsberg to national attention. Kerouac's *On the Road*, published in 1957, glorified escape from expectations and conventions. Some in the 1950s found themselves embracing Kerouac's belief that, "[t]he only people for me are the mad ones, the ones who are mad to live."

25.2 Quick Review

What forces supported conformity or rebellion in the 1950s?

Race and Civil Rights

25.3 Analyze the growth and impact of the Civil Rights Movement between 1954 and 1965.

Segregation, economic marginalization, and political disenfranchisement were reality for most African Americans in the 1950s, as they had been since the collapse of Reconstruction in the 1870s and 1880s (see Chapters 15 and 19). However, the African American community never accepted segregation or second-class citizenship, and in the 1950s, it seemed as if African American resistance to "separate but equal" burst forth in many different places at about the same time (see Map 25-3). Legal challenges to school segregation that had been building for decades achieved a major victory in 1954. Soon thereafter, long-simmering opposition to

Map 25-3 Civil Rights Events, 1953–1963.

Most, but not all, of the major events of the Civil Rights Movement took place in the states of the South. Important events, such as the one noted on the map in New York, also took place in the North, mostly after 1963.

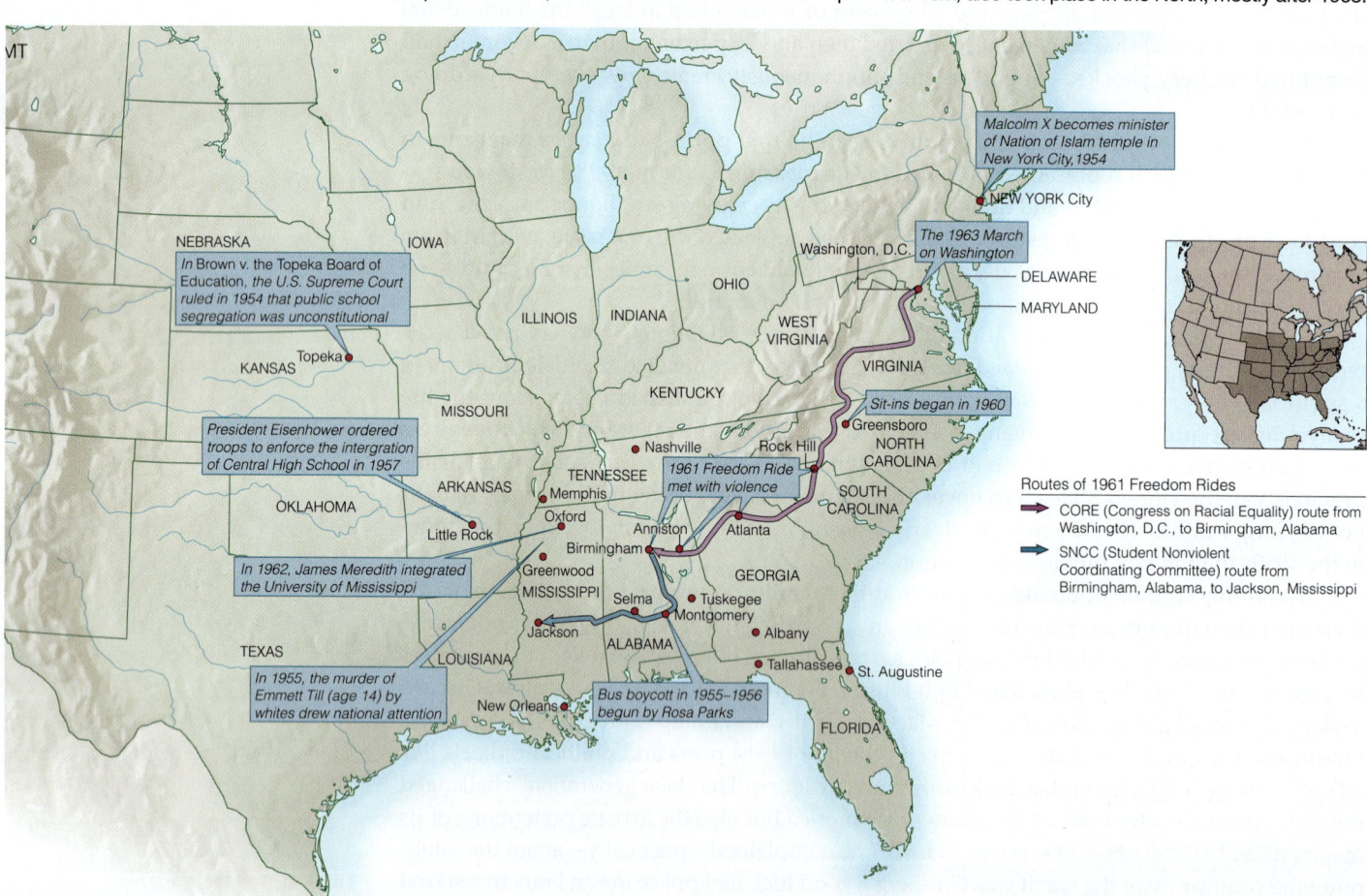

segregation in public transportation led to a yearlong bus boycott in Montgomery, Alabama. Meanwhile, young African Americans and some white supporters sat in at segregated lunch counters, organized voter registration drives, and found themselves considering significant alternatives to American culture, some in racially integrated settings and some in all-black institutions.

25.1

25.2

25.3

The Long Road to *Brown v. Board of Education*

On May 17, 1954, the United States Supreme Court announced its unanimous decision in the legal challenge to the racial segregation of public schools, a case known as ***Brown v. Board of Education***. Chief Justice Earl Warren wrote:

> We conclude that in the field of public education the doctrine of "separate but equal" has no place. Separate educational facilities are inherently unequal.

It had been a long road to that finding.

The National Association for the Advancement of Colored People (NAACP), though founded in 1909, was often only whispered about in black communities in the South throughout the 1930s, 1940s, and 1950s. In the early 1950s, Anne Moody, then a high school student in Centerville, Mississippi, asked her homeroom teacher what NAACP meant. The teacher said, "You see the NAACP is trying to do a lot for the Negroes and get the right to vote for Negroes in the South." She also warned Moody, "I shouldn't be telling you all of this. … It could cost me my job." The teacher was gone the following year.

In the 1930s, the NAACP began to challenge state "separate but equal" laws, bypassing state legislatures and governors with federal court cases arguing that the separate facilities were, in fact, far from equal. Two brilliant lawyers took charge of the NAACP legal effort—Charles Hamilton Houston, then dean of the Howard University Law School, and his former student, Thurgood Marshall. When Houston retired in 1938, Marshall, then just thirty years old, became the NAACP chief counsel, a position he held for twenty-three years. In 1961, Marshall was appointed as a federal judge serving on the U.S. Court of Appeals, and from 1967 to 1991, he served as the first African American justice of the U.S. Supreme Court.

The Houston-Marshall strategy at the NAACP was to chip away at segregation. In a 1938 case, *Missouri ex rel. Gaines v. Canada, Registrar of the University, et al.*, the U.S. Supreme Court ruled that Lloyd Gaines could not be rejected by the University of Missouri Law School on the basis of his race unless the university could offer him an equally good legal education within the state of Missouri. To offer legal education to whites but not to blacks, or to force blacks to leave the state for their education, Chief Justice Hughes said, "is a denial of the equality of legal right." In *Alston v. School Board of the City of Norfolk* in 1940, the NAACP won a ruling that said separate salary schedules for black and white teachers violated the Fourteenth Amendment. In 1950, the Court issued two rulings. In *Sweatt v. Painter*, it said that separate law schools for blacks and whites were not equal, and in *McLaurin v. Oklahoma State Regents*, it ruled that segregating graduate students violated their equal protection rights. With each case, segregation was becoming more expensive for states to maintain and the arena in which it could be exercised smaller. The time was coming for a direct challenge to *Plessy v. Ferguson*, the 1896 decision by which the Supreme Court had originally approved "separate but equal" arrangements.

While the NAACP lawyers were winning cases, students at the all-black R. R. Morton High School in Farmville, Virginia, called a strike to protest conditions at their school in 1951. Although the white school in Farmville had comfortable facilities, some classes at R. R. Morton were held in tar-paper shacks, students had to wear coats to keep warm, and the teachers had to gather wood for the wood stoves. The authorities had long promised new facilities, but construction was continually postponed.

Only after going on strike did the students appeal to the NAACP. The national organization sent word that they would consider taking the case, but only if the challenge was for completely integrated schools. The students agreed and called on the adults in their community to follow them. Thus was launched one of the five cases that would be consolidated as *Brown v. Board of Education*.

Brown v. Board of Education
A Supreme Court decision in 1954 declaring that "separate but equal" schools for children of different races violated the Constitution.

The five states whose policies were challenged in the NAACP suit hired the 1924 Democratic presidential nominee John W. Davis as their attorney to defend the separate but equal policies. However, the Supreme Court agreed with the NAACP's argument that separate education always violated the Fourteenth Amendment's guarantee of "the equal protection of the laws." The unanimous 1954 decision said, "We come then to the question presented: Does segregation of children in public schools solely on the basis of race, even though the physical facilities and other 'tangible' factors may be equal, deprive the children of the minority group of the equal educational opportunities? We believe that it does."

There were those who thought that with the *Brown* decision, the battle was over. Many years later, Kenneth Clark, whose testimony was central to the case, recalled ruefully, "How naïve I was! … I thought that within ten years or so, America would be free of it. … I expected southern states to resist, but I thought that their resistance would decrease and that we were on the road to some sort of functional democracy." It would take much more.

Some governors began massive resistance to school integration. The most dramatic took place in Little Rock, Arkansas, in the fall of 1957. Rather than allow the racial integration of previously all-white Central High School, the state's segregationist governor Orval Faubus ordered the Arkansas National Guard to stop nine African American students from enrolling in the school. In a speech the night before school was scheduled to begin, Faubus said he was making the move because of a fear of violence. "Blood will run in the streets," he said, if black students tried to enter Central High.

Nine brave young students, known as the Little Rock Nine, were scheduled to test the integration of Central High School. Elizabeth Eckford remembered the terror when she found herself face-to-face with a white mob:

> Somebody started yelling, "Lynch her! Lynch her!"
>
> I tried to see a friendly face somewhere in the mob—someone who maybe would help. I looked into the face of an old woman and it seemed a kind face, but when I looked at her again, she spat on me.

It was a harrowing experience that Eckford never forgot.

The students, the mob, and the National Guard were all recorded on national television. While President Eisenhower was no advocate of school integration, he was not about to allow an order of the U.S. Supreme Court to be flouted. He told his attorney general, Herbert Brownell, "Well, if we have to do this, and I don't see any alternative, then let's apply the best military principles to it and see that the force we send there is strong enough that it will not be challenged, and will not result in any clash." Eisenhower sent riot-trained units of the 101st Airborne. Before nightfall, a thousand U.S. soldiers were in Little Rock, securing the high school and ensuring the safety of the students.

Montgomery, Alabama

In 1955, a year and a half after the *Brown* decision, Rosa Parks finished her workday in Montgomery, Alabama, and began her bus ride home. She took a seat in the prescribed "Negro section" in the back of the bus. A few blocks later, when more whites boarded, the driver, J. P. Blake, moved the line between the sections so that all of the whites could have seats. When none of the blacks moved, Blake warned them, "You better make it light on yourselves and let me have those seats." When others moved, Rosa Parks stayed where she was. "Are you going to stand up?" Blake asked. Parks said, quite simply, "No."

Blake summoned the Montgomery police who arrested Parks. When she was allowed to call home, Parks told her mother of her arrest and her mother immediately got in touch with E. D. Nixon, the acknowledged leader of Montgomery's civil rights community, who was not a newcomer to making tough decisions. Nixon, then age fifty-six, was president of Montgomery's chapter of the NAACP. He worked as a porter on the railroad and was vice president of the Alabama branch of the Brotherhood of Sleeping Car Porters, the most powerful black-led union in the United States. He had been one of the planners of the 1941 March on

Washington. Nixon asked Clifford and Virginia Durr, Montgomery whites who were civil rights activists, to join him and the three went to the Montgomery jail to sign the bond for Rosa Parks's release. Within a few hours, Parks was free and at home.

Early in that evening, the matter could have ended. The court would probably have let Parks off with a small fine, and the segregated world of Montgomery could have returned to normal. But as Nixon and the Durrs talked with Rosa Parks, her husband, and her mother, the question arose: Was this incident the test case they had all been waiting for? In *Brown v. Board of Education* the year before, the Supreme Court had ruled that segregated *schools* were illegal. But what about transportation? If she were willing, if she could overcome her husband Raymond's fear that "[t]he white folks will kill you, Rosa," there could not be a better person than Rosa Parks for the test case they all sought.

Parks had a long history as a civil rights activist. She first tried to register to vote in 1943 when only a very tiny percentage of Alabama blacks voted. She was told she did not pass the literacy test. The same thing happened in 1944. In 1945, she hand-copied every question on the literacy test while she was taking it, in an obvious first step toward a legal challenge. Apparently the authorities wanted to avoid a legal challenge more than they wanted to avoid

The arrest of Rosa Parks in 1955 for refusing to abide by the rules of the segregated buses of Montgomery, Alabama, represented an important moment in civil rights history, one of many developments that undermined the image of the 1950s as an era of total complacency with the status quo.

her vote. She received her registration in the mail and began voting in Alabama elections in 1946. In the summer of 1955, Parks attended a desegregation workshop at Highlander. "I was forty-two years old, and it was one of the few times in my life up to that point when I did not feel any hostility from white people," Parks said.

Given her background, many have wondered whether Parks's action on the bus had been planned. She insisted it had not. But her life had prepared her for what happened. A few months later, Parks said, "There had to be a stopping place, and this seemed to have been the place for me to stop being pushed around and to find out what human rights I had, if any."

Parks, Nixon, and the Durrs retained a young African American lawyer, Fred Gray, as her attorney. Nixon began calling the local ministers including the new minister at Dexter Avenue Baptist Church, Martin Luther King, Jr., who was third on his list. Among the people Gray called that evening was Jo Ann Gibson Robinson, a professor at Montgomery's all-black Alabama State College and a leader in the black Women's Political Caucus (WPC) in Montgomery, who remembered, "Telephones jangled; people congregated on street corners and in homes and talked … [but] A numbing helplessness seemed to paralyze everyone." Without consulting other leaders, Robinson and the WPC decided to call a boycott of the Montgomery buses when Parks went on trial. She, another professor, and two students pretended that they needed to grade papers and went to their offices in the middle of the night. By 4:00 a.m. the next morning, using the school's mimeograph machine, they had prepared thousands of leaflets that said:

> Another Negro woman has been arrested and thrown in jail because she refused to get up out of her seat on the bus for a white person to sit down. … This has to be stopped. … We are, therefore, asking every Negro to stay off the buses Monday in protest.

Between 4:00 a.m. and 7:00 a.m., Robinson and her students distributed the leaflets. They finished in time for Robinson to teach her 8:00 a.m. class on schedule and then distributed more leaflets.

Robinson's leaflet fell into the hands of the white *Montgomery Advertiser*, which published news of the plan on its front page on Saturday, inadvertently helping the campaign along by spreading the news. Nearly all of Montgomery's blacks stayed off the buses that first day. At a planning meeting on Monday afternoon, Martin Luther King, Jr., then twenty-six years old, was elected president of what became the Montgomery Improvement Association (MIA). As president, King was the main speaker at a Monday evening service. He called on Montgomery's African American community to protest with courage and dignity. After King's sermon, Ralph Abernathy, minister of Montgomery's First Baptist Church,

25.1

25.2

25.3

proposed that the boycott continue until the demands—courteous treatment by the bus operators and the seating of passengers on a first-come, first-served basis, whites from the front, blacks from the back—were met. Segregation itself was not yet challenged, only the kind of humiliating enforcement of segregation experienced by Parks. From that evening it was clear; it was not to be a one-day boycott. People would wait as long as it took.

Ultimately, it took a yearlong boycott of the Montgomery buses to win the victory the black community wanted, and it took a combination of careful planning and inspirational preaching to get there. People needed courage and inspiration, but they also needed taxis and car pools to get them to work. Black-owned taxis offered reduced fares. The ministers organized car pools to help people who needed to go the longest distances.

The nation's black leadership was not enthusiastic about events in Montgomery. The Montgomery Bus Boycott was a spontaneous outburst that national leaders had played no

Thinking Historically

The Many Faces of the Civil Rights Movement

Rosa Parks's refusal to give up her bus seat in Montgomery, Alabama, in December 1955 led to a yearlong boycott of the buses, launched the career of a young Montgomery minister, Martin Luther King, Jr., and changed the course of American history. But the boycott worked only because of many who never became famous.

Besides Parks and King, some among the many who made the Montgomery boycott a national event:

- Claudette Colvin—A young African American who was arrested for refusing to give up her seat on a bus nine months before Parks but who local leaders thought was not the right candidate for a test case because she was pregnant and unmarried. Her legal appeal was later combined with that of Rosa Parks.
- E. D. Nixon—A longtime civil rights and union activist who commanded great respect in black and white communities in Montgomery.
- Clifford and Virginia Durr—White residents of Montgomery who had long supported civil rights for African Americans at considerable personal cost and who had national connections to help the local organizers.
- Fred Gray—Then a twenty-four-year-old lawyer in Montgomery who represented Rosa Parks. Gray had gone to law school with a private promise "to become a lawyer, return to Alabama, and destroy everything segregated I could find."
- Jo Ann Gibson Robinson and the members of the Women's Political Caucus—Were already urging male civil rights leaders to protest Montgomery's segregated buses.
- Ralph Abernathy—A respected senior minister and an officer of the NAACP who convinced King to support the bus boycott.
- Mother Pollard—An elderly member of King's congregation who responded to her pastor's concern that she was too old to keep walking, replying, "My feets is tired but my soul is rested."
- And thousands of additional residents of Montgomery—Committed supporters who attended

rallies, organized alternative forms of transportation, or simply walked to and from work for a year rather than break the boycott.

In thinking about how best to teach the history of the Civil Rights Movement, Diana Turk, a professor at New York University, said:

Ask most middle- and secondary-level students what they have learned about the Civil Rights Movement, and most likely they will tell you a story of great leaders who, through their bravery, and inspiring words, led millions. ... But ... much is lost when we look at history as a story of only a few individuals and their acts of heroism. As Dr. Adam Green, an historian of the black Civil Rights Movement in the United States, importantly argues, great leaders don't get very far unless they have great organizers behind them; someone needs to plan and announce boycotts and marches, set up rallies, arrange for speeches and press coverage, and spread the word about the events that together make up movements. ... Not only can a focus on organizers give students a sense of some of the important—and often forgotten—forces that helped shape history, but such an approach also can empower students to see how seemingly small, localized, and unheralded actions can truly change the course of human events.

Source: Diana Turk, Rachel Mattson, Terrie Epstein, and Robert Cohen, *Teaching U.S. History: Dialogues among Social Studies Teachers and Historians* (New York: Routledge, 2010).

Thinking Critically

1. **Comparison**
   What different roles did the diverse figures described above play in the boycott? How did their efforts reinforce each other?

2. **Argument Development**
   Defend or refute the following statement: The Montgomery Bus Boycott proves that the most important social change is produced by action on the local level.

role in organizing. Roy Wilkins, the longtime national leader of the NAACP, invited King to address the NAACP convention in San Francisco, and he expressed deep doubts about the boycott. Thurgood Marshall openly criticized King, preferring to stick with court cases. "All that walking for nothing. They might as well have waited for the court decision," Marshall said of the boycott.

But as the year wore on, the boycott had its impact. The boycott received favorable national media attention. Fundraising became easier, and King found himself becoming a national celebrity. The aged W. E. B. Du Bois wrote that, although he still had his doubts about boycotts, if King's passive resistance could undermine American racism, it would be a huge victory. On June 4, an appeals court ruled in favor of Rosa Parks, and on November 13, 1956, the United States Supreme Court concurred. Early in the morning of December 21, 1956, one year and three weeks after Rosa Parks had refused to move, King and a few others, followed by reporters, boarded the first bus of the day. "We are glad to have you," the polite driver said.

In January 1957, King, Abernathy, and some sixty black ministers created the **Southern Christian Leadership Conference**, based in Atlanta, Georgia. The MIA had been a temporary organization focused on the bus boycott. The SCLC institutionalized the energy and the planning that had started in Montgomery and created a permanent national organization and a long-term platform for King.

Southern Christian Leadership Conference (SCLC)

The leading clergy-led voice of the Southern, nonviolent Civil Rights Movement, founded in 1957 by Martin Luther King, Jr., and some sixty other black ministers, many of whom were veterans of the Montgomery Bus Boycott.

Students and Sit-Ins

On February 1, 1960, three years after the buses in Montgomery were integrated and as John F. Kennedy battled to win presidential primaries, four African American freshmen at North Carolina Agricultural and Technical College sat down at the whites-only lunch counter of the Woolworth's store in Greensboro, North Carolina. They asked politely for service and ordered coffee. After sitting at the counter all day, they still had not received their orders. Nineteen students joined the sit-in the next day, and on the third day, they numbered eighty-five. On the fourth day, more than three hundred people joined the sit-in, expanding it to another store's lunch counter. This group action was not a well-planned event. The established civil rights leaders in the NAACP and King's SCLC had not been involved and, indeed, knew nothing of it until after the fact. They struggled to decide whether to support, ignore, or lead the sit-ins. But it didn't matter what they did. The student-led sit-ins that started in Greensboro spread like wildfire across the South.

Atlanta Journal-Constitution/AP Images

The lunch counter sit-ins, launched by these students at a segregated lunch counter in Greensboro, North Carolina, in February 1960 began a new and powerful phase of the Civil Rights Movement.

25.1

25.2

25.3

25.1

25.2

25.3

Before February ended, there were sit-ins in thirty-one cities in eight Southern states. One of the largest and longest took place in Nashville, Tennessee. After hearing of the Greensboro actions, over five hundred well-dressed African American college students walked into downtown Nashville and sat down at lunch counters in all of the major stores. The Nashville police allowed a mob to beat many of the demonstrators, and more than sixty protesters were jailed in Nashville. The mayor sought compromise and agreed to appoint a biracial committee to look at segregation in the stores. The appointment of the committee was a victory long sought by Nashville's older civil rights leaders, and it had been won by the students. By July, the lunch counters in Greensboro had also become desegregated.

While many of King's peers were not sure what to make of the sit-ins, and the NAACP Legal Defense Fund was not willing to defend those arrested, King endorsed them, seeing the sit-ins as a way to confront segregation nonviolently and directly. He continued to defend the sit-ins to an older and very wary civil rights community, and the sit-ins continued to grow in significance.

From Freedom Rides to Birmingham to Washington— "I Have a Dream," 1963

While the sit-ins continued, the U.S. Supreme Court in a 1960 ruling, *Boynton v. Virginia*, declared that any segregation in interstate transportation was unconstitutional. James Farmer and others in the Congress of Racial Equality (CORE) decided to test the decision with "Freedom Rides" to hasten integration of interstate bus service and terminals through the South. They warned the attorney general and the FBI in advance. When the seven blacks and six whites on the two buses began their trip in May 1961, they encountered violence first in Rock Hill, South Carolina, where John Lewis was beaten when trying to enter a white rest room, and then in Anniston, Alabama, where one of the buses was burned and most of the riders beaten. All of the riders were beaten again when a bus reached Birmingham, Alabama—one white rider so badly he suffered permanent brain damage. An FBI informer had reported Ku Klux Klan plans to attack the Freedom Riders, but at no point did they get any federal protection. New riders who joined the effort were also beaten and arrested. Eventually, 328 Freedom Riders were arrested in the summer of 1961.

Bill Hudson/Ullstein archive/AP Images

The Birmingham, Alabama, police force used dogs to attack civil rights demonstrators, a response that brought worldwide condemnation.

When the new Kennedy administration called for a "cooling-off" period, Farmer responded that "blacks have been cooling off for 150 years. If we cool off any more, we'll be in a deep freeze." Finally, in the fall, Attorney General Robert Kennedy convinced the Interstate Commerce Commission to order that any bus or train that crossed a state line (and thus under the Constitution became subject to federal rules) could not use any segregated facilities.

In September 1962, James Meredith became the first black to enroll at the University of Mississippi, backed by a federal court order. In response, Mississippi governor Ross Barnett promised that "[n]o school will be integrated in Mississippi while I am your governor." Robert Kennedy thought he also had a private promise from Barnett to keep order on the campus, but when Barnett instead whipped up a crowd of some three thousand whites who began throwing rocks and eventually shooting, Kennedy sent federal marshals and then federal troops, who restored order at the university.

Early in 1963, King began a campaign to desegregate Birmingham, Alabama, perhaps the most segregated city in the South. He expected resistance. King was promptly arrested during a protest—and used the time to write one of his most famous publications, "Letter from Birmingham Jail." The Birmingham police, under their chief, "Bull" Connor, also arrested some three thousand protesting children and turned fire hoses and attack dogs on children and adults. Civil rights organizers also met with violent resistance elsewhere. Medgar Evers, the NAACP field secretary in Jackson, Mississippi, was murdered on his front porch that June. Riots erupted in Northern cities in July. Who knew what was coming next?

Widespread television coverage brought an international outcry about the violence in Birmingham, including criticism by the Soviet Union. President Kennedy, who had been slow to act on civil rights, but feared bad publicity especially in the context of the Cold War, introduced his long-promised civil rights bill in June 1963. Kennedy told Congress that "[t]he heart of the question is whether all Americans are to be afforded equal rights and equal opportunities." To support the proposed civil rights bill, civil rights leaders A. Philip Randolph and Bayard Rustin called for a March on Washington. On August 28, 1963, more than twenty years after Randolph first proposed a march on Washington, and one hundred years after Abraham Lincoln signed the Emancipation Proclamation, over 200,000 Americans marched in the nation's capital and listened to speeches at the Lincoln Memorial.

The keynote address of the March on Washington was delivered by Martin Luther King, Jr. In words that have become immortal, King declared that in spite of all the injustice, "I still have a dream," that the situation in America could change. In the cadences of traditional black preachers, using words from Katherine Lee Bates, Thomas Jefferson, and the biblical prophet Isaiah, King preached the hope that, in America, black people and white people could, indeed, be sisters and brothers.

Martin Luther King's "I Have a Dream" speech is now iconic, but in August 1963, it took courage to make that speech not only because civil rights workers and leaders were being beaten and killed, as King would be, but also because many would think such hopes foolish and empty. Even as King spoke, it was unclear whether Kennedy or the Congress would do much to expand freedom or pass a civil rights bill.

Martin Luther King, Jr., at the 1963 March on Washington.

25.1

25.2

25.3

The Student Nonviolent Coordinating Committee and Mississippi

On Easter weekend of 1960, some of the students who had been participating in sit-ins across the South gathered at Shaw University in Raleigh, North Carolina. Ella Baker, who helped organize the Raleigh meeting, later recalled, "Just as the sit-ins had skyrocketed

Student Nonviolent Coordinating Committee (SNCC)

Black civil rights organization founded in 1960 that drew heavily on younger activists and college students.

or escalated without rhyme or reason, so too the response to the concept of a conference escalated beyond our expectations." James Lawson, who had played a major role in the sit-in movement in Nashville and had been expelled from the Vanderbilt University Divinity School for his efforts, also joined the Raleigh conference. He told the students that their actions were "a judgment upon middle-class conventional, halfway efforts to deal with radical social evil." The students voted to form their own organization rather than affiliate with either the SCLC or the NAACP. Thus, the **Student Nonviolent Coordinating Committee (SNCC)** was born.

No one did more to shape SNCC than Ella Baker. Baker had worked for the NAACP in the 1940s. Martin Luther King recruited her to the SCLC in the 1950s, but she found herself deeply frustrated by the male dominance of the minister-led SCLC. Her own philosophy was that "[p]eople have to be made to understand that they cannot look for salvation anywhere but to themselves." John Lewis, the youngest speaker at the March on Washington and another SNCC founder, said, "We all recognize the fact that if any radical social, political, and economic changes are to take place in our society, the people, the masses must bring them about." Like many in SNCC, Lewis was distrustful of any single charismatic leader, even King. In the sit-in movement and in SNCC, Baker and Lewis found like-minded souls.

Bob Moses arrived in Atlanta in the summer of 1960 to volunteer with SNCC during his vacation from his job as a teacher in New York City. As Moses traveled through the rural South, he met some amazing people, like Amzie Moore, who lived far from the centers of civil rights activity. Moses described meeting Moore:

> He was the only adult I met on this trip who had clearly fixed the students in his sights. It was as if he had been sitting there in Cleveland [Mississippi] watching the student movement unfold, waiting for it to come his way, knowing it had to eventually come, and planning ways to use it in light of his fifteen year effort, since World War II, at making changes in the cotton plantation land of the Mississippi delta.

Moses would encounter more people like Moore on his travels, and they changed him.

Moses learned that while Moore appreciated the legal work of the NAACP, integration was not his priority. His passion was the vote. Living in a congressional district that was two-thirds black, it was obvious to Moore what the vote could do. Moses wrote to the SNCC office in Atlanta, "Amzie thinks, and I concur, the adults here will back the young folks but will never initiate a program strong enough to do what needs to be done." Thus was born SNCC's focus on a massive student-led campaign for the vote. In 1961, Moses returned to Mississippi to work full-time on voter registration for SNCC.

In September 1961, Herbert Lee, a supporter of the voter registration effort in Amite County, Mississippi, was shot by E. H. Hurst, a white state representative. Hurst admitted that he had shot Lee but was never prosecuted for the murder. Other murders followed.

Even when the threat of violence and murder was not imminent, people who had lived with segregation and violence all their lives were reluctant to challenge the system. In the winter of 1963–1964, SNCC developed a plan to bring a thousand mostly white college students to Mississippi to help with the voter registration effort and to focus national attention on the denial of rights in Mississippi. Some SNCC field organizers worried that so many whites would undermine the strength of the black community. On the other hand, grassroots leaders like Fannie Lou Hamer argued, "If we're trying to break down this barrier of segregation, we can't segregate ourselves." In June 1964, thousands of student volunteers, white and black, arrived for what became Mississippi Freedom Summer to register local African Americans to vote and to demonstrate to the nation what an interracial coalition looked like. They were met with considerable hostility. Three of the volunteers, James Chaney, a black, and Andrew Goodman and Michael Schwerner, both white, were killed in late June near Philadelphia, Mississippi. There were also tensions within the movement, yet Mississippi Freedom Summer garnered national publicity for voting rights and changed the lives of many who participated.

As more blacks registered to vote, they also organized the **Mississippi Freedom Democratic Party (MFDP)** to challenge the official all-white Mississippi delegation for the August 1964 Democratic Convention at which Lyndon Johnson, then president, was to be

Mississippi Freedom Democratic Party (MFDP)

A separate Democratic delegation, launched as a result of the SNCC-led voter registration campaign, that challenged the right of the regular, all-white delegation to represent Mississippi at the 1964 Democratic Convention.

American Voices

Fannie Lou Hamer, "Testimony to the Credentials Committee," 1964

When Fannie Lou Hamer testified at the national Democratic Convention, she had come a long way from an SNCC voter registration meeting. "Until then," she said, "I'd never heard of no mass meeting and I didn't know that a Negro could register and vote. ... When they asked for those to raise their hands who'd go down to the courthouse the next day, I raised mine. Had it up as high as I could get it."

It was the 31st of August in 1962 that eighteen of us traveled twenty-six miles to the county courthouse in Indianola [Mississippi] to try to register to become first-class citizens.

We was met in Indianola by policemen, Highway Patrolmen, and they only allowed two of us in to take the literacy test at the time. After we had taken this test ... we continued on to Ruleville ... where I had worked as a timekeeper and sharecropper for eighteen years. I was met there by my children, who told me that the plantation owner was angry because I had gone down to try to register. ...

He said, "If you don't go down and withdraw your registration, you will have to leave." Said, "Then if you go down and withdraw," said, "you still might have to go because we are not ready for that in Mississippi."

And I addressed him and told him and said, "I didn't try to register for you. I tried to register for myself."

I had to leave that same night. ...

[Hamer also described her subsequent arrest:]

I was carried to the county jail and put in the booking room. ...

I was carried out of that cell into another cell where they had two Negro prisoners. The State Highway Patrolmen ordered the first Negro to take the blackjack [a wooden club].

The first Negro prisoner ordered me, by orders from the State Highway Patrolman, for me to lay down on a bunk bed on my face.

I laid on my face and the first Negro began to beat ... I began to scream and one white man got up and began to beat me in my head and tell me to hush. ...

I was in jail when Medgar Evers was murdered.

All of this is on account of we want to register, to become first-class citizens. And if the Freedom Democratic Party is not seated now, I question America. Is this America, the land of the free and the home of the brave, where we have to sleep with our telephones off the hooks because our lives be threatened daily, because we want to live as decent human beings, in America? Thank you.

Source: http://americanradioworks.publicradio.org/features/sayitplain/flhamer.html, downloaded July 8, 2011.

Thinking Critically

1. **Analyzing Primary Sources**
   What does the document tell you about Hamer's historical situation and her motives in registering to vote?

2. **Contextualization**
   What developments in the Civil Rights Movement created the situation in which Hamer spoke?

William J. Smith/AP Images

SOURCE: Fannie Lou Hamer (1917-1977) Testimony Before the Credentials Committee, Democratic National Convention Atlantic City, New Jersey - August 22, 1964. Retrieved from: http://americanradioworks.publicradio.org/features/sayitplain/flhamer.html

nominated for reelection. Just weeks before the national convention, hundreds of newly registered Mississippi voters, having been turned away from the regular all-white Democratic Party meetings in Mississippi, met in Jackson and elected sixty-eight delegates to the convention.

The MFDP succeeded in raising the denial of voting rights in Mississippi to national attention even though its delegation was not seated at the national convention. The convention made Fannie Lou Hamer, a forty-seven-year-old Mississippi sharecropper and spokeswoman for MFDP, a national voice. Bob Moses described the MFDP delegates as "sharecroppers, domestic workers, and farmers" who were asking the national Democratic Party to truly be "the party of such people" while also "taking the first step toward gaining control over their lives."

The North and Malcolm X

By the 1960s, half of the nation's African Americans lived in the North, most in racially segregated urban neighborhoods. While the hopes of blacks in the South generally focused on ending the brutal segregation and on winning the right to vote, the hopes of Northern blacks focused on ending segregated housing patterns, poor-quality schooling, and economic marginalization. One of the most prominent voices for Northern urban blacks was Malcolm X. As Marcus Garvey had done for a previous generation, Malcolm spoke of pride, self-sufficiency, and self-determination.

Malcolm was born Malcolm Little in Omaha, Nebraska, in 1925. He remembered the grinding poverty, racism, and violence of Depression-era America.

As a young adult, Malcolm pursued a life of crime and in February 1946, just before his twenty-first birthday, received a ten-year sentence for a string of burglaries. In his *Autobiography*, he said, "I had sunk to the very bottom of the American white man's society."

While he was in prison, Malcolm experienced a religious conversion and joined the Nation of Islam, or the Black Muslims as they were commonly known. When he was released in 1952, he moved to Detroit and was soon named assistant minister at Detroit Temple Number One. The Black Muslims believed that it was important to reject traditional last names—which they saw as slave names since many came from former slave owners—and so Malcolm Little became Malcolm X. His message as a minister was, "We didn't land on Plymouth Rock, my brothers and sisters—Plymouth Rock landed on *us*! … It was a mix of pride and separation from white people—the 'white devils'—along with a call for total allegiance to Allah and Allah's Messenger Elijah Muhammad."

Malcolm disdained integration and the southern Civil Rights Movement. While he was gaining fame as "the fiery Black Muslim," Malcolm was also starting to have his doubts about Elijah Muhammad. Early in 1964, he broke with the Nation of Islam and set off on a pilgrimage to Mecca as is required of every devout Muslim man. In Mecca, Malcolm found himself among Muslims from all over the world. He was transformed by the experience. When a fellow pilgrim asked him what about the Hajj had impressed him the most, Malcolm answered, "The *brotherhood*! The people of all races, colors, from all over the world coming together as *one*! It has proved to me the power of the One God." No longer would he preach separation for its own sake. He was not any less militant, but Malcolm returned from Mecca as El-Hajj Malik El-Shabazz, a devout traditional Muslim.

When he returned to New York in 1964, Malcolm explained his new beliefs. He said of his experience in Mecca, "In the past, yes, I have made sweeping indictments of *all* white people. I never will be guilty of that again—as I know now that some white people *are* truly sincere, that some truly are capable of being brotherly toward a black man." He was willing to join interracial coalitions to achieve immediate goals and would work within as well as against the political system.

Malcolm was not willing to adopt King's nonviolence and believed African Americans needed to defend themselves. When he heard Fannie Lou Hamer describe the beating she had received, he said, "When I listened to Mrs. Hamer, a black woman—could be my mother, my sister, my daughter—describe what they had done to her in Mississippi, I asked myself how in the world can we ever expect to be respected … and we do nothing about it?"

He was not the advocate of violence that others portrayed him to be, but he would never adopt King's commitment to nonviolence. At one point he said, "Let sincere whites go and teach non-violence to white people!"

After his break with the Nation of Islam, he established his own independent Muslim Mosque Incorporated to preach what he believed was true Islam as opposed to that taught by the Black Muslims. He also established a political organization, the Organization of Afro-American Unity (OAAU), to advance his political agenda. His top priority, he said, was to submit "the case of the American Negro before the United Nations." Rather than focus on federal legislation, Malcolm believed that African Americans had a case to bring their continuing marginalization before the UN, and with the support of African and Middle Eastern nations, he was confident they would win.

More important than any organization, however, Malcolm fostered a new sense of pride in a generation of northern African Americans. He challenged the quality of education in black communities. He led demonstrations against police violence. He called on African Americans to "control the politics in his own residential areas by voting … and investing in the businesses." He had a vision of African Americans making international alliances with the people of the then newly independent African nations and with the Muslim world. As the scholar Manning Marable said of him, "Malcolm's great strength was his ability to speak on behalf of those to whom society and state had denied a voice due to racial prejudice."

The new Malcolm was willing to accept white coworkers, but not to be led or controlled. He dreamed that the day might come when "in our mutual sincerity we might be able to show a road to the salvation of America's very soul." Malcolm was assassinated by Nation of Islam followers in February 1965. But he would continue to inspire great hopes long after he was gone.

A highly controversial figure in his day, Malcolm X (1925–1965) was an eloquent speaker and writer, a passionate activist, a courageously outspoken champion of black people, and a critic of American racism. Today he is an iconic figure memorialized in poems, song, films, books, and operas.

25.3 Quick Review

Why were organizations like SNCC, CORE, the SCLC, and the NAACP essential to the Civil Rights Movement? Why were individual actors, from those who marched to those who organized to those who gave speeches, all essential?

Conclusion

The 1950s was a decade of contrasts. For many, they were the complacent decade when Dwight Eisenhower presided over a nation that had won World War II and in which many were happy to move to new suburban homes and domestic contentment. At the same time, the continuing Cold War with the Soviet Union and the threat of the hydrogen bomb greatly influenced U.S. foreign and domestic policy throughout the 1950s. Especially after the launch of the Soviet satellite *Sputnik* in 1957, the space race with the Soviet Union prompted Americans to panic about the state of its technology and its education system. Among African Americans, the many-faceted Civil Rights Movement transformed their lives and U.S. practices of segregation.

During the Eisenhower administration (1953–1961), the United States pursued policies that attempted to minimize the costs of the Cold War, protect the non-Communist world from Communist infiltration, and avoid armed confrontation. Key pieces of Eisenhower's foreign policy included the threat of "massive retaliation" with hydrogen bombs and the extensive use of spying and covert operations in foreign countries. When the Soviet Union launched the first space satellite, the American government responded by creating NASA to manage space exploration and by establishing new domestic programs linking education to national defense.

The 1950s were relatively peaceful and prosperous for many Americans. The economy continued to grow, and many experienced a substantial increase in family income. Americans also became much more active in religious organizations during the period. At the same time, television came to dominate American popular culture. Most of the programming of the 1950s sought to reaffirm the suburban lifestyles of the white middle class, and new thirty-second television commercials encouraged Americans to buy everything from Alka-Seltzer to automobiles. The automobile also rose to prominence in 1950s America, giving rise to new industries to support cars and to an interstate highway system. However, America's love affair with the automobile required more and more highway construction and a steady supply of cheap gasoline—an issue that would come to dominate American politics.

In the 1950s, the modern Civil Rights Movement began to challenge the segregation, marginalization, and political disenfranchisement that had been commonplace for African Americans for almost a century. After decades of court challenges by the NAACP, the U.S. Supreme Court finally ruled in 1954 that racial segregation of public schools was unconstitutional. Civil rights protesters also successfully boycotted segregation of the public transportation system in Montgomery, Alabama, and conducted sit-ins demanding the integration of lunch counters across the nation. The newly created Student Nonviolent Coordinating Committee worked for voting rights in the South.

A very different civil rights leader emerged in the North. Malcolm X became a prominent Northern voice for the nation's African Americans. He rejected the integration-focused strategy of Southern civil rights leaders and spoke of pride, self-sufficiency, and self-determination for blacks free from white interference. Malcolm was assassinated in February 1965, but the Civil Rights Movement continued to press for full equality on many different fronts throughout the 1960s.

Chapter Review

In what ways was the United States a different country in 1960 from that in 1950? How did domestic and international events influence these changes in American society?

Chapter 25 Summary and Review

Eisenhower's America, America's World

25.1 **Explain the continuation of the Cold War under a new Republican administration.**

Summary

Postwar foreign policy was profoundly shaped by the possibility of nuclear war. Eisenhower's foreign policy centered on two key elements: the threat of massive nuclear retaliation and the use of covert operations. Under Eisenhower, the CIA was given the task of destabilizing and overthrowing foreign governments that were deemed unfriendly to U.S. interests. In some areas such as Indochina, the United States took the place of declining European imperial powers. The Soviet launch of *Sputnik* sparked U.S. entry into the "space race." Over the course of Eisenhower's eight years in office, efforts toward better relations between the United States and the Soviet Union moved forward in fits and starts, with both sides remaining wary of the other. In 1960, John F. Kennedy won a narrow victory over Richard Nixon, which signaled to many Americans that a generational shift had occurred in American politics.

Review Questions

1. Argument Development
   What were Eisenhower's overarching foreign policy objectives? How successful was he in achieving those objectives?

2. Contextualization
   Why did the United States and the Soviet Union find it so difficult to move past their mutual distrust and build a less confrontational relationship?

A Culture on the Move

25.2 **Explain the impact of cultural and technological changes on the country.**

Summary

The United States underwent dramatic social and cultural changes over the course of the 1950s. Television quickly became an American institution and helped create a shared national culture. The popularity of automobiles led to the creation of an interstate highway system, which in turn created new industries, altered community development patterns, and changed the way Americans worked and lived. The number of Americans who were members of churches and other religious organizations grew substantially. The intense cultural pressure to conform provoked dissent and rebellion across many cultural outlets, especially music and literature.

Review Questions

3. Contextualization
   How do you explain the origins of the religious boom of the 1950s? What influences might the Cold War have had on the boom?

4. Argument Development
   Figures like Elvis Presley and Allen Ginsberg were seen as rebels of the postwar period. What exactly were they rebelling against?

Race and Civil Rights

25.3 **Analyze the growth and impact of the Civil Rights Movement between 1954 and 1965.**

Summary

In the 1950s, African Americans and their supporters launched a multipronged movement to combat segregation and discrimination. Decades of sustained effort by the NAACP and other organizations culminated in the 1954 Supreme Court ruling in *Brown v. Board of Education* that overturned the doctrine of "separate but equal." Implementation of the *Brown* decision faced intense resistance from many white Southerners. The Montgomery Bus Boycott focused attention on segregation and discrimination in public transportation and made Martin Luther King, Jr., a national figure. Student activists played crucial roles in the civil rights protests of the early 1960s, particularly through sit-ins, Freedom Rides, and black voter registration. In the North, Malcolm X offered an alternative to the southern Civil Rights Movement that rejected nonviolence and had its roots in black nationalism.

Review Questions

5. Continuity and Change over Time
   How is the white Southern opposition to *Brown v. Board* part of a very long story about efforts to maintain a segregated society?

6. Comparison
   Compare and contrast Malcolm X and Martin Luther King, Jr. What were the most important similarities and differences in their responses to racial discrimination and segregation?

1. Preparing to Write: Plan Your Argument

Long Essay Question—Evaluate the extent to which there are similarities in mass culture during the 1920s and the 1950s.

One way to structure your argument is by the topics music, broadcasting, and literature. Within each section, you can compare and contrast. A Venn diagram can help you plan. Note that when you do plan, go beyond cataloging similarities and differences and get to the "So what?" question. What is something interesting that comes out of this comparison? Why does this comparison matter? Your answers to these questions can be the basis of your thesis.

2. Preparing to Write: Organize Your Evidence

Document-Based Question—Evaluate the extent to which the direct action strategy shaped the Civil Rights Movement from 1955 to 1965.

You can begin by developing a thesis. (As you survey the evidence, feel free to look ahead to the story of the Selma March and the Voting Rights Act in Section 26.3.) How can Fannie Lou Hamer's account from "American Voices" in Section 25.3 help support your thesis? As you explain how, address how the context of the previous ten years is important in understanding her testimony.

Chapter 26
Lives Changed
1961–1968

Bernie Boston/The Washington Post/Getty Images

This widely publicized picture of an antiwar demonstrator putting a flower in the end of a rifle at the October 1967 March on the Pentagon reflects some of the deepest divisions of the 1960s.

Chapter Objective

Demonstrate an understanding of the unique time known as "the sixties."

⌄ Learning Objectives

New Voices, New Authorities

26.1 Explain the growing social protest in books, films, and student movements starting in the early 1960s.

Camelot, the White House, and Dallas—The Kennedy Administration

26.2 Analyze the successes and failures of the Kennedy administration and how they interacted with popular culture in the United States.

The Coming of Lyndon B. Johnson

26.3 Analyze the successes and failures of the Johnson administration in terms of the two issues that dominated his years in office—the launching of the Great Society programs and the war in Vietnam.

In 1960, while Kennedy and Nixon contested the presidency, a handful of white students organized **Students for a Democratic Society (SDS)**. SDS represented a new birth of activism on the part of white young people just as the Student Nonviolent Coordinating Committee (SNCC) had given voice to the activism of African American students (see Chapter 25). The birth of groups like SDS and SNCC guaranteed that the 1960s would not be as quiet as the 1950s. As Bob Dylan, the best-known folk singer of the early 1960s, sang, "The times they are a-changing'."

Student protesters and folk singers were far from the only signs that something new was brewing in American culture after 1960. New literature signaled numerous changes. Between 1961 and 1963, new books challenged fundamental issues—the ways cities were developing, the pollution of the environment, and the quiet desperation of many women's lives.

The new president also represented a generational change in American politics, and there would be many more political changes to come. This chapter traces the dynamic changes that some Americans embraced, others rejected, but few ignored as the United States experienced the decade known to many simply as "the sixties."

New Voices, New Authorities

26.1 **Explain the growing social protest in books, films, and student movements starting in the early 1960s.**

Though it was formative for many, the Civil Rights Movement was only one of many challenges to American culture in the 1960s. Writers and artists had often been uncomfortable with the conformity of the 1950s, and their uneasiness took on new forms as the new decade began. Small political movements burst onto a larger stage. The result was a number of books, films, and songs that reflected and helped shape a rapidly changing culture, while wide-ranging protest movements, often led by students, changed not only college campuses but also the country.

Books, Films, Music

Jane Jacobs was a writer and activist in New York's Greenwich Village when she wrote *The Death and Life of Great American Cities* in 1961. In the opening line of that book, Jacobs said, "This book is an attack on current city planning and rebuilding." Indeed, it was an amazingly successful attack. Reflecting on the book's impact, one urban planner wrote, "When an entire field is headed in the wrong direction … then it probably took someone from outside to point out the obvious." After Jacobs, city planners in New York and most cities turned away from massive highway development, sprawling suburbs, and isolated urban high-rise buildings to focus on smaller, more neighborhood-friendly options. Projects to bulldoze slums and build highways were replaced in the 1960s by the redevelopment of existing urban neighborhoods. Jacobs did not bring about this change single-handedly, but her book was a guidebook to a new generation of urban planners.

Rachel Carson's *Silent Spring* is often called the bible of the conservation movement. Other people, dating back to Theodore Roosevelt, talked about conserving rather than taming nature, but Carson gave the preservation movement a new focus in the 1960s. While earlier conservation efforts focused on protecting land from development, Carson described in graphic detail what pesticides were doing to birds and animals.

Michael Harrington's *The Other America*, also published in 1962, is sometimes credited with launching the Kennedy-Johnson War on Poverty. Harrington's popular book voiced a growing concern, urging a new look at the urban and rural poverty that had gone unnoticed in the affluent 1950s, and the critic Dwight McDonald convinced President Kennedy to read it. Harrington put a human face on the way poverty was hidden in modern America, writing, "The poor still inhabit the miserable housing in the central area. . . . The failures, the unskilled, the disabled, the aged, and the minorities are right there, across the tracks, where they have always been. But hardly anyone else is. … They have no face; they have no voice." The War on Poverty began to change that reality in 1964 and 1965.

26.1

26.2

26.3

Pictorial Press Ltd/Alamy Stock Photo

Rachel Carson's research into the disastrous environmental impact of DDT and other chemicals was published as a book, *Silent Spring*, in 1962. The book and her subsequent efforts have been credited as part of the beginning of the modern environmental movement.

Students for a Democratic Society (SDS)

A student organization, founded in 1960, to give voice to a new wave of student protest.

Betty Friedan's *The Feminine Mystique*, published in 1963, played an equally central role in the development of the new women's movement of the late 1960s and early 1970s (see Chapter 27). *The Feminine Mystique* named what Friedan called the "problem that has no name": the "comfortable concentration camp" where white middle-class suburban women lived.

Published in England in 1963, though only later in the United States, a much more personal book, *The Bell Jar*, by the Boston-born poet Sylvia Plath (then living in England), told a story that reflected Plath's own life—most of all, as she wrote to her mother, how "isolated a person feels when having a breakdown." Though Plath was reflecting on a serious case of depression, which later took her life, *The Bell Jar*, like *The Feminine Mystique*, struck a nerve among many women who had been pushed by their culture to accept the role of homemaker and helper to a successful husband. In the late 1960s and early 1970s, a generation of women found multiple ways to break out of this and other oppressive lifestyles.

26.1
26.2
26.3

Thinking Historically

Rachel Carson's *Silent Spring*, 1962

Rachel Carson grew up in a rural community northeast of Pittsburgh on the Allegheny River. As an adult, she worked for the federal Fish and Wildlife Service and in 1951 published The Sea Around Us, *a description of ocean life. The book was a great success, and Carson then decided to study the impact of DDT and other chemicals on the environment. The result was* Silent Spring, *which changed the way many Americans thought about the environment. Carson warned:*

Since the mid-1940s over 200 basic chemicals have been created for use in killing insects, weeds, rodents, and other organisms described in the modern vernacular as "pests," and they are sold under several thousand different brand names.

These sprays, dusts, and aerosols are now applied almost universally to farms, gardens, forests, and homes—nonselective chemicals that have the power to kill every insect, the "good" and the "bad," to still the song of birds and the leaping of fish in the streams, to coat the leaves with deadly film, and to linger on in the soil—all this though the intended target may be only a few weeds or insects. Can anyone believe it is possible to lay down such a barrage of poisons on the surface of the earth without making it unfit for all life? They should not be called "insecticides," but "biocides."

Carson was criticized by the chemical industry. President Kennedy, however, was impressed with the book and ordered his Science Advisory Committee to review it. Kennedy subsequently banned domestic use of DDT, and in 1970, President Nixon created the Environmental Protection Agency.

Source: Rachel Carson, *Silent Spring* (Boston: Houghton Mifflin, 1962).

Thinking Critically

1. **Analyzing Primary Sources**

   Who do you think Carson's primary audience was? How might Carson have responded to critics in the chemical industry? How might people's jobs or political views have impacted their point of view regarding Carson's work?

2. **Continuity and Change over Time**

   How were the conservation efforts inspired by Carson different from earlier conservation efforts such as those of Teddy Roosevelt?

Each of these books sold thousands, sometimes hundreds of thousands, of copies. They were read by college students and people of every age, and were discussed on the radio and television, in newspaper editorials, in sermons in religious communities, and around family dinner tables, bringing their ideas to many who never read them. Each book reflected changes that were already under way and, at the same time, each speeded change.

Joan Baez and Bob Dylan, singing together at the 1963 Newport Folk Festival, represented a new folk music that was often linked directly to protest movements.

Films and music had possibly even more influence on Americans. In the 1960s, films and music took on a new and harder edge. Stanley Kubrick's *Dr. Strangelove* portrayed the leaders of the United States and the Soviet Union as crazed militarists willing to destroy the world. Later in the decade, *Bonnie and Clyde* (1967), *The Wild Bunch*, and *Easy Rider* (both 1969) showed a level of violence not previously seen in films, reminding audiences that this world was still a very violent one.

Many who had enjoyed the provocative rock 'n' roll sexuality of Elvis in the 1950s listened to the provocative protest folk songs of Bob Dylan and Joan Baez in the early 1960s and later to the drug-influenced acid rock of Jimi Hendrix, Pink Floyd, and the Grateful Dead in the later 1960s. Change, protest, and disengagement were increasingly reflected in film and song.

Protest songs and angry movies, however, did not completely dominate the media in the 1960s. The sentimental celebration of love and marriage, *The Sound of Music* (1965), earned $100 million, the highest gross income of any movie up to that time. *The Adventures of Ozzie and Harriet* continued to be one of the most popular TV series up to 1966. In addition, the traditional music on the *Lawrence Welk Show* and the symphonic pop music of Henry Mancini competed with folk and rock throughout the decade. The sixties were far from a unified decade, in culture or politics, but the very depth of the disunity was one of the hallmarks of the times.

The Student Movement of the 1960s

Universities had long been the location for challenges to the norms of the larger society. During the Great Depression of the 1930s, there were many student demonstrations. But the sheer numbers of students and the new attitudes of the baby boom generation who came to college in the 1960s transformed college life. In 1947, as a result of the GI Bill, college enrollments reached a historic high, and they continued to grow in each following decade.

Budgets for higher education grew even faster than enrollments. As sociologist and 1960s student activist Todd Gitlin noted, "By 1960 the United States was the first society in the history of the world with more college students than farmers." Ten years later, the nation had three times as many students as farmers. Although most of the students of the late 1940s and 1950s had been relatively quiet, the students of the 1960s were not.

Students who had founded the Students for a Democratic Society (SDS) in 1960 met at Port Huron, Michigan, in 1962 to draft a statement of their beliefs. The 1962 Port Huron statement, of which Tom Hayden, then a graduate student, was the prime author, began, "We are people of this generation, bred in at least modest comfort, housed now in universities, looking uncomfortably to the world we inherit." Recognizing their baby boom origins, the statement continued, "Many of us began maturing in complacency," but then, "[a]s we grew, however, our comfort was penetrated by events too troubling to dismiss … the Southern struggle against racial bigotry [and] the enclosing fact of the Cold War." The Port Huron statement noted "a yearning to believe there is an alternative to the present, that something can be done to change circumstances in the school, the work places, the bureaucracies, the government. … It is to this latter yearning, at once the spark and engine of change, that we direct our present appeal." The spark and the "yearning to believe there is an alternative to the present" would characterize the decade of the 1960s for many, especially the young.

Not long after SDS was launched, another student movement emerged at the University of California at Berkeley. In the fall of 1964, the Berkeley administration issued a directive that student organizations that were raising funds for off-campus causes such as civil rights using tables set up on the university grounds had to move those efforts off campus. Opposition to the directive quickly united students. When petitions and meetings with the university administration did not resolve the issue, a group of students, some of whom had spent the previous summer in the South as part of Mississippi Freedom Summer, called for civil disobedience in Berkeley.

Students brought their tables back to campus and waited to see what would happen. Before long, campus police arrived and arrested Jack Weinberg, who had been sitting at one of the tables, placing him in a police car. Quickly, some three thousand students surrounded the car, and for the next thirty-two hours, while Weinberg sat in the car, speaker after speaker used the top of the car as a platform. The long spontaneous rally launched the Free Speech Movement at Berkeley.

In December of that year, at a much larger student rally on the Berkeley campus, Mario Savio, a junior philosophy major who emerged as the prime voice of the student protest during the siege of the police car, told his fellow students, "There's a time when the operation of the machine becomes so odious … you've got to put your bodies upon the gears and upon the wheels, upon the levers, upon all the apparatus and you've got to make it stop." Hundreds marched into the administration building to stop the university's wheels. They sat in for two days until arrested. Berkeley remained a center of student protest.

26.1 Quick Review

How did newly critical books and films, changes in popular music, and student protest symbolize the changes coming to the United States in the early 1960s?

26.1

26.2

26.3

26.1

26.2

26.3

Camelot, the White House, and Dallas— The Kennedy Administration

26.2 Analyze the successes and failures of the Kennedy administration and how they interacted with popular culture in the United States.

The student protests were but one aspect of the changes taking place in the early 1960s. The January 1961 inauguration of John F. Kennedy (referred to often as JFK) brought the youngest president elected in the nation's history to replace the oldest who had served up to that time. A new generation was taking charge of the country from college campuses to the White House. Kennedy partisans remembered his years in office as "one brief shining moment"—to cite the lines of the then-popular *Camelot*, a Broadway play about medieval glory to which the Kennedy's glamour was often compared. Certainly John Kennedy, his young and attractive wife, Jacqueline Bouvier Kennedy, and their extended family made for a dramatic comparison with the sometimes dowdy Eisenhowers. They were able to project an image of glamour, youth, vigor (the president's favorite word, pronouncing it with his Boston accent as "vigah"), and wit. Kennedy loved to spar with the press and they with him. During the Kennedy years, the White House was the scene of gala events, concerts, and dinner parties not seen in Washington for some time. The hopes and expectations for change that arrived with Kennedy were unmistakable.

The New Frontier

Civil rights advocates also had high hopes for the Kennedy administration, believing that the new president, who had gone out of his way as a candidate to support Martin Luther King, Jr., would do more to support the cause of civil rights than Eisenhower. The Kennedy administration created a Committee on Equal Employment Opportunities headed by Vice

AP Images

Jacqueline Kennedy and her husband made the White House a center of grace and culture as in this reception honoring Nobel Prize winners, including the poet Robert Frost and the novelist Pearl Buck.

President Johnson to look into discrimination in hiring. They hired blacks in the federal government, including some in high positions in the civil and foreign service. JFK nominated African Americans, including Thurgood Marshall, to federal judgeships. During the presidential campaign in 1960, Kennedy promised to introduce a new federal civil rights bill if elected. But throughout 1961 and 1962, no such bill emerged from the White House. He also had promised to end racial discrimination in federal housing with the "stroke of a pen," but when no order emerged, civil rights organizers started sending thousands of pens to him.

Kennedy remained slow to move on civil rights. He could count votes in the Congress, and Southern senators with high seniority made congressional action hard to imagine. The Kennedys were also good at gauging voter interest, and in 1961 and 1962, not that many white voters seemed interested in civil rights issues. At the same time, J. Edgar Hoover hated Martin Luther King, Jr., and was convinced that he was a sexual degenerate and a Communist. He had tapes to prove extramarital activity on King's part, if nothing to show that he was a Communist. Hoover also had tapes to prove President Kennedy's considerable extramarital activities, which may well have made both Kennedy brothers reluctant to challenge Hoover, who they allowed to tap King's telephones. Whatever the reasons, the vaunted Kennedy vigor was not brought to civil rights.

In other areas, Kennedy's **New Frontier**, as he called his domestic policy, was more successful. Working closely with House Speaker Sam Rayburn, the administration was able to win an increase in the federally mandated minimum wage. At their urging, Congress also provided funds for job training and tougher regulations for testing new drugs before they went on the market. JFK was the first president since Herbert Hoover to include no women in the cabinet, but he appointed Eleanor Roosevelt to head the Presidential Commission on the Status of Women, which recommended federal laws against sex discrimination. Kennedy issued executive orders ending sex discrimination in the federal civil service and signed the 1963 Equal Pay Act, which mandated equal pay for equal work. In part because of a mentally ill sister, Kennedy cared deeply about mental health and, at his urging, Congress passed the Mental Retardation Facilities and Community Mental Health Act in 1963, which funded support for mental health programs.

In May 1961, Kennedy, who had been critical of the lack of interest in space exploration by the Eisenhower administration, advocated a significant increase in funding for the National Aeronautics and Space Administration (NASA) and made a promise that within ten years the United States would safely land a man on the moon. Although Kennedy did not live to see the promise fulfilled, in 1969, the nation celebrated that accomplishment.

The chair of his Council of Economic Advisers, Walter Heller, convinced Kennedy that a tax cut would stimulate the economy, leading to greater prosperity for Americans and improved standing of the Kennedy administration with voters. Kennedy fought hard for the tax cut and won. Nevertheless, as a whole, the domestic record was disappointing. The *New York Times* for November 12, 1963, said, "Rarely has there been such a pervasive attitude of discouragement around Capitol Hill. … This has been one of the least productive sessions of Congress within the memory of most of its members."

Religion, Education, and the Courts

Just as Kennedy had his reasons for not wanting to deal with civil rights, he also had very strong reasons for not wanting to deal with the issue of religion. As the first Catholic to be elected president, he wanted to steer clear of anything that might imply his religion was influencing his work. But as with civil rights, issues of religion were bubbling.

On June 25, 1962, the U.S. Supreme Court announced its decision in the case of *Engel v. Vitale*. By a 6–1 vote, the Court declared that schools in New York State could not open the school day with a prayer the state government had recommended. The specific prayer was of relatively recent origin. As the Cold War led to a fear of "godless communism," the New York State Board of Regents, which had responsibility for all public schools in the state, recommended—but did not require—opening the school day with prayer and then composed a suggested one. The prayer was bland, and any students who objected could be excused when it was recited. Nevertheless, there were problems. Nonbelievers did

---

26.1

26.2

26.3

New Frontier

The name given to the domestic programs of the Kennedy administration (1961–1963).

Engel v. Vitale

U.S. Supreme Court decision that banned mandated prayers or devotional Bible reading in American public schools.

not want to say any prayer. Devout believers found the vague prayer close to blasphemy. When Joseph and Daniel Roth asked to be excused from their Long Island classroom during the prayer, they were taunted. Their father, Lawrence Roth, challenged the prayer in court. As the case was combined with others and moved through the courts, it generated public attention and anger. In the end, Justice Hugo Black spoke for the Supreme Court majority in saying, "We think that the constitutional prohibition against laws respecting an establishment of religion must at least mean that in this country it is no part of the business of government to compose official prayers."

A year later, the Court went further, and in a 1963 decision, *Abington School Board v. Schempp*, the Court ruled that any devotional reading of scriptures or recitation of prayers was unconstitutional. The Court went out of its way to insist that the academic study of religion, including the study of the Bible "for its literary and historic qualities," not only was constitutional but also was to be encouraged. However, it was not the business of government, the Court said, to lead devotional activities.

The Supreme Court's decisions provoked a firestorm. Many claimed that the Court was "legislating God out of the public schools." New York congressman Frank J. Becker proposed an amendment to the Constitution to allow voluntary prayer and Bible reading. The evangelist Billy Graham said, "The trend of taking God and moral teaching from the schools is a diabolical scheme." Alabama governor George Wallace said, "I don't care what they say in Washington, we are going to keep right on praying and reading the Bible in the public schools of Alabama." While Catholics had once opposed devotional activities in public schools, sure that they would be Protestant, New York archbishop Francis Cardinal Spellman now said he was "shocked and frightened" by the Court's decisions. The decisions were the beginnings of a cultural war that would last for decades.

Kennedy's Foreign Policy—From the Bay of Pigs to the Cuban Missile Crisis

In a private conversation with his defeated rival, Richard Nixon, President Kennedy asked Nixon, "Foreign affairs is the only important issue for a president to handle, isn't it?" Kennedy said he really didn't care about the minimum wage "compared with something like Cuba." While Americans receiving minimum wage might care a great deal about it, Kennedy's focus was, indeed, Cuba, Germany, Vietnam, China, and perhaps most of all the Soviet Union. In his inaugural address, Kennedy had promised to "pay any price, bear any burden, meet any hardship, support any friend, oppose any foe to assure the survival and success of liberty." He came to office a devout Cold Warrior and remained one.

The first test of Kennedy's Cold War resolve came early. The corrupt government of Cuban dictator Fulgencio Batista had been overthrown at the beginning of 1959, late in Eisenhower's second term. The new revolutionary government led by Fidel Castro was very popular in the United States during its first few months in office. Castro was welcomed in the United States and even appeared on the *Ed Sullivan Show*. Organized crime, which had enjoyed a haven for gambling and prostitution in Cuba under Batista, was driven out by Castro to the applause of most Americans. However, the Cuban-American relationship quickly soured. The new revolutionary government executed a number of Batista supporters—too many, most Americans thought. As part of its land reform efforts, the Castro government seized the island's large commercial enterprises, including vast holdings of American sugar and oil companies. Unhappy business interests—legitimate and illegitimate—began a public relations campaign against the new Cuban government. Castro's Communist leanings also became clearer as Cuba developed close ties with the Soviet Union. Before long, Soviet military advisors arrived in Cuba. By the time Kennedy came to office in January 1961, many considered Cuba to be a virtual satellite of the Soviet Union. The Eisenhower administration had developed plans to train a volunteer force to invade the island. Influential people, including JFK's father, former ambassador Joseph P. Kennedy, urged Kennedy to take action. While some advisors had reservations, Allen Dulles, the head of the Central Intelligence Agency (CIA), was a strong advocate, and Secretary of Defense McNamara and the Joint Chiefs of Staff approved the invasion.

On April 15, 1961, less than three months after JFK took office, American-based planes bombed Cuba. Two days later, a brigade of 1,400 U.S. volunteer troops landed at the **Bay of Pigs** on Cuba's south coast. The plan was for the force to connect with Cuban anti-Castro forces, which the CIA was convinced were ready to rise up against the regime. In fact, no internal revolt sprang up. Cuban defenses were strong. When the attackers called for further air support from the United States, Kennedy refused. He had become convinced that the attack was doomed. Within hours, 114 of the invaders were killed and 1,189 taken prisoner. The Bay of Pigs fiasco was a huge embarrassment for Kennedy. He took personal responsibility for the failure. He also fired Allen Dulles. For the rest of his term, Kennedy would be more cautious and less willing to trust advisors in the CIA.

Kennedy's first summit with Soviet leader Nikita Khrushchev took place in June 1961 in Vienna, just two months after the Bay of Pigs crisis. The meeting did not go well. Khrushchev gloated over the Soviet Union's success in getting the first man into space when Yuri Gagarin orbited the earth in April. He also made threatening comments about Berlin. Khrushchev seemed to believe that the new president was weak and could be browbeaten. In fact, his actions only strengthened Kennedy's inclination to show he could be tough. Two months later, Khrushchev ordered the construction of what came to be known as the **Berlin Wall** to separate the Soviet zone of the city from the western zone and similar barriers separating all of East Germany from West Germany. German Communists complained that their Socialist system provided free education for people who then took their skills west to make more money. After August 1961, no such movement, nor family visits or other travel, were possible.

By fall, Berlin had become very tense. Some Kennedy advisors suggested that the United States should use force to stop construction of the Berlin Wall. Others wondered whether access would be blocked as it was at the time of the Berlin Airlift. By the end of October, U.S. and Russian tanks faced off in Berlin. Some wondered whether World War III was about to begin. Eventually, the United States and the Soviet Union compromised. Kennedy acknowledged that he would "rather have a wall than a war," and Khrushchev did not try to close off access to Berlin as Stalin had done. While the city remained a flash point, and the Berlin Wall stayed in place until November 1989, the crisis passed.

The third major foreign policy crisis of the Kennedy administration—and the most dangerous—took place in October 1962. Again, the focus was Cuba. After the U.S. failure in the Bay of Pigs invasion, Cuban-Russian ties grew stronger and the Soviets sent more military personnel to Cuba. In the summer of 1962, the Soviets began building missile bases in Cuba that could house medium-range missiles pointed at the United States. As U.S. reconnaissance flights showed proof of the missiles in Cuba, it became clear that a major crisis—the **Cuban Missile Crisis**—was brewing.

In this crisis atmosphere, Kennedy convened an "Executive Committee" of the National Security Council. For thirteen tense days in October 1962, these advisors debated the next U.S. step. Moderates led by UN Ambassador Adlai Stevenson urged restraint. Why panic about a new missile site, they asked, when the United States had missiles in Turkey and there were enough submarine-based missiles to destroy the planet? Hard-liners, including former secretary of state Dean Acheson and National Security Adviser McGeorge Bundy, urged an immediate U.S. attack on the missile site. A third group, led by Robert Kennedy, opposed a surprise strike, which, RFK said, would make his brother "the Tojo [the Japanese premier who ordered the attack on Pearl Harbor] of the 1960s." The president agreed with his brother's position and overruled the hard-liners, but he was also determined to be tough.

On October 22, President Kennedy informed Khrushchev in both a diplomatic communication and a prime-time television speech that the United States would enforce a complete "quarantine" against future military shipments to Cuba and that the United States would meet any Soviet retaliation anywhere in the world with a "full retaliatory response." The stakes could not be higher. If a Soviet ship ran the blockade, it would be fired on by the United States. If the Soviets made a military move, the United States was prepared to fire missiles. Many worried that the world was on the brink of nuclear war. The next morning, as the first Soviet ships approached, people held their breath. Then the Soviet freighters turned around. Secretary of State Dean Rusk said, "We're eyeball to eyeball, and the other fellow just blinked."

26.1

26.2

26.3

Bay of Pigs

A 1961 invasion of Cuba by anti-Castro rebels, backed by the Kennedy administration, that was quickly defeated, much to Kennedy's embarrassment.

Berlin Wall

A substantive partition built by East Germany on instructions from the Soviet Union that cut off all travel between East and West Berlin from 1961 to 1989.

Cuban Missile Crisis

A tense standoff between the United States and the Soviet Union in October 1962 during which each country stood on the brink of nuclear war over the placement of Soviet missiles in Cuba.

An American surveillance plane took pictures like this one of missile facilities in Cuba that deeply worried the Kennedy administration.

Behind the scenes, Kennedy and Khrushchev had come to an agreement. The Soviets agreed to remove the missiles in return for an end to the quarantine of the island and a promise that the United States would not invade. The United States also agreed to remove its missiles from Turkey but did not announce its decision. An unthinkable war had been avoided. Both leaders quickly took steps to avoid a repeat of the crisis, and new communication systems—especially a "hot line" from the Pentagon and White House to the Kremlin—were set up so there would be no delay in communication in any future crisis.

Some military leaders and Cuban exiles were furious at Kennedy. U.S. Air Force General Curtis LeMay (who had commanded the bombing of Tokyo in 1945) stunned the president when he told him, "It's the greatest defeat in our history, Mr. President. ... We should invade today." Others wondered whether Kennedy allowed his machismo to get the best of him when the missiles in Cuba were no more of a threat than others already in place and hardly worth a world war.

In spite of the 1960 campaign rhetoric in which Kennedy had accused Eisenhower of allowing a "missile gap" to develop between the United States and the Soviet Union, once in office, Kennedy acknowledged that no such gap existed. Nevertheless, the Kennedy administration increased military spending from $47.4 billion when it took office to $53.6 billion in its last budget. The United States expanded the number of Polaris submarines armed with missiles as well as the number of land-based missiles in the United States. Each side in the Cold War had enough missiles to destroy the world multiple times.

The administration created a new "flexible response" policy as an alternative to Eisenhower's "mutually assured destruction." They gave high priority to creating "counterinsurgency" forces called the Green Berets that could engage in small-scale military operations in hot spots around the world. In planning for Cuba, where the administration had a special interest, they developed Operation Mongoose, a secret CIA program to destabilize the Castro regime by contaminating Cuban sugar, causing explosions in Cuban factories, and developing at least thirty-three plans to assassinate Castro, all of which failed.

In addition to Kennedy's efforts to contain communism, the administration launched a new effort at peace in Laos, support for the U.S. Agency for International Development (AID), and efforts at economic reform in Latin America and elsewhere. Kennedy also launched the **Peace Corps**, through an executive order, to recruit young idealistic Americans to spend two years abroad as volunteers working on education and development projects. In the spring of his first year in office, the president, joined by First Lady Jacqueline Kennedy, dazzled Europe.

Nearing the end of his first term, however, Kennedy's foreign policy legacy was mixed. Chester Bowles, who served for a time as undersecretary of state in the Kennedy administration, said that the Kennedy inner circle were "full of belligerence" and "sort of looking for a chance to prove their muscle." A nuclear-armed world was a dangerous place to do such a thing. Nevertheless, in November 1963, in spite of ongoing tensions in Southeast Asia, Berlin, and Cuba, JFK was still immensely popular in many parts of the world, and the world was at peace. The president turned his attention to his 1964 reelection campaign.

Peace Corps

A program launched by the Kennedy administration to recruit young idealistic Americans to spend two years abroad as volunteers working on education and development projects.

Dallas, Conspiracies, and Legacies

The Kennedy team wanted to ensure that Texas, home of the vice president, stayed Democratic in 1964. But the Democratic Party in Texas was deeply divided and Kennedy was not popular in there. Some Texans, indeed, had a deep visceral hatred for him. In November 1963, Kennedy dreaded the trip he needed to make to build his standing in the Lone Star State.

After the president and Jackie Kennedy arrived in Dallas on November 22, 1963, they rode into the city center in a caravan, the president and First Lady along with Texas governor John Connally and his wife in the first car, Vice President Johnson in the next one. A little after noon, as they passed the Texas School Book Depository, several shots rang out. One wounded Connally. Two hit the president. A back brace he wore for constant back pain held him erect and the second shot hit his head. By the time the president's car reached the nearest emergency room, the president was dead. A Catholic priest offered the last rites.

Vice President Lyndon Johnson had been right behind Kennedy's car and quickly understood what had happened. In the afternoon, Johnson, flanked by his wife, Lady Bird, and by Jacqueline Kennedy, with JFK's blood still on her dress, took the presidential oath of office. Then they flew to Washington. Kennedy's death provoked an outpouring of national grief. Suddenly, the youthful vigor that the president had projected, and the hopes that many Americans had projected onto him, seemed to dim.

Lyndon Johnson insisted that the presidential party wait until Kennedy's coffin was brought to Air Force One, still parked at the airport where it had arrived that morning, before taking the oath of office on board the presidential plane.

Lee Harvey Oswald was arrested for the murder. His fingerprints were on the gun and he had easy access to the window where the shots were fired. Two days later, another troubled man, Jack Ruby, shot Oswald in the Dallas police station. Many suspected a widespread conspiracy. President Johnson asked Supreme Court Chief Justice Earl Warren to lead

26.1

26.2

26.3

a high-level bipartisan commission to find out the truth. The commission's report—known as the Warren Report—concluded that Oswald acted alone. Not everyone was convinced; no one could confirm for sure the whole story behind Kennedy's death. Whatever the truth, a very different kind of person became president on November 22, one who would lead the administration and the country with a dramatically different style and set of priorities.

26.2 Quick Review

What were the major accomplishments and frustrations of the Kennedy administration?

The Coming of Lyndon B. Johnson

26.3 Analyze the successes and failures of the Johnson administration in terms of the two issues that dominated his years in office—the launching of the Great Society programs and the war in Vietnam.

John F. Kennedy had been born to wealth and had attended Harvard College. As a child he had met Franklin D. Roosevelt because his father was Roosevelt's ambassador to Great Britain. He was elected to Congress as a war hero after his small boat, *PT-109*, had been sunk in the Pacific during World War II, and he had served eight years in the U.S. Senate before becoming president. Kennedy was handsome and charismatic, important factors in his election and continuing popularity.

Lyndon Johnson was born to poverty in the Texas hill country northwest of San Antonio and grew up in a small house in Johnson City when there were no sidewalks or electricity. His tough and slightly wild father served in the Texas legislature, trying hard to make ends meet, and his strong-willed mother yearned for a better life. LBJ, as he was often called, attended Southwest Texas State Teachers College. He arrived in Washington as a congressional secretary a year before Roosevelt was elected and managed to meet FDR, whom he idolized and who in 1935 appointed the then twenty-six-year-old LBJ as the director of the National Youth Administration for the state of Texas. Johnson worked harder than any other NYA state director, got important services for Texas, and never forgot the value of government when he saw the New Deal bring jobs, electricity, and hope to people living isolated lives in rural poverty.

Johnson had a long and distinguished career in Congress before becoming vice president. He was first elected to the House of Representatives in 1937. He campaigned tirelessly and worked equally tirelessly once in office, building strong ties and coalitions. LBJ and his wife, Lady Bird, became a family for the sometimes lonely bachelor Sam Rayburn, another Texan, who served as Speaker of the House for all but four years between 1940 and 1961. LBJ lost a primary race for a Senate seat in 1941 but won the seat in 1948. Once in the Senate, Johnson built connections to the powerful committee chairs. In 1953, at the age of forty-five, he was elected Democratic leader in the Senate. In 1955, he suffered a severe heart attack, recovered quickly, and kept working, kept building coalitions, becoming known for the "Johnson treatment," when he would grab a colleague by the coat lapels and hold his face an inch away while using anger, humor, and statistics to win a wavering vote. He was highly respected for his ability to get things done in the Senate, even if he was often feared and seldom liked. Few said he was handsome or charismatic. Everyone said he was effective.

Johnson hated his tenure as vice president. Many of Kennedy's inner circle, especially Attorney General Robert Kennedy, made sure he was kept out of the most significant decisions. Once he became president, LBJ desperately wanted to be loved as Kennedy had been, but most of all was determined to get things done in a way that Kennedy had not been able to do. On the domestic front, he succeeded masterfully at moving his agenda along before slowly sinking into the morass of Vietnam.

The famous Johnson treatment often involved very close face-to-face encounters, as here with President Johnson seeking support from his mentor, Senator Richard Russell of Georgia, who would not support the president on the civil rights bill.

The War on Poverty and the Great Society

In his first speech as president, five days after Kennedy was shot, LBJ mourned with the nation, but he also demonstrated a confident leadership that the country was looking for. Johnson told the Congress that he was determined to continue the "Kennedy dream" of education, jobs, care for the elderly, and "equal rights for all Americans." One could question whether, given his focus on foreign policy, those goals had actually been Kennedy's dream, but they would certainly be Johnson's. Johnson insisted that "[n]o memorial or oration or eulogy could more eloquently honor President Kennedy's memory than the earliest possible passage of the civil rights bill for which he fought so long." Congress was being put on notice that the former powerful Democratic majority leader of the Senate, now president, was determined to see his legislation passed.

Later, after he left office, Johnson explained his approach to the presidency. "If it's really going to work, the relationship between the President and the Congress has got to be almost incestuous. He's got to know them even better than they know themselves. And then, on the basis of this knowledge, he's got to build a system that stretches …, from the moment a bill is introduced to the moment it is officially enrolled as the law of the land." And that was exactly what Johnson did. He made sure he knew who would support each bill, knew what the specific desires were of those who might be brought to support a measure, and knew how to cajole those who did not want to support it. He rewarded supporters with phone calls, personal notes, White House invitations, and special services in their states and districts, and he never hesitated to punish opponents. He came to office with a Democratic majority in both houses of Congress and a nation mourning a fallen president. He used that circumstance, plus his incredible legislative skill, to move significant legislation through an often reluctant Congress.

Johnson's first agenda was the stalled civil rights bill. Everyone expected the bill that Kennedy had submitted to be watered down. Johnson, normally the great compromiser, would not allow any tampering with the bill. He was determined to keep every section intact. He broke with his Senate mentor, Richard Russell of Georgia, who led the opposition to the bill, and, instead, made an alliance with the Republican Senate minority leader, Everett Dirksen of Illinois. With Dirksen's help, Republicans and Democrats overcame a Russell-led filibuster. The most sweeping civil rights bill since Reconstruction was passed and signed by Johnson on July 2, 1964. It not only included provisions for equal access and equal opportunity but also specifically forbade discrimination in employment based on race, color, religion, and national origin as well as outlawed discrimination based on sex, a clause that later feminists would use most effectively. The law established a new Equal Employment Opportunity Commission to ensure enforcement.

As Johnson pushed hard for the Civil Rights Act of 1964, he also tackled a broader agenda. In his first State of the Union speech in January 1964, Johnson said, "This administration, today, here and now, declares unconditional war on poverty in America." Then in May, he used the commencement speech at the University of Michigan to describe what he called the **Great Society**, which would be how he described all of his domestic programs. Kennedy had already started efforts to attack poverty in the United States, but Johnson, the New Dealer from Texas, had seen what federally financed rural electrification did to change the lives of poor people and was passionate (see Map 26-1, p. 790). He idolized Franklin Roosevelt and wanted to imitate him. He also knew that if he wanted to remain in office, he would have to face a skeptical electorate in only eleven months and he wanted to present a solid track record.

The first legislation of the War on Poverty was passed by Congress in August 1964. It included provision for many of the programs later associated with the Great Society, including Volunteers in Service to America (VISTA), a domestic peace corps that recruited young people to work for a year serving in high-poverty urban and rural settings; a Neighborhood Youth Corps to provide jobs for poor youth (modeled on the Civilian Conservation Corps of the New Deal era); work study loans and grants to support college students; small-business loans; community action programs directed at building up grassroots organizing ventures; Head Start to provide poor children with the same sort of readiness for kindergarten that their more well-off counterparts got at home; Neighborhood Legal Services, which provided

The Great Society

The name Lyndon Johnson gave to his far-reaching domestic program, which included federal aid to education, Medicare and Medicaid health insurance, immigration reform, and before long, the Voting Rights Act.

Map 26-1 Americans in Poverty.

This map shows the percentage and distribution of Americans living below the poverty line at the end of the 1960s.

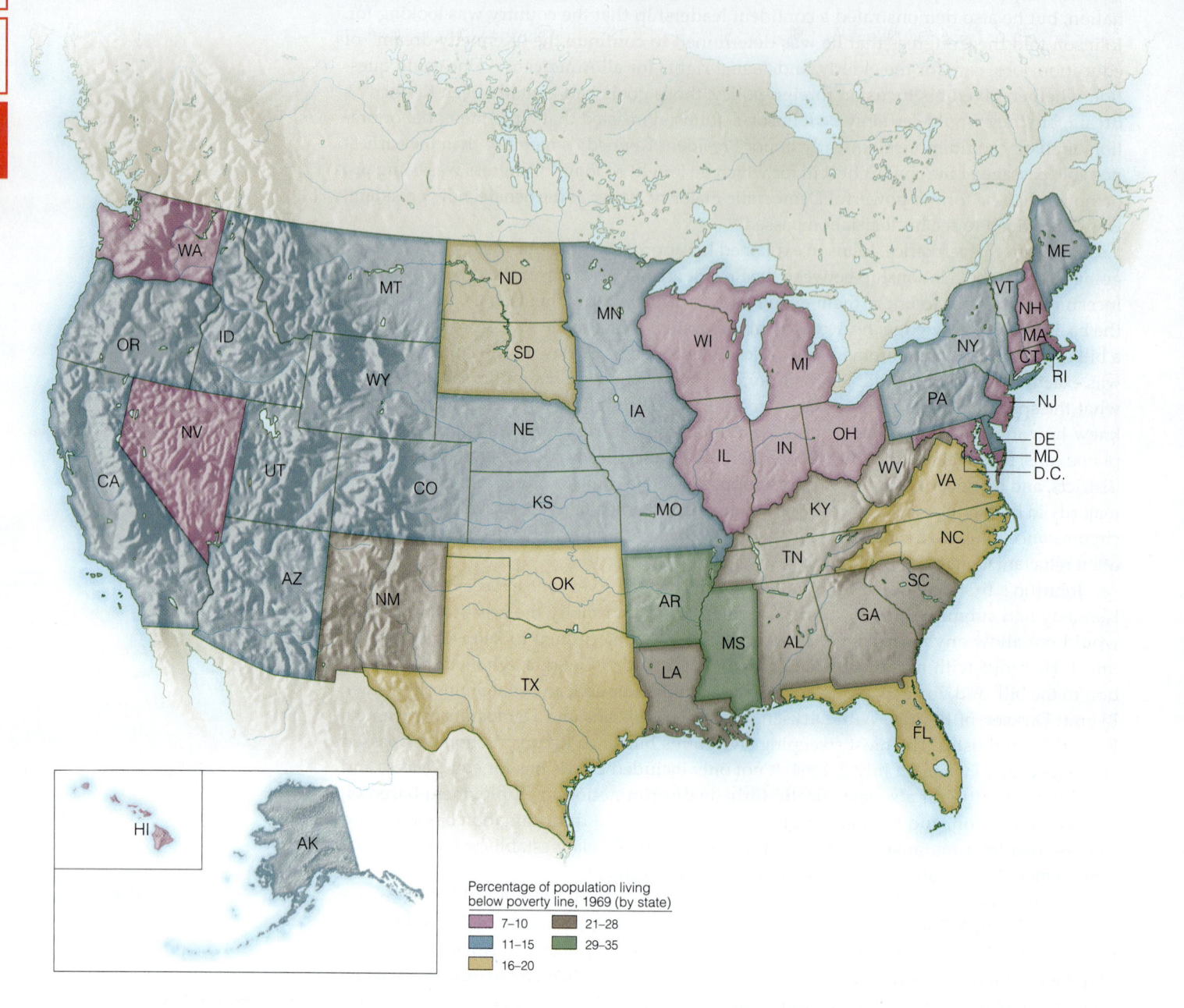

Percentage of population living
below poverty line, 1969 (by state)

▮	7–10	▮	21–28
▮	11–15	▮	29–35
▮	16–20		

government-funded lawyers for the poor; and to coordinate all of these ventures, an Office of Economic Opportunity. This impressive agenda was only a first step for Johnson, but to do more, he needed to be elected in his own right.

Johnson wanted to not only win election in 1964 but also win with such a mandate that nothing could stand in the way of his programs. Before he could do that, however, Johnson had to face a divided Democratic Party, a Republican opponent, and his own inner demons. Johnson's insecurities ran deep. He knew that the Kennedy family despised him. He knew that he did not have their urbane sophistication and that, a century after the Civil War, much of the country still distrusted Southerners. He also knew—powerfully so—that he had become president—the office he had wanted all his life—only through a terrible tragedy.

Despite his concerns, however, Americans saw LBJ as the sitting president who had taken command of the situation when JFK was killed, and Johnson had no serious resistance to the 1964 nomination. Notwithstanding, Johnson was under great pressure to name

American Voices

Lyndon B. Johnson, "Great Society Speech," 1964

Six months after he had taken the oath of office in Dallas, Lyndon Johnson gave the commencement address at the University of Michigan. He used the speech to outline the Johnson plan for the Great Society—to improve the quality of life for all Americans.

I have come today from the turmoil of your Capital to the tranquility of your campus to speak about the future of your country. …

… For in your time we have the opportunity to move not only toward the rich society and the powerful society, but upward to the Great Society. The Great Society rests on abundance and liberty for all. It demands an end to poverty and racial injustice, to which we are totally committed in our time. But that is just the beginning.

The Great Society is a place where every child can find knowledge to enrich his mind and to enlarge his talents. …

So I want to talk to you today about three places where we begin to build the Great Society—in our cities, in our countryside, and in our classrooms. …

Our society will never be great until our cities are great. Today the frontier of imagination and innovation is inside those cities and not beyond their borders.

New experiments are already going on. It will be the task of your generation to make the American city a place where future generations will come, not only to live but to live the good life. …

A second place where we begin to build the Great Society is in our countryside. We have always prided ourselves on being not only America the strong and America the free, but America the beautiful. Today that beauty is in danger. The water we drink, the food we eat, the very air that we breathe, are threatened with pollution. Our parks are overcrowded, our seashores overburdened. Green fields and dense forests are disappearing. …

A third place to build the Great Society is in the classrooms of America. There your children's lives will be shaped. Our society will not be great until every young mind is set free to scan the farthest reaches of thought and imagination. We are still far from that goal. …

These are three of the central issues of the Great Society. …

So, will you join in the battle to give every citizen the full equality which God enjoins and the law requires, whatever his belief, or race, or the color of his skin?

Will you join in the battle to give every citizen an escape from the crushing weight of poverty?

Will you join in the battle to make it possible for all nations to live in enduring peace—as neighbors and not as mortal enemies?

Will you join in the battle to build the Great Society, to prove that our material progress is only the foundation on which we will build a richer life of mind and spirit?

Source: Lyndon B. Johnson, Speech to the Graduating Class, University of Michigan, Ann Arbor, May 22, 1964, Public Papers of the Presidents of the United States, Lyndon B. Johnson, Book I (1963–1964), pp. 704–707.

Thinking Critically

1. **Contextualization**

   How much did the voices of protest, which were so strong in the United States in the 1960s (see Chapter 25 and the start of this chapter), shape the context for Johnson's agenda?

2. **Comparison**

   Knowing that Johnson idolized Franklin Roosevelt, what parallels do you see between the Great Society and the New Deal? What important differences?

Attorney General Robert Kennedy as his running mate. There was a logic to the move; Bobby (as he was always known) was keeper of the Kennedy legacy and his nomination would unite the party. Still, as Johnson later wrote, "With Bobby on the ticket, I'd never know if I could be elected on my own." In addition, Johnson deeply disliked Bobby Kennedy. He was convinced that Bobby had tried to derail his own vice presidential nomination in 1960. Eventually, LBJ informed Bobby that he would not be his running mate and, instead, supported him in a successful run for the U.S. Senate from New York. Johnson selected liberal Minnesota senator Hubert Humphrey to be his vice president. Humphrey, though more liberal than Kennedy or Johnson, was also deeply loyal to Johnson, perhaps even to a fault.

The most serious challenge to Johnson's easy nomination came from the Mississippi Freedom Democratic Party (MFDP), in which grassroots civil rights activists sought the convention seats of the regular Mississippi delegation that had been elected in white-only caucuses (see Chapter 25). Although Johnson was a supporter of civil rights, he was concerned that, if the "regular" Mississippi delegates were unseated by the Mississippi Freedom delegates and walked out, and those from Alabama and other nearby states joined them, then it would threaten the Democrats' hold on several Southern states. Johnson did not want to risk a repeat of the 1948 Dixiecrat revolt. Neither Johnson nor other party leaders understood the depth of anger that stirred the MFDP protest, nor did they see, as the MFDP leaders did, the way in which the movement represented a new form of grassroots democracy. Neither the choice of running mate nor the MFDP challenge hurt Johnson's election chances, but both illustrated deep divides in American politics that even Johnson's masterful negotiating skills could not bridge.

The Republican Party was deeply divided in 1964. The original front runner for the Republican nomination, New York's liberal governor Nelson Rockefeller, had left his wife of many years to marry a younger woman. At that point, the country had never elected a divorced person as president. There was also significant conservative opposition to Rockefeller's nomination. Many conservative Republicans were determined that in 1964 the party would nominate a "real conservative," and Rockefeller's main opponent for the nomination was the conservative Arizona senator Barry Goldwater.

Goldwater, an affable and tolerant individual, had friends across the political spectrum and spurned personal racial prejudice. However, he opposed civil rights legislation as an invasion of personal freedom. He felt the same way about the graduated income tax and most other government programs. Further, he called for a more aggressive opposition to communism, even in places where Communist regimes were well established, saying that America "could lob one into the men's room at the Kremlin." He won most of the primary contests, and when the Republican Convention met in San Francisco, the delegates were so committed to him that they shouted down Nelson Rockefeller. When Goldwater spoke, he said, "Let me remind you that extremism in defense of liberty is no vice … and that moderation in pursuit of justice is no virtue." It was just what the delegates wanted to hear. It was less popular, however, with the wider electorate.

The Democrats made good use of Goldwater's statements, developed a sophisticated television advertising campaign, and painted Goldwater as a dangerous man. Johnson won in a landslide. As he left the inaugural ball in January 1965, Johnson told his staff, "Don't stay up late. There's work to be done. We're on our way to the Great Society." The next day that work started.

In the spring of 1965, the triumphant Johnson pushed four major pieces of legislation through Congress in addition to a raft of other bills that, on their own, would have been considered significant with any other Congress. The core Great Society legislation of 1965 included federal aid to education, Medicare and Medicaid, immigration reform, and the Voting Rights Act.

Johnson knew that federal aid to education had been blocked for many years by civil rights activists out of the fear that aid might go to segregated schools and by a deadlock between Catholic representatives, who would not support aid unless it went to parochial as well as public schools, and many Protestant representatives, who would never support aid to Catholic schools. Johnson was determined to break the deadlock. The Civil Rights Act of 1964 solved the first issue since it made it illegal for any segregated institution to receive federal aid. Johnson solved the divide on religion with a policy by which federal education funds would follow the child, whichever school the child was in. The Elementary and Secondary Education Act was submitted to Congress in January 1965 and passed in three months. Johnson signed it at a ceremony in front of a school that he had once attended, with one of his former teachers sitting beside him.

Every Democratic president since Franklin Roosevelt had also sought to provide federal health insurance, especially for the elderly. A coalition led by the American Medical Association, fearing government control of medical practices, stopped every effort. However, half of all Americans over age sixty-five had no health insurance and they, too, were a powerful constituency. Within months of being proposed, Congress created Medicare, offering basic medical insurance to everyone over sixty-five. Arkansas congressman Wilbur Mills, a close Johnson ally, added a provision to the Medicare bill, creating Medicaid, which provided federal funding for medical insurance to Americans living in poverty. For some old and poor people, the resulting Medicare and Medicaid legislation enabled the first visit to a medical doctor in their lives.

Even though there was not a lot of pressure to reform the nation's immigration laws in the 1960s, Johnson was determined to make immigration reform a part of the Great Society. The highly restrictive laws of 1921 and 1923 drastically limited immigration, virtually cutting off anyone from eastern Europe, Africa, or Asia (see Chapter 21). Pressure for change came from New York representative Emanuel Celler, who had tried and failed to get an exception to the old and restrictive "national origin" quotas so that Jews could flee Nazi Germany and who was now determined to change the law (see Chapter 23).

The Immigration Act of 1965 abolished the old quotas, though it hardly made immigration easy. The legislation held the total number of immigrants at 290,000 (the number who were expected annually under the old law), but established priorities for education and skills rather than national origin. The law also provided an important loophole, allowing immigration above the new quota for close relatives of U.S. citizens, including foreigners who married a citizen. Although little change was expected when the legislation was signed, the new immigration law represented the beginning of a significant new era of immigration, one that matched and then exceeded the number of immigrants who came to the United States from 1890 to 1920.

The fourth major piece of legislation that Congress enacted in 1965 was the Voting Rights Act. As 1965 began, Johnson did not have additional civil rights legislation on his agenda. The Civil Rights Act of 1964 was the most significant congressional intervention in civil rights since Reconstruction. Johnson wanted to focus in 1965 on other aspects of his Great Society and did not relish another round of conflict with Richard Russell and other Southern senators. Civil rights leaders, however, did not mean to take a back seat to anyone else's agenda.

Martin Luther King, Jr., decided to create a national confrontation around the right to vote (see Chapter 25). The 1964 Civil Rights Act banned segregation in public accommodations and the use of federal funds for any segregated institution, but it did not address the right to vote. In many parts of the Deep South, more than 90 percent of blacks were kept off the voting rolls. As they had for decades, county voting registrars used literacy tests and other techniques to make it extremely hard for a black person to register to vote, and, as Fannie Lou Hamer's eloquent testimony at the 1964 Democratic Convention showed, when legal techniques failed, outright violence was used. The Mississippi Freedom Democratic Party may not have gotten seated at that 1964 convention, but they had made an impression on many Americans. King and the SCLC were determined to keep the issue of the vote for African Americans alive. When they selected Selma, Alabama, as the site for a major confrontation, SNCC, which had focused on voting rights from its founding, agreed to join. Segregation in Selma was rigid, despite the Civil Rights Act. The city of 29,000 included 15,000 blacks of voting age. Only 355 of those black citizens were registered to vote.

The demonstrations in Selma, Alabama, and the violent response shocked the world. On Sunday, March 7, as the Selma marchers began to cross the Edmund Pettus Bridge, sheriff's deputies charged them on horseback, clubbing people right and left. John Lewis, the head of SNCC (and a future member of Congress), was one of several people who were knocked unconscious. Pictures of "Bloody Sunday," as the day became known, were shown around the world. Two weeks later, marchers, now protected at Johnson's directive by the Alabama National Guard, finally completed a march to the state capital of Montgomery. That evening, the marchers happily sang, "We have overcome." But the same evening, KKK members followed one of the marchers' supporters, Viola Liuzzo of Detroit, as she drove black marchers home from the event, and those Klan members killed her. The country had had enough of this sort of violence.

Only a week after the Bloody Sunday march, Johnson went before Congress to give one of his most memorable speeches. He told Congress and the nation:

> This time, on this issue, there must be no delay, no hesitation, and no compromise.... Because it is not just Negroes, but really it is all of us who must overcome the crippling legacy of bigotry and injustice. And we shall overcome.

Hearing the first president from the South since the Civil War speak uncompromisingly of the right to vote while using the words of the Civil Rights Movement's hymn moved many to tears.

The Voting Rights Act, which with unrelenting pressure from Johnson passed Congress by overwhelming majorities, gave the U.S. Department of Justice the right to intervene in any county where 50 percent or fewer of the eligible voters were registered—virtually all of the Deep South. Agents could monitor literacy or other tests and if necessary appoint new federal registrars. On August 6, 1965, Johnson signed the law in the same room where Lincoln had signed the Emancipation Proclamation 102 years earlier (see Map 26-2).

With the Voting Rights Act, the Immigration Act, Medicare and Medicaid, and the Elementary and Secondary Education Act, and a host of other measures, Johnson was doing what he knew how to do best, getting federal legislation, federal money, and federal enforcement powers to address specific issues. He was certainly not without his critics. Many worried that the education funds were being used to expand already bloated school bureaucracies. Medicare and Medicaid seemed to be a huge new federal program that would eventually bankrupt the country. The Civil Rights Act and Voting Rights Act, though popular, also created disaffection with Johnson and the Democratic Party that would, as Johnson knew, turn many Southerners into Republicans.

Johnson's personality was also a problem. Although he was a master of legislation and gave some of the most memorable speeches of any president, he was also a very difficult person. He could be crude and cruel, especially to those closest to him. George Reedy, who served as Johnson's press secretary and saw him close up, said, "[A]s a human being he was a miserable person—a bully, sadist, lout, and egoist. ... [H]is lapses from civilized conduct were deliberate and usually intended to subordinate someone else do to his will." Such behavior might be effective when arm-twisting was needed to get a bill through Congress, but it also left precious little reservoir of goodwill when Johnson got into trouble. After 1965, Johnson got into a lot of trouble, especially in foreign policy.

Reflecting on the Johnson administration, Averill Harriman, a senior advisor to every president from Roosevelt to Johnson, said, "LBJ was great in domestic affairs. ... [I]f it hadn't been for ... Vietnam he'd have been the greatest President ever." In analyses of the Johnson presidency, "If it hadn't been for Vietnam" is a steady refrain. The war in Vietnam destroyed national support for Johnson and the Great Society. The war divided Americans as no war since the Civil War. Opposition to and support for the war created a new political divide within the country and destroyed many long-standing allegiances. Cynicism about the con-

Map 26-2 The Impact of the Voting Rights Act.

This map shows the significant increase in African American voter registration between 1960 and 1966 as a result of the Voting Rights Act.

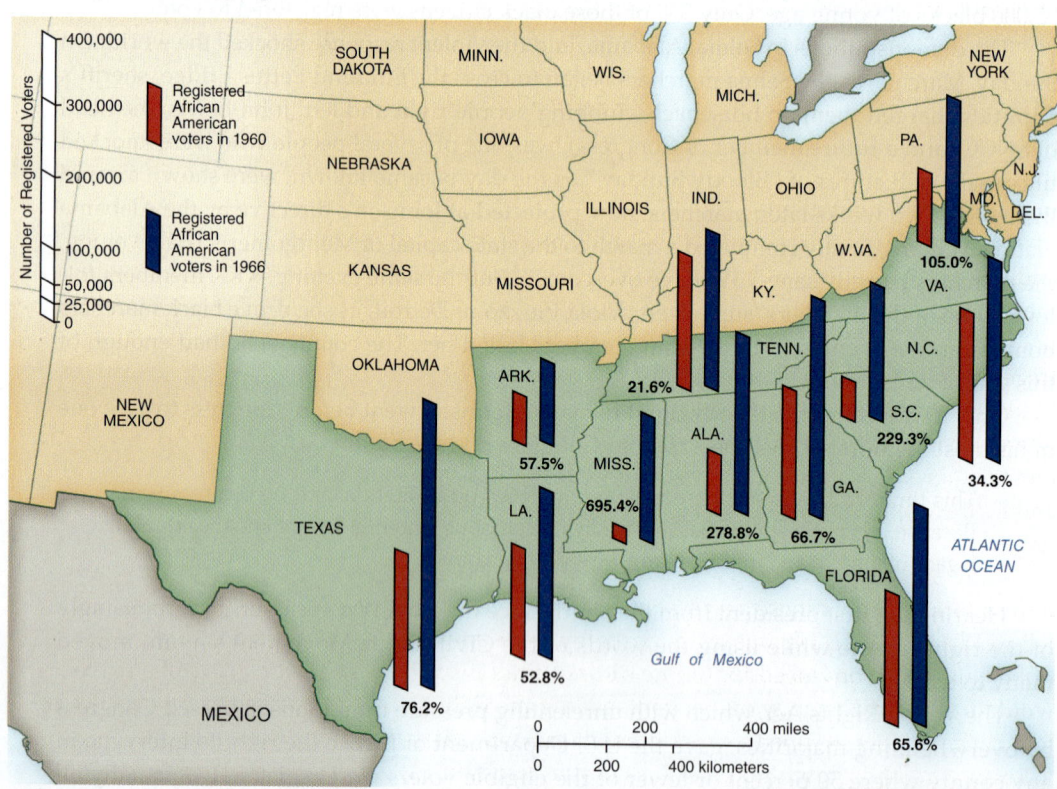

duct of the war became cynicism about government itself and eventually all authorities. The war cost fifty-eight thousand American lives, and many thousands more were wounded in body and mind in the turmoil of Vietnam. Whatever one's ultimate judgments about the U.S. effort in Vietnam, it is impossible to understand the history of the United States in the late 1960s and beyond without understanding the impact of that war.

26.1

26.2

26.3

Vietnam

Kennedy's foreign policy priorities were Cuba and Berlin. Until the final weeks of his life, he did not pay a lot of attention to Vietnam. When Kennedy became president, the United States had fewer than one thousand troops in Vietnam, sent to train the South Vietnamese army. Slowly, JFK authorized small increases not only to train troops but also to join them on combat missions against infiltrators from the North Vietnamese Army (NVA) and their allied South Vietnamese insurgents organized as the National Liberation Front (NLF). So-called counterinsurgency and strategic hamlet programs were designed to find and destroy enemy forces. Unfortunately, the violence of these missions and the corruption of the South Vietnamese regime under the leadership of the increasingly despotic Ngo Dinh Diem undermined popular support. Diem was part of a Catholic elite minority in a country where the majority was Buddhist. Although his Christianity and his anti-communism made him an appealing figure in the United States, his despotic and corrupt administration alienated many Vietnamese.

In the summer of 1963, fierce protests were mounted within South Vietnam against the Diem regime. Quang Duc, a Buddhist monk, burned himself to death on June 11 to protest conditions, and more protests and self-immolations followed. Kennedy's new ambassador to Vietnam, Henry Cabot Lodge, Jr., lost all faith in Diem and, with Kennedy's tacit agreement, supported a military coup against Diem. The CIA-backed coup took place on November 1, and Diem and his brother were killed, something Kennedy had not necessarily expected. And then, three weeks later, Kennedy was dead. Some seventeen thousand U.S. military "advisors" were in Vietnam.

As he became president, LBJ wanted to use the office to focus on domestic policy. From the beginning, however, he felt he could not ignore Vietnam, and, he insisted, "I am not going to be the President who saw Southeast Asia go the way China went [to communism]." It was a fateful vow. Equally fateful was the fact that, on balance, Johnson himself was as insecure about foreign policy as he was secure about domestic policy. Winning a war was a very different thing from getting Congress to pass a bill. LBJ kept Kennedy's foreign policy advisors, and most of them were convinced that communism had to be contained around the globe. If Communist North Vietnam threatened non-Communist South Vietnam, then, they believed, the United States needed to protect the non-Communist south, however unpalatable the fight might be.

Plans for expanding the war were on Johnson's desk from the day he became president and, although he eventually implemented them, he did delay expanding the U.S. involvement in Vietnam (see Map 26-3, p. 796). He wanted to defeat Barry Goldwater in the 1964 elections, and part of his strategy was to paint Goldwater as a crazy warmonger. He also wanted to get the Great Society legislation through Congress. Even so, Johnson said in retrospect, "I knew from the start that I was bound to be crucified either way I moved. If I left the woman I really loved—the Great Society—in order to get involved with that bitch of a war on the other side of the world, then I would lose everything at home. … But if I left that war and let the Communists take over South Vietnam, then I would be seen as a coward and my nation would be seen as an appeaser."

Johnson convinced himself that being "seen as an appeaser" in Vietnam would lead to new Soviet and Chinese aggression elsewhere, just as appeasement with Germany had led to World War II. He was intimidated by the Kennedy legacy of toughness in foreign policy and was convinced that, if he did not find a way to save South Vietnam, "[t]here would be Robert Kennedy out in front leading the fight against me, telling everyone that I had betrayed John Kennedy's commitment to South Vietnam … that I was a coward." For a Texan who had grown up on stories of the heroes of the Alamo, being called a coward

26.1

26.2

26.3

Map 26-3   The War in Vietnam.

Vietnam, South and North, and sites of major battles in the U.S.-led war.

was simply beyond contemplation. Johnson's fear proved to be ironic since, four years later, Robert Kennedy would run as an antiwar candidate against Johnson.

Throughout 1964, LBJ increased the military advisors modestly, from seventeen thousand to twenty-three thousand, but he did all he could to keep Vietnam off of the front pages in the year of the election. The one big exception came on August 1, when there were reports that a North Vietnamese torpedo boat fired on the U.S. destroyer *Maddox*. Johnson ordered an immediate military response. Johnson also went to Congress and asked for a resolution granting him the right to use "all necessary measures" to repel any attacks against the U.S. forces in Vietnam. The **Gulf of Tonkin Resolution** passed easily—unanimously in the House and with only two dissenting votes in the Senate—and in later years, it was this resolution, rather than any further congressional action, that presidents Johnson and Nixon used to prosecute the war. Only many years later did historians discover that there was no

Gulf of Tonkin Resolution

Legislation passed by Congress in 1964 that allowed the United States to use force to protect U.S. interests in Vietnam.

solid evidence that anything had been fired at the *Maddox* or that a second destroyer had come to aid it during the August encounter, but Johnson got the power he wanted.

After Johnson's inauguration in January 1965, the military situation in South Vietnam deteriorated badly—North Vietnamese forces controlled perhaps half the land and people of the south. Johnson's key foreign policy advisors, especially Secretary of State Dean Rusk and Secretary of Defense Robert McNamara, urged a major escalation of U.S. involvement. Some, especially Undersecretary of State George Ball, opposed escalation but, in early 1965, most were calling for more troops.

In February 1965, Johnson said, "I can't ask our American soldiers out there to continue to fight with one hand tied behind their backs," and launched a major bombing campaign against North Vietnam to stop the flow of supplies to the south. As the bombing expanded—3,600 runs in April, 4,800 by June—the United States also sent more ground forces to protect the American air base at Da Nang. Once there, these troops also engaged in battle and then needed more troops to support them. Fifty-thousand troops were in Vietnam by April 1965, and the number rose to 75,000 by midsummer. By July, Secretary McNamara, noting that the bombing alone was not defeating the northern forces, urged that the U.S. troop strength be increased from 75,000 to more than 200,000. Johnson agreed. But he did not want to go to Congress for authorization, fearing that it would disrupt the Great Society legislation. So he quietly asked for an additional appropriation for the war and announced a troop increase at a midday news conference devoted to other issues. The result was that although Johnson won short-term success for his domestic programs, he planted the seeds of long-term distrust.

For the next two years, combat in Vietnam expanded. Eventually, half a million U.S. troops were in Vietnam. Numbers at that level could be sustained only by an increased military draft. Deferments became difficult to get, especially for minority and working-class men. Casualty numbers also grew, undermining morale among the troops and at home. Costs mushroomed. In 1965, the military budget was $49.6 billion; by 1968, it was $80.5 billion. Try as they might, the U.S. commanders could not get the South Vietnamese

US Army Photo/Alamy Stock Photo

U.S. soldiers often flew in and out of combat on helicopters—choppers—that also served as backup and rescue for them. But the fighting on the ground was hot, dirty, and dangerous and, to many, also pointless.

army to play a major role in the war. They avoided battle when they could and seemed to have an uncanny way of knowing where danger was and leaving those sites to the Americans.

As U.S. soldiers did more of the fighting, they also saw less purpose to what they were doing. Troops went out on search-and-destroy missions, and then came back to their bases with little to show other than a list of enemy soldiers killed. One soldier asked, "What am I doing here? We don't take any land. … We just mutilate bodies." An American officer, speaking of his company's attack on the village of Ben Tre, which was suspected of harboring NLF supporters, said, "We had to destroy the village in order to save it." Destroying villages to "save" them, marching into the jungle, engaging in battles with enemy forces—battles that the U.S. troops almost always won—but then coming back to their bases while the enemy forces reorganized in the jungle were strategies that seemed pointless to most soldiers. The U.S. commander in Vietnam, General William Westmoreland, kept providing optimistic reports. Few were convinced.

Racial tensions often exploded in Vietnam. In 1965, 12.6 percent of the troops were black but 24 percent of combat deaths were of black soldiers. Black soldiers, who knew that civil rights workers were being killed in Alabama and Mississippi at home, believed that they were often being sent on the most dangerous missions. Many became increasingly angry at their fellow troops, at their officers, and at the war.

While morale disintegrated on the ground in Vietnam, public support for the war also evaporated. By launching the war quietly, Johnson had not built public support. Many Americans had a natural tendency to support the president and the troops at first, but that support declined rapidly. Vietnam was the nation's first televised war. Television did not actually show a lot of combat; many of the battles were at night or far from cameras. Nevertheless, footage of troops going into combat as well as pictures of dead and wounded American soldiers brought the war into American living rooms as no war had been. Lack of clear progress created doubt. Opposition to the war built with each news report, each draft call, and each casualty list.

While critics have rightly pointed out that no more than 20 percent of college students took part in antiwar demonstrations, and those demonstrations were mostly on elite campuses such as the University of California at Berkeley, Columbia, and Harvard, few campuses anywhere were untouched by antiwar fervor, especially as many students worried about draft calls or felt the guilt at being protected by their student status while friends

African American troops in Vietnam, who bore a disproportional share of the fighting and dying, quickly lost faith in the effort.

American Voices

Paul Thomas Coe, "Vietnam Letters," 1969–1970

Paul Thomas Coe was a devout Mormon and a student at the University of California at Berkeley. In 1969, he lost his draft deferment. These letters reflect his experience in Vietnam.

The President of the United States March 17, 1969
To: Paul T. Coe
GREETINGS:
You are hereby ordered for induction into the Armed Forces of the United States, and to report to: Local Board No. 31 on April 16, 1969, Wednesday at 6:00 A.M. (morning) for forwarding to an Armed Forces Induction Station.

Basic Training

I'm tired of trying to rationalize things in my mind. All my beliefs seem to form a giant paradox. There is no room in my heart to justify killing, I can't ever justify the training to kill, and yet I can't justify copping out. I can't justify desertion although that seems the only logical course of action. I know inside that a time is drawing near when our families will need to draw together and the world will be in an uproar, so leaving for another country is out. The church speaks so loudly against breaking the law, and so loudly for supporting our constituted way of life that I can't justify refusing my orders. I want to do what is called of me for my country, but I can't justify the senseless loss of life. … But with every day I become more conscious of the ominous power we've given the military, and hate it so much more. …

Peace on Earth

P.T.

In Vietnam

11 September, 1970

There really isn't that much I can tell you. Rain has begun and the monsoons will be here soon. … Another thing, the chow is sorry. I mean ungood food & I'm sick of dried up burnt gristly cold roast beef, nearly every day. You'd think they'd at least learn how to cook that one thing if that's all they cook, but no not them. By the way have you taught Barb [Paul's wife] to make decent gravy yet?

Miss you Mom. Give love to all.

Paul

24 Sept. 70

Rather than go out with some battalion Recon [reconnaissance] team and sit in the rain, I joined what is called the 3rd Brigade Air Cavalry. It's an instant Recon team. They insert us into trouble spots for a day or two & then extract us … you can take anything when you know they're gonna pull you out in two days.

Just got back from a three-day mission directly west of Hue about three ridgelines east of the A Shau Valley. We were sent in there to investigate enemy supply routes. … Then we found that the LZ [Landing Zone] we were supposed to go to was ¾ up the Ridge and washed out, so nobody could get up to it. … We made it to the LZ & the Birds [helicopters] were beautiful. After circling for ten minutes they figured how to get in, but they didn't like it either because there was high ground all around. But they came in anyway about ten feet off the water … so I threw my weapon in, grabbed that skid, pulled myself to a boulder and jumped in. Felt good. Let my legs dangle out the door all the way back. …

Paul

***

DEPARTMENT OF THE ARMY
08 DEC 1970
Dear Mr. and Mrs. Coe,

By this time I am sure that you have been notified of the death of your son, Paul T. Coe. I want you to know that Paul's death came as a tragic shock to me and to all the men who knew him. On behalf of the entire company, I extend our deepest and most sincere sympathy.

On 14 November 1970, Paul was a member of a daylight patrol in the vicinity of Camp Evans, with the Headquarters Reconnaissance Platoon, when the patrol hit a booby trapped area. Your son was killed by multiple fragmentation wounds when one of the hostile booby traps exploded. I hope that it may be of some comfort to you to know that Paul died instantly and did not suffer. …

Sincerely,

FRANK A. LIGHTLE
Captain, Infantry
Commanding Officer

Source: Republished with permission of Taylor and Francis Group LLC Books from TIME IT WAS: AMERICAN STORIES FROM THE SIXTIES, Karen Manners Smith and Tim Koster, 2016; permission conveyed through Copyright Clearance Center, Inc.

Thinking Critically

1. **Analyzing Primary Sources**

   How did Coe view his military training and service? What specific factors did he mention that shaped those views? What else in Coe's historical situation might have shaped his opinions?

2. **Comparison**

   In what ways were Coe's letters similar to those written by soldiers in previous American wars? In what ways do they reflect the specific context and experiences of the war in Vietnam?

went off to Vietnam. As the war escalated, campus-based teach-ins—gatherings at which experts or better-informed students taught others about Vietnam—built antiwar sentiment. At an April 1965 March on Washington to end the war, twenty-five thousand people heard SDS president Paul Potter say, "The incredible war in Vietnam has provided the razor, the terrifyingly sharp cutting edge that has finally severed the last vestige of illusion that morality and democracy are the guiding principles of American foreign policy." In 1966, 1967, and 1968, the teach-ins became angrier and the disaffection with the government greater. As early as 1966, demonstrators were not only calling for American withdrawal from Vietnam but also waving NLF flags and chanting, "Ho, Ho Ho Chi Minh, [t]he NLF is gonna win."

Students were far from the only opponents of the war. The Women's Strike for Peace, the Fellowship of Reconciliation, and the Catholic Worker Movement were pacifist organizations who had opposed all war for decades. In addition, more religious leaders began to speak out about the specific war in Vietnam. Catholic priests Daniel and Philip Berrigan and William Sloane Coffin, the Protestant chaplain at Yale University, became leading antiwar activists.

Established civil rights groups did not want to risk a break with the Johnson administration when LBJ was doing so much to support civil rights. Even so, SNCC was the first among them to oppose the war. A 1966 SNCC position paper attacked a war "to preserve a 'democracy' which does not exist at home." In April 1967, Martin Luther King, Jr., stood in the pulpit at New York's Riverside Church to tell the Civil Rights Movement and the nation that he had come to see that the war was sending poor and black Americans eight thousand miles away to fight for rights that they did not have in the United States. "Somehow this madness must cease," he pleaded.

As the war continued, some opponents took their opposition to a new level. When some 35,000 demonstrators surrounded the Pentagon and tried to disrupt daily business in Washington in October 1967, the government reacted harshly with mass arrests of the protestors. Between 50,000 and 100,000 young men left the United States, most of them moving to Canada, to avoid serving in a war they thought was wrong. Many of those who moved to Canada eventually returned to the United States, especially after presidential pardons granted by presidents Ford and Carter, but some 50,000 Americans became permanent residents of Canada as a result of the Vietnam War while others stayed in neutral nations like Sweden.

In 1967, a group of young men in San Francisco announced that they were staying in the United States but refusing to cooperate with the military draft in any way. "We will renounce all deferments and refuse to cooperate with the draft in any manner, at any level," they said. Draft resistance, and a willingness to be arrested for the act, was a new stage in the protest movement. Later, Dr. Benjamin Spock (whose book on child care had been the bible for the parents of many of those now refusing the draft) and Rev. William Sloane Coffin were arrested for urging draft resistance.

Still others tried different forms of direct action to try to stop the war. In May 1969, opponents of the war, including some religious leaders, walked into offices of Dow Chemical Company, which made the napalm jelly that was used to burn, kill, and maim in Vietnam, and poured blood into filing cabinets and on office equipment to disrupt the workings of the offices.

While opposition to the war in Vietnam broadened, Johnson isolated himself with trusted advisors. He agonized about casualty reports, wept while signing letters of condolence to those who had lost a loved one in the war, and regularly got up at 4:00 and 5:00 a.m. to check on casualty figures. He never seriously considered changing course and stopped talking to those who suggested that he should. He authorized the CIA, which was only supposed to operate abroad, to spy on American antiwar leaders who he became convinced were Communists, and he authorized the FBI to infiltrate and disrupt the antiwar movement. Johnson brought the army commander in Vietnam, General Westmoreland, to Washington, D.C., in November 1967 to tell Americans that there was "light at the end of the tunnel" in Vietnam. By that time, fewer Americans were convinced.

Library of Congress Prints and Photographs Division, Warren K. Leffler [LC-DIG-ds-07432]

As the war in Vietnam wore on, more and more people—often led by high school and college students—took part in antiwar demonstrations, demanding an end to the hostilities and a more peaceful world.

When Historians Disagree

Could—or Should—the United States Have Won in Vietnam?

Historians have long disagreed sharply on how to understand the U.S. experience in Vietnam. They disagree about alternative courses of action, especially about the question of whether the United States could have "won" the war, and what the outlines and costs of a U.S.

victory might have been. Recent history—and the war in Vietnam is still relatively recent history—is always especially contentious, and the history of the war in Vietnam will probably remain so for years to come.

Guenter Lewy, *America in Vietnam*. New York: Oxford University Press, 1978, pp. v–vii, pp. 430–439.

To a large number of Americans the Vietnam war represents not only a political mistake and national defeat but also a major moral failure. …

It is the reasoned conclusion of this study … that the sense of guilt created by the Vietnam war in the minds of many Americans is not warranted and that the charges of *officially condoned* illegal and grossly immoral conduct are without substance. …

The decisive reason for the growing disaffection of the American people was the conviction that the war was not being won and apparently showed little prospect of coming to a successful conclusion. …

The U.S. in the years from 1954 to 1975 could have pursued policies different from those actually followed. What if, instead of making a piece-meal commitment of military resources and adopting a policy of gradualism in their use, America had pursued a strategy of surprise and massed strength at decisive points? What if the mining of North Vietnamese harbors had taken place in 1965 instead of 1972? What if the U.S. from the beginning had implemented a strategy of population security …? What if Vietnamization had begun in 1965 rather than 1968? While one cannot be sure that these different strategies, singly or in combination, would necessarily have brought about a different outcome, neither can one take their failure for granted.

George C. Herring, *America's Longest War: The United States and Vietnam, 1950–1975*. New York: McGraw-Hill, 1978; Third edition, 1996, pp. x–xii, 298–299.

Why did the United States make such a vast commitment in an area of so little apparent importance? What did it attempt to do during the quarter century of its involvement there? Why, despite the expenditure of more than $150 billion, the loss of more than 58,000 lives, the application of its great technical expertise, and the employment of a huge military arsenal, did the world's most powerful nation fail to achieve its objectives and suffer its first defeat in war, a humiliating and deeply frustrating experience for a people accustomed to success? What have been the consequences for Americans, Vietnamese, and others of the nation's longest and most divisive war? …

I believe now, as I did then, that U.S. intervention in Vietnam was based on a policy fundamentally flawed in its assumptions and major premises. I do not believe that the war could have been won in any meaningful sense or at a moral or material cost that most Americans would—or should—have found acceptable. …

Given these harsh realities, the American effort to create a bastion of anticommunism south of the seventeenth parallel was probably doomed from the start. The United States could not effect the needed changes in South Vietnamese society without jeopardizing the order it sought, and there was no long-range hope of stability without revolutionary change.

Thinking Critically

1. **Analyzing Secondary Sources**

   What further evidence would you need to be convinced by Lewy's conclusion that with a different policy the war in Vietnam might have been won? What further evidence would you want to agree with Herring that there is no way the war could have been won?

2. **Argument Development**

   Do you agree with Levy or Herring or neither? How would you frame your own historical interpretation of the U.S. war in Vietnam? What is the central argument you would make? What evidence would you use to support it?

1968

In 1968, the growing tensions in America exploded. Few were untouched by the anger and fear that the year provoked.

Two months after General Westmoreland's optimistic assessment, the light at the end of the tunnel in Vietnam dimmed considerably. On January 30, 1968, the first day of Tet, the Vietnamese lunar new year, North Vietnamese and NLF forces attacked everywhere across

26.1

26.2

Tet Offensive

A significant North Vietnamese assault on American bases across Vietnam.

26.3

South Vietnam, all at once. They blew a hole in the wall surrounding the American embassy in Saigon and came close to getting into the inner compound. They attacked the distant Marine post at Khe Sanh. They took control of the old Vietnamese capital city of Hue. And they attacked American and South Vietnamese forces all over the country. Eventually, the **Tet Offensive** was beaten back, at terrible cost to the North Vietnamese. By one estimate, the North lost 40,000 troops compared with 2,300 South Vietnamese and 1,100 Americans. Even so, the North had won an important victory. Public trust in Westmoreland and Johnson was never restored. The president and the general had said that the United States was winning the war, but now it certainly looked like it was losing. Johnson's popularity dropped from its already low 40 percent approval rating to 26 percent. Walter Cronkite, the anchor of the CBS Evening News and perhaps the most trusted journalist in the country, who had maintained careful neutrality in his reporting, traveled to Vietnam after Tet and returned to tell his viewers, "It seems more certain than ever that the bloody experience of Vietnam is to end in a stalemate." Many agreed.

When Westmoreland responded to the Tet Offensive by asking for even more troops, beyond the 525,000 Americans already in Vietnam, Johnson's new secretary of defense, Clark Clifford, told the president, "We seem to have a sinkhole. ... I see more and more fighting with more and more casualties on the U.S. side and no end in sight to the action." Secretary of State Rusk, long a supporter of the war, recommended a bombing halt and an offer of negotiations with North Vietnam. Johnson hated the advice, but he could no longer ignore it.

Johnson's lack of popularity was also catching up with him. Everyone assumed that, as an incumbent president, Johnson would easily win nomination for another term. But the antiwar mood was growing, in the country and in the Democratic Party. On March 12, 1968, in the nation's first primary vote in New Hampshire, Minnesota senator Eugene McCarthy, who had become a strong opponent of the war, won 42 percent of the votes against LBJ's 49 percent. Many who had participated in antiwar demonstrations decided to be "clean for Gene" and campaign door-to-door in New Hampshire. They found a ready electorate, people of many different persuasions, including those who were fed up with the seemingly endless war and those who were frustrated because LBJ seemed unwilling either to commit the force needed to win or to withdraw. The New Hampshire vote was far too close for a sitting president.

Even worse than the challenge from McCarthy, at least from Johnson's perspective, was one from New York senator Robert Kennedy, whom Johnson loathed. Bobby Kennedy realized that McCarthy's win meant LBJ could be defeated for the nomination and that, since McCarthy had opened the way, it was a good time to challenge him. While McCarthy was little-known, Bobby was perhaps the best-known politician in the country. Soon after the New Hampshire vote, Kennedy announced that he was entering the contest. For many who opposed the war, wanted further social change, and dreamed of a return to the glory days of the JFK presidency, Bobby's 1968 campaign was a dream come true. His campaign struck an emotional chord among both supporters and opponents—seldom seen in American politics.

On March 31, 1968, just weeks after the New Hampshire vote, Johnson gave a nationally televised speech. He announced plans to reduce the bombing as "the first step to deescalate the conflict." He called on Ho Chi Minh to "respond positively and favorably to this new step for peace." Then he surprised the country, and perhaps himself, by adding, "I shall not seek, and will not accept, the nomination of my party for another term as your president." Johnson, the ultimate politician, knew that public trust was essential to govern. And by March 1968, he had lost that trust. North Vietnam did respond, and the road to peace had begun. It would be a long and painful road, however, one that would last far beyond the end of Johnson's term. Johnson's career and his hopes for the country had become casualties of Vietnam—though very far from the only casualties.

Four days after Johnson's surprise announcement, Martin Luther King, Jr., was shot and killed in Memphis, Tennessee, where he was supporting a strike by the city's garbage collectors. With the murder of King, the leading spokesperson for nonviolence, many felt that the cause of nonviolence itself had been damaged. Riots erupted all over America. Police arrested twenty thousand people in 130 cities in the week following King's assassination. Forty-six people, forty-one of them black, were killed. Urban America seemed to be coming unglued.

The riots that followed King's death reflected the deep anger in much of the African American community. In Oakland, California, Huey Newton and Bobby Seale had founded the Black Panther Party for Self-Defense in 1966. Newton and Seale insisted that urban police forces had become occupying armies in the black community. Following a California law then in place allowing unconcealed weapons, the Panthers conducted their own armed patrols of Oakland as a defense. Such an armed presence, however, almost assured violence. A seventeen-year-old Panther, Bobby Hutton, was killed the same month as King. Many more Panthers would be killed in subsequent years. The Panthers always remained a tiny fringe group, as popular for their swagger as for their breakfast programs and their commitment to armed self-defense. Even so, while small, they were a symbol that many blacks embraced—a move away from the self-sacrificing nonviolence of King to a more angry and militant stance.

Two weeks after King's death and the urban riots, students at Columbia University, led by the SDS chapter, took over the president's office and refused to leave. Four buildings were held by white students and a fifth building, separately, by black students. The Columbia sit-in was a protest over the university's war-related research and a university plan to build a new gymnasium in the park that separated the university from the African American community of Harlem. In addition, it reflected far-reaching anger toward all authorities. After eight days, the university administration called on the police to clear the buildings and they did. The violence of the police move onto the campus—during which more than a hundred demonstrators were injured—also pointed to the deep fault lines in the nation. The mostly working-class white police were furious at the white students, whom they considered privileged snobs. The student revolt at Columbia was one of many. Students protesting the war or local issues took over buildings, held mass rallies, disrupted classes, and burned war-related research materials on more than 150 campuses in the 1968–1969 academic year.

In the face of this violent—some said crazy—time in American history, Bobby Kennedy continued his campaign for the presidency. He not only championed the antiwar cause but also befriended César Chávez of the Farm Workers Union, rural whites in Appalachia, Puerto Rican immigrants living in New York City, American Indians on isolated reservations, and urban blacks in city after city, as no candidate had ever done. On June 5, Kennedy won the California Democratic primary but moments afterward was shot by an Arab nationalist. He died days later. As with King, many hopes died with Kennedy.

When the Democratic National Convention met in Chicago in August 1968, Kennedy was dead. The McCarthy campaign had been sidelined. The party nominated Hubert Humphrey, LBJ's loyal vice president, who had not entered a single primary. Humphrey had long been a darling of the liberal wing of the party, but his silence on Vietnam and his steadfast loyalty to the increasingly unpopular Johnson meant that he had lost the trust of many.

While the convention met to hear speeches and act on the nomination, protests erupted inside and outside the convention hall. Many delegates protested on the floor of the convention itself. Huge demonstrations were also planned for Chicago during convention week by demonstrators who had their own divisions. One faction, led by longtime pacifist David Dellinger, wanted a nonviolent but militant protest against the war, LBJ, and Humphrey. Another group, of whom Tom Hayden and Rennie Davis of the SDS were the most prominent, wanted a more direct confrontation, which they knew might provoke police violence. Finally, a group who called themselves Yippies, led by Abbie Hoffman and Jerry Rubin, believed that the best way to protest was to make fun of the Democrats and the Chicago police in every way possible.

Chicago's mayor, Richard Daley, was determined to quash all demonstrations. As the convention met, the police attacked the demonstrators with tear gas and billy clubs in the glare of television cameras. They attacked delegates. They attacked the press. Nationally known reporters Dan Rather and Mike Wallace were both roughed up. As crowds chanted

San Francisco Examiner/AP Images

Black Panther Party founders Huey P. Newton and Bobby Seale. The Panthers advocated a radical economic, social, and educational agenda that made it the target of a determined campaign of suppression and elimination by the police and the FBI.

26.1

26.2

26.3

26.1

26.2

26.3

Bettmann/Getty Images

In what was later termed a "police riot" by an investigating commission, Chicago police officers attacked and beat demonstrators at the 1968 Democratic National Convention.

"The whole world is watching," the violence in Chicago was broadcast around the world. One McCarthy delegate described what he saw from his hotel window: "Cops chased kids off into the park and out of sight among the trees, emerged with one cop dragging a boy or girl by the leg and another cop running alongside clubbing in the groin. A man tried to carry a bleeding woman into the hotel, and they were both clubbed and thrown into the wagon."

In the aftermath of the convention, a commission appointed to investigate what had happened described it as a "police riot." The fact that this could happen, with "the whole world watching," represented how deeply divided Americans were in 1968.

The November 1968 presidential election presented three choices. First was Hubert Humphrey and his vice presidential nominee, Maine senator Edmund Muskie, a ticket that barely seemed to limp out of the Chicago convention. Humphrey said later, "My wife and I went home [from the convention] heartbroken, battered, and beaten."

The Republican Party emerged from its summer convention as united as the Democrats were divided. Richard M. Nixon, the second candidate, who had lost to John Kennedy in 1960, spent the intervening eight years quietly laying the groundwork for a political comeback. He collected many political debts and cashed them all in to win the 1968 nomination on the first ballot. His running mate was Maryland governor Spiro Agnew, who had once been seen as a liberal but who, especially after the Baltimore riots following King's death, became a voice of white backlash against what he called the "circuit-riding, Hanoi-visiting, caterwauling, riot-inciting, burn-America-down" types in the black and white communities. Nixon announced a "secret plan" to end the war in Vietnam and otherwise ran a carefully scripted, television-savvy, and very expensive campaign. The Republicans outspent the Democrats almost two to one.

Third was candidate Governor George Wallace of Alabama, who had made his name blocking school integration and who launched a strong third-party campaign. To the surprise of many, he qualified for the ballot in all fifty states. Wallace and his running mate, Air Force General Curtis LeMay, had support, ranging from the most conservative groups in the country—including the KKK and the John Birch Society—to the many white Southerners opposed to racial integration to many in the North who were appalled by riots and antiwar demonstrations. With comments like "If any demonstrator ever lays down in front of my car, it'll be the last car he'll ever lay down in front of," Wallace courted what he called the "law and order" vote.

In early fall, it seemed as if Nixon was unstoppable. Nixon's major theme "Working Americans have become the forgotten Americans," his promise to do something different in Vietnam (no one knew what), and his success in representing anti-Johnson sentiment without getting specific all worked in his favor. An early poll gave him 43 percent of the vote to Humphrey's 28 percent and Wallace's 21 percent. Humphrey, however, ran a surprisingly strong campaign. He tried to repair the Democratic coalition, distanced himself from Johnson, and reached out to his longtime supporters. At the same time, Nixon struck some as too smooth, and a vote for Wallace seemed a wasted vote. By election day, the polls said the race between Humphrey and Nixon was too close to call.

Nixon won the November election, by a close vote of 37.7 million to 37.1 million, while Wallace took almost 10 million votes. Nixon's electoral college lead was greater: 301 to 191. The Democrats retained both houses of Congress, however. Humphrey won 97 percent of the black vote but only 35 percent of the white vote. Between them, Nixon and Wallace had won 57 percent of all of the votes, a significant backlash against Johnson's huge 1964 victory, against the war, and against the demonstrators who opposed it. In 1968, Americans were more deeply divided by race and class and region than they had been in many years, and anything approaching national consensus was a distant dream. The election results also showed that Vietnam would remain an unsolved issue for a new administration.

26.3 Quick Review

How did the war in Vietnam impact Great Society programs, the Johnson presidency, and the country?

Conclusion

In contrast to the 1950s, the 1960s ushered in a period of intense and very widespread unrest, activism, and social upheaval that in one way or another touched most people. Writers and artists began to criticize many aspects of American culture and helped set in motion the modern ecological conservation movement, the feminist movement, a new focus on poverty, and a vocal antiwar movement. Perhaps the most iconic of these movements was the student movement. In 1960, a small group of white students formed Students for a Democratic Society, which along with the African American–led Student Nonviolent Coordinating Committee sought to end war, racial injustice, and economic inequality.

President John F. Kennedy and his wife, Jacqueline Kennedy, brought youth, charm, and energy to the White House. Kennedy was preoccupied with Cuba, Germany—especially Berlin—and the Soviet Union. After the failed Bay of Pigs invasion in 1961, Cuban ties to Russia grew. The Soviets sent military personnel to the Caribbean island, and in 1962, the Russians began building bases in Cuba for housing missiles capable of reaching the United States. A clash between the United States and the Soviet Union seemed inevitable, but the two nations avoided a potentially cataclysmic confrontation.

In November 1963, Kennedy was assassinated and Lyndon Johnson became president. Unlike his predecessor, Johnson was remarkably successful in advancing his domestic policy goals, which he called the Great Society. During his tenure, Congress passed the Civil Rights Act, a new immigration law, and the Voting Rights Act, as well as created Medicare and Medicaid health insurance and greatly expanded federal aid to education and the poor. Still, Vietnam remained a problem, and as Johnson steadily increased U.S. involvement on that front, opposition to the war intensified at home.

In 1968, mounting tensions in American society exploded. In the midst of the violence, at home and abroad, Johnson announced that he would not seek another term as president. Four days afterward, Martin Luther King, Jr., was assassinated and race riots broke out across the country. Two months later, Robert Kennedy was shot and killed. At the 1968 Democratic National Convention, protests erupted outside the convention hall, and the police attacked demonstrators as well as onlookers in what was later called a "police riot." The presidential race of 1968 was a very close one, and the tumultuous year ended with the election of Republican Richard Nixon to the presidency.

Chapter Review

The 1960s have been seen as a decade of protests. How did the nature of these protests change from the early to the late 1960s?

New Voices, New Authorities

26.1 **Explain the growing social protest in books, films, and student movements starting in the early 1960s.**

Summary

The 1960s saw widespread challenges to the conformity of the 1950s. Writers and artists produced works that reflected and shaped a rapidly changing culture. Writers challenged conventional thinking on a wide variety of public policy issues, including city planning, the environment, poverty, and gender roles. Politics made its way into popular films and music, although a great deal of popular entertainment remained traditional and uncontroversial. At the same time, college students began questioning American institutions and articulating the viewpoint of a new generation.

Review Questions

1. Contextualization
   What might explain the dramatic impact in the 1960s of books like Michael Harrington's *The Other America*? Why did similar books published in the 1950s have less influence?

2. Continuity and Change over Time
   What changes in American society were reflected in popular film and music in the 1960s? In what ways did popular entertainment also reflect social and cultural continuity?

Camelot, the White House, and Dallas—The Kennedy Administration

26.2 **Analyze the successes and failures of the Kennedy administration and how they interacted with popular culture in the United States.**

Summary

Despite John F. Kennedy's popular image, the Kennedy administration had surprisingly few legislative victories and gave a higher priority to foreign policy than domestic concerns. While civil rights advocates had high hopes for the Kennedy administration, JFK pursued a cautious course, launching few initiatives, at the same time being careful not to alienate Southern members of Congress or to get too far ahead of American public opinion. While the Kennedy administration made some gains in other areas of domestic concern, his overall record is more notable for its inactivity. Kennedy was as reluctant to engage with the issue of religion in American life as he was to grapple with civil rights. Nonetheless, a series of Supreme Court rulings established a sharper division between church and state, angering many Americans in the process. In contrast to his passivity on domestic issues, Kennedy was committed to taking an active role in fighting the Cold War. JFK's initial forays into foreign policy were not promising. The Bay of Pigs was a fiasco, and Kennedy's 1961 summit with Khrushchev did not go well. The 1962 Cuban Missile Crisis brought the world to the brink of nuclear war. All in all, JFK's foreign policy legacy was mixed. The Kennedy administration was cut short by the assassination of the president in November 1963, which produced a tremendous outpouring of public grief. Many Americans were unconvinced by the official finding that Lee Harvey Oswald was the sole person responsible for Kennedy's death.

Review Questions

3. Argument Development
   How do you explain Kennedy's modest list of domestic accomplishments? Why do you think he enjoys a much better reputation today than his record would seem to support?

4. Causation
   What assumptions about the Cold War helped shape Kennedy's foreign policy?

5. Contextualization
   What does the public response to the Supreme Court's rulings in *Abington School Board v. Schempp* and *Engel v. Vitale* tell us about the society and culture of the United States in the 1960s?

The Coming of Lyndon B. Johnson

26.3 **Analyze the successes and failures of the Johnson administration in terms of the two issues that dominated his years in office—the launching of the Great Society programs and the war in Vietnam.**

Summary

Lyndon Johnson's childhood experience with poverty and his remarkable effectiveness as a member of Congress prepared him to advance an ambitious domestic agenda as president. Johnson worked closely with Congress to pass landmark civil rights legislation, launch a war on poverty, and implement his vision for a Great Society. LBJ's domestic agenda gathered momentum after his landslide victory in 1964. The core Great Society legislation of 1965 included federal aid to education,

Medicare and Medicaid, immigration reform, and the Voting Rights Act. As significant as Johnson's domestic victories were, they were undermined by the war in Vietnam. The war divided the country, destroyed support for Johnson's domestic agenda, and led to widespread cynicism in American society about authority in general and government in particular. At first, Johnson hesitated to expand the war, but became convinced that the momentum behind the Great Society initiative would stall if South Vietnam fell. With the military situation in Vietnam deteriorating rapidly, Johnson began a rapid escalation of U.S. troops in Vietnam in 1965. Increasing the U.S. troop presence did not bring victory, however, and military morale declined along with public support for the war. The 1968 Tet Offensive destroyed the last vestiges of public confidence in Johnson's conducting of the war, and LBJ decided not to seek a second term as president. The assassinations of Martin Luther King, Jr., and Robert Kennedy plunged the nation into even greater uncertainty and unrest. Divisions within the Democratic Party, highlighted by the violence at the Democratic Convention, opened the door for Republican Richard Nixon's victory in the 1968 presidential election.

Review Questions

6. Comparison
Compare and contrast Johnson's and Kennedy's domestic policy. What is similar about their goals? Why do you think LBJ was much more effective in getting so much major legislation passed?

7. Causation
What impact did developments in the war in Vietnam have on domestic politics in the United States during the 1960s?

8. Argument Development
What divisions in American society were revealed by the events of 1968?

1. Preparing to Write: Close in the Conclusion

Long Essay Question—Evaluate the extent of change in the use of federal power to promote greater racial equality from 1945 to 1965.

As you will recall, there are a few good ways to close your argument in a brief conclusion. It might be effective to tie this story to the larger narrative about the expanding moral responsibility of the federal government. Remember to reference your thesis in this explanation.

2. Preparing to Write: Support Your Assertion

Short-Answer Question—Using the excerpts from "When Historians Disagree" in Section 26.3, answer (a), (b), and (c).

a. Briefly explain ONE major difference between Lewy's and Herring's historical interpretations about American involvement in Vietnam.

b. Briefly explain how ONE specific historical event or development during the age that is not mentioned directly in the excerpts could be used to support Lewy's interpretation.

c. Briefly explain how ONE specific historical event or development during the age that is not mentioned directly in the excerpts could be used to support Herring's interpretation.

You will recall that for each of the three responses, you can make your assertion in the first sentence and then explain your reasoning in the next two sentences. At first, it might seem difficult to support Lewy's interpretation since so much of his excerpt is filled with counterfactuals. However, he also makes the point that "the sense of guilt created by the Vietnam war in the minds of many Americans is not warranted." You can support this statement by defending the moral purpose of the war, explaining how it fit into our wider Cold War commitments.

Chapter 27
Rights, Reaction, and Limits 1968–1980

Bettmann/Getty Images

Widely diverse groups of Americans began to protest conditions and policies that they found intolerable. Among them, members of the American Indian Movement took over the closed prison on Alcatraz Island in San Francisco Bay, claiming it as "surplus federal land" that rightly belonged to them.

Chapter Objective

Demonstrate an understanding about the mix of liberalism and conservatism that emerged after 1968.

 Learning Objectives

The New Politics of the Late 1960s

27.1 Explain Nixon's policies and politics, domestic and international.

The Movements of the 1960s and 1970s

27.2 Analyze the many political and cultural movements that followed in the track of the Civil Rights Movement.

The Culture Wars of the 1970s

27.3 Analyze the reaction to the liberal and radical politics of the 1960s and 1970s and the growth of new militant conservative movements.

Politics, Economics, and the Impact of Watergate

27.4 Explain the political impact of Watergate and subsequent developments that set the stage for the "Reagan Revolution."

Basic contradictions in American life came to the surface between 1968 and 1980. The new Republican president, elected thanks to a backlash against the unresolved war in Vietnam, initially widened the war. Nixon, elected with conservative support, also began a new era of relations with Communist China and signed some of the most far-reaching social legislation in history. While the civil rights and antiwar movements splintered, more Americans began demanding their rights in other areas. A women's movement transformed intimate relationships as well as the work world and American culture. The civil rights campaigns of Latinos, Asians, American Indians, gay men, and lesbians also made their impact on American society.

Public discourse became more divisive and angry after 1969. The new vice president, Spiro T. Agnew, called protesters "nattering nabobs of negativism." A new conservative ideology emerged, built on Barry Goldwater's campaigns and on cultural issues, which included opposition to the Equal Rights Amendment and the growth of a new "religious right." Before the decade was over, the United States was defeated in Vietnam; Richard Nixon had resigned in disgrace; his appointed successor, Gerald Ford, was defeated in his bid for reelection; and his successor Jimmy Carter was also defeated in his reelection attempt. The decade was one that held much anger, much sordidness, and few moments of greatness.

The New Politics of the Late 1960s

27.1 **Explain Nixon's policies and politics, domestic and international.**

Early in 1969, Kevin Phillips, a special assistant during Richard Nixon's successful presidential campaign, published *The Emerging Republican Majority*. Phillips analyzed what he saw as the significance of the election and focused on two major changes in American politics. The new Republican Party, Phillips said, was based in "the rising insurgency of the South, the West, the New York City Irish, and middle-class suburbia." Phillips offered a detailed statistical analysis to show that the suburbs especially were overwhelmingly middle class, white, and Republican.

The 1968 election, as Phillips described it, was a reaction against the Civil Rights Movement, which had generated considerable anger in white America and a repudiation of Johnson's Great Society. Expanded government programs and services offended people who wanted small government, who distrusted an intrusive state, and who feared racial integration.

Many found the analysis convincing even though Phillips did not assess the impact that the war in Vietnam had on the politics of 1968. Even so, many, including Lyndon Johnson, attributed the 1968 Democratic presidential losses to the war. While antiwar protesters were furious at Johnson and the Democrats for continuing the war, many other Americans were angry that the war was not being won. Anger at antiwar dissidents also ran deep. For a substantial number of Americans, celebrations of freedom from restraint—political, cultural, and sexual—were abhorrent.

The Roots of the Conservative Reaction of the 1960s

While the suburban-based conservatism was new, it was deeply rooted in the early development of suburbia. Some Americans had long disagreed with the direction of the country. William F. Buckley's conservative journal, the *National Review*, appeared in 1955. Ayn Rand's novel *Atlas Shrugged* appeared in 1957, the themes of which argued that any interference with individual rights would destroy human freedom. Ministers such as James Fifield at the First Congregational Church in Los Angeles preached that "[t]he blessings of capitalism come from God."

As late as 1960, there were plenty of conservatives and liberals in both parties. After the 1960 election, however, the two parties began to move in opposite directions, and over time, most liberals moved to the Democratic Party while most conservatives became Republicans. The drift toward fairly rigid and uniform positions in each party was already clear

Significant Dates

1969	Nixon is inaugurated as president
	Stonewall Inn riot
	Neil Armstrong becomes the first person to walk on the moon
	Woodstock, New York, Music and Art Fair
	Moratorium, largest antiwar demonstration in U.S. history
1970	First Earth Day celebration
	Forty-six women employees sue *Newsweek*
	U.S. invasion of Cambodia
	Kent State and Jackson State demonstrations
1972	First issue of *Ms.* magazine
	Nixon visit to China
	Nixon signs Title IX banning sex discrimination in higher education
	Watergate break-in
	Congress sends Equal Rights Amendment to the states
	Phyllis Schlafly launches STOP ERA
	Nixon defeats McGovern for president
1973	Last U.S. combat troops leave Vietnam
	Supreme Court's *Roe v. Wade* decision
	American Indian Movement occupies Wounded Knee
	Vice President Spiro Agnew resigns and is replaced by Gerald Ford
1974	Richard Nixon resigns; Gerald Ford becomes president
1975	Communist forces occupy Saigon; Vietnam War ends
1976	Carter defeats Ford in presidential election
1978	Camp David peace talks lead to Camp David Accords
	United States normalizes diplomatic ties with China

(continued)

27.1

27.2

27.3

27.4

by the late 1960s. In the 1960s and 1970s, the conservative shift among Republicans was led by Arizona senator Barry Goldwater, who emerged as the hero of the conservative wing of the Republicans. In his first Senate campaign in 1952, Goldwater asked audiences, "Do you believe in expanding federal government? … Do you want federal bureaus and federal agencies to take over an ever-increasing portion of your life?" If the answer was "no," then, Goldwater said, he was their man. In 1960, he criticized Eisenhower as representing a "dime store New Deal." He criticized the U.S. Supreme Court's *Brown v. Board of Education* decision as an unconstitutional federal intervention in the rights of states, and he voted against the 1964 Civil Rights Act, saying that the race relations issue "is best handled by the people directly concerned." His book, *The Conscience of a Conservative*, published in April 1960, spoke to a white middle class that was unhappy with taxes and government intrusion, no longer interested in the New Deal safety net, frightened by the Civil Rights Movement, and fiercely anti-Communist. It was this conservative movement that took over the Republican Party in 1964, even though their hero went down to defeat.

Four years later in 1968, it was Goldwater's philosophy, not Eisenhower's, that Richard Nixon used to make his comeback. Nevertheless, Nixon's actual presidency contradicted his campaign assertions. Richard Nixon was a jumble of insecurities and contradictions. His insecurities and his sense that there were many enemies about to attack him made it hard for Nixon to build warm personal relationships or inspire the broad popularity of presidents like Eisenhower or Kennedy. He isolated himself and often lied to hide the inner workings of his administration. Even though he had been elected as the voice of those who had supported Goldwater, his administration would be relatively liberal. Many federal programs were still popular, and Nixon was happy to support them and reap the political benefit even as he attacked liberals and liberalism as a way to win yet other voters to his side.

Nixon Domestic Policies—Liberal Legislation, Conservative Politics

Although a self-proclaimed conservative, Nixon seemed to some to be a liberal in disguise. In July 1969, Nixon led the celebrations when John F. Kennedy's goal was achieved and Neil Armstrong became the first person to walk on the moon, propelled there by American technology. In spite of the revulsion against LBJ, the 1968 election retained many Great Society Democrats in Congress. Congressional Democrats and the Republican president worked together to pass significant legislation. Johnson's 1965 Voting Rights Act was renewed in 1970. New federal funds were provided for a "war on cancer" and other medical research. Offended when she heard a group of school superintendents dismiss the educational needs of girls, Representative Edith Green of Oregon, joined by Representatives Patsy Mink of Hawaii and Shirley Chisholm of New York, proposed Title IX, which was added to the Civil Rights Act in 1972, banning sex discrimination in higher education—not only in sports but also in all college and university activities, and Nixon signed the law. Funds for Medicare, Medicaid, and Social Security were increased. Federal affirmative action regulations were toughened by Nixon's Department of Labor.

Nixon did much more than any of his predecessors to strengthen environmental protection. While the Kennedy and Johnson administrations had pressed passage of the Clean Air Act, Clean Water Act, and Endangered Species Act, it was under Nixon that the new cabinet-level Environmental Protection Agency (EPA) was created as well as the Occupational Safety and Health Administration (OSHA). The 1973 Endangered Species Act expanded protection for animals and plants. New Clean Air and Clean Water acts mandated the cleanup of polluted areas without regard to the cost.

Nixon also approved government support of arts and culture, particularly regional art programs and folk art. When Nixon took office, the annual budget of the National Endowment for the Arts (NEA) was $7.7 million. Many worried that Nixon, who had never shown any appreciation of art, would cut the budget, but he proposed increases each year. By the time he left office, the NEA budget was over $60 million, almost a tenfold increase.

Nixon championed the Family Assistance Plan (FAP) that was designed by Daniel Moynihan—then a Nixon policy advisor and later a Democratic senator. It would have replaced Aid to Families with Dependent Children (known simply as "welfare" to most) with a guaranteed annual income. FAP was defeated by a combination of liberals who thought it did not provide enough money to people in poverty and by conservatives who thought it expanded government handouts. Nixon also proposed a system of federally mandated health insurance, the only Republican to do so. Overall federal spending for people in poverty rose by some 50 percent, and total federal spending for social insurance (which always includes more middle-class than poor beneficiaries) rose from $27.3 billion in the year Nixon took office to $64.7 billion at the time of his second inauguration.

It is impossible to call anyone who presided over such spending a conservative. Nixon could be seen as the last of the New Deal presidents, and many Goldwater conservatives saw him that way and were furious with him. From Nixon's perspective, the programs were popular, he basked in the praise he received, and he remained confident that the Goldwater conservatives were certainly not going to desert the Republican Party for the Democrats.

However, Nixon was an unusually ruthless "win-at-all-costs" politician more than he was either a liberal or conservative. If a policy like increasing Social Security benefits or launching the EPA brought him votes, he was all for it. If fanning the flames of divisiveness brought more votes, Nixon fostered division. He encouraged Vice President Agnew's attacks on protesters and experts. Nixon himself condemned protesters as "the vicious and lawless elements in our society."

In planning his reelection campaign, Nixon and his campaign manager, former attorney general John Mitchell, developed a "Southern Strategy" to win over Wallace voters. The administration slowed enforcement of federal guidelines for school desegregation and courted segregationist politicians. When officials in the Justice Department sought to enforce desegregation rules, Nixon wrote to John Ehrlichman, his closest aide, "Do what the law requires and not *one bit more.*" He approved a plan that would involve the CIA and FBI in illegal bugging and wiretapping. He maintained a "Freeze List" of those who must never be invited to the White House and a larger "Enemies List," including reporters, politicians, and others, who should be watched regularly.

International Issues—Vietnam, China, and Beyond

Before he left office, LBJ had reduced the bombing of North Vietnam and begun the **Paris Peace Talks**. Even so, the war itself dragged on. In his presidential campaign, Nixon had promised a "secret plan" to end the war, but the end was a long time coming. Nixon and his national security advisor, Henry Kissinger, had a habit of bypassing the State Department and sometimes even their own staff. In Vietnam and other foreign policy arenas, the Nixon-Kissinger policies were the closely guarded work of these two men.

THE CONTINUING SAGA OF VIETNAM   In the first months of the Nixon-Kissinger tenure, the Paris Peace Talks went nowhere. Nixon expanded the bombing of North Vietnam and started bombing supply routes and North Vietnamese enclaves in neutral Cambodia. In the next four years, from early 1969 until the bombing ended in December 1972, more U.S. bombs were dropped on Cambodia than were dropped by the United States during World War II. The expanded bombing did nothing to break the will of the North Vietnamese leadership, though damage and civilian casualties were high. The bombing of Cambodia took a higher toll.

A year after the bombing began, Cambodia's prime minister, Lon Nol, overthrew the chief of state, Prince Sihanouk. From his exile in China, Sihanouk then urged Cambodians to join the anti-American Communist resistance, the Khmer Rouge. The result was a devastating civil war in theretofore relatively peaceful Cambodia. When the Khmer Rouge—a very different Communist insurgency from that in Vietnam—defeated the Lon Nol government, they launched a decade of horror in which they tried to turn the clock back to "Year Zero" and make Cambodia a preindustrial state. In the process, they killed teachers or anyone showing signs of American, Vietnamese, or Western education or influence. Perhaps a quarter of all Cambodians died, and many who survived had then to live through years of fourteen-hour workdays and constant hunger. Ironically, the horror of the Khmer Rouge rule in Cambodia ended only when Vietnam invaded the country in 1978.

Paris Peace Talks

Talks with North Vietnam that led to an agreement by the Nixon administration to withdraw all U.S. troops from Vietnam in 1972.

Vietnamization

The policy of turning the fighting of the Vietnam War over to South Vietnam in exchange for greater U.S. financial support.

While Nixon and Kissinger expanded the bombing, they sought to withdraw American ground troops from Vietnam. It was, after all, sending young Americans to Vietnam that was fueling most of the resistance to the war. In May 1969, the administration announced plans to change the draft regulations so a new lottery system would give young men a better sense of the odds of their being called while reducing the overall size of the call-up "pool." Eventually, the Nixon administration moved from a draft to an all-volunteer army to reduce public resistance to Vietnam and future wars.

The administration's new policy was called **Vietnamization**. Money and arms would be sent to the South Vietnamese government so more and better-trained Vietnamese troops might replace American troops. In 1969, the South Vietnamese army expanded from 850,000 to 1,000,000 troops while the first 25,000 U.S. troops were withdrawn. In the years that followed, fewer and fewer American troops were stationed in Vietnam. However, the people of South Vietnam had never embraced the war with the enthusiasm that either the South Vietnamese or American governments wanted, so it was difficult for the South Vietnamese government to rely on their loyalty.

Maintaining the morale of the U.S. troops who remained in Vietnam was very difficult. The war seemed to have no purpose. Those on leave sometimes refused to return. Desertions spiked as soldiers sought asylum in Canada or Sweden. In Vietnam, there were near-mutinies as soldiers refused to fight for strategic positions that seemed to have no value; "fragging" of officers—sometimes lethal attacks on officers by enlisted men—increased dramatically with over one thousand reported between 1969 and 1972. Racial tensions among the troops escalated. Drug use increased. By one estimate 40,000 of the 250,000 troops remaining in Vietnam in 1971 were using heroin. Protests against the war mounted within the army itself.

After 1968, protests against the war were larger and angrier than ever. In the fall of 1969, 600,000 to 750,000 people gathered on the Washington Mall to protest the war. When Nixon confirmed that U.S. troops had invaded Cambodia in April 1970, protests took place

John Filo/Premium Archive/Getty Images

The killing of four protesting students at Ohio's Kent State University, followed by the killing of two more at Jackson State in Mississippi, changed the nation's mood. The country was fighting a distant war while disagreements about that war were leading Americans to shoot and kill other Americans at home.

27.1

27.2

27.3

27.4

on 350 college campuses around the country. A quarter of all the nation's college students may have been involved. On May 4, Ohio National Guard troops opened fire at protesters at Kent State University, killing four. Two days later, local police killed two protesting students at historically black Jackson State College in Mississippi. In April 1971, one thousand veterans of the war camped out in Washington to protest the war while they read the names of dead buddies and flung medals on the Capitol steps. One of the veterans, twenty-seven-year-old John Kerry—a future senator and presidential candidate—testified before the Senate Foreign Relations Committee. He asked, "How do you ask a man to be the last man to die for a mistake?"

President Nixon insisted that the protests made no impact on him. When students from a number of universities gathered in May 1970 to remember the four who died at Kent State, construction workers jumped into the crowd, hitting the students with their hard hats. A few days later, officials of the construction unions presented Nixon with an honorary hard hat, which he accepted as a "symbol, along with our great flag, for freedom and patriotism to our beloved country." A *Newsweek* poll reported that 58 percent of Americans blamed the Kent State students for the violence, only 11 percent the National Guard. The same poll showed that 50 percent of Americans approved the invasion of Cambodia while 39 percent opposed it. The anger swirling around the war took many forms, not only protest against the war but also anger at the protesters and anger at two presidential administrations as much for the failure to expand the war as for making war in the first place.

Then, as the 1972 presidential election approached, the United States and North Vietnam, meeting at the until then unproductive Paris Peace Talks, agreed to a compromise. Henry Kissinger, in private meetings with the North Vietnamese negotiators, agreed that North Vietnamese troops in South Vietnam could remain there pending a final resolution. Le Duc Tho, the North Vietnamese negotiator at the talks, agreed that the South Vietnamese Thieu government could stay in place pending the resolution and that American prisoners of war—mostly bomber pilots, some of whom had been held for years—would be returned. On October 31, 1972, Kissinger announced, "Peace is at hand." It turned out to be a premature announcement. South Vietnamese president Thieu, who had not been informed of the changing U.S. position, objected to the continued presence of North Vietnamese troops, and after Nixon had won a second term on November 7, he backed Thieu. The war continued.

In December 1972, after his reelection, Nixon expanded the bombing of the North. More bombs were dropped in the twelve-day "Christmas bombing" than in the previous three years. In January 1973, peace talks led back to the same agreement as had been considered in October, in spite of Thieu's continuing skepticism. On January 27, 1973, a cease-fire took effect; U.S. combat troops soon left the country. American prisoners of war were returned and went home. The direct U.S. involvement in Vietnam was over. The United States continued to provide aid for the Thieu government, kept advisors in South Vietnam, and bombed supply routes in Cambodia. But without U.S. fighting forces, the South Vietnamese government lost ground and would lose more ground in the years ahead.

CHINA While the war to stop a Communist victory in Vietnam continued, Nixon, in perhaps the most surprising move of his administration, began to normalize U.S. relations with Communist China. Ever since the Communist victory in 1949, the People's Republic of China and the United States had remained deeply hostile to each other. The United States continued to recognize the Chinese government-in-exile on the island of Taiwan as the official government of China, in spite of the fact that the Communist government based in Beijing ruled the land. Then in July 1971, National Security Adviser Kissinger made a secret trip to China and laid the groundwork for a highly publicized trip by President Nixon to China in February 1972. Nixon's every move was televised, including his handshake with Chairman Mao Zedong, his toasts with Premier Zhou Enlai, and his tour of the Great Wall.

The trip had a number of substantive benefits for all concerned. From Nixon's perspective, he got a promise that China would not intervene in Vietnam. China got a promise of a smaller U.S. military presence in Taiwan. Both countries established new diplomatic channels and expanded trade and travel opportunities. For China, the trip also meant an end to decades of isolation, and for Nixon, it was a public relations boost at the beginning of an election year. Long after the trip, Nixon said, "This was the week that

27.1

27.2

27.3

27.4

President Richard Nixon, who had made his reputation as a staunch anti-Communist, ended years of hostility between the United States and Communist China with his February 1972 trip that included meetings with top Chinese leaders and this toast with Chinese premier Chou En-lai (Zhou Enlai).

Pictorial Press Ltd/Alamy Stock Photo

changed the world ... a bridge across 16,000 miles and 22 years of hostilities." In a tense world, it certainly began a new era of cooperation and coexistence.

EXPANDED FOREIGN DEALINGS   While Nixon's trip to China received the most publicity, U.S. dealings with the Soviet Union may have been more substantive. In September 1970, Nixon and Soviet premier Leonid Brezhnev came to an agreement about Cuba. While the Soviet Union continued to provide Cuba with aid and the United States continued its embargo on trade with the island, relations thawed considerably when the Soviets agreed to suspend building a submarine base there and the United States promised there would not be another invasion of the island.

A year later, the United States and Soviet leaders reduced tensions in Berlin. In May 1972, Nixon traveled to Moscow for a meeting with Brezhnev in which they agreed to a **Strategic Arms Limitation Treaty (known as SALT I) and an Anti-Ballistic Missile Treaty (ABM),** which began the process of reducing the world's supply of nuclear weapons.

Other elements in the Nixon-Kissinger foreign policy were less successful. The Six-Day War in the Middle East had taken place in June 1967, a year and a half before Nixon's election, but the new administration had to deal with the outcome. In the 1967 war, using American-supplied weapons but keeping the Americans in the dark about their intentions, Israel attacked Egypt and Syria. The Egyptian army was devastated, and Israeli troops came close to overthrowing the government of Syria until stopped by the United States at the insistence of the Soviets, who used the hotline between Washington and Moscow for the first time. Israel seized forty-two thousand square miles and tripled its size.

Nixon supported friendly Arab governments, especially the then "twin pillars" of Saudi Arabia and Iran. Nixon was delighted that with their oil money—much of it U.S. supplied through massive oil purchases—Saudi Arabia and Iran could also handle their own defense and purchase American arms. When a crisis emerged in Jordan in the summer of 1970, Israel and the United States jointly defended a friendly government there. But real peace in the Middle East remained elusive.

Nixon and Kissinger sought to project American influence in other parts of the world with mixed results. They disliked India's prime minister Indira Gandhi and believed that India was intent on an alliance with the Soviet Union. Although Gandhi could be difficult and Indian links to the Soviet Union were real, the long-term result was a U.S. policy to strengthen ties to a military dictatorship in Pakistan. The alliance led the United States to support that government when it tried to put down a rebellion in the Bengali region

Strategic Arms Limitation Treaty (known as SALT I) and an Anti-Ballistic Missile Treaty (ABM)

Major treaties negotiated with the Soviet Union to reduce the world's supply of nuclear weapons.

that cost perhaps a million lives. It would be a long time before Indian or Bengali people warmed to the United States.

In Chile, the United States tried hard to keep a Marxist Salvador Allende from winning the 1970 election. When he did win, the CIA kept trying to destabilize the Allende government. The efforts worked, and Allende was overthrown and killed in a military coup in 1973. The U.S.-backed military forces that overthrew the democratically elected government launched Chile on a course of years of tyranny and terror.

Finally in August 1971, almost three decades after the World War II leaders, meeting at Bretton Woods, New Hampshire, had made the U.S. dollar the currency against which all other would be pegged as a way to stabilize exchange rates (see Chapter 24), Nixon announced a "**New Economic Policy**" and ended that practice. In the future, the dollar would float freely in relationship to other international currencies. Nixon hoped that by cutting the dollar loose from other currencies, the new exchange rates would make it easier for people in other countries to buy U.S. goods. He wanted to bolster the economy before the 1972 election, and the economy received a valuable jolt. The long-term result of ending the stability in international exchange rates was less certain.

New Economic Policy

A policy that ended the decades-long plan in which all other currencies would be based on the U.S. dollar.

27.1

27.2

27.3

27.4

27.1 Quick Review

Nixon's policy has been described as liberalism at home and a tough Cold War stance abroad. Explain why you would agree or disagree with this view.

The Movements of the 1960s and 1970s

27.2 **Analyze the many political and cultural movements that followed in the track of the Civil Rights Movement.**

The Civil Rights Movement had captured the country's attention in the 1950s and 1960s, but it was not until the late 1960s and 1970s that many other groups of Americans formed their own movements to demand new rights and freedoms. Women, Latinos, American Indians, Asians, and members of the white counterculture all formed their own organizations, made their own demands, and pushed the society to acknowledge their concerns between 1968 and 1980.

The Women's Movement

Through the 1960s, the place of women in society remained surprisingly unchanged and unconsidered from what it had been in the 1950s. Newspapers still ran separate listings for male and female jobs. Only a token number of women were admitted to law, medical, or other professional schools. Policies that would be unbelievable only a short time later, like a rule in many places that husbands had to sign off on a wife's credit card application, were still the norm. In November 1964, Stokely Carmichael made his infamous comment, "The position of women in SNCC is prone." Women who went to Mississippi to fight for civil rights ended up doing domestic chores as well as organizing, and women in the antiwar movement found it very difficult to be seen as credible leaders. Women did not like what they saw in these circumstances.

Women also began running for office in larger numbers than ever before. Only a tiny number of women served in state legislatures or Congress before the late 1960s. Nevertheless, during the 1960s, momentum grew as more women, and a more diverse group of women, started running for and winning elections. More women were elected to Congress, including Patsy Mink (D-Hawaii) in 1965, the first Asian woman, and Shirley Chisholm (D-New York), the first African American woman in 1969. In 1971, Congresswomen Chisholm, Mink, Bella Abzug, and other women in elective and appointed offices created the National Women's Political Caucus (NWPC), a bipartisan organization to encourage

Jesse-Steve Rose/The Image Works

In the 1970s, many women came together to protest inequality, raise consciousness, and change the ways men and women interacted in American society.

women to seek office. In 1972, Chisholm also ran for president and carried 151 delegates in the Democratic National Convention. In 1975, Ella Grasso was elected governor of Connecticut, the first woman to be elected a state governor who was not following her husband.

At the end of the 1960s, some younger women began consciousness-raising groups, discussing their experiences as women as well as the emotional, political, and economic toll that sexism was taking in their lives. Like the students who founded SNCC, these younger women had far less patience with working "inside the system" than their elders. Some began to separate from larger organizations and political movements, while others also separated from the men with whom they were previously aligned politically or personally.

A month after the violent demonstrations at the Democratic Convention in Chicago in 1968, Robin Morgan began organizing women to disrupt the Miss America Pageant in Atlantic City, New Jersey. The pageant was very popular in the 1950s and 1960s. Women representing each state were judged for their beauty and poise. "Miss America was perfect for us lefty Women's liberationists," Morgan insisted. "She touched capitalism, militarism, racism, and sexism, all in one fell swoop." Women who came to Atlantic City had a "Freedom Trash Can" in which they threw underwire bras, constricting girdles, copies of *Playboy* magazine, and other symbols of women's oppression. When the *New York Post* carried the story, the editors wanted to make a comparison to draft card burning, and erroneously coined the term "bra burning," though as far as anyone knows, no bras were burned in Atlantic City or at any other women's event.

A short time later, the Office of Federal Contract Compliance at the Department of Labor supported Bernice "Bunny" Sandler when she filed a complaint against the University of Maryland after she had been turned down for a faculty appointment because, she was told, "Let's face it, Bunny, you come on too strong for a woman." The case eventually became a nationwide class action suit against university discrimination.

In August 1970, moderate and radical feminists came together to celebrate the fiftieth anniversary of the women's suffrage amendment. On Women's Strike for Equality Day, fifty thousand women marched down New York's Fifth Avenue, including Congresswoman Bella Abzug, National Organization for Women founder Betty Friedan, and newer leaders such as Gloria Steinem and Kate Millett.

Joining Friedan and Pauli Murray, the cofounders of NOW, younger women like Kate Millett, Germaine Greer, and Gloria Steinem began their activist careers at the end of the 1960s, bringing the issues of women's struggles and women's rights to the foreground. In 1970, Florence Howe founded the Feminist Press to reissue the work of earlier feminist writers and publish the work of new women authors. In Massachusetts, twelve women founded the Boston Women's Health Book Collective and published a small booklet, *Women and Their Bodies*, in 1970. An expanded version, *Our Bodies, Ourselves*, became a best seller. A group of African American feminists calling themselves the Combahee River Collective—in honor of a Civil War battle led by Harriet Tubman—issued a statement in 1977, saying, "Black, other Third World, and working women have been involved in the feminist movement from its start," and they wanted to be sure that "elitism within the movement" did not marginalize them. The poetry of the black lesbian feminist Audre Lorde began to gain wide circulation.

In 1972, Gloria Steinem, who had become a major voice of women's liberation, sometimes to the irritation of Betty Friedan, launched *Ms.* magazine, which turned into a mass-market success when it sold 250,000 copies in its first eight days. Although too tame for some, and too much of a one-woman show for others, *Ms.* remained a voice of new ideas and important, challenging thinking. It also successfully encouraged a switch from "Mrs." and "Miss" to the marriage-neutral term "Ms." that matched the equally neutral "Mr."

Other women were lobbying state legislatures to make abortions legal. Among them was a young attorney, Sarah Weddington, who took on a Texas case that would eventually change the abortion laws of the United States. The U.S. Supreme Court heard the initial arguments of the case of *Roe v. Wade* in the spring of 1972. Jane Roe was a fictitious name to protect the plaintiff's identity. In January 1973, the Court announced the 7–2 decision that the right to privacy prevented any state from outlawing abortion in the first two trimesters of a woman's pregnancy. *Roe v. Wade* would lead to battles about abortion and the role of the courts for decades.

Still other women endeavored to change their working conditions or to open new careers to women. In 1973, Boston office workers organized a group they called "9 to 5," which became a union. Using new federal laws against workplace discrimination, women also entered nontraditional careers in business and the construction trades that had been closed to them. Women began to appear as plumbers, bus drivers, and senior business executives.

The leaders of NOW, especially Pauli Murray, were determined to revive the struggle for an Equal Rights Amendment to the U.S. Constitution. An Equal Rights Amendment (ERA) was first proposed by the Women's Party in the early 1920s, immediately after the success of the women's suffrage amendment. By the 1970s, it seemed like the next logical step. Newly elected representative Shirley Chisholm gave a passionate speech, "Equal Rights for Women," to the House in 1969. NOW began serious lobbying of the Senate in 1970. The ERA passed by a vote of 354 to 24 in the House and 84 to 8 in the Senate. President Nixon endorsed the amendment, which said simply, "Equality of rights under the law shall not be denied or abridged by the United States or by any state on account of sex." As we will see, however, as it moved through state legislatures for ratification, the ERA fell victim to a much changed political atmosphere.

The United Farm Workers, 1965–1970

César Chávez began organizing in the grape-growing town of Delano, California, in 1961. He was soon joined by Dolores Huerta. The Farm Workers Association (FWA), which later became the **United Farm Workers** union, drew on both the community organizing model developed by Saul Alinsky in Chicago and on the older tradition of a mutual benefits association within the Catholic Church. Catholic priests and nuns, Protestant ministers, and members of the United Auto Workers Union all helped the FWA grow. College students, many fresh from campus-based protest and civil rights activity, joined the effort. It was a powerful coalition, stretching far beyond the small towns of California's little noticed agricultural regions.

In September 1965, Chávez, Huerta, and Larry Itliong, a leader of the Filipino farmworkers, planned a coordinated effort by Filipino and Latino organizers and called a major strike for the fall harvest in Delano. A meeting of 1,200 Mexican American workers on September 16, 1965, began with a chant "Viva la Huelga! Viva la Causa!" The drawn-out Delano strike and subsequent grape boycott had begun and received widespread support across the country. It took five years, but on July 29, 1970, the Delano grape growers signed a contract recognizing the farmworkers union as their bargaining agent. Chávez declared, "From now on, all grapes will be sweet."

The American Indian Movement—From Alcatraz to Wounded Knee

In November 1969, American Indians began a year-and-a-half siege of the abandoned federal prison on Alcatraz Island that gained national attention. Earlier, in 1964, Vine Deloria, a thirty-year-old Standing Rock Sioux, won leadership of the National Congress of American Indians, which had been founded in 1944 to support the development of Indian tribal governments. A new direction began for the nation's largest Indian organization. The **American Indian Movement (AIM)** was founded in Minneapolis among urban Indians in the late 1960s, but become a major force on the reservations in the 1970s, making some of its leaders like Russell Means and Dennis Banks national figures.

27.1

27.2

27.3

27.4

Roe v. Wade

The U.S. Supreme Court's landmark 1973 decision declaring antiabortion laws unconstitutional and protecting a woman's right to choose.

United Farm Workers

A union of migrant workers of California, which bargained for better salaries and working conditions.

American Indian Movement (AIM)

The most widely recognized of several Native American civil rights organizations in the 1970s.

Annie Wells/Los Angeles Times/Getty Images

A charismatic union leader César Chávez, working closely with Dolores Huerta, became the face of the organizing effort among California migrant workers, especially the grape pickers. After his death in 1993, Chávez was often memorialized in murals and posters. Now in her late eighties, Huerta remains active in labor and women's movements today.

American Voices

Three Views on Women's Rights

When Betty Friedan and Pauli Murray launched NOW in 1966, they wanted the equivalent of the NAACP for women—a national organization to lobby, raise issues in the media, and reach a wide audience. In 1969, Shulamith Firestone spoke for more radical feminists through the Redstockings Manifesto. While NOW blamed a system of oppression, Redstockings blamed men. Phyllis Schlafly challenged both and specifically the momentum building for an Equal Rights Amendment.

National Organization for Women, Statement of Purpose, 1966

We, men and women who hereby constitute ourselves as the National Organization for Women, believe that the time has come for a new movement toward true equality for all women in America, and toward a fully equal partnership of the sexes, as part of the world-wide revolution of human rights now taking place. ...

WE BELIEVE that the power of American law, and the protection guaranteed by the U.S. Constitution to the civil rights of all individuals, must be effectively applied and enforced to isolate and remove patterns of sex discrimination, to ensure equality of opportunity in employment and education, and equality of civil and political rights and responsibilities on behalf of women. ...

WE REJECT the current assumptions that a man must carry the sole burden of supporting himself, his wife, and family, and that a woman is automatically entitled to lifelong support by a man upon her marriage; or that marriage, home and family are primarily a woman's world and responsibility—hers, to dominate, his to support. We believe that a true partnership between the sexes demands a different concept of marriage, an equitable sharing of the responsibilities of home and children, and the economic burdens of their support.

Source: National Organization for Women Statement of Purpose (1966), reprinted with permission. This is a historical document and may not reflect the current language or priorities of the organization.

Redstockings Manifesto (excerpt), July 7, 1969

Women are an oppressed class. Our oppression is total, affecting every facet of our lives. We are exploited as sex objects, breeders, domestic servants, and cheap labor. We are considered inferior beings, whose only purpose is to enhance men's lives. Our humanity is denied. Our prescribed behavior is enforced by the threat of physical violence.

Because we have lived so intimately with our oppressors, in isolation from each other, we have been kept from seeing our personal suffering as a political condition. This creates the illusion that a woman's relationship with her man is a matter of interplay between two unique personalities, and can be worked out individually. In reality, every such relationship is a class relationship,

and the conflicts between individual men and women are political conflicts that can only be solved collectively.

We identify the agents of our oppression as men. Male supremacy is the oldest, most basic form of domination. All other forms of exploitation and oppression (racism, capitalism, imperialism, etc.) are extensions of male supremacy: men dominate women, a few men dominate the rest. All power structures throughout history have been male-dominated and male-oriented. Men have controlled all political, economic, and cultural institutions and backed up this control with physical force. They have used their power to keep women in an inferior position. *All men* receive economic, sexual, and psychological benefits from male supremacy. *All men* have oppressed women.

Source: The Redstockings Manifesto first appeared as a mimeographed flyer, desinged for distribution at women's liberation events. To read the full manifesto and see other materials from the 1960s rebirth years of feminism from the Redstockings Women's Liberation Archives for Action, go to www.redstocking.org, or write to PO Box 744 Stuyvesant Station, New York, NY 10009.

Phyllis Schlafly, "What's Wrong with 'Equal Rights' for Women?", February 1972

Of all the classes of people who ever lived, the American woman is the most privileged.

We have the most rights and rewards, and the fewest duties. ...

Women's lib is a total assault on the role of the American woman as wife and mother, and on the family as the basic unit of society.

Why should we trade in our special privileges and honored status for the alleged advantage of working in an office or assembly line? Most women would rather cuddle a baby than a typewriter or factory machine. Most women find that it is easier to get along with a husband than a foreman or office manager.

Women's libbers do *not* speak for the majority of American women. American women do *not* want to be liberated from husbands and children. We do *not* want to trade our birthright ... for the mess of pottage called the Equal Rights Amendment.

Source: *Phyllis Schlafly Report* 5, no. 7 (February 1972).

Thinking Critically

1. **Comparison**

   What did each document seem to say about the role that the institution of marriage plays, or potentially plays, in American society? How would you describe the differences?

2. **Contextualization**

   What do you think was the intended audience for each of the three documents?

In 1973, traditionalists among the Sioux on the Pine Ridge Reservation in South Dakota staged a dramatic takeover of the village of Wounded Knee, site of the massacre of 1890. Dennis Banks and Russell Means became the spokespersons for AIM and dared the federal government to repeat the attack. The standoff lasted seventy-one days as AIM held the town while agents of the U.S. Marshall Service and the FBI surrounded them. In May, after an FBI agent had been seriously wounded and two AIM members killed, both sides agreed to

27.1

27.2

27.3

27.4

Bettmann/Getty Images

The occupation of Wounded Knee, site of the 1890 massacre, took on great symbolic significance for many American Indians.

end the siege, and the Sioux won a government agreement to reconsider the treaty rights of the Oglala Sioux.

Another demonstration soon followed when Indians staged a sit-in at the Bureau of Indian Affairs offices in Washington, D.C. In 1975, two FBI agents were killed in another standoff at Pine Ridge, and one of the AIM leaders, Leonard Peltier, was arrested and sentenced to prison for life, although his involvement in the violence and the verdict in his case remain hotly contested more than forty years later.

The upsurge of Indian activity at Alcatraz, Wounded Knee, the Bureau of Indian Affairs office in Washington, and elsewhere gained more than publicity. In 1970, the Nixon administration negotiated the return of the Blue Lake in New Mexico, considered sacred by the Taos people, to the Taos Pueblo. In 1971, the Alaska Native Claims Settlement Act was passed by Congress, resolving long-standing land disputes. The 1972 Indian Education Act also provided funds for new schools that would be under tribal control. In 1973, the government began again to recognize Indian tribes as legitimate agents, starting with the Menominees in Wisconsin.

Asian Civil Rights

The 1970s were also a time in which the nature of American racial diversity began to change. In 1965, when Lyndon Johnson signed a new immigration law, only 5 percent of immigrants to the United States were from Asia. In the 1970s, that number climbed to 50 percent. Small Japanese and Chinese communities grew dramatically, while immigrants began to arrive from India, Pakistan, and Korea. After the end of the war in Vietnam, many Vietnamese refugees came to the United States and created new lives and communities here. Especially in Hawaii and California, the growing Asian population changed state and local politics. Wing F. Ong was the first Chinese American and the first Asian American elected to a state office when he joined the Arizona legislature in 1946, but the numbers grew rapidly. Daniel Inouye served in the U.S. Senate from Hawaii from 1963 to 2012. Most elected Asians were Democrats, but Republican Asians, both with roots in India, were elected as governors of Louisiana and South Carolina, and more Asians continued to run and win office elsewhere.

While elective politics has been a major focus of organizing in the diverse Asian communities, it is not the only one. The Asian American Legal Defense and Education Fund, modeled on civil rights organizations among other ethnic groups, has been active especially in representing young people who were profiled for racial, ethnic, or religious reasons. It has been an especially important organization for Asians who are Muslim or, in the case of Sikh's, are not Muslim but perceived to be by too many others. Although Asians have been coming to North America long before there was a United States, the majority of the country's growing Asian population are immigrants or the children of immigrants from the post-1965 era.

Changing Issues of Race and Diversity in the 1970s

The most dramatic scenes of the black Civil Rights Movement in the 1950s and 1960s took place in the South. In the 1970s, integration efforts moved north. Although Boston had a national reputation for liberalism, Boston's tightly knit ethnic neighborhoods could be hostile to outsiders. In 1974, federal courts found that the Boston School Committee (the local name for the school board) had engaged in a deliberate policy of redrawing school district lines to maintain racial segregation, and the court ordered an immediate integration of the schools, transferring students across the city by bus, for the opening of school in the fall of 1974. Boston exploded. It was many years before peace returned to the Boston schools.

While Boston was split over school integration, New York was split over a proposal developed by community leaders, the mayor, and the Ford Foundation for local community control of public schools. In certain "experimental districts," in predominantly Puerto Rican

Thinking Historically

The Young Lords Party and the Origin of Political Movements in the 1970s

Historians have debated why so many different political movements—among women, Latinos, American Indians, gay men and lesbians, and others—emerged in the late 1960s and 1970s. In the 1950s and early 1960s, the Civil Rights Movement focused on the black freedom struggle. A new white student movement emerged in the 1960s. In the next ten years, it seemed, every group of Americans was starting to demand its own rights and to challenge social injustice wherever it was found.

One of these new movement groups was the Young Lords Party, a Puerto Rican group that came into existence in New York City in 1969. Pablo Guzmán, one of the founders of the Young Lords, remembered their origins. His description of the diverse forces that led them to organize sheds light on the experience of many other groups.

In Guzmán's account, the Young Lords began with a street protest in the summer of 1969:

> All we had been trying to do after sweeping up the streets on previous Sundays was talk with sanitation about once-a-week pickups and nonexistent trash cans, and about how to decently treat people asking for help instead of blowing them off."

Guzmán and his friends thought that, if protests helped win victories for the African American community, it only made sense to use the same tactic for their own community. But when the protest produced an angry police presence, they decided it was time to recruit more support: "It was the summer of 1969, and the first stateside organization of radical young Puerto Ricans was announcing itself—we hoped—as a political force."

They quickly learned about La Raza Unida (the people united) that was emerging among Mexican Americans in the West and especially about the Black Panther Party, the militant black organization, on which the Young Lords would model themselves. They were also influenced by international connections in a world where many were challenging American dominance. Guzmán

had spent a semester studying in Mexico. He said, "I left as Paul Guzman, a nervous only-child of a Puerto Rican-Cuban mother and a Puerto Rican father ... I came back to the states as Pablo Guzmán."

While other groups influenced young urban Puerto Ricans like Guzmán, there were also other roots to the protest movement, as Guzmán reflected:

> But it didn't come from nowhere—my parents and my grandparents, after all, had first instilled in me a sense that there was far too long a history of injustice in this society. "Only," as my father would say later at my trial, "your mother and I never thought you would actually try to do something about it. Not on such a scale, anyhow."

But with deep roots in their own communities and with the inspiration of seeing others, the Young Lords, like the American Indian Movement or the gay men of the Stonewall Inn, were not going to remain quiet in the face of what they saw as significant injustice.

Note: Today, Pablo Guzmán is a senior journalist with CBS news.

Source: Pablo Guzmán, *Village Voice*, March 21, 1995.

Thinking Critically

1. **Comparison**

   How does Guzmán's description compare with the emergence of other movements described in this chapter?

2. **Analyzing Primary Sources**

   How did Guzmán describe the impact that his family history and the larger historical situation in which he lived had on what he did?

East Harlem, and an African American neighborhood in Brooklyn, local school boards were elected and given powers previously held by the central office. When the Brooklyn board transferred twelve white teachers out of the district in May 1968, the overwhelmingly white New York teachers union called a citywide strike that lasted for much of the 1968–1969 school year, crippled the schools, and exacerbated racial tensions in New York.

In other cities such as Detroit, Cleveland, Baltimore, St. Louis, Milwaukee, and Buffalo, whites virtually deserted the city for the suburbs. As a result, more African Americans were elected to the office of mayor. Richard Hatcher had been elected mayor of Gary, Indiana, and Carl Stokes mayor of Cleveland, Ohio, in 1967; Tom Bradley was elected in Los Angeles, Coleman Young in Detroit, and Maynard Jackson in Atlanta, all in 1973; and Walter Washington in Washington, D.C., in 1974.

Blacks and Latinos also began to seek opportunities in higher education in numbers never seen before. A growing black middle class could afford college in substantial numbers for the first time, and Johnson-era affirmative action programs opened doors. But some whites felt that affirmative action subjected them to "reverse discrimination." The arguments about affirmative action came to a head when Allan Bakke, a white applicant, was rejected for admission to the medical school at the University of California at Davis in 1973. Bakke sued, claiming that he had been denied because the university held 16 percent of the slots for minority students. In the U.S. Supreme Court's **Bakke decision** in June 1978, four justices ruled that race-based programs were illegal and that the university had discriminated against Bakke while four justices ruled that race-based affirmative action was constitutional. The ninth justice, Lewis Powell, joined with those ordering Bakke's admission, but on much more limited grounds. Powell said that an individual could not be excluded solely on the basis of race, but that race could be a consideration. One law professor remarked, "It was a landmark occasion, but the court failed to produce a landmark decision."

In 1974, the U.S. Supreme Court in *Lau v. Nichols* ruled that school districts must make accommodations for students who came to school not speaking English. These accommodations could include English-immersion programs or full bilingual programs. They could not, as San Francisco had been doing, simply tell a non-English speaker like Kenny Lau to make the best of it and learn English on his own. A year later, in November 1975, Congress passed and President Ford signed the Education for all Handicapped Children Act requiring the "least restrictive" possible accommodation for students with special needs.

As immigration from Asia and Latin America increased significantly after 1965, new immigrants came from many parts of Asia, Mexico, many countries of Central and South America, and the racially diverse islands of the Caribbean. With this growing racial diversity, interracial marriages became more common. A child with one Asian parent and one parent from Central America was not adequately described with traditional ethnic labels.

Bakke Decision

The U.S. Supreme Court's 1978 decision that limited, but did not end, affirmative action programs to achieve racial diversity in a university's student body.

Out of the Closet—Stonewall and Gay/Lesbian Rights

The *New York Times* for June 29, 1969, carried an article that said:

> Hundreds of young men went on a rampage in Greenwich Village shortly after 3 a.m. yesterday after a force of plainclothes men raided a bar that the police said was well known for its homosexual clientele.

Something shifted that night when a group of gay men at the Stonewall Tavern in New York City's Greenwich Village, whom the police assumed would submit quietly to arrest as they had in the past, refused to do so. Many who had long kept their identities hidden stood up. Many would never return to a closeted life. Many around the country would join them. In the 1970s, gay liberation became a political movement. And the rebellion at the Stonewall Tavern has been honored as one of the key starting moments.

While the American Psychological Association (APA) had traditionally defined homosexuality as "a form of mental illness," pressure from outside and from within its own ranks led to a 1973 change when its board voted to remove homosexuality from its list of psychiatric disorders. "We will be removing one of the justifications for the denial of civil rights to individuals whose only crime is that their sexual orientation is to members of the same sex," an APA leader said.

27.1

27.2

27.3

27.4

Throughout the 1970s, more and more gay men and lesbians came out of hiding—"out of the closet"—to demand equal rights.

Woodstock Music and Art Fair

A countercultural music festival, held near Woodstock, New York, that attracted an audience of over 400,000 in 1969.

In November 1974, Elaine Nobel was elected to the Massachusetts state legislature as the first openly lesbian or gay state representative in the United States. The following January, Minnesota state senator Allan Spear announced that he, too, was gay and, inspired by Nobel, would no longer keep his sexual orientation a secret. Then in 1977, Harvey Milk, a gay man, was elected to the San Francisco Board of Supervisors, symbolizing the radical change that was taking place.

A Counterculture and Its Critics—Sex, Drugs, and Rock 'n' Roll

The summer after Richard Nixon's inauguration, more than 400,000 young Americans gathered on August 15–17, 1969, on a farm in Bethel, New York, for the **Woodstock Music and Art Fair**. Many more would have attended if massive traffic jams and rain-induced mud had not made travel to Woodstock exceedingly difficult. Those who attended Woodstock heard Janis Joplin, Jimi Hendrix, and Jefferson Airplane as well as folk performers, including Joan Baez. Many smoked marijuana, swam in the nude, and generally enjoyed a weekend free from the constraints of traditional society. If any event stands as a symbol of the counterculture of the late 1960s, Woodstock was that event. It was also a symbol that stood closer to the end of the counterculture's life than the beginning.

Several factors helped create the counterculture's hippies of the 1960s. One was the creation of hallucinogenic drugs. The creation of a diethylamide of lysergic acid (LSD) by Albert Hoffman (no relation to Abbie Hoffman), who was seeking a way to treat schizophrenia, set a new generation on a drug-assisted search for vision quests and heightened ecstasy in body and soul. LSD was popularized by Timothy Leary and Ken Kesey as the key to the ultimate revelation or a way to "blow your mind." Music was also essential to the counterculture. Rock 'n' roll had gone through extraordinary changes in the 1960s. Two British rock groups, the Beatles and the Rolling Stones, became huge hits in the United States in the early 1960s with music that mocked mainstream music, including songs like "A Hard Day's Night." Bob Dylan moved from folk music to rock. His "Like a Rolling Stone" moved to number one on the charts. In "Sgt. Pepper's Lonely Hearts Club

The Woodstock festival of 1969 was a three-day celebration of new freedoms that were already passing for many.

Band" and their first movie, *Yellow Submarine*, the Beatles embraced the psychedelic world. Finally, anger at a war that seemed always to be escalating led some, notably Abbie Hoffman and Jerry Rubin, to conclude that the best protest was street theater and humor that mocked those who they thought were leading the country to ruin.

If the counterculture had a physical home, it was in San Francisco's Haight-Ashbury district from 1966 to 1969. In Haight-Ashbury, the counterculture ruled its own small domain. Street theater could be seen on every corner. A group called the Diggers gave out free food. Relationships were casual and informal. Drugs were easily available. The summer of 1967 was declared the "summer of love," and young people from every corner of the United States streamed into "the Haight" to "make love, not war." But drugs led to too many emergency room visits and violence. Rock heroes Janis Joplin and Jimi Hendrix both died of drug overdoses in 1970 and Jim Morrison died in 1971, each twenty-seven years old. Venereal disease spread rapidly. The free food disappeared, and the street actors went elsewhere. Utopia, it seemed, could not last long.

27.2 Quick Review

How might an historian account for the many political and cultural movements that emerged in the 1960s and 1970s?

The Culture Wars of the 1970s

27.3 **Analyze the reaction to the liberal and radical politics of the 1960s and 1970s and the growth of new militant conservative movements.**

In the 1970s, the United States was a deeply divided nation. Among activist women there were major conflicts between feminist and antifeminist groups. Conservative Protestants, Catholics, and Jews found new common ground, often in opposition to liberals in their own traditions. The nation's deep racial divides shifted as various groups representing specific ethnicities—whites, blacks, Latinos, Asians, and American Indians—moved in different directions.

Phyllis Schlafly and the Defeat of the Equal Rights Amendment

Perhaps no one symbolized the new political situation, what some have called the culture wars of the 1970s, as much as Phyllis Schlafly. Schlafly was born Phyllis Stewart in a middle-class family in St. Louis, Missouri, in August 1924, three years after Betty Friedan, another child of the Midwest. However, their paths diverged dramatically. Schlafly was deeply influenced by her Roman Catholic background and the commitment to individual responsibility she was taught as a child. Throughout the 1940s and 1950s, Schlafly was a conservative activist within the Republican Party. She organized grassroots efforts for Barry Goldwater and wrote *A Choice, Not an Echo*, an attack on liberals within the Republican Party.

After the Goldwater defeat, a new opportunity opened for her. In December 1971, Schlafly was invited to a debate in Connecticut. She wanted to focus on national defense, but was told that the focus would be the **Equal Rights Amendment** that was being debated at that time in the U.S. Senate. Schlafly had no opinion of the amendment, but agreed to read up on it before coming to Connecticut. She did, and the result was her decision to make opposition to the ERA her prime focus.

In 1972, as Congress was voting on the ERA, Schlafly began arguing that equal rights actually meant diminished rights for women and launched the STOP ERA initiative. Schlafly pulled in women whom she knew from anti-Communist organizing. By early 1973, STOP ERA had chapters in twenty-six states. Eventually, thirty-five states ratified the

Phyllis Schlafly gave hundreds of speeches, like this one at the Illinois state capitol building, convincing enough states to defeat the proposed Equal Rights Amendment to the U.S. Constitution.

Bettmann/Getty Images

Equal Rights Amendment

A proposed amendment to the U.S. Constitution giving women equal rights with men; ratified by thirty-five states, three short of the needed number.

27.1

27.2

27.3

27.4

Map 27-1 Support of and Opposition to the ERA.

Although the majority of state legislatures voted to approve the proposed Equal Rights Amendment to the Constitution, the amendment fell three states short of the required three-fourths approval.

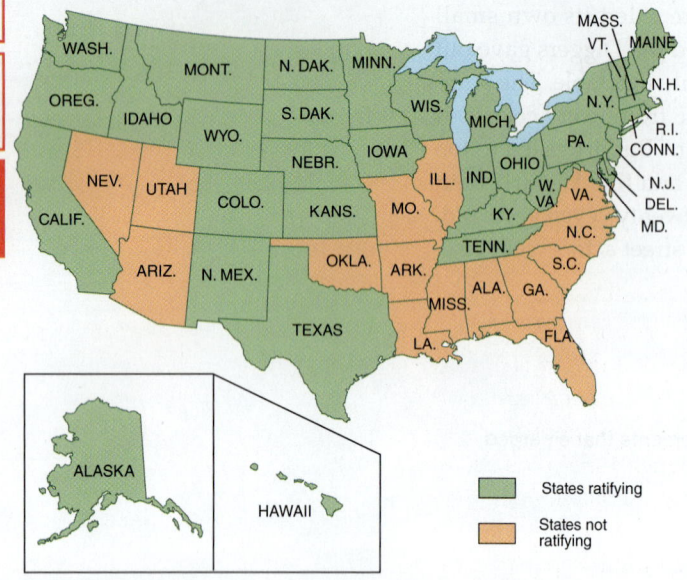

States ratifying

States not ratifying

Moral Majority

One of the first large-scale organizations of the emerging "religious right," which organized support for conservative candidates and was a major force in American politics in the early 1980s.

ERA, but it fell three short of the required thirty-eight states and was not added to the Constitution (see Map 27-1). Schlafly claimed much of the credit for its defeat. New cultural issues, including opposition to feminism, to abortion rights, to homosexual rights, and to the defense of prayer in school, as well as a particular definition of morality and law and order in the larger society, became the keys to a new conservative constituency and, for Phyllis Schlafly, a new career as an activist. For the Republican Party, they would be the keys to victory in several future election cycles.

The Rise of the Religious Right

Looking back at the 1972 election, Charles Colson, one of Nixon's prime advisers said, "It was ... the first time in modern American political history that social issues became dominant." They would become even more dominant in later campaigns.

In 1978, Pat Robertson, who had founded the Christian Broadcasting Network in 1960, said that if traditionalist Catholics and evangelical Protestants, long distrustful of each other, could come together, "We have enough votes to run the country." These were fighting words and they made Robertson a central player in the religious right in the 1980s.

By far the most powerful expression of the growing religious right in the 1970s was a new organization, the **Moral Majority**, founded by Reverend Jerry Falwell, pastor of the Thomas Road Baptist Church in Lynchburg, Virginia, which claimed 17,000 members. Falwell was also president of Liberty Baptist College (later Liberty University) and host of the television *Old Time Gospel Hour*, which ran on three hundred stations for an audience of some 1.5 million people.

The Moral Majority was, Falwell said, "pro-life, pro-family, pro-morality, and pro-American." It was anti-ERA, in favor of prayer in schools, the teaching of alternatives to evolution, and like some earlier secular conservative movements, intensely anti-Communist. Falwell opposed U.S. foreign policy that favored the relaxation of tensions with the Soviet Union and called on the nation's leaders to fight communism. He said, "Our government has the right to use its armaments to bring wrath upon those who would do evil." Falwell, who had opposed civil rights in the 1960s, said, "If you would like to know where I am politically, I am to the right of wherever you are. I thought Goldwater was too liberal." The Moral Majority helped register perhaps two million new voters before the 1980 election. They were a force to be reckoned with.

27.3 **Quick Review**

Were the culture wars of the 1970s—STOP ERA and the Moral Majority—reactions to earlier liberalism or something new in American culture and politics? Support your answer.

Politics, Economics, and the Impact of Watergate

27.4 Explain the political impact of Watergate and subsequent developments that set the stage for the "Reagan Revolution."

U.S. leadership and the U.S. economy faltered in the 1970s. The three presidents who served during that decade were ultimately viewed as flawed or weak. Nixon was driven from office in a scandal called Watergate. His successor, Gerald Ford, disappointed many, particularly for pardoning Nixon, and Ford's successor, Jimmy Carter, was unable to pull a nation out of a crisis with Iran and out of a gas-shortage crisis at home. The country, desperate for strong leadership, put its faith in a movie-star-turned-politician, Ronald Reagan, to start a new decade.

The Economic Context

The 1950s and 1960s had been decades of almost constant economic growth. During the 1960s, the nation's poverty rate dropped from 22.2 percent to 12.6 percent. The income of many Americans rose dramatically. More Americans had more to spend and more financial security than in any previous generation. While the 1970s did not see anything like a return to the financial distress of the 1930s, they were not such good times. The sense of decline was widespread.

Although the U.S. economy grew in the 1960s, the economies of other countries, especially Germany and Japan, grew more quickly. U.S. corporations failed to invest in research and development as much as companies in competing countries. Americans began buying foreign-made goods that were less expensive or of better quality. U.S. manufacturers moved production to other countries where wages were lower, costing U.S. workers their jobs. In 1971, for the first time since 1900, the United States imported more than it exported.

Throughout the 1970s, unemployment continued to be much higher than in the 1960s. While high unemployment normally meant low inflation, inflation also remained high during the decade, and the combination came to be known as "stagflation." To keep taxes low and foster public support for the Great Society, while also increasing military spending for Vietnam, Lyndon Johnson had allowed government debt to grow dramatically. Nixon also did little to reduce government debt, using government programs to build popularity while keeping taxes low for the same reason. The result was continued inflation in spite of the unemployment. When federal officials tried to reduce unemployment by providing stimuli to the economy, inflation got worse. When they cut spending, unemployment soared. The country began to talk about a "misery index"—the combined harm done by unemployment and inflation. Between March and December 1974, the Dow Jones Industrial Average fell from 892 to 577, a major loss for investors.

The economy was further undermined by a rapid rise in energy costs. In retaliation for U.S. support for Israel during the Yom Kippur war in October 1973, Arab members of the Organization of the Petroleum Exporting Countries (OPEC) raised the price of oil on the world market. Oil, which had sold for $1.77 a barrel in October 1973, rose to $12 a barrel by the spring of 1974. Suddenly, gasoline and heating oil were very expensive. Presidents Nixon, Ford, and Carter were all bedeviled by public anger over long lines at gas stations, something Americans had not experienced since World War II. Average Americans saw their disposable income decline as more money had to be spent to keep their cars running and their houses warm.

American automakers were slow to anticipate the impact of the rising prices for gasoline and kept making only large gas-guzzling cars. As a result, sales of Japanese imports, Toyotas, Hondas, and Datsuns, which had held only a small share of the U.S. auto market, soared. Steel mills, tire manufacturers, auto parts makers, and, of course, Ford, Chrysler, and General Motors, all cut back and laid off workers. Unemployment rose, especially in the Northeast and Midwest, a region that took on the new name of the **Rust Belt**. A 1976 *New York Times* series described the shift from the old industrial Northeast and Midwest to the South and Southwest: "All day and through the lonely night the moving vans push southward, the fourteen-wheeled boxcars of the highway, changing the demographic face of America." The **Sun Belt** states of the South and Southwest, which had been growing since World War II and which became even more popular with the widespread use of air-conditioning that followed the prosperity of the 1950s, boomed.

The rapid decline of the so-called Rust Belt and the equally rapid growth of the South and Southwest Sun Belt reflected many changes within the United States in the 1970s. The South itself had certainly changed. It was no longer the rigidly racially segregated economic backwater it was in the 1950s. Indeed, the South was more racially integrated than the North. Tanya Tucker's 1974 song, "The South Is Gonna Rise Again," told her audience that

27.1

27.2

27.3

27.4

Rust Belt

States of the Northeast and Midwest that had traditionally been the nation's manufacturing heartland but where older industries including steel making and automobile production moved out, often overseas, leaving rusting factories and high unemployment.

Sun Belt

States of the Southwest and West where warmer weather appealed to many and the advent of air-conditioning made living much more comfortable with a resulting population boom as newer industries relocated and families moved in large numbers.

the South would rise, "but not the way they thought it would back then. I see everybody hand-in-hand." In the new economy, Tucker sang, "I see sons and daughters of sharecroppers but they're not pickin' cotton anymore." But they were also not joining unions, and wages in the South stayed lower than in the North. Elected representatives of the new South tended to oppose what they saw as an intrusive government.

For some, the rise of the air-conditioned "Sun Belt" stretching from the Old Confederacy through the Southwest of Arizona and California, was a chance for a fresh start in fast-growing cities like Houston, Texas, or Phoenix, Arizona, and the suburbs around them. For others, especially those left behind in the North, it was a disaster. In 1975–1976, New York City suffered a major financial crisis. When the decline in city tax revenue and federal aid meant that the city could not pay its bills, it was forced to lay off 3,400 police officers, 1,000 firefighters, and 4,000 hospital workers. Cleveland eventually defaulted on its debts in 1978. Throughout the North, city services declined and crime spiraled.

There seemed to be relatively little that the federal government could do through the 1970s to change the economic situation or address stagflation. Tax cuts, proposed by every administration, did not have the impact that some hoped and, in the absence of corresponding cuts in federal spending, which were highly unpopular, tended to fuel further inflation. Americans found themselves in an unaccustomed era of limits, and they regularly took their anger out on political leaders of both parties.

Watergate and the End of the Nixon Presidency

When he was reelected in November 1972, Nixon seemed to be at the peak of his powers. In fact, he was beginning a long slow decline that would make his second term a torture for him, his administration, and, ultimately, the country until he finally resigned in disgrace in August 1974.

Watergate

The crisis that began with an illegal break-in at the Democratic Headquarters in the Watergate apartment complex and ended with Richard Nixon's resignation.

The constitutional crisis known as **Watergate** began with a simple burglary in June 1972. As the election campaign heated up, the special operations group known as "the plumbers" was set up within the ill-named Committee to Re-elect the President (CREEP). G. Gordon Liddy, leader of the plumbers recommended to CREEP's director, former attorney general John Mitchell, and his deputy Jeb Stuart Magruder, that they break into the offices of Democratic Committee chair Lawrence O'Brien, which were housed in the Watergate complex in Washington, D.C., to put a tap on his telephone. Mitchell and Magruder approved the plan, but the plumbers were caught. Police found an address book on the burglars that included a number for E. Howard Hunt, a former plumber now working for CREEP, and both Hunt and Liddy were soon arrested as coconspirators in the break-in.

The White House dismissed the whole thing as a "third-rate burglary." If Nixon had simply admitted the stupidity and fired Hunt and Liddy, perhaps even Mitchell and Magruder, the issue might have ended there. But such a move was not Nixon's style. His orders to his chief aide, Haldeman, were to "play it tough" and, most fatefully, to order the CIA to stop an FBI investigation of the burglary. In those moves, the grounds for the eventual impeachment of the president were laid since the CIA order to the FBI was an obstruction of justice.

While the Democratic candidate George McGovern tried to raise the issue during the fall campaign, not much came of it. But when Hunt and Liddy went to trial in front of federal district judge John J. Sirica, the judge determined that there was more to the case than a simple burglary. In addition, two *Washington Post* reporters, Carl Bernstein and Robert Woodward, began a search for more information, including the cultivation of a secret source who they called Deep Throat. (Only decades later was it revealed that Deep Throat was Mark Felt, deputy director of the FBI, who was angry that the FBI had been ordered out of the case and angry at Nixon for passing him over for the director's position when the FBI's longtime director J. Edgar Hoover died.)

In January 1973, just as Nixon began his second term, the Watergate burglars were found guilty in federal court. Sirica gave them all maximum sentences, but promised to reconsider if they would break their silence. One of the burglars, James McCord, started to talk to federal prosecutors. By April, not only McCord but also John Dean, Nixon's White House lawyer, and Deputy Campaign Director Magruder were talking to the grand jury.

They also talked to staff of a Senate Select Committee, chaired by Senator Sam Ervin of North Carolina. At that point, several of Nixon's closest advisors, including Haldeman and Ehrlichman, resigned. Still, proof of the president's knowledge or involvement of the affair was lacking. Then in May, the Ervin Committee started to hold televised hearings, and the nation first watched McCord accuse Dean and Mitchell, and then watched Dean accuse the White House. They also learned that Nixon had secretly taped conversations in the Oval Office to preserve a record for his memoirs.

By fall, Ervin, Sirica, and Archibald Cox, a Justice Department special prosecutor, all demanded the Oval Office tapes. Nixon refused to turn them over, claiming "executive privilege," the right of the president to keep White House deliberations confidential. On October 20, the president ordered his attorney general, Elliot Richardson, to fire Cox as special prosecutor. Richardson refused, and Nixon fired Richardson, then fired Deputy Attorney General William Ruckelshaus. Finally, the third-ranking person at the Justice Department, Robert Bork, fired Cox. The moment was known as the "Saturday Night Massacre." Nixon surrendered only some of the tapes, including one from days after the break-in that had an "accidental" eighteen-and-one-half-minute erasure. Public opinion started turning against the president.

The administration, so thoroughly embroiled in scandal and secrecy, was not able to pursue much else in foreign or domestic policy. It was in the middle of the Watergate crisis that Arab leaders, angry at Nixon's efforts first to reduce the dollar's value in international exchange rates (since oil was paid for in U.S. dollars) and then to support Israel, retaliated by increasing the cost of oil by some seven times. When in June 1974 Nixon tried to deflect his domestic troubles with another dramatic international trip—to Moscow to meet with Soviet leaders—the summit produced no meaningful results.

In the meantime, things seemed to go from bad to worse for the president. In October 1973, Vice President Spiro Agnew was convicted of soliciting kickbacks and forced to resign. Following the terms of the Twenty-Fifth Amendment to the Constitution added in 1967, Nixon nominated House Republican leader Gerald Ford as vice president. Ford, a popular leader with no particular ties to the White House, was quickly confirmed. As the investigation uncovered more of Nixon's dealings, the president responded, "I am not a crook." It was a low point in presidential history. But more was to come.

In March 1974, Haldeman, Ehrlichman, and former attorney general Mitchell were indicted. Federal courts ordered that the White House tapes be turned over to the courts and to the House committee, which had begun drawing up charges that would lead to the impeachment of the president. Nixon appealed the decision about the tapes. On July 24, the Supreme Court ruled that Watergate was a criminal matter and executive privilege did not apply. The tapes had to be handed over. On July 27, Democrats and many Republicans on the House committee began voting to recommend the impeachment of the president for obstruction of justice.

Rather than face the full House vote and the trial in the Senate, both of which he now knew he would lose, Nixon went on television on the evening of August 8 and told the nation, "I have never been a quitter. To leave office before my term is completed is abhorrent to every instinct in my body. But as president, I must put the interest of America first. ... Therefore, I shall resign the Presidency effective at noon tomorrow."

As the Nixon family began a sad journey to their home in San Clemente, California, Gerald Ford was sworn in as president. The nation breathed a sigh of relief that a long and distracting ordeal was over. Conservative columnist James J. Kilpatrick wrote, "The swearing-in of Gerald Ford can't come one hour too soon." At noon on April 9, Chief Justice Warren Burger, just after administering the presidential oath to Ford, turned to Pennsylvania senator Hugh Scott and said, "Hugh, it worked. Thank God it worked." Burger was celebrating the victory of the Constitution. Ford tried hard to live up to the trust that people, liberal and conservative, now placed in him. But he did not inherit an easy situation.

Gerald Ford

Gerald Ford entered the White House with high approval ratings. He also inherited an economy that was staggering from inflation and unemployment as well as an international scene that included the last stages of the defeat of South Vietnam. Fortunately for him, there

27.1
27.2
27.3
27.4

was a sense of bipartisan goodwill in his early days in office. George Reedy, a staunch Democrat and former press secretary for Lyndon Johnson, said, "Ford is one of the very few men in public life whose absolute honesty I do not question." Such a reputation was a precious, if limited, asset as Ford faced the nation's problems that were now his.

Ford came from Grand Rapids, Michigan. He had been an Eagle Scout, a star football player at the University of Michigan in the 1930s, and a Navy veteran of World War II. Like several other World War II veterans, including Kennedy and Nixon, Ford entered politics soon after the war, winning a seat in the House of Representatives in 1948. He gained a reputation for hard work and honesty and was elected House minority leader in 1965. Even so, not everyone respected him. Lyndon Johnson said that the House minority leader had played football once too often without a helmet. Before and during his presidency, he was often portrayed as long-winded and bumbling.

The new president believed that his top priority was to heal a wounded nation. A month after taking office, he made a controversial proposal that draft evaders be given amnesty in return for alternative service as a way to heal the divisions of the Vietnam War. Ford gave Richard Nixon a "full, free, and absolute pardon" for any crimes committed during his administration. Some hinted that Ford had made a deal with Nixon, but the new president insisted during and after his term in office that his top priority was healing the country, which included moving beyond Watergate.

Ford was convinced that the best way to counter inflation and unemployment was to get government spending under control and reduce the federal deficit. Congress, however, was very reluctant to accept any of Ford's proposals to cut federal spending. By January 1975, as the economy continued to worsen, Ford supported a tax cut. Congress approved an even larger cut than Ford had requested, and he reluctantly signed the popular bill in March 1975. He then proceeded to infuriate Democrats by vetoing a number of federal spending bills. Throughout most of the rest of his term, Ford and the Congress battled over tax and spending issues, both sides wanting tax cuts, but Ford insisting they be offset by spending cuts. Each side was determined to blame the other for ongoing economic woes and to claim the credit when the economy did improve modestly in late 1975 and early 1976. However, no one could claim that the economy was healthy during Ford's term.

Détente

The policy of building better understanding and a more peaceful relationship between the United States and the Soviet Union.

In addition to economic challenges, Ford had also inherited a number of foreign policy crises. The Cold War was still very real, and when the Soviet Union expelled the author Aleksandr Solzhenitsyn in February 1974, public opinion in the United States was inflamed, undermining some of Nixon's **détente** efforts to build a new and better relationship with the Soviet Union. Ford calmed U.S.-Soviet relations when he met with Soviet premier Leonid Brezhnev and signed the Helsinki Accords, promising peaceful resolution of outstanding issues and new scientific cooperation. The Middle East, however, remained tense, and India tested its first nuclear weapon in May 1974. In addition, Kissinger, whom Ford had retained as secretary of state, supported a military coup in Argentina in 1976, as he had in Chile in 1973.

Most frustrating, however, was Vietnam. The last U.S. troops had been out of Vietnam for more than a year when Ford took office, but military advisors, CIA, and State Department officers remained, and the United States continued to provide crucial aid. Congress was out of patience with the war. In March 1975, Ford briefly considered a recommendation from Kissinger to resume the bombing of North Vietnam but ultimately rejected it. Nevertheless, he was furious when in April Congress refused his request for emergency military aid to South Vietnam. In early 1975, the pro-American government of Laos fell to communists. In early April, the pro-American Lon Nol government of Cambodia fell to the Khmer Rouge. On April 29, 1975, the government of South Vietnam surrendered. As North Vietnamese tanks crashed through the gate

On April 9, 1974, Gerald Ford was sworn in as president of the United States just after Richard Nixon had resigned and departed from the White House grounds.

American Voices

Gerald R. Ford, Remarks upon Taking the Oath of Office as President, 1974

When Richard Nixon resigned as president on August 9, 1974, Gerald Ford became president. Moments after being sworn in, he spoke to the nation:

Mr. Chief Justice, my dear friends, my fellow Americans:

The oath that I have taken is the same oath that was taken by George Washington and by every President under the Constitution. But I assume the Presidency under extraordinary circumstances never before experienced by Americans. This is an hour of history that troubles our minds and hurts our hearts. …

I am acutely aware that you have not elected me as your President by your ballots, and so I ask you to confirm me as your President with your prayers. And I hope that such prayers will also be the first of many. …

I believe that truth is the glue that holds government together, not only our Government but civilization itself. That bond, though strained, is unbroken at home and abroad.

In all my public and private acts as your President, I expect to follow my instincts of openness and candor with full confidence that honesty is always the best policy in the end.

My fellow Americans, our long national nightmare is over.

Our Constitution works; our great Republic is a government of laws and not of men. Here the people rule. But there is a higher Power, by whatever name we honor Him, who ordains not only righteousness but love, not only justice but mercy.

As we bind up the internal wounds of Watergate, more painful and more poisonous than those of foreign wars, let us restore the golden rule to our political process, and let brotherly love purge our hearts of suspicion and of hate. …

God helping me, I will not let you down.

Thank you.

Source: Downloaded July 1, 2011, from www.fordlibrarymuseum.gov/library/speeches/740001.asp.

Thinking Critically

1. **Contextualization**

   Beyond the Nixon resignation, what "extraordinary circumstances" might Ford be referring to?

2. **Comparison**

   Why might Americans be willing to trust Gerald Ford's words after the dishonesty of the Johnson and Nixon administrations? Why not?

---

of the presidential palace in Saigon and the last U.S. helicopters took off from the roof of the American Embassy, there was little Ford could do but attempt the rescue of some Vietnamese orphans, mostly children born as a result of relationships between Vietnamese women and U.S. service personnel. The long American presence was over. South Vietnam disappeared and the Communist government renamed Saigon as Ho Chi Minh City.

As the 1976 presidential election approached, Ronald Reagan, the popular two-term governor of California, challenged Ford in the Republican primaries. Reagan was staunchly anti-Communist, attacking Ford and Kissinger for yielding too much to the Soviet Union, and he appealed to conservative voters. But Reagan was not able to dislodge a sitting president. Ford sought to unify the party by replacing his current (appointed) vice president, former New York governor Nelson Rockefeller, on the ticket with a more conservative candidate, Kansas senator Robert Dole, whom Reagan liked.

Democrats believed that after Watergate, and especially after Ford's pardon of Nixon, 1976 was to be their year, and they waged a vigorous campaign. At the beginning of the primary season, former Georgia governor Jimmy Carter was considered a long shot in a race that involved some of the nation's best-known leaders, including Washington senator Henry Jackson and Representative Morris Udall of Arizona. To the surprise of many, Carter won primary after primary and went on to a first-ballot nomination. He selected the well-known liberal senator from Minnesota, Walter Mondale, as his vice president.

Carter started the race with a twenty-point lead in the polls, but Ford was a better campaigner than many expected. In the end, Carter's focus on the continued high inflation and unemployment, the "misery index," the lingering national anger about Watergate, and Carter's success in positioning himself as the outsider won the election. The final vote was very close, with Carter winning 50 percent of the popular vote to Ford's 48 percent. Ford took his loss in stride, saying, "I want to be remembered as … a nice person, who worked at the job, and who left the White House in better shape than when I took over." Most agreed he deserved that tribute. Many also looked forward to a more wholesale change of national management in January 1977.

27.1

27.2

27.3

27.4

As the last helicopters left the roof of the U.S. Embassy in Saigon in 1975, hundreds of Vietnamese who had supported the U.S. effort tried to get out. Most were left behind.

Bettmann/Getty Images

Jimmy Carter's Difficult Years—Gas Lines, Inflation, Iran

By tradition, after taking the oath of office at the Capitol, a new U.S. president leads the inaugural parade back to the White House. Normally, the president rides in a limousine, but in 1977, Jimmy Carter chose to walk so he could be closer to the people, something that Carter very much wanted to have as a hallmark of his presidency. In the long campaign, Carter promised "never to tell a lie or to make a misleading statement." After the lies and cover-up of Watergate and Lyndon Johnson's "credibility gap," Carter was a refreshing change and walking to the White House was an important symbol of a different time to come.

Jimmy Carter was born in 1924 in the still rigidly segregated South, in the small town of Plains, Georgia. His father was a successful farmer, but Plains was a small place, and Carter left it to attend the U.S. Naval Academy at Annapolis, Maryland. After his navy service, Carter returned to Plains to run the family peanut farm and soon entered politics, serving in the Georgia state senate in the 1960s. In 1970, he was elected governor of Georgia. Some civil rights leaders never trusted Carter. But in his inaugural address as governor, he said, "The time for racial discrimination is over." As governor, Carter courted the King family and created a biracial coalition that he thought should be typical of the "New South," which he sought to represent.

Jimmy Carter and his wife, Rosalynn, were deeply religious, active members of their Southern Baptist Church in Plains and later in Washington, D.C., where Carter taught a Sunday school class. Carter's Christian faith reassured some and worried others, but his unapologetic sincerity and his equally clear commitment to the separation of church and state—uninterested in imposing his beliefs on others—tended to win him respect.

Carter's openness, his down-home style, and his fresh approach heightened his popularity. Two months into his administration, the new president had an extraordinary 75 percent public approval rating. The new administration knew from the beginning that the economy was the key to any success they would have. In spite of some modest improvements, stagflation remained a reality, and the rising costs from the energy crisis seemed to grow worse by the minute. During his first year in office, Carter proposed a large economic stimulus package that included $4 billion for public works programs. Although an economic conservative, Carter was willing to risk inflation to get a sluggish economy moving and put more Americans back to work. He also sought to end government regulations that he thought got in the way of a more robust economy. He signed the Airline Deregulation Act, which ended government control of airline prices with significant benefit to consumers. Later in his term, he also supported an expansion of the food stamp program to provide food to the hungry and stimulate the economy.

Carter appointed former Republican cabinet member James Schlesinger as his special advisor on energy—later secretary of energy when Congress approved the new cabinet department—and told Schlesinger to come up with a comprehensive energy plan, and do so in three months. Schlesinger did, and Carter appeared on television to tell the nation of his new proposals, which included a "gas guzzler tax" on high-mileage cars, tax credits for conservation, and a total of 113 separate proposals to reduce energy consumption and increase its availability. *Newsweek* summarized the speech this way: "Some of the time he was Jimmy the evangelist, preaching to a nation living in energy sin. Then he was Jimmy the engineer, rattling off statistics and throwing around terms like retrofitting and cogeneration. And then he was Jimmy the leader, summoning the nation to fight the 'moral equivalent of war.'" Unfortunately for Carter, the energy plan had been developed in secret, and the Congress was far from enthusiastic about it.

Carter also tried to deal with both unemployment and inflation, but by the fall of 1978, he had become convinced that he had to make inflation his top priority. Robert Strauss, a special counselor in the White House, tried with some success to "jawbone" business and labor (persuade them through public appeals) to keep wage increases and prices down. Later in 1978, Carter appointed Alfred Kahn to institute wage and price freezes. Still, inflation increased. As Americans used credit cards to keep up with the increases in costs, credit card and other consumer debt grew from $167 billion when Carter took office to $315 billion in 1979, further fueling the inflationary spiral. Only late in Carter's presidency did inflation decline when Paul Volcker, chair of the Federal Reserve Board, dramatically shrank the nation's money supply, but that achievement, too, was at great cost to Carter's popularity, particularly because it caused a major upsurge in unemployment.

Fueling the inflationary spiral, and causing a crisis of its own, the price of fuel just kept going up. In March 1979, the nuclear reactor at Three Mile Island in central Pennsylvania malfunctioned and the reactor core began to melt down. More than 100,000 Pennsylvania residents were required to flee. The disaster led to a national fear of nuclear energy. No new nuclear plants were built in the United States, leading to increased dependence on oil (see Map 27-2). However, oil was a volatile source of energy. The United States had long since ceased being able to produce all of the oil it needed and imported a significant amount

27.1

27.2

27.3

27.4

Map 27-2 Nuclear Plants around the United States.

By 1980, the United States had 103 nuclear reactors that produced power for commercial use, supplying approximately 20 percent of the nation's electricity. After the crisis at Three Mile Island, that number would not grow.

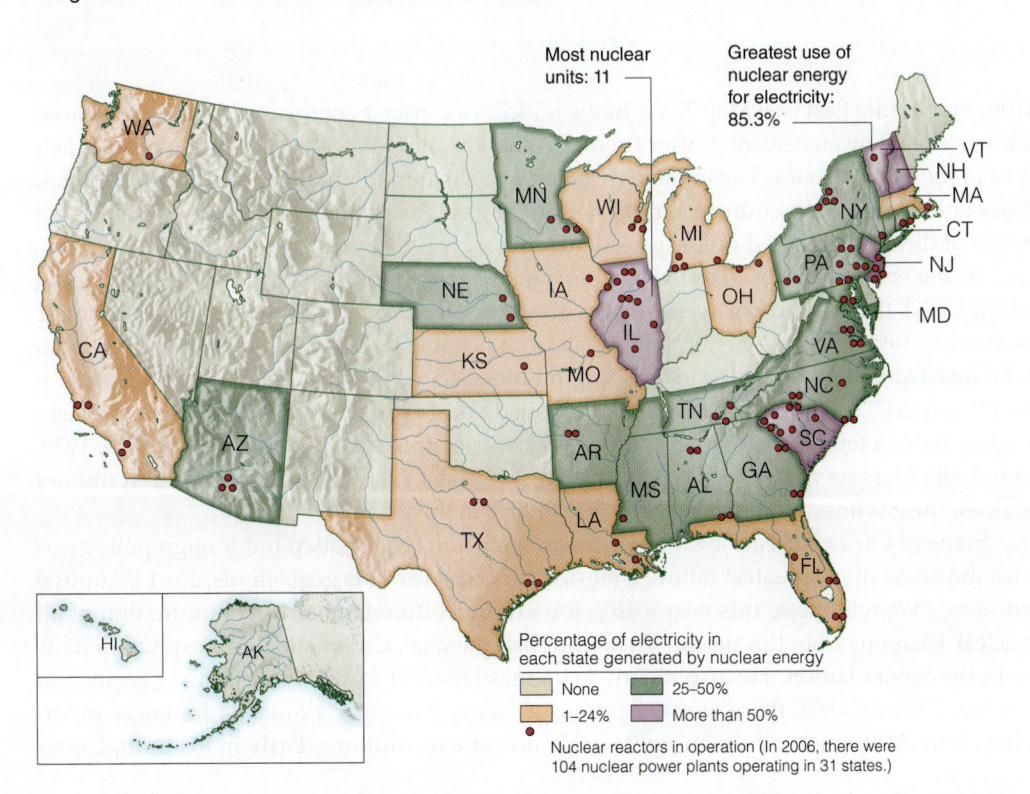

Percentage of electricity in each state generated by nuclear energy

- None
- 1–24%
- 25–50%
- More than 50%
- Nuclear reactors in operation (In 2006, there were 104 nuclear power plants operating in 31 states.)

Map 27-3 Oil-Producing Nations.

As the United States became more and more dependent on imported oil, it became deeply engaged with the sometimes unstable nations that produced the bulk of the world's supply.

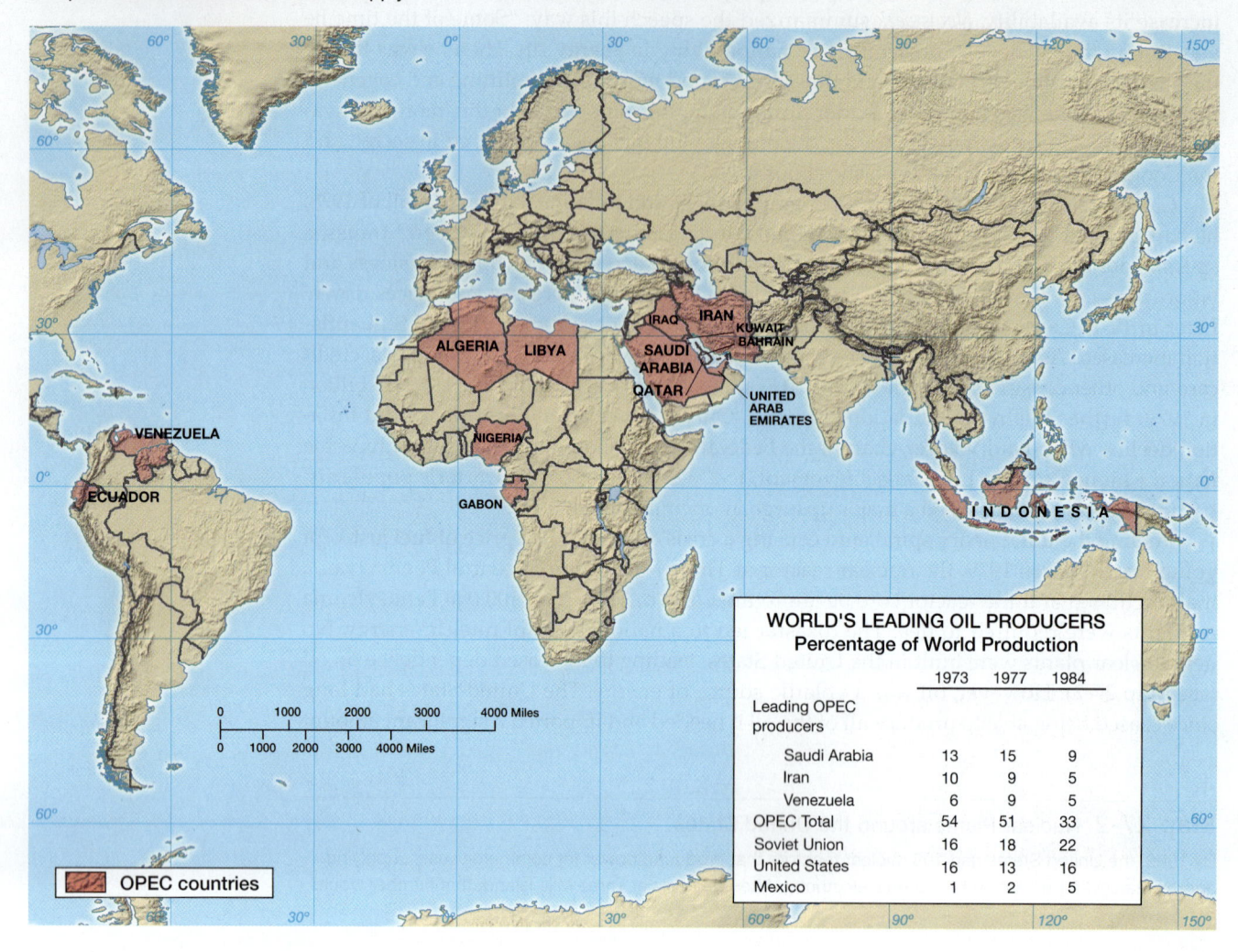

WORLD'S LEADING OIL PRODUCERS
Percentage of World Production

	1973	1977	1984
Leading OPEC producers			
Saudi Arabia	13	15	9
Iran	10	9	5
Venezuela	6	9	5
OPEC Total	54	51	33
Soviet Union	16	18	22
United States	16	13	16
Mexico	1	2	5

OPEC countries

from the Middle East (see Map 27-3). In the middle of Carter's energy crisis, OPEC increased the price of oil by 60 percent. Carter predicted that the move would cost 800,000 people their jobs in the United States. The immediate result was further inflation and very real shortages. Gas stations across the country simply ran out of gas. The public uproar was palpable, and much of the anger focused on the president.

At the end of June 1979, as Carter returned from foreign policy triumphs—the signing of the SALT II arms control agreement with the Soviet Union in Vienna and an economic summit in Tokyo, Japan—he received a call from his pollster and confidant Patrick Caddell who insisted that Carter come to Washington immediately, saying, "You have no idea how bad it is here." The president canceled a planned vacation in Hawaii and headed to Washington. After a ten-day retreat at Camp David, Carter spoke to the nation on July 15, 1979, about what he saw as its "crisis of confidence." It was a visionary statement, but it did not shorten the gas lines or improve Carter's standing in the polls.

Some of Carter's greatest early successes came in foreign policy, but foreign policy was also the arena of his greatest failures. He announced one of his goals in his short inaugural address: "We will move this year a step toward our ultimate goal—the elimination of all nuclear weapons from this earth." To accomplish the goal, Carter sought to expand détente with the Soviet Union. He also meant to increase respect for human rights at home and abroad. Under Carter, there would be none of Henry Kissinger's *Realpolitik* stances in foreign affairs that ignored human rights or democratic institutions. Early in his term, Carter took a number of steps in all of these directions. He quickly pardoned draft evaders from the Vietnam era. He halted production of the B-1 bomber, which was planned as a more advanced, and expensive, version of the B-52. He ended development of the neutron bomb. He also established full diplomatic relations with the People's Republic of China, furthering the new relationship that Nixon had begun. In 1978, Carter won Senate ratification of treaties for the eventual turnover of the Panama Canal to the Republic of Panama. All of these moves brought harsh critiques, but most Americans supported them.

Carter's greatest foreign policy triumph was the signing of the **Camp David Accords** between Egypt and Israel in September 1978. Carter was determined to be a Middle East peacemaker. He visited both Egypt and Israel and then invited Menachem Begin of Israel and Anwar Sadat of Egypt to come to the presidential retreat at Camp David for thirteen days in September 1978. Carter remembered, "The easy, gentle atmosphere was very helpful. It kept tensions down." After some very tough negotiations, the leaders achieved a major breakthrough. The Camp David Accords included formal recognition of the state of Israel by Egypt while Israel agreed to return the Sinai Peninsula to Egypt.

Carter was dogged in his pursuit of détente with the Soviet Union. In June 1979, Carter negotiated the SALT II agreement, which built on earlier agreements and placed a limit on the numbers of missiles and bombers each side would have. It was an important development; however, the effort at détente was undermined by events halfway around the world. In December 1979, the Soviet Union invaded Afghanistan to protect a beleaguered pro-Soviet government there. Carter saw the vastly expanded Soviet presence in Afghanistan as a violation of the decades-old American policy of containing Soviet communism. He ended the export of grain to the Soviet Union and ordered a U.S. boycott of the 1980 summer Olympic Games scheduled for Moscow. In spite of the fact that more than sixty other nations honored the Olympic boycott, it was a deep disappointment to athletes who had been preparing for years to compete. Carter's moves hurt his popularity at home and undermined his efforts toward détente.

Carter's worst foreign policy disaster, however, was with Iran. In January 1979, the government of the shah of Iran (who had been installed by a U.S.-backed coup in the 1950s) was overthrown. Ayatollah Ruhollah Khomeini, the exiled leader of the Muslim radicals, returned to Iran and created an Islamic Republic with a government that was based on religious law and that gave religious leaders like Khomeini ultimate authority. When in October the ailing shah was admitted to the United States for medical treatment, Khomeini and his followers were furious. On November 4, 1979, a mob stormed the U.S. Embassy in Tehran, taking sixty-six Americans hostage.

The **Iranian hostage crisis** became the dominant event of Carter's last year in office. The government froze Iranian assets in the United States, expanded the pressure on Iran, and tried every way possible to negotiate the release of the American hostages. In April 1980, feeling that negotiations were a failure, Carter approved an attack on Iran to rescue the hostages. The attack was a failure as a sandstorm and hydraulic problems disabled some of the helicopters and another crashed into a cargo plane. Eight Americans were killed, but none got close to the hostages. Secretary of State Cyrus Vance resigned in protest. Later that year, after Iraq attacked Iran, the Iranian government agreed to negotiate, but the process was slow. Only on the day Carter left office in January 1981, and after Reagan had taken the oath of office, were the hostages released.

Handout/MCT/Newscom

Carter's greatest triumph was presiding over a new peace treaty between Anwar al-Sadat of Egypt and Menachem Begin of Israel.

27.1

27.2

27.3

27.4

Camp David Accords

An agreement between Israel and Egypt, brokered by President Carter, that brought mutual recognition between the countries and a step toward peace in the Middle East.

Iranian hostage crisis

The invasion of the American embassy in Iran by revolutionary guards who then took sixty-six hostages, holding them from November 1979 until January 1981.

27.1

27.2

27.3

27.4

The Coming of Ronald Reagan

Carter's problems with the economy, energy, and hostages formed the backdrop to the 1980 election campaign. Within the Democratic Party, there was great unease with the president. His cautious economic policies and determination to balance the federal budget alienated liberals. His go-it-alone style alienated Congress. Massachusetts senator Edward "Ted" Kennedy challenged Carter in the primaries. Public opinion polls showed a two-to-one preference for Kennedy, last of the charismatic Kennedy brothers, over Carter. But Kennedy never seemed able to articulate the reasons he was challenging Carter. And for all of his popularity, memories persisted of the time in 1969 when Kennedy had driven a car off a bridge near Chappaquiddick on Martha's Vineyard and left a young woman, Mary Jo Kopechne, to drown. In the end, Carter defeated Kennedy for the nomination. Kennedy supported Carter in the general election, but the wounds of a tough primary fight remained. Carter stayed close to the White House and focused on the hostage crisis. The president who once prided himself on his openness and accessibility now adopted a "Rose Garden Strategy," leaving his office only rarely, even to campaign.

The Republicans entered the campaign with great confidence. The contest for the nomination quickly came down to one between former California governor and movie actor, Ronald Reagan, and former CIA director and U.S. ambassador to China, George H. W. Bush. Bush fought a tough campaign, calling Reagan's economic plan "voodoo economics." But Reagan was hugely popular with conservatives, who were known as the "Republican base." He was also an effective and articulate campaigner and easily won the nomination. Reagan named Bush as his running mate. Conservatives, who had felt marginalized since Barry Goldwater's loss in 1964, believed that their day had come. Reagan was an effective campaigner, impressing many with his sunny optimism. In the one presidential debate that was held, Reagan scored points with his poise and his response "There you go again" to a Carter critique. Reagan won in a landslide. The Republicans gained thirty-four seats in the House, though it still had a Democratic majority, but they took over the Senate with a 53 to 47 majority that included the defeat of Democratic stalwarts Frank Church of Idaho and George McGovern of South Dakota. The Democratic Speaker of the House, Tip O'Neill, said of the election, "A tidal wave hit us." Bill Moyers, who had served in the Johnson administration, said, "We didn't elect this guy [Reagan] because he knows how many barrels of oil are in Alaska. We elected him because we want to feel good." The 1980s and the time of the "Reagan Revolution" would be a very different one from the decade that had just ended.

Blindfolded American hostages are paraded outside the U.S. Embassy in Tehran by their militant captors after Iranian students stormed the embassy in November 1979. Sixty Americans and forty nationals from other countries were taken by the students and held captive inside the embassy.

Bettmann/Getty Images

27.4   Quick Review

What factors made it hard for Ford and Carter to win popular approval? What could each have done to be more effective during their terms in office?

Conclusion

Public discourse in the United States, which had been heated in the 1960s, became even more divisive and angry after 1968. In the 1970s, new Civil Rights Movements emerged as women, gays and lesbians, Latinos, Asians, and American Indians began to demand equality and fair treatment. A new movement among white youth who were angry and disaffected with American society also grew rapidly. Against this expanding civil rights backdrop, a new conservative ideology surfaced, focusing on religion, morality, and culture. Compared with the 1950s and 1960s, the 1970s ushered in an economic downturn that undercut the security of many Americans. The 1970s also gave rise to political turmoil as one president was forced to resign in disgrace and two others lost their bids for reelection.

The new Civil Rights Movements of the 1970s resulted in advancements for many Americans. Women achieved improved working conditions and social status. Filipino and Mexican American farmworkers successfully bargained for recognition of a union in California. American Indians staged protests at Alcatraz, Wounded Knee, and the offices of the Bureau of Indian Affairs, achieving modest gains with respect to civil rights and tribal autonomy. Asians ran for and won political offices as never before. Gay and lesbian Americans began to step out of the closet, and the modern gay rights movement was born. At the same time, traditional conservatives were bewildered and angered by the rapidly shifting culture of the United States, and the so-called culture wars began. The "moral majority" organized a political response to repudiate both the civil rights agendas of the 1960s and 1970s and a changing social scene they did not like.

The Republican Party became increasingly conservative in the 1970s, but Richard Nixon was an inconsistent conservative. During Nixon's tenure, Title IX was added to the Civil Rights Act, the Environmental Protection Agency and the Occupational Safety and Health Administration were created, and overall government spending to aid the poor rose significantly. On the international front, Nixon authorized a relentless bombing campaign against North Vietnam and secretly expanded the fighting into Cambodia. At the same time, Nixon sought to withdraw all ground troops from Vietnam. Despite the war in Vietnam, Nixon normalized relations with Communist China and successfully negotiated two treaties with the Soviet Union designed to reduce the supply of nuclear weapons. Ultimately, the Watergate scandal ended Nixon's presidency. When Vice President Gerald Ford took office, he hoped to heal a wounded nation, but controversial domestic decisions and multiple foreign policy crises seriously damaged the effectiveness of his administration.

In 1976, Jimmy Carter, a little-known governor from Georgia, was elected president, defeating Ford. Carter successfully brokered a peace between Egypt and Israel. Nonetheless, ongoing economic problems at home—inflation, a high unemployment rate, and gas shortages—and his failure to secure the release of American hostages in Iran resulted in Carter's stunning reelection defeat to Ronald Reagan in 1980.

Chapter Review

As the Civil Rights Movement expanded from the Black freedom struggle to encompass many different groups, how did these different groups define the rights they wanted? What were the similarities and differences in their demands? How do you account for the political dissatisfaction with presidents Nixon, Ford, and Carter? How were the issues the three faced similar? How were they different?

Chapter 27 Summary and Review

The New Politics of the Late 1960s

27.1 Explain Nixon's policies and politics, domestic and international.

Summary

The late 1960s saw the emergence of a conservative backlash against the social and cultural changes of the 1960s. This new conservatism was rooted in the development of white suburban culture. Conservatism came to be associated with the Republican Party and with the political ideology of Barry Goldwater. Conservative forces propelled Richard Nixon to the White House, but his administration pursued a relatively liberal domestic agenda, working with liberal Democrats in Congress to pass Title IX, create the Environmental Protection Agency and the Occupational Safety and Health Administration, and to increase funding for the arts. Nonetheless, Nixon employed a "Southern Strategy" in his 1972 reelection campaign, pursuing policies that played to the racial fears of conservative Southern white voters. Nixon and Kissinger's approach to the war on Vietnam centered on expanded bombing, including bombing of neutral Cambodia, and the gradual withdrawal of American troops. The shift in policy was accompanied by even greater domestic conflict over the war. In 1973 a cease-fire agreement was reached and American troops left Vietnam. As American involvement in the war in Vietnam wound down, Nixon pursued a new relationship with China and worked to reduce tensions between the United States and the Soviet Union. Nixon-Kissinger initiatives in the Middle East and South America were less successful.

Review Questions

1. **Argument Development**
   How do you explain the fact that Nixon's relatively liberal domestic agenda was accompanied by a Southern Strategy focused on conservative voters?

2. **Comparison**
   Compare and contrast Nixon and Johnson's Vietnam War strategies. How do you account for the differences?

3. **Contextualization**
   Why do you think Nixon, who had the reputation of being a fierce anti-Communist, pursued a policy of détente?

The Movements of the 1960s and 1970s

27.2 Analyze the many political and cultural movements that followed in the track of the Civil Rights Movement.

Summary

Inspired by the Civil Rights Movement of the 1950s and 1960s, a variety of groups pushed for greater legal and social equality in the 1960s and 1970s. The women's movement moved forward on a number of fronts. More women, and a more diverse group of women, started running for and winning elections. At the end of the 1960s, some younger women began consciousness-raising groups, discussing their experiences as women and the emotional, political, and economic toll that sexism was taking in their lives. The success of NOW and *Ms.* magazine demonstrated that feminism had entered the mainstream. The 1960s also saw farmworkers organize to protect their collective interests. Led by César Chávez, Dolores Huerta, and others, farmworkers made significant gains. The founding of the American Indian Movement signaled a new direction in Indian activism. Dramatic protest actions drew attention to American Indians, their concerns, and their status. The huge influx of Asian immigrants established organizations to protect their civil rights. The black Civil Rights Movement entered a new phase in the 1970s. School integration efforts moved north. Black politicians were elected to high office in many cities, and affirmative action became a central issue in the national debate over race in America. The 1969 confrontation between gay men and the New York City police at the Stonewall Inn marked the beginning of gay liberation movement. The counterculture of the 1960s celebrated new values associated with a new generation and rejected the culture and traditions of the 1950s. But at the moment of the movement's signature event, Woodstock, the counterculture had already started to decline. Ultimately, the movement became a victim of its own excesses.

Review Questions

4. **Contextualization**
   Why do you think so many social movements emerged at this particular moment in American history?

5. **Continuity and Change over Time**
   How did the struggle for African American rights change over the course of the 1960s? Why did it change?

The Culture Wars of the 1970s

27.3 Analyze the reaction to the liberal and radical politics of the 1960s and 1970s and the growth of new militant conservative movements.

Summary

In the 1970s, the United States was a deeply divided nation, one in which differences over fundamental social and cultural values were at the heart of political debate. Phyllis Schlafly led the conservative backlash against feminism and the Equal Rights Amendment. Schlafly's activism was part of a larger conservative movement centered on opposition to feminism, opposition to abortion rights, opposition to homosexual rights, defense of prayer in school, and an insistence on moral and legal absolutism. Religious conservatives claimed a central place in the conservative movement and in the Republican Party. The rise of the religious right was epitomized by the success of Jerry Falwell's Moral Majority. The emergence of the religious right took place against a backdrop of growing religious diversity.

Review Question

6. Contextualization
What connections can you make between the defeat of the Equal Rights Amendment and the larger cultural and political trends of the 1970s?

Politics, Economics, and the Impact of Watergate

27.4 **Explain the political impact of Watergate and subsequent developments that set the stage for the "Reagan Revolution."**

Summary

The political turmoil of the 1970s took place against a backdrop of a changing global economic situation that adversely affected the United States. While the U.S. economy continued to grow in the 1960s, the economies of other countries, especially Germany and Japan, grew more quickly. As the United States lost its competitive edge, unemployment and inflation began to rise. The economy was further undermined by a rapid rise in energy costs, brought on by the policies of the Organization of the Petroleum Exporting Countries (OPEC). When American automakers failed to adapt to high gasoline prices, their share of the American car market fell. There seemed to be relatively little that the federal government could do through the 1970s to change the economic situation. American economic problems were compounded by political turmoil. The Watergate break-in and the cover-up that followed brought down the Nixon presidency. Nixon's successor, Gerald Ford, battled Congress over tax and spending issues, as both sides blamed the other for the

country's economic problems. Ford's decision to pardon Nixon remains controversial. Jimmy Carter defeated Ford in a close election in 1976, but he could not heal the economy or solve the country's energy problems. Carter had a number of foreign policy successes, most notably the Camp David Accords, but the Iranian hostage crisis dominated his last year in office and contributed to his defeat by Ronald Reagan in 1980. Reagan's election marked a major turning point in American politics, as conservatives rose to prominence in American government.

Review Questions

7. Argument Development
Presidential policies had helped ailing economies in the past. Why couldn't any of the three presidents of the 1970s turn around the economy?

8. Causation
Between 1960 and 1980, Americans' faith in the power of government had dropped precipitously. What were the most significant factors that led to such a drastic change in sentiment?

1. Preparing to Write: Develop Your Thesis

Long Essay Question—Evaluate the extent of similarities in federal environmental policies from the early 1900s and the 1960s/early1970s.

For this response, you may want to use the format, "Although X, Y." For the first part of your response, you can identify similarities. But the focus here—as with most Comparison questions—should be on the differences. As you note the central nature of the differences, briefly share why such significant differences exist.

2. Preparing to Write: Support Your Assertion

Document-Based Question—Evaluate the extent to which the women's rights movement influenced the social and political status of women from 1966 to 1980.

Write a topic sentence for the first section, which could discuss general goals for the movement as well as early attempts to organize. In "American Voices" from Section 27.2, you will find a statement of purpose from the National Organization for Women's (NOW). Use it to support your topic sentence. As you do, integrate discussion of the authors' point of view.

Section I: Multiple-Choice Questions

Questions 8.1–8.3 refer to the following excerpt.

"I am fully aware of the broad implications involved if the United States extends assistance to Greece and Turkey, and I shall discuss these implications with you at this time. ...

To ensure the peaceful development of nations, free from coercion, the United States has taken a leading part in establishing the United Nations. ... We shall not realize our objectives, however, unless we are willing to help free peoples to maintain their free institutions and their national integrity against aggressive movements that seek to impose upon them totalitarian regimes. This is no more than a frank recognition that totalitarian regimes imposed on free peoples, by direct or indirect aggression, undermine the foundations of international peace and hence the security of the United States. ... I believe that it must be the policy of the United States to support free peoples who are resisting attempted subjugation by armed minorities or by outside pressures. I believe that we must assist free peoples to work out their own destinies in their own way. I believe that our help should be primarily through economic and financial aid which is essential to economic stability and orderly political processes."

—President Truman, Address to Congress, 1947

8.1   Which nation is providing the "outside pressures" referred to by Truman?

  a. Germany
  b. U.S.S.R.
  c. Japan
  d. China

8.2   The policy articulated by Truman in this speech eventually led to which of the following?

  a. U.S. involvement in Vietnam
  b. Détente with China
  c. Decolonization in Asia and the Middle East
  d. Decreased American influence in Latin America

8.3   Critics of U.S. implementation of the Truman Doctrine would argue that the United States did not "support free peoples who are resisting attempted subjugation by armed minorities or by outside pressures." Which of the following would best support their argument?

  a. CIA efforts to overthrow democratically elected officials in South America
  b. U.S. involvement in the Korean War against the North Koreans
  c. U.S. support of Diem, a Catholic, in majority-Buddhist Vietnam
  d. Truman's support of Greece and Turkey to keep them free of communism

Questions 8.4–8.5 refer to the following graph.

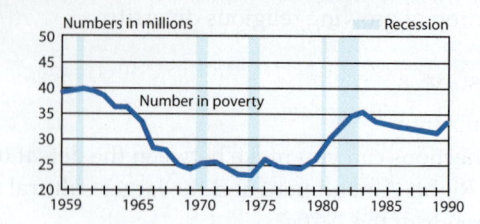

Figure 27-1 U.S. Census Bureau, Current Population Survey, 1960–2012 Annual Supplement.

8.4   The portion of the graph from the 1960s supports which of the following arguments?

  a. War has a positive influence on the economy.
  b. Tax cuts have the greatest impact on employment numbers.
  c. Federal programs can help the neediest.
  d. Environmental laws do not harm the economy.

8.5   Which of the following was a contributing factor that helps explain the trend shown in the graph that begins in the 1970s?

  a. A rise in oil prices
  b. The end of the Vietnam War
  c. An increase in immigration
  d. The decline of social protest groups

Questions 8.6–8.7 refer to the following excerpt.

"A knowledgeable and engaged president Kennedy spent as much or more time on Cuba as on any other foreign-policy problem. Cuba stood at the center of his administration's greatest failure, the Bay of Pigs, and its alleged greatest success, the missile crisis. Why did President Kennedy and his chief advisers indulge such an obsession with Cuba and direct so many U.S. resources to an unrelenting campaign to monitor, harass, and ultimately destroy Havana's radical regime? ... Overarching all explanations for the Kennedy's obsession with Cuba is a major phenomenon of the second half of the twentieth century: the steady erosion of the authority of imperial powers. ... The strong currents of decolonization, anti-imperialism, revolutionary nationalism, and social revolution, sometimes in combination, undermined the instruments the imperial nations had used to maintain control and order. The Cuban Revolution exemplified this process of breaking up and breaking away. American leaders reacted so hostilely to this revolution ... because Cuba, as symbol and reality, challenged U.S. hegemony in Latin America."

—Thomas Paterson, historian, "Fixation with Cuba," published in 1989

8.6 Which of following factors contributed most directly to the developments described in the excerpt?

   a. Commitment to international aid

   b. Détente

   c. The military industrial complex

   d. Containment

8.7 Paterson refers to "[t]he strong currents of decolonization, anti-imperialism, revolutionary nationalism, and social revolution." Which of the following pieces of evidence would best support his contention?

   a. South Vietnam's alliance with the United States

   b. President Truman's commitment of support for Greece and Turkey

   c. Indochina's desire to be free of French control

   d. President Eisenhower's policy of massive retaliation

Questions 8.8–8.9 refer to the following excerpt.

"We are people of this generation, bred in at least modest comfort, housed now in universities, looking uncomfortably to the world we inherit.

   When we were kids the United States was the wealthiest and strongest country in the world. ...

   As we grew, however, our comfort was penetrated by events too troubling to dismiss. First, the permeating and victimizing fact of human degradation, symbolized by the Southern struggle against racial bigotry, compelled most of us from silence to activism. Second, the enclosing fact of the Cold War, symbolized by the presence of the Bomb, brought awareness that we ourselves, and our friends, and millions of abstract "others" we knew more directly because of our common peril, might die at any time. We might deliberately ignore, or avoid, or fail to feel all other human problems, but not these two, for these were too immediate and crushing in their impact, too challenging in the demand that we as individuals take the responsibility for encounter and resolution."

—Students for a Democratic Society (SDS), "Port Huron Statement," 1962

8.8 Which of the following strategies best reflects the way the men and women who affiliated with the SDS tried to take responsibility for the major issues they faced in the years after the Port Huron statement was issued?

   a. Protesting U.S. involvement in Vietnam

   b. Collaborating with the FBI to expose Communists

   c. Campaigning for Republican candidate Richard Nixon

   d. Opposing environmental legislation

8.9 Members of the SDS would most likely support which of the following?

   a. The Sun Belt Migration

   b. The American Indian Movement

   c. Increased military spending

   d. Decreased domestic spending

Section II: Short-Answer Questions

8.10 Using the map preceding page, answer (a), (b), and (c).

    a. Briefly explain how ONE major historical factor contributed to the development depicted in the map.

    b. Briefly explain ONE specific effect that resulted from the development depicted in the map.

    c. Briefly explain ANOTHER specific effect that resulted from the development depicted in the map.

8.11 Using the following image, answer (a), (b), and (c).

Sam Myers / AP Images

Crowd protesting the first black family to move into Levittown, Pennsylvania, a formerly all-white suburb, 1957.

    a. Briefly explain ONE major difference in how American and national identity is defined by Americans, as depicted in the image.

    b. Briefly explain ANOTHER major difference in how American and national identity is defined by Americans, as depicted in the image.

    c. Briefly explain how this image fits in the context of suburbanization.

Section III: Long Essay Questions

Directions: Answer Question 8.12 **or** 8.13. (Suggested writing time: 40 minutes) In your response you should do the following.

- Respond to the prompt with a historically defensible thesis or claim that establishes a line of reasoning.

- Describe a broader historical context relevant to the prompt.

- Support an argument in response to the prompt using specific and relevant examples of evidence.

- Use historical reasoning (e.g., comparison, causation, continuity or change over time) to frame or structure an argument that addresses the prompt.

- Use evidence to corroborate, qualify, or modify an argument that addresses the prompt.

8.12 Evaluate the extent to which antiwar protests shaped U.S. Vietnam policy from the years 1965 to 1975.

8.13 Evaluate the extent to which the growth of Christian evangelism fostered change in American politics from 1950 to 1980.

Section IV:

Read on MyHistoryLab

Document-Based Question: The 1960s

Part 9

Certainty, Uncertainty, and New Beginnings, 1980 to the Present

Luis M. Alvarez/AP Images

Chapter 28
The Reagan Revolution 1980–1989

American Photo Archive/Alamy Stock Photo

No American president since Franklin Roosevelt has so dominated the nation's politics and, indeed, culture as Ronald Reagan, shown here at his inauguration in 1981.

Chapter Objective

Demonstrate an understanding of the changes in government, in the economy, and in the larger society in the times known as the Reagan Revolution.

 ## Learning Objectives

A Rapidly Changing U.S. Government

28.1   Explain Reagan's impact on the United States and the world.

The Changing Nature of the American Economy

28.2   Explain internal and international economic developments that shaped the United States.

Changes in the Rest of the Country

28.3   Explain cultural changes in the United States during the 1980s.

The voters who gave Ronald Reagan his margin of victory over Jimmy Carter in 1980 were a diverse lot. Working-class whites, North and South, sometimes called "Reagan Democrats," were alienated by the civil rights and protest movements of the 1960s and 1970s. Many feared crime, which they tended to see as a "black issue," and wanted a champion of "law and order." The coalition also included middle-class and upper-middle-class suburbanites in revolt over taxes, especially rising property taxes, and government regulations that they thought were intrusive. The antitax movement led to the passage of Proposition 13 in California in 1978, a law sponsored by a private citizen, Howard Jarvis, which significantly cut California's property taxes and ultimately the state's vaunted government services. Other states copied Proposition 13, reducing taxes and public services. A third group of Reagan supporters were social conservatives—Catholics and Protestants associated with the religious right—for whom the key issues were their opposition to abortion, sexual and reproductive freedoms, gay rights, and the teaching of evolution as well as their desire for prayer in the public schools. In seeking to limit abortion or gay rights, the social conservatives wanted a more activist government, even if they otherwise favored a smaller government and lower taxes.

With the 1980 election, it seemed that larger numbers of Americans were in the mood for more conservative times and a generally less active federal government. Many of the diverse groups that supported Reagan also shared a staunch hostility to communism and believed that presidents from Franklin Roosevelt to Richard Nixon had been too soft. They were united in their anger at those they considered elitist—celebrities in Hollywood, the media, universities, and the federal government. In Ronald Reagan, the former actor and two-term governor of California, they found a hero who, they believed, would not disappoint them. This chapter is a look at the Reagan Revolution, the wide-ranging changes in the federal government, in U.S. international relations, and in American culture that took place while Ronald Reagan was president, some with his support and some in spite of his best efforts.

A Rapidly Changing U.S. Government

28.1   **Explain Reagan's impact on the United States and the world.**

Many federal government programs that dated from the New Deal changed drastically during what came to be known as the **Reagan Revolution**. By the end of the eight years that Ronald Reagan was president, taxes took less of people's incomes; the federal debt ballooned; a fifty-year period in which labor unions could rely on a friendly government came to an end; and the percentage of the population in labor unions, especially in the private sector, continued its precipitous decline. The Cold War, which had been the dominant element in U.S. foreign policy since the end of World War II, also ended. Both the Republican and Democratic parties emerged from the Reagan Revolution more conservative than they had been. Supporters and detractors all agreed that the presidency of Ronald Reagan was a significant turning point in the United States.

Ronald Reagan and the Reagan Coalition

When Ronald Reagan became president, he was only one month short of his seventieth birthday, the oldest man elected to the office up to that time. Reagan was born in the small town of Tampico, Illinois, in 1911. His father was a shoe salesman and an alcoholic who was unsuccessful in his search for better jobs until he was hired by the New Deal's WPA. His mother, who worked as a seamstress, was a religious woman who made sure that the young Ronald and his brother were brought up in church. He said of his childhood, "We didn't live on the wrong side of the tracks, but we lived so close we could hear the whistle real loud." Handsome and popular, Reagan was elected high school class president and then student body president at Eureka College in Illinois.

Soon after college, and after a brief stint as a sports announcer in Iowa, Reagan left the Midwest for Hollywood where he appeared in fifty-three films between 1937 and 1953.

Reagan Revolution

Major changes in American politics under the leadership of Ronald Reagan, including cuts in taxes and domestic spending and increased military spending.

It was steady work and it paid well. Reagan later said that he generally made two pictures per year, earning $300,000 to $400,000 per film, and would have worked harder to make more pictures if not for the high tax bite. The work took Reagan a long way from the marginal economic status of his childhood. He married and later divorced Jane Wyman, whose Hollywood career was more successful than his; he would be the first divorced person elected president. He was popular in Hollywood and was elected president of the Screen Actors Guild from 1947 to 1952, a position he used to identify suspected Communists in the film industry. When he became U.S. president, he was the first former union president to do so. During his Hollywood years, Reagan remained a Democrat, voting for Harry Truman in 1948 and against Richard Nixon for the Senate in 1950.

In 1952, he married Nancy Davis and left a declining Hollywood career to become a spokesperson for the General Electric Company, serving as the TV host of the General Electric Theater program from 1954 to 1962. Working for GE, he also gave pep talks to workers at GE plants, touted GE products, and gave speeches about the corporation's views on taxes and government regulation. In his GE career, as in Hollywood, Reagan mastered the art of connecting with audiences, especially maintaining a relaxed and genial presence in the face of lights, crowds, and distractions as well as delivering content from a script. While at GE, he also changed his party registration from Democrat to Republican.

By the time Reagan left GE in 1962, he was as well known for his political views as his acting. He supported Barry Goldwater in 1964. In a standard stump speech that came to be known simply as "the speech," Reagan said that the choice facing Americans was "whether we believe in our capacity for self-government or whether we abandon the American Revolution and confess that a little intellectual elite in a far-distant capital can plan our lives for us better than we can plan them ourselves." The speech did not elect Goldwater, but it did bring Reagan to the attention of a crucial audience—rich Republican conservatives who agreed to back him if he would run for governor of California in 1966. The incumbent governor, Democrat Edmund G. "Pat" Brown, a tough campaigner who had defeated Richard Nixon in 1962, was seeking a third term in 1966. Reagan defeated him in the fall election and won reelection as governor in 1970.

Reagan talked a more conservative line than he practiced as governor. While he was tough on student protests, raised tuition at California's public colleges and universities, and ousted Clark Kerr as the president of the University of California, he was willing to compromise with a Democratic legislature on other matters. He raised taxes to cover a budget shortfall as well as signed bills supporting liberalized abortion rights and bilingual education. Some of his conservative supporters were nervous about his positions but valued his skill as a campaigner. As a conservative governor of the nation's largest state, Reagan quickly became a presidential contender. He almost defeated Gerald Ford for the 1976 Republican nomination and easily defeated George H. W. Bush to win the 1980 nomination and then the presidential election against Jimmy Carter. As president, Reagan did not disappoint most of his supporters.

Reaganomics—Supply-Side Tax Cuts, Military Growth, and Electoral Politics

Reagan came to office with three priorities: increasing military spending to ensure that the United States was significantly stronger than the Soviet Union, cutting domestic spending and government-sponsored social programs, and cutting the federal income tax. He was willing to compromise on almost everything else.

The antitax crusade had helped elect Reagan, and he surrounded himself with advisors who developed new economic theories to defend a tax cut even as he sought increased military spending. Reagan justified the tax cut with an economic theory known as **supply-side economics**. As defined by Republican congressman Jack Kemp and Democratic senator Lloyd Bentsen, *supply-side* referred to stimulating the economy, not by means of federal spending—the traditional approach since the New Deal—but, rather, by cutting taxes so that people would have more to spend to foster private investment that might then lead to the creation of new jobs.

supply-side economics

An economic theory arguing that, to stimulate the economy, the best intervention is a tax cut that would stimulate the "supply side."

28.1

28.2

28.3

Tax cut proponents also cited what is called the "Laffer curve." Developed in the 1970s by Jude Wanniski, a correspondent for the *Wall Street Journal*, and economist Arthur Laffer, the curve meant to show that higher taxes reduced government income by reducing the incentive to work and earn taxable wages. At the extreme ends, the curve made complete sense. Zero tax would not impact the will to work in any way, and a 100 percent tax would certainly stifle most enterprise. But the point in between, where taxes really cut into the will to work and where decreased tax rates might actually increase government income, was hard to pinpoint.

When Reagan first called for a 30 percent tax cut and used Laffer and the supply-side arguments to justify his position, his main rival for the 1980 Republican nomination, George Bush, called it "voodoo economics," and Jimmy Carter called Reagan's tax plans "rebates for the rich, deprivation for the poor, and fierce inflation for all of us." But after he became president, Reagan dismissed criticism, saying of the economists who challenged his ideas, "They're the sort of people who see something works in practice and wonder if it works in theory." In spite of a lack of evidence in either practice or theory, the president made a tax cut his first priority, and in August, forty-eight congressional Democrats—their Democratic colleagues called them "boll weevils"—joined the Republican minority to pass a cut in federal income taxes that reduced the top rate on individual income from 70 to 50 percent. The president won the first of his goals—the implementation of "Reaganomics," as his economic policy came to be called—in less than one hundred days in office.

In addition to the tax cut, Congress passed a modified version of Reagan's budget. He did not get all the cuts he wanted, but the new federal budget reduced domestic spending significantly. Reagan also used his administrative authority to cut additional federal programs, including food stamps and other programs for the poor as well as Social Security benefits for people with disabilities. Some 500,000 people were removed from the Social Security disability list. Another 300,000, who had been employed through the Carter administration's Comprehensive Employment and Training Act (CETA), lost their government-sponsored jobs. The cuts were not the wholesale abolition of welfare that Reagan advocated, but they represented a substantial cut in the federal safety net that had been growing since the 1930s. At the same time, some programs, such as Aid to Families with Dependent Children (AFDC) and federal tax credits for the poor, actually expanded during the Reagan years.

George Lane/AP Images

The Reagan cuts in domestic programs, including health insurance benefits for the elderly through Medicare, were not done without protest, as shown here. But few protests had a major impact on the cuts themselves.

While campaigning for the presidency, Reagan also promised to expand the military so the United States would, without question, be the most powerful nation on earth. As a candidate, he said, "You spend what you need." As president, he got congressional approval to develop a new B-2 bomber as well as cruise and MX missiles and to expand the navy. During his first term in office, from 1981 to 1985, the total defense spending of the United States rose by 34 percent, from $171 billion to $229 billion.

Within months of the new administration coming to office, Americans understood that the change in Washington was significant. In addition to the tax cuts and expanded military spending, the new administration showed its attitude when the members of the Professional Air Traffic Controllers' Organization (PATCO)—the people who guide airplanes on take-off and landing—went on strike. The president told the members of the union, who were federal employees, that they had forty-eight hours to go back to work or they would be fired. When almost two-thirds of PATCO members stayed out on strike, Reagan fired all eleven thousand of them. They permanently lost their jobs, and the union was destroyed. People worried about the safety of air travel with so many veteran controllers gone, but the signal was clear. Organized labor, used to having a friend in the White House, was demoralized. Other strikes were also defeated, including an especially bitter one by the meatpackers at the Hormel plant in Minnesota in 1985–1986. Union membership dropped from one-fourth of the U.S. workforce to one-sixth during Reagan's two terms. Organized labor, long a major force in American society, was on a long, slow decline, something that delighted the president and his conservative backers even as it had a real impact on the wages of many workers, both union members and others, who benefited when unions successfully negotiated higher salaries.

In the short term, the Reagan initiatives did not improve the nation's economy. The president strongly supported Federal Reserve Chair Paul Volcker, whom Carter had appointed. Both presidents told Volcker to curb inflation no matter what the cost. Volcker did, with tough policies that sent unemployment above 10 percent in 1982, the highest since the Great Depression of the 1930s. Many people lost jobs, and new jobs were often in low-paying service sectors of the economy. Homelessness doubled while Reagan was in office, from an estimated 200,000 to 400,000. The recession of the early Reagan years hurt the president's popularity, and the Republicans lost seats in Congress in the 1982 elections. By 1983, the national economy started to improve and continued to do so through the last five years of Reagan's tenure. Economists argued whether the improvement was due to the tax cuts or expanded military spending, but a strong economy made Reagan more popular.

One result of the Reagan economic agenda was rapid growth in the federal deficit. The tax cut did not bring in as much new revenue as estimated, while the expansion of military spending more than offset cuts in domestic programs. The total federal deficit nearly tripled during the Reagan years, from $914 billion to $2.7 trillion. More than one supporter saw the deficit as Reagan's greatest failure. The United States, which had been a major creditor nation since World War I, became the world's largest debtor nation. The government kept borrowing money to cover the federal deficit while individuals borrowed money—often by running up huge credit card debts. Daniel Patrick Moynihan, once an advisor to Richard Nixon and who was a Democratic senator from New York throughout the Reagan years, warned that the huge deficits virtually guaranteed that new federal initiatives to improve the lives of average or poor citizens were now off the table.

As Reagan faced reelection in 1984, the Democrats selected former vice president Walter Mondale, after an intense primary battle with Colorado senator Gary Hart. In historic move, Mondale asked New York representative Geraldine Ferraro to be his running mate, the first time a woman was on the ticket of a major political party. At seventy-three, Reagan seemed old, especially when in one debate with Mondale he seemed to lose track of a story he was telling. Reagan dismissed the issue, saying, "I will not make age an issue in this campaign. I am not going to exploit, for political purposes, my opponent's youth and inexperience."

Reagan could not so easily dismiss other issues, however. Labor unions almost unanimously supported Mondale, although because of Reagan's policies they had far

28.1

28.2

28.3

less clout. Most African Americans supported Mondale, continuing a move by black voters to the Democratic Party that was speeded by Reagan's inattention to their needs. Moreover, Reagan's silence on the rising epidemic of AIDS, a new and deadly disease, created some of his toughest enemies. Even social and religious conservatives who had flocked to Reagan in 1980 were disappointed. He had done little more than talk about many of their issues such as school prayer during his first term. As president, he never gave a speech to an antiabortion audience. However, conservatives did not have another candidate.

By 1983, the economy started to turn around, helping Reagan. More Americans had jobs, and people were buying more goods, often on credit, including personal computers, video cassette recorders (VCRs), and telephone answering machines, none of which had been available in the 1970s.

Reagan also benefited from an upsurge of popular patriotism that he had helped to foster. The space shuttle program had been years in the making since the days when Americans worried about *Sputnik* and Soviet leadership in space, but Reagan benefited when the first space shuttle was successfully launched in April 1981. Reagan's tough line with the Soviet Union pleased anti-Communists, and the fact that at the end of his first term he was the first president since Herbert Hoover never to have met with a Soviet leader did not worry them. In June 1984, Reagan traveled to France for the fortieth anniversary of the D-Day landing that ended World War II. In a series of events carefully scripted by his communications director, Michael Deaver, he led a series of jubilant and patriotism-filled celebrations honoring veterans and American power. Later that summer, the Olympics were held in Los Angeles, and Reagan led the celebrations, emphasizing how far the country had come since the boycott of the games in Moscow only four years before. Reagan's wealthy supporters also gave him a huge financial edge over Mondale.

Perhaps most of all, Reagan's own sunny disposition made people like him. His TV ads reinforced Reagan's message that it was *"Morning Again in America."* His optimism was on full display when on March 30, 1981, Reagan was shot while leaving a speaking event. His press secretary, James Brady, was severely wounded and permanently disabled. Few knew at the time how seriously the president had been wounded when a bullet lodged in his left lung and he bled heavily. But just before entering surgery, Reagan looked at his wife, Nancy, and said, "Honey, I forgot to duck," and then asked the surgeons, "Please tell me you're all Republicans." That sort of pluck made him popular even with people who disagreed with his policies. In addition, his speaking style was extraordinary. His many years as an actor paid off. His friends called him "The Great Communicator," and even his toughest opponents admired him. The Democratic Speaker of the House, Tip O'Neill, who tangled with Reagan on many occasions, said of him, "He may not be much of a debater, but with a prepared text he's the best public speaker I've ever seen. … I'm beginning to think that in this regard he dwarfs both Roosevelt and Kennedy."

In the November 1984 vote, Reagan carried every state except Mondale's home state of Minnesota and the District of Columbia and won almost 60 percent of the popular vote. While Republicans continued to control the Senate 53 to 46, the Democrats controlled the House 252 to 182.

A year after the election, a group of Democrats, including Representative Richard Gephardt of Missouri and Governor Bill Clinton of Arkansas, organized the Democratic Leadership Council. These "New Democrats" argued that there was more to the election than Reagan's personal popularity and that the Democratic Party was not going to win elections until it moved closer to the conservative mainstream. The creation of the Democratic Leadership Council was high tribute to the conservative shift in American opinion that constituted the heart of the Reagan Revolution and signaled a move away from traditional New Deal Democratic values that included significant government services, especially for those in need, and support for labor unions.

As Reagan entered his second term, people expected a repeat of the first. Reagan's top priority remained reducing taxes, and in the mid-1980s, many Democrats agreed. A bipartisan coalition passed the Tax Reform Act of 1986, which cut the number of tax brackets from fourteen to two, with tax rates of 15 and 28 percent, respectively, while

Morning Again in America
The campaign slogan of Ronald Reagan's reelection effort in 1984.

closing many tax loopholes. Led by the president, who had begun his first term cutting the tax rate for the wealthiest Americans from 70 to 50 percent, the government had now cut it to 28 percent.

After the 1986 tax bill passed, Reagan devoted more and more of his time to foreign policy. He continued to appoint conservative judges and to support deregulation and the shrinking of the federal government, but he did not present major domestic policy initiatives in his last two years in office. Reagan had come to office a devout Cold Warrior. But before he left office, he presided over the greatest change in U.S.–Soviet relationships since Franklin Roosevelt had granted U.S. recognition to the Soviet Union in the 1930s.

Expanding the Cold War—From Star Wars to Iran-Contra

When Ronald Reagan became president in January 1981, he was more sophisticated as a politician than many of his detractors (and some of his supporters) admitted. Nevertheless, he had not spent much time outside of the United States and did not know much about foreign policy. He was served by a series of weak national security advisors as well as two secretaries of state, two secretaries of defense, and a strong director of central intelligence, William Casey, all of whom disliked each other intensely, kept major developments secret from each other, and at times implemented contradictory policies. First Lady Nancy Reagan also took an active role in policy discussions, especially when she feared that conservative ideologues were taking her husband in an unnecessarily hard-line direction. It was not an administrative structure leading to crisp and clear decision making. However, in the midst of apparent chaos, Reagan himself appeared to have been a far stronger leader than perceived, one who determined the main aspects of his foreign policy even as he left the details of implementation to others.

EFFORTS TO UNDERMINE COMMUNISM   Reagan's fierce anticommunism, which first developed when he battled with perceived Communists in the film industry in the 1940s, was reinforced by his religious faith, which was offended by Communist atheism. He saw communism as "the focus of evil in the modern world," and the United States as the exceptional carrier of goodness—the "shining city on a hill." He disliked the long-standing policy of containment that had been at the core of American foreign policy from Truman to Carter. He did not want merely to contain communism where it was. He wanted to undermine existing Communist governments.

During his first term, Reagan was harshly critical of the Soviet Union. Despite that fierce anticommunism, however, Reagan had a great horror of nuclear war. His firm belief was that a nuclear war could "never be won and must never be fought." Nevertheless, in a 1983 speech to Christian evangelicals, Reagan referred to the Soviet Union as "**the evil empire**." A year later, in August 1984, thinking that the microphone was turned off, Reagan said, "My fellow Americans, I am pleased to tell you today that I've signed legislation that will outlaw Russia forever. We begin bombing in five minutes." It was a joke, but the Soviets found it frightening. Reagan also ordered a massive arms buildup. Worried about U.S. vulnerability and believing that any negotiations needed to be from a position of strength, Reagan supported annual increases in the military budget between 1981 and 1986. He arranged the deployment of new intermediate-range missiles in Europe in 1983 and resisted talks with Soviet leaders.

In 1981, as protest movements spread in Poland and the Polish Communist government instituted martial law, Reagan imposed sanctions on the Soviet Union: an end to landing rights in the United States for the Russian airline Aeroflot, a ban on the sale of equipment for a Soviet natural gas pipeline, and—at the petty level—termination of the special parking privileges of Soviet ambassador Anatoly Dobrynin in the State Department garage. The administration secretly funneled some $20 million to Solidarity, the Polish protest movement, through the Vatican Bank, with the approval of Polish pope John Paul II.

the evil empire

A phrase that Reagan used for the Soviet Union in particular and all Communist countries in general.

In March 1983, Reagan, against the almost unanimous advice of his foreign policy team, who seldom agreed on anything, announced that the United States was going to develop a **Strategic Defense Initiative (SDI)**. As the president described it, SDI would use U.S. technological know-how to create a series of space stations armed with lasers that would destroy any enemy missiles fired at the United States. He thought that the long-standing U.S. policy dating to the Eisenhower administration of mutually assured destruction in which each superpower had the ability to retaliate after a nuclear attack was essentially a commitment to mutual suicide. In 1979, Edward Teller, the lead scientist in the development of the hydrogen bomb, told Reagan that for all its missiles, the United States had virtually no defense against incoming ones. As president, Reagan was determined to create one, to make Soviet missiles "impotent and obsolete."

Senior advisors worried that SDI would be expensive, impractical, and a needless escalation of the Cold War. Critics called the whole system "Star Wars," and worried that it would militarize space, drain the treasury, and ultimately turn out to be ineffective. Military contractors, however, loved SDI. The president was committed, and throughout his two terms, research and development of the system continued.

Only long after Reagan left office did it become clear how deeply fearful Soviet leaders were of the Reagan rhetoric and arms buildup, especially SDI. The Soviets feared that SDI would make them vulnerable to a U.S. attack, one they could not resist if they could not retaliate. In September 1983, a Soviet satellite mistook blips for incoming U.S. missiles and the country went on full military alert. Only the courage of a young Soviet officer, who believed that there was a computer error and who overrode the system, appears to have avoided a World War III with millions of deaths in both countries. The Cold War had never been so dangerous.

MANAGING RELATIONS IN THE MIDDLE EAST   As the United States focused on the Soviet Union, the Reagan foreign policy advisors also viewed the rest of the world through the prism of the Cold War, sometimes with disastrous results. Regarding the Middle East, Reagan came to office with a generally pro-Israel point of view, a perspective that was supported by many Christian evangelicals in his political base. His team believed that Jimmy Carter's Camp David Accords had tilted U.S. policy too closely toward Egypt and wanted to correct the balance. At the same time, they saw Israel, Egypt, Jordan, and Saudi Arabia as U.S. allies and were prepared to sell military aircraft to the Saudis and to supply Israel with jet bombers and military hardware. Their goal was to create a strong buffer in the Middle East against Syria and Iraq, both of which were viewed as Soviet client states (see Map 28-1, p. 850).

In Afghanistan, Reagan expanded the Carter-era efforts to resist the Soviet occupation. In 1983 and 1984, the United States provided significant aid to the Mujahedeen opposition, whom Reagan called "freedom fighters." In 1985, when the Soviets escalated their involvement, Reagan ordered his military to do "what's necessary to win," and the United States began supplying the Afghan resistance with antiaircraft missiles and satellite-based intelligence on Soviet troop movements. Eventually, the Soviets withdrew from Afghanistan, leaving the CIA-backed Taliban in control of the country, a development that came with significant long-term consequences not only for the people of Afghanistan but also for the United States.

Libya's longtime leader Muammar Gaddafi had come to power in 1969, long before Reagan's time. Most of his North African neighbors found him to be a troublemaker, but he especially liked to create trouble for the United States. Reagan was determined to respond. In 1981, the U.S. Navy conducted exercises off the Libyan coast, and when Libyan jets attacked, the navy shot them down. As terrorism expanded across the Middle East, Reagan was sure Gaddafi was behind much of it. When a TWA flight was hijacked in June 1985 and a West German discotheque was bombed in December of that year, killing one U.S. soldier, Reagan retaliated. In April 1986, the United States bombed Gaddafi's headquarters in Tripoli, destroying much of the Libyan air force and killing some thirty civilians including Gaddafi's fifteen-month-old adopted daughter. For a time, Libya was quiet, but in December 1988, a Pan Am flight was blown up over Lockerbie, Scotland, and the plot was again traced to Libya. Nevertheless, Gaddafi maintained his hold on power until 2011.

28.1

28.2

28.3

Strategic Defense Initiative (SDI)

President Reagan's program to defend the United States with sophisticated technologies that some thought as unworkable, also known as "Star Wars."

Map 28-1 The United States and the Middle East.

Events in the Middle East, Afghanistan, and northern Africa involved the United States in a series of crises during the 1980s that would only expand in the 1990s.

Although the hostage crisis with Iran ended the day Reagan came to office in January 1981, the United States remained hostile to Iran because of the crisis. When Iran and Iraq went to war against each other in September 1980, the United States tended to wish both sides ill. However, as the war continued, members of Reagan's National Security Council (NSC) became convinced that it might be possible to support moderates within the Iranian government and build a new U.S. relationship by supplying Iran with weapons. The United States also had good reason to believe that Iran had influence with forces in Lebanon that were holding seven U.S. citizens hostage. NSC staff, led by National Security Advisor Robert McFarlane, argued Iran might help free the hostages, which was a high priority for the president. Carrying forged Irish passports and traveling under assumed names, McFarlane and his deputy, Lieutenant Colonel Oliver North, secretly visited Tehran. In spite of U.S. policy never to negotiate for the release of hostages and despite its official arms embargo of Iran, the United States sold over two thousand missiles to Iran in 1985 and 1986. It was the beginning of the greatest foreign policy misadventure of the Reagan administration.

Reagan and his advisors were further pulled into Middle East conflicts when Israel invaded Lebanon in June 1982. Israel's goal was to attack the presence of the Palestine Liberation Organization (PLO) in Lebanon and create a buffer against Syria. Reagan did not object, though he tried to get Israel to limit its engagement. Later that year, the United States sent a detachment of Marines to join an international peace effort in Lebanon. In October 1983, a truck loaded with TNT drove into the U.S. barracks, killing 241 Marines. Americans, including the president, were horrified at the loss of life. The purpose the Marines were supposed to serve was always vague, and after the tragedy, the administration announced that the Marines were to be "redeployed" to ships off the coast, where they moved in 1984.

In response to the experience in Lebanon, Defense Secretary Caspar Weinberger and his top military advisor and future chair of the Joint Chiefs of Staff, Colin Powell, crafted what became known as the Powell Doctrine. Henceforth, they said, U.S. soldiers would be sent overseas only as a last resort and only if the mission was clearly defined, attainable, supported by the public, and included an exit strategy, none of which had been true in the case of the deployment in Lebanon. The new restrictions would be honored more clearly in some cases than others. Toward the end of the Reagan administration, when Palestinians in the Gaza Strip and West Bank territories under the control of Israel rose up in what they called the *intifada* (or "shaking off"), the United States did little beyond urge both sides to negotiate.

DEALING WITH PERCEIVED THREATS IN LATIN AMERICA U.S. policy in Central America, especially in El Salvador, Honduras, and Nicaragua, was also shaped by the Cold War. Since the 1920s, Democratic and Republican administrations depended on a series of Latin American dictators to create a safe climate for U.S. business and ensure that there was no Communist influence in the government of their countries. What they did to their own citizens was of less concern to American authorities. By the time Reagan had come to office, the longtime dictator in Nicaragua, Anastasio Somoza, had been overthrown by a popular uprising, and the totalitarian regime in El Salvador was seriously threatened by similar opposition. Fearing Communist influence in such popular uprisings, the Reagan administration supported the besieged government of El Salvador and sought to overthrow the new government of Nicaragua (see Map 28-2).

Jeane Kirkpatrick, Reagan's United Nations ambassador, said that Central America was "the most important place in the world for us." Kirkpatrick also outlined a key Reagan policy of differentiating between authoritarian governments such as that of El Salvador, which Kirkpatrick said could in time be reformed into democracies, and totalitarian governments—particularly, the government of the Soviet Union and its client states—which she claimed would never change. Under the policy, the United States would provide support for the former and opposition to the latter.

Map 28-2 The United States and the Americas.

During the Reagan and first Bush administrations, the United States intervened several times in the Caribbean and Central America, most of all in Nicaragua and El Salvador.

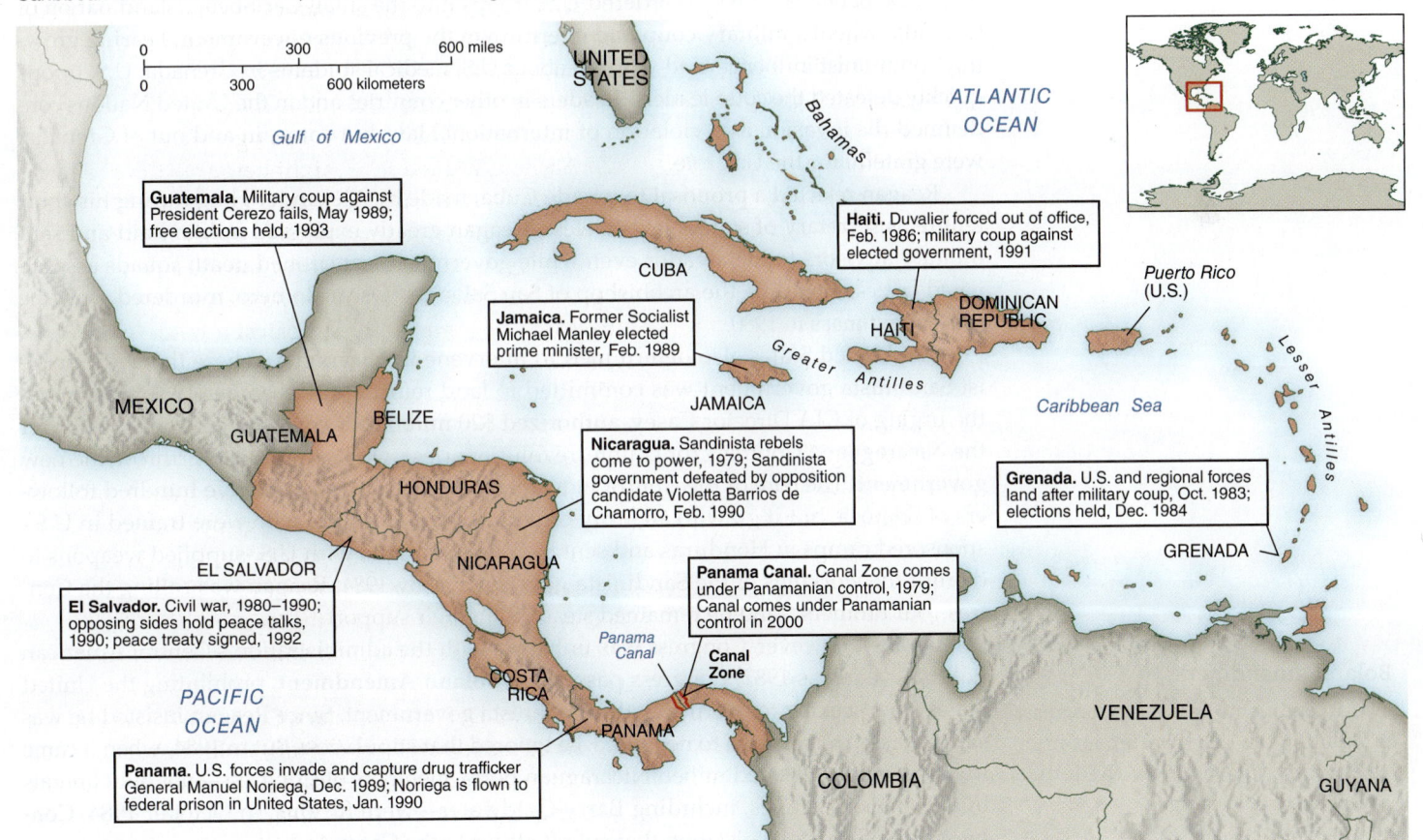

Jeane Kirkpatrick served as U.S. ambassador to the United Nations during Reagan's term in office. Kirkpatrick outlined a key Reagan-era belief that authoritarian governments could be reformed while totalitarian governments could not. Skeptics wondered about the difference.

In October 1983, Reagan ordered U.S. troops into the small Caribbean island nation of Grenada, where a military coup had overthrown the previous government. Fearing growing Communist influence, and worried about U.S. medical students in Grenada, U.S. troops quickly defeated the coup leaders. Leaders in other countries and in the United Nations condemned the invasion as a violation of international law, but some, in and out of Grenada, were grateful for the U.S. role.

Reagan rejected a proposal to invade Cuba, made by Alexander Haig during his short tenure as secretary of state. Nevertheless, Reagan greatly expanded military aid and sent military advisors to El Salvador even while government-sanctioned death squads assassinated critics, including the archbishop of San Salvador, Oscar Romero, murdered while he was saying mass in 1980.

The United States also determined to intervene in Nicaragua, where the new Socialist Sandinista government was committed to land reform. In December 1981, Reagan, at the urging of CIA Director Casey, authorized $20 million for covert operations to support the Nicaraguan "Contras" (or counterrevolutionaries), who sought to overthrow the new government. The core of the Contra movement was a group of some five hundred followers of Somoza, but it grew to an army of perhaps ten thousand who were trained in U.S.-sponsored camps in Honduras and sent back to Nicaragua with U.S.-supplied weapons to disrupt the workings of the Sandinista government. By 1984, Reagan was calling the Contras "our brothers," and he remained steadfast in their support.

Boland amendment

Two amendments passed by Congress, prohibiting the U.S. government from attempting to overthrow the leftist government of Nicaragua.

By 1984, however, Congress was unhappy with the administration's Central American policy. As early as 1982, Congress passed the **Boland Amendment**, prohibiting the United States from seeking to overthrow the Sandinista government. Since Reagan insisted he was simply trying to get them to negotiate, he ignored that stipulation. But in 1984, when it came to light that the CIA had mined Nicaraguan ports, members of Congress—not only liberals but also conservatives, including Barry Goldwater—were furious. In October 1984, Congress passed stricter legislation that cut off all aid to the Contras.

But Reagan did not give up easily. The president encouraged efforts of a young National Security Council staffer, Oliver North, to find new sources of aid, though it was never clear how much Reagan knew of the details of North's enterprise. Since Congress had banned government aid to the Contras, North sought donations from friendly governments in Taiwan, Brunei, and Saudi Arabia and from wealthy private U.S. citizens like beer magnate Joseph Coors. At least $50 million in such aid was delivered to the Contras.

Seeking to expand the aid, North and his mentor Casey had what they termed a "neat idea." The United States was secretly selling arms to Iran. What if, they thought, the United States could make a profit on the clandestine arms shipments to Iran, and then use the funds to support the Contras? Congress would not have to appropriate any money, and no one needed to know.

The complex arrangement did not remain secret for long. In October 1986, an American cargo plane loaded with military supplies for the Contras was shot down in Nicaragua. The Sandinista government let the world know that, in spite of the two Boland Amendments, the United States was still providing significant aid to the Contras. A month later a Beirut, Lebanon, newspaper published an account, based on Iranian sources, of U.S. arms sales to Iran and the link to hoped-for hostage releases. People soon connected the two, and the scandal quickly became known as the "arms for hostages" deal or simply as "**Iran-Contra**." The matter was serious. In selling arms to Iran and in funding the Contras, U.S. laws had been broken, laws that the White House clearly knew existed. Some in Congress talked of impeachment. As with Nixon at Watergate, the question was "what did the president know and when did he know it."

As the details of U.S. activity began to emerge, the president insisted that the government "did not, repeat, did not trade arms or anything else for hostages." He also asked Attorney General Ed Meese to investigate. Oliver North immediately began to shred documents in his office. Meese reported to the president that North had, in fact, not only sold arms to Iran—presumably to free hostages—but also used the profits to aid the Contras. National Security Advisor John Poindexter met with Reagan, confirmed that Meese was right, and resigned. Reagan asked former Texas senator John Tower to lead an investigation. A special prosecutor, Lawrence Walsh, was appointed, and Congress held hearings.

Iran-Contra

A plan to secretly sell arms to Iran in exchange for the release of hostages held in Lebanon and to use the profits to provide aid to the Contra forces of Nicaragua.

In his testimony before Congress regarding the Iran-Contra investigation, Oliver North looked and sounded like a hero to many, in spite of the fact that he had obviously broken the law.

Reagan eventually had to admit, "I told the American people I did not trade arms for hostages. My heart and best intentions still tell me that it is true, but the facts and evidence tell me it is not." Many were shocked that an administration that talked so much about law and order was doing so many illegal things. Reagan clearly knew about the illegal sale of arms to Iran and the arms-for-hostages deals. Many also suspected that he knew about the transfer of funds to the Contras, although that was never proved. Poindexter and North insisted that the decision rested with them alone. Not everyone was convinced, but no "smoking gun" was found. North managed to testify brilliantly before Congress, portraying himself as a well-meaning patriot, and though Reagan's approval rating plummeted, talk of impeachment ended.

Walsh continued his investigation after Reagan left office and eventually secured the indictment of several officials, but Reagan's successor, George H. W. Bush, pardoned them. In 1994, Walsh concluded that Reagan probably should have been impeached, but by then, he was retired and ill. Iran-Contra seriously damaged Reagan's reputation. As Reagan entered his last two years in office, many considered his foreign policy efforts to be a failure. Between 1987 and 1989, however, the president accomplished his great foreign policy triumph.

Ending the Cold War

During his first term, as Reagan talked tough and launched the arms buildup, he also refused to meet with Soviet leaders. Leonid Brezhnev, who had led the Soviet Union since Nikita Khrushchev was deposed in 1964, died in 1982. His successor, Yuri Andropov, died two years later, and the next leader, Konstantin Chernenko, died a year after that. Reagan said, "How am I supposed to get anyplace with the Russians ... if they keep dying on me?" Then in 1985, a new and very different leader, Mikhail Gorbachev, came to power in the Soviet Union.

After a succession of hard-line Communists who were aging and ill, Gorbachev represented a new younger generation of reform-minded Soviet leaders who saw how desperately their country needed change. Top-down Soviet-style planning was strangling the economy. Matching the United States in military matters took a huge percentage of their nation's limited wealth. The disastrous meltdown of the nuclear reactor at Chernobyl just after Gorbachev came to office further convinced him of the need for change. Gorbachev could be as charming and optimistic as Reagan, but he was also a devoted Communist and a very tough leader. He called for major changes: *perestroika*, reform of the Soviet economic system while maintaining communism, and *glasnost*, more openness and freedom for Soviet citizens. He quickly concluded that matching the U.S. arms buildup was going to bankrupt the Soviet Union, and he sought a way to end the arms race.

After his reelection in 1984, Reagan was also ready to talk. By 1985, he had achieved the military buildup that he wanted and could negotiate from a position of strength. U.S. allies, especially those in Europe who lived on the front line of any conflict, were tired of Cold War tensions and increased pressure on the United States for a different policy. Nancy Reagan nudged her husband away from the hard-liners in his administration. Reagan also knew that his Cold War credentials gave him room to maneuver that another leader might not have.

By 1985, Reagan and Gorbachev were ready to work together. British prime minister Margaret Thatcher, known as the Iron Lady because of her ability to stand up to pressure, was a close ally and friend of Reagan. She assured him that Gorbachev was someone "with whom we can do business." Reagan and Gorbachev began a private correspondence and then met for the first time in November 1985 at Geneva where they agreed in general to a reduction in nuclear arms. The following October, they met again at Reykjavik, Iceland. There, in a small house on the ocean, they got to know each other. They talked about their lives—Gorbachev had once wanted to be an actor—their grandchildren, and their hopes for the future. At one point, they frightened their respective staff when they reached a tentative agreement to abolish *all* nuclear weapons by 2000 and then moved the date back to

perestroika

Russian for "restructuring," efforts to make the Soviet economic and political systems more modern, flexible, and innovative.

glasnost

Russian for "openness," encouragement of new ideas and easing of political repression in the Soviet Union.

1995. That agreement floundered over Gorbachev's insistence that they include SDI and Reagan's refusal. The Reykjavik summit ended in anger over Star Wars and without any agreement, but the two men had established a personal bond.

In June 1987, Reagan traveled to Berlin, the flashpoint of the Cold War. Facing the Berlin Wall at the Brandenburg Gate, he demanded, "Mr. Gorbachev, tear down this wall!" The speech, which sounded much more like Reagan's old-line anticommunism than the new thaw in U.S.–Soviet relations, seemed to have been as much an effort to reassure the president's conservative critics as an actual demand. In fact, the steps that Reagan and Gorbachev were taking would lead to the end of the wall within two years, just after Reagan left office.

Soon after Reykjavik, the Soviet physicist Andrei Sakharov convinced Gorbachev that SDI would not work and could safely be ignored. The two leaders then authorized further negotiations on offensive weapons that led to a treaty dramatically reducing intermediate-range nuclear forces (INF) and to onsite inspections so rigorous that they frightened the American CIA.

Critics in both countries thought the leaders were moving too fast. In the Senate, North Carolina's Jesse Helms tried to stop any new treaty, and Howard Phillips of the Conservative Caucus called the president a "useful idiot for Soviet propaganda." Gorbachev, for his part, had to deal with military and civilian attacks for his "capitulationist line" toward the United States. Even so, the momentum was not going to be stopped.

At their next summit in Washington, D.C., in December 1987, Reagan signed the INF Treaty in a well-publicized ceremony, and Gorbachev met and mingled with American crowds like a U.S. politician. The two seemed at ease with each other. When Reagan included one of his favorite sayings, "trust, but verify," in his remarks, Gorbachev interjected, "You repeat that at every meeting." People celebrated "Gorby fever." The Senate ratified the INF Treaty by a large vote in May 1988. The two countries also made significant progress in resolving the conflicts in Nicaragua and Afghanistan, plans for joint space missions, cultural and student exchanges, and emigration and human rights. They jointly sponsored a UN resolution calling for an end to the Iran-Iraq war. The same month that the Senate ratified the INF Treaty, the two leaders met for a fourth time in Moscow. They walked through Red Square, called each other "old friends," and talked with Russian citizens. When asked about his earlier Cold War speeches, Reagan said they were from "another time, another place." Before Reagan left Moscow, the United States and Soviet Union had essentially normalized their relationship. For all intents and purposes, the Cold War was over.

Ira Schwartz/AP Images

This picture of Soviet premier Mikhail Gorbachev and U.S. president Ronald Reagan in Moscow's Red Square would have dumbfounded most Americans only a few years earlier.

28.1
28.2
28.3

The Strained Election of 1988

As a candidate in the Republican primaries in 1980, George Bush had called Ronald Reagan's economic plans "voodoo economics." While Democrats had a field day with the term, once he became Reagan's vice president Bush was a loyal member of the Reagan team, so loyal that some thought he had disappeared, but those who thought that way underestimated him considerably.

George Herbert Walker Bush was a child of privilege. His father was a successful banker and Republican senator from Connecticut. Bush attended private schools and expected to attend Yale when World War II intervened. While Ronald Reagan made war movies in Hollywood for the government, Bush flew more than fifty combat missions in the South Pacific and was shot down twice. After the war, he married Barbara Pierce, attended Yale, and then moved to Texas to make his fortune in the oil business. He served two terms in

28.1

28.2

28.3

When Historians Disagree

Did Ronald Reagan End the Cold War?

Historians agree that on entering the White House in 1981, Ronald Reagan took a tougher line on the Cold War than his predecessors and that, a little less than eight years later, he and Soviet leader Mikhail Gorbachev were strolling through Red Square together calling each other "old friends." But historians continue to have sharp debates about the particular role that Reagan played in these extraordinary changes. Did he "win" the Cold War? Was he merely a bystander to events unfolding in Russia? How important was the personal chemistry between Reagan and Gorbachev? On these and many related questions, there is no agreement, and historians represent very different views.

Peter Schweizer, *Reagan's War*. New York: Random House, 2002, pp. 280–284.

Those virtues that Reagan so admired—courage and character—are what the nearly half-century battle against communism required most of him. Beginning in Hollywood and throughout his presidency, Reagan was always willing to speak the truth about communism....

In retrospect, it is clear that Reagan was largely correct about communism and his critics were wrong. Soviet communism was the threat that he claimed it was and was vulnerable in the way he said it would be. He was on the correct side of the great battles of his forty-year struggle against communism. Moscow and its supporters did try to gain a level of control in Hollywood; the peace movement in the 1970s and 1980s was being influenced by the Soviet Union; and Moscow and Havana did have plans to subvert Central America. Archives in the former Soviet bloc settle these debates....

No American throughout the history of the Cold War up until Reagan had been willing to make rolling back and defeating communism a primary goal. Even anti-Communists like Richard Nixon subscribed to the seductive idea that stability was most important and that a healthy Soviet Union was important for long-term peace. But Reagan understood that communism by its nature was a danger to peace because it relied on fear and external enemies to maintain its legitimacy....

How did Reagan contribute to the demise of the Soviet empire? You can draw up a scorecard and count the economic costs that Reagan's policies placed on a struggling Soviet economy....

Or you can look at the body blows that the Soviet empire suffered. Military defeat in Afghanistan ... the survival and eventual triumph of Solidarity in Poland. In both of these cases, Reagan proved decisive in victory.

Since the end of the Cold War, a debate has raged about how it ended. One person who never got wrapped up in this debate was Ronald Reagan. One of the last items to be removed from his Oval Office desk in January 1989 was a small sign that read: "It's surprising what you can accomplish when no one is concerned about who gets the credit."

Michael Schaller, "Reagan and the Cold War," in Kyle Longley, Jeremy D. Mayer, Michael Schaller, and John W. Sloan, *Deconstructing Reagan: Conservative Mythology and America's Fortieth President*. Armonk, NY: M.E. Sharp, 2007, pp. 3, 30, 36.

Popular memories of Ronald Reagan focus on his embrace of free markets at home and strident anticommunism abroad. To many Americans, his unapologetic celebration of patriotism and military fortitude not only made the nation safer, but also in the words of British prime minister Margaret Thatcher, won the Cold War "without firing a shot." ... In contrast to this claim of cause and effect, most historians dispute the assertion that communism was on a victory roll in 1981 and that Reagan's policies led directly to Soviet collapse a decade later....

During 1987, events pushed both Gorbachev and Reagan toward a more cooperative relationship.... Gorbachev hoped to slash Soviet defense spending (an estimated 25 percent of gross national product, as compared to 3 percent in the United States) to free resources for economic restructuring. He hoped that democratic reforms would both mobilize support for his leadership and win concessions from Washington....

[U.S. secretary of state] Schultz and other moderates now advising Reagan saw this new Soviet stance as something of a lifeline for a president floundering in the Iran-contra scandal and watching his public approval ratings falling sharply.

... Yet instead of encouraging Gorbachev's democratic reforms and efforts to build international cooperation, in public and private venues Reagan took to boasting that his hard line had forced a Soviet retreat....

By the time the Soviet Union dissolved in December 1991, new threats had emerged in the post-Cold war world. George Kennan, the architect of containment, spoke to this fact in an opinion piece he published in the New York Times on October 28, 1992. It was "simply childish," Kennan asserted, to say that Reagan's policies achieved victory. The United States had not "won" the long struggle that cost both sides so dearly. Each bore responsibility for its inception and duration. Politicians should pause before patting themselves on the back.

Thinking Critically

1. **Analyzing Secondary Sources**

   To what degree might either Schweitzer or Schaller, or both, be expressing a personal point of view about Ronald Reagan rather than a historical argument based on the best evidence? What evidence would you want to see before making a decision?

2. **Argument Development**

   Knowing what you know now about the end of the Cold War, how would you make a counterargument to one or both authors based on available evidence?

the House of Representatives from Houston. He was defeated when he ran for the Senate in 1970 but was subsequently appointed head of the Republican Party, nominal U.S. ambassador to China after the Nixon trip, and head of the CIA for Gerald Ford.

The conservative wing of the Republican Party never trusted Bush, especially after his "voodoo economics" remarks, but also because of his lack of enthusiasm for their social issues. Disappointed that Reagan had not done more to support the social issues that were near and dear to them, some conservatives thought that 1988 was their chance.

American Voices

Jesse Jackson and Pat Robertson—Presidential Candidates, 1988

Pat Robertson was the most conservative candidate to seek the Republican nomination in 1988 and Jesse Jackson the most liberal to seek the Democratic. Both were Baptist ministers. Both lost to more moderate candidates and endorsed them, but each also had a significant impact on their respective party platform. In speeches to their conventions, they outlined their own views.

Jesse Jackson, 1988 Democratic National Convention Address	Pat Robertson, 1988 Republican National Convention Address
When I look out at this convention, I see the face of America: Red, Yellow, Brown, Black, and White. We're all precious in God's sight—the real rainbow coalition.... When I was a child growing up in Greenville, South Carolina, and grandmamma could not afford a blanket, she didn't complain … she took pieces of old cloth … sewed them together into a quilt, a thing of beauty and power and culture. Now, Democrats, we must build such a quilt. Farmers, you seek fair prices, and you are right—but you cannot stand alone. Your patch is not big enough. Workers, you fight for fair wages, you are right—but your patch, labor, is not big enough. Women, you seek comparable worth and pay equity … Head Start, and day care and prenatal care on the front side of life, relevant jail care and welfare on the back side of life, you are right—but your patch is not big enough. Students, you seek scholarships, you are right—but your patch is not big enough. Blacks and Hispanics, when we fight for civil rights, we are right—but our patch is not big enough. Gays and lesbians, when you fight against discrimination and a cure for AIDS, you are right—but your patch is not big enough.... But don't despair. Be as wise as my grandmamma. Pull the patches and the pieces together, bound by a common thread. When we form a great quilt of unity and common ground, we'll have the power to bring about health care and housing and jobs and education and hope to our Nation. We, the people, can win.	Four years ago the keynote speaker at the Democratic National Convention told us that America was a tale of two cities—the "haves" and the "have-nots." The rich and the poor. The upper class and the lower class. … The Democrats have given us a clear picture of their city. They offer unlimited government, massive transfers of wealth from the productive sector of society to the nonproductive, and ever-increasing regulation of the daily lives of the people and their children. In the city of the Democratic Party, the liberal mindset reigns supreme. Criminals are turned loose and the innocent are made victims. Disease carriers are protected and the healthy are placed at great risk. In the Democrat's city, welfare dependency flourishes and no one is held accountable for his or her behavior. Society is always to blame. In the Democrat's city, the rights of the majority must always take a back seat to the clamorous demands of the special interest minorities. And yet, in their city it is always the majority that must pay the bills, through higher and higher taxes. … Ladies and Gentlemen, the Republican Party wants to write a tale of another city. … We see a city set on a hill. A shining light of freedom for all of the nations to see and admire. A city made great by the moral strength and self-reliance of her people.

Source: Jesse Jackson, 1988 Democratic National Convention Address, downloaded July 26, 2011, from www.americanrhetoric.com/speeches/jessejackson1988dnc .htm; Pat Robertson, 1988 Republican National Convention Address, downloaded July 26, 2011, from www.patrobertson.com/Speeches/PresidentialBidEnded.asp.

Thinking Critically

1. **Comparison**
   What did each speaker see as the fundamental source of America's strength? How did they differ? Were there ways in which their views were similar?

2. **Analyzing Primary Sources**
   What light do these two speeches shed on the historical situation of the time and on the fundamental ideological divisions in American politics in the late 1980s and early 1990s?

28.1

28.2

28.3

And Democrats, convinced that Reagan was more personally popular than his programs, believed that the end of his second term would be their chance to retake the White House. Neither challenge succeeded.

In the Republican Party, the conservative but genial Kansas senator Robert Dole challenged the vice president. And Pat Robertson, the extremely conservative religious broadcaster and head of the Christian Broadcasting Network, who had strongly supported Ronald Reagan, now resigned his ordination as a Baptist minister and campaigned for the nomination. Robertson felt that it was time to take the religious right's social and cultural issues into a presidential campaign. While Bush won the nomination on the first ballot, he embraced many of Dole's and Robertson's issues, invited a conservative, Indiana senator J. Danforth Quayle—whom many considered to be a lightweight—to be his running mate, and made a speech he would later regret, telling the Republican Convention, "Read my lips. No new taxes."

Sensing possible victory, many Democrats sought the nomination. Colorado senator Gary Hart, an initial front-runner, was forced out of the race after he was photographed on the yacht *Monkey Business* with the model Donna Rice—not his wife—sitting on his lap. The nomination battle came down to a contest between the Reverend Jesse Jackson, a longtime civil rights leader, and Massachusetts governor Michael Dukakis. Jackson was extremely popular in some circles and reviled in others. He was the first African American candidate to win presidential primaries in southern states, winning five. But in the end, Dukakis won the Democratic nomination. He summed up his campaign when he told the Democratic convention, "This election is not about ideology, it's about competence."

Dukakis entered the fall campaign with a seventeen-point lead in the polls, but the lead quickly evaporated in what turned into a very nasty battle. Dukakis's focus on competence did not make for an inspiring campaign. The Bush camp, led by Lee Atwater, ran TV ads featuring a black convicted criminal, Willie Horton, who had killed a man and raped a woman while on furlough from a Massachusetts prison. The fact that many states, including Reagan's California, had furlough policies did not make a difference. The appeal to fear was strong. In the end, Bush swamped Dukakis by a vote of almost 49 million to 42 million and 426 to 111 electoral votes and won the presidential term he had long sought.

> **28.1** Quick Review
>
> How successfully did Ronald Reagan fulfill his initial goals? How did his goals change during his term in office?

The Changing Nature of the American Economy

28.2 Explain internal and international economic developments that shaped the United States.

Presidential candidates, economists, and families who gathered around the dinner table or the TV trays in the living room all debated the nature of the economic changes that were taking place in the 1980s as "Reaganomics" led to tax cuts, a reduction in government services, and fewer government regulations. Late in his term, in July 1987, President Reagan proposed what he called an Economic Bill of Rights that included "freedom to enjoy the fruits of one's labor ... free from excessive government taxing, spending and borrowing by the government ... the freedom to own and control one's property ... freedom to participate in a free market ... and to achieve one's full potential without government limits on opportunity." It was a philosophy that Reagan seemed to embody in his own life story. Yet by 1987, some Americans were beginning to have second thoughts.

Kevin Phillips, who helped Republican presidential campaigns from Nixon to Reagan, was among them. In his book *Boiling Point*, he described what he saw as Reagan's term came to an end. Reagan had been elected in 1980, Phillips said, because government was "fairly in disrepute for its swollen size and record of aggravating rather than solving problems." He continued, saying that with the cuts in taxes and government programs, however, "[h]igh-income persons did not suffer, but middle-class voters usually worried when federal and state reductions went too far" (see Figure 28-1).

One of the striking features of the economy of the 1980s was the extraordinary fortunes made by a few individuals. In the 1980s, Ivan Boesky anticipated corporate takeovers and mergers, buying stock just before it increased in value with stunning regularity. In December 1986, Boesky was honored with a cover photo in *Time* magazine, and by 1987, he had earned a total of more than $200 million.

Michael Milken, an investor for the firm Drexel Burnham Lambert who specialized in so-called junk bonds, earned much more. Junk bonds were high-risk investments that could pay high yields. Milken arranged investments in gambling casinos and technology startups as well as "leveraged buyouts" in which investors would buy a controlling share of a company—using loans arranged by Milken—and thereby take it over in spite of the will of its owners and managers. In 1987, his estimated income for that one year was $550 million.

Boesky, Milken, and other slightly lesser figures were the heroes of the 1980s. In a speech to business students at the University of California, Berkeley, Boesky said, "I think greed is healthy. You can be greedy and still feel good about yourself." But Kevin Phillips noted, "By early 1990 *The New York Times* noted that Wall Street found an unnerving whiff of populism in the public's anger over junk-bond pioneer Michael Milken's $550-million-a-year salary."

Federal employees at the Security and Exchange Commission (SEC) became suspicious that anyone could have as much success as Boesky in guessing the direction of stock values year after year. An SEC investigation showed that Boesky was indeed getting illegal insider information about corporate takeovers and mergers. When he was charged with breaking the law, Boesky implicated Milken, whose illegal dealings were even more complex. Boesky was eventually fined $100 million, half of his fortune; Milken paid over $1.1 billion; and both served almost two years in federal prison. In the 1987 movie *Wall Street*, the villain Gordon Gekko gave a "greed is good" speech, based on Boesky's Berkeley talk, which became a symbol of an era.

It was not only a few highfliers who got into trouble in the late 1980s, however. Throughout much of the 1970s, the Dow Jones Industrial Average had hovered just under 1,000 (that is, the average value of a share on the list was $1,000; see Chapter 22). In 1980, the average crossed the magic 1,000 line to 1,100, and from there it just kept going up along with public optimism. By 1987, the average was above 2,500. Then in October 1987, the bottom fell out as it had done before. On October 19, known as "Black Monday," the market fell by 508 points, closing below 2,000. The next day, the Federal Reserve Bank, seeking to avoid a repeat of the 1929 crash, responded, pumping millions of dollars into the market. Consumer confidence returned and the market stabilized, but in one day, American stocks had dropped $500 billion in their value, and many investors lost their savings.

Among the victims of Black Monday was the nation's savings and loan industry. In 1982, as part of the Reagan efforts to deregulate government, most of the restrictions on

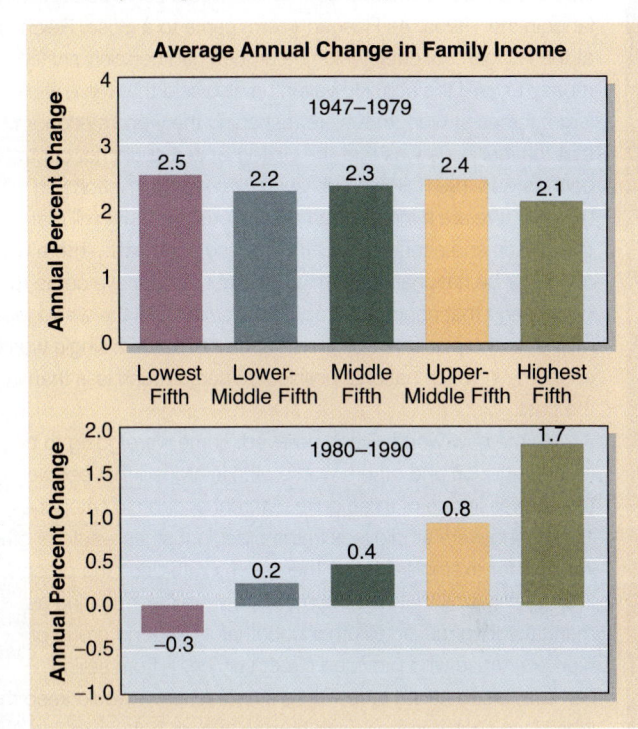

Figure 28-1 Real Family Income, 1980–1990.

As this chart shows, between 1947 and 1979, Americans of all classes saw an increase of 2.1 percent to 2.5 percent in their income. Between 1980 and 1990, however, the poorest fifth of Americans got poorer, the middle groups barely held their own, and the top fifth got much more wealthy.

28.1

28.2

28.3

28.1
28.2
28.3

Thinking Historically

A Changing World Economy

Robert Reich, a respected economist, would serve as secretary of labor in the 1990s. As Reagan's term came to a close, Reich looked at the Reagan tax cuts, which he argued had certainly shifted money toward the rich. However, he also said that there were larger forces at work that were reshaping the world's economy and that the real issue was that the United States could not control its economy. In 1991, Reich published *The Work of Nations*, in which he said, "We are living through a transformation that will rearrange the politics and economics of the coming century. ... There will no longer be national economies, at least as we have come to understand that concept." Trade, finance, indeed the whole job market of the planet, Reich insisted, had become a single worldwide economy in which national policies mattered much less than in the past.

In the new world, Reich believed, some were going to be much better off and others worse off. He argued that people found themselves in one of three quite different economic categories. Those who were employees in the older industries—auto or steel workers for example—found themselves with declining prospects. Well-paying jobs that had been secure were disappearing as manufacturing moved to other countries. A second group of workers, those who provided direct services—from selling hamburgers to health care workers to teachers—would keep their jobs since such services were hard to export, but would find their futures relatively flat. And finally, in the third category, those Reich called "symbolic analysts" the scientists, inventors, developers, and money managers, would do quite well, indeed better than ever before. For example, Reich noted:

> In 1960, the chief executive of one of America's 100 largest nonfinancial corporations earned, on average, $190,000 or about forty times the wage of his average factory worker. After taxes, the chief executive earned only twelve times the factory worker's

wages. By the end of the 1980s, however, the chief executive earned, on average, more than $2 million—ninety-three times the wages of his (rarely her) average factory worker. After taxes, the chief executive's compensation was about seventy times that of the average factory worker.

Clearly the Reagan tax cuts had something to do with the change, but not everything.

For Reich, the larger issue was the shift from a national American economy to a unified world economy:

> All Americans used to be in roughly the same economic boat. Most rose or fell together. ... We are now in different boats, one sinking rapidly [the industrial workers], one sinking more slowly [service workers], and the third rising steadily [that of managers and inventors].

In the economy that Reich described, Americans would compete, not with each other, but with people in the same sort of work around the world. Not everyone agreed with Reich, but it was hard to look at the nation at the end of the 1980s and not conclude that some, indeed, were sinking and others were rising quite spectacularly.

Source: Robert B. Reich, *The Work of Nations: Preparing Ourselves for 21st Century Capitalism* (New York: Vintage Books, 1991), pp. 7 and 208.

Thinking Critically

1. **Comparison**
   How does Reich's economic analysis compare with either defenders or critics of Reagan's economic policies?

2. **Contextualization**
   How does Reich help place the changing American economy of the 1980s in an international context?

savings and loan associations were removed. They were allowed to invest not only in houses and cars, which they had long done, but also in risky oil and gas ventures, real estate developments, and even junk bonds like those sold by Michael Milken. They attracted many more depositors by paying previously unheard of high levels of interest. They made huge fortunes for their executives and investors. But when the stock market, junk bonds, and then housing prices collapsed in the late 1980s, the savings and loan industry found itself in serious trouble with investments that were not worth what they owed to depositors. Some 1,200 of the nation's 4,000 savings and loans required federal help or went out of business. Since the federal government guaranteed savings and loan deposits as they did bank deposits, the government—and taxpayers—were left with the cost, which came to $500 billion or $2,000 for every American. Further investigations showed that U.S. senators had done special favors for the savings and loan industry and six senators were censured. Savings and loan owners who made fortunes were found to have stolen from their companies. William Crawford, a California official charged with investigating the scandal, said, "The best way to rob a bank is to own one."

28.1

28.2

28.3

Peter Morgan/AP Images

The stock market crash of October 19, 1987, set off panicked selling as did every stock market crash.

28.2 Quick Review

How did government policies and changes in the worldwide economic structure impact the average American in the 1980s?

Changes in the Rest of the Country

28.3 **Explain cultural changes in the United States during the 1980s.**

On April 5, 1985, Michael Jackson, the most successful American rock star of the 1980s, joined in a concert, originally planned by Bob Geldof and Midge Ure, Irish and Scottish musicians, respectively, to raise funds for famine relief in Africa. The concert was broadcast around the world and raised $44 million in a production that included Jackson, Lionel Richie, Bob Dylan, Ray Charles, Billy Joel, Cyndi Lauper, Bette Midler, Willie Nelson, Paul Simon, Bruce Springsteen, Stevie Wonder, and Tina Turner.

Three months later, on July 13, 1985, some 100,000 people attended one of two simultaneous rock concerts held in Philadelphia, Pennsylvania, and London, England. Another 1.5 to 1.9 billion people around the world watched the concerts on TV or listened on radio. At the July concert, Jackson, his guests, and an audience of many million sang We Are the World.

These Live Aid concerts eventually raised over $80 million for Africa. Subsequent concerts raised more money, dollars that made a real difference in feeding people. The fundraising concerts also symbolized new international connections. With new high-speed communications, people in various geographical locations could listen to the same concert at the same time as no previous generation had. They could also transfer money, hold meetings, and plan new enterprises, creating a worldwide culture and economy. Given the speed of travel, it did not take much longer for people to visit new places, transmit diseases, or start a new life halfway around the world.

Popular Culture—Music, Television, Theater

In addition to the famine-relief fund-raising—which was badly needed—the 1985 concerts also symbolized the way American musicians had come to dominate the world. Michael Jackson, Bruce Springsteen, and Cyndi Lauper first emerged in the 1970s and 1980s.

28.1

28.2

28.3

Ebet Roberts/Getty Images

Some of the nation's best-known musicians, such as Lionel Richie, Dionne Warwick, Bob Dylan, and others, performing at "Live Aid '85" "Concert on July 13, 1985, at John F. Kennedy Stadium in Philadelphia, Pennsylvania.

They were joined in these concerts by others, Ray Charles, Bob Dylan, and Tina Turner, who had been international figures since the 1950s or 1960s. They represented diverse musical styles from Turner's start in rhythm-and-blues to Charles's jazz, to Lauper's rock, but all had become cultural icons from major world cities to isolated rural villages in Asia, Africa, and tiny Pacific islands.

The popularity of American musicians was made possible, in part, by rapidly changing technologies. Michael Jackson insisted that We Are the World be released at exactly 3:50 p.m. Greenwich Mean Time (10:50 a.m. on the East Coast of the United States) in eight thousand radio stations around the world. The technology to transmit the music to all of these stations was new. When the Live Aid concerts were held in July 1985, one of the musicians, Phil Collins, managed to perform in person at both the London and the Philadelphia concerts thanks to the supersonic Concorde plane that brought him across the Atlantic faster than the speed of sound. Music Television (MTV) began broadcasting in August 1981 and built a worldwide audience for rock music. Generating these huge audiences would not have happened without the nonstop broadcasting of music videos aimed at audiences in the twelve- to thirty-four-year-old demographic who made up the bulk of those who attended the concerts or listened to the broadcasts. And after We Are the World had been released, it and other music from the concerts was listened to over and over by individuals using Sony Walkman personal stereos, first sold in 1979, or Sony compact disc (CD) players, which produced far better quality than older tapes and records. American music of the 1980s could be heard worldwide because American—and Japanese—technology made possible the easy and cheap distribution of quality musical sounds.

The music of the 1980s also connected with Americans, especially young Americans, and their counterparts around the globe. It was their generation's challenge to the traditional culture and its music. Where jazz, rock, and folk music all began as protests, against musical and political systems, so the music of the 1980s was its own form of protest. African American artists dominated the music, but they were not alone. Tina Turner, an African American, who with her husband had headlined the Ike and Tina Turner Revue in the 1950s and 1960s, emerged after her divorce as a force in her own right in the 1980s, celebrating her energy and her sexuality with recordings like *Private Dancer* in 1984. A younger white woman, Madonna, celebrated her sometimes off-the-wall sexuality in releases such as her 1984 album, *Like a Virgin*. A new generation, the children of the baby boomers, was creating a new music and a new culture of its own in the 1980s and making sure that its country, and the world, listened.

The 1980s were one of the most successful decades in the history of the film industry. The most popular film of the decade was *E.T., the Extra-Terrestrial*, a story produced by Steven Spielberg about a small creature from outer space who liked candy and wanted to "phone home." Other highly successful films of the decade included *The Empire Strikes Back* (1980); *Return of the Jedi* (1983) in George Lucas's Star Wars trilogy; *Batman*; *Ghostbusters*; and the Indiana Jones movies, *Raiders of the Lost Ark* (all in 1981) and *Indiana Jones and the Last Crusade* (1989). There were also more violent movies such as *Terminator* (1984) with Arnold Schwarzenegger and the Rambo films with Sylvester Stallone. While both Schwarzenegger and Stallone played classic "good guys," the films had plenty of blood and violence. Spike Lee directed films such as *Do the Right Thing*, which explored serious issues in a thoughtful way. Martin Scorsese's *The Last Temptation of Christ*, released in 1988, generated critical acclaim but also demonstrations in front of theaters, with its portrayal of Jesus as a man with ordinary temptations. As with music, so with films, technology expanded beyond anything previously thought possible. People still watched movies in theaters, but they also watched them at home as VCRs made it possible for films to be distributed not only to the local theater but also to the local living room where people could watch at their leisure.

The most successful TV series of the 1980s, *The Cosby Show*, reflected an updated version of the 1950s family shows. But the family in *The Cosby Show*, the Huxtables, was led by an African American doctor, played by Cosby. The focus on a successful African American family in the mainstream of America, and their warm acceptance by viewers, was a clear shift. In contrast, when the lead character of *Murphy Brown*, played by Candice Bergen, had a child without being married and indicated that the father's identity was not important, Vice President Dan Quayle criticized the show.

African American artists and writers also came to play a dominant role in theater and literature in the 1980s. The playwright August Wilson began producing a series of plays that explored the black experience from 1900 to 2000, including *Ma Rainey's Black Bottom* in 1985 and *Fences* in 1986. Toni Morrison's novel *Beloved*, published in 1987, explored the evils of slavery and eventually won the Nobel Prize for Literature.

Culture Wars—The Christian Coalition and Other Critics

The cultural developments of the 1980s and 1990s in music, drama, and creative writing also produced a considerable critical response. Looking at the era, Robert Bork, a conservative legal scholar who had been denied a position on the Supreme Court by a Senate vote in 1987, published *Slouching toward Gomorrah* in 1996 in which he blamed a decline he saw in American culture on the nation's "enfeebled hedonistic culture," its "uninhibited display of sexuality," and its "popularization of violence." Many other authors, liberal and conservative, worried about what the liberal African American journalist Carl Rowen called the "sexual rot and gratuitous violence" that led to "decadence, decay, and self-destruction." In 1985, "Tipper" Gore, whose husband was then Democratic senator from Tennessee, co-founded the Parents Music Resource Center after hearing her eleven-year-old daughter listen to music that she deemed profane by the recording artist Prince.

The religious right was made up of people who were increasingly angry at many of the cultural trends of the 1980s and 1990s. The Moral Majority, the major political organization of the religious right, declined in

Opposition to abortion became one of the major rallying cries of the growing religious right.

Eve Arnold/Magnum Photos

28.1

28.2

28.3

the late 1980s and disbanded in 1989 (see Chapter 27). Some commentators thought that decline would be the end of religious conservatism as a political force. They could not have been more mistaken. After Pat Robertson lost his campaign for the Republican nomination in 1988, he helped launch a new conservative religious and political organization: the Christian Coalition.

Robertson hired a young veteran of the College Republican National Committee, Ralph Reed, to run the Christian Coalition on a day-to-day basis. Reed brought a steady hand as well as organizational and fund-raising skills to the Christian Coalition that the Moral Majority never had. He was a young fresh face and managed to portray himself as a moderating influence on the more extreme Robertson.

Pat Robertson was born in 1930. His father was a conservative Democratic U.S. senator from Virginia from 1946 to 1966. Robertson earned a law degree from Yale before studying for the Baptist ministry. He founded the Christian Broadcasting Network and *The 700 Club*, a religious talk show that reached millions, before he began his more overt political campaigning. In running for president and then launching the Christian Coalition, Robertson sought to resist what he saw as the increased secularization of American culture and avert what he saw as God's coming judgment on the nation's sins. Another evangelical minister, describing Robertson's supporters, said, "They have a bunker mentality. They feel modernity is against them—in matters dealing with sex, crime, pornography, education."

Ralph Reed, born in 1961, was a generation younger than Robertson. He was fascinated with the mechanics of politics, put off by the religious right because of their amateurishness, and determined that the Christian Coalition would be an effective organization. The two made a strong team. By 1992, the Christian Coalition had more than 150,000 members and controlled the grassroots Republican Party in several states.

By the mid-1990s, every Republican candidate for president was courting the Christian Coalition and Reed could say, "We have gained what we have always sought, a place at the table, a sense of legitimacy." His goal was more than legitimacy, however. Reed and Robertson wanted to shape the nation's political agenda, from the grass roots up as much as from the top down. Their impact throughout the 1990s testified to the coalition's power.

Religious conservatives were not the only critics of American culture in the 1980s and 1990s. Robert Bellah, a liberal sociologist, argued in his 1986 book, *Habits of the Heart*, that Americans were becoming individualistic and consumption oriented and were losing their ability to work together for the common good. A decade later in 1995, a Harvard scholar, Robert Putnam, published *Bowling Alone* in which he explored the impact of individualism. Americans who, in the past, joined churches, social and service organizations, and bowling leagues, now stayed home to watch television, spent less time in face-to-face gatherings of any sort, and even if they went out to a bowling alley, now did it alone. Some critics thought that Putnam and Bellah romanticized the past, but few dismissed their worries.

New Immigrants, New Diversities

In the 1980s and 1990s, many who lived in the United States were very recent arrivals. In 2000, 28.4 million people, or 10.4 percent of the population of the United States, were foreign born. This increase was a significant change from the 4.7 percent who were foreign born in 1970 and marked the end of almost fifty years of very tough immigration restrictions. When Congress passed and Lyndon Johnson signed the Immigration and Nationality (Hart-Celler) Act in 1965, no one expected it to have a major impact on the overall numbers of people coming to the United States (see Chapter 26). They could not have been more wrong. The 1965 law capped the number of immigrants at the same place as the older law. But in addition to the numerical limits in the 1965 law, it provided for family reunion. If one member of a family was a legal resident or citizen of the United States, then that member could bring his or her family, regardless of the caps. By the 1990s, two-thirds of all immigrants to the United States were coming as part of family reunions.

28.1

28.2

28.3

Official government numbers showed the impact of the changes brought about by the law:

4.5 million immigrants in the 1970s

7.3 million immigrants in the 1980s

9.1 million immigrants in the 1990s

In addition, by most estimates, between 250,000 and 350,000 came to the United States every year without official documentation. In 2000, the U.S. population stood at 281 million, including some 28 million who had come between 1970 and 2000—more individuals than at any other thirty-year time span in the nation's history.

The new immigrants who came between 1970 and 2000 also came from places different from immigrants of earlier eras. Before 1924, when the United States virtually closed its doors to immigrants (see Chapter 21), most immigrants had come from Europe or, unwillingly, from Africa. After 1980, most new immigrants came from Latin America and Asia. Between 1980 and 2000,

2 million people came to the United States from Europe (mostly from
    former Soviet states),

5.7 million people came from Asia,

4 million people came from Mexico,

2.8 million people came from Central America and the Caribbean,

1 million came from South America,

600,000 came from Africa, and

250,000 came from Canada.

By any counting, they were reshaping the country.

Immigrants moved to every part of the United States. Meatpacking plants in Kansas, potato farms in Maine, and agribusiness in southern Indiana all depended on recent immigrants who were willing to do hot, dirty, and generally low-paying work. The majority of immigrants, however, settled in relatively few areas, especially the states of California, Texas, Florida, New Jersey, Illinois, and New York. By 2000, California's population was 27 percent foreign born as a result of a major influx of new immigrants and a modest white exodus.

Many immigrants also came to the United States without official approval (some called them "undocumented," others just "illegal"). The borders with Mexico and Canada were hard to guard, and many simply walked across. Others came on tourist visas and never left. In 1986, Congress passed legislation that President Reagan signed, giving anyone who had been in the United States since 1982 the right to seek amnesty, and 1.7 million people, most from Mexico, took advantage of the law.

Debates about immigration became intense. In campaigning for the Republican presidential nomination in 1992, Patrick Buchanan staked out his anti-immigrant views. He said, "Our own country is undergoing the greatest invasion in its history, a migration of millions of illegal aliens yearly from Mexico. … A nation that cannot control its own borders can scarcely call itself a state any longer." In 1986, almost three-quarters of California voters approved a law that made English the "official language" of the state. While the law had little formal meaning, it was a slap at those who spoke other languages. Some labor union leaders and workers, white and black, complained that new immigrants were taking their jobs or depressing wages in whole industries.

The sign at this vigil in Echo Park, Los Angeles, reads, "This fruit is the product of immigrants' labor." Members of the city's Latino community bless fruit baskets as they protest a state crackdown on undocumented immigration and the increase of border patrol guards.

Damian Dovarganes/AP Images

On the other hand, defenders of immigration argued that the American economy was dependent on immigrants who were willing to take jobs—in restaurants, agriculture, and home health care—that few native-born Americans were willing to do. Would the crops get harvested, the meat packaged, the dishes washed, and the elderly cared for if immigrants, documented and undocumented, were forced to leave? Immigrants are generally younger than the average population, pay taxes, and contribute to the Social Security system, though in the case of those who are undocumented, they may never collect benefits. Some studies indicate that immigrants are more highly educated, more likely to be in stable families, and less likely to be engaged in crime, though other scholars disputed those numbers. While the arguments continued, people kept coming.

American Indians in the 1980s—Casinos and Rebirth

While their numbers were drastically reduced by war and disease, American Indian tribes have survived and sometimes thrived in spite of the difficulties. As restrictions on teaching American Indian languages, culture, and religion were lifted in the 1940s, 1950s, and 1960s, a surprising reservoir of an earlier cultural heritage resurfaced. For some tribes, Coyote is the perfect symbol of Indian life. Coyote is the trickster who disappears and reappears as he needs to in order to survive and thrive in new contexts. At the Spirit Mountain Casino, which is operated by the Grand Ronde Reservation in western Oregon State, a picture of Coyote dominates the gambling hall and the tribal logo. It is a fitting symbol of how a casino has given new life to a tribe.

Gambling transformed many American Indian communities in the 1980s. While often a subject of derision, gambling brought prosperity to many tribes that had experienced only poverty. Two federal court cases, *Seminole Tribe of Florida v. Butterworth* in 1981 and *California v. Cabazon Band of Mission Indians* in 1987, made it difficult for states to limit gambling on Indian reservations. Some of those who controlled the gambling industry did not like the idea of new competitors, and Donald Trump complained about "equal treatment under the law." But the United States had always used a different set of laws for Indians, and treaty rights created a unique situation. In the court cases, tribes and their attorneys argued that the treaty rights creating the reservations gave them all the powers of any sovereign state to handle their own affairs. To regularize the new industry that was emerging, Congress passed the Indian Gaming Regulatory Act (IGRA) in 1988, and Reagan signed it. A new industry was born, one that brought prosperity to some tribes, even though others did not or could not take advantage of the boom in gambling.

The Pequots Foxwoods Casino produced almost $900 million in 1994, and the tribal council used the money to create other job-producing enterprises, including a silica mine and a printing plant. They bought the former Electric Boat shipyard that helped maintain the U.S. nuclear submarine fleet. Their goal was long-term economic development that was not dependent only on the gambling industry. Other tribes did the same. The Oneida Tribe of Wisconsin used the income from its slot-machine complex near Green Bay to open a chain store and a high-tech research and development firm. The Choctaws of Oklahoma used income from a bingo parlor in Durant to build a manufacturing plant, hotels, and the Choctaw Nation Travel Plaza, which earned $1.4 million per month in 1992.

The new wealth allowed tribes to design their own museums, support retention of tribal languages, and maintain aspects of their culture that were otherwise being lost. They also allowed tribes to expand schools, provide new job-training programs and health services, and generally support their members. Indians who had drifted away from reservations were now returning, a change since the 1950s when a government Urban Relocation Program had led perhaps half of all American Indians to move from reservations to cities. Others who were part Indian were now claiming their Indian ties. Determining who was, and was not, a member of a specific tribe became a complex issue for some. R. David Edmunds, an ethnohistorian who himself is part Cherokee, wrote that traditionally no one questioned tribal membership: "If the Shawnees said you were Shawnee, you *were* Shawnee." By the 1990s, however, such issues had become more complex, and tribes sometimes had to make difficult decisions. Nevertheless, the new prosperity was significant.

American Voices

Caridad Ríos, Adela Aguirre, and Saša Savić Talk about Their Immigrant Experiences in the United States

No single immigrant experience stands for the hundreds of thousands of people who have moved from crisis, poverty, or war to make new lives in the United States. These brief interviews with Caridad Ríos, a forty-year-old native of Lake Chapala, Jalisco, Mexico; Adela Aguirre, also from Mexico; and Saša Savić from the former Yugoslavia describe some common experiences.

Caridad Ríos: I don't believe I'll ever return to my country, because of them [her children]. Because how could I leave them? For better or worse they need their mother here, even if they're grown. ... This country is made up of immigrants. From the earliest times, immigrants came. ... This country belongs to the whole world. ... I have worked, now I am receiving food stamps, but who cares? I have worked, I have contributed here.

Adela Aguirre: [speaking of Chinese immigrant women at the workshop she attended] The first time ... that I began to notice, that I said that yes, they also feel bad, they also have problems. They also go through what I'm going through, so Adela, what are you complaining about? Yes. That was when I began to get more interested in everything. It was when I began to pay more attention to them. Because I said, I have to learn from them. I have to learn a lot from all my *compañeras*, but even more from them [the Chinese women]. First of all, because they are another, they are another nationality, they have other customs, they have another language. And maybe the nicest thing they made me learn was just that, that I realized that there are people, of whatever origin or whatever nationality that will help you, will motivate you.

Saša Savić: Basically I was raised in a middle-class family in the former Yugoslavia. My father was an officer in the army. So when I finished high school I served in the army, because it was mandatory for everybody to serve for one year. So I did that and coming out of the army there was a lot of political problems in the country. The country was in turmoil; everybody wanted to separate from each other. So since I'm from a mixed marriage—my father is Serbian and my mother Croatian—it was impossible to choose a side and say, "okay, I want to fight in the Serbian army against Croatians or the Croatian army against Serbians." So we decided to elope; my girlfriend at the time and I decided to get married and to try to come to this country. It was very hard to get a visa at the time. ... Because we said we wanted to go there on our honeymoon, we were granted a visitor visa.

Source: Caridad Rios and Adela Aguirre in Kathleen M. Coll, Remaking Citizenship: Latina Immigrants & New American Politics (Stanford: Stanford University Press, 2010).

Thinking Critically

1. **Analyzing Primary Sources**

   What was the historical situation in the home country (Savić) or in the United States (Rios and Aguirre) that made all three want to live their lives in the United States?

2. **Argument Development**

   Defend or refute the following statement: The essential motives, experiences, and expectations of immigrants to the United States have changed very little over the centuries.

AIDS and the Gay Community

In 1980, Acquired Immune Deficiency Syndrome (AIDS) was an unknown disease. In June 1981, the Centers for Disease Control (CDC), the U.S. government's key agency for monitoring the spread of disease, reported AIDS for the first time. Later studies found that AIDS may have infected people in the United States as early as 1969, but only in the 1980s did Americans learn about what would quickly become a terrible new scourge, first identified among gay men.

By May 1982, the *New York Times* carried a story, "New Homosexual Disorder Worries Officials." At first, health officials did not know what the disease was. They were starting to discover that a cluster of symptoms were appearing in certain groups of people, especially homosexual men and intravenous drug users, but it took some time to understand what was happening. The symptoms were terrible: tumors, breathing difficulty, difficult digestion, and eventually, death. By 1984, researchers discovered the infectious agent, the human immunodeficiency virus (HIV), and understood that they were not dealing with a few isolated cases but, rather, a growing worldwide pandemic. In 1985, the CDC recorded 5,600 deaths from AIDS. Three years later, 61,816 had died of AIDS. By then, researchers had also concluded that HIV was spread through contact with bodily fluids, especially but not exclusively through sex or through sharing needles or even blood transfusions that brought the blood of an infected person into contact with another. People with many sexual partners and people who routinely shared needles were especially susceptible. HIV, they also concluded, could not be spread by a hug, by touching the same material, or through the air, but many people panicked and would not come near anyone suspected of carrying the disease.

As HIV-AIDS spread—the CDC confirmed 98,835 cases by 1988—the famous and the unknown were afflicted. The actor Rock Hudson, who often played tough heterosexual male roles but was gay, announced in July 1985 that he had been suffering from AIDS since 1984. Many, including Hudson's good friend Ronald Reagan, were stunned. Hudson died in 1985. Arthur Ashe, a famous tennis star, announced in April 1992 that he had contracted AIDS through a blood transfusion in the mid-1980s, and he died in February 1993. In 1987, a previously unknown teenager, Ryan White, became a national voice for AIDS victims. White, who suffered from hemophilia, had contracted AIDS from blood treatments, but was then ostracized and expelled from school in his hometown of Kokomo, Indiana. He died in April 1990. White's gentle personality made him a hero. In addition to White, Ashe, and Hudson, thousands of other Americans were suffering and dying. In some communities with large groups of gay men, especially San Francisco's Castro district and New York City's Greenwich Village, it seemed as if a whole community was dying, and those who survived spent their time caring for the sick and attending funerals.

As people understood more about the disease, they also turned to the federal government for action. The government could not stop AIDS, but it could fund research that might lead to treatment and cure. The government could also spread information more effectively than any other agency, especially as it became known that using condoms during sex resulted in significantly safer if not completely safe sex and that using sterilized needles and not sharing them offered significant protection for drug users. But the call for government action crashed into the ideology of many of the leading players in the Reagan administration. The president's director of communications, Patrick Buchanan, had once said, "The poor homosexuals. They have declared war on nature and now nature is exacting an awful retribution." Other Reagan supporters, including Secretary of Education William Bennett, may not have agreed with Buchanan, but they strongly opposed supporting condom use. Requests by scientists at the CDC for more research funds were routinely denied.

When the U.S. surgeon general C. Everett Koop, himself very conservative on matters of sex education, decided that it was his duty to get information out to the public on the dangers of AIDS and how to reduce those dangers, he said he realized, "I would have to skate fast on thin ice to get by political appointees who placed conservative ideology over saving lives." After Koop issued his first report, members of the Domestic Policy Council suggested "revisions" that Koop believed would undermine its effectiveness. Only in 1987 did Reagan speak publically about AIDS for the first time. Breaking a silence that had irritated many, including Nancy Reagan, the president called AIDS "public enemy Number One," but he continued to refuse to acknowledge or meet Ryan White or mention condoms until after he left office in 1989.

Across the country, gay and lesbian organizations, especially ACT-UP shown here, demonstrated to demand more funding for research into the causes and cures for AIDS as well as support for immediate help to AIDS victims.

Bettmann/Getty Images

Gay activists became increasingly militant. In the fall of 1987, ACT-UP (AIDS Coalition to Unleash Power) staged a massive demonstration of 500,000 people in New York City. In addition, ACT-UP and other organizations, including the American Foundation for AIDS Research, continued to lobby for better public education, which in the 1990s was very effective. Eventually in 1992, Congress appropriated approximately $2 billion for AIDS research. While no cure or medical prevention has yet been discovered, important advances in the treatment of AIDS came as a result. AIDS had once been a death sentence, but by 2000, many with AIDS were living long and full lives as long as they continued to monitor their treatments carefully. In combining issues of medical science, health, sexuality, and drug use, the AIDS epidemic illustrated a tangle of cultural issues facing the nation as it entered the 1990s.

> ## 28.3 Quick Review
>
> How did cultural—and technological—changes in the United States in the 1980s impact each other and government policy?

Conclusion

Ronald Reagan came to office in 1981 with three key priorities: increase military spending, cut domestic spending and social programs, and cut the federal income tax. During the Reagan administration, all three goals were met. The Republican and the Democratic parties both became more conservative. Many New Deal programs were eliminated or drastically modified, and the combination of tax cuts and military spending increased the national debt.

Reagan and his advisors rejected the idea that federal spending was the best way to stimulate a sluggish economy. Instead, they sought to foster private investment and create new jobs by cutting taxes. Relying on what they called supply-side economics, Reagan drastically reduced both taxes and domestic expenditures. Reagan's initiatives, at first, did very little to improve the nation's economy. During his first term, unemployment, inflation, and the national debt all rose steadily. But, by 1983, the economy seemed to be improving, although the drastic fall in stock value in 1987 and the subsequent savings and loan crisis suggested that the U.S. economy was in trouble again.

Reagan came to office focused on moving beyond the containment policies of his predecessors and destabilizing Communist governments where they existed. The United States also intervened in both overt and covert ways in many countries in the Middle East and Latin America to prevent what they feared might be the spread of communism. Later in his administration, the efforts to build new contacts within Iran and to fund the opposition to the Nicaraguan government led to what was known as the Iran-Contra scandal, which seriously undermined the administration's credibility and foreign policy record. As part of his anticommunism agenda, Reagan also initiated the Strategic Defense Initiative (SDI), or Star Wars, with the intention of destroying any Soviet missiles in space before they could strike the United States. While SDI greatly troubled the Soviets, it was never a viable technology. Surprisingly, given his hard-line stance against communism, Reagan forged a diplomatic relationship with Soviet leader Mikhail Gorbachev. Before he left office, Reagan and Gorbachev had essentially brought the forty-year-long Cold War to an end.

In the 1980s, the culture wars began to dominate American politics as changes in technology and communications brought the world closer together and new forms of music and entertainment, much of it of American origin, dominated the world's culture. At the same time, the religious conservatives of the Christian Coalition were alarmed by liberalizing cultural trends and by the ways that immigration was transforming the country. By the end of the decade, the country had been rocked by the AIDS epidemic, which some tried to ignore but which was, indeed, one of the great public health crises in history.

> ## Chapter Review
>
> How did American culture and politics change during the 1980s with the advent of the Reagan Revolution and so many other changes at the same time?

Chapter 28 Summary and Review

A Rapidly Changing U.S. Government

28.1 Explain Reagan's impact on the United States and the world.

Summary

As an actor and spokesman for General Electric, Ronald Reagan developed his talent for connecting with audiences. That talent proved enormously valuable when Reagan entered politics. Reagan's two terms as governor of California established him as a major player in conservative politics. His victory in the 1980 presidential election was built on a diverse coalition that included three main groups: disaffected working-class whites, antitax and regulation suburbanites, and social conservatives. As president, Reagan had three priorities: increase military spending, cut domestic spending and social programs, and cut the federal income tax. Reagan also pursued staunch antiunion policies as president. Relying on supply-side economics, Reagan argued that tax cuts would actually increase government revenue. Reagan was able to implement much of his tax and spending program, but instead of increasing government revenue, it led to ballooning deficits. An improving economy, a surge in popular patriotism, and Reagan's skill as a campaigner propelled him to a landslide victory in the election of 1984. Much of his second term was dominated by foreign policy. Reagan's foreign policy was shaped by anticommunism and a desire to reduce the threat to the United States posed by nuclear weapons. Both priorities were reflected in Reagan's Strategic Defense Initiative (SDI). The Reagan administration tended to see developments in the Middle East and Latin America through the prism of the Cold War and pursued policies that were meant to counter Soviet expansion and influence. Reagan's efforts to evade legal restrictions on U.S. aid to anticommunism forces in Nicaragua and on the sale of arms to Iran led to the Iran-Contra scandal. The rise of Mikhail Gorbachev to power in the Soviet Union created an opportunity for Reagan to make real progress in nuclear arms reduction. Negotiations between the two leaders resulted in important reductions in intermediate-range nuclear missiles and to the normalization of relations between the United States and the Soviet Union. Running a campaign that embraced the conservative social and economic agenda, George H. W. Bush defeated Democrat Michael Dukakis in the 1988 presidential election.

Review Questions

1. Causation
   Why did working-class whites, a demographic that had traditionally voted Democratic, throw their support behind Reagan at the polls? What caused this important political shift that began in the 1960s?

2. Argument Development
   What was it about Reagan's style and communication that made him so appealing to voters?

The Changing Nature of the American Economy

28.2 Explain internal and international economic developments that shaped the United States.

Summary

By the end of Reagan's second term, some Americans were beginning to have second thoughts about the benefits of tax cuts and deregulation. The immense fortunes accumulated by a small number of individuals inspired both admiration and concern as income inequality increased in the United States. Deregulation contributed to insider trading and the collapse of the savings and loan industry. The cost of such financial malfeasance was born by taxpayers.

Review Question

3. Argument Development
   Why or why not was Reaganomics a successful economic policy?

Changes in the Rest of the Country

28.3 Explain cultural changes in the United States during the 1980s.

Summary

In the 1980s, popular culture took on a global dimension, with American music and musicians playing a dominant role in the new world culture. Technology played a central role in making this development possible. Technology also changed the way that people viewed movies and television. Meanwhile, the religious right led the backlash against the cultural developments of the 1980s and 1990s. In the 1990s, Pat Robertson's Christian Coalition rose to the forefront of the movement and became a powerful player in Republican politics. The late 1900s saw a surge in immigration, largely from Latin America and Asia. Debates about immigration, particularly illegal immigration, intensified and gained new prominence in American politics. During the same decades, America's original inhabitants struggled to maintain their distinct identity and heritage. Some American Indian tribes gained new prosperity as the result of the Indian Gaming Regulatory Act. The emergence of AIDS as a major threat to public health galvanized the gay community.

Under Reagan, the federal government did very little to limit the spread of the disease or to seek treatment options. Aggressive lobbying by AIDS activists, however, led to significant federal involvement starting in 1992 and to important progress in combating AIDS.

Review Questions

4. Causation

What role did technology play in the spread of American popular culture around the world in the 1980s?

5. Continuity and Change over Time

How did the Christian Coalition help change the identity of the Republican Party?

1. Preparing to Write: Plan Your Argument

Long Essay Question—Evaluate the extent of change in U.S. Cold War foreign policy during the period 1945 to 1989.

Design a time line that runs from 1945 to 1989. Below the time line, note what is constant in this period. Above the time line, track how the general U.S. policy looks different under different presidencies. You will not be able to discuss every

president. Instead, consider anchoring this discussion in three presidents: Truman, Nixon, and Reagan. As you note the differences, be sure to explain why the policy changes. From here, you can develop a thesis statement and an outline of the rest of your argument. In your topic sentences, address the featured history reasoning skill, in this case, "Continuity and Change over Time."

2. Preparing to Write: Establish Context in Your Introduction

Long Essay Question—Evaluate the extent to which there were similar causes for immigration to the United States in the late 1800s/early 1900s and the late 1900s.

Recall that when a question asks you to "evaluate the extent" of similarities, it is implied that you can discuss differences. After you develop a thesis, think about how you can establish context to open your essay. A brief discussion about the pull of the American dream that runs across generations? However you begin, establish that context in the first few sentences of your introduction, and then finish with your thesis.

Chapter 29
A New World Order
1989–2001

Greg Gibson/AP Images

Bill Clinton, here surrounded by an enthusiastic crowd of supporters, was enormously effective as a political campaigner.

Chapter Objective

Demonstrate an understanding of the changes in the United States as the threat of communism ended, new foreign problems arose, and new economic and technological issues shaped the country.

∨ Learning Objectives

The First Bush Administration, 1989–1993
29.1 Explain the New World Order that George Bush described.

The Clinton Presidency
29.2 Analyze the impact of the Clinton presidency and the Clinton–Gingrich conflict on the country.

Technology Dominates an Era
29.3 Analyze the changes in technology and their impact on U.S. culture.

Beyond Clinton—The Coming of George W. Bush
29.4 Explain the 2000 election results and the initial domestic agenda of the new administration.

At the Berlin Wall, which had divided the city for almost thirty years, people from east and west greeted each other and celebrated a new freedom.

Oliver Gerhard/imageBROKER/Alamy Stock Photo

On Inauguration Day, January 20, 1989, as Ronald Reagan left the White House, the nation was prosperous, his loyal vice president was replacing him, and perhaps even more significant, the long Cold War with the Soviet Union seemed to be coming to an end. George H. W. Bush would lead the nation in a very different international context from any predecessor since World War II. In April 1989, just after Bush's inauguration, the Communist government of Poland, with Gorbachev's permission, legalized the prodemocracy Solidarity and agreed to free elections. In June, for the first time in history, a Communist government was voted out of office and yielded power peacefully to its non-Communist successor. That fall, Hungary followed the same course and ousted its Communist government. Demonstrations in East Germany led to a change in leadership, and on November 9, the Berlin Wall that had divided the city, and Europe, for almost thirty years came down. With the fall of the Berlin Wall, Berliners who had never met each other embraced and celebrated. Leaders of East and West Germany talked of unification, which came two years later. In December, Czechoslovakia inaugurated a non-Communist government.

What had begun as a conversation between two leaders in a house in Iceland in 1986 had become, by 1989, what the new president called "a new world order." The end of the Cold War drastically changed U.S. foreign policy and allowed people to see the world differently. At the same time, rapid advances in technology changed the lives of almost every American. Tracing the changes in U.S. foreign policy and politics in the post–Cold War world as well as the domestic changes, especially those brought about by technology in the decade after the Cold War ended, is the initial focus of this chapter.

In spite of George H. W. Bush's considerable success with foreign policy, he ran into difficulty on the domestic front. In 1992, he was replaced by William J. (Bill) Clinton who, in spite of several problems of his own, managed to serve a full two terms and leave the economy much better than he found it. Nevertheless, in 2000, the nation turned again to a Republican, the former president's son, George W. Bush, who launched his own domestic agenda before having his administration overtaken by international issues.

Tiananmen Square

Prodemocracy demonstrations involving thousands of young Chinese students.

The First Bush Administration, 1989–1993

29.1 Explain the New World Order that George Bush described.

Few people came to the White House as well prepared to manage the rapid changes in the international situation as George H. W. Bush. As a former U.S. ambassador to China, former head of the CIA, and former vice president, he knew the key players and understood the context of events as well as anyone. Unlike his predecessor, Bush came to office with a prime interest in foreign policy. It was an expertise that might serve him well in the rapidly changing world of the 1990s. The United States was also changing, economically and technologically, but President Bush was less prepared to deal with some of the rapid domestic changes that were taking place, which in the end cost him a second term in office.

Foreign Policy between 1989 and 1993

Bush and his foreign policy team—Secretary of State James Baker, Secretary of Defense Richard Cheney, National Security Advisor Brent Scowcroft (a retired air force general), and Joint Chiefs of Staff Chair General Colin Powell—were initially skeptical of the agreements by which Reagan and Gorbachev had sought to end the Cold War, and they did not propose to reduce defense spending. However, the pace of international developments only accelerated after Bush took office. Bush maintained a hands-off policy toward the dissolution of Soviet control in Eastern Europe. He said that the United States did not want to "poke a stick in the eyes of Mr. Gorbachev." But he insisted, in spite of pleas by Gorbachev and European leaders, that Germany had the right to be united and that the new nation should be part of NATO. Bush showed less inclination to state a position when Lithuania declared independence in March 1990, leaving it to the Lithuanians and the Soviets to work out the terms of their own agreement.

While Gorbachev and Bush got to know each other, Gorbachev's own hold on power weakened. Hardliners within the Kremlin blamed Gorbachev for weak leadership as Soviet control of Eastern Europe ended. In August 1991, old-line Communists staged a military coup and arrested Gorbachev. Boris Yeltsin, the president of the Russian Republic, the largest and most powerful of the fifteen Soviet Republics that made up the Soviet Union (or Union of Soviet Socialist Republics, the U.S.S.R.), helped defeat the coup leaders, and Gorbachev was freed and restored to power within days. However, the restoration was short lived. In December 1991, Gorbachev announced that the Union of Soviet Socialist Republics, which had governed Russia and its neighbors since 1917, was no more. Former Soviet Republics savored their independence. Gorbachev's position simply disappeared. At the Kremlin, the red hammer and sickle flag was replaced with the blue flag of the Russian Republic. The prime enemy of the United States through forty-five years of Cold War had simply disappeared (see Map 29-1).

While Eastern Europe went through its dramatic changes, the other Communist giant, China, was also changing. As a former ambassador to China, Bush thought he knew the country well and wanted to build closer ties. But he was taken by complete surprise in the spring of 1989, when Chinese students gathered in **Tiananmen Square** in the heart of China's capital, Beijing, to protest the Communist Party's tight hold and to demand more democratic governance and greater individual freedom. Such protests were unheard of in Communist China. By May, as protests had spread to two hundred other Chinese cities, the government declared martial law and then in June sent tanks and army units into Tiananmen Square, killing perhaps three thousand students and injuring three times as many. The Communist government of China was not about to follow Russia's peaceful transition to a different social system. The world, including President Bush, was horrified. For the rest of his term, Bush was torn about whether to join other nations in protest or seek to maintain and expand ties with China. The result was an unclear and inconsistent China policy.

In August 1990, the Bush foreign policy team was confronted by another surprising crisis in yet another part of the world. On August 1, Iraqi dictator Saddam Hussein ordered an attack on Iraq's smaller neighbor, Kuwait, and quickly took control of the country. Kuwait had been part of Iraq until 1961, and Hussein insisted he was simply reuniting what should

29.1

29.2

29.3

29.4

Map 29-1 Europe after Communism.

The map of Europe was radically rearranged after the Soviet Union broke apart in 1991 into independent republics and the nations of Eastern Europe claimed their independence from Russian domination.

never have been divided. The U.S. ambassador to Iraq, April Glaspie, had told Hussein that the United States had "no opinion" on Iraq's border dispute with Kuwait, but she never meant that statement to mean the United States would allow Iraq to swallow its neighbor. Both Iraq and Kuwait were among the world's largest oil producers, and Iraqi control of Kuwait meant that an Iraqi dictator, whom the United States did not trust, was in control of 20 percent of the world's oil.

Bush announced, "This will not stand." The United States negotiated with Hussein but also began military planning. Bush gained the support of Syria, Egypt, and Saudi Arabia in insisting that Iraq must leave Kuwait. In November, the UN Security Council authorized the use of force if negotiations did not succeed. While there was significant opposition in the United States to any intervention, negotiations faltered and Congress authorized the use of force, though in the Senate the vote was a close 52–47.

On January 17, 1991, the U.S.-led **Operation Desert Storm** began. An air war showered missiles and bombs on the Iraqi forces in Kuwait and destroyed communications

Operation Desert Storm

Code name for the successful offensive against Iraq by the United States and its allies in the 1991 Persian Gulf War.

In a very short war in early 1991, U.S. troops landed in Kuwait and quickly secured its independence from Iraq.

Patrick Downs/AP Images

and electrical systems in Iraq. On February 24, U.S. Marines from bases in Saudi Arabia landed in Kuwait and in one hundred hours of battle drove the Iraqi forces out of the country. Kuwait was reestablished as an independent country and a close U.S. ally. Fearing unnecessary carnage and not wanting a U.S. occupation of Iraq proper, Bush then halted all military operations. The war was over. It seemed an easy military victory, but it was not without costs.

Within Iraq, rebellions broke out against Hussein's rule. While Bush hoped they would succeed, he was not willing to intervene. He did, however, take action to protect the Kurdish minority in a new autonomous region within northern Iraq, announcing a "no fly zone" in which the United States would shoot down any Iraqi planes over that area, but opposition forces in the rest of the country, expecting U.S. aid that never came, were slaughtered by Hussein's troops. A U.S. boycott of Iraq led to widespread suffering within the country. Finally, the staging of U.S. troops in Saudi Arabia, site of the holiest places in the Muslim world, stirred anger among devout Muslims who hated the idea of non-Muslims in that region. Among those who were angry was Osama bin Laden, a Saudi who founded al-Qaeda, a terrorist organization, to retaliate against both Saudi Arabia and the United States.

Meanwhile, closer to home, Panama's dictator, Manuel Noriega, had received CIA support to oppose Communists in the region, but he had also gotten rich through drug trafficking and had become a brutal dictator. When his party lost a presidential election in May 1989, Noriega annulled the election. Knowing that the Carter-era treaty meant that the Panama Canal was going to be returned to Panama, Bush took no chances. On December 20, a U.S. assault team landed in Panama and took control of the country. They restored the democratically elected president of Panama, Guillermo Endara, and eventually arrested Noriega as a drug dealer and imprisoned him in Florida.

The Bush team also made other international efforts that had mixed results. The administration negotiated a **North American Free Trade Agreement (NAFTA)**, which would eliminate tariffs between the United States and Canada and Mexico, but Senate confirmation of the treaty was slow in coming. When Somalia, a nation in northeast Africa, was threatened by famine and chaos, the United States sent twenty-eight thousand peacekeeping troops but could not effect large-scale changes. To the surprise of many of its own citizens, Yugoslavia, which had been relatively stable since the end of World War II, disintegrated into ethnic hostility between its Eastern Orthodox Serbian, Roman Catholic Croatian, and Bosnian Muslim communities. In response to the new crisis in Yugoslavia, the United States supported a UN peacekeeping mission, which was ineffective, and an arms embargo. Even with the Cold War over, the world remained a confusing and dangerous place.

North American Free Trade Agreement (NAFTA)

Agreement reached in 1993 by Canada, Mexico, and the United States to substantially reduce barriers to trade.

Education, Legislation, and the Supreme Court

In his inaugural address, George Bush angered the outgoing Ronald Reagan by saying that it was time "to make kinder the face of the Nation and gentler the face of the world." He also continued the Reagan assault on big government, insisting that the new "kindness" must come from a "thousand points of light," emerging from local nongovernmental groups around the country rather than from federal government programs.

Bush called himself an "education president." Where Reagan sought to abolish the Department of Education, Bush convened the nation's governors at an "Education Summit" in Charlottesville, Virginia, in the fall of 1989. The plan that emerged from Bush's partnership with the governors, who were led by Arkansas governor Bill Clinton, was called America 2000. It sought to improve the nation's schools by setting new national standards for all students.

Bush also supported two other pieces of legislation that would have far-reaching results. He supported the **Clean Air Act**, which toughened air quality standards and pollution controls. It would put into effect huge changes in industry and begin to shift more attention to environmental issues. He also led the fight for the **Americans with Disabilities Act (ADA)**, which passed Congress in 1990. The ADA outlawed discrimination in employment, public services, and public accommodations for people with disabilities. It not only transformed the face of American buildings, which now had to provide wheelchair ramps, elevators, and appropriate lavatories for those with physical disabilities, but also put in motion changes in hiring practices and services that would benefit all those with disabilities.

Bush's first appointment to the Supreme Court, David Souter, drew little controversy. Souter turned out to be a more liberal judge than many expected, probably including Bush, especially when he voted to affirm the Court's *Roe v. Wade* decision in 1992. When Thurgood Marshall retired, Bush stirred considerable controversy by nominating Clarence Thomas. Thomas, like Marshall, was an African American, but while Marshall had been known as "Mr. Civil Rights" and was probably the most liberal member of the Court in many years, Thomas was known as an unusually conservative Republican. In his confirmation hearings, Thomas was accused of sexual harassment by Anita Hill, a black law professor and former member of Thomas's staff. Hill offered explicit testimony as to what Thomas had said and done, which was highly embarrassing to Thomas and his supporters. Hill was attacked in turn by conservatives, and Thomas called the assault a "high-tech lynching for uppity blacks," but when he was confirmed by the narrowest of Senate votes, 52 to 48, many women concluded that the male senators did not take sexual harassment seriously.

Clean Air Act

Passed by Congress in 1990 as amendments to an earlier act; required substantial restrictions on air pollution.

Americans with Disabilities Act (ADA)

Legislation that significantly expanded physical access and improved legal options for people with disabilities.

Joe Marquette/AP Images

The Supreme Court's 1973 *Roe v. Wade* decision, stating that the right to privacy guaranteed in the Constitution protects a woman's right to choose an abortion, remained controversial and impacted American politics for decades to come, most of all in terms of the appointment of every new Supreme Court justice.

While Thomas took his seat on the Court, more women ran for and won elective office the following year than in any previous time, increasing their numbers in the Senate, the House, and state legislatures.

Race: From Rodney King to O. J. Simpson

In March 1991, Rodney King, an African American, failed to stop for police on the Foothill Freeway near San Fernando, California. Los Angeles Police Department (LAPD) officers gave chase for eight miles and finally arrested King. When King resisted arrest, four police officers beat him as he lay on the ground. A nearby resident used a home video camera to record the arrest and beating, and the video was quickly distributed around the nation. People were outraged. Although King had resisted arrest, the officers had continued to beat him long after he was subdued.

The four officers on the video were arrested. Their attorneys argued that they could not get a fair trial in Los Angeles and the trial was moved to the suburban city of Simi Valley, thirty miles from Los Angeles. The result was that the officers faced a mostly white jury, likely to be more friendly to them than any in Los Angeles County. In April 1992, the jury found three of the officers not guilty and deadlocked on the fourth. The acquittal released pent-up anger in the black community in Los Angeles. Riots lasting four days resulted in 53 deaths, 2,300 injuries, and $1 billion in property damage. Black and Latino rioters targeted whites and Asians in their neighborhoods, perhaps especially Korean store owners. A video from the riot showed a white truck driver being pulled out of his cab and beaten. Only the intervention of other blacks, who got the driver to a hospital, saved his life. For many, the arrest of King, the trial, and the riot that followed illustrated just how deeply lines were still drawn between races in the United States in the 1990s.

While the events around King got the headlines, scholars and activists debated the state of race relations. Some observed that despite what happened, much had changed since the 1950s when blacks were legally barred from white schools, white bus seats, and all-white polling places in many parts of the country. Orlando Patterson, a Harvard sociologist, wrote, "Relations between ordinary Afro-Americans and Euro-Americans are, in fact, the best they have ever been, although still far from ideal." Other scholars were less sure, noting that events like the beating of Rodney King and data about the educational experience of many black and Latino students confirmed that much had not changed. Andrew Hacker, a political scientist, wrote that "a huge racial chasm remains, and there are few signs that the coming century will see it closed."

In 1994, another trial illustrated the depth of the racial divide. O. J. Simpson, a celebrated African American Hall of Fame former football star, was arrested in June after his former wife, Nicole Brown, who was white, and her white friend Ron Goldman were found stabbed to death just outside her condominium in an exclusive neighborhood of Los Angeles. The evidence against Simpson seemed strong, but black and white Americans saw it differently. In one poll, 63 percent of whites thought he would get a fair trial, while 69 percent of blacks thought he would not. The trial was a media circus. Simpson's lead attorney, Johnnie Cochran, a tough African American trial lawyer, proved that the investigation of Simpson by the Los Angeles police was filled with racist assumptions, although he did not prove Simpson's innocence. When in October 1995 a jury acquitted Simpson of the murder charge, a majority of blacks agreed with the verdict. Most whites were stunned. Regardless of whoever killed Brown and Goldman, the Simpson trial showed that Americans of different races were deeply divided in how they viewed the criminal justice system in the 1990s.

Economic Troubles and the Election of 1992

Bush's greatest political failure was his inability to manage the U.S. economy. After 1990, the economy went into a serious recession. During 1991 and 1992, AT&T fired 100,000 workers, GM fired 74,000, and two major airlines, Pan Am and Eastern, went bankrupt, throwing more out of work. People blamed the president. Bush seemed out of touch, a perception that did not help his political standing.

Bush's economic problems became an even worse political liability when he decided, in the face of the rapidly increasing government debt, that he needed to raise taxes in spite

29.1

29.2

29.3

29.4

Wally McNamee/Corbis Historical/Getty Images

President Bush, future president Clinton, and independent candidate Ross Perot debated in the lively 1992 presidential campaign.

of his promise not to do so. When the top tax bracket was increased from 28 to 31.5 percent, the *New York Post* headline said, "Read my lips: I lied." Conservative Republicans never forgave Bush.

With the Republican Party in not-quite-open revolt and the nation's economy in trouble, Democrats smelled victory in the 1992 election. Arkansas governor Bill Clinton soon emerged as a Democratic front-runner. When Clinton lost the New Hampshire Primary, he called himself the "comeback kid," and campaigned harder than ever. Clinton grew up in poverty but excelled in school and won scholarships to Georgetown University, was awarded a Rhodes scholarship to Oxford, and then went on to Yale Law School. At Yale, he also met and married fellow student Hillary Rodham. He was charismatic on the campaign trail. As one of the founders of the Democratic Leadership Council, he was a moderate who distanced himself from his party's more liberal members. Clinton also had his weaknesses. The explanations he gave for his rumored womanizing, draft dodging, and one-time marijuana smoking were never convincing and he earned the name "Slick Willie." But he was a tough campaigner who would not quit. He won the Democratic nomination, asked Tennessee senator Al Gore, a fellow baby boomer, to be his running mate, and kept his campaign focused. A sign in the Clinton campaign headquarters reading "It's the economy, stupid" said it all.

An independent candidate also entered the race, eccentric billionaire H. Ross Perot. Perot described the deficit as being "like a crazy aunt we keep down in the basement. All the neighbors know she's there but nobody wants to talk about her." He said that Bush's NAFTA treaty would produce a "giant sucking sound" of American jobs leaving the country. Although given virtually no chance of winning, Perot was the most popular third-party candidate in many years.

Bush was challenged for the Republican nomination by conservative commentator Pat Buchanan, known as the "pit bull of the Right." Bush easily defeated Buchanan for the nomination, but the attack weakened the president. The conservative dominance of the 1992 Republican convention, especially the vocal role of religious conservatives like Buchanan, alienated moderate voters. Throughout the fall campaign, the president seemed disengaged. It was not a close contest. Clinton won almost forty-five million votes to Bush's thirty-nine million. Surprisingly, Perot won almost twenty million votes, hurting Bush more than Clinton. Democrats retained control of the Senate 57 to 43 and the House 258 to 176.

29.1

29.2

29.3

29.4

29.1 Quick Review

How did the nation's foreign and domestic policy evolve over the course of George H. W. Bush's presidency?

The Clinton Presidency

29.2 **Analyze the impact of the Clinton presidency and the Clinton–Gingrich conflict on the country.**

Clinton came to office with high hopes. He idolized John F. Kennedy and wanted to be remembered as another Kennedy. Clinton, the first baby boomer president, replaced Bush, the last of eight presidents who had served in World War II. He saw his coming to office as a generational change and told the country, "Today, a generation raised in the shadows of the Cold War assumes new responsibilities." He set an activist agenda, saying, "We must invest more in our own people, in their jobs, in their future, and at the same time cut our massive debt." Clinton did cut the federal deficit, dramatically. Success on other fronts, however, was more elusive.

The Early Clinton Agenda: It's Still—Mostly—the Economy

Clinton knew that he owed his election to the poor state of the nation's economy and that he would be reelected in 1996 only if the economic picture brightened. Having campaigned as a moderate Democrat, he surprised many when he made health-care reform his first major policy initiative. Clinton, however, was convinced that reforming the nation's chaotic health insurance system would provide a significant jolt to the economy and that providing insurance for the thirty-five million Americans who had no insurance would help close the growing gap between rich and poor.

In spite of personal tensions in their marriage, Bill and Hillary Clinton were a close political team, sometimes compared with Franklin and Eleanor Roosevelt. The president appointed his wife, along with trusted associate Ira Magaziner, to lead a task force to redesign the nation's health-care system. Unfortunately, the Clinton-Magaziner team made two significant errors. First, their final 1,342-page report was too long and far too complicated. Second, while they consulted hundreds of experts in developing the report, they failed to consult with Congress. In 1993, Clinton said, "If I don't get health care, I'll wish I didn't run for President." In the end, he did not get it. Conservatives in the Republican minority, led by Congressman Newt Gingrich from Georgia, attacked the plan. Representatives of physicians and the insurance industry criticized the plan with TV ads and heavily financed congressional lobbying. Without strong support from a large segment of the population or the Democratic majority in Congress, the plan was doomed. In August 1994, the president announced that he was dropping the plan. It had not yet reached a single vote in Congress.

Other issues also made life difficult for Clinton. When Clinton tried to fire longtime staff members of the White House travel office for alleged improprieties, he was blocked and accused of trying to give those jobs to friends. When he tried to fulfill a campaign promise to end the ban on gay men and lesbians serving in the armed forces, he was blocked again. The resulting compromise of "Don't ask, don't tell," in which officers would not ask about sexual orientation and soldiers and sailors would keep their sexual orientation hidden or face discharge, satisfied no one.

Only weeks into the new presidency, Clinton's administration had to handle an unexpected confrontation. In Waco, Texas, cult members led by David Koresh had blockaded themselves in their group's compound. A gun battle with agents of the FBI and Bureau of Alcohol, Tobacco, and Firearms on February 28 led to a seven-week stand-off. When the FBI became convinced that children in the compound were being abused, they attacked. Koresh

29.1

29.2

29.3

29.4

ordered the compound burned, and he and more than eighty of his followers, including twenty-one children, were killed. It was a horrible outcome that brought significant criticism of the administration and especially of Janet Reno, the new attorney general who had approved the raid.

Clinton had more success on other fronts. Within two weeks of taking office, he signed the Family and Medical Leave Act, which Bush had vetoed twice. The law guaranteed up to twelve weeks of unpaid leave for family medical emergencies and pregnancy. In his campaign, he had promised to develop a national service plan, and Congress quickly approved Clinton's AmeriCorps, which encouraged volunteerism and promised financial support for college costs to those who gave a year of national service. In September 1994, the first twenty thousand AmeriCorps volunteers were sworn in. Congress also authorized $2 billion for **Goals 2000**, the Clinton version of Bush's America 2000 education plan to set national educational standards in core academic subjects. In addition, Congress approved a modest ban on semiautomatic assault weapons and a "Freedom of Access to Clinic Entrances Act" that required antiabortion protesters to keep some distance from medical clinics or places of worship. During his first two years, the Senate confirmed two of Clinton's Supreme Court nominees, Ruth Bader Ginsburg and Stephen Breyer. With their confirmation, the Court's conservative drift seemed to stop.

In addition, Clinton was convinced that the huge deficit, which had grown substantially under Reagan and Bush, was creating a drag on the American economy. He was also anxious to establish his political credentials as a moderate. In August 1993, less than seven months into office and with the health-care bill still pending, Congress passed Clinton's first budget. The budget infuriated conservatives because it included a tax increase, and it infuriated liberals because it did little for federal programs. The administration's goal was simple: balance the federal budget and lower the federal debt. Clinton succeeded, and during his term in office, the total federal spending as a share of the U.S. gross domestic product dropped from 21.5 percent to 19.1 percent. Starting in 1998, real surpluses allowed a major reduction in the federal debt.

Immediately after the Clinton's budget passed Congress, he turned his attention to getting congressional approval of the North American Free Trade Agreement (NAFTA), which had been negotiated by George Bush. Few gave NAFTA much chance for approval. Labor unions hated the treaty because it proposed to reduce all trade barriers between the United States, Canada, and Mexico, and the unions feared it would cost jobs. Ross Perot had based his third-party campaign on opposition to NAFTA and had succeeded in winning 19 percent of the vote. Nevertheless, Clinton believed that free trade and the development of an unfettered global economy was the key to long-term prosperity. Many economists agreed, believing that, in a global economy, most forms of protectionism hurt everyone and free and open trading arrangements bolstered commerce and eventually everyone's well-being. Clinton allied with Republicans in Congress, and against some of his closest Democratic allies, to get the treaty passed, and he signed it in December 1993.

As a moderate, Clinton sought to undercut Republican efforts to differentiate themselves from him, which Republicans found infuriating. Under the leadership of a Georgia congressman, Newt Gingrich, and Dick Armey and Tom DeLay of Texas, House Republicans planned for the 1994 midterm elections. The House of Representatives had enjoyed a Democratic majority and a Democratic Speaker for sixty of the sixty-four years between 1930 and 1994. While the Senate and the White House changed hands, the House seemed permanently Democratic. But a new generation of representatives, coming mostly from suburban districts, especially in the South, where there had been few Republicans elected until the 1970s, were determined to create a Republican majority in the Congress and enact their agenda. They were very successful. In November 1994, thirty-four Democrats were defeated in their bids for reelection, a new Republican majority took control, and Gingrich became the Speaker of the House.

"The Era of Big Government Is Over"

With the new Republican majority and Newt Gingrich as the new Speaker coming to power at the end of Clinton's second year in office, the chance for significant legislative victories

Goals 2000
Legislation that set tough new goals over the coming decades to improve the quality of American schooling.

Not all Americans supported the NAFTA trade agreement. Many feared it would cost a significant number of jobs in the United States.

Jim West/Alamy Stock Photo

for Clinton virtually disappeared. Clinton would spend much of the next six years either trying to hold on to past Democratic victories or doing what he and his closest political advisor, Dick Morris, called "triangulating," finding a third point between increasingly conservative Republicans and increasingly liberal Democrats to stake out their own position, one that sometimes undercut both.

The biggest battle between the Clinton administration and the Gingrich Republicans came in late 1995, only months into the tenure of the new Congress. After several months of budget battles, Congress passed a budget that included cuts in social programs. Clinton vetoed the budget with the result that the government was briefly without a budget, forcing a partial government shutdown for six days in November. After temporary legislation reopened government offices, the Republican House passed a budget with even further cuts, reducing funds for food stamps, Medicare, and other domestic program. Republican leaders proudly announced, "This is a fundamental change in the direction of government." Clinton again vetoed the budget, and on December 16, the government shut down for twenty-one days. Federal employees went without their paychecks; national parks and "nonessential" government offices closed. Only in January was a compromise reached that restored most of the cuts. Most political observers thought Clinton had won the battle, painting Gingrich as an extremist.

In the context of this tense budget debate, Clinton went to Congress in January 1996 to give his annual State of the Union message. He announced, "The era of Big Government is

American Voices

Republican "Contract with America," 1994

Contests for seats in the U.S. House of Representatives are traditionally local. In the 1994 campaign, however, 337 Republican candidates endorsed a common platform in a dramatic ceremony on the Capitol steps. Their "Contract with America" represented the voice of conservative Americans.

As Republican Members of the House of Representatives and as citizens seeking to join that body we propose not just to change its policies, but even more important, to restore the bonds of trust between the people and their elected representatives. ...

Thereafter, within the first 100 days of the 104th Congress, we shall bring to the House Floor the following bills, each to be given full and open debate, each to be given a clear and fair vote and each to be immediately available this day for public inspection and scrutiny.

1. **THE FISCAL RESPONSIBILITY ACT:** A balanced budget/tax limitation amendment. ...

2. **THE TAKING BACK OUR STREETS ACT:** An anticrime package including stronger truth-in-sentencing ... and cuts in social spending from this summer's "crime" bill to fund prison construction and additional law enforcement. ...

3. **THE PERSONAL RESPONSIBILITY ACT:** ... cut spending for welfare programs, and enact a tough two-years-and-out provision with work requirements to promote individual responsibility.

4. **THE FAMILY REINFORCEMENT ACT:** Child support enforcement, tax incentives for adoption, strengthening rights of parents in their children's education ... to reinforce the central role of families in American society.

5. **THE AMERICAN DREAM RESTORATION ACT:** A $500 per child tax credit... [and] provide middle class tax relief.

6. **THE NATIONAL SECURITY RESTORATION ACT:** No U.S. troops under U.N. command... strengthen our national defense and maintain our credibility around the world.

7. **THE SENIOR CITIZENS FAIRNESS ACT:** Raise the Social Security earnings limit. ...

8. **THE JOB CREATION AND WAGE ENHANCEMENT ACT:** Small business incentives, capital gains cut and indexation... , to create jobs and raise worker wages.

9. **THE COMMON SENSE LEGAL REFORM ACT:**... Stem the endless tide of litigation.

10. **THE CITIZEN LEGISLATURE ACT:** A first-ever vote on term limits.

Source: Downloaded from http://www.nationalcenter.org/ ContractwithAmerica.html, August 2, 2011.

Thinking Critically

1. **Comparison**
   What fundamental principles and assumptions link the ten initiatives included in the contract? How do you trace their roots in U.S. history?

2. **Analyzing Primary Sources**
   To which audiences was the contract meant to appeal? Which audiences were most likely to find it objectionable?

29.1

29.2

29.3

29.4

Denis Paquin/AP Images

Backed by 337 Republican candidates for Congress, then Republican minority leader Newt Gingrich announced a unified campaign platform, a "Contract with America," on which all would campaign for election to the House of Representatives in the 1994 elections. The result was the election of a Republican majority that made Gingrich the first Republican Speaker of the House in decades.

over." Many Democrats wondered who had really won the budget showdown. Clinton had already promised that one of his major policy goals for 1996 was to "put an end to welfare as we know it." After vetoing more conservative legislation, in August 1996, Clinton signed a bill that replaced the federal government's long-standing Aid to Families with Dependent Children (AFDC) program with temporary assistance that prevented most people, except the disabled, from receiving more than two years of assistance, with a five-year lifetime maximum. New York senator Daniel Moynihan called the result, which dropped millions from eligibility, the "most brutal act of social policy since Reconstruction." Fortunately, the economy was experiencing a boom time when the law was passed; the minimum wage was raised, and there were jobs to be found, at least in the short run. The long-term cost to some of the nation's poorest people was a different matter.

Clinton took other positions that disappointed liberals. He signed the **Defense of Marriage Act**, which said no state was required to recognize a same-sex marriage from another state. Since no state yet allowed same-sex marriage when the law passed, it was a symbolic move, but for gay and lesbian voters who had supported Clinton, it was a frustrating limitation that would have a greater impact in future years.

In spite of the Republican gains in the 1994 elections, the 1996 presidential election was seldom in doubt. The Republicans nominated Senator Robert Dole, a decorated World War II hero and a longtime Washington insider who preferred compromise to Gingrich-style conflict. Dole had a good sense of humor but was not a strong campaigner. Clinton adopted many Republican issues and campaigned energetically. Clinton's fund-raising ability meant that the two parties were closely matched in funds, whereas Republicans had traditionally outspent Democrats by a two-to-one margin. Perot again ran as an outsider. Clinton won

Defense of Marriage Act

Legislation that required the federal government to ignore provisions of any state act recognizing same-sex marriages; was declared unconstitutional by the U.S. Supreme Court in 2013.

49 percent of the vote to Dole's 40 percent. Perot's vote dropped to less than 9 percent. Clinton coasted to a second term, but with Republican majorities in both houses of Congress.

In the post–Cold War era, other trends were reshaping the American political scene. By the 1990s, the majority of Americans lived in suburbs, up from only a quarter of the population in the 1950s. The combination of suburbanization and the Voting Rights Act typically led to the nation's urban centers electing liberal Democrats, often African Americans or Latinos who reflected their district's majority, and the surrounding suburbs electing white conservatives who reflected those districts. State legislatures often drew district lines in ways that virtually assured Republican control of some congressional districts and Democratic control of others. Especially in the South and West, Republican victories often came at the cost of moderates of either party, with the result that, as the Republican Party got more conservative, the Democratic Party got more liberal.

Since 1900, if not earlier, the Republican Party represented the elite—major corporate executives, Wall Street investors, and small-town business leaders. The Democrats were the party of the working class, especially union members. The New Deal Coalition, which had kept Congress solidly Democratic for so long, included union members, urban immigrants (especially the Irish), and the white South. During the New Deal, most African American voters, who had traditionally been Republicans, shifted to the Democratic Party. However, by the time Clinton came to office, much had changed. Many white Southerners had turned against the Civil Rights Movement, which they associated with the Democrats, and had become Republicans. Many white workers in the North, especially those in ethnic enclaves, were making the same transition for the same reason. In addition, union membership had fallen to below 10 percent of nongovernment workers, reducing the impact of unions in elections and the union vote. At the same time, more and more middle- and upper-middle-class professionals, including teachers, journalists, lawyers, and many in high-tech industries, supported the more liberal policies of the Democrats. In contrast to either 1930 or 1960, when if one knew a person's income, one could make a good guess as to his or her political party preference, no such guess was possible in 1990.

As the political divisions between the two parties grew sharper, the political discourse of the country grew more caustic. Angry talk radio shows drew huge audiences. Rush Limbaugh, who called women activists "feminazis" and environmentalists "environmental wackos," drew an audience of twenty million. The National Rifle Association stridently attacked any politician of either party who voted for any gun control. Common Cause sought to speak for a liberal perspective. Few spoke for moderation or even good manners. Respectful differences did not sell radio advertising. Likewise, respecting differences did not win political debates in Washington in the 1990s.

Small Wars and Dangerous Terrorists— Clinton's Foreign Policy

Clinton once said, "Foreign policy is not what I came here to do." Nevertheless, as president, he could not ignore the rest of the world. His proudest foreign policy accomplishment came early, with the passage of NAFTA, but it was far from his last foreign engagement.

Early in his first term, in September 1993, Israeli prime minister Yitzhak Rabin and Palestine Liberation Organization (PLO) leader Yasser Arafat shook hands in the White House after signing the **Oslo Accords**, which Norway had helped to broker. The Oslo agreement led to a suspension of the *intifada*, the Palestinian uprising that had been going on since 1987. The PLO recognized Israel's right to exist and renounced terrorism, while Israel agreed that the PLO would assume governing authority in parts of the West Bank and Gaza Strip. It was an optimistic moment for peace in the Middle East that ended all too soon when an outraged Israeli assassinated Rabin.

In 1993, events in Somalia and Haiti demanded attention. Bush had initially sent troops to Somalia to help secure peace in that war-torn region of Africa, and Clinton authorized 440 elite troops. When American troops sought to capture a warlord who had ordered the killing of Pakistani UN troops, two U.S. Black Hawk helicopters were shot down in Mogadishu and eighteen Americans were killed; the body of one was dragged through the streets

Oslo Accords

A 1993 agreement between Israel and the Palestine Liberation Organization (PLO) in which Israel agreed that the PLO could govern the West Bank and Gaza Strip in exchange for PLO recognition of Israel's right to exist.

of the city. Clinton immediately withdrew all Americans. In Haiti, when demonstrators blocked the landing of U.S. peacekeepers in Haiti, Clinton did not persist, in spite of his desire to support the democratically elected president Jean-Bertrand Aristide.

In light of experiences in Somalia and Haiti, Clinton took an even more cautious stand in Rwanda when civil war broke out in April 1994. For one hundred days, Hutus butchered perhaps 800,000 Tutsi and moderate Hutus who had tried to stop the genocide. The United States and the world did virtually nothing, although perhaps 70 percent of the Tutsi population was killed. After he left office, Clinton said that his failure to act in Rwanda was his greatest regret, but there was little support for intervention in 1994.

At the same time, the former Yugoslavia was continuing to come apart. Slobodan Milošević, the nationalist leader of Serbia, wanted to create a new "pure" Serbian nation. He led a slaughter in which perhaps 200,000 Bosnian Muslims were killed by Bosnian and Serbian nationalists. Some 6,000 UN peacekeepers were held as virtual prisoners while the slaughter went on (see Map 29-2).

While the United States and most of Europe did nothing, the battle continued. Finally, in the summer of 1995, Clinton ordered the bombing of Serbian positions. When in July 1995 Serbia forced forty thousand Muslim refugees out of a UN safe area around Srebrenica, and then murdered some seven thousand Muslim men and boys, Clinton determined that further action was needed. In August, the United States joined with other NATO forces in massive air strikes on Bosnian Serb positions. The bombing and NATO support for Croatian and Bosnian Muslim ground forces led Milošević to agree to join negotiations at the Wright-Patterson Air Force Base in Dayton, Ohio. The **Dayton Peace Accords** led to a significant reduction of the conflict, the placement of sixty thousand NATO soldiers in Bosnia, including twenty thousand Americans, and the eventual war crimes trial of Milošević. In June 1999, the American commander in Europe, General Wesley Clark, convinced Clinton

Dayton Peace Accords

A November 1995 agreement that began the process to bring peace to the former Yugoslavia.

Map 29-2 Yugoslavia Comes Apart.

In 1991–1992, the nation of Yugoslavia, which had been created in the aftermath of World War I, came apart as ethnic rivalries burst into warfare.

New nations seceding from Yugoslavia
- Former Yugoslavia
- Serbia
- Slovenia
- Croatia
- Bosnia and Herzegovina
- Kosovo
- Macedonia

that the United States needed to intervene again to stop Serbian aggression in the province of Kosovo where Muslims made up 90 percent of the population. A bombing raid on the Serbian capital of Belgrade resulted in a bomb falling on the Chinese Embassy, which killed several staff members and deeply hurt U.S.–Chinese relations.

Iraq also remained an issue, even though the war with Iraq over Kuwait was over before Clinton came to office. After the CIA concluded that Saddam Hussein had tried to arrange the assassination of former president Bush, Clinton ordered a missile strike on Baghdad that destroyed the country's intelligence headquarters. The government also continued to monitor potential terrorist activity emanating from Iran or North Korea, both of which were seeking to develop nuclear weapons.

In his efforts at foreign relations, Clinton also tried to broker peace agreements. In 1995, he sought to recognize the government of Vietnam and supported a mission by three veterans of the Vietnam War then serving in the U.S. Senate, Democrats John Kerry of Massachusetts and Robert Kerrey of Nebraska and Republican John McCain of Arizona, all of whom testified that there were no remaining prisoners of war in Vietnam and urged reconciliation. In addition, he worked for peace in Northern Ireland and in 1994 appointed former U.S. senator George Mitchell as special envoy. Mitchell helped broker the **Good Friday Accords** of 1998, a promising breakthrough in war-torn Ireland.

Good Friday Accords

A 1998 peace agreement to bring a peaceful settlement to the long-standing battles between Catholic and Protestant factions in Northern Ireland.

Terrorism at Home and Abroad

Terrorism, both domestic and foreign, posed unique challenges because terrorists were difficult to find, to predict, and to deal with. While international terrorist acts deeply frightened the United States, a new form of domestic terrorism stunned the nation. The actions of the FBI in Waco, Texas, had infuriated Timothy McVeigh and Terry Nichols, who believed that the FBI attack needed to be avenged. They managed to build a powerful truck bomb, and on April 19, 1995, McVeigh drove the bomb to the parking lot of the Alfred P. Murrah Federal Building in Oklahoma City and detonated it. The resulting blast killed 168 people, including a number of children in a day-care center. The bombing was the largest terrorist attack in U.S. history up to that time. McVeigh and Nichols were eventually captured, and McVeigh was executed, but government officials and the public knew that they were not the only Americans so disaffected that they might turn to violence.

Four years later, two deeply disaffected teenagers, Eric Harris and Dylan Klebold, whose journals reflected their fascination with the Oklahoma City bombing, went on a rampage at their high school in Littleton, Colorado. Their deadly rampage was one of many similar school shootings, often in suburban or rural areas and often initiated by disturbed and angry males who sought revenge against teachers and more popular students and the fleeting fame that came with such actions.

In February 1993, only a month after Clinton took office, Muslim terrorists bombed the World Trade Center in New York City, killing six. Over one thousand people were injured in the blast and five thousand were evacuated from the buildings. The bombing had been fueled by anger at the United States over its support for Israel and over the fact that U.S. troops had been stationed in Saudi Arabia near Muslim holy places. Some of the terrorists involved had gotten training from the terrorist group known as al-Qaeda.

The leader of al-Qaeda was a rich Saudi, Osama bin Laden, who had been expelled from his home country for his terrorist leanings and then expelled from Africa, where he had been living. He landed in Afghanistan and supported the Taliban government. In February 1998, when bin Laden called for a holy war against the West, the CIA estimated that he had some 15,000 followers, though little was known about the hard-to-find organization. In August 1998, al-Qaeda operatives managed to bomb the U.S. embassies in both Kenya and Tanzania. Most of the 223 killed and 4,500 wounded were African civilians working in or around the embassies, though 12 Americans were also killed. In October 2000, another al-Qaeda bomb ripped a hole in the hull of the navy's USS *Cole* while it was anchored in a port in Yemen. Seventeen sailors were killed. In all, some 90 Americans were killed by foreign terrorists, mostly bin Laden's al-Qaeda, during the Clinton years. Far worse was to come in 2001, but the warning signs were there.

Thinking Historically

The Causes of the Columbine Shootings

After the shooting rampage at Columbine High School in Littleton, Colorado, people tried to make sense of what happened and why. Neal Gabler, writing for the Los Angeles Times, *asked readers to locate the tragedy in cultural and historical context:*

Of all the bizarre sidelights to the horrifying massacre at Columbine High School in Littleton, Colo., Tuesday, the most bizarre may have been the story of the students trapped inside the school who called local TV stations on their cell phones and provided brief commentaries on the action. According to one report, they signed off only because they feared the intruders might be watching television themselves and thus discover the whereabouts of the cell-phone users. All of which suggests that even for the perpetrators and their victims, television was the great mediator. …

But tragedies like this are media events not only because the media immediately latch onto them. Often they are media events in two far more important senses: first, because the perpetrators usually seem to have modeled their behavior after certain figures in the popular culture and, second, because the rampages seem ultimately to have been staged for the media on the assumption that if you kill it, they will come. Or, put another way, what we witnessed at Littleton was not just inchoate rage. It was a premeditated performance in which the two gunmen roamed the school dispatching victims, whooping with delight after each murder. Without pop culture, the slaughter would have been unimaginable. …

[Dylan Klebold and Eric Harris] worshipped Adolf Hitler, loved Goth music, and had a special fondness for Marilyn Manson, the mordant rockstar whose satanic persona is designed to scandalize parents of his fans. In short, Harris and Klebold were creatures of pop culture. …

When you live within a virtual reality, you have to expect some addled individuals won't accept the difference between the movie or video screen and the screen of life.

Source: Neal Gabler, "Becoming Your Fantasy in Virtual Munich Beer Hall," *Los Angeles Times*, April 25, 1999, reprinted in Stuart A. Kallen, editor, *The 1990s* (San Diego, CA: Greenhaven Press, 2000), pp. 85–89.

Thinking Critically

1. **Comparison**
   What do you think about Gabler's description of teen culture in the age of the Internet? How might the culture be different without the technology?

2. **Contextualization**
   What other factors should Gabler include in seeking to understand the Columbine shooting in the context of the 1990s?

29.1
29.2
29.3
29.4

Everett Collection Historical/Alamy Stock Photo

The October 2000 bombing of the American destroyer USS *Cole* in Yemen was one of several terrorist attacks against the United States during Clinton's years in office.

Scandal and Impeachment

On January 21, 1998, the *Washington Post* carried a story that surprised, but probably did not shock, the nation. The president of the United States had been involved in an affair with a young White House intern and had lied about it to his wife, to his administration, to the press, and under oath. In the months that followed, the young intern, Monica Lewinsky, and the sexual escapades of Bill Clinton, remained front-page news.

Kenneth Starr, a zealous lawyer and former Republican solicitor general, was appointed as an independent prosecutor in 1994 to look into accusations that the president and Hillary Clinton's land dealings in a development at the Whitewater River in Arkansas had been improper. He spent the next four years, and a significant amount of taxpayer money, investigating but never discovered evidence of a crime. Starr had also been an advisor to the legal team assembled for a sexual harassment suit brought against Bill Clinton by Paula Corbin Jones, an Arkansas state employee who claimed that, while Clinton was governor, he had ordered a state trooper to bring her to his hotel room and sought sexual favors. Because of the trooper's role, the affair came to be known as "troopergate."

By late 1997, both the Paula Jones lawsuit and the Whitewater investigation were causing only limited political damage to the president. Then the situation changed rapidly. A disgruntled former White House staffer, Linda Tripp, secretly recorded the conversations as Lewinsky shared intimate details of her relationship with the president. For Starr, the tapes proved that the president had lied under oath and perhaps also urged Lewinsky to lie, both federal crimes that could lead to impeachment.

Clinton denied the whole story. At a press conference a few days after the *Washington Post* story broke, he said, "I did not have sexual relations with that woman, Ms. Lewinsky." Hillary Clinton denounced Starr as being part of a "vast right-wing conspiracy" and said— accurately—that he "has literally spent four years looking at every telephone call we've made, every check we've ever written, scratching for dirt."

In the summer of 1998, Lewinsky told a federal grand jury about her affair with the president and produced a semen-stained dress that she had saved. Backed into a corner, on August 17, Clinton told a federal grand jury that he had engaged in an "inappropriate" relationship with Lewinsky. That evening, he gave a TV speech in which he said, "I did have a relationship with Ms. Lewinsky that was not appropriate. ... It constituted a critical lapse in judgment and a personal failure." And he admitted he had "misled people, including even my wife." But he also insisted that the Starr investigation had "gone on too long, cost too much, and hurt too many innocent people."

Many, even among Clinton's closest supporters, were furious, if not at the affair, then at the lying. At a time when the country needed to deal with its economy and the terrorist attacks abroad, the president was distracted and untrustworthy. In December, the House of Representatives, with its Republican majority, voted to impeach Clinton on the grounds that he had committed perjury in his original testimony to a federal grand jury and had sought to obstruct justice in the Paula Jones case. It was only the second time in U.S. history that a president had been impeached. (Nixon resigned before an impeachment vote.) According to the Constitution, removing the president is a two-part process. The House must vote impeachment—essentially the same as a grand jury indictment—then the House acts a prosecutor while the Senate acts as the jury, with the chief justice of the Supreme Court presiding. On February 12, 1999, the Senate rejected the charges against Clinton by a vote of 55 to 45 for the perjury charge and 50 to 50 for the obstruction of justice charge, a very safe margin since a two-thirds vote was required to convict. Five to ten Republicans joined all of the Democrats in voting not guilty on the two charges. Clinton could focus again on being president. The Starr investigation cost $60 million.

Speaker Gingrich had been among the president's harshest critics, but the impeachment did not turn out well for Gingrich. Just before the impeachment vote, Republicans lost five seats in the November midterm congressional elections. It was the first time since 1934 that the party holding the White House showed gains in midterm elections. But the Speaker, who had been an avid prosecutor of the president, was further hurt by the revelation that he, too, had been having an extramarital affair with a young staff aide. He resigned as Speaker and announced that he would leave the House. The newly elected Republican Speaker, Robert Livingston of Louisiana, turned out to also be having an affair and he, too, resigned.

While many in the media were fascinated by the whole case, the American public was surprisingly indifferent. Even if many did not approve of an extramarital affair, it did not seem as big an issue as it might once have been. Clinton was hardly the first president to stray from his marriage vows. Perhaps more important, the nation was prosperous and at peace in 1999. Clinton seemed to be doing his job, whatever his personal life. As the case wound down, Starr's approval rating was 19 percent. Clinton's seldom dropped below 55 percent in his second term.

The Prosperous 1990s

Although an economic downturn brought Clinton to office, an economic upsurge kept him there. After Clinton's second year in office, the U.S. economy started to grow, and it did not stop growing for the next six years. Most Americans were better off at the end of Clinton's term than they had been at the beginning. The signs of the new prosperity were everywhere. Of the nation's 107 million households, 106 million had a color TV by 2000, 96 million had a VCR or DVD player, 92 million a microwave, and 81 million had air-conditioning. Houses were larger than ever before. Americans were eating better as fresh, local, and seasonal foods became more widely available and more popular.

The prosperity of the 1990s was the result of many factors. Clinton's budget, which brought down the federal deficit and produced the first federal budget surpluses in decades, made more money available for investment and spending and kept interest rates low. Experts argued about whether Clinton's free-trade policies, like NAFTA, were helping or hurting the economy. Changes in agriculture made farms and farmers more productive so fewer people, working less land, could produce more food—and more variety of foods—than ever before—enough to feed the United States and much of the rest of the world. The boom in technology was producing many new products and cutting the costs of items such as TVs and computers that were already on the market. Indeed, technologically enhanced economic productivity was probably the single largest driver of the economic prosperity of the 1990s. In addition, easily available personal credit, at low interest rates, fed the consumer spending and consumer confidence, even though it allowed people to pile up worrisome levels of debt. In his last State of the Union message in January 2000, Clinton was able to say, "Never before has our nation enjoyed, at once, so much prosperity and social progress with so little internal crisis and so few external threats." No wonder the president remained popular and the people of the United States relatively happy.

29.2 Quick Review

Were Clinton's high approval ratings justified, based on his domestic and foreign policy accomplishments? Why or why not?

Technology Dominates an Era

29.3 **Analyze the changes in technology and their impact on U.S. culture.**

While Americans battled over elections and a host of social issues, a small group of Americans were transforming the world in a very different way. In the 1990s, computer use and technological innovation—from connections to the Internet to the use of cell phones—became widespread in the United States. In his 2011 biography of Steve Jobs, perhaps the foremost innovator in the competitive field of those who fundamentally changed the ways

29.1

29.2

29.3

29.4

Americans communicated with each other and the world around them, Walter Isaacson wrote:

> Jobs stands as the ultimate icon of inventiveness, imagination, and sustained innovation. ... [He and colleagues at Apple] developed not merely modest product advances ... but whole new devices and services that consumers did not yet know they needed.

If one wants to understand how technology changed the United States in the years after 1990, it is important to understand the impact of Jobs and people like him.

The Birth of New Technologies

During World War II, the military sought ways to speed the mathematical calculations to send a shell in exactly the right direction to hit an enemy target. These first computers were exactly what the name implied: machines that computed distance, velocity, and air pressure to get a shot where it was intended to go. After the war, the U.S. Army's 1946 ENIAC computer, known as the "giant brain," performed ballistic calculations in thirty minutes that had taken twelve hours for humans to perform. With its 17,468 vacuum tubes, it was also the largest electronic apparatus on the planet. Throughout the 1950s and 1960s, similar large mainframe computers became common throughout American military bases, universities, and industry.

Postwar inventions made it possible to move from large mainframe computers to personal computers. In 1947, the Bell Labs invented transistors that could replace bulky and unreliable vacuum tubes. In 1958, Jack Kilby at Texas Instruments found a way to construct a transistor and the circuitry needed to launch the pocket calculator. In 1968, Robert Noyce and Gordon Moore founded Intel to market a microprocessor that was key to personal computers. The computer giants of the day—Burroughs, Univac, NCR Corporation, Control Data Corporation, and Honeywell—dismissed Intel. Within a decade, Intel would outpace all of them.

In January 1975, the first personal computer, the MITS Altair 8800, went on the market. The MITS company promised investors it would sell at least two hundred Altair computers. It quickly sold several thousand. The Altair had its problems. MITS shipped the computer as a kit, and the buyer needed to assemble it. One early purchaser, Steve Dompier of Berkeley, California, reported enthusiastically that his Altair had arrived "in the mail at 10 a.m. and thirty hours later it was up and running with only one bug in the memory." Not everyone, however, had thirty hours to dedicate to making the new computer work. Those who did manage to successfully assemble their computers quickly realized the Altair's second problem: it didn't actually *do* much on its own. With no keyboard, no screen, and no disk drive,

The ENIAC computer, created in 1946 and huge by later standards, allowed the army more computational possibilities than ever before imagined.

the Altair consisted of a case, a series of switches, and lights. It could do some things—solve mathematical problems as well as keep and sort lists. Dompier even found a way to link it to a radio and turn data into music. This was a machine for dedicated enthusiasts, not the general public.

One especially enthusiastic group in the San Francisco Bay area called themselves the Homebrew Club. As self-described geeks, they wanted to have fun with the machines, but they also had a political agenda. They were rebels against the large government, universities, and corporations that dominated society and used technology, especially the giant mainframe computers, to do so. Homebrew wanted a world in which the individual with a personal computer was more powerful than the corporation or the military or the university with its giant computers. Ted Nelson, another Bay Area geek, wrote in his 1974 self-published *Computer Lib/Dream Machines* that it was time to "liberate" the computer and put its power into everyone's hands, just as a "decade earlier, students had demonstrated in Berkeley with signs that said (mocking the instructions on cards then used in mainframe computers), 'Human Being: Do not bend, spindle, or mutilate.'" Steve Wozniak and Steve Jobs were part of Homebrew. They decided that they should market their own kit that could outperform the Altair. They sold their first Apple I computer in 1976. However, to accomplish all they wanted—to make the computer truly a popular device that everyone could use—they needed something simpler and easier than the Altair or the Apple I. Jobs studied the styling of popular European toasters and mixers in the kitchen department at Macy's in San Francisco and designed the plastic case for what became the Apple II. The two also designed new uses for the Apple. The Apple II could be connected to a TV or a stand-alone screen and used to play computer games. It could be used for spreadsheets and word processing. Small businesses could do their own financial analysis.

Jobs and Wozniak also courted investors, including two Silicon Valley engineers, Mike Markkula and Michael Scott, who formed the core of the new Apple Company that launched the Apple II computer in 1977. Apple was a huge success. Apple Computer's revenue went from $800,000 in 1977 to $48 million in 1979, and it was only the beginning.

IBM, the largest of the computer companies, realized the money to be made in personal computers and was determined that "Big Blue," as IBM was known, not be left behind. In the 1970s, IBM's money and power came from its manufacture of office machines (the name IBM actually meant something—International Business Machines), including popular typewriters, and from leasing the large mainframe computers used by corporations and government agencies.

In the summer of 1980, IBM created a special task force independent of all the normal routines of the company to create a personal computer (PC) that could compete head-to-head with Apple. The task force did its work in twelve months, and the first IBM PC went on the market in August 1981. It was a huge hit. IBM made $43 million from its PC division in the first year, and the profits were soon in the billions.

The core of the IBM PC was Intel's microprocessor, a power supply from Zenith, and printers from Epson. The design team turned to a Seattle-based upstart known as Micro-soft (later simply Microsoft), led by computer enthusiasts Bill Gates and Paul Allen, for the software for the PC.

Gates and Allen had written a class-scheduling program for their own high school while students there. In 1975, Gates, like the people at Homebrew, became fascinated with the Altair. He dropped out of Harvard and moved to Albuquerque, New Mexico, where the Altair was manufactured. He and Allen began writing software for the Altair and founded their company, Micro-soft, in April 1975. While Homebrew wanted to share all information freely, making personal computers part of a "people's revolution," Gates saw the potential for profit. He wrote a 1976 open letter condemning information sharing as "theft." Software, Gates insisted, should be as closely held as any computer hardware. When the IBM team approached him, Gates assured them he could produce what they needed. He bought another operating system, the "Quick and Dirty

Science and Society/SuperStock

The Apple II, designed by Steve Jobs and Steve Wozniak, had expanded computing capabilities for both personal and business use.

Operating System" (QDOS), adapted it to the needs of the IBM PC, and renamed it the MS-DOS (or Microsoft Disk Operating System). Rather than sell the system to IBM, Gates licensed the MS-DOS system and received royalties on every IBM PC sold. The foundation was laid by 1980 to make Bill Gates the richest person on the planet within a decade.

By 1979, even before IBM set its team to work, Steve Jobs was looking for ways to improve the Apple II. He visited the research offices of the Xerox Corporation, Xerox PARC, which was something of a mecca to computer developers. The staff was intrigued but wary of the upstart Jobs. At Xerox, Jobs saw an engineer, Larry Tesler, working with a small box that he used to move a cursor around on a computer screen. Tesler called it a "mouse," and with it, he could click on icons, open and close "windows" on the screen, and give the machine commands. The mouse was slow and bulky. The engineers at Xerox were not quite sure what to do with it. Soon, Xerox withdrew from the personal computer business—though it made a fortune selling printers that linked to PCs made by others. But Jobs felt like he had seen the future. He set a team to work designing a very different and more user-friendly mouse, and the Macintosh computer that went on sale in 1981 transformed the industry with its easy-to-operate system guided by a handheld mouse that replaced the need to key in commands.

A Connected Nation

By the 1990s, the personal computers that were being produced by Apple and IBM, as well as the systems such as those made by Microsoft that made them useful, were providing people with the ability to read, write, calculate, and do much more at speeds never before thought possible. Nevertheless, for the most part, these amazing machines each still stood alone. As early as the 1940s, dreamers like Vannevar Bush, founder of the National Science Foundation, were imagining a day when, through connected systems, "[t]he patent attorney has on call the millions of issued patents. . . . The physician, puzzled by a patient's reactions . . . runs rapidly through analogous case histories." But only in the 1990s did it become possible for most people to make meaningful connections between individual computers—to share information, seek information, and combine information in heretofore unimaginable ways. Those connections were made possible by the development of the **Internet**, a massive network of smaller networks joined together. Many separate developments created the Internet.

President Kennedy and his secretary of defense Robert McNamara were preoccupied with the question of how the president could maintain communication with the nation's far-flung military installations if a nuclear war actually happened and knocked out the nation's highly centralized telephone network. To solve the problem, the Pentagon turned to researchers at the RAND Corporation, and a RAND employee, Paul Baran, led the team to solve the problem. A decade later, on August 27, 1976, in the parking lot of Zott's Beer Garden near Stanford University, a team of Stanford researchers sent a message from a computer in a van to another computer they had placed inside the bar. The message was received, and the first data transmission had taken place over a network. A much more sophisticated system came quickly.

A next crucial step in connecting computers was the development of the World Wide Web, which was achieved by Tim Berners-Lee. Berners-Lee was an English physicist working at the international physics lab in Switzerland, known as CERN, where he noted that the various scientists from different countries could not share information from computer to computer. His goal was to find a way to connect computers and share information, lots of information.

In 1990, Berners-Lee found a way to create a common system so the information within files could easily be shared from computer to computer. He created a language for formatting files in hypertext so they could be read in the same way by the sending and receiving computers, and he called the language Hypertext Markup Language, or HTML. In addition, he developed a method of moving files of information, which he called the **World Wide Web (WWW)**, although in the beginning, it connected only the computers within the laboratories at CERN. By the end of 1990, the World Wide Web was up and running within the

Internet

The system of interconnected computers and servers that allows the exchange of e-mail, posting of websites, and other means of instant communication.

World Wide Web (WWW)

Since 1991, a protocol for information use on the Internet.

29.1

29.2

29.3

29.4

small research community at CERN. By August 1991, it was being made available at select Internet sites around the world, and by 1992, it was being used by more and more people who received hypertext information through the Internet.

In the early 1990s, Berners-Lee made another crucial decision. Although he could have gotten rich off of his invention, he insisted that the World Wide Web would be free. On April 30, 1993, CERN announced that anyone, anywhere in the world could use the Web without payment of royalties or legal constraints. The information superhighway, as Tennessee senator Al Gore would call it, was launched. (Gore did not "invent" the Internet, but he did coin the term "information superhighway" in 1990 and sponsored legislation to support it in Congress.)

People needed the right software on their computers to connect to the World Wide Web. One of the earliest software programs, and the first to be available at no cost, was produced by Marc Andreessen, a twenty-one-year-old computer science major at the University of Illinois. In January 1993, he posted an announcement that said, "By the power vested in me by nobody in particular, alpha/beta version of 0.5 of NCSA's Motif-based information system and World Wide Web browser, X Mosaic, is hereby released... Cheers, Marc." Andreessen then moved to California and was recruited by venture capitalist Jim Clark to develop a more sophisticated connection system, and in October 1994, Netscape was launched as a browser. Soon thousands of people in the United States and around the world were connecting to the Internet for the first time using Netscape Navigator. Other systems, America Online (AOL) and Yahoo!, soon followed. Before long, Bill Gates was leading Microsoft in the development and distribution of its own Web browser. By 1998, over 45 million people—quite a jump from 15,000 in 1990—were connected to the World Wide Web. People could shop, do research, listen to music, or tour the world, without leaving the comfort of their own homes.

E-mail messages began replacing telephone calls and office memos in the late 1990s. Ray Tomlinson, a researcher working at the Defense Department, inaugurated the use of @ as the core of an e-mail address. In the 1990s, people embraced the opportunity to send and receive messages at times of their own convenience rather than to have to answer the telephone.

The Dot-com Bubble and Its Eventual Burst

Just as the world of electronic communications was being born in the 1990s, many people decided that the key to making a fortune was investing in the enterprise. As had happened many times before (see Chapter 22 on the stock market crash of 1929), overeager investors created a bubble that eventually burst.

In March 2000, an article in *Barron's*, the respected business magazine, asked, "When will the Internet Bubble burst?" A week later, *Business Week* ran a story on Internet stocks called "Wall Street's Hype Machine." Investors, some of whom were already beginning to have their own worries, paid attention. At the end of March and all through April 2000, stocks in high-technology companies fell dramatically. Between March 10 and April 14, Yahoo! fell from 178 to 116. By the end of December 2000, nearly every technology company was down significantly. Some, like Amazon.com, recovered. Others did not. The value of specific parts of the new electronic world had shrunk, but the new electronic order was just beginning.

Google Becomes a Verb

In September 1998, two Stanford University graduate students, Larry Page and Sergey Brin, launched a new company in a garage in Menlo Park, California. They called their company Google. Page and Brin first met at Stanford in 1995, and by 1996, they had decided to search for and find information through the still-new World Wide Web. Other search engines predated Google, and others rose to challenge its dominance, but it quickly became the leader. As early as December 1998, a computer magazine was reporting Google's "uncanny knack" for producing good information very quickly, and by 2001, one could search for information on Google in twenty-six languages.

29.1

29.2

29.3

29.4

By December 2001, Page and Brin's company had scanned or indexed three billion webpages, almost 80 percent of the total then in existence. And as the number of webpages grew, Google kept scanning and indexing. When someone in any corner of the globe typed a question or a name or a topic into the google.com search page, a series of interconnected computers at Google headquarters in Mountain View, California, scanned the data and presented a list of websites to the searcher. With the advent of Google, virtually all of the knowledge available anywhere on the Internet was available at the click of a few key strokes to everyone, not just computer geeks with unlimited time and patience.

Google never charged for its services, which along with its speed, was a key to its popularity. The company's main source of revenue came from advertisements. Hotels in London may pay to get top billing when someone does a search of "London," while sporting goods companies may pay for top billing when a search is done for "sneakers." In 2004, Google launched Google Books. The company signed agreements with a number of prominent libraries, including Harvard, the Library of Congress, and the New York Public Library, to digitize *all* of their holdings. The books whose copyrights had expired would be made available online. Books still under copyright—which included most books—would have only small selections available, considered "fair use," and readers would be referred to the publisher for more. Authors and publishers were nervous about the fact that the whole book would be stored in Google's electronic archives, but John L. Hennessy, the president of Stanford University and a member of Google's board of directors, said, "We need to rethink our copyright framework that is still a remnant of the past." The nature of copyrights and, indeed, the printed page would be in for dramatic changes.

The Y2K Scare of January 1, 2000

As the nation prepared for the calendar change from 1999 to January 1, 2000, people were strangely preoccupied with their computers. The fear of what was sometimes called the "Y2K problem" or the "Millennium bug" illustrated how completely the United States had already become dependent on computers by 2000.

The Y2K problem was relatively simple. Beginning in the 1970s, computer programmers began using a two-digit code for the date. Rather than take up additional memory for 1978, they shortened the space for the year to two digits. Everyone—and every machine— knew that "78" meant 1978. But as 2000 got closer, some computer researchers began to get very nervous. If on New Year's Day 2000 the computers suddenly thought it was 1900, who knew what might happen in term of systems malfunctioning.

The U.S. Department of Defense worried about crucial information systems shutting down. Banks worried that their accounts could be lost. Electric companies worried that the electric grid, now completely computer controlled and monitored, could shut down. Hospitals worried that everything from heart monitors and breathing machines to the electricity and air conditioning in the operating rooms could stop. Internet-based businesses might not be able to operate. Ultimately, very little went wrong. Monitoring equipment in nuclear power plants in Japan failed but was repaired within a few hours. Bus ticket validation machines in Australia failed. In several countries, some cell phones stopped taking messages. In the United States, slot machines in Delaware stopped and the Naval Observatory clock briefly said that it was January 1, 19100. The problems, however, hardly resulted in the end of the world as some had feared.

Some insisted that the whole Y2K crisis had been a distraction and was merely a way to sell lots of new computers. Others knew how much work it had taken to avoid a crisis. Paul Saffo, director of the Institute for the Future in Menlo Park, California, said, "This was not hype. This was not software consultants trying to create a full employment act for themselves. This really could have screwed up our lives, and you know, a whole bunch of little geeks saved us." David Eddy, a computer programmer in Boston who first coined the term "Y2K crisis," said, "The reason nothing bad happened was that so many people put so much work into it."

A lot of money was spent on Y2K preparation, perhaps $100 billion in the United States and $300 billion worldwide. Old computers and operating systems were replaced. By 1999,

American Voices

Peter de Jager and Richard Bergeon, *Countdown Y2K: Business Survival Planning for the Year 2000*, 1999

As more people realized the seriousness of what could happen to the nation's computers on January 1, 2000, many people began to worry. At the end of the 1990s, publications like this one by de Jager and Bergeon raised the alarm.

Introduction: Houston, We Have a Problem

It's New Year's Day 2000 and you're headed to your best friend's house to watch football. You're in a hurry because you don't want to miss kickoff, and you have to stop at the nearest cash machine first, because you promised to bring the beer. But instead of cash, the ATM commandeers your card, rudely informing you that it has expired.

Furious, but knowing you won't get much help on a holiday, you head to the nearest 7-11 intending to pay for your refreshments with a credit card. Pulling up to the store, you think a lot of people have the same idea, because there's a long line at the checkout counter. But the problem is not a run on beer; instead, you find out, the cash register is not working. The word, as it reaches you at the end of the line, is that the cash register is computer-based and requires a valid date to start up. And for some reason, it won't. "Some reason" is the Year 2000 problem, Y2K for short.

The preceding hypothetical—but probable—scenario is just the tip of the iceberg, and if collective public denial continues, it is an iceberg that will sink titanic computer systems worldwide. Like the unheeded warnings of disaster on the oceanliner *Titanic*, the alert to the Year 2000 problem has been sounded. ... The truth is, the Year 2000 problem will affect each of us, personally and professionally.

Source: Peter de Jager and Richard Bergeon, *Countdown Y2K: Business Survival Planning for the Year 2000* (Boston: John Wiley & Sons, 1999).

Thinking Critically

1. **Comparison**
   How do de Jager and Bergeon seek to use a historical comparison to alert their readers to the seriousness of the Y2K problem?

2. **Analyzing Primary Sources**
   How would you describe the authors' purpose in writing this article in 1999? Given what you know about the outcome, did they succeed in their purpose?

29.1

29.2

29.3

29.4

the United States and the world had become deeply dependent on computers, the Internet, the World Wide Web, and related technology, most of which had not even existed twenty or thirty years earlier, and could not risk a shutdown.

The Latest Technology—Winners, Losers, and Change Agents

Soon after 2000, the fast-paced technological changes were producing some clear winners: companies like Google and Microsoft and the thousands of engineers and inventors who worked in places like Silicon Valley in California or Seattle, Washington. There were also clear losers.

When the Sony Walkman cassette tape player appeared in 1979, it seemed part of a never-ending expansion of the music industry. People could buy music and listen as they walked or worked. By 2001, however, the music industry was in deep trouble. In the 1990s, the best-selling album sold fifteen million copies. In 1999 alone, the music industry reported profits of $14.6 billion, but in retrospect, that point was the peak year for the industry's profits. That number would fall to $6.3 billion in 2009. It was just too easy to download music, share it, and give it away. In 2001, representatives of the music industry were successful in a lawsuit closing Napster, one of the first vehicles for downloading music, which had been launched in 1999, but other technology made it easier and easier to download music without paying. If the industry was going to survive after 2001, then it would need to find a new way to create, market, and profit from music products.

Newspapers went through similar losses. After 2000, newspaper advertising, which generates most of newspaper revenue, fell dramatically, as did the actual sales of newspapers. Circulation kept dropping for most newspapers and some, like the *Los Angeles Times* and the *Boston Globe*, lost perhaps a third of all subscribers between 2000 and 2010. Many of these papers began small online versions, but readers had already become accustomed to accessing other news sites that had been designed specifically for online readers.

Newspapers have yet to recover. Some have adapted well with strong electronic editions. Others have not.

Many people also began to worry about the loss of privacy that can accompany growing information technology. Certainly, Google held a lot of information, not just on products but on people who search for information. E-mail was much easier to hack into and read than traditional letters or telephone calls, an issue that would create major political embarrassments to political leaders and the U.S. government in the future. Federal laws for the protection of privacy, especially for letters sent through the U.S. mail, did not apply to much of the new technology. Mobile phones made it easy to call from anywhere, but they also made it easy for people to track anyone's location. Privacy, as civil libertarians had traditionally defined it, was fast changing.

In the decades after 2001, technology kept changing the way people lived their lives and interacted with others. A world without e-mail or without the ability to search the World Wide Web or listen to music or follow one's friends on Facebook became virtually unimaginable. Yet before the 1990s, such a world did not exist. In that decade, the foundation for the technological future was set.

> ### 29.3 Quick Review
>
> Is the expansion of technology beneficial to people, businesses, and/or governments? Why or why not?

Beyond Clinton—The Coming of George W. Bush

29.4 Explain the 2000 election results and the initial domestic agenda of the new administration.

Bush v. Gore—The Election and the Court Case of 2000

The Constitution prevented Clinton, who still had a remarkably high approval rating, from running for a third term in 2000. The logical candidate for the Democratic nomination was Vice President Al Gore. During the eight years that Gore served as vice president, he established a solid reputation with special expertise in government operations, the use of the Internet, and the environment. Gore's 1992 book, *Earth in the Balance*, described "humankind's assault on the earth." Although Gore had worked with Clinton for eight years, he and the president were never especially close, and Gore had been deeply offended by the Monica Lewinsky affair. He selected Connecticut senator Joseph Lieberman as his running mate, the first Jew to be on a major party's national ticket.

The two leading candidates for the Republican nomination were George W. Bush, the governor of Texas and the son of the former president, and Arizona senator John McCain. McCain was considered more liberal than Bush who called himself a "compassionate conservative." By March, Bush had wrapped up the nomination. He asked former secretary of defense Dick Cheney be his vice presidential nominee.

Gore made a fateful decision to distance himself from Clinton and did not call on the president to do much campaigning. He campaigned in favor of tough gun control legislation and for women's right to choose on abortion decisions, and he promised to keep the Social Security trust fund in a "lock box" separate from the rest of the federal budget. Many, even among his supporters, found him to be stiff and "wooden," hardly the relaxed and at-ease campaigner that Bill Clinton had been.

Bush promised a major tax cut, giving the current budget surplus back to the people. He favored allowing people to invest some of their Social Security contributions in their

29.1

29.2

29.3

29.4

own stock market accounts. He promised to reform public education. He told the country that he was "a uniter, not a divider," and would work with Democrats and end the divisive partisanship in Washington. In a not-so-subtle reference to the Lewinsky affair, he promised to restore "honor and dignity" to the presidency. He talked openly about how he had overcome his own alcoholism and about his born-again Christian faith. He was a surprisingly strong campaigner in spite of his tendency to mangle the English language with statements like, "Families is where our nation finds hope, where wings take dreams."

Two other candidates also entered the race: Ralph Nader, running on the Green Party ticket, and Patrick Buchanan, running a conservative and anti-immigrant campaign. Although Nader and Buchanan might take crucial votes away from either candidate, no one gave them a chance of winning.

As the polls closed on November 7, 2000, the deciding vote came down to Florida. Gore had won a small majority in the overall vote—a final count of 50,992,335 for Gore versus 50,455,156 for Bush. However, American presidential contests are decided by electoral votes, and whoever won Florida's electoral vote would win the presidency (see Map 29-3). At one point, the major TV networks, using exit polls, announced that Gore had carried Florida. Later they announced that Bush had won. By midmorning the next day, everyone agreed that the election was too close to call. It would stay that way for the next thirty-six days.

Problems with Florida's election procedures became apparent. Both campaigns assembled teams of attorneys. Some African American voters had been intimidated or turned away from the polls. In other places where votes were counted by punch cards fed into voting machines, cards with "hanging chads," that is, cards that were not punched all the way through, were not counted. When Gore asked for a recount in four counties where the errors seemed especially glaring, the Bush lawyers challenged him in court. After the Florida Supreme Court sided with Gore, the Bush team took the case to the U.S. Supreme Court. On December 12, the Supreme Court ruled in a 5-to-4 decision that a recount in only four counties violated the equal protection of the law and that, given the time that had elapsed, all recounts in Florida must cease. The next day Gore conceded the election. All five of the justices who voted to end the recount had been appointed by Reagan or the first president Bush. The other four justices were scathing in their dissent. The Court's senior justice John

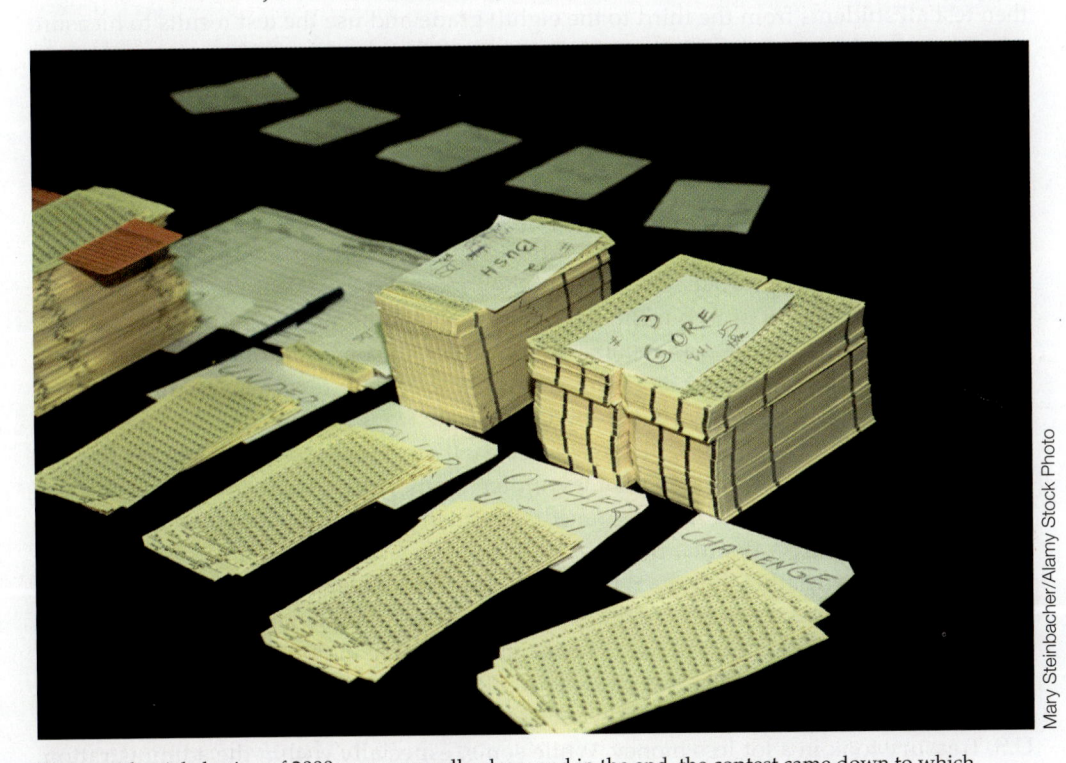

Mary Steinbacher/Alamy Stock Photo

The presidential election of 2000 was unusually close, and in the end, the contest came down to which candidate won the state of Florida. A recount there involved examining many ballots for potential irregularities until the U.S. Supreme Court, in a 5–4 decision, ordered the recount suspended, resulting in a victory for George W. Bush.

29.1

29.2

29.3

29.4

Map 29-3 The Election of 2000.

The presidential election of 2000 reflected how deeply divided the United States had become. The Northeast and West leaned Democratic, while the nation's midsection plus the South leaned Republican. Though Gore won the popular vote, Bush ultimately carried the Electoral College by three votes after he was awarded the Florida vote.

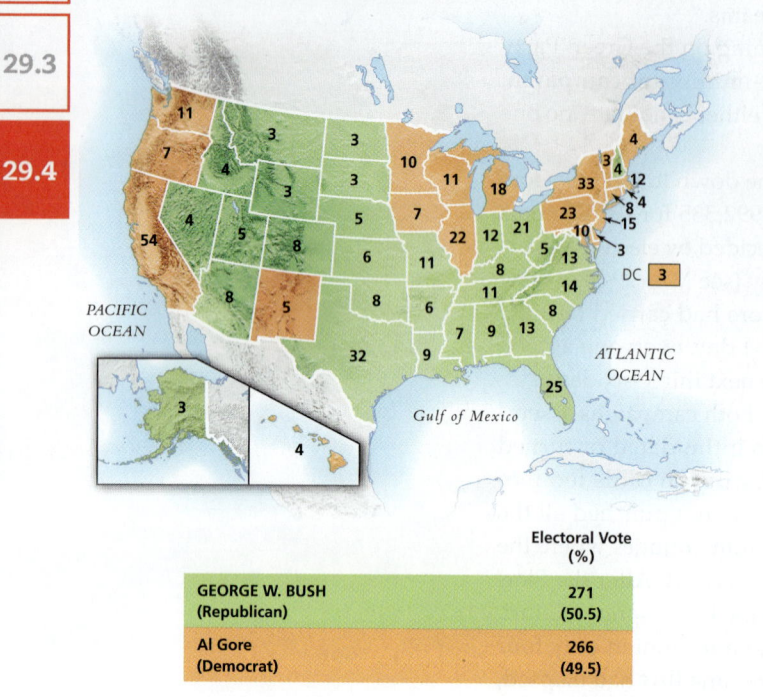

	Electoral Vote (%)
GEORGE W. BUSH (Republican)	271 (50.5)
Al Gore (Democrat)	266 (49.5)

No Child Left Behind

Federal legislation requiring that all students be tested and that schools show "adequate yearly progress" in the test scores of all students.

Paul Stevens, who had been appointed by Gerald Ford, said, "Although we may never know with complete certainty the identity of the winner of this year's Presidential election, the identity of the loser is perfectly clear. It is the Nation's confidence in the judge as an impartial guardian of the rule of law."

The George W. Bush Presidential Agenda

Given how close the election had been, many expected a cautious start for the new administration, but once in office in January 2001, George W. Bush did not waste any time implementing his own agenda. He selected a cabinet with more racial minorities and more women than any previous one, but they were a very conservative lot.

Three days after the inauguration, Bush announced that he would use the upcoming renewal of the Elementary and Secondary Education Act, first passed under Lyndon Johnson in 1965 (see Chapter 26) to change the course of federal education policy. He had campaigned on a promise to address what he called the "soft bigotry of low expectations" for poor students, and he acted quickly on that promise. He called his new proposal **No Child Left Behind** and announced he would seek a bipartisan education reform that would be "the cornerstone of my administration." In spite of the highly partisan split around his election, two of the most liberal Democratic members of Congress, Massachusetts senator Edward M. Kennedy and California House representative George Miller played key roles in developing the act and shepherding it through Congress. The core of No Child Left Behind was a requirement that, to receive federal funds, states must develop clear standards, then test all students from the third to the eighth grade and use the test results to measure whether individual schools and districts were making "adequate yearly progress" (AYP) in improving the education of all students and closing the "achievement gap." Although many supported the legislation, its implementation quickly generated criticism of the amount of testing involved, the constraints imposed by the regulations, and the lack of funding available for implementation.

Bush moved with equal speed on his other top priority, an across-the-board tax cut. During the campaign, he had insisted that the Clinton budget surpluses should be given directly back to taxpayers. Alan Greenspan of the Federal Reserve Board told Congress that Bush's proposed tax cut of $1.6 trillion over ten years would not harm the economy and might do some good. There was general consensus about some sort of cut, and Bush was able to sign a phased-in tax cut of $1.4 trillion on June 7, 2001, less than five months after the inauguration. The new law cut the highest tax rate from 39.6 percent to 35 percent—a significant cut, though still above the Reagan rates. It also created a new lower tax bracket of only 10 percent for the working poor, exempted many people from any federal tax, and phased out inheritance taxes. Almost immediately, many taxpayers received rebate checks. Cutting taxes was a very popular policy.

The tax cut legislation, however, posed two serious problems. The first was that most of the major cuts were to be phased in, and people were impatient. Pressure mounted to speed up the implementation of the tax cuts, and in less than two years, Bush proposed and Congress passed the Jobs and Growth Tax Relief Reconciliation Act of 2003, which speeded tax reductions significantly. The second problem was that, with reduced taxes, the U.S. Treasury took in a lot less money. While some, especially within the administration, argued that the tax cuts were stimulating the economy and creating jobs, most economists outside of government saw little evidence for the claim. Both sides had to acknowledge that the tax cuts—along with significantly increased spending by the administration, especially after 9/11—were creating a growing federal deficit. The surpluses of the late Clinton years

29.1

29.2

29.3

29.4

Nati Harnik/AP Images

American classrooms like this one were transformed by the expectations included in the No Child Left Behind legislation. In this 2003 photo, Rod Paige, secretary of the Department of Education under George W. Bush, answers questions from students during a visit to the Skinner Magnet Center in Omaha, Nebraska.

disappeared. For the rest of the Bush term, the federal deficit grew significantly. Some, like Vice President Dick Cheney, said, "Deficits don't matter." Economists and many leaders of both parties were less sure.

Education reform and tax cuts were both enacted during Bush's first year. A number of other policy initiatives were also enacted, some very quickly. Bush came to office committed to what he called "faith-based initiatives." He believed that religious communities were often better than the federal government at delivering direct human services. Nine days after the inauguration, he proposed what he called "charitable choice" legislation that would allow religious groups to apply for federal funds as long as they were not to be used for worship or proselytizing. While legislation made it through the House, two different bills were blocked in the Senate. In frustration, Bush issued executive orders in December 2002 that prohibited federal agencies from discriminating against religious charities and established faith-based offices in several cabinet departments. For some religious communities, the faith-based initiatives created an especially friendly atmosphere.

Bush had also campaigned on a promise to reform Social Security, giving individuals greater choice in the investment of the funds they contributed to the Social Security system. While other priorities dominated his early years, he did not forget the issue. Bush devoted a significant amount of his 2005 State of the Union speech—the first of his second term—to his proposal to allow more choice in the use of Social Security funds. By 2005, however, Bush was distracted by war, and Democrats were far less willing to give in to the president's initiatives. Little movement happened on allowing greater choice in Social Security, and after the 2008 financial crisis, when people realized that such choices might have been financially devastating, the idea died.

Bush had little patience with conservationists. He signed legislation allowing drilling in the Arctic National Wildlife Refuge in Alaska and supported offshore oil exploration. He did not move on environmental issues or global warming. Because of his own religious convictions, he opposed stem cell research in spite of dramatic appeals from many, including Nancy Reagan. His appointments, especially to the federal courts, tended to be very conservative. While the 2000 presidential election had been fought almost exclusively over domestic issues, and the first acts of the new administration confirmed that focus, the events of September 11, 2001, changed everything. In the next chapter, we turn to that tragic day and its aftermath.

29.4 Quick Review

How did George W. Bush's campaign promises translate to his actual domestic policies once he was president?

Conclusion

In 1989, the Cold War came to an end and "a new world order" began to take shape. When George H. W. Bush took office in 1989, he was well positioned to see the United States through the dissolution of the Soviet Union and the end of the Cold War. But as soon as the Cold War had ended, other international crises began. Bush sent U.S. troops to Iraq to protect the independence of Kuwait, ordered the overthrow of Panamanian dictator Manuel Noriega, and sent peacekeeping troops to both Somalia and Yugoslavia. Amid this international turmoil, the Bush administration also had to confront the increasing threat of nonstate terrorist organizations.

While Bush focused on international issues, the U.S. economy fell into a recession, and when he raised taxes, despite an earlier promise not to do so, the conservative wing of the Republican Party was furious. Division within the Republican Party and the troubled economy allowed Democratic candidate Bill Clinton, whose campaign team motto was "It's the economy, stupid," to defeat Bush in his bid for reelection.

Clinton initially focused on two issues: the economy and the nation's health-care system. He managed, with the help of a Democratic-controlled Congress, to balance the federal budget, lower the national debt, and secure approval for the North American Free Trade Agreement (NAFTA), but his health-care plan faltered before it reached the U.S. Congress for a vote. Two years into Clinton's first term, Republicans took control of the House of Representatives, forcing him to further moderate his positions. In his remaining six years in office, Clinton worked with Republicans to limit some budget cuts, end the nation's traditional welfare system, and pass the Defense of Marriage Act. Although Clinton faced impeachment stemming from charges that he had lied under oath about a sexual affair, he remained popular.

Dramatic developments in technology launched a new information era in the 1990s. Personal computers, which first became available in the 1980s, became commonplace in the 1990s. New companies such as Apple, Microsoft, and Google emerged, and existing companies such as IBM and Xerox adapted to changing technologies. In the 1990s, developments such as the Internet and the World Wide Web allowed people to connect and communicate at speeds never before thought possible. By the end of the decade, technology had become so pervasive in American life that many feared a catastrophic Y2K problem if computers malfunctioned on January 1, 2000. In addition, concern grew about the computer's impact on a range of existing institutions from the music industry to books and newspapers and on personal privacy. Nevertheless, by 2001, it was clear that the transformation of life as a result of technology was here to stay.

The 1990s concluded with one of the strangest presidential elections in American history. It took over one month and a decision of the U.S. Supreme Court to determine that George W. Bush, not Al Gore, would succeed Clinton as president. Once in office, the Second President Bush quickly implemented a major piece of education reform legislation and a significant tax cut. He also focused on "faith-based initiatives," allowing public funds to be used by religious institutions.

Chapter Review

How did changes in the 1990s and early 2000s connect the United States to the rest of the world to an extent unimagined at the beginning or in the middle of the 1900s?

Chapter 29 Summary and Review

The First Bush Administration, 1989–1993

29.1 **Explain the New World Order that George Bush described.**

Summary

George H. W. Bush's primary interest was foreign policy. The Bush team was initially skeptical of the speed with which Reagan and Gorbachev had reached agreements. The collapse of Soviet control over Eastern Europe and the subsequent dissolution of the Soviet Union itself left a vastly different world in their wake. At the same time, China's Communist leaders had no intention of relaxing their authority as Gorbachev did in the Soviet Union. Bush wanted closer diplomatic and commercial ties with China, but the Chinese crackdown on internal protest and dissent left the future of U.S.–China relations uncertain. In the Middle East, the Iraqi occupation of Kuwait led to war between Iraq and a U.S.-led international coalition. While victory in the Persian Gulf War was swift and involved relatively little loss of American lives, the long-term consequences of the war would prove profound. In domestic affairs, Bush placed a high priority on education, led the fight for the Americans with Disabilities Act, and supported the Clean Air Act. At the same time, he continued the Reagan assault on big government and nominated Clarence Thomas to the Supreme Court. Racial issues became a central part of the Thomas nomination hearings along with the issues of gender discrimination and sexual harassment, and the Rodney King incident and the O. J. Simpson trial illustrated how deeply lines were still drawn between races in the United States in the 1990s. A weak economy and Bush's decision to raise taxes left him politically vulnerable, allowing a relatively unknown governor, Bill Clinton, to win the White House in 1992.

Review Questions

1. **Comparison**
   Compare and contrast the global situation faced by the United States in 1980 and 1990. What challenges and opportunities did the changed world present to the Bush administration?

2. **Contextualization**
   What did the Thomas nomination hearings, the Rodney King incident, and the O. J. Simpson trial indicate about the state of race and gender relations in the United States at the end of the 1900s?

The Clinton Presidency

29.2 **Analyze the impact of the Clinton presidency and the Clinton–Gingrich conflict on the country.**

Summary

Bill Clinton's first term in office produced mixed results. On the one hand, he secured the passage of a deficit-reducing budget, AmeriCorps, the Family and Medical Leave Act, Goals 2000, and the North American Free Trade Agreement. On the other hand, his health-care plan was defeated, he was forced into a compromise on gays in the military, and in 1994, the Republicans took control of the House of Representatives. Clinton won a battle with House leaders over a government shutdown resulting from budget impasses, but moved to the right in a number of ways, lending his support to new limits on federal welfare and to the Defense of Marriage Act. Clinton won reelection in 1996, but the Republicans gained majorities in both houses of Congress. Throughout the 1990s, partisan divisions grew sharper as the Republican Party became more conservative and the Democratic Party became more liberal. Clinton emphasized domestic policy, but he was forced to deal with events in the Middle East, the former Yugoslavia, Haiti, and central Africa. During Clinton's presidency the threat of terrorism, both foreign and domestic, grew. An impeachment trial that was centered on Clinton's affair with Monica Lewinsky deflected Clinton's attention during his second term, but did not result in his conviction. Despite the ups and downs of Clinton's personal political fortunes, the 1990s were a prosperous decade.

Review Question

3. **Contextualization**
   Why did Clinton, a Democratic president, support and even initiate a series of center-right policies?

Technology Dominates an Era

29.3 **Analyze the changes in technology and their impact on U.S. culture.**

Summary

The 1990s and early 2000s were marked by new technologies that would transform the world. While postwar governments and universities played the dominant role in the development of mainframes, individual entrepreneurs spearheaded the development of personal computers. The growing dependency of the United States and the world on computers was underscored by the Y2K scare of January 1, 2000. The development of the Internet and the World Wide Web multiplied the power of computers and facilitated the creation of dense connections between organizations and individuals. As was the case with computers, the Internet grew out of the search for military applications of new technology. Unwarranted investor enthusiasm for new and untested Internet business models led to a stock bubble and the dot-com crash of early 2000. The rise of Google to worldwide prominence underscored the power of the Internet to disseminate information. The Internet and personal computing posed economic challenges and opportunities, allowing some industries to grow rapidly and forcing others to reconsider long-standing business models.

Review Question

4. Argument Development
Defend or refute the following statement: "The advent of the Internet was the most important advance in communications technology since the invention of the printing press."

Beyond Clinton—The Coming of George W. Bush

29.4 **Explain the 2000 election results and the initial domestic agenda of the new administration.**

Summary

The prosperity of the Clinton years was not enough to guarantee Vice President Al Gore victory in the 2000 presidential election. Court challenges to Gore's request for a recount of votes in Florida went all the way to the Supreme Court, where the Court ruled by a 5–4 margin in favor of George W. Bush. In office, Bush sought and found bipartisanship with No Child Left Behind, while much of the rest of his agenda pleased conservatives. Bush's tax cuts were at the center of his domestic agenda. They were quite popular with voters and helped stimulate the economy, though they added to an already-growing federal deficit.

Review Question

5. Comparison
In what ways were George W. Bush's domestic policies similar to Clinton's, and in what ways were they different?

1. Preparing to Write: Support Your Assertion

Short-Answer Question—Using the following excerpts, answer (a), (b), and (c).

"[W]ithin the first 100 days of the 104th Congress, we shall bring to the House Floor the following bills. …

"1. THE FISCAL RESPONSIBILITY ACT
A balanced budget/tax limitation amendment. …
"3. THE PERSONAL RESPONSIBILITY ACT

… [C]ut spending for welfare programs, and enact a tough two-years-and-out provision with work requirements to promote individual responsibility."

—**Republican "Contract with America," 1994**

"We know big Government does not have all the answers. We know there's not a program for every problem. We know, and we have worked to give the American people a smaller, less bureaucratic Government in Washington. And we have to give the American people one that lives within its means. The era of big Government is over. But we cannot go back to the time when our citizens were left to fend for themselves."

—**President Bill Clinton, State of the Union Address, 1996**

a. Briefly explain ONE important similarity between the "Contract with America" and President Clinton's speech.
b. Briefly explain ONE important difference between the "Contract with America" and President Clinton's speech.
c. Briefly explain ONE factor that accounts for the similarities that you indicated in (a).

For each response, make your assertion in the first sentence and explain your reasoning in two additional sentences. While most comparisons of Republican and Democratic views from a particular age are almost always marked by stark differences, the 1990s are unique in that President Clinton determined that to succeed politically, he had to "triangulate" by developing positions somewhere between those of the two parties. However, as you study the excerpts, you will see that the position Clinton took curiously leaned closer to the Republican Party than to his own. Why do you think that is? What does it tell us about the state of politics from 1980 to 2000?

2. Preparing to Write: Closing in the Conclusion

Long Essay Question—Evaluate the extent to which there are similarities in U.S. foreign policy during the 1920s/1930s and the 1990s.

After you develop a thesis that would answer this question, consider how you would write a conclusion that both revisits your argument while at the same time closes it. Unlike the 1920s, the United States accepts its role as the leader of the free world in the 1990s, but in both cases, it is a challenge to develop a consistent policy. One way to close is to place these two periods in the larger context of a cycling American foreign policy.

Chapter 30
Entering a New Time, 2001 to the Present

Chao Soi Cheong/AP Images

The September 11, 2001, terror attack on the World Trade Center in New York and the Pentagon in Washington, D.C., was a tragedy that shaped American politics and the lives of many individual Americans.

Chapter Objective

Demonstrate an understanding of the most recent history of the United States from September 11, 2001, to the present.

Learning Objective

The Impact of September 11, 2001

30.1 Analyze the impact of 9/11 on the nation, the presidency of George W. Bush, and Bush administration policies around the world.

Difficult Years on the Domestic Front

30.2 Explain the impact of Hurricane Katrina on the Gulf Coast and the costs and consequences of the 2008 financial crisis.

The Obama Years

30.3 Analyze the reasons for the successes and failures of the Obama administration and changes in the American culture while he was president.

New Liberals, New Conservatives, Election Surprises

30.4 Analyze the most recent political developments in the United States from the Tea Party movement to the election of Donald Trump as president in 2016.

Tuesday morning on September 11, 2001, dawned clear and beautiful on the East Coast of the United States. President George W. Bush was in Florida, reading to a class of second graders as part of his effort to build support for the No Child Left Behind legislation, while First Lady Laura Bush was meeting with Democrat champion Senator Edward Kennedy to discuss the bill. Most Americans were going about their business at the beginning of another workweek as memories of summer vacations faded. At 7:59 a.m., American Airlines Flight 11 took off from Boston's Logan International Airport bound for Los Angeles. In the minutes that followed, United Airlines Flight 93 left Newark for San Francisco; American Flight 77 left Washington, D.C., for Los Angeles; and United Flight 175 left Boston for Los Angeles. None of those four flights made it to their intended destination.

On each of the four planes, just minutes after takeoff, hijackers took control of the flight using box cutters—then legal to carry onto a plane—as weapons. As terrified crew and passengers used cell phones to call relatives and authorities, the planes turned back toward the East Coast. At 8:46 a.m., American Flight 11, crashed into the North Tower of the World Trade Center. Seventeen minutes later, United Flight 175 crashed into the South Tower of the Trade Center. At 9:37 a.m., American Flight 77 crashed into the Pentagon. By this time, passengers on United Flight 93 had learned from cell phone calls that they were part of a massive terrorist plot. As the plane headed for Washington, D.C., heroic passengers overpowered the hijackers and the plane crashed in a field in Somerset County, Pennsylvania. And history took a dramatic turn.

Many acts of heroism occurred on that September 11 morning. Betty Ong, a flight attendant on American Airlines Flight 11, stayed on her cell phone, reporting minute by minute until the plane crashed into the World Trade Center. In New York City, Nick Gerstle, a technician for Verizon, joined some New York firefighters who found two trapped New York City police officers. He heard the officers say, "Please! Don't let us die!" And they didn't. Julia Martinez and Margaret Espinoza were paraprofessionals—teacher aides—at the High School for Leadership and Public Service, which was only a block away from the World Trade Center. They began moving two wheelchair-bound students out of the chaos, found their way blocked by debris, and, with the aid of two strangers, simply picked up the girls and carried them to safety. This chapter focuses on the two decades after that tragic day during which many public and personal events were shadowed by what came to be called simply 9/11.

The Impact of September 11, 2001

30.1   **Analyze the impact of 9/11 on the nation, the presidency of George W. Bush, and Bush administration policies around the world.**

In the first hours after the horrific crashes, no one knew what to make of the attack. On first hearing the news on radio or TV, most people had the same reaction as Florence Engoran, who worked in the South Tower of the World Trade Center. When she arrived at her office on the fifty-fifth floor, someone said, "A small plane hit the other building." She remembered, "I wasn't especially upset by the news," and tended to agree with her coworker who said, "Oh, just sit down, let's keep working. We have to get out some focus reports." Within minutes, however, as she saw flames and heard another crash, Engoran realized that something much more serious was happening. Although she was five months pregnant, Engoran headed for the stairs and walked down the fifty-five flights. Before she made it to the bottom, the lights were off and the stairwell was filled with dust, but she made it. Most of those working in the buildings made it out. But many did not. Handicapped people who could not walk down the stairs were stuck. People on the higher floors could not get past the fires. Some seventy-eight police officers and four hundred firefighters who had responded to the emergencies remained in the buildings trying to evacuate people when the structures collapsed. It all happened very fast. At 9:58 a.m., just one hour after the crash, the South Tower of the World Trade Center collapsed floor by floor, showering a wide area with rubble. Thirty minutes later, the North Tower also collapsed. What had been two of the tallest buildings in the world that morning were now simply a giant hole in the ground.

30.1

30.2

30.3

30.4

The worst violence on U.S. soil since the Civil War had just taken place. Nearly 3,000 people died—246 passengers on the planes; 2,600 at the World Trade Center, a few of which were unlucky passersby; and 125 people at the Pentagon. The fear, loss, anger, and fortitude generated from that day would shape a new reality for the nation.

At 9:30 a.m., the Federal Aviation Administration grounded all flights within the United States. For the week that followed, the skies would be clear of everything but high-flying military planes. Airports would be eerily quiet. At a little after 1:00 p.m., President Bush, just nine months into his first term, addressed the nation from an air force base in Louisiana, telling people that massive security measures were in effect and that the United States would "hunt down and punish those responsible for these cowardly acts," though at that point no one was quite sure who they were. At 8:30 p.m., President Bush spoke to the nation for a second time, this time from the Oval Office, asking for prayers for the families and friends of the victims and again promising retaliatory action. Ground Zero was still a mass of burning rubble and would be for weeks. The Pentagon fire was contained, but not under control. The nation tried to make sense of what had happened.

Finding the Terrorists—al-Qaeda, the Taliban, Afghanistan

In the initial confusion of the morning of September 11, no one was quite sure who was behind the attack. By early afternoon, George Tenet, the director of the CIA, informed President Bush that while the agency was still investigating, all the evidence pointed to an attack by al-Qaeda, ordered by its leader, Osama bin Laden. By late that evening, when the president met with what he then called his "war council," they all agreed that plans needed to be developed to punish those behind the attack.

On September 20, President Bush spoke to a joint session of Congress. He said of the government of Afghanistan, "They will hand over the terrorists, or they will share their fate." And he told the rest of the world, "Either you are with us, or you are with the terrorists." There would be no neutrals in the coming war on terror. The president insisted, "The enemy of America is not our many Muslim friends. It is not our many Arab friends. Our enemy is a radical network of terrorists, and every government that supports them." Nevertheless, the militant tone of the speech, while reassuring some, worried many. In the immediate aftermath of the attacks, international support and sympathy for the United States was high. Even nations long hostile to the United States such as Syria were expressing support. But with Bush's response, some of the support began to fade.

By the time Bush spoke, CIA and U.S. Army forces had been dispatched to Pakistan and Uzbekistan to prepare for an attack on Afghanistan, whose Taliban government was protecting bin Laden and al-Qaeda. In early October, the United States attacked sites within Afghanistan while building on-the-ground alliances with Afghan warlords who were hostile to the Taliban regime. On November 9, the northern city of Mazar-e-Sharif fell to the U.S.-led coalition forces, and a few days later, the Taliban government fled the capital of Kabul. By early December, the United States and its local allies were in control of the country, and on December 22, Hamid Karzai, a leader of one of the anti-Taliban factions, was installed as the new leader of Afghanistan. For the most part, however, the Taliban and al-Qaeda leaders had escaped.

Many Afghans celebrated the defeat of the austere and tyrannical Taliban even as they kept a wary eye on the Americans and on each other. Late in 2001, U.S.-backed forces attacked the remaining al-Qaeda strongholds in a region of mountainous caves known as Tora Bora. Perhaps a quarter of all al-Qaeda and Taliban operatives were killed or captured, but the rest, including bin Laden and his chief lieutenant, Ayman al-Zawahiri, escaped into the lightly governed provinces on the Pakistani side of the border from which they continued to operate with considerable freedom. The United States did not track bin Laden down until May 2011, almost ten years later.

In the aftermath of the attack, President Bush, under considerable pressure from families of victims, appointed a special commission to study the **9/11 attack** and make recommendations regarding future policy. The chair of the commission, former Republican governor of

9/11 attack

The attack of September 11, 2001, on the World Trade Center and the Pentagon organized by al-Qaeda.

American Voices

September 11, 2001, Artie Van Why

Everyone who lived through September 11, 2001—near or far from the different events—had their own experience, one they will not forget. Artie Van Why came from Montgomery County, Maryland. After ten years pursuing a stage career in New York City, he went to work for a New York law firm. In June 2001, the firm moved to a building directly across the street from the World Trade Center. He was at work in the firm's word processing center on the morning of 9/11. His reflections began as notes to friends, became a well-received play, and finally a book from which the following firsthand account is taken.

I don't remember which came first, the shudder of the building or the loud sound. They probably came at the same time. …

In whatever the order, there was a loud boom; our building shook, and then there was quiet. My coworkers and I looked at one another.

I remember saying, "What was that?" Someone else asked, "Was that thunder?" … Had something possibly exploded? … One of our phones rang, and it was our supervisor, calling from home. She screamed to the person who answered something about seeing it on TV and for us to, "Get out of the building!" …

As I passed through the revolving door and out onto the street, it was like stepping into a snowstorm. Everything was white. The sidewalks and the streets—as far as I could see—were covered with what looked like a surreal blanket of fresh fallen snow. Paper of all sorts and sizes was scattered everywhere, coming down from the sky all around me, like bizarre flakes. There were whole sheets of paper and scraps of paper and bits of paper floating down from as far up as I could see. I had never seen so much paper.

I took the few steps that brought me to Church Street. I stood in front of the World Trade Center, between the Millennium Hotel and the Century 21 store. I noticed other objects and forms and substances on the ground—clumps of insulation, chunks of what looked like plasterboard. My attention left the ground though, as with those few steps toward Church Street, my head tilted upward, finally letting the north tower become my focus. Oh my God! What was supposed to have been just a small hole made by a little plane was a huge canyon blasted into the side of the tower. Smoke, the thickest and blackest I've ever seen, billowed from the gaping wound. Flames of the brightest oranges and reds shot out from the blackness. …

[After the collapsing of the twin towers, Van Why began walking to his apartment in Midtown.]

There was an obvious stillness in the air as the hordes of us walked, dazed and shocked, uptown. Thousands of us. Strangers. A mass of silent humanity walking together.

I remember seeing a woman's high-heel shoe, lying in the street, and wondering if she was still walking with just one shoe on. …

How arbitrary it all had been as to who had died, who had lived. There were the incredible stories of people walking from the rubble, the stories of people who should have been there that morning but weren't, the stories of the people who shouldn't have been down there, but were.

You know, I don't believe I had witnessed the wrath of anyone's God that morning. What I had been a witness to when I looked up at those burning towers was the ultimate evil that man is capable of. The evidence of just how deep hatred could run, how far it could go.

But I had also been a witness to something else that day—down on the ground. I witnessed the ultimate goodness of man, the evidence of how strong courage could be, to what lengths it would go.

I believe God was in the hands of everyone who reached out to help someone else. He was in the arms of people on the streets as they embraced one another. He was in the tears of strangers who cried together. He was in all the lives that were given in the line of duty, in the acts of heroism. He was in the hearts of the people across the country who, as they watched the horror from afar, felt compassion.

Source: Van Why, Artie. "That Day in September: *A Personal Remembrance of 9/11*," *Lulu.com*, Copyright © 2006. Used by permission.

Thinking Critically

1. **Analyzing Primary Sources**

   How does the point of view of someone who experienced the terror and courage of 9/11 illuminate your understanding of history? How might it compare with the memory of others who were farther away?

2. **Comparison**

   How does Van Why's account of 9/11 compare with other stories you have heard or read of the events on that day?

New Jersey Thomas Kean, and vice chair Lee H. Hamilton, former Democratic representative from Indiana, were careful to say, "We write with the benefit and handicap of hindsight." Nevertheless, they noted significant mistakes. They reported that while presidents and CIA directors are inundated with information, a lot of information had pointed to a possible large-scale al-Qaeda attack. As early as December 1998, the CIA's Presidential Daily Brief for Bill Clinton noted that there was evidence that "suggests bin Laden and his allies are preparing for attacks on the U.S., including an aircraft hijacking." A report to George W. Bush on August 6, 2001, included a detailed note headlined, "bin Laden Determined to Strike in U.S." "The most important failure," they concluded, "was one of imagination. We do not believe leaders understood the gravity of the threat." The terrorist danger from

While the defeat of the Taliban brought new opportunities to many Afghans, especially women, who could again study in school and take jobs, it did not bring stability to the country.

bin Laden and al-Qaeda had barely come up during the 2000 presidential campaign. Before 2001 was over, the response to terror dominated all other news.

The War on Terror at Home

The *Report of the 9/11 Commission* made recommendations to tighten security within the United States and abroad. However, they noted, "Many of our recommendations call for the government to increase its presence in our lives. ... Therefore, while protecting our homeland, Americans should be mindful of threats to vital personal and civil liberties." Whether the Bush administration, or the Obama administration that followed, kept the right balance has been a subject of continuing debate.

Even before the Commission finished its work, Congress, at Bush's request, passed the **USA PATRIOT Act**, which the president signed on October 26, 2001. The act expanded the authority of the Department of Justice to search telephone, e-mail, medical, financial, and library records without a court order and to increase monitoring of the U.S. borders and of noncitizens within the country. It also gave the Department of the Treasury the right to monitor financial records and bank transactions. In the midst of the fears generated by 9/11, the PATRIOT Act passed by large majorities in both houses of Congress. Most defended the law's provisions as necessary at a time of national emergency. Nevertheless, some were deeply troubled by the bill. Richard Armey, a conservative Republican member of the House, insisted that the act expire in five years. Wisconsin liberal Democratic senator Russell Feingold, the only member of the Senate to vote against the law, said, "Some have said rather cavalierly that in these difficult times, we must accept some reduction in our civil liberties in order to be secure. Of course, there is no doubt that if we lived in a police state, it would be easier to catch terrorists. ... But that probably would not be a country in which we would want to live."

The debate about the PATRIOT Act continued long after it passed. In January 2003, the American Library Association, worried about increasing searches of library records, condemned the PATRIOT Act as "a present danger to the constitutional rights and privacy rights of library users." Others disagreed. John Yoo, a U.S. Department of Justice attorney, and Eric Posner, a law professor, wrote a piece for the American Enterprise Institute in

USA PATRIOT Act

Legislation that sought to protect Americans by authorizing significant new data gathering by the federal government.

30.1

30.2

30.3

30.4

December 2003 in which they said, "If the act marginally reduces peacetime liberties, this is a reasonable price to pay for a valuable weapon against al-Qaeda." While the debate continued, President Bush signed a renewed version of the PATRIOT Act in March 2006, and President Barack Obama signed two further extensions of the law in 2010 and 2011 and a modified version in 2015 that extended most provisions through 2019.

The Wars in Afghanistan and Iraq

From the moment the first plane hit the World Trade Center, some in the administration were convinced that Iraq's Saddam Hussein was somehow behind the attack or at least allied with al-Qaeda. Deputy Secretary of Defense Paul Wolfowitz insisted that Iraq had to be dealt with if terrorism was to be defeated. Vice President Cheney supported a U.S. attack on Iraq. Others urged caution. The CIA and others in the National Security Council initially found no "compelling case" against Iraq. Indeed, evidence showed considerable antipathy between the very religious al-Qaeda and a secular leader like Saddam Hussein. In the immediate aftermath of 9/11, the focus stayed on the al-Qaeda strongholds in Afghanistan (see Map 30-1). However, the issue of Iraq never went away.

British prime minister Tony Blair supported plans for an attack on Iraq, but Jack Straw, Blair's foreign minister, insisted, "Saddam was not threatening his neighbors, and his WMD [weapons of mass destruction] capability was less than that of Libya, North Korea, or Iran."

Map 30-1 Afghanistan and Iraq.

After a 2001 attack on the Taliban government of Afghanistan, the United States turned its attention to Iraq, which it attacked in 2003.

Under a sign proclaiming "Mission Accomplished," President Bush announced the end of combat operations in Iraq on May 1, 2004. The worst of America's difficulties in Iraq, however, were just beginning.

As talk of a possible U.S. attack on Iraq circulated, an article appeared in the *Wall Street Journal* on August 15, 2002, by Brent Scowcroft, who had been the national security advisor in the administration of the first President Bush. Scowcroft wrote, "Don't attack Saddam." He urged instead that the United States should "be pressing the United Nations Security Council to insist on an effective no-notice inspection regime for Iraq." Some speculated that Scowcroft's article was, in fact, a warning from Bush's father (the first President Bush)—a close friend of Scowcroft—but if it was, it came too late.

In January 2002, just four months after the attacks in New York and Washington, D.C., Bush gave his State of the Union message in which he singled out Iraq, along with Iran and North Korea, as an "axis of evil." Bush said, "Iraq continues to flaunt its hostility toward America and to support terror. … This is a regime that has something to hide from the civilized world."

After considerable debate, Congress voted to authorize the use of military force if diplomacy with Iraq failed. The resolution passed the Senate by a vote of 77 to 23 and the House by 296 to 133. While almost everyone supported the invasion of Afghanistan and the attack on al-Qaeda, divisions ran deep about Iraq. A young Barack Obama had not yet been elected to the Senate, but he told a rally, "This is a dumb war."

After the congressional vote, Colin Powell took the arguments to the United Nations Security Council. Powell put his personal prestige on the line to convince the Security Council of the need to topple Saddam Hussein's government. The vote was 15 to 0 in favor. France, Russia, and China, all of which had grave reservations about a war in Iraq, hoped that the authorization would force Iraq to agree to tougher inspections to avoid an invasion. With authorization from Congress and the UN, the United States, allied with a coalition of other countries, most of whom sent only token forces, went to war and toppled Saddam Hussein with lightning speed.

On March 19, 2003, U.S. forces began the war using bombers—over 1,500 flights a day—plus launching navy cruise missiles. The U.S. military called it "shock and awe." After the air attack, ground forces moved across the country. By the first week in April, the airport at Baghdad fell to U.S.-led troops and U.S. tanks roared into the capital city. The Iraqi minister of information was captured, most of the rest of the leadership fled, and Saddam Hussein was a fugitive in the country he had long dominated. U.S. and British casualties were very low. The war, it seemed, had been won skillfully. On May 1, President Bush flew to an aircraft carrier and announced, "Major combat operations in Iraq have ended. In the battle of Iraq, the United States and our allies have prevailed." He later wished he had made a less dramatic announcement.

Securing a country as large and as tightly regulated as Iraq was no easy task. Many Iraqis who were delighted to see Hussein gone were uneasy about the role of foreign troops in their country. An Iraqi professor told American reporter Anne Garrels, "You understand, you will now have to be in complete control, and we will resent you every step of the way." In fact, the United States never sent enough forces to manage the country once the old government had been removed. Very little planning had gone into preparation for the post-invasion world of Iraq. Condoleezza Rice, then the national security advisor, said, "The concept was that we would defeat the army, but the institutions would hold, everything from ministries to police forces." It did not happen.

As soon as the old authority was gone, looters stole computers, televisions, and metal from government buildings to be sold for scrap. At the Central Bank, looters drilled into the vaults and ran out with the money, much of it in U.S. dollars or euros that could not be traced. They broke into the National Museum and carried off fifteen thousand ancient objects of extraordinary value.

Defense Secretary Rumsfeld responded, "Stuff happens." Most Iraqis and people around the world were less understanding. One military advisor said, "We're incompetent as far as they're concerned."

In May 2003, Secretary Rumsfeld appointed a U.S. diplomat, L. Paul "Jerry" Bremer, as head of the **Coalition Provisional Authority (CPA)** to bring order to Iraq. Bremer was an experienced diplomat, but he was not familiar with the Middle East. He set up his head-quarters in the fortified "Green Zone," a former Hussein palace, and issued two orders that in retrospect seemed a serious mistake. Modeling the first order on the de-Nazification of Germany after World War II, Bremer ordered the de-Baathification of Iraq. The Baath Party had been Hussein's political party, the only one allowed in the country. Government officials—senior officials, police officers, and teachers—were required to be members. The order that no member of the Baath Party could work in the new administration immediately threw some thirty thousand to fifty thousand out of work. The idea that ministries or the police could quickly be up and running was gone.

A week later, Bremer dissolved the Iraqi army. The initial U.S. plans for a postwar government had focused on removing a few generals and then reestablishing the army since it was solid and had discipline as well as credibility inside Iraq. With his order, Bremer dissolved this source of structure and order. He also infuriated some 400,000 Iraqi soldiers who thought they had been promised that, if they would not resist the Americans, they could keep their jobs after the war. Now they were out of their jobs and had lost their pensions, but still had access to arms.

As it became clear that the United States could not maintain order, Iraqis not only became angry at the Americans but also became angry at one another. Hussein's dictatorship had maintained tight control. Now within weeks, members of the Sunni Muslim minority, of which Hussein was a part and which had been the nation's elite, were attacked by members of the Shiite Muslim majority. The Sunnis fought back. On August 29, two car bombs killed moderate Shiite leader Ayatollah Mohammad Baqir al-Hakim and 124 of his followers and destroyed the mosque where they were worshipping. While Sunnis and Shiites fought in the center and south of the country, Iraqi Kurds in the north, who had been protected for twelve years by the "no fly zone," now fought to maintain their autonomy. Reprisal followed reprisal and the Americans were caught in the middle of it. More American soldiers were killed between May and October of 2003 in "postwar" fighting than from March to May of that year in the actual invasion.

Between 2003 and 2004, U.S. forces searched the country, trying to find weapons of mass destruction and the escaped dictator Saddam Hussein. In spite of the fact that those weapons had been one of the prime reasons for going to war, none were ever found. Hussein apparently had wanted to keep up the pretense that they existed to frighten the United States and his old enemies like Iran. In fact, the weapons were not there. Bush wrote in his *Memoirs*, "In retrospect, of course, we all should have pushed harder on the intelligence and

Coalition Provisional Authority (CPA)

The temporary governing authority for Iraq set up after the U.S. invasion in March and April 2003.

revisited our assumptions." However, Hussein himself was found not far from his hometown of Tikrit in December 2003. After an extended trial, Hussein was executed by the U.S.-backed provisional government of Iraq in December 2006.

As Iraq spiraled into civil war, U.S. soldiers complained that they had no training for serving as an occupying force. Electricity worked in Baghdad for perhaps eight hours a day, even in the summer when air-conditioning was desperately needed. Oil was being pumped only at very low levels.

By late summer 2003, Hussein's prisoners had been freed from the **Abu Ghraib prison**, and the U.S. military was using the prison to hold some four thousand prisoners of their own. They had orders from the Pentagon to "get information" from the new prisoners. In the search for information, they humiliated prisoners by keeping some naked in front of female guards, by piling them on top of each other, and by making them crawl and bark. U.S. troops took pictures of what they were doing. In April 2004, the whole sordid mess at Abu Ghraib came to light. CBS News, the *New Yorker* magazine, and news organizations around the world, including Arab news sources like *Al Jazeera*, showed the pictures and reported what was happening at Abu Ghraib. Hearing the reports, U.S. General James Mattis responded, "When you lose the moral high ground, you lose it all."

A year after the invasion, the U.S. commanding officer, General Ricardo Sanchez, described the situation as a "civil war" and added, "What's more, we had created these conditions ourselves." Paul Bremer said, "We've become the worst of all things—an ineffective occupier."

At home in the United States, opposition to the war and the occupation was growing. There were no weapons of mass destruction. There was no order in Iraq. There was no end in sight.

The war in Iraq dominated U.S. elections. In the 2004 presidential contest, the Democrats nominated a Vietnam-era war hero, Senator John Kerry of Massachusetts, after a spirited contest with Howard Dean, the governor of Vermont. Although the Dean campaign's success at raising funds and recruiting volunteers through the Internet did not lead to his nomination, it transformed future political campaigns. Once Kerry secured the Democratic nomination, the party united behind him. Kerry had voted for the war, but he had become a major critic. He called the war and the subsequent U.S. occupation of Iraq a "colossal blunder," and said that the president was "deliberately misleading the American people." Bush responded that the "world is better off without Saddam Hussein." Outside political groups supporting Bush sought to tarnish Kerry's military record. Although Kerry had struck a chord with his criticism, he was not a strong campaigner. In the end, the president won by a very small margin of 62 million to 59 million or 50.7 percent of the popular vote to Kerry's 48.3 percent. The electoral vote was also close: 286 to 251. Nonetheless, Bush won a second term. Republicans also maintained control of Congress.

By 2006, the war's cost in lives and dollars was a top issue in the midterm election. Democrats won a majority in both houses of Congress and Democrat Nancy Pelosi replaced Republican Dennis Hastert as Speaker of the House of Representatives, the first woman in history to serve as Speaker. Two new women were added to the Senate, bringing the total of women to sixteen—a then all-time high. Many thought the Republicans were going to be in trouble in the 2008 presidential election. President Bush would face an unfriendly Congress during his last two years in office.

Abu Ghraib prison

An Iraqi prison taken over by U.S. forces after the invasion.

30.1

30.2

30.3

30.4

Iraqi detainees wait to be released at Abu Ghraib prison, west of Baghdad in Iraq, June 2006. Pictures taken in Abu Ghraib prison of tortured prisoners circulated around the world, including the Muslim Middle East, inflaming anti-American sentiment.

Wathiq Khuzaie/Getty Pool/AP Images

30.1

30.2

30.3

30.4

the surge

In January 2007, a new American commander in Iraq, General David Petraeus, led an additional thirty thousand troops to take control of the countryside and create a level of stability and public trust in the United States, not seen since the invasion of 2003.

Looking at the situation in Iraq in 2006, one American official said, "We've taken Samarra four times, and we've lost it four times. … We need a new strategy." In November 2006, after the midterm elections, President Bush fired Defense Secretary Rumsfeld and replaced him with Robert Gates, a less ideological administrator. A new U.S. ambassador to Iraq, Ryan Crocker, who spoke Arabic and who knew the Middle East well, was appointed. General David Petraeus was made the overall commander of military forces in the region. He developed a very different strategy in Iraq. First there was "**the surge**," an infusion of an additional thirty thousand U.S. troops to provide strength in numbers. Petraeus placed units in population centers with orders to get to know and protect the Iraqi people to find out what their complaints were and try to respond. If troops took control of an area, they stayed and tried to build a new infrastructure. Troops felt vulnerable, and losses were high. Slowly, however, the troops and the Iraqi government began to take control of the country. By fall, one journalist reported from Baghdad, "Some shops stay open until late in the evening. Children play in parks, young women stay out after dark, restaurants are filled with families, and old men sit at sidewalk cafes playing backgammon and smoking shisha pipes." It was a peace of sorts, though Iraq was still a very violent place.

30.1 Quick Review

In what ways did the war on terror dominate domestic and international issues during George W. Bush's presidency?

Difficult Years on the Domestic Front

30.2 Explain the impact of Hurricane Katrina on the Gulf Coast and the costs and consequences of the 2008 financial crisis.

While the war in Iraq dominated much of the political discussion in the United States, it was far from the only event of the later years of the Bush administration. Debates continued about Bush's education and tax policies. Perhaps most of all, the weather and the bursting of the bubble of real estate speculation dominated George W. Bush's second term.

Hurricane Katrina and Its Aftermath

Hurricane Katrina

A massive storm that hit New Orleans and the Gulf Coast in August 2005, leading to widespread death and destruction.

Early Monday morning August 29, 2005, **Hurricane Katrina**, one of the most powerful and deadly hurricanes in American history, hit New Orleans and the Gulf Coast of Louisiana, Mississippi, and Alabama. Hurricanes have naturally pounded Florida and the Gulf Coast since long before the first Europeans or Africans arrived, but Katrina was a natural disaster compounded by human failure. The result was hours and days of anguish for many, over 1,800 deaths, and more than $75 billion in damage.

It started raining in Biloxi, Mississippi, around 5:00 p.m. on Sunday, August 28, 2005. By 9:00 p.m., it was raining in New Orleans and the wind was starting to pick up. Weather forecasters had realized that Hurricane Katrina might be the "big one," the hurricane that people in the area long feared, and they told people to prepare with increasing urgency. Nevertheless, neither the mayor of New Orleans nor the governors of Louisiana or Mississippi issued mandatory evacuation orders.

When Katrina hit, the hurricane's winds splintered buildings, toppled power lines, collapsed highway bridges, tore off part of the roof of the New Orleans Superdome where many had sought refuge, and stirred up waves on Lake Pontchartrain that weakened the levees. The wind also drove a huge surge of water onto the shore and up the Mississippi River. Winds blew steadily at 150 miles per hour. Sometime between 3:00 and 5:00 a.m., the levees on the 17th Street Canal gave way. New Orleans lost electric power at 5:15 a.m. and telephone service at 7:11 a.m. As the weakened levees failed, a wall of water poured

Marko Georgiev/Getty Images

Lower Ninth Ward residents stranded on the roof of their homes await rescue. The death and destruction that came with Hurricane Katrina was unimaginable to most Americans.

into neighborhoods where it rose rapidly, destroyed buildings, and trapped people in upper floors and attics.

The Lower Ninth Ward had been a working-class African American community for generations. Churches thrived, as did neighborhood bars offering jazz, blues, and iconic New Orleans–style music. The area was seven feet below sea level, but the levees were designed to keep the water out. People in the Lower Ninth Ward had few options other than trying to ride out the storm. When the levees broke, most of the Lower Ninth Ward was under water.

Few failed to notice that the worst scenes of suffering and death that resulted from Katrina were in African American communities. The New Orleans Police Department was part of the problem. Many of the officers simply deserted their posts. Some of those who remained offered heroic help, but others were eventually convicted of criminal activity. In addition, the Federal Emergency Management Agency (FEMA) failed to live up to its responsibilities. FEMA had been created during the Carter administration to coordinate the diverse federal agencies that might be needed in the case of a natural disaster. However, for too long during Katrina and its aftermath, FEMA did nothing. FEMA staff were asking, "Why aren't we getting the orders? Why isn't this being treated like a real emergency?" FEMA's director in 2005, Michael Brown, was a political appointee with no experience in managing any disasters. When Brown assured Mississippi governor Haley Barbour that "FEMA had lots of hurricane practice in Florida," Barbour responded, "I don't think you've seen anything like this." It was one of the kinder statements Brown heard that week as people waited for federal help that did not come.

By Wednesday, August 31, two days after the storm, two hospitals in New Orleans, Charity and University, lost their generators. It was over one hundred degrees in the hospitals. With no electricity, staff and volunteers used hand pumps to keep oxygen flowing to desperately ill people. With virtually no water or supplies, only the most rudimentary medical aid was possible. Those in the Superdome were trying to survive in horrifying, primitive conditions with no sanitation and dead bodies lying exposed in hallways. Not until Thursday were thousands of people finally evacuated to Houston, Texas, where shelter was offered. New Orleans never returned to its pre-Katrina population, and years after the storm, whole neighborhoods were virtually abandoned even as others, like the Ninth Ward, slowly rebuilt and came back to life.

The Financial Crisis of 2008

The headline in the *Wall Street Journal* for Monday, September 15, 2008, was double the normal size and ran across all six columns of the paper. It said:

> CRISIS ON WALL STREET AS LEHMAN TOTTERS, MERRILL IS SOLD
> AND AIG SEEKS TO RAISE CASH

By the time most people read the paper, Lehman had declared bankruptcy. Bank of America bought Merrill Lynch, and bankers and federal authorities were trying to save the American International Group (AIG). Before the day was over, the stock market fell by 504.48 points. It would fall much further.

In one extraordinary weekend, Saturday and Sunday September 13 and 14, 2008, most of the nation's leading bankers and senior government officials, led by Secretary of the Treasury Henry "Hank" Paulson, tried to salvage the American economy. Although the government and the bankers failed to save Lehman Brothers, they avoided a far worse fate of massive bankruptcies and the coming of a second Great Depression. Nevertheless, they did not succeed in saving the thriving economy of the last two decades.

The extent of the **financial crisis of 2008** came as a surprise, even to Treasury Secretary Paulson, who had warned that a crisis was coming since becoming the top federal financial official in July 2006 and to Timothy Geithner, who would be treasury secretary in the Obama administration but was then the head of the New York Federal Reserve Bank. The size and complexity of the crisis that hit the country in 2008 was much more severe than they would have predicted.

The economy had been growing rapidly since the early 1990s. Interest rates had remained low in part because of policies at the Federal Reserve Bank; in part because of the Clinton-era efforts to cut the size of the federal deficit; and in part because bankers and governments in Asia, especially China, were willing to make low-interest loans to Americans and European borrowers, particularly to finance their purchases of Asian goods.

During the 1990s and early 2000s, because of policies fostered by the Clinton and Bush administrations, bankers got much more freedom from federal regulations than had been the case in any period since the Depression—freedom that some thought led directly to the crisis of 2008. In 1999, with bipartisan support, Congress passed the Gramm-Leach-Bliley Act, which repealed a section of the 1933 Glass-Steagall Act. Glass-Steagall, which was passed at the height of the Great Depression, created the Federal Deposit Insurance Corporation (FDIC) to provide federal insurance for bank accounts but also required that insured banks not use their money to speculate, that is, to make risky investments. For decades, insured banks provided mortgages to families that wanted to buy a home, usually up to 80 percent of the price of a house, so people could pay off their homes over a twenty- to thirty-year time span. Banks were cautious in making loans, insisting on detailed documentation of a family's ability to pay back the loan. Most of the time, a bank that issued a mortgage continued to hold it until the loan was paid off.

Investment banks, such as Lehman Brothers and Goldman Sachs, were free to speculate on the stock market or in other less secure but possibly more profitable investments, but they were not federally insured; investors were risking their own money, not that of the taxpayers. What had been a hard-and-fast divide between investment and commercial banks in 1933 had been slowly eroding and, after 1999, had become a very porous wall.

Two further developments changed the way banks operated and mortgages were issued in the United States. President George W. Bush talked of an "ownership society" in which

financial crisis of 2008

A significant economic downturn that began with the housing mortgage market and ultimately led to high unemployment.

30.1

30.2

30.3

30.4

Americans would be invested in their communities because they owned their own homes. Liberal Democrats like Massachusetts representative Barney Frank insisted that mortgages be available to allow poorer people to own their own homes.

At the same time, banks found new ways to handle—and increase the profits from—home mortgages. Rather than issue a mortgage and then hold it, banks divided mortgages into small shares—"sliced and diced" them, as some said—and then sold the mortgage shares, at a profit, to many different banks and investors. As a result, banks could invest in pieces of many different mortgages in ways that seemed to lower the risk of individual mortgage defaulting since investors held portions of many mortgages rather than the whole amount of a few. With political pressure at high levels to help more people become home owners, interest rates at a low level, and mortgages easier than ever to sell to other banks, mortgage lenders began issuing mortgages to people who never before would have been eligible. They issued mortgages with no down payment and no required documentation of income or ability to pay in what became known as the "subprime mortgage market." With such easy funding available, sellers found they could ask higher prices for homes, and housing prices climbed at an extraordinary rate.

Between 2001 and 2006, housing prices kept rising, interest rates stayed low, and bankers made a lot of money. The investment bank Goldman Sachs generated an average income of $661,000 per employee in 2007. Goldman's chief, Lloyd Blankfein, earned $54 million that year. Mortgages were no longer merely for primary residences but were also for investment. People bought houses, then quickly sold them for higher amounts, a process known as "flipping." Everyone seemed to be making money, and many argued that only fools were left out of the process. The situation was a classic bubble very much like every other bubble, including the stock market bubble of 1929 and the dot-com bubble of the 1990s.

In 2006, housing prices stopped rising. People who had bought houses they could not afford with the plan to "flip" them could not sell them. People who had bought homes with flexible interest rates, thinking that they would refinance for a lower rate later, could not find a new mortgage. Many started defaulting on loans. As defaults grew, banks who held the mortgages started to get into trouble. Even in situations where mortgages had been "sliced and diced," banks that owned slices of many unpaid mortgages found themselves in trouble. Initially, most people thought the crisis would be limited to a few mortgage lenders who had taken too many risks. They were wrong.

Before long, it became clear that large and supposedly stable investment banks like Lehman and Goldman Sachs, which held portions of many sliced loans, were in a lot of trouble. Bankers who had taken risks throughout their careers, confident that there was always a way out, could not find a way out of the crisis. While Treasury Secretary Paulson was trying to maintain confidence in the fall of 2008, he privately asked his wife, "What if the system collapses?"

In the end, the nation's financial system did not collapse. But it did not resume the financial health or confidence that had characterized most of the 1990s and early 2000s. At the end of September, Secretary Paulson and congressional leaders put together Troubled Asset Relief Program (TARP) legislation to stop the continuing financial collapse. When TARP was put to a vote in the House of Representatives, in spite of the support of leaders of both parties, the bailout was rejected by a 228 to 205 vote. Many in both parties did not think it was the government's business to use taxpayer money to bail out investors who had taken too many risks. Immediately after the vote, the Dow Jones Industrial Average lost another 777 points, the biggest one-day drop ever. Another report indicated that 159,000 jobs had been lost in September. The crisis was spreading far beyond the banks. As credit and confidence dried up, people saw jobs, savings, and pensions disappear. The American economy seemed to be teetering badly. Finally, on Friday October 3, under pressure from President Bush and from both major presidential candidates,

Jeff Grace/LA OPINION/Newscom

Inflated housing prices and problems with home mortgages helped cause the financial crisis of 2008. As a result, many people were evicted or forced to sell homes they could no longer afford, which produced a glut in the housing market and a significant drop in home prices and values.

Congress passed the TARP legislation. The law created a $700 billion fund to buy troubled assets from the banks and stabilize the system. "We have shown the world that the United States will stabilize our financial markets and maintain a leading role in the global economy," Bush said.

In May 2009, Congress created a Financial Crisis Inquiry Commission to hold hearings and study the crisis. At one hearing, in June 2010, the financier Warren Buffett was asked who was to blame. "[I]t's a little bit like Cinderella at the ball," Buffett said. "People may have some feeling that at midnight it's going to turn to pumpkin and mice, but it's so darn much fun. ... There's no villain." Others thought there was some specific blame to be assigned. People blamed Lehman Brothers and other banks. They blamed the auditing companies that should have looked more closely at the account books of the banks. They blamed the repeal of Glass-Steagall since the old law would have prevented banks from speculation. And many saw the crisis as one more in the sad long line of investment bubbles that, when they burst, hurt not only those caught up in the speculation but also the economy of the whole nation and, indeed, of the world. Certainly, the crisis could have been worse, and the work of the treasury secretary and the TARP legislation may have kept the country from another Great Depression. However, as Congressman Barney Frank said of Paulson's efforts, "You don't get any credit for disaster averted."

After 2008, unemployment rates stayed stubbornly high. In 2009 and 2010, the United States had an official unemployment rate of 10 percent, and if one counted discouraged and part-time workers, it was closer to 16 percent. Those who lost their jobs were out of work for increasingly longer periods of time. High unemployment creates its own negative cycle. For the unemployed, it is devastating. When unemployed people do not buy cars, computers, and refrigerators, the whole economy slows down.

The crisis of 2008 also brought other economic problems to light. Three months after the collapse of Lehman Brothers, a New York financier, Bernard Madoff, was arrested and charged with securities fraud. Madoff's Investment Securities Company was, in reality, a giant Ponzi scheme (see Chapter 21). Madoff delivered grand returns on investments made with his company, but it turned out that Madoff simply used newly invested funds to pay out high returns on older funds. He did not invest, or even save them. As long as more money kept coming in, Madoff was able to keep up the illusion of amazing success, and investors were happy. When the nation's finances seized up in the fall of 2008, Madoff was not able to keep the investments coming in, and without them, the payments could not keep going out, and the whole house of cards collapsed. Madoff was sentenced to 150 years in prison; investors lost between $10 and $17 billion.

In May 2011, another highly regarded investor, Raj Rajaratnam, head of the Galleon Group, a multibillion-dollar hedge fund, or speculative investment group, was convicted of fourteen counts of securities fraud for bribing corporate employees to provide inside information that allowed Galleon to "guess" future stock values and make a fortune. By 2011, business leaders, and especially investors, were not highly regarded by a large segment of the American public.

Business leaders were not the only ones held in low esteem, however. Why, people asked, did the government officials bail out banks and the auto industry but not individuals who had lost jobs or were about to lose homes? Why was so much taxpayer money needed to stabilize investment banks when bankers were still getting huge bonuses but unemployment stayed stubbornly high? Were the high officials in the Treasury Department really on the side of the average American? Some wondered when the real recovery would begin. Some wondered whether the United States was at the beginning of a permanent decline while other nations, especially perhaps China, might replace it as the world's leading financial powerhouse.

30.2 Quick Review

How did the response to Hurricane Katrina and the financial crisis of 2008 lead to a new level of distrust of government?

The Obama Years

30.3 Analyze the reasons for the successes and failures of the Obama administration and changes in the American culture while he was president.

Barack Obama was elected as a U.S. Senator from Illinois, just as George W. Bush won a second term in 2004. Many noticed Obama's upset win in a seven-way Illinois Democratic primary, his "politics of hope" keynote speech at the 2004 Democratic convention, his telegenic appearance, and his ability to rally people. He was born a biracial child to an African father and a white mother from the American heartland, was a community organizer in Chicago, graduated from Harvard Law School, and was a Illinois state senator before his election to the U.S. Senate.

Nevertheless, Obama was a Senate freshman when Majority Leader Harry Reid called him in for a meeting. Heading to the meeting, Obama told his scheduler Robert Gibbs, "I wonder what we screwed up." But afterwards, a stunned Obama told Gibbs, "Harry wants me to run for president.. . . He really wants me to run for president."

Reid had noticed Obama's ability to connect with voters. Reid also worried that the frontrunner for the Democratic nomination in 2008, Hillary Clinton, was deeply unpopular with many voters despite her obvious competence and experience. Party leaders, desperate for another candidate, thought they had found one in Obama.

The Election of 2008

In modern American politics, being anointed by the party's leaders is a far cry from being nominated. Running for high office required Obama and the other candidates to slog through months of primary elections, including the Iowa caucuses and the New Hampshire primary in January and February, until the midsummer nominating convention. All along the way, voters were more than happy to overrule the party elite.

Senator Obama visited Netscape founder Marc Andreessen (see Chapter 29) and told him that he wanted to run the most sophisticated digital campaign on record. Andreessen was impressed that "the Senator was personally interested in the rise of social networking, Facebook, YouTube, and user-generated content." With the help of the Internet, Obama was able to raise twice the funds of his main rival, Hillary Clinton, and go on to win the nomination in spite of a long and bruising race.

The battle for the Republican nomination was as hard fought. President Bush could not run for a third term, and his popularity had sunk as a result of the war and financial crisis. Arizona senator John McCain was the frontrunner throughout the campaign. McCain had almost defeated Bush for the nomination in 2000 and was a war hero—having been a prisoner of war in Vietnam. He also had a hair-trigger temper and had experienced an ugly divorce before remarrying. Nevertheless, McCain's reputation as a moderate and an independent meant that he would not be tarred with all of Bush's troubles. In spite of several primary challengers, McCain won key Republican primaries, and the Republican nomination. The only remaining question was who he would select to be his running mate.

McCain needed a game-changing move. He selected the forty-four-year-old governor of Alaska, Sarah Palin. She was popular in Alaska and had conservative Republican credentials. Palin became a campaign sensation, but her lack of familiarity with national politics and her feuding with the McCain campaign staff probably hurt as much as it helped. When Obama asked Delaware senator Joseph Biden to be his running mate, the contrast between someone with decades of national experience and Alaska's twenty-month governor could not have been greater, even considering that Obama himself was still in his first term in the Senate.

The September financial crisis played to Obama's strengths. McCain always said that economic issues were not his strong point. In contrast, Obama had a good grasp of economic issues and spent his time learning from people like Bush's treasury secretary Paulson and Federal Reserve chair Ben Bernanke, both of whom came to respect him. At the same time, the economy and the war in Iraq continued to hamper the Republicans. On Election Day, Obama defeated McCain by 53 percent to 46 percent of the vote, carrying 365 electoral votes to McCain's 173 votes. The nation, which had fought a civil war and witnessed a long civil

In November 2008, Barack Obama, born in 1961 in Hawaii to a father from Kenya and a mother from Kansas, became president of the United States—a time of celebration for many.

health-care reform

The top priority of the Obama administration to provide universal health care for all Americans.

rights movement over issues of race, had just elected its first African American president. Some argued that the election proved that the nation had transcended the long-simmering issue of race. Others were not so sure and saw Obama as a unique individual whose election did not change as much as hoped.

Obama's Agenda—Stimulus, a Health Plan, and Economic Reform

President-elect Obama asked his former primary opponent Hillary Clinton to serve as his secretary of state and she did. In addition, he knew that while the TARP bailout of the banks had been a first step, much more needed to be done.

Obama was famous for his use of a Blackberry and an iPhone during his Senate career and his presidential campaign. Bemoaning the need to give up his iPhone for security reasons once elected president, Obama continued to use a Blackberry as well as his personal Twitter account, his MacBook Pro, and an iPad 2. The world of high technology arrived in the White House in January 2009.

Immediately on taking office in January 2009, Obama proposed the American Recovery and Reinvestment Act as a way to move beyond the Bush-sponsored TARP legislation, and like TARP, it passed within weeks. The act pumped money into the economy, providing funds for road improvements, railroads, and unemployment benefits, not just for stability as TARP had done. The Recovery and Reinvestment Act was standard economics, an effort to "prime the pump" and get the economy moving by spending funds so employment would rise, private spending would pick up, and the government could step back. Unfortunately for Obama, the emergency spending piled further debts on top of those already in place, and many began to worry about the cost, especially when not enough people saw the immediate benefit.

Obama also moved quickly to implement what he hoped would be his signature initiative: health care for all Americans. From Harry Truman on, every Democratic administration sought to implement **health-care reform**, but every effort had failed. Obama wanted to be the Democrat who accomplished it. After a long and bitter fight, he was able to sign the Patient Protection and Affordable Care Act on March 23, 2010. The law quickly became known as Obamacare, first by critics, though the president soon embraced the term. Unlike the stimulus legislation, however, health care was a long fight, filled with compromises. It dominated the Congress that came to office with Obama. The Republican minority was dedicated to defeating the measure while many Democratic senators demanded special concessions and exemptions to win their support. The result was that the historic health-care legislation passed with only Democratic votes and only after a long political process that discouraged almost everyone. The new law required every American to have health insurance; prohibited insurance companies from excluding anyone, including those with preexisting conditions; provided government subsidies for those who have trouble buying insurance; and penalized employers not offering health insurance. A number of state attorneys general challenged the legislation in court, but in the spring of 2012, the U.S. Supreme Court in a split decision upheld the law. Surprising its supporters, the law ended up being a political liability for a Democratic president and his party in the midterm elections of 2010 and the presidential elections of 2012 and 2016. Only after the 2016 election brought the country a Republican president and majority in Congress did many realize how many people were helped by the legislation and how difficult it was to replace.

Early in the implementation of the Recovery and Reinvestment Act, the administration invested significant funds in support of education reform. The Common Core State Standards were originally launched by state governors and superintendents to ensure a common experience of students across the nation, but the standards lost favor as they came to be seen as a federal intrusion, especially after the Obama administration invested so much in the implementation process.

Only in 2015 did the administration finally achieve a replacement for the unpopular Bush-era No Child Left Behind Act. The new law, called the Every Student Succeeds Act, gave states much greater leeway in the implementation of policies even as it maintained the basic goals of the earlier legislation. It was ironic that an administration that had used the tools of No Child Left Behind to try to reshape American education supported legislation that shifted so much power out of the federal government and to the individual states.

One of Obama's other major goals was termed the DREAM Act, a law meant to grant permanent legal status to children who were undocumented immigrants and those who had served in the military. When it became clear in 2011 that the logjam in Congress meant that no bill would emerge, the president implemented part of the act through a 2012 administrative action, but a court challenge stopped the presidential directive before it could be enforced. In fact, the Obama administration deported more undocumented people than any previous administration, and some called the president the "deporter in chief." Immigration was a major issue in the campaign to succeed Obama and, it seemed, was bound to remain a contentious issue after Obama left office.

After the passage and implementation of the stimulus bill, which was Obama's initial response to the financial crisis of 2008, he wanted to make more systemic changes in the role of government as economic stabilizer. The Dodd-Frank bill, named for its Senate and House sponsors, was signed in 2010. It created complex layers of reporting and a number of new agencies, including the relatively popular Consumer Financial Protection Bureau to oversee credit card and mortgage borrowing and the Financial Stability Oversight Council to ensure there was no repeat of the bubble of 2008. The new law involved detailed reporting procedures for businesses, something that cost Obama support on Wall Street, but critics said it did not have the teeth of the kinds of legislation that had been passed in the New Deal.

While Obama had significant legislative victories, especially given the fact that Republicans were in charge of the House of Representatives for six of his eight years in office, he was not always viewed as a highly effective president. Obama was one of the most stirring orators in history, but he stayed removed from the day-to-day give-and-take of politics, which limited his ability to get things done. He left office with very high public approval but a sense that he might have done more.

The Rise of the Tea Party, Occupy Wall Street, and Divided Government

In part because of anger at the health-care legislation, in part because of fears about the growing national debt, and in part because of a long-standing bias among Americans against big government, the huge plurality with which Obama came to office started to evaporate rapidly.

Less than a year after Obama's inauguration, the growing voter anger became apparent to the nation, particularly after one of the icons of American liberalism, Massachusetts senator Edward M. Kennedy, died of a brain tumor in August 2009. Kennedy had served in the U.S. Senate since 1962, the fourth-longest Senate career in U.S. history. A special election was called to fill Kennedy's unexpired term, and almost everyone assumed that whoever received the Democratic nomination would get the job. But a little known Republican state senator, Scott Brown, campaigned hard, promising to be the crucial vote to sustain a filibuster in the Senate against the health-care legislation. To the surprise of many, Brown won. Although he was not able to stop the passage of the health-care law, Brown's election was a sign that something was shifting in American politics. It was not the first such sign.

Only weeks after Obama's inauguration, protests were springing up in many different places. In Seattle, a twenty-nine-year-old woman, Keli Carender, organized a small protest rally about "the spending," whether it was Bush's TARP or Obama's stimulus. Carender told a small crowd that "I started thinking, what are we getting ourselves into? It didn't make sense to me to be spending all this money when we don't have it." Then, a little while later, on February 19, 2009, a financial news commentator, Rick Santelli, said that Obama's

30.1

30.2

30.3

30.4

30.1

30.2

30.3

30.4

The Tea Party movement named itself after those who had dumped tea in Boston Harbor in 1773 rather than pay a tax on it. Many in the modern movement shared the antitax, antigovernment sentiments of the earlier Tea Party, while some dressed the part.

stimulus efforts were "promoting bad behavior" if they bailed out "the losers" who had offered or taken out mortgages that they could not afford. Santelli said, "We're thinking of having a Chicago **Tea Party** in July." And the name took hold.

In September 2010, between seventy thousand and ninety thousand demonstrators converged on Washington, D.C., to protest the health-care legislation and government spending, especially the bailouts of banks and, later, auto manufacturers. Some wore tricorn hats to symbolize their link to the original Boston Tea Party. Some, alluding to fears that the health-care legislation would limit treatments, carried signs that said, "Pull the plug on Obama, not Grandma." Tea Party candidates challenged Republicans in primary elections all through 2009 and 2010 and sometimes defeated long-standing Republican moderates. In November 2010, with solid Tea Party support, Republicans took control of the House of Representatives and made gains in the Senate. But the Tea Party candidates were of a different sort than the older Republicans, not only more conservative but also far less willing to compromise.

The Tea Party was fueled by fear about the debt, uncertainty about the economy, and anger at big institutions, most of all the federal government but also corporations and universities. Many in the Tea Party were distrustful of nearly all government programs, especially those designed to help the poor or minority groups. It quickly became clear that the Tea Party was not going away, even though its membership might be filled with internal contradictions. Tea Party members disliked government but wanted their Social Security checks to arrive on time; they hated the new health-care act but loved their Medicare cards. When the outgoing Congress repealed the "Don't Ask, Don't Tell" ban on gay and lesbian personnel serving in the military in late 2010, the Tea Party was divided about its response; neither the Tea Party nor the Republicans made it a major issue. Still, the Tea Party, with its focus on economic issues and anger at big government, was a powerful group.

In the summer of 2011, the new Tea Party–fueled Republican majority in the House of Representatives brought the country to the brink of financial default as they refused until the last minute to raise the nation's borrowing capacity. Standard & Poor's, one of the nation's leading auditing agencies, lowered the U.S. credit rating for the first time in history because of the government's seeming inability to deal with the federal debt.

As if in response to the Tea Party, a new movement of students and other young people also emerged to protest conditions in the country. While the Tea Party took a conservative

Tea Party

A protest group whose members sometimes modeled themselves on the Tea Party of the American Revolution and objected to the rising federal debt, Obamacare, and most government regulation.

stance on economic issues, **Occupy Wall Street** was closer to the left on most issues. In September 2011, a group of young people held a rally near Wall Street in Lower Manhattan and then moved into nearby Zuccotti Park where they planned to stay. A Canadian publication, *Adbusters*, had been calling for just such a move, and by late September it was a reality. The rallying cry of Occupy Wall Street was "We are the 99%" to differentiate themselves from the richest 1 percent, including the bankers who surrounded them in Lower Manhattan. Although those gathering in protest consistently refused to issue a manifesto or platform, Occupy was an angry response to the financial crisis and the growing gap

Occupy Wall Street

A protest group that protested the rising level of student debt, the lack of job opportunities, and the fact that the economy seemed stacked in favor of the rich.

30.1

30.2

30.3

30.4

Thinking Historically

Same-Sex Marriage

On June 26, 2013, in a 5–4 opinion in the case of **United States v. Windsor***, the U.S. Supreme Court declared a significant part of the Defense of Marriage Act (DOMA) unconstitutional. Writing for the majority, Justice Anthony Kennedy said, "DOMA's principal effect is to identify a subset of state-sanctioned marriages and make them unequal. … This places same-sex couples in an unstable position of being in a second-tier marriage."*

The decision was not without debate. Four justices opposed the majority. Writing for the minority, Justice Antonin Scalia said that the Court should never have taken on the case and, further, that the decision would lead inevitably to the Supreme Court's declaring all state laws against gay marriage to be invalid, which is exactly what the Court did in June 2015. In the 2015 case, **Obergefell v. Hodges**, the Court, also in a 5–4 vote, legalized gay marriage in all fifty states. Justice Kennedy again wrote the majority opinion, adding that the decision granted same-sex marriages "equal dignity in the eyes of the law," fulfilling a basic constitutional safeguard.

In both cases, the majority opinion became the law of the land. After 2015, same-sex marriage was legal everywhere in the United States.

When the Congress passed and President Bill Clinton signed the Defense of Marriage Act in September 1996, no state recognized same-sex marriage. But fearing the potential of same-sex marriage, the Republican Congress passed the Defense of Marriage Act and the Democratic president signed it. As a result, federal law said that no matter what a state did, in the eyes of the federal government (for federal income tax, for federal pensions, for benefits for spouses of government employees and armed forces personnel and many related matters), a state-sanctioned same-sex marriage was invalid.

Nevertheless, as some feared and others hoped, states started to act on their own. In 2003, the Massachusetts Supreme Judicial Court declared that state laws prohibiting same-sex marriage were invalid in that state and gay and lesbian couples began getting married there. State courts in other states, including California, Connecticut, and Iowa, issued similar rulings. Then in 2009, the Vermont legislature sanctioned same-sex marriage, New York followed in 2011, and in 2012 Washington, Maine, and Maryland passed similar laws. By the time *Obergefell v. Hodges* came before the Court, the majority of states allowed same-sex marriage and only fifteen had outright bans.

MARCIO SANCHEZ/POOL/EPA/Newscom

Activists Phyllis Lyon and Del Martin became the first same-sex couple to be married in San Francisco on February 12, 2004. In June 2013, the U.S. Supreme Court said that same-sex couples could not be denied federal marriage benefits.

Same-sex marriages, illegal in every part of the United States as late as 2002, were recognized everywhere in 2015. The issue had been a major one in earlier elections, especially in 2004, and Obama was the first president to support it—though only when he ran for reelection in 2012—but after 2015, the issue virtually disappeared as a major divide. Although many Republicans still opposed same-sex marriage, and nearly all Democrats including all the 2016 candidates supported it, even its opponents seldom made a major issue of the topic by 2016. Opinion polls indicated that the majority of the American people agreed with the new policies. It was a rapid and dramatic change in American culture.

Thinking Critically

1. **Comparison**
   How would you compare the political mood in the United States when the Defense of Marriage Act was passed in 1996 and when it was declared unconstitutional in 2015?

2. **Contextualization**
   What other developments in American culture and political debate might help explain decisions like those of the Massachusetts Supreme Court, the Vermont legislature, or in 2013 and 2015, the U.S. Supreme Court?

United States v. Windsor

30.1 A June 2013 Supreme Court decision that declared Americans in same-sex marriages had the same federal rights as all other married citizens.

30.2

Obergefell v. Hodges

30.3 A Supreme Court case, decided in 2015 in a 5–4 vote, which legalized gay marriage in all fifty states.

30.4

between rich and poor in the country. They condemned the huge level of college debt that many young people were carrying and the difficulties for a new generation in getting jobs.

Before long, Occupy movements were springing up all around the country—Occupy Los Angeles, Occupy Oakland, Occupy Denver, Occupy Boston, and Occupy Rochester. In November, some three months after the encampment at Zuccotti Park began, New York police cleared the park. But the Occupy movement was far from over. Through the winter and the following years, Occupy held rallies, meetings, and planning sessions.

The Election of 2012

As President Obama and the Democrats looked to the 2012 election, they did so with considerable optimism. The worst of the financial crisis seemed to be past, and the wars in Iraq and Afghanistan were at least winding down. U.S. intelligence had finally tracked down Osama bin Laden and he was killed in a raid in 2011. At the same time, the president and his party were aware of some significant liabilities. The economy remained far from robust; the health-care law—which some now called Obamacare—remained unpopular, especially among people who resented all forms of government intrusion in their lives. Many of those who had voted for the first time in 2008 to support Obama were disillusioned with the slow pace of change and might well not bother to vote in 2012. It was going to be a close contest.

The battle for the Republican nomination was a long one. Former Massachusetts governor Mitt Romney was always one of the frontrunners. But a number of other candidates, including former Minnesota governor Tim Pawlenty, former Speaker Newt Gingrich, businessman Herman Cain, and Representative Michele Bachmann, gave Romney a strong challenge. In the end, Romney won the nomination and asked Congressman Paul Ryan, who had earned his conservative credentials with a series of tax-cutting proposals, to be his running mate.

One of Romney's great strengths, his years of business experience, came to hurt him as Democrats exploited the numbers of layoffs that had taken place in Romney-owned companies. Obama won by a solid 51 percent to 47 percent majority and carried 332 electoral votes to Romney's 206 (see Map 30-2). The Congress, however, remained divided, with Democrats having a majority in the Senate and Republicans in the House.

Map 30-2 The Election of 2012.

This map captures the extent of Obama's presidential election triumph and underscores the realignments of Republican red states and Democratic blue states.

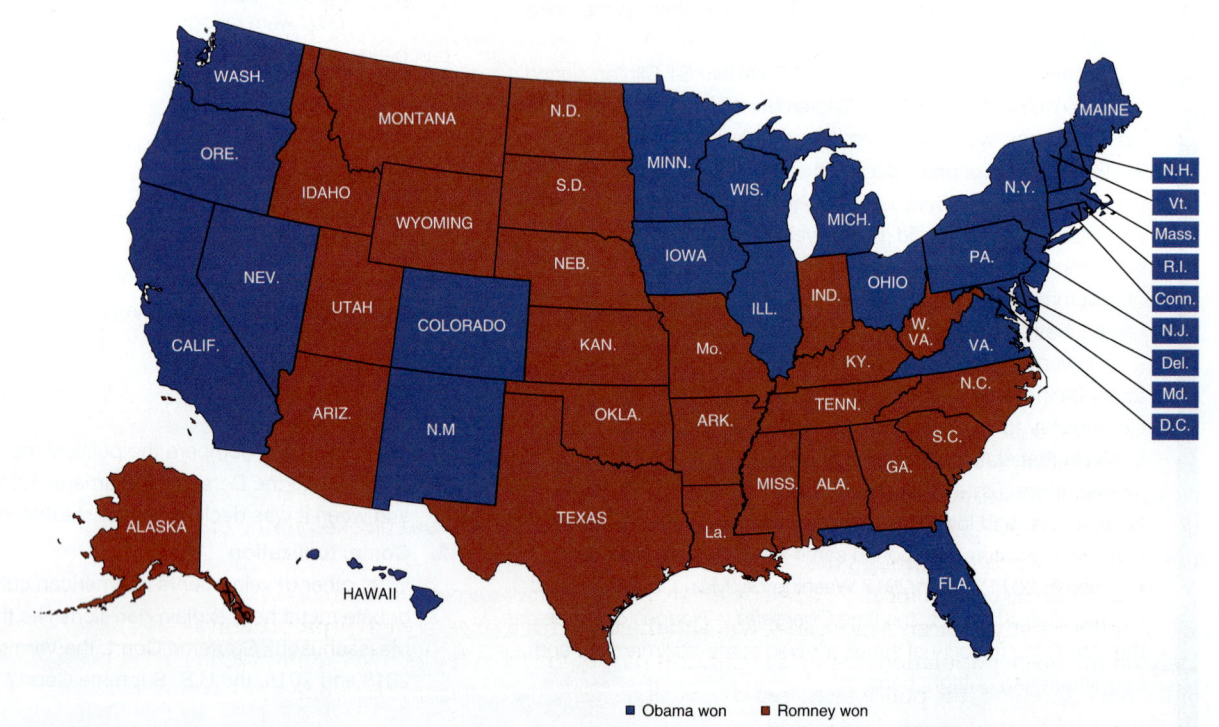

■ Obama won ■ Romney won

Soon after the inauguration, Obama said he would use executive authority to institute action on climate change and quickly issued tough new limitations on emissions. As he faced a divided Congress through his second term, the president turned more and more to executive authority to get things done on climate, immigration, and a number of other issues. Supporters of what the president was doing were thrilled to see a more activist White House, while critics worried about growing independent presidential power and what it might mean for the future.

30.1

30.2

30.3

30.4

30.3 Quick Review

How have domestic issues contributed to divisions in the government and the country during Obama's time in office?

New Liberals, New Conservatives, Election Surprises

30.4 Analyze the most recent political developments in the United States from the Tea Party movement to the election of Donald Trump as president in 2016.

In the years after 2012, the United States remained a very divided place. Although the divide was strong between Republicans and Democrats, each party also had bitter internal divisions. And the divides seemed to be everywhere. Many Americans said they had lost faith in both political parties and in most elected leaders.

The significant divide of race showed no signs of being healed. With the election, and reelection, of the nation's first African American president, some had hoped that there could be a new "post-racial" era, but events across the country during Obama's second term showed that hope to be illusory. In addition, the economic recovery after 2008 was not spread at all evenly. While some prospered, quickly returning to or surpassing their pre-2008 economic status, many other Americans, across racial and ethnic groups, found themselves stuck with stagnant or falling wages. A nation that had long seen itself as middle-class was now divided between a few who were very comfortable or extremely wealthy and a larger number who felt their economic prospects dimming if not outright disastrous. Especially with the growth of the Latino population, Americans of European American background were becoming a minority—slowly in some places and very rapidly in others such as California. Those who had long thought of the nation as a white and Christian country sometimes found it difficult to adjust. And all of the tensions fed each other and made it even more difficult for healing to take place or national policy to be made.

Black Lives Matter

In August 2014, a town most Americans had never heard of, Ferguson, Missouri, became a flash point for the nation's ongoing racial crisis. A young black man, Michael Brown, was shot and killed by a Ferguson police officer. In the aftermath of the shooting, Brown's body was left on the street for over four hours while his parents were kept away at gunpoint. The black community in Ferguson exploded, and soon, people were coming from across the United States to support them. The anger shocked the nation as protesters held vigils but also challenged the police directly, picketed the police headquarters, and blocked traffic on Interstate 70, which ran through the city.

Part of the issue was local. The nearly all-white police force was seen as an occupying army in the mostly African American town, and the town used fines, levied disproportionately on the black population, to pay a significant part of the town budget. In the aftermath of Brown's shooting, the police increased the tensions, defacing memorials set up for Brown and using rubber bullets on demonstrators.

Events in Ferguson dominated the news, as reports of other blacks suffering at the hands of white police officers had not. Past tensions between African American communities and many mostly white police forces had fueled the growth of the Black Panther Party in the 1970s and convulsed many cities in the 1980s, 1990s, and early 2000s. But from the summer of 2014 onward, something new was happening—in the attention being paid to the issue, the level of anger and resistance in black communities, the ways new technologies made information available, and the size of the response. The advent of new smartphones meant that many citizens could make video images and distribute them. Many more people than before were appalled at the police violence that they saw, which began leading to mass protests, especially when, in most cases, the police officers involved were never charged. In July 2014, just before the events in Ferguson, Eric Garner, who had been selling cigarettes on the streets of New York's Staten Island, was arrested and killed when the arresting officer held him in a chokehold. A video of the arrest went viral as Garner pleaded for his life, saying again and again, "I can't breathe," before his death. Athletes wore T-shirts saying "I can't breathe" and New Yorkers joined in protest. In the course of 2014, there were more deaths. Twelve-year-old Tamir Rice was shot and killed while playing with a toy gun in Cleveland, Ohio. Tanisha Anderson was killed when another Cleveland officer slammed her to the ground and her head hit the concrete. The following year, Freddie Gray was killed in Baltimore, Maryland. Videos, Twitter communications, Facebook posts, and a generalized sense of outrage all helped spread the response.

A new decentralized organization, Black Lives Matter, had been created in response to the killing of an unarmed black teenager, Trayvon Martin, in 2013, but in the summer of 2014, it became the voice of a new political movement, a voice that was amplified across the nation through social media. Demanding an end to police brutality everywhere, Black Lives Matter was highly decentralized but very effective. Sounding much like those who organized the Student Nonviolent Coordinating Committee and lunch-counter sit-ins in the 1960s, Johnetta Elzie, a young resident of Ferguson, said, "The youth leading this movement is important because it is our time. For so long the elders have told us our generation doesn't fight for anything, or that we don't care about what goes on in the world. We have proved them wrong." Another speaker told a forum in Ferguson, "This ain't your grandparents' civil rights movement." Even as they built on a long line of civil rights efforts, the many diverse leaders of Black Lives Matter were determined to strike out in a new way that fit their generation.

Economic Troubles, Economic Stagnation, and a Divided Nation

Most economists agree that sometime after 1970, a sixty-year trend toward greater economic equality came to an end, and inequality—the differences in salaries and in net worth between the rich and everyone else—began to grow. They also agree that, after the economic crisis of 2008, inequality became much greater than ever. In August 2016, the Congressional Budget Office issued a report noting that the top 10 percent of the population now holds about three-quarters of total family wealth, on average about $4 million per family; a middle group owns about a quarter of total family wealth, or $36,000 per family; and the bottom half of the population is simply in debt, about $13,000 in debt on average per family. Different reports give different numbers, but few disagree about the general pattern. While economists differ on exact numbers and on the reasons they give for the cause of this development, very few, whether conservative or liberal, disagree about the reality.

At the same time, many Americans do not need an economist to tell them that their economic prospects are not good—neither as good as those of their parents' generation nor as good as they had hoped. Many young people blame the huge increase in college debt, one of the issues that fueled Occupy Wall Street. Others blame the growth of free trade and the end of trade barriers that had protected American workers and American jobs—though this issue is hotly debated. Others blame the rapid decline in organized labor and the fact that more and more jobs do not have union salaries or union benefits. Finally, some economists

American Voices

Understanding Black Lives Matter

Black Lives Matter is a loose coalition of mostly young activists who are committed to ending police violence in black communities and to building a new civil rights movement in the United States. Describing themselves, the Black Lives Matter website says:

> When we say Black Lives Matter, we are broadening the conversation around state violence to include all of the ways in which Black people are intentionally left powerless at the hands of the state.

Many of the Black Lives Matter leaders speak of their frustration with an older generation of civil rights leaders. The coalition rejects what they see as the old ways of the movement that kept straight black men in the front, and they insist:

> Black Lives Matter affirms the lives of Black queer and trans folks, disabled folks, Black-undocumented folks, folks with records, women and all Black lives along the gender spectrum. It centers those that have been marginalized within Black liberation movements.

* * *

Keeanga-Yamahata Taylor, a Princeton University scholar sympathetic to the movement, describes the birth of Black Lives Matter:

> Every movement needs a catalyst, an event that captures people's experiences and draws them out from their isolation into a collective force with the power to transform social conditions. Few could have predicted that white police officer Darren Wilson shooting Mike Brown would ignite a rebellion in a small, largely unknown Missouri suburb called Ferguson. For reasons that may never be clear, Brown's death was a breaking point for the African Americans of Ferguson but also for hundreds of thousands of Black people across the United States.

* * *

Studying the Black Lives Matter movement, Deen Freelon, Charlton D. McIlwain, and Meredith D. Clark see it as a significant example of the power of newer media to support various liberation movements. They write:

> In the United States, police violence against people of African descent is nothing new. But widespread public use of mobile phone cameras and social media has recently thrust the issue into the national spotlight like never before. Videos, images, and text narratives of violent encounters between police and unarmed black people circulated widely through news and social media in the summer of 2014, galvanizing public outrage. …

"#Blacklivesmatter" and "Black Lives Matter" are not synonyms. The Twitter hashtag was created in July 2013 by activists Alicia Garza, Patrisse Cullors, and Opal Tometi in the wake of George Zimmerman's acquittal for second-degree murder of unarmed Black teenager Trayvon Martin. For more than a year, #Blacklivesmatter was only a hashtag, and not a very popular one; it was used in only 48 public tweets in June 2014 and in 398 tweets in July 2014. But by August 2014 that number had skyrocketed to 52,288 partly due to the slogan's frequent use in the context of the Ferguson [Missouri] protests.

* * *

While the rallying cry "black lives matter" struck a chord among many, others found themselves fearful of the anger and the potential for separatism. Some whites insisted, "All lives matter," but many African Americans responded, "Yes, but it is black lives that are threatened by police violence and that is what we are talking about right now." In July 2016, former New York mayor Rudy Giuliani lashed out at Black Lives Matter after five Dallas policemen were killed by a lone black shooter. The killings were condemned by Black Lives Matter, but Giuliani said the movement had painted a target on the police and ignored black-on-black crime. On CBS's Face the Nation, *the former mayor continued:*

> When you say black lives matter, that's inherently racist. … Black lives matter. White lives matter. Asian lives matter. Hispanic lives matter. That's anti-American, and it's racist.

The divisions over race, dating back to the landing of the first enslaved Africans in the early 1500s, did not seem about to end in the early 2000s.

Sources: www.blacklivesmatter.com/about, downloaded August 26, 2016; Keeanga-Yamahtta Taylor, *From #BlackLivesMatter to Black Liberation* (Chicago: Haymarket Books, 2016), p. 153; Deen Freelon, Charlton D. McIlwain, and Meredith D. Clark, "Beyond the Hashtags: #Ferguson, #Blacklivesmatter, and the online struggle for offline justice" (Washington, DC: Center for Media and Social Impact, 2016); Megan Twohey, "Rudolph Giuliani Lashes Out at Black Lives Matter," *New York Times*, July 10, 2016.

Thinking Critically

1. **Comparison**
   How do you account for the huge differences in perspective between #BlackLivesMatter and Mayor Giuliani? How much is an issue of race? How much is related to other factors?

2. **Contextualization**
   How does the context of other developments during the Obama years—new media as well as changes in race relations—impact all of these statements?

insist that, though inequality is rising, many are actually better off than in the past, though others dispute that claim.

Most statistics point to a general stagnation in salaries among the vast majority of Americans. But it is not just salaries that seem to be stuck. The sociologist Arlie Russell Hochschild reports that a large number of people fear a range of forces, cultural eclipse

Janine Wiedel Photolibrary/Alamy Stock Photo

In the summer and fall of 2014, a new political movement, Black Lives Matter, often led by young women, galvanized African American communities across the United States as protests of the killing of blacks by police escalated.

along with economic decline and a sense that the government has betrayed them. This level of alienation is especially true among working-class whites and males but includes a good number of women; it is also true among people who feel that the bailout saved the banks but did not help them and among those who believe that many upper-middle-class professionals are doing quite well but look down on others. In addition, the sense of alienation is fueled by the fact that, far too often, Americans speak only to people like themselves and do not meet or mingle or listen to people of other races or economic brackets. The nation seems divided by class, by geography, and by basic attitudes toward the government and toward other Americans.

The Angry Election of 2016

In the midst of many debates—about politics, about race, about economics—the United States turned to another presidential election to be held in November 2016. The midterm elections of 2014 had brought Republican majorities to both houses of Congress, but both parties were as divided internally as they were from each other. Republican House Speaker John Boehner was forced out by conservatives in his own caucus in 2015 because he seemed too willing to compromise. Both parties saw the rise of so-called outsider candidates in 2016. Even though the platforms of the two major outsiders could not have been more different, there was a sense of rebellion in the air.

Among the Democrats, Hillary Clinton was the clear frontrunner for the 2016 presidential nomination, though some worried that she had also been the frontrunner in 2008 yet had lost the nomination to a then newcomer, Barack Obama. By 2016, Clinton had gained significant stature—she had served as Obama's secretary of state for his first term—but she also had some new concerns to overcome, including the attack on Benghazi, Libya, in which the U.S. ambassador was killed while she was secretary of state and her use of a private e-mail server rather than the secure government one. Nevertheless, early on she seemed like the only serious candidate in the field, and the strength of her political and financial support kept other possible challengers out of the race.

Clinton was challenged by two less-well-known candidates, Martin O'Malley, former Maryland governor, and Bernie Sanders, an Independent senator from Vermont and

30.1

30.2

30.3

30.4

self-described democratic socialist who normally sided with Democrats in the Senate and was running for the Democratic nomination. While O'Malley dropped out early, Sanders became a surprisingly strong challenger. Sanders campaigned on the slogan "a future to believe in," promising to widen Obamacare into a guaranteed medical program for all, to address the nation's growing income inequality through programs to close the gap, and to end what he called a corrupt campaign finance system that supported pro-business candidates in both parties. He was surprisingly popular, drawing huge crowds and becoming the first candidate in history to receive financial support from more than one million donors, mostly in small amounts. He rejected all large corporate support. He connected with white working-class voters, but trailed significantly among black voters. In the end, he could never overcome Clinton's institutional support and lead in fund-raising and recognition. At the Democratic Convention in July, Sanders endorsed her in a strong speech while insisting that "the political revolution continues" and maintaining his own organization. Clinton selected Virginia senator Tim Kaine as her vice presidential running mate and entered the fall campaign with a strong lead.

The Republican field was much more wide open with no clear frontrunner. Some thought that former Florida governor Jeb Bush would emerge as a consensus candidate, but though he received strong financial backing, he never took off with Republican primary voters. The field was crowded and early primary debates had as many as ten speakers on stage, with others in the wings, wanting to be there. Two Republican senators, Marco Rubio of Florida and Ted Cruz of Texas, were stronger than Bush in that crowded field, and some thought one of them would eventually emerge as the nominee. To the surprise of many, however, Donald Trump, a New York businessman and reality TV star, with no experience in elective office, won the most votes in primary after primary. Bernie Sanders ran well to the left of Hillary Clinton and the Democratic primaries; in contrast, Trump ran well to the right of most Republican candidates on some issues and toward a traditionally left stance on others. He was as strongly anti–free trade as Sanders was and, like Sanders among the Democrats, Trump tapped into the sense of alienation and "being left behind" that many voters—most of all white poor and working-class voters—felt. But quite unlike Sanders, Trump was also extremely anti-immigrant, especially attacking Muslim immigrants. At one point, he said he would bar all Muslims from entering the United States and at another promised to deport all eleven million undocumented (or illegal) immigrants currently in the United States and promised to build a wall to stop immigration from Mexico.

Most thought that Trump was too extreme a candidate to win the nomination, but his extremism, his anti establishment rhetoric, and, some said, his not-very-hidden racism connected with a significant number of primary voters—more voters than any other single Republican candidate. By the end of the primaries, it was clear that the outside candidate had won the nomination against former governors and senators. Trump selected Indiana governor Mike Pence, a nationally known conservative, as his running mate.

Right up to the Republican nominating convention in Cleveland in August 2016, Republican nominee Mitt Romney along with many other moderate Republicans did everything they could to stop the nomination. Former presidents George Bush, father and son, announced that they would not vote for Trump. Former nominee John McCain said that Trump had "fired up the crazies," but finding himself in a tough reelection battle for his Arizona Senate seat, endorsed him anyway. Most other current elected officials, from House Speaker Paul Ryan on down did the same thing. The fall election—pitting Hillary Clinton against Donald Trump—promised to be one of the most difficult on record.

In the fall of 2016, while the election was fought out, the country seemed caught in a moment of unusual malice. Candidates and their supporters displayed strong dislike of the other side that reached heights not seen in decades. More than almost any time since the Civil War, different Americans heard the news from different sources and, indeed, heard different news. Trump supporters chanted "lock her up" at political rallies, believing that Clinton's use of her private e-mail account was not only a serious mistake—which many believed it was—but also a crime. Many within Trump's base saw Clinton and the Democratic Party as elite snobs out of touch with many Americans' economic pain or, perhaps even more, many Americans' anger at being dismissed as not worthy of serious consideration. In contrast, Clinton supporters, including President Obama, feared Trump in a way that they had not feared previous Republican candidates. Trump's promise to build a wall all along the border with Mexico to stop immigration seemed outlandish, his anti-Muslim rhetoric seemed to play directly into the hands of Muslim extremists while alienating the majority of Muslims in the United States and the world, his continued demeaning comments about women frightened a wide range of women and led many women and men to oppose him, his willingness to humiliate people with disabilities and his very personal attacks on members of the media seemed out of bounds for any candidate, while his dismissal of concerns about climate change and his hair-trigger temper worried many who thought about the future of the planet and the control of the nuclear codes. On the other hand, every one of these positions seemed to solidify Trump's popularity with his core supporters.

At the same time, Americans thought about many things besides politics, and important community ties survived the turmoil. *New York Times* columnist Nicholas Kristof reminded readers that in the midst of an angry election, many Americans found ways to be generous. Kristof reported on an India-born Muslim, Malik Waliyani, who had recently bought a gas station and convenience store in Georgia but found his new business burglarized and damaged. It was not clear whether Waliyani's Muslim faith had been an issue in the destruction, but when the members of the Smoke Rise Baptist Church heard what happened and their pastor said, "Let's shower our neighbor with love. … Our faith inspires us to build bridges, not to label people," over two hundred church members bought gas and goods from Waliyani, letting him know they cared. As Kristof concluded, "Good people, like the members of Smoke Rise Baptist, are reweaving our nation's social fabric even as it is being torn."

In the weeks before the election, the nation's social fabric continued to tear. The candidates Hillary Clinton and Donald Trump met for three increasingly tense debates and, by the end, had dispensed with the usual handshakes and signs of comity. When stories of hugely demeaning comments and actions by Trump toward many women emerged, some Republicans distanced themselves from him and Clinton's lead widened, though Trump dismissed the comments as "locker room talk." Then a week before the election, the director of the FBI announced that he had found new material and was reopening the investigation into Clinton's use of her private e-mail account. The investigation was completed in only a few days and no new evidence of wrong doing was found, but the news seemed to slow Clinton's momentum.

Finally, as the long and angry campaign came to an end in the evening of November 8, 2016, it became clear that nearly all pollsters and commentators had been wrong. While Clinton carried the nation's cities—from New York to Atlanta to Chicago as well as smaller ones—and liberal states from Massachusetts to California, Trump carried the suburbs, most of the South, and surprisingly large majorities in rural areas everywhere (see Map 30-3). Clinton won almost three million more votes than Trump, but given the power of suburbs and rural areas in the Electoral College, Trump's victory in the electoral count that mattered was clear. The final popular vote was 65,844,610 for Clinton but 62,979,636 for Trump. In the Electoral College, however, Trump won 306 votes to 232 for Clinton. It was the third time in U.S. history that a Republican had won the electoral vote in spite of a Democrat winning the popular vote.

Trump's supporters saw the vote as a victory for the people who, like themselves, had been forgotten in a fast-changing America—a mostly older, often rural or suburban, and overwhelmingly white group. Clinton's supporters feared that the election had been determined by people who were afraid of a rapidly developing ethnic diversity of the country, discomfort with their candidate's gender, and nostalgia for an earlier time in the nation's history. They also worried about the mental stability of the president-elect and the anger that he and his supporters brought to the nation.

Christian Gooden/Tribune Content Agency LLC/Alamy Stock Photo

During the Fall 2016 campaign, Democratic nominee Hillary Clinton and Republican nominee Donald Trump participated in three increasingly tense debates that highlighted differences in their political philosophies and in their personal styles.

Whatever people's opinions, on January 20, 2017, Donald J. Trump was inaugurated as the forty-fifth president of the United States. The inner circle of his advisors seemed to represent a mix of some deeply ideologically conservatives, traditional politicians, and his family. His cabinet nominees were mostly highly successful business leaders who had made their fortunes and were now joining the team of another unusually successful businessman. They were largely white males, more so than any presidential cabinet since Ronald Reagan.

Richard Ellis/Alamy Stock Photo

After a hard-fought and close contest with Hillary Clinton, Donald Trump became the forty-fifth president of the United States on January 20, 2017.

Map 30-3 The Two Americas of 2016.

As this map shows, in the 2016 election, although Hillary Clinton won some three million more votes than Donald Trump, her voters were clustered in a few parts of the United States—mostly large urban areas and the West Coast. More sparsely populated parts of the nation voted for Trump by large majorities, which accounts not only for the land areas shown here but also for his victory in the all-important Electoral College in spite of his loss of the popular vote.

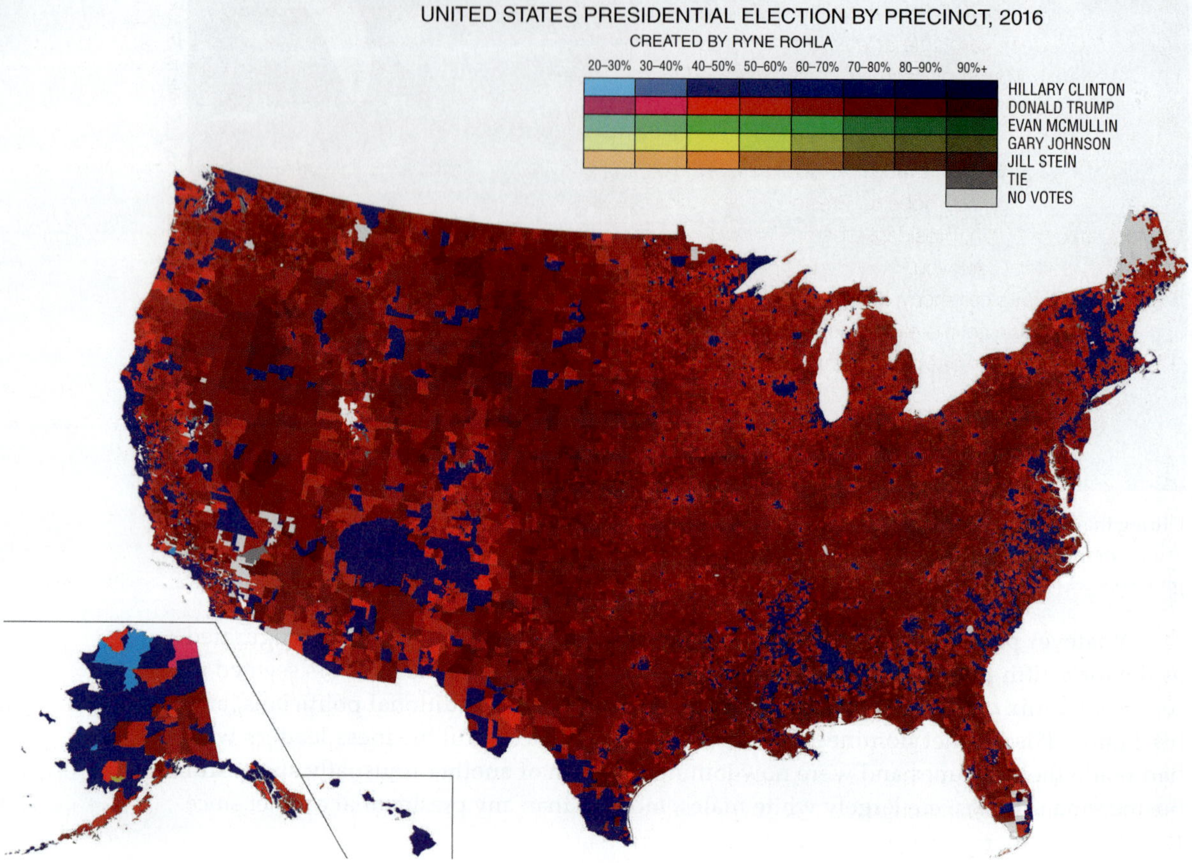

UNITED STATES PRESIDENTIAL ELECTION BY PRECINCT, 2016

CREATED BY RYNE ROHLA

20–30%	30–40%	40–50%	50–60%	60–70%	70–80%	80–90%	90%+	
								HILLARY CLINTON
								DONALD TRUMP
								EVAN MCMULLIN
								GARY JOHNSON
								JILL STEIN
								TIE
								NO VOTES

Ryne Rohla, National Precinct Map, 2016 Presidential General Election Maps. http://rynerohla.com/index.html/election-maps/2016-presidential-general-election-maps/Used with permission.

On Sunday, January 21, 2017, the day after the inauguration, the nation saw a unique response—a series of women-led marches across the nation, and indeed all around the world—protesting the policies that the new president had promised, especially his hostility to Muslims, to immigrants, and to women's rights. A small group of younger women had begun planning for such a demonstration immediately after the November vote, and by January, the expected crowd grew and grew—from early estimates of under 200,000 to the well over 500,000 in Washington, D.C., alone. While Trump had won the election especially because of his strong support in small towns and rural areas, the 500,000 to 1 million women and men who marched in Washington, D.C., were joined by 450,000 who marched in New York City and 175,000 in Boston but also 200 in Abilene, Texas; 500 in Bismarck, North Dakota; 7,200 in Birmingham, Alabama; 300–500 in Sheboygan, Wisconsin; and 3 hardy souls who marched in Nebraska City, Nebraska. In addition, thousands of others marched in cities around the world. All told, some 3 million to 5 million protesters marched in demonstrations across the nation and many others in numerous countries. Speaker after speaker at the Women's Marches made it clear that the new president was not going to have the honeymoon given to some of his predecessors and that whatever came next, the president's policies were going to be met with resistance at every turn. Bipartisanship in politics or national unity on almost any topic seemed a distant dream.

American Voices

Two Americas—2017

To the surprise of many, President Trump used his inaugural address to speak to the anger and alienation of his core constituency with little attention to unifying themes. The Women's March of January 21 represented a very different set of voices in the country. Speaker after speaker announced their commitment to resist the ideology and policies of the new administration, among them, a young actress, political activist, and daughter of Honduran parents—perhaps best known for her role in the TV series Ugly Betty—*thirty-two-year-old America Ferrera.*

Donald J. Trump, Inaugural Address, January 20, 2017

Chief Justice Roberts, President Carter, President Clinton, President Bush, President Obama, fellow Americans, and people of the world: Thank you. …

Today's ceremony, however, has very special meaning. Because today we are not merely transferring power from one administration to another, or from one party to another—but we are transferring power from Washington, D.C. and giving it back to you, the American People.

For too long, a small group in our nation's Capital has reaped the rewards of government while the people have borne the cost. Washington flourished—but the people did not share in its wealth. Politicians prospered—but the jobs left, and the factories closed.

The establishment protected itself, but not the citizens of our country. Their victories have not been your victories; their triumphs have not been your triumphs; and while they celebrated in our nation's capital, there was little to celebrate for struggling families all across our land.

That all changes—starting right here, and right now, because this moment is your moment: it belongs to you. … January 20th, 2017, will be remembered as the day the people became the rulers of this nation again. The forgotten men and women of our country will be forgotten no longer. …

Americans want great schools for their children, safe neighborhoods for their families, and good jobs for themselves. These are the just and reasonable demands of a righteous public.

But for too many of our citizens, a different reality exists: Mothers and children trapped in poverty in our inner cities; rusted-out factories scattered like tombstones across the landscape of our nation; an education system flush with cash, but which leaves our young and beautiful students deprived of knowledge; and the crime and gangs and drugs that have stolen too many lives and robbed our country of so much unrealized potential.

This American carnage stops right here and stops right now. . . .

And now we are looking only to the future. We assembled here today are issuing a new decree to be heard in every city, in every foreign capital, and in every hall of power.

From this day forward, a new vision will govern our land.

From this moment on, it's going to be America First.

Sources: Donald J. Trump, Inaugural Address, January 20, 2017. Retrieved from: www.whitehouse.gov/inaugural-address

---

America Ferrera, Speech at the Women's March, January 21, 2017

My name is America Ferrera. And I am deeply honored to march with you today as the chair of the artists' table, as a woman and as a proud first-generation American born to Honduran immigrants.

It's been a heart-rending time to be both a woman and an immigrant this country. Our dignity, our character, our rights have all been under attack, and a platform of hate and division assumed power yesterday. But the president is not America. His Cabinet is not America. Congress is not America. We are America! And we are here to stay!

We march today for our families and our neighbors, for our future, for the causes we claim and for the causes that claim us. We march today for the moral core of this nation, against which our new president is waging a war.

He would like us to forget the words *"Give me your tired, your poor, your huddled masses yearning to be free,"* and instead take up a credo of hate, fear and suspicion of one another.

But we are gathered here and across the country and around the world today to say, Mr. Trump, we refuse.

We reject the dehumanization of our Muslim mothers and sisters.

We demand an end to the systemic murder and incarceration of our black brothers and sisters.

We will not give up our right to safe and legal abortions.

We will not ask our LGBTQ families to go backwards.

We will not go from being a nation of immigrants to a nation of ignorance.

We won't build walls, and we won't see the worst in each other.

And we will not turn our backs on the more than 750,000 young immigrants in this country currently protected by DACA.

"Together we, all of us, will fight, resist and oppose every action that threatens the lives and dignity of any and all of our communities," America concluded. "Marchers, make no mistake. We are, every single one of us, on attack. Our safety and freedom are on the chopping block and we are the only ones who can protect one another. If we do not fight together… we will lose together."

Sources: America Ferrera, Speech at the Women's March, January 21, 2017. Used by permission.

Thinking Critically

1. Contextualization

In what specific ways does President Trump's 2017 speech reflect the themes of the 2016 presidential election? In what ways does Ferrera's speech reflect the Clinton campaign or something different?

2. Comparison

Note at least one similarity and one difference between President Trump's vision for the future of the United States and that of America Ferrera.

Jeff Grossman/WENN Ltd/Alamy Stock Photo

The day after President Trump's inauguration, hundreds of thousands of women and men participated in Women's Marches in cities across the United States and around the world to protest his announced policies.

30.4 Quick Review

Describe the major divisions in the United States after 2001—racial, economic, political, and cultural.

Conclusion

In the days after the September 11 attacks, the Bush administration immediately developed a strategy to punish those responsible. U.S. forces invaded Afghanistan, which was protecting Osama bin Laden and al-Qaeda, and quickly overthrew the Taliban regime there. Although the United States had forced a change in government in Afghanistan and had killed or captured many al-Qaeda operatives, others including bin Laden escaped into Pakistan. It took another ten years to find bin Laden; meanwhile, insurgents continued to engage the U.S. military and destabilize Afghanistan and other parts of the world.

While the United States waged war in Afghanistan, the Bush administration turned its attention to Iraq. Despite the lack of compelling evidence that Iraq was connected to the September 11 attacks, the United States and Great Britain obtained UN and congressional approval for an invasion, based on alleged Iraqi possession of weapons of mass destruction. Major combat operations in Iraq ended quickly, but the United States was ill prepared to serve as an occupying force, and Iraq quickly descended into civil war. By 2004, public opinion was turning against the war. U.S. casualties were high, Iraq was in chaos, and no weapons of mass destruction were ever found. Still, the U.S. mission in Iraq continued.

In Bush's second term, domestic problems also plagued the Bush administration. In 2005, the federal response to Hurricane Katrina was wholly inadequate, and after 2008, the U.S. economy was in a deep recession.

The 2008 presidential election culminated in the election of the nation's first African American president, Barack Obama. Obama moved quickly to address the financial crisis, but although the economy was eventually stabilized, unemployment remained high. The Obama administration's highest priority was to get Congress to approve a federal health insurance system, which was signed into law in 2010. In the midst of a very slow recovery in which ordinary Americans suffered greatly, new protests, including the Tea Party and the Occupy Wall Street movements, emerged to express voter dissatisfaction with continual war and with the economic meltdown. Obama won a second term in November 2012, but the political divisions in the country and in Washington continued. In the midst of this strengthening divide, the U.S. Supreme Court declared that same-sex marriage was a right everywhere in the country in 2015. Although the Court's decision was accepted by many, it greatly disturbed some, who resisted strongly. In addition, Obama's historic election and reelection had not meant that the nation had entered a "post-racial" era; indeed, the issue of race came to the foreground when in 2014 and 2015 a number of African Americans were killed by white police officers. A new organization, Black Lives Matter, promised the beginning of a new and different civil rights movement. The nation remained deeply divided on social, economic, and political issues throughout Obama's second term, and lasting resolutions seemed hard to find. In the election of 2016, many of the issues that had been bubbling up—anger about economic disparities, cultural alienation, gender, race, and immigration—all came to the foreground of national politics in an unusually nasty contest in which Donald Trump was elected. The divisions, turmoil, and deep concerns continued, however, and, indeed, even the social fabric that holds Americans together seems to be in for trying times.

Chapter Review

How did the election of 2016 encompass issues that had plagued the United States since 2000? How was it different?

Chapter 30 Summary and Review

The Impact of September 11, 2001

30.1 Analyze the impact of 9/11 on the nation, the presidency of George W. Bush, and Bush administration policies around the world.

Summary

The terrorist attacks of September 11, 2001, the worst attack on the United States in history, led to profound changes in the federal government and in U.S. foreign policy. In the immediate aftermath of the attacks, President Bush called for a global war on terror and identified Afghanistan as the war's first important battlefield. Afghanistan's Taliban government was quickly toppled, but the early gains there would prove largely illusory. Nonetheless, in the aftermath of 9/11, foreign policy issues dominated Bush's presidency. At home, the PATRIOT Act expanded the powers and authority of the Department of Justice, many claimed at the expense of civil liberties. Overseas, the Bush administration, ignoring critics who pointed out the dangers involved in invading Iraq and who cast doubt on the administration's justifications for the war, proceeded to invade Iraq. As was the case in Afghanistan, the existing regime was quickly toppled, but securing the peace proved far more difficult than the administration had predicted. Poor planning by the administration and insufficient American troops contributed to Iraq's spiral into chaos and civil war. Revelations about conditions in Abu Ghraib prison damaged U.S. credibility around the world, and by 2004, American public opinion was turning against the war. Despite the fact that Bush secured a second term in the 2004 presidential election, opposition to the war continued to mount, and Republican defeats in the 2006 midterm elections signaled trouble ahead for the Republicans in the 2008 presidential election.

Review Questions

1. Causation
Describe the effects that the 9/11 attacks had on the psyches of Americans.

2. Argument Development
How do you think President Bush's decision to invade Iraq will be viewed by future historians?

Difficult Years on the Domestic Front

30.2 Explain the impact of Hurricane Katrina on the Gulf Coast and the costs and consequences of the 2008 financial crisis.

Summary

Hurricane Katrina was a natural disaster compounded by human failure. The storm devastated the entire Gulf Coast, but in the storm's aftermath, it became clear that the worst scenes of suffering and death were in New Orleans' poor black communities. Failures and delays on the part of the New Orleans Police Department and the Federal Emergency Management Agency (FEMA) only made the suffering worse. A few years later, a financial panic on Wall Street shook the American economy. The crisis resulted from two related developments. First, deregulation broke down the divide between investment and commercial banks, which allowed financial institutions to become more closely interconnected and encouraged such institutions to take greater risks. Second, financial institutions changed the way they issued and invested in home mortgages, changes that encouraged the growth of a housing bubble. Swift federal intervention saved the economy from collapse, but substantial damage had been done. In the coming years, unemployment increased and the economy slowed down.

Review Questions

3. Causation
How did human failure contribute to the death and destruction caused by Hurricane Katrina?

4. Argument Development
Was TARP an effective or ineffective government solution to the 2008 financial crisis?

The Obama Years

30.3 Analyze the reasons for the successes and failures of the Obama administration and changes in the American culture while he was president.

Summary

In 2006, with the encouragement of senior Democratic officials, Barack Obama made the decision to challenge Hillary Clinton for the 2008 Democratic presidential nomination. Obama emerged victorious after a hard-fought primary campaign that did not wrap up until June. The Republicans nominated John McCain. Trailing in fund-raising and public opinion, McCain selected Sarah Palin as his running mate in an effort to shake up the race and to energize his conservative base. The performance of the two candidates during the September financial crisis convinced many voters that Obama was the right person to solve the country's economic problems, and Obama won a clear victory in November. Despite the passage of stimulus legislation, the economy continued to struggle during Obama's first term. Passage of the Affordable Care Act was a major legislative accomplishment, but it did not help Obama's public approval ratings. The Obama administration also reformed No Child Left Behind by giving more power to the states, while Democrats in Congress crafted Dodd-Frank to add layers of regulation to the mortgage process in an effort to avoid a repeat of the crisis of 2008. Anger within the conservative wing of the Republican Party led to the emergence of the Tea Party, a loose coalition of irate, disaffected, and highly conservative voters. The Tea Party was fueled by fear about the debt, uncertainty about the economy, and anger at big institutions, most of all the federal government but also corporations and universities. The Tea Party played a central role in the 2010 midterm elections and secured the election of a conservative, uncompromising, Republican majority in the House of Representatives. On the other end of the political spectrum, participants in the Occupy Wall Street movement focused their anger on growing income inequality. In the 2015 case *Obergefell v. Hodges*, the Supreme Court ruled that states could not ban same-sex marriage, reflecting the rapidly changing public opinion on this issue. As the 2012 election neared, many believed that conditions were ripe for the Republicans to retake the White House. Despite conservative misgivings, the Republicans nominated former Massachusetts governor Mitt Romney. Romney's weakness as a candidate and a strong showing by Obama's supporters combined to seal Obama's reelection. With a divided Congress and political rancor making the prospects of major legislation slim, Obama's turned to the use of executive order in his second term.

Review Questions

5. Contextualization
What does Obama's election in 2008 and reelection in 2012 tell us about the state of race relations in the United States in the early 2000s?

6. Comparison
Compare and contrast the goals of the Tea Party and Occupy Wall Street.

New Liberals, New Conservatives, Election Surprises

30.4 Analyze the most recent political developments in the United States from the Tea Party movement to the election of Donald Trump as president in 2016.

Summary

After the 2012 election, the United States found itself deeply divided in a number of ways. Just years after the election of the nation's first African American president, it was obvious the country had not progressed as much on racial matters as originally thought. The emergence of Black Lives Matter underscored this realization as the grassroots movement protested the killing of African Americans at the hands of police across the country. Middle-class Americans grew frustrated with economic inequality and wages that had remained stagnant for decades. All of the tension seemed to come to a head in the

bitter, divisive election of 2016. After fending off the insurgent campaign of Bernie Sanders and his enthusiastic supporters, Hillary Clinton won the Democratic nomination. The Republican contest was even more hotly contested, and against all odds, the outsider who was very familiar to Americans, Donald Trump, won the nomination. The general election was one like no other in recent history. Supporters of each candidate were fueled by sheer hatred of the other side. Clinton was the front-runner, but Trump's controversial statements did not sink his candidacy as many expected. And his controversial positions on issues such as immigration only brought him closer to his base. Defying the polls, Trump emerged as the winner of the electoral vote, while Clinton won the popular one. It was a crushing defeat for Democrats but a triumphant one for Trump voters who felt that someone finally understood and represented them. The day after Trump was sworn in as president before a crowd of supporters, Women's Marches took place everywhere across the country as the left registered a loud protest against the policies of the new president. The two days symbolized just how divided the country was, and few could envision how the divide could be bridged anytime soon.

Review Questions

7. Argument Development
"This ain't your grandparents' civil rights movement." was a comment made about Black Lives Matter. What does it mean?

8. Comparison
Compare Trump's connection to his base with Andrew Jackson's connection to his.

1. Preparing to Write: Support Your Assertion

Document-Based Question—Evaluate the extent to which U.S. foreign policy was similar at the beginning of the Cold War and the beginning of the war on terror.

After you develop a thesis statement for this question, use the passages from President Bush's September 20, 2001, speech in Section 30.1 as evidence to support your argument. Focus on Bush's main message and include discussion of how his historical situation (context) shaped it.

2. Preparing to Write: Organize Your Evidence

Long Essay Question—Evaluate the extent to which economic and social factors shaped U.S. political movements from 2008 to 2016.

For this question, the first section of your essay's body could explain how the transformation played out on the political left, while the second half could explain how the change played out on the right. Create a t-chart and title the sides Left and Right. On the left side, identify specific evidence that explains the election of President Obama and the rise of the populist movements Occupy Wall Street and Black Lives Matter. On the right side, identify specific evidence that explains the rise of the Tea Party and the election of President Trump. From your evidence, you can develop a thesis.

Section I: Multiple-Choice Questions

Questions 9.1–9.3 refer to the following excerpt.

"Ubiquitous computers will … come in different sizes, each suited to a particular task. My colleagues and I have built what we call tabs, pads and boards: inch-scale machines that approximate active Post-It notes, foot-scale ones that behave something like a sheet of paper (or a book or a magazine). …

Obtaining information will be trivial: 'Who made that dress? Are there any more in the store? What was the name of the designer of that suit I liked last week?' The computing environment knows the suit you looked at for a long time last week because it knows both of your locations, and, it can retroactively find the designer's name even if it did not interest you at the time. …

Most important, ubiquitous computers will help overcome the problem of information overload. There is more information available at our fingertips during a walk in the woods than in any computer system, yet people find a walk among trees relaxing and computers frustrating. Machines that fit the human environment, instead of forcing humans to enter theirs, will make using a computer as refreshing as taking a walk in the woods."

—Mark Weiser, "The Computer for the 21st Century,"
Scientific American, 1991

9.1 An implication of Weiser's argument is that computer technology will

   a. become increasingly integrated into our daily lives

   b. take the place of many outdoor activities

   c. have the effect of keeping people from reading great books and going to museums

   d. damage our culture irreparably by diminishing person-to-person contact

9.2 In noting that "[o]btaining information will be trivial" about products like dresses, Weiser was most likely arguing that computer technology will

   a. replace salespeople in retail stores

   b. increase the variety of products available

   c. enable Americans to have wider participation in the world economy

   d. diminish the lives of Americans since they will be able to order products directly from dressmakers

9.3 Which of the following sources from the 2000s would most likely support Weiser's argument in the excerpt?

   a. A report on the distracting effects of personal devices

   b. Sales figures from dress and suit retailers

   c. A poll that asks Americans the degree to which increased access to information has improved their lives

   d. Data from phone companies on the amount of time devices are used and when they are used

Questions 9.4–9.6 refer to the following excerpt.

"[W]ithin the first 100 days of the 104th Congress, we shall bring to the House Floor the following bills, each to be given full and open debate, each to be given a clear and fair vote and each to be immediately available this day for public inspection and scrutiny.

1. ***The Fiscal Responsibility Act:*** *A balanced budget/tax limitation amendment and a legislative line-item veto. …*

2. ***The Taking Back Our Streets Act:*** *An anticrime package including stronger truth-in- sentencing, 'good faith' exclusionary rule exemptions, effective death penalty provisions, and cuts in social spending from this summer's 'crime' bill to fund prison construction. …*

3. ***The Personal Responsibility Act:*** *Discourage illegitimacy and teen pregnancy by prohibiting welfare to minor mothers and denying increased AFDC for additional children while on welfare. …*

4. ***The Family Reinforcement Acts:*** *Child support enforcement, tax incentives for adoption, strengthening rights of parents in their children's education, stronger child pornography laws. …*

5. ***The National Security Restoration Act:*** *No U.S. troops under U.N. command and restoration of the essential parts of our national security funding."*

—Republican Contract with America, 1994, United States
Republican Party

9.4 The proposed Personal Responsibility Act reflected which of the following Republican beliefs about Democratic programs?

   a. Not enough legislation was aimed at helping the needy.

   b. The programs were counterproductive in fighting poverty.

   c. The programs were not adequately funded.

   d. The scope of the programs needed to be widened.

9.5 Which of the following best describes the overarching goals of the Republican Party in the late 1900s?

   a. The United States must play a greater role in world affairs.

   b. The free market needs regulation to effectively serve the people.

   c. The size and scope of government needs to be reduced.

   d. The immigration system needs to become stricter.

9.6 Which of the following statements about Republican initiatives from the late 1900s is true?

   a. Much of the legislation that aimed to eliminate existing programs went nowhere because these programs were popular with voters.

b. Their wide popularity led to Republicans dominating presidential elections during this period.

c. They grew out of the assumption that the previous Congresses had placed too much emphasis on "family values" at the expense of more substantive legislation.

d. Most proposals reflected the Republican Party's move to the left.

Questions 9.7–9.8 refer to the following excerpt.

"Considered in its entirety, the Tea Party is neither a top-down creation nor a bottom-up explosion. This remarkable political outpouring is best understood as a combination of three intertwined forces. Each force is important in its own right, and their interaction is what gives the Tea Party its dynamism, drama, and wallop. Grassroots activism is certainly a key force, energized by angry, conservative-minded citizens who have formed vital local and regional groups. Another force is the panoply of national funders and ultra-free-market advocacy groups that seek to highlight and leverage grassroots efforts to further their long-term goal of remaking the Republican Party, pushing it towards the hard right on matters of taxation, public spending, and government regulation. Finally, the Tea Party cannot be understood without recognizing the mobilization provided by conservative media hosts who openly espouse and encourage the cause. From Fox News to right-wing radio jocks and bloggers, media impresarios have done a lot to create a sense of shared identity that lets otherwise scattered Tea Parties get together and feel part of something big and powerful. Media hosts also put out a steady diet of information and misinformation—including highly emotional claims—that keep Tea Party people in a constant state of anger and fear about the direction of the country and the doings of government officials."

—Theda Skocpol and Vanessa Williamson, *The Tea Party and the Remaking of Republican Conservatism*, 2013

9.7 When Skocpol and Williamson wrote "the Tea Party is neither a top-down creation, nor a bottom-up explosion," they made the point that the Tea Party

a. is made up of not just poor people; in fact, some members are quite affluent

b. did not "burst on the scene," but actually has a long history going back many decades

c. has sincere grassroots activists, but much of the money that funds its activities comes from very wealthy conservative sources

d. has many members that are seriously confused about their own origins

9.8 In discussing the role of conservative media, Skocpol and Williamson are highlighting the fact that

a. it made military spending a national issue

b. the two parties were able to find common ground on many, but not all, issues

c. it brought civility to public discourse

d. debates over the size and scope of government remained divisive

---

Section II: Short-Answer Question

Question 9.9 refers to the following excerpt.

"The "one big thing" Reagan knew was the power and value of human freedom, which proved to be the defining principle of his worldview. It guided what he thought about domestic politics and was central to his vision for the world. For more than thirty years, Reagan embraced a vision for dealing with the Soviet Union and ending the Cold War that was remarkably consistent and proved to be decisive. People who note his apparent lack of interest in the details of diplomacy, missile throw weights, and international law fail to see his larger strategic vision. Details that animate so many in the word of politics, academe, and journalism did not interest him so much as the "metaphysics" of the Cold War."

—Peter Schweizer, *Reagan's War*, 2003

9.9 Using the excerpt above, answer (a), (b), and (c).

a. Briefly explain how ONE specific domestic policy during the period 1981 to 1989 could be used to support Schweizer's interpretation.

b. Briefly explain how ONE OTHER specific foreign policy during the period 1981 to 1989 could be used to support Schweizer's interpretation.

c. Briefly explain how ONE specific historical event or development during the period 1981 to 1989 that is not explicitly mentioned in the excerpt could be used to contradict Schweizer's interpretation.

Section III: Long Essay Questions

Directions: Answer Question 9.10 **or** Question 9.11 (Suggested writing time: 40 minutes) In your response you should do the following.

- Respond to the prompt with a historically defensible thesis or claim that establishes a line of reasoning.

- Describe a broader historical context relevant to the prompt.

- Support an argument in response to the prompt using specific and relevant examples of evidence.

- Use historical reasoning (e.g., comparison, causation, continuity or change over time) to frame or structure an argument that addresses the prompt.

- Use evidence to corroborate, qualify, or modify an argument that addresses the prompt

9.10 Evaluate the extent to which there are similarities in the way technology impacted American society in the late 1800s/early 1900s and the late 1900s/early 2000s.

9.11 Evaluate the extent to which there are similarities in the way immigration impacted American society in the late 1800s/early 1900s and the late 1900s/early 2000s.

Section IV:

Read on MyHistoryLab

Document-Based Question: Competing Political Visions

The Constitution of the United States of America

We the people of the United States, in order to form a more perfect union, establish justice, insure domestic tranquillity, provide for the common defense, promote the general welfare, and secure the blessings of liberty to ourselves and our posterity, do ordain and establish this Constitution for the United States of America.

ARTICLE I

Section 1. All legislative powers herein granted shall be vested in a Congress of the United States, which shall consist of a Senate and House of Representatives.

Section 2.
1. The House of Representatives shall be composed of members chosen every second year by the people of the several States, and the electors in each State shall have the qualifications requisite for electors of the most numerous branch of the State legislature.
2. No person shall be a representative who shall not have attained to the age of twenty-five years, and been seven years a citizen of the United States, and who shall not, when elected, be an inhabitant of that State in which he shall be chosen.
3. Representatives and direct taxes[1] shall be apportioned among the several States which may be included within this Union, according to their respective numbers, which shall be determined by adding to the whole number of free persons, including those bound to service for a term of years, and excluding Indians not taxed, three fifths of all other persons.[2] The actual enumeration shall be made within three years after the first meeting of the Congress of the United States, and within every subsequent term of ten years, in such manner as they shall by law direct. The number of representatives shall not exceed one for every thirty thousand, but each State shall have at least one representative; and until such enumeration shall be made, the State of New Hampshire shall be entitled to choose three, Massachusetts eight, Rhode Island and Providence Plantations one, Connecticut five, New York six, New Jersey four, Pennsylvania eight, Delaware one, Maryland six, Virginia ten, North Carolina five, South Carolina five, and Georgia three.
4. When vacancies happen in the representation from any State, the executive authority thereof shall issue writs of election to fill such vacancies.
5. The House of Representatives shall choose their speaker and other officers; and shall have the sole power of impeachment.

Section 3.
1. The Senate of the United States shall be composed of two senators from each State, chosen by the legislature thereof,[3] for six years; and each senator shall have one vote.
2. Immediately after they shall be assembled in consequence of the first election, they shall be divided as equally as may be into three classes. The seats of the senators of the first class shall be vacated at the expiration of the second year, of the second class at the expiration of the fourth year, and of the third class at the expiration of the sixth year, so that one third may be chosen every second year; and if vacancies happen by resignation, or otherwise, during the recess of the legislature of any State, the executive thereof may make temporary appointments until the next meeting of the legislature, which shall then fill such vacancies.[4]
3. No person shall be a senator who shall not have attained to the age of thirty years, and been nine years a citizen of the United States, and who shall not, when elected, be an inhabitant of that State for which he shall be chosen.
4. The Vice President of the United States shall be President of the Senate, but shall have no vote, unless they be equally divided.
5. The Senate shall choose their other officers, and also a president pro tempore, in the absence of the Vice President, or when he shall exercise the office of the President of the United States.
6. The Senate shall have the sole power to try all impeachments. When sitting for that purpose, they shall be on oath or affirmation. When the President of the United States is tried, the chief justice shall preside: and no person shall be convicted without the concurrence of two thirds of the members present.
7. Judgment in cases of impeachment shall not extend further than to removal from office, and disqualification to hold and enjoy any office of honor, trust or profit under the United States: but the party convicted shall nevertheless be liable and subject to indictment, trial, judgment and punishment, according to law.

Section 4.
1. The times, places, and manner of holding elections for senators and representatives, shall be prescribed in each State by the legislature thereof; but the Congress may at any time by law make or alter such regulations, except as to the places of choosing senators.
2. The Congress shall assemble at least once in every year, and such meeting shall be on the first Monday in December, unless they shall by law appoint a different day.

Section 5.
1. Each House shall be the judge of the elections, returns and qualifications of its own members, and a majority of each shall constitute a quorum to do business; but a smaller number may adjourn from day to day, and may be authorized to compel the attendance of absent members, in such manner, and under such penalties as each House may provide.
2. Each House may determine the rules of its proceedings, punish its members for disorderly behavior, and, with the concurrence of two thirds, expel a member.
3. Each House shall keep a journal of its proceedings, and from time to time publish the same, excepting such parts as may in their judgment require secrecy; and the yeas and nays of the members of either House on any question shall, at the desire of one fifth of those present, be entered on the journal.
4. Neither House, during the session of Congress, shall, without the consent of the other, adjourn for more than three days, nor to any other place than that in which the two Houses shall be sitting.

Section 6.
1. The senators and representatives shall receive a compensation for their services, to be ascertained by law, and paid out of the Treasury of the United States. They shall in all cases, except treason, felony, and breach of the peace, be privileged from arrest during their attendance at the session of their respective Houses, and in going to and returning from the same; and for any speech or debate in either House, they shall not be questioned in any other place.
2. No senator or representative shall, during the time for which he was elected, be appointed to any civil office under the authority of the United States, which shall have been created, or the emoluments whereof shall have been increased, during such time; and no person holding any office under the United States shall be a member of either House during his continuance in office.

Section 7.
1. All bills for raising revenue shall originate in the House of Representatives; but the Senate may propose or concur with amendments as on other bills.
2. Every bill which shall have passed the House of Representatives and the Senate, shall, before it become a law, be presented to the President of the United States; If he approves he shall sign it, but if not he shall return it, with his objections, to that House in which it shall have originated, who shall enter the objections at large on their journal, and proceed to reconsider it. If after such reconsideration two thirds of that House shall agree to pass the bill, it shall be sent, together with the objections, to the other House, by which it shall likewise be reconsidered, and if approved by two thirds of that House, it shall become a law. But in all such cases the votes of both Houses shall be determined by yeas and nays, and the names of the persons voting for and against the bill shall be entered on the journal of each House respectively. If any bill shall not be returned by the President within ten days (Sundays excepted) after it shall have been presented to him, the same shall be a law, in like manner as if he had signed it, unless the Congress by their adjournment prevent its return, in which case it shall not be a law.
3. Every order, resolution, or vote to which the concurrence of the Senate and the House of Representatives may be necessary (except on a question of adjournment) shall be presented to the President of the United States; and before the same shall take effect, shall be approved by him, or being disapproved by him, shall be repassed by two thirds of the Senate and House of Representatives, according to the rules and limitations prescribed in the case of a bill.

---

[1] See the Sixteenth Amendment.
[2] See the Fourteenth Amendment.
[3] See the Seventeenth Amendment.
[4] See the Seventeenth Amendment.

Section 8. 1. The Congress shall have the power To lay and collect taxes, duties, imposts, and excises, to pay the debts and provide for the common defense and general welfare of the United States; but all duties, imposts, and excises shall be uniform throughout the United States.

2. To borrow money on the credit of the United States;

3. To regulate commerce with foreign nations, and among the several States, and with the Indian tribes;

4. To establish a uniform rule of naturalization, and uniform laws on the subject of bankruptcies throughout the United States;

5. To coin money, regulate the value thereof, and of foreign coin, and fix the standard of weights and measures;

6. To provide for the punishment of counterfeiting the securities and current coin of the United States;

7. To establish post offices and post roads;

8. To promote the progress of science and useful arts, by securing for limited times to authors and inventors the exclusive right to their respective writings and discoveries;

9. To constitute tribunals inferior to the Supreme Court;

10. To define and punish piracies and felonies committed on the high seas, and offenses against the law of nations;

11. To declare war, grant letters of marque and reprisal, and make rules concerning captures on land and water;

12. To raise and support armies, but no appropriation of money to that use shall be for a longer term than two years;

13. To provide and maintain a navy;

14. To make rules for the government and regulation of the land and naval forces;

15. To provide for calling forth the militia to execute the laws of the Union, suppress insurrections and repel invasions;

16. To provide for organizing, arming, and disciplining the militia, and for governing such part of them as may be employed in the service of the United States, reserving to the States respectively, the appointment of the officers, and the authority of training the militia according to the discipline prescribed by Congress;

17. To exercise exclusive legislation in all cases whatsoever, over such district (not exceeding ten miles square) as may, by cession of particular States, and the acceptance of Congress, become the seat of the government of the United States, and to exercise like authority over all places purchased by the consent of the legislature of the State in which the same shall be, for the erection of forts, magazines, arsenals, dockyards, and other needful buildings; and

18. To make all laws which shall be necessary and proper for carrying into execution the foregoing powers, and all other powers vested by this Constitution in the government of the United States, or any department or officer thereof.

Section 9. 1. The migration or importation of such persons as any of the States now existing shall think proper to admit, shall not be prohibited by the Congress prior to the year one thousand eight hundred and eight, but a tax or duty may be imposed on such importation, not exceeding ten dollars for each person.

2. The privilege of the writ of habeas corpus shall not be suspended, unless when in cases of rebellion or invasion the public safety may require it.

3. No bill of attainder or ex post facto law shall be passed.

4. No capitation, or other direct, tax shall be laid, unless in proportion to the census or enumeration herein-before directed to be taken.[5]

5. No tax or duty shall be laid on articles exported from any State.

6. No preference shall be given by any regulation of commerce or revenue to the ports of one State over those of another: nor shall vessels bound to, or from, one State be obliged to enter, clear, or pay duties in another.

7. No money shall be drawn from the treasury, but in consequence of appropriations made by law; and a regular statement and account of the receipts and expenditures of all public money shall be published from time to time.

8. No title of nobility shall be granted by the United States: and no person holding any office of profit or trust under them, shall, without the consent of the Congress, accept of any present, emolument, office, or title, of any kind whatever, from any king, prince, or foreign State.

Section 10. 1. No State shall enter into any treaty, alliance, or confederation; grant letters of marque and reprisal; coin money; emit bills of credit; make any thing but gold and silver coin a tender in payment of debts; pass any bill of attainder, ex post facto law, or law impairing the obligation of contracts, or grant, any title of nobility.

2. No State shall, without the consent of the Congress, lay any imposts or duties on imports or exports, except what may be absolutely necessary for executing its inspection laws: and the net produce of all duties and imposts laid by any State on imports or exports, shall be for the use of the treasury of the United States; and all such laws shall be subject to the revision and control of the Congress.

3. No State shall, without the consent of the Congress, lay any duty of tonnage, keep troops, or ships of war in time of peace, enter into any agreement or compact with another State, or with a foreign power, or engage in war, unless actually invaded, or in such imminent danger as will not admit of delay.

ARTICLE II

Section 1. 1. The executive power shall be vested in a President of the United States of America. He shall hold his office during the term of four years, and, together with the Vice President, chosen for the same term, be elected, as follows:

2. Each State shall appoint, in such manner as the legislature thereof may direct, a number of electors, equal to the whole number of senators and representatives to which the State may be entitled in the Congress: but no senator or representative, or person holding any office of trust or profit under the United States, shall be appointed an elector.

The electors shall meet in their respective States, and vote by ballot for two persons, of whom one at least shall not be an inhabitant of the same State with themselves. And they shall make a list of all the persons voted for, and of the number of votes for each; which list they shall sign and certify, and transmit sealed to the seat of the government of the United States, directed to the president of the Senate. The president of the Senate shall, in the presence of the Senate and House of Representatives, open all the certificates, and the votes shall then be counted. The person having the greatest number of votes shall be the President, if such number be a majority of the whole number of electors appointed; and if there be more than one who have such majority, and have an equal number of votes, then the House of Representatives shall immediately choose by ballot one of them for President; and if no person have a majority, then from the five highest on the list the said House shall in like manner choose the President. But in choosing the President, the votes shall be taken by States, the representation from each State having one vote; a quorum for this purpose shall consist of a member or members from two thirds of the States, and a majority of all the States shall be necessary to a choice. In every case after the choice of the President, the person having the greatest number of votes of the electors shall be the Vice President. But if there should remain two or more who have equal votes, the Senate shall choose from them by ballot the Vice President.[6]

3. The Congress may determine the time of choosing the electors, and the day on which they shall give their votes; which day shall be the same throughout the United States.

4. No person except a natural born citizen, or a citizen of the United States, at the time of the adoption of this Constitution, shall be eligible to the office of President; neither shall any person be eligible to the office who shall not have attained to the age of thirty-five years, and been fourteen years a resident within the United States.

5. In case of the removal of the President from office, or of his death, resignation, or inability to discharge the powers and duties of the said office, the same shall devolve on the Vice President, and the congress may by law provide for the case of removal, death, resignation or inability, both of the President and Vice President, declaring what officer shall then act as President, and such officer shall act accordingly until the disability be removed, or a President shall be elected.

6. The President shall, at stated times, receive for his services a compensation which shall neither be increased nor diminished during the period for which he shall have been elected, and he shall not receive within that period any other emolument from the United States, or any of them.

7. Before he enter on the execution of his office, he shall take the following oath or affirmation:—"I do solemnly swear (or affirm) that I will faithfully execute the office of President of the United States, and will to the best of my ability, preserve, protect and defend the Constitution of the United States."

Section 2. 1. The President shall be commander in chief of the army and navy of the United States, and of the militia of the several States, when called into the actual service of the United States; he may require the opinion in writing, of the principal officer in each of the executive departments, upon any subject relating to the duties of their respective offices, and he shall have power to grant reprieves and pardons for offenses against the United States, except in cases of impeachment.

2. He shall have power, by and with the advice and consent of the Senate, to make treaties, provided two thirds of the senators present concur; and he shall nominate, and by and with the advice and consent of the Senate, shall appoint ambassadors, other public ministers and consuls, judges of the Supreme Court, and all other officers of the United States, whose appointments are not herein otherwise provided for, and which shall be established by law; but the Congress may by law vest the appointment of such inferior officers, as they think proper, in the President alone, in the courts of laws, or in the heads of departments.

3. The President shall have power to fill up all vacancies that may happen during the recess of the Senate, by granting commissions which shall expire at the end of their next session.

---

[5] See the Sixteenth Amendment.

[6] Superseded by the Twelfth Amendment.

Section 3. He shall from time to time give to the Congress information of the state of the Union, and recommend to their consideration such measures as he shall judge necessary and expedient; he may, on extraordinary occasions, convene both Houses, or either of them, and in case of disagreement between them with respect to the time of adjournment, he may adjourn them to such time as he shall think proper; he shall receive ambassadors and other public ministers; he shall take care that the laws be faithfully executed, and shall commission all the officers of the United States.

Section 4. The President, Vice President, and all civil officers of the United States, shall be removed from office on impeachment for, and conviction of, treason, bribery, or other high crimes and misdemeanors.

ARTICLE III

Section 1. The judicial power of the United States shall be vested in one Supreme Court, and in such inferior courts as the Congress may from time to time ordain and establish. The judges, both of the Supreme and inferior courts, shall hold their offices during good behavior, and shall, at stated times, receive for their services, a compensation, which shall not be diminished during their continuance in office.

Section 2. 1. The judicial power shall extend to all cases, in law and equity, arising under this Constitution, the laws of the United States, and treaties made, or which shall be made, under their authority;—to all cases of admiralty and maritime jurisdiction;—to controversies to which the United States shall be a party;[7]—to controversies between two or more States;—between a State and citizens of another State;—between citizens of different States;—between citizens of the same State claiming lands under grants of different States, and between a State, or the citizens thereof, and foreign States, citizens or subjects.

2. In all cases affecting ambassadors, other public ministers and consuls, and those in which a State shall be party, the Supreme Court shall have original jurisdiction. In all the other cases before mentioned, the Supreme Court shall have appellate jurisdiction, both as to law and fact, with such exceptions, and under such regulations as the Congress shall make.

3. The trial of all crimes, except in cases of impeachment, shall be by jury; and such trial shall be held in the State where the said crimes shall have been committed; but when not committed within any State, the trial shall be such place or places as the congress may by law have directed.

Section 3. 1. Treason against the United States shall consist only in levying war against them, or in adhering to their enemies, giving them aid and comfort. No person shall be convicted of treason unless on the testimony of two witnesses to the same overt act, or on confession in open court.

2. The Congress shall have power to declare the punishment of treason, but no attainder of treason shall work corruption of blood, or forfeiture except during the life of the person attained.

ARTICLE IV

Section 1. Full faith and credit shall be given in each State to the public acts, records, and judicial proceedings of every other State. And the Congress may by general laws prescribe the manner in which such acts, records and proceedings shall be proved, and the effect thereof.

Section 2. 1. The citizens of each State shall be entitled to all privileges and immunities of citizens in the several States.[8]

2. A person charged in any State with treason, felony, or other crime, who shall flee from justice, and be found in another State, shall on demand of the executive authority of the State from which he fled, be delivered up to be removed to the State having jurisdiction of the crime.

3. No person held to service or labor in one State under the laws thereof, escaping into another, shall, in consequence of any law or regulation therein, be discharged from such service or labor, but shall be delivered up on claim of the party to whom such service or labor may be due.[9]

Section 3. 1. New States may be admitted by the Congress into this Union; but no new State shall be formed or erected within the jurisdiction of any other State, nor any State be formed by the junction of two or more States, or parts of States, without the consent of the legislatures of the States concerned as well as of the Congress.

2. The Congress shall have power to dispose of and make all needful rules and regulations respecting the territory or other property belonging to the United States; and nothing in this Constitution shall be so construed as to prejudice any claims of the United States, or of any particular State.

Section 4. The United States shall guarantee to every State in this Union a republican form of government, and shall protect each of them against invasion; and on application of the legislature, or of the executive (when the legislature cannot be convened) against domestic violence.

ARTICLE V

The Congress, whenever two thirds of both Houses shall deem it necessary, shall propose amendments to this Constitution, or, on the application of the legislatures of two thirds of the several States, shall call a convention for proposing amendments, which in either case shall be valid to all intents and purposes, as part of this Constitution, when ratified by the legislatures of three fourths of the several States, or by conventions in three fourths thereof, as the one or the other mode of ratification may be proposed by the Congress; Provided that no amendment which may be made prior to the year one thousand eight hundred and eight shall in any manner affect the first and fourth clauses in the ninth section of the first article; and that no State, without its consent, shall be deprived of its equal suffrage in the Senate.

ARTICLE VI

1. All debts contracted and engagements entered into, before the adoption of this Constitution, shall be as valid against the United States under this Constitution, as under the Confederation.[10]

2. This Constitution, and the laws of the United States which shall be made in pursuance thereof; and all treaties made, or which shall be made, under the authority of the United States, shall be the supreme law of the land; and the judges in every State shall be bound thereby, any thing in the Constitution or laws of any State to the contrary notwithstanding.

3. The senators and representatives before mentioned, and the members of the several State legislatures, and all executive and judicial officers, both of the United States and of the several States, shall be bound by oath or affirmation to support this Constitution; but no religious test shall ever be required as a qualification to any office or public trust under the United States.

ARTICLE VII

The ratification of the conventions of nine States shall be sufficient for the establishment of this Constitution between the States so ratifying the same.

Done in Convention by the unanimous consent of the States present the seventeenth day of September in the year of our Lord one thousand seven hundred and eighty-seven, and of the independence of the United States of America the twelfth. In witness whereof we have hereunto subscribed our names.
[Signatories' names omitted]

Articles in addition to, and amendment of, the Constitution of the United States of America, proposed by Congress, and ratified by the legislatures of the several States, pursuant to the fifth article of the original Constitution.

AMENDMENT I

[First ten amendments ratified December 15, 1791]
Congress shall make no law respecting an establishment of religion, or prohibiting the free exercise thereof; or abridging the freedom of speech, or of the press; or the right of the people peaceably to assemble, and to petition the government for a redress of grievances.

AMENDMENT II

A well regulated militia, being necessary to the security of a free State, the right of the people to keep and bear arms, shall not be infringed.

AMENDMENT III

No soldier shall, in time of peace be quartered in any house, without the consent of the owner, nor in time of war, but in a manner to be prescribed by law.

AMENDMENT IV

The right of the people to be secure in their persons, houses, papers, and effects, against unreasonable searches and seizures, shall not be violated, and no warrants shall issue, but upon probable cause, supported by oath or affirmation, and particularly describing the place to be searched, and the persons or things to be seized.

AMENDMENT V

No person shall be held to answer for a capital or otherwise infamous crime, unless on a presentment or indictment of a grand jury, except in cases arising in the land or naval forces, or in the militia, when in actual service in time of war or public danger; nor shall any person be subject for the same offense to be twice put in jeopardy of life or limb; nor shall be compelled in any criminal case to be a witness against himself, nor be deprived of life, liberty, or property, without due process of law; nor shall private property be taken for public use, without just compensation.

AMENDMENT VI

In all criminal prosecutions, the accused shall enjoy the right to a speedy and public trial, by an impartial jury of the State and district wherein the crime shall have been committed, which district shall have been previously ascertained by law, and to be informed of the nature and cause of the accusation; to be confronted with the witnesses against him; to have compulsory process for obtaining witnesses in his favor, and to have the assistance of counsel for his defense.

AMENDMENT VII

In suits at common law, where the value in controversy shall exceed twenty dollars, the right of trial by jury shall be preserved, and no fact tried by a jury shall be otherwise reexamined in any court of the United States, than according to the rules of the common law.

---

[7] See the Eleventh Amendment.

[8] See the Fourteenth Amendment, Sec. 1.

[9] See the Thirteenth Amendment.

[10] See the Fourteenth Amendment, Sec. 4.

AMENDMENT VIII

Excessive bail shall not be required, nor excessive fines imposed, nor cruel and unusual punishments inflicted.

AMENDMENT IX

The enumeration in the Constitution of certain rights shall not be construed to deny or disparage others retained by the people.

AMENDMENT X

The powers not delegated to the United States by the Constitution, nor prohibited by it to the States, are reserved to the States respectively, or to the people.

AMENDMENT XI [JANUARY 8, 1798]

The judicial power of the United States shall not be construed to extend to any suit in law or equity, commended or prosecuted against one of the United States by citizens of another State, or by citizens or subjects of any foreign State.

AMENDMENT XII [SEPTEMBER 25, 1804]

The electors shall meet in their respective States, and vote by ballot for President and Vice President, one of whom, at least, shall not be an inhabitant of the same State with themselves; they shall name in their ballots the person voted for as President, and in distinct ballots the person voted for as Vice President, and they shall make distinct lists of all persons voted for as President and of all persons voted for as Vice President, and of the number of votes for each, which lists they shall sign and certify, and transmit sealed to the seat of the government of the United States, directed to the President of the Senate;—The President of the Senate shall, in the presence of the Senate and House of Representatives, open all the certificates and the votes shall then be counted;—The person having the greatest number of votes for President, shall be the President, if such number be a majority of the whole number of electors appointed; and if no person have such majority, then from the persons having the highest numbers not exceeding three on the list of those voted for as President, the House of Representatives shall choose immediately, by ballot, the President. But in choosing the President, the votes shall be taken by States, the representation from each State having one vote; a quorum for this purpose shall consist of a member or members from two thirds of the States, and a majority of all the States shall be necessary to a choice. And if the House of Representatives shall not choose a President whenever the right of choice shall devolve upon them, before the fourth day of March next following, then the Vice President shall act as President, as in the case of the death or other constitutional disability of the President. The person having the greatest number of votes as Vice President shall be the Vice President, if such number be a majority of the whole number of electors appointed, and if no person have a majority, then from the two highest numbers on the list, the Senate shall choose the Vice President; a quorum for the purpose shall consist of two thirds of the whole number of Senators, and a majority of the whole number shall be necessary to a choice. But no person constitutionally ineligible to the office of President shall be eligible to that of Vice President of the United States.

AMENDMENT XIII [DECEMBER 18, 1865]

Section 1. Neither slavery nor involuntary servitude, except as a punishment for crime whereof the party shall have been duly convicted, shall exist within the United States, or any place subject to their jurisdiction.

Section 2. Congress shall have power to enforce this article by appropriate legislation.

AMENDMENT XIV [JULY 28, 1868]

Section 1. All persons born or naturalized in the United States, and subject to the jurisdiction thereof, are citizens of the United States and of the State wherein they reside. No State shall make or enforce any law which shall abridge the privileges or immunities of citizens of the United States; nor shall any State deprive any person of life, liberty, or property, without due process of law; nor deny to any person within its jurisdiction the equal protection of the laws.

Section 2. Representatives shall be apportioned among the several States according to their respective numbers, counting the whole number of persons in each State, excluding Indians not taxed. But when the right to vote at any election for the choice of electors for President and Vice President of the United States, representatives in Congress, the executive and judicial officers of a State, or the members of the legislature thereof, is denied to any of the male inhabitants of such State, being twenty-one years of age, and citizens of the United States, or in any way abridged, except for participating in rebellion, or other crime, the basis of representation there shall be reduced in the proportion which the number of such male citizens shall bear to the whole number of male citizens twenty-one years of age in such State.

Section 3. No person shall be a senator or representative in Congress, or elector of President and Vice President, or hold any office, civil or military, under the United States, or under any State, who having previously taken an oath, as a member of Congress, or as an officer of the United States, or as a member of any State legislature, or as an executive or judicial officer of any State, to support the Constitution of the United States, shall have engaged in insurrection or rebellion against the same, or given aid or comfort to the enemies thereof. But Congress may by a vote of two thirds of each House, remove such disability.

Section 4. The validity of the public debt of the United States, authorized by law, including debts incurred for payment of pensions and bounties for services in suppressing insurrection or rebellion; shall not be questioned. But neither the United States nor any State shall assume or pay any debt or obligation incurred in aid of insurrection or rebellion against the United States, or any claim for the loss or emancipation of any slave; but all such debts, obligations, and claims shall be held illegal and void.

Section 5. The Congress shall have the power to enforce, by appropriate legislation, the provisions of this article.

AMENDMENT XV [MARCH 30, 1870]

Section 1. The right of citizens of the United States to vote shall not be denied or abridged by the United States or by any State on account of race, color, or previous condition of servitude.

Section 2. The Congress shall have power to enforce this article by appropriate legislation.

AMENDMENT XVI [FEBRUARY 25, 1913]

The Congress shall have power to lay and collect taxes on incomes, from whatever source derived, without apportionment among the several States, and without regard to any census or enumeration.

AMENDMENT XVII [MAY 31, 1913]

The Senate of the United States shall be composed of two senators from each State, elected by the people thereof, for six years; and each senator shall have one vote. The electors in each State shall have the qualifications requisite for electors of the most numerous branch of the State legislature.

When vacancies happen in the representation of any State in the Senate, the executive authority of such State shall issue writs of election to fill such vacancies: Provided, That the legislature of any State may empower the executive thereof to make temporary appointments until the people fill the vacancies by election as the legislature may direct.

This amendment shall not be so construed as to affect the election or term of any senator chosen before it becomes valid as part of the Constitution.

AMENDMENT XVIII[11] [JANUARY 29, 1919]

After one year from the ratification of this article, the manufacture, sale, or transportation of intoxicating liquors within, the importation thereof into, or the exportation thereof from the United States and all territory subject to the jurisdiction thereof for beverage purposes is hereby prohibited.

The Congress and the several States shall have concurrent power to enforce this article by appropriate legislation.

This article shall be inoperative unless it shall have been ratified as an amendment to the Constitution by the legislatures of the several States, as provided in the constitution, within seven years from the date of the submission hereof to the States by Congress.

AMENDMENT XIX [AUGUST 26, 1920]

The right of citizens of the United States to vote shall not be denied or abridged by the United States or by any State on account of sex.

Congress shall have the power to enforce this article by appropriate legislation.

AMENDMENT XX [JANUARY 23, 1933]

Section 1. The terms of the President and Vice President shall end at noon on the 20th day of January and the terms of Senators and Representatives at noon on the 3d day of January, of the years in which such terms would have ended if this article had not been ratified; and the terms of their successors shall then begin.

Section 2. The Congress shall assemble at least once in every year, and such meeting shall begin at noon on the 3d day of January, unless they shall by law appoint a different day.

Section 3. If, at the time fixed for the beginning of the term of President, the President-elect shall have died, the Vice President-elect shall become President. If a President shall not have been chosen before the time fixed for the beginning of his term, or if the President-elect shall have failed to qualify, then the Vice President-elect shall act as President until a President shall have qualified; and the Congress may by law provide for the case wherein neither a President-elect nor a Vice President-elect shall have qualified, declaring who shall then act as President, or the manner in which one who is to act shall be selected, and such person shall act accordingly until a President or Vice President shall have qualified.

Section 4. The Congress may by law provide for the case of the death of any of the persons from whom, the House of Representatives may choose a President whenever the right of choice shall have devolved upon them, and for the case of the death of any of the persons from whom the Senate may choose a Vice President whenever the right of choice shall have devolved upon them.

---

[11] Repealed by the Twenty-first Amendment

Section 5. **Section**s 1 and 2 shall take effect on the 15th day of October following the ratification of this article.

Section 6. This article shall be inoperative unless it shall have been ratified as an amendment to the Constitution by the legislatures of three-fourths of the several States within seven years from the date of its submission.

AMENDMENT XXI [DECEMBER 5, 1933]

Section 1. The Eighteenth Article of amendment to the Constitution of the United States is hereby repealed.

Section 2. The transportation or importation into any State, Territory, or possession of the United States for delivery or use therein of intoxicating liquors in violation of the laws thereof, is hereby prohibited.

Section 3. This article shall be inoperative unless it shall have been ratified as an amendment to the Constitution by conventions in the several States, as provided in the Constitution, within seven years from the date of the submission thereof to the States by the Congress.

AMENDMENT XXII [MARCH 1, 1951]

No person shall be elected to the office of the President more than twice, and no person who has held the office of President, or acted as President, for more than two years of a term to which some other person was elected President shall be elected to the office of the President more than once.

But this article shall not apply to any person holding the office of President when this article was proposed by the Congress, and shall not prevent any person who may be holding the office of President, or acting as President, during the term within which this article becomes operative from holding the office of President or acting as President during the remainder of such term.

This article shall be inoperative unless it shall have been ratified as an amendment to the Constitution by the legislatures of three-fourths of the several States within seven years from the date of its submission to the States by the Congress.

AMENDMENT XXIII [MARCH 29, 1961]

Section 1. The District constituting the seat of Government of the United States shall appoint in such manner as the Congress may direct.
A number of electors of President and Vice President equal to the whole number of Senators and Representatives in Congress to which the District would be entitled if it were a State, but in no event more than the least populous State; they shall be in addition to those appointed by the States, but they shall be considered, for the purposes of the election of President and Vice President, to be electors appointed by a State; and they shall meet in the District and perform such duties as provided by the twelfth article of amendment.

Section 2. The Congress shall have power to enforce this article by appropriate legislation.

AMENDMENT XXIV [JANUARY 23, 1964]

Section 1. The right of citizens of the United States to vote in any primary or other election for President or Vice President, for electors for President or Vice President, or for Senator or Representative in Congress, shall not be denied or abridged by the United States or any State by reason of failure to pay any poll tax or other tax.

Section 2. The Congress shall have power to enforce this article by appropriate legislation.

AMENDMENT XXV [FEBRUARY 10, 1967]

Section 1. In case of the removal of the President from office or of his death or resignation, the Vice President shall become President.

Section 2. Whenever there is a vacancy in the office of the Vice President, the President shall nominate a Vice President who shall take office upon confirmation by a majority of both Houses of Congress.

Section 3. Whenever the President transmits to the President pro tempore of the Senate and the Speaker of the House of Representatives his written declaration that he is unable to discharge the powers and duties of his office, and until he transmits to them a written declaration to the contrary, such powers and duties shall be discharged by the Vice President as Acting President.

Section 4. Whenever the Vice President and a majority of either the principal officers of the executive departments or of such other body as Congress may by law provide, transmit to the President pro tempore of the Senate and the Speaker of the House of Representatives their written declaration that the President is unable to discharge the powers and duties of his office, the Vice President shall immediately assume the powers and duties of the office as Acting President.

Thereafter, when the President transmits to the President pro tempore of the Senate and the Speaker of the House of Representatives his written declaration that no inability exists, he shall resume the powers and duties of his office unless the Vice President and a majority of either the principal officers of the executive departments or of such other body as Congress may by law provide, transmit within four days to the President pro tempore of the Senate and the Speaker of the House of Representatives their written declaration that the President is unable to discharge the powers and duties of his office. Thereupon Congress shall decide the issue, assembling within forty-eight hours for that purpose if not in session. If the Congress, within twenty-one days after receipt of the latter written declaration, or, if Congress is not in session, within twenty-one days after Congress is required to assemble, determines by two-thirds vote of both Houses that the President is unable to discharge the powers and duties of his office, the Vice President shall continue to discharge the same as Acting President; otherwise, the President shall resume the powers and duties of his office.

AMENDMENT XXVI [JUNE 30, 1971]

Section 1. The right of citizens of the United States who are eighteen years of age or older to vote shall not be denied or abridged by the United States or by any State on account of age.

Section 2. The Congress shall have power to enforce this article by appropriate legislation.

AMENDMENT XXVII[12] [MAY 7, 1992]

No law, varying the compensation for services of the Senators and Representatives, shall take effect until an election of Representatives shall have intervened.

[12] James Madison proposed this amendment in 1789 together with the ten amendments that were adopted as the Bill of Rights, but it failed to win ratification at the time. Congress, however, had set no deadline for its ratification, and over the years—particularly in the 1980s and 1990s—many states voted to add it to the Constitution. With the ratification of Michigan in 1992 it passed the threshold of 3/4ths of the states required for adoption, but because the process took more than 200 years, its validity remains in doubt.

Sources

Chapter 1 The World Before 1492

The Peopling of North America

Daniel K. Richter, *Facing East from Indian Country: A Native History of Early America* (Cambridge; Harvard University Press, 2001) is an especially useful source for all early American Indian history. See also James Wilson, *The Earth Shall Weep: A History of Native America* (New York: Grove Press, 1998); and Elsie Clews Parsons, *Pueblo Indian Religion*, (Lincoln: University of Nebraska Press, 1939, 1996). Some have also argued that the Indians of the Americas were actually descendants of ancient travelers across the Atlantic from Africa or Europe or a mix of these with the earlier arrivals from Asia. See for example, Ivan van Sertima, *They Came before Columbus: The African Presence in Ancient America* (New York, 1976) and Vine Deloria, Jr., *Red Earth, White Lies: Native Americans and the Myth of Scientific Fact* (New York: Scribner, 1988). The debate, while important, involves scholars and time periods far beyond the scope of this book. For earlier North American communities see, George R. Milner, *The Moundbuilders: Ancient Peoples of Eastern North America* (London: Thames & Hudson, 2004); Sally A. Kitt Chappell, *Cahokia: Mirror of the Cosmos* (Chicago: University of Chicago Press, 2002); Timothy R. Pauketat, *Ancient Cahokia and the Mississippians* (Cambridge, England: Cambridge University Press, 2004); William C. Foster, *Historic Native Peoples of Texas* (Austin: University of Texas Press, 2009); and Stephen H. Lekson, *The Architecture of Chaco Canyon* (Salt Lake City: The University of Utah Press, 2007); Robert W. Patch, *Maya and Spaniard in Yucatan, 1648–1812* (Stanford: Stanford University Press, 1993); Leslie G. Cecil & Timothy W. Pugh, editors, *Maya Worldviews at Conquest* (Bounder: University Press of Colorado, 2009). See also the journal *Science Advances* for May 2016 for information on recent discoveries in Florida.

Diverse American Communities in the 1400s

Richter, *Facing East from Indian Country: A Native History of Early America* is a prime source for this material. See also Theda Perdue, *Cherokee Women: Gender and Culture Change, 1700–1835* (Lincoln: University of Nebraska Press, 1998); James Wilson, *The Earth Shall Weep: A History of Native America* (New York: Grove Press, 1998); Ruth Underhill, Religion Among American Indians," in Roger C. Owen, James F. Deetz, and Anthony D. Fisher, editors, *The North American Indians: A Sourcebook* (New York: The Macmillan Company, 1967); William Prescott, *History of the Conquest of Mexico* (New York: Modern Library, no date, probably 1844); Carroll L. Riley, *The Kachina and the Cross: Indians and Spaniards in the Early Southwest* (Salt Lake City: University of Utah Press, 1999); George R. Milner, *The Moundbuilders: Ancient Peoples of Eastern North America* (London, England: Thames & Hudson, 2004); Charles C. Mann, *1491: New Revelations of the Americas Before* Columbus (New York: Alfred A. Knopf, 2005); William W. Warren, *History of the Ojibway People*, second edition, edited by Theresa Schenck (Minneapolis, Minnesota Historical Society Press, 2009, originally 1885); Samuel Eliot Morison, *The European Discovery of America: The Northern Voyages, A. D. 500–1600* (New York: Oxford University Press, 1971); John A. Crow, *The Epic of Latin America*, fourth edition (Berkeley: University of California Press, 1992).

A Changing Europe in the 1400s

For an excellent study of the philosophical and theological foundation of medieval Europe's economy, and the leaders who changed all of that, see Robert L. Heilbroner, *The Worldly Philosophers* (New York: Touchstone, 1999). For a useful discussion of the debates about Prince Henry's motivation, especially among Portuguese historians, see John Thornton, *Africa and Africans in the Making of the Atlantic World, 1400–1800* (Cambridge, England: Cambridge University Press, second edition, 1998); Carlos Fuentes, *The Buried Mirror: Reflections on Spain and the New World* (Boston: Houghton Mifflin, 1999); Matt S. Meier and Feliciano Ribera, *Mexican Americans/ American Mexicans: From Conquistadors to Chicanos* (New York: Hill and Wang, 1993), pp.17–18. For changes in ship building and navagaton see Lincoln Paine, *The Sea & Civilization: A Maritime History of the World* (New York: Vintage Books, 2015).

Africa in the 1400s

Ralph A. Austen, Trans-Saharn *Africa in World History* (New York: Oxford University Press, 2010); Ousmane Oumar Kane, *Beyond Timbuktu: An Intellectual History of Muslim West Africa* (Cambridge: Harvard University Press, 2016); John Thornton, *Africa and Africans in the Making of the Atlantic World, 1400–1800* (Cambridge, England: Cambridge University Press, second edition, 1998); Basil Davidson, F. K. Buah, J. F. Ade Ajayi, *A History of West Africa*, 1000–1800 (London: Longman, 1996); and Eric Wolfe, *Europe and the People without History* (Berkeley: University of California Press, 1982).

Asia in the 1400s

David K. Yoo and Eiichiro Azuma, editors, *The Oxford Handbook of Asian American History* (New York: Oxford University Press, 2016); Louise Levathes, *When China Rules the Seas* (New York: Simon and Schuster, 1994); Jared Diamond, *Guns, Germs, and Steel* (New York: W. W. Norton, 1997, 2005); J. H. Elliott, *Empires of the Atlantic World: Britain and Spain in America, 1492–1830* (New Haven: Yale University Press, 2006).

Chapter 2 First Encounters, First Conquests, 1492–1607

Columbus and the Columbian Exchange, and Early Conquests

Carlos Fuentes, *The Buried Mirror: Reflections on Spain and the New World* (New York: Mariner Books, 1999); Irving Rouse, *The Tainos: Rise and Decline of the People Who Greeted Columbus* (New Haven: Yale University Press, 1992); Oliver Dunn and James E. Kelley, Jr., translators, *The Diario of Christopher Columbus's First Voyage to America, 1492–1493*, abstracted by Fray Bartolome de las Casas (Norman: University of Oklahoma Press, 1988); Jared Diamond, *Guns, Germs, and Steel: The Fates of Human Societies* (New York: W. W. Norton, 1997, 2005); Alfred W. Crosby, *Ecological Imperialism: The Biological Expansion of Europe, 900–1900* (Cambridge: Cambridge University Press, 1986); and Alfred W. Crosby, Jr., *The Columbian Exchange: Biological and Cultural Consequences of 1492* (Westport, Connecticut: Greenwood Press, 1972); E. T. Jones, "Alwyn Ruddock: 'John Cabot and the Discovery of America," *Historical Research* 81 (2008), pp. 224–254; downloaded February 26, 2012; Hugh Tomas, "The Conquest," in *Aztecs* (London: The Royal Academy, 2002); *Letters of Amerigo Vespucci, and Other Documents Illustrative of his Career* (Cambridge, England: Cambridge University Press, 2010); Thomas Bender, *A Nation Among the Nations: America's Place in World History* (New York: Hill and Wang, 2006); Bartolome de las Casas, *History of the Indies*, translated and edited by Andree Collard (New York: Harper & Row, 1971; Juan Friede and Benjamin Keen, *Bartolome de Las Casas in History: Toward an Understanding of the Man and His Work* (DeKalb: Northern Illinois University Press, 1971); Erika Lee, *The Making of Asian America: A History* (New York: Simon & Schuster, 2015).

A Divided Europe—The Impact of the Protestant Reformation

For material on the Protestant Reformation see Diarmaid MacCulloch, *The Reformation: A History* (New York: Viking Penguin, 2004); and two earlier but still excellent sources Hans J. Hillerbrand, *The Protestant Reformation*, revised edition (New York: Harper Perennial, 2009); Williston Walker, *A History of the Christian Church*, third edition, revised by Robert T. Handy (New York: Charles Scribner's Sons, 1970).

Exploration and Encounter in North America: The Spanish

Juan Ponce de Leon, fundador y primer gobernador del pueblo puertorriquêno, descubridor de la Florida y del Estrecho de las Bahamas (Barcelona, Espana, Editorial Universitaria, Universidad de Puerto Rico, 1971); "Ponce de Leon, Juan," Encyclopedia Britannica, from Encyclopedia Britannica Online. http://search.eb.com/eb/articles?tocid-9060663. See also Jane Landers, "Free and Slave," in Michael Gannon, The New History of Florida (Gainesville: University of Florida Press, 1996); Alex D. Krieger, *We Came Naked and Barefoot: The Journey of Cabeza de Vaca Across North America* (Austin: University of Texas Press, 2002); *The Journey of Alvar Nunez Cabeza de Vaca and His Companions from Florida to the Pacific, 1528–1536*, translated from his own narrative by Fanny Bandelier, edited with an introduction by Ad F. Bandelier (New York: Allerton Book Co., 1922); Robert Silverberg, *The Pueblo Revolt* (Lincoln: University of Nebraska Press, 1970); John L. Kessell, "To See Such Marvels with My Own Eyes: Spanish Exploration in the Western Borderlands," *The Coronado Expedition From the Distance of 460 Years*, edited by Richard Flint and Shirley Cushing Flint (Albuquerque: University of New Mexico Press, 2003); Gloria A. Young and Michael P. Hoffman, editors, *The Expedition of Hernando de Soto West of the Mississippi, 1541–1543* (Fayetteville, The University of Arkansas Press, 1993); Lawrence A. Clayton, Vernon James Knight, Jr., and Edward C. Moore, editors, *The De Soto Chronicles: the Expedition of Hernando De Soto to North America in 1539–1543* (Tuscaloosa: The University of Alabama Press, two volumes, 1993); James Wilson, *The Earth Shall Weep: A History of Native America* (New York: Grove Press, 1998); Harry Kelsey, *Juan Rodriquez Cabrillo* (San Marino, CA: Huntington Library, 1986); Albert Manucy, *Sixteenth Century St. Augustine: The People and Their Homes* (Gainesville: University Press of Florida, 1997); "Florida," Encyclopedia Britannica Online, http://search.eb.com/ebi/articles?tocld=200862; Eugene Lyon, "Settlement and Survival," in Michael Gannon, editor, *The New History of Florida* (Gainesville: University Press of Florida, 1996); David K. Yoo and Eiichiro Azuma, editors, *The Oxford Handbook of Asian American History* (New York: Oxford University Press, 2016).

Exploration and Encounter in North America—The French

Samuel Eliot Morison, *The European Discovery of America: The Northern Voyages, A.D. 500–1600* (New York: Oxford University Press, 1971); Roger Riendeau, *A Brief History of Canada* (Markham, Ontario: Fitzhenry and Whiteside, 2000).

Exploration and Encounter in North America—The English

Karen Ordahl Kupperman, *The Jamestown Project* (Cambridge: Harvard University Press, 2007); Tony Horwitz, *A Voyage Long and Strange* (New York: Henry Holt, 2008).

Chapter 3 Settlement, Alliances, and Resistance, 1607–1718

The English Settle in North America

J.H. Elliott, *Empires of the Atlantic World: Britain and Spain in America, 1492–1830* (New Haven: Yale University Press, 2006) is an excellent source for early English settlement.

See also Karen Ordahl Kupperman, The Jamestown Project (Cambridge: Harvard University Press, 2009); Nathaniel Philbrick, *Mayflower: A Story of Courage, Community, and War* (New York: Viking Penguin, 2006); Edmund S. Morgan, *American Slavery, American Freedom: The Ordeal of Colonial Virginia* (New York: W. W. Norton, 1975/2003); Samuel Eliot Morison, *Builders of the Bay Colony* (Boston: Houghton Mifflin, 1930, revised, 1958); John Winthrop, *History of New England from 1610 to 1649*, ed. James Savage (Boston: Little, Brown, 1853); Ira Berlin, *Many Thousands Gone: The First Two centuries of Slavery in North America* (Cambridge: Harvard University Press, 1998).

England's Wars, England's Colonies

The story of England's civil war has been told many times from many perspectives. For understanding the religious nature of the conflict I have turned to Williston Walker, *History of the Christian Church*, third edition (New York: Scribners, 1970); J. Franklin Jameson, *Narratives of New Netherlands, 1609–1664* (New York: Charles Scribner's Sons, 1909); Eric Homberger, *The Historical Atlas of New York City* (New York: Henry Holt, 2005.); Berlin, *Many Thousands Gone: The First Two Centuries of Slavery in North America.*

France Takes Control of the Heart of the Continent

Craig Brown, editor, *The Illustrated History of Canada* (Toronto, Key Porter, 2002). See also David Hackett Fischer, *Champlain's Dream* (New York: Simon & Schuster, 2008). Charles J. Balesi, *The Time of the French in the Heart of North America* (Chicago: Alliance Francaise, 2000), Olivia Mahoney, *Chicago: Crossroads of America* (Chicago: Chicago History Museum, 2006); Francis Parkman, *La Salle and the Discovery of the Great West*, two volumes, (Boston, 1902, reprinted New York: AMS Press, 1969); Reuben Gold Thwaites, editor, *Travels and Explorations of the Jesuit Missionaries in New France, 1610–1791*, Vol. LXV, *Lower Canada, Mississippi Valley, 1696–1702* (Cleveland: The Burrows Brothers, 1900); Ned Sublette, *The World That Made New Orleans* (Chicago: Lawrence Hill, 2008); Charles E. Champan, *A History of California: The Spanish Period* (New York: The Macmillan Company, 1930).

Developments in Spanish Colonies North of Mexico

J.H. Elliott, *Empires of the Atlantic World: Britain and Spain in America, 1492–1830* (New Haven: Yale University Press, 2006); Robert Silverberg, *The Pueblo Revolt* (New York,: 1970; reprint Lincoln: The University of Nebraska Press, 1994); Franklin Folsom, *Indian Uprising on the Rio Grande: The Pueblo Revolt of 1680* (Albuquerque: University of New Mexico Press, 1973, 2000,); Charles Wilson Hackett, *Revolt of the Pueblo Indians of New Mexico* (Albuquerque: University of New Mexico Press, 1942).

Chapter 4 Creating the Culture of British North America, 1689–1754

England's Glorious Revolution and the Rights of Englishmen, 1689

Elliott, *Empires of the Atlantic World*; John Locke, *Second Treatise on Government* (originally 1689; reprinted Arlington Heights, IL: Crofts Classics, 1982).

The Plantation World—From a Society with Slaves to a Slave Society

Ira Berlin, *Many Thousands Gone: The First Two centuries of Slavery in North America* (Cambridge: Harvard University Press, 1998); Edmund S. Morgan, *American Slavery, American Freedom: The Ordeal of Colonial Virginia* (New York: W. W. Norton, 1975/2003); John Barbot, "A Description of the Coasts of North and South Guinea," (1682) in Thomas Astley and John Churchill, editors, *Collection of Voyages and Travels* (London, 1732), cited in Steven Mintz, editor, *African American Voices: A Documentary Reader, 1619–1877* (Malden, MA: Wiley-Blackwell, 2009), pp. 42–45; Edwin G. Burrows and Mike Wallace, *Gotham: A History of New York City to 1898* (New York: Oxford University Press, 1999); Jill Lepore's *New York Burning: Liberty, Slavery, and Conspiracy in Eighteenth-Century Manhattan* (New York: Random House, 2005).

Stability and Instability in the American and British World

Mary Beth Norton, *In the Devil's Snare* (New York: Random House, 2002); Gordon S. Wood, *The Americanization of Benjamin Franklin* (New York: Penguin Books, 2004); Benjamin Franklin, *Autobiography*; Jane Kamensky, "The Colonial Mosaic, 1600–1760," in Nancy F. Cott, editor, No Small Courage: *A History of Women in the United States* (New York: Oxford University Press, 2000); Mari Jo Buhle, Teresa Murphy, Jame Gerhard, *Women and the Making of America* (Upper Saddle River, NJ: Pearson, 2009); "The Letterbook of Eliza Lucas Pinckney, 1742," in Paul G. E. Clemens, editor, The Colonial Era: A Documentary Reader (Malden, MA: Blackwell, 2008); Navigation Act of 1660 and Gottlieb Mittelberger, *Journey to Pennsylvania in the Year 1750 and Return to Germany in the Year 1754* in Louis B. Wright and Elaine W. Fowler, English Colonization of North America (New York: St. Martin's Press, 1968); Sydney E. Ahlstrom, *A Religious History of the American People* (New Haven: Yale University Press, 2004); Hasia R. Diner, *A New Promised Land: A History of Jews in America* (New York: Oxford University Press, 2000); Clarence H. Faust and Thomas H. Johnson, editors, *Jonathan Edwards* (New York: The American Writers Series, 1935), pp. 159–163; Jonathan Edwards, *A Treatise Concerning Religious Affections* (Boston: S. Kneeland and T. Green, 1746, reprinted and edited by John E. Smith, New Haven: Yale University Press, 1959); Thomas Bender, *A Nation Among the Nations* (New York: Hill and Wang, 2006); Elliott, *Empires of the Atlantic World*; Leonard Labaree, et al, editors, *The Papers of Benjamin Franklin* (New Haven: Yale University Press, 1959–).

The International Context

Thomas Bender, *A Nation Among the Nations* (New York: Hill and Wang, 2006); Elliott, *Empires of the Atlantic World*; Wood, *The Americanization of Benjamin Franklin*; Leonard Labaree, et al, editors, *The Papers of Benjamin Franklin* (New Haven: Yale University Press, 1959–); Wright and Fowler, *English Colonization of North America.*

Chapter 5 The Making of a Revolution, 1754–1783

Preludes to Revolution

Material on the French and Indian War is from William M. Fowler, Jr., *Empires At War: the French and Indian War and the Struggle for North America, 1754–1763* (New York: Walker & Company, 2005). See also Daniel K. Richter, *Facing East from Indian Country: A Native History of Early* America (Cambridge: Harvard University Press, 2001). Richter's perceptive interpretation of the experience of American Indians is a key resource for understanding this material.

"The Revolution Was in the Minds of the People"

Gary Nash, *The Unknown American Revolution: the Unruly Birth of Democracy and the Struggle to Create America* (New York: Viking, 2005) is especially helpful for understanding the diverse voices of the revolutionary era. For a different perspective see Gordon S. Wood, *The Radicalism of the American Revolution* (New York: Random House, 1991). See also Bernard Bailyn, *The Intellectual Origins of the American Revolution* (Cambridge: Harvard University Press, 1992). An excellent new source on urban street resistance to British authority can be found in Benjamin L. Carp, *Rebels Rising: Cities and the American Revolution* (New York: Oxford University Press, 2007). In order to explore these topics further see also Merrill Jensen, *Tracts of the American Revolution* (New York: Bobbs-Merrill, 1967), Jeremy Black, *Revolutions in the Western World 1775–1825* (Hants, England: Ashgate, 2006), Edwin S. Gaustad, *A Documentary History of Religion in America to the Civil War* (Grand Rapids, MI: William B. Eerdmans, 1993), Carl Bridenbaugh, *Mitre and Sceptre* (1962), Mari Jo Buhle, Teresa Murphy, Jane Gerhard, *Women and the Making of* America (Upper Saddle River, NJ: Pearson Prentice Hall, 2009), Alfred W. Blumrosen and Ruth G. Blumrose, *Slave Nation: How Slavery United the Colonies & Sparked the American Revolution* (Naperville, IL: Sourcebooks, 2005), Phillis Wheatley, "To the Right Honourable William, Earl of Dartmouth, His Majesty's Principal Secretary of State for North America," *The Poems of Phillis Wheatley*, and Lemuel Haynes, "Lexington, Massachusetts, 1775," both in Herb Boyd, *Autobiography of a People* (New York: Doubleday, 2000). For art see Jane Kamensky, *The World of John Singleton Copley* (New York: W.W. Norton, 2017).

The War for Independence

Robert Middlekauff, *The Glorious Cause: The American Revolution, 1763–1789* (New York: Oxford University Press, 2005) is a thorough source on the Revolutionary War. Nathaniel Philbrick's recent *Valiant Ambition: George Washington, Benedict Arnold, and the Fate of the American Revolution* (New York: Viking, 2016) tells a detailed story of the rivalries and frustrations that were part of living through and fighting the Revolution. See also David McCullough, *John Adams* (New York: Simon & Schuster, 2001), Joseph J. Ellis, *American Sphinx: The Character of Thomas Jefferson* (New York: Alfred A. Knopf, 1997), *Common Sense* is worth reading carefully. I have been guided in analysis here by my own reading of the pamphlet and by Gregory Tietjen's introduction to the 1995 edition, Thomas Paine, *Common Sense* (New York: Barnes & Noble, 1995); Richard Archer, *As if An Enemy's Country: The British Occupation of Boston and the Origins of Revolution* (New York: Oxford University Press, 2010); John Shy, *A People Numerous and Armed: Reflections on the Military Struggle for American Independence* (New York: Oxford University Press, 1976); Charles Royster, *A Revolutionary People at War: The Continental Army and American Character* (1979). Elizabeth F. Ellet, *The Women of the American Revolution* (New York: Charles Scribner, 1852) is a goldmine of material on the ways many different women experienced the revolution. For women's experience see also Marylynn Salmon, "The Limits of Independence: 1760–1800," in Nancy F. Cott, editor, *No Small Courage: A History of Women in the United States* (New York: Oxford University Press, 2000).

Chapter 6 Creating a Nation, 1783–1788

The State of the Nation at War's End

David McCullough's *John Adams* (New York: Simon & Schuster, 2001) was on the top of the bestseller charts, followed not far behind by Joseph J. Ellis' *Founding Brothers* (New York: Alfred A. Knopf, 2000). Also very helpful in understanding the "founding fathers" is Ellis' *American Sphinx*. Philip S. Foner, ed., *The Complete Writings of Thomas Paine*, (New York: Citidal Press, 1945), Vol. II, pp. 243, 286–287. The description of the Newburgh Conspiracy is taken from Richard H. Kohn, *Eagle and Sword: the Federalists and the Creation of the Military Establishment in America, 1783–1802* (New York: The Free Press, 1975), pp. 17–39. Kohn's work remains the best study of this and several other military developments in the earliest years of the Republic. For Shay's Rebellion, see David P. Szatmary, *Shay's Rebellion: The Making of an Agrarian Insurrection* (Amherst: University of Massachusetts Press, 1980) and Leonard L. Richards, *Shay's Rebellion: the American Revolution's Final Battle* (Philadelphia: University of Pennsylvania Press, 2002). For an Indian perspective on the new U.S. government, see Daniel K. Richter, *Facing East from Indian Country: A Native History of Early* America (Cambridge: Harvard University Press, 2001), p. 164. Richter's perceptive interpretation of the experience of American Indians is a key resource for understanding this material and also William L. Stone, *Life of Joseph Brant—Thayendanegea*, (New York: Alexander V. Blake, 1838) two volumes, Vol. II, pp. 237–239. Ira Berlin, *The Making of African America: The Four Great Migrations* (New York: Viking, 2010) is a terrific source on the African American experience in the early Republic. See also Benjamin Banneker to Thomas Jefferson, August 19, 1791 in Herb Boyd, editor, *Autobiography of a People: Three Centuries of African American History Told by Those Who Lived It* (New York: Random House, 2000), pp. 52–55; Phyllis Wheatley to Rev. Samson Occom, New London, Connecticut, February 11, 1774, in Julia Reidhead, editor, *The Norton Anthology of American Literature*, Fifth Edition (New York: W.W. Norton, 1998), Vol. I, pp. 838–839; and *Memoirs of the Life of Boston King, a Black Preacher*, 1798. I have used multiple sources in seeking to understand women's experience during and after the Revolution including Mary Beth Norton, *Liberty's Daughters: The Revolutionary Experience of American Women, 1750–1800* (Boston: Little, Brown, 1980), pp. 209–242; Mary Beth Norton, *Founding Mothers & Fathers: Gendered Power and the Forming of American Society* (New York: Random House, 1996), pp. 404–405; Mari Jo Buhle, Teresa Murphy, and Jane Gerhard, *Women in the Making of America* (Upper Saddle River, NJ: Pearson, 2009), pp. 77–97; Marylynn Salmon, "The Limits of Independence, 1760–1800," in Nancy F. Cott, editor, *No Small Courage: A History of Women in the United States* (New York: Oxford University Press, 2000), pp. 116–126; see quote on p. 120; and Dorothy A. Mays, *Women in Early America: Struggle, Survival and Freedom in a New World* (Santa Barbara, CA: ABC-CLIO, 2004), p. 179.

Creating a Government: Writing the U.S. Constitution

I have used three main sources in telling the story of the writing and adoption of the Constitution: Richard Beeman, *Plain, Honest Men: the Making of the American Constitution* (New York: Random House, 2009), Woody Holton, *Unruly Americans and the Origins of the Constitution* (New York: Hill and Wang, 2007), and Max Ferrand, *The Framing of the Constitution of the United States* (New Haven: Yale University Press, 1913). Material on the state conventions can be found in Beeman pp. 386–411. See also Max Farrand, editor, *The Records of the Federal Convention of 1787*, 4 vols. (New Haven, 1911–1937) ; Merrill Jensen, editor, *The Documentary History of the Ratification of the Constitution* (Madison, WI: 1976), XIV.

Chapter 7 Practicing Democracy, 1789–1800

Convening a Congress, Inaugurating a President, Adopting a Bill of Rights

Richard Labunski, *James Madison and the Struggle for the Bill of Rights* (New York: Oxford University Press, 2006), pp. 178–185, 187–204;, 278–280; Richard Beeman, *Plain, Honest Men: the Making of the American Constitution* (New York: Random House, 2009), pp. 413–414; John Ferling, *The Ascent of George Washington: The Hidden Political Genius of an American Icon* (New York: Bloomsbury Press, 2009), pp. 278–307.

Creating an Economy: Alexander Hamilton and U.S. Economic System

Ron Chernow, *Alexander Hamilton* (New York: Penguin Books, 2004) is a valuable source of information on Hamilton's life and economic views. See especially pp. 286–295, 291–331, 344–361, 370–381.

Setting the Pace: The Washington Administration

Ron Chernow, *Washington: A Life* (New York: the Penguin Press, 2010) is a useful new biography of George Washington. Also very useful is John Ferling, *The Ascent of George Washington: The Hidden Political Genius of an American Icon* (New York: Bloomsbury Press, 2009), especially pp. 287–289, 317–323, 330. There are many sources on Washington's second term diplomatic maneuvers. I have relied especially on George C. Herring, *From Colony to Superpower: U.S. Foreign Relations Since 1776* (New York: Oxford University Press, 2008), pp. 56–92.

The Birth of Political Parties: Adams and Jefferson

There are many useful descriptions of the election of 1796 and Adams's inauguration. See especially Gordon S. Wood, *Empire of Liberty: A History of the Early Republic* (New York: Oxford University Press, 2009), pp. 206–216; David McCullough, *John Adams* (New York: Simon & Schuster, 2001), pp. 458–471; Ferling, pp. 347–350. For the Quasi-War with France, see George C. Herring, *From Colony to Superpower: U.S. Foreign Relations Since 1776* (New York: Oxford University Press, 2008), pp. 83–92; Wood, *Empire of Liberty*, pp. 209–275; McCullough, pp. 467–536. The best source on the election of 1800 is Edward J. Larson, *A Magnificent Catastrophe: the Tumultuous Election of 1800, America's First Presidential Campaign* (New York: The Free Press, 2007). As the subtitle indicates, this book is a study of just the topic of this section of the chapter. See also Wood, pp. 276–314; McCullough, pp. 535–559.

Chapter 8 Creating a New People, Expanding the Country, 1801–1823

Jefferson and the Republican Ideal

Gordon S. Wood, *Empire of Liberty: A History of the Early Republic, 1789–1815* (New York: Oxford University Press, 2009) is a first rate overview of the culture and political life of the U.S. in the Jeffersonian era and beyond. It has served as my prime source for much of this material. See especially, pp. 276–356 and 576–619. Annette Gordon-Reed and Peter S. Onuf, *"Most Blessed of the Patriarchs": Thomas Jefferson and the Empire of the Imagination* (New York: W. W. Norton, 2016) is a terrific recent study of Jefferson. For Jefferson's relationship with Sally Hemings, see Annette Gordon-Reed, *The Hemingses of Monticello: An American Family* (New York: W. W. Norton, 2008).

The Ideal of Religious Freedom

For religious developments in the era an excellent place to start is Sydney E. Ahlstrom, *A Religious History of the American People*, Second Edition (New Haven: Yale University Press, 2004), pp. 429–454. See also Alice Felt Tyler, *Freedom's Ferment: Phases of American Social History from the Colonial Period to the Outbreak of the Civil War* (New York: Harper & Row, 1944); Thomas L. Webber, *Deep Like the Rivers: Education in the Slave Quarter Community, 1831–1865* (New York: W. W. Norton, 1978), pp. 80–81, 191–206; Ira Berlin, *The Making of African America: The Four Great Migrations* (New York: Viking, 2010), p. 93; John Hope Franklin and Alfred A. Moss, Jr., *From Slavery to Freedom: A History of African Americans*, Seventh Edition (New York: Alfred A. Knopf,

1994), pp. 100–103; Hasia R. Diner, *A New Promised Land: A History of Jews in America* (New York: Oxford University Press, 2003), pp. 17–21.

Beyond the Mississippi: The Louisiana Purchase and the Expedition of Lewis and Clark

George C. Herring, *From Colony to Superpower: U.S. Foreign Relations Since 1776* (New York: Oxford University Press, 2008), pp. 101–109; Wood, *Empire of Liberty*, pp. 357–399; Ned Sublette, *The World That Made New Orleans: From Spanish Silver to Congo Square* (Chicago: Lawrence Hill Books, 2008), especially pp. 106–111 and 161–164; Mari Jo Buhle, Teresa Murphy, and Jane Gerhard, *Women and the Making of America* (Upper Saddle River, NJ: Pearson Prentice Hall, 2009), pp. 115–117. For the Lewis and Clark expedition's story, I have relied primarily on Frederick E. Hoxie and Jay T. Nelson, editors, *Lewis & Clark and the Indian Country: The Native American Perspective* (Urbana: University of Illinois Press, 2007) and the classic *Journals of Lewis and Clark*, edited by Bernard DeVoto (Boston: Houghton Mifflin, 1953). For two very different views of the expedition see also Alvin M. Josephy, Jr., *Lewis and Clark Through Indian Eyes* (New York: Vintage, 2006) and Stephen E. Ambrose, *Undaunted Courage: Meriwether Lewis, Thomas Jefferson, and the Opening of the American West* (New York: Simon & Schuster, 1996).

The War of 1812: "Mr. Madison's War"

The story of the War of 1812 is told in many places. I have drawn primarily on Herring, *From Colony to Superpower*, pp. 93–133; Wood, *Empire of Liberty*, pp. 659–700; Thomas Bender, *A Nation Among the Nations: America's Place in World History* (New York: Hill & Wang, 2006), pp. 106–115. The material on Tecumseh and the Prophet is from John Sugden, *Tecumseh: A Life* (New York: Henry Holt, 1997), by far the best of many biographies of the Indian leader.

Expanding American Territory and Influence

Herring, *From Colony to Superpower*, pp. 134–175; Wood, *Empire of Liberty*, p. 370; Daniel K. Richter, *Facing East from Indian Country. A Native History of Early America* (Cambridge: Harvard University Press, 2001), pp. 226–236; Sellers, pp. 181–185.

Chapter 9 New Industries, New Politics, 1815–1828

Creating the Cotton Economy

Daniel Walker Howe, *What Hath God Wrought: The Transformation of America, 1815–1848* (New York: Oxford University Press, 2007), Gene Dattel, *Cotton and Race in the Making of America: the Human Costs of Economic Power* (Chicago: Ivan R. Dee, 2009), and Sven Beckert, Empire of Cotton (New York: Random House, 2014) are all essential reading for understanding the impact of cotton on the United States in the early 1800s. See also Henry Bibb, *Narrative of the Life and Adventures of Henry Bibb* (New York: Published by the Author, 1849), pp. 114–118, cited in Sean Patrick Adams, *The Early American Republic: A Documentary Reader* (Malden, MA: Wiley-Blackwell, 2009), pp. 99–101; "R" in the *Voice of Industry*, March 26, 1847, cited in Philip S. Foner, editor, *The Factory Girls* (Urbana: University of Illinois Press, 1977), pp. 87–88 as well as the rest of that volume; Phyllis Deane, *The First Industrial Revolution* (Cambridge: Cambridge University Press, 2nd edition, 1979); Angela Lakwete, *Inventing the Cotton Gin* (Baltimore: Johns Hopkins University Press, 2003); Constance McL. Green, *Eli Whitney and the Birth of American Technology* (Boston: Little, Brown, 1956);. Ira Berlin, *The Making of African America: The Four Great Migrations* (New York: Viking, 2010), pp. 99–130; Charles Ball, *Fifty Years in Chains; or, The Life of An American Slave* (New York: H. Dayton, 1860), pp. 28–31, 240–241, 280; Harriet H. Robinson, *Loom and Spindle: Or Life Among the Early Mill Girls* (New York, 1898; reprinted Kailua, HI: Press Pacifica, 1976); Alan J. Singer, *New York and Slavery: Time to Teach the Truth* (Albany: State University of New York press, 2008), pp. 89–93. For the story of the packet ships see Stephen Fox, *Transatlantic: Samuel Cunard, Isambard Brunel, and the Great Atlantic Steamships* (New York: Harper Collins, 2003), pp. 3–7.

Commerce, Technology, and Transportation

In addition to Howe, *What Hath God Wrought*, Charles Sellers, *The Market Revolution: Jacksonian America, 1815–1846* (New York: Oxford University Press, 1991) is essential reading for this material. See also Carol Sheriff, *The Artificial River: The Erie Canal and the Paradox of Progress, 1817–1862* (New York: Hill and Wang, 1996); Washington Irving, The Sketch Book (New York, 1819). Gordon Wood's Introduction to *Empire of Liberty* tells the Rip Van Winkle story and its implications for a changing America very well. For the story of Ichabod Washburn see Joyce Appleby, *Inheriting the Revolution: The First Generation of Americans* (Cambridge: Harvard University Press, 2000), p. 9. See also Sellers, pp. 152–157.

From the Era of Good Feeling to the Politics of Division

Howe, *What Hath God Wrought* and Sellers, *The Market Revolution* are also essential reading for understanding the politics of the 1820s. For further detail see Joseph J. Ellis, *American Sphinx: The Character of Thomas Jefferson* (New York: Random House, 1996), pp. 316–317; Jon Meacham, *American Lion: Andrew Jackson in the White House* (New York: Random House, 2008), pp. 41–49.

Chapter 10 Democracy in the Age of Jackson, 1828–1844

Jacksonian Democracy, Jacksonian Government

Jon Meacham, *American Lion: Andrew Jackson in the White House* (New York: Random House, 2008) is an excellent political biography of Jackson. To understand the opposition to Jackson it is useful to read David S. Heidler and Jeanne T. Heidler, *Henry Clay: The Essential American* (New York: Random House, 2010). For an overview of the Jacksonian era an excellent source is Daniel Walker Howe, *What Hath God Wrought:*

The Transformation of America, 1815–1848 (New York: Oxford University Press, 2007); William G. McLaughlin's *Cherokee Renascence in the New Republic* (Princeton: Princeton University Press, 1986).remains the best story of the Cherokee experience in the half century leading up to Removal. Also important is Theda Perdue, *Cherokee Women* (Lincoln: University of Nebraska Press, 1998); Howe, *What Hath God Wrought*, pp. 342–357 and 414–423 and Meacham, *American Lion: Andrew Jackson in the White House*, pp. 141–145. De Tocqueville quote is from Alexis de Tocqueville, *Democracy in America* (originally 1835; reprinted New York: Penguin Books, 2003), p. 380, pp. 463–464; Charles Sellers, *The Market Revolution: Jacksonian America, 1815–1846* (New York: Oxford University Press, 1991).

Democratized Religion: The Second Great Awakening

Sydney E. Ahlstrom, *A Religious History of the American People* (New Haven: Yale University Press, 2004), pp. 385–647; Jon Butler, *Awash in a Sea of Faith: Christianizing the American People* (Cambridge: Harvard University Press, 1990), p. 289; Timothy L. Smith, "Protestant Schooling and American Nationality, 1800–1850," *Journal of American History*, Vol. 53 (1966–67), pp. 679–694; Whitney R. Cross, *The Burned-Over District: The Social and Intellectual History of Enthusiastic Religion in Western New York, 1800–1850* (Ithaca, NY: Cornell University Press, 1950), especially pp. 151–169; Charles G. Finney, *Memoirs* (New York, 1876), p. 24; Mari Jo Buhle, Teresa Murphy, Jane Gerhard, *Women in the Making of America* (Upper Saddle River, NJ: Pearson Prentice Hall, 2009), p. 199; James W. Fraser, *Pedagogue for God's Kingdom: Lyman Beecher And The Second Great Awakening* (Lanham, MD: University Press of America, 1985); Louis Menand, *The Metaphysical Club* (New York: Farrar, Straus and Giroux, 2001), pp. 16–22; Ralph Waldo Emerson, "An Address Delivered before the Senior Class in Divinity College, Cambridge, Sunday Evening 15 July, 1838," included in Nina Baym, *The Norton Anthology of American Literature*, Fifth Edition, Vol. I (New York: W. W. Norton, 1998), pp. 1114–1126. There have been several excellent accounts of America's nineteenth-century communitarian movements including Dolores Hayden, *Seven American Utopias: The Architecture of Communitarian Socialism, 1790–1975* (Cambridge: MIT Press, 1976); J. Stein, *The Shaker Experience in America* (New Haven: Yale University Press, 1992); Spencer Klaw, *Without Sin: The Life and Death of the Oneida Community* (New York: Penguin Press, 1993); John Humphrey Noyes, *History of American Socialisms*; (1870); Robert Owen, *The Life of Robert Owen by Himself* (1920; first published in 1857); Charles Nordhoff, *The Communistic Societies of the United States* (1875); and Alice Felt Tyler, *Freedom's Ferment* (Minneapolis: University of Minnesota Press, 1944).

Democratized Education, Democratized Art: The Birth of the Common School, American Painting and Photography

Catharine Beecher, "An Essay on the Education of Female Teachers (New York: Van Nostrand & Dwight, 1835); Margaret A. Nash, *Women's Education in the United States, 1780–1840* (New York: Palgrave Macmillan, 2005); Kathryn Kish Sklar, *Catharine Beecher: A Study in American Domesticity* (New York: W. W. Norton, 1973); Anne Firor Scott, "The Ever Widening Circle: The Diffusion of Feminist Values from Troy Female Seminary," *History of Education Quarterly* (Spring, 1979), 3–25; James W. Fraser, *Preparing America's Teachers: A History* (New York: Teachers College Press, 2007); Polly Welts Kaufman, *Women Teachers on the Frontier* (New Haven: Yale University Press, 1984); Carl F. Kaestle, *Pillars of the Republic: Common Schools and American Society, 1780–1860* (New York: Hill and Wang, 1983); Wayne Urban and Jennings Wagoner, *American Education: A History* (New York: Routledge, 2008); Michael Katz, *The Irony of Early School Reform* (Cambridge: Harvard University Press, 1968). Judith H. O'Toole, *Different Views in Hudson River School Painting* (New York: Columbia University Press, 2005); Beaumont Newhall, *The History of Photography: From 1839 to the Present*, fifth edition (New York: Museum of Modern Art, 1982).

Chapter 11 Manifest Destiny—Expanding the Nation, 1830–1853

Manifest Destiny: The Importance of an Idea

Anders Stephanson, *Manifest Destiny: American Expansionism and the Empire of Right* (New York: Hill and Wang, 1995); Frederick Merk, *Manifest Destiny and Mission in American History: A Reinterpretation* (New York: Alfred A. Knopf, 1963); Robert W. Merry, *A Country of Vast Designs: James K. Polk, the Mexican War and the Conquest of the American Continent* (New York: Simon and Schuster, 2009); Daniel Walker Howe, *What Hath God Wrought: The Transformation of America, 1815–1848* (New York: Oxford University Press, 2007), pp. 702–722; George C. Herring, *From Colony to Superpower: U.S. Foreign Relations Since 1776* (New York: Oxford University Press, 2008), pp. 173–184. See also Antonio Maria Osio, *The History of California: A Memoir of Mexican California*, translated and edited by Rose Maria Beebe and Robert M. Senkewicz (Madison: University of Wisconsin Press, 1996), p. 247; William C. David, *Lone Star Rising: the Revolutionary Birth of the Texas Republic* (New York: Free Press, 2004), pp. 213–224, 1–27, 73; Gregg Cantrell, *Stephen F. Austin: Empresario of Texas* (New Haven: Yale University Press, 1999), pp. 104–201, 348–364; Rodolfo F. Acuna, *Occupied America: A History of Chicanos*, Seventh Edition (Boston: Longman, 2011), pp. 39–43. The web site www.uselectionsatlas.org/TESULTS/national is a very helpful resource for tracking the breakdown of votes in all presidential elections from 1789 to the present.

The U.S. War with Mexico, 1846–1848

For the U.S. War with Mexico, see especially Robert W. Merry, *A Country of Vast Designs: James K. Polk, the Mexican War and the Conquest of the American Continent* (New York: Simon and Schuster, 2009) and Daniel Walker Howe, *What Hath God Wrought: The Transformation of America, 1815–1848* (New York: Oxford University Press, 2007),

pp. 731–791. See also John Quincy Adams cited in Nash Candelaria, *Not By The Sword* (Tempe, AZ: Bilingual Press, 1982), p. 1; Roy P. Basler, editor, *Abraham Lincoln: His Speeches and Writings* (Cleveland: World Publishing, 1946), p. 202; Henry David Thoreau, *On the Duty of Civil Disobedience* (1848, republished New York: Macmillan, 1962); Carlos R. Herrera, "New Mexico Resistance to U.S. Occupation," in Erlinda Gonzales-Berry and David R. Maciel, editors, The Contested Homeland: A Chicano History of New Mexico (Albuquerque: University of New Mexico Press, 2000); Ronald Takaki, *A Different Mirror: A History of Multicultural America* (Boston: Little Brown, 1993), p. 168–171; Norman Graebner, *Empire on the Pacific: A Study of American Continental Expansion* (New York, 1955); Alan Rosenus, *General Vallejo and the Advent of the Americans* (Berkeley, CA: Heyday Books, 1999), pp. 105–119; Mariano G. Vallejo, "What the Gold Rush Brought to California," in Valeska Bari, *The Course of Empire, First Hand Accounts of California in the Days of the Gold Rush of '49* (New York: Coward-McCann, 1931), pp. 55–56; Leonard Pitt, *The Decline of the Californios: A Social History of the Spanish-Speaking Californians, 1846–1890* (Berkeley: University of California Press, 1966, 1998); Genaro M. Padilla, *My History, Not Yours: The Formation of Mexican American Autobiography* (Madison: University of Wisconsin Press, 1993); Douglas Monroy, *Thrown Among Strangers: the Making of Mexican Culture in Frontier California* (Berkeley: University of California Press, 1990); Lisbeth Haas, *Conquests and Historical Identities in California, 1769–1936* (Berkeley: University of California Press, 1995); and Ramon A. Gutierrez and Richard J. Orsi, editors, *Contested Eden: California Before the Gold Rush* (Berkeley: University of California Press, 1998); Susan Lee Johnson, *Roaring Camp: The Social World of the California Gold Rush* (New York: W. W. Norton, 2000).

West into the Pacific

Eric Jay Dolin, *Leviathan: A History of Whaling in America* (New York: W. W. Norton, 2007); Herman Melville, *Moby Dick* (New York: Harper and Brothers, 1851); Jim Murphy, *Gone A-Whaling: The Lure of the Sea and the Hunt for the Great Whale* (New York: Houghton Mifflin, 1998); George C. Herring, *From Colony to Superpower: U.S. Foreign Relations Since 1776* (New York: Oxford University Press, 2008). See also materials at the New Bedford Whaling Museum www.whalingmuseum.org.

Chapter 12 Living in a Nation of Changing Lands, Changing Faces, Changing Expectations, 1831–1854

A Different People—The Changing Face of the American People in the 1840s and 1850s

Ronald Takaki, *Strangers From A Different Shore: A History of Asian Americans* (New York: Little, Brown, 1989); Iris Chang, *The Chinese in America* (New York: Viking, 2003); Erika Lee, *The Making of Asian America: A History* (New York: Simon & Schuster, 2015); Jay P. Dolan, *The Irish Americans: A History* (New York: Bloomsbury Press, 2008); Martha Hodes, *The Sea Captain's Wife* (New York: W. W. Norton, 2006); Stanley K. Schultz, *Culture Factory: Boston Public Schools, 1789–1860* (New York: Oxford University Press, 1973); Fray Angelico Chavez. *But Time and Chance: The Story of Padre Martinez of Taos, 1793–1867* (Santa Fe, New Mexico: Sunstone Press, 1981); Rodolfo F. Acuna, *Occupied America: A History of Chicanos*, Seventh Edition (Boston: Longman, 2011); Mari Jo Buhle, Teresa Murphy, Jane Gerhard, *Women and the Making of America* (New York: Pearson Prentice Hall, 2009); George C. Herring, *From Colony to Superpower: U.S. Foreign Relations Since 1776* (New York: Oxford University Press, 2008); Slavery in the United States, 1840s and 1850s; David Brion Davis, *Inhuman Bondage: The Rise and Fall of Slavery in the New World* (New York: Oxford University Press, 2006); Ira Berlin, *The Making of African America: the Four Great Migrations*, Chapter Three, "The Passage to the Interior (New York: Viking, 2010); Eugene D. Genovese, *Roll, Jordan, Roll: The World the Slaves Made* (New York: Vintage, 1976); Harriet Jacobs, *Incidents in the Life of a Slave Girl* (original 1861; Mineola, NY: Dover Publications, 2001); Elizabeth Fox-Genovese, *Within the Plantation Household: Black and White Women of the Old South* (Chapel Hill: University of North Carolina Press, 1988); Timothy S. Huebner, "Roger B. Taney and the Slavery Issue: Looking beyond—and before—*Dred Scott*," *The Journal of American History* 97:1 (June 2010), pp. 17–38; Elizabeth Fox-Genovese and Eugene D. Genovese, *Slavery in White and Black* (New York: Cambridge University Press, 2008); John Hope Franklin and Loren Schweninger, *Runaway Slaves: Rebels on the Plantation* (New York: Oxford University Press, 1999); Harriet Jacobs, "Incidents in the Life of a Slave Girl," in Herb Boyd, editor, *Autobiography of a People* (New York: Doubleday, 2000) cited in pp. 90–92; David E. Swift, *Black Prophets of Justice: Activist Clergy Before the Civil War* (Baton Rouge: Louisiana State University Press, 1989); Frederick Douglass, *Narrative of the Life of Frederick Douglass: An American Slave* (1845; reprinted Cambridge: Harvard University Press, 1967);. Biographical information on Tubman is taken primarily from Nancy A. Davidson, "Harriet Tubman," in *Notable Black American Women*, edited by Jessie Carney Smith (Detroit: Gale Research, 1992), pp. 11151–1155 and Judith Nies, *Seven Women: Portraits from the American Radical Tradition* (New York: Viking, 1977), pp. 34–59; Donald E. Williams, Jr., *Prudence Crandall's Legacy* (Middletown, CT: Wesleyan University Press, 2014). See also Sarah Bradford, *Harriet Tubman: the Moses of Her People* (1886; reprint New York: Corinth, 1961). For slave revolts, see Herbert Aptheker, *American Negro Slave Revolts* (New York, 1943); David Robertson, *Denmark Vesey: The Buried Stories of America's Largest Slave Rebellion and the Man Who Led It* (New York: Alfred A. Knopf, 1999); and Manning Marable and Leith Mullings, *Let Nobody Turn Us Around: Voices of Resistance, Reform, and Renewal: An African American Anthology* (Lanham, MD: Rowman & Littlefield, 2000), pp. 35–36 and "The Statement of Nat Turner, 1831," in Marable and Mullings, *Let Nobody Turn Us Around*, p. 37. David Walker, *David Walker's Appeal in Four Articles; Together with a Preamble, to the Coloured Citizens of the World, but in Particular and Very Expressly, to those of the United States of*

America (Boston: Revised and published by David Walker, 3rd ed, 1830), reprinted in Marable and Mullings, *Let Nobody Turn Us Around*, pp. 23–35; Henry Highland Garnet, "An Address to the Slaves of the United States of America," 1843 reprinted in Marable and Mullings, Let Nobody Turn Us Around, pp. 58–63. Manisha Sinha, *The Slave's Cause: A History of Abolition* (New Haven: Yale University Press, 2016) is an excellent new study of the abolitionist movement as is Eric Foner, *Gateway to Freedom: The Hidden History of the Underground Railroad* (New York: W. W. Norton, 2015) for that topic. The best current biography of William Lloyd Garrison is Henry Mayer, *All on Fire: William Lloyd Garrison and the Abolition of Slavery* (New York: St. Martin's Press, 1998). For evangelical abolitionists see Gilbert H. Barnes, *The Antislavery Impulse, 1830–1844* (New York: American Historical Association, 1933, reprinted 1964) and Gilbert H. Barnes and Dwight L. Dumond, eds., *Letters of Theodore Dwight Weld, Angelina Grimke Weld, and Sarah Grimke, 1822–1844*, 2 vols. (1934, reprint Gloucester, MA: Peter Smith, 1965).

New Strength for American Women
The best current account of the Seneca Falls Convention is Judith Wellman, *The Road to Seneca Falls: Elizabeth Cady Stanton and the First Woman's Rights Convention* (Urbana: University of Illinois Press, 2004). See also Elizabeth Cady Stanton, Susan B. Anthony, and Matilda Joslyn Gage, editors, *A History of Woman Suffrage*, vol. I (Rochester, NY, 1881); Elizabeth Cady Stanton, *Eighty Years & More: Reminiscences 1815–1897* (T. Fisher Unwin, 1898, republished Boston: Northeastern University Press, 1993); Sarah M. Grimke, *Letters on the Equality of the Sexes and the Condition of Women* (Boston: Isaac Knapp, 1838), reprinted in Nancy F. Cott et al, editors, *Roots of Bitterness: Documents of the Social History of American Women* (Boston: Northeastern University Press, 1996), pp. 123–127. For an excellent recent overview of the work of both sisters see the preface to also Gerda Lerner, *The Feminist Thought of Sarah Grimke* (New York: Oxford University Press, 1998), pp. 3–46. For the classic study of the Grimke-Weld work, see Gilbert H. Barnes and Dwight L. Dumond, editors, *Letters of Theodore Dwight Weld, Angelina Grimke Weld and Sarah Grimke: 1822–1844*, 2 vols. (1934, reprint, Gloucester, MA. Peter Smith, 1965). See also Elizabeth Ann Bartlett, editor, *Sarah Grimke, Letters on the Equality of the Sexes and Other Essays* (New Haven: Yale University Press, 1988); Gerda Lerner, editor, *The Feminist Thought of Sarah Grimke* (New York: Oxford University Press, 1998) and Gerda Lerner's *The Grimke Sisters from South Carolina: Rebels against Slavery and for Woman's Rights* (Boston: Houghton Mifflin, 1967). My interpretation of the Grimkes rests primarily on Lerner's important biographical work on their lives. For Sojourner Truth see *The Anti-Slavery Bugle*, June 21, 1851, cited in Manning Marable and Leith Mullings, editors, *Let Nobody Turn Us Around* (Lanham, MD: Rowman & Littlefield, 2000), pp. 67–68. I think there is reason to doubt some later versions of the speech that were rendered in the dialect of southern blacks because Truth spoke all of her life with the Dutch accent of her native Hudson Valley.

Chapter 13 The Politics of Separation, 1850–1861
From Union to Disunion
James McPherson, *Battle Cry of Freedom: The Civil War Era* (New York: Oxford University Press, 1988) is an excellent source on the tensions leading up to the Civil War as it is on the war itself. For the compromises and tensions of the 1850s see also David S. Heidler and Jeanne T. Heidler, *Henry Clay: The Essential American* (New York: Random House, 2010); "The Compromise of 1850," The Library of Congress American Memory Historical Collection, www.loc.gov/rr/program/bib/ourdocs/Compromsie1850.html; Craig Miner, *Seeding Civil War: Kansas in the National News, 1854–1858* (Lawrence: University Press of Kansas, 2008).

Bleeding Kansas and Dred Scott v. Sanford
McPherson, *Battle Cry of Freedom*; Timothy S. Huebner, *The Taney Court: Justices, Rulings, and Legacy* (ABC-CLIO, 2003).

The Economy, the Panic of 1857, and the Lincoln-Douglas Debates
David Brion Davis, *Inhuman Bondage: The Rise and Fall of Slavery in the New World* (New York: Oxford University Press, 2006); Lisa Clayton Robinson, "Uncle Tom's Cabin," *Africana: The Encyclopedia of African and African American Experience, Second Edition*, edited by Kwame Anthony Appiah, edited by Henry Louis Gates Jr. Oxford African American Studies Center, http://www.oxfordaasc.com/article/opr/t0002/e3928 (accessed Sat Oct 9, 2010); Wendy Wagner, "Uncle Tom's Cabin," *The Oxford Companion to United States History*, edited by Paul S. Boyer, Oxford African American Studies Center, http://www.oxfordaasc.com/article/opr/t119/e1567 (accessed Sat Oct 9, 2010); Michael Winship, "Uncle Tom's Cabin: History of the Book in the 19thCentury United States," http://utc.iath.virginia.edu/interpret/exhibits/winship/winship.html (accessed Fri Oct 8, 2010); "Article XIV-Editorial Miscellany," De Bow's Southern and Western Review, March 1853 http://utc.iath.virginia.edu/saxon/servlet/SaxonServlet?source-utc/sml/responses/proslav/p (accessed Fri Oct 8, 2010); Marc Egnal, *Clash of Extremes: The Economic Origins of the Civil War* (New York: Hill and Wang, 2009); Aaron W. Marrs, Railroads in the Old South: Pursuing Progress in a Slave Society (Baltimore: The Johns Hopkins University Press, 2009); Abraham Lincoln, "Speech delivered at Springfield, Illinois, at the close of the Republican State Convention," June 16, 1858, "First Debate, at Ottawa, Illinois, August 21, 1858," "Letter to Doctor C. H. Ray, November 20, 1858," "Letter to Salmon Portland Chase, June 9, 1859," in Roy P. Basler, editor, *Abraham Lincoln: His Speeches and Writings* (Cleveland: World Publishing, 1946); Doris Kearns Goodwin, *Team of Rivals: the Political Genius of Abraham Lincoln* (New York: Simon & Schuster, 2005), pp. 140–210; Edward l. Ayers, *In the Presence of Mine Enemies: The Civil War in the Heart of American, 1859–1863* (New York: W. W. Norton, 2003).

From John Brown to the Secession of the South
Doris Kearns Goodwin, *Team of Rivals: The Political Genius of Abraham Lincoln* (New York: Simon & Schuster, 2005); McPherson, *Battle Cry of Freedom*; Alexander K. McClure, *Old Time Notes of Pennsylvania* (Philadelphia: J. C. Winston Company, 1905, pp. 360362 cited in Edward L. Ayers, *In the Presence of Mine Enemies: The Civil War in the Heart of America, 1859–1863* (New York: W. W. Norton, 2003); Eric Foner, *The Fiery Trial: Abraham Lincoln and American Slavery* (New York: W. W. Norton, 2010).

Chapter 14 And the War Came: The Civil War 1861–1865
Fort Sumter to Antietam, 1861–1862
These accounts of the Civil War are taken primarily from James McPherson, *Battle Cry of Freedom: The Civil War Era* (New York: Oxford University Press, 1988). See also the National Park Service Battle Summaries of every Civil War battle http://www.nps.gov/hps/abpp/civil.htm

The Emancipation Proclamation
The Most useful source on Lincoln's thinking and the Emancipation Proclamation is Eric Foner, *The Fiery Trial: Abraham Lincoln and American Slavery* (New York: W. W. Norton, 2010); See also Edward L. Ayers, *In the Presence of Mine Enemies: the Civil War in the Heart of America, 1859–1863* (New York: W. W. Norton, 2003); John Hope Franklin and Alfred A. Moss, Jr., *From Slavery to Freedom: A History of African Americans*, Seventh Edition (New York: Alfred A. Knopf, 1994); James Oakes, *Freedom National: The Destruction of Slavery in the United States, 1861–1865* (New York: W. W. Norton, 2013).

The Home Front—Shortages, Opposition, Riots, and Battles
For the impact of the war on civilians, see Drew Gilpin Faust, *Mothers of Invention: Women of the Slaveholding South in the American Civil War* (Chapel Hill: University of North Carolina Press, 1996) as well as McPherson, *Battle Cry of Freedom* and Ayers, *In the Presence of Mine Enemies* and http://www.nps.gov/history/hps.abpp/civil.htm. For an excellent way the death toll of the Civil War changed American attitudes towards death, see Drew Gilpin Faust, *This Republic of Suffering: Death and the American Civil War* (New York: Vintage Books, 2008).

From Gettsburg to Appomattox and Beyond
James McPherson, *Battle Cry of Freedom*; Eric Foner, *The Fiery Trial*; Drew Gilpin Faust, *Mothers of Invention*; Drew Gilpin Faust, *This Republic of Suffering*; Kenneth M. Ludmerer, *Learning to Heal: The Development of American Medical Education* (Baltimore: Johns Hopkins University Press, 1985); Sean Conant, editor, *The Gettysburg Address* (New York: Oxford University Press, 2015); Ulysses S. Grant, *Memoirs and Selected Letters* (originally 1885, republished New York: Library of America, 1990); Martha Hodes, *Mourning Lincoln* (New Haven: Yale University Press, 2015).

Chapter 15 Reconstruction, 1865–1877
Federal Reconstruction Policy
By far the best source on federal Reconstruction policy is Eric Foner, *Reconstruction: America's Unfinished Revolution, 1863–1877* (New York: Harper & Row, 1988); See also Eric Foner, *The Fiery Trial*; John David Smith, *Black Voices From Reconstruction, 1865–1877* (Gainesville: University Press of Florida, 1997); Francis E. Abernethy, Patrick B. Mullen, Alan B. Govenar, editors, *Juneteenth Texas: Essays in African American Folklore* (Denton; University of North Texas Press, 1996); Henry Mayer, *All on Fire: William Lloyd Garrison and the Abolition of Slavery* (New York: St. Martin's Press, 1998); F. Douglass, "What the Black Man Wants:' Sojourner Truth , 1867 speech in New York City, reprinted in Herb Boyd, editor, *Autobiography of a People* (New York: Anchor Books, 2000); and for election results www.uselectionatlas.org/RESULTS/national.php?year=1868&off=0&f=1 and www.uselectionatlas.org.

The Impact of Reconstruction
Foner, *Reconstruction*, remains a key work. See also Steven Hahn, *A Nation Under Our Feet: Black Political Struggles in the Rural South from Slavery to the Great Migration* (Cambridge: Harvard University Press, 2003); William L. Clay, *Just Permanent Interests: Black Americans in Congress, 1870–1992* (New York: Amistad Press, 1993),; John David Smith, *Black Voices From Reconstruction, 1865–1877* (Gainesville: University Press of Florida, 1997); W. E. B. DuBois, *Black Reconstruction in America* (1903, reprinted Boston: Bedford Books, 1997); W. E. B. DuBois, *The Souls of Black Folk* (1903, reprint New York: Crest, 1961); Brenda Stevenson, editor, *The Journals of Charlotte Forten Grimke* (New York: Oxford University Press, 1988); James D. Anderson, *The Education of Blacks in the South, 1860–1935* (Chapel Hill: University of North Carolina Press, 1988); Frederick Douglass, *Narrative of the Life of Frederick Douglass: An American Slave* (1845; Cambridge: Harvard University Press, 1967); Maria S. Waterbury, *Seven Years Among the Freedmen*, cited in Nancy Hoffman, *Woman's "True" Profession: Voices from the History of Teaching* (New York: Feminist Press, 1981); Rupert Sargent Holland, editor, *Letters and Diary of Laura M. Towne* (1912; reprint New York: Negro Universities Press, 1969); and especially Ronald E. Butchart, *Schooling the Freed People: Teaching, Learning, and the Struggle for Black Freedom, 1861–1876* (Chapel Hill: University of North Carolina Press, 2010).

Terror, Apathy, and the Creation of the Segregated South
See Foner, *Reconstruction*; Nicholas Lemann, *Redemption: The Last Battle of the Civil War* (New York: Farrar, Straus and Giroux, 2006); Mary Drake McFeely and William S. McFeely, "Chronology" in Ulysses S. Grant, *Memoirs and Selected Letters* (New York: The Library of American, 1990); Charles Lane, *The Day Freedom Died: The Colfax*

Massacre, the Supreme Court, and the Betrayal of Reconstruction (New York: Henry Holt, 2008); Frances Smith Foster, "Introduction" to Frances E. W. Harper, Iola Leroy (1892; reprinted New York: Oxford University Press, 1988); and C. Vann Woodward, The Strange Career of Jim Crow (New York: Oxford University Press, 1966). See also "Speech on September 3, 1868, before the Georgia State Legislature," and Frances Ellen Watkins Harper, "An Address Delivered at the Centennial Anniversary of the Pennsylvania Society for Promoting the Abolition of Slavery, 1875," reprinted in Manning Marable and Leith Mullings, editors, Let Nobody Turn Us Around: An African American Anthology (Lanham, MD: Rowman & Littlefield, 2000), pp. 131–134 and pp. 138–143.

Chapter 16 Conflict in the West, 1865–1912
The Tribes of the West and the U.S. Government

Two excellent studies of the Comanche Empire are, Pekka Hamalainen, The Comanche Empire (New Haven: Yale University Press, 2008) and S.C. Gwynne's Empire of the Summer Moon ();Robert M. Utley, The Indian Frontier, 1846–1890, Revised Edition (Albuquerque: University of New Mexico Press, 1984); Joan Waugh, U.S. Grant: American Hero, American Myth (Chapel Hill: University of North Carolina Press, 2009); Thomas Powers, The Killing of Crazy Horse (New York: Alfred A. Knopf, 2010); Nathaniel Philbrock, The Last Stand: Custer, Sitting Bull, and the Battle of the Little Bighorn (New York: Viking, 2010); Ellen Fitzpatrick, History's Memory: Writing America's Past, 1880–1980 (Cambridge: Harvard University Press, 2004); David Wallace Adams, Education for Extinction: American Indians and the Boarding School Experience, 1875–1928 (Lawrence: University Press of Kansas, 1995); Francis Paul Prucha, The Great Father: The United States Government and the American Indians, 2 vols. (Lincoln, 1984),

The Impact of the Transcontinental Railroad, 1869

Richard White, Railroaded: The Transcontinentals and the Making of Modern America (New York: W. W. Norton, 2011); Craig Miner, The Most Magnificent Machine: America Adopts the Railroad, 1825–1862 (Lawrence, University Press of Kansas, 2010).

The Transformation of the West

Clyde A. Milner II, Carol A. O'Connor, Martha A. Sandweiss, The Oxford History of the American West (New York: Oxford University Press, 1994); Lewis Atherton, The Cattle Kings (Bloomington: Indiana University Press, 1961); E. E. Dale, The Range Cattle Industry, 2nd. ed. (Norman: University of Oklahoma Press, 1960); Rosenbaum, Mexicano Resistance in the Southwest; Andrew Bancroft Schlesinger, "Las Gorras Blancas, 1889–1891," The Journal of Mexican American History I:2 (Spring 1971), 94–97.

Chapter 17 The Gilded Age: Building a Technological and Industrial Giant and a New Social Order, 1876–1913
Technology Changes the Nation

The Free Library of Philadelphia, Centennial Exhibition Digital Collection http://libwww.freelibrary.org/CenCol/exh-org.htm downloaded November 29, 2010; Sean Dennis Cashman, America in the Gilded Age: From the Death of Lincoln to the Rise of Theodore Roosevelt, Third Edition (New York: New University Press, 1993); Pauline Maier, Merritt Roe Smith, Alexander Keyssar, Daniel J. Kevles, Inventing America: A History of the United States (New York: W. W. Norton, 2006), pp. 632–634; Jackson Lears, Rebirth of a Nation: The Making of Modern America, 1877–1920 (New York: HarperCollins, 2009).

Corporations and Monopolies

H. W. Brands, American Colossus: The Triumph of Capitalism, 1865–1900 (New York: Doubleday, 2010); T. J. Stiles, The First Tycoon: The Epic Life of Cornelius Vanderbilt (New York: Alfred A. Knopf, 2009); Jackson Lears, Rebirth of a Nation: The Making of Modern America, 1877–1920 (New York: Harper, 2009).

Lives of the Middle Class in the Gilded Age

H. W. Brands, American Colossus: The Triumph of Capitalism, 1865–1900 is also important for understanding daily life. See also George M. Marsden, Understanding Fundamentalism and Evangelicalism (Grand Rapids, MI: William B. Eerdman's, 1991); George M. Marsden, Fundamentalism and American Culture, Second Edition (New York: Oxford University Press, 2006); Sean Dennis Cashman, America in the Gilded Age: From the Death of Lincoln to the Rise of Theodore Roosevelt. For middle class women, Karen Manners Smith's chapter, "New Paths to Power, 1890–1920," in Nancy F. Cott, editor, No Small Courage: A History of Women in the United States (New York: Oxford University Press, 2000) is a goldmine of information. See also Carroll Smith-Rosenberg, Disorderly Conduct: Visions of Gender in Victorian America (New York: Oxford University Press, 1985) and Frances B. Cogan, All-American Girl: The Ideal of Real Womanhood in Mid-Nineteenth-Century America (Athens: University of Georgia Press, 1989); William Leach, Land of Desire: Merchants, Power, and the Rise of a New American Culture (New York: Random House, 1993).

Immigration

Ronald Takaki, A Different Mirror: A History of Multicultural America (Boston: Little, Brown, 1993); Hamilton Holt, editor The Life Stories of Undistinguished Americans as Told by Themselves (originally 1906, republished New York: Routledge, 2000); David Von Drehle, Triangle: The Fire That Changed America (New York: Atlantic Monthly Press, 2003); "Italians," in Stephan Thernstrom, editor, Harvard Encyclopedia of American Ethnic Groups (Cambridge: The Belknap Press of Harvard University, 1980); Iris Chang, The Chinese in America: A Narrative History (New York: Viking, 2003); Herbert J. Gans, The Urban Villagers: Group and Class in the Life of Italian-Americans (New York: The Free Press, 1962); Hasia R. Diner, Roads Taken: The Great Jewish Migrations to the New World and the Peddlers Who Forged the Way (New haven: Yale University Press, 2015); http://www.ellisisland.org/genealogy/ellis_island_history.sap, retrieved December 12, 2010; http://www.TaylorStreetArchives.com, retrieved December 12, 2010; http://faculty.marianopolis.edu/c.belanger/quebechistory/readings/leaving.htm, retrieved December 12, 2010.

Chapter 18 Responses to Industrialism, Responses to Change, 1877–1914
Conflict in the New South

Edward L. Ayers, The Promise of the New South, 15th Anniversary Edition (New York: Oxford University Press, 2007).

The Politics of Conflict—From Populist Movement to Populist Party

Charles Postel, The Populist Vision (New York: Oxford University Press, 2007); Michael Kazin, The Populist Persuasion (New York: Basic Books, 1995).

Worker Protest and the Rise of Organized Labor

Nell Irvin Painter, Standing at Armageddon: The United States, 1877–1919 (New York: W. W. Norton, 2008); Michael A. Bellesiles, 1877: America's Year of Living Violently (New York: The New Press, 2010); James Green, Death in the Haymarket: A Story of Chicago, the First Labor Movement and the Bombing that Divided Gilded Age America (New York: Random House, 2006); Nick Salvatore, Eugene V. Debs: Citizen and Socialist (Urbana: University of Illinois Press, 1984); Elliott J. Gorn, Mother Jones: The Most Dangerous Woman in America (New York: Hill & Wang, 2001); J. Anthony Lukas, Big Trouble (New York: touchstone, 1997); Patrick Renshaw, The Wobblies: the Story of the IWW and Syndicalism in the United States (Chicago: Ivan R. Dee, 1967, 1999); David Von Drehle, Triangle: The Fire that Changed America (New York: Atlantic Monthly Press, 2003); Philip Foner, Women and the American Labor Movement (New York: Free Press, 1980); Thomas G. Andrews, Killing for Coal: America's Deadliest Labor War (Cambridge: Harvard University Press, 2008).

Chapter 19 Progressive Movements, Progressive Politics, 1879–1917
The Revolt of the Intellectuals

Nell Irvin Painter, Standing at Armageddon: The United States, 1877–1919 (New York: W. W. Norton, 2008); Louis Menand, The Metaphysical Club (New York: Farrar, Straus and Giroux, 2001). A number of earlier works are also helpful in understanding the emergence of progressivism including, Samuel Hays, The Response to Industrialism (1957); Robert Wiebe, The Search for Order (1967), Gabriel Kolko, The Triumph of Conservativism (1963); Richard Hofstadter, The Age of Reform (1955); Henry George, Progress and Poverty: An Inquiry into the Cause of Industrial Depressions and of Increase of want with Increase of Wealth (originally 1879, reprinted New York: The Modern Library, 1929), pp. 3, 5, 405.

The Transformation of the Cities

Jay P. Dolan, The Irish Americans: A History (New York: Bloomsbury Press, 2008); William L. Riordon, Plunkitt of Tammany Hall (originally 1905, New York; E. P. Dutton, 1963); Richard Hofstadter, The Age of Reform: From Bryan to F.D.R. (New York, 1955); Lincoln Steffens, The Autobiography of Lincoln Steffens (New York: The Literary Guild, 1931); Allan Nevins, Grover Cleveland: A Study in Courage (1932); Don Lochbiler, "The Shoemaker Who Looked Like a King," from the Detroit News, Michigan History archive, http://apps.detnews.com/apps/history/index.php?id=175, downloaded December 28, 2010; "Samuel M. Jones," and "Brand Whitlock," Ohio Historical Society, Ohio History Central, http://www.ohiohistorycentral.org, downloaded December 28, 2010; John Dewey, The School and Society (Chicago: University of Chicago Press, 1899); David Tyack & Elisabeth Hansot, Managers of Virtue: Public School Leadership in America, 1820–1980 (New York: Basic Books, 1982); Mari Jo Buhle, Teresa Murphy, and Jane Gerhard, Women and the Making of America (Upper Saddle River, NJ: Pearson Prentice Hall, 2009); Edwin S. Gaustad, A Documentary History of Religion in America Since 1865 (Grand Rapids: William B. Eerdmans, 1998); Jane Addams, Twenty Years at Hull House (originally published 1910, republished New York; Penguin Putnam, 1961); Jane Addams, Democracy and Social Ethics (New York: Macmillan, 1913); Jane Addams, The Spirit of Youth and the City Streets (New York: Macmillan Company, 1909; Champaign: University of Illinois Press, 1972); Allen F. Davis, Spearheads for Reform: The Social Settlements and the Progressive Movement (New York: Oxford University Press, 1967); Lawrence A. Cremin, The Transformation of the School: Progressivism in American Education, 1876–1957 (1961).

Progressive Politics on the National Stage

Edmund Morris, Theodore Rex (New York: Random House, 2001); Sean Dennis Cashman, America in the Gilded Age: From the Death of Lincoln to the Rise of Theodore Roosevelt, third edition (New York: New York University Press, 1993); Douglas Brinkley, The Wilderness Warrior: Theodore Roosevelt and the Crusade for America (New York: Harper Collins, 2009); James Chace, 1912: Wilson, Roosevelt, Taft & Debs—the Election That Changed the Country (New York: Simon & Schuster, 2004); John Milton Cooper, Jr., Woodrow Wilson: A Biography (New York: Alfred A. Knopf, 2009).

Chapter 20 War in the Progressive Era, 1890–1919

The most useful source for all parts of this chapter is George C. Herring, *From Colony to Superpower: U.S. Foreign Relations Since 1776* (New York: Oxford University Press, 2008). See also Jay P. Dolan, *The Irish Americans: A History* (New York: Bloomsbury Press, 2008); Adam Hochschild, *King Leopold's Ghost: A Story of Greed, Terror, and Heroism in colonial Africa* (Boston: Houghton Mifflin, 1998); Sydney E. Ahlstrom, *A Religious History of the American People* (New Haven: Yale University Press, 2004); Sean Dennis Cashman, *America in the Gilded Age: From the Death of Lincoln to the Rise of Theodore Roosevelt*, Third Edition (New York: New York University Press, 1993); Michael McGerr, *A Fierce Discontent: The Rise and Fall of the Progressive Movement in America* (New York: Oxford University Press,); John Milton Cooper, Jr., *Woodrow Wilson: A Biography* (New York: Alfred A. Knopf, 2009); and Adam Hochschild, *To End All Wars: A Story of Loyalty and Rebellion, 1914–1918* (New York: Houghton Mifflin Harcourt, 2011).

Chapter 21 Living in Good Times, 1919–1929
The Prelude—The Red Summer of 1919
Frederick Lewis Allen, *Only Yesterday: An Informal History of the Nineteen-Twenties* (New York: Harper & Row, 1931); Nancy F. Cott, editor, *No Small Courage: A History of Women in the United States* (New York: Oxford University Press, 2000); Vicki L. Ruiz, *From Out of the Shadows: Mexican Women in Twentieth Century America* (New York: Oxford University Press, 2008).

The 1920s—The Exuberance of Prosperity
Peter H. Lindert and Jeffrey G. Williamson, *Unequal Gains: American Growth and Inequality since 1700* (Princeton: Princeton University Press, 2016); Michael A. Lerner, *Dry Manhattan: Prohibition in New York City* (Cambridge: Harvard University Press, 2007); Daniel Okrent, *Last Call: The Rise and Fall of Prohibition* (New York: Scribner, 2010); Thomas M. Coffey, *The Long Thirst: Prohibition in America: 1920–1933* (New York: W. W. Norton, 1975); Linda Gordon, *Woman's Body, Woman's Right: A Social History of Birth Control in America* (New York: Penguin Books, 1977); James Reed, *From Private Vice to Public Virtue: The Birth Control Movement and American Society Since 1930* (New York: Basic Books, 1978); George Chauncey, *Gay New York: Gender, Urban Culture, and the Making of the Gay Male World, 1890–1940* (New York: Basic Books, 1994); Pauline Maier, Merritt Roe Smith, Alexander Keyssar, Daniel j. Kevles, *Inventing America: A History of the United States*, second edition (New York: W. W. Norton, 2006).

The 1920—The Conflicts about American Ideals
David J. Goldberg, *Discontented America: The United States in the 1920s* (Baltimore: The Johns Hopkins University Press, 1999); John M. Barry, *Rising Tide: The Great Mississippi Flood and How It Changed America* (New York: Simon & Schuster, 1997); Adam Cohen, *Imbeciles: The Supreme Court, America Eugenics, and the Sterilization of Carrie Buck* (New York: Penguin Press, 2016); Daniel J. Kevles, *In the Name of Eugenics: Genetics and the Uses of Human Heredity* (New York: Knopf, 1985); *Race and Membership in American History: The Eugenics Movement* (Boston: Facing History and Ourselves); Aristide R. Zolberg, *A Nation By Design: Immigration Policy in the Fashioning of America* (Cambridge: Harvard University Press, 2006); Michael Innis-Jimenez, *Steel Barrio: The Great Mexican Migration to South Chicago, 1915–1940* (New York: New York University Press, 2013); Mae M. Ngai, *Impossible Subjects: Illegal Aliens and the Making of Modern America* (Princeton: Princeton University Press, 2004); E. David Cronon, *Black Moses: The Story of Marcus Garvey* (Madison: University of Wisconsin Press, 1955, 1969); and John Hope Franklin and Alfred A. Moss, *From Slavery to Freedom: A History of African Americans* (New York: Alfred A. Knopf, 1994).

Harding, Coolidge, and Hoover—The Politics of the 1920s
Phillip G. Payne, *Dead Last: The Public Memory of Warren G. Harding's Scandalous Legacy* (Athens: Ohio University Press, 2009); William Leach, *Land of Desire: Merchants, Power, and the Rise of a New American Culture* (New York: Random House, 1993).

Chapter 22 Living in Hard Times, 1929–1939
The Coming of the Great Depression
John Kenneth Galbraith, *The Great Crash, 1929* (originally 1955, republished Boston: Houghton Mifflin, 1997); Michael Bernstein, *The Great Depression: Delayed Recovery and Economic Change in America, 1929–1939* (1987); David Burner, *Herbert Hoover: A Public Life* (New York: Knopf, 1979); William J. Barber, *From New Era to New Deal: Herbert Hoover, the Economists, and American Economic Policy, 1921–1933* (Cambridge: Cambridge University Press, 1985).

New Deal
Anthony J. Badger, *FDR: The First Hundred Days* (New York: Hill & Wang, 2008); Irving Bernstein, *A Caring Society: The New Deal, the Worker, and the Great Depression* (Boston: Houghton Mifflin, 1985); Ira Katznelson, *Fear Itself: The New Deal and the Origins of Our Time* (New York: W. Wl Norton, 2013); Lewis Meriam, et al., *The Problem of Indian Administration* (Baltimore: Johns Hopkins University Press, 1928); John Hope Franklin and Alfred A. Moss, Jr., *From Slavery to Freedom: A History of African Americans*, seventh edition (New York: Knopf, 1994); Sarah Jane Deutsch, "From Ballots to Breadlines: 1920–1940," in Nancy F. Cott, editor, *No Small Courage: A History of Women in the United States* (New York: Oxford University Press, 2000), p. 457–460; Timothy Egan, *The Worst Hard Time* (Boston: Houghton Mifflin, 2006); Joe Klein, *Woody Guthrie: A Life* (New York: Random House, 1980), pp. 112–141; John Steinbeck, The Grapes of Wrath (New York: the Viking Press, 1939); Manuel G. Gonzales, *Mexicanos: A History of Mexicans in the United States* (Bloomington, University of Indiana Press, 2009); David

M. Kennedy, *Freedom From Fear: The American People in Depression and War, 1929–1945* (New York: Oxford University Press, 1999), pp. 254–257; Linda Gordon, *Dorothea Lange: A Life Beyond Limits* (New York: W. W. Norton, 2009); Eric Foner, *The Story of American Freedom* (New York: W. W. Norton, 1998); Sidney Fine, *Sit-Down: The General Motors Strike of 1936–1937* (Ann Arbor: University of Michigan Press, 1969); Kim Phillips-Fein, *Invisible Hands: The Businessmen's Crusade Against the New Deal* (New York: W. W. Norton, 2009); James MacGregor Burns, *Roosevelt: The Lion and the Fox* (New York: Harcourt Brace, 1956).

The Deep Roots of War—The United States, Europe, and Asia
In my description of the roots of World War II, I have depended primarily on David M. Kennedy, *Freedom From Fear: The American People in Depression and War, 1929–1945* (New York: Oxford University Press, 1999) and George C. Herring, *From Colony to Superpower: U.S. Foreign Relations Since 1776* (New York: Oxford University Press, 2008).

Chapter 23 Living in a World at War, 1939–1945
Preparedness and Isolation 1939–1941
David M. Kennedy, *Freedom From Fear: The American People in Depression and War, 1929–1945* (New York: Oxford University Press, 1999) and George C. Herring, *From Colony to Superpower: U.S. Foreign Relations Since 1776* (New York: Oxford University Press, 2008).

Mass Mobilization in a Society at War
Kennedy and Herring remain the key sources for all sections of this chapter. See also Tom Brokaw, *The Greatest Generation* (New York: Random House, 1998); Charles E. Francis, *The Tuskegee Airmen* (Boston: Branden Publishing Company, 1993); Zachary Bullock, "Teaching Objection: How Textbooks Distort and Lie About Conscientious Objection to World War II," *Rethinking Schools*, Vol. 23, No. 3 (Spring, 2009); See individual biographies in www.navajocodetalkers.org (downloaded May 1, 2011) and www.nps.gov/pwro/collection/website (downloaded April 15, 2011); A. Philip Randolph, in Herb Boyd, *Autobiography of a People* (New York: Anchor Books, 2001), pp. 309–310; John Hope Franklin and Alfred A. Moss, Jr., *From Slavery to Freedom: A History of African Americans*, seventh edition (New York: Alfred A. Knopf, 1994), pp. 436–437; Allan Berube, *Coming Out Under Fire: The History of Gay Men and Women in World War II*,. Twentieth Anniversary Edition (Chapel Hill: University of North Carolina Press, 2010); Peter Irons, *The Courage of Their Convictions: Sixteen Americans Who Fought Their Way to the Supreme Court* (New York: Penguin Books, 1990).

Industrial Strength, Industrial Prosperity
Again, Kennedy and Herring are key.

Winning a World War—North Africa, Europe, Asia, the Pacific, 1943–1945
In addition to Kennedy and herring see Michael Norman and Elizabeth M. Norman, *Tears in the Darkness: The Story of the Bataan Death March and its Aftermath* (New York: Farrar, Straus and Giroux, 2009); Elliott Johnson, "D-Day and All That," an interview in Studs Terkel, *"The Good War"* (New York: The New Press, 1984), pp. 254–264; Felix L. Sparks, "An Oral History," interview by William C. McClearn, *The Colorado Lawyer*, Vol. 27, No. 10 (October, 1998), downloaded from www.cobar.org May 8, 2011; U.S. Holocaust Museum www.ushmm.org downloaded May 7, 2011.

Chapter 24 The World the War Created, 1945–1952
The United States in 1945
James T. Patterson, *Grand Expectations: The United States, 1945–1974* (New York: Oxford University Press, 1996); David Halberstam, *The Fifties* (New York: Random House, 1993); Elaine Tyler May, *Homeward Bound: American Families in the Cold War Era*, Revised Edition (New York: Basic Books, 2008); Lisabeth Cohen, *A Consumers' Republic: The Politics of Mass Consumption in Postwar America* (New York: Vintage Books, 2004); Kenneth T. Jackson, *Crabgrass Frontier: The Suburbanization of the United States* (New York: Oxford University Press, 1985); Nicholas Lemann, *The Promised Land: The Great Black Migration and How It Changed America* (New York: Vintage, 1992); Isabel Wilkerson, *The Warmth of Other Suns: The Epic Story of America's Great Migration* (New York: Random House, 2010); Ira Berlin, *The Making of African America: The Four Great Migrations* (New York: Viking, 2010); Stanley Meisler, *United Nations: The First Fifty Years* (New York: The Atlantic Monthly Press, 1995); Alfred E. Eckes, Jr., *A Search for Solvency: Bretton Woods and the International Monetary System, 1941–1971* (Austin: University of Texas Press, 1975); Robert L. Heilbroner, *The Worldly Philosophers: The Lives, Times, and Ideas of the Great Economic Thinkers*, seventh edition (New York: Touchstone, 1995).

The Cold War Begins
James T. Patterson, *Grand Expectations: The United States, 1945–1974* (New York: Oxford University Press, 1996); George C. Herring, *From Colony to Superpower: U.S. Foreign Relations Since 1776* (New York: Oxford University Press, 2008); John Lewis Gaddis, *The United States and the Origins of the Cold War, 1941–1947* (New York: Columbia University Press, 1972); Arnold A. Offner, *Another Such Victory: President Truman and the Cold War, 1945–1953* (Stanford: Stanford University Press, 2002); Thomas G. Paterson, editor, *Cold War Critics: Alternatives to American Foreign Policy in the Truman Years* (Chicago: Quadrangle Books, 1971); Richard Hofstadter, *The Paranoid Style in American Politics and Other Essays* (Cambridge: Harvard University Press, 1996).

Politics, 1948–1952

James T. Patterson, *Grand Expectations: The United States, 1945–1974* (New York: Oxford University Press, 1996).

Chapter 25 Complacency and Change, 1952–1965

Eisenhower's America, America's World

James T. Patterson, *Grand Expectations: The United States, 1945–1974* (New York: Oxford University Press, 1996); George C. Herring, *From Colony to Superpower: U.S. Foreign Relations Since 1776* (New York: Oxford University Press, 2008); Theodore H. White, *The Making of the President, 1960* ().

A Culture on the Move

James T. Patterson, *Grand Expectations: The United States, 1945–1974* (New York: Oxford University Press, 1996); David Halberstam, *The Fifties* (New York: Random House, 1993)

Race and Civil Rights

Richard Kluger, *Simple Justice: A History of "Brown v. Board of Education" and Black America's Struggle for Equality* (New York: Alfred A. Knopf, 1975); Anne Moody, *Coming of Age in Mississippi* (New York: Laurel, 1968); Cynthia Stokes Brown, editor, *Ready from Within: Septima Clark and the Civil Rights Movement* (Trenton, NJ: Africa World Press, 1990); John Hope Franklin and Alfred A. Moss Jr., *From Slavery to Freedom: A History of African Americans*, seventh edition (New York: Alfred A. Knopf, 1994); Henry Louis Gates Jr. and Cornel West, *The African American Century* (New York: The Free Press, 2000); Taylor Branch, *Parting the Waters: America in the King Years, 1954–1963* (New York: Simon & Schuster, 1988); Taylor Branch, *Pillar of Fire: America in the King Years, 1963–1965* (New York: Simon & Schuster, 1998); Kenneth B. Clark, interview in Studs Terkel, *Race: How Blacks and Whites Think and Feel About the American Obsession* (New York: New Press, 1992); Daisy Bates, *The Long Shadow at Little Rock* (Fayetteville: the University of Arkansas Press, 1962); James M. Washington, editor, *A Testament of Hope: The Essential Writings and Speeches of Martin Luther King, Jr.* (San Francisco: Harper San Francisco, 1986); Manning Marable, *Malcolm X: A Life of Reinvention* (New York: Viking, 2011); Malcolm X, *The Autobiography of Malcolm X* (New York: Grove Press, 1965); Kofi Natambu, *The Life and Work of Malcolm X* (Indianapolis: Alpha Books, 2002).

Chapter 26 Lives Changed, 1961–1968

New Voices, New Authorities

James T. Patterson, *Grand Expectations: The United States, 1945–1974* (New York: Oxford University Press, 1996); Todd Gitlin, *The Sixties: Years of Hope, Days of Rage* (New York: Bantam Books, 1987); Jane Jacobs Obituary, *New York Times*, April 25, 2006; Michael Harrington, *The Other America* (New York: Macmillan, 1962); Mark Hamilton Lytle, *The Gentle Subversive: Rachel Carson, Silent Spring, and the Rise of the Environmental Movement* (New York: Oxford University Press, 2007); Priscilla Coit Murphy, *What a Book Can Do: The Publication and Reception of Silent Spring* (Amherst: University of Massachusetts Press, 2005).

Camelot, the White House, and Dallas—The Kennedy Administration

Arthur M. Schlesinger, Jr., *A Thousand Days: John F. Kennedy in the White House* (Boston: Houghton Mifflin Company, 1965); Frederick Kempe, *Berlin 1961: Kennedy, Khrushchev, and the Most Dangerous Place on Earth* (New York: G.P. Putnam's Sons, 2011); James T. Patterson, *Grand Expectations: The United States, 1945–1974* (New York: Oxford University Press, 1996).

The Coming of Lyndon B. Johnson

For the most thorough although sometimes quite biased and still incomplete study of LBJ, see Robert Caro's multi volume political biography, *The Years of Lyndon Johnson* including *The Path to Power* (New York: Alfred A. Knopf, 1982), *Means of Ascent* (1989), *Master of the Senate* (2002), *The Passage of Power* (2012); see also Doris Kearns, *Lyndon Johnson and the American Dream* (New York: St. Martin's Press, 1976); Todd Gitlin, *The Sixties: Years of Hope, Days of Rage* (New York: Bantam Books, 1987); Alexander Bloom and Wini Breines, editors, *"Takin' it to the Streets": A Sixties Reader* second edition (New York: Oxford University Press, 2003); George C. Herring, *From Colony to Superpower: U.S. Foreign Relations Since 1776* (New York: Oxford University Press, 2008); John Hagan, *Northern Passage: American Vietnam War Resisters in Canada* (Cambridge: Harvard University Press, 2001).

Chapter 27 Rights, Reaction, and Limits, 1968–1980

The New Politics of the Late 1960s

Kevin P. Phillips, *The Emerging Republican Majority* (New Rochelle, NY: Arlington House, 1969); Lisa McGirr, *Suburban Warriors: The Origins of the New American Right* (Princeton: Princeton University Press, 2001); Kim Phillips-Fein, *Invisible Hands: The Businessmen's Crusade Against the New Deal* (New York: W. W. Norton, 2009); Bruce J. Schulman, *The Seventies: The Great Shift in American Culture, Society, and Politics* (Cambridge, MA: Da Capo Press, 2002); George C. Herring, *From Colony to Superpower: U.S. Foreign Relations Since 1776* (New York: Oxford University Press, 2008); Joel Brinkley, *Cambodia's Curse: The Modern History of a Troubled Land* (New York: Public Affair, 2011).

The Movements of the 1960s and 1970s

Susan Brownmiller, *In Our Time: Memoir of a Revolution* (New York: Delta, 1999); Sara M. Evans, *Tidal Wave: How Women Changed America at Century's End* (New York: Free

Press, 2003); and Nancy F. Cott, editor, *No Small Courage: A History of Women in the United States* (New York: Oxford University Press, 2000); Barbara Smith, *All the Women Are White, All the Blacks are Men, But Some of Us Are Brave: Black Women's Studies* (New York: the Feminist Press, 1982); Florence Howe, *A Life in Motion* (New York: The Feminist Press, 2011). For the development of *Our Bodies, Ourselves*, see www.ourbodiesourselves.org/about/history.asp, downloaded July 10, 2011; Katherine Hanson, Vivian Guilfoy, and Sarita Pillai, *More Than Title IX: How Equity in Education Has Shaped the Nation* (Lanham, MD: Rowman & Littlefield, 2009); Marshall Ganz, *Why David Sometimes Wins: Leadership, Organization, and Strategy in the California Farm Worker Movement* (New York: Oxford University Press, 2009); Ronald B. Taylor, *Chavez and the Farm Workers* (Boston: Beacon Press, 1975); Mark Day, *Forty Acres: Cesar Chavez and the Farm Workers* (New York: Praeger, 1971); Ronald Takaki, *A Different Mirror: A History of Multicultural America* (Boston: Little, Brown, 1993); J. Craig Jenkins, *The Politics of Insurgency: The Farm Worker Movement in the 1960s* (New York: Columbia University Press, 1985); Paul Chaat Smith and Robert Allen Warrior, *Like a Hurricane: The Indian Movement from Alcatraz to Wounded Knee* (New York: The New Press, 1996); William Hagan, *American Indians* (Chicago: University of Chicago Press, 1961, 1993); Erika Lee, *The Making of Asian America: A History* (New York: Simon & Schuster, 2015); David K. Yoo and Eiichiro Azuma, *The Oxford Handbook of Asian American History* (New York: Oxford University Press 2016); Joseph M. Cronin, *Reforming Boston Schools, 1930 to the Present: Overcoming Corruption and Racial Segregation* (New York: Palgrave, 2011); Jerald E. Podair, *The Strike That Changed New York: Blacks, Whites, and the Ocean–Hill Brownsville Crisis* (New Haven: Yale University Press, 2002); Shirley Brice Heath and Milbrey W. McLaughlin, editors, *Identity and Inner-City Youth: Beyond Ethnicity and Gender* (New York: Teachers College Press, 1993); Allen J. Matusow, *The Unraveling of America: A History of Liberalism* (New York: Harper & Row, 1984); Todd Gitlin, *The Sixties: Years of Hope, Days of Rage* (New York: Bantam, 1987, 1993).

The Culture Wars of the 1970s

Donald T. Critchlow, *Phyllis Schlafly and Grassroots Conservatism: A Woman's Crusade* (Princeton: Princeton University Press, 2005); Phyllis Schlafly, *Feminist Fantasies* (Dallas: Spence publishing Company, 2003); Catherine E. Rymph, *Republican Women: Feminism and Conservatism From Suffrage Through the Rise of the New Right* (Chapel Hill: The University of North Carolina Press, 2006); Leon Friedman and William F. Levantrosser, *Richard M.. Nixon: Politician, President, Administrator* (New York: Greenwood Press, 1991); Nancy F. Cott, editor, *No Small Courage: A History of Women in the United States* (New York: Oxford University Press, 2000), pp. 529–586; Edwin Gaustad and Leigh Schmidt, *The Religious History of America* (New York: Harper Collins, 2002), pp. 329–427; Bruce J. Schulman, *The Seventies: The Great Shift in American Culture, Society, And Politics* (New York: DeCapo Press, 2002).

Politics, Economics, and the Impact of Watergate

James T. Patterson, *Restless Giant: The United States from Watergate to Bush v. Gore* (New York: Oxford University Press, 2005); Timothy Moy, "Culture, Technology, and the Cult of Tech in the 1970s," in Beth Bailey & David Farber, editors, *America in the Seventies* (Lawrence: University Press of Kansas, 2004); Johnny Ryan, *A History of the Internet and the Digital Future* (London, England: Reaktion Books, 2010); Roy A. Allan, *A History of the Personal Computer: The People and the Technology* (London, Ontario, Canada: Allan Publishing, 2001); Malcolm Gladwell, "Annals of Business, Creation Myth: Xerox PARC, Apple, and the Truth about Innovation," *The New Yorker* (May 16, 2011), pp. 44–53; Jimmy Carter, *White House Diary* (New York: Farrar, Straus, and Giroux, 2010).

Chapter 28 The Reagan Revolution, 1980–1989

A Rapidly Changing U.S. Government

James T. Patterson, *Restless Giant: the United States From Watergate to Bush v. Gore* (New York: Oxford University Press, 2005); Robert Dallek, *Ronald Reagan: The Politics of Symbolism*, With a New Preface (Cambridge: Harvard University Press1984, 1999); John Ehrman and Michael W. Flamm, *Debating the Reagan Presidency* (Lanham, MD: Rowman & Littlefield, 2009); George C. Herring, *From Colony to Superpower: U.S. Foreign Relations Since 1776* (New York: Oxford University Press.

The Changing Nature of the American Economy

Kevin Phillips, *Boiling Point: Republicans, Democrats, and the Decline of Middle-Class Prosperity* (New York: Random House, 1993); Robert B. Reich, *The Work of Nations* (New York: Random House, 1991); James B. Stewart, *Den of Thieves* (New York: Simon & Schuster, 1991); Kathleen Day, *S & L Hell* (New York; W. W. Norton, 1993).

Changes in the Rest of the Country

Ed Ward, Geoffrey Stokes, and Ken Tucker, *Rock of Ages* (New York: Rolling Stone Press, 1986); Haynes Johnson, *Sleepwalking Through History* (New York: Anchor Books, 1992); Stuart A. Kallen, *A Cultural History of the United States Through the Decades: The 1980s* (San Diego, CA: Lucent Books, 1999); Justin Watson, *The Christian Coalition: Dreams of Restoration, Demands for Recognition* (New York: St. Martin's Press, 1997); Jonathan Zimmerman, *Whose America? Culture Wars in Public Schools* (Cambridge: Harvard University Press, 2002); Aristide R. Zolberg, *A Nation by Design: Immigration Policy in the Fashioning of America* (Cambridge: Harvard University Press, 2006); Daniel J. Tichenor, *Dividing Lines: the Politics of Immigration Control in America* (Princeton: Princeton University Press, 2002); Christopher L. Miller, "Coyote's Game: Indian Casinos and the Indian Presence in Contemporary America," in Sterling Evans, editor, *American Indians in American History, 1870–2001* (Westport, CT: Praeger, 2002); M.E. Melody and Linda M. Peterson, *Teaching America About Sex: Marriage Guides and Sex Manuals from the Late Victorians to Dr. Ruth* (New York: New York University

Press, 1999); C. Everett Koop, *Koop: The Memoirs of America's Family Doctor* (New York: Random House, 1991); James T. Patterson, *Restless Giant: the United States From Watergate to Bush v. Gore* (New York: Oxford University Press, 2005).

Chapter 29 A New World Order, 1989–2000

The First Bush Administration

James T. Patterson, *Restless Giant: the United States From Watergate to Bush v. Gore* (New York: Oxford University Press, 2005); George C. Herring, *From Colony to Superpower: U.S. Foreign Relations Since 1776* (New York: Oxford University Press; Stephen Thernstrom and Abigail Therntrom, *America in Black and White: One Nation, Indivisible* (New York: Simon & Schuster, 1997); Gary Orfield and Dean Whitla, "Diversity and Legal Education: Student Experiences in Leading Law Schools," downloaded August 1, 2011 from https://gseis.ucla.edu/faculty/members/orfield;

The Clinton Presidency

Haynes Johnson, *The Best of Times: America in the Clinton Years* (New York: Harcourt, 2001); Major Garrett, *The Enduring Revolution: How the Contract with America Continues to Shape the Nation* (New York: Crown Forum, 2005); James T. Patterson, *Restless Giant: the United States From Watergate to Bush v. Gore* (New York: Oxford University Press, 2005).

Technology Dominates an Era

Walter Isaacson, *Steve Jobs* (New York: Simon & Schuster, 2011); Y2K, though considered a significant issue at the time, has received remarkably little historical attention. American Radio Works offered a thoughtful five year retrospective, "The Surprising Legacy of Y2K" including reporting by Catherine Winter, Chris Farrell, and Ochen Kaylan from which much of this material is taken. See http://americanradioworks.publicradio.org/features/y2k/a..html, downloaded August 6, 2011. See also Robert L. Mitchell, "Y2K: the good, the bad and the crazy," *Computerworld*, December 28, 2009, http://www.computerworld.com/s/article/print/9142555/Y2K_The_good_the_bad_and_the_crazy?taxonomyName=Management+and+Careers&taxonomyId=14, downloaded August 6, 2011; John Cassidy, *dot.con: The Greatest Story Ever Sold* (New York: HarperCollins, 2002); Joe Saltzman, "Instant Communications Across Cyberspace," and David Brin, "Personal Privacy Lost to Technology," both in Stuart A. Kallen, editor, *The 1990s* (San Diego, CA: Greenhaven Press, 2000); Ken Auletta, *Googled: The End of the World As We Know It* (New York: Penguin, 2009); Johnny Ryan, *A History of the Internet and the Digital Future* (London, England: Reaktion Books, 2010); John Brownlee, "President Obama Wishes He Had Cooler Tech in the Oval Office," Geek.com, April 17, 2011.

The George W. Bush Presidential Agenda

George W. Bush, *Decision Points* (New York: Crown, 2010); Matthew Eshbaugh-Soha and Tom Miles, "George W. Bush's Domestic Policy Agenda," *The American Review of Politics*, Vol. 29, (Winter, 2008–2009), pp. 351–369 and http://millercenter.org/president/gwbush/essay/biography/print, downloaded August 6, 2011.

Chapter 30 Entering a New Time, 2001– to the Present

The Impact of September 11, 2001

Damon DiMarco, *Tower Stories: An Oral History of 9/11* (Santa Monica, CA: Santa Monica Press, 2007); Thomas H. Kean and Lee H. Hamilton, *The 9/11 Report: The National Commission on Terrorist Attacks Upon the United States*, issued July 22, 2004 (New York: St. Martin's Press, 2004); American Library Association, "Resolution on the USA Patriot Act and Related Measures that Infringe on the Rights of Library Users," adopted January 29, 2003; John Yoo and Eric Posner, "The Patriot Act Under Fire," American Enterprise Institute, December 1, 2003; Terry H. Anderson, *Bush's Wars* (New York: Oxford University Press, 2011); George C. Herring, *From Colony to Superpower: U.S. Foreign Relations Since 1776* (New York: Oxford University Press, 2008); George W. Bush, *Decision Points* (New York: Crown Publishers).

Difficult Years on the Domestic Front

Douglas Brinkley, *The Great Deluge: Hurricane Katrina, New Orleans, and the Mississippi Gulf Coast* (New York: Harper Perennial, 2007).
Andrew Ross Sorkin, *Too Big to Fail* (New York: Penguin Books, 2009, 2010); The National Commission on the Causes of the Financial and Economic Crisis in the United Stated, *The Financial Crisis Inquiry Report* (New York: Public Affairs, 2011); Robert B. Reich, *Aftershock: The Next Economy & America's Future* (New York: Vintage Books, 2011); and George Packer, "A Dirty Business," *The New Yorker*, June 27, 2011, pp. 42–55.

The Obama Years

Morton Keller, *Obama's Time: A History* (New York: Oxford University Press, 2015); Jonathan Chait, *Audacity: How Barack Obama Defied His Critics and Created A Legacy That Will Prevail* (New York: Custom House, 2017); Glenda Elizabeth Gilmore and Thomas J. Sugrue, *These United States: A Nation in the Making, 1890 to the Present* (New York: W. W. Norton, 2015); John Heilemann and Mark Halperin, *Game Change: Obama and the Clintons, McCain and Palin, and the Race of a Lifetime* (New York: Harper Perennial, 2010); Kate Zernike, *Boiling Mad: Inside Tea Party America* (New York: Times Books, Henry Holt, 2010); Jill Lepore, *The Whites of Their Eyes: The Tea Party's Revolution and the Battle Over American History* (Princeton: Princeton University Press, 2010); Todd Gitlin, *Occupy Nation: The Roots, the Spirit, and the Promise of Occupy Wall Street* (New York: HarperCollins, 2012).

New Liberals, New Conservatives, New Elections

Keeanga-Yamahtta Taylor, *From #BlackLivesMatter to Black Liberation* (Chicago: Haymarket Books, 2016); Michelle Alexander, *The New Jim Crow: Mass Incarceration In the Age of Colorblindness* (New York: the New Press, 2012); Peter H. Lindert and Jeffrey G.; Williamson, *Unequal Gains: American Growth and Inequality Since 1700* (Princeton: Princeton University Press, 2016); Robert J. Gordon, *The Rise and Fall of American Growth: The U.S. Standard of Living Since the Civil War* (Princeton, Princeton University Press, 2016); Arlie Russell Hochschild, *Strangers in Their Own Land* (New York: The New Press, 2016); James W. Ceaser, Andrew E. Busch, and John J. Pitney, Jr., *Defying the Odds: The 2016 Elections and American Politics* (Lanham, MD: Roman & Littlefield, 2017).

Index